SOCIOLOGY

SECOND EDITION

John J. Macionis

Kenyon College

Prentice Hall, Englewood Cliffs, New Jersey 07632

Library of Congress Cataloging-in-Publication Data

Macionis, John J.
    Sociology/John J. Macionis.—2nd ed.
       p.   cm.
    Bibliography: p. 644
    Includes indexes.
    ISBN 0–13–823287–3
    1. Sociology.   I. Title.
    HM51.M166 1989   88–21832
    301—dc19   CIP

Acquisitions editor: Nancy Roberts
Development editor: Susanna Lesan
Editorial/production supervision: Serena Hoffman
Interior design: Judith A. Matz-Coniglio
Cover design: Bruce Kenselaar
Manufacturing buyer: Peter Havens
Photo researchers: Sheryl Mannes and Anita Dickhuth
Photo editor: Lorinda Morris-Nantz
Cover art: WPA mural, Coit Tower, San Francisco
Cover photo: Ellis Herwig/Stock, Boston

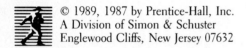 © 1989, 1987 by Prentice-Hall, Inc.
A Division of Simon & Schuster
Englewood Cliffs, New Jersey 07632

Printed in the United States of America

10 9 8 7 6 5 4 3 2

ISBN 0-13-823287-3

PRENTICE-HALL INTERNATIONAL (UK) LIMITED, *London*
PRENTICE-HALL OF AUSTRALIA PTY. LIMITED, *Sydney*
PRENTICE-HALL CANADA INC., *Toronto*
PRENTICE-HALL HISPANOAMERICANA, S.A., *Mexico*
PRENTICE-HALL OF INDIA PRIVATE LIMITED, *New Delhi*
PRENTICE-HALL OF JAPAN, INC., *Tokyo*
SIMON & SCHUSTER ASIA PTE. LTD., *Singapore*
EDITORA PRENTICE-HALL DO BRASIL, LTDA., *Rio de Janeiro*

Brief Contents

Contents

Boxes

SOCIAL POLICY

SOCIETY IN HISTORY

PROFILE

CLOSE-UP

Preface

This text has been conceived, written, and produced with a keen awareness of its audience: undergraduate college and university students beginning the study of sociology. One of the greatest challenges in writing an introductory text is addressing the diversity of students enrolled in this course. Indeed, this is a diversity I know first-hand, having taught for almost twenty years in a wide range of academic settings, including large universities, small private colleges, community colleges, and even a prison and a police academy. A text that acknowledges the great diversity of the academic community is not only attractive to the various segments, but is richer for them all because it truly represents the diversity of North American society.

Most sociologists would probably agree that there is little in the discipline that is inherently beyond the understanding of any undergraduate student. At the same time, *how* material is presented—in terms of explanation and example—is crucial in an introductory text. I have labored to present the discipline comprehensively and clearly, so that students of all ages, social backgrounds, and career interests can share the vital insights and excitement of sociology.

THE ORGANIZATION OF THIS TEXT

Part I systematically introduces *the foundations of sociology*. First and foremost, sociology is a perspective—an invigorating point of view that illuminates familiar social patterns in a new and instructive way. The sociological perspective is the focus of Chapter 1, and this discussion is carried through the entire text. Because sociology also includes a vast enterprise of scientific research, Chapter 2 introduces the logic of science and the major methods used to investigate human society. These methods are illustrated by important pieces of sociological research, so that research strategies come to life. As readers learn what sociologists *do*, they become better able to critically evaluate what they read in subsequent chapters. Chapters 1 and 2 also explain that sociology is concerned with values as well as facts. From the outset, many sociologists

have been moralists as well as scientists, and fascinating controversies at the center of the discipline are explored throughout this book.

Part II presents *the foundations of social life*. Chapter 3 explores the central concept of culture, emphasizing not only the many ways of life that make up our world, but also the social diversity found within American society. Chapter 4 presents four visions of society developed by major social thinkers who have had an enormous influence on sociology. This unique chapter can be used in its entirety to introduce prominent thinkers whose ideas will appear in many subsequent chapters. Alternatively, its four sections can be assigned individually according to an instructor's specific needs. Chapter 5 focuses on socialization—the ways in which people gain their humanity as they learn to actively participate in society. Chapter 6 provides a close-up look at the patterns of social interaction that make up our everyday lives. Chapter 7 offers full-chapter coverage of groups and organizations, and Chapter 8 completes the unit by explaining how the operation of society promotes both deviance and conformity.

Part III provides a detailed analysis of *social inequality*. Because of its importance, two chapters are devoted to social stratification. Chapter 9 introduces major concepts and describes systems of social inequality in a world context. Chapter 10 highlights patterns of social inequality and their consequences in American society. Race and ethnicity—important dimensions of both social inequality and social diversity—are discussed in Chapter 11. Chapter 12 explains the biological foundations of sex and sexuality, and how societies incorporate them into gender stratification. The elderly—a rapidly growing segment of American society—are given full-chapter coverage in Chapter 13.

Part IV engages in a wide-ranging discussion of *social institutions*. These include the family (Chapter 14), education (Chapter 15), religion (Chapter 16), politics and government (Chapter 17), and the economy and work (Chapter 18). The growing concern over health and medical care is reflected in full-chapter coverage of this topic (Chapter 19).

Part V focuses on important dimensions of *social change*. Chapter 20 discusses the historical and contemporary impact of population growth and urbanization throughout the world. Chapter 21 explains how people provoke (and resist) change through various forms of collective behavior and social movements—in the past, the present, and the future. Chapter 22 completes the unit with a systematic analysis of the dimensions of social change in the United States and in other societies, emphasizing the distinctive qualities of the modern world.

FEATURES OF THIS TEXT

Chapter Introductions. One of the most popular features of the first edition has been the brief vignettes that open each chapter. In this revision, opening vignettes spark the interest of the reader and introduce an important theme that is carried through the chapter.

Learning Aids. Throughout the text, **key concepts** are identified when first introduced by boldfaced type, followed by a precise definition. An alphabetical listing of key concepts appears at the end of each chapter, and again in the **Glossary** at the end of the book. Each chapter also includes a numbered **Summary** to help students review the material and assess their comprehension. Also at the end of each chapter is a list of **Suggested Readings** that describes books of importance and highlights the most recent publications on the topic at hand.

Illustrations. Much thought has gone into providing a program of photography and artwork that will enrich students' learning. Dramatic photographs and socially significant works of art have been carefully selected and reproduced in full color. These images do more than add to the visual appeal of the text; they help readers see how the ideas in the book apply to themselves and to the larger world. In addition, clear and lively graphics throughout the text present data efficiently.

Multitheoretical Analysis. The major theoretical paradigms in sociology that are introduced in Chapter 1 are used to provide a broad analysis of topics in subsequent chapters. The structural-functional, social-conflict, and symbolic-interaction paradigms are each presented as part of a full sociological analysis. In addition, social-exchange analysis, ethnomethodology, cultural ecology, and sociobiology are included in a number of

chapters. Chapter 4 amplifies this text's commitment to introducing students to social theory in that it allows readers to become familiar with the ideas of social thinkers *before* their work is discussed in later chapters. This chapter, which may be assigned as a whole or in parts throughout the course, details the approach and significant ideas of important classical theorists (Karl Marx and Max Weber) and influential contemporary theorists (Gerhard and Jean Lenski and Talcott Parsons).

Recent Sociological Research. Sociology is continuously renewing and revising its ideas as a result of ongoing research. This text blends classical statements in sociology with the latest research, as reported in leading publications in the field. On average, almost 60 percent of the citations in each chapter represent material published since 1980.

Contemporary Focus on Women and Men. In addition to the full chapter on the important concepts of sex and gender, *every* chapter reflects ways in which the issues under discussion affect the lives of men and women. A special effort has been made to incorporate sociological research by women.

Boxes. Although boxes are common to most good introductory texts, this text provides a wealth of uncommonly good boxes. They are integral parts of the text and bring life and substance to important issues. *Profile* boxes introduce fifteen men and women who have shaped the development of sociology. Rather than lumping such biographical introductions together in Chapter 1 as some other texts do, this text incorporates profile boxes into the chapter in which a particular sociologist's work is discussed in detail. *Cross-Cultural Comparison* boxes reflect the strongly comparative character of this text, examining the fascinating cultural diversity found around the world. *Sociology of Everyday Life* boxes provide an opportunity for readers to see how the sociological perspective encourages new understandings of familiar processes and events. *Social Policy* boxes highlight controversial issues in American society that affect the lives of us all. *Society in History* boxes link the present to the past, showing that modern social patterns are often quite unlike those taken for granted in earlier generations. Finally, *Close-Up* boxes provide analysis and illustration of key ideas and arguments. All boxes have been designed from the outset as integral parts of the text and should be read as they appear in the chapter.

CHANGES IN THIS EDITION

As a teacher of sociology, I could not help being deeply gratified by the warm reception given the first edition of *Sociology*—by all accounts, the most successful new introductory text in sociology in a decade. Hundreds of instructors and students have shared their reactions to the text, pointing out its strengths as well as making constructive suggestions. With these generous comments in mind, I have critically evaluated every page of the book with the goal of making the second edition significantly better than the first. Important changes include the following:

New Chapters on Social Organization. "Social Interaction in Everyday Life" (Chapter 6) expands earlier material to provide a new chapter devoted entirely to micro-level issues. Beyond discussion of status and role, the social construction of reality, and the presentation of self, it offers new sections on ethnomethodology and encountering strangers in urban life. In addition, this chapter now includes a sociological analysis of humor, an issue that is rapidly gaining attention but has not received coverage in other introductory texts.

"Groups and Organizations" is now an expanded, full chapter (Chapter 7). Included is more material on group conformity, networks, and formal organizations. New sections contrast bureaucracy and small groups, investigate the power structure of organizations, and explore efforts to humanize bureaucracy. Special efforts are made to help students apply sociological insights to their own lives within an increasingly bureaucratized society.

Reordering of Chapters. Socialization is now discussed in Chapter 5, so that Part II concludes with a more logical flow of material from micro concerns to macro issues.

New Topics. Beyond those mentioned above, this edition of *Sociology* includes new material on such topics as the medicalization of deviance (Chapter 8), ideology and institutional support for social inequality (Chapter 9), the expansion of low-paying jobs during the 1980s (Chapter 10), and the new reproductive technologies that are changing the family (Chapter 14). Throughout the text, there is more material on corporate America and expanded coverage of global issues. Chapters 18 and 22 now provide an even broader discussion of modernization theory and dependency theory than before.

The Latest Statistical Data. This revision provides not only the most recent research findings, but also the latest statistical data available as of mid-1988. In many cases, this means that 1987 or even 1988 data are provided.

Concise and Clear Definitions of Concepts. This revision is the result of a line-by-line effort to improve the wording and construction of ideas. Special attention has been given to making the conceptual clarity and accuracy of this text second to none.

SUPPLEMENTS

This text is the heart of a complete learning package that includes an *Annotated Instructor's Edition*—the first of its kind in a sociology text. The AIE is the complete text with two major additions: (1) an *Instructor's Manual* bound directly into the front of the book, and (2) teaching annotations prepared by the author printed at the top of the page. These annotations provide a wealth of ideas and resources to improve classroom teaching and discussion. Full details on how to use the AIE to advantage are found in the preface to the *Instructor's Manual*.

The *Instructor's Manual* was prepared by Professor Edward L. Kain (Southwestern University). It provides a detailed outline of each chapter, a wide range of suggested lecture plans, topics for class discussion, topics for essay examinations and research projects, and a list of suitable films. Instructor's annotations throughout the text indicate how the IM can be used easily and effectively.

The *Study Guide and Workbook*, prepared by Professor Virginia McKeffery-Reynolds (Northern Illinois University), provides the student with an opportunity to review key ideas in each chapter of the text. Exercises and self-tests allow the student to assess personal learning continually as the course proceeds. A version of this study guide is available on computer disk for both the IBM PC and the Apple II family of personal computers.

The *Test Item File*, prepared by Professor Richard Bucher (Community College of Baltimore), provides 2000 objective test questions. These items are available on diskette for both the IBM PC and the Apple II family of personal computers, as well as in a bound booklet.

A set of nine *Interactive Simulations* for the IBM PC and the Apple II family of personal computers were prepared by a team headed by Professor Byron Matthews (University of Maryland at Baltimore County). A Demonstration Disk containing brief versions of these simulations is available for preview through local Prentice-Hall representatives, and a license for free use of the complete set is available upon adoption of the text.

The *Film Guide*, revised by Professor Peter Remender (University of Wisconsin at Oshkosh), is a useful guide to films for each chapter of this text. It includes instructions for obtaining films and suggestions for integrating them into classroom discussion.

New to this edition of *Sociology* is Prentice-Hall's *Video Lecture Series*. A VHS cassette offers topic introductions on "The Sociological Perspective" and "Social Stratification" by John Macionis, a lecture on "Culture" by David Popenoe, plus lectures on "Collective Behavior" and "Deviance" by Erich Goode. These video vignettes can be used with Chapters 1, 3, 5, 8, 9, and 21 of this text and are free to adopters.

Video Supplements. Adopters of this text may choose from a wide range of video cassettes suitable for classroom use. See any Prentice-Hall representative for details.

ACKNOWLEDGMENTS

The conventional practice of designating a single author obscures the fact that the efforts of dozens of women and men are reflected in a book. Prentice Hall editor Bill Webber's steady support and boundless enthusiasm contributed greatly to the success of the first edition. Similarly, developmental suggestions made then by Kathleen Hall are still evident in this revised edition. Many members of the Prentice Hall sales staff, and especially Robert Thoresen, have offered constructive suggestions that have improved this edition of the text. Nancy Roberts, sociology editor at Prentice Hall, deserves credit for overseeing the revision of this text. She consistently held this project to the highest standards, and I trust that she will not be disappointed.

The editorial production of *Sociology* was directed by Serena Hoffman, whose skillful management made a complex task seem easy. Barbara Heir coordinated the revision of the supplements package. The design of the text was the creative work of Judy Matz-Coniglio. Careful copy editing of the manuscript was provided by Carol Freddo. Lorri Morris-Nantz, Sheryl Mannes, and Anita Dickhuth served as photograph researchers. Terri Peterson was responsible for developing the marketing program for this book. I also wish to extend my sincere thanks to Ed Stanford, John Isley, Susan Willig, Vicki Tandler, and Kathleen Dorman, all of whom provided important support that made this a better book.

The process of critical review is indispensible to the development of any text. The following people have served as reviewers of part or all of this project:

David Ashley
Nijole Benokraitis, University of Baltimore
Paul R. Benson, Tulane University
Charles Bolton, Portland State University
Jean H. Cardinalli, Monroe County Community College
Frank Clemente, Pennsylvania State University
Peter Conrad, Brandeis University
Harold Cox, Indiana State University
Sheila Cordray, Oregon State University
Harrold Curl, Mount Vernon Nazarene College
Dennis K. Dedrick, Georgetown College
John Farley, Southern Illinois University
Joe R. Feagin, University of Texas
Juanita M. Firestone, University of Texas at Austin
Alvin J. Fischer, Camden County College
Don C. Gibbons, Portland State University
Norval D. Glenn, University of Texas
H. James Graham, Mott Community College
Marshall J. Graney, University of Tennessee
Linda M. Grant, Southern Illinois University
L. Sue Greer, University of Pittsburgh
Patricia A. Guartney-Gibbs, University of Oregon
Maureen Hallinan, University of Notre Dame
Charles L. Harper, Creighton University
Jessie D. Harper, St. Cloud State University
Cedric Herring, Texas A&M University
Gary Hodge, Collin County Community College
Kathy Hughes, Henderson Community College
Janet C. Hunt, University of Maryland
Norris R. Johnson, University of Cincinnati
Ronald L. Johnstone, Central Michigan University
Ross A. Klein, Skidmore College
Marlene Lehtinen, University of Utah
Hugh F. Lena, Providence College
Larry Lyon, Baylor University
Wilfred G. Marston, University of Michigan
John D. McCarthy, Catholic University
Meredith B. McGuire, Montclair State College
Virginia McKeefery-Reynolds, Northern Illinois University
Dwayne Monette, Northern Michigan University
Wilbert E. Moore, University of Denver
Peter Morrill, Bronx Community College
Charles W. Mueller, University of Iowa
Anthony M. Orum, University of Texas

Dorothy M. Roe, Milwaukee Area Technical College
Howard Sacks, Kenyon College
Beth Anne Shelton, State University of New York at Buffalo
Anson Shupe, University of Texas
Karen Cole Smith, Sante Fe Community College
Eve Spangler, Boston College
Michael Stein, University of Missouri
George F. Stine, Millersville University
Teresa A. Sullivan, University of Texas
Verta Taylor, The Ohio State University
Vickie H. Taylor, Danville Community College
Kendrick S. Thompson, Northern Michigan University
Susan Tiano, University of New Mexico
Andrew Treno, Clarke College
Theodore C. Wagenaar, Miami University
Pamela Barnhouse Walters, Indiana University
Philo C. Wasburn, Purdue University
David L. Westby, Pennsylvania State University
John Wilson, Duke University

In addition, I owe thanks to the following colleagues for sharing their wisdom in ways that have improved this book: Kipp Armstrong, Bloomsburg State College; Carolie Coffey, Cabrillo College; Gerry Cox, Fort Hays State University; Harold Curl, Mount Vernon Nazarene College; Helen Rose Ebaugh, University of Houston; Charles Frazier, University of Florida; Steven Goldberg, City College, City University of New York; Jeffery Hahn, Mount Union College; C. Allen Haney, University of Houston; Peter Hruschka, Ohio Northern University; Glenna Huls, Camden County College; Harry Humphries, Pittsburgh State University; Patricia Johnson, Houston Community College; Irwin Kantor, Middlesex County College; Thomas Korllos, Kent State University; Don Luidens, Hope College; Larry Lyon, Baylor University; Li-Chen Ma, Lamar University; Toby Parcel, The Ohio State University; Virginia Reynolds, Indiana University of Pennsylvania; Laurel Richardson, The Ohio State University; Len Tompos, Lorain County Community College; Christopher Vanderpool, Michigan State University; and Stuart Wright, Lamar University. Special thanks are due to Ed Kain, Southwestern University, who prepared the Instructor's Manual and provided suggestions for the Instructor's Annotations in the text.

I also wish to thank members of my department at Kenyon College—Rita Kipp, George MacCarthy, Esther Merves, Howard Sacks, Ed Schortman, Ken Smail, Dave Suggs, and Pat Urban—for sharing ideas and for occasionally putting up with an overstressed colleague.

This edition of *Sociology* has again benefited from the critical editorial eye of Amy Marsh Macionis, who is also responsible for preparing the indexes. Carol A. Singer, Government Documents Librarian at Kenyon College, provided research assistance and is responsible for the presence of only the latest statistical data in this revision.

Finally, from the outset some six years ago, Susanna Lesan of Prentice Hall's editorial and production staff has committed an inordinate amount of her time, energy, and enthusiasm to this book. As is the case with many in her profession, her work is sometimes taken for granted. But not this time. For all the Saturdays at the office, for all the hours on the phone, for all the good judgment and the good friendship, this edition of *Sociology* is affectionately and respectfully dedicated to Susy Lesan.

About the Author

John J. Macionis (pronounced ma-SHOW-nis) is a native of Philadelphia, Pennsylvania. He received his bachelor's degree from Cornell University and his doctorate in sociology from the University of Pennsylvania. He is the author of articles and papers on topics such as community life in the United States, interpersonal relationships in families, effective teaching, and humor. An area of particular interest is urban sociology; he is coauthor of a well-received text, *The Sociology of Cities*. He has also coedited the new companion volume to this text: *Seeing Ourselves: Classic, Contemporary, and Cross-Cultural Readings in Sociology*.

John Macionis is currently associate professor of sociology at Kenyon College in Gambier, Ohio. He recently served as Chair of the Anthropology-Sociology Department, as Director of Kenyon's multidisciplinary program in humane studies, and as Chair of Kenyon's faculty.

Professor Macionis teaches a wide range of upper-level courses, but his favorite course is Introduction to Sociology, which he teaches every semester. He enjoys extensive contact with students on his home campus, as a frequent visitor to other campuses, and as a regular participant in teaching programs abroad.

CHAPTER 1

The Sociological Perspective

"Any unit in the vicinity of 50 East 79th Street, respond to report of gunshot in apartment 17-B." The crackling voice on the car radio brings the police officers suddenly to life; the apartment house in question is two short blocks straight ahead. Guiding the patrol car through the traffic and waves of pedestrians common to a summer evening on the Upper East Side of Manhattan, the two officers are there in a minute. Leaving the car double-parked with emergency lights ablaze, they dash through the lobby of the tall apartment house and into the elevator. Nervous and silent, they rise to the seventeenth floor, unsure of what will confront them when the doors open. Seconds later, they are surrounded by a group of people swarming around the entrance to apartment 17-B. The excited chatter ends abruptly as the two officers approach.

"I'm the manager," one woman announces. "There's no answer—I've been banging on the door. Here's the key."

The people in the hallway press in behind the officers as they cautiously enter the apartment, their fingers poised above their service revolvers. But there is no need to draw their guns. On the floor of the living room directly in front of them lies the lifeless body of a middle-aged man. He is dressed in pajamas and a robe, and a small-caliber pistol lies a few inches from his right hand.

The Importance of Perspective

Here we have presented a hypothetical incident, an apparent suicide on a summer evening in New York.* More specifically, this incident has been described from the vantage point of police officers responding to a radio call. This *perspective*—or point of view—is probably easy for anyone to assume. Although few people have actually worked as police officers, almost everyone knows at least something about police work from newspaper reports, movies, television, and personal observations. In a situation of this kind, the job of the police officer is to make an official report describing the event—noting what happened, when, and, if possible, how. From the perspective of a police officer, the crucial facts about this incident would no doubt be the identity of the victim, the address, the time, where the body was found, and the presence of the pistol as the apparent cause of death.

Consider now the same event from a second perspective, that of the deceased man's psychiatrist. Upon learning of this death, what facts would stand out in the psychiatrist's mind as most important? Perhaps the psychiatrist would recall unfortunate events in the dead man's youth, his long struggle with depression, and his

---

* The general idea behind this example has been used in the classroom by E. Digby Baltzell.

previous impulses toward suicide. Notice that from the psychiatrist's point of view the crucial facts are quite different from those identified by the police officers.

A sociologist would make use of yet another perspective. Reading about the man's death, a sociologist might note that he was male, Protestant, wealthy, and unmarried. These facts would probably be ignored by the police officers and the psychiatrist. The police officers focus on certain facts that apply only to this one situation. Similarly, the psychiatrist thinks in terms of the personal traumas that may have contributed to this particular suicide. In contrast, the sociologist is not interested in how or why any *particular* individual commits suicide as much as in why suicide is more characteristic of some *categories* of people than others. These three points of view applied to one situation illustrate that, to a large degree, *perspective is the basis of "reality."*

THE SOCIOLOGICAL PERSPECTIVE

A distinctive perspective is fundamental to the discipline of **sociology,** which is defined as *the scientific study of society and the social activity of human beings.* As an academic discipline, sociology is continually adding to a body of knowledge about how human beings think and act as social creatures. Sociologists derive this knowl-edge from research conducted according to a variety of procedures, many of which are described in Chapter 2. As explained later in this chapter, sociologists also make use of various theoretical approaches to guide their inquiry. But all sociologists use one basic perspective in their quest to understand the social world.

Seeing the General in the Particular

Sociologists are interested in how and why certain categories of people—in the example just described, such categories include males, Protestants, the wealthy, and the unmarried—tend to think and act in similar ways. As Peter Berger (1963) suggests, this characteristic of the sociological perspective can be described as *seeing the general in the particular.* All disciplines attempt to see how particular facts may be the basis of general patterns; sociology takes this approach to studying human social behavior.

Emile Durkheim, an early and influential French sociologist, pioneered the study of suicide in the late nineteenth century (1966; orig. 1897). At that time, suicide was often viewed as simply a matter of an individual's moral weakness. But Durkheim was able to demonstrate that suicide was more common among some categories of people than among others. He theorized that people who are *socially integrated*—that is, strongly bound to

Adopting a perspective places us in a particular position in relation to any topic of study. The sociological perspective does not reveal all that is true, but it is one vital means to understand the world.

Table 1–1	SUICIDE IN THE UNITED STATES, 1984			
	Males		**Females**	
	Whites	Blacks	Whites	Blacks
Number of suicides per 100,000 people	21.3	10.6	5.9	2.2

SOURCE: U.S. National Center for Health Statistics, 1987.

others by ties of affection and obligation—are less likely to commit suicide than those who are more socially isolated.* He was led to this conclusion through an examination of recorded instances of suicide in various regions of France and Central Europe. These records revealed that the suicide rates for certain categories of people—males, Protestants, the wealthy, and the unmarried—were higher than for other categories of people—females, Catholics and Jews, the poor, and the married. Durkheim explained the patterns in terms of the relative social integration of these categories of people. Within male-dominated societies such as those of Europe, females are less independent than males and more mindful of the expectations of others. Catholic and Jewish beliefs encourage strong social ties and group conformity, whereas Protestant beliefs emphasize individual freedom of thought and action. Wealthy people have a far wider range of personal choices than do the poor, whose freedom is limited by their poverty. Finally, unmarried people are less socially integrated than those who are bound to others by marriage and family responsibilities.

Almost a century later, the available statistics on suicide in the United States still support Durkheim's analysis (Breault, 1986). The data presented in Table 1–1 show that in 1984 there were just over 21 suicides for every 100,000 white males; in contrast, there were only about one-fourth as many suicides among white females. Among blacks, the suicide rate among males was almost five times as high as among females. Notice, too, that for each sex the suicide rate for whites is higher than for blacks. Following Durkheim's analysis, we can conclude that the higher suicide rate among whites—and particularly white males—is due to their greater wealth and power within American society. As Durkheim explained, poorer people and those with limited social

* This discussion is a much abbreviated account of Durkheim's considerably more complex analysis of suicide.

ited social choices are more socially integrated than people with greater individual freedom.

In this way, Durkheim demonstrated how general social patterns can affect the actions of particular individuals. Thus his research is a classic illustration of how the sociological perspective reveals the general in the particular. The box on p. 4 provides a more recent example of how general social patterns have affected the particular decisions of a category of well-known Americans.

Seeing the Strange in the Familiar

The sociological perspective can also be described as *seeing the strange in the familiar*. This does not mean that sociologists focus on the bizarre elements of society. Rather, the sociological perspective involves detaching oneself from familiar explanations of the social world in order to gain new insights that at first may seem somewhat strange. Using the sociological perspective leads, in the words of Peter Berger, to the conclusion that "things are not what they seem" (1963:23).

Most people in American society today take the social world so much for granted that they barely "see" it at all. Therefore, using the sociological perspective to take a fresh look at society generally requires a bit of practice. Gradually, however, people find that the sociological perspective reveals facts quite different from those often described as "common sense." Some students enter a first course in sociology with a vague understanding that sociology is, in one way or another, the complicated study of the obvious. The following examples should convince you that what the sociological perspective reveals is actually quite different from what most people would claim to be the "obvious" facts of social life.

Why Did You Come to This Particular College?

Without using a sociological perspective, students are likely to answer this question with diverse, matter-of-fact answers:

I wanted to stay close to home.
This college has the best women's basketball team.
A journalism degree from this school will ensure a good job.
My girlfriend goes to school here.
I wasn't accepted at the school I really wanted to attend.

SOCIOLOGY OF EVERYDAY LIFE

The Name Game: The Social Background of Celebrities

On July 4, 1918, twins were born to Abe and Becky Friedman in Sioux City, Iowa. The first to be born was named Esther Pauline Friedman; her sister was named Pauline Esther Friedman. Today, these women are "household names" in the United States. But as celebrities, they are known as Ann Landers and Abigail Van Buren.

The Friedman sisters are hardly the only Americans who have changed their names to further their careers—a practice especially common among celebrities. At first glance, this may seem to be simply a matter of particular preferences. However, the sociological perspective suggests that a more general pattern is operating. Looking through the names below, notice how men and women of many different backgrounds have adopted English-sounding names. This reflects the fact that American society has long accorded great social prestige to those of Anglo-Saxon background.

How many of these well-known entertainers can you identify?

1. Michael James Vijencio Gubitosi	1. Robert Blake
2. Betty Persky	2. Lauren Bacall
3. Margarita Carmen Cansino	3. Rita Hayworth
4. Anna Maria Italiano	4. Anne Bancroft
5. Frederick Austerlitz	5. Fred Astaire
6. Lucille Le Sueur	6. Joan Crawford
7. Anthony Benedetto	7. Tony Bennett
8. Issur Danielovitch Demsky	8. Kirk Douglas
9. Mladen Sekulovich	9. Karl Malden
10. Dino Crocetti	10. Dean Martin
11. Allan Stewart Konigsberg	11. Woody Allen
12. Gerald Silberman	12. Gene Wilder
13. Eugene Maurice Orowitz	13. Michael Landon
14. Bernadette Lazzarra	14. Bernadette Peters
15. Karen Ziegler	15. Karen Black
16. Henry John Deutschendorf, Jr.	16. John Denver
17. Ramon Estevez	17. Martin Sheen
18. Walter Matasschanskayasky	18. Walter Matthau

Such responses are quite meaningful to the people expressing them, and because they are familiar, there is nothing startling about any of them. Although such responses may be valid, however, they are certainly incomplete. The sociological perspective reveals something very important that such explanations omit.

To approach this question sociologically, we must first take a step back from reasons that apply to *particular* people and seek more *general* explanations. First of all, let us consider what students as a *category* of people have in common. Simple observation provides one characteristic. Although people of all ages attend college, most students are relatively young—generally between eighteen and twenty-four years of age. A social pattern in American society links college attendance to this period of life. Something more is involved, however, because most Americans today between the ages of eighteen and twenty-four are *not* enrolled in college. In 1985, only 37 percent of Americans within the college-age bracket were actually attending college (U.S. National Center for Education Statistics, 1987). Now college students begin to look like a more unusual category of people: generally young, but representing not much more than one-third of their age group.

In addition, college students in the United States tend to come from families with considerable social privi-

People the world over fashion their appearances and engage in patterns of behavior that those in other societies may find strange or even incomprehensible. We are no different, taking our own way of life for granted. Sociology offers fresh and unexpected insights about the familiar social world.

lege and substantial income. In 1985, the typical college student between eighteen and twenty-four years of age was from a family with an income of about $30,000—several thousand higher than the average income for all American families (U.S. Bureau of the Census, 1986e, 1987g). Looking more closely, we see that some college students have far more economic advantages than others do. Because most of the costs of a college education in the United States are paid by students and their families, more income means more choice about what college to attend. Some colleges are much more expensive than others are; in addition, going away to school costs more than attending college while living at home. In short, many college students end up at schools corresponding to their social background.

Three-fourths of the more than 12 million college students in the United States attend schools that receive government funding (U.S. National Center for Education Statistics, 1985). These schools include locally funded community colleges, which generally offer two-year programs, and four-year state colleges. In both cases, 1987 tuition for students living at home averaged about $1,000 while the costs of room and board brought the yearly total to between $5,000 and $6,000. Private four-year colleges and universities, however, were even more expensive: tuition and the costs of room and board aver-

Because they are usually a small minority, black students may become keenly aware of social patterns that members of the white majority take for granted. This is a common experience of blacks who attend expensive, private colleges.

aged about $12,000 a year and, at the most expensive schools, was about $18,000 annually (U.S. Education Department, 1986; Anderson, 1987). Not surprisingly, then, students from families of more modest means are likely to attend local two-year colleges or four-year state schools. Many of the growing number of older students in the United States have job and family responsibilities; as a result, they are likely to attend relatively inexpensive colleges that are near home and that allow part-time and evening enrollment. Private four-year colleges and universities are generally within the financial means only of students from families with considerable income (Ballantine, 1983).

To Americans who embrace the commonsense view that our society offers "equal opportunity for all," whether and where one attends college may be seen as simply a matter of personal choice. Thus, stating that more general social forces are at work may initially seem strange. But the sociological perspective reveals that social background has a powerful influence on every individual's personal decisions.

Why Do People Get Divorced?

Familiar explanations for divorce are that people fall out of love, or that relationships succumb to tensions caused by financial problems, pressures at work, alcoholism, or infidelity. These reasons are certainly real, in that they describe the troubles of particular people. But more reasons than these are involved, as indicated by the rising divorce rate in the United States. As Figure 1–1 shows, the divorce rate in the United States increased tenfold between 1890 and 1987. Change in the divorce rate certainly reflects choices made by particular women and men, yet the fact that the divorce rate has risen dramatically during this century suggests that more general social forces are also at work. One important change in American society during this period (discussed at length in Chapter 12) has been the growing number of women in the labor force. In 1900, about one in five American women worked outside the home; by 1987, well over half (56 percent) of American women did so. This fact, along with the women's movement, more educational opportunity, and technological advances in birth control, has provided women today with a far wider range of choices and opportunities. Similarly, as discussed in Chapter 14, divorce no longer carries the sinful stigma it had a century ago. As a result, both women and men feel less bound to remain in unsatisfying marriages.

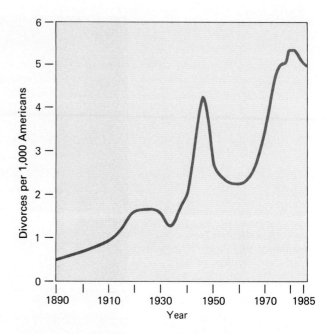

Figure 1–1 The Divorce Rate for the United States, 1890–1987

A closer look at Figure 1–1 also shows that the divorce rate declined somewhat during the 1930s and rose sharply during the mid-1940s. Individual choices were certainly involved in these patterns, but, once again, more general social patterns were also important. The 1930s was a decade of economic depression, which greatly limited the opportunities of Americans and made spouses more dependent on each other. Thus divorce became less likely. On the other hand, the early 1940s brought the Second World War, which separated millions of American couples for several years. Many marriages were unable to survive this separation, so the divorce rate was unusually high for several years after the war.

In sum, familiar explanations for divorce provide an incomplete picture of this important issue. The sociological perspective reveals that general patterns within society as a whole often set the stage for the choices made by particular men and women.

Depersonalizing the Personal

Especially in individualistic North American society, human beings tend to understand their lives in very personal terms. We feel, think, and act as individual human beings. We emphasize the importance of choice in our lives, claiming, for example, "I went to college because I wanted to be a veterinarian," or "My parents decided to get a divorce because they fought all the time." Our everyday awareness carries a heavy load of personal responsibility, so that we kick ourselves when things go wrong and pat ourselves on the back when we enjoy success. But when we step back from the familiar world of individual choices and personal responsibility, we see that general social forces act on everyone, making our individual lives less distinctive than we may have imagined.

What could be more personal than suicide? Surely, taking your own life is among the most individualistic of all actions, carried out for reasons that seem highly personal. Perhaps this is the reason that Emile Durkheim chose to examine suicide: he wanted to demonstrate that impersonal social forces are at work even in the apparent isolation of a self-destructive act. How else can the fact that suicide rates are higher or lower for various categories of people be explained? Similarly, anyone who has gone through a divorce knows that it is a profoundly personal experience, commonly fraught with disorientation, hurt, anger, and uncertainty. To those involved, *their* divorce may seem like the *only* divorce. It would sound strange to them to hear that what they are enduring is a "sociological phenomenon." Proud of our individuality, even in painful times, we resist the idea that we act in socially patterned ways and that social forces guide us in certain directions.

Human beings do have considerable autonomy, but we are deeply affected by the values, beliefs, and patterns of behavior that characterize the society we live in. To be convinced of this fact, you have only to imagine how different your life would be had you been born in ancient China, medieval England, or modern Ethiopia. The sociological perspective helps us to "depersonalize the personal" by revealing that our personal lives are shaped by impersonal forces that have preceded us and will remain long after we are gone.

The Sociological Perspective in Everyday Life

As we have explained, the common sense of most Americans tends to overlook the power of social forces. But even before we take a first course in sociology, some kinds of situations do prompt us to view the world sociologically.

Confronting Other Societies

A foreign exchange student newly arrived on an American college campus is likely to notice social patterns that Americans take for granted. The strangeness of the surroundings helps a foreigner see that people's behavior is not only a result of individual choice, but also reflects patterns of the larger society. In the same way, of course, traveling abroad heightens the awareness of social patterns among Americans. Just as important, confronting other societies often prepares us to look at American society with new eyes when we return home. A similar broadening of perspective occurs when we confront unfamiliar social environments within our own society—visiting strange neighborhoods, for example, or meeting people whose beliefs and patterns of behavior are different from our own.

Being an Outsider: Race, Sex, and Age

Sociologists often use the term **social marginality** to refer to *being excluded from social activity as an "outsider."* All people experience social marginality from time to time; for some categories of Americans, however, being an outsider is commonplace. The more common their experience of social marginality, the more they are likely to make use of the sociological perspective.

No black person, for example, could live very long in the United States without being aware of how much the social significance of race can affect personal experiences. But because white people constitute the dominant majority of American society, whites think about race only occasionally. When they do think about it, they may consider race an issue that applies only to black people rather than also to themselves. This social blindness probably accounts for the fact that some whites occasionally accuse nonwhites of exaggerating the importance of race. But within a primarily white society, nonwhites are forced to be more aware of race than are whites.

In a similar way, women of all races are more likely to see the world sociologically than are men. For the past two decades, women who have personally experienced some of the limitations that American society imposes on females have been getting together to compare notes. The result has been a growing awareness that a woman's experience of social inequality is not merely personal, but is also a reflection of powerful social forces. Some men, because of their dominant social position, have failed to see patterns of sexual inequality. Like the whites noted above, they have sometimes accused

women of exaggerating the problem. In the 1970s, American women described their growing recognition of sexual inequality as "consciousness raising"; this could also be viewed as an example of social marginality fostering the development of a sociological perspective.

The elderly often perceive social patterns more acutely than young people do. While this may be partly due to the wisdom gained over a lifetime, also important is the fact that the elderly often experience considerable social marginality. As Chapter 13 explains further, Americans tend to define growing old as the loss of the capacity to engage in many important human activities—including physical recreation, work, and even sex. Since most elderly people are indeed physically and mentally capable of all these activities, they come to understand more clearly than the young how much society defines what individuals are and how they should think and act (Comfort, 1980; Myerhoff, 1980).

In short, people who are placed on the outside of social life—because of such factors as race, sex, or age—are likely to be more aware of social patterns that others take for granted. They have stepped back from society (perhaps more accurately, society has stepped back from them) and therefore have a more sociological view of the world. A heightened sociological awareness can also characterize *insiders* who are brought into contact with outsiders.

Because elderly Americans are often viewed as social outsiders, they tend to be more sociological in their outlook than younger people. In Japan, however, the elderly play a more central part in social life; as a result, they probably adopt a sociological perspective less readily.

Periods of Social Crisis

American sociologist C. Wright Mills (1959) suggested that some periods in history foster a more widespread use of the sociological perspective than others do. In this century, the 1930s stand out as a decade of heightened sociological awareness. The Great Depression followed the stock market crash of 1929, resulting in unemployment for about one-fourth of the labor force in the United States. Under such circumstances, most unemployed workers could not help but see general social forces at work in their individual lives. Rather than claiming, "Something is wrong with *me*; I can't find a job," they were likely to say, "The economy has collapsed; there are no jobs to be found!"

People very quickly develop a sociological perspective when the established patterns of society began to shake and crumble. The decade of the 1960s was another period when the sociological awareness of Americans was enhanced. The civil rights, women's liberation, antiwar, and hippie movements all challenged accepted social patterns in a highly visible way. This social climate

American society encourages a belief in the "self-made man," which may explain our tendency to perceive disadvantaged people as personally undeserving.

called attention to the ways in which personal experiences were being shaped by forces beyond people themselves: the political, economic, military, and technological elements of "the system." Although the merits of these movements may be debated, it is indisputable that, by pointing to social forces that affect the lives of all Americans, they all contained an element of the sociological perspective.

As these everyday examples suggest, an introduction to sociology is an invitation to learn a new way of looking at patterns of social life that have become so familiar that they are almost invisible. At this point, we might well consider whether this invitation is worth accepting. In other words, what are the benefits to you of learning to use the sociological perspective?

The Benefits of the Sociological Perspective

The benefits of studying sociology are not likely to be exactly the same for everyone. The specific knowledge that has been amassed within sociology is immense and can be readily applied to our lives in countless ways. There are, however, four general ways in which the sociological perspective can enrich our lives.

The first benefit is epitomized by Peter Berger's (1963) assertion that society is often not what it appears to be. In every society in the world, people come to accept as "true" certain ideas and perceptions of themselves. Whether or not these perceptions are factual, they form the basis of people's reality. *The sociological perspective challenges our familiar understandings of the world, so that we can take a new and critical look at what has been assumed to be "true."*

For Americans, one important example of a widespread "truth" is what may be called the belief in the "autonomous individual." This means that we tend to think that people live rather independently of one another, and that they are personally responsible for whatever fate may befall them. Furthermore, Americans tend to emphasize the importance of success in terms of having a comfortable home, a respectable occupation, and a high income. As a result, we often praise particularly successful people as being somehow "better" than those who have not fared as well. They are thought to work harder and, perhaps, to be more intelligent. On the other side of the coin, people who do not measure up to the American view of "success" are perceived as personally undeserving and less able. A sociological approach encourages us to ask whether these beliefs are actually true and, to the extent that they are not, why they are so widely held.

We have already provided evidence that individuals are not nearly as autonomous as American common sense suggests. To a large degree, the relative success of any American is shaped by such factors as sex, race, age, and social background. This means that taking a highly individualistic view of society will lead to giving too much credit to some people for their achievements, just as it encourages the unrealistic practice of blaming others for their apparent "personal failures." We may also wonder if the American conception of "success" is the only ground on which to judge others, as well as to judge ourselves.

The second benefit of learning to use the sociological perspective follows from the fact that the earth is host to a remarkable variety of human social life. North Americans represent only about 5 percent of the world's population, and, as Chapter 3 explains, throughout the rest of the world people live in ways that differ dramatically from our own. Therefore, as Joel Charon (1982) suggests, the sociological perspective reveals that to be different from others is not to be "wrong" in any absolute sense. Within any society, people form conceptions of the proper way to live. But taking historical and cross-cultural variations into account, there are countless competing versions of what is proper. *The sociological perspective reveals to us the vast range of human diversity.* This recognition is the first step toward making personal decisions about how to live our own lives.

The third benefit provided by the sociological perspective involves understanding that—right or wrong—American society operates in a particular and deliberate way. No one is able to live with complete disregard for society's "rules of the game." In the game of life, we may decide how to play our cards, but it is society that deals us the hand. The more effective player is generally one who better understands how the game works. Here again, sociology is valuable. *The sociological perspective allows us to understand the constraints and opportunities that affect our lives.* Knowledge of this kind is power. Through it, we come to understand what we are likely and unlikely to accomplish for ourselves, and we are able to see how the goals we adopt can be realized more effectively.

The fourth benefit of the sociological perspective involves the impact that any individual can have on the larger society. Those who have little awareness of how society operates tend to passively accept the status quo. *The sociological perspective enables us to be more active participants in society.* For some, this may mean embracing society as it is; others, however, may try to change society in some regard. The discipline of sociology advocates no one particular political orientation. Indeed, sociologists are widely spread across the political spectrum. But evaluating any aspect of society depends on the ability to identify social forces and to assess their consequences. Some thirty years ago, C. Wright Mills (1959) pointed out the importance of what he termed the *sociological imagination* in helping people to actively confront the forces of society. The box explains further.

THE ORIGINS OF SOCIOLOGY

Having described sociology's distinctive perspective, we can turn to the history of the discipline. Sociology is one of the youngest academic disciplines—far younger than history, physics, or economics, for example. It was only about 150 years ago that many new ideas about society began coming together to form a systematic discipline that studies society. Auguste Comte, a French social thinker, gave the discipline its name in 1838; he is widely regarded as "the father of sociology."

People have had a deep interest in society since the beginning of human history, but the sociological perspective is a relatively recent development, as is the scientific approach to knowledge on which sociological research is based.

Science and the Development of Sociology

The nature of society was an issue of major importance in the writings of brilliant thinkers of the ancient world, including the Greek philosophers Plato (427–347 B.C.E.) and Aristotle (384–322 B.C.E.).* Similarly, the Roman emperor Marcus Aurelius (121–180), the medieval theologian St. Thomas Aquinas (*c.* 1225–1274), the great English playwright William Shakespeare (1564–1616), and a host of others reflected about human society in their writings. Yet, as Emile Durkheim noted toward the end of the last century, none of these social thinkers approached society with a sociological point of view.

> Looking back in history . . . we find that no philosophers ever viewed matters [with a sociological perspective] until quite recently. . . . It seemed to them sufficient to ascertain what the human will should strive for and what it should avoid in established societies. . . . [T]heir aim was not to offer us as valid a description of nature as possible, but to present us with the idea of a perfect society, a model to be imitated. (1972:57; orig. 1918)

In other words, prior to the birth of sociology, philosophers, theologians, and other thinkers were primarily concerned with imagining the "ideal" society. Some, of course, wrote to provoke their audiences to think about the world, or merely to entertain. But none attempted an analysis of society *as it was.* This is what marked the birth of sociology: pioneers of the discipline such as Auguste Comte and Emile Durkheim reversed these priorities. Although they were certainly concerned with how human society could be improved, their major goal was to understand how society actually operates.

The key to distinguishing between understanding what society *ought to be* and what society *is* lies in the

---

*Throughout this text, the abbreviation B.C.E. designates "before the common era." This terminology is used in place of the traditional B.C. (meaning "before Christ") as a reflection of the religious plurality of American society. Similarly, in place of the traditional A.D. (*anno Domini*, or "in the year of our Lord"), the abbreviation C.E. ("common era") is employed.

Understanding Society: The Key to Understanding Ourselves

The American sociologist C. Wright Mills (1916–1962) described the perspective of sociology as "the sociological imagination." He maintained that this new point of view benefits individuals by helping them to see how their personal lives are shaped by larger social forces. In short, Mills argued, we cannot fully understand ourselves without understanding the society in which we live.

When a society becomes industrialized, a peasant becomes a worker; a feudal lord is liquidated or becomes a businessman. When classes rise or fall, a [person] is employed or unemployed; when the rate of investment goes up or down, a [person] takes new

heart or goes broke. When wars happen, an insurance salesman becomes a rocket launcher; a store clerk, a radar man; a wife lives alone; a child grows up without a father. Neither the life of an individual nor the history of a society can be understood without understanding both.

Yet [people] do not usually define the troubles they endure in terms of historical change. . . . The well-being they enjoy, they do not usually impute to the big ups and downs of the society in which they live. Seldom aware of the intricate connection between the patterns of their own lives and the course of world history, ordinary [people] do not usually know what this connection means for the kind of [peo-

ple] they are becoming and for the kinds of history-making in which they might take part. They do not possess the quality of mind essential to grasp the interplay of [individuals] and society, of biography and history, of self and world. . . .

What they need . . . is a quality of mind that will help them to [see] . . . what is going on in the world and . . . what may be happening within themselves. It is this quality . . . that . . . may be called the sociological imagination.

SOURCE: C. Wright Mills, *The Sociological Imagination* (New York: Oxford University Press, 1959), pp. 3–5.

---

development of a scientific approach to knowing. As Chapter 2 describes in detail, there are many ways to understand the world. During the medieval period in Europe, people's view of humanity was heavily shaped by religion. Society was widely held to be an expression of God's will—at least insofar as human beings, under the guidance of the church, were capable of fulfilling a divine plan. Gradually, however, science—based on identifying facts through systematic observation—was growing in importance. Through the efforts of early scientists such as the Polish astronomer Copernicus (1473–1543), the Italian astronomer and physicist Galileo (1564–1642), and the English physicist and mathematician Sir Isaac Newton (1642–1727), a scientific understanding of the natural world emerged. Not surprisingly, within a century after Newton, sociology became established as a scientific approach to the study of society.

Reflecting on the origins of scientific sociology, Comte (1975; orig. 1851–1854) suggested that organized efforts to understand the world have historically become more scientific as they have progressed through three stages of development. In his "law of the three stages," Comte identified these stages as theological, metaphysical, and scientific.

In the study of society, the earliest, *theological stage* is based on understanding society as a reflection of supernatural forces such as the will of God. The belief in a divine plan for human society dominated the ancient world and most of the feudal period of European history.

During the final centuries of the feudal era in Europe, the theological approach to society gradually gave way to what Comte termed the *metaphysical stage*, in which abstract forces (such as "human nature") were thought to confer a basic character on society. The metaphysical approach to understanding society is exemplified by the writings of the English philosopher Thomas Hobbes (1588–1679), who suggested that society was a reflection of a human nature that was innately selfish. Notice that both the theological and the metaphysical approaches do not focus attention on society itself, but on factors that are believed to shape society—God's will in the theological view, and human nature in the metaphysical.

The last few centuries have seen the dawning of what Comte characterized as the final, *scientific stage* in humanity's long quest to understand society. Comte believed that a scientific approach focuses attention di-

Auguste Comte (1798–1857)

Growing up in the shadow of the French Revolution, which brought sweeping changes to France, was certainly reason enough to become fascinated with society. Thus Auguste Comte soon left a conservative, small-town family and journeyed to Paris. There he spent most of his life observing and reflecting on the human drama that was all around him. From the Greek and Latin words meaning "the study of society," Comte described his work as "sociology."

The twin foundations of Comte's work were to use science to understand how society operates, and then to apply this knowledge to the practical task of social reform. During his lifetime, scientists were becoming increasingly sophisticated in studying nature. Why not, Comte reasoned, apply the same scientific methods to understanding human society?

Clearly, Comte believed that social laws characterize society just as nature is governed by physical laws. The search for these social laws led him to focus on what he called *social statics*—how society operates as a cohesive system of many interrelated parts—and *social dynamics*—how society changes in an orderly way.

Few sociologists today would agree that society operates according to absolute and invariable laws comparable to those of nature. Yet most sociologists do accept that the study of society should be concerned with both social stability and social change. Most sociologists also agree that sociology should be based, as much as possible, on scientific methods.

---

rectly on society instead of on external forces that, in earlier eras, were believed to be the cause of social patterns. The scientific approach is based on the assertion that society, like the physical world, operates according to its own internal forces and patterns. Comte looked forward, therefore, to nothing less than a gradual understanding of all the laws of social life. This approach is often called **positivism,** which may be defined as *the assertion that science, rather than any other type of human understanding* (such as religious faith), *is the path to knowledge.*

When sociology became established as an academic discipline in the United States at the beginning of this century, early sociologists such as Lester Ward (1841–1913) were strongly influenced by Comte's ideas. Even today, more than a century after Comte's death, most sociologists continue to view science as a crucial element of sociology. But many contemporary sociologists caution that science cannot be applied to the social world in the same way that it is applied to the physical world. As we shall explain in Chapter 2, the causes of human behavior are often far more complex than the causes of events in the natural world. In other words, human beings are more than physical objects; they are creatures with considerable imagination and spontaneity whose behavior can never be fully explained by any scientific "laws of society."

Social Change and the Development of Sociology

The gradual development of science in Europe was one important foundation of sociology. But something more was involved: revolutionary change in European society itself (Nisbet, 1966). The increasing importance of science is but one dimension of the modernization of Europe. Social change is continuous, of course, but European societies experienced striking transformations during the seventeenth and eighteenth centuries. In the midst of especially rapid social change, people were less likely to take society for granted. Indeed, as the social ground shook under their feet, they focused more and more on society, which stimulated the emergence of the sociological perspective.

Revolutionary change at this time involved three related dimensions. First, various technological innovations in eighteenth-century Europe led to the appearance of factories. This new way of producing material goods soon gave rise to an *industrial economy*. Second, factories located within cities drew millions of people from the countryside, where agriculture had been the traditional livelihood. As a result, the growth of industry was accompanied by the explosive *growth of cities*. Third, the development of the economy and the growth of cities were linked to changes in *political ideas*. We shall briefly describe these three dimensions in turn.

The rise of the industrial economy.   During the Middle Ages in Europe, people who were not working in agriculture typically worked at home in small-scale *manufacturing* (a word derived from Latin words meaning "to make by hand"). Thus homes were more than residences; they were also centers of commercial endeavors such as baking, making furniture, and sewing garments. Early in the eighteenth century, something new appeared in England—the factory. Factories were centers of production in which new sources of energy, including steam power, were harnessed to large machines. Various material goods began to be mass produced rather than being made by hand one at a time.

Factories became the core of an expanding industrial economy, causing changes that were broader still. As factories spread throughout Europe, they shook the medieval society to its foundations. One important change was the gradual demise of life within small, highly personal villages. As historian Peter Laslett points out, there had been almost no impersonal relationships in medieval society: "There were no hotels, hostels, or blocks of flats for single persons, very few hospitals and none of the kind we are familiar with, almost no young men and women living on their own" (1984:11). Although societies in medieval Europe were certainly characterized by conflict as well as cooperation, their social world was exceedingly personal. People lived and worked within small communities in which traditions were well established and the inhabitants knew one another personally.

The coming of factories, however, drew people from all across Europe to the growing cities, where jobs were more plentiful. Here they became part of a largely anonymous industrial work force. Instead of working within the personal relationships of the family, they now worked for strangers—the owners and managers who controlled the factories.

The overall result of the development of the industrial economy was the breakdown of a long-established way of life within countless small communities. As factories drew people from the countryside, cities began to grow rapidly.

The growth of cities.   The factories that sprouted across England and other areas of Western Europe became

The Industrial Revolution drew people in Europe and North America away from small towns to large industrial cities. This disruption of traditional social patterns stimulated the development of the discipline of sociology.

magnets attracting people in need of work. As the English textile industry grew in importance, land previously used for farming was transformed into grazing land to raise sheep—the source of wool. In the process of what is known as the "enclosure movement," countless people were pushed from the countryside and flooded into the cities in search of employment in factories.

Not surprisingly, industrial cities rapidly grew to unprecedented size. Most medieval European cities had been small towns by today's standards: small, self-contained worlds built within defensive walls. Even by 1700, at the beginning of the industrial era, London was the largest city in Europe with a population of only about 500,000. Within two centuries, however, London's population grew *thirteen times* larger, reaching almost 6.5 million (Chandler & Fox, 1974). Manchester, another of England's early industrial cities, grew almost fivefold during the first half of the nineteenth century. Similar urban growth took place across the European continent as cities became centers of the new industrial economy.

Life within these expanding cities was markedly different from life in the hinterland. Not only was the environment far less personal, but the tremendous influx of people simply overwhelmed the capacity of cities to absorb them. Widespread social problems—including pollution, crime, and inadequate housing—fostered concern about the state of society, further stimulating the development of the sociological perspective. The great English writer Charles Dickens was keenly aware of the changes (not all of which were for the better) wrought by the explosive growth of cities. The box provides an excerpt from one of his novels of that time.

Political changes.   As we noted earlier, medieval society was widely viewed as an expression of divine will. The feudal nobility claimed to rule by "divine right," and the entire social order was understood as the natural expression of God's plan for humanity. Under these circumstances, social patterns were largely taken for granted. Relationships within the family and the social ties that linked lord and serf, priest and parishioner, were as little noticed as the air people breathed (Nisbet, 1966:108). Political ideas were largely a matter of identifying the moral obligation of each person to others, depending on the individual's position in the larger scheme of life. Such a view of society is clearly evident in lines from the old Anglican hymn "All Things Bright and Beautiful":

> *The rich man in his castle,*
> *The poor man at his gate,*
> *He made them high and lowly*
> *And ordered their estate.*

In the midst of these marked changes in the economy and the rapid growth of cities, changes in political thought were inevitable. In contrast to the political conservatism that had characterized the medieval era, from the sixteenth century onward critics maintained a spirited attack on the view that society was an expression of divine will. The character of society, and the responsibilities of the individuals who composed it, became matters of intense debate. In the writings of English thinkers such as Thomas Hobbes (1588–1679), John Locke (1632–1704), and Adam Smith (1723–1790), we find less concern with the moral obligations of individuals to society,

SOCIETY IN HISTORY

London: Urban Chaos and the Sociological Perspective

In this selection from one of his well-known novels, Charles Dickens reveals how the striking changes in nineteenth-century Europe fostered growing awareness of society, often in terms of explicit social criticism.

[Harriet Carker] often looked with compassion, at such a time, upon the stragglers who came wandering into London, by the great highway hard-

by, and who, footsore and weary, and gazing fearfully at the huge town before them, as if foreboding that their misery there would be but as a drop of water in the sea, or as a grain of sea-sand on the shore, went shrinking on, cowering before the angry weather, and looking as if the very elements rejected them. Day after day, such travellers crept past, but always, as she thought, in one direction—always towards the town. Swallowed up

in one phase or other of its immensity, towards which they seemed impelled by a desperate fascination, they never returned. Food for the hospitals, the churchyards, the prisons, the river, fever, madness, vice, and death—they passed on to the monster, roaring in the distance, and were lost.

SOURCE: Charles Dickens, *Dombey and Son* (London: Oxford University Press, 1974; orig. 1848), p. 462.

and an increasingly pronounced view of society as the product of individual self-interest. The key phrases in the new political climate were *individual liberty* and *individual rights*. The Declaration of Independence—the document celebrating the separation of the American colonies from England and strongly reflecting the ideas of John Locke—is a clear statement of these new political ideas; it holds that all people have "certain unalienable rights," including "life, liberty, and the pursuit of happiness." The political revolution in France that began soon afterward in 1789 was, of course, an even more dramatic effort to break with political and social traditions.

These changes—the rise of an industrial economy, explosive urban growth, and revolutionary political ideas—were important dimensions of the rapid transformation of the Western world from medieval traditionalism to modernity. As he surveyed his own society after the French Revolution, the French social and political thinker Alexis de Tocqueville was guilty of only slight exaggeration when he exclaimed that these changes had amounted to "nothing short of the regeneration of the whole human race" (1955:13; orig. 1856). Because the familiar world of the past had altered so quickly and so dramatically into the strange world of modernity, people had become much more aware of the social forces affecting their personal lives.

In this context, it is easy to see why Auguste Comte and other pioneers soon developed the new discipline of sociology. Similarly, there is little surprise that sociology developed *where* it did. Rather than arising everywhere in Europe, sociology was stimulated most in precisely those societies that had experienced the social changes we have described to the greatest extent. In France, Germany, and England—where social transformation had been truly revolutionary—sociology flowered by the end of the nineteenth century. Conversely, in societies touched less by these momentous events—including Portugal, Spain, Italy, and Eastern Europe—there was little development of the sociological perspective.

Many of the crucial ideas within the discipline of sociology can also be traced to rapid social change. Many, if not most, of the early sociologists found the drastic social changes in Europe to be deeply disturbing. One response—illustrated by the ideas of Comte—was conservative, fearing that people, overpowered by change and uprooted from long-established local communities, were losing the traditional supports of family, community, and religion. Sociologists who followed Comte's

lead took strong exception to those who viewed society as simply an expression of individual self-interest. Rather, these sociologists maintained, social bonds such as family and neighborhood were the basic units of society. It would have made no more sense to Comte to think of society only in terms of individuals than it would to us to think of this book only in terms of its component atoms. In short, Comte shared with many other early sociologists a belief that society is a complex whole that is more than just the people it contains.

Another response to the massive changes we have described was more radical, as illustrated by the writings of the German social thinker Karl Marx (1818–1883), whose ideas are introduced at length in Chapter 4. Sociologists who have been influenced by Marx have also been critics of modern social patterns. In their case, however, the concern is not over the dissolution of traditional social patterns so much as over the fact that the great wealth produced by the Industrial Revolution has remained in the hands of a small proportion of people.

Clearly, there are differences between the political positions implied by the ideas of Auguste Comte and Karl Marx. But, for the present, notice what they have in common. As sociologists, they shared—and sociologists today continue to embrace—a focus not on individuals so much as on the social patterns that link people into an ongoing society. The major topics of sociology that are explored in subsequent chapters of this book—including culture, social class, race, ethnicity, gender, the family, and religion—are all concerned with the ways in which individuals are joined—and also divided—within the larger arena of society.

In sum, the birth of sociology, its scientific method of study, and its emphasis on social patterns rather than on the individual are all related to the historical changes that shaped the modern world.

SOCIOLOGICAL THEORY

As indicated earlier in this chapter, the discipline of sociology involves more than a distinctive point of view. The sociological perspective provides new insights into countless familiar situations; but linking specific observations together in a meaningful way involves another element of the discipline, theory. In the simplest terms, a **theory** is *an explanation of the relationship between two or more specific facts*. To illustrate the use of theory in sociology, recall Emile Durkheim's study of suicide.

Durkheim attempted to explain why some categories of people (males, Protestants, the wealthy, and the unmarried) have higher suicide rates than others (females, Catholics, the poor, and the married). To do so, he linked one set of facts—suicide rates—to another set of facts—the level of social integration characteristic of these various categories of people. Through systematic comparisons, Durkheim was able to develop a theory of suicide, namely, that people with low social integration are more prone to take their own lives.

To provide another illustration, how might we explain the sociological observation that college science courses in the United States typically contain more men than women? One theoretical approach would suggest that the sciences are more attractive to males than to females; perhaps males simply have a greater innate interest in science. Another possibility is that American society encourages males to develop an interest in science while simultaneously discouraging this interest in females. A third theoretical approach would suggest that the educational system has some formal or informal policy that limits the enrollment of women in science courses.

As this example shows, there is usually more than one theoretical explanation for any particular issue. Therefore, the ability to link facts together into a meaningful theory does not in itself mean that the theory is correct. In order to evaluate contrasting theories, sociologists make use of various methods of scientific research, which will be described in detail in Chapter 2. As sociologists use these scientific methods to gather more and more information, they are able to confirm some theories while rejecting or modifying others. In the early decades of this century, for example, several sociologists interested in the rapid growth of cities developed theories that linked city living to distinctive patterns of human behavior, such as pronounced impersonality and even mental illness. As we shall explain in Chapter 20, however, research completed during subsequent decades has found that living in a large city does not necessarily result in social isolation, nor does it diminish mental health. Within any discipline, therefore, theory is never static; because sociologists are continually carrying out research, sociological theory is always being refined.

In attempting to develop theories about human society, sociologists face a wide range of choices. What issues should they choose to study? What facts should they link together to form theories? Questions such as these are not answered in a haphazard fashion; rather, theory building is guided by a general framework that sociologists call a theoretical paradigm. Following the ideas of George Ritzer (1983), a **theoretical paradigm** is *a fundamental image of society that guides sociological thinking*.

As our earlier discussion of the ideas of two of sociology's founders—Auguste Comte and Karl Marx—suggested, not all sociologists base their work on the same image of society. Some emphasize the fact that societies often remain remarkably stable over time; others focus on social change. Similarly, while some direct attention to ways in which people are united through their common membership in a single society, others emphasize how society divides people according to sex, race, or social class. Moreover, while some sociologists define their goal as explaining the operation of society as it exists, others encourage what they consider to be desirable social change. Finally, while some sociologists address the operation of society as a whole, others find the patterns of individual interaction within specific situations more interesting.

In short, all sociologists do not agree about what the most interesting or useful questions are, and even when they do agree on the questions, they often disagree on the answers. This does not mean, however, that sociological theory is utter chaos, because sociologists tend to organize their work by using one or more of three major theoretical paradigms.

The Structural-Functional Paradigm

The **structural-functional paradigm** is *a theoretical framework based on the view of society as a system of many different parts that work together to generate relative stability*. As its name suggests, this theoretical paradigm has two components. First, it assumes that society is composed of **social structure**, defined as *relatively stable patterns of social behavior*. The most important social structures are major parts of society such as the family, religion, politics, and the economic system. Second, each element of social structure is understood within this paradigm in terms of its **social functions,** which refer to *consequences for the operation of society as a whole*. Thus each part of society has one or more important functions that are necessary for the society to persist, at least in its present form.

It should be evident that the structural-functional paradigm is partly rooted in the ideas of Auguste Comte. Another who advanced this theoretical approach was the English sociologist Herbert Spencer (1820–1903). Spencer was a serious student of both the human organ-

Herbert Spencer (1820–1903)

Herbert Spencer was born in the midst of the Industrial Revolution that was transforming England. The rapid changes of the time led him to devote much of his life to the study of society.

Spencer shared with Auguste Comte a belief that society operated according to fixed laws, as well as a desire to understand these laws through scientific research. Spencer's view of society was also deeply influenced by his contemporary, Charles Darwin (1809–1882), who proposed that living organisms evolve over time to better survive in their environment. Similarly, Spencer believed societies would evolve according to the principle of "the survival of the fittest"—a phrase widely attributed to Darwin but actually first used by Spencer. This view of society, which came to be known as *social Darwinism*, was based on the idea that, over many generations, the most intelligent, ambitious, and productive people would survive, while those who were less able would die out. This led Spencer to foresee a society that steadily improved according to its own evolutionary operation.

Ultimately, Spencer found himself at odds with Comte's earlier belief that sociology could be used to guide social reform. Spencer strongly opposed any such efforts simply because he thought they would only interfere with society's own process of evolution. Thus he remained hostile to charity and any governmental action to assist the poor, which he viewed as favoring the weakest members of society and causing society as a whole to deteriorate.

Spencer's views were appalling to some, but they won widespread support among the growing number of wealthy industrialists in England and the United States who opposed government intervention of any kind on behalf of workers and the poor. By the end of the nineteenth century, however, social Darwinism had become discredited, not only as a remarkably heartless view of society, but also as a position with little basis in scientific fact.

---

ism and society, and he asserted that the two have much in common. The human body, for example, has a number of important structural parts, such as the skeleton, the musculature, and the internal organs, which include the brain, heart, and lungs. All of these body parts are *interdependent*, and every bone, muscle, and organ has a function that contributes to the survival of the human organism. In the case of human society, all its elements, especially its social institutions, are interdependent structural parts that function together to keep society operating. A sociologist guided by the structural-functional paradigm is likely to ask such questions as: "What social patterns tend to persist in human societies?" and "How does each pattern function to keep the society operating?"

Several decades after the death of Comte, Emile Durkheim continued the development of the structural-functional paradigm in France. Like Spencer, his English counterpart, Durkheim maintained that each element of society helps society to continue over time. As will be described at length in Chapter 16, Durkheim was particularly concerned with how morality and religion could serve as a foundation of common values promoting social integration.

As sociology developed within the United States, many of the ideas of both Herbert Spencer and Emile Durkheim were carried forward by Talcott Parsons (1902–1979), the major proponent of the structural-functional paradigm in American sociology. Parsons's analysis of society will be described in detail in Chapter 4.

A contemporary American sociologist whose work has largely been guided by the structural-functional paradigm is Robert K. Merton (1910–   ). One of Merton's (1968) important contributions has been to show that any part of society can have many functions, some of which are more readily recognized than others. This idea led him to distinguish between two kinds of functions. The **manifest functions** of any element of social structure are *consequences that are recognized and intended by people within the society.* On the other hand, any part of society may also have **latent functions,** which are *consequences that are largely unrecognized and unintended.* The rapid proliferation of motor vehicles during this century provides a simple illustration of this distinction. The manifest function of a motor vehicle is to transport people and goods from one place to another; this is certainly what people think about when they buy a car or a truck. But motor vehicles also have important latent functions. They allow people to travel about in relative isolation, reinforcing the American emphasis on personal independence. Automobiles also have the latent function of being what we commonly call a *status symbol.* The owners of expensive foreign cars such as Volvos or BMWs, for example, may be perceived as having more sophisticated tastes—and certainly larger bank accounts—than the owners of domestic economy cars such as Cavaliers.

Furthermore, although the structural-functional paradigm tends to emphasize the useful consequences of any social pattern for all of society, Merton points out that not every element of social structure is necessarily useful. In other words, any particular pattern may have **social dysfunctions,** which are *undesirable effects on the operation of society.* One of the dysfunctions of having more than 170 million motor vehicles in the United States is the problem of air pollution, which is especially serious in many large cities. It is also undeniable that

In less than a decade, the Ford assembly line in Highland Park, Michigan, produced over one million automobiles. Although the automobile greatly improved life in North America, cars also proved to have undesirable consequences for American society that few anticipated.

the greater physical mobility afforded by motor vehicles has contributed to a weakening of traditional families, a change that has been lamented by many Americans.

According to structural-functional analysis, any social pattern that becomes predominantly dysfunctional can be expected to change over time. For example, the problem of air pollution created by the use of millions of motor vehicles has resulted in technological changes that have reduced the amount of toxic emissions from each car.

The structural-functional paradigm has had a very strong influence on the discipline of sociology. In fact, until quite recently, structural-functionalism was often described as "mainstream sociology." In the last several decades, however, the structural-functional paradigm has been subjected to increasing criticism. Its critics point out that this theoretical paradigm focuses attention on ways in which society is unified, while tending to ignore social divisions within the population based on such factors as social class, race, and sex. In addition, the structural-functional emphasis on social stability tends to push aside concern for the important process of social change. Both of these criticisms are reflected in the growing importance of another theoretical orientation in sociology—the social-conflict paradigm.

The Social-Conflict Paradigm

The **social-conflict paradigm** is *a theoretical framework based on the view of society as a system characterized by social inequality and social conflict that generate social change.* As this definition indicates, the social-conflict paradigm is based on an image of society that differs considerably from that of structural-functionalism. The structural-functional paradigm views society as a relatively stable, well-integrated system; accordingly, it minimizes the divisive consequences of social inequality. In contrast, the social-conflict paradigm highlights the extent to which society is divided by social class, race, ethnicity, sex, and age. Sociologists guided by this paradigm view patterns of social inequality as resulting from the unequal distribution of valuable resources—money, education, social prestige—among different categories of a population.

The structural-functional paradigm acknowledges that some social patterns can be dysfunctional as well as functional for society. The social-conflict paradigm, however, emphasizes that virtually all social patterns are useful *to some people* while being harmful to others.

To illustrate, consider an issue that will be discussed at length in Chapter 15: the practice in American secondary schools of placing some students in academic tracks and others in vocational tracks. The structural-functional paradigm would draw attention to ways in which society as a whole benefits from providing different types of education to students with different records of academic achievement and varying abilities. This would seem to be useful for everyone in society. The social-conflict paradigm provides a contrasting insight: this practice benefits some and harms others, as it perpetuates patterns of social inequality.

Research in the United States has shown that students placed in college-preparatory tracks are typically from more privileged families. As they eventually become part of the minority of Americans who have a college education, they are likely to enter occupations that will provide them with prestige and a high income, thus extending to their children the privileges enjoyed by their parents. The vocational tracks, however, are often filled with students from less privileged backgrounds, sometimes with little regard for their actual abilities. They receive no preparation for college, and thus, like

Karl Marx stands out as a thinker for whom ideas about the world were necessarily fused with action intended to improve the human condition.

their parents before them, they are likely to enter occupations that provide little prestige and income. Furthermore, research shows that the standardized tests used to measure "academic ability" are often designed and worded in a way that is understood by white people from well-to-do backgrounds who speak standard English, but can be confusing to intelligent Americans of other backgrounds (Bowles & Gintis, 1976; Oakes, 1982, 1985).

In practice, then, the social-conflict paradigm approaches any issue by asking such questions as: "Which categories of people benefit from particular social arrangements? Which lose out?" Insofar as social patterns provide more benefits to some people than to others, this approach leads sociologists to view society as an arena in which the interests of some categories of people are opposed to those of other categories of people. Moreover, dominant categories—the rich in relation to the poor, whites in relation to nonwhites, and males in relation to females—typically attempt to protect their privileges by strongly supporting the status quo. Those with fewer privileges can be expected to counter these efforts by attempting to bring about a more equitable distribution of social resources. This is the basis for social conflict in the United States, which has historically taken the form of strikes and other kinds of labor unrest, the civil rights movement, and the more recent women's liberation movement. Overall, then, rather than viewing society as existing in a state of relative stability, the social-conflict paradigm asserts that society is likely to experience continual social conflict and change.

Finally, many sociologists who make use of the social-conflict paradigm not only attempt to understand society as it is, they also try to transform society to achieve greater social equality. This was the goal of Karl Marx, the social thinker who has had a singularly important influence upon the development of the social-conflict paradigm in sociology. Marx had little patience with those who sought to use science only to understand how society works. In a well-known declaration (which can be seen today on his monument in London's Highgate Cemetery), Marx maintained that "The philosophers have only *interpreted* the world, in various ways; the point, however, is to *change* it."

The Symbolic-Interaction Paradigm

The third theoretical paradigm in sociology differs from the two we have already introduced in a major respect. The structural-functional and social-conflict paradigms share a **macro-level orientation,** meaning *a concern with large-scale patterns that characterize society as a whole.* Both approach society as you might investigate a city from the windows of a helicopter—noting, for example, that highways facilitate the flow of traffic from one place to another, or that there are striking contrasts between the neighborhoods of the rich and the poor. The symbolic-interaction paradigm, on the other hand, has a **micro-level orientation,** meaning *a concern with small-scale patterns of social interaction within specific settings.* To continue the illustration, you might explore a city in this way at street level, noting, for example, social patterns that characterize the interaction of individuals in public parks, or situations in which people may act friendly or indifferent toward one another as they pass on the street. The **symbolic-interaction paradigm,** then, is *a theoretical framework based on the view of society as a highly variable product of the continuous interaction of individuals in various settings.*

The symbolic-interaction paradigm helps to overcome a limitation typical of all macro-level approaches to understanding society. Society is indeed composed of broad social patterns, such as "the family" and "social inequality." Yet in a more fundamental sense, society is based on *people* engaging one another in social interaction. Moreover, human beings do not experience society as an abstract system; to each of us, society is a collection of specific social experiences in our daily lives. Thus the major contribution of the symbolic-interaction paradigm is that it draws attention to the fact that society is composed of the countless everyday social actions and reactions of human beings.

How do the everyday lives of human beings provide the foundation of society? The answer, which will be discussed in detail in Chapter 3, is that people interact with one another in terms of *symbolic* meanings. Only in rare situations do they respond to each other directly, as when someone ducks to avoid a punch. More commonly, human beings respond to others according to their subjective understanding of what they perceive. For example, a poorly dressed man on a city street may be defined as "just a bum looking for a handout," and as a result be ignored. On the other hand, the man could be defined as a "fellow human being in need," which would provoke a different response from passersby. Similarly, a police officer walking nearby may generate a sense of security in some pedestrians and a feeling of nervous anxiety in others. Sociologists guided by the symbolic-interactional approach view society as a complex mosaic of subjective perceptions and responses.

The development of the symbolic-interaction paradigm was greatly influenced by Max Weber (1864–1920), a German sociologist who emphasized the importance of understanding society as it is subjectively perceived by individuals. Weber's approach to understanding society is considered at length in Chapter 4.

From this foundation, a number of sociologists later developed a number of related approaches to understanding society. Chapter 5 includes a discussion of the ideas of American sociologist George Herbert Mead (1863–1931), who explored how the human personality gradually emerges as a result of social experience. Chapter 6 presents the work of American sociologist Erving Goffman (1922–1980). Goffman's approach to understanding society is described as *dramaturgical analysis* because he emphasized the ways in which human beings—like actors on a stage—deliberately act to foster certain impressions in the minds of others. Other sociologists, including George Homans (1910–) and Peter Blau (1918–), have developed an approach to understanding social behavior called *social-exchange analysis.* This is an attempt to identify how individuals interact on the basis of concern for what each one stands to gain and lose from others. In Chapter 14, this approach is applied to the process of courtship, in which individuals typically seek to marry a person who offers to them at least as much—in terms of physical attractiveness, intelligence, and social background—as they offer in return.

The structural-functional paradigm, the social-conflict paradigm, and the symbolic-interaction paradigm are the three major frameworks that guide the efforts of sociologists to develop an understanding of society. Their important characteristics are summarized in Table 1–2. In the examination of any social issue, each theoretical paradigm provides only part of a complete sociological analysis. The greatest benefits come from linking the sociological perspective to all three, as we shall now illustrate by an analysis of the significance of sports in American society.

Sports: An Illustration of the Three Theoretical Paradigms

Sports are a prominent element of life in North America. Almost every American has engaged in some type of sports. From the earliest grades, sports make up part of the educational programs, and many adults continue to participate in sports well into old age. In the United States, the sale of sporting goods is a multibillion-dollar

Table 1–2 THE THREE MAJOR THEORETICAL PARADIGMS: A SUMMARY

Theoretical Paradigm	Orientation	Image of Society	Illustrative Questions
Structural-functional	Macro-level	A system of interrelated parts that is relatively stable based on widespread consensus as to what is morally desirable; each part has functional consequences for the operation of society as a whole	How is society integrated? What are the major parts of society? How are these parts interrelated? What are the consequences of each for the operation of society?
Social-conflict	Macro-level	A system characterized by social inequality; any part of society benefits some categories of people more than others; conflict-based social inequality promotes social change	How is society divided? What are major patterns of social inequality? How do some categories of people attempt to protect their privileges? How do other categories of people challenge the status quo?
Symbolic-interaction	Micro-level	An ongoing process of social interaction in specific settings based on symbolic communication; individual perceptions of reality are variable and changing	How is society experienced? How do human beings interact to create, sustain, and change social patterns? How do individuals attempt to shape the reality perceived by others? How does individual behavior change from one situation to another?

industry. Moreover, millions of Americans observe and discuss sporting events each year. The importance of sports is also evident in the fact that television carries more than three hours of sports into American homes each day, and the results of sporting events are a major part of reports in the news media (Coakley, 1986).

What new insights can the sociological perspective provide about this important and familiar element of American society? Each of the three major theoretical paradigms in sociology provides part of the answer.

The Functions of Sports

Structural-functional analysis directs attention to various functions of sports for society as a whole. The manifest functions of sports include providing a form of recreation and a relatively harmless way to "let off steam," and contributing to the physical fitness of the population. Sports have important latent functions as well, from bringing people together to form social relationships to generating tens of thousands of jobs. But perhaps the most important latent function of sports is fostering specific attitudes and patterns of behavior that are central to the operation of American society.

For example, success in sports depends on developing personal skills through discipline and effort, which are important in achieving success in other areas of social life as well. The ability to engage in teamwork and to play by the rules are other important social skills that are developed through participation in sports and taught by example to those who observe sporting events. Probably most important in American society, sports generate the sense of personal competition that Americans value so much in their emphasis on being a winner (Spates, 1976a; Coakley, 1986). Vince Lombardi once said, "Winning is not everything, but making the effort to win is." He was talking about football, but his words fairly describe a society in which individuals typically strive to advance their own interests—often at the expense of others.

Evidence to support this connection between sports and society is also found by looking at societies other than our own. Those that place less emphasis on personal competition, such as the People's Republic of China, engage in few of the aggressive types of sports so popular in North America. Research has also shown that, among technologically primitive societies, those that are more warlike have more aggressive sports than do those that are more peaceful (Sipes, 1973).

Team sports in the United States have traditionally been a male activity. In recent decades, however, many more females have been participating.

Sports may also have dysfunctional consequences for society. For example, some colleges and universities in the United States are so intent on fielding winning teams that they recruit students for their athletic ability rather than for their academic aptitude. This may adversely affect the academic standards of the school, and also leave the athletes themselves little time to devote to their studies. Len Bias, the University of Maryland basketball star who tragically died from cocaine use in 1986, earned no academic credits at all during the previous semester—a situation far from rare among athletes whose practice sessions may consume four or five hours a day (Bingham, 1987). The tragedy of Len Bias is all the greater because he was one of the few—perhaps one in a hundred male college players—to earn a professional sports contract. For too many others, the long-term benefits of attending college may be meager. As sociologist Harry Edwards points out about his own university, "I've known athletes . . . who are functional illiterates who have been here for four years. If this is going on at [the University of California at] Berkeley, which is supposed to have such integrity, imagine what's going on at the jock-factory schools" (cited in Bowen, 1985:64).

In sum, the structural-functional paradigm illuminates the fact that sports have numerous functional consequences for the operation of society. The most important of these is probably the illustration of important ideas on which a society is based. Within American society, these ideas include the importance of competition and personal success.

Sports and Social Conflict

A social-conflict analysis of sports might begin by pointing out that sports are part of broader patterns of social inequality in American society. Some sports—such as tennis, swimming, golf, and skiing—involve considerable expense, so participation is largely limited to the well-to-do. Not surprisingly, the sports that attract the largest followings—football, baseball, and basketball—are those that are accessible to people of more modest means. In other words, the favorite sports of particular people are likely to reflect general patterns of economic inequality.

Sports within the United States are also overwhelmingly oriented toward males. Sexual discrimination has traditionally limited the opportunity of American females to participate in most sports, even when they have the talent, interest, and economic means to do so. When the first modern Olympic Games were held in 1896, for example, women were excluded from all competition (Mangan & Park, 1987). Until quite recently, girls were barred from Little League teams in most parts of the country. The exclusion of females has been defended by ungrounded sexual stereotypes that claim girls either lack the ability to engage in sports or risk losing their femininity if they do so. Joan Benoit, a gold medalist marathon runner in the 1984 Olympic games, conceded that becoming a serious athlete seemed wrong for an American woman: "When I first started running I was so embarrassed I'd walk when cars passed me. I'd pretend I was looking at the flowers" (cited in Coakley, 1986:115).

Thus we can understand the social pattern within American society by which males are encouraged to be athletes, while females are expected to be attentive observers and cheerleaders. Only a generation ago, few women in the United States and Canada were involved in professional sports, and even today most school sports programs provide more funds to athletic programs for males than to those for females. But the fitness movement and political efforts by women resulting in government legislation have reduced this inequity so that the number of high-school women in sports programs increased from about 300,000 in 1970 to 1.8 million by 1984 (Coakley, 1986:116). In addition, more women now play professionally in such sports as basketball, golf, and tennis. Still, women continue to take a backseat to men in professional sports—particularly in those that provide the most earnings and social prestige.

There is considerable truth to the observation that nonwhites in American society have enjoyed a greater opportunity to earn high incomes in professional sports

Sociologist Harry Edwards has helped officials of professional baseball to recognize and respond to the social barriers that generally excluded nonwhites from management positions.

than in other occupations. This is a relatively recent development, however. In professional baseball, the first of the major American sports to admit nonwhite players, it was only in 1947 that Jackie Robinson broke the "color line." By 1985, however, blacks accounted for one in five professional baseball players, just over half of all football players, and three-fourths of all basketball players (Coakley, 1986:145).

According to sociologist Harry Edwards (1973), the increasing proportion of black males in professional sports is largely due to the fact that individual athletic performances can be measured precisely. For this reason, white prejudice cannot easily diminish the achievement of nonwhite athletes. Nonetheless, racial discrimination continues to shape professional sports in the United States. For example, while nonwhite players are now common, virtually all managers and owners of sports teams are white. In 1987, Al Campanis, a vice-president of the Los Angeles Dodgers baseball team, stated on national television that while blacks are good athletes, they may lack the "necessities" to become team managers and executives. The furor that followed this racist remark revealed to Americans that, forty years after Jackie Robinson's great achievement, nonwhites continue to be excluded from professional sports beyond the playing fields. In 1987, for example, there was not a single black manager in major-league baseball nor a single head coach in professional football (Lenihan, 1987). In response, Peter Ueberroth, the baseball commissioner, recently announced the hiring of sports sociologist Harry Edwards

as a special consultant to help black and Hispanic former players find new jobs in baseball management (Litsky, 1987).

Furthermore, nonwhite players are unlikely to play in the starring positions in professional sports. For example, in 1986, 70 percent of black players in the major leagues played in the outfield (Staples, 1987). Figure 1–2 shows the proportion of white and black players in the various positions within professional baseball, football, and basketball. Clearly, in all three sports, the more central positions have the highest proportion of white players.

On a broader level, the social-conflict paradigm raises the question of what category of people benefit

Participating in a particular sport is not simply a matter of personal choice. The summer Olympics typically include athletic events such as track and field, which are accessible to people of all social backgrounds. The winter Olympics, however, include sports such as figure skating and skiing, which require considerable financial resources. For this reason, nonwhite Americans—more often poor than whites—participate in greater numbers in the summer Olympics.

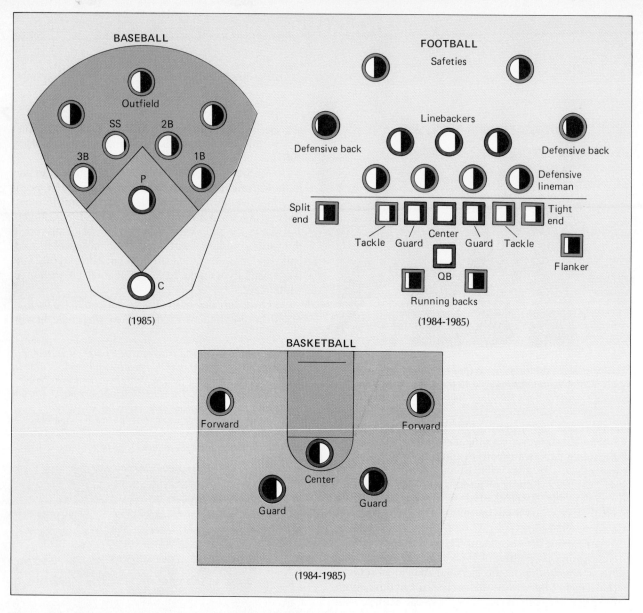

Figure 1–2 Race and Professional Sports: Patterns of Discrimination

These three diagrams indicate the proportion of white and black players in the three major professional sports in the United States. In each case, the central positions—outlined in red—have the highest proportion of white players. (Coakley, 1986)

most from the operation of professional sports teams. Although millions of Americans watch professional sports, the vast profits these teams produce are enjoyed by the small number of people—predominantly white males—who own teams as they would any other piece of property. Though the people living in a city may speak of a professional team as "ours," the reality is that the team is controlled by an owner who would not hesitate to move it to another city in search of higher profits.

In the last decade or so, professional athletes have managed to gain a larger share of the vast profits their sports earn. By the late 1980s, for example, the average salary of major-league baseball players had risen above $350,000—six times more than the average a decade earlier, and far higher than salaries earned by even the baseball greats of past decades. Nonetheless, baseball and other professional sports provide the chance to earn a high income to only a tiny proportion of nonwhite Americans. Furthermore, in all professional sports, the lion's share of both power and profits continues to be held by the few owners.

In sum, the social-conflict paradigm illuminates the ways in which professional sports are characterized by patterns of social inequality. As noted earlier, sports may reflect the importance of competition and achievement in American society, but they also reveal extensive sexual and racial inequality.

Sports as Interaction

Any sports event is also a complex pattern of social interaction. In part, the behavior of participants is guided by their assigned positions and by the rules of the game. But sports, like all human behavior, are also partly spontaneous. For this reason, each game is a unique event that unfolds in ways that cannot be predicted. According to the symbolic-interaction paradigm, sports are an ongoing process rather than an abstract "system."

The symbolic-interaction paradigm also draws attention to the fact that each player is likely to understand the game and other team members somewhat differently. This is especially true with regard to competition—a key element in American sports. Not every individual reacts to a highly competitive situation in the same manner. For people who have very competitive personalities, the heightened pressure that accompanies a sports event increases motivation to perform well. Some may even play the game simply to have the opportunity to compete against—and outperform—opponents. For others, however, love of the game may be greater than the need to be a winner; these people may actually perform less well under pressure. Still others use sports to build personal friendships; they may fear that competition will serve to alienate players from one another (Coakley, 1986).

Although observers tend to think of a team as a single entity, team members are distinct human beings who are likely to interact according to the various perceptions they have of one another—including prejudices and personal jealousies as well as respect. The inclusion of black athletes in professional sports in the United States, for example, did not generally diminish teamwork on the field. However, the interaction of white and black players off the field has often revealed less social solidarity (Edwards, 1973).

A particular player's subjective perception of the game may change significantly over time. Any rookie, for example, can be expected to experience considerable anxiety about entering the big leagues and to feel quite self-conscious during the first few games. In time, however, a more comfortable sense of really being a member of the team may emerge. This process of coming to feel at home in professional sports was slow and agonizing for Jackie Robinson, who initially was only too aware that many white players, and millions of white baseball fans, resented his presence in major-league baseball (Tygiel, 1983). In time, however, his outstanding performance as a player and his polite and cooperative manner off the field won him the respect of the entire nation.

Furthermore, although sports teams are composed of people with varied motives and perceptions of one another, each player is expected to display team spirit and all the other elements of good sportsmanship. Following the dramaturgical analysis of Erving Goffman (1959), we can say that professional athletes typically attempt to conform to ideal expectations of the athlete as honest, hard-working, and, above all, committed to the team's success. In reality, of course, many fall quite short of these ideals. For instance, frequent news accounts since the mid-1980s have documented the involvement of both amateur and professional athletes with illegal drugs. The reputation of many professional baseball players suffered when evidence indicated that some had sold illegal drugs and that a far larger number had regularly played while under the influence of cocaine or other drugs. Mandatory drug testing in sports is, in part, a controversial effort to restore the ideal image of athletes in American society.

In sum, the social-interaction paradigm draws attention to the fact that individuals shape society, just as they are, in turn, shaped by society. Therefore, a sports event, like any social situation, is never entirely predictable. Furthermore, the participants in sports can be expected to have subjective perceptions of the game and one another that vary from person to person and change over time.

As this three-part analysis of sports suggests, sociology involves a distinctive perspective that seeks to identify general patterns in the behavior of particular individuals. Moreover, the discipline has historically evolved several different theoretical paradigms that direct attention to various dimensions of social life. These differences do not imply that any one theoretical paradigm is more right or wrong than any other. For a number of social issues, the application of different theoretical paradigms generates interesting debates and controversies, many of which will be described in later chapters. To understand all the various insights that the sociological perspective offers requires becoming familiar with them all.

SUMMARY

1. Reality is largely a matter of perspective. The sociological perspective provides the means to recognize that the lives of individuals are shaped by the forces of society.

2. Because the sociological perspective directs attention to the fact that general social forces shape particular life experiences, this point of view may be described as "seeing the general in the particular."

3. Emile Durkheim's research on suicide demonstrates that general social forces shape particular life experiences by showing that a highly personal action such as suicide is more common among some categories of people than among others.

4. The impact of social forces on individual lives goes largely unrecognized in American society. Therefore, by revealing the operation of social forces in everyday life, the sociological perspective can also be described as "seeing the strange in the familiar."

5. The sociological perspective sometimes arises naturally. Entering another society is likely to provoke awareness of social forces. Similarly, categories of people who experience social marginality in a society are likely to perceive the effects of social forces more than others do. During periods of social crisis, everyone is more likely to view the world sociologically.

6. There are four general benefits to using the sociological perspective. First, it upsets our familiar understandings of the world, encouraging critical evaluation of "truths" we may have unthinkingly accepted. Second, the sociological perspective makes us aware of the diversity of human social behavior. Third, we come to understand the constraints and opportunities that affect our lives. Fourth and finally, the sociological perspective allows us to be more active participants in society.

7. Auguste Comte gave sociology its name in 1838. While previous social thought had focused on what society ought to be, sociology was based on the use of scientific methods to understand society as it is.

8. The emergence of sociology was also a reaction to the rapid transformation of European society during the seventeenth and eighteenth centuries. The rise of an industrial economy, the explosive growth of cities, and the emergence of new political ideas combined to direct attention to the operation of society.

9. The observations made by the sociological perspective are linked together in terms of sociological theory. This process is guided by each of three theoretical paradigms.

10. The structural-functional paradigm is a framework for explaining how various social structures are integrated and how each functions to promote the stable operation of society as a whole. This theoretical paradigm tends to minimize the extent of social inequality and social change.

11. The social-conflict paradigm is a framework for exploring patterns of social inequality that generate conflict within a society and promote social change. This theoretical paradigm tends to minimize the extent of social integration and social stability.

12. In contrast to these two macro-level theoretical paradigms, the symbolic-interaction paradigm is a micro-level framework for studying patterns of individual interaction within specific situations. At this level of analysis, society is seen as highly variable and constantly changing.

13. The three major theoretical paradigms provide different—and complementary—sociological analyses of sports. The structural-functional paradigm emphasizes that sports encourage patterns of behavior that contribute to the overall operation of society. The social-conflict paradigm links sports to patterns of social inequality. The symbolic-interaction paradigm directs attention to the fact that sports—like all of social life—are based on the partly spontaneous interplay of individual human beings.

14. No one of these theoretical paradigms is more right or wrong than either of the other two. Rather, each directs attention to different dimensions of any social issue. The greatest benefits of using the sociological perspective are derived from applying all three paradigms.

KEY CONCEPTS

latent functions the unrecognized and unintended consequences of any social pattern

macro-level orientation a concern with large-scale patterns that characterize society as a whole

manifest functions the recognized and intended consequences of any social pattern

micro-level orientation a concern with small-scale patterns of social interaction within specific settings

positivism the assertion that science, rather than any other type of human understanding, is the path to knowledge

social-conflict paradigm a theoretical framework based on the view of society as a system characterized by social inequality and social conflict that generate social change

social dysfunctions the undesirable consequences of any social pattern

social functions the consequences of any social pattern for the operation of society

social marginality exclusion from social activity as an "outsider"

social structure relatively stable patterns of social behavior

sociology the scientific study of society and the social activity of human beings

structural-functional paradigm a theoretical framework based on the view of society as a system of many different parts that work together to generate relative stability

symbolic-interaction paradigm a theoretical framework based on the view of society as a highly variable product of continuous interaction of individuals in various settings

theoretical paradigm a fundamental image of society that guides sociological thinking

theory an explanation of the relationship between two or more specific facts

SUGGESTED READINGS

The two paperbacks listed below are readable classics that describe the sociological perspective and the benefits of learning to think sociologically.

C. Wright Mills. *The Sociological Imagination.* New York: Oxford University Press, 1959.

Peter Berger. *An Invitation to Sociology.* Garden City, NY: Anchor Books, 1963.

This paperback provides an introduction to the discipline with an emphasis on the symbolic interaction paradigm and sociology's applications to our everyday lives.

David A. Karp and William C. Yoels. *Sociology and Everyday Life.* Itasca, IL: F. E. Peacock, 1986.

In this book, the author convincingly shows how social forces operate on a disadvantaged segment of American society to promote criminal activity.

Eleanor M. Miller. *Street Woman.* Philadelphia: Temple University Press, 1986.

This recent sociological analysis of suicide in modern Japan supports Durkheim's contention that social forces are at work even in the most personal of actions.

Mamoru Iga. *The Thorn in the Chrysanthemum: Suicide and Economic Success in Modern Japan.* Berkeley: University of California Press, 1986.

George C. Homans, a well-known American sociologist, wrote the following book after retirement to reflect on his discipline, American society, and how his own life was shaped by membership in one of Boston's most privileged families.

George Caspar Homans. *Coming to My Senses: The Autobi-*

ography of a Sociologist. New Brunswick, NJ: Transaction Books, 1984.

The following two books describe the history of sociology. The first is a general intellectual history of the discipline with extensive discussion of sociology's European roots. The second details the development of American sociology at the University of Chicago in the years after World War I.

Martin Bulmer. *The Chicago School of Sociology: Institutionalization, Diversity, and the Rise of Sociological Research.* Chicago: The University of Chicago Press, 1984.

Randall Collins and Michael Makowsky. *The Discovery of Society.* New York: Random House, 1984.

A comprehensive sociological analysis of sports is found in this paperback:

Jay J. Coakley. *Sport in Society: Issues and Controversies.* 3rd ed. St. Louis: Times Mirror/Mosby College Publishing, 1986.

This useful paperback book for the beginning student includes a discussion of theoretical paradigms in sociology as well as information about how to gather data for writing papers:

Pauline Bart and Linda Frankel. *The Student Sociologist's Handbook.* 4th ed. New York: Random House, 1986.

Information about career possibilities and other practical applications of the discipline of sociology is found in the following publication:

American Sociological Association. *Careers in Sociology.* Washington, D.C., 1984.

第三次全国人口普查
簇桥公社锦江大队第一普查组
流动登记站

CHAPTER 2

Sociological Investigation

On a summer afternoon in 1958, a young sociologist on vacation in Maine stopped in Brunswick, the site of Bowdoin College. E. Digby Baltzell was intending simply to look up a few facts in the small college's library when something unforeseen occurred. As he entered the library, he faced full-size portraits of three men who had been among the greatest American achievers of their age: Nathaniel Hawthorne, author of *The Scarlet Letter* and other classic works of American literature; Henry Wadsworth Longfellow, whose famous poems include "The Song of Hiawatha"; and Franklin Pierce, fourteenth president of the United States. All three graduated from Bowdoin College in the class of 1825.

Baltzell is a graduate of the University of Pennsylvania in Philadelphia, a school many times larger than Bowdoin. As he stood in Bowdoin's modest library looking at the fine portraits, his sociological imagination was aroused: "No three individuals of comparable stature had ever graduated from my own university or from any other college in the state of Pennsylvania. Why?" (1979:ix–x)

A routine trip to the library thus opened up a world of questions in the mind of one sociologist: How could such a small college have produced a number of great achievers, the likes of whom had never been seen in the entire history of a far larger, and highly prestigious, university? What historical differences might affect pat-terns of achievement within New England, on the one hand, and Pennsylvania, on the other?

In an effort to answer these questions, E. Digby Baltzell began a long course of sociological investigation, and we shall look at his findings later in this chapter. For the moment, however, we can note that Baltzell's efforts consumed many years of carefully planned research. Using the sociological perspective, he studied the historical differences in patterns of achievement among the natives of the regions surrounding Boston and Philadelphia. The final result of his efforts was the award-winning book *Puritan Boston and Quaker Phila-delphia* (1979), a classic example of sociological thinking.

Baltzell's work illustrates the use of more than the sociological perspective. It is also an excellent example of what this chapter is about: sociology as scientific investigation. Many people think of scientific research only in terms of laboratory experiments involving expensive equipment, but as the account of Baltzell's visit to Bowdoin suggests, sociological investigation is not restricted to a laboratory. In fact, one of the most exciting aspects of sociological investigation is that it can take place almost anywhere, at any time.

We are all continual observers of social life. Standing in line in the school cafeteria, lying on the grass in a public park, or just sitting on the porch watching people walk by—in fact, wherever we may be—we are in a position to observe the social world around us. Sociology offers us a means not only to observe, but also to understand the social patterns of which we are a part.

THE BASICS OF SOCIOLOGICAL INVESTIGATION

Three basic requirements underlie the process of sociological investigation. We have already suggested the first: *Look at the social world surrounding you*. But, as Chapter 1 explained, simply "looking" is not enough. You must become aware of social patterns, seeing general form in the multitude of particular events that make up any social landscape. This occurs as you adopt the second basic requirement of sociological investigation: *Use the perspective of sociology*. As you do so, the familiar world suddenly becomes strange, full of curious patterns of behavior.

Notice how E. Digby Baltzell did exactly this when he entered the library at Bowdoin College. He could have admired the handsome portraits on the wall, then walked over to the bookshelves, found what he was looking for, and gone on his way. But the sociological perspective deepened Baltzell's vision so that something unexpected emerged from an otherwise ordinary situation. This brings us to the third requirement for being a sociological investigator: *Be curious and ask questions. What* are the characteristics of our social world? *How* did they come to exist? *Who* benefits from some particular social patterns? And *why*?

These three requirements—looking at the world around you, using the sociological perspective, and asking questions—are fundamental to sociological investigation. Important as these requirements are, however, they are only the beginning. They make you aware of the social world; they stimulate your curiosity; they get you started asking questions. But then there is the often much more difficult matter of finding the answers. To understand what is involved in finding an answer to a sociological question, we must first consider how we come to recognize any piece of information as being "true."

Ways of Knowing

What do we mean when we say that we "know" something? "Knowing" can, of course, mean any number of things. First, we can know something on the basis

Although science has become central to the world view of most Americans, religion is still the dominant force in the lives of many people, such as these Hasidic boys in Brooklyn, New York.

of personal experience. Caught in a thunderstorm, for example, we would be able to testify to the personal experience of feeling wet. Second, we can also come to know something on the basis of faith—acceptance of a truth that transcends our personal experience (O'Dea & Aviad, 1983). Belief in God, for example, is generally not based on direct personal experience, but most Americans accept the existence of God all the same and express this belief in various forms of religious activity. Third, we come to know other things because some recognized expert attests to their truth. When we want to know how to spell a word correctly, for example, a look in a dictionary will satisfy us because we presume that the editors of a dictionary know how to spell words. The fourth basis for knowing is agreement among people around us about what constitutes the "facts." North Americans "know" that sexual intercourse among young children is wrong, because such activity is held to be a taboo by virtually everyone within our culture. But among the Trobriand Islanders of New Guinea, children may engage in sexual intercourse before they become teenagers, with the approval of their parents. Especially in traditional societies, agreement concerning preferred ways of living is a most important basis of "truth."

Imagine that you are an agricultural expert serving

as a Peace Corps volunteer in the midst of a small, traditional society. Early in your visit, you go out into the fields and observe local farmers placing a dead fish directly on top of the ground where each seed is planted. Curious about this practice, you are told that the fish are gifts to the god of the harvest; your host adds, in a tone of warning, that one year when no fish were caught to use as gifts, the corn harvest was much worse than usual.

According to your host's system of knowledge, the use of fish as gifts to the harvest god makes sense. But, with your scientific training in agriculture, you would probably see a different "truth" in this situation: the decomposing fish fertilize the ground so that it produces a better crop of corn.

Knowledge about the chemical benefits of fertilizer represents science, the fifth basis of knowing. **Science** can be defined as *a logical system that bases knowledge on facts derived from direct, systematic observation.* Instead of being based on personal experience or faith, the supposed wisdom of "experts," or simply general agreement, scientific knowledge is based on **empirical evidence**—that is, *the results of systematic procedures that we are able to verify with our senses.*

This does not mean, of course, that even members of technologically advanced societies routinely reject all ways of knowing except science. A medical researcher seeking an effective treatment for cancer, for example, may still count on her tastebuds to know if she has seasoned a meal correctly, practice her religion as a matter of faith, seek the advice of experts in making financial decisions or in raising children, and derive many of her values and attitudes from those around her. Yet neither her own opinions nor those of others— the basis of what we commonly call "common sense"— are fundamentally important to her work as a scientist. As we suggested in the last chapter, common sense is often an incomplete—and sometimes a misleading— guide to understanding society.

Common Sense versus Scientific Evidence

Here are seven statements that many North Americans consider "true" on the basis of common sense. Each is at least partly contradicted by evidence derived from scientific investigation.

1. *Children from the slums are far more likely to break the law than are children from well-to-do families.* As

we shall see in Chapter 8, young people of all social classes engage in delinquency. Children from less socially privileged backgrounds, however, are more likely to become involved with law enforcement officials. Therefore, their delinquency is more likely to show up in official crime statistics.

2. *The United States and Canada are middle-class societies in which most people are more or less socially equal.* The distribution of income throughout the population of North America is actually very unequal. In fact, the richest 5 percent of the population have more than half of the total wealth in the United States. We shall explore this issue in detail in Chapter 10.

3. *Most poor people do not want to work even though they have the opportunity to do so.* Studies of the poor in America do not bear this out. As we shall see in Chapter 10, most of the poor in the United States are actually children and elderly people.

4. *Differences in the social behavior of males and females are "just human nature."* What we call "human nature" is in fact a product of the society in which we are raised, as Chapter 3 will explain. And, as we shall see in Chapter 12, some other societies' definitions of "masculine" and "feminine" vary from those our society takes for granted.

5. *People's personalities change as they grow old; they lose many former interests and become especially concerned about poor health.* As we shall see in Chapter 13, scientific study of the process of aging reveals that our personalities actually change very little as we grow old. Although the standards of our society may suggest that elderly people should be less socially active, most older people themselves seek to maintain a high level of social involvement. Problems of personal health do increase in old age, but the majority of the elderly do not suffer from serious health problems.

6. *Most people marry because they are in love.* Research has shown that in most of the world, marriage actually has very little to do with love. Moreover, as explained in Chapter 14, in societies that do recognize love as important, people are likely to decide that they "love" someone who is socially defined as a suitable marriage partner.

7. *Our schools attempt to develop the intellectual potential of all children.* Actually, as we shall see in Chapter 15, the opportunities for learning within our schools vary significantly according to the social background of students. Right from the earliest grades, students from more privileged social backgrounds receive better educa-

tions than do others, and college attendance is limited to a minority of our population.

The Value of Scientific Understanding

As adults, we are constantly bombarded by information. Newspapers, television, and our friends tell us "what's what," but unless we are willing to believe everything we read and hear, we must learn to separate what is true from what is not.

Sociology's basis in science provides guidelines by which to judge the truth of various "facts" we encounter. Like all forms of knowledge, science has its limitations, but science does help us evaluate many kinds of information more accurately. Thus, as the perspective of sociology raises questions about the operation of society, science provides a means of finding answers.

THE ELEMENTS OF SCIENCE

Although many ways of knowing are important to our everyday lives, sociology does not accept them as true unless they can be verified scientifically. Sociologists see society in much the same way that natural scientists see the physical world—as composed of identifiable parts that exist in specific relationship to one another. Thinking scientifically, then, every society is a complex system of interrelated parts, each one of which is linked in specific ways to others. As social scientists, we attempt to specify *what* these parts are and *how* they are interrelated.

Taking this approach, a sociologist might ask questions such as:

What segments of the population are most likely to vote in national elections?
Are abused children more likely than others to become child abusers themselves?
Are city dwellers less neighborly than people living in rural areas?

Notice how each of these questions links parts of the social world together. The goal of sociological investigation is to provide specific answers to such questions by gathering empirical evidence.

The following sections of this chapter describe in detail a number of important elements of scientific inves-

tigation. First we shall consider the important ideas of *concept* and *variable*.

Concepts and Variables

Sociology uses concepts to identify the elements that make up a society. A **concept** is *an abstract idea that represents an aspect of the world, inevitably in a somewhat ideal and simplified form*. Sociologists make use of concepts when they describe human beings in terms of their "social class," "sex," "religion," and "ethnicity."

A concept can have a value that varies from case to case, in much the same way that price in a supermarket varies from item to item. When we use the concept "social class," for example, we might designate a particular person as "upper class," "middle class," "working class," or "lower class." When "social class" or any other concept is characterized by varying values, it can also be called a **variable**—defined as *a concept that has a value that varies from case to case*.

Closely related to the use of variables is the process of **measurement**, meaning *the process of determining the value of a variable in a specific case*. "Weight" is a familiar concept that can be used as a variable because its value varies from case to case. To determine the specific value of this variable in your own case, you would engage in a simple process of measurement by stepping on a scale. Many variables in sociology, however, are not so easily measured.

For example, how would you measure something as complex as "social class"? In everyday life, we do this crudely in a number of ways: looking at how a person dresses, listening to patterns of speech, or noting where someone lives. More systematically, sociologists often compile information such as a person's income, occupation, and education in designating a specific social class. But here we face a problem: a variable can sometimes be measured in more than one way. A particular man may have a very high income; on these grounds we might define him as "upper class." Yet he may earn his high income selling automobiles; on the basis of his occupation, then, he would appear to be "middle class." Finally, he might have only an eighth-grade education, which suggests that he be considered "lower class." To resolve this particular dilemma, sociologists may combine income, occupation, and education into a single composite measurement of social class that we shall describe in Chapter 10.

Three Statistical Measures

We often describe a number of people, objects, or figures in terms of averages: the average grade on the sociology exam; our favorite basketball player's average this season; the average American's viewpoint on some issue. Sociologists actually can use three different statistical measures to describe what is average—that is, what is typical for some subject of interest. Assume that we wish to describe the average salary of seven city council members with the following incomes:

$14,250 $64,000
$21,750 $23,000
$23,000 $14,000
$18,500

The simplest of these three statistical measures is the **mode,** defined as *the value that occurs most often.* In this example, the mode is $23,000, since that value occurs twice, while the others occur only once. If each value were to occur only once, there would be no mode; if two values each occurred twice, there would be two modes. The mode is easy to identify; yet because it tells us little about *all* the values, it is rarely used in sociological research.

A more commonly used statistical measure is the **mean,** which is *the arithmetic average,* calculated by adding the numerical values of all cases and dividing by the total number of cases. The sum of the seven incomes here is $178,500, which we divide by 7 to arrive at a mean income of $25,500. Notice, however, that the mean income is actually higher than the income of six of the seven members of the council. This is because one member has an income ($64,000) that is considerably higher than the incomes of the other six. The mean thus has the drawback of being strongly influenced by any extremely high or low value, and will therefore give a somewhat distorted picture of a distribution of values that has any extreme scores. For this reason, sociologists often avoid using this measure.

The **median** is *the value that occurs midway in a series,* that is, the middle case. Here the median income for the seven people is $21,750, since three incomes are higher and three are lower. (If there were an even number of cases, the median would be halfway between the two middle cases.) In this example, the median actually gives the most typical picture of the income of the group as a whole. When a large number of cases is involved, extreme scores are common; since the median is not influenced by such extreme cases, this measure is the one most widely used by sociologists to describe what is average. Throughout this book, you will find the median used to describe a number of variables of sociological interest.

Specifying exactly what is being measured in assigning a value to a variable is called **operationalizing the variable.** This is an important part of all research because how a variable is operationalized (that is, exactly what is being measured) obviously affects what the value of the variable turns out to be. When they report the results of their research, sociologists should carefully explain how all variables used in a study were operationalized so that others will understand exactly how conclusions were reached.

Throughout this book, we shall describe society in terms of many different variables. Of course, we cannot describe everyone as an individual, but we can use statistical measures that efficiently describe a large number of people in terms of a single value. The box introduces several commonly used statistical measures.

Reliability and Validity of Measurement

Careful operationalization of variables is the first step in carrying out useful measurement in social research. But the quality of measurement in science is based on two other considerations, the reliability and the validity of the measurement process. **Reliability** is *the quality of consistency in measurement.* If the social class of the same person were measured several times (by the same or different researchers) and each time the same value was assigned, this measurement would be considered to be reliable. A process of measurement that is not reliable is of little use in sociology—just as a scale that gave inconsistent readings of weight would be useless to a physicist.

Even if measurement does produce consistent results (and is thus reliable), the measurement is not necessarily valid. **Validity** means *the quality of measurement afforded by actually measuring what one intends to measure.* Say you want to measure how religious people are, and decide to do so by asking how often they attend religious services. In other words, you assume that the more often people attend religious services, the more religious they are. Yet this may well yield an invalid picture of "religiosity," because what you are actually measuring is "attendance at religious services," which may have little to do with belief in God or other dimensions of religious faith. While it may yield consistent results (thus being "reliable"), such a measurement may actually measure something other than what we wish (and thus may lack validity). Because the process of measurement is fundamental to sociological investigation, reliability and validity are important issues in all research.

Relationships among Variables

The real payoff in sociological investigation comes from using the logic of science to determine the relationships among variables. Any variable may be related to another in a number of ways. Ideally, scientific investigation seeks to specify the relationship between two variables in terms of **cause and effect,** which means that *change in one variable is caused by change in another.* A familiar cause-and-effect relationship occurs when we put a tray of water into the freezer. The lower temperature causes a change in the state of the water, which turns to ice. In this case, *the variable that has caused the change* (the lower temperature of the freezer) is called the **independent variable.** *The variable that is changed* (the state of the water) is called the **dependent variable.** The value of the second variable, in other words, is dependent on the value of the first. Sociologists often describe variables as "independent" or "dependent" to place them in relation to one another. Keep in mind, however, that *no* dimension of social life can be completely explained by any single cause (or independent variable).

Just because two variables can be shown to be related, however, does not mean that a relationship of cause and effect exists. In some cases, two variables may appear to vary together, while actually neither one affects the other at all. For example, the salaries of professional athletes have risen as the number of automobiles in the United States has also grown; yet these two phenomena are hardly related.

As a more complex example, consider the observation that rates of juvenile delinquency are higher among people who live in crowded housing. In this example, we shall operationalize the variable "juvenile delinquent" to mean a person under the age of eighteen having a police record, and operationalize the variable "crowded housing" to mean living with less than a set amount of square feet of living space per person. On the face of it, we might be tempted to conclude that crowded housing causes tensions that promote juvenile delinquency. Understood this way, "crowded housing" is treated as an independent variable, and "juvenile delinquency" would be the dependent variable. But *does* crowded housing cause juvenile delinquency?

In this case, we know that two variables—the extent of crowding and rates of juvenile delinquency—vary together. *When two variables are shown to vary together,* they are said to demonstrate **correlation.** We know there is a correlation between these two variables, shown in Part (a) of Figure 2–1 on page 35. But does this, in itself, mean that crowding *causes* delinquency? It is possible, but there are other possibilities as well. An alternative explanation is suggested by thinking for a minute about what kind of people may *both* live in very crowded housing *and* be more likely to have police records. In simple terms, the answer is people with less power and choice in our society, the poor. Thus the fact that crowded housing and juvenile delinquency tend to be found together may mean that both factors are caused by the third factor, poverty (Fischer, 1984). The relationship among the three variables is shown in Part (b) of Figure 2–1. When two variables are correlated (in this case, crowding and delinquency), but each is independently caused by some third variable (in this case, income), the two have no causal link to each other. Their relationship is therefore described as a *spurious correlation.*

Identifying a correlation as spurious is often a tricky task, but one that can be solved through the use scientific **control,** in this case meaning *the ability to neutralize the effect of one variable so that the relationship among other variables can be more precisely determined.* In the example we have been using, we might examine housing density and delinquency while controlling the effect of income. In practice, this simply means observing the relationship between delinquency and density for persons of only one income level. In this way, we could see if people of one income level living in more crowded conditions have higher delinquency rates than others of the same income level who are not subject to such crowding. If they do, we will have evidence to support the conclusion that crowded homes do in fact cause

(a)

Density of living conditions ←— Correlation —→ Delinquency rate

If two variables vary together, they are said to be correlated. In this example, density of living conditions and juvenile delinquency increase and decrease together.

(b)

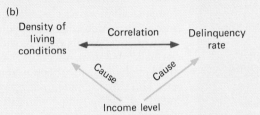

Density of living conditions ←— Correlation —→ Delinquency rate

Cause   Cause

Income level

Here we consider the effect of a third variable: income level. Low income level may cause <u>both</u> high density living conditions <u>and</u> a high delinquency rate. In other words, as income level decreases, both density of living conditions and the delinquency rate increase.

(c)

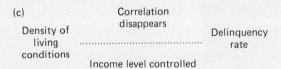

Correlation disappears

Density of living conditions .... Delinquency rate

Income level controlled

If we control income level—that is, examine only cases with the same income level—do those with higher-density living conditions still have a higher delinquency rate? The answer is <u>no</u>. There is no longer a correlation between these two variables.

(d)

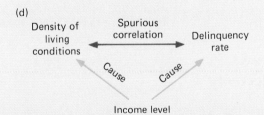

Density of living conditions ←— Spurious correlation —→ Delinquency rate

Cause   Cause

Income level

This leads us to conclude that income level is a cause of both density of living conditions and the delinquency rate. The original two variables (density of living conditions and delinquency rate) are thus correlated but neither one causes the other. Their correlation is therefore <u>spurious</u>.

Figure 2–1 Correlation and Cause: An Example

delinquency. If they do not, we can rule out a cause-and-effect relationship between the two.

In other words, the way to see if an observed correlation is spurious is to hold constant the effects of any third variable that we suspect might be a cause of both the original variables, and then see if there continues to be a correlation between the two original variables. Part (c) of Figure 2–1 illustrates how this might be done. (Researchers have shown that most, although perhaps not all, of the relationship between crowding and social problems does disappear if the effects of income are controlled.) So we have now sorted out the relationship among the three variables, as illustrated in Part (d) of Figure 2–1. Crowded housing and juvenile delinquency have a spurious correlation, and we have reason to think that a higher level of both is caused by a lower level of income.

In summary, correlation means only that two variables vary together in some measurable way. Cause and effect, however, involves not only correlation, but also change in one of the variables actually causing change in the other. To conclude that a relationship of cause and effect exists, three factors must be demonstrated: (1) the two variables are correlated; (2) the independent (or causal) variable precedes the dependent variable in time; and (3) no evidence exists that a third variable is responsible for a spurious correlation between the two.

Understanding cause and effect is the goal of science, but doing so is extremely difficult, even under laboratory conditions. Outside the laboratory a simple incident such as an automobile accident is the outcome of countless causal factors that can never be predicted or controlled.

The Samoa Controversy: Personal Values, Social Science, and Politics

Margaret Mead (1901–1978) is widely recognized as the most important of all American anthropologists. (Like sociology, anthropology is the study of human behavior, but with a focus on preindustrial rather than modern societies.) Mead's influence extended well beyond academic circles because she wrote a number of best-selling books about cultural patterns around the world. Several years after her death, however, her work became the center of controversy. It raises questions about how personal values may shape research, and how research findings are used to influence public policy.

Mead began her career by studying how children grew up in Samoa, an island in the South Pacific. Her research emphasized that, far from being a product of biological maturation, the process of growing up varies significantly from one culture to another. In taking this position, Mead was placing herself on one side of a raging debate as to whether biology or the environment has a greater influence on human behavior.

One of the pioneers of research about human societies was Margaret Mead, who began her study of Samoa in the South Pacific at the age of twenty-three.

At the time of her work, the dominant view among scientists (especially those in the natural sciences) was that human behavior reflected biological forces. There were important political consequences of this view, including the belief that some categories of people were biologically superior to others. Thus, for example, many proponents of this position were strong supporters of legislation restricting immigration to America of peoples they viewed as "inferior."

A leading figure on the other side of the debate was Mead's graduate school professor, Franz Boas. He shared with Mead the belief that environment, rather than biology, is the primary architect of human behavior. Not surprisingly, scientists on this side of the debate feared that what they viewed as false biological doctrine was being used to justify unfair social policies.

Margaret Mead's first book, *Coming of Age in Samoa*, provided powerful support for the environmental side of what came to be known as the "nature-nurture debate" (see Chapter

Identifying cause-and-effect relationships is valuable because it makes possible the scientific goal of using some facts to predict others. In the natural sciences, demonstrating cause-and-effect relationships is sometimes relatively easy, since the use of laboratories can ensure extensive control of a number of variables. The sociologist faces a more difficult task. In a world of countless social forces, to which each of us may react in a unique way, relationships of simple cause and effect are rarely found. Sometimes sociologists must be satisfied with demonstrating only correlation. When relationships of cause and effect can be shown, they are usually complex, involving a large number of variables.

Objectivity

Assume that ten people who work for a magazine in Minneapolis are given the assignment of putting together a story about the best restaurant in that city. With their employer paying all the expenses, they set out for a week of fine dining. When they get together to compare notes, will one restaurant be the clear choice of them all? Perhaps, but that hardly seems likely.

Science requires that all concepts be carefully operationalized in advance. In this case, however, each of the ten people might decide that "best restaurant" means something different. For one, the best restaurant might

5). After concluding that growing up in Samoa was attended by little of the turbulence typical of adolescence in the United States, Mead claimed that environment must take precedence over biology in shaping human behavior. She subsequently made similar claims regarding the significance of sex: environment, and not biology, was responsible for how masculine and feminine behavior were defined. Thus no category of people is innately superior to any other.

Along with the work of other researchers, Mead's research was responsible for the decline of biological views of human behavior by the middle of this century. Yet shortly after her death, another researcher, who had also conducted research in Samoa, claimed that Mead's conclusions did not square with the facts. Derek Freeman, in a stinging criticism entitled *Margaret Mead and Samoa: The Making and Unmaking of an Anthropological Myth*, argues that Mead misrepresented Samoan society by imposing her personal politics on the facts she chose to emphasize. According to Freeman, Samoan society

is not the stress-free way of life that Mead described, but a competitive arena that reflects universal biological forces found throughout the human species.

Scholars are divided as to where the truth lies. To some, Mead was a young (twenty-three years of age when she arrived in Samoa in 1925) and unseasoned researcher who was encouraged by her teacher Franz Boas to go out and find the "ammunition" needed to do battle with those who endorsed a biological view of human behavior. Her conclusions are too "neat," the argument goes, suggesting that she saw only what she was looking for in her research. Thus her work must be viewed as personal politics as much as scientific facts.

To others, Freeman is the villain in the controversy. While acknowledging that Mead's work is not immune to criticism (after all, her Samoa study was completed more than fifty years ago, when research techniques were relatively primitive), her conclusions are held to be mostly sound. It is Freeman, Mead's defenders charge, who is rigidly committed

to a largely biological view of humanity, so that he has put his own "spin" on the facts.

There is, certainly, some truth in both sides of this recent controversy. No doubt, too, personal ambition has played a part: Mead would hardly have wanted to challenge the views of her teacher; Freeman, on the other hand, gained both wealth and fame by attacking the work of a great scientist. On one point, however, there can be agreement: in a political world, complete objectivity is an elusive goal in research, as the potential always exists for results to be colored by the personal politics (and the personal ambition) of researchers.

SOURCE: Based on Margaret Mead, *Coming of Age in Samoa* (New York: Dell, 1961 [orig. 1928]); Derek Freeman, *Margaret Mead and Samoa: The Making and Unmaking of an Anthropological Myth* (Cambridge: Harvard University Press, 1983); John Leo, "Bursting the South Sea Bubble," *Time*, Vol. 121, No. 7 (February 14, 1983): 68–70; and Annette B. Weiner, "Ethnographic Determinism: Samoa and the Margaret Mead Controversy," *American Anthropologist*, Vol. 85, No. 4 (December 1983): 909–919; Lowell Holmes, "A Tale of Two Studies," *American Anthropologist*, Vol. 85, No. 4 (December 1983):929–935.

be a place that serves good home cooking at reasonable prices; for another, the choice might turn on a rooftop view of the city; for yet another, gourmet French cuisine might be the deciding factor. Like so many other things in our lives, the best restaurant may well be mostly a matter of individual taste.

Personal values may be fine when it comes to restaurants, but they pose a problem to scientific investigation. This does not mean that sociologists or other scientists do not have personal opinions about whatever they study; they usually do. But science demands that researchers try to eliminate personal biases that may affect their observations. The scientific ideal is **objectivity,** *a*

state of complete personal neutrality in conducting research. In sociology, however, and in other disciplines as well, objectivity is an elusive goal. Complete objectivity on the part of a researcher is rare (if not impossible), but at the very least researchers should try to become aware of any personal biases they may have and to state them explicitly along with their findings. In this way, readers of the research can exercise appropriate caution in accepting the conclusions.

The relationship between personal values and scientific study was a primary focus in the work of the influential German sociologist Max Weber (1946; orig. 1918). He did not doubt that the personal values of the sociologist play some part in sociological investigation, at least in the selection of topics to be studied. Why, after all, would one person choose to study hunger in America, another to study patterns of political participation in Canada, and yet another to study religious cults? Clearly these topics have personal relevance to those who invest a good bit of their time and energy in studying them. In short, all researchers undertake studies that are *value-relevant*—what has personal significance.

Weber argued, however, that once we have settled on a topic, we must suspend our personal values in pursuit of the facts *as they are* and not attempt to describe the world as we think *it should be*. This distinction between *what is* and *what ought to be* was, for Weber, the essential difference between the world of science and the world of politics. To live up to this ideal of scientific investigation is, of course, no easy matter. Research almost always has political implications, and, like all human beings, researchers may have many strong opinions. But scientists, Weber believed, must have an open mind, ready to accept the results of their investigations *whatever they may be*. Only then can they approach the goal of research that is *value-free*.

Even those sociologists who accept Weber's ideas, however, can never be entirely aware of their own biases. Our social identities affect the ways we think, how we see the world, and what we find to be morally good or socially dangerous. There, too, sociologists are not average people; most are male, white, natives of urban areas, and highly educated. In addition, although the opinions of sociologists cover the full political spectrum, sociologists generally tend to be more liberal than the population as a whole, as well as more liberal than members of many other academic disciplines (Wilson, 1979). As researchers, sociologists of all political persuasions must be on guard against the effects of personal biases on their work. As a consumer of that research, you should be aware of biases introduced by researchers, and also of how *your own* personal biases may influence your understanding of whatever you read.

A common way to limit the distortion to research caused by personal values is **replication** of research, meaning that *other researchers repeat the same study*. If others obtain the same results, we are more confident that the original research was conducted objectively. Perhaps the reason that scientific investigation is called *re*search is the fact that replication is so common. If the original research and the replications are carried out as objectively as possible, with careful use of concepts, clear statements of how variables are operationalized, valid

and reliable measurement, and precise specification of the relationships among variables, then all researchers should reach the same conclusions. If conclusions differ, however, we have reason to suspect that at least one of the studies has been tainted by personal biases. The box describes a recent controversy that illustrates the difficulty of achieving objectivity in research.

SOME LIMITATIONS OF SCIENTIFIC SOCIOLOGY

Science is a tool vital to sociology. But, as Chapter 1 indicated, science developed largely through the study of the *natural world*. Researchers who attempt to scientifically study the *social world* commonly face several problems not encountered by natural scientists.

1. *Since the causes of human behavior are generally more complex than the causes of natural events, sociologists can only rarely make precise determinations of cause and effect. Thus human behavior cannot be predicted with the precision of the natural sciences.* Astronomers are able to predict the behavior of the heavenly bodies with remarkable precision; they know years in advance, for example, when Halley's comet will next be visible from the earth. People, however, have minds of their own, so that no two individuals are likely to react to the same social surroundings the same way. Therefore, while sociologists often speak of "probabilities," they can rarely speak of "certainties"—especially with regard to the behavior of a specific individual.

2. *We all react to the world around us, so the mere presence of sociological investigators may affect the behavior that the researcher is trying to study.* An astronomer can gaze through a telescope at the stars and have no effect whatever on them, but people often react to being studied. Some may become anxious or defensive; others may try to "help" the researcher by providing the answers or actions that they think are expected of them.

3. *Social patterns vary greatly around the world and are constantly changing; what is true in one place or time may not hold true in another.* Atoms and molecules do not consciously shape their environment; human beings do, in remarkably variable ways. The laws of physics hold anywhere and at any time. Our understanding of human behavior, however, must acknowledge human diversity and remain subject to revision as ways of life change over time.

4. *Because sociologists are part of the social world they study, objectivity in social research presents special problems.* Chemists, for example, are not usually affected personally by what goes on in test tubes; sociologists, however, live in the society they study. Therefore, sociologists may face greater difficulties in controlling—or even in recognizing—personal values that may distort their work.

The Importance of Subjective Interpretation

Important as objectivity is in sociological investigation, science cannot eliminate all elements of subjectivity from the work of sociologists. Indeed, as the Margaret Mead–Derek Freeman controversy suggests, complete objectivity in research is an ideal rarely, if ever, achieved. But in the minds of some sociologists, eliminating all subjectivity from research would not be desirable even if it were possible. Two arguments support this position.

First, science is fundamentally a series of procedures—rather like a recipe used in cooking—that guides the work of the researcher. But more than recipes are required to become a great chef; similarly, understanding scientific procedures will never, by itself, produce a great sociologist. In both cases, what is also required is an inspired personal imagination. Robert Nisbet (1970) has pointed out that the source of the greatest human insights has not been science itself, but the lively thinking of creative human beings. Thus the contributions of Albert Einstein as a physicist or of Max Weber as a sociologist result not only from their skillful use of the scientific method, but also from their curiosity and imagination.

Second, science is insufficient for comprehending the vast and complex range of human motivations and feelings, including greed, love, pride, and despair. While science can help us gather facts about human behavior, it can never fully embrace the process by which human beings build a world of subjective meanings (Berger &

This celebrated photograph of a golf swing by Harold E. Edgerton suggests an important lesson about sociological investigation: Analyzing patterns of human behavior is of little value without also understanding the meanings that motivate the action.

Kellner, 1981). Moreover, no scientist's data speak for themselves; sociologists are always faced with the ultimate task of *interpretation*: creating meaningful explanations of the facts that confront them. In this sense, sociology is an art as well as a science.

Politics and Ethics in Sociology

Most sociologists accept Weber's position that, ideally, politics has no place in sociology. Most also agree that Weber's goal of a value-free sociology is more easily stated than achieved. Some sociologists go further, however, maintaining that sociologists cannot, and should not even try to, eliminate the effect of political values on their work.

Alvin Gouldner (1970a, 1970b), for example, has argued that a value-free sociology is an impossibility, a "storybook picture" of social research. All aspects of social life—from national decision making to the everyday relationships between women and men—inevitably have political implications. This is simply because all social life contains the dimension of power, and any particular social arrangement is likely to benefit some people more than others. Thus, Gouldner continues, there is no way to remove politics from social analysis; all research is shaped by political values and has political consequences. But, he concludes, sociologists do have some choice in the matter since they can decide what values are worth supporting. Although this viewpoint is not limited to sociologists of any one political orientation, it is especially strong among those influenced by the ideas of Karl Marx. As noted in Chapter 1, Marx asserted that while understanding the world is important, the crucial task is to change it (1972:109; orig. 1845).

Political considerations of this sort suggest that research does have the power to affect the lives of people for good or ill. Researchers must therefore be concerned with how they conduct their research as well as with their conclusions. The American Sociological Association—the major professional association of sociologists in North America—has published a set of formal guidelines for the conduct of research (1984). As we have already seen, technical competence and objectivity are of paramount importance in conducting all research. Sociologists must also strive to protect the rights, privacy, and safety of anyone involved in a research project. Sociologists are obligated to terminate any research—however useful its possible results—if they note potential danger to participants. In cases of even minimal danger, sociolo-

gists must ensure in advance that all participants understand and accept the risks. All subjects in research are entitled to full anonymity, even if sociologists come under legal pressure to release confidential information. Sociologists must not use their role as researchers to obtain information for purposes other than sociological investigation. Sociologists' work is properly intended to increase our knowledge about society, and not, for example, to assist anyone's political aims or business ambitions. If sociologists become affiliated with any private or public agency, they must disclose this information to those who participate in the research and, in subsequent publications, to the public as a whole. Prior to agreeing to work for any private or public agency, a sociologist must find out what, if any, conditions will be imposed upon the research process. Money or other forms of support should be refused if their acceptance will create pressure to violate any of the ethical guidelines mentioned here.

Research carried out in other societies can raise special ethical problems. The type of inquiry taken for granted in one society may constitute an invasion of privacy in another. Some sociological research may have a bearing on political events in the foreign country; sociologists must not engage in research that might increase tensions within another society or among nations.

Having completed their research, sociologists should report their findings in full, with a precise description of how the study was conducted. They should make their data widely available, so that others have the opportunity to replicate the research. Especially if research may affect public policy, sociologists should clearly indicate their organizational affiliations and sources of funding, attempt to provide all possible interpretations of their data, and point out the limitations of their conclusions (American Sociological Association, 1984).

THE METHODS OF SOCIOLOGICAL RESEARCH

Four research methods are widely employed in sociological investigation. A **research method** is *a strategy for carrying out research in a systematic way*—comparable to a blueprint used in building or a pattern used in sewing. The four methods discussed here are all expressions of the logic of science. They differ, however, in the specific ways in which observations are made and in the kinds of questions they help us answer. No method is always better or worse than any other; each has charac-

Natural disasters, such as the earthquake that destroyed part of Mexico City in 1985, provide opportunities for field research that could never be created in a laboratory.

teristic strengths and weaknesses that make it particularly suitable for certain kinds of research.

Experiments

The logic of science is clearly expressed in the **experiment**—*a method that seeks to specify cause-and-effect relationships among variables.* Experimental research, in other words, is *explanatory* in character, attempting to show what factors in the social world cause change to occur in other factors. Experiments are typically based upon the test of a specific **hypothesis**—*a theoretical statement of a relationship between any facts or variables.* The goal of an experiment is to find out whether or not the hypothesis is supported by empirical evidence. Thus an experiment involves three steps: (1) the dependent variable is measured; (2) the dependent variable is exposed to the effects of the independent variable; and, (3) the dependent variable is measured again to see what (if any) change has taken place.

Conducting experiments requires careful control of all factors that might have some effect upon what is being measured. This is easier to do in a laboratory—an artificial setting specially constructed for this pur-

pose—than in the field. But field experiments have the advantage of allowing researchers to observe subjects in their natural setting. In addition, field experiments can investigate the effects of factors (such as natural disasters) that could never be artificially created in a laboratory (Erikson, 1976). On the other hand, most field experiments are difficult to replicate because similar conditions may never occur again. In comparison, laboratory experiments are relatively easy to replicate.

In the field or in the laboratory, the danger always exists that subjects will change their behavior if they are aware of being part of a research project. In the late 1930s, the Western Electric Company asked a team of researchers to attempt to identify factors affecting workers' productivity at its Hawthorne factory near Chicago (Roethlisberger & Dickson, 1939). The researchers conducted a series of experiments, in one case testing the hypothesis that increasing the available lighting would raise productivity. First they measured the productivity of the workers (the dependent variable), then they increased the lighting (the independent variable), and finally, they measured the productivity of the workers again. As expected, productivity had increased. But then the lighting was reduced and, surprisingly, productivity increased again. The researchers were then faced with evidence that did not support their initial hypothesis; if lighting was not causing the productivity rate to go up, what was?

In time, the researchers realized that simply knowing that their performance was being studied by researchers had caused the workers to increase their productivity. This led sociologists to use the term **Hawthorne effect** to indicate *distortion in research caused by the awareness of subjects that they are the focus of study.*

A Laboratory Experiment: The Stanford County Prison

Social scientists sometimes design experiments within artificially constructed "laboratories" that resemble places generally unavailable for research. The prison system has long been a topic of interest to many sociologists, but opportunities to carry out research within prisons are limited. Philip Zimbardo nonetheless sought to investigate the issue of prison violence and to evaluate common stereotypes about its causes: that prisoners, as criminals, are in jail precisely because they are prone to antisocial behavior, and that prison guards are the kind of people who enjoy pushing others around and who routinely take out their own frustrations on the prisoners.

Zimbardo suspected that such commonsense explanations were misleading. He believed that, placed within the prison setting, even the healthiest and most emotionally stable people would be prone to violent behavior. Zimbardo proposed an alternative explanation in the form of the following hypothesis: *The conditions of prisons themselves—not the personalities of the people involved—are the major cause of prison violence.* Thus the prison itself was viewed as the independent variable capable of causing changes in the dependent variable, human violence.

In order to test this hypothesis, Zimbardo's team of researchers designed a fascinating experiment (Zimbardo, 1972; Haney, Banks, & Zimbardo, 1973). They placed an ad in a local newspaper in Palo Alto, California, offering young men $15 a day to help with a two-week research project. Seventy young men responded; all were local college students from families in the United States and Canada. Each student was given a series of physical and psychological tests. The researchers selected twenty-four people who seemed to be exceptionally healthy, both physically and mentally. Then the men were randomly assigned to two groups; half were designated "prisoners" and half became "guards." The guards and prisoners were to spend the next two weeks in the "Stanford

County Prison," an approximation of a prison specially constructed in the basement of the psychology building on the Stanford University campus.

The "prisoners" were not prepared for what happened next: an unexpected arrest by the Palo Alto police at their homes. They were searched, handcuffed, and taken to the local police station, where they were fingerprinted. Then they were transported to the "prison" on the Stanford campus. There each prisoner met the rest of his fellows, as well as those assigned to guard the prison. The "guards" had been warned about the potential danger of working in the prison, and were told to keep the prison secure at all times. Zimbardo and his associates sat back with a video camera to see what would happen next.

What actually happened was a little more than anyone had bargained for. Within a very short period of time, the researchers could see that the participants were taking their roles all too seriously. Both the "guards" and the "prisoners" began to act so much like stereotypical guards and prisoners that they were quickly losing touch with all they had learned throughout their lives about basic human decency. The guards showed increasing hostility toward the prisoners, insulting them, forcing them to engage in humiliating tasks such as cleaning out toilets with their bare hands, and even physically abusing them. For their part, the prisoners became increasingly self-absorbed and hostile to one another.

Zimbardo's "mock prison" study demonstrated that young men instructed to assume the roles of guards and prisoners soon displayed extreme hostility toward one another.

Within the first four days, five prisoners had to be removed from the study "because of extreme emotional depression, crying, rage and acute anxiety" (1973:81). Before the end of the first week, the researchers had to cancel the experiment because hostility between the two groups had become so intense. Zimbardo explains (1972:4): "The ugliest, most base, pathological side of human nature surfaced. We were horrified because we saw some boys (guards) treat others as if they were despicable animals, taking pleasure in cruelty, while other boys (prisoners) became servile, dehumanized robots who thought only of escape, of their own individual survival and of their mounting hatred for the guards."

The results of this experiment appear to support Zimbardo's hypothesis that the causes of prison violence lie in the social character of prisons themselves, rather than in the personalities of guards and prisoners, as common sense might suggest. The researchers had effectively controlled this variable by carefully selecting in advance only young men who were models of psychological health.

This research is also significant in terms of its political and ethical implications. Zimbardo's findings raise obvious questions about the way we as a society operate prisons, and suggest the need to drastically reform our prison system in order to curb the kind of violence the researchers witnessed. Zimbardo's research also indicates the dangers of subjecting research participants to highly stressful situations that may threaten their physical or mental well-being. Such dangers may not always be predictable (Zimbardo apparently did not expect his research to unfold the way it did) or as immediately apparent as they were in this case. Researchers have an obligation to consider carefully the potential for harm to subjects at all stages of their research and to end a study, as Zimbardo responsibly did, if subjects appear to be psychologically or physically threatened.

Survey Research

A **survey** is *a method of sociological investigation in which individuals provide responses to a series of items or questions*; it is the most widely used of all research methods in sociology (Wells & Picou, 1981). Surveys are particularly useful when we are seeking answers to specific questions, especially when what we want to know cannot be observed directly, such as the political preferences and religious beliefs of individuals, or the private lives of married couples. Because surveys typically involve a number of different variables, they—like experiments—are appropriate for conducting *explanatory research* in which we attempt to specify the relationship among several variables in terms of correlation or cause and effect. Surveys are also commonly used in *descriptive research*, in which a sociologist simply attempts to describe the social patterns that characterize some geographical location (such as an ethnic neighborhood) or some category of people (such as gamblers in casinos).

Population and Sample

In survey research, a **population** is defined as *all the people about whom a researcher gathers information*. We might wish, for example, to discover the proportion of people who have completed college among those living in a particular city. In this case, all the people in the city would represent the survey population. Large-scale survey organizations often seek such information on a national scale. The most familiar examples are polls that are taken during political campaigns. In this type of survey, every adult in the country would constitute the population. Contacting such a vast number of people would require far more time and money than most researchers are likely to have, however. To get around this problem, they use a **sample**—*a representative part of the entire population*—in their study. The precise proportion of a population represented by a sample varies. Polling organizations such as that led by George Gallup (see box on p. 44) are able to represent the entire population of the United States with a carefully selected sample of about fifteen hundred people.

The logic of sampling is really very simple, and is something we use, at least in a crude form, all the time. Imagine walking around at a party and noticing that five or six people are obviously bored to the point of distraction. If you were to conclude that the party is a flop, you would be making an inference about everybody (the "population") on the basis of observing only some of the people (the "sample"). But how can we know if those in a sample actually represent the entire population?

The representativeness of a sample depends on how the members of that sample are selected. Samples are drawn in several ways, but the most common technique is *random sampling*, which is based on the mathematical laws of probability. People are selected from an entire population in such a way that every person has the same chance of being selected. A simple and familiar example of random selection is the operation

SOCIOLOGY OF EVERYDAY LIFE

National Political Surveys

Almost 90 million people in the United States voted in the presidential election of 1984. There was little suspense about the outcome because before the first vote had been cast, election polls had predicted the landslide victory of Ronald Reagan, which was confirmed soon afterward.

Such polls, now a routine part of American politics, provide strong evidence of the accuracy of surveys. On the basis of information obtained from as few as fifteen hundred people, pollsters are usually able to predict the outcome of elections within about 2 percentage points. How can two thousand people tell us how 90 million are likely to vote? The key to accurate prediction is selecting a sample representative of the population as a whole, and pollsters today have highly refined techniques for doing just that.

National polls of this kind have not always been so precise. In 1936, a poll carried out by the *Literary Digest* predicted that Republican Alfred E. Landon would defeat Franklin Delano Roosevelt by a considerable margin. When the votes were in, Alf Landon had actually lost the election by about the same margin as Walter Mondale lost to Ronald Reagan in 1984. The reason for the embarrassingly incorrect results published by the *Literary Digest* was that the magazine's sample was simply not representative of the voting population. The *Digest* mailed survey ballots to some 10 million people (far more than would be included in a poll today), using names obtained from telephone listings and automobile registrations. In doing so, they ran into two major problems. First, the survey return rate was low: only about 20 percent of the people responded. Even more important, the sample was considerably biased. After all, 1936 was a period of severe economic depression; those who had a telephone or a car were more affluent than the average American and therefore more likely to vote for a Republican candidate.

While the incorrect prediction made by the *Literary Digest* did nothing for the popularity of that magazine (which soon went out of business), another poll had accurately predicted the decisive Roosevelt victory. That survey was conducted by George Gallup (1902–1984), who was just beginning his career and who went on to become the best-known national survey researcher in the United States.

SOURCE: Information on Gallup and the *Literary Digest* poll adapted from Earl Babbie, *The Practice of Social Research* (Belmont, CA: Wadsworth, 1983), pp. 141–143.

---

of a raffle, in which the names of a small number of winners are pulled out of a box containing the names of all entries. If every entry did not have an equal chance of selection, we would hardly consider the drawing to be fair. The same general principle applies to random sampling in sociological research. Sociologists, however, are unlikely to create a random sample by pulling names out of a hat; computers are used to randomly select subjects from a population.

Novice researchers sometimes make the mistake of thinking that contacting people haphazardly—by, say, walking up to people on the street—will produce a random sample. This, unfortunately, is not the case. Imagine standing on a city street corner, clipboard in hand, seeking information from people who pass by. Even if you were able to speak with everyone who walked past you, your sample would not represent the entire population because, wherever you were in the city, some kinds of people would be more likely than others to be on that street. Moreover, you would probably find some kinds of people more approachable than others, and there would be some you would positively want to avoid. For a sample to be truly random, every member of the population must have an equal chance of being selected.

Quota sampling, on the other hand, does not make use of the laws of probability. Instead, the researcher purposefully selects sample subjects who have important characteristics typical of the population as a whole. A quota sample would have the same percentages of, for example, males and females, homeowners and apartment dwellers, as the total population. Generally, a quota sample does not represent the entire population as well as a random sample does because it is based on only a limited number of population characteristics, while random selection automatically includes all variations in the population.

Sometimes quota sampling is combined with random selection. In this case, the population is divided into categories (say, males, females, Hispanics, blacks, and whites), and separate random samples are drawn for each category of the population. This technique, called *stratified sampling*, increases the certainty that each category of the population will be included in the sample in the same proportion that it occurs in the population as a whole.

The main advantage of using any sampling technique rather than contacting the entire population is a considerable savings in time and expense. If the sample is carefully selected, we can assume that the results obtained will be representative of the entire population.

Questionnaires and Interviews

Selecting the subjects who will be contacted is only the first step in carrying out a survey. Also required is a specific way to ask questions and record answers. Two commonly used techniques are questionnaires and interviews.

A **questionnaire** is *a series of questions or items to which subjects are asked to respond.* In most cases, possible responses to each item are provided so that answering involves only selecting the best response (the format is similar to multiple-choice examination ques-

tions). Analyzing the results of the survey is easy because the possible responses have been limited by the researcher. A questionnaire that provides such a set of responses to the subject has a *closed-ended format.*

In some cases, however, a researcher might want to let people respond in an entirely free way. In an *open-ended format*, subjects are able to express their responses however they wish, which captures subtle shades of opinion. Of course, the researcher later has to make sense out of what can be a bewildering array of answers.

How to present the questions to subjects is a major decision in every study that uses a questionnaire. Most often, a questionnaire is mailed to respondents, who are asked to complete the form and then to return it to the researcher, usually also by mail. This technique is called a *self-administered survey*. When subjects respond to such questionnaires, no researcher is present, of course; so the questionnaire must be prepared in an attractive way, with clear instructions and questions that are easy to understand. In self-administered surveys, it is especially important to pretest the questionnaire with a small group of people before sending it to all subjects in the study. The small investment of time and money involved can help prevent the costly problem of finding out—too late—that instructions or questions were not clear to respondents.

Making use of the mail has the significant advan-

Self administered surveys, which can be completed by subjects on their own, enable researchers to collect information from many people without the investment of a great deal of time or money. Interviews in the field have the advantage of allowing the researcher to discuss an issue in depth with the subject, but can be time-consuming and expensive.

tage of bringing a large number of people over a wide geographical area into the study at relatively little expense to the researcher. But one drawback of using the mail is the characteristically low rate of returned questionnaires. On the average, fewer than half the people who receive questionnaires in sociological research complete and return them. And even a 50 percent return rate is likely to require follow-up mailings to coax reluctant subjects to return questionnaires. Of course, only subjects who are capable of completing a questionnaire can be included in self-administered research. Young children could not be expected to do so, nor could many hospital patients. Moreover, estimates suggest that perhaps one-third of American adults have too much difficulty with reading and writing to complete a questionnaire on their own (Kozol, 1985a).

Researchers may also make use of the **interview** (sometimes called an *interview-survey*), which is *a questionnaire administered personally to the subject by the researcher*. Interviews are especially useful if the items have an open-ended format, because the researcher can ask follow-up questions, both to probe a bit more deeply and to clarify the subject's responses. The researcher must be sure not to influence a subject's responses, however; sometimes even raising an eyebrow as a person begins to answer a question can be enough to change a response. The advantage of an interview is that a subject is more likely to complete a questionnaire if contacted personally by the researcher. One disadvantage is that tracking people down and personally interviewing them is costly and time-consuming, especially if all subjects do not live in the same area.

Whether or not a questionnaire is personally administered, the way questions are worded can have a surprisingly significant effect on the answers given. Words or phrases that have an emotional impact are sure to influence the subject's response. For example, someone who might agree with the statement "I approve of having my child taught by people representing a variety of political opinions" might very well respond negatively to the same statement rephrased to read: "I would approve of having my child taught by a communist." Similarly, "women who receive public assistance" is more neutral than the phrase "welfare mothers." Sometimes the wording of questions suggests what other people think, and therefore encourages the subject's agreement. People would be more likely to respond affirmatively to the question "Do you *agree* that the police force is doing a good job?" than they would to the question "Do you *think* that the police force is doing a good job?"—simply

because the phrase "do you agree" suggests that most other people endorse the statement. An even more neutral wording of this question might be "How would you rate the job that the police are doing?" In short, researchers should try to avoid any language that introduces a prejudgment or suggests the "correct" response.

Researchers should also avoid questions that are actually two questions in one, for example, "Do you think that the government should spend less money for military defense and spend more for domestic social programs?" The problem here, of course, is that a subject could very well agree with only part of the question, so that saying either yes or no would distort the actual opinion the researcher is seeking.

Surveys at Work: A Study of American Couples

Couples are a basic social unit in most societies of the world. In 1975, two American sociologists, Philip Blumstein and Pepper Schwartz, began a large and complex investigation of couples in the United States: how they make decisions, what importance sex has in their lives, and how factors such as jobs and money shape their relationships. This research culminated in the publication of *American Couples* (1983), a book that provides many rich insights into close human relationships.

Blumstein and Schwartz operationalized the concept *couple* to mean two individuals who (1) live together and (2) have had a sexual relationship for at least some of the time they have been together. Aware that previous sociological research had considered primarily married couples, they enlarged their focus to include cohabiting heterosexual couples as well as male and female homosexual couples.

Blumstein and Schwartz faced a mammoth task in gathering information on a topic involving tens of millions of Americans—especially since some of the information involved normally private matters such as sexual relationships. Their study is an excellent example of how questionnaires and interviews can be used to generate information on a complex issue.

Building a Sample. Ideally, researchers might seek to draw a random sample from a listing of the complete population of all American couples. No such listing is available even for married couples; and Blumstein and Schwartz were aware that many homosexual men and women are quite secretive about their relationships, fearing negative public reaction to their sexual preference. Lacking a complete listing of their study population, they could not obtain a precisely representative sample, but they employed several strategies to make their sample as representative as possible.

First, Blumstein and Schwartz acquired as many subjects as they could, because the larger the number of subjects in the sample, the more representative of the population it is likely to be. They were fortunate in the early phase of their research to have the help of the mass media. Word of their research was carried in national news reports, and they appeared on several national television shows. They welcomed volunteer subjects and were soon swamped with offers to participate from couples across the country. In response to such requests, they sent questionnaires by return mail.

Second, Blumstein and Schwartz tried to ensure that all categories of couples were included in the study. Even a large sample is not representative if some categories of people are more likely to volunteer their participation than others. Heterosexual couples are probably more likely than homosexual couples to volunteer in this way. Blumstein and Schwartz made use of contacts within the homosexual communities of Seattle (the city in which they both lived and worked) and also San Francisco (in which many homosexuals are open about their sexual preference.) They also asked initial participants to suggest others who might be willing to join the research. This procedure, often called *snowball sampling*, usually causes the number of participants to increase quickly.

Third, to broaden the range of participants even further, Blumstein and Schwartz appeared before a variety of civic associations (Democratic and Republican organizations, the PTA, service organizations such as the Rotary Club and the Junior League, and various churches and synogogues), indicating their need for participants and leaving questionnaires to be completed by those who wished to do so.

Fourth and finally, the researchers attempted to engage the interest of the general public by walking through neighborhoods telling about their research and by leaving flyers in public places such as supermarkets and movie theaters. In the end, the researchers distributed almost twenty-two thousand questionnaires.

While Blumstein's and Schwartz's sample was certainly large and diverse, there was no guarantee that their rather informal sampling strategy would produce a sample precisely representative of the entire population of American couples. As they proceeded, the researchers were mindful of this issue, and attempted to identify any systematic distortion that their recruitment of participants might have introduced. Researchers have the re-

sponsibility to include such an assessment as part of their final report, and Blumstein and Schwartz made the following evaluation:

> [The sample] does not represent all of the couples in the United States, and it would be misleading if our findings were applied to all groups within the country. For instance, a large number of our couples come from the New York, San Francisco, and Seattle areas. More important, our couples are primarily white and disproportionately well educated. We have more high salaries and prestigious occupations among our couples than would be found in the general population. Thus, we need to be tentative about applying our findings to working-class or poor people, or people with only a grade-school education (1983:548).

Notice that such limiting factors do not substantially reduce the value of the researcher so long as researchers carefully assess and report what population their sample represents.

The Use of Questionnaires. Since there was such a large number of participants, Blumstein and Schwartz chose to use a questionnaire to collect information. Because they had many specific questions for the subjects, the questionnaire was long—some thirty-eight pages— and therefore had to be carefully prepared and clearly worded. Furthermore, they made use of a closed-ended format to lessen the work of compiling the results.

From the almost twenty-two thousand questionnaires Blumstein and Schwartz distributed, more than twelve thousand were returned—a return rate of about 55 percent, which is unusually good, especially in light of the length of the questionnaire. Blumstein and Schwartz suggested several reasons that the rate was not higher. Some couples were no longer together when they received the questionnaires. Sometimes both partners did not complete the questionnaires as requested. Follow-up mailings (which would probably have increased the return rate) were impossible because, in keeping with ethical guidelines about protecting the privacy of participants, all records of names and addresses were destroyed so that no information could be linked with a specific person.

The Use of Interviews. Blumstein and Schwartz used the interview method to gain a deeper understanding of the lives of couples in their study. For example, the researchers wanted to gather information on the history of each couple's relationship, a topic that could not be explored easily using a questionnaire. Because of the time needed to locate subjects and to conduct the interviews, Blumstein and Schwartz needed the help of a research staff in this phase of their study. In all, researchers interviewed 320 couples for periods of time ranging from two and one-half to four hours.

Because the researchers wished to personally interview subjects rather than use the telephone, the couples to be interviewed were selected from three limited areas, the regions surrounding Seattle, San Francisco, and New York City. As in their use of questionnaires, Blumstein and Schwartz were concerned about the representativeness of their interview sample and made use of the system of stratified sampling. The researchers used variables such as education, duration of the relationship, and sexual preference to establish many categories of couples, then randomly selected a smaller number of couples from each category. Thus the couples finally selected for interviews would be more likely to resemble the entire study population.

Members of the research team traveled to the home of the couple to ensure that participants would be as comfortable as possible and also to spare them any unnecessary inconvenience. Partners were interviewed separately as well as together, since one person would often be willing to discuss topics that the other partner would attempt to avoid. So two researchers were involved in each interview. Interviewing one partner out of the other's hearing was often a problem in smaller homes; as Blumstein and Schwartz reported, "Some couples had only one suitable room, and so several interviews were conducted without heat, or with a flashlight, in backyards and even bathrooms. We came to call these our bathtub interviews" (1983:20).

These interviews contributed depth and detail to the research that would not have been possible if Blumstein and Schwartz had used only questionnaires. In this part of the research as well, Blumstein and Schwartz were careful to treat all information confidentially. While being careful not to influence the responses of the participants, the interviewers encouraged openness by being nonjudgmental about what each participant revealed. In the end, the research team concluded that they had learned many things that each participant had never revealed to anyone else. This was a further reason to ensure that the privacy of each person was fully protected, and the content of each interview was not even shared with the person's partner.

Findings. Among the most interesting of Blumstein's and Schwartz's findings was the link between money and power. Despite the common view that the force of love usually leads to a balance of power between partners, they found that the partner with the higher income generally has more power in the relationship. Interestingly enough, this pattern does not hold among couples composed of homosexual women. Because American women do not usually judge their personal worth by their income, Blumstein and Schwartz reasoned, lesbians in couples do not usually assess each other on such grounds.

Another interesting finding concerned the likelihood of people having a sexual relationship outside the couple, which Blumstein and Schwartz describe with the neutral term "nonmonogamy." As you can see in Table 2–1, in all types of partnerships the likelihood of nonmonogamy increased over time, yet the likelihood also varies by type of relationship. Married couples are the least likely of all types of couples to be nonmonogamous. Among cohabiting heterosexuals, however, the likelihood of sex outside the relationship is far greater. Further differences emerge among homosexual couples, none of whom (by law) can marry. Lesbians have a slightly lower rate of sexual involvement outside their relationships than do cohabiting heterosexuals. Gay men, on the other hand, were found to be the most likely of all categories of couples to have other sexual relationships (although, as noted in Chapter 19, the AIDS epidemic soon changed this pattern). Other results of Blumstein and Schwartz's portrayal of Americans' close relationships in the 1980s are presented in Chapter 14.

Participant Observation

Participant observation is *the systematic observation of people while taking part in their activities, usually in a natural setting.* This research method is useful for studying social life within virtually any setting, ranging from gambling casinos to religious seminaries. Participant observation is also widely used by cultural anthropologists to study other societies. Cultural anthropology is closely related to sociology, except that while sociologists typically focus their attention on their own society, cultural anthropologists apply the method of participant observation—which they call *fieldwork*—to small, technologically primitive societies. In both disciplines, researchers compile descriptions of various social settings: cultural anthropologists describe an unfamiliar culture in an *ethnography*; a sociologist may study a particular category of people or a particular setting as a *case study*.

CLOSE-UP

Tips on Reading Tables

A table provides a great deal of information in a small amount of space, so learning to read tables can increase your reading efficiency. When you spot a table, look first at the title to see what information it contains. In Table 2–1, for example, the title is presented at the top, indicating that the table reports the sexual activity of American couples. In many cases, the title of a table will also indicate all the variables that are used in organizing the data. Here sexual patterns are described in terms of three additional variables: (1) the type of relationship involved (married couples, cohabiting heterosexual couples, and homosexual couples); (2) the duration of the relationship (under 2 years, 2–10 years, over 10 years); and (3) the sex of the respondent (males and females).

These three variables form the three major parts of the table, and six categories of people are found within each part. For each category, the proportion of people who reported sexual activity outside of the relationship is presented, along with the proportion that reported no such activity. For each category, two percentages are presented, adding up to 100 percent.

Looking at the first part of the table, we can see that 13 percent of females married for less than two years reported sexual activity outside of their relationship, while 87 percent reported no such activity. For women married between two and ten years, 22 percent reported being nonmonogamous, while 78 percent reported no instance of nonmonogamy. The same percentages hold for women married for more than ten years. Comparable information is provided for the other categories of people as well.

The information in this table leads to several conclusions. First, we can see that for each type of relationship, the longer the couple has been together, the more likely the people involved are to be nonmonogamous. Second, for each type of relationship, males are more likely than females to be nonmonogamous. Third, the likelihood of nonmonogamy varies among the different types of couples. Overall, married couples are the least likely to be nonmonogamous; cohabiting heterosexual couples are somewhat more likely to be nonmonogamous. Notice, finally, that the pattern among homosexuals differs sharply by sex. Gay males are the most likely of all couples to be nonmonogamous; the proportion of nonmonogamous lesbians is higher than that of married females and slightly lower than that of cohabiting heterosexual females.

Table 2–1 SEXUAL ACTIVITY AMONG AMERICAN COUPLES, BY TYPE OF RELATIONSHIP, DURATION OF RELATIONSHIP, AND SEX OF RESPONDENT

Married Couples				Cohabiting Heterosexual Couples				Homosexual Couples			
Years Together	Reported Sexual Activity outside Relationship			Years Together	Reported Sexual Activity outside Relationship			Years Together	Reported Sexual Activity outside Relationship		
	Females		Males			Females		Males			Females		Males	
	Yes	No	Yes	No		Yes	No	Yes	No		Yes	No	Yes	No
Under 2	13%	87%	15%	85%	Under 2	20%	80%	21%	79%	Under 2	15%	85%	66%	34%
2–10	22	78	23	77	2–10	42	58	47	53	2–10	38	62	89	11
Over 10	22	78	30	70	Over 10*	no data		no data		Over 10	43	57	94	6

* Too few cohabiting couples had been together for more than ten years.

SOURCE: Adapted from Philip Blumstein and Pepper Schwartz, *American Couples* (New York: William Morrow, 1983), p. 276. © 1983 by Philip Blumstein and Pepper W. Schwartz. Adapted by permission of William Morrow & Co.

Sociologists are likely to choose the method of participant observation when they have only a vague understanding of the social life they wish to investigate; thus studies of this kind are termed *exploratory* and *descriptive*. They usually begin with few, if any, specific hypotheses to test; in some cases, researchers may not even know at the outset what the important questions will turn out to be. Compared to experiments and survey research, then, participant observation has fewer hard-and-fast rules. The research plan must initially be flexible enough to adapt to unexpected circumstances. At the outset a researcher simply seeks to gain entry into what may be an unfamiliar social setting. In time, the researcher's observations give rise to many specific questions, which are systematically answered so that a detailed description of a way of life gradually emerges.

As its name suggests, participant observation has two sides. On the one hand, gaining an "insider's" look depends on becoming a participant in the setting—"hanging out" with others, attempting to act, think, and even feel the way they do. In contrast to other research methods, participant observation requires a researcher to become immersed in a social setting, not for a week or two, but usually for a period of years. On the other hand, during that time the researcher must strive to maintain the role of "observer"—one who stands back from the action—applying the sociological perspective to patterns of behavior that others take for granted. The researcher must keep a careful, daily record, called *field notes*, of exactly how the research proceeds. Incorporated into the final report of the research, these notes allow others to understand not only a researcher's conclusions, but also how they were obtained. As you can see, the two roles required of the researcher—"insider" participant and "outsider" observer—are not always easy to combine.

Obviously, the results of a participant–observer study depend more on the personal interpretations of the researcher than would the results obtained through other research methods. Participant observation is therefore a type of **qualitative research,** meaning *research based heavily on subjective impressions.* In contrast, surveys are an example of **quantitative research,** which *emphasizes the analysis of numerical data.* Because personal impressions play such a central role in participant observation, this method may be criticized as lacking scientific rigor. Yet its personal approach is also a strength; while a highly visible team of sociologists attempting to administer formal surveys may disrupt many social

settings, a sensitive participant–observer can often gain considerable insight into people's natural behavior.

A Case Study: Street Corner Society

An early study using the method of participant observation that is today considered a sociological classic was conducted in the late 1930s by William Foote Whyte. As a graduate student at Harvard University, Whyte was fascinated by the lively street life of a nearby, rather run-down section of Boston. He decided to undertake a study of this neighborhood, for which he used the pseudonym "Cornerville" to protect the privacy of its inhabitants.

Cornerville was the home of first- and second-generation Italian immigrants. Many were poor and in several other ways quite different from the upper-middle-class neighbors among whom Whyte had lived all his life. To many Bostonians, Cornerville was a place to be avoided: a poor, chaotic slum that was the home of racketeers. But Whyte was not willing to accept what many people "knew" about Cornerville. His curiosity led him to find out for himself exactly what kind of life actually went on inside the community. Whyte wanted to see firsthand how the people of Cornerville lived, how they organized their daily lives, and how their world made sense to them.

During the four years that culminated in the publication of his influential book *Street Corner Society* (1981; orig. 1943), Whyte found that many of the stereotypes about Cornerville—that it was a disorganized "slum," for example—were dead wrong, at least from the point of view of its inhabitants. He discovered that the community was highly organized, with its own code of values, its own complex social structure, and its own kinds of social conflicts.

Whyte's experience in Cornerville demonstrates some of the advantages of the participant-observation method as well as some of its pitfalls. Whyte could have taken his clipboard and questionnaire to one of Cornerville's community centers and asked local residents to tell him about their lives. Or he could have asked members of the community to come to his office at Harvard for interviews. In either case, the information he gathered would certainly have been misleading because, as we have already seen, the awareness of being observed often alters the behavior of people being studied. Indeed, many of the residents of Cornerville might have been unwilling to talk to him at all under those circumstances. Whyte realized that he had to downplay his role of observer if people were to be comfortable in his presence. He therefore tried to become part of Cornerville's everyday social patterns.

One night early in his study, Whyte joined a group of people in Cornerville who frequented a gambling establishment. After listening to a man tell a long tale about how gambling was organized, Whyte commented naively, "I suppose the cops were all paid off?" The man's reaction taught Whyte something about the tension between being a participant and being an observer:

> The gambler's jaw dropped. He glared at me. Then he denied vehemently that any policeman had been paid off and immediately switched the conversation to another subject. For the rest of that evening I felt very uncomfortable.

> The next day [a local acquaintance] explained the lesson of the previous evening. "Go easy on that 'who,' 'what,' 'why,' 'when,' 'where' stuff, Bill. You ask those questions and people will clam up on you. If people accept you, you can just hang around, and you'll learn the answers in the long run without even having to ask the questions." (1981:303)

Gaining insider status—becoming a participant—was thus the crucial first step in Whyte's research. But how could an upper-middle-class Anglo-Saxon graduate student from Harvard become part of the life of a poor Italian immigrant community like Cornerville?

Whyte faced the problem of "breaking in" that is common to participant-observation research. Trying to gain entry to a strange social environment can be embarrassing—and sometimes even dangerous, as Whyte soon found out. Unsure about how he should approach the people of Cornerville, Whyte received some questionable advice from a young instructor at Harvard. Why not, the friend suggested, drop into the local bars, offer to buy a young woman a drink, and encourage her to talk about life in Cornerville? Thinking that this might be worth a try, Whyte entered a bar one evening, but could find no women alone. Presently, however, he noticed one man talking with two women—providing him with what he thought was a good opportunity:

> I approached the group and opened with something like this: "Pardon me. Would you mind if I joined you?" There was a moment of silence while the man stared at me. Then he offered to throw me down the stairs. I assured him that this would not be necessary, and demonstrated as much by walking right out of there without any assistance. (1981:289)

Conducting research depends on gaining access to people of interest. For this reason, more sociological studies have focused on relatively poor and powerless Americans than on those of greater wealth and power.

This experience taught Whyte another important lesson: the researcher must be sensitive from the outset to the danger of imposing in any way upon the subject. Attempting to force an entry in the way Whyte did is not only awkward for the researcher, but represents an unfair intrusion into the lives of other people.

Fortunately, Whyte's research soon took a decided turn for the better when he met a young man named "Doc" in the local settlement house. Whyte explained his interest in conducting a study of Cornerville and his difficulty of getting started to Doc, who took Whyte under his wing and promised to introduce him as a friend to others in the community. This was the real beginning of Whyte's research because, with Doc's help, he soon became a regular among the people of the community.

Whyte's friendship with Doc illustrates the importance that a *key informant* can play in field research. Key informants not only give a researcher entree into a community, but often also make suggestions as to how and where to go about finding specific information. The use of a key informant has its dangers, however. If Whyte had to avoid the problem of becoming too much of an observer, he also had to guard against becoming too much of a participant. A researcher may be tempted to become "one of the people" in order to experience their way of life in the most natural way. But a researcher who becomes too personally involved in the social setting risks losing the detachment necessary to make systematic, objective observations.

Too much personal involvement can also limit a researcher's exposure to the community as a whole. Most social settings are composed of many smaller groups of people who form social cliques. A sociologist who is not openly identified as a researcher not only violates the ethical guideline prohibiting any misrepresentation of one's role, but also runs the risk of being perceived as a member of one or another of these cliques and losing access to other members of the community. A key informant, for example, may know only part of the community. Relying too heavily on this one person may skew the researcher's perceptions of the community. Thus, while a key informant may be invaluable at the outset, the participant-observer must soon seek a broad range of contacts.

Whyte was able to do this, and he soon recognized that Cornerville was hardly the stereotypical disorganized slum it was believed to be by so many Bostonians. Many immigrant members of the community participated in a wide range of civic associations in the hope of becoming "established" Americans. Moreover, a number of their children were in college with a eye toward future success. To be sure, there were social divisions in Cornerville, as there are in virtually every community. Yet Whyte was able to see that this distinctive section of Boston was composed mostly of people who, though poor, were working hard to build a future for themselves.

Perhaps more than any other method of sociological investigation, participant observation places a tremendous responsibility on the single researcher. Although in some cases research of this kind is carried out by a team of researchers, more often only a single person is involved. Thus, throughout the study, efforts to perceive the entire community as completely and objectively as possible are of paramount importance.

Secondary Analysis

Each of the three major methods of conducting sociological investigation we have considered so far involves researchers personally collecting their own data. Doing so is not always possible, however, or even necessary. In many cases, sociologists engage in **secondary analysis,** which is *the independent analysis of data originally collected by other researchers.*

The data most widely used in this way are statistics gathered by agencies within the governments of many countries. The Bureau of the Census (a branch of the U.S. Department of Commerce) is continuously gathering information about the population of the United States, which includes a wide range of variables of interest to the sociologist. Similar information is also available from Statistics Canada, a branch of the Canadian government. Information about many other societies in the world can be found in the publications of various agencies of the United Nations. A wide range of published information of this kind can be obtained from most college libraries.

Secondary analysis may also involve one researcher using data originally collected by other sociologists. The major advantage of using available data—whether government statistics or the results of other research studies—is that it saves the researcher the time and money needed to personally collect the necessary information. Using data collected by others means that sociologists can undertake certain kinds of research that would otherwise be impossible. Moreover, the quality of data available from government agencies is generally better than what most individual researchers could hope to obtain, at least without considerable expense.

Still, secondary analysis has characteristic problems. For one thing, the researcher may not know how accurate the data are. Was information gathered in a systematic way that encouraged unbiased responses? Was all information accurately recorded? Once the decision to use available data has been made, it is usually not feasible to address these questions. At the very least, however, the researcher must be aware of the potential for error and distortion.

Emile Durkheim's nineteenth-century study of suicide, described in Chapter 1, is one of the best-known sociological investigations making use of existing records. But Durkheim's research also illustrates the potential for error. He used official records indicating the number of suicides among various segments of European society. But whether a death was actually a suicide is often uncertain. Many accidents may be incorrectly classified as suicides; perhaps more commonly, actual suicides may be recorded as accidents or deaths due to other causes.

Sociologists today make extensive use of official statistics concerning the frequency of various crimes in the United States, yet they are always on guard against distortions in these statistics. Researchers have learned, for example, that many crimes are not reported to the police; and, to make this problem more complex, the rate of reporting varies according to the type of crime. Homicides, for example, are very likely to come to the attention of the police, while rapes have long been significantly underreported. Researchers sometimes collect their own data to check the accuracy of official crime statistics, recognizing that the value of available data depends on having some idea of how accurate they are.

A second problem with the use of available data is that often they were collected for purposes different from those of a subsequent researcher. Questions may have been phrased and presented to respondents in a way not exactly suited to the current researcher's goals, or the subjects might not be the current researcher's ideal sample. Obviously, we are dealing with a "trade-off" here. The usefulness of the data must be balanced against the ease by which they are obtained. Therefore, whenever researchers use information collected by others, they must interpret the data with care and in a way suitable to their goals. An example of this process is the research conducted by E. Digby Baltzell, which we introduced at the beginning of this chapter.

Using Available Data:
Religious Values and Achievement

E. Digby Baltzell's visit to the library of Bowdoin started him thinking about why such a small school had produced a number of graduates who made a significant mark on the history and culture of the United States. Baltzell's hunch was that New England in general had produced far more than its share of national leaders in diverse fields such as politics, law, and the arts, while his native Pennsylvania had produced few such people. Was this actually true? And if so, why?

In dealing with historical questions of this kind, Baltzell (1979) realized that he would have to rely on information compiled by others. Thus he turned to the *Dictionary of American Biography*, a twenty-volume source of biographical information on over thirteen thousand men and women. Baltzell knew that by using this source he was limiting himself to considering only those people the editors of the *Dictionary* believed worthy of inclusion. But despite the editors' possible bias, he believed that there was no better source of the information he needed. Baltzell's next step was to determine the extent of each person's achievement. How could one person be compared to another? A clue to a solution lay in the statement by the book's editors that the length of each biography was proportional to the person's achievement. All such ratings are open to argument, but Baltzell knew he could hardly have done better starting from scratch.

Baltzell then identified the seventy-five Americans with the longest biographies, and a striking pattern began to emerge. Massachusetts came out on top, with twenty-one of the seventy-five longest biographies; overall, the New England states had thirty-one such entries. In contrast, Pennsylvania had only two of the longest biographies; and the entire Middle Atlantic region had only twelve. Next Baltzell noted that almost all the great achievers from Massachusetts were from a very small area in and around the city of Boston. Furthermore, using length of biography as a measure of achievement, he found that the outstanding families from the Boston area had achieved far more than those from Philadelphia. At this point he realized that his original suspicion had been well-founded: New England had indeed produced far more eminent Americans than had the Middle Atlantic region.

What might explain the high level of achievement in such a small part of America and the corresponding lack of achievement in the region surrounding Baltzell's own city of Philadelphia? Baltzell drew inspiration from one of the classic studies carried out by the German sociologist Max Weber (1958; orig. 1904–5). In this study (which is described at length in Chapter 4), Weber found that different religious ideas have a powerful effect on patterns of individual achievement. Baltzell realized that religion could have planted the seeds of two different attitudes toward achievement in Bostonians and Philadelphians.

Both cities were originally founded by members of religious groups persecuted in England. The early Puritans of Boston were strong believers in the innate sinfulness of human beings and used their families, churches, and schools to exercise strict control over people's behavior. Hard work and social prominence were ways of glorifying God, as well as signs that a person had received God's blessing. Thus Puritanism encouraged a hierarchical and highly disciplined way of life in which personal achievement was vigorously sought and highly respected.

In contrast to the Puritans, the Quakers who founded Philadelphia believed that human beings are inherently good. Thus they did not see the need for strong social institutions to "save" individuals from sinfulness. Moreover, believing all people to be equal, the Quakers established a way of life in which personal modesty was highly valued and in which no one sought to stand apart from others. Thus the environment of Quakerism discouraged people from the kind of public achievement that was actively sought in Boston.

Baltzell conceived of Boston and Philadelphia in terms of a historical experiment. Each city, he maintained, could be thought of as a "test tube": Puritanism was introduced into one, Quakerism into the other. From our vantage point at the end of the twentieth century, we can see what "chemical reactions" occurred in each case. Baltzell's findings clearly suggest that religion did have a significant impact on individual achievement in Boston and Philadelphia. Of course, he did not claim that Puritanism was in any absolute sense "better" than

Quakerism; he merely demonstrated that these two religions represented social forces that shaped the lives of individual human beings in very different ways.

Keep in mind that the historical data Baltzell compiled do not, in any absolute sense, *prove* the conclusions he reached about the importance of religion to social achievement. Baltzell's theory is certainly consistent with the data, but research usually produces results that can be understood in more than one way. In this case, for example, we might wonder if the standards used by the editors of the *Dictionary of American Biography* favor the Puritan style of living and thus diminish the importance of Quaker contributions. Alternatively, perhaps early in our country's history the Puritans were able to establish a dominant position in many areas of American life which they jealously and successfully defended against others—Quakers included—in the decades that followed. Baltzell, of course, considered such possibilities, but ended by arguing eloquently in support of the importance of religion to historical patterns of achievement. Still, his study serves to remind us that scientific research inevitably contains the subjective element of interpretation.

Four major methods of sociological investigation have now been introduced, and are summarized in Table 2–2. A final consideration involved in the use of scientific methods is how the specific facts obtained through sociological investigation are related to theory.

Table 2–2 FOUR RESEARCH METHODS: A SUMMARY

Method	Application	Advantages	Limitations
Experiment	For explanatory research that specifies relationships among variables; generates quantitative data	Provides greatest ability to specify cause-and-effect relationships; replication of research is relatively easy	Laboratory settings have artificial quality; unless research environment is carefully controlled, result may be biased
Survey	For gathering information about issues that cannot be directly observed, such as attitudes and values; useful for descriptive and explanatory research; generates quantitive or qualitative data	Sampling allows surveys of large populations using questionnaires; interviews provide in-depth responses	Questionnaires must be carefully prepared and may produce low return rate; interviews are expensive and time-consuming
Participant Observation	For exploratory and descriptive study of people in a "natural" setting; generates qualitative data	Allows study of "natural" behavior; usually inexpensive	Time-consuming; replication of research is difficult; researcher must balance roles of participant and observer
Secondary Analysis	For exploratory, descriptive, or explanatory research whenever suitable data are available	Saves time and expense of data collection; makes historical research possible	Researcher has no control over possible bias in data; data may not be suitable for current research needs

THE INTERPLAY OF THEORY AND METHOD

The methods of sociological investigation we have described serve as guides toward the discovery of facts about our social world. Facts, however, are not the final goal of research; as suggested in Chapter 1, what we are really after is the development of theory—a system of ideas that serves to link together a number of specific facts into meaningful understanding.

When using any of the methods of sociological investigation, a researcher attempts to connect specific observations or facts to social theory. This process involves two types of logical thinking. **Deductive logical thought** *begins with general ideas about the world that must be subjected to scientific evaluation to see whether they are correct*. To do this, general ideas are used to state a specific, testable hypothesis linking two or more variables together. The researcher then chooses an appropriate method for collecting evidence that may or may not support the hypothesis. If the evidence does support the hypothesis, the value of the initial theory is strengthened; if it does not, the theory must be revised or perhaps rejected entirely. The deductive logical model, then, proceeds from the general (theory) to the specific (facts used for evaluation).

Philip Zimbardo's "Stanford County Prison" experiment illustrates the operation of this model. Zimbardo began with the general idea that prisons themselves affect human behavior. He then designed a specific hypothesis that extremely healthy young men placed in a prison setting would display violent behavior in a short time. Zimbardo was able to confirm this hypothesis by demonstrating the negative effects of prison on human behavior. Had his experiment produced different results, his original theory would clearly have required reformulation.

A second type of logical thought works in the other direction. **Inductive logical thought** *begins with specific observations that the researcher attempts to link together into a general theory*. In other words, a researcher is faced with facts that initially cannot be explained and uses inductive reasoning to organize these facts into a broader statement about human behavior.

E. Digby Baltzell's research provides an illustration of the inductive logical model. He began with the observation that one New England college had produced a surprising number of high achievers. He then collected more information on two regions of the United States and gradually saw a distinctive pattern emerging. Finally,

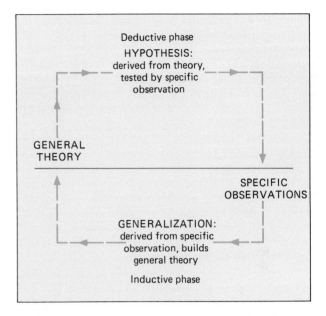

Figure 2–2   Deductive and Inductive Logical Thought

he interpreted this pattern as evidence of the importance of religious values to historical achievement.

In most cases, however, researchers make use of both types of logical thought, as presented in Figure 2–2. Researchers often begin with general ideas that lead (deductively) to hypotheses, which in turn are evaluated on the basis of specific observations. These observations then lead (inductively) to modifying the original ideas into a somewhat different theory.

THE STEPS IN SOCIOLOGICAL INVESTIGATION

The following nine steps are general guidelines for carrying out any research project in sociology.

1. *Define the topic you wish to investigate.* The ideas for social research can come to you anywhere and at any time if you remain curious and observe the world around you from the sociological perspective. As Max Weber suggested, the issue chosen for study is likely to have some personal significance to you.

2. *Find out what has already been written about the topic.* You are probably not the first person to have an

interest in the particular issue. Spend enough time in the library to learn what theories and methods of sociological investigation have been applied to your topic. Theory guides the kinds of questions you ask, and research methods provide strategies for finding answers. In looking over the research that has already been done on the topic, be especially mindful of problems that may have come up before.

3. *Assess the requirements for carrying out research on the topic.* What resources are necessary to support your research? How much time will you need? Can you do the work yourself? If not, how much help will you need? What expenses will you have along the way? What sources of funding might be available to support your research? It is important that you be able to provide answers to all of these questions before you actually begin to design the research project.

4. *Specify the questions you are going to ask.* Are you seeking to explore an unfamiliar social setting? To describe some category of people? Or to investigate the link between several variables? If your study is exploratory, what general questions will guide your work? If it is descriptive, what specific characteristics are you going to describe and for what population? If your study is explanatory, what hypothesis will you be testing? How do you plan to operationalize each variable?

5. *Consider the ethical issues involved in the research.* Not every study will raise major ethical issues, but you should be sensitive to this matter at the outset of your research. Will you promise anonymity to the subjects? If so, how will you ensure that anonymity will be maintained? Can your research cause harm to anyone? How might you design the study to minimize the chances for such harm?

6. *Decide what research method you will use.* At this point you are planning the actual strategy for carrying out the research. Keep in mind that the appropriate method is largely related to the kind of questions you will be asking as well as to the resources available to support your research. Consider all major research strategies—as well as innovative combinations of approaches—before deciding how to proceed.

7. *Put the method to work to gather data.* The collection of data is carried out according to the research method you have chosen. Be sure to record all information accurately and in a way that will make sense to you later (it may be some time before you actually write up the results of your work).

This painting by René Magritte suggests that insight is the ultimate goal of sociological investigation. It is achieved only by combining research skills with human imagination.

8. *Interpret the findings.* Organize your data in terms of the questions that concerned you initially and decide what answers the data suggest. If your study involved a specific hypothesis, the data should provide you with a basis to confirm, reject, or modify the hypothesis. Keep in mind that there may be several ways to interpret the results of your study, consistent with different theoretical paradigms, and you should consider them all. Also be on guard against the ever-present danger that your personal values or your expectations at the outset will affect how you make sense out of the data you have collected.

9. *Consistent with your findings, what are your conclusions?* Prepare a final report indicating what you have learned from the research. Consider the contributions of your work both to sociological theory and to improving sociological methods of research. What is the value of your research to other people in general? Finally, evaluate your own work. Did the research work out as you had hoped? What questions are left unanswered? Note any ways in which your own biases may have affected your conclusions.

SUMMARY

1. Sociology is more than a perspective; it is also a form of investigation that uses the logic of science to learn about the social world.

2. Science is an important foundation of all sociological research and, more broadly, a valuable means of evaluating information we encounter every day.

3. There are three basic requirements for sociological investigation: (1) being aware of the larger social world; (2) using the sociological perspective; and (3) being curious and asking questions about society.

4. There are many different ways of knowing, including personal experience, faith, acceptance of information provided by experts, and social agreement. Science represents an approach to knowing that is based on empirical evidence, and as such, may contradict our common sense.

5. Science makes use of concepts and variables. Concepts are abstract ideas that represent elements of society; concepts that vary in value are called variables. Measurement is the process of determining the value of a variable in any specific case. Sound measurement has the qualities of reliability and validity.

6. Science seeks to specify the relationship among variables. Ideally, researchers seek relationships of cause and effect in which one factor (the independent variable) is used to predict change in another factor (the dependent variable). In many cases, however, sociological investigation can only demonstrate that two variables vary together—a relationship called correlation.

7. Science demands objectivity on the part of a researcher. While issues chosen for investigation may reflect personal interests (which Weber described as "value-relevant" research), personal values and biases are—ideally—suspended in conducting the research ("value freedom").

8. Scientific research developed primarily through study of the natural world. Although science can be used to study social behavior, it has important limitations in such studies.

9. Curiosity and imagination, necessary for all successful research, spring from the human mind and not from science. Moreover, all human reality is based on patterns of meaning. The process of interpretation is therefore part of all sociological investigation.

10. Although most sociologists endorse Weber's ideal of value-free research, many believe that all research inevitably involves political values. Some even argue that sociological research should encourage desirable social change.

11. All sociological research has ethical implications—the potential to affect participants and others for good or ill. Sociological researchers must understand they have a professional responsibility to conduct all research according to recognized ethical guidelines.

12. Experiments are a method of sociological investigation in which researchers attempt to specify the relationship between two (or more) variables. Although the ideal form of the experiment is usually carried out in a laboratory that affords maximum control over the environment, experiments can also be conducted in the field.

13. Surveys are a research method by which a researcher obtains responses from subjects to a series of items or questions. Surveys often involve various sampling techniques as well as the use of questionnaires and interviews.

14. Participant observation is a method of sociological investigation that involves direct observation of a social setting for an extended period of time. The researcher is both a participant in the setting and a careful observer of it.

15. Secondary analysis, or making use of available data, is the fourth major method of sociological investigation. Although researchers must ensure that available data are suitable for their particular purposes, this approach affords considerable savings in time and money.

16. Theory and research are closely interrelated. Deductive thought is the logical process by which general theoretical ideas generate a hypothesis that is subject to

evaluation according to the specific facts produced by research. Inductive thought is the logical process by which specific observations and research findings lead to formulating more general theoretical ideas. Most sociological investigation is characterized by both types of logical thought.

KEY CONCEPTS

cause and effect a relationship between two variables in which change in one (the independent variable) causes change in another (the dependent variable)

concept an abstract idea that represents some element of the world

control the ability to neutralize the effect of one variable so that the relationship among other variables can be more precisely determined

correlation a relationship between two (or more) variables in which they vary together with no demonstrated relationship of cause and effect

deductive logical thought a logical process that begins with general ideas that generate specific hypotheses subject to scientific evaluation

dependent variable a variable that is changed by another (independent) variable

empirical evidence what we can observe or otherwise verify with our senses

experiment a method of sociological investigation that seeks to specify cause-and-effect relationships among variables

Hawthorne effect distortion in research caused by the awareness of subjects that they are the focus of study

hypothesis a theoretical statement of the relationship between any facts or variables

independent variable a variable that causes change in another (dependent) variable

inductive logical thought a logical process that begins with specific observations that are linked together into a general theory

interview questions administered personally to the subject by the researcher

mean the arithmetic average of a series of numbers, calculated by dividing the sum by the number of cases

measurement the process of determining the value of a variable in a specific case

median the value that occurs midway in a series of numbers

mode the value that occurs most often in a series of numbers

objectivity the state of complete personal neutrality in conducting research

operationalizing a variable specifying exactly what is to be measured in assigning a value to a variable

participant observation a method of sociological investigation involving the systematic observation of people while taking part in their activities, usually in a natural setting

population all people about whom research gathers information

qualitative research research based heavily on subjective interpretation

quantitative research research that emphasizes analysis of numerical data

questionnaire a series of questions or items to which subjects are asked to respond

reliability the quality of consistency in measurement

replication the process by which a study is repeated by other researchers

research method a strategy for carrying out research in a systematic way

sample a representative part of a population

science a logical system that bases knowledge on facts that are derived from direct, systematic observation

secondary analysis a method of sociological investigation involving the independent analysis of data originally collected by other researchers

survey a method of sociological investigation in which individuals provide responses to a series of items or questions

validity the quality of measurement afforded by actually measuring what one intends to measure

variable a concept that has a value that varies from case to case

SUGGESTED READINGS

The following books introduce the process of sociological investigation in terms that are easy for beginning students to understand:

> Morton M. Hunt. *Profiles of Social Research: The Scientific Study of Human Interactions*. New York: Russell Sage Foundation/Basic Books, 1986.

> Walter L. Wallace. *Principles of Scientific Sociology*. Hawthorne, NY: Aldine, 1983.

> Earl Babbie. *The Practice of Social Research*. 4th Edition. Belmont, CA: Wadsworth, 1986.

Like artists, social researchers are constantly reflecting on their work and honing their skills. These two books provide personal insights into what it means to become involved in sociological investigation.

> Shulamit Reinharz. *On Becoming a Social Scientist: From Survey Research and Participant Observation to Experimental Analysis*. New Brunswick, NJ: Transaction Books, 1984.

> William Foote Whyte in collaboration with Kathleen King Whyte. *Learning from the Field: A Guide from Experience*. Beverly Hills, CA: Sage, 1984.

This book is a collection of essays that explores the neglected issue of how the sex and marital status of researchers can affect the research process.

> Tony Larry Whitehead and Mary Ellen Conaway, eds. *Self, Sex, and Gender in Cross-Cultural Fieldwork*. Urbana, IL: University of Illinois Press, 1986.

All researchers need to develop skills to communicate their findings to others in a comprehensive and interesting way. These two books (the second aimed at more advanced writers) can help you to do just that.

> The Sociology Writing Group. *A Guide to Writing Sociology Papers*. New York: St. Martin's Press, 1986.

> Howard S. Becker, with a chapter by Pamela Richards. *Writing for Social Scientists: How to Start and Finish Your Thesis, Book, or Article*. Chicago: University of Chicago Press, 1986.

Research is often the basis for evaluating various kinds of social programs. This book explores how sociological investigation can assess the consequences of social welfare programs.

> Daniel Glaser. *Evaluation Research and Decision Guidance: Correctional, Addiction Treatment, Mental Health, Education, and Other People-Changing Agencies*. New Brunswick, NJ: Transaction Books, 1987.

The relationship between research and politics and personal values continues to be a central concern in sociology. The first book listed below is one of the best efforts to explore this controversy-filled area. The second is a recent history of the discipline that suggests that particular social values and priorities deeply influenced the work of pioneering sociologists.

> Alvin W. Gouldner. *The Coming Crisis of Western Sociology*. New York: Avon Books, 1970.

> Arthur J. Vidich and Stanford M. Lyman. *American Sociology: Worldly Rejections of Religion and Their Directions*. New Haven: Yale University Press, 1985.

The ethics of research—particularly with regard to the method of participant observation—is the focus of this paperback collection of essays.

> Martin Bulmer, ed. *Social Research Ethics: An Examination of the Merits of Covert Participant Observation*. New York: Holmes and Meier, 1982.

CHAPTER 3

Culture

A small aluminum motorboat chugged steadily along the muddy Orinoco River, deep in the vast tropical rain forest of southern Venezuela. French anthropologist Napoleon Chagnon was nearing the end of a three-day journey to the home territory of the Yąnomamö, one of the few technologically primitive societies remaining on earth.

Some twelve thousand Yąnomamö live in scattered villages along the border between Venezuela and Brazil. The Yąnomamö way of life contrasts sharply with our own. They are spirit worshippers who have no form of writing. Until recent contact with outsiders, they used rudimentary weapons such as the bow and arrow to hunt for food. Thus Chagnon would be as strange to them as they to him.

By two o'clock in the afternoon, Chagnon had almost reached his destination. The hot sun made the humid air all the more uncomfortable. The anthropologist's clothes were soaked with perspiration; his face and hands were swollen from the bites of innumerable gnats that swarmed around him. But he hardly noticed, preoccupied with the fact that, in just a few moments he was to meet people unlike any he had ever known.

Chagnon's heart pounded as the boat slid onto the riverbank near a Yąnomamö village. Sounds of activity came from nearby. Chagnon and his guide climbed from the boat and walked toward the village, stooping as they pushed their way through the dense undergrowth. Chagnon describes what happened next:

> I looked up and gasped when I saw a dozen burly, naked, sweaty, hideous men staring at us down the shafts of their drawn arrows! Immense wads of green tobacco were stuck between their lower teeth and lips making them look even more hideous, and strands of dark green slime dripped or hung from their nostrils—strands so long that they clung to their [chests] or drizzled down their chins.

> My next discovery was that there were a dozen or so vicious, underfed dogs snapping at my legs, circling me as if I were to be their next meal. I just stood there holding my notebook, helpless and pathetic. Then the stench of the decaying vegetation and filth hit me and I almost got sick. I was horrified. What kind of welcome was this for the person who came here to live with you and learn your way of life, to become friends with you? (1983:10)

Fortunately for Chagnon, the Yąnomamö villagers recognized his guide and withdrew their weapons. Although reassured that he would at least survive the afternoon, Chagnon was still shaken by his inability to make any sense of the people surrounding him. And this was to be his home for a year and a half! He wondered why he had forsaken physics to study human culture in the first place.

There are now over 5 billion people living on our planet. We are all *Homo sapiens*—members of a

Anthropologists seek to understand ways of life that may differ greatly from their own. At times, this may be personally hazardous; it always produces some degree of culture shock.

single biological species. Even so, we can be overwhelmed by the differences that distinguish us from one another, differences not of biology but of culture. Upon his arrival at the Yanomamö village, Chagnon experienced a severe case of **culture shock**: *the personal disorientation that may accompany entry into an unfamiliar social world.* Like most of us, Chagnon had been raised to keep his clothes on, even in hot weather, and to use a handkerchief when his nose was running—especially in front of others. The Yanomamö clearly had other ideas about how to live. The nudity that embarrassed Chagnon was the Yanomamö's customary manner of going about. The green slime hanging from their nostrils was one effect of a hallucinogenic drug commonly used among friends, as we might share beer or wine. The "stench" from which Chagnon recoiled in disgust no doubt smelled like "Home Sweet Home" to the inhabitants of that Yanomamö village.

Human beings the world over have very different ideas about what is pleasant and unpleasant, polite and rude, true and false, right and wrong. All these differences, created by one biological species, are expressions of human culture.

WHAT IS CULTURE?

Culture may be defined as *the beliefs, values, behavior, and material objects shared by a particular people.* Sociologists distinguish between **nonmaterial culture**: *the intangible creations of human society* (such as ideas and beliefs), and **material culture**: *the tangible products of human society* (ranging from armaments to zippers). The terms *culture* and *society* are used in much the same way, but their precise meanings are slightly different. Culture is a way of life a number of people have in common. A society is a group of people who interact with one another within a geographical or political boundary and who share a culture. Obviously, neither society nor culture can exist without the other.

In everyday terms, culture is reflected in what we wear to work, when and what we eat, and how we enjoy spending our free time. In addition, our culture leads us to sleep in houses of wood and brick, while people of other cultures live in igloos of ice or teepees made of animal skins. Culture provides the framework within which our lives become meaningful, based on standards of success, beauty, and goodness, and reverence for a god or gods, the forces of nature, or long-dead ancestors. Culture also shapes our personalities—what we commonly (yet inaccurately) describe as "human nature." The Yanomamö are fierce and warlike, and they strive to develop these "natural" qualities in their children. The Tasaday of the Philippines, in contrast, have been described as so peace-loving that their language has no word for violence. Both the American and Japanese cultures stress achievement and hard work; but Americans value self-assertion and competition, while the Japanese emphasize cooperation and self-denying obedience to authority. In short, our culture affects virtually every dimension of our lives, from our facial expressions to our family life.

Notice that sociologists use the concept of culture in a broader sense than most other people do. When we talk about "culture" in everyday conversation, we usually mean such highly regarded areas of life as literature, music, and other arts. Speaking sociologically, however, culture refers to *everything* that is part of a people's way of life—not just an award-winning novel, gourmet cuisine, and ballet, but also jokes shared among friends, fast food, and break-dancing. In short, culture encompasses all the patterns of life within a society.

None of these patterns is "natural" in human beings, although most people around the world view their particular way of life as just that. Human beings are born with the capacity to create culture, and learn to do so as members of a society. Although a great deal of every culture is transmitted from generation to generation, every element of culture is a human product that is subject to change.

The deliberate, flexible, and diverse qualities of culture are uniquely human. Most other living creatures—be they amoebas, ants, or antelopes—behave in remarkably uniform ways. Their way of life is largely shaped by biological forces and changes only over long periods of time. A few animals—most notably chimpanzees and other related primates—appear to have the ability to create rudimentary forms of culture, such as the use of tools, and to teach such skills to their offspring. But the creative ability of human beings to shape their world far exceeds that of any other form of life, so that *only humans rely on culture rather than instinct to ensure the survival of their kind* (Harris, 1987).

To understand how this came to be, we must briefly review the long history of our species on the earth.

Human Intelligence and Culture

In a universe scientists estimate to be 15 billion years old, our planet is a relatively young 4.5 billion years of age, and the human species is a wide-eyed infant of 40,000. We can trace our ancestry to the first forms of life that emerged a billion years after the earth was formed. Our history took a crucial turn when the primate order of mammals developed only some 65 million years ago.

In the millions of years that followed, the early primates (whose present-day descendants also include monkeys and apes) evolved into the most intelligent of life forms, with the largest brains relative to body weight of all living creatures. Our human line diverged from that of our closest primate relatives, the great apes, about 12 million years ago. Our common lineage is apparent, however, in noteworthy characteristics that the human species shares with the chimpanzees, gorillas, and orangutans of today: great sociability, leading to affectionate and long-lasting bonds with others for purposes of child rearing and mutual protection; the ability to walk upright (normal in humans, but less commonly used by other primates); and hands that can grasp and manipulate objects with great precision.

Fossil records place the emergence of the first species of life with clearly human characteristics at about 2 million years ago. These distant ancestors had the mental capacity to develop a primitive form of culture, including the use of fire, tools, weapons, and crude shelters. Such achievements may seem modest, but they mark a major event in human history. At this point, our ancestors had embarked on an evolutionary course in which culture—made possible as the human brain enlarged—became the primary strategy for human survival.

It is worth pausing here to emphasize how recently in the long history of our universe our earliest direct ancestors emerged. To make this more clear, Carl Sagan (1977) has suggested that we consider the entire 15-billion-year history of our universe to be a single calendar year. The life-giving atmosphere of our planet did not develop until the fall of that year, and the earliest forms of human beings did not appear until December 31, the last day of the year, at about 10:30 at night! Yet not until much later—about 250,000 years ago, or minutes before the end of Sagan's "year,"—did the earliest members of our own biological species emerge. These *Homo sapiens* (derived from Latin meaning "thinking man") continued to evolve until, 40,000 years ago, human beings who looked very much like ourselves lived on the earth (Ember & Ember, 1985). With brains as large as our own, these "modern" *Homo sapiens* were able to develop culture at a rapid pace, as the wide range of tools and cave art from this period suggests. However the emergence of what we call civilization, based on permanent settlements and specialized occupations, began in the Middle East only about 12,000 years ago (Hamblin, 1973; Wenke, 1980). In terms of Sagan's "year," this flowering of human culture occurred during the final *seconds* before midnight on New Year's Eve. Our modern industrial way of life has existed for only some 300 years—just a final millisecond in Sagan's "year."

What does this vast history tell us about culture? First, human culture is linked to the biological evolution of human beings. The human ability to purposefully create a way of life—as opposed to merely responding to biological forces—developed extremely slowly over millions of years. Second, the creation of culture only became possible when the brain size of our ancestors increased. Biological forces that we commonly call *instincts* gradually diminished as human beings gained the mental capacity to fashion their natural environment for themselves. At this point, human nature was no longer instinct but culture, setting us apart from other forms of life (Barash, 1981). An important human trait ever since has been creativity, which explains today's fascinating (and, as Napoleon Chagnon's experiences show, sometimes disturbing) diversity in human ways of life.

THE COMPONENTS OF CULTURE

Although their contents vary greatly, all cultures have five components in common: symbols, language, values, norms, and material culture. We shall begin with the one that underlies the rest: symbols.

Symbols

In the simplest terms, a **symbol** *is anything that carries a particular meaning recognized by members of a culture.*

In every society, elites use distinctive adornment to convey a message of power and prestige. But this practice takes different forms, as shown by a comparison of monarchs from the United Kingdom, Nigeria, and Iran.

Sounds, images, objects, and human action can all serve as symbols. The words on this page are just ink on paper, but they are also symbols because they represent something more. Even the wink of the eye is a symbol that can serve as an expression of interest, understanding, or insult.

Symbolic meanings are the basis of every culture, providing the foundation of the reality we experience in any social situation. Because we take the symbols of our own culture for granted, we are usually unaware of how vital they are. One way to recognize their importance, however, is to use symbols inconsistent with usual cultural patterns. Imagine, for example, the congregation's response to a priest who appeared in church dressed like a Hell's Angel.

Another way to understand the power of symbols is to enter an unfamiliar culture. A frequent reason for experiencing culture shock is that we cannot properly interpret the meaning of the symbols around us. Like

Napoleon Chagnon confronting the Yąnomamö, we feel lost, unsure of how to act, and sometimes frightened—a consequence of being outside the symbolic web of culture that unites individuals in meaningful social life.

Symbols vary across cultures, so that an action or object with important symbolic meaning in one culture may have a very different meaning, or no meaning at all, in another. To people in Japan as well as North America, a baseball bat symbolizes a favorite sport; but the Yąnomamö would probably see it as a well-carved club that arouses thoughts of hunting or war. The Stars and Stripes flying in front of the post office symbolizes "the home of the free and the brave" to people in the United States, but the home of the "capitalist imperialists" to most citizens of the Soviet Union. Thus symbols that bind together members of one culture also serve to separate the various cultures of the world from one another.

Any number of behaviors that seem insignificant to us may have symbolic meanings that are actually offensive to people of other cultures. For example, Americans often sit with one leg draped casually across the other—to us, simply a matter of comfort. Yet doing so exposes the bottom of one's foot, which to a member of an Islamic culture in the Middle East is an insult. (Further illustrations of this problem are presented in the box.) To some degree, symbolic meanings also vary among different categories of people in a single society. Owning an expensive foreign car may seem unpatriotic to an auto worker in Detroit, but to a young banker in California the car may symbolize the fact that she is on her way up the career ladder. Similarly, opening a door for a woman may be thought of as an act of courtesy by many men, yet symbolize male dominance to many women.

Cultural symbols often change over time. Blue jeans were first worn as sturdy clothing by people engaged in manual labor. For generations they were identified with the working class. In the 1960s, however, they became popular among students—many of them affluent—as a symbol of the rejection of conventional cultural patterns. In the 1970s, "designer jeans" became fashionable (and often expensive) symbols of the latest trend in clothing.

In sum, symbols are the means by which human beings make sense of their lives. In a world of cultural diversity, the use of symbols may cause embarrassment and even conflict, but without symbols our existence would be meaningless indeed.

CLOSE-UP

Helen Keller: Becoming Part of a Symbolic World

The most important day I remember in all my life is the one on which my teacher, Anne Mansfield Sullivan, came to me. I am filled with wonder when I consider the immeasurable contrast between the two lives which it connects. It was the third of March, 1887, three months before I was seven years old. . . .

Have you ever been at sea in a dense fog, when it seemed as if a tangible white darkness shut you in, and the great ship, tense and anxious, groped her way toward the shore with plummet and sounding line, and you waited with beating heart for something to happen? I was like that ship before my education began, only I was without compass or sounding-line, and had no way of knowing how near the harbour was. "Light! give me light!" was the wordless cry of my soul, and the light of life shone on me in that very hour. . . .

The morning after my teacher came she led me into her room and gave me a doll. The little blind children at the Perkins Institution had sent it and Laura Bridgman had dressed it; but I did not know this until afterward. When I had played with it a little while, Miss Sullivan slowly spelled into my hand the word "doll." I was at once interested in this finger play and tried to imitate it. When I finally succeeded in making the letters correctly I was flushed with childish pleasure and pride. Running downstairs to my mother I held up my hand and made the letters for doll. I did not know that I was spelling a word or even that words existed; I was simply making my fingers go in monkey-like imitation. In the days that followed I learned to spell in this uncomprehending way a great many words, among them *pin*, *hat*, *cup* and a few verbs like *sit*, *stand* and *walk*. But my teacher had been with me several weeks before I understood that everything has a name.

One day, while I was playing with my new doll, Miss Sullivan put a big rag doll into my lap also, spelled "d-o-l-l" and tried to make me understand that "d-o-l-l" applied to both. Earlier in the day we had had a tussle over the words "m-u-g" and "w-a-t-e-r." Miss Sullivan had tried to impress it upon me that "m-u-g" is *mug* and that "w-a-t-e-r" is *water*, but I persisted in confounding the two. In despair she had dropped the subject for the time, only to renew it at the first opportunity. I became impatient at her repeated attempts and, seizing the new doll, I dashed it upon the floor. I was keenly delighted when I felt the fragments of the broken doll at my feet. Neither sorrow nor regret followed my passionate outburst. I had not loved the doll. In the still,

dark world in which I lived there was no strong sentiment or tenderness. I felt my teacher sweep the fragments to one side of the hearth, and I had a sense of satisfaction that the cause of my discomfort was removed. She brought me my hat, and I knew I was going out into the warm sunshine. This thought, if a wordless sensation may be called a thought, made me hop and skip with pleasure.

We walked down the path to the well-house, attracted by the fragrance of the honeysuckle with which it was covered. Someone was drawing water and my teacher placed my hand under the spout. As the cool stream gushed over one hand she spelled into the other the word *water*, first slowly, then rapidly. I stood still, my whole attention fixed upon the motions of her fingers. Suddenly I felt a misty consciousness as of something forgotten—a thrill of returning thought; and somehow the mystery of language was revealed to me. I knew then that "w-a-t-e-r" meant the wonderful cool something that was flowing over my hand. That living word awakened my soul; gave it light, hope, joy, set it free! There were barriers still, it is true, but barriers that could in time be swept away.

SOURCE: Helen Keller, *The Story of My Life* (New York: Doubleday, Page and Company, 1903), pp. 21–24.

Language

All human cultures organize symbols into **language**—*a system of symbols with standard meanings that allows members of a society to communicate with one another.* All cultures have a spoken language, although some

lack a system of writing. The Yąnomamö, for example, communicate entirely with spoken words.

Sharing beliefs, thoughts, and feelings with others is the basis of culture, and it is language that makes this possible. Humans who for one reason or another have not learned to use language experience considerable social isolation, buffeted by nameless sensations they do not understand. The box presents the familiar story of Helen Keller; born deaf and blind, Keller learned language when she was seven years old, and the resulting change in her world was profound.

Language—in a sense, our cultural heritage in coded form—is the most important means of **cultural transmission,** *the process by which culture is passed from one generation to the next.* Every word we speak is rooted in the lives of those who came before us, much as our bodies still contain the genes of our ancestors. Once we have learned the meaning of the symbols used in language, we have access to the accumulated knowledge of centuries.

For most of human history, culture has been directly transmitted through personal communication. It was not until about five thousand years ago, in fact, that writing was commonly used, and then it was known only to a tiny proportion of people (Haviland, 1985). Two centuries ago, only a small fraction of the North American population was literate. Even today, some 25 million adults in the United States cannot read and write and must rely on what anthropologists call the *oral tradition.* This is a considerable handicap since writing is an increasingly important means of communication in most human societies.

Language is also the foundation of human imagination. Because language involves connecting symbols in virtually infinite combinations, we have the capacity to conceive of alternatives to our ordinary perceptions of the world. If we were unable to imagine our world in different symbolic terms, our lives would lack the vital dimensions of purposeful change and creative variety.

Is Language Uniquely Human?

Are speech and writing unique to human beings? The sounds and other physical signals animals make to one another can be viewed as a form of language; but these are largely instinctual, and most nonhuman creatures lack the mental capacity to understand or create a symbolic system of communication as complex as human language. Still, research has shown that a few animals have at least some ability to use symbols in the process of communicating with one another and with humans.

Allen and Beatrice Gardner taught a chimp named Washoe to use 160 different words of the American Sign Language. Washoe was able not only to attach signs to objects but also to put signs together into new and meaningful combinations. For example, when a researcher

Although chimps are physically incapable of human speech, researchers have trained them to recognize and respond to hundreds of images. This shows that humans are not the only species with the capacity for language.

known to Washoe as Susan stepped on Washoe's doll, Washoe gave a series of responses: "Up Susan; mine, please up; gimme baby; shoe up; please move up." Other studies have shown that chimps understand complex instructions such as "You insert banana in pail, apple in dish" (Gardner & Gardner, 1969; Premack, 1976; Harris, 1987).

More recently reported research contains even more remarkable conclusions. E. Sue Savage-Rumbaugh claims that a four-year-old pygmy chimpanzee named Kanzi not only has spontaneously created simple sentences, but also has gained the capacity to respond to spoken English she has not heard before. For example, if asked with no physical gestures whatever, "Will you get a diaper for your sister?" Kanzi is able to do so—a feat until now undocumented among nonhuman primates (Eckholm, 1985).

Chimpanzees do not have the physical ability to form the consonant sounds made by humans. But these recent achievements suggest that we should not chauvinistically assume only humans have any claim to culture. Since they have a limited ability to use symbols, some other species must be viewed as capable of at least rudimentary cultural patterns.

The Sapir-Whorf Hypothesis

In the English language, crystals of frozen water that fall from the sky are called *snow*. An English-speaking skier may also distinguish between *powder* and *corn snow*. Partly melted snow piled up in gutters we call *slush*. But, in general, we use one word for all types of snow. Eskimos, on the other hand, have many words precisely distinguishing various forms and consistencies of snow— falling snow, drifting snow, damp snow, dry snow, and so forth. Does this difference in vocabulary mean that our perceptions of a winter day in the Arctic would differ from those of an Eskimo companion?

We tend to assume that the more than one thousand languages used on earth describe a single reality shared by all people, and that a sentence translated from English to Swahili retains its original meaning. But this assumption was challenged by two anthropologists who specialized in linguistic studies, Edward Sapir and his student and colleague Benjamin Whorf (Sapir, 1929, 1949; Whorf, 1956).

Sapir and Whorf suggested that language is more than simply attaching labels to parts of the "real world." According to them, language actually stands between us and the world, determining what our "reality" is. This is so, in part, because every language has words or expressions that have no precise counterpart in another symbolic system. In addition, each language fuses symbols to particular emotions. Thus, as multilingual people can attest, the reality of a given social situation varies according to whether a person "experiences" it in English, Spanish, German, or some other tongue (Falk, 1987). Formally, then, the **Sapir-Whorf hypothesis,** as this idea has come to be called, holds that *we know the world only in terms that our language provides*. Making use of different systems of language, a Turk, a Brazilian, and a Filipino actually live in "distinct worlds, not merely the same world with different labels attached" (Sapir, 1949:162).

North American culture makes use of a complex system of numbers through which we experience reality in precise numerical terms. When we look at our weekly paychecks, for example, we are likely to be sure that every penny we expect to receive is there. The Yanomamö, on the other hand, have only three numbers in their language, corresponding to "one," "two," and "more than two" in English (Chagnon, 1983). The Yanomamö lack symbols to distinguish between, say, 100 and 150. Of course, our own language limits us in different ways. Much of our thinking about warfare is based on traditional conceptions of military superiority as a source of national security. In an age of nuclear weapons capable of ending life on this planet in a matter of minutes, however, does building more and more weapons to ensure military "superiority" increase our security or undermine it? Are we even able to comprehend the consequences of the use of this military "superiority"?

The Sapir-Whorf hypothesis is a valuable insight, but should not be interpreted to mean that human beings are absolutely constrained to understand the world in only one way. Except for the disabled, human beings have five senses and great mental capacity. This allows us to perceive and understand even things for which our own language has no specific word, although we may have to make a greater effort to do so. Thus our system of language generates strong *tendencies* to understand the world in a particular way, rather than *determining* how we do so.

Furthermore, the relationship between a culture's language and its view of reality is not a matter of simple cause and effect. The Sapir-Whorf hypothesis suggests that language shapes culture as a whole; yet a number of other factors within a culture affect its language. For example, the increasing use of computers has led to new words and phrases such as *bytes, interface,* and *random access memory*. Similarly, as more technologically advanced people gradually intrude into the South American rain forests, the Yanomamö will probably need to specify quantities more precisely, and will probably create a more complex number system to do so.

Culture and language are thus interrelated, and change in either one is likely to affect the other. The desire for greater equality in a predominantly white society led Afro-Americans to replace the word *Negro* with the word *black*. After more than twenty years of increasing usage, the new term has helped improve white people's perceptions of black Americans. For generations, adult males in English-speaking societies have been called *men*, while adult females have often been referred to condescendingly as *girls*. The recent emphasis on calling women *women* is both a cause and an effect of the changing position of women in our culture.

Values

Values are *standards by which members of a culture define what is desirable or undesirable, good or bad, beautiful or ugly* (Williams, 1970:27). They are not descriptive statements but evaluations and judgments, from the standpoint of the culture, of what ought to be. These broad principles are reflected in virtually every aspect of a people's way of life.

All of us have built our own views of ourselves and the world on the values of our culture, often without being aware we have done so. While growing up, we learned from our families, schools, and religious institutions how to think and act in ways valued by our culture, what personal goals are defined as worthy, and how to properly relate to our fellow human beings.

In a society as large and diverse as the United States, of course, few cultural values are shared by everyone. Over the centuries, people from all over the world have entered the United States and, as a result, our culture has become a mosaic of different values. Still, like every other culture, it has a large number of values that most people recognize and that tend to persist over time. A number of values—most of them established early in our society's history by the original English settlers—remain strong enough today to be described as "dominant American values."

American Values

According to Robin Williams (1970), the following ten values are among the most important within American culture.

1. *Equal opportunity.* Americans tend to value providing everyone with the opportunity to get ahead, although everyone is not expected to end up in the same situation. In other words, while Americans do not believe that everyone should have the same amount of wealth or education, we do believe that the opportunity to acquire these things should be equally available to all. Many Americans have traditionally believed that such equality of opportunity does exist in our society, and that personal achievement is limited only by an individual's abilities and desire.

2. *Achievement and success.* American culture is competitive; that is, the belief is that each person should receive only what is deserved on the basis of individual talent and initiative. Occupation is perhaps the most important area in which Americans measure achievement and success. Thus many Americans assume that a physician has more innate ability and drive than a nurse.

3. *Activity and work.* American culture encourages action over reflection, and we Americans actively attempt to manipulate and control the environment to serve our interests. For this reason, we often take a dim view of cultures that appear more easygoing.

4. *Efficiency and practicality.* Americans value activity that solves problems and produces the greatest results in the least amount of time. "Building a better mousetrap" is praiseworthy in our culture, especially when done in the most "cost-effective" way.

5. *Progress.* Americans are generally optimistic about themselves and their future. We tend to believe that the present is better than the past, that the future is likely to be better still, and that the "very latest" is the "very best." American supermarkets are full of products that are advertised as "new and improved." Relatively few items are praised for being "old-fashioned," although in a society that changes as rapidly as our own, there is always some tendency to cast a nostalgic eye on the "slower and simpler" ways of the past.

6. *Science.* Americans believe that science provides the most effective way to address problems. We expect the work of scientific experts and technologists to continually improve our lives. We like to think of ourselves as rational people, and tend to devalue emotions and intuition as sources of knowledge.

7. *Material comfort.* We are a culture of consumers, eager to acquire material things of all kinds. Most Americans define the good life in terms of having many possessions. Celebrations, from birthdays to religious holidays, are occasions to present others with material goods.

8. *Democracy.* Americans believe that each individual has political rights that cannot be overridden by others. Ideally, our political system is based on the participation of all adults through the process of elections. Similarly, our economy is based on providing products and services that meet the needs of a broad range of selective, individual consumers.

9. *Freedom.* Closely related to democracy, this cultural value is based on the belief that each person has the right of free expression. Furthermore, although Americans recognize that everyone has responsibilities and obligations to others, we also believe that individuals should be free to pursue their own goals without unreasonable interference from the government or other people.

10. *Racism and group superiority.* Although expressing a commitment to the values of equality and freedom, Americans often link personal worth to membership in particular social categories based on ethnicity, race, social class, or sex. Thus, while Americans like to think of themselves as equals, some of us are "more equal than others."

Values in Action: The Games People Play

Dominant American values have pervasive effects even when we are least aware of them. A good illustration of this process is in the games we play as children. Although childhood games may seem simply a way of having fun, they also provide important lessons in what a culture defines as important.

James Spates (1976a) has used the sociological perspective to reveal that a number of familiar children's games reflect and promote important cultural values. In the game King of the Mountain, for example, Spates finds a clear expression of competition as a prominent value in American culture:*

> In this game, the King (winner) is the one who scrambles to the top of some designated area and holds it against all challengers (losers). This is a very gratifying game from the winner's point of view, for one learns what it is like (however brief is the tenure at the top before being thrown off) to be an unequivocal success, to be unquestionably better than the entire competition. (1976a:286)

Each player thus attempts to become number one at the expense of all other players. As we all know, success is not without its costs, and King of the Mountain teaches us about these costs as well.

> The King can never relax in such a pressurized position and, psychologically, constant vigilance is very difficult to endure for long. Additionally, the sole victor is likely to feel a certain alienation from his peers: whom can he trust? Truly, "it is lonely at the top."

If King of the Mountain expresses our cultural emphasis on winning, other children's games conversely teach us the plight of being a loser. Tag and Keep Away are probably the best examples of games of this kind. Spates notes that in the game of Tag, the person designated "It" becomes the loser. The "It" player is singled out as lacking the ability to be a member of the group—an experience so difficult to bear that often other players will eventually allow themselves to be tagged just to end "It's" ordeal. All players thus learn the importance of competing successfully, as well as the dangers of not fitting in with the group.

With such observations in mind, we can more easily understand the prominence of competitive team sports in American culture and why athletes such as tennis champion Chris Evert and baseball great Pete Rose are celebrated as cultural heroes.

_____

* The excerpt presented here has been slightly modified on the basis of unpublished versions of this study, with the permission of the author.

There is often a very serious side to play. For instance, King of the Mountain imparts important lessons about success and power.

Value Inconsistency and Value Conflict

Within any society, the values held by different categories of people are likely to reveal some variation from the dominant cultural values. Age, sex, ethnicity, race, and social class all affect the experiences of individuals and therefore the values they are likely to hold. As members of many different social categories, we may also experience inconsistency in our personal values. An upper-class homosexual male may experience conflict between our culture's standards of masculinity and his own personal expressions of sexuality, as well as between his class privilege and the underdog status he holds as a member of a sexual minority. This example also suggests that the dominant culture often defines a particular category of people in a way that conflicts with how they wish to define themselves. Homosexual men and women have recently become more active in opposing the traditional (and often quite distorted) stereotypes of themselves presented in conventional cultural images.

Even the dominant values of a culture sometimes contain contradictions (Lynd, 1967; Bellah et al., 1986). Americans frequently find themselves torn between the "me first" attitude of an individualistic, success-at-all-costs orientation and the often contradictory need for a sense of belonging and community. In addition, the value Americans place on equality or opportunity for all has long been in conflict with a tendency to promote or degrade others on the basis of their race, sex, or social background.

Such value conflicts inevitably cause strain in most of us, leading to awkward balancing acts or rationalizations in our views of the world. We may decide that some values are more important than others; for example, we may choose to maximize our own achievement even though we know that doing so will limit opportunities available to others. Or we may simply deny that there is any value conflict at all. As we shall see in detail in Chapter 9, Americans often minimize the fact that social inequalities in the United States greatly inhibit the opportunities of some individuals to achieve what our culture defines as success. We may overlook the contribution family wealth and power make to one student's ability to complete a college education and go on to a prestigious career, and see another student's need to leave school to help support a family as an indication of personal failure. Thus, in an effort to downplay the inequality of opportunity that does exist in America, we may hold to the common sentiment that "It doesn't matter what kind of family you were born into; if you have the desire to get ahead, you certainly can!" This assertion is inconsistent with the facts; yet because they desire to resolve value conflicts, many people are likely to believe it all the same.

Norms

For most of our history, Americans have viewed sex as appropriate within marriage, and then largely for the purpose of having children. By the 1960s, however, sex had become widely redefined as a form of recreation, perhaps involving people who otherwise knew little of each other. By the mid-1980s, the rules of sex had changed once again. In the face of growing fears of sexually transmitted diseases, the "sexual revolution" was coming to an end, with Americans tending to limit their sexual activity to one partner (McKusick, et al., 1985; Smilgas, 1987).

Such patterns illustrate the operation of what sociologists call **norms**, *rules and expectations by which a society guides the behavior of its members*. Some norms are *proscriptive*, mandating what we must *not* do. For example, Americans are now cautioned to avoid casual sex. Other norms are *prescriptive*, stating what we *must* do. Following practices of "safe sex," for instance, has been broadly promoted in recent years.

Some norms apply to virtually every social situation. For example, we expect children to comply with parental demands at home and in public. Other norms, however, vary from situation to situation. It is perfectly acceptable, and even expected, that people applaud at the end of a musical performance; but applauding a priest or rabbi at the end of a religious service would violate norms that apply to a religious setting. In the same way, the norms that guide our behavior at a library, a formal dinner party, and a rock concert are all somewhat different.

Mores and Folkways

Not all cultural norms have the same degree of importance. William Graham Sumner (1959; orig. 1906), an early American sociologist, used the term **mores** (pronounced more-ays, a plural form of the rarely used singular word *mos*) to refer to *norms that have great moral significance*. Proscriptive mores—often referred to as *taboos*—would include the American expectation that adults not have sexual relations with children. Mores can also be prescriptive, as in the expectation that people in public places wear sufficient clothing to conform to the American "standard of decency."

Because of their importance within the cultural system, mores usually apply to anyone in any situation, and most people believe that conformity to mores is crucial to the existence of society as we know it. Consequently, a violation of mores generally provokes strong negative sanctions from others. For example, we consider the right to one's property to be an important expression of American mores. Consequently, from early childhood, we learn that theft is a serious violation of norms, and one that can disrupt established social relations. For this reason, mores are usually supported by *law*—norms that are formally enacted through a political process so they can be enforced by the power of the state.

Sumner used the term **folkways** to designate *norms that have little moral significance*. Standards of etiquette and appearance are examples of folkways. We may tease a friend who appears slovenly dressed, but the way a person chooses to dress is usually a matter of taste rather than morality. Unlike mores, folkways are highly variable from one situation to another, so that while we might enjoy being rowdy at a soccer game, we do not usually act that way aboard an airliner.

Violations of folkway typically elicit only mild social reactions. For example, a male who does not wear a tie to a formal dinner party would be violating situational folkways; he might be the subject of some comment, but probably no one would take direct action against him. On the other hand, if he were to arrive at the dinner party wearing *only* a tie, he would be violating cultural mores and would likely become the target of serious negative sanctions.

The operation of norms shows us that culture is not simply patterns of human behavior, but is also the arbiter of what is right and wrong. Knowing that others share these standards makes possible a sense of security and trust in our personal interactions. Norms are thus part of the symbolic road map of culture, guiding us as to what is expected in social situations.

Social Control

The operation of norms promotes conformity. When approaching a movie theater, for instance, we take our place at the end of the ticket line without thinking much about it. But consider the angry mutterings if we were to push directly to the front of the line. Someone might even bark, "Just what do you think you're doing!" If we were to apologize for our mistake, offer a reasonable explanation, and go to the end of the line, the expressions of outrage might turn to nods of approval. Such negative and positive responses from others, termed *sanctions*, reward us for conformity and punish us for deviance. Sanctions may be applied informally, as in this example, or in more formal ways, ranging from grades in school to arrest by the police and imprisonment by courts of law. Sanctions are the basis for a culture's system of **social control**: *various means by which members of society encourage conformity to cultural norms.*

The enforcement of norms does not depend entirely on the reaction of others. Recall a situation in which you were alone and did something you knew was wrong. Perhaps as a child you took something that belonged to someone else. Even if no one ever found out about it, you probably reacted negatively to your own behavior. As we come to believe in most of the norms of our culture, in other words, we usually respond *to ourselves* just as someone else observing our behavior would. This is a result of *internalizing* cultural norms—that is, incorporating norms into our own personalities. The evidence that we have done so lies in our experience of *guilt*—the negative judgment we make of ourselves for having violated a norm—and *shame*—the painful acknowledgment of others' disapproval.

"Ideal" versus "Real" Culture

Norms are not descriptions of actual behavior as much as statements about how we *should* behave as members

The "dress for success" idea is largely a matter of conforming to established folkways. Women who enter occupations traditionally held by men sometimes adopt patterns of dress that resemble those of their male colleagues.

of a culture. Like values, norms are ideals that only imperfectly correspond to actual behavior. Sociologists therefore distinguish between **ideal culture,** *social patterns consistent with cultural values and norms,* and **real culture,** designating *social patterns that actually occur.* This distinction is useful when we consider, for example, that while the vast majority of Americans acknowledge the importance of sexual fidelity in marriage, roughly one-third of married people are sexually unfaithful to their spouses at some point in their marriage. Such contradictions are common to all cultural systems, as suggested by the old saying "Do as I say, and not as I do."

Moreover, like all elements of cultural systems, norms vary over time and among different segments of the population. The cultural values and norms brought to North America by English settlers centuries ago continue to shape American life, but many of our current interpretations of them would seem strange indeed to Sir Walter Raleigh or Abigail Adams. Immigrants have introduced such a variety of cultural patterns into our society that real American culture is far more diverse than any single description can convey.

Material Culture

In addition to intangible cultural elements such as values and norms, every culture includes a wide range of tangible human creations that sociologists refer to as *artifacts.* The Yanomamö build huts and make hammocks from materials gathered in the forest around them. They hunt and defend themselves with bows and arrows, fashion distinctive tools to use in raising crops, and paint their bodies with pigments of various colors. All these forms of material culture among the Yanomamö may appear as strange to us as their nonmaterial culture— including their language, values, and norms.

Despite their obvious differences, material and nonmaterial elements of culture are closely related. An examination of any cultural system indicates that material culture is an expression of cultural values. Warfare is a major part of Yanomamö life, in which men pride themselves on being aggressive and able to successfully meet whatever challenges may confront them. The value placed on militaristic skills is reflected in the attention the Yanomamö give to making weapons. The poison tips of their arrows are highly valued possessions.

In the same way, the material elements of our own culture reflect the values we consider important.

The value we place on individuality and independence, for instance, is obvious in our preference for privately owned automobiles over mass transportation. Over 130 million automobiles are registered in the United States today, which is one car for every licensed driver and more than one car for every two Americans. This means that at any given moment every American could climb into a car—and *nobody* would have to sit in back!

Material culture reflects not only cultural values but also **technology,** which is *the application of cultural knowledge to the task of living in a physical environment.* Think of technology as a bridge between the world of nature and the world of culture. The Yanomamö, for example, have a relatively primitive technology, meaning that their way of life is strongly shaped by the forces of nature. Thus they make simple shelters and weapons, and they produce food through small-scale planting and hunting. In contrast, technologically advanced societies (such as those of North America) have considerable ability to reshape nature according to their own cultural values.

Because we highly value our own sophisticated technology, Americans may judge cultures with more primitive technology as less advanced. There is some evidence to support such a judgment. If we use average life expectancy as the measure of a society's quality of life, our technology seems to have served us well. American males born in 1985 can expect to live, on the average, over seventy-one years; American females, over seventy-eight years (U.S. Bureau of the Census, 1987). This represents an increase in life expectancy of more than 50 percent since the turn of the century. In contrast, Napoleon Chagnon estimated that the life expectancy of the Yanomamö is less than forty years.

We must take care, however, to avoid self-serving judgments about the quality of life of people whose cultures differ from our own. Although the Yanomamö are quite eager to gain some of the advantages of modern technology (such as steel tools and shotguns), it may surprise you to learn that they are generally well fed by world standards, and are quite satisfied with their lives (Chagnon, 1983). We must also bear in mind that while our advanced technology has produced timesaving devices that reduce work and seemingly miraculous forms of medical treatment, it has also contributed to unhealthy levels of stress and created weapons capable of destroying in a flash everything that humankind has managed to achieve.

Finally, technology is another cultural element that varies substantially even within American society. Although many of us may not be able to imagine life without a stereo, television, and microwave oven, some members of our society cannot afford such items, and still others oppose them on principle. The Amish are a case in point, as the box explains.

CULTURAL DIVERSITY: MANY WAYS OF LIFE IN ONE WORLD

Between 1820 (when the government began keeping track of immigration) and 1985, over 50 million people came to the United States. Earlier in this century, most came from Europe; by the mid-1980s, one-half million people were entering the United States every year, mostly from Asia and Latin America (Fallows, 1983; U.S. Bureau of the Census, 1987g). This large-scale immigration has made the United States a land of cultural diversity.

Our cultural variation also reflects our multiple geographical regions, religions, and lifestyles. Although sociologists sometimes speak of the "cloth of culture," a more accurate description of our culture might be "patchwork quilt." Thus to understand our culture, we

Artists help shape the image we have of our own way of life. Many have portrayed the culture of privileged people. This painting, "Pharmaceuticals" by Mexican artist Diego Rivera (1886–1957), depicts life from the point of view of those with fewer advantages.

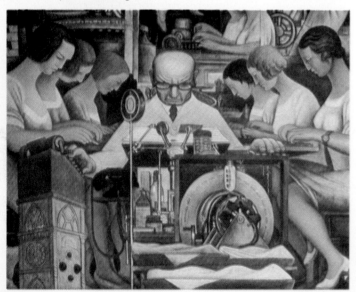

must move beyond a focus on dominant cultural patterns to a consideration of cultural diversity.

Subcultures

Sociologists use the term **subculture** to refer to *cultural patterns that differ from the dominant culture in some distinctive way.* Age, ethnicity, social class, and lifestyle all encourage the formation of subcultures within a society. Occupations also foster such subcultural differences as specialized language, as anyone who has ever spent time with race-car drivers, jazz musicians, or even sociologists can attest. Residents of rural areas may mock the ways of "city slickers," who in turn deride their "country cousins." Sexual preference generates yet another subculture in our society, especially in cities such as San Francisco, Los Angeles, and New York, where large numbers of gay men and women live.

Most present-day societies are composed of many subcultures based on ethnicity. Consider Yugoslavia, a nation in southeastern Europe that is a rather extreme case. This one small country (roughly the size of the state of Wyoming, with a population of about 25 million) makes use of two alphabets, has three major religions, speaks four major languages, contains five major nationalities, is divided into six separate republics, and absorbs cultural influences from seven other nations with which it shares borders. How does American culture compare to that of Yugoslavia?

We learn as children that the United States is a "melting pot" in which people of many nationalities are blended together into "Americans," sharing a single culture. But ethnicity and race have generated greater cultural diversity—and sometimes greater controversy—than this official history suggests. In recent years, cultural distinctiveness seems to have gained in popularity. Many who have come to North America from other cultures do not want to renounce their traditional ways of life and blend into the mainstream.

In 1984, Congress began to debate legislation that would make English the national language of the United States. That this issue should even arise may surprise us, since the English language has been one of the major components of American culture for hundreds of years. Yet, at the beginning of this decade, some 23 million people—about 11 percent of the population—spoke a language other than English in their homes. And their number is steadily increasing toward an estimated 40

CROSS-CULTURAL COMPARISON

The Amish: Rejecting Modern Technology

Westward from the rolling farmlands of central Pennsylvania, through Ohio, Indiana, and southern Ontario, live some 100,000 Old Order Amish—inhabitants of North America since the colonial era who have always stood apart from the dominant culture of this continent.

The Amish are descendants of sixteenth-century Germans who joined religious movements that opposed the established society of their day. Religious and political persecution drove them from their homelands, and many eventually resettled in the New World. Compared to the society around them, the Amish have changed little over the centuries. To most North Americans they are "relics of the past who live an austere, inflexible life dedicated to inconvenient and archaic customs" (Hostetler, 1980:3–4).

The Amish are distinguished by their plain, old-fashioned forms of dress and by the horses and buggies they use for transportation. Devoutly religious, they are committed to their families and to their small, stable communities which make no use of electricity or gasoline-powered vehicles. The Amish have strongly resisted being drawn into the larger society around them, striving instead to be

A *small society within a wider culture that embraces technological progress, the Amish deliberately maintain their traditional cultural patterns, including the same means of transportation used in centuries past.*

self-sufficient and to retain as much as possible their ancestors' way of life. The Amish view of the world is captured in the phrase "The old is the best, and the new is of the devil" (1980:10–11).

The Amish way of life is highly personal. Their settlements are limited in size to the number of people who can work and worship together in close, lasting relationships. The Amish have a secure sense of belonging to a culture in which they are personally known and cared for, and

in which they find a strong identity and sense of purpose. Although Amish life demands a conformity that can be a strain to some, most Amish people are satisfied to model themselves on those who have gone before them. As much as possible, they attempt to educate their children themselves rather than expose them to outside influences. They view science and technology as forces that threaten to dilute and ultimately destroy their cherished way of life.

For much of their history in North America, the Amish have been of little interest to others. In recent decades, however, their existence has become more widely known, and they now endure thousands of outsiders who come as tourists to examine these strange people who seem to live in the past. Is this interest simply a passing phenomenon? Or does our heightened curiosity about the Amish suggest that they may have something to teach the rest of us? Perhaps in the Amish, many of us can see "islands of sanity in a culture gripped by commercialism and technology run wild" (1980:4).

SOURCE: Based on John A. Hostetler, *Amish Society*, 3rd ed. (Baltimore: The Johns Hopkins University Press, 1980).

---

million by the beginning of the next century. Table 3–1 indicates which languages are spoken in homes across the United States. In areas of the United States with large concentrations of non–English-speaking people, ethnic subcultures often prompt parents to insist that their children be provided with a bilingual education in public schools. The box on p. 77 presents some dimensions of this complex and controversial issue.

Canada has long faced an especially serious problem because it is a society where two major cultural groups—those of English ancestry and those of French ancestry—live together. Of 25 million Canadians, about 67 percent speak only English, and 18 percent speak only French, and the remaining 15 percent are bilingual. The French-speaking minority experiences certain social and economic disadvantages in a society where English

Table 3–1 LANGUAGE AS AN INDICATOR OF CULTURAL DIVERSITY IN THE UNITED STATES

Language Spoken at Home	Approximate Number of People
English	190,187,000 (89.0%)
Most common languages other than English	23,060,000 (11.0%)
Spanish	11,116,000
Italian	1,618,000
German	1,587,000
French	1,551,000
Polish	821,000
Chinese	630,000
Philippine languages	474,000
Greek	402,000
Portuguese	352,000
Japanese	337,000
Korean	267,000
Vietnamese	194,000

SOURCE: U.S. Bureau of the Census, *Statistical Abstract of the United States 1985*, 105th ed. (Washington, DC: U.S. Government Printing Office, 1984), Table 43, p. 36.

"Skinheads" embrace cultural patterns that are significantly at odds with dominant American values and norms. The resurgence of racial violence that occurred in the United States during the 1980s suggests that even countercultures never exist entirely apart from the larger culture.

culture predominates. Although Canada officially recognizes both cultural groups by having two national languages, conflict between English-speaking and French-speaking Canadians continues (Esman, 1982).

Countercultures

Cultural differences within a society may also represent active opposition to at least some aspects of the dominant culture. A **counterculture** is defined as *cultural patterns that are strongly at odds with the dominant culture.* Those members of society who embrace countercultural patterns are likely to lead some members of a society to question the morality of the majority; not surprisingly, the majority may be swift to direct the forces of social control against them, from negative coverage in the mass media to police action.

In many societies, countercultures are linked to youth (Spates, 1976b, 1982, 1983). Most of us are familiar with several youth-oriented countercultures that were widely publicized during the 1960s. The hippies challenged the competitive, individualistic, and materialistic values of mainstream American society. Instead, they favored a collective and cooperative lifestyle in which

"being" was more important than "doing," and personal qualities such as "expanded consciousness" were more prized than material possessions. Such differences led many hippies to "drop out" of the larger society, often to form large countercultural communities. The Haight-Ashbury district of San Francisco was perhaps the best-known hippie community in the world.

During the same period, other countercultures reflected active opposition to the American political system and its actions abroad, especially the war in Vietnam. Political organizations such as Students for a Democratic Society (SDS) organized protest marches, while even more radical groups carried out sporadic acts of violence against what they viewed as an unjust and militaristic society. Similarly, the Black Panthers armed themselves in revolt against what they saw as the racism of American culture.

Countercultures develop their own distinctive folkways, including styles of dress, forms of etiquette and recreation, and tastes in music. Many members of the 1960s countercultures wore blue jeans and "ethnic" clothing to symbolize their identification with the "com-

Bilingual Education: The Debate over Cultural Diversity

As millions of immigrants came to North America a century ago, their children entered schools that were intent on teaching them English. Never mind that the children believed themselves to be Greek, Chinese, or Lebanese, or that their parents never spoke English at home. Schools were an important means of transforming the new immigrants into Americans.

In recent decades, growing cultural diversity has caused Americans to reconsider the issue of what languages will be used in schools. By the mid-1980s, more than 5 million children in U.S. schools spoke a native language other than English. The vast majority of them were from Spanish-speaking homes, but dozens of other ethnic groups were also represented. The Bilingual Education Act, passed by Congress in 1968, mandates that children who do not speak English at home can request to be educated in their own language as they simultaneously learn to speak English. As a result, American schools now teach children in some 125 different languages—from Spanish to Haitian Creole, Hmong, Khmer, and Ulithian. Many immigrants also request schools to instruct their children in their own cultural heritage.

Proponents claim several advantages for bilingual education. First, unless children who do not speak English are taught in their native languages (while they also study English), they will quickly fall behind their English-speaking peers. Second, bilingual programs make school more interesting to children who have not yet learned to speak English proficiently, which helps ensure that they will complete their education. Third, children of diverse cultural backgrounds who are encouraged to appreciate their heritage gain a sense of pride in themselves and become better citizens as adults.

Critics, however, see a number of drawbacks to bilingual education. First, providing instruction to some 5 million students in over one hundred languages is terribly expensive; the annual cost of doing so approaches $2 billion. Second, schools cannot always find teachers able to speak the children's languages, especially those spoken by the most recent immigrants to the United States. California, for example, has been successful in employing only about half the teachers it needs for its bilingual programs. Third, some critics fear that bilingual programs will retard the rate at which children in families new to America enter the cultural mainstream. In other words, students who do not learn to use English proficiently may find their future job prospects greatly reduced.

Whatever the costs or problems involved in bilingual education, there is evidence that children do indeed learn better in school if taught in their native language. At the same time, bilingual education is a deliberate means of enhancing—rather than diminishing—the cultural diversity of the United States, and for this reason it is likely to remain controversial. At the heart of the problem is not simply educational policy, but the broader issue of cultural diversity. While some regard cultural differences as good in and of themselves, other Americans believe that this kind of diversity should not be officially encouraged. Schools have become the battleground where Americans struggle with the problems raised by the continuing fact that our nation is built on an enormous range of cultural diversity.

SOURCES: Based on "Battle over Bilingualism," *Time*, September 8, 1980, pp. 64–65; Edward B. Fiske, "One Language or Two? The Controversy over Bilingual Education in America's Schools," *The New York Times*, November 10, 1985, Sect. 12, pp. 1, 45.

mon people" of our society, and listened to rock and roll music, which then had little of the middle-class respectability it enjoys today.

Although perhaps less evident today than in the 1960s, countercultures still flourish in the United States and abroad. In the United States, the Ku Klux Klan and other white supremacist groups promote violence and racial hatred in order to protect what they see as "real American values." In Europe, North America, and elsewhere, young "punks" express their contempt for established culture through provocative styles of music and appearance—shaved heads or multicolored hairstyles, black leather and chains—that are exceedingly distasteful to most people in their societies.

Cultural Change

Anyone who has looked through a family photo album showing how grandparents lived years ago can have no doubt that cultures undergo significant change. In our day-to-day existence, we may not notice changes because we are busy living our lives, not observing them. Cultural changes are usually evident only over a period of years. Consider, for example, changes in the American family over the past half century. Government statistics (U.S. Bureau of the Census, 1986a; U.S. National Center for Health Statistics, 1987b) show that the divorce rate is now more than twice as high as it was in 1940, when a family composed of a bread-winning father, a housewife mother, and their children was the norm. Between 1970 and 1986, the number of single-parent households more than doubled, so that today a majority of children in the United States can expect to live with only one parent before they reach the age of eighteen. Moreover, women have become a much larger proportion of the labor force in recent decades, and more of them are deciding to marry and have children later in life than they once did, or remaining single, but perhaps having children all the same.

Table 3–2 illustrates some of the cultural changes half a century can bring. In 1924, Robert and Helen Lynd looked at the lives of high-school students in Muncie, Indiana; more recently, Theodore Caplow and Howard Bahr (1979) did the same thing to see what had changed in a city long believed to be typical of the United States. Table 3–2 shows that while there was little change in some beliefs and attitudes of Muncie students, many other opinions were quite different. Thus profound cultural changes can occur within a single lifetime.

The fact that women's increased participation in the labor force is associated with changing patterns of marriage illustrates the principle of **cultural integration:** *that the various parts of a cultural system are extensively interrelated.* This means that change in one part of the cultural system is likely to be accompanied by changes in other parts of the system. Not all parts of the cultural system are subject to change at the same rate, however. William Ogburn (1964) has observed that the material elements of culture (such as the medical technology that has created "test-tube babies") change more rapidly than the nonmaterial elements (such as values concerning family life). Ogburn called this pattern **cultural lag:** *inconsistencies within a cultural system resulting from the unequal rates at which different cultural elements*

Table 3–2 CHANGES IN AMERICAN NORMS AND BELIEFS OVER A FIFTY-YEAR PERIOD

Norm or Belief	Percentage of Respondents Agreeing	
	1924	1977
"The theory of evolution offers a more accurate account of the origin and history of mankind than that offered by a literal interpretation of the first chapters of the Bible."	28	50
"Christianity is the one true religion and all peoples should be converted to it."	94	38
"It is wrong to go to movies on Sunday."	33	6
1924: "The Allied Governments in the World War were fighting for a wholly righteous cause." 1977: "In the Viet Nam war the United States was fighting for a wholly righteous cause."	83	36
"The United States is unquestionably the best country in the world."	92	78
"Every good citizen should act according to the following statement: 'My country—right or wrong.' "	61	49
"A citizen of the United States should be allowed to say anything he pleases, even to advocate violent revolution, if he does no violent act himself."	20	47
"It is entirely the fault of a man himself if he does not succeed."	47	47
"The fact that some men [1977: "people"] have so much more money than others shows that there is an unjust condition in this country which ought to be changed."	30	34

SOURCE: Theodore Caplow and Howard M. Bahr, "Half a Century of Change in Adolescent Attitudes: Replication of a Middletown Survey by the Lynds," *Public Opinion Quarterly,* Vol. 43 (1979), pp. 1–17.

change. In a culture that now has the technical ability to allow one woman to give birth to a child by using another woman's egg that has been fertilized in a laboratory, how are we to apply the traditional terms *motherhood* and *fatherhood?*

Three general processes cause change within a culture. First is *invention,* the process of creating new cultural elements—video games, political parties, or polio vaccines, for example. The telephone (1876), the airplane (1903), and the aerosol spray can (1941) are inventions that have had a tremendous impact on our culture. The process of invention occurs constantly, as indicated by the thousands of applications received by the United States Patent Office each year.

Discovery is the second, closely related cause of cultural change. It involves recognizing and understanding something already in existence—from a distant star, to the foods of a foreign culture, to the muscle power of American women. Discovery is often the result of scientific research; many medical breakthroughs happen this way. Yet discovery can also occur quite by accident, as when Marie Curie unintentionally left a rock on a piece of photographic paper in 1898 and thus discovered radium.

The third cause of cultural change is *diffusion*, the spread of both material and nonmaterial elements from one cultural system to another. The presence of missionaries, as well as anthropologists such as Napoleon Chagnon, introduced a number of new cultural elements to the Yąnomamö. Many elements of American culture have spread throughout the world through diffusion: jazz music, with its roots deep in the culture of black Americans; computers, first built in the mid-1940s in a Philadelphia laboratory; and even the United States Constitution, on which several other countries have modeled their own political systems.

Many Americans are surprised to learn how much of our own culture actually came from elsewhere as a result of cultural diffusion. Ralph Linton's classic essay in the box on p. 80 reveals that even a half century ago our culture was much less all-American than we might have imagined.

Ethnocentrism and Cultural Relativity

A question in the popular game Trivial Pursuit asks which beverage is most popular among Americans. Milk? Soft drinks? Coffee? The answer is actually *soft drinks*, but any of the beverages mentioned seems perfectly appropriate to members of our culture.

If the Masai of eastern Africa were to join the game, however, their answer might well be "Blood!" To us, of course, the idea of drinking blood is revolting, if not downright unnatural. On the other hand, nothing is more "natural" to Americans than drinking milk—a practice unappealing to billions of people in the world (including the Chinese).

This example raises a most important question: How can we come to terms with other people's ways of living when they offend our own ideas of what is proper? As we saw earlier, culture is the basis not only

for our perceptions of the world, but also for our sense of right and wrong. It is no wonder, then, that we experience discomfort—and sometimes even disgust—when we encounter cultural patterns that differ radically from our own.

Recall how even Napoleon Chagnon, trained as an anthropologist to have an open mind, first reacted to the Yąnomamö as "naked, sweaty, and hideous." Later he found that some of the Yąnomamö's cultural practices challenged his own sense of morality. For example, Yąnomamö men, who dominate Yąnomamö women, share their wives sexually with younger brothers or friends. From the Yąnomamö point of view, this common practice represents friendship and generosity. From *our* point of view, however, it can be understood only as a perversion of moral standards that is grossly unfair to women.

Anthropologists and sociologists caution us against **ethnocentrism,** which is *the practice of judging another culture by the standards of our own culture.* The tendency to be ethnocentric is perhaps inevitable because our understanding of the world is so closely tied to our own particular way of life. Yet it results in unfair evaluation of an unfamiliar culture because that which is judged is not understood in its own cultural terms. Ethnocentrism is a two-way street, of course. Just as we tend to define those who differ from us in negative terms, so others may judge us. The Yąnomanö, for example, initially considered Napoleon Chagnon to be a "subhuman foreigner who had come to live among them" (Chagnon, 1983:14).

An alternative to ethnocentrism is **cultural relativism,** *the practice of judging any culture by its own standards.* Cultural relativism is often a difficult attitude to achieve, since it requires not only understanding the values and norms of another culture, but also suspending those of the culture we have known all our lives. Still, the effort is worth making for reasons of goodwill or self-interest. As the advancing technology of transportation and communication makes our world seem smaller, our need to gain an understanding of other cultures increases. A decade ago, sociologists Thomas and Margarita Melville began a consulting firm to help American businesses deal with members of other cultures. According to the Melvilles, American business people abroad create needless difficulties for themselves by assuming that those who do not live according to American standards "don't know what they are doing, and therefore are stupid and immoral" (Lenz, 1984). Clearly, such attitudes lose us prestige as well as business abroad.

CLOSE-UP

"One Hundred Percent American"

There can be no question about the average American's Americanism or his desire to preserve this precious heritage at all costs. Nevertheless, some insidious foreign ideas have already wormed their way into his civilization without his realizing what was going on. Thus dawn finds the unsuspecting patriot garbed in pajamas, a garment of East Indian origin; and lying in a bed built on a pattern which originated in either Persia or Asia Minor. He is muffled to the ears in un-American materials: cotton, first domesticated in India; linen, domesticated in the Near East; wool from an animal native to Asia Minor; or silk whose uses were first discovered by the Chinese. All these substances have been transformed into cloth by methods invented in Southwestern Asia.

On awakening he glances at the clock, a medieval European invention, uses one potent Latin word in abbreviated form, rises in haste, and goes to the bathroom. Here, if he stops to think about it, he must feel himself in the presence of a great American institution: he will have heard stories of both the quality and frequency of foreign plumbing and will know that in no other country does the average man perform his ablutions in the midst of such splendor. But the insidious foreign influence was invented by the ancient Egyptians, the use of glazed tiles for floors and walls in the Near East,

porcelain in China, and the art of enameling on metal by Mediterranean artisans of the Bronze Age. Even his bathtub and toilet are but slightly modified copies of Roman originals. The only purely American contribution to the ensemble is the steam radiator, against which our patriot very briefly and unintentionally places his posterior. . . .

Returning to the bedroom, the unconscious victim of un-American practices removes his clothes from a chair, invented in the Near East, and proceeds to dress. He puts on close-fitting tailored garments whose form derives from the skin clothing of the ancient nomads of the Asiatic steppes and fastens them with buttons whose prototypes appeared in Europe at the close of the Stone Age. This costume is appropriate enough for outdoor exercise in a cold climate, but is quite unsuited to American summers, steam-heated houses, and Pullmans. Nevertheless, foreign ideas and habits hold the unfortunate man in thrall even when common sense tells him that the authentically American costume of G-string and moccasins would be far more comfortable. He puts on his feet stiff coverings made from hide prepared by a process invented in ancient Egypt and cut to a pattern which can be traced back to ancient Greece, and makes sure they are properly polished, also a Greek idea. Lastly, he ties about his neck a strip of bright-colored cloth

which is a vestigial survival of the shoulder shawls worn by seventeenth-century Croats. He gives himself a final appraisal in the mirror, an old Mediterranean invention, and goes downstairs to breakfast. . . .

Breakfast over, he places upon his head a molded piece of felt, invented by the nomads of Eastern Asia, and, if it looks like rain, puts on outer shoes of rubber, discovered by the ancient Mexicans, and takes an umbrella, invented in India. He then sprints for his train—the train, not the sprinting, being an English invention. At the station he pauses for a moment to buy a newspaper, paying for it with coins invented in ancient Lydia. Once on board he settles back to inhale the fumes of a cigarette invented in Mexico, or a cigar invented in Brazil. Meanwhile, he reads the news of the day, imprinted in characters invented by the ancient Semites by a process invented in Germany upon a material invented in China. As he scans the latest editorial pointing out the dire results of our institutions of accepting foreign ideas, he will not fail to thank a Hebrew God in an Indo-European language that he is a one hundred per cent (decimal system invented by the Greeks) American (from Americus Vespucci, Italian geographer).

SOURCE: Ralph Linton, "One Hundred Percent American," *The American Mercury*, Vol. XL, No. 160 (April 1937), pp. 427–429.

But is cultural relativism the entire solution to the controversies raised by cultural diversity? Besides routinely offering their wives as sexual partners to other men, Yąnomamö men are quite brutal to women, often reacting with violence when a woman commits some apparent social impropriety. Chagnon reports cases of men shooting women with arrows and otherwise seriously mutilating them. Even in the unlikely event that Yąnomamö women accept this sort of treatment, should we adopt the culturally relative view that such practices are morally right as long as the Yąnomamö themselves accept them?

The fact that there is but one human species leads us to suspect that there must be some basic standards of conduct that are "fair" for people everywhere. But what are they? How can we resist the tendency to put forward our own standards of fair play as applicable to everyone else? Sociologists have no clear answer to this dilemma, yet in a world in which societies come into increasing contact amidst ever-present problems of hunger and war, this is an issue well worth careful thought.

THEORETICAL ANALYSIS OF CULTURE

Culture provides us with the means to understand ourselves and the world around us. Sociologists and anthropologists, however, have the special task of understanding culture. Of course, something as complex as culture cannot be fully understood in terms of any one theoretical approach. Consequently, we will present several widely used approaches.

To make sense of culture as a broad system of symbols, values, and norms, we must adopt a macrolevel sociological viewpoint. You will recall that there are two such theoretical paradigms within sociology, the structural-functional paradigm and the social-conflict paradigm. Each provides valuable insights about culture.

Structural-Functional Analysis

The structural-functional paradigm is based on a vision of culture as a highly integrated system that is relatively stable over time. Within this system, any single element, or *cultural trait*, is understood in terms of its functional contribution to the operation and perpetuation of the culture as a whole. Cultural change is understood as the result of either cultural diffusion (related, perhaps, to immigration) or invention and discovery within the culture. In general, however, the structural-functional paradigm draws our attention to stability rather than to change.

Structural-functionalism regards values as the foundation of a cultural system (Parsons, 1964). In this sense, structural-functionalism draws on the philosophical doctrine of *idealism*, which holds that ideas (rather than, for example, patterns of material production) are the basis of human reality. Therefore, as noted earlier, we can expect cultural values to be expressed in a wide range of social activities. Games, for instance, are cultural traits with the function of teaching important values that support the continued operation of the culture. Obviously, values also serve to bind the members of a society together.

To illustrate the application of this paradigm, con-

Sociologists caution against being ethnocentric, but point out that cultural relativism also has dangers. During the 1930s and 1940s, the Nazis enjoyed considerable popular support in Germany and Austria while they conducted programs of systematic violence and murder against men, women, and children alike.

sider once again the culture of the Amish, which was described earlier. Slowly working hundreds of acres of farmland with a horse and plow, and rejecting electricity and a host of other modern conveniences, makes little sense to most Americans. We can make a meaningful interpretation of such practices, however, by considering the purpose these cultural traits serve in Amish society. Hard work—usually outside the home for men and inside for women—is an important means of maintaining the Amish value of discipline. Long days of shared labor, along with meals and recreation at home, enhance the solidarity of the family. By using traditional technology and avoiding modern conveniences, the Amish are able both to maintain the value of self-sufficiency and to preserve their distinctive way of life (Hostetler, 1980).

As noted in Chapter 1, elements of a culture can also have dysfunctional consequences. In the case of the Amish, the degree of conformity demanded by the community can generate strains within and among individuals, who inevitably have their personal differences. In extreme cases, specific cultural practices may even lead to a community's destruction. Consider the Shakers, another countercultural religious group that flourished in the nineteenth century. This culture prohibited sexual relations among its members. Although they were able to survive for decades by assimilating new members from the outside world, the Shakers' failure to reproduce themselves ultimately led to their disappearance.

The structural-functional paradigm also leads us to expect that all cultures would have at least some traits in common, since all cultures are created by human beings with many of the same basic needs and life experiences. The term **cultural universals** refers to *traits found in all cultures of the world*. George Murdock (1945), who conducted a comparative examination of hundreds of different cultures, found dozens of general traits common to all, although specific patterns often differed considerably from one culture to another. One example of a cultural universal is the family, which functions everywhere to control sexual reproduction and to oversee the upbringing of children. Another is funeral rites, which are a response to the fact that humans everywhere must deal with the reality of death. Jokes exist everywhere, at least partly because they provide a relatively safe means of relieving stress. Yet, as Chapter 6 explains, jokes don't travel well, so what is funny to us may puzzle, or even offend, members of other cultures.

Evaluation. The structural-functional paradigm usefully suggests how cultures are organized systems that attempt to meet human needs. Since all cultures are created by one species, they have much in common. At the same time, since there are many ways to meet almost any human need, cultures around the world reveal striking diversity. An important limitation of structural-functional analysis is its tendency to stress a society's dominant cultural patterns and to direct less attention to cultural diversity *within* a society. This is especially true with regard to cultural differences that arise from social inequality. In addition, the structural-functional paradigm tends to emphasize cultural stability, drawing less attention to cultural change.

Social-Conflict Analysis

The social-conflict paradigm suggests that we view culture not as a well-integrated system but as a dynamic arena of social conflict generated by inequality among categories of people. This paradigm draws attention to the ways in which cultural patterns serve the needs of some members of society at the expense of others.

Unlike structural-functionalism, which accepts certain cultural values as given, the social-conflict paradigm critically asks why these values exist. What forces in society are responsible for generating one set of values and not another? How do the values that characterize a particular culture support patterns of social inequality? Sociologists who make use of this paradigm, especially those who have been influenced by the work of Karl Marx, argue that values are themselves shaped by other cultural elements—particularly a culture's system of economic production. In this sense, the social-conflict paradigm is related to the philosophical doctrine of *materialism*, which holds that the ways people deal with the material world (industrial capitalism in the United States, for example) have a powerful effect on all other dimensions of their culture. Such a materialist approach contrasts to the idealist leanings of structural-functionalism.

Social-conflict analysis holds that the competitive and individualistic values of American culture are a reflection of our capitalist economy, in which factories and other productive enterprises are privately owned. The social prominence of those who control production reinforces the American belief that the rich and powerful have more talent and discipline than other people, and therefore they deserve social privileges. Because of this belief, people are likely to accept capitalism as "natural," despite the fact that it generates great disparity in the material advantages enjoyed by various people.

Social inequalities cause continual strain and disruption that, over time, are likely to result in cultural change. People with few social resources promote a transformation of society that those who benefit from the current system can be expected to resist. The civil rights movement and the women's movement are two recent examples of change generated by disadvantaged segments of American society, both of which have met with opposition by defenders of the status quo.

Evaluation. The strength of the social-conflict paradigm is that it reveals that cultural systems fail to address the needs of all members of society equally. Just as important, this orientation suggests that cultural elements serve to maintain the dominance of some people over others. One consequence of this social inequality is that cultural systems generate forces that promote change. A limitation of the social-conflict paradigm is that it tends to stress the divisiveness of culture, directing less attention to the ways in which cultural patterns integrate all members of society. This suggests the importance of using *both* the social-conflict paradigm and the structural-functional paradigm to gain a fuller understanding of culture.

Naturalist Analysis

Two other theoretical paradigms, cultural ecology and sociobiology, also help us gain a broader understanding of culture. Rooted in the natural sciences, both extend sociological analysis by emphasizing that human culture is created within the natural world. Thus they may be called *naturalist analyses of culture.*

Cultural Ecology

Ecology is a branch of the natural sciences that explores the relationship between a living organism and its natural environment. **Cultural ecology** is thus defined as *a theoretical paradigm that explores the interrelationship of human culture and the physical environment.* This paradigm directs attention to how characteristics of the physical environment, such as climate and the availability of food, water, and other natural resources, may shape cultural patterns.

Consider the case of India, a nation with widespread hunger and malnutrition where the norms of the predominantly Hindu culture prohibit the killing of cows because they are considered sacred animals. To North Americans this prohibition is puzzling, since

In India, a land in which many people go hungry, cows are venerated by Hindus and are therefore not used as a source of food. Cultural ecologists point out that cows make other, more important, contributions to Indian society.

beef is one of our major foods. Is the prohibition against killing cows simply a rather arbitrary religious belief? Marvin Harris (1975) believes the matter is more complex. As part of India's ecological system, he suggests, the cow has an importance that greatly exceeds its value as a source of food.

Harris points out, first, that cows do not threaten human beings by competing for food, since most of the grasses they consume have no nutritional value to humans. But, more important, cows provide two resources of great value to Indians: oxen (the neutered offspring of cows) and manure. With little industrial technology, Indian farmers cannot afford the high costs of farm machinery. Oxen-driven plows are thus as important to Indian agriculture as tractors are to American agriculture. Given Indians' reliance on oxen in farming, it would hardly make sense for them to kill cows. In addition, cows annually produce millions of tons of manure, which is burned as fuel (India has little oil, coal, or wood) and processed into building material. To kill cows, then, would deprive millions of Indians of homes and a source of heat. Thus we can see why the great ecological liability of cow slaughtering is forbidden by Hindu values and norms.

Evaluation. Cultural ecology adds a dimension to our understanding of culture that is neglected by both sociological paradigms noted earlier: the important interplay between culture and the natural environment. The strength of this approach lies in explaining how cultural patterns can be linked to the limitations that confront human beings living within a particular physical environment. A limitation of the cultural-ecology paradigm is that the physical environment rarely shapes cultural patterns in a simple or direct way. More correctly, the cultural and physical worlds interact, each shaping the other. An additional limitation of this approach is that some cultural elements are more readily linked to the physical environment than others.

Sociobiology

Since its origin in the nineteenth century, sociology has had a rather uneasy relationship with biology. In part, this uneasiness is due to rivalry between two disciplines that attempt to explain human life. A more important source of friction, however, is the fact that in the past some biological interpretations of human behavior—for example, those purporting to explain why certain people engage in criminal activity or why one race enjoys a position of dominance over another—were expressions of ethnocentrism rather than legitimate science. Early sociologists often provided evidence to refute such thinking.

By the middle of this century, sociologists had succeeded in demonstrating that culture rather than biology was the major force shaping human lives. Within the last decade, however, new ideas linking human behavior to the principles of biological evolution have revived old debates. This research has created **sociobiology**: *a theoretical paradigm that seeks to explain cultural patterns as the product, at least in part, of biological causes.* As you might expect, many sociologists have greeted this new paradigm with considerable skepticism. Sociobiology certainly has its limitations, but it may also provide helpful insights into human culture.

Sociobiology and Human Evolution

Our understanding of the development of life on earth is based largely on the theory of evolution first put forward by Charles Darwin in 1859 in his book *Origin of Species.* Darwin believed that living organisms change over long periods of time as a result of the process of *natural selection,* which is a matter of four simple principles. First, all living organisms live and reproduce within a natural environment. Second, within each species there is a certain degree of random variability in genes, the basic units of life that carry characteristics of one generation into the next. Third, this random genetic variation can be thought of as the way in which a species "tries out" new life patterns in a particular environment. As a result of this variation, some organisms will more successfully survive by transmitting their genes to offspring more efficiently than other organisms do. Fourth and finally, the gene-linked characteristics associated with greater success in reproduction are likely, over thousands of generations, to become common within a species; genetic characteristics that do not aid survival are likely to disappear.

In short, Darwin asserted that a natural environment selects some gene-based characteristics over others on the basis of how well they contribute to reproductive success. As selected genetic traits become more pronounced over time, *adaptation* of a species to its environment occurs, and these characteristics taken together can be described as the "nature" of the organism.

Applying Sociobiology to Human Culture

The brilliance of Darwin's insights lies in their ability to explain much of the behavior of nonhuman organisms. But we get into murkier water when we attempt to apply these principles to human beings.

Scientists have long recognized that the behavior of nonhumans is regulated by encoded genetic programs. The behavior of ants or bees, for example, obviously reveals a remarkable degree of uniformity. The complex behavior of such insects is accurately described as "social" because individual ants or bees perform interrelated, specialized tasks, and these patterns of behavior continue over long periods of time. Although ants and bees do form "societies," they do not have the capacity to use symbols, and thus they lack culture. They do not creatively fashion their life patterns as we do; rather, they are prisoners of their own biology (Berger, 1967).

But what of human beings? We know that cultures around the world are strikingly different from one another, and that all cultures are themselves internally diverse and change over time. Yet we also know that the various cultures of the world are not nearly as different as they *could be,* as evidenced by numerous cultural universals. Such cultural universals are particularly intriguing to sociobiologists. If human beings are entirely free to create culture in any imaginable way, why do we find some cultural patterns everywhere? Perhaps, sociobiologists reason, the answer lies in the fact that people everywhere are members of a single biological species. Perhaps our biological characteristics have some influence on the culture we create.

Why is sugar sweet? Sociobiologist David Barash asks this simple question, bringing to mind the fact that human beings the world over favorably distinguish foods that taste sweet from those that taste sour. Chemically, the answer is that sugar tastes sweet because it contains sucrose. But from the sociobiological point of view, Barash offers another explanation:

> What is the evolutionary explanation for sugar's sweetness? Clearly, just as beauty is in the eye of the beholder, sweetness is in the mouth of the taster. To anteaters, ants are "sweet";

A *widespread pattern in many cultures is for males to be more forward than females in initiating heterosexual relationships. Sociobiology suggests that this cultural pattern—part of the so-called "double standard"—emerged because males and females benefit from distinctive reproductive strategies.*

anteaters may even find sugar bitter—certainly they don't like it as much as we do. The reason is clear enough: we are primates, and some of our ancestors spent a great deal of time in trees, where they ate a great deal of fruit. Ripe fruit is more nutritious than unripe, and one thing about ripe fruit is that it contains sugars. It doesn't take much imagination to reconstruct the evolutionary sequence that selected for a strong preference among our distant ancestors for the taste that characterized ripe fruit. Genes that influenced their carriers to eat ripe fruit and reject the unripe ultimately made more copies of themselves than did those that were less discriminating. (1981: 39)

Sociobiologists extend this line of argument to include many other forms of human behavior. Sex, for example, is certainly "sweet" to human beings, as it is to all forms of life. The surface explanation for this basic fact is simply that sex feels good. But *why* does it? From a sociobiological point of view, the reason is that sex is vital to the process of reproducing our genes in the next generation. There is no surprise here. But what about the way in which males and females characteristically approach sexuality?

We are all aware of what has been traditionally described within our culture as the "double standard," that is, the pattern by which males generally engage in sexual activity more freely than females do. Indeed, men are often allowed, and even encouraged, to "sow their

wild oats," while women are expected, and even constrained, to be far more discriminating about how often and with whom they engage in sexual relationships. Sociobiologists note with interest that this pattern is not limited to our culture. As sex researcher Alfred Kinsey put it, "Among all people everywhere in the world, the male is more likely than the female to desire sex with a variety of partners" (cited in Barash, 1981:49).

Following the sociobiological argument, nature has assigned females and males very different parts to play in the reproductive process. Females bear children that result from the joining of a woman's egg with a man's sperm. But there are striking differences in the value of a single sperm to the male and a single egg to the female. One male releases millions of sperm in a single ejaculation—technically speaking, enough "to fertilize every woman in North America," according to Barash (1981:47). Women, on the other hand, produce far fewer eggs. So, in principle at least, men are biologically capable of fathering thousands of offspring, while women are able to bear a much smaller number of children. From a strictly biological point of view, then, males are likely to reproduce their genes most efficiently through a strategy of sexual promiscuity. But this strategy does not serve the reproductive interests of women. Each of a woman's relatively few pregnancies demands much more of her; she must carry the child for the duration of the pregnancy, give birth, and nurse the child afterward. Thus efficient reproductive activity on the part of the female may be to select a male whose own qualities will contribute to her child's ability to survive and reproduce most successfully (Remoff, 1984). There is no doubt that the double standard is a cultural pattern linked to the historical domination of females by males (Barry, 1983). But sociobiology suggests that this pattern—like many others—has an underlying biological logic. Simply put, it has developed widely around the world because males and females everywhere have benefited from different reproductive strategies.

Evaluation. Because sociobiology is a relatively new approach to understanding culture, its value is not yet entirely clear. Potentially, sociobiology may offer insights about the biological roots of some cultural patterns—especially cultural universals. At present, however, sociobiology remains controversial.

First, because so-called biological facts have historically been used (or more precisely, *mis*used) to justify placing one race or sex in a position of social disadvantage, sociobiology can be suspected of attempting to do the same thing. However, sociobiology has no connection to an earlier biology's claims that any one race, for example, is innately superior or inferior to another. On the contrary, sociobiology serves to unite rather than divide humanity by asserting that all humans are members of a single species, sharing the same evolutionary history.

Sexism—the assertion that males are inherently superior to females and are therefore justified in having greater social power—is also not part of sociobiological thinking. Sociobiology does rest on the assumption that, from a biological standpoint, men and women are distinctive in ways that no culture is ever likely to eliminate completely—if, in fact, any culture intended to. Sociobiology would have to be considered sexist in this limiting sense of recognizing sex-linked human difference. As Barash points out, however, sexism is based not on the recognition of biological *differences* between males and females per se, but rather on the assertion that males are somehow *better* or *more worthy* than females. Biologically, however, both sexes are equally vital to the reproduction of the human species.

Second, sociobiology may be criticized for lacking scientific proof of its claims. Some sociobiologists, including Edward O. Wilson (1975, 1978), who is generally considered to be the founder of this field of study, believe that future research is likely to provide the evidence necessary to demonstrate the biological roots of human culture.

Nonetheless, it is highly doubtful that biological forces will ever be shown to *determine* human behavior; human behavior is *learned* within a system of culture. More likely, the value of sociobiology will be in showing, as David Barash suggests, that biological forces make some cultural patterns more common than others. This is because, given our evolutionary history, some cultural patterns are simply easier to learn than others. (For example, it is easy to learn to like what our bodies tell us is sweet.) For this reason, Barash describes the forces of biology as "whisperings" within us that create a tendency for humans to develop some cultural patterns rather than others. Biological forces in human beings, he claims, can be compared to "throwing a paper airplane in a strong wind" (1979:39). The wind represents our cultural environment, which is capable of subverting any tendency we may have acquired over our evolutionary history. The development of birth control techniques, for example, has allowed people in many cultures to separate sex from reproduction and therefore to develop sexual attitudes very different from those that prevailed in the past.

Sociobiologists would argue that some cultural patterns (such as the double standard) may be so rooted in our evolutionary past that they would be very difficult to eliminate. Further cultural developments will either prove or disprove this assertion. For now, we can say that the forces of culture represent a far greater influence on human behavior than do the forces of biology.

Still, biology is very much a part of human beings. We are, after all, living creatures whose large brains are the foundation of our creation of culture as a means of survival. In this sense, the forces of "nature" (our biological being) and "nurture" (what we learn within a cultural environment) are more intertwined than in opposition. As noted earlier, *culture is our nature* (Berger, 1967; Lewontin et al., 1984).

The final value of both these naturalist analyses lies in showing us that, while we create a highly variable world of symbols and meaning that we call *culture*, we do so in the context of the natural world. We live in ecological relationship both to other forms of life and to natural resources. Furthermore, naturalist analyses remind us that the ability to create many different cultures results from the transformation of our species throughout our evolutionary past—a long history that in some ways may still be imprinted on our patterns of culture. Sociological and naturalist interpretations of human culture are not irreconcilable, nor are they necessarily even inconsistent. Each provides us with a partial understanding of our world of culture, and we can increase our understanding by making use of them both.

CULTURE AND HUMAN FREEDOM

We have now completed a broad examination of human culture, which shapes who we are and how we understand the world around us. The final task of this chapter is to consider the individual in the midst of culture. Does the power of culture always have beneficial consequences for human beings?

Culture as Constraint

During the long course of human evolution, culture has developed as the human strategy for survival within the natural world. But necessary though culture is for the human species, it can have negative consequences for some people. The extensive social inequality supported by American culture is a case in point. Although our culture provides great privilege to some, as we shall see in detail in Chapter 10, tens of millions of Americans face a variety of problems associated with poverty. Moreover, women of all social classes have often felt powerless in the face of cultural patterns that reflect male power and privilege.

Specific cultural patterns can also have widespread negative consequences. The value American culture places on competitive achievement encourages us to strive for excellence, yet this value also serves to isolate us from one another. Material comforts do improve our lives in many ways, yet a preoccupation with objects may divert us from the security and satisfaction that comes from close relationships with others and a strong

religious faith. Our emphasis on personal freedom provides a great deal of privacy and autonomy, but at the expense of a sense of community in which the problems of life are shared among many people, rather than shouldered by lone individuals (Slater, 1976; Bellah et al., 1986).

While culture is as necessary to human beings as biological instinct is to other forms of animal life, it can detract from our well-being. Yet a fundamental difference between human beings and other animals gives us reason to see the world of culture in a more positive light, as we shall now explain.

Culture as Freedom

In certain ways, human beings may appear to be prisoners of their culture, just as ants or bees are prisoners of their biology. But careful thought about the ideas presented in this chapter suggests that this is not exactly true. Over millions of years of human evolution, humans developed culture as a way to survive effectively in the natural environment. Culture gradually took our species out of a world shaped largely by biology into a world we can shape for ourselves.

Although culture may seem to oppose human interests at times, it reflects the human capacity to be creative, to shape and reshape the world according to our own goals, interests, and choices. The evidence to support this conclusion lies all around us: great cultural diversity exists within our own society, and rich cultural variety is found around the world. Furthermore, culture is not static, but is everywhere changing. Thus, if culture sometimes takes the form of constraint, it is also a continual source of human opportunity. The more we are able to discover about the operation of our culture, the greater will be our ability to make effective use of the freedom it offers us.

SUMMARY

1. Culture refers to the patterned way of life of human beings; although some animals have rudimentary forms of culture, only human beings rely on culture for survival.

2. Culture emerged over the long course of human evolution as the human brain gradually enlarged. The first cultural elements came into existence between about 2 million and 40,000 years ago. However, the more

complex patterns of culture that we call civilization emerged only between 5,000 and 10,000 years ago.

3. Culture is based on symbols, attaching significance to objects and patterns of behavior. Language is the most important expression of cultural symbolism; it transmits culture in the present and also from generation to generation.

4. All cultures are built upon values, standards that shape our orientation to the world around us.

5. All cultures also contain norms that guide human behavior. Mores are norms of high moral significance; folkways are norms of low moral significance in which greater individual discretion is allowed.

6. Values and norms provide statements of ideal culture; in practice, real culture varies considerably from these standards.

7. Cultural systems also contain material creations that reflect cultural values. Material culture is the product of a culture's technology.

8. Cultures contain significant internal variation. Subcultures are cultural patterns that differ from the dominant culture; countercultures are cultural patterns that are strongly at odds with the dominant culture.

9. Culture is never static; invention, discovery, and diffusion all generate cultural change. Not all parts of a cultural system change at the same rate, however, which causes cultural lag.

10. Having learned the standards of our own culture, we often evaluate other cultures ethnocentrically. The alternative to ethnocentrism is cultural relativism, by which different cultures are understood in terms of their own standards.

11. The structural-functional paradigm emphasizes the extent to which culture is a relatively stable system of interrelated parts. Any specific cultural element is understood in terms of its function in maintaining the entire cultural system.

12. The social-conflict paradigm draws attention to the extent to which a cultural system is a dynamic arena of social inequality and conflict.

13. The cultural-ecology paradigm explores the ways in which patterns of human culture are shaped by the natural environment.

14. Like cultural ecology, sociobiology is a "naturalistic" paradigm that explores ways in which patterns of human culture may emerge in response to subtle biological forces that have developed over the long course of human evolution.

15. Culture can serve as a constraint on human needs and ambitions; yet since culture is a human creation, human beings have the capacity to shape and reshape their cultural world to better realize their own needs.

KEY CONCEPTS

counterculture cultural patterns that are strongly at odds with the dominant culture

cultural ecology a theoretical paradigm that explores the interrelationship of human culture and the physical environment

cultural integration the principle that the various parts of the cultural system are extensively interrelated

cultural lag inconsistencies within a cultural system resulting from the unequal rates at which different cultural elements change

cultural relativism the practice of judging any culture by its own standards

cultural transmission the process by which culture is passed from one generation to the next

cultural universals traits found in all human cultures

culture the beliefs, values, behavior, and material objects shared by a particular people

culture shock the personal disorientation that may accompany entry into an unfamiliar social world

ethnocentrism the practice of judging another culture by the standards of our own culture

folkways norms that have little moral significance and about which greater personal discretion is allowed

ideal culture social patterns consistent with cultural values and norms

language a system of symbols with standard meanings that allows members of a society to communicate with one another

material culture tangible elements of culture such as clothing and cities

mores norms that have great moral significance, the violation of which is usually met with vigorous reaction

nonmaterial culture intangible elements of culture such as values and norms

norms rules and expectations by which a society guides the behavior of its members

real culture actual social patterns that are typically only an approximation of ideal cultural norms

Sapir-Whorf hypothesis the assertion that people perceive the world only in terms of the symbols provided by their language

social control the process by which members of a culture encourage conformity to cultural norms

sociobiology a theoretical paradigm that seeks to explain cultural patterns as the product, at least in part, of biological causes

subculture cultural patterns that differ from the dominant culture in some distinctive way

symbol anything that carries a particular meaning recognized by members of a culture

technology the application of cultural knowledge to the task of living in a physical environment

values culturally defined standards of desirability, goodness, and beauty that serve as broad guidelines for social life

---

SUGGESTED READINGS

Napoleon Chagnon's account of the Yąnomamö is extremely interesting, both as a description of a culture very different from our own and as the story of carrying out fieldwork in a most unfamiliar setting.

Napoleon A. Chagnon. *Yąnomamö: The Fierce People.* 3rd ed. New York: Holt, Rinehart and Winston, 1983.

Cannibalism is a practice almost impossible for Westerners to comprehend. Yet, as this book explains, consuming human beings is quite acceptable within some cultures.

Peggy Reeves Sanday. *Divine Hunger: Cannibalism as a Cultural System.* Cambridge, UK: Cambridge University Press, 1986.

This paperback presents the "tough guy" (and much rarer, the "tough gal") in American culture. Including popular "tough guys" of today and of the past, this paperback explores America's "ambivalent love affair with strength."

Rupert Wilkinson. *American Tough: The Tough-Guy Tradition and American Character.* New York: Harper & Row, 1986.

One criticism of American culture concerns the extent to which males have historically shaped the lives of women. The growing awareness of the power of women to shape their own lives within a traditionally male world is the subject of this readable paperback.

Anne Wilson Schaef. *Women's Reality: The Emerging Female System in a White Male Society.* Minneapolis: Winston, 1981.

This recent analysis of American culture emphasizes the conflict between values of individualism and achievement, on the one hand, and a sense of community, on the other.

Robert N. Bellah, Richard Madsen, William M. Sullivan, Ann Swidler, and Steven M. Tipton. *Habits of the Heart: Individualism and Commitment in American Life.* New York: Harper & Row, 1986.

Music is a powerful force within a cultural system. This book describes the lives and music of four popular musicians who helped develop the "protest song" in opposition to many dominant cultural values.

Wayne Hampton. *Guerrilla Minstrels: John Lennon, Joe Hill, Woody Guthrie, Bob Dylan.* Knoxville, TN: The University of Tennessee Press, 1986.

Irish travelers represent a long-established subculture that is explored through the story of one of its members.

Sharon Gmelch. *Nan: The Life of an Irish Traveling Woman.* New York: W. W. Norton, 1986.

Why have firearms had such a strong presence in the cultural history of the United States? This paperback uses the sociological perspective to provide an answer.

William R. Tonso. *Gun and Society: The Social and Existential Roots of the American Attachment to Firearms.* Lanham, MD: University Press of America, 1982.

Since language is the key to culture, the history of the English language in the United States—in all its variety—helps to explain the interaction of various cultural forces in American history.

J. L. Dillard. *Toward a Social History of American English* (with a chapter on Appalachian English by Linda L. Blanton). New York: Mouton Publishers, 1985.

Marvin Harris has used the cultural-ecology paradigm to explain a number of apparently strange cultural practices found around the world. The following book provides fascinating reading:

Marvin Harris. *Good to Eat: Riddles of Food and Culture.* New York: Simon and Schuster, 1986.

The first of the following books is a direct and enjoyable account of sociobiology, exploring patterns of behavior among humans as well as other animals. The second is a critical response to sociobiology.

David Barash. *The Whisperings Within: Evolution and the Origin of Human Nature.* New York: Penguin Books, 1981.

R. C. Lewontin, Steven Rose, and Leon J. Kamin. *Not in Our Genes: Biology, Ideology, and Human Nature.* New York: Pantheon, 1984.

CHAPTER 4

Society

In the classic eighteenth-century novel *The Life and Adventures of Robinson Crusoe*, Daniel Defoe tells the story of a shipwrecked sailor stranded alone on an island in the middle of the ocean. Crusoe managed to gather supplies from the wreckage of the ship, and he constructed shelter and discovered food on the island. Over the months that followed, he attempted to recreate many elements of his native English culture: keeping track of time, observing the Sabbath, fashioning clothing from animal skins, and even making an umbrella to protect himself from the sun.

Why would a writer of this age describe a "society" built on the efforts of a single individual? Perhaps the answer lies in important social changes at that time. Rather than a reflection of divine will, human society was becoming understood as the complex interaction of distinct individuals. In short, *Robinson Crusoe* is more than an adventure story; it is Defoe's comment about a society increasingly built on individual self-interest.

Society can be defined as *people who interact with one another within a limited territory and who share a culture*. But what exactly does this deceptively simple term mean? In this chapter, four major social theories guide an investigation of the character of human society. Each identifies and links together major parts of society; each also describes societies of the past and how they have changed. At the same time, each emphasizes some-

what different facts, so that a careful examination of all four theories will provide a more complete understanding of human society.*

Gerhard and Jean Lenski describe changing types of human societies over a period of roughly ten thousand years, from the earliest groups of people who banded together to hunt and gather food, to highly industrialized societies such as those of North America. In the Lenskis' view, the primary factor that distinguishes one type of society from another is technology, and technological innovation often has revolutionary consequences for society as a whole. Karl Marx also understood human history as a long and complex process of social change. For Marx, however, social conflict, rooted in the way in which human beings produce material goods, was crucial to understanding how society works and why it changes. Max Weber acknowledged the importance of productive forces, but he sought to demonstrate the power of human ideas to shape society. Weber believed that modern society is based on a rational and scientific process of thought that has led to the form of social organization he called

---

* The sociologists included in this chapter were selected to provide the broadest range of ideas about human society. Of course, other theorists are extensively discussed in various chapters—see, for example, the account of Emile Durkheim's thought in Chapters 1, 8, 16, and 22.

bureaucracy. Talcott Parsons addressed the basic question of how something as complex as human society is possible in the first place. He identified what he believed were the basic requirements for the operation of society, and also explained social change as a process by which the internal structure of a society becomes increasingly complex.

The four analyses of society presented in this chapter provide answers to several important questions: How do societies differ and how is modern industrial society distinctive? How and why do societies change? What do all societies have in common? The theorists included in this chapter provide somewhat different answers to these questions. As their ideas are discussed, therefore, major similarities and differences in their theories will be highlighted.

GERHARD AND JEAN LENSKI: SOCIOCULTURAL EVOLUTION

For hundreds of years, a small society called the Ona lived at the southernmost tip of South America. Surviving by gathering vegetation and hunting game, the Ona may well have observed the Portuguese explorer Ferdinand Magellan sail in 1520 through the straits that now bear his name. Although their technologically primitive society endured for many centuries with little change, the encroachment of technologically more advanced people gradually deprived them of their land. Many Ona gave up their traditional way of life; others fell victim to foreign diseases. The death of the last full-blooded member of the Ona was recorded in 1975 (Lenski & Lenski, 1987:127–129).

Most people who live in the industrialized world of rapid transportation and instant global communication would regard the Ona as only a curious vestige of the past. But the contrast between societies such as our own and those of extinct or vanishing peoples such as the Ona provokes a number of questions about the character and meaning of human society. Gerhard and Jean Lenski have described the great differences among societies that have existed throughout human history. They explain how technologically simple societies such as the Ona—the only type of human society until about ten thousand years ago—have been transformed into the industrial societies common in much of the world today.

In analyzing human society, the Lenskis use an approach that is called **sociocultural evolution,** defined as *the process of social change and development in human societies that results from gaining new cultural information, particularly technology* (Lenski & Lenski, 1987:75). Sociocultural evolution is closely related to cultural ecology (described in Chapter 3) in that it focuses on the interrelationship of a society and its physical environment. In addition, this approach draws on the biological concept of evolution to suggest that societies, like living species, change over time as the effects of specific innovations ripple through them. In particular, the Lenskis see technology as vitally important in shaping cultural patterns. Societies with primitive technology can support only a small population engaging in a highly limited way of life. Technologically advanced societies, however, can become extremely large and engage in highly diverse activities.

The Lenskis also point out that the amount of technological information within a society is related to the rate at which social change is likely to occur. Because of their primitive technologies, societies such as the Ona change only slowly. On the other hand, in highly industrialized societies, change is so swift that people may experience dramatic transformations within their lifetimes. Consider some familiar elements of North American culture that would probaby puzzle, or even alarm, people who lived just a few generations ago: test-tube babies, genetic engineering, the threat of nuclear holocaust, computers, electronic surveillance, transsexualism, space shuttles, and artificial hearts (Lenski & Lenski, 1982:3).

As a society's technological information expands, the processes of invention, discovery, and diffusion (described in Chapter 3) become more rapid. In other words, a single technological advance can reshape a culture as it is applied to many existing cultural elements. Of course, societies sometimes resist the effects of technological change; Americans, for example, have been reluctant to develop nuclear power. But, in general, this connection between technology and social change has been found through much of human history.

On the basis of the Lenskis' work, we can distinguish four general types of societies according to their technology: hunting and gathering societies, horticultural and pastoral societies, agrarian societies, and industrial societies.*

---

* This account is limited to the major types of societies described by the Lenskis.

Gerhard Lenski (1924–   ) and Jean Lenski (1928–   )

Gerhard Lenski is an American sociologist well known for his research on the topics of religion and social inequality. Jean Lenski is a writer and poet who has worked closely with her husband in sociological research. Together, they have written at length about the issue of sociocultural evolution.

The Lenskis' ideas about society and social change have much in common with those of Marvin Harris, whose ecological analysis of culture was described in Chapter 3. Cultural ecology, as you will recall, explains how specific cultural patterns help a society to survive in a particular natural environment. Similarly, sociocultural evolution explores the changing ways in which a specific element of culture—technology—is used by a society in the production of important material resources from the natural environment.

Cultural ecology and sociocultural evolution are different, however, in one important respect. Cultural ecology emphasizes that the natural environment can shape cultural patterns. The Lenskis' model of sociocultural evolution also states that societies are influenced by their natural environments—but asserts that this is more true of some societies than of others. Because they have little ability to manipulate the environment, technologically primitive societies are influenced the most by their natural surroundings. More technologically advanced societies have a far greater ability to shape the natural world according to their own designs. Therefore, technologically primitive societies are mostly alike, with some variations as a result of differing natural environments. Technologically advanced societies, in contrast, reveal the striking cultural diversity described in Chapter 3.

Hunting and Gathering Societies

A **hunting and gathering society** is a *society that uses simple technology to hunt animals and gather vegetation.* From the emergence of the first human beings on earth until about ten thousand years ago, all humans lived within hunting and gathering societies. Such societies remained common until several centuries ago, although only a few persist today, including the Pygmies of central Africa, the Bushmen of southwestern Africa, the Aborigines of Australia, the Kaska Indians of northwest Canada, and the Tasaday of the Philippines.

At this early stage of sociocultural evolution, the inefficiency of food production demands that the primary activity be the search for game and edible plants. Hunters and gatherers in harsh environments must spend a great deal of time acquiring food; those in areas lush with vegetation and game, however, may enjoy a considerable amount of leisure. Since food production requires a large amount of land, hunting and gathering societies are spread widely and contain only several dozen people. They are also typically nomadic, moving on after they deplete the vegetation in one area or in the pursuit of migratory animals. Although they periodically return to earlier sites, they rarely form permanent settlements.

Hunting and gathering societies are typically organized around the family. The family obtains and distributes food, teaches necessary skills to children, and pro-

In technologically primitive societies, successful hunting by males is typically a source of high prestige. However, the gathering of vegetation by females is a more abundant and dependable source of nutrition.

tects its members. While the range of activities in hunting and gathering societies is quite limited, some specialization is linked to age and sex. The very young and the very old are expected to contribute only what they can, while healthy adults secure most of the food. The gathering of vegetation—the primary food source—is typically carried out by women, while men do most of the hunting. Therefore, males and females have somewhat *different* positions, but hunters and gatherers probably see men and women as *equal* in social importance (Leacock, 1978).

Some individuals within hunting and gathering societies enjoy more social prestige than others. Male hunters with exceptional skills, for example, are admired, as are women who are unusually productive in gathering vegetation. There are, however, few formal positions of leadership. In most hunting and gathering societies, one person assumes the position of shaman, or spiritual leader, but the benefits of doing so are limited to greater prestige rather than more material possessions. Furthermore, even a shaman must help procure food. Overall, then, the social organization of hunting and gathering societies is relatively simple and egalitarian.

Hunting and gathering peoples rarely turn their primitive weapons—spears, the bow and arrow, and stone knives—to the task of warfare. However, their simple

way of life renders them vulnerable to the forces of nature. Storms and droughts, for instance, may destroy the plants and animals that serve as their food supply. Similarly, they have few effective means to deal with accident and disease. Such high risks lead hunting and gathering peoples to cooperate and share food—a strategy that increases the society's ability to survive. Nonetheless, many members do not outlive childhood, and perhaps half of all adults die before reaching the age of twenty (Lenski & Lenski, 1987:105).

In modern times, the encroachment of advanced societies has limited the migration of hunting and gathering societies, and within the areas that remain to them, the risk of depleting game and vegetation is high. The Lenskis doubt that any hunting and gathering society will survive into the twenty-first century. Fortunately, study of their way of life has produced valuable information about humanity's sociocultural history and our fundamental ties to the natural world.

Horticultural and Pastoral Societies

Between ten thousand and twelve thousand years ago, the technology of *horticulture*—allowing the cultivation of plants—slowly began to change the character of many hunting and gathering societies. The **horticultural society** developed: *a society that cultivates plants using hand tools*. The transition from hunting and gathering to horticulture was gradual, spanning thousands of years. Horticulture first emerged in fertile regions of the Middle East and Southeast Asia. Through cultural diffusion, horticultural technology—based on the hoe and the use of the digging stick to punch holes in the ground for seeds—had spread as far as Western Europe and China by about six thousand years ago. In Central and South America, the cultivation of plants appears to have emerged independently about nine thousand years ago, although horticulture was less efficient there because of the rocky soil and mountainous terrain.

Not all societies were quick to abandon hunting and gathering in favor of horticulture. Hunters and gatherers who enjoyed a plentiful supply of vegetation and game probably found little reason to embrace the new technology (Fisher, 1979). The Yąnomamö, described in Chapter 3, illustrate the common practice of incorporating horticulture into the more traditional pattern of hunting and gathering (Chagnon, 1983). Then, too, in particularly arid regions of Africa, Europe, and Asia, horticulture was of relatively little value. People in these regions developed the **pastoral society**, *a society whose livelihood is based on the domestication of animals*. In some cases, horticulture and pastoralism were combined to produce more stable sources of food. There are numer-

ous examples today of horticultural-pastoral societies in South America, Africa, the Middle East, and Asia.

The domestication of plants and animals was a technological advance that transformed societies in several ways. One result was the production of more material resources, so that societies became larger, containing populations well into the hundreds. Societies that emphasized pastoralism remained largely nomadic, moving their settlements as their herds migrated to fresh grazing lands. Those that emphasized horticulture formed settlements of several hundred people, moving only when the soil became depleted. As trade linked settlements, multicentered societies were formed with an overall population that often exceeded five thousand.

The domestication of plants and animals enabled societies to generate a *material surplus*—more resources than were necessary to sustain day-to-day living. As a result, not everyone had to produce food; some people could perform specialized activities such as creating crafts, engaging in trade, or serving as full-time priests. In comparison to hunting and gathering societies, horticultural and pastoral societies are marked by far more social complexity.

Although variable, religious beliefs among hunting and gathering societies center on the conviction that numerous spirits inhabit the world. Among the less technologically advanced horticultural societies, ancestor worship is common. In more advanced horticultural

Pastoral people continue to flourish today in many North African societies.

societies, a conception of God as Creator is often found. In societies that are predominantly pastoral, the belief in God as Creator is also common, but God is perceived as directly involved in the well-being of the society as a whole (Lenski & Lenski, 1987). This view of God is widespread within American society today, which is explained by the fact that two of the major religions of North America—Christianity and Judaism—emerged among pastoral peoples.

The technological capacity to produce a surplus of food also results in pronounced patterns of social inequality within horticultural and pastoral societies. As some families produce more food than others, they assume positions of relative privilege and power and form alliances with other privileged families, so that social advantages endure over many generations.

Once a small number of families comes to exercise control over an increasingly large society, a rudimentary form of government emerges. However, there are technological limitations to the extent of this power. Without, for example, the ability to communicate or to travel quickly, it is possible to directly control only a small number of people. Furthermore, the exercise of power often breeds opposition, and there is evidence of frequent revolts and other forms of political conflict in these societies.

In sum, the domestication of plants and animals enabled societies to become much more productive than they could have through reliance on hunting and gathering. But advancing technology does not produce purely beneficial consequences. The Lenskis suggest that technological progress may be accompanied by ethical regression. The production of more goods has historically been accompanied by less willingness to share resources among all members of a society. Moreover, this stage in sociocultural evolution is marked by the emergence of slavery, more frequent warfare, and, in a few cases, cannibalism.

Agrarian Societies

About five thousand years ago, further technological advance led to the emergence of the **agrarian society**, which is *a society that engages in large-scale agriculture based on the use of plows drawn by animals.* Agrarian societies first appeared in the Middle East, but this technology was gradually adopted throughout the world. The Lenskis argue that the animal-drawn plow, along with other technological advances that occurred at about the same time—including the invention of the wheel, writing,

The Great Pyramids, constructed with human labor some 4,500 years ago, remain as evidence of the expanding technology of early agrarian societies, as well as of their characteristic social inequality.

and numbers, and the expanding use of metals—caused changes in human societies so profound that this era in human history is widely regarded as "the dawn of civilization" (1987:166).

The animal-drawn plow was a far more efficient means to produce food than the hand tools used for cultivation in horticultural societies. Aeration of the soil as it was turned by the plow also increased soil fertility. Land could be farmed continuously for many decades, permitting permanent settlements. Irrigation also developed in many societies about this time. The large food surpluses produced by agriculture, combined with the use of animals and wagons for transportation, allowed agrarian societies to become far larger both in population and in geographical size. Representing an extreme case, the Roman Empire at its height (about 100 C.E.) had a population of roughly 70 million and encompassed some 2 million square miles (Stavrianos, 1983; Lenski & Lenski, 1987).

The greater surplus of food produced by agriculture enables a larger part of the population to engage in specialized activities other than farming. Skills once common to most members of society—such as clearing land, building, processing food, and engaging in trade—become the basis of distinct occupations. Money replaces

Plants, Technology, and the Status of Women

The evidence suggests that women made a greater contribution to food production than men did in the early stages of sociocultural evolution. Hunters and gatherers valued meat highly, but the hunting carried out primarily by males did not provide a dependable source of food. Thus the gathering of vegetation, mostly by females, was the primary means of ensuring survival.

The tools and seeds used in horticulture developed under the control of women because they already had primary responsibility for providing and preparing food. Although men probably did most of the work of clearing land, women planted and tended the crops. Then the harvest provided work for everyone—male and female, young and old.

When cultivation was under the control of women, men assumed most of the responsibility for trade and tending herds of animals. About five thousand years ago, an important cultural invention took place—the development of metals. This invention spread by cultural diffusion, primarily through the network of male traders. It seems all but certain that males, who were already managing animals, were responsible for hitching the metal plow to cattle, initiating the transition from horticulture to agriculture. As this happened, men for the first time moved into a dominant position in the production of food. As Elise Boulding explains, the result was a decline in the social position of women:

> The shift of the status of the woman farmer may have happened quite rapidly, once there were two male specializations relating to agriculture: plowing and the care of cattle. This situation left women with all the subsidiary tasks, including weeding and carrying water to the fields. The new fields were larger, so women had to work just as many hours as they did before, but now they worked at more secondary tasks. . . . This would contribute further to the erosion of the status of women.

SOURCES: Based on Elise Boulding, *The Underside of History* (Boulder, CO: Westview Press, 1976), pp. 161–163; also Elizabeth Fisher, *Woman's Creation* (Garden City, NY: Anchor Press/Doubleday, 1979).

---

barter as the primary means of economic exchange—with the advantage, as the Lenskis point out, of allowing anyone to engage in business with virtually anyone else (1978:185). The expansion of trade is also historically linked to the growth of large cities as economic and political centers. Ancient Rome contained roughly 1 million people—a size unprecedented in the ancient world. Cities in modern agrarian societies such as India and Egypt are now many times that size. As economic activity expands among a growing population, social life in agrarian societies becomes more individualistic and impersonal.

Dramatic patterns of social inequality are common to agrarian societies. In many cases—including the United States early in its history, especially the South—a large proportion of the population are slaves or peasants who work under the control of elites. Freed from the need to work, elites are able to engage in the study of philosophy, art, and literature. This probably explains how culture, in the common sense of the term, became associated with privileged segments of society.

In horticultural societies, the social position of women is high since they have much of the responsibility for producing food. In agrarian societies, however, men typically have a position of clear social dominance (Boulding, 1976; Fisher, 1979). The box provides a closer look at the declining social position of women over the course of sociocultural evolution.

Religion often reinforces a social hierarchy in which males are preeminent by presenting God in masculine terms. More generally, religion tends to reinforce the power of existing elites by propagating the belief that people are morally obligated to carry out their assigned tasks and to support the elite with some of what they produce. The pharaoh in ancient Egypt and the emperor in China were perceived by their peoples as nothing less than gods who were to be served in any way they wished. Similarly, religion has supported the practice of slavery. In America and elsewhere, slavery was justified in the eyes of elites through the belief that God had wisely placed "childlike" human beings in the care of their owners. Even in the early twentieth century, the czar was held in awe by much of the Russian population.

Within agrarian societies, then, the power of elites tends to greatly expand. At the same time, these societies may reach empire proportions, making the task of ruling them increasingly complex. In order to control such large societies, elites need the services of a wide range of administrators. As the economy expands, therefore, the political system becomes established as a distinct part of society.

In sum, the Lenskis describe agrarian societies as characterized by marked patterns of social and cultural diversity. In addition, more significant differences are formed among agrarian societies than among horticultural and pastoral societies. This is because advancing technology provides greater control over the natural world. Able to make more use of the creative elements of human culture, agrarian societies exhibit striking diversity.

Industrial Societies

An **industrial society,** such as the United States or Canada, is *a society that uses sophisticated machinery powered by advanced fuels to produce material goods.* The muscle power of humans and animals is no longer the primary means of producing material goods, and tools and machinery become more complex and efficient owing to the incorporation of metal alloys such as steel. The steam engine (first coupled to machinery in England in 1765) efficiently mechanized many productive tasks previously done by hand. But this was just the beginning of the *Industrial Revolution,* which ushered in the final stage of the Lenskis' model of sociocultural evolution. As shown in Figure 4–1, the rate of technological innovation continued to increase rapidly throughout the nineteenth century, producing vast social changes and, as noted in Chapter 1, stimulating the birth of sociology itself. Within another century, railroads and steamships revolutionized transportation, and tall buildings supported by steel frames formed towering skylines of cities in Europe and North America.

By the beginning of the twentieth century, automobiles were further changing Western societies and electricity was becoming a part of everyday life. New forms of communication such as the telephone, radio, and television were gradually making a large world seem smaller and smaller. Within the last two generations, this process of innovation has escalated so that humans now fly great distances—often faster than the speed of sound—and even routinely fly away from the planet entirely. This is a remarkable fact when we consider that in all of human history until about seventy-five years ago, human beings traveled no faster than about thirty-five miles an hour—the speed of a steam locomotive or a fast horse. In recent years, computers have revolutionized humanity's ability to process information. Nuclear power, used for destruction ten years before it was used to generate electricity, has perhaps forever changed how we think about the world.

In contrast to agrarian societies, where many occupations are carried on within the home, the industrial society's development of large machinery led to the creation of factories. Individuals who had worked primarily within the family became industrial workers linked to many others only by economic necessity. Lost in the process were many traditional values, beliefs, and customs that had guided agrarian life for centuries.

Industrialism has generated societies of unparalleled size. Although the health of people living in industrial cities was initially poor, a rising standard of living and advancing health-related technology gradually resulted in the control of diseases that had for centuries caused high death rates for children and adults alike.

Figure 4–1   The Increasing Rate of Technological Innovation

This figure illustrates the increasing rate of technological innovation in Western Europe after the beginning of the Industrial Revolution in the mid-eighteenth century. Technological innovation occurs at an accelerating rate because each innovation combines with existing cultural elements to produce many further innovations. (Lenski & Lenski, 1987:67).

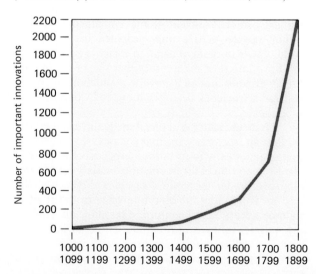

Technology can threaten as well as serve humanity. The utter destruction of the Japanese city of Nagasaki in 1945 by the armed forces of the United States—using a single, "primitive" nuclear bomb—is a grim reminder of the horrors of modern warfare.

As a result, average life expectancy in industrial societies significantly increased, leading to population growth. Industrialization has also brought about a greater concentration of population. Within agrarian societies, population is usually dispersed over the land, with only about 10 percent of people living in cities. The urban proportion of industrialized societies, on the other hand, now generally exceeds 75 percent.

Occupational specialization, which increased over the long course of sociocultural evolution, is now more pronounced than ever. Indeed, in industrial societies, people often identify one another in terms of what they do for a living rather than in more personal terms. Similarly, cultural values have become more varied. As we described in Chapter 3, the societies of North America contain numerous subcultures and countercultures that are often strikingly different from one another.

Within industrial societies, the family has lost much of its traditional significance as the center of social life. It is no longer the major setting for economic production, education, and religious activity. The increasing numbers of single people, divorced people, and single-parent families also reflect the effects of technological advance, as Chapter 14 describes in detail.

The Lenskis suggest that when a society first becomes industrialized, the benefits of advancing technology are enjoyed by only a small part of the population. The majority—especially the urban industrial workers—frequently live in poverty. Over time, however, the benefits of industrial societies are extended. Economic, social,

and political inequality in industrial societies today is probably less than it was a century ago. The need for an increasingly literate and skilled workforce accounts for the leveling of the dramatic social inequality common to agrarian societies. Education has become more widespread, and political rights have been widely extended throughout most industrial societies. For example, even a century ago, only a few women in isolated areas of the United States could vote. With the passage of the Nineteenth Amendment to the Constitution in 1920, women were afforded voting rights equal to men; in Canada, women voted in national elections two years earlier. This pattern of increasingly broader political participation is common to industrialized societies, as recently illustrated by the widespread demands for democratic reforms in Korea, a recently industrializing nation. A summary of the characteristics of industrial societies in relation to the three other types identified by the Lenskis is presented in Table 4–1.

The power of industrial societies is unparalleled in human history; but also, ironically enough, so is their vulnerability to fears and dangers that our agrarian ancestors could not have imagined. Greater individualism affords real benefits, but as we shall explain in Chapter 22, it has also deprived people of the traditional sense of community that characterized agrarian societies. Furthermore, humanity's ability to manipulate nature has not been all to the good, as witness the staggering problem of environmental pollution. Perhaps most important, although industrial societies engage in warfare far less

Table 4—1 SOCIOCULTURAL EVOLUTION: A SUMMARY

Type of Society	Historical Period	Productive Technology	Population Size
Hunting and Gathering Societies	Only type of society until about 10,000 years ago; still common several centuries ago; the few examples remaining today are threatened by extinction	Primitive weapons	25–40 people
Horticultural and Pastoral Societies	From about 10,000 years ago, with decreasing numbers after about 3000 B.C.E.	Horticultural societies use hand tools for cultivating plants; pastoral societies are based on the domestication of animals	Settlements of several hundred people, interconnected to form societies of several thousand people
Agrarian Societies	From about 5,000 years ago, with large but decreasing numbers today	Animal-drawn plow	Millions of people
Industrial Societies	From about 1750 to the present	Advanced sources of energy; mechanized production	Millions of people

frequently than do societies with less developed forms of technology, war now poses unimaginable horrors. Should the current weapons of war ever be used, human life could be forever extinguished or, less drastically, regress to preindustrial forms. In some respects, technological advances have brought people the world over closer together, creating a "global village." What remains, of course, are the daunting problems of establishing peace and justice—problems that technology alone can never solve.

KARL MARX: SOCIAL CONFLICT

Karl Marx was born in Germany in the early nineteenth century, when the Industrial Revolution was radically transforming the agrarian societies of Europe. Marx spent most of his adult life in London, then the capital of a vast British Empire. Colonies around the world supplied England's industrial economy with raw materials and served as markets for British and manufactured goods.

London was a huge metropolis where the extremes of wealth and poverty were obvious to all. A few aristocrats and industrialists enjoyed barely imaginable wealth and privileges, while the majority of the population labored long hours for low wages, lived in slums, and suffered from poor nutrition and disease.

Marx was both saddened and angered by the social inequities he saw all around him. The technological miracles of industrialization had done little to improve the conditions of life for the majority. To Marx, this represented a fundamental contradiction: how could a society that was so rich have a majority who were so poor? Just as important, how could this situation be changed? Many people, no doubt, think of Karl Marx as a man determined to tear societies apart; but actually he was motivated by compassion for humanity and sought to help a society already badly divided find a new and just unity.

The key to Marx's thinking is the idea of **social conflict**, which means *struggle among segments of society over valued resources*. In fact, the social-conflict paradigm in sociology is based heavily on the ideas of Karl Marx.

Table 4—1 (CONTINUED)

Type of Society	Settlement Pattern	Social Organization	Examples
Hunting and Gathering Societies	Nomadic	Family-centered; specialization limited to age and sex; little social inequality	Pygmies of central Africa Bushmen of southwest Africa Aborigines of Australia Tasaday of the Philippines
Horticultural and Pastoral Societies	Horticulturalists form relatively small permanent settlements; pastoralists are nomadic	Family-centered; religious system begins to develop moderate specialization; increased social inequality	Middle Eastern societies about 5,000 B.C.E. Various societies today in New Guinea and other Pacific islands Yąnomanö today in South America
Agrarian Societies	Cities become common, though they generally contain only a small proportion of the population	Family loses significance as distinctive religious, political, and economic systems emerge; extensive specialization; increased social inequality	Egypt during construction of the Great Pyramids Medieval Europe Numerous nonindustrial societies of the world today
Industrial Societies	Cities now contain most of the population	Distinct religious, political, economic, educational, and family systems; highly specialized; marked social inequality persists, diminishing somewhat over time	Most societies today in Europe and North America Japan

Social conflict can, of course, take many forms: individuals may quarrel, some colleges have long-standing rivalries, and nations occasionally go to war. For Marx, however, the most significant form of social conflict arises from the way a society produces material goods.

In the nineteenth-century European societies familiar to Marx, the system of material production was industrial capitalism, which exists today in various forms in North America, Western Europe, and many other societies. Within this system, Marx designated a small part of the population as **capitalists**—*those who own factories and other productive enterprises.* Capitalists seek profits by selling products for a price greater than the costs of production. Most people within the society are the industrial workers Marx termed the **proletariat**—*those who provide the labor necessary for the operation of factories and other productive enterprises.* Workers offer their labor in exchange for the wages necessary to live. In Marx's analysis, social conflict between capitalists and workers is an inevitable result of the productive process itself. To maximize profits, capitalists try to minimize wages, generally their single greatest expense. Competi-

tion encourages capitalists to keep wages as low as possible. Workers, on the other hand, want wages to be as high as possible. Since profits and wages draw upon the same economic resources, social conflict results. Marx argued that this conflict could be ended only by fundamental changes in the capitalist system, changes he believed would eventually occur.

Marx's analysis of society is a form of the philosophical approach called *materialism* because it emphasizes how the system of producing material goods shapes all of society. By this, Marx did not mean that once the economic system is established, the rest of society—including cultural values, politics, and family patterns—falls into place in a direct chain of cause and effect. Rather, like all macro-level theorists, Marx saw society as a system of many interrelated parts, each having an effect on all the others. But just as the Lenskis argue that technology is a crucial force that affects all dimensions of society, so Marx argued that the economic system is of special importance in shaping society:

> [T]he economic structure of society [is] the real foundation [of society]. . . . The mode of production in material life

Karl Marx (1818–1883)

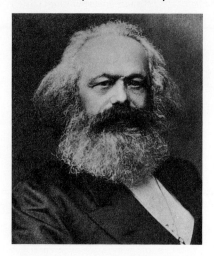

Few names evoke such strong responses as that of Karl Marx. Many consider him a genius and a prophet, others see only evil in his ideas. Marx is, in any event, the social thinker who has had the greatest impact on the world's people. Today, roughly one-fourth of humanity lives in a society that considers itself Marxist.

Controversy surrounded Marx even during his own lifetime. Born in Trier (now in West Germany), he received a doctorate in Berlin in 1841 and soon began working as a newspaper editor. But his relentless criticism led to conflict with government authorities, and he moved to Paris. Subsequently, his controversial activities forced him to leave France as well. He resettled in London, where he lived for the rest of his life.

Along with Emile Durkheim and Max Weber, Marx is one of the major figures in the development of European sociology. However, his ideas received relatively little attention in American sociology until the 1960s. The reason for this neglect surely lies in Marx's explicit criticism of industrial-capitalist society. Early American sociologists frequently dismissed his ideas as mere "politics" rather than serious scholarship. As noted in Chapter 2, however, some measure of values and ethics is present in every

social analysis. But while most sociologists heeded Weber's call for a value-free sociology by attempting to minimize or conceal their own values, Marx's work is explicitly value-laden. What set him apart from others was that he called for the radical reorganization of society. As we have come to recognize the extent to which values affect all ideas, Marx's social analysis has finally received the attention it deserves as an important part of sociology in North America.

According to Marx, ideas should never be separated from political action. He did not wish simply to offer an interpretation of society; he wanted to help people understand the destructive effects of industrial capitalism so that they could change society in order to better meet the needs of the vast majority.

SOURCE: Based in part on George Ritzer, *Sociological Theory* (New York: Alred A. Knopf, 1983), pp. 63–66.

---

determines the general character of the social, political, and spiritual processes of life. (1959:43; orig 1859)

Marx therefore saw the economic system as the *infrastructure* of society—its foundation—and other social institutions, such as the family, the political system, and religion, as society's *superstructure*—meaning that they are built on this foundation and extend the significance of the economic system into all areas of social life. This important idea is illustrated in Figure 4–2. In practical terms, then, each social institution in an industrial-capitalist society reinforces the control of that society by the capitalists, who run the economy. For example, the legal system serves the interests of capitalists by protecting private property and allowing workers to be hired and fired at the discretion of those who own factories.

Most members of industrial-capitalist societies do not view their legal system, or any other part of society, as part of an ongoing social conflict. Indeed, individual rights to private property are taken for granted as "natural." To illustrate, Americans commonly think that some people live in poor-quality housing because they cannot afford something better, and would hardly expect anyone to provide better housing for them unless doing so would be profitable. Likewise, people who are out of work are likely to be seen as lacking the skills or the motivation to become employed. Marx argued that this kind of thinking is molded by our capitalist society, resting on "truths" defined by a social system in which human well-being is based on the operation of the marketplace. Such "truths," he insisted, are actually questionable products of a specific social context. Poor housing and

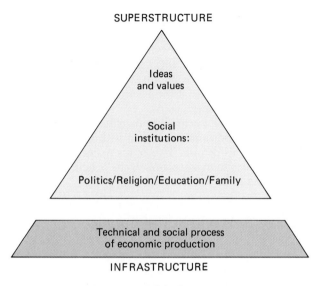

SUPERSTRUCTURE

Ideas
and values

Social
institutions:

Politics/Religion/Education/Family

Technical and social process
of economic production

INFRASTRUCTURE

Figure 4–2 Karl Marx's Model of Society

*This diagram illustrates Marx's materialist approach: that the
process of economic production shapes the entire society.
Economic production involves both technology (industry, in
the case of capitalism) and social relationships (for capitalism,
the relationship between the capitalists, who control the process,
and the workers, who are simply a source of labor). Upon this
infrastructure, or economic foundation, are built the major
social institutions, as well as core cultural values and ideas.
Taken together, these additional social elements represent the
society's superstructure. Marx maintained that all the other
parts of the society are likely to operate in a manner consistent
with the economic system.*

unemployment are not inevitable; they are merely one
set of human possibilities generated by capitalism (Cuff
& Payne, 1979).

This led Marx to the idea of **false consciousness:**
*the belief that the shortcomings of individuals themselves,
rather than society, are responsible for many of the personal problems that people experience.* Marx used this
concept to suggest that industrial capitalism itself was
the cause of many of the social problems he found all
around him. False consciousness makes people incapable
of perceiving the real cause of their suffering, and thus
renders them unable to address social problems actively
and effectively. At the same time, Marx believed that
false consciousness could be overcome. In short, people
could become aware of how their lives were shaped by
industrial capitalism and then act to improve their circumstances.

Social Change

Like the Lenskis, Marx studied the nature and causes
of social change, noting that while change is often gradual
or evolutionary, it is sometimes rapid enough to be called
revolutionary. Marx was well aware that social change
was partly caused by technological advance. However,
he emphasized the greater importance of social conflict
in transforming societies.

Marx believed that the earliest human societies
(hunters and gatherers in the Lenskis' analysis) were characterized by primitive communism. The word *communism* means simply that the production of food and other
material goods is a cooperative effort shared more or
less equally by everyone. While each person in the earliest
societies had personal belongings, the resources of nature
were available to everyone rather than privately owned.
For this reason, and because all members of the society
carried out much the same tasks, social conflict of the
kind common to more technologically advanced societies
was impossible.

Horticulture was a technological advance that introduced significant patterns of social inequality to human societies. Within horticultural, pastoral, and early
agrarian societies—which Marx described simply as the
"ancient world"—warfare produced military captives who
typically became slaves. Supported by the political state,
a small elite (the "masters") used the labor of these slaves
to produce riches for themselves. Slaves and masters
were thus locked into an irreconcilable pattern of social
conflict (Zeitlin, 1981).

As elites amassed greater wealth through the development of agriculture, patterns of social conflict persisted
much as before. In later agrarian societies—such as those
of Europe between about the twelfth and the eighteenth
centuries—serfs, whose social position was only slightly
better than that of slaves, worked the lands owned by
the nobility. Church and state were closely allied in
that era; both law and religion supported feudalism by
defining the existing social order as an expression of
God's will. For Marx, such a system amounted to little
more than "exploitation, veiled by religious and political
illusions" (Marx & Engels, 1972:337; orig. 1848).

Gradually, however, new productive forces
emerged within medieval agrarian societies. Trade expanded steadily through the centuries, and was generally
conducted by peasants who had settled in the cities and
managed to become free of feudal obligations to the
nobility. In this way, a new social category was formed—
the *bourgeoisie* (a French word meaning "of the town").

The bourgeoisie gained wealth as they exchanged goods for profits within a market system. By the mid-eighteenth century, the Industrial Revolution was introducing sophisticated machinery and new sources of energy into the productive process. Ownership of the factory system turned the bourgeoisie into true capitalists who had enough wealth and power to rival the old feudal nobility. Ultimately, the nobility were overwhelmed, and the capitalists took control of the emerging industrial-capitalist societies of Europe.

This revolutionary transformation illustrates Marx's contention that social conflict generates social change. The bourgeoisie emerged in agrarian societies, developing out of the oppressed serfs. The wealth of the bourgeoisie was not based on the feudal system of agricultural production, however, but on commercial trade. As trade expanded, so did the power of the bourgeoisie. Ultimately, the Industrial Revolution gave the bourgeoisie the power they needed to overthrow the feudal nobility and take control of society for themselves. While technological advance was an important part of this change, the feudal system was ultimately overthrown from below as a result of class conflict between the bourgeoisie and the nobility.

Just as the bourgeoisie that emerged in agrarian societies rose to power along with industrial capitalism, Marx claimed that the proletariat or industrial workers spawned by industrial capitalism would ultimately gain the power to create yet another social revolution. The proletariat emerged as English capitalists converted fields once tilled by serfs into grazing land for sheep. To the capitalists, sheep were more valuable than people, since they provided the wool needed for the growing textile industries. Deprived of their livelihood, peasants had

little choice but to migrate to the cities to seek work in factories. In this way, the stage was set for another historical confrontation between those who controlled economic production—in this case, the capitalists—and those exploited by the economic system—the proletariat. This confrontation is at the heart of Marx's analysis of industrial capitalism.

Marx's goal was to illuminate the destructive characteristics of industrial capitalism with the intention of encouraging its demise. Two of his major ideas—social class and alienation—explain why he believed this social system had to be overthrown.

Social Class and Social Conflict

"The history of all hitherto existing society is the history of class struggles." With this observation, Marx (and his collaborator Friedrich Engels) began their best-known statement, the "Manifesto of the Communist Party" (1972:335; orig. 1848). The idea of social class is at the heart of Marx's concern with social conflict. Within industrial capitalism, as in earlier types of society, the two major social classes are based on the position people have in the system of material production. The capitalists and the proletariat, Marx explained, are the historical descendants of dominant and subjugated classes in earlier types of societies: masters and slaves in the ancient world, and nobility and serfs in the feudal world. In each case, one class controls the other as productive property.

Social conflict, then, is nothing new. Under feudalism, however, serfs were bound to the nobility by long-rooted tradition that emphasized personal ties between nobles and serfs and the moral obligation of serfs

Artists depicted the ample evidence of the numbing poverty that was commonplace in the rapidly growing cities of the nineteenth century. To Karl Marx, this posed a contradiction: industrial technology for the first time promised material plenty for all, yet capitalism concentrated this wealth in the hands of a few.

to carry out their assigned work. Industrial capitalism dissolved those ties, creating a new, impersonal relationship between the classes that Marx described in the "Manifesto" as based only on "naked self-interest" and "callous cash payment." Under industrial capitalism, therefore, social conflict between the two classes was more obvious to all.

In Marx's analysis, social class is more than just a description of people's relationship to the system of material production. Classes inevitably foster social conflict, as those who are exploited engage in political action to better meet their needs and those with great privileges typically oppose political action directed at change. But despite the fact that industrial capitalism had brought class conflict more out in the open, Marx recognized that social change was a difficult process. First, he claimed, workers must *become aware* of their shared oppression within the productive process. Second, they must organize to *take direct action* to address their problems. In other words, they must recognize that their plight is not a matter of personal failings (as capitalist cultural beliefs suggest), nor even the fault of other workers with whom they compete for jobs. Rather, it is the consequence of industrial capitalism itself. In short, workers must gain a bit of the sociological perspective to see how social forces have placed them in the same situation. In doing so, they replace false consciousness with **class consciousness**: *the recognition by workers of their unity as a class in opposition to capitalists and, ultimately, to capitalism itself.* Because the inhumanity of early capitalism seemed so obvious to Marx, he believed that industrial workers would inevitably organize in opposition to industrial capitalism. In doing so, they would cease to be merely a social class *in* themselves and become a social class acting *for* themselves.

And what of the other major social class—the capitalists? Their formidable wealth and power, protected as it is by the institutions of society, might seem invulnerable. But Marx saw a weakness in the capitalist armor. Capitalists are motivated by a desire for personal gain and fear the competition of other capitalists. Thus Marx thought that capitalists would be more reluctant than the proletariat to band together, even though they, too, have common interests. Furthermore, he believed, the capitalist system itself operates to ultimately undermine the power of the capitalists. By competing with one another, capitalists keep wages low and thereby encourage workers to join together into a social class actively opposed to industrial capitalism. Thus, Marx claimed, capitalists contribute to their own undoing in the long run.

Alienation of the Proletariat

Marx believed that workers would be provoked into open revolt by their suffering under industrial capitalism. This leads to his consideration of alienation within society.

Marx used the term **social alienation** to mean *the experience of powerlessness in social life.* To Marx, social alienation is a direct result of the operation of industrial capitalism: workers, dominated by capitalists and dehumanized by their jobs, find little satisfaction in their lives and feel individually powerless to improve their situation. A major contradiction in capitalist society, according to Marx, is that as human beings have used advanced technology to gain increasing power over the world, the productive process itself has increasingly exerted power over human beings. The result is that workers find the conditions of industrial-capitalist production very unsatisfying. They feel themselves to be only a commodity, a source of labor, bought by capitalists when necessary and discarded when no longer needed. Marx cited four ways in which industrial capitalism alienates workers.

Alienation from the act of working. Ideally, work is satisfying to human beings as a means to meet their needs and develop their potential. But without a voice in what is produced or how production takes place, what worker is likely to be happy? Furthermore, work in industrial-capitalist societies is often tedious, involving countless repetitions of a specific task requiring no imagination or creativity. The fact that much human labor in industrial societies has been replaced by machines would hardly have surprised Marx. As far as he was concerned, capitalism had turned human beings into machines long ago.

Alienation from the products of work. The products of workers' labor belong not to them, but to the capitalists, who do not produce the products but dispose of them in exchange for profits. Thus, Marx concluded, the more workers put into the products of their labor, the more they lose.

Alienation from other workers. Marx thought that productive activity should be cooperative, affirming the bonds that unite people into a society. Within industrial capitalism, however, he believed that workers cannot act cooperatively. They are forced to compete with one another to find work, and their social contacts typically provide little companionship. In the box on p. 106, an automobile worker and a telephone receptionist describe their lives in terms that illustrate Marx's insights.

Social Alienation Within Industrial Capitalism

These excerpts from the book *Working* by Studs Terkel illustrate how workers may experience social alienation in their jobs.

Twenty-seven-year-old Phil Stallings is an auto worker in a Ford Motor Company assembly plant in Chicago.

I start the automobile, the first welds. From there it goes to another line, where the floor's put on, the roof, the trunk, the hood, the doors. Then it's put on a frame. There is hundreds of lines. . . . I stand in one spot, about two- or three-feet area, all night. The only time a person stops is when the line stops. We do about thirty-two jobs per car, per unit. Forty-eight units an hour, eight hours a day. Thirty-two times forty-eight times eight. Figure it out. That's how many times I push that button.

The noise, oh it's tremendous. You open your mouth and you're liable to get a mouthful of sparks. (Shows his arms) That's a burn, these are burns. You don't compete against the noise. You go to yell and at the same time you're straining to maneuver the gun to where you have to weld.

You got some guys that are uptight, and they're not sociable. It's too rough. You pretty much stay to yourself. You get involved with yourself. You dream, you think of things you've done. I drift back continuously to when I was a kid and what me and my brothers did. The things you love most are what you drift back into.

Lots of times I worked from the time I started to the time of the break and I never realized I had even worked. When you dream, you reduce the chances of friction with the foreman or the next guy.

It don't stop. It just goes and goes and goes. I bet there's men who have lived and died out there, never seen the end of the line. And they never will—because it's endless. It's like a serpent. It's just all body, no tail. It can do things to you. . . .

Twenty-four-year-old Sharon Atkins is a college graduate working as a telephone receptionist for a large midwestern business.

I don't have much contact with people. You can't see them. You don't know if they're laughing, if they're being satirical or being kind. So your conversations become very abrupt. I notice that in talking to people. My conversation would be very short and clipped, in short sentences, the way I talk to people all day on the telephone. . . .

You try to fill up your time with trying to think about other things: what you're going to do on the weekend or about your family. You have to use your imagination. If you don't have a very good one and you bore easily, you're in trouble. Just to fill in time, I write real bad poetry or letters to myself and to other people and never mail them. The letters are fantasies, sort of rambling, how I feel, how depressed I am.

. . . I never answer the phone at home.

SOURCE: Studs Terkel, *Working* (New York: Pantheon Books, 1974), pp. 57–59; 221–222. © 1974 by Pantheon Books, A Division of Random House, Inc.

Alienation from humanity. Industrial capitalism alienates workers from their human potential. Marx argued that a worker "does not fulfill himself in his work but denies himself, has a feeling of misery rather than well-being, does not freely develop his physical and mental energies, but is physically exhausted and mentally debased. The worker, therefore, feels himself to be at home only during his leisure time, whereas at work he feels homeless" (1964a:124–125; orig. 1844). In other words, productive activity, ideally an expression of the best qualities in human beings, is perverted by industrial capitalism to express the worst aspects of human life.

Although workers experience alienation as a personal problem, Marx maintained that it is really a consequence of industrial capitalism. But he believed industrial workers could overcome their alienation by uniting into a true social class that was aware of the cause of its problems and prepared to change society.

Revolution

The only way out of the trap, contended Marx, was for workers to change society. He envisioned a more humane and egalitarian type of productive system, which he termed *socialism.* Marx had no illusions about the obstacles to a socialist revolution, but he was disappointed that workers in England did not join together to end industrial capitalism during his lifetime. Still, believing deeply in the basic immorality of industrial capitalism, he was sure that, in time, the working majority would understand that they held the key to a better future in their own hands. This transformation would certainly be revolutionary, and perhaps even violent. In the end, however, a socialist society based on meeting the needs of all would emerge.

For Marx, a socialist society promised an end to the social conflict that turns one part of society against another. The discussion of social stratification in Chapter 9 will reveal more about changes in industrial-capitalist societies since Marx's time, and why the revolution he longed for has not yet taken place. For now, we will use Marx's own words to sum up his hope for the future (1972:362; orig. 1848): "The proletarians have nothing to lose but their chains. They have a world to win."

MAX WEBER: THE RATIONALIZATION OF SOCIETY

Max Weber combined a keen interest in law, economics, religion, and history to produce what many regard as the most significant contribution to sociology by an individual. Weber's ideas influenced all three of sociology's major theoretical paradigms and are so wide-ranging that they are difficult to summarize in simple terms. Nonetheless, all of his work was an attempt to learn what is distinctive about modern society. Here we shall briefly consider two of Weber's most important contributions: the process he called *rationalization* and its relationship to social change, and the type of *rational organizations* he considered to be characteristic of modern society.

Weber's analysis of society reflects the philosophical approach called *idealism* because it emphasizes the importance of human ideas in shaping society. Like the

Lenskis, he believed technology was responsible for important social patterns. He also shared many of Marx's ideas about social conflict (see Chapter 9). But he departed from a materialist analysis by arguing that societies differ primarily in terms of the ways in which human beings think about the world around them. For Weber, human consciousness—ideas, beliefs, and values—was as important as technology and social conflict in causing social change. Thus he saw modern society as the result of *new ways of thinking* as well as new technology and systems of material production. Weber's emphasis on nonmaterial elements of culture in contrast to Marx's focus on material culture has led his work to be described as "a debate with the ghost of Karl Marx" (Cuff & Payne, 1979:73–74).

Weber was particularly concerned with how individuals attach meaning to their actions. He believed strongly in the importance of objective research methods (as discussed in Chapter 2), but he maintained that a scientific analysis of human behavior is insufficient to explain the form a society takes and why it changes. One must also understand the intangible, subjective forces that shape social life. Weber stressed the importance to sociological research of **verstehen** (a German word meaning "insight" and "empathic understanding"), which is defined as *the effort to learn how individuals in a particular social setting understand their own actions.* Weber believed, in other words, that understanding human motivations is as important to sociology as observing human behavior.

In his study of society, Weber made use of the **ideal type:** *an abstract description of any social phenomenon in terms of its essential characteristics.* He employed ideal types to categorize and compare many specific patterns of human thought and behavior. In this way, he was able to identify the essential characteristics of, say, Protestants that set them apart from members of other religions, or to explain how modern society differs from feudal society. An ideal type has much in common with

Socialist revolutions did occur as Marx expected, but not in the industrial-capitalist societies of Western Europe. Rather, beginning with the Russian Revolution in 1917, shown here, they have occurred largely in agrarian societies.

Max Weber (1864–1920)

To be called a "sociologist" probably would have offended Max Weber. Not that he was indifferent to the study of society; indeed, he spent most of his life doing just that. But Weber's contribution to our understanding of humanity is so broad and rich that no single discipline can properly claim him.

Weber was born into a prosperous German family. His father was a government official who later achieved considerable power on the national political scene. His mother was devoutly religious and preoccupied with her own salvation.

Weber earned a degree in law and began a legal career, but his curiosity transcended any single field of study. His writings reflect an enormous range of interests, including history, economics, and religion as well as sociology.

There is little doubt that Weber's personal life strongly influenced his development as a sociologist. His mother's devout Calvinism must surely have motivated him to pursue the study of world religions, especially the connection between Calvinism and the rise of industrial capitalism. From his father, Weber clearly gained an interest in the operation of bureaucracy and political life.

Weber was both a scholar and a politician. He experienced conflict between the two, however, since one demands reflection and impartiality, while the other requires action based on strong personal conviction. Weber may never have entirely resolved this dilemma, although he attempted to by insisting that sociology be conducted in a value-free manner, while encouraging all individuals to become involved in politics as private citizens.

For many reasons, Weber's life was not entirely happy. He endured conflict with his parents and later suffered for years from psychological problems that sharply limited his ability to work. Even so, the exceptional number of major studies he produced has led many to regard him as the most brilliant sociologist in history.

the more familiar idea of stereotype, in that both are abstract exaggerations of reality. Unlike a stereotype, however, an ideal type is largely factual and is not unfairly positive or negative (Theodorson & Theodorson, 1969:194). In Weber's use, the word *ideal* carries no evaluative connotations such as "good" or "the best"; any social phenomenon—criminality as well as religion—can be described using an ideal type.

Rationality and Industrial Capitalism

With its emphasis on patterns of thought, Weber's analysis of the transformation of European society from feudalism to industrial capitalism differs from the theories of the Lenskis and Marx. Weber claimed that feudal society was based on **tradition**—*sentiments and beliefs about*

the world that are passed from generation to generation. Within a traditional society, human thought and action strongly reflect the past. Moreover, a social pattern is held to be right and proper precisely because it has existed for so long.

In contrast, Weber argued, modern society had become characterized by **rationality**—*deliberate, matter-of-fact calculation of the most efficient means to accomplish any particular goal.* A rational view of the world is largely indifferent to the past; patterns of thought and behavior are adopted on the basis of their present, practical consequences. In modern society, politics, business, and even personal relationships are calculated activities designed to produce specific results.

In Weber's view, industrial capitalism developed as part of what he called the **rationalization of society**, meaning *the change from tradition to rationality as the* *characteristic mode of human thought.* Modern society, he claimed, had become "disenchanted" as sentimentality and religious faith gave way to rationality and a greater reliance on scientific methods.

While recognizing that technological advance is an important dimension of social change, Weber maintained that technological innovation can be encouraged or hindered by the way people in a society understand their world. He noted that although many societies of the world held the technological keys to industrialism, the Industrial Revolution had occurred only in some areas of Western Europe (1958; orig, 1904–1905). Weber explained this curious fact by pointing out that only in Western Europe did a rational view of the world develop. Without such a rational view of the world, he concluded, the development of industrial technology would seem of little significance.

Marx, of course, claimed that industrial capitalism was anything but rational, since this system failed to meet the needs of most of the population. But from Weber's point of view, industrial capitalism is the essence of rationality because it is based on the pursuit of profit through deliberately calculated action. Furthermore, within a highly rational culture, individuals are keenly aware of what is in their best interest. Thus, without denying the existence of social conflict as emphasized by Marx, Weber believed that rationality was a more important force in shaping modern society (Gerth & Mills, 1946:49).

Protestantism and Capitalism

Weber began his analysis of the importance of rationality in modern society by noting that industrial capitalism developed primarily in areas of the world where Calvinism—a Christian religious denomination that emerged as part of the Protestant Reformation—was widespread. This was a crucial observation because Weber also knew that Calvinists, as an ideal type, approached life in a highly disciplined and rational way.

Central to the religious views spread by John Calvin (1509–1564) is the doctrine of *predestination.* This means that God, with complete control over the universe, has selected some people for salvation and others for eternal damnation. Because an individual's fate had been predestined before birth, Calvinists believed that there was nothing people could do to alter their destiny. Neither could individuals know what their fate was to be. One certainty, however, was that their fate was a matter of

unequaled importance, for what hung in the balance was nothing less than heavenly glory or hellfire for all of eternity.

The central question that framed the life of Calvinists, then, was their eternal fate. But how was the individual to know this fate? Calvinists gradually came to an answer of sorts: the individual chosen for everlasting salvation could expect to prosper in this world. While not entirely logical, this assertion appealed to people anxious about their eternal destiny. Worldly prosperity became a sign—if not proof—of salvation, and as Calvinists became absorbed in a quest for worldly success, they emphasized rationality, discipline, and hard work. They pursued prosperity, not essentially to be rich, but to carry out God's will as effectively as possible. In Weber's terms, they viewed their work as a divine "calling." Furthermore, if they were successful, they reinvested their profits in their business, since to spend money self-indulgently would certainly be sinful. Nor were Calvinists prompted to share their wealth with the poor. Tending to view poverty as a sign of rejection by God, they reasoned that not even God's elect could do anything to help the poor. In short, Calvinists deliberately and piously used their wealth to generate more wealth, practicing personal thrift and quickly embracing the technological advances that accompanied the Industrial Revolution.

According to Weber, other religions of the world—including Catholicism, which had dominated Europe before the Protestant Reformation—encouraged a more traditional, "otherworldly" acceptance of one's lot on earth in hopes of greater rewards in the life to come. In contrast, Calvinists believed that their duty was to strive for success in all endeavors in order to fulfill God's plan. And so it was, Weber explained, that within a few centuries industrial capitalism became well established in areas of northwestern Europe in which Calvinism was strong.

Weber's study of Calvinism is strong evidence of the power of ideas—which Marx considered to be merely a reflection of the process of material production—to shape all of society. Still, Weber's theory can be criticized for implying a rather simple causal model of the development of capitalism. This was certainly not Weber's intention; indeed, his work was partly a reaction to what he considered to be Marx's tendency to explain modern society simplistically in terms of economic forces. Thus his concern with the power of ideas should be viewed as an effort to broaden Marx's vision of society. Later in his career, in fact, Weber (1961; orig. 1920) stressed that the development of industrial capitalism was exceedingly complex, involving both economic and legal factors in addition to a distinctive world view (Collins, 1986).

Weber continued to believe, however, that the crucial characteristic of the modern world was rationality. When the religious calling that so motivated the early Calvinists gradually weakened, he noted, industrial capitalism continued to thrive on personal discipline, but in search of profit for its own sake rather than for the glory of God. This, of course, is the essence of the world becoming "disenchanted." In sum, the social qualities of early Calvinism, stripped of their explicitly religious character, are at the heart of what Weber held to be the distinctive organizational feature of the modern world: bureaucracy.*

Rationality and Modern Society

Weber believed that a rational world view not only encouraged the Industrial Revolution, but also defined the character of modern society. As early as the horticultural era, societies began to develop deliberate means to administer their diverse activities. As societies became larger and more complex, administrative organizations also grew in size. In feudal Europe, for example, the Catholic Church was an enormous organization with thousands of officials who maintained its political and religious influence. Still, Weber argued, all elements of traditional social organization reflected a traditional world view rather than rationality.

Truly efficient social organization became possible in Western societies only in recent centuries, Weber claimed, as a rational world view replaced traditionalism. The type of social organization commonly called *bureaucracy* emerged as a result of the rationalization of society and is closely linked to industrial capitalism.

In simple terms, **bureaucracy** is defined as *an organizational model rationally designed to perform complex tasks efficiently*. The complex affairs of modern society are typically carried out by large-scale organizations structured in a bureaucratic way—business corporations, government agencies, labor unions, and universities, to cite a few examples. In noting characteristics of bureaucratic organizations, Weber was able to identify crucial principles of modern social organization (1946:196–204; orig. 1921).

---

* This discussion has benefited from the ideas of Chris Wright, University of Aberdeen, Scotland.

Specialization. In traditional societies, all individuals usually engage in many of the same activities. The rational organization of modern society, however, separates human activity into numerous specialized tasks and responsibilities, which correspond to various formally recognized *offices*. A college, for example, contains numerous offices, including those of the president, deans, faculty, and athletic coaches. Each officer carries out specific tasks in a deliberate way.

Hierarchy of formal offices. Power in modern societies corresponds in large measure to hierarchically arranged offices. Within specific organizations officers are supervised and controlled by those in higher positions. The bureaucratic hierarchy typically resembles a pyramid— the higher the level of responsibility, the fewer offices there are. In vertical channels of communication, directives from officers with greater decision-making power flow downward to others who carry out the specific tasks; reports on work accomplished flow upward to supervisors.

Rules and regulations. To early Calvinists, discipline was rooted in religious belief. Within the disenchanted modern world, discipline is encouraged by extensive organizational rules and regulations. Rewards and punishments—including promotion and dismissal—encourage adherence to organizational norms. Discipline allows the organization to operate in a predictable fashion, with the goal of efficiency.

Technical competence. With the cultural value of efficiency, modern social organization is based on recruiting people who have the necessary training and technical competence. Within organizations, individual performance is routinely evaluated to ensure that any bureaucratic officer is capable of meeting organizational goals. Advancement to positions of greater importance is generally based on a record of high achievement in positions of lesser responsibility. Having undertaken the extensive training necessary to hold an official position, individuals enter into their employment as a "career," the modern counterpart of a "calling."

Impersonality. Weber pointed out that since feelings and emotions are often not expressions of rationality, they are opposed to rational social organization. In traditional societies, all organizations are based on personal relationships and the central organization is the family. In contrast, rationality in modern society is expressed by the demand that officials treat all people and situations impartially and according to organizational rules. Therefore, for example, a professor is expected to grade a student on the basis of performance, not personal feelings. Nor

Like Karl Marx, Max Weber saw modern society as alienating. As this painting by George Tooker suggests, however, alienation was more a result of rigid bureaucratic organization than a consequence of social inequality.

is likely to be modified if doing so will make the organization even more efficient. In contrast, traditional social organization, which places little emphasis on efficiency, is typically hostile to change and remains stable over long periods of time. Thus Weber asserted that rationality has done for organizational efficiency what industrialization has done for the production of material goods:

> The decisive reason for the advance of bureaucratic organization has always been its purely *technical* superiority over any other form of organization. The fully developed bureaucratic apparatus compares with other organizations exactly as does the machine with the nonmechanical modes of production. (1978:973; orig. 1921)

Rationality and efficiency also have a natural affinity to capitalism, as Weber noted:

> Today, it is primarily the capitalist market economy which demands that the official business of public administration be discharged precisely, unambiguously, continuously, and with as much speed as possible. Normally, the very large capitalist enterprises are themselves unequalled models of strict bureaucratic organization. (1978:974; orig. 1921)

Alienation of the Bureaucrat

In ideal terms, then, bureaucracies are organizations of unparalleled efficiency. Indeed, Marx reached much the same conclusion about industrial capitalism as a system of material production. At the same time, however, Marx was aware of the destructive effects of this economic system on human beings, as we have already described. Weber, too, saw in bureaucratic organization the cause of alienation.

Rules and regulations demand that people be treated as cases rather than as individuals. In addition, specialized organizational tasks may involve tedious repetition. And perhaps most important, human spontaneity and creativity can be stifled by bureaucratic formality. In fact, much of Weber's writing reveals a pessimism about modern life based on the fear that, rather than serving the interests of humanity, bureaucracies might become a modern form of enslavement. In language that is reminiscent of Marx's description of the human toll of industrial capitalism, Weber described modern humanity in terms of the alienated bureaucrat: "only a small cog in a ceaselessly moving mechanism which prescribes to him an endlessly fixed routine of march" (1978:988; orig. 1921). Comparing modern organizations to "machines" in which individuals are "chained"

can bureaucratic leaders pass their power on to their sons and daughters. Any personal motives that influence the behavior of an officer are likely to be defined as a conflict of interest between the individual and the organization.

Formal, written communications. In contrast to the informal, face-to-face patterns of communication in traditional societies, modern society makes use of formal, written documents. Such documents are maintained over time, becoming the "files" that Weber argued are the heart of any bureaucratic organization. The importance of formal documents lies in the fact that organizational activity is in principle not spontaneous and personal, but meant to conform to formal policies regarding goals and the means to achieve them. Such records enable the bureaucratic organization to persist in predictable fashion despite changes in personnel.

Bureaucracy and Rationality

In Weber's view, bureaucracy is the inevitable consequence of a rational world view because each organizational element is deliberately designed to achieve a specific purpose and to increase the efficiency of the organization. In addition, any rationally enacted policy

Talcott Parsons (1902–1979)

Talcott Parsons is at once the most influential American sociologist of this century and one of the least read.

Parsons's Paradox begins in the mid-1920s, when the young man traveled to Germany for graduate study. Particularly drawn to Alfred Weber, Parsons also absorbed much of older brother Max Weber's social thought. Of course, Parsons could hardly escape the influence of the other German giant of sociology, Karl Marx. However, he subsequently dismissed most of Marx's ideas. He certainly rejected Marx's materialist conception of society in favor of Max Weber's idealist view of the centrality of ideas and values in shaping society.

In spite of positioning himself on one side of a number of intellectual debates, Parsons imagined that he could fashion a single, grand theory of society. Attempting to fuse the wide range of sociological approaches was certainly an ambitious undertaking; those who were less generous called it pretentious.

Parsons did manage to draw together many diverse ideas, but his theory making was always guided primarily by the structural-functionalist paradigm. The paradox of his career is this: Though he had immense influence by midcentury, rather than unifying the discipline, he provoked the rapid development of other theoretical approaches—notably the symbolic-interaction paradigm and the social-conflict paradigm (Adriaansens, 1979). Furthermore, as interest in these other approaches grew, Parsons's influence tended to subside.

---

to their activity despite their efforts to "squirm free," Weber feared that the logical end point of a rational world view would be the reduction of people to mere robots.

TALCOTT PARSONS: THE FUNCTIONS OF SOCIETY

How is something as complex as human society possible? Answering this question was the life work of Talcott Parsons. Parsons was especially concerned with understanding how each element of social structure contributed to the stable operation of society; therefore, he made extensive use of the structural-functional paradigm. In brief, Parsons's view of society is the following:

1. *Society is a system of functionally interrelated parts.* The many different parts of society are interdependent and function to maintain the operation of society as a whole.

2. *Society is generally stable over time.* The parts of a society are integrated in a state of equilibrium that enhances stability over considerable periods of time.

3. *Society changes in an orderly fashion.* The functional integration of the parts of society discourages random or chaotic social change. Societies change in order to operate more efficiently, primarily by developing greater internal differentiation.

All of the macro-level explanations of human society presented in this chapter identify major parts of society, their interrelationships, and their consequences. The Lenskis describe how technology has shaped social patterns over human history, Marx was concerned with social classes and resulting social conflict, and Weber explained how a distinctive world view shaped modern society. What sets the work of Parsons apart is his key assertion that society is a well-integrated system in which every social pattern makes a functional contribution to the operation of society as a whole. In addition, Parsons's analysis raises perhaps the most general—and in many ways, the most difficult—of all the issues considered in this chapter. He attempted to explain how the vastly complex phenomenon of human society is possible in the first place, how society as a complex system operates, and how and why societies change.

To address these questions, Parsons developed a number of related theoretical arguments, many of which were modified over his long career. Here we shall consider only a few of his most basic ideas, beginning with the necessary conditions for the survival of society.

The Functional Requirements of Society

Parsons (1951) claimed that every society must satisfy four functional requirements in order to exist. In other words, these are basic tasks that any society must successfully perform.

1. *Adaptation*. A society must adapt to the physical environment in order to survive. Parsons suggested that any society's first task is to produce and distribute the material resources (food and shelter are important basic examples) necessary to sustain the lives of its members.

2. *Goal attainment*. Once a society has satisfied the basic physical needs of its members, its second general task is to develop and address other societal goals. These might include raising people's standard of living and managing relations with other societies. Once various goals are identified, their relative importance must be assessed and organized efforts must be undertaken to achieve them.

3. *Integration*. For any goal to be achieved, a society must establish some form of internal organization. Modern societies especially contain a large number of people who engage in many highly specialized activities. The efforts of all members of the society must be directed and coordinated if goals are to be realized.

4. *Pattern maintenance*. Integrating people's efforts depends on motivating everyone to conform to established patterns of thinking and acting. In other words, the members of a society must share largely the same cultural values and observe the same cultural norms. That ensures that social patterns will be maintained with minimal disruption.

Taking another step in Parsons's analysis, we may ask: How does a society ensure that each of the four functional requirements will be effectively addressed? Parsons suggested that modern societies contain five basic internal parts, or social institutions, that address these

tasks (Parsons & Smelser, 1965). A **social institution** is defined as *a major structural part of society that addresses one or more of its basic needs*. First, adaptation is achieved through the operation of a society's economy—the social institution primarily concerned with obtaining necessary resources from the physical environment and distributing them in some orderly way to the population. Second, goal attainment is addressed through the political institution. The selection of social goals and the means for their implementation is the primary function of politics. Third, the integration of society is enhanced politically through law, as well as by the educational institution, which provides culturally appropriate knowledge and training to members of society. Fourth, pattern maintenance is promoted by two additional social institutions—religion and the family—which instill in individuals recognition of culturally approved values and norms.

In reality, of course, all social institutions contribute at least something to meeting each of the four functional requirements. Parsons's point, however, is that each social institution plays a somewhat specialized part in the general process of ensuring the survival of society.

The Four-System Hierarchy

Parsons also viewed society as having four major systems or levels, each linked in a general way to one of the four functional requirements (Parsons, 1951; Parsons & Shils, 1951). He maintained that the four systems have varying degrees of importance for the operation of society, so he presented them as four levels in a hierarchy, as illustrated in Figure 4–3. This vertical representation of society is roughly analogous to a standing human being. The physical environment is the ground on which society is based, since human beings are fundamentally biological creatures. Overhead is the vast and mysterious universe, drawing us upward from our biological roots as we search for the significance of human existence. According to Parsons, all social life is ultimately an attempt to solve problems of meaning. Thus Parsons's four systems of society rise between the ground and the stars, so to speak. Each system is based on more simple systems beneath it and shaped by more sophisticated systems above it.

1. *The behavioral system*. Because human beings are biological creatures, Parsons claimed that society is rooted in the biological existence of the human species. The behavioral system refers to meeting the survival needs

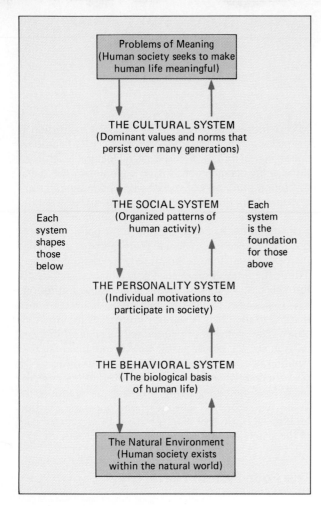

Figure 4-3   The Four-System Hierarchy

(Parsons, 1966:28)

of human beings and is therefore related to the functional requirement of adaptation.

2. *The personality system.* While biological existence is the basis of human personality, Parsons believed that biology plays little part in shaping the human personality. Although each individual is in some ways unique, everyone's self-concept and view of the world are socially formed. The personality system refers to the ways in which individuals are motivated to band together, working cooperatively to meet their goals. In this way, the personality system is related to the functional need of goal attainment.

3. *The social system.* Within any society, people interact with one another according to established patterns of social norms. Parsons called these organized patterns of behavior the social system. Through the operation of the social system, society addresses the functional requirement of integration.

4. *The cultural system.* The cultural system includes all the symbols created by human beings in an attempt to find meaning in their lives. Parsons considered the cultural system to be the most powerful force in human society. Especially important are dominant cultural values, transmitted from generation to generation, that guide a society in developing and perpetuating an organized social structure. The cultural system addresses the functional requirement of pattern maintenance.

Because the cultural system is of the greatest importance, its influence flows down through the other systems of society (as illustrated in Figure 4–3), affecting social patterns, shaping personality, and giving meaning to human existence. In addition, each system is the foundation on which the system above is constructed. In other words, there can be no personality without biological existence, no social system without motivated personalities, and no cultural system without integrated social living.

The Evolution of Societies

Parsons's identification and analysis of the major structural parts of society in terms of their functional interrelationships led him to emphasize social order and stability. In doing so, he received substantial criticism for allegedly neglecting the issues of social conflict and social change that so preoccupied other sociologists. Although Parsons never devoted very much attention to social conflict, toward the end of his career he did develop a model of social change in evolutionary terms.

Parsons's (1966) analysis of social change is similar to the Lenskis' model of sociocultural evolution in that it argues that societies become more advanced over time. But while the Lenskis' analysis of social change emphasizes the consequences of technological innovation, Parsons's analysis presents social change as a process of *differentiation*, by which the parts of a society become increasingly numerous and specialized.

In simple terms, the process of differentiation means that, over time, one general part of society develops into two or more specialized parts that meet society's needs more efficiently. In hunting and gathering societies, for example, the family addresses all four of Parsons's functional requirements of society. Over time, however, distinct religious, political, economic, and educational institutions become separate from the family. Once it has distinct social institutions, each addressing a different basic task, a society is able to carry out the four functional requirements more efficiently.

In intermediate societies, distinct religious institutions exist along with the family system.

Using this basic model, Parsons identified three types of societies: primitive, intermediate, and modern. These should be viewed as very general stages that human societies pass through over time.

Parsons's *primitive societies* correspond roughly to hunting and gathering societies and early horticultural and pastoral societies as described by the Lenskis. Primitive societies, Parsons noted, have no distinct religious, political, economic, and educational institutions. Rather, all social needs are addressed within the family.

Internal differentiation begins within what Parsons described as *intermediate societies*, which correspond to more advanced horticultural and pastoral societies and early agrarian societies in the Lenskis' analysis. Initially, these societies have only limited internal differentiation—usually a religious system distinct from the family. In time, rudimentary political and economic institutions develop, although they remain partly under the control of the family. It is within agrarian societies that the political institution becomes distinct from the family. As Parsons explains, this is partly because of the greater size of agrarian societies and partly because of the development of writing, which fosters the growth of political administration.

What Parsons called *modern societies* emerge with extensive development of distinct social institutions. By the time of the Industrial Revolution, the economy was becoming separate from the family, as productive work moved out of the home and into factories. Within a century or so, the demand for a better-trained labor force resulted in the emergence of the educational institution as the last differentiated sphere. Within modern societies, therefore, there are five major social institutions: the family, religion, the political system, the economy, and the educational system.

In Parsons's view, the process of increasing internal differentiation is synonymous with the advance of society.

In what Parsons termed primitive societies, social organization is limited to family groups.

In modern societies, many institutions exist as distinct arenas of life. In London and other modern cities, one finds churches, schools, business areas, residential neighborhoods, government offices, and military districts.

This is because differentiated societies can more efficiently address the four functional requirements (adaptation, goal attainment, integration, and pattern maintenance). In primitive societies, as noted, all the functional requirements are addressed within the family. But as societies evolve toward intermediate and modern forms, these functional requirements become the focus of distinct social institutions. As explained previously, the economy is of primary importance for adaptation; politics addresses the task of goal attainment; religion and education address the need for societal integration. In modern societies, then, the function of the family is primarily that of pattern maintenance. Parsons believed that distinct social institutions respond to the four functional requirements better than the family does by itself. Thus, he concluded, modern society, in which all five social institutions have developed, is the most advanced of the three societal types.

Parsons had the most positive view of social change among the social thinkers we have considered in this chapter. The Lenskis caution that societies with advanced technology are not necessarily better in any other sense. Marx was critical of societies throughout human history, and claimed that social conflict is most intense within modern industrial-capitalist societies. Although Weber recognized the organizational efficiency of modern bureaucratic society, he was deeply fearful that human beings would become lost within a maze of organizational rules and structures. In contrast, Parsons seemed to see modern societies as truly better than earlier types. As a result of gaining greater overall efficiency, he claimed, modern society relieves individuals of many mundane tasks that burdened their ancestors. In addition, he suggested, a highly differentiated society supports greater cultural diversity, encourages greater tolerance, and enhances individual freedom (Alexander, 1984). Finally, the widespread literacy characteristic of modern societies allows more people access to what their culture has to offer.

Despite Parsons's belief that modern society provides a higher quality of life, he was not uncritical of modern society. Within a highly differentiated society, he pointed out, individuals face a potentially overwhelming range of personal choices. Furthermore, he emphasized that integration is a far greater problem in modern society than in less differentiated societies in which all activities take place within the family. Nonetheless, in relation to the other social thinkers we have considered, Parsons clearly held the most optimistic view of modern society.

FOUR VISIONS OF SOCIETY

At the beginning of this chapter, we presented several important questions about the operation of human society. To conclude, we shall highlight the answers to these questions provided by the four visions of society we have examined.

How Do Societies Differ and How Is Modern Society Distinctive?

All of the social thinkers we have presented address this question. For Gerhard and Jean Lenski, societies throughout human history differ primarily in terms of their productive technology. Modern societies are distinc-

tive, in the Lenskis' view, primarily in their use of industrial technology. Karl Marx reached much the same conclusion, pointing to historical differences in the productive system. But Marx was less concerned with these differences than with showing that material production in all historical societies (except for the most primitive hunters and gatherers) generates social conflict. For Marx, modern society is distinctive only in that social conflict has become more obvious. In contrast to Marx, Max Weber emphasized the characteristically different modes of human thought in societies through history. Feudal societies, he claimed, were traditional, while modern societies have a distinctively rational view of the world. Finally, for Talcott Parsons, historical differences among societies depend on their degree of internal differentiation. The family dominates primitive societies, whereas modern societies have distinct social institutions.

How and Why Do Societies Change?

Here again, the social thinkers we have considered provide different insights. The Lenskis claim that social change is primarily a matter of technological innovation that, over time, alters a society in a revolutionary way. Marx pointed to social conflict as the cause of social change; the struggle between social classes is the force that has pushed societies toward revolutionary reorganization. Weber sought to counter Marxist materialism with an idealist view, showing that modes of thought are also important to social change. He demonstrated how the rational thinking characteristic of Calvinism had contributed to the Industrial Revolution, and how rationality has generated extensive bureaucratic organization in modern societies. Finally, although he was more concerned with social stability than with social change, Parsons theorized that social change resulted from the process of internal differentiation that increased a society's ability to survive. Societies change, he concluded, because greater internal complexity allows them to operate more efficiently.

What Do All Societies Have in Common?

It is in response to this question that the social thinkers we have considered show the greatest differences. The Lenskis clearly see the historical differences among various types of societies as more striking than their commonalities. They explain that all societies engage in material production, but *how* they do so is quite variable. Marx provided a more direct answer to this question: All societies (except for the most primitive type) are characterized by social conflict. In other words, regardless of their productive technology, societies place one category of people in opposition to another. Weber avoided directly answering the question—his comparative approach led him to dwell more on the fascinating differences among societies—but he certainly would have agreed with the Lenskis that technology is important to all societies. And like Marx, he recognized historical patterns of social conflict. Yet he often found the world views of various societies he studied so different that he hedged on formulating generalities that would deemphasize this variety. Parsons, however, considered this question of commonality essential. In response, he specified four functional prerequisites that all societies must address.

Finally, we have also found different assessments of modern society and its likely future among these social thinkers. The Lenskis are careful to avoid equating technological advance with overall quality of life, yet they do indicate that industrial societies provide many advantages, including a higher standard of living and a much longer life span. Moreover, as technology continues to advance, we can expect societies of the future to experience further—perhaps revolutionary—changes. Marx found little to celebrate in modern society; yet he looked to the future for a final resolution of historical class conflict as socialism placed the productive system under the control of all the people. Weber believed a socialist revolution would do little to eliminate the dehumanizing aspects of widespread bureaucracy. Indeed, he feared that socialist revolution might even expand the power of large-scale organizations. Thus his view of modern society and the future is probably the most pessimistic of all. Parsons, in contrast, was decidedly optimistic. He maintained that modern society provides the highest quality of life in history. Not only does it meet basic social needs more effectively, but it also gives individuals more education and greater freedom than they ever enjoyed before. There is little doubt that Parsons expected the quality of human life to continue to rise.

The significant differences among these four approaches to understanding society do not mean that any of them is, in an absolute sense, right or wrong. Society is an exceedingly complex phenomenon, and the work of these social thinkers draws attention to various parts of a vast picture.

SUMMARY

Gerhard and Jean Lenski

1. The Lenskis' model of sociocultural evolution is based on the assertion that social change is primarily the result of technological advance. Technological advance also increases the rate of social change.

2. Hunting and gathering societies, extending from earliest human history to the present, contain only several dozen people who are nomadic. Virtually all social activities take place within the family. Hunting and gathering societies are rapidly disappearing from the world.

3. In horticultural societies, which emerged about ten thousand years ago, women used hand tools for cultivation. These societies contain several hundred people in a single settlement linked by trade to other settlements. Pastoral societies, in which animals are domesticated, engage in extensive trading networks, but remain nomadic. Greater social inequality and warfare are common in both types of societies.

4. In agrarian societies, which emerged about five thousand years ago, men use animal-drawn plows for agriculture. Some of these societies reached empire proportions and contained large permanent settlements. Agrarian societies are characterized by greater specialization, money, and marked social inequality.

5. Industrial societies, first arising only about 250 years ago in Europe, make use of advanced sources of energy as well as sophisticated machinery. In these societies, social change is the most rapid. Most of the population lives in and around cities, and many social activities take place in distinct institutional spheres apart from the family.

6. Technological advance does not always result in improvement in other dimensions of social life. Historically, technological advance has generated greater social inequality, and today, advanced technology has created unprecedented environmental dangers and weapons of war that threaten the entire planet.

Karl Marx

7. Marx understood society and social change in terms of inequality and social conflict between social classes, which are defined by their relation to the process of

producing material goods. Thus his social-conflict analysis of society is also materialist.

8.   Social conflict has characterized human history except for the earliest hunting and gathering societies. In "ancient" societies, social conflict involved masters and slaves; in agrarian societies, nobility and serfs; in industrial-capitalist societies, the bourgeoisie and the proletariat.

9.   To Marx social class implied more than simply people's position in the process of material production. A true social class is aware of its interests and acts to improve its social position.

10.   The industrial-capitalist system alienates workers in four ways: from the act of working, from the products of work, from other workers, and from human potential.

11.   Although he recognized the obstacles to their doing so, Marx believed that industrial-capitalist workers would replace false consciousness with class consciousness and ultimately act to overthrow the industrial-capitalist system.

Max Weber

12.   Weber's contribution to sociology is wide-ranging, but his emphasis is on the importance of the subjective meaning of human behavior.

13.   Weber's idealist approach claimed that ways of thinking have a powerful effect on society and social change.

14.   In contrast to the importance of tradition in feudal society, modern society is based on rational thought. Weber described this transformation as the rationalization of society.

15.   Weber demonstrated the power of ideas to help change society in his analysis of the links between Calvinism and the rise of industrial capitalism.

16.   Rationality in modern society is the basis of bureaucracy. The major characteristics of this form of organiza-

tion are specialization of activities, hierarchical arrangement of offices, extensive rules and regulations, emphasis on technical competence, impersonality, and formal, written communication.

17.   Weber was aware of the human costs of bureaucratic efficiency. Individuals are often treated as cases, and rigid rules can stifle human creativity. Weber's overall view of modern society is largely negative.

Talcott Parsons

18.   Parsons viewed society as a system of interrelated parts existing in a state of equilibrium and order. His analysis emphasizes the functional significance of various parts of society.

19.   All societies must address four functional requirements for survival: adaptation, goal attainment, integration, and pattern maintenance. In modern societies, various social institutions function to meet each of these needs.

20.   All societies contain four conceptually distinct levels of social life: the behavioral system, the personality system, the social system, and the cultural system. In Parsons's hierarchical order, each system has increasing power to shape society as a whole; all, however, are essential to the operation of society.

21.   Parsons identified three historical types of societies: primitive, intermediate, and modern. These are distinguished by their relative degree of internal differentiation. In primitive societies, the family is the single social institution; modern societies have five major social institutions: the family, religion, the political system, the economy, and the educational system.

22.   Parsons viewed modern society postively because he believed it provided the highest quality of human life. He was aware, however, that members of modern societies face unique problems of integration.

KEY CONCEPTS

agrarian society a society that engages in large-scale agriculture based on the use of plows drawn by animals

bureaucracy an organizational model rationally designed to perform complex tasks efficiently

capitalists those who own factories and other productive enterprises

class consciousness the recognition by workers of their unity as a social class in opposition to capitalists and to capitalism itself

false consciousness the belief that the shortcomings of individuals themselves, and not society, are responsible for many of the personal problems that people experience

horticultural society a society that cultivates plants using hand tools

hunting and gathering society a society that uses simple technology to hunt animals and gather vegetation

ideal type an abstract description of any social phenomenon in terms of its essential characteristics

industrial society a society that uses sophisticated machinery powered by advanced fuels to produce material goods

pastoral society a society whose livelihood is based on the domestication of animals

proletariat those who provide the labor necessary for the operation of factories and other productive enterprises

rationality deliberate, matter-of-fact calculation of the most efficient means to accomplish any particular goal

rationalization of society the change from tradition to rationality as the characteristic mode of human thought

social alienation the experience of powerlessness in social life

social conflict struggle among segments of society over valued resources

social institution a major structural part of society that addresses one or more of its basic needs

society people who interact with one another within a limited territory and who share a culture

sociocultural evolution the process of social change resulting from gaining new cultural elements, particularly technology

tradition sentiments and beliefs about the world that are passed from generation to generation

verstehen a German word meaning the effort to learn how individuals in a particular social setting understand their own actions

---

SUGGESTED READINGS

A comprehensive account of Gerhard and Jean Lenski's analysis of the history of human societies is found in the following textbook:

Gerhard Lenski and Jean Lenski. *Human Society: An Introduction to Macrosociology.* 5th ed. New York: McGraw-Hill, 1987.

A detailed and critical account of the consequences of the Industrial Revolution for human society is found in this brief but worthwhile book.

Richard J. Badham. *Theories of Industrial Society.* New York: St. Martin's Press, 1986.

One of the best sources of essays by Karl Marx and Friedrich Engels is the following paperback:

Robert C. Tucker, ed. *The Marx-Engels Reader.* 2nd ed. New York: W. W. Norton, 1978.

The ideas of Karl Marx, especially with regard to issues of morality and justice, are presented in this recent book:

Steven Lukes. *Marxism and Morality.* Oxford, UK: Clarendon Press, 1985.

Perhaps Max Weber's best-known study is his analysis of Protestantism and capitalism. This paperback can be readily understood by the beginning student, and provides valuable insights into not only Western society but Weber's approach to sociology as well.

Max Weber. *The Protestant Ethic and the Spirit of Capitalism.* New York: Charles Scribner's Sons, 1958 (orig. 1904–05).

This paperback, by a noted contemporary sociologist, explores the ideas of Max Weber with a focus on many previously neglected issues.

Randall Collins. *Weberian Sociological Theory.* Cambridge, UK: Cambridge University Press, 1986.

Talcott Parsons's work is not easy reading, but it is worth the effort. These two paperbacks are a good place to start. The first provides an overview of his vision of society; the second focuses on societal evolution.

Talcott Parsons. *The System of Modern Societies.* Englewood Cliffs, NJ: Prentice-Hall, 1971.

Talcott Parsons. *Societies: Comparative and Evolutionary Perspectives.* Englewood Cliffs, NJ: Prentice-Hall, 1966.

Two good, general sources for Parsons's ideas on human society are the following:

Francois Bourricaud. *The Sociology of Talcott Parsons.* Chicago: The University of Chicago Press, 1981.

Pat N. Lackey. *Invitation to Talcott Parsons' Theory.* Houston: Cap and Gown Press, 1987.

This paperback is a series of essays with a single theme: that sociological theory has lost some vitality over the course of the last century as many sociologists are reluctant to acknowledge the moral significance of sociological thinking.

Mark L. Wardell and Stephen P. Turner, eds. *Sociological Theory in Transition.* Boston: Allen & Unwin, 1986.

CHAPTER 5

Socialization

On a cold winter day in 1938, a concerned social worker paid a call to a farmhouse in rural Pennsylvania and found a five-year-old girl hidden in a second-floor storage room. The child, whose name was Anna, was wedged into an old chair with her arms tied above her head so that she could not move. She was dressed in only a few filthy garments, and her arms and legs were like matchsticks—so thin and frail that she could not use them (Davis, 1940:554).

Anna's situation was both moving and tragic. She was born in 1932 to an unmarried woman of twenty-six who lived with her father. Enraged by his daughter's "illegitimate" motherhood, he initially refused to even have the child in his house. Anna was therefore taken to a children's home in a nearby city shortly after her birth. But Anna's mother was unable to pay for her care, so the child was moved from one stranger's house to another for a period of several months. Finally, not yet six months of age, Anna was brought back to live with her mother and grandfather.

At this point, her ordeal intensified. Because of the grandfather's continuing hostility, Anna's mother kept her in a room that resembled an attic, providing almost no attention and just enough milk to keep her alive. Anna stayed in that room, with essentially no human contact, for five years.

Upon reading of the discovery of Anna, sociologist Kingsley Davis traveled immediately to see the child, who had been taken by local authorities to a county home for children. He was appalled by her condition: Anna was emaciated and devoid of strength. Just as important, she displayed none of the social qualities that are commonly associated with being human. Anna did not speak, smile, laugh, or even show anger. She was completely apathetic, as if the people caring for her did not even exist. Not surprisingly, then, they concluded initially—but incorrectly—that Anna was deaf and blind (Davis, 1940).

THE IMPORTANCE OF SOCIAL EXPERIENCE

Here is a case, at once deplorable and fascinating, of a human being deprived of virtually all social experience. Anna was physically alive, but she was clearly not a human being in the full sense of those words. Such an incident reveals the power of human society to endow biological creatures with the capacity for thought, emotion, and meaningful action. Deprived of social contact, Anna was simply an *object* rather than a *person*. In short, no one can become fully human in the absence of social experience.

121

This chapter examines the way in which we become social beings. This is the importance of **socialization,** defined as *a lifelong process of social interaction by which individuals develop their human potential and learn the patterns of their culture.* Socialization is a vital foundation of our humanity. As the unfortunate case of Anna shows us, in the absence of socialization, a human being is little more than a living organism. Unlike other species of life for which behavior is determined biologically, human beings require social learning in order to gain the capacity to survive. And beyond mere survival, social experience provides the foundation of personality. **Personality** is a concept that embraces broad patterns of our social humanity; in the simplest terms, it is defined as *the organized system of personal thoughts, feelings, and behavior.* Personality includes how we think about the world and about ourselves, how we respond emotionally to various situations and to other people, and how we act within our daily lives. Only through the development of personality do people become distinctive human beings, while at the same time sharing culture as members of a society. The absence of social experience eliminates the possibility for the development of personality.

Social experience is vital not only for the realization of personality, but also for the continuation of society. A society has a life that extends both forward and backward in time, far beyond the life span of any individual. As described in Chapters 3 and 4, every society must teach something of its past and present way of life to its new members. The complex and lifelong process of socialization is the fundamental way in which culture is transmitted from one generation to another (Elkin & Handel, 1984).

Human Development: Nature and Nurture

Virtually helpless at birth, the human infant needs care and nourishment from others to survive. A child also relies on others to learn patterns of culture. Although a case like Anna's makes these facts very clear, for many years the importance of social experience to individual development was obscured by an unfounded belief that human behavior could be explained almost entirely in biological terms.

Chapter 3 explained how an understanding of the genetic foundation of behavior developed in the mid-nineteenth century, largely based on the work of Charles Darwin. In brief, Darwin's theory of evolution held that a species gradually changes over many generations as genetic variations lead to more successful survival and reproduction. As Darwin's influence grew, his ideas were applied to the understanding of human behavior. "Naturalists" argued that human behavior is based in biology and explained every pattern of human behavior as an instinct supposedly natural to the human species. By the latter part of the nineteenth century, virtually all human behavior was understood in this way—and such notions are still with us. It is sometimes claimed, for example, that our economic system is a reflection of "instinctive human competitiveness," or that some people are "born criminals." Similarly, females are often alleged to be naturally more intuitive and emotional, and males naturally more self-controlled and rational (Witkin-Lanoil, 1984).

The naturalist argument has also been widely used to explain variations in the characteristic behavior of different societies. After centuries of world exploration and empire building, Western Europeans were well aware of how different one society could be from another. Usually, they attributed these differences to biological characteristics rather than viewing them as simply cultural variations. We have already noted the common tendency of people in every society to evaluate alien cultural patterns as deficient, on the basis of the standards of their own culture. In past centuries, it was even more common to interpret these differences in terms of biological evolution. Thus Europeans and North Americans viewed the members of technologically less advanced societies as human beings who were biologically less evolved. This self-serving and ethnocentric view, of course, provided an important justification for colonial practices. It is easy to enter another society, exploit its resources, and perhaps enslave its people if you believe that they are not truly human in the same sense that you are.

In the twentieth century, such naturalistic explanations of human behavior were challenged. Psychologists such as John B. Watson (1878–1958) claimed that patterns of human behavior are conditioned by the environment. Watson's theory, known as *behaviorism*, explains specific behavior patterns as the result of learning within a social environment rather than as the result of biological instincts. Watson (1930) differed radically from the naturalists, first of all, by asserting that human beings of all cultures have the same biological foundation. Therefore, he rejected the idea that variations in human behavior were based on differences in evolutionary progress or biological instincts. Instead, he viewed human behavior

as malleable, open to the influence of any imaginable environment:

> Give me a dozen healthy infants . . . and my own specified world to bring them up in, and I will guarantee to take any one at random and train him to become any type of specialist that I might select—doctor, lawyer, artist, merchant-chief, and yes, even beggar-man and thief—regardless of his talents, penchants, tendencies, abilities, vocations, and race of his ancestors. (1930:104)

Watson was aware that he was somewhat overstating his case, but he was convinced that the widespread view that linked human behavior to biology was fundamentally in error and that nurture—or learning—was a far more powerful influence.

Watson's assertions gradually received more and more support from other researchers. By the first decades of this century, anthropologists had amassed considerable information on patterns of behavior within societies the world over. These patterns are highly variable, even among societies that have much the same level of technological development. This variation is inconsistent with the belief that human behavior is rooted in the biology of the species. An outspoken proponent of the "nurture" view of human behavior, noted anthropologist Margaret Mead argued, "The differences between individuals who are members of different cultures, like the differences between individuals within a culture, are almost entirely to be laid to differences in conditioning, especially during early childhood, and this conditioning is culturally determined" (1963:280; orig. 1935).

Thus, over the course of this century, biological explanations of human behavior have lost most of their former eminence. Today social scientists are cautious about describing any human behavioral trait as instinctive. Even the development of sociobiology, discussed in Chapter 3, has not challenged the conclusion that human behavior is primarily a consequence of learning within a cultural system. This does not mean that biology has no part in human behavior. Obviously, all social life depends on the functioning of the human body. We also know that children share some of the biological traits of their parents. The clearest case of hereditary transmission involves elements of physical appearance—such as height, weight, hair and eye color, and facial features. Heredity probably also has some importance in the transmission of intelligence and personality characteristics (such as how one reacts to stimulation). The potential to excel in such activities as art and music may also have a genetic component. Overall, however,

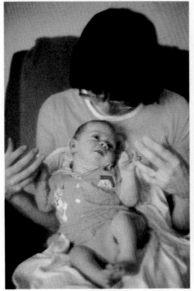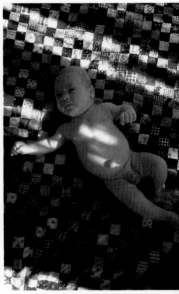

Reflexes are distinctive behavior patterns present at birth in infants that enhance the likelihood of survival. The sucking reflex, which in some cases begins even before birth, is clearly related to gaining nourishment. The grasping reflex can be triggered by placing an object such as a finger or pencil in an infant's palm, causing the hand to close. This reflex, which applies to the foot as well, generally disappears during the first year of life. The Moro reflex occurs when an infant is startled, causing the arms to spread and fingers to stretch, quickly followed by a relaxation of the arms and a closing of the hands. Scientists speculate that this reflex originated among human ancestors so that a falling baby would grasp the body hair of a parent.

there is little doubt that personality development is influenced more by the environmental forces of nurture than by the biological forces of nature. Furthermore, even if a dimension of human potential *is* inherited, whether or not it is developed depends upon social experiences (Plomin & Foch, 1980; Goldsmith, 1983).

As suggested in Chapter 3, human nature is the creation, learning, and modification of culture. Thus, rather than being in opposition, human nature and nurture are actually inseparable.

Margaret Mead, a pioneer in the study of cultural conditioning, is shown here on a visit in 1953 to the Manus of the Admiralty Islands.

Social Isolation

For obvious ethical reasons, researchers cannot conduct experiments involving the social isolation of human beings. Consequently, much of what we know about the effects of social isolation has come from rare cases of children unfortunately placed in isolation by their families. But even these cases pose problems for researchers, who—like Kingsley Davis—typically enter the picture at the end of an ordeal and have to piece together what happened over a period of years. For this reason, research into the effects of social isolation has made use of animals.

Studies with Nonhuman Primates

Nonhuman primates have been used to explore the consequences of social isolation. Classic research of this kind was carried out by psychologists Harry and Margaret Harlow (1962). The Harlows placed rhesus monkeys—whose behavior is in some ways surprisingly similar to that of human beings—in various conditions of social isolation to observe the consequences.

A key finding was that complete social isolation for a period of even six months (while being provided with adequate nutrition) was sufficient to produce serious disturbances in the monkeys' development. When subsequently introduced to others of their kind, these monkeys showed considerable fear and were unable to defend themselves when other monkeys acted aggressively toward them.

The Harlows also placed infant rhesus monkeys in cages with an artificial mother constructed of wire mesh and a wooden head, with the nipple of a feeding tube where the breast would be. Monkeys subjected to prolonged isolation under these circumstances survived physically, but they, too, were subsequently unable to interact with other monkeys. However, when the artificial mother was covered with soft terry cloth, the infant monkeys clung to it and appeared to derive some emotional satisfaction from the closeness, which lessened the negative effects of their social isolation. The Harlows concluded that a crucial part of normal emotional development is receiving affectionate cradling as part of mother-infant interaction.

The Harlows also made two other discoveries. First, monkeys deprived of mother-infant contact but having plenty of contact with other infant monkeys did not suffer adversely. This shows that it is the lack of all social experience, rather than the specific absence of maternal contact, that produces devastating effects. Second, the Harlows found that infant monkeys socially isolated for short periods of time (about three months) eventually regained normal emotional patterns after rejoining other monkeys. Thus they concluded that the effects of short-term isolation can be overcome; longer-term isolation, however, appeared to cause irreversible emotional damage to the monkeys.

Long-Term Effects of Social Isolation in Children

The case of Anna, described at the beginning of this chapter, is the best-known instance of the long-term social isolation of a human infant. After her discovery, Anna was taken from her family and lived for almost a year in a county home, where she received basic medical attention and regular social contact. When Kingsley Davis (1940) visited Anna in the county home only ten days after she had been placed there, he noted evident improvement: she was more alert and showed some human expression, even smiling with obvious pleasure. During the next year, Anna made slow but steady progress, showing increasing interest in other people and gradually gaining the ability to walk. She was finally experiencing the humanizing effects of socialization, evident in the fact that she displayed more and more familiar human characteristics. After being placed in a foster home, Anna enjoyed the constant attention of another person, and a year after the end of her ordeal she was able to feed herself, walk alone for short distances, and play with toys.

Consistent with the observations of the Harlows, however, it was becoming apparent that Anna's five years of social isolation had left her permanently damaged. At the age of eight she had the mental and social development of a typical child of a year and a half. Only as she approached the age of ten did she show the first signs of using language. We can only speculate as to her ultimate development, however, because at the age of ten Anna died of a blood disorder, possibly related to her long years of abuse.

A second, quite similar case reveals more about the long-range effects of social isolation. At about the same time that Anna was discovered, another girl around the same age was found under strikingly similar circumstances. After over six years of virtual isolation, this girl—known as Isabelle—revealed the same lack of human responsiveness that had characterized Anna (Davis, 1947). Unlike Anna, though, Isabelle was the object of intensive efforts by psychologists to aid her development. One week after this program began, Isabelle was attempting to speak, and a year and a half later, her vocabulary was approaching two thousand words. The psychologists concluded that Isabelle had managed to progress through what is normally about six years of

Harry and Margaret Harlow found that physical contact with an artificial "mother" provides emotional satisfaction to infant rhesus monkeys and lessened the detrimental effects of social isolation.

development in two years of intensive effort. By the time she was fourteen, Isabelle was attending sixth-grade classes in school, apparently well on her way to at least an approximately normal life.

A final case of childhood isolation involves a thirteen-year-old girl in California who was isolated in a small room from the age of about two (Pines, 1981). Upon discovery, her condition was similar to that of the other two children we have described. She was emaciated (weighing only fifty-nine pounds) and had the mental development of a one-year-old. Genie, as she came to be known, was afforded intensive treatment under the direction of specialists and is alive today. Yet even after years of care, her ability to use language is no better than that of a young child (Pines, 1981).

Such tragic cases clearly demonstrate the crucial importance of social experience for the development of human personality. Furthermore, consistent with the Harlows' research with rhesus monkeys, there may be a point at which social isolation in human infancy results in developmental damage that cannot be fully repaired. Precisely what this point is remains unclear from the small number of cases that have been studied. Yet some researchers now suspect that without social experience leading to the development of language in early childhood, the human brain loses much of its capacity for subsequent development (Pines, 1981).

UNDERSTANDING THE SOCIALIZATION PROCESS

Socialization is a highly complex process, so that, much like the approaches to understanding society that were presented in Chapter 4, explanations of socialization differ in approach and emphasis. The following sections present the ideas of several twentieth-century thinkers who have had the greatest influence on our understanding of the process of socialization.

Sigmund Freud: The Elements of Personality

Sigmund Freud (1856–1939), who spent most of his life in Vienna, lived during the period in which Europeans viewed human behavior as a reflection of biological forces. Freud was trained in the natural sciences and began his career as a physician. His importance today, however, is based on his contributions to the understanding of human personality. Freud's greatest achievement was the development of psychoanalysis, a form of treatment for psychological problems that involves exploring the operation of the unconscious mind through intensive dialogue between therapist and client. The focus here is on those aspects of Freud's work that have a direct bearing on the process of socialization.

Basic Human Needs

Freud believed that biological factors play an important part in the human personality, although he did not share the view that human behavior reflects the operation of biological instinct. True, he did use the term *instinct*, but he was referring to very general human needs in the form of *urges* or *drives*. Freud ultimately decided that there are two basic human needs. First, he claimed, all people have a basic need for human bonding, which he described as the life instinct, or *eros*. Second, he made the controversial claim that people also have an aggressive drive, which he called the death instinct, or *thanatos*. Clearly, Freud conceived of these two basic drives as opposing one another. He claimed that although

people were not necessarily aware of this tension within them, both basic drives provided the general foundation for human lives.

Freud's Model of Personality

Freud attempted to incorporate both basic needs and the forces of society into an overall model of personality. In this model, the human personality is composed of three conceptual parts: id, ego, and superego. Freud claimed that the **id** represents *the human being's basic needs*, which are primarily unconscious and demand immediate satisfaction. Rooted in the biological organism, the id is present at birth, which means that a newborn infant is basically a bundle of needs—for attention, touching, food, and so forth—that seek satisfaction. Since social life does not allow the individual to continuously seek personal physical satisfaction, the id's desires inevitably come up against the resistance of society, which may help to explain why the first word a child learns is often "no." The child must therefore learn to approach the world realistically. This is accomplished through the ego, the second part of the personality, which becomes differentiated from the id. The **ego** represents *the conscious attempt to balance the innate pleasure-seeking drives of the human organism and the demands*

More than a century after his birth, the ideas of Sigmund Freud continue to influence our understanding of human personality. His daughter, Anna Freud, shown here with her father in 1913, also contributed to the development of psychoanalysis.

and realities of society. In a sense, the ego is the way we come to terms with the fact that we can't have everything we want. Finally, the human personality develops the **superego,** which is *the presence of culture within the individual.* The superego may be thought of as an understanding of *why* we can't have everything we want. It is based on internalized values and norms, and is basically the same as conscience. The superego develops first as a recognition of parental demands, but gradually enlarges its scope as the child learns that parental control is largely a reflection of the moral demands of the larger cultural system.

Initially, then, a child experiences the world as physical sensations linked to need satisfaction. With the gradual development of superego, however, the child begins to understand the world not simply in terms of physical pleasure and pain, but also in moral terms of right and wrong. In other words, initially a child can feel good only in the physiological sense, but later a child learns to feel good for behaving in culturally appropriate ways, and to feel bad (the experience of guilt) for having failed to do so.

If the ego successfully mediates between the opposing forces of the id and the superego, the personality of the individual is considered to be well adjusted. If the conflict is not successfully mediated, in Freud's view, the resulting imbalances can lead to personality disorders. Freud stressed that childhood is a critical period for the formation of an individual's basic personality orientation, and that imbalances and conflicts experienced during that stage of life can linger as an unconscious source of personality problems later on.

Freud termed society's attempts to control the drives of each individual *repression.* In his view, some repression is inevitable since society cannot permit all the individual's needs to be met without some compromise. Often this compromise takes the form of redirecting individual energy into socially approved forms of expression. This process, which Freud called *sublimation,* transforms a fundamentally selfish drive into a more socially acceptable form. For example, the sexual needs of the individual may lead to marriage, or the individual's aggressive urges may be expressed in the socially acceptable form of competitive sports.

Freud's work was highly controversial within his own lifetime and remains so today. His own European society vigorously repressed human sexuality, so that few of his contemporaries were prepared to accept sexuality as basic to humanity. Recently, Freud's thinking has also been criticized for allegedly representing a distorted and unfair attitude toward women (Donovan & Littenberg, 1982). Although Freud's thinking about socialization has been overshadowed by the ideas of others, his conception of the internalization of social norms and especially his emphasis on the importance of childhood experiences in the formation of personality remain significant contributions.

Jean Piaget: Cognitive Development

During his long life, Jean Piaget (1896–1980) became one of the foremost psychologists of the century. Much of his thinking centered on human *cognition*—the process of human thought and understanding. Early in his career, Piaget systematically observed the behavior of his own three children and became fascinated not just with *what* they knew, but with *how* they understood the world. This led him to theorize that children organize their world in characteristic ways corresponding to their age. He identified four major stages of cognitive development, which he claimed reflected biological maturation as well as increasing social experience. Progressing through these stages, the child not only learns an increasing amount of information, but also comes to organize knowledge in new and different ways.

The Sensorimotor Stage

The first stage of human development in Piaget's model is the **sensorimotor stage**—*the level of human development in which the world is experienced only through the senses in terms of physical contact.* In this stage, which corresponds roughly to the first two years of life, the infant explores the world through touching, poking, sucking, and listening. By about four months of age, children discover that their own bodies are something separate from the larger environment. Within the first year of life, they also achieve the realization of what Piaget termed *object permanence.* Adults know, for example, that when someone walks out of the room, that person is simply elsewhere, but the infant may respond as if the person no longer exists. Only with time do children become aware that the existence of something does not depend on their direct sensory contact with it. Until attaining this awareness, of course, a child does not comprehend the world as an orderly and trustworthy environment.

Although children's efforts at imitating the actions or sounds of others become more sophisticated during the sensorimotor stage, they do not have the capacity to use symbols. Thus very young children cannot engage in thought. They know the world only in terms of direct physical experience.

The Preoperational Stage

The second stage described by Piaget is the **preoperational stage,** which refers to *the level of human development in which language and other symbols are first used.* The preoperational stage typically begins by the age of two and extends to about the age of seven. Using symbols, children can now experience the world mentally—that is, they can conceive of something without having direct sensory contact with it. They also gain the ability to distinguish between their ideas and objective reality. They cease to believe that their dreams are real, and are able to recognize the element of fantasy in fairy tales (Kohlberg & Gilligan, 1971; Skolnick, 1986). Unlike adults, however, they are able to attach names and meanings to objects within their environment only in very specific terms. A child may describe a specific toy, for example, but be unable to describe the qualities of toys in general.

Furthermore, without the ability to use concepts apart from specific objects, a child cannot conceive of objects abstractly in terms of size, weight, and volume. One of Piaget's best-known experiments provides an illustration. He placed two identical glasses filled with the same amount of water on a table and asked several children aged five and six if the amount in each was the same. They acknowledged that it was. The children then watched Piaget take one of the glasses and pour its contents into a much taller, narrower glass, so that the level of water in that glass was higher than the water in the other glass. He asked if one glass held more. The typical answer of the five- and six-year-olds was that the taller glass held more water. But children over the age of seven, who are able to think in more abstract terms, were typically able to see that the amount of water remained the same.

During the preoperational stage of development, children also have a very egocentric view of the world (Damon, 1983). For example, you may have noticed young children placing their hands in front of their faces and exclaiming, "You can't see me!" They assume that if they cannot see you, then you must be unable to see them. This illustrates that they perceive the world only from their own vantage point and cannot imagine that a situation may appear different to another person.

In Piaget's well-known experiment, children over the age of seven (in the concrete operational stage of development) were able to recognize that the quantity of liquid remained the same when poured from a wide beaker into a tall beaker.

The Concrete Operational Stage

The third stage in Piaget's model is the **concrete operational stage,** *the level of human development characterized by the use of logic to understand objects or events, but not in abstract terms.* Within this stage, which typically corresponds to the years between about seven and eleven, children make significant strides in their ability to comprehend and manipulate their environment. They begin to think logically, connecting events in terms of cause and effect. In addition, they attach more than one symbol to a particular event or object. For example, if you were to say to a girl of six, "Today is Wednesday," she might respond, "No, it's my birthday!"—indicating that she is able to think of an event in terms of only one symbol. Within a few years, however, she would be able to respond by saying, "Yes, and this Wednesday is also my birthday!" However, during the concrete operational stage, the thinking of children remains centered on concrete objects and events. They may understand that hitting their brother without provocation is unfair, but they are unable to discuss situations in which hitting a brother *would be* fair. Another important development during the concrete operational stage is that children lose their previously egocentric outlook and are able to imaginatively put themselves in the position of another person. Thus they can perceive a situation from another's point of view. As we shall explain shortly, this ability is the foundation for engaging in complex activity, such as games, with a number of other people.

The Formal Operational Stage

The fourth stage in Piaget's model is the **formal operational stage,** which is *the level of human development characterized by highly abstract thought and the ability to imagine alternatives to reality.* Beginning at about the age of twelve, children have the capacity to think of themselves and the world in highly abstract terms rather than only in terms of concrete situations. If, for example, you were to ask a child of seven or eight, "What would you like to be when you grow up?" a typical answer might be a concrete response such as "A teacher," "A doctor," or "An airplane pilot." Once the final stage of cognitive development is attained, however, the child is capable of making an abstract response, such as, "I would like a job that is challenging." At this point, the child is no longer bound by reality, but is able to imagine and evaluate various hypothetical alternatives. For this reason, children entering the stage of formal operations often develop an interest in imaginative literature, such as science fiction (Skolnick, 1986). The capacity for abstract thought also allows the child to comprehend metaphors. Hearing the phrase "Joan is just spinning her wheels" might lead a younger child to look outside to the street, but the older child will understand that Joan is simply not getting anywhere in some particular situation.

Piaget apparently believed that human beings in every culture progress sequentially through the four stages described above. But he also noted that the precise age at which each stage of development is reached varies from person to person, depending on innate mental ability and the intensity of social learning. Furthermore, not everyone should be expected to achieve the final formal operational stage. For instance, people within traditional societies that change very slowly may have difficulty imagining a life different from their own. Even in the United States, according to some research, perhaps 30 percent of thirty-year-olds have not reached the formal operational stage (Kohlberg & Gilligan, 1971:1065). This underscores once again the importance of social experience in the development of personality. People who are not exposed to highly creative and imaginative thinking are unlikely to develop this capacity in themselves.

More than Freud, who viewed human beings as buffeted by the opposing forces of biology and society,

Piaget believed that the human mind has the potential to be active and creative. In other words, Piaget believed that people have considerable ability to shape their own social world. This important idea is found throughout the work of George Herbert Mead, whose ideas are presented next.

George Herbert Mead: The Social Self

What exactly is social experience? How does social experience make us fully human? Such fundamental questions guided the work of George Herbert Mead, who is introduced in the box on p. 130. Within the discipline of sociology, Mead is widely regarded as having made the greatest contribution to explaining the process of socialization.

Mead's analysis (1962; orig. 1934) has often been described as *social behaviorism,* which suggests a connection with the behaviorist ideas of psychologist John B. Watson, described earlier. The two men were close friends who shared many ideals, and Mead echoed Watson's view of the environment as a powerful influence on human behavior. But Mead saw basic errors in Watson's approach. Watson focused on behavior itself, ignoring mental processes because he thought they could never be studied scientifically. Watson thus assumed that the behavior of humans and of other animals was essentially the same. Mead acknowledged that the scientific study of the human mind is difficult, but maintained that mental activity is precisely what distinguishes human behavior from that of other animals.

The Self

In Mead's analysis, the basis of human existence is the **self**—*the individual's awareness of being a distinct entity in the midst of society.* He considered the self to be inseparable from society, a connection that can be explained in a series of steps. First, Mead asserted that the self emerges as a result of social experience. Thus he believed that the self is not based in biology, is not the same as the body, and does not exist at birth. Mead rejected the position that human personality and behavior are an expression of biological drives (as asserted by Freud) or develop as a result of biological maturation (as Piaget claimed). For Mead, the self develops only as the individual engages in social experience with others. In the absence of such experience—as demonstrated by cases of isolated children—the body may grow but no self will emerge.

George Herbert Mead (1863–1931)

George Herbert Mead was born to a Massachusetts family that was part of the academic establishment of the day. His mother served for ten years as president of Mt. Holyoke College, and his father was both a minister and a professor.

Both parents were very religious, creating a home environment in which Mead was not very comfortable. Several years after finishing college, he began to study philosophy—an approach to ethical matters he found more to his liking. After a period of study in Germany, Mead began his teaching career at the University of Michigan in 1891.

At this point, many of the questions that were to guide the rest of his working life began to take form. Mead was especially influenced by the psychologist John Watson and the sociologist Charles Horton Cooley. Mead incorporated ideas from a num- ber of different disciplines into an understanding of the social act and the development of individual personality, which he called the *self*. He carried on this work after he moved to the University of Chicago in 1894, where he spent the rest of his life.

The discussion of Mead's ideas in this section of the chapter focuses on his contribution to understanding the process of human socialization. In addition, Mead's view of society as a complex, ongoing process based on the interaction of individuals served as the foundation of the symbolic-interaction paradigm in sociology.

SOURCE: Partly based on James A. Schellenberg, *Masters of Social Psychology* (New York: Oxford University Press, 1978), pp. 38–62.

The second step in Mead's analysis is his explanation of social experience as the exchange of symbols—meanings shared by people engaged in social interaction. A wave of the hand is a symbol, as is a word or a smile. Thus, while Mead agreed with Watson that human behavior can be shaped through manipulating the environment, he maintained that this does not describe what is distinctively human in our behavior. A dog, for example, can be trained to respond to a specific stimulus; but the dog does not attach meaning to this behavior. Human beings, on the other hand, perceive their own behavior, and that of others, in terms of meanings and are as sensitive to intention as to action. In short, a dog can respond to *what you do*, but a human being also has the capacity to respond to *what you have in mind* as you do it.

A brief example can clarify this important distinction. By making use of reward and punishment, you can train a dog to walk out on the porch and bring back an umbrella. But the dog cannot understand the intention behind the command. Thus, if the dog cannot find the umbrella, it will not return with a raincoat instead. Human beings would do this because they are able to understand actions in terms of underlying intentions.

The third step in Mead's analysis is his assertion that by trying to understand the intentions of others, people are able to assume one another's point of view. And by imaginatively putting ourselves in the other person's place, we are able to anticipate the other person's response to us. Before we can engage in a simple social act such as throwing a ball to a friend, for instance, we have to imagine the friend's response to us—the act of catching our own throw. In this way, Mead explained, social interaction involves seeing ourselves as others see us—a process that he termed "taking the role of the other."

The Looking-Glass Self

Charles Horton Cooley, one of Mead's colleagues, broadened the idea of "taking the role of the other" by suggesting that others represent a looking glass in which we are able to imagine ourselves according to how they react to us. Cooley (1964; orig. 1902) used the phrase **looking-glass self** to mean that *the conception we have* of our self is derived from the responses of others to us. In other words, in social interaction, others serve as a mirror, allowing us to see ourselves as we imaginatively place ourselves in their role. Both Cooley and Mead agreed that the ability to take the role of the other is based on the use of symbols and is the foundation of the self and all social experience.

The I and the Me

Mead described the self as two related parts. First, there is the *self as subject*, which initiates action. This reflects Mead's view of human beings as innately active and spontaneous in their environment, initiating social interaction with others. For simplicity, he called this subjective element of the self the *I* (the subjective form of the personal pronoun). All spontaneous action of the human being is thus understood as the operation of the I. Second, there is the *self as object*, that is, how we imagine ourselves from the perspective of someone else. Mead called this objective element of the self the *me* (the objective form of the personal pronoun). In other words, the self is both a subject initiating interaction with others (the I) and an object to itself (the me) through the process of taking the role of the other. All social experience, then, is a continuous interplay of the I and the me: we are spontaneous and creative as well as guided by the responses of others to our own actions.

Mead stressed that *thinking* is also social experience, even when we are alone. Our thoughts are partly creative (representing the I), but thinking also allows us to become objects to ourselves (representing the me) as we imagine how others would respond to our ideas. In thought as in social interaction, then, human beings are self-conscious.

Mead's concepts of the I and the me are sometimes confused with Freud's concepts of the id and the superego. In fact, the two pairs of ideas are more different than they are alike. First, as we earlier indicated, Freud rooted the id in the biological organism, while Mead rejected any link between the self and biology. It is true that both Freud's concept of the superego and Mead's concept of the me reflect the power of society to shape the personality. Yet even here there is an important difference. For Freud, id and superego were locked in continual combat; Mead, however, understood the I and the me as working closely together. Furthermore, while Freud viewed the superego as repressive, Mead understood the me as providing a gratifying sense of direction to human behavior (Meltzer, 1978).

Development of the Self

Mead linked the development of the self to gaining a more sophisticated ability to take the role of the other. Like Freud and Piaget, Mead recognized early childhood as the crucial period during which the self takes form. Unlike Piaget, however, he did not describe the development of self in terms of stages linked closely to age. This difference is explained by the fact that Piaget emphasized biological maturation as important to personality development, while Mead consistently minimized the importance of biological forces. Thus Mead thought that the self became increasingly complex over time simply as the result of more and more social experience.

Mead claimed that very young children, lacking extensive social experience, respond to others only in terms of *imitation*. At this point, no self exists because children only mimic the behavior of others without understanding underlying intentions. Therefore, this first stage of behavior is a matter of crude replication rather than interaction based on symbols.

As children learn to use language and other symbols, however, the self begins to emerge in the form of *play*. Now children recreate complex patterns of behavior they observe around them in the form of role playing. At first, role playing involves single roles modeled on specific people—such as parents or other primary group members—whom sociologists now describe as *significant others*. We are all familiar, for example, with the way children can take on the role of mother or father in their play. Such play gives them the opportunity to learn to imagine the world from one other person's point of view.

As children gain further social experience, they learn to simultaneously take the roles of many others in a single situation. This indicates that the self is becoming more complex, able to initiate different actions in response to different others. This makes possible moving from simple play involving one role to more complex *games* involving many roles at one time. Mead's distinction between play and games in the development of self is illustrated in the box.

A final step in the development of self is the ability of children to respond to themselves from the point of view of society in general. As Figure 5–1 suggests, this amounts to the ability to take the role of many others in many different situations at once. More simply, this means that children gradually become aware that people throughout their society recognize many of the same cultural norms and values. As these norms and values

"Peek-a-boo" reveals the inability of very young children to "take the role of the other." Children reason that, since they cannot see you, you must not be able to see them. "Dress-up" is a form of play common among children learning to assume the role of another, often that of a parent. Complex team sports require players to simultaneously take the role of many other people. Thus, such games as soccer occur only among older children who have gained considerable social experience.

are incorporated into the self, children begin to respond to themselves as they imagine *any* other person in *any* situation would. Mead used the term **generalized other** to refer to *widespread cultural norms and values that are used as a reference in evaluating ourselves.*

Mead emphasized that the emergence of self is the foundation of the socialization process. But this does not mean that socialization ends with the full emergence of the self. On the contrary, Mead viewed socialization as a lifelong process in which changing social experiences would continuously reshape every individual. Moreover, he understood socialization as a two-way process: just as we are shaped by society, so we act back to shape the world around us. In other words, human beings are both active and creative, and play a large part in their own socialization. Because the individual and soci-

The self is able to simultaneously
take the role of:

recognizing the "general other"	many others	in	many situations
engaging in games	many others	in	one situation
engaging in play	one other	in	one situation
engaging in imitation	no ability to take role of other

FIGURE 5–1 Building on Social Experience: Mead's Theory of Self

Play and Games in Mead's Analysis of Socialization

Learning to take the role of the other begins as a child engages in play. Play involves imaginatively taking on the role of one other person, such as mother, father, doctor, or soldier. Two children playing Doctor, for example, may dress as doctor and patient, experiencing the world as each imagines this "other" does.

As they gain more social experience, children move from play to games. Unlike play, a game typically involves many children playing different roles. Games therefore require the more complex social process of simultaneously viewing oneself through the eyes of many others. A baseball fan, Mead often turned to

sports to illustrate his ideas. Imagine, then, that you are playing shortstop in a softball game. With one out in the inning and a runner on first base, the batter hits a ground ball to you, setting up the classic double-play situation. In order to respond, you have to imagine yourself through the eyes of a number of others. The fielder at first base does not expect you to throw the ball there; but the fielder at second base *does* expect a throw, and as quickly as possible. At the same time, however, you have to view this process through the eyes of the runner moving toward second base. If this player looks able to beat the throw, you should throw to first instead. But

even that choice is contingent on how close the batter now is to first base. In other words, to decide how to respond to any situation within a game, you have to take the role of many others at the same time.

Since children of four or five years of age usually have not had sufficient social experience to simultaneously assume the roles of many others, they may be able to play catch with one other person, but be unable to engage in the more complex social interaction characteristic of a game such as softball.

SOURCE: For suggestions here and throughout this part of the chapter, I am grateful to Howard Sacks of Kenyon College.

ety act on each other, Mead claimed that the individual self is certainly influenced—but never rigidly determined—by the larger society.

SPHERES OF SOCIALIZATION

To say that socialization is a lifelong process means simply that we are affected in at least some small way by every social experience we have. In modern industrial societies, several distinct spheres of social life have special importance for the ongoing socialization of individuals.

The Family

The family is the most important social setting in which socialization takes place. During at least the first several years of life, for most individuals, the family *is* the social world. Only when children start school do they typically spend a great deal of time away from their families. As we have seen, infants are almost entirely dependent on others to meet their various needs, and this responsibility

almost always falls on the family. Therefore, the family is the original primary group for most people. The intensive social experiences that occur within the family form the foundation of our personalities, however much we may change in later life. The family is largely responsible for the process of cultural transmission by which values and norms are taught to new members of the society and incorporated into individuals' sense of themselves. Although parents never completely determine the development of their children, critical dimensions of self-concept such as attitudes, interests, goals, beliefs, and prejudices are acquired within the family.

What families teach to their children is not all intentional. Children learn constantly from the kind of environment that is unconsciously created by the adults in their family. Whether children believe themselves to be weak or strong, smart or stupid, loved or simply tolerated—and whether they believe the world to be trustworthy or dangerous—is largely a consequence of this early environment.

The family is also the sphere of social life in which we first learn what our culture considers to be appropriate attitudes and behavior for males and females. From infancy, boys and girls receive both conscious and unconscious instruction from their parents and other family members in how to be "masculine" and "feminine" (Tavris & Wade, 1984; Witkin-Lanoil, 1984). As noted in Chapter 3, much of what we consider to be innate in ourselves is actually a product of culture, incorporated into our personalities through socialization. Sex-role socialization has always been one of the family's most important functions.

Of course, ideas of "proper child rearing" vary greatly; generally, however, research suggests that parental attention to children encourages their social development. For example, the extent to which children receive physical contact, verbal stimulation, and responsiveness from their parents is related to their rate of intellectual growth (Belsky, Lerner, & Spanier, 1984).

The family is important to the socialization process not simply for shaping the personality, but also for providing children with a social position. In other words, parents not only bring children into the physical world, they also place them within society. Many ascribed characteristics—such as social class, religion, race, and ethnicity—are directly conferred on children by their families and become part of their concept of self. Long before each one of us was old enough to know it, we had taken a place within the structure of society that was determined by our family. True, we can either accept or attempt to change this original social placement, but we will certainly have to deal with it throughout our lives. The social position we receive from our families can influence virtually every dimension of our existence.

In addition to affecting the amount of material resources that are available to us, the social class of our families is related to many of the values and orientations we have toward the world. Melvin Kohn (1977) conducted interviews with working-class and middle-class parents in the United States to study how social class affects what children learn as they grow. He found that working-class parents tend to stress behavioral conformity in rearing their children. Middle-class parents, on the other hand, are typically tolerant of a wider range of behavior and show greater concern for the intentions and motivations that underlie their children's actions. Kohn explained this difference in terms of the education and occupations typical of parents in each social category. Working-class parents usually lack higher education and often have jobs in which they are extensively supervised and expected to do as they are told. Therefore, they tend to develop similar expectations of obedience and conformity in their children. In contrast, middle-class parents usually have more formal education and work

in occupations that give them more autonomy and encourage the use of imagination. These parents are therefore likely to encourage the same qualities in their children. Such differences in patterns of socialization can have important long-term effects on children's ambition. As we suggested in Chapter 1, middle-class children are more likely than working-class children to go to college, and they are more confident of succeeding both in college and in their careers (Wilson, 1959; Ballantine, 1983). In sum, parents tend to prepare their children to follow in their footsteps, adapting to the constraints or freedoms of their inherited social positions.

Schooling

When formal schooling begins, unfamiliar people and experiences introduce several new elements into the socialization process. In school, children learn to interact with other people who are not (at least initially) part of their primary group, and who may have social backgrounds that differ from their own. As children encounter greater social diversity, they are likely to become more aware of their own social categories. For example, one study of children in kindergarten showed that white and black children tended to form play groups based on race (Finkelstein & Haskins, 1983). Similarly, boys and girls tend to form distinct play groups, reinforcing the importance that our culture attaches to sex (Lever, 1978).

The most widely recognized contribution of schooling to the socialization process is teaching children a wide range of knowledge and skills. In the early grades, these are basic skills such as reading, writing, and arithmetic. Later, secondary schools and colleges teach highly specialized knowledge and skills that are needed to function in a complex industrial society that has many specialized productive roles.

What children learn in school is not limited to the recognized curriculum, however. What is often called the *hidden curriculum* teaches them important cultural values. As discussed in Chapter 3, for example, school activities such as spelling bees and sports teach children competitiveness and the value of success. Children are also taught in countless subtle ways that their society's way of life—including its political and economic systems—is both practically and morally good. In addition, schools further socialize children into their culturally approved sex roles. As Raphaela Best (1983) points out, instructional activities for boys and girls often differ, encouraging boys to engage in more physical activities and to spend more time outdoors, and inducing girls to engage in more sedentary activities, including helping the teacher with various housekeeping chores. Such differences related to sex continue throughout the process of formal education. For example, college women may be urged to select majors in the arts or humanities, while college men may be encouraged to study the physical sciences.

Another important part of the hidden curriculum of early schooling is the experience of being evaluated in tasks such as reading and athletic performance on the basis of universal standards rather than on the basis of particular personal relationships, as is often the case in families. Such impersonal evaluation is a continual experience within American schools and has a strong impact on how children come to view themselves. At the same time, the confidence or anxiety that children develop at home can have a significant effect on how well they perform in school (Belsky, Lerner, & Spanier, 1984). Furthermore, the school is probably the first bureaucracy that children encounter. The school day is based on a strict time schedule, so children experience impersonal regimentation for the first time and learn what it is like to be part of a large organization.

As noted in Chapter 4, structural-functionalist sociologist Talcott Parsons argued that education plays a vital part in promoting social integration. From this point of view, schools not only help children adjust to living within a large, impersonal world, but also teach them the knowledge and skills necessary for the successful performance of adult roles. On the other hand, the social-conflict paradigm suggests that schooling encourages children to support the status quo. American education, for example, teaches the benefits of capitalism and the existing political system. Moreover, as Chapter 15 describes in detail, schooling tends to perpetuate social inequality by linking gender and social class to the extent and type of education that children receive.

Peer Groups

By the time children start school, they have discovered another new setting for social activity in the **peer group,** *people with common interests and social position who are usually of the same age.* A young child's peer group is generally drawn from neighborhood playmates; later, peer groups are composed of friends from school and recreational activities.

The peer group differs from the family and the school in that it allows children to engage in many activities without the direct supervision of adults. In fact, young people often form peer groups because they afford an escape from some of the obligations imposed on them by teachers and parents. Within the peer group, children have considerable independence, and this gives them valuable experience in forging social relationships on their own and developing a sense of themselves apart from their families. Peer groups also provide the opportunity for members to discuss interests that may not be shared by parents (such as styles of dress and popular music) as well as topics young people may wish to avoid in the presence of parents and teachers (such as drugs and sex).

The greater autonomy of the peer group makes possible activity and learning that would not be condoned by adults. No doubt this is why parents have long expressed concern about who their children's friends are. They often prefer that their children associate only with others of the same social background, in the hope that the peer group will reinforce, rather than undermine, what children learn at home. In a society that is changing rapidly, however, peer groups often rival the influence of parents. This is simply because when social patterns change quickly, the interests and attitudes of parents and children may differ considerably—as suggested by the familiar phrase "the generation gap." The importance of the peer group is typically greatest during adolescence, when young people are beginning to break away from their families and think of themselves as responsible adults. It is especially during this period of life that peer groups exert strong pressure on members toward conformity. Conforming to the peer group eases some of the anxiety provoked by breaking away from the family.

The conflict between parents and peers in the socialization process may be more apparent than real, however, for even during adolescence children remain strongly influenced by their parents. While peer-group influences may be strong with regard to such short-term concerns as style of dress and musical taste, parents continue to shape the long-term aspirations of their children. For example, one study found that parents had more influence than even best friends on young people's educational aspirations (Davies & Kandel, 1981).

Finally, a neighborhood or school typically contains numerous peer groups that form a complex social mosaic. As described in Chapter 7, people often perceive their own peer group in positive terms while viewing others negatively. Therefore, many peer groups may have importance in the socialization process. Individuals may seek to conform to their own groups while forming an identity in opposition to various other groups. In some cases, too, people may be strongly influenced by peer groups that they would like to join. For example, upon entering a new school, a young man with a desire to excel at basketball may wish to become part of the basketball players' social crowd. He may therefore attempt to conform to what he sees as the social patterns of this group in the hope of eventual acceptance. This represents what sociologists call **anticipatory socialization**, *the process of social learning directed toward assuming a desired status and role in the future.* Another example of anticipatory socialization might involve a young lawyer who hopes to eventually become a partner in her law firm. By adopting the attitudes and behavior of other partners, she hopes to encourage her acceptance into this exclusive social group.

The Mass Media

The **mass media** are *channels of communication directed to vast audiences within a society.* Common to industrial societies, the mass media include television, radio, newspapers, and magazines. All of these constantly present us with information of all kinds and, as a result, have an enormous effect on our attitudes and behavior. The mass media often claim to present world events in a factual manner. However, a number of sociologists have argued that they tend to present the interests of established elites in a favorable light, while portraying those who challenge the system in negative terms (Gans, 1980; Parenti, 1986), as the box illustrates.

First developed in 1939, television rapidly became part of the American way of life after 1950. Then, only about 9 percent of American households had one or more television sets, but by the late 1970s, this proportion had increased to 98 percent where it remains today. The average household television is turned on for seven hours a day (U.S. Bureau of the Census, 1987g). Before children learn to read, watching television has become a regular part of their routine. By the age of three, many children in the United States have become avid television watchers, and American schoolchildren actually spend more hours in front of a television than they do in school (Anderson & Lorch, 1983; Singer, 1983). Television may very well consume more of children's time than interacting with parents. Clearly, television is the most influential mass medium and a powerful force in the socialization process (Singer & Singer, 1983).

Like the other mass media, television is not *interactive*, meaning that although it has an effect on us, we are not able to immediately respond to those who direct its content. Television is therefore far more than a source of entertainment; it is also a means of programming our attitudes and beliefs. For example, television has traditionally portrayed men and women according to cultural stereotypes, showing, for example, males in positions of power and women only as mothers or subordinates (Cantor & Pingree, 1983; Ang, 1985). As Chapter 12 describes in detail, advertising in the mass media has also traditionally presented males and females in stereotypical ways (Courtney & Whipple, 1983). Similarly, television shows have long portrayed relatively affluent families in favorable terms, while suggesting that less affluent people (such as Archie Bunker in *All in the Family*) are ignorant and wrongheaded (Gans, 1980). In addition, the members of racial and ethnic minorities have been, until recently, all but absent from television. The successful 1950 comedy *I Love Lucy*, for example, was shunned by all the major television producers because it featured Desi Arnaz—a Hispanic—in a starring role. Blacks and other minorities are now more visible on television because advertisers have come to recognize the marketing advantages of appealing to these large segments of American society (Wilson & Gutiérrez, 1985). Even so, minorities still tend to be portrayed in ways that are most attractive to white middle-class Americans (consider, for example, *The Cosby Show*, which portrays a well-to-do black family). Just as important, television programming also influences us through what it ignores, such as the lives of the poor and the large homosexual minority in the United States. By avoiding these segments of American society, American television programming sends the message that they don't matter or—even more incorrectly—that they don't exist.

There is a lively continuing debate among sociologists and psychologists regarding the overall impact of television on human behavior. Of particular concern is the steadily increasing level of television violence. There is now considerable research evidence suggesting that violence in programming fosters violent behavior among viewers (Goldsen, 1978; National Institute of Mental Health, 1982).

Television has unquestionably enriched American culture in many respects, bringing into our homes a wide range of entertainment and educational programming. Furthermore, it is a "window on the world" that has increased our awareness of diverse cultures and provided a means of addressing current public issues. At

SOCIOLOGY OF EVERYDAY LIFE

The News as Socialization

Except for what is presented as editorial comment, we tend to think of news reports as factual. Herbert Gans, however, suggests that the content of the news is highly ethnocentric, teaching us the goodness of our own way of life.

Like the news of other countries, American news values its own nation above all, even though it sometimes disparages blatant patriotism. This ethnocentrism comes through most explicitly in foreign news, which judges foreign countries by the extent to which they live up to or imitate American practices and values, but it also underlies domestic news. Obviously, the news contains many stories that are critical of domestic conditions, but these conditions are almost always treated as deviant cases, with the implication that American ideals, at least, remain viable. The Watergate scandals were usually ascribed to a small group of power-hungry politicians, and beyond that to the "Imperial Presidency"—but with the after-

thought, particularly following Richard Nixon's resignation, that nothing was fundamentally wrong with American democracy even if reforms were needed.

The clearest expression of ethnocentrism, in all countries, appears in war news. While reporting the Vietnam War, the news media described the North Vietnamese and the National Liberation Front as "the enemy," as if they were the enemy of the news media. Similarly, weekly casualty stories reported the number of Americans killed, wounded, or missing, and the number of South Vietnamese killed; but the casualties on the other side were impersonally described as "the Communist death toll" or the "body count."

Again, as in war reporting everywhere, the committing of atrocities, in this case by Americans, did not get into the news very often, and then only toward the end of the war. Seymour Hersh, the reporter credited with exposing the My Lai massacre, had con-

siderable difficulty selling the story until the evidence was incontrovertible. The end of the war in Vietnam was typically headlined as "The Fall of South Vietnam," with scarcely a recognition that by other values, it could also be considered a liberation, or in neutral terminology, a change in governments. (1980:42–43)

Similar political labels are used to distinguish between allies and enemies of the United States in current world conflicts. For example, why do Americans distinguish between the "military forces" of Israel and "terrorists" sponsored by Libya? Between the "insurgents" fighting the established government in El Salvador and the "freedom fighters" seeking to topple the governments in Nicaragua and Afghanistan?

SOURCE: Herbert J. Gans, *Deciding What's News: A Study of CBS Evening News, NBC Nightly News, Newsweek and Time* (New York: Vintage Books, 1980).

the same time, television remains the subject of controversy insofar as it distorts our social relations by supporting traditional stereotypes and promoting violence.

Finally, the advertising on which the mass media depend for revenues attempts to manipulate our attitudes and behavior so that we discover "needs" that can only be satisfied through purchasing a particular product. The tremendous advertising budgets of major corporations suggest that these efforts are, in general, quite successful. Advertising instructs us, for example, that neighbors and friends may talk behind our backs if our bathrooms are not spotlessly clean, that we "have bad breath more often than we may think," that "wetness" under the arms is bad, although "moisturizing" the face is good. In sum, advertising has a great deal to do not only with

the way we view the world, but also with how we manage our homes and think about ourselves (Goldsen, 1978).

Public Opinion

Public opinion is defined as *the attitudes of people throughout a society about one or more controversial issues.* Although primary groups have the greatest importance in the process of socialization, our attitudes and behavior are also influenced by what we perceive to be the opinions of other members of our society. As will be seen in the discussion of Solomon Asch's (1952) research in Chapter 6, people often conform to the attitudes of others—even strangers—to avoid being singled out as different. The mass media provide numerous accounts of the latest trends, and there is little doubt that many Americans seek to conform to such patterns. For example, the clothing industry's success in marketing new fashions several times a year illustrates people's tendency to adopt—within their financial means—what the trend makers present as desirable.

Our parents, teachers, and peers are also important in presenting public opinion to us. As George Herbert Mead suggested, what others think—or what we *think* they think—has an important effect on how we perceive both them and ourselves. Because public opinion tends to reflect the dominant values and norms of a society, those who do differ in some way from the majority may be defined in negative terms. Widespread American opinion suggests that if we are homosexual, we are "sick," that males who are noncompetitive "lack character," and that females who are assertive are "pushy." Thus people who fail to conform to cultural patterns may develop a sense of being social outsiders. As we shall explain in Chapter 8, public opinion may judge nonconformity such a serious matter that nonconforming individuals may be viewed by society, and by themselves, as deviants. No one, of course, ever conforms completely to the dominant values and norms. Ironically, many people who publicly display conformity to cultural patterns experience private anxiety about their failure to live up to ideal cultural expectations.

Within complex, industrial societies, socialization takes place in a wide range of settings. In addition to those we have described, there are religious organizations, the workplace, and social clubs. More generally, since socialization is based on all social experience, this process actually occurs *everywhere*. For this reason, socialization inevitably involves inconsistencies; even within the family, we may learn different information from various family members. Thus socialization is not a simple process of learning, but a complex balancing act in which individuals encounter a wide range of ideas in the process of forming their own distinctive personality.

SOCIALIZATION AND THE LIFE CYCLE

Although most discussions of socialization focus on childhood, socialization is actually a process of becoming that continues throughout our lives. Our experiences are socially structured during different stages of the life cycle—commonly understood to include childhood, adolescence, adulthood, and as a final stage of adulthood, old age. Socialization has distinctive characteristics within each stage.

Childhood

Charles Dickens's classic novel *Oliver Twist* is set in London in the early part of the nineteenth century, when the Industrial Revolution was bringing sweeping changes to English society. Oliver's mother died in childbirth and, barely surviving himself, he began life as an indigent orphan, "buffeted through the world—despised by all, and pitied by none" (Dickens, 1886:36; orig. 1837–1839). What little pleasure Oliver Twist received in his early years came through charity. Long before he reached the age when we expect a young person to seek employment, he began a life of toil and drudgery in a workhouse, working long hours in exchange for filthy shelter and meager food.

Had Oliver Twist been born to an aristocratic family, his life would have been far easier. In one sense, however, he was fortunate to have survived at all in a society in which perhaps one-fifth of all children died in their first year of life. Until this century, therefore, parents were less concerned with *how* their children would grow up than with *whether* they would grow up at all (Skolnick, 1986:19).

In American culture today, *childhood*—roughly the first twelve years of life—is defined as a period of freedom from the responsibilities of the adult world. But during the Middle Ages in Europe—and, as *Oliver Twist* testifies, long afterward—children's lives were very much like those of adults. Historian Philippe Ariès (1965) explains that medieval Europe had no conception of childhood; as soon as children were able to survive without constant care, they became part of adult society. In practice, this meant that children often worked long hours, just as most adults did. This pattern persists in preindustrial societies today. Throughout Latin America, Africa, and Asia, children often begin working as early as four or five years of age.

This may seem startling because our common sense suggests that children are very different from adults—inexperienced in the ways of the world and biologically immature. In technologically advanced societies, children are typically socialized to dress and behave differently from adults and are protected from adult concerns such as work and sex. But far from being an inevitable consequence of biological maturation, the characteristics of childhood—and even whether it exists at all—are largely a matter of social definition. The variation in cultural conceptions of childhood shows that what is considered to be natural in one society need not be viewed as such in other societies. The box on p. 140 provides an example.

Recently, sociologists and psychologists have found evidence that—especially in relatively affluent families—childhood is becoming shorter and shorter. In other words, children are being subjected to mounting pressures to dress, speak, and act like adults (Elkind, 1981; Winn, 1983). Evidence of the "hurried child" pattern includes ten-year-old boys in designer jeans, and girls of the same age adorned with jewelry and makeup. The mass media now introduce into the child's world sexuality, violence, and a host of other issues that were considered to be adult topics only a generation ago. Young children may routinely watch films that graphically depict violence and listen to rock music that contains sexually explicit lyrics. Pressure to grow up quickly is also exerted in the home because greater numbers of mothers work, requiring children to fend more for themselves. Furthermore, today's parents are often delighted if their children can read, spell, or discuss world events before their peers can do these things, believing that this indicates greater intelligence. This is a view that was uncommon even a century ago. Schools also encourage rapid maturation by emphasizing achievement, which reflects positively on both the child and the school. In the view of child psychologist David Elkind (1981), the "hurried child" pattern is a recent—and detrimental—change in American society's conception of childhood that results in children being confronted with issues they have little basis for understanding, let alone successfully resolving.

Adolescence

As childhood emerged as a distinct stage of life in industrial societies, *adolescence* came to be recognized as a buffer stage between childhood and adulthood corresponding roughly to the teenage years.

We generally associate adolescence with emotional and social turmoil; young people experience conflict with their parents and attempt to develop their identity and find their place within adult society. Since adolescence is commonly linked to the onset of puberty—the point

"Maids of Honor," by seventeenth-century Spanish painter Diego Velazquez, suggests that childhood as a stage of life did not exist during the Middle Ages in Europe.

at which the individual becomes biologically capable of reproduction—we often attribute much of the social turmoil of this stage of life to physiological changes. However, the sociological perspective suggests that the instability of adolescence reflects inconsistencies in the socialization process. For example, adults expect adolescents to be increasingly self-reliant and responsible for themselves, yet adolescents are considered unequipped for the adult occupations that would give them financial independence from their parents. Adolescents also receive inconsistent messages about sexuality—encouraged from the sex-oriented mass media to be sexually active and simultaneous messages of restraint from adults. Consider, also, that an eighteen-year-old male may have the adult responsibility of going to war thrust upon him, while simultaneously being denied the adult right to

Among some American families today, the "hurried child" pattern encourages children as young as six to look and act like adults.

drink alcohol. In 1971, with the passage of the Twenty-sixth Amendment to the United States Constitution, eighteen-year-olds of both sexes were given the right to vote. In the late 1980s, on the other hand, the government has pressured states to adopt a drinking age of twenty-one. Unquestionably, biological changes mark the onset of adolescence, but the social ambiguities of this stage of life are increased by contradictions in the social definition of adolescents; no longer children, they are not yet considered adults.

For this reason, too, the experience of stormy adolescence varies according to social background. Young people from working-class families often move directly into the adult world of work and parenthood after they complete high school. However, those from wealthier families typically have the resources to put off adulthood as they attend college and perhaps graduate school, which may extend adolescence into the later twenties and even the thirties (Skolnick, 1986).

Further evidence that adolescence is not inherently

CROSS-CULTURAL COMPARISON

Discontinuities Between Childhood and Adulthood

Anthropologist Ruth Benedict argued that in many respects American culture defines children and adults in opposing terms. This is a common pattern in industrial societies, and is based on the fact that socialization is a lengthy process in which children must learn complex knowledge and skills before they are able to function as adults. Thus there is a considerable amount of discontinuity in the transition from childhood to adulthood, evident in the fact that children are defined as "irresponsible" and "submissive," while adults are defined as "responsible" and "dominant." However, this opposition between stages of life is not found in many preindustrial societies, in which cultural definitions of children and adults are much the same.

To illustrate, while Americans de-

fine adults as "sexual," children are defined as "sexless." Among the Zuni—a Native American society of New Mexico—childhood sexuality is discouraged, but not because it is considered morally wrong. Rather, the Zuni emphasize the reproductive significance of sex, so they see little point in children engaging in it before they reach the age of puberty. Even more different from the American point of view are the Melanesian cultures of Southeast New Guinea. Benedict found that these cultures view sexual activity among children as quite acceptable. Rather than reacting with alarm to childhood sexual activity, adults typically laugh it off, believing that for biologically immature children, no harm can result.

The more a culture defines childhood and adulthood in similar terms,

the more socialization simply builds on a foundation begun early in life. In American society, however, opposing conceptions of childhood and adulthood introduce discontinuities into the socialization process. This means that what is *learned* during early socialization must be *unlearned* at a later time. Perhaps, Benedict suggested, we can understand the widespread sexual anxieties among adults in our culture as a result of discontinuity in socialization:

> The adult in our culture has often failed to unlearn the wickedness or the dangerousness of sex, a lesson that was impressed upon [the child] strongly during [the] most formative years. (1938:165)

SOURCE: Ruth Benedict, "Continuities and Discontinuities in Cultural Conditioning," *Psychiatry*, Vol. 1 (May 1938): 161–167.

a confusing stage of life is provided by cross-cultural research. When anthropologist Margaret Mead studied the culture of the Samoan Islands in the 1920s, for example, she found that boys and girls received very little adult attention until they were in their midteens, at which point they were simply defined as adults. In the Samoan culture, childhood and adulthood were not defined in strong opposition, so the transition between the two stages of life was easily achieved (M. Mead 1961; orig. 1928).

We might ask why our own society insists on deferring adult status for such a long time. Part of the answer is that industrial societies are based on highly specialized roles, many of which require extensive education and training. As discussed in Chapter 15, industrial societies now legally require adolescents to attend school at least through their midteens. Furthermore, as noted earlier, young people with the financial resources to do so may complete additional years of higher education, in the process further deferring their transition to full adulthood. At the other end of the social spectrum, poor children—especially poor black children—experience an extended adolescence because our society fails to provide them with the financial security of a job.

Adulthood

At the age of thirty-five, Eleanor Roosevelt, one of the most widely admired American women, wrote in her diary: "I do not think I have ever felt so strangely as in the past year . . . all my self confidence is gone and I am on the edge, though I never was better physically I feel sure" (cited in Sheehy, 1976:260). What explains Eleanor Roosevelt's self-doubt? Perhaps she was troubled by the attention her husband was paying to another, younger woman; perhaps as she looked into the future, she could not see what challenges or accomplishments might bring a sense of satisfaction to her life. As she experienced what we might today describe as a "midlife crisis," there was much that she could not foresee. Although her husband, Franklin Delano Roosevelt, was shortly to suffer the crippling debilities of poliomyelitis, his rising political career would lead ultimately to thirteen consecutive years as his country's president. And Eleanor Roosevelt would become perhaps the most active and influential of all first ladies. After her husband's death, she remained influential in politics and served as a delegate to the United Nations. When she died in 1962, three United States presidents attended her funeral.

Eleanor Roosevelt's life illustrates two major characteristics of the stage of life that we call *adulthood*, which in our culture typically begins at some point during the twenties. First, adulthood is the period during which most of life's accomplishments typically occur. In other words, having been socialized into society's conception of adulthood, people embark upon careers and raise families of their own. Second, especially in the later years of adulthood, people are likely to engage in reflection, evaluating what they have been able to accomplish, sometimes with the sobering realization that some of the idealistic dreams of their youth will never be realized.

Early Adulthood

By the beginning of adulthood, personalities have been largely formed, although marked transformations in an individual's social environment—such as unemployment, divorce, or serious illness—may result in significant personal changes (Dannefer, 1984). Early adulthood—until about the age of forty—is generally a time of working toward many goals set earlier in life. Young adults assume a host of day-to-day responsibilities that in the past were taken care of by their parents or others. Even those who have been able to attend college have often learned little about how to meet many of these new demands. In beginning a family, we draw on the experience of having lived within the family formed by our parents, but as children we may have understood little about adult responsibilities. In addition, socialization during early adulthood typically involves learning patterns of intimate living with another person who may have just as much to learn. Early adulthood is also a period of learning to juggle conflicting goals and interests (Levinson et al., 1978). Emotional bonds may link us to parents and home towns, but job opportunities may draw us elsewhere. Careers make tremendous demands on our time and energy—resources that may be needed for establishing satisfying relationships with family members and friends. Women, especially, face the realization that "doing it all" can be extremely difficult, since in our culture they are still expected to assume primary responsibility for child rearing and household chores, even when they have demanding occupations outside the home. In short, women are often caught between the traditional femin*ine* patterns that they learned as children and the more contemporary femin*ist* patterns they learned as adults (Sexton, 1980; cited in Giele, 1982:121).

Later Adulthood

Young adults usually cope with these tensions optimistically, with high hopes about the future. But in later adulthood—after the age of about forty—marked changes for the better in life circumstances are less likely. The distinctive quality of later adulthood is thus a greater degree of reflection, as people assess what they have achieved in light of their earlier expectations. In addition, people become more aware of the fragility of health—not typically a major concern in youth. Women who have spent the first part of their adulthood raising a family can find later adulthood especially trying. Children have grown up and require less attention, husbands are absorbed in their careers, so that women may find spaces in their lives that are difficult to fill. Women who get divorced during later adulthood may experience serious economic problems (Weitzman, 1985). For all of these reasons, many women begin careers in later adulthood; in fact, during the first half of the 1980s, women between thirty-five and forty-four years of age were the fastest-growing segment of the American labor force (U.S. Bureau of the Census, 1987g). But neither education nor a career is easy after several decades of working primarily in the home.

The traditional conception of femininity also stresses the importance of physical attractiveness. Both older men and older women face the reality of physical decline, but our society's traditional socialization of women has made good looks so crucial that wrinkles, weight gain, and loss of hair are generally more traumatic for women than for men. Men, of course, have their own particular difficulties. Some must face the fact that they have achieved only limited success and their careers are unlikely to change dramatically over the rest of their working lives. Others, realizing that the price of career success has been neglect of other dimensions of their personal development, harbor deep uncertainties about their self-worth even in the face of praise from others (Farrell & Rosenberg, 1981).

Eleanor Roosevelt's midlife crisis may well have involved some of the personal transitions we have described. But her own life also illustrates the fact that the greatest productivity and personal satisfaction may occur in later adulthood. Socialization in America's youth-oriented culture has convinced many people that life ends after forty. As the average life expectancy and average age of Americans has increased, however, such limiting notions about later life have begun to change. Although major life transformations become less likely with the passing of time, the potential for learning and new beginnings continues all the same.

Old Age and Dying

Old age, beginning in about the mid-sixties, is the final years of adulthood and of life itself. Here again, societies attach different meanings to a time of life. In preindustrial societies, old age typically brings considerable influence and respect. As explained in Chapter 13, this is because the elderly usually control land and other forms of wealth, and also because in societies that change slowly, they represent a lifetime of wisdom. Thus, although the elderly face many challenging transitions, they are in a position to make important decisions for younger family members (Sheehan, 1976; Hareven, 1982).

In industrial societies, however, the fact that younger people typically work apart from the family lessens the influence of the elderly. Also, in a rapidly changing society, older people tend to be defined as marginal or even obsolete. They are thought to be unaware of new trends and fashions, and their wisdom is often seen as irrelevant to the social world of younger people. As we have already noted, industrial societies, including those in North America, are characterized by a youth orientation in which the physical beauty, the high level of physical activity, and the attitudes of the young are the standards by which everyone is judged.

It is likely, however, that this youth orientation will diminish as the proportion of old Americans steadily increases. The percentage of Americans over the age of sixty-five has risen almost threefold since the beginning of this century; today there are more Americans in old age than in their teens. Moreover, as average life expectancy increases, more and more Americans will live well past the age of sixty-five. Looking to the next century, the Census Bureau (1984) predicts that the fastest-growing segment of our population will be those over eighty-five. It is projected that there will be almost seven times as many people over that age a century from now as there are today.

At present, socialization within old age differs in an important way from socialization during the earlier stages of life. For the young, advancing age typically means entering new roles and taking on new responsibilities. Old age, however, involves the opposite process: leaving roles that have long provided a sense of social identity and a source of meaningful activity. Retirement is one clear example. Although retirement sometimes fits the common image of being a period of restful activity after years of work, it often produces a sense of detachment from familiar routines, if not outright boredom. Like any transition in life, retirement demands that a person *learn* to participate in society in new and different ways while simultaneously *unlearning* patterns and routines of earlier stages in life. And we must not overlook the transition that is required of the nonworking wife or husband who must change routines to accommodate a spouse now spending more time in the home.

Throughout most of human history, death commonly struck people during all stages of life, and often quite early—a consequence of widespread disease linked to a low standard of living, accidents, and primitive medical technology. In industrial societies, however, although death can still occur at any time (especially among the poor), it is usually linked to old age. Therefore, even though more and more Americans reaching the age of sixty-five can look forward to decades of life, patterns of socialization in old age cannot be separated from the ultimate recognition of impending death.

After observing many dying people, Elisabeth Kübler-Ross (1969) described death as a typically orderly transition involving five distinct stages. Because American culture tends to ignore the reality of death, people's first reaction to the prospect of their own death is usually *denial*. This involves flatly discounting the inevitability of death and avoiding situations or circumstances that might suggest the contrary. The second stage is *anger*; the person has begun to accept the fact of impending death, but views it as a gross injustice. In the third stage, anger gives way to *negotiation*, the attitude that death may not be inevitable and that a bargain might be struck with God to allow life to continue. The fourth stage is *resignation*, often accompanied by psychological depression. Finally, adjustment to death is completed in the fifth stage, *acceptance*. At this point, rather than being paralyzed by fear and anxiety, the person sets out to constructively use whatever time remains to put personal affairs in order.

Of course, everyone reacts to impending death in a somewhat different manner. People confronted with terminal illness in midlife, for example, are likely to experience more denial and anger than people in their eighties, who have suffered a long, steady physical decline. As the proportion of Americans in old age increases, we can expect attitudes toward death to change. Today, for example, death is more widely discussed than it was earlier in this century, and many people view death as preferable to months or even years of suffering and social isolation in hospitals and rest homes. In addition, married couples are now likely to anticipate their own deaths with discussion and planning. This may ease somewhat the disorientation that usually accompanies the death of a spouse—a greater problem for women who, on the average, outlive their husbands.

This brief examination of major life stages leads to two general conclusions. First and most important, although linked to the biological process of aging, the essential characteristics of each stage of life are a construction of society. Each stage of the life cycle illustrates the social structuring of experience. Life patterns therefore differ among people of different age categories in one society, just as any one stage of life may be experienced differently within various cultures. Second, each period of the life cycle presents characteristic problems and transitions that involve learning something new and, in many cases, unlearning what has become familiar. Socialization is thus not confined to any single period in life, but is a lifelong process of interaction between an individual and the larger society.

SOCIALIZATION WITHIN TOTAL INSTITUTIONS

So far, this chapter has focused on the process of socialization as it applies to the vast majority of people living within familiar settings. For some 700,000 Americans, however, a special type of socialization takes place because they are confined—often against their will—within such settings as prisons and mental hospitals. Prisons and mental hospitals are examples of a **total institution,** defined as *a setting in which individuals are isolated from the rest of society and controlled and manipulated by an administrative staff.*

According to Erving Goffman (1961), total institutions have three distinctive characteristics. First, they encompass the entire lives of their residents, including eating, sleeping, working, and playing. Second, they subject all their residents to standardized activities, food, and sleeping quarters. Third, they subject residents (who are often described as *inmates*) to formal rules and rigid scheduling of all activities from eating to showering. Furthermore, inmates are continually supervised by members of the administrative staff, who exercise power over them much as adults in our society monitor the activities of young children.

Total institutions rigidly control the social environment of inmates as a deliberate effort at **resocialization:** *socialization at odds with past social experience that may radically alter the individual's personality.* The power of a total institution to reshape personality lies in the fact that inmates are completely cut off from the outside world and under the virtually total control of others. This is typically accomplished through the use of physical barriers such as outside walls (usually with barbed wire and guard towers), barred windows, and locked doors. In this way, the inmates' entire social world can be manipulated by the administrative staff to produce change—or at least compliance—in the inmate.

Resocialization is a two-part process. First, the staff attempts to destroy the new inmate's conception of self. This is accomplished through a series of experiences that Goffman describes as "abasements, degradations, humiliations, and profanations of self" (1961:14). For example, inmates are required to surrender personal possessions—including clothing and grooming articles—that are normally used to maintain a person's distinctive "presentation of self." In their place, inmates receive standard-issue items that make everyone more alike. In addition, inmates are typically given standard haircuts, so that, once again, what was distinctive becomes uniform. The staff also uniformly processes new inmates by searching, weighing, fingerprinting, and photographing them, and by issuing them a serial number. Individuals also surrender the right to privacy—often evident in demands that they undress publicly as part of the admission procedure—and learn that their living quarters are subject to routine searches and inspections. These "mortifications of self" serve to undermine the sense of identity and personal autonomy that the inmate typically brings to the total institution from the outside world.

The second part of the resocialization process involves efforts to systematically rebuild a different self. The staff manipulates inmates through a system of rewards and punishments. Being allowed to keep a book or having extra cigarettes may seem trivial from the vantage point of outsiders, but in the rigidly controlled environment of the total institution, such privileges can be powerful motivations toward conformity. On the other side of the coin, privileges can be quickly withdrawn and—in more serious cases—inmates can be subjected to physical pain and social isolation. Furthermore, the duration of stay in a prison or mental hospital is often related to the degree of cooperation with the staff. Goffman emphasizes that demands for conformity in a total institution may involve motivation as well as outward behavior. A person who displays no outward violation of the rules, in other words, may still be subjected to punishment for having "an attitude problem."

Resocialization in a total institution may considerably change the inmate. The complete rebuilding of a person's self is an extremely difficult task, however, and no two people are likely to respond to the environment of any total institution in precisely the same way (Irwin, 1980). Therefore, while some inmates may experience "rehabilitation" or "recovery" (meaning they change according to the official purposes of the staff), others may gradually sink into an embittered state because of the perceived injustice of their incarceration. As noted in Chapter 2, prisons subject inmates to an environment that is frequently both violent and dehumanizing. Furthermore, over a considerable period of time, the rigidly controlled environment of a total institution may render people incapable of the independent action required for social life in the outside world. Such individuals can be described as having become *institutionalized.*

In total institutions as elsewhere, people build a sense of self on the basis of social experience. In all social settings, people incorporate norms and values into their personalities and develop a self-image on the basis of what they perceive to be the attitudes of others toward them.

SOCIALIZATION AND HUMAN FREEDOM

This chapter has explained how society, through the process of socialization, shapes how we think, feel, and act. If society has this power over us, are we free in any meaningful sense? The final section of this chapter provides a closer look at this important question.

Children as well as adults throughout North America enjoy watching the Muppets, stars of television and film. Observing the antics of Kermit the Frog, Miss Piggy, and the rest of the troupe, one might almost believe that these puppets—with their wide range of human expressions—are real rather than passive objects animated by movements that originate backstage. The sociological perspective reveals that human beings are like puppets in that we respond to the backstage influences of society. The discussion of socialization in this chapter suggests that society not only influences our behavior but also shapes our very being.

But an understanding of the process of socialization also reveals that the analogy between human beings and puppets ultimately breaks down. Viewing human beings as the puppets of society leads into the trap that Dennis Wrong (1961) has called an "oversocialized" conception of the human being. In part, Wrong wishes to remind us that we are biological as well as social creatures—a point that was emphasized by Sigmund Freud. In describing human drives, Freud was not arguing that human behavior is a direct result of biological forces, but rather suggesting that highly general needs (for human bonding and, more controversially, for aggression) exist within the human species. To the extent that any biological force has an impact on our being, we can never be entirely shaped by society.

The fact that human beings may be subject to *both* biological and social influences, however, hardly supports the notion of human freedom. Here is where the ideas of George Herbert Mead are of crucial importance. Mead recognized the power of society to act on human beings, but argued that human spontaneity and creativity (conceptualized in the I) cause human beings to continually *act back* on society. On this basis, the process of socialization affirms the ability of human beings to make choices for themselves. Within society, human beings are continually engaged in reflection, evaluation, and action. Therefore, although the process of socialization may initially suggest a similarity between human beings and puppets, Peter Berger points out that "unlike the puppets, we have the possibility of stopping in our movements, looking up and perceiving the machinery by which we have been moved" (1963:176). In doing so, we can act to change society—if we wish, to pull back on the strings. This reaffirms our individual autonomy. As Berger adds, the more we are able to utilize the sociological perspective to recognize how the machinery of our society works, the freer we can be.

SUMMARY

1. Socialization is the process by which social experience provides the individual with qualities and capacities that we associate with being fully human. For society as a whole, socialization is the means of teaching culture to each new generation.

2. In the nineteenth century, patterns of human behavior were widely believed to be an expression of human nature in the form of instincts. Today, human qualities are understood to be mainly a result of nurture rather than nature. Human nature is, therefore, the creation of culture in highly variable ways.

3. The importance of social experience is evident in the lack of human development characteristic of socially isolated children. Some evidence suggests that if early childhood is devoid of social experience, some permanent limitation in language acquisition—and thus other social learning—may result.

4. Sigmund Freud described the human personality as composed of three conceptual parts. The id represents general human needs, which Freud claimed were innate. The superego represents cultural values and norms as internalized by the individual. The needs of the id and the cultural restraints of the superego are mediated by the operation of the ego.

5. Jean Piaget believed that human development is the result of both biological maturation and increasing social experiences. He asserted that socialization involves four major stages of development—sensorimotor, preoperational, concrete operational, and formal operational.

6. To George Herbert Mead, the process of socialization is based on the emergence of the self, which he believed is entirely the result of social experience. Mead emphasized the importance of learning to take the role of the other—a process evident in children's play and games. He viewed the self as partly spontaneous (the I) and partly guided by the reaction of others (the me).

7. Charles Horton Cooley used the term *looking-glass self* to recognize that our conception of ourselves is influenced by our perceptions of how others respond to us.

8. The family is usually the first setting of socialization, and has primary importance for initially shaping a child's attitudes and behavior. The child also receives many ascribed statuses from the family.

9. The school exposes children to greater social diversity and introduces them to the experience of being evaluated on the basis of universal standards of performance. In addition to formal lessons, the hidden curriculum teaches cultural definitions of race and gender and fosters support for the existing political and economic system.

10. In peer groups, the child is subject to less adult

supervision than in the family and in school. Peer groups take on increasing significance in adolescence, often rivaling the family in importance to the socialization process.

11. The mass media, especially television, have considerable importance in the socialization process. The fact that children spend more time watching television than attending school has sparked controversy—particularly with regard to aggressive behavior, which, according to research, is encouraged by the violent content of much television programming.

12. Public opinion is also important in the socialization process. Although people are more influenced by primary groups, attitudes and values that are widespread in society are also important in shaping individual thoughts and actions.

13. As is true of all stages of the life cycle, the characteristics of childhood—and even its very existence—are the result of social definition. During the medieval era, European societies did not recognize childhood as a stage of life. In contrast, industrial societies such as the United States define childhood and adulthood in opposing terms.

14. Americans define adolescence as the transition between childhood and adulthood. While adolescence is often a difficult period for Americans, this is not the case in all societies.

15. During early adulthood, socialization involves settling into careers and raising families. Later adulthood is often marked by considerable reflection about earlier goals in light of actual achievements.

16. Old age involves many transitions, including loss of occupational status and establishing new patterns of social life. While the elderly typically have high prestige in preindustrial societies, industrial societies are more youth-oriented. Death usually occurs in old age; adjustment to the death of a spouse (an experience more common to women) and acceptance of the inevitability of one's own death are part of socialization in old age.

17. Inmates of total institutions such as prisons and mental hospitals have all their social experiences within a single physical setting under the control of organizational officials. Total institutions often have the goal of resocialization—radically changing the individual's personality.

18. Socialization demonstrates the power of society to shape our thoughts, feelings, and actions. Yet, as George Herbert Mead pointed out, the relationship between self and society is a two-way process: each shapes the other within ongoing social interaction.

KEY CONCEPTS

anticipatory socialization the process of social learning directed toward assuming a desired status and role in the future

concrete operational stage Piaget's term for the level of human development characterized by the use of logic to understand objects or events, but not in abstract terms

ego Freud's designation of the conscious attempt to balance the pleasure-seeking drives of the human organism and the demands and realities of society

formal operational stage Piaget's term for the level of human development characterized by highly abstract thought and the ability to imagine alternatives to reality

generalized other G.H. Mead's term for widespread cultural norms and values that are used as a reference in evaluating ourselves

id Freud's designation of the human being's basic needs

looking-glass self Cooley's term for a conception of self derived from the responses of others to us

mass media channels of communication directed toward a vast audience within a society

peer group people with common interests and social position who are usually of the same age

personality the organized system of personal thoughts, feelings, and behavior

preoperational stage Piaget's term for the level of human development in which language and other symbols are first used

public opinion the attitudes of people throughout a society about one or more controversial issues

resocialization socialization at odds with past social experiences that may radically alter the individual's personality

self the individual's awareness of being a distinct entity in the midst of society

sensorimotor stage Piaget's term for the level of human

development in which the world is experienced only through the senses in terms of physical contact

socialization a lifelong process, based on social interaction, by which individuals develop their human potential and learn the patterns of their culture

superego Freud's designation of the presence of culture within the individual in the form of internalized values and norms

total institution a setting in which individuals are isolated from the rest of society and controlled and manipulated by an administrative staff

---

SUGGESTED READINGS

A general overview of many of the issues discussed in this chapter is found in the following book:

Frederick Elkin and Gerald Handel. *The Child and Society: The Process of Socialization.* 4th ed. New York: Random House, 1984.

George Herbert Mead's analysis of the development of self is presented in this paperback, compiled after Mead's death by many of his students.

George Herbert Mead. *Mind, Self, and Society from the Standpoint of a Social Behaviorist.* Charles W. Morris, ed. Chicago: University of Chicago, 1962; orig. 1934.

The first of the two books listed below is a classic study of the history of the family, including changing conceptions of childhood and related patterns of socialization. The second book describes the recent development of the "hurried child" pattern in the United States.

Philippe Ariès. *Centuries of Childhood: A Social History of Family Life.* New York: Vintage Books, 1965.

David Elkind. *The Hurried Child: Growing Up Too Fast Too Soon.* Reading, MA: Addison-Wesley, 1981.

This book is a collection of fourteen essays that share a concern for the distinctive elements of socialization among black children.

Harriette Pipes McAdoo and John Lewis McAdoo, eds. *Black Children: Social, Educational, and Parental Environments.* Beverly Hills, CA: Sage Publications, 1985.

This paperback uses the social-conflict paradigm to analyze the mass media in the United States. Parenti asserts that the mass media are not the liberal influence many claim them to be, but rather support the American capitalist economic system.

Michael Parenti. *Inventing the News: The Politics of the Mass Media.* New York: St. Martin's Press, 1986.

How have the mass media shaped the way Americans perceive minority groups? This book explores images of four categories of Americans—blacks, Latinos, Native Americans, and Asians—as they are presented by the mass media.

Clinty C. Wilson II and Félix Gutiérrez. *Minorities and Media: Diversity and the End of Mass Communication.* Beverly Hills, CA: Sage Publications, 1985.

Dallas is a popular television show, not only in the United States, but in Europe as well. This paperback provides a European perspective on *Dallas* and what it conveys about American society.

Ien Ang. *Watching Dallas: Soap Opera and the Melodramatic Imagination.* New York: Methuen, 1985.

While still in her early twenties, Margaret Mead completed what is probably the best-known book in anthropology. In this paperback, she argues that the problems of youth are socially created rather than rooted in biology.

Margaret Mead. *Coming of Age in Samoa.* New York: Dell, 1961; orig. 1928.

As noted in the box on page 36, Derek Freeman has sparked a lively debate by criticizing Margaret Mead's Samoa research, questioning her research methods as well as many of her conclusions.

Derek Freeman. *Margaret Mead and Samoa: The Making and Unmaking of an Anthropological Myth.* Cambridge, MA: Harvard University Press, 1983.

The following two books examine patterns of socialization in the middle years of life. The first provides extensive research on the lives of men; the second is a collection of essays that focus on the lives of women.

Michael P. Farrell and Stanley D. Rosenberg. *Men at Midlife.* Boston: Auburn House Publishing Company, 1981.

Janet Zollinger Giele, ed. *Women in the Middle Years: Current Knowledge and Directions for Research and Policy.* New York: John Wiley and Sons, 1982.

Personality is shaped by the particular times in which we live. How the 1960s influenced a generation of Americans is suggested by this historical look at a turbulent decade.

Joan Morrison and Robert K. Morrison. *The Sixties Experience: Sights and Sounds of the Decade of Change in the Words of Those Who Lived It.* New York: Times Books, 1987.

The following book examines the process of socialization, emphasizing characteristic differences in the social experiences of females and males:

Carol Gilligan. *In a Different Voice: Psychological Theory and Women's Development.* Cambridge, MA: Harvard University Press, 1982.

CHAPTER 6

Social Interaction in Everyday Life

Alice thought she had never seen such a curious croquet-ground in her life; it was all ridges and furrows; the balls were live hedgehogs, and the mallets live flamingos, and the soldiers had to double themselves up and to stand upon their hands and feet, to make the arches. . . .

The players all played at once without waiting for turns, quarreling all the while, and fighting for the hedgehogs; and in a very short time the Queen was in a furious passion, and went stamping about, and shouting "Off with his head!" or "Off with her head!" about once a minute. . . .

"I don't think they play at all fairly," [Alice said], "and they all quarrel so dreadfully one can't hear oneself speak—and they don't seem to have any rules in particular; at least, if there are, nobody attends to them—and you've no idea how confusing it is." . . .

The confusion of Lewis Carroll's "Alice in Wonderland" is easy to understand; she has difficulty making sense out of behavior that appears to lack any pattern. For people to feel secure in a social setting, there must be at least some apparent rules of behavior. Chapter 5 examined the process of socialization—how we learn to participate in social interaction while simultaneously developing a self. This chapter further explores social interaction, focusing on many familiar situations in our everyday lives. We shall find that human behavior is far from the chaotic experience of the Queen's croquet game. On the contrary, the sociological perspective reveals that our everyday lives are composed of many, often complex, patterns and processes.

THE STRUCTURE OF SOCIAL INTERACTION

Because society is an organized system, as discussed in the last chapter, it is not surprising that social interaction is patterned. Society is, after all, built on countless interactions among individual human beings, and, as described in Chapter 3, human beings have the capacity to act with almost infinite variety. In the absence of social patterns, people would indeed find social life confusing. Culture provides guidelines for everyday life in the form of values and norms.

To illustrate, consider the familiar setting of an American college classroom. Entering the classroom, students could do almost anything—begin to sing or throw a football around the room—but, guided by the social norms that apply to that setting, they routinely take their seats, perhaps talking quietly among themselves, and await the arrival of the professor. Even though professors are defined as being in charge of the class, they too are bound by cultural norms, so they begin to teach from a position at the front of the room while facing the class.

Certainly, no two students or teachers behave in precisely the same ways; yet social behavior in one American classroom is remarkably like that in any other. In spite of personal differences, individuals who enter the classroom behave like "professors" or "students." This fact is clearly evident to people who return, after many years, to a school they once attended. The school may be filled with unfamiliar faces, but the social patterns remain much the same. In other words, even though different people come and go from this setting, there is a social structure to the classroom that persists over time. In the same way, although every family is composed of different individuals, the behavior of "mothers," "fathers," "brothers," and "sisters" is also largely patterned according to cultural norms.

Social Structure and Individuality

The assertion that human behavior is socially patterned often provokes some initial resistance. Living in a culture that prizes individual autonomy, few Americans readily admit to being part of any kind of system. Rather, we tend to emphasize individual responsibility for behavior and highlight the unique elements of our personalities. The fact that we behave in patterned ways, however, does not threaten our individuality. Quite the opposite: individuality is encouraged by social structure.

First, and more generally, our humanity involves much more than physical existence. As Chapter 5 explained, becoming fully human is possible only through interaction with others. Within social life, distinct personalities emerge as people blend their unique qualities with the values and norms of the larger culture.

Second, and more specifically, not knowing the rules that apply to any social setting inhibits us from freely expressing ourselves. The social world can be disorienting, even frightening, when behavioral guidelines are unclear. Without this knowledge, we may feel too uncomfortable to express our unique personalities with confidence.

To illustrate, consider the common experience of going alone to a party given by people we do not know well. Entering such a setting—and not knowing quite what to expect—is likely to cause some anxiety. Such situations generally provoke self-consciousness as we try to make a favorable impression, looking to others for clues about what sort of behavior is expected of us. Only after we understand the behavioral standards that apply to the setting are we likely to feel comfortable enough to "act like ourselves."

Of course, social structure also places some constraints on human behavior. By guiding behavior within culturally approved bounds, established social patterns discourage what is culturally defined as unconventional. Traditional values and norms in the United States and Canada, for example, still reflect the expectation that males will be "masculine" (physically strong, self-assertive, and rational) and that females will be "feminine" (physically weak, self-effacing, and emotional). The structure of society exerts pressure on individuals to fit into one or the other of these categories, ignoring the fact that most people have both "masculine" and "feminine" qualities (L. Bernard, 1980). In this and many other ways, social structure can limit any individual's freedom to think and act in ways that may be personally preferred. In addition, as we shall see in Chapter 8, the failure to conform to established social patterns may lead to being defined by others as deviant.

Keep in mind, however, that social structure guides rather than rigidly determines human behavior. A cello and a saxophone are each designed to make only certain kinds of sounds. In an analogous fashion, social structure is a design that produces a certain kind of behavior. But, like musical instruments, any social situation can be "played" in a wide range of creative ways.

Status

Having described the structured character of everyday social interaction, we shall now present several of its characteristic components. Among the most important is **status,** which refers to *a recognized social position that an individual occupies within society.* Every status involves a number of rights, duties, or expectations that guide social interaction. Sociologists therefore use this term rather differently from its everyday meaning of "prestige," as in the case of a bank president having "more status" than a bank teller. Speaking sociologically, both "bank president" and "bank teller" are statuses because they represent socially defined positions. At the same time, it is true that social statuses are characterized by *ranking,* in that some have far more prestige and power than others.

What happens in virtually any social setting is guided by the statuses that people occupy. Within the college classroom, for example, social interaction is based on two major statuses—professor and student. Interaction within families also reflects various statuses, including mother, father, son, and daughter. In each case, a status serves to define the relationship between various individuals, thereby forming patterns in social life. Students are aware of their various rights and responsibilities in relation to professors; similarly, professors pattern their behavior in relation to their students. A status, then, is a social definition of who and what we are in relation to specific others.

Since people are linked to others in many different social situations, each person occupies many statuses simultaneously. The term **status set** refers to *all the statuses a particular person holds at a given time.* A girl is a daughter in relation to her parents, a sister to her siblings, a friend to those in her social circle, and a goalie to members of her hockey team. Status sets are complex, and they are also changeable. A child becomes an adult, a student becomes a lawyer, and people marry to become husbands and wives, sometimes to become single again as a result of death or divorce. Joining an organization or finding a job enlarges one's status set; withdrawing from activities diminishes it. Individuals gain and lose many statuses over a lifetime.

Statuses involve more than social positions in relation to others; they play an important part in how people define themselves. Occupational status, for example, is a major element of most Americans' self-concept. Long after retirement, a man may still think of himself as a minister and be similarly defined by others.

Ascribed Status and Achieved Status

Sociologists use a helpful distinction to describe how people obtain various statuses. An **ascribed status** is *a social position that is received at birth or involuntarily assumed at a later point in the life course.* Examples of statuses that are commonly ascribed at birth are being a son, a Hispanic, a female, or the Prince of Wales. Becoming a teenager, a senior citizen, or a widow or widower are examples of statuses ascribed as part of the aging process. Any ascribed status is a social position about which the individual has little or no personal choice.

On the other hand, an **achieved status** refers to *a social position that is assumed voluntarily and that reflects a significant measure of personal ability and effort.* Examples of achieved statuses are being an honors student, an Olympic athlete, a husband or wife, a computer programmer, or a thief. In each case, the individual has at least some significant choice in the matter.

One problem with this distinction, however, is that many statuses are actually the result of *both* ascription and achievement. More specifically, people's ascribed statuses influence the statuses they are likely to achieve. As noted in Chapter 1, many people who are college students were born into relatively privileged families, so that gaining the status of student was the result of ascription as well as achievement. More generally, a person born into a family of high social position has numerous advantages that are likely to result in such achieved statuses as being a well-paid professional and a member of an exclusive social club—each a status that would be far more difficult to obtain for a person born without such privileges.

Master Status

Although a person usually holds many statuses at one time, one status often has far greater significance than any of the others. A **master status** is *a status that has exceptionally great significance for shaping a person's entire life.* A master status, therefore is usually a crucial element of a person's self-concept and social identity.

Furthermore, such a status can be either mostly ascribed or mostly achieved. Within American society, a person's occupation—largely a matter of achievement—is usually important enough to be considered a master status. This is because occupation conveys so much information, including some idea of a person's education, income and, of course, family background. For this reason, adults typically introduce themselves to others by stating their occupations along with their names. Other master statuses, however, are based on ascription. Being a Rockefeller, for instance, may be the single fact that stands out in the minds of acquaintances. Serious disease can also be the basis of a master status. Many cancer patients are avoided even by past friends; for victims of acquired immune deficiency syndrome (AIDS), disease is commonly a master status, resulting in marked social isolation. In addition, other highly visible ascribed characteristics such as sex, ethnicity, and even physical appearance often function as master statuses. People who are strikingly good-looking or unusually ugly, extremely heavy or exceptionally thin, are sometimes seen by others primarily in physical terms, to the exclusion of their other personal qualities. Whatever their personal abilities, women are devalued within most societies of the world,

A physical disability could become a master status, but this need not be the case for those who minimize its effects on their lives.

including the United States and Canada, while men enjoy greater prestige and opportunities simply because of their sex. Likewise, those with severe physical disabilities may feel dehumanized because in the minds of some people they represent little more than their handicaps. In the box, several physically disabled people describe how this can be so.

Race also has traditionally been a master status in American society. A striking illustration of the operation of race as a master status is the life and death of Dr. Charles Drew, a medical surgeon who was largely responsible for the establishment of blood banks—lifesaving supplies of blood available to hospitals across the United States. In 1950, while driving to a medical conference in Alabama, Dr. Drew was seriously injured in an automobile accident. He was taken to a local hospital that was then restricted to white patients. Although he was known to be a distinguished physician and scientist, the question of whether a black man should be admitted to the hospital was raised. In the end, the hospital did decide to treat Dr. Drew, but, tragically, did not have the blood plasma that might have saved his life. This incident suggests that some people might have been prepared to overlook Dr. Drew's accomplishments as a physician and to respond to him simply on the basis of his race (Low & Clift, 1981; Logan, 1982).

Role

A second major component of social interaction is **role**, which refers to *patterns of behavior corresponding to a particular status.* Ralph Linton (1937) described a role as the *dynamic* expression of a status. Every status involves various rights and duties; in other words, those who hold the status are expected to behave in particular ways. Therefore, a student has a role that involves patterned interaction with professors and other students, and which reflects the academic demands made by the college. As Linton explained, while individuals *occupy* a status, they *perform* a role. Cultural norms suggest how a person who holds a particular status *ought* to act, which is often called a *role expectation*. As noted in Chapter 3, however, real culture only approximates ideal culture; therefore, actual *role performance* usually varies somewhat from role expectation. In addition, of course, insofar as values and norms vary throughout a society, people may perform comparable roles quite differently.

Like status, a role is *relational* in that it organizes our behavior toward some other person. The role that

Physical Disability as Master Status

The following excerpts are from interviews with four people with physical disabilities. Each suggests that a physical disability can shape a person's life, insofar as the person is defined by others as being "different."

Kimberly Ann Grant, age nineteen, lives in Alexandria, Virginia, and has cerebral palsy:

People notice a lot of things. They notice that I walk funny and have scars over my legs, and have crutches. They stare at me a lot. When I went to Springfield Mall with my mother and sister, my mom was going shopping and I was going someplace else. My sister finds this person staring at me, and then she says to me, "Kim, I am so mad that someone has stared at you." I don't feel as bad if someone stares. I try to ignore it, forget about it, and pretend they aren't there.

Now in his late thirties, David Clark was stricken with polio when he was ten months of age. He lives and works in Corning, New York.

All the stares you get from the public used to really bother me when I was younger. But either it doesn't happen as much nowadays, or parents have taught their children better about disabilities, or else I'm older and more immune to it, I don't know, It doesn't bother me now like it used to; it used to really bother me. But I really think people are better educated now about disabilities and they don't look as much and make you feel like you're a freak, which is the way I felt when I was younger and they were looking at you like you didn't belong there, what's your problem?

Donna Finch is twenty-nine years old, holds a master's degree in social work, and lives with her husband and son in Muskogee, Oklahoma. She is also blind.

Most people don't expect handicapped people to grow up, they are always supposed to be children. . . . [Y]ou aren't supposed to date, you aren't supposed to have a job, somehow you're just supposed to disappear. I'm not saying this is true of anyone else, but in my own case I think I was more intellectually mature than most children, and more emotionally immature. I'd say that not until the last four or five years have I felt really whole.

Rose Helman is an elderly woman living near New York City. She has spinal meningitis and is also blind.

You ask me if people are really different today than in the 20s and 30s. Not too much. They are still fearful of the handicapped. I don't know if *fearful* is the right word, but uncomfortable at least. But I can understand it somewhat; it happened to me. I once asked a man to tell me which staircase to use to get from the subway out to the street. He started giving me directions that were confusing, and I said, "Do you mind taking me?" He said, "Not at all." He grabbed me on the side with my dog on it, so I asked him to take my other arm. And he said, "I'm sorry, I have no other arm." And I said, "That's all right, I'll hold onto the jacket." It felt funny hanging onto the sleeve without the arm in it.

SOURCE: Michael D. Orlansky and William L. Heward, *Voices: Interviews with Handicapped People* (Columbus, OH: Charles E. Merrill, 1981), pp. 85, 92, 133–134, 172. Copyright 1981. Reprinted by permission of the publisher.

corresponds to the status of parent, for example, is ideally defined in terms of responsibilities toward a child. Correspondingly, the role of son or daughter is ideally defined in terms of obligations toward a parent. There are countless other examples of roles paired in this way: the behavior of wives and husbands is performed in relation to each other, as is the behavior of physicians and patients and of professors and students.

Because individuals occupy many statuses at one time—a status set—they perform multiple roles. Yet a person has even more roles than statuses because any one status involves performing several roles in relation to various other people. Robert Merton (1968) introduced the term **role set** to identify *a number of roles attached to a single status.* Figure 6–1 illustrates the status set and corresponding role sets of one individual. Four statuses are presented, each linked to a different role set. First, this woman occupies the status of "wife." Corresponding to this status is a role set that includes her behavior toward her husband (which we might call the "conjugal role") and her responsibilities in maintaining the household (the "domestic role"). Second, she also holds the status of "mother." Part of this role set is the care of children (the "maternal role") and activities in

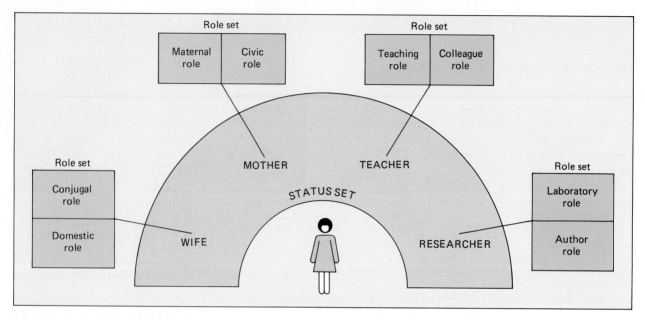

Figure 6–1 Status Set and Role Set

various organizations such as the PTA (the "civic role"). Third, as a teacher, she interacts with students (the "teaching role") as well as with other professors (the "colleague role"). Fourth, as a researcher, she gathers information (the "laboratory role") that is the basis for her publications (the "author role"). Figure 6–1 is, of course, only a partial listing of this individual's status set and role sets; a person generally occupies dozens of statuses at one time, each linked to a role set.

Conflict and Strain

As this example suggests, performing the various roles that make up an array of role sets is not always easy. Indeed, sometimes the roles that are attached to different statuses demand patterns of behavior that we find to be incompatible. In the example used in Figure 6–1, note that all of the roles shown—wife, mother, teacher, researcher—involve demands on a person's limited time and energy. As working mothers can testify, carrying out the role of parent as well as the role of breadwinner can be difficult. Sociologists use the concept of **role conflict** to refer to *incompatibility among the roles corresponding to two or more statuses.* We experience role conflict when we find ourselves unable to perform all the roles that correspond to the many statuses we hold at any point in time.

Even a single status may leave a person with the feeling of being pulled in several directions at once. This is because many roles linked to a particular status may make competing demands on us. The concept of **role strain** designates *incompatibility among roles corresponding to a single status.* Consider the status of "mother" used in the example. A mother may seek to be a good friend to her child, maintaining a close relationship as a confidante. At the same time, however, a mother's responsibility to appropriately discipline her child may demand that she maintain some measure of personal distance. In short, performing the roles attached to even one status may involve something of a "balancing act" as we attempt to satisfy various duties and obligations that are difficult to combine.

There are several ways in which individuals typically deal with problems associated with multiple roles. Probably the simplest approach to reducing role conflict is to decide that some roles are more important than others. A new mother, for instance, might devote most of her efforts to parenting and put her career on hold, at least for the present. Of course, resolving role conflict in this way depends upon being able to *afford* to disengage from work—an option unavailable to many mothers.

Therefore, another common means to deal with role conflict is what Robert Merton (1968) described as "insulating" roles from one another. In this case, no role is discarded, but people "compartmentalize" their lives so that roles linked to one status are performed in one setting for one part of the day, while those corresponding to another status dominate activity elsewhere or at some other time. This is the pattern whereby people try to leave their jobs behind them when they go home to assume the responsibilities of spouse or parent.

A common approach to reducing the problem of role strain is emphasizing one dimension of a particular role, while withdrawing from another dimension with which it conflicts. In this way, for example, a parent may decide that maintaining a close and trusting relationship with a child is more important than enforcing cultural norms as a disciplinarian.

Role conflict and role strain frequently arise within industrial societies because people routinely assume many statuses and perform an even greater number of roles. Indeed, as we shall see presently, how we behave in one particular setting is not always how we appear to be in some other situation. Even so, it would be incorrect to conclude that social structure is therefore

When individuals have to perform several roles simultaneously, they may experience role conflict, as in the case of this mother trying to juggle her roles as parent and worker.

a troublesome characteristic of human behavior. Certainly social life in modern societies is complex and sometimes problematic. But status and role are the means by which relationships are organized and clarified so that social interaction can proceed in a relatively efficient manner.

The Social Construction of Reality

Some fifty years ago, the Italian playwright Luigi Pirandello skillfully applied the sociological perspective to social interaction. In *The Pleasure of Honesty*, Angelo Baldovino—a brilliant man with a rather checkered past—enters the fashionable home of the Renni family and introduces himself in a most peculiar way:

> Inevitably we construct ourselves. Let me explain. I enter this house and immediately I become what I have to become, what I can become: I construct myself. That is, I present myself to you in a form suitable to the relationship I wish to achieve with you. And, of course, you do the same with me. . . . (1962:157–158)

This curious statement suggests that while social interaction is guided by status and role, each human being has considerable ability to shape patterns of interaction with others. What we perceive as the "reality" of society may seem to be fixed. After all, society existed long before we were born, affects us throughout the course of our lives, and continues after we die. But bear in mind that society is also the behavior of countless creative people. Just as society affects the individual, so does the individual affect society (Berger & Luckmann, 1967).

The phrase **social construction of reality** refers to *the process by which individuals creatively shape reality through social interaction*. This is an important foundation of the symbolic-interaction paradigm in sociology, as described in Chapter 1. In this light, Angelo Baldovino's statement suggests that in an unfamiliar situation, quite a bit of "reality" is not yet clear in anyone's mind. Consequently, Baldovino takes advantage of his ability to "present himself" in terms that he thinks are suitable to his purposes. As others do the same, reality is socially constructed. What is unusual about Baldovino is that people are not generally aware of creating society in this way, and even when they are, they are seldom so "up front" about their deliberate efforts to foster an impression.

Social interaction, then, is a process of negotiation that generates a changing reality. In many cases, interaction results in general agreement as to how a situation should be defined. In fact, almost all situations involve at least some such consensus. But it is unlikely that participants in any social situation will have precisely the same perception of the reality that is constructed. This is because social interaction brings together people with different purposes and interests, each of whom can be expected to seek a somewhat different shaping of reality.

Consider, for example, the familiar case of a motorist being stopped by a police officer. The police officer often initiates the encounter with a request to see a driver's license and automobile registration. While this may be perceived as both reasonable and polite, it also carries an important message between the lines:

"I am the one who is in control here."

The officer is then likely to state the reason for pulling the car over in the first place:

"I stopped you because you were traveling forty-five miles per hour in a twenty-five zone."

The motorist, of course, may or may not be willing to accept this definition of the situation. A common response might be:

"Was I really going that fast? Gee, I don't think so—in fact, I was just passed by several cars going much faster!"

In responding this way, the motorist gently resists the officer's assertion. But this is done without explicitly stating that the officer is incorrect, which could provoke the officer into a firmer response. In other words, the motorist implies: "Perhaps I was exceeding the speed limit, but I didn't do this intentionally, and there are other people more deserving of your attention." The motorist's objective, obviously, is to define the situation as one of lesser importance: perhaps deserving of a warning but not a ticket. However, the final word in defining this situation goes to the police officer, who holds a status that provides greater power (Molotch & Boden, 1985).

Driving away with a ticket, the motorist knows all too well that the results of this process of negotiation can be very real. W. I. Thomas (1966:301; orig. 1931) succinctly expressed this insight in what has come to be known as the **Thomas theorem**: *situations that are defined as real are real in their consequences.* Applied

to social interaction, Thomas's insight means that although reality may initially be "soft" as it is fashioned through the creative negotiation of various parties, it can become "hard" in its effects. If Angelo Baldovino succeeds in convincing others that he is intelligent and trustworthy, for example, he will be treated as such in subsequent social interactions. If people do not buy his act, they will consider him a dishonest fool, whatever he may think of himself.

The Importance of Culture

Human beings construct the reality that they experience through their interaction, but do so in ways that are at least somewhat predictable. In other words, rather than fashioning reality "out of thin air," human creativity draws on what is available in surrounding culture. This means, for example, that the construction of social experience in ancient Greece was significantly different from that common in Iran today. In the same way, of course, the social experiences of Iranians may seem foreign indeed to many Americans.

Perhaps it is because socially constructed realities are guided by culture that, in all societies, they are typically regarded as "given" or "natural." This is, of course, the essence of the Thomas theorem, which claims the emerging social world is "real" to those who fashion it. One of the benefits of the sociological perspective is the constant reminder that humans have made (and can remake) the surrounding social world.

In addition, given differences in cultural context, any object or human action is subject to differing interpretations. The meanings attached to the two sexes, stages of the life cycle, or even the days of the week vary according to cultural context. In a recent study, for example, Wendy Griswold (1987) asked people from different cultures—the West Indies, Great Britain, and the United States—to read several novels and offer their understanding of them. She found that culture served as the basic "blueprint" with which people constructed meaning. The result is that what people see in a book—or in any social situation—is guided by the culture with which they fashion their realities.

The fact that people of the world construct reality in ways that are often strikingly different helps to explain the experience of "culture shock" well known to the traveler. Keep in mind, too, that within a single society diverse values and norms as well as differences of wealth can lead to the construction of highly variable realities.

Ethnomethodology

It is hardly surprising that human beings take for granted most of the reality they create. After all, what would social life be like if we questioned every situation we experienced? There is, however, an approach within sociology that attempts to understand everyday life precisely by challenging patterns of conventional behavior.

Ethnomethodology is this approach, one of several that fall within the general symbolic-interaction paradigm. The term itself has two parts: the Greek "ethno" refers to patterns of culture or the understandings of their surroundings that people share, and "methodology" designates a system of methods or principles. Putting these together leads to defining **ethnomethodology** as *the study of the everyday, commonsense understandings that people have of the world around them.*

The term *ethnomethodology* was coined in the 1950s by Harold Garfinkel (1917–), a sociologist who was dissatisfied with the views of society that were widespread within the discipline at that time. Rather than seeing society as a broad "system" with a life of its own (as, for example, Talcott Parsons tended to do, as Chapter 4 explained), Garfinkel looked at familiar everyday experiences to see how people are constantly engaged in formulating understandings of particular settings (Heritage, 1984). People readily expect certain behavior when sitting down to dinner in a restaurant, when beginning to take a final examination, or when driving onto a freeway. As important as such conventional understandings may be, however, Garfinkel (1967) maintained that few people ever think much about them.

In the rebellious social climate of the 1960s, Garfinkel developed a distinctive technique for making clear what the typically unacknowledged patterns of everyday life are: *break the rules*. In other words, he reasoned, there is no better way to tease out the conventional realities than to deliberately ignore them.

Following their teacher's lead, Garfinkel's students set out to map the patterns of everyday life by deliberately refusing to "play the game." Some entered stores and insisted on bargaining for items with standard prices, others recruited people into simple games (such as tic-tac-toe) only to intentionally flout the rules, still others initiated conversations and slowly moved closer and closer until they were almost nose to nose with their quarry. At the very least, intentional rule violation was met with bewilderment; often "victims" were provoked to anger. One of Garfinkel's students reported, for exam-

Norms govern social behavior in virtually every setting, although we don't often think very much about them. Breaking the rules and observing the reactions of others is one means of making the norms of everyday life more clear.

ple, the following exchange initiated by an acquaintance (1967:44):

Acquaintance: "How are you?"

Student: "How am I in regard to what? My health, my finances, my school work, my peace of mind, my . . ."

Acquaintance (now red in the face and suddenly out of control): "Look! I was just trying to be polite. Frankly, I don't give a damn how you are."

In each case, Garfinkel maintains, a deliberate lack of social cooperation may allow the researcher to see more clearly the unspoken rules of everyday life. Moreover, the importance of these rules is indicated by the fact that people find their violation unpleasant, even threatening.

The provocative character of ethnomethodology, coupled with its focus on commonplace experiences, has led some sociologists to view this approach as less-than-serious research. Even so, ethnomethodology has certainly succeeded in demonstrating the often unrecognized patterns of everyday life, which others have explored in detail.

Dramaturgical Analysis: "The Presentation of Self"

Erving Goffman (1922–1980) shared with Garfinkel a concern for the patterned character of everyday life. Goffman agreed that people socially construct reality, and he attempted to show that in doing so, we have much in common with actors performing on a stage. Thus, calling to mind a director scrutinizing the action in a theater, Goffman termed his approach to understanding everyday life **dramaturgical analysis,** defined as *the analysis of social interaction in terms of theatrical performance.*

Dramaturgical analysis provides a fresh look at two now-familiar concepts. A status is very much like a part in a play, and a role can be compared to a script that supplies dialogue and action to each of the characters. The various settings in which roles are performed can be compared to the stage of a theater, and the action that occurs is observed by various audiences. The heart of Goffman's analysis is the process he called **the presentation of self,** which means *the ways in which individuals, in various settings, attempt to create specific impressions in the minds of others.* This process is also known as *impression management,* and contains a number of common elements (Goffman, 1959, 1967).

Performances

As individuals present themselves to others, consciously and unconsciously they convey information about how they wish to be understood. Goffman called these efforts, taken together, a *performance.* Dress, tone of voice, gestures, and the objects people carry with them are all part of a performance. Another important element of any performance is its physical location. Since cultural norms vary from setting to setting, individuals perform according to the social context. People who are joking loudly on the sidewalk, for example, are likely to assume a more reverent manner when they enter a church. Just as important, individuals often design settings, such as their home or office, to invoke the reactions they desire in others. Like a stage, a setting can be used to enhance an individual's performance by providing numerous specific pieces of information.

Consider, for example, how a physician's office influences patterns of social interaction. This setting is carefully crafted by the physician and the medical staff to convey appropriate information to their audience of patients. Physicians enjoy considerable prestige and power in American society. Usually, this is conveyed to others as soon as they enter the office by the fact that the physician is nowhere to be seen. Instead, within what Goffman describes as the "front region" of the setting, the patient encounters a receptionist. This person functions as a gatekeeper, deciding if and when the patient can meet the physician. A simple survey of the doctor's waiting room, with patients (often impatiently) waiting to gain entry to the inner sanctum at the direction of the staff, leaves little doubt that the medical team is in control of events.

The physician's private office constitutes the "back region" of the setting. Here are found various props, such as medical books and one or more framed degrees, that serve as a further reminder that the physician, and not the patient, has the specialized knowledge necessary to guide their social interaction. Notice, too, that the physician usually receives the patient while sitting behind a large desk—a symbol of power—and the patient is provided with only a chair. Slightly changing the seating arrangement could considerably lessen the hierarchical impression. The physician could sit down next to the patient on a couch, for instance, putting both people on more equal terms.

Although the physician's manner may be friendly, the numerous degrees on the wall establish her qualifications to take charge of the interaction with her patient.

SOCIOLOGY OF EVERYDAY LIFE

The Gynecological Examination: A Dramaturgical Analysis

Erving Goffman explains how individual performances convey specific information to an audience. Sociologist Joan Emerson points out, however, that performances can sometimes be understood in more than one way. She claims that there are situations in which ambiguity can be especially disruptive, and which therefore require special dramaturgical efforts to ensure that the information a performance conveys is understood correctly.

The gynecological examination of female patients by male physicians is one such precarious situation. Emerson systematically observed seventy-five such examinations and concluded that the gynecological exam may be misinterpreted by patients. The basis of the problem is that a male physician must touch the genitals of a female patient. Ambiguity arises from the fact that in other settings, such behavior between males and females is defined as either a consensual sexual relationship or a sexual assault. However, neither of these situational definitions is acceptable in the case of a medical examination. Therefore, the medical staff must carefully structure their personal performances to remove sexual connotations as completely as possible so the patient will define the situation as a clearly medical procedure in which her dignity is fully respected.

Emerson notes several ways in which the medical staff attempt to do this. First, the examination is restricted to a specific setting used for no other purpose—a room whose decor and equipment evoke only a medical definition of the situation. All personnel wear medical uniforms, never clothing that could be worn in other, nonmedical situations. The medical staff also try to make the patient feel that such examinations are simply routine rather than highly unusual, which from the patient's point of view they actually are.

Rapport between physician and patient is important, but this should be established before the examination begins. Once the examination starts, the performance of a male physician must be very matter-of-fact, suggesting to the patient that examining the genitals is no different from examining any other part of the body. A female nurse is usually present during the examination. Her manifest function is to assist the physician, but she also serves the important latent function of dispelling any impression that the situation involves a man and woman "alone in a room" (Emerson, 1970:81). The nurse usually initiates the procedure with a soothing phrase such as "The doctor wants to take a peek at you now." Once the examination is under way, however, all members of the medical staff are careful to use only language that is both technical and impersonal. They avoid any mention of topics that would be discussed in other settings. Moreover, they address the woman being examined only in impersonal terms, reflecting her status as patient. Rather than speaking about "*your* vagina," for example, the physician refers, more technically, to "*the* vagina."

Moreover, phrases such as "let your knees fall apart" are used in place of such sexually loaded language as "spread your legs" (Emerson, 1970:81–82). Finally, physical contact between the physician and the patient is limited to what is medically necessary.

Issues of this kind are not part of traditional medical education in the United States. This is unfortunate because, as Emerson's analysis shows, understanding the *sociological* process that occurs in the examination room is just as important as mastering the *medical* skills involved. But the importance of sociological insights is gradually being recognized by medical professionals. At the Southwestern Medical School in Dallas, Texas, for example, Professor David Hemsell urges his medical students to gain a better understanding of this process from the female patient's point of view by actually climbing onto an examination table and placing their feet in the metal stirrups with their legs apart. Hemsell claims, "The only way to understand women's feelings is to be there." He adds that "you can see the impact of being in that position hit them in the face like a two-by-four." Imagine the even greater impact if male medical students were required to do this without wearing their trousers.

SOURCES: Joan P. Emerson, "Behavior in Private Places: Sustaining Definitions of Reality in Gynecological Examinations," in H. P. Dreitzel, ed., *Recent Sociology*, Vol. 2 (New York: Collier, 1970), pp. 74–97; Professor Hemsell's work is described in *Mother Jones*, December 1984), p. 9.

The physician's appearance and manner convey still more information. The usual costume of white lab coat may have the practical function of keeping clothes from becoming soiled, but its primary function is to let others know at a glance the physician's status. A stethoscope around the neck or a black medical bag in hand serves the same purpose. The highly technical terminology used by the physician, while occasionally necessary, often mystifies the patient. In this sense, *mystification* is the deliberate practice of using technical language that is understood by some but not by others in order to reinforce a hierarchy within any situation. The use of the title "Doctor" by patients who, in turn, are often addressed by only their first names also serves to underscore the physician's position of dominance.

The overall message of a physician's performance is clear: "I can help you, but you must agree that I am in charge." Of course, not all medical situations are so easily defined. In some special cases, medical performances generate ambiguity in the minds of patients, which can cause misunderstanding and unnecessary discomfort. The box presents a dramaturgical analysis of a sensitive medical situation familiar to women.

Nonverbal Communication

Novelist William Sansom provides the following description of a fictional Mr. Preedy—an English vacationer on a beach in Spain:

He took care to avoid catching anyone's eye. First, he had to make it clear to those potential companions of his holiday that they were of no concern to him whatsoever. He stared through them, round them, over them—eyes lost in space. The beach might have been empty. If by chance a ball was thrown his way, he looked surprised; then let a smile of amusement light his face (Kindly Preedy), looked around dazed to see that there *were* people on the beach, tossed it back with a smile to himself and not a smile *at* the people. . . .

. . . [He] then gathered together his beach-wrap and bag into a neat sand-resistant pile (Methodical and Sensible Preedy), rose slowly to stretch his huge frame (Big-Cat Preedy), and tossed aside his sandals (Carefree Preedy, after all). (1956; cited in Goffman, 1959:4–5)

Through his performance, Mr. Preedy offers a great deal of information about himself to anyone who cares to observe him. Yet notice that this information is conveyed without his uttering a single word. This fictional portrait illustrates the process of **nonverbal communication,** which is *communication using body movements, gestures, and facial expressions rather than spoken words.*

Nonverbal communication is largely based on the use of the body to convey information to others, as suggested by the more common phrase *body language.* Facial expressions are crucial to nonverbal communication. Smiling, for example, is a symbol of pleasure, although we distinguish between the casual, lighthearted smile of Kindly Preedy on the beach, a smile of embarrassment,

Facial gestures are central to nonverbal behavior, and smiling is probably the most important gesture of all. We recognize dozens of distinctive smiles, each conveying a different meaning. Here we see the "shy smile" often associated with the young, the "triumphant smile" that typically follows a victory, and the "inviting smile" that welcomes further interaction.

and the full, unrestrained smile we often associate with the "cat who ate the canary." Other facial expressions are used to convey an almost limitless range of human emotions, including anger, confusion, disgust, pain, indifference, sadness, and seriousness of purpose.

Eye contact is another very significant element of nonverbal communication. In general, eye contact is an invitation to further social interaction. An individual across the room "catches our eye," for instance, and a conversation begins. Avoiding the eyes of another, in contrast, discourages communication. Our hands speak for us, too. Hand gestures commonly used within our culture can convey, among other things, an insult, a request for a ride, an invitation to someone to join us, or a demand that others stop in their tracks. Gestures of this kind are commonly used to supplement spoken words. Pointing in a menacing way at someone, for example, gives greater emphasis to a word of warning, as a shrug of the shoulders adds an air of indifference to the phrase "I don't know," and rapidly waving the arms lends urgency to the single word "Hurry!"

Like all symbols, nonverbal communication is largely culture-specific. A smile indicates pleasure the world over, but many gestures that are significant within North American culture mean nothing—or something very different—to members of other cultures. Indeed, as discussed in Chapter 3, a gesture indicating praise in North America may convey a powerful insult to those who "read" the performance according to a different set of rules.

The examples of nonverbal communication presented so far are elements of a deliberate performance. Nonverbal communication is often difficult to control, however. Sometimes, in fact, verbal communication (information we give) is contradicted by nonverbal cues (information we give off). Listening to her teenage son's explanation for returning home at a late hour, for instance, a mother begins to doubt his words because he is unable to hold eye contact. The guest on a television talk show claims that his recent divorce is "the best thing that ever happened to me," yet the nervous swing of his leg suggests otherwise. In this manner, nonverbal communication may provide clues to verbal deception, in much the same way that a lie detector measures the subtle physical changes in breathing, perspiration, and blood pressure that accompany telling lies. Does this mean that careful observers can detect dishonesty in another's performance? Paul Eckman believes they can, as the box on p. 162 explains.

Idealization

Goffman suggests that many performances attempt to *idealize* a person's social image. Whatever their actual motives and intentions may be, people usually want to convince others that they are abiding by ideal cultural standards. Idealization is easily illustrated by returning to the world of physicians and patients.

Within the hospital, physicians engage in a routine commonly described as "making rounds." Entering the room of a patient, the physician often stops at the foot of the bed and silently examines the patient's chart. After a moment or two, physician and patient briefly converse. In culturally ideal terms, this routine involves a concerned physician coming to make a personal inquiry into a patient's condition.

In fact, something less ideal is often going on. A physician who sees perhaps thirty-five patients a day is unlikely to remember very much about most of them. Immediately reading the chart is therefore an opportunity to rediscover the identity of the patient and recall the patient's medical problems. Openly revealing the extent to which medical care is impersonal would undermine the culturally ideal perception of the physician as deeply concerned about patients' welfare. The process of idealization also helps to explain the common pattern by which patients assume that "what the doctor orders" must be in their own best interest. No doubt this is often the case. But, as Chapter 19 suggests, prescribing drugs, admitting patients to hospitals, and performing various types of surgery are actions commonly made by physicians with a keen awareness of what's in it for themselves (Kaplan et al., 1985).

Idealization is woven into the fabric of everyday life in countless ways. Physicians and other professionals typically attempt to idealize their motives for entering into their chosen careers. They assert their work is an effort to "make a contribution to science," to "answer a calling from God," or to "serve the community." Rarely do such people suggest that their motives are often less honorable: to seek a high income or to enjoy the power over others that these occupations provide. Similarly, most of us smile and make polite remarks to people we do not like. Because such ideal cultural patterns are expected, they often go largely unnoticed. Even when we suspect that others are putting on an act, we are unlikely to openly challenge their performance for reasons we shall now explain.

SOCIOLOGY OF EVERYDAY LIFE

Telling Lies: Clues to Deceit

On September 15, 1938, Germany's chancellor Adolf Hitler and Britain's prime minister Neville Chamberlain met for the first time, as the world looked on with the hope of avoiding war. Although his plans to begin World War II were already well under way, Hitler assured Chamberlain that peace could be preserved. Chamberlain believed what he heard, writing soon afterward that "in spite of the hardness and ruthlessness I thought I saw in his face, I got the impression that here was a man who could be relied upon when he had given his word" (Eckman, 1985:15–16). In retrospect, of course, Chamberlain should have paid less attention to the message Hitler *gave* and more to the contradictory signals he *gave off*.

Can the careful observer tell if another person is lying? The task is difficult because there is no bodily gesture that directly indicates deceit, as, for example, a smile indicates pleasure. On the other hand, any would-be deceiver faces a problem. Because any performance involves so many pieces of information, few people can be confident of presenting a full performance without allowing some element of contradictory information to raise the observer's suspicions. Therefore, Paul Eckman believes that deceit can be detected by examining a complete performance with an eye for any discrepancies in the information that is conveyed.

More specifically, Eckman suggests one can detect deception by directing attention to four types of information provided by a performer. The first is *language*, the major channel of communication in social interaction. Words are relatively easy for a liar to manipulate; they are readily rehearsed in the mind prior to being presented. Lies are often revealed, however, by simple slips of the tongue—words that the performer did not mean to say. For example, a young man who is deceiving his parents by claiming that his roommate is a male friend rather than a female lover might inadvertently use the word *she* rather than *he* in a conversa-

tion. The more complicated the deception, of course, the more likely a performer will introduce contradiction into what is said.

A second means of communicating is *voice*—meaning all the characteristics of speech other than words. Voice includes the tones and patterns of speech, which often contain clues to deception because they are harder for a person to control. When attempting to hide a powerful emotion, for example, a person's voice is likely to tremble. Similarly, the rate of speech may become unusually fast (suggesting anger) or slow (suggesting sadness). In other cases, inappropriate pauses between words—or nonwords, such as *ah* and *ummm*—may suggest discomfort.

Third, the *body* can "leak" information that a performer consciously wishes to conceal. Subtle body movements, for example, may suggest nervousness, as can sudden swallowing or more rapid breathing. These are usually good indications of deception because they are extremely difficult

Embarrassment and Tact

The haughty pinnacle of fashion enters the room with her slip showing; the eminent professor consistently mispronounces a simple word; the visiting dignitary rises from the table to speak, unaware that his napkin still hangs from his neck. As carefully as individuals may craft their performances, slipups of this kind frequently occur. They may result in *embarrassment*, which in a dramaturgical analysis means recognizing that a poor performance has failed to convince an audience. As Goffman suggests, embarrassment is the experience of "losing face."

Embarrassment is an ever-present danger in social interaction. This is because, first, idealized performances typically contain an element of deception. Second, since performances are extremely complex, any inconsistent piece of information can render an entire performance inauthentic in the eyes of an audience.

A curious fact about social interaction is how often an audience chooses to overlook flaws in a person's performance in order to avoid introducing embarrassment into a social situation. Pointing out that a woman's slip is showing is usually appropriate only if doing so is likely to spare her greater embarrassment. Indeed, in Hans Christian Andersen's classic fable "The Emperor's New Clothes," the child who blurts out that the emperor is actually naked is scolded for being rude.

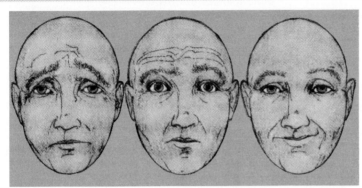

Telling lies is difficult because few people can skillfully manipulate their facial gestures. The grief in Figure A is probably genuine, since few people can intentionally lift the upper eyelids and inner corners of the eyebrows in this way. Likewise, the fear and apprehension in Figure B also appears genuine, since intentionally raising the eyebrows and pulling them together in this way is also extremely difficult. In contrast, the asymmetrical smile in Figure C is probably a phony expression of pleasure since, for most people, genuine pleasure is expressed by a "balanced" smile.

for the individual to control. In other cases, *not* using the body in a usual manner to enhance words—as in the case of a person making an effort to fake excitement—may suggest deception.

Fourth, uncontrollable *facial expressions* also provide clues to deception. A person trying to appear happy while actually feeling sad, for example, is likely to "flash" momentary frowns to observers as concealed emotion leaks through the performance. Raising and drawing together the eyebrows is a sign of fear or worry that is virtually impossible for most people to accomplish voluntarily. If this expression appears while a person claims to be at ease, deception is probably taking place.

These brief examples suggest that lies can be detected, although the ability to notice the relevant clues usually requires training. As parents know with regard to their children, clues to deception are easier to spot in people whose patterns of speech and behavior are familiar. Furthermore, clues to deception are more prevalent when a person is trying to contain strong emotions. Some cases of deception, in other words, can be unmasked more readily than others. Many people who have unusual ability to carefully manage their verbal and nonverbal performances (including both those with theatrical training and those who have spent many years deceiving others) can be quite successful in their deceptions. There are, in short, good liars and bad liars.

SOURCE: Adapted from Paul Eckman, *Telling Lies: Clues to Deceit in the Marketplace, Politics, and Marriage* (New York: W. W. Norton, 1985).

People not only ignore flaws in a performance, they often help another person recover from them. Goffman suggests that this is the meaning of *tact*, which from a dramaturgical point of view is helping another person "save face." After hearing an offensive racial slur, for instance, people may be tactful in a variety of ways. No response at all may signal that they wish to pretend the statement was never made. Mild laughter may indicate they wish to dismiss what they have heard as a joke. Or a listener may simply respond, "Bill, I know you don't mean that"—thereby suggesting that one part of a performance does not reflect on the actor's overall social image.

Why is tact so common? The answer lies in the fact that people usually take situational reality quite seriously, so that when embarrassment occurs, discomfort results not just for one person but for *everyone*. Just as members of a theater audience feel uneasy when an actor forgets a line, people who observe a poor performance are reminded of how fragile their own performances often are. Through their performances, human beings construct social reality, which is like a dam holding back a sea of potentially chaotic alternatives. Should one person's performance spring a leak, others can be expected to tactfully assist in making repairs. After all, everyone is engaged in jointly building reality, which no one wants to be suddenly swept away.

Goffman's research shows that although individuals

interact with a considerable degree of individuality and spontaneity, everyone's social interactions are constructed out of similar patterned elements. Almost four hundred years ago, Shakespeare wrote:

> All the world's a stage,
> And all the men and women are merely players.
> They have their exits and their entrances,
> And one man in his time plays many parts.

Human behavior is certainly not as rigidly scripted as a stage performance. Yet, in a lifetime, each individual does play many parts in ways that combine social structure with expressions of a unique personality. As Goffman concludes, even if human behavior is not exactly a matter of stage and script, there is still a good bit of truth to Shakespeare's observation (1959:72).

INTERACTION IN EVERYDAY LIFE: TWO ILLUSTRATIONS

Several important ways of understanding social interaction have now been presented. In the final sections of this chapter, these ideas will be applied to two everyday situations.

The Urban World: Encountering Strangers

The United States is a nation of city slickers: about three of every four Americans live in urban places. This means that, for most of us, everyday life involves interacting with *strangers*, people about whom we know very little. Potentially, at least, encountering strangers is unsettling. Not having interacted with a person before, how do we know what behavior to expect? What behavior is appropriate on our part? In short, encountering strangers raises the general problem of constructing a meaningful reality in a largely undefined situation.

Lyn Lofland notes that city dwellers have always faced the problem of making sense of reality in the midst of public anonymity. But she claims that constructing meaning is not as difficult as it may seem, because city life also provides urbanites with important clues to the social identity of strangers. These clues are visual, so that they are immediately available before interaction is initiated. In her book *A World of Strangers* (1973),

Lofland argues that identity clues are of two types; one was more important to city dwellers in the past, one is more relevant to urbanites today.

Cities of the Past: The Importance of Personal Appearance

Before the Industrial Revolution transformed Western Europe and North America in the eighteenth and nineteenth centuries, cities were generally much smaller than they are today. For this reason, cities were not quite the world of strangers that we face; people were likely to know at least something about many others they encountered on the streets. Yet the streets of the cities of the past were a striking mix of humanity. This apparent chaos, Lofland states, could easily overpower the individual, as the accompanying box explains.

In part, the chaos of preindustrial cities reflects the fact that cities have always concentrated social activity in a limited physical area. But as the box illustrates, preindustrial cities also brought together many *different* human activities into public places, so that a street or plaza might be used for teaching, selling, begging, lounging, stealing, and almost anything else, all at the same time. Adding further to the complexity of everyday life, people of all social backgrounds were mixed together throughout most of the city.

Lofland's historical research suggests that people developed a characteristic way of coping with this apparent confusion. They built a meaningful reality through attention to important visual clues. *People who were not known personally were categorized on the basis of their appearance.* This was possible in preindustrial cities because what Goffman called "presentations of self" corresponded closely to the important statuses that people held. Cultural norms—and often even the law—demanded that nobles dress in ways that set them clearly apart from men and women who were "commoners," so social identity was as obvious as the styles and fabrics of people's garments. Members of religious groups had their distinctive garb, so their identity was also evident at a glance. Likewise, butchers, physicians, lawyers—members of virtually all trades and professions—appeared in public distinctively clothed and adorned. Even those who had been convicted of some offense could often be identified simply by "looking them over": many such people displayed visible mutilations or brandings that had been inflicted according to their crime.

In this way, Lofland concludes, people walking the streets of preindustrial cities may have encountered

The Chaotic Preindustrial City

The following description, based on Lyn Lofland's book *A World of Strangers*, lets us imagine the striking mixture of human activities that was commonly found on city streets before the Industrial Revolution. Larger cities today are centers of social diversity because they cover hundreds of square miles and may contain more than a million people. But in small preindustrial cities, the experience of social mixture reached chaotic levels because people made greater use of the streets and other public places, and all sorts of events were clustered in a town center not much larger than what we would call a single neighborhood.

Picture yourself, then, dropped by means of a time machine in the midst of some mythical preindustrial city. You are struck, first of all, by the sheer amount of activity there. Merchants, operating out of little cubbyholes, have spread their wares in the street. Next to them, a school of some type appears to be in session and you wonder how the students can concentrate. A wandering vendor is coming toward you, shouting out the wonders of his wares, and out of the hubbub of the street noises, you can make out the shouts of other wandering vendors moving through other streets. Someone stops a vendor and they begin haggling over the price of an item. Here and there, such an encounter has drawn a crowd of people, many of whom shout insults back and forth.

Down the same street, a beggar with obviously sightless eyes and a face scarred by burns continuously calls out for aid. You note, in fact, that the streets are teeming with beggars. Some appear to be members of religious orders, others are lame

"The Fight of Carnival and Lent," by Pieter Breughel (1525–1569) illustrates the social chaos of preindustrial cities.

or maimed, but many seem to have no bodily afflictions. Some are adults, others are children. Wandering actors, street singers, and storytellers attract crowds with their performances. In one nearby plaza, you note a public reader who seems to drone on and on about absolutely nothing, and you marvel at the patience of his listeners.

Suddenly a town crier appears, shouting to all he passes that a fire is under way at such and such a place. Following the crowd, you arrive at the scene and watch people attempt to control the flames. No one special seems to be in charge, and efforts to contain the fire appear hopeless. People running for water to a nearby fountain must contend with men and women who are bathing, washing clothes, and exchanging gossip.

Then, pushing its way through the crowd, comes an enclosed litter. It is being carried by four huge men

and is richly appointed. Surrounding it are four other men carrying weapons. Much of the crowd makes way for the litter as it passes. Those who are slow to move are roughly pushed aside by the guards. You cannot see inside, but are told that this litter is carrying one of the city's elite.

At this point, you may well have had enough. The multiplicity of sights and sounds, the pushing and shoving and shouting of the crowd, the smells—particularly the smells— all of this has become "too much." Too many people are crowded into too small a space, simply jumbled together—rich and poor, healthy and diseased, young and old, houses and businesses, the public and the private. All seems disorder. All seems chaos.

SOURCE: Adaptation of Lyn Lofland, *A World of Strangers: Order and Action in Urban Public Space* (New York: Basic Books, 1973), pp. 30–33.

strangers not knowing *who* they were, but in little doubt about *what* they were because of their distinctive appearances. With such clues to social identity, of course, interaction (or avoidance) could proceed appropriately.

Cities of the Present: The Importance of Location

You may have already recognized that personal appearance is less useful as a clue to social identity today than it was before the Industrial Revolution. Strict social codes no longer demand that wealthier people dress one way and people of more modest incomes another. Nor does appearance any longer distinguish people of specific occupations. In addition, mass production has spread clothing and jewelry fashions that at least look like those once restricted to the elite few. Fashion trends also play a part, sweeping vast numbers of people from many social backgrounds into similar ways of dressing and grooming.

The overall result is that urbanites look much more alike today than they did centuries ago. Certainly, in cities containing both rich and poor, people today can and do make inferences about the social identity of strangers from their appearance. But Lofland contends that appearance now conveys less information about someone's social identity. Furthermore, today's urbanites typically live in much larger cities. In the course of a single day, one might expect to encounter thousands—even tens of thousands—of strangers. How, then, can meaningful interaction proceed?

Lofland answers that today's city dwellers order their surroundings, just as urbanites always have. But we now rely extensively on a visual clue to the social identity of strangers that was largely absent in cities of the past. *People who are not known personally can be categorized according to their spatial location.* In other words, how to proceed in the presence of strangers depends largely on *where* the interaction takes place. This is so because industrial cities have developed into a mosaic of many different districts or neighborhoods. This happened as industrial technology—trolleys, railroads, and automobiles—caused cities to grow larger and aided the movement of certain categories of people or particular kinds of social activities to distinctive areas. Therefore, just as personal appearances were often a matter of custom and law in the past, so norms and zoning laws shape today's cities into many different social worlds.

All this means that any particular public space is likely to be used for only a few activities, mostly by one category of people. Imagine entering a residential

Even without personal knowledge of strangers, we often infer their social identity from the location. Most New Yorkers will readily recognize these "business types" common to the Wall Street district.

neighborhood in New York, Chicago, or Los Angeles that is filled with expensive high-rise housing attended by doormen in formal uniforms. In such a location, the people on the streets—perhaps walking dogs, dashing out for a small purchase, or returning from a parking garage—are likely to have many of the same social characteristics. The fact that most of us can readily visualize what such people might look like, Lofland maintains, means that location provides us with clues to identify strangers and guide social interaction. In any given location—whether it be the area we have just described, a poor inner-city neighborhood, a distinctive ethnic community, or the city's downtown financial district—we have some idea of what kinds of people we are likely to encounter and what social patterns typically occur.

In sum, urbanites have always made use of visual clues in constructing social reality and in fashioning their "presentations" to others. What has changed is simply how this is done. Lofland notes a final difference: today's larger and more populous cities generally offer a wider range of personal choices about how to live, an idea captured in the modern term *lifestyle*. In other words, today's cities—with their wide range of distinctive social environments—contain more kinds of people and activities, and provide more tolerance for the particular choices people make. At least within the limits of available resources, modern urbanites have more opportunities to construct their social realities than people had in the past.

Humor: Playing with Reality

Humor is a part of everyday life for virtually everyone. Comedians stand out among our favorite entertainers, most newspapers contain cartoon pages, and even professors and the clergy are likely to include humor in their performances. But like much of everyday life, humor is largely taken for granted. While everyone laughs at a joke, few people think about why something is funny or why humor appears to be a universal element of social life. Here we will apply many of the ideas developed in this chapter to the topic of humor.[*]

Humor as Contrasting Versions of Reality

Humor is derived from the contrast of two incongruous realities. Generally, one socially constructed reality can be termed *conventional* because it is consistent with what values and norms lead people in some situation to expect. The other reality can be called *unconventional* because it represents a significant violation of cultural patterns. Humor, therefore, arises from ambiguity and "double meanings" involving two differing definitions of a situation. Consider the following examples by Henny Youngman (1987), master of the simple joke:

> A guy comes up to me in New York and asks "How do I get to Carnegie Hall?" I say, "Practice! Practice!"

> In Washington, somebody asks, "How do you get to the White House?" I tell 'em, "Make promises! Tell lies!"

In each of these jokes, the first line represents a conventional reality. Someone has asked for directions, leading the listener to expect to hear a detailed account of streets and turns. However, the unconventional response contained in the second line opposes the conventional expectation. Playing on the ambiguity of the phrase "get to," the response refers not to street directions but to career goals. The foundation of all humor is placing two contrasting realities together in this way.

The same simple pattern is evident in the well-known "knock-knock" jokes. Here is one example.

> "Knock knock."
> "Who's there?"
> "Howard."
> "Howard who?"
> "Fine thanks, and yourself?"

---

[*] The ideas contained in this discussion are those of the author (1987), except where otherwise noted. Although the author believes that this is the first attempt to explore humor in this way, the general approach is drawn from the ideas of others that have been presented in this chapter, notably those of Erving Goffman.

Comedians construct contrasting versions of reality—the foundation of humor—in various ways. Perhaps the most common format for comedy is the "funnyman-straightman" team, illustrated here by Lucille Ball and Desi Arnaz. Other comedians, working alone, create characters that spoof symbols of conventional society, such as Don Mondello's portrayal of Father Guido Sarducci.

In this joke, the first four lines represent a conventional conversation in which one person seeks to identify another at the door. The humor is introduced with the final line that contains the unconventional response. Generally, the more powerful the opposition between the conventional and unconventional realities, the greater the potential for humor. When telling jokes, people can strengthen this opposition with careful attention to the words they use and the timing of each part of the delivery. The goal of powerful opposition between the contrasting realities also suggests the reason that we describe the ending of a joke as the *punch line*.

The Dynamics of Humor: "Getting It"

Someone who does not understand both the conventional and unconventional realities embedded in a joke offers the typical complaint: "I don't get it." The significance of "getting" the humor, then, is a matter of understanding the two realities involved well enough to perceive their incongruity.

There is often something more involved, however. All of the information necessary to get the joke may not be explicitly stated. Therefore, the audience must pay attention to the stated elements of the joke and then inferentially complete the joke in their own minds. You will have to engage in this process in order to get the following joke that we imagine people in Afghanistan might tell in the wake of the invasion of their country by the Soviet Union:

> "What's the difference between a dead dog lying in the road and a dead Russian soldier lying in the road?"
> "I don't know. What is the difference?"
> "There are skid marks in front of the dog . . ."

Three pieces of information are explicitly stated here: (1) a dog lies dead in the road, (2) a Russian soldier lies dead in the road, and (3) there are skid marks in front of the dog. In order to get this joke, however, you must draw out two other pieces of information: we infer that there are no skid marks in front of the soldier, leading to the further conclusion that a passing Afghan driver struck the Russian soldier *deliberately*. Now we have a powerful contrast between a conventional reality ("deliberately killing someone is wrong") and an unconventional reality ("except for Afghans killing Russian soldiers"). The result, of course, is humor.

One might wonder why an audience is commonly required to make this sort of effort in order to understand a joke. The answer is that this practice pays dividends in audience response. Simply put, a listener's reaction to the joke is heightened by the pleasure of having completed the puzzle necessary to get the joke. This pleasure is partly a matter of satisfaction at one's mental abilities. In addition, getting the joke confers a favored "insider" status on the listener within the larger audience. On the other side of the coin, we can understand the frustration that accompanies not getting a joke: the fear of mental inadequacy coupled to a sense of being socially excluded from the pleasure that others share. Not surprisingly, "outsiders" in such a situation may fake getting the joke, or they may quietly ask "insiders" to explain the joke to end their sense of being left out.

The Topics of Humor

As a means of playing with reality, humor is framed against what is conventional within any culture. Therefore, since people the world over differ in what they hold to be conventional, so do they differ in what they find to be funny. Musicians often travel to perform for receptive audiences around the world, suggesting that music may be the "common language" of humanity. But comedians rarely do so, demonstrating that humor does not travel well.

What is humorous to the Chinese, then, may be lost on most Americans. In the same way, different categories of people in one society may find humor in different situations. To some extent, New Englanders, southerners, and westerners have their own brands of humor, as do people of different ethnic backgrounds, people of different ages, and people in various occupations.

In all these cases, however, humor deals with topics that lend themselves to double meanings—in short, humor is closely tied to what is controversial. For example, the first jokes many of us learned as children were probably concerned with what Americans tend to define as a childhood taboo: sex. The mere mention of "unmentionable acts" or even parts of the body can bring paralyzing laughter to young faces.

This is also the reason that a thin line separates what is funny from what is considered "sick." In fact, the word *humors* was used during the Middle Ages to refer to a balance of bodily fluids that determined a person's health or sickness. In most cultural settings, not always taking seriously conventional definitions of reality (in other words, having a "sense of humor") is valued. But, at the extreme, never taking conventional reality seriously is to risk being considered mentally ill.

Even in less serious instances, a person may be admonished for telling a "sick" joke, often the result of taking lightly a situation that is expected to be treated with reverence. There are some topics, in other words, that any culture expects to be understood in only one way; consequently, they are defined as "off limits" for humor. Examples of such off-limits topics are people's religious beliefs and a tragic accident resulting in loss of life.

The functions of humor

As a means of expressing that which opposes cultural convention, humor can be valuable to any social system. Following structural-functionalist analysis, the universal-

Because humor involves challenging conventional social realities, "outsiders"—particularly religious and racial minorities—have always been disproportionately represented among America's comedians. The Marx Brothers, sons of poor Jewish immigrants, delighted in revealing the pretentions of the Protestant upper class. A similar pattern was employed by black comedian Eddie Murphy, shown here in a movie role being arrested for trespassing on a millionaire's estate in Beverly Hills.

ity of humor reflects its function as a social "safety valve" allowing the release of potentially disruptive sentiments. Jokes express sentiments that might be dangerous if taken seriously, as consideration of racial and ethnic jokes readily suggests. Called to account for saying something that could be defined as offensive, a person may diffuse the situation by simply stating, "I didn't mean anything by what I said, it was just a joke!" Likewise, a person who would be justified in taking offense at another's behavior may use humor as a form of tact, smiling, as if to say, "I could be angry at this, but I choose not to take seriously what you have done."

Humor and conflict

Humor is also an expression of conflict among various categories of people. Males and females, blacks and whites, and rich and poor tend to endorse somewhat different definitions of reality. Consequently, members of one such category can use humor to call into question the interests of those they oppose. Men who tell jokes about feminists, for example, are almost certainly expressing hostility to the interests of women (Benokraitis & Feagin, 1986). Similarly, jokes at the expense of homosexuals reveal the tensions that surround sexual orientation in American society.

These very different issues—encountering strangers and humor—are but two of the countless dimensions of everyday life. They have in common the ability to illustrate how people in social interaction construct a world of meaning. They also suggest the value of the sociological perspective for understanding our everyday lives.

SUMMARY

1. Social interaction is creative and spontaneous, but it also involves patterns that are called social structure. By guiding behavior within culturally approved bounds, social structure helps to make situations understandable to participants.

2. A major component of social structure is status. Within an entire status set, a master status may have great importance for a person's social identity.

3. In principle, an important distinction is made between ascribed status and achieved status. In practice, however, almost all statuses reflect some combination of both ascription and achievement.

4. Role is the dynamic expression of a status. Like statuses, roles are relational, guiding people as they interact with one another.

5. The roles that correspond to two or more statuses may be incompatible, giving rise to role conflict. In a similar way, incompatibility among the different roles that are linked to even one status (the role set) can generate role strain.

6. The phrase "social construction of reality" conveys the important idea that people build the social world as they interact with one another.

7. The Thomas theorem points out that although reality is a human creation, it is real in its consequences for those involved.

8. People are creative in generating social reality, but they do so within the context of their culture and available social resources.

9. Ethnomethodology is the study of how people build understandings of everyday social situations. This approach often reveals how situations are defined by violating patterns of expected behavior.

10. Dramaturgical analysis explores how people construct personal performances from patterned elements. This approach to understanding everyday life makes use of ideas derived from theatrical performances.

11. People make use of language, nonverbal behavior, and deliberately fashioned physical settings in their performances. Often these performances attempt to idealize personal intentions.

12. All social behavior carries the ever-present danger of embarrassment. Often others respond to a "loss of face" with tact.

13. Encountering strangers has always been a common everyday experience, especially in cities. In the past, people identified strangers largely in terms of their appearance. Today, the location of interaction is an important clue to social identity.

14. Humor is based on the contrast between conventional and unconventional social realities. Because humor is framed by the larger culture, people the world over often find humor in very different situations.

KEY CONCEPTS

achieved status a social position that is assumed voluntarily and that reflects a significant measure of personal ability and effort

ascribed status a social position that is received at birth or involuntarily assumed at a later point in the life course

dramaturgical analysis the analysis of social interaction in terms of theatrical performance

ethnomethodology the study of the everyday, common-sense understandings that people have of the world around them

master status a status that has exceptionally great significance for shaping a person's entire life

nonverbal communication communication using body movements, gestures, and facial expressions rather than spoken words

presentation of self the ways in which individuals, in various settings, attempt to create specific impressions in the minds of others

role patterns of behavior corresponding to a particular status

role conflict incompatibility among the roles corresponding to two or more statuses

role set a number of roles attached to a single status

role strain incompatibility among roles corresponding to a single status

social construction of reality the process by which individuals creatively shape reality through social interaction

status a recognized social position that an individual occupies within society

status set all the statuses a particular person holds at a given time

Thomas theorem the assertion that situations that are defined as real are real in their consequences

SUGGESTED READINGS

This paperback provides many examples of rich insights about everyday life that the sociological perspective offers.

David A. Karp and William C. Yoels, *Sociology and Everyday Life.* Itasca, IL: Peacock, 1986.

These two classics in sociology are easily understood and readily available in paperback.

Erving Goffman. *The Presentation of Self in Everyday Life.* Garden City, NY: Doubleday Anchor Books, 1959.

Peter L. Berger and Thomas Luckmann. *The Social Construction of Reality: A Treatise in the Sociology of Knowledge.* Garden City, NY: Doubleday Anchor Books, 1967.

At the end of his career, Erving Goffman wrote this book to apply dramaturgical analysis to spoken communication.

Erving Goffman. *Forms of Talk.* Philadelphia: University of Pennsylvania Press, 1981.

Written sources all but ignore the everyday lives of women, especially black women in America. This paperback is an oral history of one black woman's life as told to her sociologist granddaughter.

Mamie Garvin Fields with Karen Fields. *Lemon Swamp and Other Places.* New York: Free Press, 1985.

Despite its centrality to our lives, human emotion is often overlooked in sociological analysis. A notable exception is the following paperback:

William H. Frey II with Muriel Langstreth. *Crying: The Mystery of Tears.* Minneapolis: Winston Press and Harper & Row, 1985.

Physical attractiveness is a topic of growing interest in social science. A good introduction to this area of study is this book.

Elaine Hatfield and Susan Sprecher. *Mirror, Mirror . . . The Importance of Looks in Everyday Life.* Albany, NY: SUNY Press, 1986.

This paperback explores the ideas of Harold Garfinkel, architect of ethnomethodology.

John Heritage. *Garfinkel and Ethnomethodology.* Cambridge, UK: Polity Press, 1984.

In the decades since World War II, shopping malls have become the new American "Main Street." This paperback examines this familiar social setting.

Jerry Jacobs. *The Mall: An Attempted Escape from Everyday Life.* Prospect Heights, IL: Waveland Press, 1984.

Art is an important dimension of everyday life that is examined sociologically in this paperback.

Arnold Hauser. *The Sociology of Art.* Chicago: University of Chicago Press, 1982.

Counseling is one important application of the social construction of reality. This book explores one of the most difficult counseling situations: when a client resists the assistance of the professional counselor.

George A. Harris and David Watkins. *Counseling the Involuntary and Resistant Client.* College Park, MD: American Correctional Association, 1987.

CHAPTER 7

Groups and Organizations

On March 8, 1965, a young marine named Philip Caputo landed at Danang, Vietnam. Sixteen months later, his tour of duty completed, he returned to the United States. He had made it. He was home. But he would never be the same. A decade later, telling the story of his time in Vietnam, Caputo (1977:xiv–xv) wrote:

> . . . an honorable discharge released me from the Marines and the chance of dying an early death in Asia. I felt as happy as a condemned man whose sentence has been commuted, but within a year I began growing nostalgic for the war.

> Other veterans I knew confessed to the same emotion. In spite of everything, we felt a strange attachment to Vietnam and, even stranger, a longing to return. The war was still being fought, but this desire to go back did not spring from any patriotic ideas about duty, honor, and sacrifice, the myths with which old men send young men off to get killed or maimed. It arose, rather, from a recognition of how deeply we had been changed, how different we were from everyone who had not shared with us the miseries of the monsoon, the exhausting patrols, the fear of a combat assault on a hot landing zone. We had very little in common with them. Though we were civilians again, the civilian world seemed alien. We did not belong to it as much as we did to that other world, where we had fought and our friends had died. . . .

. . . [I also want] to describe the intimacy of life in infantry battalions, where the communion between men is as profound as any between lovers. Actually, it is more so. It does not demand for its sustenance the reciprocity, the pledges of affection, the endless reassurances required by the love of men and women. It is, unlike marriage, a bond that cannot be broken by a word, by boredom or divorce, or by anything other than death. Sometimes even that is not strong enough. Two friends of mine died trying to save the corpses of their men from the battlefield. Such devotion, simple and selfless, the sentiment of belonging to each other, was the one decent thing we found in a conflict otherwise notable for its monstrosities.

In these words Philip Caputo describes the power of social experience—even in the midst of violence—to fuse individual beings together in ways that change everyone involved. Notice how he writes of *we* contrasted to *them*; how he stresses the sense of *belonging* shared with the soldiers around him, the sense of *intimacy*, *bonding*, and *devotion*.

Social life is more than the interaction of individuals, the focus of Chapter 6. It is also the process of participating in something larger than ourselves. One type of larger collectivity is the *social group*, illustrated by the countless clusters of soldiers whose identities were fused by the experiences of a battlefield. Also of increasing importance for modern social life is the *formal organization*. Such organizations include the Marine Corps, business corporations, universities, and volunteer associations such as the American Red Cross. This chapter explores both social groups and formal organizations.

SOCIAL GROUPS

Virtually no one lives without some sense of belonging and identification with other people. Or, more simply, almost everyone participates in *social groups*. A **social group** is defined as *two or more people who have a high degree of common identity and who interact on a regular basis*. As earlier chapters have explained, human beings are social creatures. Not surprisingly, then, we join together in couples, families, circles of friends, platoons, churches, businesses, clubs, and numerous large organizations. Whatever form social groups may take, they are composed of people who share awareness of common membership based on shared experiences, loyalties, and interests. In short, even as they are aware of their individuality, the members of social groups also think of themselves as a special "we."

Of course, in the broadest sense, everyone in a society can be described as one very large social group distinct from all others: Americans, for example, have a social identity apart from Russians. But, strictly speaking, sociologists do not consider an entire society to be a social group because most of its members do not know each other personally or interact with one another on a regular basis.

Groups, Aggregates, and Categories

A sense of belonging, reinforced by regular social interaction, distinguishes the members of a social group from other collections of people that they may superficially resemble. The term *aggregate* refers to a number of people who are in the same place at the same time, but who interact little, if at all. Nor do the individuals who make up an aggregate have a sense of belonging together. People riding together on a subway are an example of an aggregate; they are not a social group.

A number of people can also be identified in terms of some common status, such as being "mothers," "soldiers," "homeowners," or "Roman Catholics." Such a common status is the basis of a *category* rather than a social group. People who constitute a category may be aware that they share some trait with others, but most of them are strangers who never socially interact.

People within some aggregates and categories can become a social group, but only if circumstances cause them to develop a feeling of common identity and to socially interact over a period of time. This may happen, for instance, to people stalled for hours in a subway car beneath the streets of New York City, or to soldiers assigned to the same unit. Overall, unlike an aggregate or a category, a social group is more than the sum of its parts. Its members recognize a social group as a distinctive entity unto itself.

Primary and Secondary Groups

Several times a day, one person greets another with a smile and a simple phrase such as "Hi! How are you?" Of course, an honest reply to this question might be expected, but not often. Usually, the other person responds with a well-scripted "Fine, and how are you?" In most cases, providing a complete account of how one *really* is doing would lead the other person to make a hasty and awkward exit.

Charles Horton Cooley (1864–1929)

Charles Horton Cooley spent his childhood in Ann Arbor, Michigan— then a small town—where his father was an influential lawyer, professor, and judge. Cooley left home to attend college, then returned to Ann Arbor for graduate study at the University of Michigan. He remained there as a member of the university's faculty from 1892 until his death.

Cooley's major contribution to sociology was exploring the character of the primary group. This interest was probably based on his personal experiences growing up during a time of great change in America. Small-town life was giving way to the fast-paced impersonality of industrial cities. Like Auguste Comte (introduced in Chapter 1), Cooley worried about the declining importance of many social patterns that had traditionally bound people together. The individualism and competition that he saw coming to dominate American society made him uneasy. He was convinced that small, cooperative social groups were of crucial importance to every human being. Without them, he believed, people would lack a sense of belonging and would be unlikely to develop attitudes encouraging fair play.

Cooley seems to have hoped that the primary group could preserve many of the traditional values of a more socially cohesive way of life in the midst of a rapidly changing society.

SOURCES: Adapted from Lewis A. Coser, *Masters of Sociological Thought: Ideas in Historical and Social Context*, 2nd ed. (New York: Harcourt Brace Jovanovich, 1977), Chap. 8; and Philip Rieff, "Introduction," in Charles Horton Cooley, *Social Organization* (New York: Schocken Books, 1962), pp. v–xx.

The extent of personal concern for others in social interaction was used by Charles Horton Cooley to draw a distinction between two general types of social groups. The **primary group** is *a typically small social group in which relationships are both personal and enduring.* Within primary groups, people have strong and lasting personal loyalties that Cooley designated as *primary relationships.* The members of primary groups typically share many activities and spend a great deal of time together, so that they come to know one another very well. Just as important, they are likely to display genuine concern for one another's welfare. The family is perhaps the most important primary group within any society.

Cooley applied the term *primary* to social groups of this kind because they are among the first groups we experience in life. Furthermore, as Chapter 5 explained, they are of primary importance in shaping our personal attitudes and behavior. Primary groups are also central to our social identity, which is why members of any primary group almost always think of themselves as "we."

The strength of primary relationships gives individuals considerable comfort and security, which is clearly evident in personal performances, as described in Chapter 6. Within the familiar social environment of family or friends, people tend to feel they can be themselves without worrying about being continually evaluated by others. At the office, for example, people are often self-conscious about their clothing and behavior; at home, they feel free to dress and act more or less as they wish.

Members of primary groups certainly provide many personal benefits to one another, including financial as well as emotional support. But people generally perceive the primary group as an end in itself rather than as a means to other ends. Thus, for example, family members or close friends are expected to help each other move into a new apartment without monetary payment. At the same time, primary group members usually do expect that such help will be mutual. A person who consistently helps a friend who never returns the favor is likely to feel used and to question the depth of the friendship.

Because primary relationships are valued in themselves rather than as a means toward some goal, members of primary groups are not viewed as interchangeable with other people. We usually do not care who cashes our check or approves a loan for us at the bank. But in primary groups—especially the family—the emphasis on personal emotions and loyalty means that, for better or worse, we feel bound to particular others. Although brothers and sisters may experience periodic conflict, they always remain brothers and sisters.

A contrasting type of social group is the **secondary group,** which is defined as *a typically large and impersonal social group based on some special interest or activity.* Within a secondary group, individuals share situational ties that are called *secondary relationships.* Not surprisingly, secondary groups are typically larger than primary groups. For example, individuals who work together in an office, enroll in the same college course, or belong to a particular political organization usually constitute a secondary group.

The opposite of the characteristics that describe primary groups apply to secondary groups. Secondary relationships involve little personal knowledge and weak emotional ties. They vary in duration, but are usually short-term, beginning and ending without particular significance. It is certainly true that some people work in an office for decades with the same co-workers, but a more typical example of secondary relationships is students in a college course who may not see one another after the semester ends. Because secondary groups are limited to a single specific activity or interest, their members have little chance to develop a deep concern for one another's overall welfare. Secondary groups are therefore less significant than primary groups for personal identity. Although people in a secondary group sometimes think of themselves in terms of "we," the boundary that distinguishes members from nonmembers is usually far less clear than it is in primary groups.

Nothing said so far is meant to imply that secondary groups are unimportant to people. They may lack the special significance of primary groups, but secondary groups are often valued as a means of achieving certain specific ends. If relationships within primary groups have a *personal orientation,* those within secondary groups have a *goal orientation.* Nor are secondary relationships always formal and unemotional. On the contrary, a moment's reflection suggests that social interaction with fellow students, co-workers, and business contacts can be quite enjoyable. Simply bear in mind that personal pleasure is not what prompts the formation of secondary groups in the first place. In sum, while members of a primary group have personal importance on the basis

of *who they are,* members of secondary groups have significance on the basis of *what they can do for us.*

We have already suggested that individuals in primary groups are likely to be sensitive to patterns of *social exchange*—how benefits received by one member compare to those received by another—although such considerations are generally not of crucial importance. Within secondary groups, however, exchange is very important. In business transactions, for example, people are keenly aware of what they receive for what they offer. Likewise, the secondary relationships that often characterize neighbors are based on the expectation that any neighborly favor will be reciprocated in the future.

The goal orientation of secondary groups diverts the focus of social interaction from personal matters to mutually beneficial cooperation. With the wish to maximize these benefits, members of secondary groups are likely to craft their performances carefully, and usually expect others to do the same. Therefore, the secondary relationship is one in which the question "How are you?" may be politely asked without really wanting an answer.

The concepts of primary group and secondary group are descriptively summarized in Table 7–1. Because these two types of social groups have been presented in general terms, neither concept is likely to precisely describe actual social groups in anyone's life. Some family relationships, for example, are more primary than others are, and not all business relationships are equally secondary. The accurate way to use these concepts, then, is to describe any actual social group as being *relatively* primary or secondary.

Table 7–1 PRIMARY GROUPS AND SECONDARY GROUPS: A SUMMARY

	Primary Group	Secondary Group
Quality of relationships	Personal orientation	Goal orientation
Duration of relationships	Usually long-term	Variable; often short-term
Breadth of relationships	Broad; usually involving many activities	Narrow; usually involving few activities
Subjective perception of relationships	As an end in itself	As a means to an end
Typical example	Families; close friendships	Co-workers; political organizations

Group Leadership

Leadership is one important element of group dynamics, which refers to the manner in which groups operate. Social groups vary in the extent to which they designate one or more members as *leaders*, with responsibility to direct the activities of all members. Some friendship groups grant no one the clear status of leader, while others do. Within families, parents generally share leadership responsibilities, although husband and wife sometimes disagree about who is really in charge. In many secondary groups, such as a business office, leadership is likely to involve formal status with clearly defined roles.

There are several different ways in which a person may become recognized as the leader of a social group. In the family, traditional cultural patterns confer leadership on the parents, though more often on the male as head of the household if two spouses are present. In other cases, such as friendship groups, one or more persons may gradually emerge as leaders, although there is typically no formal process of selection. In larger secondary groups, leaders are usually formally chosen through election or recruitment.

Leaders are often thought to be people with unusual personal ability, but decades of research have failed to produce consistent evidence that there is such a category as "natural leaders." It seems that there is no set of personal qualities that all leaders have in common. Rather, virtually anyone may be recognized as a leader depending on the particular needs of a group (Ridgeway, 1983).

Furthermore, although we commonly think of social groups as having a single leader, research suggests that there are typically two different leadership roles that are likely to be held by different individuals (Bales, 1953; Bales & Slater, 1955). The first is **instrumental leadership,** which refers to *leadership that emphasizes the completion of tasks by a social group.* Group members look to instrumental leaders to "get things done." The second is **expressive leadership,** defined as *leadership that emphasizes the collective well-being of the members of a social group.* Expressive leaders are less concerned with the performance goals of a group than they are with providing emotional support to group members and attempting to minimize tension and conflict among them. Members look to expressive leaders for personal support and to maintain stable relationships within the group.

Because their concern is mainly with performance, instrumental leaders are likely to have a rather secondary relationship to other group members. They give orders and may discipline those who inhibit attainment of the group's goals. Expressive leaders, on the other hand, cultivate more personal or primary relationships with others in the group. They offer sympathy when someone experiences difficulties or is subjected to discipline, are quick to lighten a serious moment with humor, and try to resolve any problem that threatens to divide the group. As the differences in these two roles suggest, expressive leaders generally receive more personal affection from group members. Instrumental leaders, if they are successful in promoting group goals, may enjoy a more distant respect.

This differentiation of leadership within a social group can be illustrated by the operation of the traditional American family (Parsons & Bales, 1955). For generations, cultural norms have supported the instrumental leadership of fathers and husbands. According to this traditional pattern, men assume most responsibility for providing family income, making major family decisions, and dispensing discipline to children (and, as the dominant partner in the marriage, to wives as well). Expressive leadership within the family has traditionally been assigned to women. Mothers and wives have been expected to provide emotional support and to attempt to maintain peaceful relationships among all family members. In light of these patterns, it is not surprising that while children may have greater respect for fathers, they typically have closer personal relationships with their mothers (Macionis, 1977, 1978). Social roles within the family have been subject to some change in recent decades (as Chapter 14 will discuss in detail), so that although the separation of the instrumental and expressive leadership in the family persists, it is far less pronounced than it was in the 1950s.

Leaders are further distinguished by the extent to which they involve other group members in decision making. *Authoritarian leaders* are instrumental in their outlook, making decisions on their own and demanding strict compliance from subordinates. This style of leadership is likely to win little personal affection from group members, although the authoritarian leader may be highly effective when groups face crisis situations in which immediate decisions are necessary and group discipline must remain high. *Democratic leaders* have more expressive qualities, seeking to include all group members in the process of making decisions. While less successful in crisis situations (in which there is little time for discussion), democratic leaders are able to apply the ideas of all members to tasks requiring reflection and imagination.

Laissez-faire leaders (from the French words meaning roughly "to leave alone") tend to minimize their position and power, allowing the group to operate more or less on its own. Generally, this type of leadership is the least effective in promoting group goals. Clearly, the type of person who becomes a leader in a social group has much to do with the particular characteristics and needs of the group itself (White & Lippitt, 1953; Ridgeway, 1983).

Group Conformity

Another important dimension of group dynamics is the desire of members to conform to cultural patterns adopted by the social group. In friendship groups, for example, conformity may afford people a more secure feeling of membership. In other groups, such as the family, conformity is not a direct condition for membership, but even so, the pressure to conform can be considerable.

The demand for conformity is not limited to primary groups. Even social interaction with unfamiliar people in a group setting can generate considerable pressure toward conformity. Just how powerful these forces can be was revealed more than thirty years ago in a classic experiment conducted by Solomon Asch (1952).

Asch's Research

Asch asked a subject to join a group with six to eight others for the supposed purpose of studying visual perception. In reality, he was interested in exploring patterns of group conformity. In each trial of his study, Asch met with a small number of "subjects" to explain the research. In fact, he had already arranged with all but one of them to create a situation in which the one naive subject would experience group pressure to support conclusions that were quite unreasonable.

What actually happened was as follows. While sitting around a table, group members were asked to carefully examine sets of cards, each similar to the set shown in Figure 7–1. On the first card was a single line. This "standard" line corresponded exactly in length to one of three lines on the second card. One at a time, the people at the table were asked to state which of the three lines on the second card matched the line on the first card. Anyone with normal vision could easily see that the line marked "A" on the second card was the correct choice. Initially, the obviously correct answer was given by everyone. But then, one at a time, all of

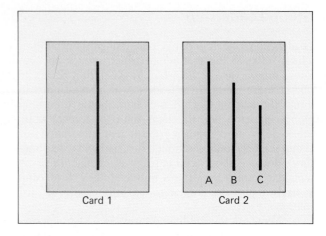

Figure 7–1   The Cards Used in Asch's Experiment in Group Conformity

(Asch, 1952:452–453).

the people collaborating with Asch started to report an obviously wrong answer. As this occurred, the unknowing subject began to look bewildered and uncomfortable, as the photos reveal. Hearing such responses created a dilemma: Should an obviously correct answer be given if doing so would cause a person to be viewed as different from others? Or should a wrong answer be given just to fit in? In performing this experiment with numerous subjects, Asch found that more than *one-third* resolved their dilemma by providing an incorrect answer. Those who did so later admitted they had had no doubt about what the right answer was, but preferred to avoid the discomfort of being different from other people—even people they did not know. Apparently, many of us are prepared to compromise our own judgment in the interests of group conformity.

Milgram's Research

In the early 1960s, Stanley Milgram—who had been a student of Solomon Asch—conducted a remarkable and controversial set of experiments at Yale University. Aware that millions of innocent people had been "slaughtered on command" during World War II, Milgram wanted to scientifically study the extent to which ordinary people would inflict suffering on others simply because an authority figure or others in a group encouraged them to do so.

In Milgram's initial research (1963, 1965; Miller, 1986), an "experimenter" greeted subjects two at a time,

In Solomon Asch's study of group conformity, the naive subject (center) becomes puzzled and uncomfortable upon realizing that his judgments differ from those of others around him.

telling them they were to engage in a study of memory. The experimenter assigned one subject the role of "teacher" and the other the role of "learner." Actually, the person assigned to be the learner was part of the study; only the person placed in the position of teacher was naive about what was really going on.

The learner was then placed in a contraption that resembled an electric chair and electrodes were attached to one arm. The experimenter instructed the teacher to read pairs of words. Subsequently, the first word of each pair was repeated and the learner was asked to recall the correct second word. As mistakes occurred, the experimenter instructed the teacher to administer a shock to the learner using a realistic-looking "shock generator." This device was marked to dispense shocks as "punishment," ranging from 15 volts (labeled "mild shock") past 300 volts (marked "intense shock") to an extreme of 450 volts (marked "Danger: Severe Shock" and "XXX"). After beginning at the lowest level, the teachers were instructed to increase the shock by 15 volts every time a mistake was made. The experimenter explained to the teacher that the shocks were "extremely painful" but caused "no permanent tissue damage."

The results were striking evidence of the ability of leaders to obtain compliance. Of the forty subjects placed in the role of teacher in the initial research, all obeyed the experimenter, even though they thought they were administering severe shocks to the learners. No one as much as questioned the procedure before 300 volts had been applied, and twenty-six of the subjects—almost two-thirds—went all the way to 450 volts.

In later research, the proportion of subjects who applied the maximum shock varied according to specific experimental conditions. But overall, Milgram found that many subjects shocked people who objected to the experiment, many shocked people who protested that they suffered from heart conditions, and many even increased the voltage as people screamed and then fell silent as if they had become unconscious. Worth noting is that subjects experienced real suffering of their own. Prodded by the experimenter to continue, they often displayed great stress in their task—which is one reason that this research has been controversial ever since. In some cases, Milgram reported, the person administering the "shocks" was "reduced to a twitching, stuttering wreck." But the subjects followed orders all the same.

Milgram—who was himself amazed and disturbed by the results—concluded that people are unlikely to question those in positions of authority, even when common sense suggests they should. Milgram then extended the research with an eye toward the earlier work of Solomon Asch, his former teacher.

Milgram wondered if Asch had found a high degree of group conformity because the task of matching lines was seen by most of the subjects as a trivial activity. What if groups pressured people to administer electrical shocks? To investigate, he repeated his experiment (1964) so that a group of three "teachers" worked together. Actually, two of the teachers were Milgram's associates, in much the same way as in Asch's earlier research. Milgram asked each of the three teachers to suggest a shock level when an error was made, with the provision that the shock actually given would be the *lowest* of the three suggestions. Thus the naive subject was in a position to decide what to do no matter what the other two said. The two teachers working with Milgram recommended increasing the shock level with each error; this was found to result in more severe shocks by the subject. The power of group conformity was evident in the fact

that subjects applied voltages three to four times higher when encouraged by others than they did when acting alone. The overall implications of Milgram's research is that people are surprisingly likely to follow the directions of "legitimate authority figures," and are also strongly influenced by others in their groups even when those others are just "ordinary people."

Janis's Research

Intrigued by the idea that people can be led to engage in behavior that violates common sense, Irving Janis (1972) examined historical documents pertaining to the actions of high governmental officials. His findings suggest that the powerful are not immune to group pressure toward conformity. Janis argued that a number of major foreign policy errors in United States history—including the failure to foresee the Japanese attack on Pearl Harbor at the beginning of World War II, the disastrous attempt to invade Cuba in 1961, and the tragic involvement in the Vietnam War—may actually have been the result of group conformity to ill-advised positions taken by the highest-ranking political leaders.

Joining together in groups is often thought to contribute to better decision making because wisdom is gained from "putting our heads together." But Janis showed that this is often not the case. First, rather than examining a problem from many points of view, groups often seek consensus. In this way, group dynamics may actually result in *narrowing* the range of options. Second, groups often develop a distinctive language, making use of key terms that favor one interpretation of events. Third, having adopted a particular position, members of the group may come to see others with more open minds as the "opposition." The result, Janis concluded, is "groupthink," meaning a reduced capacity for critical reflection.

Groupthink was evident in the decision of the Kennedy administration to launch an invasion of Cuba—a plan that failed badly and provoked international criticism of the United States. Arthur Schlesinger, Jr., former adviser to President John Kennedy, acknowledged guilt "for having kept so quiet during those crucial discussions in the Cabinet Room," but added that the group operated in such a way as to discourage anyone from speaking out against what appeared to be "nonsense" (Janis, 1972:30, 40).

More recently, groupthink was probably at work in the Iran-Contra scandal. Some members of the Reagan administration formulated a plan to sell weapons to Iran in order to encourage the release of American hostages held in Lebanon. The plan called for proceeds from the arms sale to fund the Contras, soldiers opposed to the Sandinista government in Nicaragua. As congressional hearings brought details of the episode to light during 1987, many characteristics of groupthink became evident. Officials involved in the plan—perhaps best exemplified by Lieutenant Colonel Oliver North—became single-mindedly committed to their cause, even to the point of ignoring apparent violations of law. Further, these officials made extensive use of language that supported only one interpretation of events. For example, they avoided speaking of "trading arms for hostages" in favor of "opening relations with moderates in Iran." Likewise, they replaced the terms "Contras" and "guerilla insurgents" with the more positive label "freedom fighters." Finally those who opposed the plan were viewed as "the opposition," so that vital information was denied to key administration officials such as Secretary of State George Schultz and perhaps even the president himself.

Reference Groups

There is little doubt that social groups can have a powerful influence on how each of us thinks and acts. This reflects the fact that people typically make evaluations and decisions by taking account of others, and often use social groups to which they belong for this purpose. The term **reference group** is used to designate *a social group that serves as a point of reference for individuals in evaluation and decision making.*

A young man who imagines how his family will respond to a woman he is dating is using his family as a reference group. Similarly, a banker who attempts to assess what her colleagues are likely to think about a loan policy she has developed is using her co-workers as a reference group. As these examples suggest, reference groups can be either primary or secondary. Because people are often strongly motivated to conform to a group, the effect of social groups on personal evaluations can be very significant.

Social groups can also be used as points of reference by nonmembers. For example, people going to job interviews usually anticipate how those in the organization dress and act, and adjust their personal performances accordingly. People are especially likely to use social groups they wish to join as reference groups, the process of *anticipatory socialization* described in Chapter 5. By

conforming to group social patterns, they hope to win acceptance as group members more readily.

Stouffer's Research

A classic study of reference group dynamics was conducted during World War II, when the government hired a team of sociologists to investigate the attitudes and morale of soldiers (Stouffer et al., 1949). One part of this study involved a survey asking soldiers to evaluate the chances of promotion for an able person in their branch of the service. Common sense would suggest that soldiers in a branch of the service with a relatively high promotion rate would be most optimistic about their chances of promotion. Yet the reverse was actually found; those in branches of the service with relatively *lower* promotion rates were actually more optimistic about their chances of promotion.

The researchers resolved this apparent paradox by recognizing that soldiers used specific reference groups in reaching their judgments. Those in a branch of the service with a lower promotion rate compared themselves to similar others, recognizing that although they had not been promoted, neither had others in their outfit. In this sense, they saw themselves as not so badly off, so they expressed relatively positive attitudes about promotion. Soldiers in a branch of the service with a higher promotion rate also used their own outfit as a reference group. But in this case, even if they had been promoted, they could point to some less deserving person who had also been promoted or to someone who had been promoted faster than they. Either of these situations caused them to view the promotion policy in more negative terms. The importance of Stouffer's research is that it demonstrates that we do not make judgments about ourselves in isolation, nor do we compare ourselves with everyone. Rather, we use specific social groups as standards in developing our individual attitudes.

Making use of reference groups, anyone is likely to feel "deprived" or "well off" only in relation to some particular other people. In other words, whatever anyone's situation in *absolute terms*, well-being is subjectively evaluated *relative* to some reference group. A feeling of affluence, then, is the result of evaluating one's situation relative to those who have less. Likewise, even people with an increasing income may feel deprived if they shift reference groups so that they continually compare themselves to others who have still more than they do (Merton, 1968; Mirowsky, 1987).

Ingroups and Outgroups

By the time children are in the early grades of school, much of their activity takes place within social groups. They eagerly join some groups, but avoid—or are excluded from—others. For example, girls and boys often form distinct play groups and display patterns of behavior that are culturally defined as feminine and masculine (Lever, 1978; Best, 1983).

On the basis of sex, employment, family ties, personal tastes, or some other category, people often identify positively with one social group while opposing other groups. Across the United States, for example, many high-school students wear jackets with the name of their school on the back and place school decals on car windows to symbolize their membership in the school as a social group. Students who attend another school may be the subject of derision simply because they are members of a competing group.

This illustrates an important process of group dynamics: the opposition of ingroups and outgroups. An **ingroup** is *a social group with which people identify and toward which they feel a sense of loyalty.* An ingroup exists in relation to an **outgroup,** which is *a social group with which people do not identify and toward which they feel a sense of competition or opposition.* Defining social groups this way is commonplace. A sports team is an ingroup to its members and an outgroup to members of other teams. The Democrats in a certain community may see themselves as an ingroup in relation to Republicans. In a broader sense, all Americans share some sense of being an ingroup in relation to Soviet citizens or other nationalities. All ingroups and outgroups are created by the process of believing that "we" have valued characteristics that "they" do not have.

This process of opposition serves to sharpen the boundaries among social groups, giving people a clearer sense of their location in a world of many social groups. It also heightens awareness of the distinctive characteristics of various social groups, though not always in an accurate way. Research has shown that the members of ingroups hold unrealistically positive views of themselves and unfairly negative views of various outgroups (Tajfel, 1982). Ethnocentrism, for example, is the result of overvaluing one's own way of life, while simultaneously devaluing other cultures as outgroups.

Furthermore, members of outgroups are often socially excluded on the grounds of negative stereotypes. This process is particularly damaging when an ingroup has greater social power than an outgroup it opposes—as is the case of English-speaking versus French-speaking Canadians and whites versus nonwhites in the United States.

Whites have traditionally viewed nonwhites in negative terms and subjected them to social disadvantages. Blacks, Hispanics, Asians, and Native Americans who seek to share the privileges of whites sometimes struggle to overcome negative self-images based on stereotypes held by the majority. The operation of ingroups and outgroups is therefore often influenced by patterns of social inequality in the larger society. While this process may have the positive consequence of fostering group loyalty, it can also generate considerable social tension and conflict.

The popularity of jeans and other articles of clothing among young people is partly explained by the desire to display ingroup solidarity.

The Importance of Group Size

Being the first person to arrive at a party affords the opportunity to observe a fascinating process in group dynamics. When fewer than about six people interact in one setting, a single conversation is usually maintained by everyone. But with the addition of more people, the discussion typically divides into two or more conversations. This example is a simple way of showing that size has important effects on the operation of social groups.

The basis for this dynamic lies in the mathematical connection between the number of people in a social group and the number of relationships among them, as shown in Figure 7–2. Two people are joined by one relationship; adding a third person results in three relationships, a fourth person yields six. As additional people are added one at a time—according to what mathematicians call an *arithmetic increase*—the number of relationships increases very rapidly—in what is called a *geometric increase*. By the time six people have joined one conversation, there are fifteen different relationships among them, which explains why the conversation usually divides at this point.

Social dynamics within the smallest social groups was of special interest to the German sociologist Georg Simmel. Simmel (1950; orig. 1902) used the term **dyad** to designate *a social group with two members*. In North American society, love affairs, marriages, and the closest friendships are dyadic. Simmel pointed out that having only two members confers two specific qualities on a social group.

First, dyads are characteristically less stable than social groups with a large number of members. Since it is based on a single relationship, a dyad requires the active participation of both members. A unique characteristic of a dyad is that the withdrawal of either person results in the group's demise. Consequently, members of a dyad are usually aware that continual effort is necessary to sustain the group's vitality. Because marriage is a dyad of great importance to society, the personal bond between two spouses is reinforced with legal and often religious ties. In this special case, in other words, society provides extra support to maintain the dyadic group in the event that personal interest declines. A large group, in contrast, has more inherent stability. A volunteer fire company, for example, is based on the activity of many people, so the indifference of even several members would not cause the group to collapse.

Second, Simmel noted that a dyad is the type of

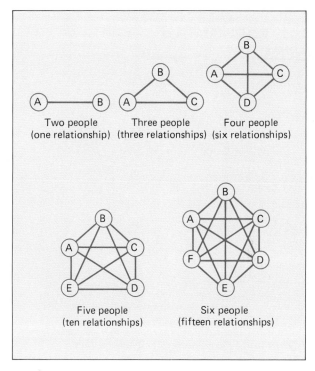

Figure 7–2 Group Size and Relationships

social group in which members experience the greatest intensity of social interaction. Since there is only one relationship, neither member shares the attention of the other with anyone else. For this reason, dyads also have the potential to be the strongest social bonds that we experience in our lives. Because marriage in our culture is dyadic, husbands and wives are, ideally, united by powerful emotional ties. As will be explained in Chapter 14, however, marriage in much of the rest of the world can involve more than two people. When it does, the attention of the spouses is divided among many relationships, so that their marriage is typically less emotionally intense than a dyadic one.

Simmel claimed that a **triad**—*a social group with three members*—is also unstable, although for a different reason. A triad contains three relationships, each uniting two of the three members. Thus any two members of a triad can form a coalition against the third member and usually get their way because they are a majority of the group. More generally, any two members of a triad may intensify their relationship, transforming the triad into a dyad that excludes the third person. This often takes place, for example, among three roommates

A distinctive characteristic of a triad is that the social bond between two of the members can exclude the third.

at college. If a triad is to persist, care must be taken to include all three members in many routine activities. If romantic interest blossoms between two members of a triad, transformation to a dyad is likely, since the two members now have a powerful bond that neither shares with the third person. The likelihood that this change will occur is suggested by the common phrase "two's company; three's a crowd."

A triad does benefit from a source of stability not found in a dyad, however. If the relationship between any two of the group's members becomes strained, the third member can serve as a mediator to restore the group's vitality. In the same way, members of a dyad (such as a married couple) may temporarily seek to include a third person (a trusted friend or counselor) in the group in an effort to resolve tensions between them.

An interesting example of small-group dynamics is the birth of the first child to a couple. Following Simmel's analysis, as the dyadic couple becomes a triadic family, each parent now shares the attention of the other with the child. Certainly, this causes resentment in some cases. On the other hand, the birth of a child may provide a welcome common focus for the activities of both husband and wife, who today carry on a significant part of their lives separately outside the home.

Social groups with more than three members tend to be more stable because the lack of interest on the part of one or even several members does not directly threaten the group's existence. Furthermore, larger social groups tend to develop a more formal social structure— a variety of statuses and roles, and often rules and regulations—which stabilizes their operation. However, larger social groups inevitably lack the intense personal relationships that are possible only in the smallest groups.

Is there an ideal size for a social group? The answer, of course, depends on the group's purpose. The dyad offers unsurpassed emotional intensity, while a group of several dozen people is likely to be more stable and also able to accomplish larger and more complex tasks. In general, however, research suggests that about five people is the size that generates the highest degree of satisfaction among group members. This is because smaller social groups require much more effort on the part of each person, while larger ones are typically much more impersonal (Slater, 1958; Ridgeway, 1983).

Networks

The term **social network** designates *a web of social ties that links people, but with less common identity and less social interaction than are typical of a social group.* A social network resembles a social group, in other words, in that it links people in relationships. But unlike group members, those connected by a network usually have little sense of membership. Moreover, unlike a group, a network brings people into only occasional contact with one another. Finally, networks have no clear boundaries, as groups generally do. A group may take the form of a "circle of friends," but a network is better described as expanding outward from an individual like a "social web" in which most people are connected only indirectly through others.

Social ties within networks may be relatively primary, as among people who attended college together and have since maintained friendships by mail and telephone. More commonly, however, network ties are extremely secondary relationships that involve little personal knowledge. A social network may also contain people we *know of*—or who *know of us*—but with whom we interact infrequently, if at all. As one woman with a widespread reputation as a community organizer explains, "I get calls at home, someone says, 'Are you Roseann Navarro? Somebody told me to call you. I have this problem . . .'" (Kaminer, 1984:94). For this reason social networks may be described as clusters of weak ties (Granovetter, 1973).

Even though social ties within networks may not be strong, these relationships are a valuable resource that can be used to personal advantage. Perhaps the most common example of the power of networks is finding a job. The scientific genius Albert Einstein sought employment for a year after completing his schooling to no avail; he succeeded only when the father of one of his classmates put him in touch with the director of an office who was able to provide a job (Clark, 1971; cited in Fischer, 1977:19). Thus, even in the case of a person with extraordinary ability, *who* you know may be just as important as *what* you know.

Nan Lin and his associates (1981) produced evidence of the extent of such network-based opportunities. Conducting a survey of 399 men in an urban area of the United States, Lin found that almost 60 percent had used social networks in finding a job; this approach was much more common than any other. But although social networks may be widespread, Lin found that they do not provide equal advantages to everyone. These networks afforded the greatest advantages to men whose fathers held important occupational positions. This reflects the fact that networks tend to contain people with similar social characteristics and social rank, thereby helping to perpetuate patterns of social inequality.

Recent research by Peter Marsden (1987) indicates that larger social networks tend to contain people who are younger, more formally educated, and living in urban areas. While the networks of men and women do not differ significantly in size, women were found to include more relatives in their networks. There is no surprise,

Networks are often a source of power. Exclusive social clubs have traditionally reinforced the advantages of some categories of Americans.

then, in the fact that women have long expressed dismay at being excluded from powerful "old-boy networks" that help men to maintain their dominant position in North American society. In response, women have recently begun building networks of their own. Women's networks are of special importance in the work world. This is because female workers of all kinds—from the assembly line to the executive office—are often isolated in settings where men outnumber them and have more power than they do. Female social networks provide the support and camaraderie, as well as the business contacts, that women might otherwise lack (Speizer, 1983).

FORMAL ORGANIZATIONS

Large social groups such as corporations or branches of government differ from small friendship groups or families in more respects than just numbers of members. Their greater size, of course, renders social relationships more impersonal. But even more is involved, since large social groups also have a complex, formal character. Sociologists, therefore, use the concept **formal organization** to refer to *a large, secondary group that is formally organized to facilitate achieving its goals.*

With almost 250 million members, American society faces countless complicated tasks ranging from providing health care to delivering the mail. Most of these are carried out by large, formal organizations. The United States government, the largest formal organization in America, employs over 5 million people in various agencies and the military services, both within the United States and abroad. Each government agency contains many smaller formal organizations that address specific tasks. Such large social groups develop lives of their own, somewhat independent of their particular members. In other words, people come and go, but the statuses they fill and the roles they perform remain largely unchanged over many years.

Types of Formal Organizations

Formal organizations differ among themselves, which has led sociologists to develop various classification schemes. On the basis of the different kinds of ties between an organization and its members, Amitai Etzioni (1975) has identified three types of formal organizations: normative, coercive, and utilitarian.

Normative Organizations

People join *normative organizations* in order to pursue some goal they believe to be morally worthwhile, receiving personal satisfaction and social prestige for their efforts rather than monetary reward. For this reason, normative organizations are also commonly called *voluntary associations*. In the United States, examples of normative organizations are community service groups (such as the PTA, the Lions Club, the League of Women Voters, Red Cross, and United Way), political parties, religious organizations, and numerous other organizations concerned with specific social issues. The United States has often been described as a society of "joiners," and Americans participate, usually on a part-time basis, in tens of thousands of normative organizations. Because women have historically been excluded from much of the paid labor force, they have traditionally played a greater part than men have in civic and charitable organizations.

Coercive Organizations

Etzioni claims that people are forced to join *coercive organizations* as a form of punishment (prisons) or treatment (mental hospitals). Since people usually resist such confinement, most coercive organizations have a distinctive physical character, making use of locked doors, barred windows, and security personnel (Goffman, 1961). The goal of coercive organizations is at the very least to segregate people as "inmates" or "patients" for a period of time. At the most, coercive organizations attempt to radically alter people's attitudes and behavior. Recall from Chapter 5 the power of coercive organizations—which are also called *total institutions*—to transform a human being's overall sense of self.

Utilitarian Organizations

Etzioni distinguishes *utilitarian organizations* by the material benefits they provide to their members. Large business enterprises, for example, are organized to generate profits for their owners and income in the form of salaries and wages for their employees. Joining utilitarian organizations is largely a matter of individual choice, although in modern societies dominated by formal organizations, many people must join one utilitarian organization or another in order to make a living. Therefore, although utilitarian organizations certainly involve greater individual freedom than coercive organizations, they provide

less freedom than normative organizations. Membership in utilitarian organizations is generally full time and may last for many years, sometimes for a person's entire working life.

Keep in mind that a particular formal organization may be any one of these three types from the point of view of people holding different statuses. A mental hospital, for example, is a coercive organization to a patient, a utilitarian organization to a psychiatrist, and a normative organization to a part-time hospital volunteer.

Bureaucracy

The origins of formal organization can be traced back thousands of years to early attempts at administering religious and political affairs. In simple terms, organizational innovations extended the control of rulers over millions of people living in vast areas. The benefits of formal organization to elites also included the ability to undertake monumental tasks never before possible. Consider, for example, the single task of building a pharaoh's pyramid in Egypt about 2500 B.C.E. Such a task—which still ranks among the "wonders of the ancient world"—demanded formal organizations to supervise and control thousands of workers engaged in many different activities.

But for centuries, organizational innovation proceeded slowly. The major factor impeding the development of formal organizations was the traditional character of preindustrial societies. This meant that long-established values and beliefs placed greater importance on "God's will" or the whims of a monarch than on organizational efficiency. Only within the last several centuries did this change in Western societies. In response to the Industrial Revolution and what Max Weber described as a "rational world view," the form of organizational structure called *bureaucracy* emerged in Europe and North America.

In Chapter 4, **bureaucracy** was defined as *an organizational model rationally designed to perform complex tasks efficiently*. The essence of bureaucratic organization is deliberately enacting policies that control organizational operations. By doing this, the organization intends to become as efficient as possible in reaching its goals. To appreciate the advantages of bureaucratic organization, consider the telephone system in the United States. Each of over 150 million telephones is able to reach any of the others at any time within seconds. This is, of course, a major technological feat beyond the imagination of people who lived in the ancient world. Even two centuries ago, communication over just several hundred miles required days. Certainly, the installation and maintenance of all these telephones, and over one billion miles of wire and other equipment needed to operate them, are costly. But just as important is the organizational task of keeping track of every telephone call for which a charge is made—noting which phone called which other phone, when, and for how long—and presenting all this information to millions of telephone users in the form of a monthly bill. A task of this kind clearly requires a special form of organizational structure.

Characteristics of Bureaucracy

What are the organizational characteristics that make the efficient completion of such tasks possible? As you will recall from Chapter 4, Max Weber (1978; orig. 1921) pointed to six distinctive qualities of bureaucratic organization. These qualities represent the *ideal* form of bureaucracy, which is only approximated by actual formal organizations.

According to Weber, *specialization* is a first key characteristic of bureaucratic organization. This means that all individuals do not engage in many of the same, general activities, as was the case in societies through most of human history. Rather, bureaucratic organization requires that individuals perform distinctive tasks that often correspond to organizational offices.

Second, the offices in a bureaucratic organization not only have different responsibilities but are arranged in a *hierarchy*. This means that each person is supervised

Max Weber imagined that the principles of bureaucratic organization would eventually be applied throughout society. What we call fast food is created by specialists who perform rigidly defined tasks within a hierarchy. Greater efficiency—and, of course, uniformity—is the result.

by "higher-ups" in the organization, and may also supervise others in lower positions. Virtually all employees in a bureaucratic organization are keenly aware of their own power and responsibility relative to others.

Third, Weber emphasized that tradition carries little weight in bureaucratic organizations. Rather, rationally enacted *rules and regulations* guide the work of all employees. The overall purpose of these rules and regulations is to exercise control over the organization's own operation and, as much as possible, its larger environment. In ideal terms, a bureaucratic organization seeks to operate in a completely predictable fashion.

Fourth, employees of bureaucratic organizations are expected to have the necessary *technical competence*. This represents a sharp break with the practice through most human history of favoring relatives over strangers. In Cooley's terms, however, bureaucracies are large secondary groups in which *who* you are is ignored in favor of *what* you can do.

Fifth, the *impersonality* of bureaucratic organizations is also evident in the performance of one's duties. Any officer is expected to act in response to impersonal rules rather than personal feelings. In principle, then, each client, supervisor, or subordinate is treated uniformly according to organizational regulations. This is, of course, the reason for the common image of the "faceless bureaucrat."

Sixth, bureaucratic organizations make use of *formal, written communications*. While most social communication is casual and verbal, bureaucracy demands that people communicate deliberately and in writing. Over time, of course, this correspondence accumulates into vast records or files. Such files are vital to an organizational form in which formal policies, rather than individual personalities, provide direction to activities.

Bureaucracies versus Small Groups

Small social groups, especially primary groups, exist largely as an end in themselves. As an organizational model for large, secondary groups, bureaucracy seeks to efficiently perform complex tasks. As a form of organization, then, bureaucracy is a means to an end.

Bureaucratic organization is designed to maximize efficiency by recruiting carefully selected personnel into the organization and limiting the variable and unpredictable effects of personal tastes and opinions. In smaller, less formal social groups, members are permitted wide-ranging patterns of behavior, governed by general social norms. Individuals respond to others in the group in a

Table 7–2 SMALL GROUPS AND FORMAL
ORGANIZATIONS: A COMPARISON

	Small Groups	Formal Organizations
Activities	Members typically engage in many of the same activities	Members typically engage in various highly specialized activities
Hierarchy	Often informal or absent	Clearly defined, corresponding to offices
Norms	Informal application of general norms	Clearly defined rules and regulations
Criteria for Membership	Variable, often based on personal liking or kinship	Technical competence to carry out assigned tasks
Relationships	Variable; typically primary	Typically secondary, with selective primary ties
Communications	Typically casual and face-to-face	Typically formal and in writing
Focus	Person-centered	Task-centered

personal manner, and everyone is more or less equal in rank. Especially in primary groups, efficiency is not an important consideration because of the emphasis on personal relationships. Weber believed, however, that personal considerations compromised an organization's efficiency and concluded that a rigid and impersonal organizational system is an effective means to overcome this limitation. Table 7-2 provides a summary of contrasts between small social groups and large formal organizations.

The Informal Side of Bureaucracy

Max Weber's analysis shows bureaucracy to be highly formal—in principle, at least, every activity is deliberately regulated. In actual organizations, however, people develop many patterns of *informal behavior* that do not fit organizational rules. Sometimes informal behavior is a means of meeting a legitimate need overlooked by formal regulations. In other cases, informal behavior may violate official rules (Scott, 1981). Overall, the complexity of formal organizations is increased by the fact that the bureaucratic blueprint is not always observed in actual operations.

Organizational leadership provides one example. Power is formally attached to organizational offices, not to the people who occupy them. In practice, however, personal traits have a significant effect on patterns of leadership. Some people have more charisma or skill in interpersonal relations than others do, and they are therefore able to manage (and manipulate) people more effectively. Jimmy Carter and Ronald Reagan both made use of the formal power of the presidency. Yet Reagan's skills as "The Great Communicator" made him a more influential president—for better or worse—than Carter was.

Authoritarian, democratic, and laissez-faire types of leadership—discussed earlier in this chapter—are as much a reflection of individual personality as of any organizational plan. In addition, decision making within an organization does not always follow the formally defined hierarchy and the official rules and regulations. As the recent Iran-Contra scandal reveals, informal social networks and shared interests can lead officials to bypass the supposedly impersonal and impartial chain of command. In other cases, influential people use organizational power to advance their own interests and those of their friends. In the "real world" of organizational life, officials who attempt to operate strictly by the book may even find themselves denied the promotions and power that are often based on informal alliances. Another common, although informal, arrangement involves people in leadership positions depending on subordinates to accomplish much of their own work. Secretaries, for instance, often have more responsibility than their official job titles and their salaries suggest.

Memos and other formal, written communications are the official means by which information is disseminated throughout a formal organization. In many cases, however, individuals cultivate informal grapevines that spread information much faster, if not always as accurately. Grapevines are of particular importance to those with low standing in the organization because more powerful officials often attempt to keep important information to themselves.

Some members of formal organizations informally attempt to modify or ignore rigid bureaucratic structures as an assertion of their independence and individuality. Put another way, strict rules and regulations often provoke people to develop their own informal standards. A classic study in the 1930s revealed the operation of an informal system of norms within the Western Electric Factory in Chicago (Roethlisberger & Dickson, 1939). Although a worker was formally required to report any rule violation by co-workers, few employees at Western Electric did so. In fact, those who did report infractions were socially

Within formal organizations, a hierarchy of responsibility is often modified according to personal preferences and abilities. In the popular television show M*A*S*H, Radar O'Reilly was only a corporal, but he was largely responsible for keeping the outfit running smoothly.

isolated by other workers as "squealers" who could not be trusted. Moreover, although the company leaders sought to regulate worker productivity through formally enacted standards, workers informally evolved their own definitions of a fair day's work, criticizing those who exceeded them as "rate-busters" and others who fell short as "chiselers" (1939:522).

The existence of such informal social structures suggests that many people share Weber's fear that bureaucratic organization is dehumanizing. But such informal structures also show that human beings have the creative capacity to humanize even the most rigidly defined social situations.

Limitations of Bureaucracy

Weber's assertion that the ideal characteristics of bureaucracy promote organizational efficiency has considerable validity. Still, a number of problems and limitations characterize the operation of actual large, formal organizations. Anyone who has ever tried to replace a lost driver's license, return defective merchandise to a large company, or change an address on a magazine subscription knows that formal organizations can be maddeningly unresponsive to the individual's needs. In part, problems of this kind are caused by an organization's failure to conform to the bureaucratic ideal. In addition, of course, no organizational system is likely to completely eradicate various human failings. But Weber was aware of limitations inherent in bureaucratic organization. As he explained, in order to operate in the most efficient manner, bureaucracy must treat each situation impersonally as a standard "case." The same procedural uniformity that allows the efficient processing of large numbers of cases

curtails the organization's ability to treat special cases with individual attention.

Facts of this sort contributed to Weber's pessimism about the overall effects of bureaucratic organization on society. He feared that bureaucracy would depersonalize society, alienate people from one another, and reduce the individual human being to merely "a small cog in a ceaselessly moving mechanism" (1978:988; orig. 1921). Formal organizations may be intended to serve humanity, in other words, but Weber feared that humanity would come to serve formal organizations.

Bureaucratic organizations are consistent with many of the dominant American cultural values discussed in Chapter 3, including efficiency, practicality, and achievement. On the other hand, bureaucracy may threaten other American cultural values, such as democracy and individual freedom. Ideally, a democratic society is based on the active participation of everyone in social decision making. But bureaucratic organizations have the power to affect our lives in many ways, while we have little sense of participation in their decisions. Moreover, as described in the box, the growth of formal organizations has been accompanied by a decline in individual privacy (Long, 1967; Smith, 1979). In sum, bureaucracy may have made organizations extremely efficient in performing specific tasks, but it has had important dysfunctional consequences for individuals.

Bureaucratic Waste and Incompetence

Bureaucratic inefficiency has been described in two essays, written in a tongue-in-cheek style, yet containing some truth. C. Northcote Parkinson summarized how bureaucracies waste time, money, and human energy

The painting "Government Bureau" by George Tooker is a powerful statement about the human costs of bureaucratic efficiency whereby all people are reduced to "cases" devoid of personal distinctiveness.

according to what he termed Parkinson's Law: "Work expands so as to fill the time available for its completion" (1957:15). To illustrate, assume an office worker in a large organization is able to complete four reports in an average day. If one day this worker were to have only two reports to prepare, how long would this task take? The logical answer is half the day, but Parkinson's Law suggests that if a full day is available to complete two reports, a full day is how long the two reports will take. In other words, few members of formal organizations are likely to seek extra work to fill their spare time. Moreover, to the extent that employees follow Parkinson's Law, they will always appear busy, leading the organization to acquire additional employees. The additional time and expense required to hire, train, supervise, and evaluate a larger staff will almost certainly ensure that everyone becomes busier still, causing the cycle to be repeated over and over again. The result is that bureaucratic organizations grow but may not accomplish a greater amount of work.

Laurence J. Peter (Peter & Hull, 1969) is responsible for the Peter Principle, which states that bureaucrats are promoted until they reach their level of incompetence. This follows from the fact that an employee successful at one level in the organizational hierarchy is likely to be promoted to a higher level. Over a long period, this may happen many times, as people work their way up the organization. However, since each new position demands new skills and often greater ability, some employees eventually reach positions in which they are in over their heads. Because they are performing their present jobs poorly, they are rendered ineligible for further promotion, and are thereby doomed to a future of inefficiency. But they have enough power to protect their interests, so they will probably be able to avoid demotion or dismissal by hiding behind rules and regulations and taking credit for work actually performed by their subordinates.

Bureaucratic Ritualism

In the minds of many Americans, the term *bureaucracy* is virtually synonymous with the term *red tape*, a phrase referring to excessive concern with organizational procedures. Describing red tape as a type of group conformity that occurs within formal organizations, Robert Merton (1968) coined the term **bureaucratic ritualism** to refer to *preoccupation with rules and regulations as ends in*

Formal Organizations and Personal Privacy

A century ago, personal privacy in the United States was often a simple matter of building a fence around one's house and hanging a "Beware of the Dog" sign on the gate. But today, fences provide little protection for personal privacy. In fact, more people have access to more information about each one of us than ever before.

What has caused this change? The most important factor has been the growth of formal organizations. There is little doubt that formal organizations are an important part of our large and complex society. Almost everyone agrees that automobile drivers should be licensed, for example; but doing so requires gathering and maintaining information about everyone who legally operates a vehicle. Similarly, the income tax system, the Social Security system, and programs to provide benefits to veterans, loans to students, and payments to the poor and the unemployed all depend on government agencies having information about the American population.

Perhaps most important, the American economy operates largely on credit. In the past, local merchants routinely extended credit to customers with no more paperwork than perhaps an I.O.U. Today, however, a vast number of credit cards provide

Computers allow the collection and storage of extensive information about each of us.

credit to people who are often total strangers. As a result, credit files are filled with information about people's residence, marital status, employment, income, debts, and a variety of other facts.

Computers now allow this information to be disseminated more widely and more rapidly than ever before. Our addresses quickly become part of many different mailing lists used by businesses, and most Americans are now deluged by so-called junk mail. All kinds of information about people is shared among various organizations, often without the knowledge of the people in question. The results are not always directly

harmful, but the potential for personal damage is growing.

Although our society may depend on the collection and use of personal information by formal organizations for various purposes, some people have become alarmed at what appears to be a growing threat to personal privacy. The result is that many states have adopted laws recognizing the right of citizens to examine information about themselves contained in organizational records, such as files at their workplaces, banks, and credit bureaus. Similarly, the U.S. Privacy Act of 1974 limits the exchange of information among various government agencies to specific purposes. Just as important, citizens now have the legal right to request the information about themselves contained in most government files. After examining this information, an individual may respond with corrections that will become part of the record. Laws of this kind are effective steps in limiting organizational violations of personal privacy, but they are not likely to dramatically reduce the existing problem. Indeed, the benefits provided by formal organizations may require sacrificing a significant measure of personal privacy.

SOURCE: Based on Robert Ellis Smith, *Personal Privacy: How to Protect What's Left of It* (Garden City, NY: Anchor/Doubleday, 1979).

themselves rather than as the means to organizational goals. Bureaucratic ritualism occurs when the members of formal organizations become so intent on conforming to rules that they overlook the overall negative consequences of doing so. In addition to creating red tape that reduces performance, ritualism stifles the creativity

and imagination of an organization's members, inhibiting changes that might allow the organization to operate more efficiently in new circumstances (Whyte, 1957; Merton 1968). Bureaucratic ritualism also contributes to the alienation from self and others that Max Weber feared as a negative consequence of bureaucratic rigidity.

Bureaucratic Inertia

Weber noted that "once fully established, bureaucracy is among the social structures which are hardest to destroy" (1978:987; orig. 1921). **Bureaucratic inertia** is *the tendency of bureaucratic organizations to persist over time*. Formal organizations tend to take on a life of their own and to perpetuate themselves. Occasionally, a formal organization that has met its organizational goals will simply disband—as, for example, the anti-British Sons of Liberty did after the American Revolution. But a more common pattern is for an organization to redefine its goals in order to survive and continue to provide a livelihood for its members. The National Association for Infantile Paralysis, which sponsors the well-known March of Dimes, was created to aid in the fight against polio. After the discovery of the Salk vaccine in the early 1950s, however, this organization did not disband but simply redirected its efforts toward other medical problems (Sills, 1969). It continues to exist today.

This illustrates a common pattern: formal organizations that no longer have meaningful goals remain in operation anyway. "Sunset laws," widely enacted in the United States, require government agencies that cannot justify their existence to be dissolved. In Illinois, for example, officials who reviewed the qualifications of people who shoe horses were finally relieved of their duties well into the automobile age. In general, however, bureaucratic inertia often means that formal organizations will devise a justification for persisting long after they have outlived their usefulness.

Oligarchy

Early in this century, Robert Michels (1876–1936) pointed out the tendency of bureaucracy to spawn **oligarchy,** or *the rule of the many by the few* (1949; orig. 1911). As noted in Chapter 4, the earliest human societies did not possess the organizational means to allow a few people to rule the many. But as societies became more complex and developed formal organizations, domination by a small elite became common. According to what Michels called "the iron law of oligarchy," formal organization inevitably generates oligarchy since such organizations are structured in a hierarchical pyramid topped by only a few powerful leaders.

In Weber's terms, bureaucracy's strict hierarchy of responsibility encourages efficiency. But Michels re-

sponds that it also discourages democracy. It is true that organizational officials are expected to subordinate their personal interest to the pursuit of organizational goals according to established rules and regulations. In actual formal organizations, however, people who occupy powerful positions usually become powerful themselves. Michels emphasized that ambitious officials can use their access to information, opportunity to influence others, and numerous other advantages to promote their personal interests. Since abuse of organizational power may not be readily evident to the public at large, Michels feared that the expansion of formal organizations might undermine society's control over its elected leaders.

Sociologists still note the prevalence of oligarchy in formal organizations (Lipset, Trow, & Coleman, 1977). In the United States and Canada, competition among powerful segments of society as well as constitutional systems of checks and balances prevent at least the extremes of oligarchy found in less democratic societies. In 1974, for example, Richard Nixon was forced to resign as president of the United States. Two years later, Jimmy Carter, considered an outsider by the na-

The rise to power of Corazon Acquino in the Philippines shows that even well-entrenched rulers can be overthrown. But keep in mind that she is no "ordinary citizen," but is a member of a very wealthy and powerful family.

Rosabeth Moss Kanter (1943–   )

During the 1960s, Rosabeth Moss Kanter began her career in sociology studying communes and other utopian settlements. Now, in the 1980s, she is likely to be found in the company of many of America's most successful business executives. A profes-

sor of business administration at Harvard University, Kanter's achievements have earned nine honorary doctorate degrees, been the subject of feature articles in *Ms.* and other national publications, and ranked her among the most influential American women.

Kanter divides her career between academic duties and Goodmeasure, Inc., a consulting firm founded with her husband that now employs some forty people. She is the author of several widely read books on formal organizations that have successfully applied sociological ideas to the task of making corporations more profitable. What sociological lessons can Kanter offer to corporate executives that warrant fees of $15,000 for a single appearance? In essence, Kanter challenges conventional organizational wisdom by demonstrating that *people*—not technology or machinery—are a corporation's most important resource. In the long run, she maintains, organizational environments

that develop human potential are the foundation of successful corporations. Reflecting on her career as a sociologist, Kanter explains:

I remember when participation was what was being talked about on college campuses by Vietnam war protesters or people looking for student power. Now it's a respectable concept in corporate America, and now very large companies are figuring out how to divide themselves into small units. Many ideas and values of the '60s have been translated into the workplace. Take, for example, the right of workers to free expression, the desirability of participation and teamwork, the idea that authority should not be obeyed unquestioningly, the idea that smaller can be better because it can create ownership and family feeling. All of these are mainstream ideas.

SOURCE: Quotation from Megan Baldridge Murray, "Innovation Without Geniuses," *Yale Alumni Magazine and Journal*, Vol. XLVII, No. 6 (April 1984): 40–43; other sources include Susan McHenry, "Rosabeth Moss Kanter," *Ms.*, Vol. 13 (January 1985):62–63, 107–108.

tional political establishment, gained enough grass-roots support among the American people to carry him to the White House. So when leadership becomes unresponsive to the needs of the majority, opposition movements may arise. Sometimes these are successful—as in the overthrow of the Iranian shah, the Marcos regime in the Philippines, and the Somoza oligarchy in El Salvador. Sometimes they are not; witness the failure to date of popular opposition in Poland and South Africa.

Rosabeth Moss Kanter, introduced in the box, has pointed to other social patterns related to hierarchy in formal organizations. She notes that rank in a bureaucratic hierarchy is typically related to ascribed statuses such as sex, race, and ethnicity. People who conform to the bureaucracy's dominant social composition are

likely to form an ingroup and enjoy greater social acceptance, respect, credibility, and access to informal social networks that help to advance their careers. In the United States and Canada, of course, these people are likely to be well-to-do white males. Categories of people present in only small proportions in a formal organization tend to feel like part of a socially isolated outgroup. They are often uncomfortably visible, but are taken less seriously, and have lower chances of promotion than others. In North American society, this is the common experience of females, nonwhites, and those from economically disadvantaged backgrounds. Such people often feel that they must do twice as good a job in order to stay where they are, let alone advance to a higher position (Kanter, 1977; Kanter & Stein, 1979:137).

Opportunity and Power: Effects on Employees

Kanter also found that concentrating power and opportunity in the hands of some members of formal organizations has important consequences for everyone's on-the-job performance. People typically explain organizational performance in terms of personal qualities: those who get ahead are smart and "hustle," those who do not are less able and less motivated. But Kanter's (1977) research in a large American corporation indicated that *organizational environment* has much to do with how an employee performs. The social composition of a formal organization is one dimension of organizational environment that, as we have already seen, affects an employee's performance. In this case, being one of the dominant category of employees increases a person's respect and access to valuable social networks.

Opportunity to advance is another important dimension of an organizational environment. Kanter found that having high opportunity to advance typically turns employees into "fast-trackers" with high aspirations, positive self-esteem, and strong commitment to the organization. On the other hand, "dead-end" jobs produce only "zombies" by limiting the aspirations of employees, so that they think poorly of themselves and have little loyalty to the company.

In a similar way, Kanter determined that positions with lots of power are those in which people are likely to build high morale, to be helpful and supportive toward subordinates, and to take a generally less rigid approach to leadership. In contrast, in low-power situations, workers tend to depress morale, to jealously guard what privileges they do have, and to rigidly supervise subordinates. Table 7–3 provides a summary of Kanter's research findings.

People may praise or blame themselves for what happens on the job, but Kanter's research shows that three dimensions of organizational environment—social composition, power, and opportunity—have powerful effects on the attitude and performance of employees.

"Humanizing" Bureaucracy

The discussion above points to an important lesson: rigid adherence to bureaucratic structure can diminish the performance and morale of employees. Research by Kanter (1977, 1980, 1983) and others (cf. Peters & Waterman, Jr., 1982) shows that a growing number of Americans support the goal of **"humanizing" bureaucracy,** meaning *efforts to develop human potential in the belief that this is the primary resource of any formal organization.*

The characteristics of a more humane organizational environment follow directly from the discussion so far. First, the social composition of the organization should, ideally, make no one feel "out of place" because of such factors as sex, race, or ethnicity. This is not possible, of course, as long as some categories of people are represented within various segments of corporations in merely token numbers. In the long run, the perfor-

Table 7–3 KANTER'S RESEARCH: A SUMMARY

	Advantaged Employees	Disadvantaged Employees
Social Composition	Being represented in high proportions helps employees to more easily fit in, and to enjoy greater credibility; they experience less stress, and are usually candidates for promotion	Being represented in low proportions puts employees visibly "on display," and results in their not being taken seriously; they tend to fear making mistakes and losing ground rather than optimistically looking toward advancement
Power	In powerful positions, employees contribute to high morale and support subordinates; such employees tend to be more democratic leaders	In low-power positions, employees tend to foster low morale and restrict opportunities for subordinates to advance; they tend to be more authoritarian leaders
Opportunity	High opportunity encourages optimism and high aspirations, loyalty to organization, use of higher-ups as reference groups, and constructive response to problems	Low opportunity encourages pessimism and low aspirations, weak attachment to the job, use of peers as reference groups, and ineffective griping in response to problems

SOURCE: Based on Rosabeth Moss Kanter, *Men and Women of the Corporation* (New York: Basic Books, 1977), pp. 246–249.

mance of all employees can be expected to increase to the extent that no one is subject to social exclusion.

Second, "humanizing" bureaucracy means breaking down oligarchy by spreading power more widely. Managers cannot benefit from the ideas of employees who have no channels for expressing their opinions. Similarly, knowing that superiors are open to suggestions encourages all employees to think creatively, increasing organizational effectiveness.

Third, expanding opportunity is also basic to "humanizing" bureaucracy. Employees stuck in routine, dead-end jobs are rarely motivated to perform well. To combat this, resources should be made available to all employees for the purposes of trying out new ideas, and no position should be ruled out as the start of an upward career path.

The advantage of "humanizing" bureaucracy is as simple as it is compelling: the organization operates more effectively. Comparing forty-seven companies with rigid bureaucratic structures to competitors of similar size but with more flexible organizations, Kanter (1983) found that the latter were more profitable. She argues, therefore, that bureaucratic structure is limiting to the extent that it treats employees as something to be controlled rather than as a resource to be developed. Perhaps rigid organization made more sense in the past when the typical employee was uneducated and was little more than a source of physical labor. But today, the labor force is much more educated and better ideas are often the key to higher profits. Thus, while the basic bureaucratic model is still a general guide to efficiency and equity, evidence suggests that organizational effectiveness is enhanced by flexible management styles, coupled with efforts to spread power and opportunity more broadly throughout the organization (Kanter 1985).

Formal Organizations in Japan

In the process of recognizing the limitations of bureaucracy, attention has been drawn to different organizational models found in other societies. The interest of Americans in Japanese organizations has grown in recent decades, which is not surprising in light of the fact that this small society has had remarkable economic success in the world marketplace. Since the end of World War II, economic growth in Japan has been five times more rapid than in the United States. Moreover, although only the size of Montana, Japan's gross national product in 1985 was about one-third as large as that of the entire United States.

Formal organizations in Japan reflect that culture's emphasis on collective identity and social solidarity. While Americans have long prized rugged individualism, Japanese society is based on traditional values that unite individuals into a society that is socially unequal, yet strongly cohesive. William Ouchi explains that the collective identity of the Japanese reduces the incidence of a number of social problems common to more rootless, individualistic societies such as the United States; for example, alcoholism, drug abuse, and suicide are all relatively uncommon in Japan. Moreover, a person feels safe walking through downtown Tokyo late at night— certainly an ill-advised activity in New York, Chicago, or Los Angeles (1981:8).

This social solidarity gives formal organizations in Japan a remarkably personal quality. In the United States, even formal organizations that have "humanized" bureaucracy are built upon secondary relationships. Japanese organizations, in contrast, are based upon more primary relationships. With some exaggeration, we may describe formal organizations in Japan as extremely large primary groups.

Ouchi (1981) highlights five major distinctions between formal organizations in Japan and their counterparts in industrial societies in the West. In each case, the Japanese organization reflects that society's more collective orientation.

1. *Hiring and advancement*. In American formal organizations promotions and higher salaries are prizes won through individual competition. In Japanese formal organizations, new graduates from schools are hired together as a group and receive much the same salaries and responsibilities. As one moves ahead, so do they all. Only after many years is any individual likely to be singled out for special advancement. Because employees of the same age have much the same experience within the organization, they develop a strong sense of common identity. Just as important, Japanese employees are typically distressed at the thought of advancing at another's expense. American business leaders who establish companies in Japan only to overlook the collective orientation of Japanese workers do so at their peril, as the box on p. 197 illustrates.

2. *Lifetime security*. In the United States, only rarely do employees remain with one company for their entire working careers. In part, this is because individualistically-thinking Americans commonly move from one

3. *Holistic involvement.* In the United States, a person's working life and private life are generally separated. Japanese organizations, in contrast, are involved in all aspects of their employees' lives. Companies often provide dormitory housing or mortgages for the purchase of homes, sponsor recreational activities, and schedule a wide range of social events in which all workers participate. Employee interaction outside the workplace strengthens collective identity and also provides a chance for the Japanese worker—characteristically very respectful toward superiors on the job—to more readily voice suggestions and criticisms.

4. *Nonspecialized training.* Bureaucratic organization in the United States is based on specialized activity, so that a person's entire career often has a single focus. From the outset, a Japanese organization trains its employees in all phases of its particular operation. This is done, of course, with the expectation that employees will remain with the organization for life. Ideally, this nonspecialized training allows a worker to understand how any one job is related to all dimensions of the organization's operation. One result is that Japanese workers probably have more technical knowledge than their American counterparts (Sengoku, 1985). In addition, broad training allows the company to move employees from job to job more easily as circumstances dictate.

5. *Collective decision making.* Decision making in American organizations is typically the responsibility of a handful of executives. This fact was clearly illustrated by President Harry Truman, whose desk at the White House displayed a sign stating, "The buck stops here." The leaders of Japanese organizations also have final responsibility for their company's performance. But they encourage all workers to offer input about any issue that affects them. Similarly, Japanese companies typically contain many semiautonomous working groups within the organization. In short, rather than simply responding to the directives of superiors, all employees in Japan share managerial responsibilities.

Because of these organizational characteristics, formal organizations in Japan generate a strong sense of loyalty in all employees. In contrast to the American cultural emphasis on individual achievement, Japanese culture emphasizes the importance of working well with others. A strong sense of collective identity is therefore fostered through broader personal involvement with the organization than is typically found in the United States. Workers do not separate their personal interest from those of the organization; instead, they realize personal goals

Japanese workers are deeply involved in the operation of their companies, just as companies become involved in the lives of their workers. Group calisthenics not only improve physical and mental performance but also foster group solidarity.

company to another as a means of fulfilling personal ambitions. In addition, American companies are quick to lay off employees in the event of economic setbacks. The Japanese case, however, is quite another matter: employees are typically hired for life. This means that companies and their employees have strong, mutual loyalties. Japanese workers who have spent several years with one organization and learned its particular policies are not very attractive to other firms, even if they were to seek a new employer. Moreover, Japanese companies are able to avoid layoffs by providing other jobs in the organization, along with any necessary retraining.

The Collective Spirit of Japanese Organizations

American companies doing business in Japan must be sensitive to the differences between American and Japanese cultural values. William Ouchi illustrates this fact by recalling a visit to a new factory in Japan that was owned and operated by Americans. In this electronics company, management sought to increase worker productivity through a piecework system that linked an individual's wages to the number of electronic products she assembled. While consistent with individualistic American culture, this practice sharply opposes the collective spirit of Japanese workers.

About two months after the factory opened, the plant forewomen approached the manager on behalf of all the women working on the assembly line. "Honorable plant manager," they said with a bow, "we are embarrassed to be so forward, but we must speak with you." They reported that the entire work force was talking about quitting because of the piecework system of wages. What Americans would endorse as an effective system of individual incentives appeared to be distasteful competition to the Japanese. Why, the women asked, couldn't a more traditionally Japanese system of payment be adopted? They explained that, consistent with Japanese practice, a new worker should have her wages fixed by her age, so that an eighteen-year-old worker would be paid more than a sixteen-year-old worker. Every year on her birthday, her wages would be raised. "The idea that any one of us can be more productive than another must be wrong," the women continued, "because none of us in final assembly could make a thing unless all of the other people in the plant had done their jobs right first. To single one person out as being more productive is wrong and is also personally humiliating to us."

The company responded appropriately by changing the wage system to conform with Japanese practice.

SOURCE: Adapted from William Ouchi, *Theory Z: How American Business Can Meet the Japanese Challenge* (Reading, MA: Addison-Wesley, 1981), p. 48.

through the organization. Furthermore, the security generated by this organizational approach ensures that workers willingly share ideas with others, offer innovative suggestions, and embrace new technological developments without fear of making themselves obsolete.

Formal Organizations and Society

Formal organizations in Japan differ from Max Weber's conception of bureaucracy. As William Ouchi (1981:62–64) explains, Weber developed his analysis of bureaucracy in nineteenth-century Europe, where most businesses were still small family undertakings. He believed that primary social relationships—often in the form of nepotism and personal favoritism—were a source of organizational inefficiency. His model of bureaucracy, now well entrenched in European and North American societies, was therefore based on impersonal, secondary relationships that emphasize technical specialization, impartiality, and behavior strictly guided by rules and regulations.

In Japan, formal organizations also developed within the context of a socially cohesive society. However, the Japanese differ from Westerners in that they perceive personal social ties as an organizational asset that can be used to increase efficiency. Thus, like all of Japanese society, Japanese formal organizations have many of the characteristics of primary social groups. In Japan at least, this approach resulted in efficiency: the Japanese record of economic growth is unparalleled.

The rapid economic advancement of the Japanese has been startling enough to make Americans take seriously their way of doing things, which has contributed to efforts to "humanize" bureaucracy in the United States. But there are other reasons to carefully study the Japanese approach to formal organizations. The United States and Canada today are less socially cohesive than the more family-based society Weber knew. Thus a rigidly bureaucratic form of organization only encourages further atomization of society. Perhaps by following the lead of the Japanese, formal organizations in North America could encourage—rather than diminish—a sense of collective identity and responsibility. This might result not only in greater organizational productivity, but also in greater integration of society.

SUMMARY

1. Social groups are an important building block of all societies. Members of social groups share a common identity and frequently interact with one another.

2. A basic sociological distinction involves primary groups and secondary groups. In essence, primary groups tend to be small and person-oriented, while secondary groups are typically large and goal-oriented.

3. Leadership is an important dimension of group dynamics. Instrumental leadership is concerned with a group's goals; expressive leadership focuses on the well-being and social ties of a group's members.

4. Group conformity is a process well documented by researchers. Because they so often seek consensus, groups do not necessarily generate a wider range of ideas about an issue than individuals working alone do.

5. Reference groups are commonly used by individuals when making decisions and evaluations. Both ingroups and outgroups are commonly used in this way.

6. Georg Simmel argued that dyads—two-person groups—have a distinctive intensity, but are unstable because of the effort necessary to maintain them. Triads, or three-person groups, can easily dissolve into a dyad by excluding one member.

7. Social networks are grouplike structures in which people have little common identity and infrequent interaction.

8. Formal organizations are large, secondary groups that seek to perform complex tasks efficiently. Depending on people's reasons for participating, formal organizations can be classified as normative, coercive, or utilitarian.

9. Bureaucracy is an organizational model that has been widely adopted in the United States. In principle, bureaucratic organization allows for the efficient completion of highly complex tasks.

10. Bureaucracy is based on specialization, hierarchy, rules and regulations, technical competence, impersonal interaction, and formal, written communications.

11. In practice, bureaucratic organization has weaknesses and drawbacks, including being unable to deal efficiently with special cases, depersonalizing the workplace, and fostering ritualism among some employees. Furthermore, Max Weber recognized that bureaucratic organization is typically resistant to change.

12. Excessive formality is linked to the emergence of informal social patterns in bureaucratic settings. In some cases, such informality helps the organization achieve its goals; in other cases, workers informally violate organizational objectives.

13. Formal organizations are often oligarchies. Rosabeth Moss Kanter's research has shown that the concentration of power and opportunity within American corporations tends to diminish organizational effectiveness and limit profits.

14. Efforts to "humanize" bureaucracy are based on the assertion that people are an organization's greatest resource. Developing human resources depends on reducing the significance of ascribed statuses such as sex and race, spreading decision-making power more widely, and broadening opportunity.

15. Formal organizations in Japan differ from the Western, bureaucratic model because of the collective spirit of Japanese culture. In numerous respects, formal organizations in Japan are based on more personal ties than are their counterparts in the United States.

KEY CONCEPTS

bureaucracy an organizational model rationally designed to perform complex tasks efficiently

bureaucratic inertia the tendency of bureaucratic organizations to persist over time

bureaucratic ritualism preoccupation with organizational rules and regulations as ends in themselves rather than as the means to organizational goals

dyad a social group with two members

expressive leadership leadership that emphasizes the collective well-being of the members of a social group

formal organization a large, secondary group that is formally organized to facilitate achieving its goals

"humanizing" bureaucracy efforts to develop human potential in the belief that this is the primary resource of any formal organization

ingroup a social group with which individuals identify and toward which they feel a sense of loyalty

instrumental leadership leadership that emphasizes the completion of tasks by a social group

oligarchy the rule of the many by the few

outgroup a social group with which individuals do not identify and toward which they feel a sense of competition or opposition

primary group a typically small social group in which relationships are both personal and enduring

reference group a social group that serves as a point of reference for individuals in evaluation and decision making

secondary group a typically large and impersonal social group based on some special interest or activity

social group two or more people who have a high degree of common identity and who interact on a regular basis

social network a web of social ties that links people, but with less common identity and less social interaction than are typical of a social group

triad a social group with three members

SUGGESTED READINGS

The following texts provide a more detailed examination of many of the issues considered in this chapter:

Rhoda Lois Blumberg. *Organizations in Contemporary Society*. Englewood Cliffs, NJ: Prentice-Hall, 1987.

Cecilia L. Ridgeway. *The Dynamics of Small Groups*. New York: St. Martin's Press, 1983.

Controversy has followed the obedience experiments of Stanley Milgram for over thirty years. This book reviews Milgram's work and other studies of this kind, and tackles the broad ethical questions that such research raises.

Arthur G. Miller. *The Obedience Experiments: A Case Study of Controversy in Social Science*. New York: Praeger, 1986.

Throughout the world, women have played a large part in various informal associations. The following two books explore the interplay of women's associations and more established centers of power in developing societies.

Patricia Caplan. *Class and Gender in India: Women and Their Organizations in a South Indian City*. New York: Tavistock, 1985.

Kathryn S. March and Rachelle L. Taqqu. *Women's Informal Associations in Developing Countries: Catalysts for Change?* Boulder, CO: Westview Press, 1986.

A historical analysis of women as volunteers in many American formal organizations is found in:

Wendy Kaminer. *Women Volunteering: The Pleasure, Pain, and Politics of Unpaid Work from 1830 to the Present*. Garden City, NY: Anchor/Doubleday, 1984.

These two books represent the growing application of sociological analysis to problems of business management. The first, by one of the best-known sociologists in the area of formal organizations, explains why some corporations outperform their competitors. The second, by a noted futurist, argues that simply "doing more of the same" in a changing society is a sure path to decline for businesses.

Rosabeth Moss Kanter. *The Change Masters: Innovation for Productivity in the American Corporation*. New York: Simon and Schuster, 1983.

Alvin Toffler. *The Adaptive Corporation*. New York: McGraw-Hill, 1985.

Here is a collection of twenty-two essays about various dimensions of organizational culture:

Peter J. Frost, Larry F. Moore, Meryl Reis Louis, Craig C. Lundberg, and Joanne Martin. *Organizational Culture*. Beverly Hills, CA: Sage Publications, 1985.

This recent book contains thirteen essays that share a concern with how power is distributed and utilized within various kinds of organizations.

G. William Domhoff and Thomas R. Dye, ed. *Power Elites and Organizations*. Newbury Park, CA: Sage Publications, 1987.

This fascinating book contrasts formal organizations in the United States with those in Japan.

William Ouchi. *Theory Z: How American Business Can Meet the Japanese Challenge*. Reading, MA: Addison-Wesley, 1981.

CHAPTER 8

Deviance

Filling the grass-covered yard in front of the jail were people of the Massachusetts Bay Colony, seventeenth-century Puritans who had come to the New World with the stern hope of establishing a Kingdom of God on earth. On this summer morning, however, their minds were filled with thoughts of the devil. They awaited the appearance from inside the jail of one of their number, Hester Prynne, who had been convicted of adultery. Several of the women mused about what punishment would fit her crime. "At the very least," suggested one, "they should have put the brand of a hot iron on Hester Prynne's forehead." Even more harshly, said another, "This woman has brought shame upon us all and ought to die."

At that moment Hester Prynne emerged from the jail, clutching a small infant in her arms, and walked deliberately along Prison Lane to a platform in the nearby marketplace. Here, for a time determined by her judges, she was to endure the stares and scorn of the community. In addition, sewn to her dress "in fine red cloth, surrounded by an elaborate embroidery," was the scarlet letter A to mark her as an adulteress.

Using the sociological perspective, this scene from Nathaniel Hawthorne's *The Scarlet Letter* represents a small society responding to the existence of deviance within its ranks. As this chapter explains, however, deviance and punishment are far more complex than they may initially seem. Why, for example, does deviance arise in the first place? Are all people who violate norms defined as deviant? Who decides what rules will be used to define deviance and when they should be applied or overlooked? Why do some instances of deviance result in criminal prosecution and punishment—perhaps even the penalty of death—while other cases of deviance are viewed as trivial and go unpunished?

WHAT IS DEVIANCE?

Deviance is defined as *the recognized violation of cultural norms*. The norms of a group or an entire society shape a wide range of human activities, so the concept of deviance is correspondingly broad. One obvious and familiar type of deviance is **crime**: *the violation of norms that have been formally enacted into criminal law*. Criminal deviance is itself quite variable, ranging from minor traffic violations to serious offenses such as homicide and rape. Closely related to crime is **juvenile delinquency**: *the violation of legal standards by children or adolescents*.

Beyond crime, however, deviance includes many other types of nonconformity, from the mild to the extreme, such as left-handedness, boastfulness, and Mohawk hairstyles, as well as pacifism, homosexuality, and mental illness. Industrial societies typically contain a wide range of subcultural values and norms. Consequently, to those who conform to society's dominant cultural standards, artists, homeless people, and members of various ethnic minorities may seem deviant. In addition, the poor—whose lack of financial resources makes conforming to many conventional middle-class patterns of life difficult—are also subject to definition as deviant. Physical traits, too, may be the basis of deviance, as members of racial minorities in America know well. Men with many highly visible tattoos on their body may be seen as deviant, as are women with any tattoo at all. Even being unusually tall or short, or grossly fat or exceedingly thin, may be the basis of deviance. Physical disabilities are yet another reason for being seen by others as deviant.

Most of the examples of deviance that come readily to mind are negative—that is, people differ in some way that others evaluate negatively. Those who are set apart by closely conforming to cultural ideals, however, are also seen as deviant. Almost all of us are well aware that we commonly fall short of ideal cultural standards. In doing so, of course, we have a lot of company, making us "typical" in our shortcomings. In this context, then, an especially wholesome person may be viewed as a "goody-goody," which is at least partly deviant. In other words, such a person is simultaneously praised for embracing cultural norms and criticized for doing so to the point of being different from others (Huls, 1987).

Deviance, then, is based on any kind of difference significant enough to provoke some people to react to another as a deviant "outsider" (Becker, 1966). In addition to social isolation, deviant people are subject to social control, by which others attempt to bring them back into line. Like deviance itself, social control takes many forms. Socialization, discussed in Chapter 5, is a complex process of social control in which family, peer groups, and the mass media influence our attitudes and behavior. A more formal type of social control is the **criminal justice system**: *the formal process by which society reacts to alleged violations of the law through the use of police, courts, and punishment.* Social control is not always a negative response to deviance; it can also be a positive response to conformity. Praise from parents, high grades in school, laudatory mention in newspapers and other mass media, and positive recognition from officials in the local community are all forms of social control that encourage conformity to conventional patterns of thought and behavior.

Deviance Is a Product of Society

We tend to view deviance simply as a result of an individual's free choice or personal failings. But, as earlier chapters have emphasized, all social behavior—deviance as well as conformity—is rooted in society. This is evident in three ways.

1. *Deviance exists only in relation to cultural norms.* No thought or action is inherently deviant. Rather, it becomes so only in relation to particular norms. As noted in Chapter 3, norms vary considerably from one society to another, and most societies contain many subcultures, so that conceptions of deviance differ as well. In the traditional village communities of Sicily, for example, norms support the use of physical violence to avenge

Hairstyles, clothing, and political opinions are all dimensions of difference that set some people apart from others as deviants.

an insult to the honor of one's family (Wolfgang & Ferracuti, 1982). In this case, *not* to avenge an insult would be defined as deviant. Within most of American society, however, cultural norms do not support the use of violence in this way. Therefore, what is honorable in Sicily is likely to result in arrest and prosecution in the United States.

As cultural norms change over time, so do conceptions of deviance. In the 1920s, American cultural norms linked women's lives to the home, so that a woman who wanted to become a corporate executive, for instance, would certainly have been considered deviant. Today, however, there is widespread support for women pursuing a career outside the home (N.O.R.C., 1987). Consequently, such women are no longer defined as deviant.

2. *People become deviant as others define them that way.* We all violate cultural norms, and even the law, from time to time. For example, most of us have at some point walked around talking to ourselves, taken something that belonged to someone else, or driven another person's automobile without permission. Simply doing any of these things, however, is not sufficient to be defined as mentally ill or criminal. Whether or not a person is defined as deviant depends on the perception and definition of the situation by others—a process that is quite variable. To a large extent, in other words, being defined as deviant depends on some questionable activity being noticed by others. Even then, however, the activity may be perceived in different ways. For example, a male celebrity such as Boy George can dress like a female onstage to the praise of adoring fans, while elsewhere another man doing the same thing might well provoke a quite negative response. In short, whether or not a person is defined as deviant depends on the variable process of social definition.

3. *Both norms and the way events are defined are related to patterns of social power.* Following the ideas of Karl Marx (introduced in Chapter 4), cultural norms—especially laws—are likely to protect the interests of powerful people. For example, closing a factory that is no longer profitable is within the legal rights of a factory owner, even though doing so puts thousands of people out of work. At the same time, a less powerful person who commits vandalism that closes a factory for a single day is likely to be defined as criminal. Powerless people also may be defined as deviant for exactly the same behavior that powerful people engage in with impunity. For example, a homeless person who stands on a street corner

On May 4, 1970, National Guard troops opened fire on students who had gathered for an antiwar demonstration at Kent State University in Ohio. Four students died and nine were wounded. Widespread opinion held that this action was legitimate—if regrettable—in light of the wave of campus protests taking place at that time. None of the troops was subject to criminal prosecution for the shootings.

and denounces the city government risks arrest for disturbing the peace. On the other hand, a candidate opposing the mayor during an election campaign can do the same thing while receiving extensive police protection. In short, both cultural norms and their application are related to patterns of social inequality.

Overall, then, while commonly understood as a quality of individuals, deviance is inseparable from the operation of society.

BIOLOGICAL EXPLANATIONS OF DEVIANCE

As explained in Chapter 5, human behavior was understood—or more correctly, misunderstood—during the nineteenth century as an expression of biological instincts. Not surprisingly, then, early interest in criminality emphasized biological causes.

Early Research

In 1876, Caesare Lombroso (1835–1909), an Italian physician who worked in prisons, developed a biological theory of criminality. Lombroso described criminals as physically distinctive—with low foreheads, prominent jaws and cheekbones, protruding ears, hairiness, and unusually long arms that made them resemble human beings' apelike ancestors. In other words, he viewed criminals as evolutionary throwbacks to lower forms of life. Because of their biologically based inadequacy, Lombroso reasoned, such individuals would think and act in a primitive manner likely to run afoul of society's laws. Toward the end of his career, Lombroso acknowledged that social factors play a part in criminality. But his early claim that some people are literally born criminals was extremely popular at a time when few powerful people were inclined to face up to flaws in social arrangements (Jones, 1986).

Lombroso's findings were based on seriously flawed research methods. He failed to see that the physical characteristics he found in prison and linked to criminality also existed in the population as a whole. Early in the twentieth century, the British psychiatrist Charles Buckman Goring (1870–1919), who also worked in prisons, compared thousands of convicts and noncriminals. There was a great deal of physical variation within both groups, but Goring's research (1972; orig. 1913) revealed no significant physical differences between criminals and noncriminals of the kind suggested by Lombroso.

Delinquency and Body Structure

Although Lombroso's theory had been disproved, others continued to search for biological explanations of criminality. William Sheldon (1949) advanced the idea that body structure was significant. He described body structure in terms of three general types: *ectomorphs*, who were tall, thin, and fragile; *endomorphs*, who were short and fat; and *mesomorphs*, who were muscular and athletic. Sheldon recognized that most people are a combination of these body types, but he noted that one type often predominates. After comparing hundreds of young men—half of whom were known to have engaged in criminal activity and half of whom were believed to be noncriminal—Sheldon reported an association between criminality and the mesomorphic body type. In other words, criminality was linked to muscular, athletic body structure.

Sheldon's general conclusion was supported by subsequent research conducted by Sheldon and Eleanor Glueck (1950). The Gluecks, however, did not claim that a mesomorphic body structure is a *direct* cause of criminality. Rather, they linked this body type to personal characteristics—such as insensitivity toward others and a tendency to react aggressively to frustration—that seem likely to promote criminality. The Gluecks also noted the importance of social environment in explaining criminality; they found that young men with mesomorphic builds were typically raised with little affection and understanding from family members.

Although these findings indicate that there may be an association between body type and criminality, they do not establish any causal connection between the two. Indeed, the association may very well have a social explanation. Young men with muscular builds have the ability to be the "bullies on the block," which some of them may become (Gibbons, 1981). Moreover, expecting muscular and athletic boys to be more physically aggressive than others, people may treat them accordingly and thereby provoke the very behavior they expect.

Recent Research

Since the 1960s, increasing knowledge in the field of genetics has rekindled interest in biological causes of criminality. Research has explored the possible connection between criminal behavior and a specific pattern of chromosomes, the structures that carry the genes (see Vold & Bernard, 1986:92–99). In human development, sex is determined by chromosomes: females have two X chromosomes, while males have one X and one Y chromosome. But in perhaps one case in every thousand, a genetic mutation causes a male to have an extra Y chromosome, resulting in an XYY sex chromosome. Research has shown that males with this XYY pattern are somewhat more likely to be found in prisons and mental institutions. Initially, this was thought to be because such males were prone to violent criminal behavior (Jacobs, Brunton, & Melville, 1965), but subsequent research has refuted this conclusion, indicating only that men with the XYY pattern are significantly taller than average. Perhaps, as noted earlier, men of unusually large size are simply more likely to be seen by others as threatening (Hook, 1973). In any case, most XYY males do *not* appear to be aggressive or prone to criminal behavior.

Rather than linking deviance to a specific genetic abnormality (such as the XYY chromosome), recent research has examined the hypothesis that overall genetic composition—in combination with social influences—may explain variations in criminality within a population (Jencks, 1987). In one study, patterns of delinquency were analyzed for 265 pairs of twins using a research design that allowed variations in criminality to be attributed, on the one hand, to the social environment and, on the other hand, to the genetic structure of the individuals (Rowe, 1983; Rowe & Osgood, 1984). The researchers concluded that genetic factors combined with differences in the social environment (such as membership in a peer group that engages in criminal activity) explain a significant amount of juvenile criminality. In a recent review of research on this topic, James Q. Wilson and Richard Herrnstein (1985) conclude that biological factors have a small but real effect on whether or not individuals engage in crime. Here again, however, the social environment is viewed as crucial for encouraging or restraining any tendencies toward criminality.

Evaluation. Biological theories have attempted to explain crime in terms of characteristics of individuals themselves. The pioneering research of Lombroso suffered from flaws of scientific logic—a problem that has diminished in subsequent biological research. Nonetheless, biological research has produced a very limited understanding of the causes of crime.

The limitations follow from several characteristic weaknesses of this kind of research. First, while some studies have found biological traits to be associated with criminality, the causal connections are poorly explained. Second, because biological research has generally focused on rare cases of individual abnormality, only a small amount of crime could ever be accounted for in this way since most people who engage in criminal activity are biologically normal. Moreover, crime represents only a small portion of what is defined as deviant behavior in American society. Third, the biological approach is highly individualistic, ignoring the variable social processes that create norms and define people as deviant.

Most recent research in genetics has still not been clearly evaluated. Yet it is important to note that this work tends to place far greater emphasis on social influences on human behavior (Gibbons & Krohn, 1986; Liska, 1987).

PSYCHOLOGICAL EXPLANATIONS OF DEVIANCE

Psychological approaches to deviance generally focus on abnormalities in the individual personality. Although some abnormalities are known to be linked to heredity, psychologists view most personality disorders as a result of socialization. Since personality is shaped by social experience throughout the life cycle, deviance is understood as the result of unsuccessful socialization to cultural expectations more than the result of biological forces present at birth.

Containment Theory

Walter Reckless and Simon Dinitz (1967) used a psychological approach to explore the hypothesis that personality traits are linked to juvenile delinquency among boys. These researchers claim that various social pressures to engage in delinquent activity are widespread, but can be contained by boys who have strong moral values and a positive self-image. Reckless and Dinitz called their idea *containment theory*.

They asked teachers to identify boys of about age twelve who were likely to engage in delinquent acts and those who were not. Interviews with both the boys and their mothers provided information on each boy's self-concept—how he viewed himself and how he related to the world around him. The "good boys" seemed to have a strong conscience (or *superego* in Sigmund Freud's terminology), generally coped well with frustration, and identified positively with cultural norms and values. The "bad boys" had a weaker conscience, were less able to tolerate frustration, and did not strongly identify with cultural norms and values. About four years later, the researchers found that the "good boys" had indeed experienced fewer contacts with the police than had the "bad boys." Reckless and Dinitz concluded that this was due largely to the personality orientations of the two groups of boys that had been identified earlier. In other words, since all the boys studied were from areas in which delinquency was widespread, boys who managed to stay out of trouble were apparently those with a strong conscience and a positive self-concept, which served as "an internal buffer which protects people against [violation] of the social and legal norms" (Reckless, 1970:401).

Evaluation. Psychological research has demonstrated that personality patterns have a moderate relationship to delinquency and other types of deviance. Even so, a number of weaknesses are common to research of this kind.

First, like the biological approach, psychological theories of deviance are highly individualistic and tend to minimize the ways in which deviance is a product of society. Personality traits that are considered to be normal or abnormal vary from society to society, just as what is defined as deviant varies with cultural norms. Second, little explanation is offered for the fact that some people are defined as deviant, while others who display similar attitudes or behavior are not. Third, it is known that much crime and other types of deviance exist among those who are both powerful and highly respected, hardly the people typically defined as psychologically abnormal.

In sum, both biological and psychological approaches view deviance as an individual attribute without exploring how conceptions of right and wrong arise in the first place or investigating the deviant person's place within the larger society. The importance of a sociological analysis of deviance lies precisely in this type of investigation.

THEORETICAL ANALYSIS OF DEVIANCE

Sociological approaches to understanding deviance correspond to the major theoretical paradigms within the discipline. All three approaches view deviance in terms of the operation of society rather than in terms of traits of individuals.

Structural-Functional Analysis

The structural-functional paradigm examines how any element of society contributes to the operation of society as a whole. At first glance, deviance may seem to have no useful function; crime, for example, causes billions of dollars in property losses each year as well as death and personal injury to hundreds of thousands of people. Nonetheless, structural-functional theorists have argued that deviance makes important contributions to the continuing operation of society.

Pioneering work in exploring the functions of deviance for society was carried out by Emile Durkheim (1964a, orig. 1895; 1964b, orig. 1893). He asserted that there is nothing abnormal about deviance, since it is an integral part of all societies. More specifically, Durkheim stated that deviance has four major functions.

1. *Deviance affirms cultural values and norms.* There can be no conception of what is morally right, Durkheim maintained, without a corresponding conception of what is morally wrong. Therefore, just as no society can exist

without cultural values, so also is deviance indispensable. Even the Puritans, that small society of colonial New England in which every aspect of life was strictly guided by religious beliefs, inevitably faced deviance. In fact, Durkheim could well have had the Puritans in mind when he asked us to:

> Imagine a society of saints, a perfect cloister of exemplary individuals. Crimes, properly so called, will there be unknown; but faults which appear [insignificant] to the layman will create there the same scandal that the ordinary offense does in ordinary consciousness. . . . For the same reason, the perfect and upright man judges his smallest failings with a severity that the majority reserve for acts more truly in the nature of an offense. (1964a: 68–69)

Reacting with disapproval to homeless people serves to reaffirm the American values of achievement and personal success.

2. *Responding to deviance clarifies moral boundaries.* Durkheim argued that reacting to some people's beliefs and actions as deviant clarifies the boundaries of acceptable behavior for everyone in a society. The point at which someone's consumption of alcohol becomes a drinking problem, for example, is clarified by the response of others. Drawing on Durkheim's ideas, Kai Erikson explains:

> When a community calls [a person] to account for [deviance] it is making a statement about the nature and placement of its boundaries. It is declaring how much variability and diversity can be tolerated within the group before it begins to lose its distinctive shape, its unique identity. (1966:11)

3. *Responding to deviance promotes social unity.* People often react to a serious episode of deviance with a shared sense of moral outrage. In doing so, Durkheim pointed out, they remind themselves of the cultural norms that unite them. During the 1980s, for example, Americans have reacted to what they view as terrorist actions against the United States with a surge of patriotism.

4. *Deviance encourages social change.* Deviance suggests alternatives to existing values and norms. Although Durkheim believed that a society must develop in its members a clear understanding of moral behavior, he also recognized the need for change over time. In other words, Durkheim believed that the deviance of today might well become the norm of tomorrow (1964a:71). In the 1950s, for example, most Americans viewed rock and roll music as a corrupter of youth and an outrage against established tastes. Today, as the box on p. 208 explains, rock and roll is part of the cultural mainstream—as all-American as apple pie and one of our most profitable exports.

An illustration. Kai Erikson (1966) used records from the early Puritan settlement in Massachusetts Bay to test several of Durkheim's ideas about the functions of deviance. He discovered that there was indeed deviance in this highly religious "society of saints." Because of their rigid cultural norms, matters of religious disagreement that would hardly be defined as deviant today were considered by the Puritans to be seriously sinful. By responding to deviance within their ranks, the early Puritans affirmed their distinctive cultural values and norms.

Erikson also found that the kinds of deviance recognized by the early Puritans were related to the moral questions they faced. Early in its history, the colony had to decide whether individuals had the right to personally interpret the Bible. Ultimately, the Puritans defined those who claimed this right as deviant, and by doing so, they clarified this particular moral boundary. Through the punishment of deviant members, the early Puritans also experienced a sense of unity based on common moral values. Although initially defined as deviant, however, the idea that people should have personal freedom in their religious activities gradually became established in the United States.

Finally, in further support of Durkheim's assertion that deviance has important social functions, Erikson found that the proportion of the population of Massachusetts Bay Colony considered deviant remained stable over time, even though the actual number of offenses varied. Erikson concluded that by continually defining a small percentage of the population as deviant—although for different reasons as community morality changed—the Puritans were ensuring that the social functions of deviance would be consistently carried out.

Merton's Strain Theory

Sociologist Robert Merton (1938, 1968) claims that the operation of society actually encourages crime and other types of deviance, especially by people in certain situations. His theory begins with the observation that a cultural *goal* in American society is financial success. In addition, American culture endorses certain *means* to achieve this goal, including obtaining an extensive education and working hard at a job. But attempting to gain wealth through theft or other dishonest activities is a violation of cultural norms. Therefore, people should derive personal satisfaction not only from success, but also from playing by the rules. To the extent that society effectively socializes its members to seek cultural goals according to normative means, what Merton has termed *conformity* should result.

Because of the importance American culture places on wealth, however, even relatively successful people may seek more wealth by violating cultural norms and perhaps the law. Corporate executives, for example, may engage in dishonest business practices or embezzle company funds, and certainly many wealthy Americans misrepresent their income to the Internal Revenue Service.

Merton called this type of activity *innovation*—attempting to achieve culturally approved goals using unconventional means. In Table 8–1, innovation is described as accepting the goal of success while rejecting conventional means to that goal. Merton claims that innovation results from the "strain" experienced when

Rock and Roll: From Deviance to Big Business

Rock and roll emerged as a controversial type of American popular music in the early 1950s. First, it drew heavily on the rhythm and blues music of black America at a time when few record companies or radio stations would produce or promote black music. Second, rock and roll was at the center of the emerging youth subculture in the United States. During the 1950s, it signified rebellion against parental authority. In the 1960s, protest and drug-based psychedelic music expressed a more general criticism of American society. Third, rock and roll was largely a musical form of the poor and the working class in America and later in Europe. Thus it was discredited among more privileged people. Fourth, and probably most important, Americans viewed rock and roll as synonymous with sex—the phrase *rock 'n' roll*, in fact, originally referred to sexual intercourse. This added to its attraction among some people, but to others it was an affront to conventional morality.

While such entertainers as Perry Como and Doris Day represented conventional musical tastes of the 1950s, Elvis Presley—the first superstar of rock and roll—was dismissed by one influential critic of the times as an "unspeakably talented and vulgar young entertainer" (cited in Gillett, 1983:17). Church groups,

Elvis Presley

Lionel Ritchey

especially in the South, launched campaigns to suppress rock and roll, which they described as an attempt by blacks to corrupt white youth. In addition to the sexually suggestive gyrations of rock and roll singers, some lyrics provoked charges of obscenity. Actually, early rock and roll lyrics were mild by today's standards, but they were viewed as threatening in a decade when sex was rarely mentioned at all.

By the 1960s, however, it became obvious that great profits could be made from rock and roll, and this was the crucial factor in removing the taint of deviance from this form of music. In addition to selling millions of records, the Beatles sold hundreds of millions of dollars' worth of side-line products, made highly profitable concert tours, and released sev-

eral successful films. About the same time, Coca-Cola began to use rock and roll music in advertising, which is now commonplace.

Today, rock and roll is big business. It has grown from 5 percent of record sales in the mid-1950s to a multibillion-dollar industry that accounts for more than 80 percent of all record sales. In the late 1980s, as well, rock and roll is increasingly evident on television. Promoter Dick Clark summed up the change when he claimed, "I don't make culture, I sell it" (cited in Chapple and Garofalo, 1977:305).

SOURCES: Based on Charlie Gillett, *The Sound of the City: The Rise of Rock and Roll* (New York: Pantheon, 1983); also Steve Chapple and Reebee Garofalo, *Rock 'n' Roll Is Here to Pay: The History and Politics of the Music Industry* (Chicago: Nelson-Hall, 1977).

the value placed on wealth overpowers the norms that regulate how wealth is to be acquired. Obviously, the poor experience this strain to the extent that their aspirations for success are frustrated by a lack of educational and job opportunities. Some resort to making their own rules in the form of theft, selling illegal drugs, or other

kinds of street hustling and racketeering. The box on p. 210 describes the process of innovation in the life of notorious gangster Al Capone.

The second response described by Merton to the inability to achieve wealth through normative means is *ritualism*. In this case, people resolve the strain of not

Table 8–1 MERTON'S STRAIN THEORY
OF DEVIANCE

Individual Responses to Dominant Cultural Patterns	Cultural Goals	Cultural Means
Nondeviant Response		
Conformity	Accept	Accept
Deviant Responses		
Innovation	Accept	Reject
Ritualism	Reject	Accept
Retreatism	Reject	Reject
Rebellion	Reject current goals, but promote new ones	Reject current means, but promote new ones

SOURCE: Based on Robert K. Merton, *Social Theory and Social Structure* (New York: Free Press, 1968), pp. 230–246.

having realized the cultural goal of wealth by simply abandoning the goal. At the same time, they place greater emphasis on conforming—often compulsively—to cultural norms in order to gain respectability. Merton suggests that ritualism is a likely response by people of modest social standing who have little opportunity to gain more in life but who fear risking what they have through innovation. An illustration of this response is provided by lower-level officials in formal organizations whom Merton described as "bureaucratic ritualists" (Chapter 7). Although ritualists are deviant insofar as they give up their goal of financial success, they are often viewed as good citizens because they rigidly adhere to cultural norms.

The third response to the inability to achieve wealth is *retreatism*—the rejection of both the goals and the norms of one's culture. Retreatists are society's dropouts. This category includes some alcoholics and drug addicts, as well as many of the street people commonly found in American cities. The deviance of retreatists lies in their unconventional way of life and also in the fact that they appear to have little desire to change their situation.

The fourth response to the failure to achieve wealth is *rebellion*. Like retreatists, rebels reject both the cultural definition of success and the normative means of achieving it. Rebels, however, go further by advocating some radical alternative to the existing social order, including new cultural values and norms. Some seek to do this through political revolution, while others promote an unconventional religious group. In any case, the rebel withdraws from established society and embraces some counterculture. Because rebels advocate radical social change, they are likely to be widely viewed as deviant.

Although Merton's strain theory is an influential statement of the relationship between deviance and the operation of society, it has been subject to various criticisms. First, Merton provides only a few clues as to why an individual would choose one response to strain over another. Second, his theory cannot explain many types of deviance—for example, crimes of passion, involuntary mental illness, and homosexuality. Third, strain theory assumes that, initially at least, everyone seeks success in conventional terms of wealth. As noted in Chapter 3, however, American society exhibits considerable variability in cultural values, so there are many different conceptions of personal success.

Deviant Subcultures

A study of delinquent youth by Richard Cloward and Lloyd Ohlin (1966) extends Merton's strain theory. Cloward and Ohlin point out that criminal types of deviance can result not only from a lack of culturally approved means to achieve success, but also from the availability of unconventional means to do so. Youths who have substantial opportunities to achieve success through legitimate means can be expected to do so, while those who have relatively more illegitimate opportunities are likely to use them. Cloward and Ohlin therefore attempt to explain delinquency in terms of the relative opportunity structure available to various categories of young people.

The life of Al Capone illustrates this idea. Capone pursued a criminal career partly because, as a poor immigrant, he was denied legitimate paths to success such as a college education. In addition, however, he recognized the illegal opportunity to become successful as a bootlegger. Where such opportunities for organized innovation are more available than conventional paths to success, Cloward and Ohlin expect *criminal subcultures* to develop. Such subcultures offer the knowledge, skills, and other resources needed to succeed in unconventional ways.

Cloward and Ohlin further suggest that if such organized innovation is impossible, as it is in many very poor and highly transient neighborhoods, delinquency may arise in the form of *conflict subcultures* in which gangs view violence as a source of prestige. Finally, *retreatist subcultures* may also arise among those who

Al Capone: The Gangster as Innovator

All I ever did was to sell beer and whiskey to our best people. All I ever did was to supply a demand that was pretty popular.

In these words, Al Capone described his life as perhaps the most notorious of America's gangsters. Capone founded his criminal empire partly on Prohibition, which outlawed the sale of alcoholic beverages in the United States between 1920 and 1933. For someone willing to take the risk, there was lots of money to be made in bootlegging.

Capone rose to power and wealth at a time when tens of millions of immigrants from Europe—mostly poor but eager to share in the American Dream of success—filled American cities. Prohibition was an attempt to uphold the cultural patterns of Anglo-Saxon Protestant America against growing cultural diversity. As socially inferior people, many immigrants encountered prejudice and discrimination that made achieving success difficult.

Although the vast majority of immigrants nonetheless patiently remained conformists in Merton's terminology, others saw in organized crime a means to achieve the American Dream. So it was that Al Capone—a man of genius and ambition, born in Naples, Italy, and brought up in an Italian slum of New York City—came to dominate one of the largest criminal empires of our history, centered in Chicago.

Capone's life illustrates Merton's concept of the deviant innovator—someone who accepts the culturally approved goal of success, but rejects conventional norms because the legitimate paths to success are largely closed to him. In the words of one analyst of the American underworld:

The typical criminal of the Capone era was a boy who had . . . seen what was rated as success in the society he had been thrust into—the Cadillac, the big bank-roll, the elegant apartment. How could he acquire that kind of recognizable status? He was almost always a boy of outstanding initiative, imagination, and ability; he was the kind of boy who, under different conditions, would have been a captain of industry or a key political figure of his time. But he hadn't the opportunity of going to Yale and becoming a banker or broker; there was no passage for him to a law degree from Harvard. There was, however, a relatively easy way of acquiring these goods that he was incessantly told were available to him as an American citizen, and without which he had begun to feel he could not properly count himself as an American citizen. He could become a gangster. (Allsop, 1961:236)

Even after they got wealth and power, gangsters found that they were denied the prestige accorded to those who had succeeded in legitimate businesses. Thus many gangsters attempted to distance themselves from their poor, ethnic origins by, for instance, changing their names. Capone took his first job from an immigrant who called himself Mr. Frankie Yale. The reputed head of the national Mafia, Yale operated from an establishment on Coney Island that he named the Harvard Inn. Capone himself demanded to be called Anthony Brown for part of his life and, according to one of his associates, hired only men who displayed few of the ethnic traits he sought to leave in his past.

The Big Fellow hires nothing but gentlemen. They have to be well dressed at all times and have to have cultured accents. They always have to say "Yes, Sir" and "No, Sir" to him. (Allsop, 1961:249)

After he achieved wealth, Capone attempted to live in the manner of upper-class Americans, although he was not accepted by such people. During the Depression, he charitably provided food to many of Chicago's destitute people and, even more significantly, succeeded in having his son Anthony enrolled at Yale University. Late in life, he enjoyed attending the wedding of his son to a well-to-do woman from Nashville.

Capone was one of the most notorious American criminals of the twentieth century, yet his hopes for himself and his family were modeled on the American Dream, which he believed a disfavored immigrant could achieve only through a life of crime.

SOURCE: Kenneth Allsop, *The Bootleggers* (London: Hutchinson and Company, 1961). Other information from E. Digby Baltzell, *The Protestant Establishment* (New York: Vintage Books, 1964), pp. 214–218.

have failed to achieve any semblance of success even using criminal means. Consistent with Merton's analysis, such subcultures are supported by dropouts who may make extensive use of alcohol or other drugs.

The importance of social class in the formation of delinquent subcultures has been highlighted by Albert Cohen (1971). Cohen suggests that delinquency is pronounced among lower-class youths because they are denied the opportunity to achieve success in a conventional way. Knowing how important success is in American society, lower-class youths find little basis for self-respect in their impoverished condition. In response, they may develop a delinquent subculture based on values and norms that offer more favorable self-definitions. According to Cohen, these values and norms may oppose those of the dominant culture as they "define as meritorious the characteristics [these youths] *do* possess, the kinds of conduct of which they *are* capable" (1971:66). Because the dominant culture values the calculated pursuit of wealth, for instance, a delinquent subculture may extol stealing "for the hell of it," providing prestige in the process. Similarly, adherents to a delinquent subculture may enjoy publicly flouting conventional norms while carefully conforming to their own norms.

Walter Miller (1970) agrees that delinquent subcultures are most likely to develop in the lower classes. However, he maintains that the values and norms of delinquent gangs arise not in reaction to a middle-class way of life, but out of the daily experiences of living with relatively little money and power. He describes six focal concerns of delinquent subcultures. First is *trouble*, arising from frequent conflict with teachers and police. Second, especially among males, is *toughness*, valuing physical size, strength, and athletic skills. Third is *smartness*, the ability to succeed on the streets, to outthink or con others, and to avoid being similarly taken advantage of. Fourth is *excitement*, the search for thrills, risk, or danger to gain needed release from a daily routine that is all too predictable and unsatisfying. Fifth is a concern with *fate*, derived from the lack of control these youths feel over their own lives. Sixth is *autonomy*, or the desire to be free from control by others, which is often expressed as resentment toward authority figures.

Evaluation. Structural-functional theories provide numerous insights into the relationship between deviance and the norms and social structures of society. The pioneering work of Emile Durkheim shows how recognizing and reacting to some form of deviance can serve the basic functions of moral definition. Merton's strain theory explains how some types of deviance may arise from the fact that the goals encouraged by the dominant culture are not accessible to some people. Cloward and Ohlin, Cohen, and Miller explain further that young people who lack the culturally approved means of achieving success may generate subcultures based on unconventional patterns of thinking and acting.

One major limitation of all these theories is that they assume the existence of a single dominant cultural system of values and norms against which attitudes and behavior are defined as either conventional or deviant. More correctly, American society is a mosaic of many cultural patterns with competing ideas of what is and is not deviant. The second problem lies in the assumption of the subcultural theorists that criminality is found primarily among the relatively poor. As we shall see later, this is a questionable assumption if criminality is defined not only in terms of street crimes such as theft, but also in terms of crimes such as stock fraud. Moreover, the cultural emphasis on financial success does not necessarily motivate the poor people to engage in criminality; rather, most poorer Americans recognize the fact that they will not achieve great wealth and limit their aspirations accordingly (Thio, 1983). The third problem is that structural-functional theories imply that everyone who violates conventional cultural standards will be defined as deviant. But being defined as deviant is actually a highly complex process that involves more than simple norm violation. This issue is a crucial concern in symbolic-interaction analysis, described in the next section.

Symbolic-Interaction Analysis

The symbolic-interaction paradigm directs our attention to the complex process by which people engaged in social interaction produce a social reality that varies from situation to situation and from person to person. In the early 1950s, sociologists began to apply this theoretical orientation to the study of deviance. This led to the recognition that social norms vary considerably; therefore, definitions of deviance and conformity are applied with surprising flexibility.

Labeling Theory

The central contribution of symbolic-interaction analysis is **labeling theory,** which is *the assertion that deviance and conformity result from the process by which individu-*

als are defined or labeled by others. Labeling theory stresses the relativity of deviance; in other words, the same behavior may be defined differently from one situation to another. Howard S. Becker has therefore claimed that deviance can be defined only as "behavior that people so label" (1966:9). Consider these situations: A woman takes an article of clothing from a roommate; a married man at a convention in a distant city sleeps with a female prostitute; a member of Congress drives home intoxicated after a party. Any of these situations may or may not be defined as deviant. The first could be defined either as borrowing or as theft. The consequences of the second situation depend largely on whether the news of his behavior follows the man back home. In the third situation, the congressman might be defined as either an active socialite or a dangerous drunk. In brief, all behavior has some or no significance to others according to a variable process of detection, definition, and response.

Keep in mind that people may be negatively labeled for being involved in situations for which they had little or no responsibility. For example, women who are the victims of the violent crime of rape are sometimes subjected to deviant labeling because of the misguided assumption that they must have encouraged the offender. The victims of serious diseases may also be labeled as

The Ray brothers, who received the virus that causes AIDS from blood transfusions, became social outcasts because of unfounded fears about the disease. Their courage is evidence that people can actively resist the stigma of deviance.

deviant even though they have violated no behavioral norms at all (except perhaps the norm that one should be healthy). Cancer patients, for instance, sometimes experience intense social isolation. And as Acquired Immune Deficiency Syndrome (AIDS) has spread among Americans, a common experience of persons with AIDS is being shunned by employers, friends, and even family members.

Drawing on the ideas of George Herbert Mead (Chapter 5), labeling theory explains that other people's judgments can have a powerful influence on how we see ourselves. Embarrassed, frightened, or overly solicitous reactions can make people with physical disabilities, for example, feel less than fully human and more helpless than they really are.

Primary and secondary deviance. Edwin Lemert (1951, 1972) has explained how being labeled as deviant can change a person's subsequent behavior. Lemert calls an activity that is initially defined as deviant *primary deviance.* Once people are defined as deviant, however, this label may become part of their social identity and self-concept, leading them to fulfill the expectations of others by engaging in *secondary deviance.* In the box "Being Overweight," for instance, Joan describes how her initial labeling as a "fatty" led her to feign sickness, to lie to her mother, and to befriend others considered deviant. This behavior, of course, only served to deepen her deviant identity—both in her mind and in the minds of others.

Stigma. The development of secondary deviance marks the start of what Erving Goffman (1963) has described as a *deviant career.* Crucial to beginning a deviant career is acquiring a **stigma**—*a powerful negative social label that radically changes a person's social identity and self-concept.* The stigma of deviance operates as a master status (Chapter 6), overpowering other dimensions of social identity so that a person is "reduced in our minds from a whole and usual person to a tainted, discounted one" (1963:3). Although the stigma was created by the labeling of others, the stigmatized person (along with everyone else) often sees it as justified by personal failings.

People usually learn the meaning of a social stigma long before such a label becomes attached to themselves. As part of the process of socialization, children learn to devalue certain categories of people. Beyond lawbreakers, these may be people of certain races or social classes and those who are obese, physically disabled, or unconventional in a host of other respects.

Eventually, individuals may learn that a particular stigma applies to them personally. Confronted with a racist remark, for example, a black child must face the hard fact of being different in a personally damaging way. Or a college student, who has long been aware of the stigma attached to homosexuality, experiences the uneasy realization that she is probably a lesbian. In other cases, a stigma is attached to a person through a formal process that Harold Garfinkel (1956) calls a *degradation ceremony*. A criminal prosecution, for example, has many of the same characteristics as a high-school graduation ceremony. In both cases, people stand before the community to be formally defined as distinctive kinds of people—negatively in one case, positively in the other. The stigmatized individual thereby becomes one of a category of people who may be avoided by others. Insofar as people come to think they deserve the stigma, they may become alienated from themselves as well.

The long-term effects on self-concept of being stigmatized can be considerable. The box on p. 214 explains that even after Joan had lost weight, she still viewed herself as unattractive to other people. However, the negative consequences of a social stigma can be resisted. Many people with physical disabilities, gay people, and members of racial minorities have successfully countered stigma by recognizing and emphasizing their personal qualities in positive terms.

Being stigmatized can also lead to the process of **retrospective labeling,** which is *the interpretation of a person's past in terms that are consistent with a present deviant label* (Scheff, 1984). For example, after discovering that a man who has spent much of his life working with the Boy Scouts has sexually molested a child, others rethink his past in the light of the new revelation ("He always did spend a lot of time around young children"). This process involves selecting and interpreting facts from the person's past in a way that is consistent with the present stigma. News reports covering the shooting of Beatle John Lennon by Mark David Chapman in 1980 selectively highlighted such facts as Chapman's running away from home on several occasions, his inability to hold a job, his use of drugs, and his compulsion to emulate Lennon—even to the point of marrying a Japanese woman. Not surprisingly, one reporter concluded, "The signs of [Chapman's] disintegration had been all too clear—and altogether missed" (Mathews, 1980:35).

Labeling and mental illness. Labeling theory is particularly useful in the study of mental illness because a person's mental condition may be difficult to define.

Because he chooses to express his religious convictions in an unconventional manner, should this man's actions be labeled as mental illness?

Psychiatrists have often assumed that mental disorders have a concrete reality similar to diseases of the body. Such factors as heredity, diet, stress, and chemical imbalances in the body are known to be at least partial causes of some mental disturbances. However, much of what we label *mental illness* is a matter of social definition, depending on the response of others or our evaluation of ourselves based on what we imagine others think of us (Thoits, 1985). This suggests that defining and treating the "mentally ill" is sometimes simply a disguised attempt to enforce conformity to cultural standards.

If a woman believes that Jesus rides the bus to work with her every day, is she seriously deluded or merely expressing her religious faith in a highly graphic way? If a man refuses to bathe or observe common etiquette, much to the dismay of his family, is he insane or simply choosing to live differently from other people? Is a socially disadvantaged person who defies authority figures mentally imbalanced or expressing justifiable resentment?

Maintaining that the label of insanity is widely applied to what is actually only "difference," psychiatrist Thomas Szasz has suggested that the notion of mental illness be abandoned (1961, 1970; Vatz & Weinberg,

Being Overweight—A Study in Deviant Labeling

A female sociologist—identifying herself only as "Joan"—begins an account of her life by noting that she was born to two overweight parents. Although heavy as a young child, Joan was not aware of being overweight until the age of six, when she began school.

> In the first grade, it was painfully pointed out to me—for the first time in my life—that I was different from other children. Other children's taunts of "fatty" and "pig" first brought shock, pain, tears, and later, guilt. I remember being afraid of the other children to the point of not wanting to walk home alone, and my mother frequently walked the one block from my home to the school to get me.
>
> The teasing, however, did not cause me to stop eating for I still did not realize the connection between eating and being overweight. Instead, I started to develop two coping and protective devices which became quite elaborate later. For one thing, I started to try very hard to establish my worth in areas not related to physical attri-

butes, while at the same time avoiding activities involving my body.

Joan's "coping devices" involved actions that, ironically, deepened her deviant identity. She learned, for example, that she could avoid the embarrassment of engaging in sports (no one wanted her as a teammate) by pretending to be sick. Gradually, this use of illness expanded:

> I also learned that by being "sick" I could avoid facing other people. . . . I was in the school nurse's office almost every day while in the third grade with a wide range of ailments. . . . This game came to an abrupt end, however, when two betrayals put a stop to my friendship with the school nurse. . . . [C]hildren in the school I attended were given a general physical by the school nurse. One part of the physical was weighing each child. When the day for my turn arrived, I went to the nurse's office with my best friend. . . . Not only was the nurse horrified when the scale read 120 pounds, but my friend laughed, ran

back to our classroom, and announced the figure to everyone. I can remember feeling terribly hurt, and somehow punished for a wrong I had done.

> The other betrayal . . . took the form of the nurse starting a "fat club" based on the idea that together fat kids could lose weight if they discussed their mutual problems. I was horrified at the thought of joining a group of *them*, probably because I didn't want to admit that I was "that" fat.

Another coping mechanism Joan devised was lying. When her mother asked her how much she weighed, she gave an answer based on what she thought her mother would believe rather than revealing her actual weight. She knew her parents disliked lying, but preferred to think of herself as a liar than as a fat person. Yet, here again, her self-protective action backfired:

> Like all good things, my deception came to an end when I was discovered during a visit to the doctor for a physi-

---

1983). Illness, Szasz argues, can afflict only the body. Mental illness, therefore, is simply a myth. Being "different" in thought or action may provoke others to irritation or hostility, but it does not imply that someone is "mentally ill." Why, then, is this label applied to certain people? Szsaz claims that doing so provides a powerful justification for encouraging—or forcing—someone to change. Szasz's views are controversial; many of his colleagues reject the idea that all mental illness is a fiction. But he has also been widely praised for highlighting the danger of abusing medical practice in the interest of promoting conformity.

Further criticism of the label of mental illness was made by Erving Goffman (1961), who pointed out that

commitment to a mental institution may reflect the needs and desires of others as much as those of the patient. Goffman provides several examples of contingencies that may trigger institutionalization although they have no direct bearing on the patient's mental condition:

> . . . a psychotic man is tolerated by his wife until she finds herself a boyfriend, or by his adult children until they move from a house to an apartment; an alcoholic is sent to a mental hospital because the jail is full, and a drug addict because he declines to avail himself of psychiatric treatment on the outside; a rebellious adolescent daughter can no longer be managed at home because she now threatens to have an open affair with an unsuitable companion.

cal. Right up to the point of stepping on the scale . . . I had my mother convinced I weighed almost fifteen pounds less. The anxiety caused by the lying was terrible, but it was nothing compared to the way I felt when they found out. I cried hysterically . . . The doctor suggested that my parents send me to a psychiatrist if I couldn't diet, which they did not do. This recommendation shocked me, and I entered high school with a much different picture of myself. At last I knew I was deviant; I accepted the fact, and I began to act accordingly.

In high school, Joan continued in her deviant role, being shunned by others and having no dates with boys for three years. She tried to lose weight but failed because, she explains, she had come to accept being heavy as part of her self-image. No longer believing her weight to be the cause of her problems, she saw herself as simply an outcast in whom no one could find very much to like. This pattern continued in college, where Joan made friends with others labeled as deviant—her roommate was a woman who was partly blind and who was known to have had extensive psychiatric treatment, and another friend was physically disabled. At this point in her life, Joan was extremely unhappy:

> I think my college depression can best be summarized by the way I felt when both my roommate and my paraplegic friend had dates on Friday night and I didn't. The only outlet I found that night for the anger I felt was the candy vending machine in the basement of the dormitory. How ironic that I should perpetuate the very thing that was helping to keep me home by eating candy.

There is no happy ending to Joan's story. She has now lost a great deal of weight and gained considerable understanding of her past. Yet she finds that her deviance has become so incorporated into her self-concept that she still lives very much as she did when she was heavy:

> I now weigh 129 pounds and plan to lose at least another 10 pounds. The loss in weight, however, has not been accompanied by any increase in dates or change of mental attitude, and I fear that it is really my internal makeup that is deviant. I still feel fat, and no matter how many times my friends or parents tell me how nice I look, I don't believe them. . . . I do not know how to get dates, let alone what type of behavior is expected on a date.

> If I sound bitter, it's because I am tired of having to do all the changing. I don't like the fact that I have allowed my life to be regulated by the opinions and expectations of other people. . . . If nothing else, I hope I have shown to what extent being obese, and others' reactions to obesity, as well as the various rationalizations one entertains under these circumstances, can influence and even create a lifestyle.

SOURCE: Adapted from Anonymous, "Losing: An Attempt at Stigma Neutralization," in Jerry Jacobs, ed., *Deviance: Field Studies and Self-Disclosures* (Palo Alto, CA: National Press Books, 1974), pp. 69–72.

> . . . One could say that mental patients distinctively suffer not from mental illness, but from contingencies. (1961:135)

The label of mental illness is a severe stigma that greatly transforms the life of the person so labeled. Most of us have experienced a period of extreme stress or other mental disability; although sometimes very upsetting, such episodes are usually of passing importance. If they form the basis of a social stigma, however, they may cause the person to embark on a deviant career as a self-fulfilling prophecy (Scheff, 1984).

The medicalization of deviance. The ideas of Szasz and Goffman are a response to an important shift in understanding deviance over the last fifty years. The growing influence of medicine—particularly psychiatry—within American society has resulted in the **medicalization of deviance,** meaning *patterns of behavior previously understood in moral terms are now viewed as medical matters.* The medicalization of deviance involves a change in the labels used to designate normality or deviance. In moral terms, definitions applied to people or their behavior involve some combination of "bad" and "good." The scientific objectivity of medicine allows no such moral judgment, however. Therefore, the medicalization of deviance involves replacing moral terms with clinical terms such as "sick" and "well."

Changing views on alcoholism illustrate this process. Until the middle of this century, an alcoholic was widely viewed as morally deficient, a "drunk" too weak to resist the pleasures of drink, or simply someone without the will to act responsibly. Gradually, however, alcoholism was redefined as a medical problem. Thus alcoholism is now generally considered to be a disease, and alcoholics are defined as "sick" rather than "bad." Similarly, problematic behavior ranging from obesity to drug addiction to child abuse was, in the past, understood in terms of morality. Today, such matters are widely defined as illnesses for which the people involved require professional assistance.

A few cases are more complex, with moral and medical views alternating over time. Homosexuality, for instance, was for centuries a moral issue in American society, a straightforward case of being "bad" according to a heterosexual standard of "good." By the 1950s, however, homosexuality was rapidly becoming a medical matter. In 1952, the American Psychiatric Association (APA) officially declared homosexuality a "sociopathic personality disturbance." This declaration by medical professionals was a powerful influence on public opinion; by 1970, about two-thirds of American adults had endorsed the view that homosexuality was a "sickness that could be cured." Since that time, however, strong criticism of the idea that gay people are "sick"—along with the obvious lack of success in "curing" homosexuality—has removed much of this medical stigma. Thus, in 1974, the APA changed its position and defined homosexuality as simply a "form of sexual behavior" and not a "mental disorder" (Conrad & Schneider, 1980: 193–209). Even so, homosexuality has not become the morally neutral matter of sexual orientation that many people have advocated. Rather, provoked in part by the association of homosexuality and Acquired Immune Deficiency Syndrome (AIDS), in 1987 about three-fourths of Americans expressed the view that homosexuality is morally wrong (N.O.R.C., 1987).

The adoption of a moral or a medical approach to deviance has a number of profound consequences. First is the matter of *who responds* to deviance. Members of the community (or officials such as police) are justified in responding to an offense against common morality, as in the case of crime. Once medical definitions are applied, however, the situation comes under the control of specialists, including counselors, psychiatrists, and physicians. Second is the issue of *how people respond* to the deviant. A moral approach defines the deviant as an "offender" subject to punishment. Medically, however, a deviant is a "patient" in need of treatment. In addition, while punishment corresponds to specific violations in the past, treatment reflects the medical assessment of the entire person with an eye toward possible future deviance (von Hirsh, 1986). The third and most important difference is *the personal competence of the person labeled as deviant.* Morally, people are responsible for their behavior. That is, they may do wrong, but they at least understand what they are doing. Medically, however, "sick" people may not be responsible for what they do. Viewed as personally incompetent, they may not even understand what is in their own best interest and are therefore subject to involuntary treatment.

Interaction and Learning to Be Deviant

Edwin Sutherland (1940) suggested that, like any other type of human behavior, deviance is learned through association with other people, especially within primary groups. He claimed that socialization typically involves exposing people to ideas that encourage criminality as well as ideas that support obeying the law. Any person's likelihood of engaging in criminal activity, then, depends upon the frequency of association with people who encourage norm violation as compared to those who encourage conformity. This is Sutherland's theory of *differential association.*

Supporting Sutherland's theory is a study of drug and alcohol use among young adults in the United States (Akers et al., 1979). Responses to a questionnaire submitted to over three thousand junior and senior high-school students led researchers to conclude that the extent of alcohol and drug use was related to the degree of encouragement of such activity by others in peer groups. They found that young people learn to engage in delinquency by imitating others, receiving praise and other rewards for delinquency, and (as Sutherland emphasized) learning to define delinquency—rather than conformity to conventional norms—in positive terms. Of additional interest is Travis Hirschi's (1969) finding that delinquency is most prevalent among youths who have weaker relationships with their parents and other people who might be expected to discourage such activity.

A learning approach to deviance also explains the persistence of high rates of juvenile delinquency in specific neighborhoods (Shaw & McKay, 1972; orig. 1942). Once established, skills and attitudes favorable to deviance may be transmitted over time, often via delinquent subcultures, as described earlier. But while some deviance may arise in this way, it is clear that adolescents also develop deviant behavior independently, perhaps as an act of rebellion against parental control. In addition, many deviant acts—such as cheating on an examination or shoplifting—may be spontaneous reactions to specific situational pressures or opportunities rather than evidence of strong commitment to a deviant career. As other researchers have concluded, many young people casually drift into and out of deviant episodes, many of which are not very serious. Thus, while young people may learn patterns of deviance, they are not necessarily strongly committed to deviant activity (Matza, 1964; Elliot & Ageton, 1980).

Evaluation. Labeling theory has generated widespread interest in recent decades. Rather than focusing on the *action* itself, it emphasizes the origin of deviance in the *reaction* of other people. This approach suggests why some people are defined as deviant while others who think or behave in much the same way are not. Moreover, by developing the concepts of stigma, secondary deviance, and deviant careers, labeling theory has demonstrated how the label of deviance can be incorporated into a person's self-concept so that it may lead to subsequent deviance.

Labeling theory has several limitations, however. First, this highly relative view of deviance tends to overlook the fact that some kinds of behavior, such as homicide, are widely considered to be serious norm violations in virtually every society (Wellford, 1980). Labeling theory is therefore most useful in providing an explanation of the less serious types of deviance, such as certain kinds of sexual behavior and mental illness. The second problem is ambiguity as to the consequences of deviant labeling. On the one hand, labeling may promote deviance in the people so defined. But on the other hand, being labeled deviant may discourage people from engaging in subsequent norm violations. In other words, questions remain as to the conditions under which deviant labeling initiates a deviant career. The third problem lies in the theory's assumption that people always resist the label of deviance. While most probably do, some may actively seek to be defined as deviant (Vold & Bernard, 1986). For example, dressing unconventionally can be a deliberate means of establishing a distinctive identity, just as civil disobedience can effectively call attention to government policies. The fourth problem is that we still have much to learn about the conditions under which labels are significant in everyday life. For instance, one recent study found that the stigma of being a former mental patient resulted in social rejection only when the person was considered likely to behave dangerously (Link et al., 1987).

Sutherland's social-learning theory has had considerable influence in sociology. His basic view that deviance is learned just like any other social pattern is widely accepted, but social-learning theory provides little insight into why society's norms and laws define certain kinds of activities as deviant in the first place. This important question is addressed by social-conflict analysis, described in the next section.

Social-Conflict Analysis

The social-conflict paradigm attempts to explain deviance in terms of basic dimensions of social inequality. This approach recognizes the variable application of the label of deviance. But rather than taking a situational approach to deviance, the social-conflict paradigm links the issue of *who* as well as *what* is defined as deviant to social inequality within society as a whole.

Why, Alexander Liazos (1972) asks, do we tend to think of deviants as "nuts, sluts, and preverts?" With this question, Liazos calls attention to the tendency to define *less powerful people* as deviant. Within any large city, for example, bag ladies, unemployed men standing on street corners, and various other down-and-outers are readily defined as deviant, while affluent and well-dressed people more easily claim respectability. Similarly, the peer groups of poor youths are likely to be defined as "street gangs," while those of affluent young people are simply called "cliques."

Social-conflict theory suggests this is true for three major reasons. First, the powerful have considerable resources to resist deviant labels. For example, corporate executives who dump hazardous wastes in violation of the law are rarely held personally accountable for these acts. Protected by their good reputations as business leaders and by a staff of experienced lawyers, they usually have enough power to avoid being labeled deviant.

Second, the norms—including laws—of any society generally tend to reflect the interests of the rich and powerful. The legal right to own property is an important foundation of Western law and provides the greatest benefits to those with the most wealth. People who threaten the wealthy, either by taking their property or by advocating a more equal society, may be readily defined as "thieves" or "political radicals." As noted in Chapter 4, Karl Marx argued that all social institutions are fundamentally supportive of the capitalist economic system

Deviance is often a matter of social standing. Americans view well-to-do people as respectable, and tend to define their activities as positive or at least harmless. The actions of those with fewer privileges are more likely to be viewed as harmful and threatening.

and protect the interests of the rich, capitalist class. Richard Quinney makes the point succinctly: "Capitalist justice is by the capitalist class, for the capitalist class, and against the working class" (1977:3).

Third, the fact that laws and other norms reflect the interests of the most powerful people in a society is obscured by the widespread belief in cultural standards as simply natural and good. For this reason, while the unequal application of the law may be seen as unjust, little thought is usually given to the fact that laws themselves may be inherently unfair (Quinney, 1977).

Deviance and Capitalism

Steven Spitzer (1980) has developed a social-conflict theory of deviance based on Karl Marx's belief that norms support a society's economic system. Spitzer claims that categories of people threatening to the operation of capitalism are likely to be defined as deviant. As Spitzer explains, such *problem populations* include many different kinds of people (1980:180).

First, capitalism is based on the private control of property. Thus those who threaten the property of others—especially the poor who steal from the rich—are prime candidates for labeling as deviant. On the other hand, instances in which the rich exploit the poor are *less* likely to be defined as deviance. For example, landlords may charge poor tenants unreasonably high rents and even forcibly evict those who cannot pay without being labeled as criminal. Within capitalist society, this is simply a matter of doing business.

Second, capitalism depends on the productive labor of the majority of people. Thus those who cannot or will not work are likely to be labeled as deviant. Americans commonly think of people who are out of work—even if through no fault of their own—as deviant. The unemployed may experience personal guilt as well as public shame.

Third, capitalism depends on a socialization process that enforces a respect for figures of authority. Thus persons who resist those in authority are likely to be labeled as deviant. Examples are children who talk back to their parents and teachers or who skip school, adults who do not cooperate with employers or police, and anyone who opposes "the system."

Fourth, capitalism rests on the widespread acceptance of its norms as both natural and just. Thus those who express or promote attitudes inconsistent with the capitalist system are subject to deviant labeling. In this category are included antiwar activists, environmentalists, people who attempt to organize workers against the capitalist owners of industry, and anyone who compares capitalism unfavorably with another type of economic system.

On the other hand, persons or activities that enhance the operation of capitalism are subject to positive labeling. For example, competitive sports express the values of individual achievement and competition vital to capitalism, so athletes have long been highly praised in American society. In addition, Spitzer notes that while the use of drugs for escape from reality (especially marijuana, heroin, and the psychedelics) is likely to be defined as deviant, the use of drugs that encourage adjustment to the status quo (such as alcohol and caffeine) tends to be defined in positive terms.

The severity of the response to various problem populations depends on how much they threaten the capitalist system. For example, some mild deviance by adolescents (such as defying authority figures) is tolerated and even expected. These young people may receive only a mildly deviant label, such as "being immature" or "going through a phase." However, more serious norm violations by young people (such as theft or violence) may be stigmatized as "delinquency." Similarly, college professors who are critical of American society are generally tolerated as long as they restrict their radical views to the classroom. Should they begin giving speeches at a local factory, they would be courting a far more serious response.

Spitzer suggests that problem populations are of two general kinds. The first he describes as *social junk*, people who are a "costly yet relatively harmless burden" to capitalist society (1980:184). Within this category are those who do not actively support the capitalist system by working and who may actually be unable to provide for themselves. Such nonproductive, but nonthreatening, members of society include Merton's retreatists (for example, winos and junkies), and people who are old, physically disabled, mentally retarded, or mentally ill. These people are defined as mildly deviant and are typically subject to control by social welfare agencies.

The second kind of problem population is made up of people perceived as directly threatening to the capitalist system; they are considered to be *social dynamite*. This category includes those who have the potential to actively challenge capitalism—for example, the large numbers of unemployed people concentrated in cities, alienated youths, radicals, and revolutionaries. In Merton's terms, this category is composed of both innovators and rebels. Because they are perceived as threatening, such people are subject to control by the criminal justice system and —in times of crisis, as during the civil rights and antiwar movements of the 1960s—by military forces such as the national guard. In 1985, members of a black activist group called MOVE, considered by city officials in Philadelphia to be extremely dangerous, entered into a confrontation with hundreds of police. In a military battle in which a helicopter was used to bomb the group's house, eleven MOVE members died and an entire West Philadelphia neighborhood went up in flames (McCoy, 1986).

Following Marx's ideas, Spitzer claims that both the "social junk" and the "social dynamite" populations are produced by capitalism. Unemployment, for example, is the inevitable result of maximizing profits by using the least amount of human labor possible in producing goods and services. Poverty, which may breed despair as well as anger and activism, is a consequence of capitalism's typically unequal distribution of material resources. Creating these categories of people, capitalism must also control them. This is the function of the social

A police confrontation in 1985 with members of a deviant group left a large section of West Philadelphia in ruins. Despite extensive public injury, powerful officials responsible for actions of this kind are unlikely to be defined as criminal.

welfare system and the criminal justice system. Both systems use deviant labels to place responsibility for the social problems that "problem populations" represent on the people themselves rather than on the capitalist system. Those who receive welfare because they have no other source of income are defined as unworthy; poor people who vent their rage at being deprived of a secure life are labeled rioters; anyone who actively challenges the government is called a radical or a communist; and those who attempt to gain illegally what they cannot otherwise get for themselves are called common thieves.

In this theory, then, social control serves a twofold purpose: to manage "problem populations" so that their threat and cost to the capitalist system are minimal, and to define the source of social problems as individual failure rather than the capitalist system itself.

Deviance and the Rich: White-Collar Crime

At the end of 1986, Ivan Boesky came to the attention of Americans. Long thought to be a genius on Wall Street, Boesky had in ten years amassed a fortune of hundreds of millions of dollars through shrewd stock transactions. It turned out that he made much of his money by breaking the law. By using "insider information"—advance tips about what companies were likely to attempt takeovers of other companies—Boesky was able to buy stocks that he knew would greatly increase in value and sit back to count his profits (Russell, 1986).

During the last few years, federal officials have charged dozens of others in the financial world with illegal dealings. Such activities are an example of **white-collar crime,** defined by Edwin Sutherland in 1940 as *"crimes committed by persons of respectability and high status in the course of their occupations"* (Sutherland & Cressey, 1978:44). As the Wall Street example suggests, white-collar crime rarely involves uniformed police converging on a crime scene with drawn guns. Nor is it likely to involve violence on the part of the criminal. Thus white-collar crime does not refer to such street crimes as murder, assault, or rape that happen to be carried out by people of high social position. Rather, it refers to crimes committed by powerful people making illegal use of their occupational positions to enrich themselves or others, often causing significant public harm in the process (Hagan & Parker, 1985; Vold & Bernard, 1986). The image of Ivan Boesky at work in an office equipped with hundreds of telephone lines suggests why

such offenses are commonly termed crime in the suites as opposed to crime in the streets.

The public harm caused by the wide range of white-collar crime—including false advertising, marketing unsafe products, embezzlement, and bribery of public officials—is far greater than most Americans realize. Estimates of the costs to society of business-related crimes range between $40 billion and $200 billion a year (Bequai, 1977, cited in Reid, 1982:247; Reiman, 1984:86). This represents up to eight times the cost to Americans of all types of common theft (U.S. Federal Bureau of Investigation, 1986). Moreover, roughly 100,000 Americans die each year from illness and injury resulting from their occupational environment—a number five times greater than all the murders carried out by street criminals (Simon & Eitzen, 1982:27; U.S. Federal Bureau of Investigation, 1987).

In his pioneering study of white-collar crime, Edwin Sutherland (1940) found that all the largest commercial corporations in the United States of the time had engaged in unlawful behavior that caused considerable social harm. Yet only about one case in ten was officially treated as the criminal action of specific persons. In other words, violation of the law is defined rather differently when it is practiced by powerful members of society. Sutherland described two significant differences.

First, he noted that violations of law involving corporations are far more likely to be treated in a civil court than in a criminal court. *Civil law* refers to general laws that regulate claims for economic losses between private parties, while *criminal law* refers to specific laws that define every individual's moral responsibility to society. Under civil law, corporations may have to pay for damage or injury they have caused, but corporate leaders *as individuals* are not charged with criminal wrongdoing. Elite deviance is unlikely to result in criminal labeling.

Ivan Boesky, for example, returned some illegally made profits and paid penalties totaling $100 million, and he was sentenced to three years in jail. But relatively few white-collar criminals are jailed: in 1986, for example, there were over 12,000 people in federal prisons for drug offenses, but only 335 for embezzlement (U.S. Federal Bureau of Prisons, 1987). In fact, almost three out of four people who *are* convicted of embezzlement in the United States are placed on probation rather than being imprisoned. As a Virginia prosecutor concluded, except for the most serious cases of embezzlement, "you probably won't go to jail" (Gest, 1985:43).

The second difference Sutherland noted is that white-collar crime usually generates far less public response than street crime does. Some corporations, he found, had routinely broken the law with little or no public reaction. The public often has no information about the existence of such crimes, since what becomes public knowledge about corporate activities is largely controlled by corporations themselves. In addition, corporate crime may be said to victimize both everyone and no one. White-collar crime involves no gun in anyone's ribs; just as important, the economic costs of such crime are usually spread throughout the population.

As the "backbone of the capitalist system," corporations exert immense power over every aspect of American life, influencing the mass media as well as the political process. High corporate officials are often graduates of prestigious universities and professional schools, members of exclusive social clubs, and well connected to other powerful people in all walks of life. Many government officials are drawn from the ranks of corporate executives; after completing a period of government service, they often return to the corporate world. As governmental officials, such people frequently regulate the activities of the very corporate enterprises in which they have spent most of their working lives. It is not surprising, then, that serious episodes of white-collar crime only occasionally come to the attention of the public.

Evaluation. Social-conflict theory explains how the creation and application of laws and other cultural norms reflect inequality of wealth and power. It also shows that the criminal justice system and social welfare agencies have the political purpose of controlling categories of the population that are perceived as threatening to the capitalist system.

Like all approaches to deviance, however, social-conflict theory is subject to criticism. First, this approach tends to assume that laws and other cultural norms are created directly by the rich and powerful. But, as we shall see in Chapter 9, it is far from clear exactly which people should be considered part of the capitalist elite. Besides, the assumption that laws are directly manipulated by the rich ignores the fact that many segments of American society influence the political process. Laws protecting consumers and the environment, for example, do not directly reflect the interests of capitalists. Second, although social-conflict theory usefully points out that social injuries caused by the powerful are often overlooked, there can be little doubt that street crime also represents genuine danger to any society. Third, the assertion that criminality and other forms of deviance are a product of social inequality leads to the conclusion

Table 8–2 THREE SOCIOLOGICAL APPROACHES TO DEVIANCE: A SUMMARY

Theoretical Paradigm	Major Contribution
Structural-functional analysis	While what is deviant may vary, deviance itself is found in all societies; deviance and the social response it provokes serve to maintain the moral foundation of society; deviance can also direct social change.
Symbolic-interaction analysis	Nothing is inherently deviant, but may become defined as such through the response of others; the reactions of others are highly variable; the label of deviance can lead to the emergence of secondary deviance and deviant careers.
Social-conflict analysis	Laws and other norms reflect the interests of powerful members of society; those who threaten the status quo are likely to be defined as deviant; social injury caused by powerful people is less likely to be defined as criminal than social injury caused by people who have little social power.

that societies exhibit deviance only to the extent that they contain social inequality. This view is challenged by Emile Durkheim's earlier contention that any and all societies, regardless of their degree of social inequality, will necessarily experience some type of deviance.

The three major theoretical orientations used by sociologists to explore crime and other types of deviance have now been described. Table 8–2 provides a summary of the important contributions of each approach to understanding deviance.

Deviance and Women

Finally, it is necessary to point out that all theories of deviance presented so far tend to pay little attention to the crucial variable of sex in explanations of deviance. More precisely, most theories have been developed by males and focus on male behavior.

Robert Merton's "strain theory," for example, defines cultural goals in terms of financial success. Traditionally, however, this has been a *masculine* goal, while females sought success through marriage and raising a family. This theory, then, has questionable application to half the population (Leonard, 1982).

Labeling theory provides a framework in which sex can be shown to influence how deviance is defined. But, to date, relatively little effort has been made to do so. A notable exception is recent work by Edwin Schur (1983). Schur highlights the fact that cases of men victimizing women often involve blurred definitions of responsibility. Men who engage in sexual harassment, rape, or other assaults against women often receive only mildly deviant labels, none at all, or even positive labels. Women who are victimized in such cases, on the other hand, often have to convince an unsympathetic audience that they were not to blame for what happened.

Social-conflict analysis also has neglected the importance of sex in theory building. This approach to deviance developed largely as an alternative to structural-functionalism. Ironically, however, it typically offers no greater insights into patterns of deviance that involve women. If capitalism and the social inequality it fosters are a primary cause of crime, for example, why are women in capitalist societies far less likely than men to engage in crime?

As we turn to the issue of crime in the next section, we shall closely examine *both* male and female patterns.

CRIME AND THE CRIMINAL JUSTICE SYSTEM

Although many types of deviance are subject only to informal negative sanctions, violations of law may activate the criminal justice system. A system of this kind, backed by the power of the state, is found in every industrial society in the world.

We have defined crime as any action, or failure to act, that violates a criminal law enacted by local, state, or national political officials. The *commission* of a crime, however, has two major components. First, there is the activity itself. Under the American legal system, only action (or the failure to act) in violation of law is criminal; simply *thinking* about violating the law is not a crime. A second necessary condition of almost all crimes is criminal intent (in legal terminology, *mens rea*, or "guilty mind") on the part of the offender.

Under the law, however, intent is a variable concept that does not refer only to deliberate activity; even negligence can be the basis of criminal responsibility if a person acts (or fails to act) in a manner that may reasonably be expected to lead to a harmful result. In the case of homicide, for example, the degree of intent of the offender is reflected in distinctions made among first-degree murder, second-degree murder, and negligent manslaughter (Reid, 1982).

Types of Crime

In the United States, information on criminal offenses is gathered by the Federal Bureau of Investigation and regularly reported in a publication called *Crime in the United States*. This report presents information about two major types of serious crimes.

Crimes against the person (or simply, violent crimes) are *crimes against people that involve violence or the threat of violence*. Such crimes include *homicide* (legally defined as "the willful killing of one human being by another"), *aggravated assault* ("an unlawful attack by one person upon another for the purpose of inflicting severe or aggravated bodily injury"), *forcible rape* ("the carnal knowledge of a female forcibly and against her will"), and *robbery* ("taking or attempting to take anything of value from the care, custody, or control of a person or persons by force or threat of force or violence and/or putting the victim in fear").

Crimes against property (or simply, property crimes) are *crimes that involve theft of property belonging to others*. This type of serious crime includes *burglary* ("the unlawful entry of a structure to commit a [serious crime] or a theft"), *larceny-theft* (the unlawful taking, carrying, leading, or riding away of property from the possession of another"), *auto theft* ("the theft or attempted theft of a motor vehicle"), and *arson* ("any willful or malicious burning or attempt to burn the personal property of another"). In the United States, property crimes are about eight times as frequent as violent crimes.

While all of the crimes noted above are widely regarded as serious, this is not the case with **victimless crimes**—*violations of law in which there are no readily apparent victims*. Examples of victimless crimes are the use of illegal drugs, homosexuality between consenting adults, prostitution, and gambling. Laws designate such activities as criminal in order to uphold society's conception of morality. However, any singular conception of public morality is actually a fiction, since all of these activities are viewed as wrong by some people and right by others. Not surprisingly, then, laws regulating victimless crimes vary widely from one area to another. In the United States, gambling is legal in Nevada and part of New Jersey, but illegal elsewhere; homosexual behavior is legally restricted in about half of all states. In addition, where they do exist, laws against victimless crimes are typically enforced unevenly.

Some people argue that victimless crimes are an insignificant threat to society and that outlawing such actions as gambling and prostitution represents an attempt by some people to impose their own morality on everyone. Therefore, they propose that such actions be decriminalized and regarded as matters of personal discretion. Others respond that while such activities may not cause serious and direct harm, they do undermine established cultural values. Even if no direct harm were to result to those who smoke marijuana, for example, some people fear that complete social acceptance of this practice would lead to a radical transformation of our cultural system.

Some victimless crimes do result in other costs to society. Riding a motorcycle without a helmet is illegal in many states. Those supporting compulsory helmet laws point out that riders who do not wear helmets are more likely to suffer serious head injuries in an accident that could result in a lifetime of medical treatment, possibly provided at public expense.

Criminal Statistics

Statistics gathered by the Federal Bureau of Investigation show that crime rates increased dramatically during the 1970s, declined during the early 1980s, and have risen once again since 1984. Figure 8–1 indicates trends for violent crimes and for property crimes.

Official crime statistics are an important source of information about crime, but they are far from perfect. The biggest problem is that they include only offenses known to the police. Although the police become aware of almost all homicides, assaults—especially those which take place between acquaintances—are far less likely to be reported. Police records include even a smaller proportion of property crimes, especially when they involve items of little value. This is because people may not realize that they have been victimized, or they may assume they have little chance of recovering their property even if they notify the police.

Rape is an especially difficult case in point. Because of the traditional stigma attached to the innocent victims of this violent crime, many women have avoided reporting rape to the police. In the last decade, however, growing public support for rape victims has resulted in more offenses being reported. This is reflected in the fact that the official number of rapes increased over 40 percent between 1977 and 1987 (U.S. Federal Bureau of Investigation, 1987). Even so, it is likely that only about half of all rapes are reported to the police.

One way to evaluate the accuracy of the official crime statistics is to conduct a victimization survey in which samples of the population are asked whether they have been victims of crime. Such surveys suggest that, overall, the actual level of crime is two to three times as great as that indicated by official reports.

A Profile of the Criminal

Government statistics and sociological research afford a general description of people who commit crimes.

Age. The likelihood of engaging in serious crime is strongly related to age for all categories of the American population (Hirschi & Gottfredson, 1983; Krisberg & Schwartz, 1983). More specifically, the greatest proportion of arrests involve Americans in late adolescence and early adulthood. People between the ages of fifteen and twenty-four, which represented 16 percent of the American population in 1986, accounted for just under half of arrests for serious crimes, including 43.4 percent of all arrests for violent crimes and 50.6 percent of all arrests for property crimes.

Sex. Official statistics suggest that crime is an overwhelmingly male activity. Although males and females constitute roughly equal proportions of the population, males were about four times more likely than females to be arrested for serious crimes in 1986: 76.1 percent of arrests for property crimes were of males; 23.9 percent were of females. For violent crimes, the disparity was even greater: 89.1 percent of the arrests were of males, with females accounting for only 10.9 percent. This general pattern is striking, although some research suggests that the criminal disparity between the sexes is far less pronounced in the lower social classes (Hagan, Gillis, & Simpson, 1985).

Certain offenses, of course, are defined in such a way as to disproportionately criminalize males or females. Rape is defined so that virtually all people arrested for this crime are men. Prostitution laws, on the other hand, are far more likely to result in the arrest of women.

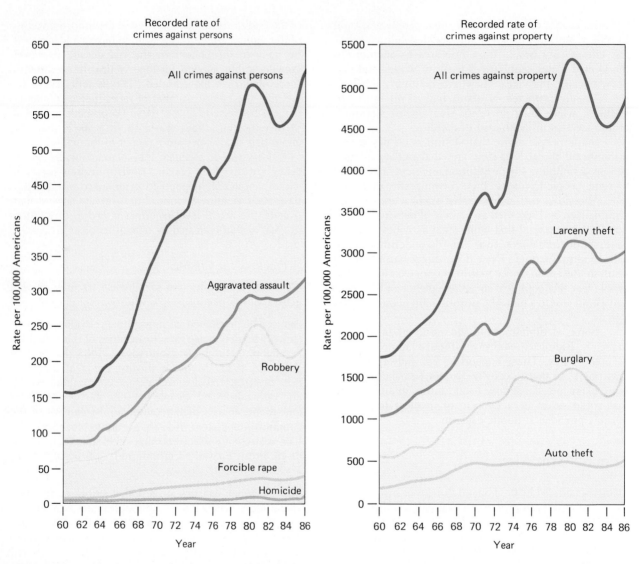

Figure 8–1 Crime Rates in the United States, 1960–1986.

Evidence suggests that the disparity in the official statistics is somewhat greater than the actual difference in male and female criminality (Cernkovich & Giordano, 1980). This may be due to the reluctance of law enforcement officials and the public as a whole to label women as criminal. It has also been suggested that the female crime rate has recently been moving closer to that of men, perhaps because of increasing sexual equality in American society. One study suggests that "as egalitarian forces expand, so too will the crime rate of the female"

(Adler & Adler, 1979:527). In support of this assertion, between 1977 and 1986 the crime rate for females rose faster (22.6 percent) than for males (17.3 percent). More recently, patterns of delinquency among daughters were found to resemble those of sons in families in which males and females tended to have equal power (Hagan, Simpson, & Gillis, 1987). Also worth noting is the fact that the greatest differences in crime rates of the two sexes are found in societies that limit the social opportunities of women the most (Blum & Fisher, 1980).

In societies such as Saudi Arabia, the fact that women have relatively little personal autonomy means that crime rates for females are extremely low.

Social class. Many Americans associate criminality with poverty, although sociological research has found that the relationship between criminality and what is commonly called social class (discussed at length in Chapter 10) is quite complex. To a large extent, the relationship depends on exactly how one defines crime.

There is general agreement that the serious crimes described earlier are more common among people of lower social standing (Wolfgang, Figlio, & Sellin, 1972; Elliott & Ageton, 1980; Braithwaite, 1981; Thornberry & Farnsworth, 1982). A similar pattern has been found in other societies as well (Clinard & Abbott, 1973). It is important to add that people of lower social standing are disproportionately the *victims* of these crimes as well.

Some sociologists, however, have challenged this link between crime and class (Tittle & Villemez, 1977; Tittle, Villemez, & Smith, 1978). They claim that the appearance of higher criminality among poorer people reflects the historical tendency for poorer people to be arrested and convicted more readily than "more respectable" people with higher social standing. As this bias in the criminal justice system has steadily lessened, the argument continues, criminality among various segments of the population has become more equal.

The evidence at hand suggests that this matter can be resolved in the following way. First, street crime does appear to be more frequent among people of lower social position, although this is not the same as stating that all or even most poor people are criminals. On the contrary, there is evidence that a large proportion of crimes are committed by a small number of hard-core offenders (Wolfgang, Figlio, & Sellin, 1972; Elliott & Ageton, 1980). Second, as John Braithwaite notes, the connection between social standing and criminality "depends entirely on what form of crime one is talking about" (1981:47). If one expands the definition of crime beyond street crime to include white-collar crime, there is little doubt that the typical criminal is not only older but also of much higher social position.

Race. The relationship between race and criminality is also quite complex. Government statistics indicate that the majority (70.6 percent) of people arrested for serious crimes in the United States in 1986 were white. At the same time, blacks were more likely than whites to be arrested for these kinds of crimes in relation to their numbers. Blacks, who are about 12 percent of the American population, accounted for about 27.7 percent of all arrests for serious crimes in 1986. For crimes against property, blacks represented 32.6 percent of all arrests. For crimes against persons, the proportion is greater still: 45.4 percent of persons arrested were black (U.S. Federal Bureau of Investigation, 1987).

Just as Americans, especially the white majority, have long linked criminality to the poor, so have they linked criminality to being black (and particularly to being young, black, and male). On the face of it, the official arrest statistics support this conclusion. Furthermore, there is ample evidence that violence is a central element of the social environment of many poor blacks (Silberman, 1980; Brown, 1984). This fact is most evident in the relative incidence of homicide among blacks and whites, as shown in Table 8–3.

For three reasons, however, no simple conclusions about crime and race are warranted. First, arrest records are not statements of proven guilt. Insofar as cultural prejudices have led the police to arrest blacks more readily than whites, or white citizens to more readily report blacks to the police as potential offenders, blacks have

Table 8–3 THE RISK OF BECOMING A MURDER VICTIM IN THE UNITED STATES

Blacks		Whites	
Males	Females	Males	Females
1 out of 21	1 out of 104	1 out of 131	1 out of 369

SOURCE: Data from Patrick A. Langan and Christopher A. Innes, "The Risk of Violent Crime," *Bureau of Justice Statistics: Special Report* (Washington, DC: U.S. Department of Justice, 1985).

been overly criminalized. The same prejudices, of course, may work in the courtroom. Even small biases on the part of law enforcement officials and the public will, in the long run, substantially distort the official record of black crime (Liska & Tausig, 1979; Unnever, Frazier, & Henretta, 1980; Smith & Visher, 1981).

The second problem is that race in the United States is closely related to overall social standing, which we have already shown affects the likelihood of engaging in street crimes. Research by Judith and Peter Blau (1982) helps to sort out the links among race, poverty, and criminality. In a study of 125 large American cities, the Blaus concluded that high rates of criminality—especially violent crime—were caused primarily by income disparity. In other words, they found little evidence to suggest that higher black criminality is due to the existence of criminal subcultures, nor did they find that poverty *in itself* accounted for much crime. The most important factor, they concluded, is relative inequality of wealth, or *poverty amidst affluence*. In a rich society, those who suffer the many daily hardships associated with poverty may experience personal despair and perceive society as unjust. This perception, the Blaus maintain, provides the impetus to crime. Because almost half of all black children grow up in poverty (in contrast to about one in six white children), and unemployment among black adults is two to three times higher than among whites, we would expect crime rates for blacks to be higher (Sampson, 1987).

The third problem, which was noted earlier, is that white-collar crimes are excluded from official statistics. Clearly, this contributes to the view of the typical criminal as not only poor but also black. When such crimes as insider stock trading, dumping industrial wastes, embezzlement, bribery, and cheating on income tax returns are included, the typical criminal turns out to be richer and more often white.

Crime in Cross-Cultural Perspective

We have seen that official criminality is highly variable within our population. But in relation to other industrialized societies, the crime rates of the United States as a whole are quite high. For example, Marshall Clinard (1978) cites Switzerland as an industrial society in which there is far less crime than in the United States. On an annual basis, he points out, only a few murders occur even in the largest Swiss cities. In contrast, New York City led all American cities with 1,582 murders in 1986; on only eight days of the year did no homicide occur. Another forty-eight cities had more than 50 murders each (U.S. Federal Bureau of Investigation, 1987:63–110). Property crimes are also far more common in the United States than in Switzerland; the American robbery rate, for example, is about twenty-five times higher (Clinard, 1978:38). Although many Western European societies have more crime than Switzerland, almost all have far less crime than the United States.

Elliot Currie (1985) suggests that America's high crime rate can be attributed to several cultural patterns that distinguish the United States from European industrial societies. He claims that American culture places such high emphasis on individual economic success that family and community life are often weakened in the process. Currie also notes that, unlike European nations, the United States has neither a government-guaranteed minimum family income level nor publicly funded child-care programs. These factors combine to weaken the fabric of society, which in Europe is a strong defense against crime. Furthermore, Currie asserts that the high level of unemployment and underemployment traditionally tolerated in the United States (and increasingly, in Western Europe as well) helps create a large and perpetually poor category of people whose opportunities to make money are often limited to crime. Perhaps the powerful American idea of individualism would promote crime no matter what policies were adopted by the government. However, Currie believes that the American emphasis on building up police forces and meting out stiff sentences in courts diverts attention from what he sees as the underlying causes of crime in American society.

All the available statistics indicate that crime rates in the nonindustrial societies of the world are also generally lower than those found in the United States. Some nonindustrial societies (in Latin America, for instance) have high rates of violent crime, but their property crime rates are generally quite low by American standards. With industrialization, however, crimes involving prop-

The police represent the most common point of contact between the public and the criminal justice system. Deciding whether to make an arrest or just talk things over is often a matter of police discretion.

erty tend to increase. This is probably because industrialization, with its emphasis on individual achievement, often disrupts the family and neighborhood relationships that have traditionally inhibited criminality (Clinard & Abbott, 1973).

Elements of the Criminal Justice System

The criminal justice system provides the formal means of reacting to crime in the United States. Important elements of this system are the police, the courts, and the punishment of convicted offenders.

The Police

The police are the most common point of contact between the public and the criminal justice system. In principle, the police maintain public order by enforcing the law in a uniform manner. In reality, however, the roughly 700,000 full-time police in the United States (in 1985) cannot effectively monitor the activities of some 240 million Americans. As a result, the police exercise considerable discretion about which situations warrant their attention and how to handle those situations.

In a study of police behavior in five cities, Douglas Smith and Christy Visher (1981) identified factors that affect typical police behavior in situations potentially defined as criminal. These researchers emphasize that once the police enter a situation, they must often act quickly. Therefore, they rely on external cues to guide their actions.

According to Smith and Visher, the legal seriousness of the offense is one important determinant of police behavior. Not surprisingly, police are more likely to make an arrest for a serious offense than for an offense that is deemed to be of minor importance. Second, police responded to the desires of the victim. In general, victims are likely to request that an arrest be made in cases of serious crime; they also do so more commonly if the suspect is male rather than female. This finding suggests one reason that males greatly outnumber females among those who are arrested. Third, police are more likely to make an arrest when dealing with uncooperative suspects. Smith and Visher report that this factor favors neither male nor female suspects, who were equally likely to act in an uncooperative manner. Fourth, the presence of bystanders increases the likelihood of arrest. Smith and Visher suggest that police wish to appear in control of a situation, so the presence of observers encourages them to act more assertively. In addition, making an arrest allows the police to redefine the stage of negotiation—that is, to move the situation from the street to the police department. Fifth and finally, Smith and Visher conclude that, all else being equal, police are more likely to arrest black suspects than white suspects. Apparently, black skin is an external cue that suggests to police either than the suspect is more dangerous or more likely to be guilty. In any event, this factor surely contributes to the disproportionately high level of arrests among blacks.

All in all, it is not surprising that the number of police relative to population is greatest in cities with high concentrations of blacks and high income disparities between the rich and the poor (Jacobs, 1979). This finding makes sense in relation to Judith and Peter Blau's (1982) conclusion that income disparity is linked to criminal violence. It would seem, then, that the police are a source of social control concentrated in areas of likely social disruption.

The Courts

After arrest by the police, a suspect's guilt or innocence is determined by a court. In principle, our court system is based on an adversarial process involving attorneys—

who represent the defendant on the one hand and the state on the other—in the presence of a judge who takes responsibility for following proper legal procedures. In practice, however, roughly 90 percent of all criminal cases are resolved prior to court appearance through **plea bargaining**—*a process of legal negotiation in which the prosecution agrees to reduce the charge against a defendant in exchange for a guilty plea.* For example, a defendant charged with burglary may agree to plead guilty to the lesser charge of possession of burglary tools; another charged with selling cocaine may agree to plead guilty to mere possession.

The major reason for the widespread use of plea bargaining is that it allows the courts to avoid the time and expense of trying most cases. A trial is largely unnecessary if there is little disagreement as to the facts of the case. Furthermore, by selectively trying only a small proportion of all cases, the courts can channel their resources into those cases deemed most important (Reid, 1982).

On the other side of the coin, defendants (some of whom may actually be innocent) are pressured to plead guilty. Insisting on a trial carries the risk of being found guilty and receiving a more severe sentence. Thus plea bargaining undercuts the right of all defendants to be tried in a court of law according to the adversarial process. According to Abraham Blumberg (1970), defendants who have little understanding of the criminal justice system, as well as those who cannot afford a good lawyer, are likely to suffer from this system of "bargain-counter justice."

Punishment

In 1831, upon conviction for the crime of setting fire to a house in an English town, a nine-year-old boy was hanged (Kittrie, 1971:103). Aside from reminding us that in the not-too-distant past children were treated very much like adults (Chapter 5), this incident raises questions about how and why a society punishes offenders. * Punishment is generally considered to provide some combination of the following four benefits to society.

---

* A surprising fact is that, at the end of 1985, two states (Indiana and Vermont) legally recognized the right to execute children as young as ten years of age; another twelve states had laws allowing the execution of offenders under eighteen years of age. Fourteen states (and the federal government) had no minimum age for executions (U.S. Bureau of Justice Statistics, 1986).

Retribution. Perhaps the most important justification for punishing offenders is **retribution,** which means *subjecting an offender to suffering comparable to that caused by the offense as an act of social vengeance.* Retribution is based on a view of society as a system of moral balance. Criminality upsets this balance, but punishment serves to restore the moral order, as suggested in the ancient dictum "An eye for an eye." Thus while a minor theft is avenged by mild punishment such as a fine or being placed on probation, a serious crime such as murder demands a long period of imprisonment or even the death of the offender.

Retribution is probably the oldest of all justifications for punishment. During the Middle Ages, crime was widely viewed as sin—an offense against God as well as society—and resulted in punishments that appear harsh by today's standards. Although retribution is sometimes criticized today because it involves no effort to reform the offender, it remains a strong justification for punishment.

Deterrence. The second justification for punishment is **deterrence,** which refers to *the attempt to reduce criminal activity by instilling a fear of being punished.* Deterrence is based on the view of human behavior as calculating and rational that emerged at the end of the Middle Ages. From this point of view, people engage in crime or other types of deviance for personal gain. If people think that deviance will result in punishment that outweighs any gain, however, such behavior is unlikely to occur.

The idea of deterrence was initially part of a reform movement that sought to curb what were perceived as excessive punishments based on retribution. Why put someone to death for an act of arson or theft, for example, if lesser suffering is sufficient to deter such crimes? As the usefulness of deterrence became more widely accepted, the execution and physical mutilation of criminals was gradually replaced by milder forms of punishment such as imprisonment.

Punishment may serve as deterrence in two ways. *Specific deterrence* demonstrates to the offender that crime does not pay, making a subsequent offense by that person less likely. Punishment is also a means of *general deterrence* in that it inhibits others who realize that the pains of punishment outweigh the pleasures of deviance.

Social protection. The third justification for punishment is *social protection*, which simply means that incarceration or execution renders an offender incapable of committing further offenses. Like deterrence, this is a rational approach to punishment that seeks to protect society from crime. In the case of incarceration, of course, social protection is limited by the fact that the vast majority of prisoners and mental patients return to society.

Rehabilitation.   The fourth justification of punishment is **rehabilitation**—*reforming the offender so that subsequent offenses will not occur.* This justification for punishment accompanied the development of the social sciences in the nineteenth century as the effects of social forces on individuals became recognized. Crime and other types of deviance came to be understood as the consequences of an unfavorable social environment, such as lack of parental supervision or poverty. But just as offenders could learn to go wrong, so could they learn to obey the rules. Therefore, prisons became *reformatories* or *houses of correction* that had as their goal the rehabilitation of offenders within a carefully controlled environment (recall Goffman's description of total institutions in Chapter 5). In principle, rehabilitation held the promise that, once released, offenders would pose little or no threat to society.

Rehabilitation is similar to deterrence in that both attempt to educate the offender to conform to conventional norms. But an emphasis on constructive improvement of the offender distinguishes rehabilitation from retribution, which simply subjects the offender to suffering. In addition, while retribution demands that the punishment fit the crime, rehabilitation links punishment to the perceived needs of the offender. Thus identical offenses might result in different punishments if offenders are thought to substantially differ.

Rehabilitation raises some difficult questions, especially in an era of "medicalizing" deviance. To what degree does society have the right to change the offender, especially in the aftermath of a relatively trivial deviant act? Does criminality—even that defined as "sick"—justify the use of behavior-modification techniques such as drugs or electric shocks? What about noncriminal deviance? Punishment in the form of enforced therapy is especially likely to occur when deviance is defined as mental illness (Kittrie, 1971). As noted earlier, this is precisely why Thomas Szasz so vigorously opposes the use of the label of insanity.

Table 8–4 provides a summary of the four justifications of punishment.

Table 8–4   FOUR JUSTIFICATIONS OF PUNISHMENT: A SUMMARY

Retribution	Probably the earliest justification. Crime is viewed as sin that can be atoned for through punishment. As a moral matter, punishment should be comparable to crime in severity.
Deterrence	An early modern approach. Crime is viewed as a social disruption, so society acts to control crime. Views people as rational and self-interested and assumes the pains of punishment need only offset pleasures of crime to deter.
Social Protection	Closely related to deterrence. Society acts to protect its members by preventing offenders from committing further crimes. Can take many forms, including incarceration and execution.
Rehabilitation	A more modern approach. Crime is viewed as the product of social problems (such as poverty) or of personal problems (such as mental illness). Offenders are reformed or subjected to medical intervention appropriate to their "sickness."

The consequences of punishment.   Although these four justifications of punishment are widely acknowledged, demonstrating the actual consequences of punishment is extremely difficult.

The value of retribution is related to Durkheim's ideas about the functions of punishment presented earlier in this chapter. Recall that Durkheim believed that responding to norm violations tends to increase people's awareness of shared moral sentiments. When society punishes a person for what it considers a moral offense, everyone experiences some sense of retribution. This is also why punishment was traditionally carried out in public. Public executions occurred in England until 1868; the last public execution in the United States took place in Kentucky in 1936. Today, however, the mass media ensure that the public is aware of executions carried out within the prison walls (Kittrie, 1971). Nonetheless, it is difficult to demonstrate scientifically that punishment upholds social morality. Moreover, punishment often advances one conception of social morality at the expense of another, as in the case of imprisoning those who object to military service.

The effectiveness of punishment as a specific deterrence is also questionable in light of the high rate of

The Death Penalty

The punishment of death—often inflicted slowly and painfully—was commonplace through much of human history. Today, legal execution is carried out in a more humane manner in the United States through (according to frequency of state laws) lethal injection (16), electrocution (15), lethal gas (8), hanging (4), and firing squad (2). Nonetheless, the death penalty remains the most controversial form of punishment. In the thirty-seven states that had a death penalty in 1985, execution was reserved for so-called capital offenses such as homicide. National surveys have found that capital punishment has the support of almost three-fourths of American adults (N.O.R.C., 1987). Yet almost all societies in Western Europe and South America have abolished the death penalty.

Defenders of the death penalty claim that executions serve the interests of society in three major ways. First, the ultimate punishment is morally justified—and perhaps even demanded—as retribution for a serious crime such as a brutal homicide. Second, the death penalty certainly addresses the issue of social protection since offenders who are executed can inflict no further social injury. Third, it is argued that capital punishment deters serious crime. In other words, if the death penalty were abolished, the homicide rate would rise.

Critics of the death penalty take issue with each of these arguments. First, if murder is morally wrong, they

Lethal injections are an increasingly common method of execution. To some, they render a necessary process more humane; others, however, oppose all forms of capital punishment.

suggest, so is killing carried out under the law. In addition, the death penalty creates the intolerable possibility that innocent people will be executed. Just as important, biases within the criminal justice system have the effect of sentencing blacks to death more readily than whites, and males more readily than females. Second, critics suggest that imprisonment of dangerous offenders is sufficient to protect society. Moreover, legally sanctioned

killing threatens society by encouraging violence as a means of solving problems. Third, critics argue that the death penalty is of questionable value as a deterrent because many killings are crimes of passion rather than rational acts.

Sociological research has provided some evidence that bears on this controversy. The justification of the death penalty as a form of retribution, of course, is a matter of moral judgment rather than factual truth—no scientist can demonstrate that killing a serious offender is right or wrong in terms of retribution. But sociological research has demonstrated that capital punishment has only limited value as a deterrent to serious crime. For example, studies have shown that the presence of the death penalty in some states has not resulted in lower homicide rates. Homicide rates do appear to decline somewhat in the month following a widely publicized execution, but this does not appear to be a very powerful effect (Stack, 1987). Finally, many societies that have no capital punishment have lower homicide rates than the United States (Sutherland & Cressey, 1978: 342–345).

Despite so little scientific evidence to support the deterrence value of the death penalty, capital punishment continues to be supported by most Americans, presumably on the grounds of retribution. This is likely to continue as long as the fear of violent crime remains high in the United States.

criminal recidivism, *subsequent offenses by people previously convicted of crimes.* Recidivism characterizes about one in every four convicted persons (Bowker, 1982; Vold & Bernard, 1986). A further problem is that about half of all crimes are not known to police, and only about one crime in five that does come to the attention of the police results in an arrest. Statistically, at least, potential offenders have good reason to believe that their crimes will never be punished. General deterrence is even more difficult to investigate scientifically since we have no way of knowing how people might act were they *not* aware of punishments applied to others. The box describes the lively debate over whether legal executions have had the intended effect of reducing capital crimes such as homicide (Glaser & Ziegler, 1974; Bowers & Pierce, 1975; Sellin, 1980; van den Haag & Conrad, 1983; Lester, 1987).

Efforts at rehabilitation have also been controversial. Prisons clearly accomplish social protection simply by keeping offenders off the streets; however, prison provides very little in the way of socially constructive learning. In fact, following Sutherland's theory of differential association, placing a person among criminals for a long period of time is likely to result in that person learning *more* criminal attitudes and skills. Prisons' potential for rehabilitation is also decreased by the widespread physical and sexual violence within them. In addition, people who are imprisoned acquire the stigma of being ex-convicts, an obstacle to successful integration into the larger society. One study involving young offenders in Philadelphia found that boys who were punished severely, and were therefore more likely to acquire a criminal stigma, later committed both more crimes and more serious ones (Wolfgang, Figlio, & Sellin, 1972).

Finally, we have already noted that only about one-third of all crimes become known to the police, and only about one-fifth of these result in an arrest. Since many arrests do not result in court convictions, only a small percentage of all crimes actually result in punishment. Therefore, one can hardly expect punishment to eliminate crime. Just as important, punishment does nothing to affect the gross disparities of wealth or other causes of crime within society itself.

SUMMARY

1. Deviance refers to a wide range of norm violations. Crime is one type of deviance, involving norms formally enacted into criminal law.

2. Deviance is related to the operation of society because (1) it exists only in relation to cultural norms, (2) it depends on a process of social definition, (3) both the creation of norms and the designation of people as offenders are influenced by the distribution of social power.

3. Biological explanations of crime began with Lombroso's research in the nineteenth century and continue today in the form of research in human genetics. Biological theories have provided relatively little understanding of crime.

4. Psychological explanations of crime and other types of deviance focus on abnormalities in the individual personality, which arise from either biological causes or the social environment. Psychological theories have been relatively successful in explaining some kinds of deviance.

5. Sociology links deviance to the operation of society rather than the deficiencies of individuals. Using the structural-functional paradigm, Durkheim pointed to several functions of deviance for society as a whole. Other contributions of structural-functional theory include Merton's strain theory and various theories of criminal subcultures.

6. The symbolic-interaction paradigm is the basis of labeling theory, which views deviance as being created through a process of social reaction and definition. Labeling theory has focused especially on secondary deviance, including the formation of deviant careers as a result of acquiring the stigma of deviance. Sutherland's differential-association theory states that deviance is learned in the same way as any other social behavior.

7. Social-conflict theory directs attention to the relationship between deviance and patterns of social inequality. Drawing on the ideas of Karl Marx, Spitzer suggests that laws and other norms reflect the interests of the most powerful people in society. Furthermore, deviant

labels are most likely to be applied to problem populations that threaten the capitalist system. Social-conflict theory also directs attention to white-collar crimes that cause extensive social harm, although the offenders are rarely defined as criminals.

8. Government statistics indicate that crime rates peak in adolescence, then drop steadily with advancing age. Males are arrested about four times as often as females.

9. People of lower social position tend to commit more street crime than Americans with greater social privilege. When white-collar crimes are included in the overall category of criminal offenses, however, this disparity is lessened.

10. Although most street crimes are committed by whites, blacks commit more crime in relation to their numbers. Eliminating all racial bias from the criminal justice system and including white-collar crimes, however, lessens this disparity.

11. The police exercise considerable discretion in their work, often relying on external cues when deciding whether to make an arrest. Research suggests that the seriousness of the offense, the wishes of the victim, the presence of bystanders, belligerence on the part of suspects, and being male and black all make arrest more likely.

12. The ideal adversarial procedure of American courts is typically replaced in practice by the system of plea bargaining. While plea bargaining allows for more efficient processing of cases, less powerful people tend to suffer from this procedure.

13. Punishment is justified in terms of retribution, deterrence, social protection and rehabilitation. The consequences of punishment are difficult to evaluate scientifically. As a result, like deviance itself, punishment is a matter of considerable controversy.

KEY CONCEPTS

crime the violation of norms that have been formally enacted into criminal law

crimes against the person (violent crimes) crimes against people that involve violence or the threat of violence

crimes against property (property crimes) crimes that involve theft of property belonging to others

criminal justice system the formal process by which society reacts to alleged violations of the law through the use of police, courts, and punishment.

criminal recidivism subsequent offenses by people previously convicted of crimes

deterrence reducing criminal activity by instilling the fear of being punished

deviance the recognized violation of cultural norms

juvenile delinquency the violation of legal standards by children or adolescents

labeling theory the assertion that deviance and conformity are the result of the process by which individuals are defined or labeled by others

medicalization of deviation viewing as medical matters patterns of behavior previously understood in moral terms

plea bargaining a process of legal negotiation in which the prosecution agrees to reduce the charge against a defendant in exchange for a guilty plea

rehabilitation reforming the offender so that subsequent offenses will not occur

retribution subjecting an offender to suffering comparable to that caused by the offense itself as an act of social revenge

retrospective labeling the interpretation of a person's past in terms that are consistent with a present deviant label

stigma a powerful negative social label that radically changes a person's social identity and self-concept

victimless crimes violations of law in which there are no readily apparent victims

white-collar crime crimes committed by people of high social position in the course of their occupations

SUGGESTED READINGS

This text provides a closer look at many of the issues discussed in this chapter, including a review of relevant theory and research.

Allen E. Liska. *Perspectives in Deviance.* 2nd ed. Englewood Cliffs, NJ: Prentice-Hall, 1987.

These two books are valuable as efforts to include women in the study of deviance. The first explains how women have been largely ignored up to the present; the second focuses labeling theory on women.

Eileen B. Leonard. *Women, Crime and Society: A Critique of Theoretical Criminology.* New York: Longman, 1982.

Edwin M. Schur. *Labeling Women Deviant: Gender, Stigma, and Social Control.* Philadelphia: Temple University Press, 1983.

This paperback examines the history and contemporary controversies surrounding punishment in the United States.

Charles W. Thomas. *Corrections in America: Problems of the Past and the Present.* Newbury Park, CA: Sage, 1987.

This text explores mental illness, including a discussion of the distribution of mental illness within the American population, and the social role of the mental patient.

Bernard J. Gallagher III. *The Sociology of Mental Illness.* 2nd ed. Englewood Cliffs, NJ: Prentice-Hall, 1987.

Poor children, the children of criminal parents, and children subject to political repression are imprisoned around the world, often in brutal environments. This book draws together reports and analyses from various societies concerning this human problem.

Katarina Tomasevski. *Children in Adult Prisons: An International Perspective.* New York: St. Martin's Press, 1986.

A thorough exploration of the issue of white-collar crime is found in the following paperback:

David R. Simon and D. Stanley Eitzen. *Elite Deviance.* 2nd ed. Boston: Allyn and Bacon, 1986.

The extent and character of police misconduct are examined in this comparative study of New York, London, and Amsterdam.

Maurice Punch. *Conduct Unbecoming: The Social Construction of Police Deviance and Control.* New York: Tavistock, 1985.

Organized crime around the world is the focus of this collection of thirteen essays.

Robert J. Kelly, ed. *Organized Crime: A Global Perspective.* Totowa, NJ: Rowman & Littlefield, 1986.

Writing that "there are a number of regions on our globe where difference of opinion is the primary cause of death," this author has woven interviews into a broad portrait of dissent in the United States.

John Langston Gwaltney. *The Dissenters: Voices from Contemporary America.* New York: Random House, 1986.

A "fence" is a buyer and seller of stolen goods. A long-time fence provides the basis for this lively look at the world of illegal business.

Darrell J. Steffensmeier. *The Fence: In the Shadow of Two Worlds.* Totowa, NJ: Rowman & Littlefield, 1986.

The deaf have long been defined as deviant by hearing people. Unusual insights into the relation between deafness and deviance can be drawn from this study of deaf people on Martha's Vineyard, Massachusetts. For some two hundred years, this island had a high rate of deafness, to the extent that deafness became part of "normal" life.

Nora Ellen Groce. *Everyone Here Spoke Sign Language: Hereditary Deafness on Martha's Vineyard.* Cambridge: Harvard University Press, 1985.

This government publication examines the victims of crime in the United States and in selected societies around the world.

Richard Block, ed. *Victimization and Fear of Crime: World Perspectives.* Washington, DC: U.S. Department of Justice, Bureau of Justice Statistics, 1984.

CHAPTER 9

Social Stratification

On April 10, 1912, the ocean liner *Titanic* left the docks of Southampton in England on its maiden voyage across the North Atlantic to New York. A proud symbol of the new industrial age, the ship boasted the most sophisticated technology of its time and towered eleven stories above the water. Twenty-three hundred passengers were on board, some of them enjoying accommodations more luxurious than most of today's travelers could imagine. The lower decks, however, were crowded with poor immigrants, journeying to what they hoped would be a better life in the United States.

On April 14, the crew received reports of icebergs in the area but paid little notice. Then, near midnight, as the ship steamed swiftly and silently westward, a lookout was stunned to see a massive shape looming out of the dark ocean directly ahead. Moments later, the ship collided with a huge iceberg, almost as tall as the *Titanic* itself, which buckled the seams in the hull along the starboard side. The sea exploded into the ship's lower levels, and within twenty-five minutes the order was given to begin deploying the lifeboats. By 2:00 A.M., the bow of the *Titanic* was already submerged and the stern was rising high above the water. There, those in the lifeboats could see hundreds of helpless passengers solemnly passing the final minutes before the ship disappeared into the frigid water (Lord, 1976).

The world was shocked by the tragic loss of over

sixteen hundred lives and by the speed with which a ship thought to be unsinkable had been claimed by the North Atlantic. Looking back at this terrible event using the sociological perspective, however, we see that some categories of passengers had much better odds of survival than others. Of those holding first-class tickets, over 60 percent survived, primarily because they were on the upper decks where warnings were sounded first and where lifeboats were most available. Only 36 percent of the

second-class passengers survived; and of the third-class passengers on the lower decks, only 24 percent escaped drowning. On board the *Titanic*, class turned out to mean more than the degree of luxury of accommodations: it was truly a matter of life or death.

This story is a dramatic illustration of the consequences of social inequality, which can make an enormous difference in the way people live—and often whether they live at all. This chapter introduces a number of major concepts and important sociological ideas concerned with social stratification. Chapter 10 continues this analysis with a focus on how social stratification shapes life in the United States.

WHAT IS SOCIAL STRATIFICATION?

Within every society, some people have more valued resources—including money, housing, education, health, and power—than others do. Patterns of this sort are commonly referred to as *social inequality*. But we must be careful to recognize that social inequality is not just a matter of *people* but also of the *society* in which they live. Therefore, sociologists use the concept **social stratification** to mean *a system by which entire categories of people within a society are ranked in a hierarchy*. To begin to understand social stratification, keep in mind four important principles.

1. *Social stratification is a characteristic of society, not simply of individuals.* Social stratification is a society-wide system that unequally distributes social resources among categories of people. In the most technologically primitive societies—the hunting and gathering societies described in Chapter 4—so little was produced that social stratification could exist in only a rudimentary form. In such a situation, whatever social inequality did exist was largely a reflection of differences among individuals: some, for example, might have enjoyed more prestige as a result of their unusual ability to procure food. In more technologically advanced societies, however, social resources are unequally distributed to various social categories in which people find themselves, often with little connection to their personal abilities.

Especially in the individualistic American culture, we easily fall into thinking about inequality in personal terms. We might say, for example, that "The people living on that side of town are lazy and content to live with very little," and contrast them to "The 'beautiful people' on the other side of town who are never satisfied with being less than the best." Without denying that personal traits play a part in shaping one's life chances, it is fair to say that social stratification involves many powerful forces that are simply beyond people's control. Did a higher percentage of the first-class passengers on the *Titanic* survive because they were better swimmers than second- and third-class passengers? Hardly. They fared better because of their privileged position on the ship. In much the same way, American children born into wealthy families are more likely than those born into poverty to be healthy and to live well into old age. Neither rich nor poor children are responsible for creating social stratification, yet this system shapes the lives of them all.

2. *Social stratification is universal and variable.* There is no case of a society completely devoid of social stratification. Though very little social stratification was found among technologically primitive societies, the historical development of productive technology has been accompanied, for better or worse, by more unequal distribution of what has been produced. But if social stratification is universal, it is also highly variable. One worldwide pattern is that social stratification within agrarian societies typically differs from that common to industrial societies. Lesser differences in systems of social inequality also distinguish the industrial societies of the world today.

3. *Social stratification persists over generations.* Social stratification is closely linked to the family, so that children assume the social positions of their parents. As described in Chapter 6, anyone's social position is, at least initially, an *ascribed status*, which is why systems of social stratification tend to have considerable stability. To some degree, however, social position is also an *achieved status* that reflects individual effort or, occasionally, sheer chance. The concept **social mobility** refers to *changes in the social position of people within a system of social stratification*.

Sometimes people experience dramatic upward social mobility. Americans celebrate the achievements of a Michael Jackson, just as many of the British express pride in the accomplishments of Prime Minister Margaret Thatcher, both of whom rose from modest beginnings to become rich and famous. Of course, people also move downward socially because of business setbacks, unemployment, or illness. But more often than not, as explained in Chapter 10, social position remains much the same over a lifetime, and children usually have roughly the same social position as their parents.

4. *Social stratification is supported by patterns of belief.* No system of social stratification is likely to persist over many generations unless it is widely viewed as fair. As noted in earlier chapters, social patterns in any society are commonly perceived as just, and often as "natural." Just as systems of social stratification differ, so do their justifications. This does not mean that everyone embraces a system of inequality to an equal degree. Typically, people with the greatest share of social privileges express the most support for their society's social stratification; those with less are more likely to challenge the system.

Systems of Caste and Class

Comparing social stratification in various societies, sociologists often distinguish systems that are relatively "open"—meaning that considerable social mobility takes place—from those that are relatively "closed"—with little social mobility (Tumin, 1985). On this basis, we can differentiate systems of *caste* from systems of *class*.

The Caste System

A **caste system** refers to *a system of social stratification based almost entirely on ascription.* In other words, caste systems are quite closed, with extremely limited social mobility. As a consequence, people are typically keenly aware of which social category they are in.

Two quite different examples of caste systems are traditional Hindu villages in rural India and the system of apartheid in South Africa. In the Indian caste system, people are born into one of several thousand caste groups—the social categories that define the individual's social position within the local community. In South Africa, the ascribed characteristics of race largely determines a person's social position. About one-seventh of South Africans are whites of European ancestry, approximately the same proportion of Americans who are of African ancestry. Yet, this minority is the dominant social category in terms of wealth and power. About three-fourths of South Africans are black and have relatively little wealth and power. The remaining population includes 3 million "coloreds"—people of mixed race—and about 1 million Asians. The box provides a closer look at the racially based system of social stratification in South Africa.

Caste systems have several other characteristics that are related to the central focus on ascription. First, the family into which a person is born has a great deal to do with a lifetime occupation. In Indian society, for instance, each caste group is traditionally linked to one type of work. The correspondence between caste group and work is far from exact, however, and some occupations (such as agriculture) are open to all. But the members of various caste groups can engage in only a limited range of work. In the same way, whites in South Africa hold almost all occupational positions that provide power and high income, while the black majority is constrained to manual labor and other undesirable occupations.

Second, because the family is the means of passing social position from one generation to the next, a rigid system of social stratification demands that people marry others of the same social position. Sociologists describe this pattern as *endogamous* marriage, in which partners marry *within* social categories rather than *between* them. The traditional pattern in India is for parents to select the marriage partners of their children, often long before the children reach adulthood. Only occasionally does a child of one caste group (usually a female) marry a person of a higher caste group (Srinivas, 1971); such marriages are rare instances of individual social mobility. In South Africa, laws forbidding sexual relationships as well as marriage between the races were eased in 1985, but with little consequence since whites and blacks are still required to live in separate areas.

Third, caste systems are supported by cultural beliefs that are often religious in character. Frequently, the entire social order is believed to be divinely sanctioned, which makes carrying out one's occupational duties and marrying correctly a moral duty (Tumin, 1985). In traditional Indian society, the higher caste groups are relatively "pure," according to Hindu religious beliefs, while lower caste groups are considered to be relatively "polluted." This is a symbolic system that serves to legitimate inequality. For example, occupations, too, are classed as relatively pure or polluted, so that engaging in an occupation beneath one's social position is defined as unclean. Similarly, the belief that a member of a higher caste can be polluted by social contact with a member of a lower caste serves to maintain social distance between the two and, of course, makes intermarriage extremely unlikely. The apartheid system in South Africa has also been maintained through the belief on the part of whites that they are morally superior to the black majority and therefore justified in dominating them.

Moral beliefs of this kind are gradually diminishing in importance in the modern world. Though caste is deeply embedded in Indian social life and persists in rural villages, the caste system is officially illegal and

CROSS-CULTURAL COMPARISON

South Africa—A Racial Caste System

At the southern tip of the African continent, South Africa is a society of about 35 million people in a territory slightly smaller than Alaska. Dutch traders established a settlement there in the mid-seventeenth century. When the British colonized the region early in the nineteenth century, the Dutch settlers moved inland. Early in the twentieth century, the British gained control of what became the Union of South Africa. In 1961, the Republic of South Africa became a politically independent nation.

In order to ensure their political control, the European white minority developed the policy of *apartheid*, or separation of the races. Long an informal practice, apartheid became a matter of law in 1948. Under this system, the black majority does not have South African citizenship, cannot own land, and has no political voice in the government. As a racially based caste, blacks are typically restricted to low-paying occupations that provide an average income only one-fourth that of whites. In the past twenty years, some 3 million blacks have been forcibly relocated to homelands—dirt-poor districts set aside to confine and control the black population. In short, in a land with extensive natural resources, blacks are constrained to poverty while most of the white minority prospers. The dominance of the white minority, which is based on the traditional view of blacks as social inferiors, is backed up by an effective police-security system. Without formal rights, blacks suspected of opposing white rule are subject to arbitrary arrest and indefinite detention.

The plight of black South Africans is evident in housing such as this.

None of this has been sufficient to keep blacks—and a growing number of sympathetic whites—from challenging the apartheid system. Violent confrontations have become more frequent in recent years, and younger blacks are growing increasingly impatient in their demands for political and economic opportunity. Some minor reforms have occurred. In 1984, South Africans of mixed race—called *coloreds*—and Asians were granted some voice in government. In addition, some "petty apartheid" regulations that separate blacks and whites in public places have ended. Blacks have also won the right to form labor unions, which has resulted in significant economic gains for some workers. Indeed, South African foreign minister Roelof Botha recently complained that Americans tend to overlook the reforms that have been made in the

system of apartheid. In addition, Botha noted, Americans seem quick to forget that it took decades to outlaw racial segregation in the United States and that it persists in some forms even today.

But the conflict in South Africa cannot be resolved by minor reforms because the racial caste system is the foundation of South African society. Whites fear—with good reason—that granting full legal rights to the black majority would destroy their privileged position. The black majority, however, appears unlikely to settle for anything less.

SOURCES: George M. Fredrickson, *White Supremacy: A Comparative Study in American and South African History* (New York: Oxford University Press, 1981); George Russell, "Railing Against Racism," *Time*, December 24, 1984, pp. 22–23; Robert B. Cullen, "The Young Lions," *Newsweek*, September 16, 1985, pp. 21–22, 25; "We Cannot Be Held to Ransom," *Time*, June 9, 1986, p. 38; Otto Friedrich, "United No More," *Time*, May 4, 1987, pp. 28–37.

the growing modernization of the country makes it increasingly impractical. Similarly, although the white minority in South Africa is attempting to hold on to its privileged position as long as possible, the system of apartheid is strongly condemned by almost every other society in the world and is slowly breaking down.

The Class System

A caste system that is suitable to stable, agrarian societies is a hindrance to industrialization, which demands new types of education and training. Thus industrialized societies are typically characterized by a **class system**—*a system of social stratification in which individual achievement is of considerable importance*. Within class systems, social categories—or classes—are not as rigidly defined as within caste systems.

Classes are less clearly defined than castes partly because of the relatively high rates of social mobility that characterize industrial societies. This greater social mobility exists for several reasons. First, the democratic political systems commonly found in industrial societies have extended political rights to more and more of the population (Glass, 1954; Blau & Duncan, 1967). While caste groups typically have different standings before the law, class systems tend to embrace the principle (although rarely the practice) of providing equal legal rights to all. Second, the industrial economy of class systems tends to encourage migration from traditional rural villages to cities. By producing more wealth and providing more opportunity for education, cities promote social mobility

In the United States, as in South Africa, nonwhites have traditionally been overrepresented in the menial occupations.

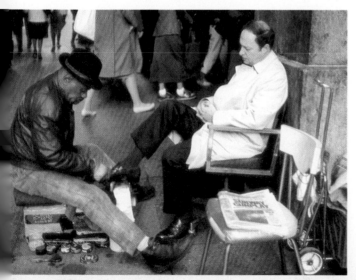

The fabulous success of entertainers such as Bruce Springsteen, whose talent enabled him to rise to superstar status, encourages Americans to believe that social position can reflect personal ability.

(Lipset & Bendix, 1967; Cutright, 1968; Treiman, 1970). Third, industrialization often attracts many immigrants to a society. Immigrants typically take low-paying jobs at the bottom of the social hierarchy, pushing others upward to occupations that provide higher income and more social prestige. Comparative research has shown that those societies with higher rates of immigration are likely to have greater social mobility (Tyree, Semyonov, & Hodge, 1979).

The greater social mobility found in class systems is linked to the belief that individual talents and abilities, rather than birth, are the crucial determinants of social position. In comparison to caste systems, occupations are not rigidly determined by ascription. In addition, although marriage usually joins people of roughly comparable social standing, parents play a smaller part in influencing their children's selection of a mate.

Another distinction between caste and class systems is their characteristic degree of **status consistency,** which means *consistency of social ranking with regard to various dimensions of social inequality*. Caste systems tend to have very high status consistency. Various caste groups differ from one another with regard to symbolic purity, wealth, and power, but any particular caste group has the same relative ranking on all these dimensions. This is another reason that social categories within caste systems are quite clearly defined. Class systems, on the other hand, have less status consistency. People tend to be socially ranked on a number of dimensions—such as amount of wealth, occupational prestige, education, and power—all of which may or may not be consistently high or low. Some people, for example, may be quite wealthy without possessing a corresponding amount of social prestige and social power. One obvious result is that the boundaries between classes are less clear than those that separate castes.

An Illustration: Great Britain

Like the United States and other Western countries, Great Britain is an industrial society with a class system. As is typical of class systems, there is some disagreement about the exact number of classes in British society, and about precisely which people belong in each one.

At the top of British society is a small upper class, probably no more than 1 percent of the population, which is composed of families that have been wealthy for many generations. Such a long period of wealth promotes high status consistency, so that upper-class Britons enjoy high prestige, are educated at expensive, elite universities, and have considerable power to shape British society.

Below the upper class is a broad range of people—perhaps one-fourth of the population—who are often lumped together as "middle class." At the high end of the middle class are the moderately wealthy, including many professionals (such as physicians and attorneys) and those successful in business. During the 1980s, the government has attempted to increase the proportion of Britons owning stocks; by 1987, estimates indicated that about 10 percent did so.* This increase has largely taken place among more wealthy members of the middle class. At the low end of the middle class are families who earn less money and who are likely to have accumulated little wealth. As is typically the case in class systems, people whose social position is near the middle tend to have somewhat lower status consistency than people at the top and those at the bottom of the hierarchy (Gilbert & Kahl, 1987). Thus middle-class Britons, like their counterparts in other industrial societies, often do not

have equal ranking with regard to dimensions of social standing such as income, education, and social prestige derived from occupation. This means, for example, that having enough income to be included in the middle class does not necessarily mean that a person has a college education or a well-regarded job.

Below the middle class, across a boundary that is difficult to place exactly, is Britain's working class. About half of the population is included in this category, typically earning rather low incomes from occupations involving manual labor. During the 1980s, although the British economy as a whole has expanded rapidly, working-class families that depend on the traditional industries such as coal mining or steel production for jobs have been hard hit by unemployment. For those affected, the minimal economic security of working-class life has worsened. Some working-class people have slipped into poverty, joining the roughly one-fourth of Britons who are economically deprived. Lower-class people—or more simply, the poor—are found in all areas of Britain, but are heavily concentrated in northern and western regions plagued by economic decline.

No understanding of Britain's class system today, however, can ignore that nation's past. Unlike the United States, Great Britain existed for many centuries as an agrarian society whose social stratification took the form of a castelike system of three *estates*. As late as the seventeenth century, British society was dominated by the nobility—the highest estate, in which wealth and power were highly concentrated. Representing about 5 percent of the population, members of the nobility owned virtually all the land, which is the basis of wealth in any agrarian society (Laslett, 1984). The ancestors of many of today's upper-class Britons were members of this nobility. Typically, the nobility engaged in no occupation at all; indeed, to be "engaged in trade" or any other type of work for income was deemed inappropriate for a noble. Well cared for by servants, the nobility had a great deal of leisure time to devote to the cultivation of refined tastes in art, music, and literature.

The estate system was maintained by the *law of primogeniture*, by which only the eldest son inherited the property of parents. This had the effect of protecting large landholdings from division among children, so that many vast estates survived for centuries. In the process, however, younger sons were forced to find other means to secure their living. Some entered the clergy—the second estate, whose power was based on extensive church ownership of land. Others became military officers or engaged in some profession. In an age when few women

---

* The proportion was reported as roughly 5 percent in 1979 (Sherrid, 1986).

could expect to earn a living on their own, the lifetime security of a noble family's daughter was typically a matter of marrying well.

Below the nobility and the clergy, the vast majority of English people formed the third estate—the commoners. Commoners typically owned little or no land, which meant most were very poor. Except for those who pursued careers in the cities, the life of the commoner involved working land owned by others and receiving little in return. Unlike the nobility and the clergy, commoners had virtually no access to education, so that they were likely to be illiterate.

As the Industrial Revolution brought a gradual end to Britain's agrarian economy, some commoners engaging in trade gained enough wealth to rival and even surpass that of the nobility. This, coupled to the extension of education and legal rights, has had the effect of blurring social distinctions. A pointed illustration of this fact is found in a recent interview of a descendant of British nobility, now making a living as a writer. Asked if Britain's castelike social barriers had finally begun to break down, she arrogantly retorted, "Of course they have, or I wouldn't be here talking to someone like you!" (New Haven *Journal-Courier*, Nov. 27, 1986).

But while Great Britain's social stratification has become more open, today's class system retains the marks of a long feudal past. First, unlike many other European societies, Britain retains a monarchy and a nobility, some of whom have great wealth that has been passed down through many generations. The British parliamentary system of government also reflects the traditional division between nobility and commoners. The House of Lords is composed of those of ascribed noble rank, although most of their power has been eroded by the more democratic cultural values of the twentieth century. Actual political control of the country resides in the House of Commons, which is made up of those who—in sociological terms—are more likely to have achieved their position through individual effort than to have assumed power solely through ascription.

The second legacy of the estate system is that social mobility in Great Britain is somewhat lower than in America (Kerckhoff, Campbell, & Winfield-Laird, 1985). In contrast to Americans, who live in a culture that strongly emphasizes individual achievement, Britons are relatively more resigned to remaining in the social position to which they were born (Snowman, 1977). Another indication of the greater rigidity of the British class system is the importance of accent as a mark of social position. A person's accent is learned over many years as part of the socialization process, and is not easily changed. Thus families of long-standing affluence tend to speak quite differently from the rest of the population.

Classless Societies

The traditional caste systems of many societies have been transformed into class systems by industrialization. Some industrial societies with socialist economies, however, claim to be classless. One example is the Union of Soviet Socialist Republics (U.S.S.R.), formed through a revolution in 1917 that ended a feudal estate system ruled by a hereditary nobility. The Russian Revolution transferred control of most farms, factories, and other means of production from private ownership to the direct control of the state. As described in Chapter 4, Karl Marx claimed that the private ownership of such productive property is the basis of social classes. The Soviet claim of being classless is therefore based on the elimination of private ownership of productive property.

But classless or not, the Soviet Union is certainly socially stratified (Lane, 1984). Occupations fall into four major categories, listed here in descending order of income, prestige, and power: (1) high government officials; (2) the Soviet intelligentsia, including lower government officials and professional workers such as engineers, scientists, college professors, and physicians; (3) manual workers in state-controlled industries; and (4) the rural peasantry. The Soviets argue that because factories, farms, colleges, and hospitals are owned and operated in the interest of all the people, Soviet society has less social inequality than capitalist societies. They also claim that the Communist Party—which controls Soviet society—attempts to ensure that no segment of the population gains disproportionate power over the others.

Critics of the Soviet Union's claim of being classless argue that occupational differences are, indeed, the basis of social classes. Just as important, they point out, is the fact that the U.S.S.R.'s extensive government bureaucracy affords overwhelming power to a small elite of politicians, military leaders, and scientists. The core of this elite are the roughly 18 million members of the Communist Party (about 6 percent of the population), many of whom enjoy privileges—such as vacation homes, chauffeured automobiles, and access to many consumer goods—not available to the larger population (Zaslavsky, 1982; Theen, 1984). In addition, the children of this elite enjoy special educational advantages and occupational opportunities. The box provides a closer look at the role of the Communist Party in the Soviet system of social stratification.

Although Soviet society cannot accurately be described as classless, the extremes of wealth and poverty in Great Britain and the United States are not found in the Soviet Union. Since elite standing in the Soviet Union is based on positions that provide power rather than great wealth, very few people enjoy a life of luxury free from work. In addition, because work is expected of, and provided for, virtually all Soviet people, there is little of the unemployment and resulting poverty that are found in the United States (Dobson, 1977).

CROSS-CULTURAL COMPARISON

The Soviet Union: Privilege in a "Classless" Society

Based on his travels in the Soviet Union, journalist David K. Shipler argues that the Communist Party plays an important role in the Soviet system of social stratification—up to a point.

Party membership, available to about 6 percent of the population, has . . . been a conduit for the rise of talent from modest backgrounds into positions of leadership, though usually in combination with higher education. Rarely, nowadays, does one find a Politburo or Central Committee member without a higher degree. . . .

Party membership alone guarantees nothing, but a nonmember is usually blocked from holding certain positions in what is called the *nomenklatura*, referring to jobs under the party's jurisdiction and control. The party makes, or at least approves, assignments in such posts as school principal and factory manager. Full-time, paid party work, as opposed to membership that is incidental to a person's main job in a school or a factory, is usually a key to perquisites such as closed shops where imported food, clothing, and electronic equipment are sold; a top spot on the long list of people waiting to buy cars; access to slightly roomier, better-built apartments; and the chance to work or travel abroad. Leading party officials, those in the Council of Ministers, and some members of the Academy of Sciences are paid

partly in "gold rubles" or "certificate rubles," coupons representing rubles exchanged for hard currency and usable in special stores selling imported goods or Soviet merchandise at reduced prices.

Party membership, acquired only upon the recommendation of Komsomol [Young Communist League] and other party officials and following a trial period, is often denied to those with some blemish on their record. The exclusivity adds luster. But nothing is categorical about the relationship between the party and the career; among successful scientists, for example, are both *partiiny* (members) and *bespartiiny* (nonmembers). Some who anticipate stepping into a garden of privilege find the fruits less succulent than imagined. This is especially so among those who remain simple card carriers, without becoming party professionals.

Sergei Polikanov, a party member, nuclear physicist, Lenin Prize winner, full member of the highly selective and elite Academy of Sciences, and head of a nuclear research laboratory at Dubna, a scientists' village north of Moscow, could not get his daughter, Katya, into an institute of psychology because she simply scored too low on the entrance examination. I'm not sure how hard he tried to use whatever pull he had—he is a rather modest man, not given to throwing his weight

around—but the fact was that Katya . . . had to go to work for a year before trying the exams again. . . .

When I asked Sergei Polikanov what privileges he got from being a party member, he couldn't think of any. In fact, his privileges—his pleasant spacious apartment in the lovely Volga River town; his large automobile; his monthly stipend above his generous salary from the academy; his tickets to the Bolshoi; his freedom to mix with Western scientists who came regularly to his institute; his access to Western scientific publications and to sophisticated equipment for his research; his occasional working trips to Western Europe—all were results of his job, his position, and his scientific skill, not of his party membership. However, without the party card he probably could not have risen to such a job. Being in the party said to his superiors, "I'm safe, you're safe, don't worry about me."

When he gave up this coveted position in an elite by becoming an open dissident, he baffled many Russian friends. One thing the citizens of the classless society understand is class.

SOURCE: David K. Shipler, *Russia: Broken Idols, Solemn Dreams* (New York: Times Books/Random House, 1984), pp. 199–200. Copyright © 1983 by David Shipler. Reprinted by permission of Times Books, a Division of Random House, Inc.

Yugoslavia is also a society organized according to Marxist principles of socialism. However, the Yugoslavs have attempted to limit the concentration of power and privilege in the hands of a government elite. In contrast to the centralized government of the U.S.S.R., a self-management system gives decision-making powers to individual factories and local communities. Like the Soviet Union, however, Yugoslavia confers the greatest power and prestige on members of the Communist Party, although party membership counts for less than it does in the Soviet Union.

How common is social mobility in the so-called classless societies such as the Soviet Union? Evidence suggests that during this century there has probably been more upward social mobility in the Soviet Union than in Great Britain or even the United States. To some extent, this is due to the absence of concentrated wealth that can be passed on from generation to generation (Parkin, 1971). But an even more important factor is the rapid industrialization and urbanization the Soviet Union has experienced during this century, which has drawn a large proportion of the working class and rural peasantry upward to occupations in factories and government (Lane, 1984).

Another factor has been the general tendency of the Communist Party to reward individual talent and ability rather than social origins (Katz, 1973). Recently, however, there are signs that social mobility is decreasing (Dobson, 1977; Shipler, 1984). This suggests that the relatively high rate of upward mobility earlier in this century may have been more a consequence of structural changes within Soviet society than a product of socialism per se (Lane, 1984).

This is an example of what sociologists call **structural social mobility,** which is defined as *social mobility on the part of large numbers of people that is due primarily to changes in the society itself, rather than to the efforts and abilities of individuals.* In general, structural social mobility is the result of broad changes in the economy of a society. In the case of Soviet society, industrialization has created a vast number of new jobs that have brought people to cities from rural areas in which farming is the primary livelihood. In much the same way, the growth of government during this century has greatly expanded occupational opportunity, especially at the higher levels. The overall effect is that, in the Soviet Union today, the population enjoys a better standard of living than was the case immediately after the Russian Revolution. As we shall see, much the same process has occurred during this century in the United States.

Institutional Support of Social Stratification

The persistence of social stratification is a topic of great interest to sociologists. On first glance, one might doubt that a society could continue without some efforts to equitably distribute its resources. But we have already seen, for example, that in Great Britain a caste system that placed most of society's wealth and power in the hands of several hundred families lasted for centuries. Just as striking is the Indian caste system in which, for some two thousand years, people appear to have accepted the idea that their lives should be shaped toward privilege or poverty by the accident of birth.

To a large extent, such persistence of social stratification is explained by the support of major social institu-

The Soviet elite is based not so much on wealth as on the enormous power wielded by the governmental bureaucracy.

tions. In effect, patterns of social inequality become "built into" a society to the point that challenging the system is both unlikely and difficult. This fact was certainly recognized by Karl Marx, whose ideas were introduced in Chapter 4. Marx's criticism of capitalism rests on the fact that the economy operates—under *normal* circumstances—to concentrate wealth among a small part of the population. This inequity persists, Marx continued, because the other social institutions serve to support economic inequality (see Figure 4–2 on p. 103). Marriage, for example, affords a means of uniting well-to-do families, so that wealth is passed from generation to generation. Similarly, the political system places the property of the rich under the protection of law and, if necessary, the police. The persistence of social stratification reflects the *institutional control of resources* by a society's elite. Under these circumstances, Marx realized, efforts to establish a new social order are difficult indeed.

But something more is involved because, although revolts and revolutions sometimes occur, history reveals that human beings are remarkably accepting of social inequality. In simple terms, inequality is not typically viewed as injustice. Quite the contrary. In virtually every society, people come to think that social stratification is a matter of fairness. Here, again, social institutions are at work. The capacity to define what is "just" or "natural" in any society represents the *institutional control of ideas*. In our own society, for instance, the educational system instructs children that their society—in most respects, at least—is a model of social good. The religious system also contributes to building "good citizens" by supporting existing social patterns as morally correct. Because culture endorses existing social relations, most people come to accept familiar patterns of social inequality. This explains why people who do challenge social stratification generally question not the system itself but their own place in it.

An important concept linking culture to social stratification is **ideology,** which refers to *ideas that reflect and support the interests of some category of a population.* Recognizing ideas as ideological, in other words, is seeing that they are political and have consequences that favor some people over others. It would be easy to perceive the political character of ideas if ideology were a simple matter of self-serving ideas generated by privileged people in a deliberate, conspiratorial fashion. But ideology is typically a matter of established cultural patterns that define certain social arrangements as "fair," so that certain categories of people are justly entitled to privileges denied to others.

To a large extent, ideology varies according to a society's level of economic and technological development. Early agrarian societies depended heavily on the labor of slaves to carry out all types of manual work. As a result, there flourished an ideological assertion that humans differed greatly in their intellectual capacities. During the celebrated "Golden Age" of ancient Greece, for example, the philosopher Aristotle (384–322 B.C.E.) expressed a common view when he said that some people deserved nothing more than slavery, while their natural "betters" were entitled to be masters. Similarly, mature agrarian societies depend on the continual performance of agricultural labor. This is ensured if people come to believe that occupation should be determined by birth and is a matter of moral necessity. Thus both the European peasant during the Middle Ages and the farmer in a traditional Indian village were likely to see the caste systems of their societies as "natural." Just as important, neither could challenge the system of social inequality without risking moral condemnation. With the rise of industrial capitalism, the interests of a new elite were reflected in cultural values celebrating individualism and achievement. Within a class system, wealth becomes almost synonymous with intelligence and hard work, just as poverty becomes a stigma of personal deficiency.

Those who gathered at Plato's fabled Academy were no cross-section of ancient Greek society. They were wealthy males—the only people that Greek society held to be capable of intellectual pursuits. Like many Americans today, they accepted the privileges as a matter of personal merit.

Ideology: Medieval and Modern Patterns

Cultural ideas that legitimate social stratification vary across history, as they do from society to society. Changing ideological patterns can be illustrated by comparing the justification for social stratification within medieval European societies to that widely applied to modern industrial-capitalist societies.

During the Middle Ages, the estate systems typical of European societies were widely viewed as legitimate on theological grounds. The social order was held to express a divine plan. Believing that they had been placed on earth to carry out God's will, people usually accepted their lot in life, which for most meant laboring in support of the agrarian system. The same view allowed others to take comfort in their privileges, for they, too, were living according to moral neces-

sity. The ideological character of this world view lies in the fact that it clearly confers great advantages on a small minority, while providing far less for the majority. The estate system was able to endure for centuries because it was linked to the will of God, as expressed in the lines of the old Anglican hymn:

The rich man in his castle,
The poor man at his gate,
He made them high and lowly
And ordered their estate.
All things bright and beautiful . . .

During the Industrial Revolution, however, newly rich industrialists gradually displaced the feudal nobility. As they did so, cultural justifications of capitalism emerged. Over time, social stratification based on the

power of birth and divine will was replaced by a new type of ideology based on individual merit. Wealth and privileges were now legitimated as rightfully falling to the talented and hard-working. On the other hand, the poor—in feudal societies, the proper objects of charitable assistance—were scorned as lacking in ambition and ability. This transformation is evident in a comment by the early-nineteenth-century German writer Johann Wolfgang von Goethe:

Really to own what you inherit,
You first must earn it with your merit.

Although the specific patterns differ, in both cases ideology serves to support a concentration of wealth, power, and prestige among the few.

The box illustrates the transformation from the medieval view of social stratification as divinely sanctioned to the more modern assertion that patterns of social inequality are just rewards for personal effort and ability.

The history of human societies clearly shows that institutional support of social stratification is powerful. But challenges to the status quo continue to arise. In such cases, institutional arrangements are called into question, and cultural "truths" become controversial as their political consequences are recognized. American women, for example, have long been deprived of opportunities both by political and familial arrangements and by the ideological notion of female inferiority. While sexual equality is not yet a reality in American society, there is little doubt that the power of patriarchy has greatly diminished during this century. The continuing struggle in South Africa provides another example of widespread rejection of patterns of social inequality. In this case, apartheid—as it has shaped the economic, political, and educational life of South Africa—has never

been widely accepted by blacks and is now losing support as a "natural" system among whites who reject ideological racism (Friedrich, 1987).

THEORETICAL ANALYSIS OF SOCIAL STRATIFICATION

Social insitutions play a major part in maintaining social stratification. But why should such patterns exist at all? Sociologists have developed two major approaches to answering this important question.

Structural-Functional Analysis

Although it differs from one society to another, social stratification is virtually universal. Structural-functional analysis attempts to explain this universality by pointing to the functional consequences that social stratification has for society as a whole.

In 1945, Kingsley Davis and Wilbert Moore first set out a theory of social stratification that has remained influential—and controversial—to this day. The Davis-Moore thesis asserts that some type of social stratification is a social necessity. It claims that occupational positions vary in their importance to society, with the most important generally requiring talents and abilities that are scarce and can be developed only through a long period of expensive education and training. In addition, such positions typically subject individuals to quite a bit of pressure and day-to-day responsibility.

In order to motivate the most able people to aspire to these important positions, society provides considerable social rewards in terms of income, social prestige, power and leisure time. To illustrate, if society considers Supreme Court justices more important than government clerks, it will give greater rewards to justices. Similarly, if the skills and training required to be a physician are more extensive than those needed to be a hospital orderly, physicians will enjoy more rewards. The result of unequal rewards is, of course, a system of social stratification. According to the Davis-Moore thesis, a society could be devoid of social stratification only if every person was equally suited to perform every occupational position.

It is important to note that Davis and Moore were not trying to *justify* social stratification; they were merely attempting to *explain* why it exists. Notice, too, that they did not specify *how much reward* should be attached to any occupational position. Their claim was simply that the necessity of having *some* system of differential rewards provides one explanation of the universality of social stratification.

Evaluation. The Davis-Moore thesis has remained influential because it addresses an important issue. Furthermore, the argument is likely to seem reasonable to many Americans. But not long after it was introduced, Melvin Tumin (1953) directed attention to what he saw as major flaws in the thesis. First, Tumin points out that the functional importance of any occupation is difficult to define precisely without taking into account the relative power of occupational groups in society. For instance, the popular assessment of physicians as very important is shaped by the bargaining power of doctors. Because doctors control the number of people entering the medical profession (through medical school admission policies), they can ensure that physicians remain much in demand. How much of this profession's importance is intrinsic, then, and how much is the result of the political policies of such organizations as the American Medical Association? Moreover, many occupational associations use considerable resources to convince the public of their importance. Furthermore, entertainers are among the highest-paid people in our society. Does this mean that Bill Cosby contributes more to American society in a one-hour nightclub performance than a justice of the Supreme Court does in a year's work? The box provides a closer look at this issue.

Second, Tumin suggests that Davis and Moore distort the consequences social stratification has for the development of some individuals' talents and abilities. The Davis-Moore thesis implies that society operates as a **meritocracy**—*a system of social stratification in which rewards are matched to personal merit*—and therefore encourages all people to develop their abilities. This may be true to a point, but Tumin claims that social stratification has even more *dysfunctional* consequences because it ensures that a great deal of talent and ability will *never* be put to use. This is because families transmit their social position from one generation to the next regardless of the merit of individuals. Moreover, the more rigid the system of social stratification, the more talent and ability that will remain undeveloped. Obviously, the extreme case is a caste system in which individuals assume occupations linked to their social position at birth. But even in more open class systems, bright and ambitious children born into poor families have

Gender plays a major part in social stratification in the United States and elsewhere. Americans are only gradually overcoming the conventional belief that women cannot assume the most responsible positions.

SOCIOLOGY OF EVERYDAY LIFE

How Much Are They Worth?

For an hour of work a Los Angeles priest earns about $3, a bus driver in San Franciso earns about $12, and a Detroit auto worker earns close to $20. John McEnroe earns about $400 for every hour he plays tennis; actor Burt Reynolds earns about $5,000 for every hour he spends making movies; singer/actress Dolly Parton earns about $25,000 for every hour she performs in Las Vegas nightclubs. Bill Cosby, 1987's highest-paid entertainer who expects to earn some $300 million just from *The Cosby Show's* reruns, demands about $100,000 an hour to take the stage.

According to the Davis-Moore thesis, occupations provide rewards according to their functional importance to the operation of society. But is an evening's performance by Bill Cosby in a nightclub worth as much to American society as a year's worth of work by a U.S. Supreme Court justice, who earns about $100,000 annually?

In practice, earnings within the market system of a capitalist economy reflect whatever a person is able to successfully demand. Therefore, star entertainers, the best professional athletes, and many business executives receive salaries fifty to one hundred times higher than the earnings of the average American. Are these people worth such salaries?

Apparently they are if they can get them.

According to a 1984 news report, Angelique Sims—a seventeen-year-old student in New York—had her doubts about the salaries received by some of America's highest-paid people. When her class met with William B. Woodside, head of a major corporation, who was earning $1 million a year, she asked him if that wasn't a lot of money to pay someone. Woodside responded that he deserved this salary because he had made his company highly profitable. But Angelique Sims was unimpressed. "I'll do your job for half your salary," she offered.

---

fewer opportunities to develop all their talents than rich children do. In the same way, half of the American population has traditionally lacked the opportunity to fully develop their abilities simply because our system of social stratification subordinates women to men—the focus of Chapter 12. In sum, Tumin argues that social

stratification ensures that while the talents and abilities of *some* people will be developed to the fullest, those of the majority will never be put to full use.

The third limitation of the Davis-Moore thesis is that it suggests that social stratification benefits all of society, ignoring the fact that social inequality has been

According to the Davis and Moore thesis, greater rewards are accorded to unusually talented people who fill important social roles. However, the fact that superstars such as Bill Cosby earn as much in an hour as members of the Supreme Court do in a year raises questions about whether profits are the best measure of what benefits society.

the basis for social conflict and even outright revolution. For this reason, the social-conflict paradigm has also been used to explain social stratification—with quite a different result.

Social-Conflict Analysis

Rather than describing the positive function of social stratification for society as a whole, social-conflict analysis views patterns of social inequality in terms of conflict between segments of society. This analysis draws heavily on the ideas of Karl Marx; an additional important contribution was made by Max Weber.

Marx's View of Social Class

As explained in Chapter 4, Marx recognized two major social classes reflecting two basic relationships to the means of production: owning productive property and laboring for others. In feudal Europe, the nobility and clergy owned the productive land, while the peasants labored to produce crops. Similarly, in class systems, the capitalists (or the bourgeoisie) own the means of industrial production, while the workers (or proletariat) supply labor. In Marx's view, the great differences in wealth and power between the two classes generate social conflict. With time, he believed, organized efforts by the working majority would lead to the overthrow of capitalism once and for all.

Marx's conflict theory of social stratification was shaped by his own observations of early capitalism in the nineteenth century, when society was clearly divided into capitalists and industrial workers. During this period in the United States, wealthy capitalists such as Andrew Carnegie, J. P. Morgan, and John Jacob Astor (one of the few very rich passengers to perish with the *Titanic*) lived in fabulous mansions filled with priceless art and staffed by dozens of servants. Their incomes were almost unimaginable, even by today's standards. Carnegie, for example, earned over $20 million in 1900, at a time when the average worker received perhaps $500 a year in wages (Baltzell, 1964).

Evaluation. Marx's analysis of social classes has had enormous influence on sociological thinking in recent decades. Still, it can be criticized for overlooking the crucial element of the Davis-Moore thesis: unequal rewards are certainly one important way to motivate people to perform social roles. As we have noted, even in the

William Balfour Ker's painting, "From the Depths," suggests that the privileges of the wealthy rest upon the poverty and suffering of others.

Soviet economy—allegedly based on Marxist principles—some occupations provide much greater rewards than others. Another common criticism of Marx's analysis is that despite striking economic inequality at the turn of the century, America never even approached the socialist revolution he predicted.

Several factors explain why the United States has never come close to having a Marxist revolution (Dahrendorf, 1959). First, the capitalist class became somewhat fragmented over time. Companies that were typically owned by *families* in the nineteenth century are today owned by a large number of *stockholders*. In addition, the executives who direct the day-to-day operations of modern corporations may or may not own a significant share of the companies they manage.

Second, the occupational structure of American society has been transformed over the last century by the so-called white-collar revolution. As Chapter 18 explains in detail, a century ago the vast majority of Americans held **blue-collar jobs:** *occupations that involve mostly manual labor*, in factories or on farms. Today, however, most of the labor force holds **white-collar jobs:** *occupations that involve mostly mental activity and skills not identified with manual labor.* Common examples of white-collar jobs are clerical, sales, or other service work in large, bureaucratic businesses. While there is a lively debate about the extent to which these new white-collar workers resemble the industrial working class described by Marx, evidence suggests that most do not think of themselves in such terms. In other words, the white-collar revolution represents structural social mobility, so that many Americans perceive their own social positions as higher than those held by their parents and grandparents. The overall result is that instead of seeing society as sharply divided between the rich and poor, as Marx did, many Americans see their society as largely middle class (Edwards, 1979; Gagliani, 1981; Wright & Martin, 1987).

Third, the plight of workers is not nearly as desperate today as it was a century ago. Workers now have considerable freedom to organize into labor unions that allow them to make demands of management backed by threats of work slowdowns and strikes. Research suggests that well-established unions have substantially improved the economic standing of many workers (Rubin, 1986). Further, labor and management now engage each other in contract negotiations on a regular basis. Thus, instead of being characterized by conflict, worker-management relations are now institutionalized.

Fourth and finally, legal protection has been widely extended during the last century. There are now laws protecting workers' rights, and workers have greater access to the legal system to see that these laws are enforced. In addition, government programs such as unemployment insurance, disability protection, and social security provide workers with far greater financial security than the capitalists of the last century were willing to grant them.

Taken together, these developments suggest that although American society remains highly stratified, some of capitalism's roughest edges have been smoothed. Consequently, social conflict today is less intense than it was a century ago.

Even so, many sociologists are unwilling to discount Marx's analysis (Miliband 1969; Edwards, 1979; Giddens, 1982; Domhoff, 1983; Stephens, 1986). They respond to the four points made above as follows. First, most corporate stock is owned by only 1 or 2 percent of Americans, an economic elite that includes many top business executives. Second, the white-collar revolution has produced jobs that in many instances provide little more income and power than factory jobs did a century ago. Also, much white-collar work is characterized by the same monotonous routine as factory work, especially the low-level clerical jobs commonly held by women. Third, while labor organizations have certainly advanced the interests of the workers over the last half century, regular negotiations between workers and management do not necessarily signal the end of social conflict. Workers must still struggle to win concessions from capitalists and, increasingly, to hold on to what they already have. Fourth, although workers have gained some legal protections unavailable a century ago, the law has done little to change the overall distribution of wealth in America and—as described in Chapter 8—the rich are still able to use the legal system to far greater advantage than the poor.

According to these critics, then, the fact that no socialist revolution has taken place in the United States does not invalidate many of Marx's observations about capitalism. American cultural values emphasizing competition and individual achievement, as well as the power of American capitalists, have successfully curbed revolutionary aspirations in this country. But as we shall see in Chapter 10, pronounced social inequality persists in American society and so does social conflict—albeit less overtly and violently than in the nineteenth century.

A summary of two contrasting approaches to social stratification is presented in Table 9–1.

Max Weber: Class, Status, and Party

As noted in Chapter 4, many of Max Weber's ideas were a critical response to the work of Karl Marx. Weber, too, understood social stratification primarily in terms of social conflict, but his analysis differs from Marx's in several important respects.

Weber considered Marx's contention that economic factors in industrial societies have produced two major, antagonistic social classes to be too simplistic. Instead, he identified three distinct dimensions of social inequality. First, he used the term *class* to refer to economic inequality. But rather than describing two major social classes, as Marx had done, Weber claimed that even workers differed among themselves in terms of their skills, so that some could command more income than others. For Weber, then, the dimension of class does not refer to neat categories but to a continuum from high to low. Weber's second dimension of inequality was *status*, which refers to an individual's degree of social prestige. Here again, there are no simple categories;

people can only be ranked in relation to one another. Third, Weber noted the importance of power, which he designated as *party*; this dimension also takes the form of a continuum from high to low.

Marx believed that social prestige and power were almost always derived from economic position; thus he saw no reason to treat them as distinct dimensions of social inequality. Weber disagreed, asserting that any individual might have quite different positions on his three dimensions of ranking. For example, a member of the clergy may accumulate little wealth but have a moderate amount of power and a great deal of social prestige. Similarly, a small-business owner may make a great deal of money, but have limited power and social prestige. Overall, then, Weber's view suggests that social stratification within class systems should not be viewed as a matter of clearly defined categories, but rather as a ranking on a multidimensional hierarchy. Sociologists today often describe such a hierarchy as **socioeconomic status**—*a composite social ranking based on various dimensions of social inequality*, including income and wealth, occupation, and education.

Weber's analysis explains the fact that class systems of industrial societies tend to have a lower degree of status consistency than the caste systems found in agrarian societies. Because people can have a varying position on each of these three dimensions of social inequality, industrial societies contain many distinctive social categories, all of which seek to pursue their own particular interests. Thus, while Marx and Weber both recognized social conflict as a prime characteristic of society, Weber saw patterns of social conflict as more variable and complex than did Marx, whose analysis was based on antagonism between two major social classes.

Weber also suggested that each of his three dimensions of social inequality has special importance in history. Agrarian societies, he claimed, place great importance on social prestige, as illustrated by the division of traditional Indian society into many caste groups with varying degrees of symbolic "purity." Newly industrialized societies generate striking economic differences within the population, raising the importance of the economic dimension of class. More mature industrial societies are characterized by the growth of large-scale formal organizations that accord tremendous power to high-ranking officials. In these societies, power becomes an increasingly important dimension of social stratification (Kerbo, 1983).

Finally, recall from Chapter 4 that Marx and Weber disagreed as to the future of industrial-capitalist societies. Because Marx based his analysis of social stratification on economics, he believed that social inequality could be largely eliminated by the abolition of private ownership of productive property. Weber doubted that overthrowing capitalism would greatly diminish social stratification in modern societies, where an increasingly important dimension of social inequality is power derived from one's position within formal organizations. Thus, even in a socialist society such as the Soviet Union, some people still have much more power than others because of their position in the massive governmental system.

Table 9–1 TWO EXPLANATIONS OF SOCIAL STRATIFICATION: A SUMMARY

Structural-Functional Paradigm	Social-Conflict Paradigm
1. Social stratification keeps society operating. The linkage of greater rewards to more important social positions benefits society as a whole.	Social stratification is the result of social conflict. Differences in social resources serve the interests of some and harm the interests of others.
2. Social stratification encourages a matching of talents and abilities to appropriate positions.	Social stratification ensures that much talent and ability within the society will not be utilized at all.
3. Social stratification is both useful and inevitable.	Social stratification is useful to only some people; it is not inevitable.
4. The values and beliefs that legitimate social inequality are widely shared throughout society.	Values and beliefs tend to be ideological; they reflect the interests of the more powerful members of society.
5. Because systems of social stratification are useful to society and are supported by cultural values and beliefs, they are usually stable over time.	Because systems of social stratification reflect the interests of only part of the society, they are unlikely to remain stable over time.

SOURCE: Adapted in part from Authur L. Stinchcombe, "Some Empirical Consequences of the Davis-Moore Theory of Stratification," *American Sociological Review*, Vol. 28, No. 5 (October 1963): 808.

Evaluation. Weber's analysis of social stratification as a multidimensional social hierarchy has had great appeal to many sociologists who recognize that social classes in the United States and other industrial societies are difficult to distinguish from one another in precise terms. At the same time, other sociologists (particularly those most influenced by the ideas of Karl Marx) emphasize that though social class boundaries have blurred over time in industrial societies, patterns of social stratification are striking all the same.

As Chapter 10 explains in detail, the most privileged Americans enjoy far greater financial resources, social prestige, and power than the majority of the American population do. In addition, a significant minority of the American population are quite poor and barely able to meet their day-to-day needs. Moreover, despite some degree of social mobility—which tends to make social classes less clearly defined—social position in American society is largely passed from generation to generation. Thus critics of Weber's approach to social stratification argue that it makes more sense to speak of *classes* in American society than of a *status hierarchy*.

The Lenskis: A Synthesis

Using Gerhard and Jean Lenski's model of sociocultural evolution presented in Chapter 4, a synthesis of the structural-functional and social-conflict analyses of social stratification can be developed (G. Lenski, 1966; Lenski & Lenski, 1987).

Because of their primitive technology, hunting and gathering societies produce little or no material resources beyond what is required for day-to-day living. Some individuals may be more successful as hunters or gatherers than others, but what they produce is generally shared. Since there is little material surplus, no categories of people are able to accumulate more resources than others. The result is that social stratification in hunting and gathering societies is minimal.

As productive technology becomes more advanced, however, societies produce surplus resources that are distributed unequally within the population. In horticultural, pastoral, and agrarian societies, people seek to increase their material wealth, and some do so more successfully than others. Over time, a small elite comes to control most of the growing material surplus, and social inequality increases. Social advantages and differences of social power typically become institutionalized, and a system of social stratification emerges.

In industrial societies, however, this process appears to reverse itself. Social inequality tends to decline because productive activity in industrial societies is highly specialized, requiring considerable education and training on the part of workers. As further technological advances make production increasingly efficient, blue-collar manual labor is gradually replaced by white-collar occupations. This means that a larger proportion of the population is able to command more social resources. In short, decreasing the intensity of social stratification over time is actually functional for industrial societies. Thus social stratification in advanced industrial societies such as the United States is somewhat less pronounced than in agrarian societies or in societies in the early stage of industrialization. Furthermore, the class system becomes characterized by more complex patterns of social inequality, so that the extent of social stratification is not always recognized. But advanced industrial societies such as the United States are still far from egalitarian, as Chapter 10 will explain in detail.

Social Stratification: Fact and Value

The year was 2081 and everybody was finally equal. They weren't only equal before God and the law. They were equal every which way. Nobody was smarter than anybody else. Nobody was better looking than anybody else. Nobody was stronger or quicker than anybody else. All this equality was due to the 211th, 212th, and 213th Amendments to the Constitution and the unceasing vigilance of agents of the Handicapper General. . . .

With these words, novelist Kurt Vonnegut, Jr. (1961) begins an imaginary description of American society a century from now, when social inequality no longer exists. The reader senses that Vonnegut is not portraying equality in positive terms; indeed, his story is a social nightmare in which every personal advantage has been neutralized by agents of the government. The most physically attractive people are required to wear masks that render them average in appearance, just as the legs of the best dancers are precisely fitted with weights to compensate for whatever natural gift sets them apart from others.

The two major theoretical approaches that have been presented suggest more than just "facts" about social stratification. Like Vonnegut's writing, they also imply evaluations. The Davis and Moore thesis, representing structural-functional analysis, argues that social stratification is necessary in a complex society because some occupational roles have greater importance than others. Patterns of social inequality, in other words, are consistent with both variation in human abilities and the variable tasks of society. Following this analysis, one would conclude that at least some degree of social stratification is necessary to the "good society." Put otherwise, one is led to imagine that pervasive social equality is not a natural state, and that it would take relentless government officials resembling the agents of Vonnegut's "Handicapper General" to achieve such a goal.

The social-conflict analysis of Karl Marx is also a mix of fact and value, albeit a different and more explicit one. Marx saw that throughout history the basic institutions of society have generated social stratification, which he condemned as a state in which the greed of the few subordinates the need of the many. He was guided by egalitarian values that, while not opposing all dimensions of human difference, held the "good society" to be one in which everyone equally shared the most important social resources. For Marx, greater equality was indeed a natural state for humanity, if only the corrupting effects of capitalism could be eliminated.

The study of social stratification is, therefore, a complex debate from which no single truth is likely to emerge. Even among people who agree on the facts, differing values often lead to opposing interpretations. This complexity is evident in the discussion of social stratification in the United States, which is the topic of Chapter 10.

SUMMARY

1. Social stratification involves ranking categories of people in a hierarchy. Social stratification is: (1) a characteristic of society that affects the lives of the entire population; (2) universal and variable in form; (3) persistent over many generations; (4) supported by cultural beliefs.

2. Caste systems, common in agrarian societies, are based almost entirely on ascription and permit very limited social mobility. Caste groups have characteristic occupations, and marriage tends to occur between people of the same social rank. Caste systems are typically supported by strong moral beliefs.

3. Class systems, common in industrial societies, place greater emphasis on individual achievement and permit considerable social mobility. There is also less status consistency than in caste systems—people may be ranked higher on one dimension of social inequality and lower on another. Thus classes are less well defined than castes.

4. Many societies with socialist economies claim to be classless. This assertion is based on the fact that productive property, argued by Karl Marx to be the basis of social classes, is collectively owned. Such societies, however, are not without social stratification.

5. The persistence of social stratification reflects the operation of various social institutions. In part, this is because institutions—such as the economic and political systems—can concentrate resources within elites. In addition, institutions—including the family, educational, and religious systems—promote ideas that legitimate patterns of social inequality. Social stratification is a matter of unequally distributed resources and also of ideology.

6. Based on structural-functional analysis, the Davis-Moore thesis states that social stratification is universal because it is functional for society. According to this thesis, social stratification encourages the most able people to assume the most important occupational positions.

7. The Davis-Moore thesis has been criticized on the grounds that (1) it is difficult to objectively determine the functional importance of any occupational position, (2) social stratification prevents many people from developing their abilities, and (3) the thesis fails to recognize that social stratification generates social conflict.

8. Karl Marx had enormous influence on the social-conflict analysis of social stratification. Marx recognized two major social classes in industrial societies: the bourgeoisie, which owns the means of production and seeks profits; and the proletariat, which provides labor in exchange for wages.

9. The socialist revolution that Marx predicted has not occurred in the United States. While some sociologists suggest that Marx's analysis was flawed, others point out that American society continues to have marked social inequality and substantial class conflict.

10. Max Weber also viewed social stratification in terms of social conflict. Unlike Marx, however, he recognized no clear social classes but pointed instead to three dimensions of social inequality: class (economic inequality), status (differences of social prestige), and party (differences of power). Weber's analysis suggests that social stratification takes the form of a multidimensional hierarchy of socioeconomic status.

11. The evolutionary approach of Gerhard and Jean Lenski provides a synthesis of the structural-functional and social-conflict views of social stratification. In technologically primitive societies, limited production of material resources results in minimal social stratification. In technologically advanced societies, social stratification is typically quite pronounced. As industrialization proceeds, however, this pattern is reversed to some extent, since less social inequality is functional for the operation of society.

12. Social stratification is a complex area of research in which any analysis is likely to be a mixture of facts and values.

KEY CONCEPTS

blue-collar jobs occupations that involve mostly manual labor

caste system a system of social stratification based almost entirely on ascription

class system a system of social stratification in which individual achievement is of considerable importance

ideology ideas that reflect and support the interests of some category of a population

meritocracy a system of social stratification in which rewards are matched to personal merit

social mobility changes in the social position of individuals within a system of social stratification

social stratification a system by which categories of people within a society are ranked in a hierarchy

socioeconomic status a composite social ranking based on various dimensions of social inequality

status consistency consistency of social ranking with regard to various dimensions of social inequality

structural social mobility social mobility on the part of large numbers of people that is due primarily to changes in society itself, rather than to the efforts and abilities of individuals

white-collar jobs occupations that involve mostly mental activity and skills not identified with manual labor

---

SUGGESTED READINGS

The following paperbacks provide a closer examination of many of the issues raised in this chapter:

Melvin M. Tumin. *Social Stratification: The Forms and Functions of Social Inequality*. 2nd ed. Englewood Cliffs, NJ: Prentice-Hall, 1985.

Anthony Giddens and David Held, eds. *Classes, Power and Conflict: Classical and Contemporary Debates*. Berkeley: University of California Press, 1982.

These two books examine the racially based conflict in South Africa. The first emphasizes the various political movements that seek an end to apartheid, the second examines the support that ideology provides to this system.

Robert Fatton, Jr. *Black Consciousness in South Africa: The Dialectics of Ideological Resistance to White Supremacy*. Albany, NY: SUNY Press, 1986.

Leonard Thompson. *The Political Mythology of Apartheid*. New Haven, CT: Yale University Press, 1985.

This paperback provides an even-handed presentation of the ideas of Karl Marx.

Robert Freedman. *The Mind of Karl Marx: Economic, Political, and Social Perspectives*. Chatham, NJ: Chatham House, 1986.

With a focus on Great Britain, this book suggests reasons for the persistence of capitalism, in spite of Marx's predictions.

Bob Carter. *Capitalism, Class Conflict and the New Middle Class*. London: Routledge & Kegan Paul, 1985.

A general analysis of social stratification in socialist societies is found in this paperback.

David Lane. *The End of Social Inequality: Class, Status and Power Under State Socialism*. Winchester, MA: Allen and Unwin, 1982.

This fascinating study of Swedish society explains how, late in the nineteenth century, the rise of a capitalist class was accompanied by a change in the entire cultural system.

Jonas Frykman and Orvar Lofgren. *Culture Builders: A Historical Anthology of Middle-Class Life*. New Brunswick, NJ: Rutgers University Press, 1987.

The meanings of social equality within three very different societies is explored in this recent book.

Sidney Verba with Steven Kelman, Gary R. Orren, Ichiro Miyake, Joji Watanuki, Ikuo Kabashima, and G. Donald Ferree, Jr. *Elites and the Idea of Equality: A Comparison of Japan, Sweden, and the United States*. Cambridge: Harvard University Press, 1987.

CHAPTER 10

Social Class in America

Two of America's greatest authors, Ernest Hemingway and F. Scott Fitzgerald, are said to have mused about social stratification. "The rich are different from other people," asserted Fitzgerald. "Yes," responded Hemingway, "they have more money."

At first glance, Hemingway may seem to have the better argument. Although he achieved both fame and fortune, Hemingway spoke as a man of modest background who had little patience with the pretensions that often accompany wealth. His views remind us that, although some Americans do have more money than others, our society has long considered citizens to be fundamentally equal. Unlike most European societies, the United States has never had a feudal aristocracy. In fact, except for our racial history, American society has known no caste system that rigidly separates categories of people.

But the position taken by Fitzgerald, a man more comfortable with the ways of the wealthy, is closer to the truth. Americans are far from equal in many vital respects. The rich enjoy not only more money, but a greater share of almost everything related to well-being. On the other hand, for millions of poor Americans, obtaining basic necessities is a daily struggle. In short, although the United States is sometimes portrayed as a "middle-class society," this chapter will explain that this is not the reality of social class in America.

If Americans tend to underestimate the extent of social inequality in the United States, perhaps we should not be surprised. First, as noted above, American society has no feudal legacy of nobility and commoners that, as noted in Chapter 9, remains evident in much of Europe. Rather, the United States was founded on the

more modern principle of equality under the law for everyone—although establishing this in practice has been a long, and still unfinished, process. Second, the American emphasis on individual autonomy and achievement often obscures the extent to which birth confers on some Americans far more advantages and opportunities than others may even imagine. Third, perceiving the full range of social inequality in America is difficult for anyone because primary groups—including family, neighbors, and friends—tend to include only those with similar social positions. Of course, daily life brings people into contact with others of varying social standing, but the full extent of these differences is usually not evident in what are often brief and impersonal interactions. Fourth and finally, since the United States is extremely wealthy compared to the rest of the world, we tend to see every American as at least fairly well off.

DIMENSIONS OF INEQUALITY

When Americans do acknowledge social stratification, they sometimes speak of a "ladder of social class" as if inequality were a matter of a single factor such as money. However, as Max Weber argued, social stratification in advanced industrial societies reflects several distinct dimensions of social inequality. The concept of *socioeconomic status,* discussed in Chapter 9, is a composite measure of social position involving such dimensions as economic resources, power, occupational prestige, and formal education.

Economic Resources and Power

There is no doubt that economic resources are quite unequally distributed within American society. One important dimension of economic inequality is **income,** meaning *occupational wages or salaries and earnings from investments.* Another, and broader, dimension of economic inequality is **wealth,** which is *the total amount of money and valuable goods that any person or family controls.*

According to government statistics, the median American family income in 1986 was $29,460 (U.S. Bureau of the Census, 1987e). Figure 10–1 presents the distribution of income for all American families. Note that the richest 20 percent of families receive 43.7 percent of income, while the poorest 20 percent receive

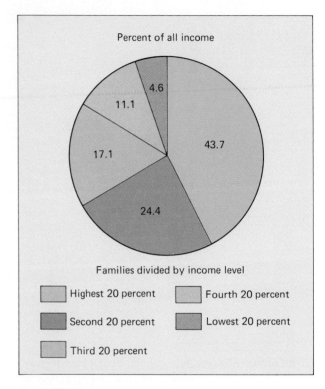

Percent of all income

4.6
11.1
17.1
43.7
24.4

Families divided by income level

Highest 20 percent   Fourth 20 percent

Second 20 percent   Lowest 20 percent

Third 20 percent

Figure 10–1   Distribution of Income in the United States.

(U.S. Bureau of the Census, 1987)

only about 4.6 percent. In addition, with about 17 percent of all income, the top 5 percent of American families receive as much as the lowest 40 percent.

But income is only part of the picture. Total wealth—in the form of stocks, bonds, real estate, and other privately owned valuables—is even more unevenly distributed. Figure 10–2 shows the approximate distribution of wealth in the United States in 1983. The richest 20 percent of American families own over three-fourths of the entire country's wealth. And most of this wealth is further concentrated in the hands of people who might be called America's "super-rich": the richest 5 percent of American families control over half the nation's wealth. And at the very top of the wealth pyramid, the richest *three* Americans have a combined wealth totaling almost $15 billion, which equals everything owned by one-half million "average" Americans (*Forbes,* 1987).

The wealth of most Americans with moderate incomes—in the second and third fifths of Figure 10–2—is far smaller, typically in the range of one year's income or about $30,000. Rather than stocks and other income-producing investments, this wealth is likely to be in the form of equity in a home and perhaps a retirement fund. For the remaining 40 percent of American families, wealth simply does not exist. In fact, the table indicates that the bottom 20 percent have financial liabilities that exceed their assets.

In American society, wealth is an important source of power; therefore, the fact that a small proportion of families control most of the wealth suggests that they also have the ability to set the agenda for all of American society. In Chapter 8, we noted that poorer Americans are more likely to be subject to punishment by the criminal justice system than wealthy Americans, who are often able to use their considerable power to avoid criminal sanctions. As Chapter 17 describes in detail, many sociologists argue that highly concentrated wealth undermines the claim that the United States is a democracy. Rather, the American political system represents the interests of a small proportion of "super-rich" families.

Occupational Prestige

In addition to being a source of income, occupation is an important basis of social prestige. Americans are widely evaluated according to their occupation, being envied and respected in some cases, and being avoided and looked down upon in others.

For over fifty years, sociologists have studied how Americans assess the social prestige of various occupations (Counts, 1925; Hodge, Treiman, & Rossi, 1966; N.O.R.C., 1987). Table 10–1 presents the results of a recent survey involving a random sample of American adults. Worth noting is the fact that most of the occupations with high prestige rankings—physician, lawyer, banker, engineer—are those that provide high incomes. This led sociologist C. Wright Mills (1956:83) to comment that "prestige is the shadow of money and power." But high social prestige can be argued to involve more than simply money, since these occupations generally demand considerable ability, education, and training. On the other hand, lower-paying occupations—salesperson, coal miner, and janitor—generally require less ability and education and provide far less occupational prestige. In general, occupational prestige rankings are much the same in all industrial societies.*

Also important is the pattern linking high social prestige to white-collar occupations, those that involve mostly mental activity free from extensive supervision by superiors. Far lower on the prestige hierarchy are blue-collar occupations that involve manual labor and are subject to at least some direct supervision. But the table suggests that the relationship between prestige and these categories of occupations is not perfect: a blue-collar locomotive engineer, for example, has more social prestige than a white-collar bank teller.

Although women are found in both white-collar and blue-collar occupations, they tend to be heavily concentrated in what are described as *pink-collar jobs* (Bernard, 1981). These are primarily service occupations—such as secretary, waitress, and beautician —that tend to fall near the bottom of the prestige hierarchy.

Figure 10–2 Distribution of Wealth in the United States, 1983

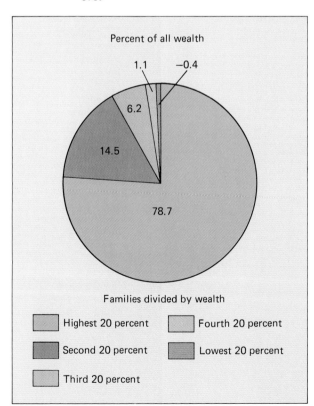

Percent of all wealth

1.1   −0.4

6.2

14.5

78.7

Families divided by wealth

Highest 20 percent   Fourth 20 percent

Second 20 percent   Lowest 20 percent

Third 20 percent

---

* I am grateful to Dr. Li-Chen Ma of Lamar University for pointing out cross-cultural material.

Table 10–1 THE RELATIVE SOCIAL PRESTIGE OF ONE HUNDRED OCCUPATIONS IN THE UNITED STATES

White-Collar Occupations	Prestige Score	Blue-Collar Occupations	White-Collar Occupations	Prestige Score	Blue-Collar Occupations
Physician	82		Bookkeeper	48	
College/university professor	78		Insurance agent	47	
Lawyer	76		Musician/composer	46	
Dentist	74			46	Secretary
Physicist/astronomer	74			44	Fireman
Bank officer	72		Adult education teacher	43	
Architect	71		Air traffic controller	43	
Aeronautical/astronautical engineer	71			42	Mail carrier
Psychologist	71			41	Apprentice electrician
Airplane pilot	70			41	
Clergy	69		Buyer/shipper, farm products	41	Farmer
Chemist	69			41	
Electrical engineer	69		Photographer	41	Tailor
Geologist	67			40	Carpenter
Sociologist	66			40	Telephone operator
Secondary school teacher	63			40	Welder
Mechanical engineer	62		Restaurant Manager	39	
Registered nurse	62		Building superintendent	38	
Dental hygienist	61			37	Auto body repairperson
Pharmacist	61			36	
Radiologic technician	61		Airline stewardess	36	Brick/stone mason
Chiropractor	60			35	TV Repairperson
Elementary school teacher	60			34	Baker
Veterinarian	60			33	Hairdresser
Postmaster	58			33	Bulldozer operator
Union official	58			32	
Accountant	57		Auctioneer	32	Bus driver
Economist	57			32	Truck driver
Draftsman	56			31	
Painter/sculptor	56		Cashier	30	
Actor	55		File clerk	30	Upholsterer
Librarian	55			29	Drill-press operator
Statistician	55			29	Furniture finisher
Industrial engineer	54			29	
Forester and conservationist	54		Retail salesperson	23	Midwife
Surveyor	53			22	Gas station attendant
Dietician	52			22	Security guard
Funeral director	52			22	Taxi driver
Social worker	52			21	Elevator operator
Athlete	51			20	Bartender
Computer specialist	51			20	Waiter/waitress
Editor/reporter	51			18	Clothing presser
	51	Locomotive engineer		18	Farm laborer
Radio/TV announcer	51			18	Household servant
Bank teller	50			17	Car washer
Sales manager	50			17	Freight handler
	49	Electrician		17	Garbage collector
	48	Aircraft mechanic		16	Janitor
	48	Machinist		14	Bellhop
	48	Police officer		09	Shoe shiner

SOURCE: Adapted from *General Social Surveys, 1972–1987: Cumulative Codebook* (Chicago: National Opinion Research Center, 1987), pp. 543–555.

Formal Education

Formal education is another important dimension of social stratification in American society. Table 10–2 describes the education of Americans aged twenty-five and over in 1985. It shows that 26.1 percent of the population had not completed a high-school education, and about 14 percent had eight years or less of schooling. While 73.9 percent of American adults had completed high school, only 19.4 percent were college graduates. So, like income, wealth, and occupational prestige, education is clearly distributed unequally in American society.

Education is important not only for its own sake, but also because it affects a person's occupation and income. Most (but not all) of the white-collar occupations shown in Table 10–1 that provide high income and social prestige require a college degree or other advanced education. Similarly, most of the blue-collar occupations that provide less income and social prestige are held by people with less education.

Ascription and Social Stratification

Within a class system such as that found in the United States, social position does reflect some measure of individual talent and effort. But ascription is also important—who we are at birth has much to do with what we become later in life.

Ancestry

Probably no single factor affects an American's social class position as much as the accident of birth. Ancestry—or social background—is responsible for our point of entry into the system of social stratification. Some Americans, including duPonts, Rockefellers, Roosevelts, and Kennedys, are known across the country and around the world simply by virtue of their family name. On a more modest scale, practically every local community in North America has several families whose wealth and power have become well established over several generations.

Just as important, what happens throughout a lifetime is influenced by the opportunities and resources present or absent at birth. The family into which one is born is closely related to one's future education, occupation, and income. For the relatively few Americans born to great riches, family wealth is passed from generation to generation: recent estimates suggest that about half of the richest Americans derived their fortunes *primarily* from inheritance (*Forbes*, 1987; Thurow, 1987). Of course, the "inheritance" of little wealth and opportunity applies in much the same way to those born to few privileges. In the United States as elsewhere, then, patterns of social stratification tend to persist over generations.

Race and Ethnicity

Race has a strong relationship to social position in American society. The median income of white families in 1986 was just over $30,800; that of black families was almost $17,600 (U.S. Bureau of the Census, 1987e). Similarly, whites have higher overall occupational standing than blacks, and slightly greater educational achievement.

Ethnic background is also related to social stratification. Traditionally, the wealthiest and most powerful Americans have been of English ancestry. Research has shown that ethnicity as well as race continues to be closely linked to overall social standing in the United States (Hirschman & Wong, 1984). A detailed examination of the importance of race and ethnicity to patterns of social inequality in America is presented in Chapter 11.

Sex

Whether one is born male or female also has important consequences for social position. Initially, this may seem strange since males and females are born into families at all levels of our system of social stratification. It is true that women born into families of high social standing have more social resources than men born into families of low social standing. But on the whole, women have

Table 10–2	EDUCATIONAL INEQUALITY IN THE UNITED STATES, 1985 (PERSONS AGED 25 AND OVER)
Not a High-School Graduate	26.1%
0–4 years	2.7
5–7 years	4.8
8 years	6.4
9–11 years	12.2
High-School Graduate	73.9
High school only	38.2
Some college (1–3 years)	16.3
College graduate or more	19.4

SOURCE: U.S. Census Bureau, 1987.

less income, wealth, occupational prestige, and slightly less educational achievement than men do (Bernard, 1981; Lengermann & Wallace, 1985). Furthermore, as will be explained later in this chapter, households headed by women are more than twelve times as likely to be poor as those headed by men. A full discussion of the link between sex and social stratification is provided in Chapter 12.

Religion

Finally, in the United States, religion is related to social standing. Among Protestant denominations, Episcopalians and Presbyterians have higher overall social standing than Lutherans and Baptists. In recent years, on the average, Jews have gained high social standing. Roman Catholics, on the other hand, have much lower overall social standing (Roof, 1979; Gallup, 1981). Thus even John Fitzgerald Kennedy—a member of one of America's wealthiest and most powerful families—became America's first Catholic president only by overcoming opposition directed at a member of a religious minority. It is not surprising, then, that many Americans have adopted a higher-ranking religion as they have moved up in the class system (Baltzell, 1979). Chapter 16 presents a closer look at the importance of religion in the American system of social stratification.

SOCIAL CLASSES IN THE UNITED STATES

As Chapter 9 explained, describing the ranking of various social categories in a rigid caste system of social stratification usually presents few problems. Painting a broad picture of social categories in a more fluid class system, however, is more difficult.

This issue brings to mind a bit of humor about a fellow who orders a pizza asking that it be cut into six slices because he isn't hungry enough to eat eight. Generally, the American class system lacks clear boundaries; therefore, we face a problem in deciding how to cut it up. Following Karl Marx, we might identify only two major social classes; yet other sociologists have suggested that there are as many as six (Warner & Lunt, 1941) or seven (Coleman & Rainwater, 1978). Another alternative, derived from Max Weber's theory of several different dimensions of social inequality, is to conclude that there are no classes at all in the United States and that the existing social inequality is actually a complex status hierarchy.

Part of the difficulty of identifying social classes reflects the relatively low level of status consistency characteristic of class systems. Especially toward the middle of the class system, a person's social position on many dimensions of social inequality may not be consistent (Gilbert & Kahl, 1987). As explained in Chapter 9, someone may have more power (as a government official, perhaps) than income and wealth. Similarly, someone who has a great deal of social prestige (for instance, as a member of the clergy) may have only moderate power and little wealth. Another factor making social classes difficult to precisely define is the considerable social mobility of a class system—which is pronounced near the middle—so that social position may change within any person's lifetime. Nonetheless, patterns of social inequality in the United States are clear enough to permit a description of four general social classes: the upper class, the middle class, the working class, and the lower class.

The Upper Class

Perhaps 3 or 4 percent of all Americans fall within the upper class. First, upper-class families have a yearly income that is, at the very least, $100,000. The "super-rich" members of the upper class may earn several million dollars or more annually. Such high income over a period of time, commonly coupled to significant inheritance of property, means that upper-class people control a vastly disproportionate share of wealth in terms of stocks and bonds, real estate, and other investments. The 1987 *Forbes* magazine profile of the richest four hundred people in America estimated their total wealth at $220 billion: the personal worth of this economic elite (including forty-nine billionaires) was a minimum of $225 million. There is little doubt that, in Marxist terms, the upper class represents capitalists who own most of the nation's productive property. Second, beyond the power inherent in their wealth, many members of the upper class have occupational positions—as top executives in large corporations and as high government officials—that give them the power to shape events in the nation and, increasingly, the entire world. Third, the upper class is highly educated, typically in the most expensive and highly regarded schools and colleges. Historically, the upper class was composed almost exclusively of white Anglo-Saxon Protestants (WASPs), although this is somewhat less true today (Baltzell, 1964, 1976).

Members of the upper class are set apart in death as they are in life. Many cities have cemeteries that contain only the rich and famous of an earlier time. Philadelphia's Laurel Hill Cemetery, shown here, has been designated a national landmark.

Upper-class people, then, enjoy the highest level of social prestige in American society. But there are social differences among even the most privileged Americans, so an important distinction is often made between the upper-upper class and the lower-upper class.

The upper-upper class. This most elite segment of the American population—often described simply as "society"—contains only about 1 percent of the population (Warner & Lunt, 1941; Coleman & Neugarten, 1971; Rossides, 1976). There is an old saying that the easiest way to get into the upper-upper class is to be born there—a fact reflected in the description of such people as "bluebloods." Ascription is evident in the fact that the great wealth of upper-upper class families is usually inherited rather than earned. For this reason, such people are often called the *old rich*—their wealth has grown old over many generations.

Life in the upper-upper class is built around highly selective social ties and memberships. These include exclusive neighborhoods, such as Beacon Hill in Boston, the Rittenhouse Square area or the Main Line in Philadelphia, the Gold Coast of Chicago, and Nob Hill in San Francisco. Schools and colleges extend this socially exclusive environment. Children are typically educated in private secondary schools with others of similar back-

ground, and continue their education at high-prestige colleges and universities. In the pattern of the European feudal aristocracy, such children study liberal arts rather than vocationally directed subjects. Social clubs and organizations further exclusivity. The women of this class, who usually have no income-producing occupations, often engage in volunteer work for charitable organizations. While helping the community, these activities also serve to maintain upper-class solidarity from generation to generation (Ostrander 1980, 1984).

The lower-upper class. The remaining 2 or 3 percent of the upper class is more precisely termed the *lower-upper class*. From the point of view of most Americans, such people are every bit as privileged as the upper-upper class just described. But there are several significant differences between these categories.

First, the primary source of wealth for those in the lower-upper class is earnings rather than inheritance. Probably most people in this category did not inherit a vast fortune from their parents, but the majority certainly inherited considerable wealth, or at least social advantages that helped them to become extremely successful in business or the professions. About half of the "super-rich" represent "new money" of the lower-upper class.

Second, even for the richest of Americans, having earned much of one's wealth may be grounds for being accorded less social prestige—especially by members of "society." Therefore, while "new rich" Americans are likely to live in very expensive houses or apartments in the most exclusive neighborhoods, they may nonetheless be excluded from the highest-prestige clubs and associations of old-monied "society."

Since membership in the lower-upper class is at least possible on the basis of achievement, upward social mobility to this point is widely considered to represent the American dream of success. The young actress who left a small town and achieved Hollywood stardom, the athlete whose years of workouts finally paid off with a million-dollar big-league contract, the clever engineer who built a computer in a garage and ten years later is managing a billion-dollar corporation—these are the sorts of achievers who become part of the lower-upper class. For this reason, Americans tend to have little interest in the upper-upper class, while paying greater attention to the "lifestyles of the rich and famous," as well as television shows such as *Dallas* and *Dynasty*. These shows portray people who are more or less like the rest of us—except that they have made a lot of money.

The distinction between the upper-upper class and

CLOSE-UP

Two Listings of Elites: The *Social Register* and *Who's Who in America*

The best indication of membership in the upper-upper class is inclusion in the *Social Register*. Simply being wealthy is not sufficient to be listed; in general, only those Americans whose families have been wealthy for several generations are likely to be included. Since membership in this part of the upper class is mostly a matter of ascription, families rather than individuals are listed in the *Social Register*. The listing for David Rockefeller, for example, indicates (1) the family address and home telephone number; (2) Mrs. Rockefeller's maiden name; (3) the names of the Rockefeller children (noting boarding schools and colleges attended); and

(4) the exclusive social clubs to which the family belongs. No mention is made of occupation, place of business, or any mark of individual achievement.

One of the best indications of personal achievement is inclusion in the national listing *Who's Who in America* (regional listings are also published that indicate a lesser degree of achievement). If the *Social Register* lists *families* on the basis of *who they are*, this book lists *individuals* on the basis of *what they have done*. Since a large number of people included in *Who's Who in America* are outstanding (and highly paid) members of high-prestige occupations, this list-

ing is a rough approximation of the lower-upper class.

Of course, some people listed in the *Social Register* are also listed in *Who's Who*. But quite different information about them is provided. David Rockefeller, for example, is also in *Who's Who*. What is given here, however, is a brief biography (such as his date of birth and educational and honorary degrees) and list of accomplishments (such as various military decorations, service to the government, several books he has written, and—most importantly—his chairmanship of the board of Chase Manhattan Bank). The address provided is his place of business.

The popularity of television programs such as Dynasty *and* Dallas *partly reflects people's desire to imagine themselves "breaking into" the upper class.*

the lower-upper class is well illustrated by comparing two listings of wealthy Americans—the *Social Register* and *Who's Who in America*. The box describes how they differ.

The Middle Class

The middle class includes 40 to 45 percent of all Americans. Because it is so large and represents the aspirations of many more people, the middle class has tremendous influence on the patterns of American culture. Television shows most often present middle-class Americans, and most commercial advertising is directed at them. Being so large, the middle class contains far more ethnic and racial diversity than does the upper class. In addition, while upper-class people (at least those within a limited geographical area) are likely to know one another, such familiarity is obviously not possible in the much larger middle class.

Roughly the top one-third of this category of Americans can be distinguished as the upper-middle class on the basis of an income that is well above average—generally in the range of $40,000 to $100,000 a year. Family income is often greater still if both husband and wife work. This allows upper-middle-class families to gradually accumulate considerable property—an elegant house in a fairly expensive area, automobiles, and some investments. Virtually all upper-middle-class people have college educations, and many have postgraduate degrees as well. Most work in white-collar occupations such as medicine, engineering, and law, or in business at the executive level. Having less wealth than members of the upper class, this category of Americans lacks the power to influence national or international events, but they often play an important part in civic and political organizations in the local community.

The rest of the middle class typically works in less prestigious white-collar occupations (such as bank teller, lower-level manager, and sales clerk) or in highly skilled blue-collar jobs. Such people sometimes have incomes as high or even higher than upper-middle-class Americans, especially if more than one family member works. However, middle-class American families usually earn between $15,000 and $40,000 a year. This roughly equals the national average (1986 median family income: $29,460) and provides a secure, if modest, standard of living. People in the middle class are generally able to accumulate only a small amount of wealth over their working lives. The goal of owning a house is achieved by most of them, however, though the house is unlikely to be in an expensive neighborhood. Most middle-class people have a high-school education, but a college degree is far from common. Reflecting their limited incomes, middle-class people who complete college generally have degrees from state-supported colleges and universities.

The Working Class

The working class contains about one-third of all Americans. Working-class people have lower incomes than those in the middle class and virtually no accumulated wealth. In Marxist terms, the working class is the core of the industrial proletariat. In general, the blue-collar occupations of the working class provide a family income between $12,000 and $25,000 a year, which is somewhat below the national average. Working-class Americans are thus quite vulnerable to financial problems caused by unemployment or illness.

Occupations of the working class include blue-collar jobs and lower-level sales and clerical positions. These jobs are typically far less personally satisfying than those held by middle-class people; the work is less interesting and challenging and is usually subject to continual supervision by superiors (Edwards, 1979). In addition, working-class jobs often provide few of the benefits, such as hospital insurance and pension programs, that give greater financial security to middle-class Americans. With little opportunity to accumulate savings, these people must plan carefully in order to afford a house. Still, about half of working-class families own their homes (typically with substantial mortgages), although their housing is usually less substantial than that of middle-class families and likely to be in lower-cost neighborhoods. Similarly, most working-class people have only a high-school education. Whereas middle-class people are able to achieve significant long-term security, working-class people get along month to month.

Another major characteristic of working-class life is the lack of power to shape events. Families typically live in modest neighborhoods because they cannot afford better housing; their children may want to attend college, but lack the money to do so. They may find little satisfaction in their jobs, but have few alternatives. Still, working-class families often express a great deal of pride in what they do have, especially in relation to those who are not working at all.

The Lower Class

Lower-class Americans—about 20 percent of the population—have unstable and insecure lives because of their low income. For this reason, they can also be described as the American poor. According to government figures, about 35 million Americans (roughly 15 percent of the population) are officially classified as poor—meaning, for an urban family of four in 1987, an annual income of $10,989 or less. Another 10 million earn only slightly more than this, and therefore live at the margins of poverty. Although most lower-class people in the United States are white, blacks, Hispanics, and other minorities are disproportionately represented. The American poor typically work in low-prestige occupations that provide low income and little intrinsic satisfaction. Their education is very limited; only some manage to complete high school, and a college degree is virtually out of reach. Many lower-class Americans have so little education that they are functionally illiterate.

In a culture that emphasizes the values of individual success and achievement, lower-class people are often seen as personally inadequate. Tragically, some of the poor come to hold such a view of themselves. But poverty is more correctly understood as a consequence of America's system of social stratification than as a reflection of personal deficiencies on the part of tens of millions of people. The lower class is also characterized by considerable social segregation, especially of the poor members of racial and ethnic minorities. This is most visible in urban areas in which large numbers of poor people live in deteriorating neighborhoods avoided by those of other social classes. Very few lower-class families ever gain the resources to purchase even the cheapest house; consequently, they typically live in undesirable low-cost rental housing.

As suggested in Chapter 9, upper-class children are socialized in an environment that attempts to develop their talents, abilities, and confidence to the fullest. In contrast, lower-class children are socialized to the hard reality of being devalued and marginal members of their own society. Observing their parents and other lower-class adults, they see little reason to be hopeful about their own future. Rather, life in the lower class demands resignation to being cut off from the resources of a rich society (Jacob, 1986).

Although some simply give up, many other poor people work desperately to make ends meet. In a participant-observation study carried out in a northern city, Carol Stack (1975) found that many of the poor did not conform to the stereotype of people lacking in initiative and responsibility. On the contrary, they devised ingenious means to survive based on mutual support. In the box, one woman in Stack's study explains how people in a poor community join together—almost like one large family—to help one another make ends meet.

CORRELATES OF AMERICAN SOCIAL STRATIFICATION

In thinking of social class in America, money, housing, and other material advantages probably come first to mind. But social stratification has even broader significance, being related to virtually every dimension of life. This section examines a number of factors related to social stratification, beginning with the crucial issue of health.

Health and Longevity

The health of the American population is closely related to social stratification. As Chapter 19 describes in detail, Americans with high incomes are about twice as likely to consider themselves to be in excellent health as people living in poverty. On the other side of the coin, only about 4 percent of high-income people describe their health as merely fair or poor, but this assessment is made by about 22 percent of poor Americans (U.S. National Center for Health Statistics, 1987a). This pattern has also been found in other societies such as Great Britain (Doyal, 1981). Just as important, children born into poor families are about 50 percent more likely to die during their first year of life than children born into more privileged families (Gortmaker, 1979). Social class is linked to life expectancy as well. For instance, black Americans born in 1985, who are about three times more likely to be poor than whites, can expect to live

SOCIOLOGY OF EVERYDAY LIFE

Being Poor Is Often Hard Work

Ruby Banks took a cab to visit Virginia Thomas, her baby's aunt, and they swapped some hot corn bread and greens for diapers and milk. In the cab going home Ruby said to me, "I don't believe in putting myself on nobody, but I know I need help every day. You can't get help by sitting at home, laying around, house-nasty and everything. You got to get up and go out and meet people, because the very

day you go out, the first person you meet may be the person that can help you get the things you want. I don't believe in begging, but I believe that people should help one another. I used to wish for lots of things like a living room suite, clothes, nice clothes, stylish clothes—I'm sick of wearing the same pieces. But I can't, I can't help myself because I have my children and I love them and I have my mother

and all our kin. Sometimes I don't have a damn dime in my pocket, not a crying penny to get a box of paper diapers, milk, a loaf of bread. But you have to have help from everybody and anybody, so don't turn no one down when they come round for help."

SOURCE: Carol B. Stack, *All Our Kin: Strategies for Survival in a Black Community* (New York: Harper and Row, 1974), p. 32.

just less than seventy years, while whites can expect to live over seventy-five years (U.S. Bureau of the Census, 1987g).

This link between health and social stratification is due, first, to the fact that nutritious foods, a safe environment, and necessary medical attention all cost money. Health-care costs have risen sharply in recent years, and now represent an expense of roughly $1,500 a year to the average American. While this much health care presents little problem to a family of four earning $50,000 a year, it is simply out of reach of one earning only $10,000. In simple terms, people of higher social position can afford to buy better health than others can.

Second, people in the lower social classes are more likely than others to live in a dangerous environment. This is true of the workplace—business offices are safer than factories and mines—as well as of neighborhoods—unsafe housing and inadequate heat are far more common among the poor than the rich or middle class. So those with the least resources face the greatest dangers both at home and at work.

Mental health is related to social class in much the same way physical health is (Link, Dohrenwend, & Skodol, 1986). Primarily because they have so much less power over their environment, one study concluded, "lower class people are exposed to more of the stressful events and situations that can lead to emotional distress than their middle and upper class counterparts" (Kessler & Cleary, 1980:476). In addition, people with greater social resources can respond more effectively when emotional disorders do appear, so they tend to recover more quickly and avoid the stigma of mental illness.

Values and Attitudes

As Chapter 3 explained, a number of dominant cultural values provide a distinctive shape to American society. Within the American population, secondary variations can be found from class to class. Americans within the upper-upper class, for example, tend to have an especially strong sense of family history since their social position is based on wealth and social prestige passed down from generation to generation (Baltzell, 1979). Many other Americans, in contrast, do not know the full names of even their four grandparents. In addition, because their social standing is mostly a matter of birth, the "old rich" tend to be understated in their manners and tastes, as if to say "I know who I am and don't have to prove anything to anyone else."

Because the class boundaries below this point are

People who are upwardly mobile are keenly aware of patterns of consumption. For them, "lifestyle" is more than simply living; it is using material things (and even pets) to make a statement about "what they have become."

less clearly defined, people in the lower-upper class and the middle classes tend to be more sensitive to patterns of consumption. The houses in which people live, the cars they drive, and the clothes they wear are often status symbols, meaning that such purchases influence a person's social position in the eyes of others. Perhaps this is why designer clothing, avoided by members of "society," is so popular among those directly below them.

Middle-class people are secure enough to be more tolerant than working-class people of controversial behavior such as premarital sexuality and homosexuality (Humphries, 1984). As suggested in Chapter 5, because they are usually subject to greater supervision and discipline, working-class people tend to emphasize conformity to conventional beliefs and practices (Kohn, 1977).

Orientation to time also has some relationship to social class. Since their social position is supported by generations of wealth, upper-class families tend to maintain a strong awareness of the past. Middle-class people, especially those who have been upwardly mobile, embody the more common American pattern of optimistically looking to the future for a better life. And the lower class has a somewhat greater orientation to the present. Edward Banfield (1974) has suggested that a present-time orientation may help keep people in poverty because it makes them less likely to plan and save and thus improve their social standing. During the 1980s, Banfield's controversial position has gained some support. It remains probable, however, that any present-time orientation characteristic of the poor comes from their realistic assessment of their limited chances of escaping poverty and attaining the American Dream, as well as their need to focus attention on the daily task of survival (Liebow, 1967; Lamar, Jr., 1985; Jacob, 1986).

Political Orientations

A general pattern in American politics is that people of higher social class tend to support the Republican Party, while those of lower social class tend to be Democrats (Wolfinger, Shapiro, & Greenstein, 1980). This is because the Republican Party has generally advanced the interests of wealthy Americans, while the Democratic Party has represented the interests of working Americans. Although the Republican Party has made gains among the working class in recent years, this overall pattern still holds.

Social standing is linked to political attitudes in several additional ways. People of higher social standing are likely to be conservative on *economic issues* because they have the most wealth to protect; for example, they tend to favor a free-market economy unregulated by government. On the other hand, high social position is related to liberal views on *social issues* such as support for the Equal Rights Amendment, abortion, and other feminist concerns. People of lower social standing show the reverse pattern: they tend to be liberal on economic issues and conservative on social issues (Nunn, Crockett, & Williams, 1978; Erikson, Luttberg, & Tedin, 1980; Syzmanski, 1983; Humphries, 1984).

With greater power in American society, people of higher social position are typically more politically active. In general, those with higher incomes, more education, and white-collar jobs vote in the greatest numbers (Wolfinger & Rosenstone, 1980). In addition, people of higher social position are more likely to belong to various voluntary associations (Hyman & Wright, 1971).

Family Life and Gender

Patterns of family life are also related to social class. This is true, first, in that marriage generally occurs between people of comparable social position (Melville, 1983). In addition, lower-class families tend to have more children than middle-class families because they marry at an earlier age and—especially among the poor—make less effective use of birth control. Upper-class families also have more children, largely because the expenses of child rearing present no hardship to them.

Patterns of child rearing also vary by social standing. Working-class and lower-class families tend to encourage their children to conform to conventional norms and obey authority figures; however, middle- and upper-class parents are typically tolerant of a wider range of behavior. This reflects parents' expectations about their children's future: those of lower social position are likely to take jobs demanding close adherence to specified rules, while those of higher social position will probably go into occupations that demand some creativity and imagination (Kohn, 1977). This general difference extends to ways in which parents typically control their children. Parents of lower social position are somewhat more likely to use physical punishment (such as spanking), while those of higher social position tend to rely more on discussion and persuasion to mold their children's behavior. The paramount difference in child-rearing patterns is that families with more social resources are better able to offer their children the opportunity to develop their talents and abilities. This is one reason, of course, that social position tends to be transmitted from generation to generation.

The relationship between spouses is also related to social class. A more rigid division of responsibilities between husband and wife is a common trait of working-class marriages, while middle-class marriages are somewhat more egalitarian (Bott, 1971). Divorce is also more common among families of lower social standing, no doubt because such factors as low income and high risk of unemployment subject these families to greater stress (Kitson & Raschke, 1981; Fergusson, Horwood, & Shannon, 1984). Finally, the number of households headed by women has been rapidly increasing during the last decade. This pattern is most prevalent among the poor—especially poor blacks—though it is showing up in higher social classes as well.

SOCIAL MOBILITY IN AMERICA

Thus far, the *static* qualities of social stratification in America have been emphasized. But since America has a class system, patterns of social inequality are also *dynamic*. In some cases, such changes take the form of individual social mobility as people move up or down as a result of their personal achievements. Earning a college degree, obtaining a higher-paying job, or succeeding in a business endeavor can result in upward social mobility; contrarily, dropping out of school, being fired from a job for poor performance, or business failure can signal downward social mobility. But, as suggested in Chapter 9, social mobility is also a matter of changes in society as a whole. During the first half of this century, for example, the economic expansion accompanying the industrialization of America raised the standard of living of millions of Americans. In this case, to draw a simple parallel, even without being very good swimmers, people were able to "ride a rising tide of prosperity." Such *structural social mobility* has been at work in the opposite direction more recently as the decline of traditional industries has forced millions of Americans to accept severe economic setbacks.

Whether caused primarily by personal achievement or primarily by changes in society as a whole, social mobility is experienced as a transition—for better or worse—in social position. In studying such patterns, sociologists draw a useful distinction between short-term and long-term transitions. **Intragenerational social mobility** takes place within a shorter time frame and is defined as *change in social position occurring during a person's lifetime*. Of even greater concern to sociologists is **intergenerational social mobility,** which refers to *change in the social position of children in relation to that of their parents*. Social mobility across generations is of particular importance because it reflects changes in society that affect virtually everyone.

Social Mobility: Myth and Reality

In few other societies do people think about social mobility as much as Americans do; in fact, moving ahead has historically been central to the American Dream. Furthermore, the assumption that society offers plenty of opportunity to improve one's social position is an important ideological support of social stratification in the United States (Kleugel & Smith, 1986).

But is social mobility as commonplace as many Americans imagine it is? Sociological research suggests that, in fact, social mobility is fairly common. Studies of intergenerational mobility using the broad categories of blue-collar and white-collar jobs (which, unfortunately, have focused almost exclusively on men) show that almost 40 percent of the sons of blue-collar workers have white-collar jobs and almost 30 percent of sons born into white-collar families have a blue-collar occupation. When more narrowly defined occupational categories are used, about 80 percent of sons show at least some social mobility in relation to their fathers (Blau & Duncan, 1967; Featherman & Hauser, 1978).

These facts support three general conclusions. First, social mobility is relatively high for American males, as we would expect in a class system. Second, at least during most of this century, social mobility has more commonly been upward than downward. This is largely a case of structural social mobility, a white-collar revolution by which white-collar jobs have steadily replaced the blue-collar and farming occupations more common several generations ago. Third, although sweeping changes are evident over many decades, social mobil-

From World War II until about 1970, American industries dominated world and domestic markets. Since then, however, a "deindustrialization of America" has brought hard times to thousands of American families. Social mobility is sometimes a matter of individual effort and luck, but more often is due to major economic changes.

ity within a single generation has usually been incremental rather than dramatic.

No patterns apply equally to *all* segments of American society, however. Black Americans have traditionally experienced significantly less upward social mobility than whites (Featherman & Hauser, 1978; Pomer, 1986), a fact all too evident in recent years. At a time when whites have benefited from an economic recovery, blacks have actually lost ground in terms of income. In 1985, about 60 percent of black Americans had *less* purchasing power than they did in 1980 (Jacob, 1986). Women represent another distinctive segment of the American population. Unfortunately, there is little research directly comparing patterns of social mobility of women and men. However, as Chapter 12 describes in detail, the majority of working women have clerical occupations (such as secretaries) and low-paying service jobs (such as waitresses). Since these jobs provide little opportunity for advancement, a reasonable conclusion is that women are also disadvantaged in terms of upward social mobility.

Finally, how does the United States compare to other industrial societies in social mobility? Because of the emphasis American culture places on individual achievement, one might expect social mobility to be more common in the United States, but comparative studies do not bear this out. Table 10–3 provides a comparative look at intergenerational social mobility in six industrial societies (Lipset & Bendix, 1967). This table shows that there were only moderate differences among the various societies. Switzerland had the most favorable picture (with the most upward mobility and the least downward mobility), while West Germany had the least positive pattern (with the least upward mobility and the most downward mobility). Notice that the United States is about in the middle in this comparison. More recent research supports the conclusion that social mobility in the United States has been comparable to that of other industrial societies in the West (McRoberts & Selbee, 1981; Kaelble, 1986).

Stratification and Mobility in Recent Decades

The American tendency to exaggerate the extent of upward social mobility (and also to minimize social movement downward) probably has its roots in historical experience. Through most of its history, the United States has been a society of expansion: westward migration lasting more than two centuries, followed by an industrial revolution during the last century. The resulting economic growth created a widespread view of American society as a land in which opportunity is bounded only by one's imagination and willingness to work. The Great Depression of the 1930s wounded but did not destroy American optimism, and prosperity returned in the 1940s, continuing through the 1960s. During this period, most Americans experienced a steadily rising standard of living.

Since then, however, the traditional confidence in upward social mobility has weakened, with some sociologists claiming that American society has entered an "age of decline" (Blumberg, 1981). Rather than expecting their standard of living to rise, a growing proportion of Americans seem to be more concerned with holding on to what they have. Even more significantly, a growing number of people may be losing the economic security long associated with middle-class living.

The basis for this change is that economic gains long taken for granted have slowed considerably. Figure 10–3 shows median family income for Americans between 1955 and 1986 in constant 1986 dollars. The pattern is clear: between 1955 and 1973, median family income for Americans grew by almost 65 percent; however, between 1973 and 1986, family income actually fell by about 2 percent (U.S. Bureau of the Census, 1987e).

The "middle-class slide." For generations, the American class system was supported by the belief that the

Table 10–3 INTERGENERATIONAL MOBILITY IN SIX INDUSTRIAL SOCIETIES

Country	Upward Social Mobility	Downward Social Mobility
Switzerland	45%	13%
France	39	20
Japan	36	22
United States	33	26
Sweden	31	24
West Germany	29	32

SOURCE: Seymour Martin Lipset and Reinhard Bendix, *Social Mobility in Industrial Society* (Berkeley: University of California Press, 1967), p. 25.

In this table, intergenerational social mobility is based on the occupation of fathers and their sons. Upward social mobility indicates a father with a blue-collar occupation and a son with a white-collar occupation. Downward social mobility indicates a father with a white-collar occupation and a son with a blue-collar occupation.

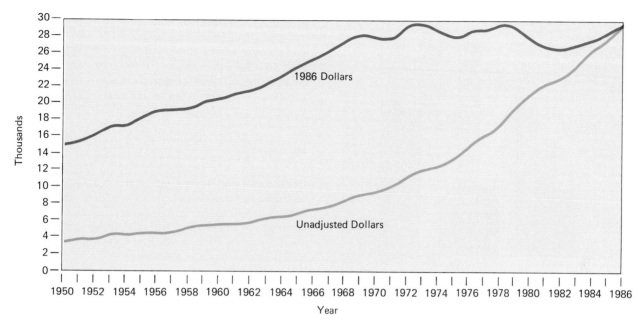

Figure 10–3   Median Family Income, 1950–1986

(U.S. Bureau of the Census)

middle class was steadily growing. Indeed, this was the case through most of this century. In addition, the rapid growth of white-collar occupations after World War II—which drew millions of Americans out of blue-collar jobs and farming—strengthened the perception that the United States was becoming more and more a middle-class society (Kerckhoff, Campbell, & Winfield-Laird, 1985).

But this upward structural social mobility began to subside during the 1970s (Pampel, Land, & Felson, 1977). In fact, the process began to *reverse* as a growing percentage of new jobs provided lower incomes. Figure 10–4 shows this turnaround. Between 1963 and 1973, almost half of new jobs were in the high-income range (more than $29,600 annually in constant 1986 dollars). Through the middle 1970s, more than 60 percent of new jobs were in the middle-income range (between $7,400 and $29,600). From 1979 to 1985, new high-income jobs fell to their lowest level, and the proportion of middle-income jobs also dropped considerably. Simultaneously, the proportion of low-income jobs more than doubled to over 40 percent. In simple terms, this means that many people—especially "average" Americans in

the middle class and working class—have suffered an economic decline. This is the economic change responsible for what is described as the *"middle-class slide."*

Many Americans are only too aware that this change has affected their lives. Far fewer people today than a generation ago expect to improve their social position. Indeed, a common fear is not being able to maintain the standard of living that people knew as children living with their parents. This problem is even more significant in light of the fact that families a generation ago were far less likely than families today to have two spouses in the labor force. Consider, as an illustration, that housing is a basic need that is becoming harder to meet. Housing prices and property taxes have risen rapidly since 1970. With little or no increase in buying power, the average American is coming to see home ownership—a basic part of the American Dream—as less likely. This is not surprising, since family income has stayed about constant while a 20 percent down payment on a typical new house has increased from roughly $5,000 in 1970 to about $20,000 in 1985 (cited in Brophy, 1986).

Of course, not all Americans have endured eco-

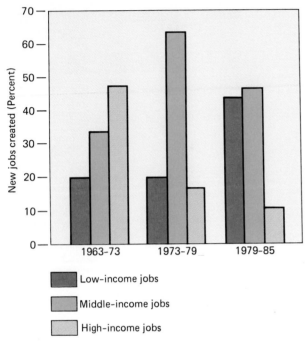

Figure 10–4 New American Jobs and Downward Mobility (Thurow, 1987)

Low-income jobs

Middle-income jobs

High-income jobs

nomic decline during the 1970s and 1980s. Indeed, the number of rich in America rose during that period, and may continue to rise even after the stock market crash of 1987. But the picture is no longer as positive for the *average* American. And for some who never had a grasp on middle-class standing, the situation is desperate. Black

Americans, for example, have strongly depended upon traditional industries such as steel for jobs. For such workers, the loss of some 3 million factory jobs since 1980 has been devastating (Jacob, 1986). As a consequence, the problem of poverty has received growing attention during the 1980s, as the next section explains.

POVERTY

Just as social stratification in America concentrates social resources in the hands of some, so it deprives others of enough resources for a secure life. Indeed, there can be no wealth and privilege without corresponding poverty and deprivation. This holds true both within American society and throughout the world.

Although *poverty* always signifies deprivation, the concept is commonly used in two different ways. **Relative poverty** refers to *a state of deprivation of social resources in relation to some standard of greater privilege.* Since all societies are stratified, relative poverty is found everywhere. Moreover, virtually anyone can be considered to be relatively poor or relatively rich according to the standard used in a comparison. A much more serious matter is **absolute poverty,** which means *a state of deprivation of social resources that is life-threatening.* Being in a state of absolute poverty is not a matter of comparing oneself with others; rather, it means that survival itself is in doubt.

Just as any one society is stratified, so is the world as a whole. Table 10–4 illustrates this pattern by present-

Underlying the "middle-class slide" is a change in the economy; high-paying industrial jobs of a generation ago are being replaced by jobs that require little skill and provide little income.

Table 10—4 INCOME AND WEALTH
IN WORLD PERSPECTIVE

Country	Gross National Product ($ billion)	Per Capita Income ($)
Industrialized Societies		
United States	3,765	13,451
Canada	340	13,000
United Kingdom	483	7,216
Soviet Union	2,067	2,600
Third World Societies		
Latin America		
Argentina	63	2,331
Bolivia	6	570
Colombia	40	1,112
El Salvador	4	854
Mexico	144	1,800
Nicaragua	4	804
Africa and the Middle East		
Cameroon	7	802
Egypt	38	686
Iran	158	2,160
Lebanon	2	1,150
Nigeria	72	750
Saudi Arabia	104	11,500
Burkina Faso (Upper Volta)	1	180
Zaire	7	127
Asia		
Bangladesh	13	119
China (People's Republic)	321	566
Kampuchea	1	100
India	200	150
Pakistan	34	280

SOURCE: U.S. Arms Control and Disarmament Agency, *World Military Expenditures and Arms Transfers 1986* (Washington, DC: U.S. Government Printing Office, 1987), pp. 59–100; *World Almanac and Book of Facts 1987* (New York: World Almanac, 1987), pp. 544–563.

This table shows gross national product (GNP) in U.S. dollars and yearly individual income for various societies. GNP data are for 1984; per capita income data range between 1981 and 1983 as available.

ing the gross national product (the total value of goods and services produced in a year) and the annual per capita income (the national average) for societies around the world. In world perspective, the United States and Canada are very rich societies. In fact, the industrialized societies of the West—often called the *First World*—are *all* quite rich. Only slightly less rich is the Soviet Union, which, along with the socialist societies of Eastern Europe, represents the *Second World*. Within these richer societies of the northern hemisphere, one can certainly speak about relative poverty, and the presence of significant hunger indicates the existence of absolute poverty for some segment of their populations. But absolute poverty is widespread in many societies of the southern hemisphere—including Latin America, Africa, the Middle East, and Asia. Taken together, these poor societies, which have experienced only limited industrialization, make up the *Third World*.

Third World Poverty

Not all Third World societies face acute problems of absolute poverty. Table 10–4 shows, for example, that oil-rich Saudi Arabia has an average personal income that is almost as high as that in the United States. But it is an exception. In many Third World societies, annual personal income is roughly equal to what an average American would earn in several days.

More than a billion people—one-fifth of the earth's population—live in absolute poverty. In the ten minutes it takes to read through this section of the chapter, about three hundred people in the world will die of starvation, three-fourths of them children. This amounts to over 15 million people each year.

Two brief comparisons will make such statistics more meaningful. At the end of World War II, the United States virtually obliterated the Japanese city of Hiroshima with an atomic bomb. The loss of life in the world from starvation, however, equals the Hiroshima death toll *every three days*. In yet other terms, it is likely that more people have died of starvation in the last five years than from all the wars, revolutions, and murders that have taken place during the last 150 years of human history (Burch, 1983).

The causes of absolute poverty on this scale are complex. First, Third World societies are generally agrarian, lacking industrial technology. Because they produce fewer resources, and also because what they produce tends to be highly concentrated within a small elite, the average person is very poor. People barely able to survive are terribly vulnerable to acts of nature such as droughts or floods, which destroy crops, and soil erosion, which destroys farmland (Barney, 1980). The recent droughts in three-fourths of the nations of Africa, for instance, have resulted in widespread starvation.

Second, as Chapter 20 explains in detail, Third World societies have the highest birth rates in the world. Low productivity and concentrated wealth make it impos-

the First World—that many critics claim adversely affects the economies of the Third World (Wallerstein, 1979; Syzmanski, 1981; Delacroix & Ragin, 1981; Harrison, 1984). As Chapters 18 and 21 explain, these multinationals exploit raw materials and cheap labor found in these countries to produce goods for rich societies. This places Third World societies in a state of economic dependency on the First World, causing an increasing economic gap between the rich and the poor nations of the world.

Some people claim that as industrialization proceeds in the Third World, the situation will improve (Rostow, 1978; Bauer, 1981). But this view has fewer supporters today than it did a decade ago. What economic growth has occurred in these societies has usually been more than offset by the rapid growth in population. As a result, the world problem of absolute poverty is likely to worsen in the years ahead. Perhaps, as some critics suggest, a drastic redistribution of world wealth may be needed to avert a catastrophe without precedent in human history.

Poverty in the United States

The United States is a rich society indeed. In fact, the personal wealth of the richest *individuals* in the United States is actually greater than the gross national product of several Third World *countries*! The income of the average American is also many times greater than that common in the Third World.

Even so, in 1985 almost 35 million people—about 14 percent of the population—in the United States were officially defined as poor, and another 12 million were close enough to the official poverty line to be considered marginally poor. In world context, most of the poor of the United States would have to be considered relatively well off, but there is more absolute poverty in American society than most people realize or than the government acknowledges. Estimates suggest that during the 1980s hunger has been the daily experience of 20 to 30 million Americans (Schwartz-Nobel, 1981; Physician Task Force on Hunger, 1987). According to the Children's Defense Fund (1985), poverty is the leading cause of mortality among young children in the United States, contributing to the deaths of perhaps ten thousand children each year. The means to eradicate this problem are certainly within reach—this organization estimates that one-half of just the *increase* in defense spending in 1986 would have been enough to rescue every child in America from poverty. Nevertheless, federal budget reductions

Poverty in the Third World falls hardest upon the children, a sobering truth strikingly portrayed by David Alfaro Siqueiros's painting "Echo of a Scream."

sible for these societies to address even the bare survival needs of their rapidly growing populations, which is why roughly one child in four dies before reaching the age of five.

The third important factor is the activity of large and powerful multinational corporations—centered in

in domestic spending during the early 1980s have hit poor people the hardest. Although programs intended to help the poor account for only about 10 percent of the federal budget, they have absorbed nearly one-third of all federal budget cuts (Interfaith Action for Economic Justice, 1984).

Who Is Poor in the United States?

Although poor people fit no single description, poverty is pronounced among certain categories of Americans.

Age. Children are more likely to be poor than Americans of any other age group—20.7 percent of those under the age of eighteen were poor in 1985. Americans over the age of sixty-five are also at greater risk of being poor—in 1985, 12.6 percent of them were officially designated as poor. Put in other terms, half of all poor people in America are either under eighteen years of age or over sixty-five.

Race and ethnicity. Almost 70 percent of all poor people are white. But in relation to their numbers, blacks are about three times as likely as whites to be poor. In 1985, 31.3 percent of all black Americans were poor, compared to 11.4 percent of whites. Poverty is also relatively high (29.0 percent) among Hispanic Americans (U.S. Bureau of the Census, 1986b).

Since both children and nonwhites are overrepresented among the poor, it is not surprising that nonwhite children are especially likely to live in poverty. Overall, about 20 percent of all Americans under 18 years of age lived in poverty in 1985, but 40 percent of Hispanic children were poor, as were 44 percent of all black children.

Sex. Poverty does not affect males and females equally. During the last few years, growing attention has been directed toward the **feminization of poverty,** which refers to *a trend by which females represent an increasing proportion of the poor.* Of all poor Americans over the age of eighteen, 62 percent are women and 38 percent are men. The problem of poverty is most serious for women who are the heads of households. They often have the financial burden of raising children, and if able to work, they typically hold low-paying jobs. About half of all poor families are households headed by a woman in which no husband is present. In marked contrast, only 4 percent of poor families are households headed by single men.

Area of residence. Poverty is found in both urban and rural areas, but not to the same degree. In 1985, 18.3 percent of Americans living outside of large urban areas were poor. In contrast, only 12.7 percent of people living in large urban areas were poor (U.S. Bureau of the Census, 1986b). This is partly because there is more wealth and often more social services in cities. Cities also have more jobs—and more different kinds of jobs—than rural areas. Thus urban areas provide relatively more opportunity for upward social mobility (Lipset & Bendix, 1967; Spates & Macionis, 1987).

People usually associate poverty with nonwhites in inner cities. But most poor people are white, and many struggle to survive in rural areas, like this family of sharecroppers in Scott County, Virginia.

Poverty: Explanations and Responses

Because America is such a rich society by world standards, explaining the presence of tens of millions of poor people is a matter of considerable importance. All sociologists agree that, along with affluence, poverty is a product of social stratification. Yet they often disagree as to how much responsibility people have for their own position in the social hierarchy. Two contrasting positions in this debate are outlined here.

The poor are primarily responsible for their poverty. During the last several centuries, the view that the poor are largely responsible for their own poverty has been widespread. This view is based on the assumption that society offers opportunity to those able and willing to take advantage of it. The poor, then, are seen as personally undeserving of a better standard of living.

In recent years, the most outspoken proponent of placing a considerable amount of blame for poverty on the poor themselves is Edward Banfield (1974). Banfield recognizes that some people—those who are too young, too old, or too sick to work—are poor through no fault of their own. But he claims that other poor people often contribute to their poverty. In simple terms, Banfield's argument is that, living in distinctive areas of cities or rural areas, the poor are guided by a distinctive lower-class culture based on a present-time orientation. This means that rather than working hard with an eye toward the future, poor people tend to live for the moment. This way of life—clearly irresponsible in Banfield's view—undermines their chance to get ahead. He asserts that the average poor person "doesn't want much success, knows he couldn't get it if he wanted to, and doesn't [even] want what might help him get success" (1974:62, quoting Herbert Hyman).

Banfield's view of the poor draws heavily on earlier research carried out by anthropologist Oscar Lewis (1961). Describing poverty in Latin America, Lewis suggested that the poor typically develop a distinctive way of life, which he called the *culture of poverty*. This involves resignation to being poor (considered a matter of fate) with little hope that the future will bring a better life. Furthermore, Lewis found that family life under conditions of poverty is likely to be anything but supportive and stable. Children grow up without the discipline and aspirations needed to make a better life for themselves, and thus a cycle of poverty is perpetuated.

This approach to explaining poverty has much in common with the structural-functional analysis of social stratification presented in Chapter 9. If we assume—

according to the Davis-Moore thesis—that some people have more talent and ability than others, and that more important occupations should provide more rewards than less important jobs do, then some amount of relative poverty would seem to be inevitable. Furthermore, this analysis suggests that the poor are largely people with the least personal merit. There is little surprise, then, in the fact that poor people typically contend with a stigma of deviance (Waxman, 1983).

Society is primarily responsible for poverty. The contrasting argument that the poor have little responsibility for their own poverty is made by William Ryan (1976). Ryan claims that by ignoring the ways in which society causes poverty, Banfield's analysis amounts to *blaming the victims* for their own suffering. In Ryan's view—which is consistent with the social-conflict analysis of social stratification—both wealth and poverty result from the unequal distribution of resources within a society. Ryan argues that there is very little economic opportunity for many Americans: this, and not the personal qualities of the poor themselves, should be the focus of attention in explaining poverty. Therefore, societies that have a very unequal distribution of wealth (such as the United States and Canada) are those that have a significant poverty problem because the system itself generates both the relatively rich and the relatively poor. On the other hand, societies that distribute wealth more equally (such as the Soviet Union and Sweden) lack these extremes.

Ryan does not deny that the poor are different in some ways from other Americans, but he claims that these differences are not *causes* of poverty as much as *consequences*. In other words, if poor people become resigned to their plight, it is because there is a real lack of opportunity in American society.

Evaluation. The explanations of poverty advanced by Banfield and Ryan are radically different. To the extent that Banfield is correct in placing most of the responsibility for poverty on the poor themselves, it would seem there is little society can do to reduce poverty. To the degree that Ryan is correct, however, poverty could be reduced by redistributing opportunity in a more equal manner. Rephrasing the Fitzgerald-Hemingway exchange recounted at the beginning of this chapter, we can see that Banfield sides with Fitzgerald by believing that "The poor are different from the rest of us." Ryan, on the other hand, echoes Hemingway's response: "Yes, they have less money." What the poor need, in Ryan's view, is simply the means of earning more income. Hopelessness, despair, and self-destructive violence are

Because of a pervasive belief that people themselves are somehow responsible for their poverty, many societies have an attitude of contempt for the "undeserving poor."

generated by poverty rather than the other way around—as illustrated by the experiences of John Coleman described in the box on p. 276.

There can be little doubt that individual ability and initiative play a part in shaping everyone's social position, at least over a lifetime. But our earlier discussion of who the poor in America actually are lends strong support to the conclusion that society is primarily responsible for poverty. The poor are not simply individuals who may lack ambition, but *categories* of people who do not have the same opportunities as others. The poor are children born into female-headed households; they are minorities who have long been denied equal participation in American society; and they are the elderly, who also have limited income through no fault of their own. Furthermore, about 40 percent of the adult poor are

actually *working poor*—people who cannot escape poverty in spite of working full-time. In part, this reflects social policy decisions such as maintaining the 1988 minimum wage level at $3.35, unchanged since 1981. At this level of pay, even two full-time workers could support a family only barely above the official poverty line. More broadly, however, the existence of millions of working poor reflects the fact that our society considers many jobs to be menial and, like the people who must perform them, undeserving of higher rewards.

Poverty, Politics, and Culture

Explanations of poverty reflect underlying political positions. One political position, consistent with the culture-of-poverty thesis, is that people have the right to as much property as they can achieve or inherit. A contrasting political position, consistent with William Ryan's explanation of poverty, holds that wealth should be distributed more equally among all members of a society. Not surprisingly, the culture-of-poverty thesis appeals most to Americans of higher social position, who would lose the most if wealth were distributed more equally. Similarly, Ryan's argument is endorsed by the poor, who would have the most to gain from radical change (Rytina, Form, & Pease, 1970).

Mainstream cultural values also affect explanations of poverty. As noted in earlier chapters, Americans tend to believe that individuals are largely responsible for their own life circumstances. No doubt, this accounts for the tendency to see successful people as personally meritorious and the poor as personally deficient. It also explains the controversial character of social welfare programs in American society. Welfare programs are defended as necessary to maintain a minimum standard of living for millions of Americans who do not have other opportunities or advantages. American cultural values that emphasize individualism, however, can lead to the conclusion that social welfare programs undermine initiative. But this ignores the vast amount of government benefits that are provided to wealthy Americans—welfare for the rich. Even as the Reagan administration was cutting social welfare programs during the early 1980s, for example, dozens of major corporations, including Boeing, General Electric, Dupont, Texaco, and Mobil, paid virtually no taxes in years in which they earned billions of dollars (Children's Defense Fund, 1985). More generally, these governmental policies are estimated to have reduced the income of each poor American by some

SOCIOLOGY OF EVERYDAY LIFE

Homeless on the Streets of New York

At the beginning of the 1980s, as the economy weakened and poverty rates rose, a term unfamiliar to many Americans gained new attention: *homelessness*. Economic decline, coupled to rising housing costs, inevitably places a home beyond the reach of more Americans. Estimates suggest that as many as 3 million Americans are homeless. They include men sleeping in doorways and women carrying all they own in a shopping bag down a busy city street. But perhaps one-third of all homeless Americans are *families* that have been pushed over the edge into homelessness by economic setbacks and policy decisions that have adversely affected poor and moderate-income people.

John R. Coleman, who spent ten years as a college president, explored the world of homeless people by living for ten days on the streets of New York. He learned that poverty can change people, and not always for the better. Here is part of his account:

> Somehow, 12 degrees at 6 A.M. was colder than I had counted on. I think of myself as relatively immune to cold, but standing on a deserted sidewalk outside Penn Station with the thought of ten days ahead of me as a homeless man, the immunity vanished. When I pulled my collar closer and my watch cap lower, it wasn't to look the part of a street person; it was to keep the wind out.

Another important lesson Coleman learned was that as one of the city's poor, he was not the same human being he had been only hours before:

> Was I imagining it, or were people looking at me in a completely different

way? I felt that men, especially the successful-looking ones in their forties and over, saw me and wondered. For the rest I wasn't there.

Entering a coffee shop for breakfast, Coleman began to realize how different he had actually become:

> The counterman looked me over carefully. When I ordered . . . he told me that I'd have to pay in advance. I did . . . but I noticed that the other customers were given checks and paid only when they left. . . . [Later] watching people come and go at the Volvo tennis tournament at Madison Square Garden, I sensed how uncomfortable they were at the presence of the homeless. Easy to love in the abstract, not so easy face to face. It's no wonder that the . . . police are under orders to chase us out of sight. . . . So far I've had eye contact with . . . three people who know me in my other life. None showed a hint of recognition.

Just as important, the experience of homelessness made Coleman perceive himself in different terms. On the second day he noted:

> Already, I notice changes in me. I walk much more slowly. I no longer see a need to beat a traffic light or be the first through a revolving door. Force of habit still makes me look at my wrist once in a while. But there's no watch there, and it wouldn't make any difference if there were. The thermometer has become much more important to me now than any timepiece could be.

One evening, Coleman sought relief from the cold on a heated grate on the street where he could sleep. Another man was already there, and of-

fered to share the space. Coleman asked him how long he had been living on the street.

> "Eleven years, going on twelve," he said.
>
> "This is only my second night."
>
> "You may not stick it out. This isn't for every man."

Ten days is certainly not enough time to learn very much about the lives of the homeless. But it was long enough for John Coleman to realize how much his self-concept would be changed by being poor. As he explains:

> Early this afternoon, I went again to [a] restaurant where I had eaten five times before. I didn't recognize the man at the cash register.
>
> "Get out," he said.
>
> "But I have money."
>
> "You heard me. Get out." His voice was stronger.
>
> "That man knows me," I said, looking toward the owner in the back of the restaurant.
>
> The owner nodded, and the man at the register said, "Okay, but sit in the back."
>
> If this life in the streets had been real, I'd have gone out the door at the first "Get out." And the assessment of me as not worthy would have been self-fulfilling; I'd have lost so much respect for myself that I wouldn't have been worthy of being served the next time. The downward spiral would have begun.

SOURCE: Excerpted from John R. Coleman, "Diary of a Homeless Man," *New York*, February 21, 1983, pp. 26–35.

$200 a year while simultaneously boosting the income of each of the richest 5 percent of Americans by over $3,000 annually (Center on Budget and Policy Priorities, 1985). Clearly, government policy has much to do with the extent of poverty in the United States. More egalitarian government policies, on the other hand, could maintain the income of all American families above the current poverty level.

American culture leads us to *personalize* our social position. Richard Sennett and Jonathan Cobb (1973) describe how working-class people tend to view their social position as a reflection of their own inadequacies—an understanding Sennett and Cobb term one of the *hidden injuries of class*. These people confess to feeling less able, less intelligent, and less significant than others who are more privileged. Similarly, people of higher social position typically explain their success in terms of personal merit. Upon graduation from college, for example, they receive congratulations and praise from families and friends. Even though a college education is virtually taken for granted among children of wealthier families and is exceptional among lower-class people, a college degree is viewed as a badge of ability attesting to the merit of the individual.

Poverty, then, is a complex problem that involves far more than the personal qualities of the poor themselves. To reduce or eliminate poverty would require changing the system of social stratification, something more privileged Americans are likely to oppose. Furthermore, our tendency to view the poor as personally deficient is deeply rooted in American culture and therefore difficult to eradicate.

SUMMARY

1. American society is characterized by pronounced economic inequality. This involves differences of income and even greater differences of wealth, and provides some Americans with far more power than others.

2. Occupational prestige is the second major dimension of social inequality in the United States. White-collar occupations generally provide more social prestige and income than do blue-collar occupations. The pink-collar occupations typically held by women provide little social prestige or income.

3. Formal education is the third major dimension of social inequality in the United States. While about three-fourths of Americans have completed high school, less than one-fifth are college graduates.

4. Social standing in the United States is related to a number of factors, including ancestry, race and ethnicity, sex, and religion.

5. The upper class is a small elite (about 4 percent) of the richest and most powerful Americans. The upper-upper class represents the old rich, whose wealth has been transmitted over several generations; the lower-upper class is the newly rich, whose primary source of wealth is earned income.

6. The middle class includes 40 to 45 percent of Americans. The upper-middle class is distinguished from the rest of the middle class by higher income, higher-prestige occupations, and more education.

7. The working class includes about one-third of Americans. With below-average income, working-class families have less financial security than those in the middle class. They commonly work in blue-collar and low-prestige white-collar jobs. Few working-class Americans have more than a high-school education.

8. The lower class represents about one-fifth of the American population. Most people in this category fall below the official poverty line or are marginally poor. Blacks, Hispanics, and other minorities are disproportionately represented in the lower class.

9. Social class affects virtually all dimensions of life, including attitudes, patterns of family life, and even personal health and life expectancy.

10. Social mobility is common in the United States, but usually only small changes occur from one generation to the next. Patterns of social mobility in the United States do not differ significantly from those in other industrial societies.

11. Since the early 1970s, changes in the American economy have resulted in a reduced standard of living for many moderate-income Americans.

12. About 1 billion people in the Third World are desperately poor. Third World poverty is linked to (1) low economic productivity, (2) large and growing populations, and (3) the operations of multinational corporations based in rich societies.

13. Some 35 million Americans are officially classified as poor. About half are children under the age of eighteen or elderly people. Most poor Americans are white, but blacks and Hispanics are overly represented among the poor. Households headed by women are especially likely to be poor. Rural people are somewhat more likely to be poor than urban people.

14. Edward Banfield suggests that much poverty is caused by the personal characteristics of the poor themselves. Opposing this view, William Ryan has argued that poverty is caused by the unequal distribution of wealth in society. Although Banfield's view is consistent with the American cultural pattern of personalizing social position, Ryan's view is closer to the truth.

KEY CONCEPTS

absolute poverty a state of deprivation of social resources that is life-threatening

feminization of poverty a trend by which females represent an increasing proportion of the poor

income occupational wages or salaries and earnings from investments

intergenerational social mobility change in the social position of children in relation to that of their parents

intragenerational social mobility change in social position occurring during a person's lifetime

relative poverty a state of deprivation of social resources in relation to some standard of greater privilege

wealth the total amount of money and valuable goods that any person or family controls

SUGGESTED READINGS

These two paperbacks provide a detailed account of many issues raised in this chapter. The first presents an overview of the class structure of the United States; the second explores how Americans evaluate patterns of social inequality.

Dennis Gilbert and Joseph A. Kahl. *The American Class Structure: A New Synthesis*. 3rd ed. Homewood, IL: Dorsey Press, 1987.

James R. Kleugel and Eliot R. Smith. *Beliefs About Inequality: Americans' Views of What Is and What Ought to Be*. Hawthorne, NY: Aldine de Gruyter, 1986.

Data on income and wealth distribution in an easy-to-understand form are found in this booklet.

Stephen J. Rose. *The American Profile Poster: Who Owns What, Who Makes How Much, Who Works Where, & Who Lives with Whom*. New York: Pantheon Books, 1986.

In this book, the author takes a probing—and often amusing—look at social differences in America.

Paul Fussell. *Class: A Guide Through the American Status System*. New York: Summit Books, 1983.

The following two books examine the American upper class. The first historically traces the development of the upper class, and draws on the research and life experiences of a sociologist who is himself one of this privileged category. The second is a detailed study of upper-class women, explaining how the lives of privileged women differ from those of privileged men.

E. Digby Baltzell. *Philadelphia Gentlemen: The Making of a National Upper Class*. Philadelphia: University of Pennsylvania Press, 1979.

Susan A. Ostrander. *Women of the Upper Class*. Philadelphia: Temple University Press, 1984.

A critical analysis of the concentration of wealth and power in American society is contained in this paperback.

G. William Domhoff. *Who Rules America Now? A View for the 80s*. Englewood Cliffs, NJ: Prentice-Hall, 1983.

The working class—often ignored in favor of the rich and the poor—is described in this paperback.

David Halle. *America's Working Man: Work, Home, and Politics among Blue-Collar Property Owners*. Chicago: University of Chicago Press, 1984.

This book describes how the decline of traditional industries in the United States has threatened the well-being of many Americans.

David Bensman and Roberta Lynch. *Rusted Dreams: Hard Times in a Steel Community*. New York: McGraw-Hill, 1987.

This book examines the "feminization of poverty"—the link between being female and being poor—in the United States and other societies.

Hilda Scott. *Working Your Way to the Bottom: The Femini-*

zation of Poverty. Boston: Routledge & Kegan Paul/Pandora Press, 1984.

This paperback provides a good introduction to the problem of world hunger.

Arthur Simon, *Bread for the World*. Rev. ed. New York: Paulist Press; Grand Rapids: Wm. B. Eerdmans Publishing Co., 1984.

This volume of fifteen papers by a number of experts examines poverty from a social policy perspective.

Sheldon H. Danziger and Daniel H. Weinberg. *Fighting Poverty: What Works and What Doesn't*. Cambridge: Harvard University Press, 1986.

The consequences of the Reagan administration's policies toward the poor are described in this book.

Tom Joe and Cheryl Rogers. *By the Few for the Few: The Reagan Welfare Legacy*. Lexington, MA: Lexington Books, 1985.

Based on information provided by the homeless themselves, the first of the following books describes the problem of homelessness in the United States. The second examines the issue from a feminist point of view.

F. Steven Redburn and Terry F. Buss. *Responding to America's Homeless*. New York: Praeger, 1987.

Sophie Watson. *Housing and Homelessness: A Feminist Perspective*. New York: Routlege & Kegan Paul, 1986.

CHAPTER 11

Race and Ethnicity

Almost forty years ago, in the city of Topeka, Kansas, a minister walked hand in hand with his seven-year-old daughter to an elementary school four blocks from their home. Linda Brown wanted to enroll in the second grade, but the school refused to admit her. Instead, public school officials required her to attend another school two miles away. This meant that she had to walk six blocks every day to a bus stop, where she sometimes waited half an hour for the bus. In bad weather, Linda Brown would be soaking wet by the time the bus came; one day she became so cold at the bus stop that she walked back home. Why, she asked her parents, could she not attend the school only four blocks away?

The answer—difficult for loving parents to give their child—was Linda Brown's introduction to the fact that her skin color made her a second-class citizen in American society. Her parents began to speak to other black people in town about the injustice of preventing black children such as Linda from enrolling in schools attended by white children. Ultimately, a suit was filed on behalf of Linda Brown and several other children, and in 1954, Linda Brown's case came before the Supreme Court of the United States. In *Brown v. the Board of Education of Topeka*, the Supreme Court ruled unanimously that racially segregated schools inevitably provide blacks with an inferior education, so that schools for black children could no longer be considered "separate but equal" to those for whites. A generation later, Linda Brown recalled this decision as a "turning point for black America" (U.S. Commission on Civil Rights, 1974:17).

More recently, Canada experienced a political crisis that had much in common with the racial issue raised by the Brown case. About two-thirds of Canadians speak only English, while one-fifth—mostly in the province of Quebec—speak only French. French Canadians gen-

Linda Brown, a key figure in the civil rights movement as a child, with her grandson today.

erally have lower social standing than the English-speaking majority. This led to a proposal that Quebec break away from the rest of Canada, which was the focus of a political referendum in 1980. When the dust settled, the voters of Quebec defeated the proposal, but not by much.

It is easy to think of the United States or Canada as a society unified by a common culture. But as the issue raised by Linda Brown suggests, race can divide a society, and as the recent events in Canada show, the same is true of ethnicity. Race and ethnicity represent dimensions of both social diversity and social inequality in all industrial societies.

Race

A **race** is *a category of people with common biological traits passed from generation to generation.* Races are commonly distinguished on the basis of skin color, hair texture, shape of facial features, and body type. In the nineteenth century, biologists identified three major racial classifications: *Caucasians,* with relatively light skin and fine hair; *Negroids,* with darker skin and coarse and curly hair; and *Mongoloids,* with yellow or brown skin and distinctive folds on the eyelids. Although all human beings are members of a single biological species, physical variability developed over thousands of generations because people live within different physical environments (Molnar, 1983). For protection from the sun in hot climates, for example, human beings developed darker skin than people living within more temperate climates.

Initially, then, physical differences among human beings were associated with geographical regions of the world. Over thousands of years, however, human beings intermarried with one another as they migrated from place to place. As a result, genetic characteristics once common to a single region spread through most of the world. Within the crossroads of the world—such as the Middle East—people display extensive genetic variation. More isolated people, such as the Japanese, have relatively less genetic variation; but no society lacks this genetic mixture. We now know, therefore, that there are no biologically pure races. Caucasians, or whites, actually display skin color that ranges from very light to very dark; and the same is true of Negroids and Mongoloids. In fact, some whites actually have darker skin and hair than some blacks! Caucasians of southern India, for example, have very dark skin, while the Negroid aborigines of Australia often have bright blond hair.

Research shows that white and black Americans are, genetically speaking, quite mixed. Over many generations, the genetic traits typical of Negroid Africans and Caucasian Europeans have combined; the Mongoloid traits of native North Americans have also spread widely through the American population. Thus many black people have a large proportion of Caucasian genes, and the opposite is true of people who appear to be white. In short, race is not a black-and-white issue.

Biological facts, however, may have little to do with cultural definitions of race. Physical traits such as skin color have erroneously been linked to such human qualities as innate mental and emotional capacities. No doubt this is the reason that people often attempt to make racial categories clearly distinct even though they

Americans commonly place people within one of these three familiar racial categories. In fact, however, there are no biologically pure races, since genes that affect physical traits have been widely mixed over countless generations.

Race—Not Always a Black-and-White Issue

Susie Phipps of Sulphur, Louisiana, had always assumed that she was white. One morning in 1978, she drove to the Louisiana Bureau of Vital Statistics in New Orleans for a birth certificate needed to obtain a passport. She was startled to see that the document listed her parents as "colored," meaning that she was legally considered to be black. Susie Phipps learned that she was not exactly who she had always thought she was. "If it was the other way around, if I was black, I'd be just as shocked and would want it fixed right," she claims.

Today Louisiana allows parents to indicate the race of their child, but when Phipps was born in the 1930s, state law defined anyone with more than one thirty-second black ancestry as black. This was an effort to keep the color line as sharp as possible in a society in which whites and blacks lived as distinct social categories.

Phipps initiated a legal case to change her racial designation. After evidence was presented that she did have one black ancestor—about 150 years ago—her request was denied.

The state of Louisiana maintained that Phipps might be as much as 17 percent black. But anthropologist Monro Edmunson testified in court that *most* American whites have more than one thirty-second black genes. Therefore, under the old Louisiana law, most of the white population of the United States would be called black!

SOURCE: Based on *People Magazine*, December 6, 1982, pp. 155–156, and subsequent news reports.

are not. Until recently, for example, the state of Louisiana defined anyone who had at least one thirty-second black ancestry as "colored." Under such laws, many people who think of themselves as white may be surprised to learn that they are legally black. The box provides a case in point.

Ethnicity

Ethnicity is defined as *a cultural heritage shared by a category of people*. Members of an *ethnic group* often share a place of ancestral origin, language, and religion, which is the basis of their collective identity. The ancestors of Polish, Hispanic, and Chinese Americans, for example, all lived in particular nations of the world, as did the forebears of French and English Canadians. English is the official language of the United States, but over 11 million Americans speak Spanish in their homes, while Italian, German, and French are each spoken in the homes of about 1.5 million Americans (see Table 3–1). The United States and Canada are also predominantly Protestant societies, but most Americans and Canadians of Spanish, Italian, and Polish ancestry are Roman Catholic, while many others of Greek, Ukranian, and Russian ancestry are members of the Eastern Orthodox Church. More than 6 million Americans (with ori-

gins in many different nations) are Jews whose ethnic identity has been strongly shaped by a common religion.

Race and ethnicity are distinct concepts: the first biological, the second cultural. But the two often go hand in hand. Asian Americans, for example, have distinctive physical traits and—for those who maintain their ancestors' way of life—cultural traits as well. Not surprisingly, then, ethnic characteristics are sometimes incorrectly viewed as racial. For example, Jews are occasionally described as a race although they are distinctive only in terms of a religious tradition as well as a history of persecution by other people (Goldsby, 1977). Ethnicity is also subject to change if people adopt a different way of life. The physical traits of race, on the other hand, persist over generations.

Minority Groups

A **minority group** is *a category of people defined by physical or cultural characteristics subject to social disadvantage*. Minority groups are of many kinds, including people with physical disabilities, political radicals, and homosexuals. But race and ethnicity are the most common bases of minority groups. Table 11–1 presents the size of various racial and ethnic groups in the United States. Minority groups have two major characteristics.

Table 11—1 RACIAL AND ETHNIC GROUPS IN THE UNITED STATES, 1980

Racial or Ethnic Classification	Approximate Number of Americans
Black	26,495,000
Hispanic	14,609,000
Mexican American	8,740,000
Puerto Rican	2,014,000
Cuban American	803,000
Other	3,051,000
Native American	1,420,000
Chinese	806,000
Filipino	775,000
Japanese	701,000
Korean	355,000
Vietnamese	262,000
Whites of European Ancestry	
English	49,598,000
German	49,224,000
Irish	40,166,000
French	12,892,000
Italian	12,184,000
Scottish	10,049,000
Polish	8,228,000
Dutch	6,304,000
Swedish	4,345,000
Norwegian	3,454,000
Russian	2,781,000
Czech	1,892,000
Hungarian	1,777,000
Welsh	1,665,000
Danish	1,518,000
Portuguese	1,024,000

SOURCE: U.S. Bureau of the Census.

Distinctive identity. First, the fact that members of a minority group have a distinctive social identity is evident in their practice of referring to themselves as "we" and "us," while designating others as "they" and "them." Because race is highly visible (and virtually impossible to change), members of racial minority groups are keenly aware of their race. Ethnicity (which can be changed) is more variable in this regard. Throughout American history, some people have downplayed their ethnicity, while others have maintained their cultural traditions and lived within ethnic neighborhoods.

Race and ethnicity are maintained over generations to the extent that people marry others like themselves.

Only a small fraction of marriages within the United States are interracial. Ethnic groups intermarry more commonly, although some cultural—and especially religious—traditions oppose marrying out of one's category. If people were to marry with no regard for race and ethnicity, of course, racial and ethnic groups would cease to exist within several generations.

Subordination. As noted in Chapter 10, race and ethnicity are part of the American system of social stratification. In addition to a distinctive identity, minority groups typically have lower incomes and less power, occupational prestige, and education. Because of this subordinate position within society, minority groups are also called *subordinate groups.*

Not *all* members of a minority group are equally disadvantaged. Within American society, for example, some blacks, Hispanics, and Armenians are very wealthy. But even those who are exceptionally well-to-do are subject to being defined as socially inferior and to being treated unfairly. Race and ethnicity often serve as a master status (as described in Chapter 6) that overpowers other personal traits.

Finally, minority groups often represent a small proportion of the population. But subordination is not the result of being a numerical minority as much as of lacking wealth and power. For example, Chapter 9 described how blacks in South Africa—a majority of the population—are grossly deprived of economic and political power by the white numerical minority. In the United States, women represent slightly more than half of the population but are still a subordinate group.

Prejudice

Prejudice is *an unfounded generalization about a category of people.* Prejudice may be directed toward people of a certain social class, sex, sexual orientation, age, political affiliation, racial or ethnic group. The word *prejudice* is closely related to the word *prejudgment,* indicating that a negative or positive attitude is formed before gaining personal knowledge of people in a social category. In general, we tend to have positive prejudices toward people like ourselves and negative prejudices toward those who are different from us. As the box suggests, within any culture prejudice may be taken for granted as natural.

The existence of prejudice is evident in a classic piece of research conducted in the 1940s by a Canadian social scientist. To one hundred hotels and resorts that advertised in a Toronto newspaper he sent two identical letters asking to reserve a room for a specific date. Both letters were mailed at the same time, but one letter used the English name Lockwood, while the other carried the German-Jewish name Greenberg. He received ninety-five responses to the first letter, all but two offering "Mr. Lockwood" a room. The second letter, however, brought only fifty-two responses, and just thirty-six offers of a room to "Mr. Greenberg." In other words, without knowing the person involved, a majority of hotel operators apparently had negative attitudes toward Jews as a category of people (Allport, 1958:4–5).

Stereotypes

A common form of prejudice is the **stereotype**—*a description of a category of people that persists even in the face of contrary evidence.* Because stereotypes often involve emotions of love (toward members of ingroups) and hate or fear (toward members of outgroups), they are hard to change even when evidence shows that they are wrong. Many people, for example, have a stereotypical understanding of the poor as lazy and irresponsible freeloaders who could support themselves if they wanted to, but choose instead to rely on welfare. As explained in Chapter 10, this stereotype does not square with the facts: most poor Americans are actually children and elderly people, and others who do work hard, but who earn little money all the same.

Stereotypes about racial and ethnic minorities are widespread in most societies. In the United States, white people often stereotype nonwhites in much the same way that wealthy people stereotype the poor: "Black people would rather be on welfare than work." Such an assertion, of course, ignores the fact that most poor people in America are white and that most blacks work as hard as anyone else and are not poor. Blacks are, however, more likely than whites to be poor—so there is sometimes a bit of truth in stereotypes. But by emphasizing some facts while ignoring others, stereotypes are a gross distortion of reality.

Racism

One of the most powerful and destructive forms of prejudice, **racism** is *the belief that one racial category is innately superior or inferior to another.* Racism involves more than the belief that one culture is better than another; it is the assertion that one part of humanity is *innately* better than another.

By the end of the nineteenth century, European societies—most notably Great Britain, France, and Spain—had established economic and political control

CROSS-CULTURAL COMPARISON

Prejudice in the United States and Yugoslavia

The author recalls a conversation during a visit to Yugoslavia:

I had joined a friend for dinner in the northern province of Slovenia—the most industrialized and wealthy part of Yugoslavia. I inquired about the relations among various ethnic minorities in Yugoslavia, which served to prod my companion to ask first about the United States.

"What is the problem between people who are black and white in your country?" he asked. "I have always heard that whites believe such bad things about blacks. This is silly—how can so many things be wrong with so many people simply because their color is different?"

I wondered how to begin explaining something as complex as the history of race relations in America to someone with little knowledge of the United States. Perhaps, I thought, some of what I had learned about Yugoslavia would allow me to draw a useful parallel. I recalled the ethnic groups living in the southern provinces of Yugoslavia, who have a religion and a rural way of life that contrast sharply with life in Slovenia.

"What about the Yugoslavs who live in the south? Why do Slovenians often speak negatively about *them?*" I asked.

"Well, of course!" he shot back. "As you learn more about Yugoslavia, you'll find that people from the south are lazy and can't be trusted. Those people don't like to work the way we do. And besides, they drink and fight all the time. Of course no one likes them."

He then sat quietly for a moment, thinking of what he had said. A bit of a smile came over his face.

"So," he began again, "enough of such things. Let us talk about something else."

over vast regions of the world. The United States had also acquired valuable possessions overseas, including Cuba, Puerto Rico, and the Philippines. Acquiring wealth from colonies often involved the ruthless oppression of other peoples. What better way to justify oppression than to believe that those subjugated are inferior beings? In much the same way, of course, many whites within the United States believed in the innate inferiority of Native Americans, whose land they usurped, and in the inferiority of black Americans, whom they forced into slavery.

In the twentieth century, racism was a foundation of the Nazi regime in Germany. Nazi racial doctrine proclaimed an "Aryan race" of blond-haired, blue-eyed Caucasians as a pure racial type—a view already noted as biological fiction. Even more troubling was the Nazi belief that this mythical Aryan race was innately superior and destined to rule the world. Nazi racism was used to justify killing "inferior beings," including some 6 million European Jews and millions of Poles, gypsies, homosexuals, and physically and mentally disabled people.

Racism is still prevalent today. Racial conflict is now common in European societies as millions of immigrants from former colonies force whites to confront greater racial and ethnic diversity (Glenn & Kennedy-Keel, 1986). As one British lawyer notes, "We haven't come to terms with the fact that black people are really here. . . . White society wants to believe it's all a bad dream—that they will wake up one morning and all the blacks will be gone. Well, it's not going to happen" (cited in Nielsen, 1984:40). Many whites in the United States also hold racist views of darker-skinned immigrants from Latin America and Asia.

Causes of Prejudice

If prejudice is not a rational assessment of facts, what are its origins? Social scientists have approached this problem in four major ways.

Scapegoat theory. The first approach, developed by John Dollard and others (1939), links prejudice to frustration. For example, if a white woman working in a textile factory is frustrated by her low wages and poor working conditions, her frustration may lead to hostility. But where should this hostility be directed? Although those who operate the factory would seem to be the most reasonable targets, expressing hostility toward powerful people is dangerous—she could lose her job. A safer course of action is to blame *powerless* people, even though there may be little rational basis for doing so. In this case, the woman might direct her hostility toward her black co-workers: "It's because there are so many blacks in this factory that we are treated like this!" This illustrates the use of a **scapegoat**—*one person or category of people unfairly blamed for the troubles of another*. Because they typically have little social power, minority groups are easily used as scapegoats.

The authoritarian personality. At the end of World War II, T. W. Adorno (1950) and a number of colleagues suggested that extreme prejudice may be a personality trait of some people but not of others. Using questionnaires and interviews, these researchers found that some people displayed strong prejudice toward many minority groups, while others revealed little prejudice against any. The prejudiced people, whom they described as having

Negative stereotypes of blacks in the United States in the nineteenth century were strengthened by popular songs such as "Jim Crow," which portrayed blacks as physically strong but intellectually weak—in short, well suited for a life of slave labor.

JIM CROW.

NEW YORK.

Published by Firth & Hall, No.1 Franklin Sq

authoritarian personalities, conformed rigidly to cultural values and believed moral issues to be a clear matter of right and wrong. In addition, such people viewed society as naturally competitive and hierarchical, with "better" people inevitably dominating those who are weaker. On the other hand, people who displayed little prejudice were less rigid in their morality and believed that, ideally, society should be relatively egalitarian. They felt uncomfortable in any situation in which some people are able to exercise power over others.

The researchers suggested that people with authoritarian personalities often had little education and many were raised by harsh and demanding parents. Faced with strong parental demands but little emotional support, children may develop considerable anger and anxiety, which leads them to be hateful and aggressive toward scapegoats—others they define as their social inferiors.

Prejudice and culture. The third approach suggests that while prejudice may be pronounced among particular people or generated by particular situations, some prejudice is a general element of culture. Ethnocentrism, discussed in Chapter 3, is one type of cultural prejudice. Using our own cultural standards, we can easily make unfairly negative evaluations of other cultures. But even within American society, dominant cultural values tend to assess some categories of people more positively than others. Emory Bogardus (1968) has examined this issue for more than forty years using the concept of *social distance*, or how closely people are willing to interact with members of various racial and ethnic categories. He asked subjects to examine a series of statements describing relationships ranging from marriage to a member of a certain category of people (low social distance) to excluding that category of people from the country (high social distance). Bogardus found that Americans tend to evaluate people of English, Canadian, and Scottish background most positively; very little social distance is expressed toward these ethnic groups. Greater social distance is expressed toward people whose background is French, German, Swedish, and Dutch. Even more negative evaluations are made of the Italians, Poles, Czechs, Jews, and Greeks. Close to the bottom of the list are blacks, Turks, Chinese, and Koreans. Those with the most positive evaluation—such as the English—are generally welcomed as family members, while others—such as blacks and Turks—are often avoided as friends. But no category of people is typically evaluated so negatively as to be excluded from the United States.

Obviously, these evaluations reflect the fact that American culture has been shaped largely by people of English ancestry, who were, after all, the original European settlers of the United States. The fact that similar evaluations are made by Americans of all races and ethnicities (except, of course, that everyone perceived little social distance from their *own* group) suggests that both positive and negative prejudices are built into American culture.

Prejudice and social conflict. The fourth approach points out that in addition to being an element of culture, prejudice is also generated by social conflict among categories of people. Prejudice arises, in other words, as a type of ideology (see Chapter 9) that justifies the oppression of minority groups.

In the United States, the enslavement of blacks greatly enriched white plantation owners in the South and white slave traders in the North. Even after slavery ended in 1865, white employers benefited from the low-cost labor of blacks and other minority groups. In the nineteenth and early twentieth centuries, many poor immigrants from Europe and Asia experienced wretched working conditions as they labored for those with greater social power. Today many impoverished immigrants from Asia and Latin America perform boring and physically exhausting jobs for the minimum wage and sometimes even less. Although law and, at times, sheer terror are used to enforce this oppression, prejudice serves as a powerful force to justify patterns of social inequality.

Following the ideas of Karl Marx, prejudice toward minority groups can be understood as serving the interests of the capitalist class. Defining minority-group workers as socially inferior justifies both low wages and poor working conditions. In addition, capitalists may encourage prejudice as a means of dividing workers so that they are less likely to organize (Geschwender, 1978). In this way, minority groups are used as scapegoats—blamed for the problems of workers that are actually caused by capitalists.

Discrimination

Closely related to prejudice is the concept of **discrimination**, which means *treating various categories of people differently*. Like prejudice, discrimination can be either positive (providing special advantages) or negative (subjecting categories of people to disadvantages). While prejudice refers to attitudes and beliefs, however, discrimination is a matter of behavior.

Prejudice and discrimination often go hand in hand. If a personnel manager is prejudiced against members of a particular minority group, she may refuse to hire them. Robert Merton (1976) describes such a person as an *active bigot* (see Figure 11–1). In some cases, however, prejudice may not lead to discrimination. If the prejudiced personnel manager knows that discriminatory hiring practices are against the law, she may put aside her prejudiced beliefs on the job, becoming the *timid bigot* in Figure 11–1. And what Merton calls *fair-weather liberals* may discriminate without being prejudiced; an unprejudiced personnel manager may discriminate because her employer wants her to do so. Finally, Merton's *all-weather liberal* lacks both prejudice and discrimination.

Like prejudice, discrimination involves more than the behavior of some individuals. **Institutional discrimination** refers to *patterns of discrimination that are woven into the fabric of society*. As the story of Linda Brown that opened this chapter indicates, social mores and laws have stood between minority groups and quality education, better jobs, decent housing, and even the right to own land and to vote. Although embracing the principle of individual equality under the law, American society has practiced both prejudice and discrimination. This paradox is perhaps most clearly evident in the fact that in World War II soldiers fought to protect American freedoms in racially segregated units of the armed forces.

Since the 1950s, legal changes have reduced—but not eliminated—overt patterns of discrimination.

Figure 11–1 Patterns of Prejudice and Discrimination
(Merton, 1976)

Does the person discriminate?

Is the person prejudiced?	Yes	No
Yes	Active Bigot (prejudiced person who discriminates)	Timid Bigot (prejudiced person who does not discriminate)
No	Fair-Weather Liberal (nonprejudiced person who discriminates)	All-Weather Liberal (nonprejudiced person who does not discriminate)

As sociologists have learned, changing the law does not always change the attitudes and behavior of individuals (Marshall et al., 1978). In part, this is because antidiscrimination laws are not always actively enforced. The 1954 Supreme Court ruling that outlawed segregated schools was greeted by widespread opposition, especially in southern states. The social separation of blacks and whites had become so deeply rooted in American society that change occurred very gradually. In fact, two decades later, educational segregation was still widespread in Topeka, Kansas (U.S. Commission on Civil Rights, 1974). Another report from Philadelphia claimed that in 1983 almost two-thirds of white students still attended racially imbalanced schools (Woodall, 1984).

Discrimination remains a problem in housing as well. The 1968 Civil Rights Act mandates a policy of "fair housing" by which the purchase or rental of housing should be equally available to all people of a given income level. Yet there is widespread evidence that housing discrimination persists. Sometimes the discrimination is overt, as in the case of a white landlord who refuses to rent an available apartment to an Asian couple, or a real estate agent who "steers" the couple toward buying a home in only Asian neighborhoods. Other cases involve de facto discrimination, in which people engage in practices that have unintended discriminatory consequences. For example, banks and other moneylending agencies may refuse to lend money to people wishing to buy a home in a neighborhood that the agency considers a poor investment risk. This may not reflect prejudice as much as sound business sense. But such actions deprive the poorer members of minority groups of the opportunity to buy a home they can afford.

A much more complex problem is poverty itself. As noted in Chapter 10, blacks are three times more likely to be poor than whites. This suggests that discrimination in terms of economic opportunity is deeply embedded in American society. As one member of Congress asked, "Can 'fair housing' come about if the economic disparity between white and black citizens is not first lessened?" (cited in Calmore, 1986:117).

Prejudice and Discrimination: The Vicious Circle

Prejudice and discrimination persist in American society because they are mutually reinforcing. W. I. Thomas offered a simple explanation of this fact, noted in Chapter

SOCIOLOGY OF EVERYDAY LIFE

Ethnic Therapy in America

According to psychologist Judith Weinstein Klein, each of us must recognize that we are "born into an ethnic, social, cultural context that affects the way we view ourselves." We can understand our personal experiences and problems, she maintains, only by realizing the importance of race and ethnicity in our lives.

This is the foundation of *ethnotherapy*, begun over a decade ago to address problems encountered by many minority group members. Therapy groups, in which a small number of people talk together under the guidance of a trained professional, reveal that many members of a particular racial or ethnic group grapple with the *same* personal problems. According to Klein, "All ethnic minorities have to deal with self-hate and feelings of inadequacy as members of American culture."

Among blacks, racism may cause repressed anger as well as uncertainty about personal capabilities. Some blacks who have been successful struggle with a sense of guilt at leaving other blacks behind.

Another therapist, Joseph Giordano, leads ethnotherapy sessions for Italian Americans. Here one important issue is the conflict between the traditional subordination of Italian women and the growing aspirations of Italian-American women. One indication of this sexual tug-of-war is the fact that in Giordano's sessions men report being married to or dating Italian-American women, while the women typically have husbands or partners who are not Italian Americans.

Among Jewish Americans, pride and respect for their religion is often tainted by self-hate: a product of being socialized within a predominantly non-Jewish society. Some express confusion and anger as they recall their past attempts to become less Jewish. One woman explained that cosmetic surgery on less than perfect noses (widely called *nose jobs*) was as common as having braces on teeth. Men and women also admit angrily confronting each other with negative stereotypes drawn from the larger society. Jewish women, accused of being self-centered, counter that Jewish men are neurotic, dependent, and unsexual.

There is an important element of the sociological perspective in ethnotherapy. To understand our own lives, we must recognize the power of society to shape our attitudes and actions.

SOURCE: Adapted from John Leo, "Therapy for Ethnics," *Time*, March 15, 1982, p. 42.

---

6 as the Thomas theorem: if situations are defined as real, they are real in their consequences (1966:301; orig. 1931).

This important idea has two parts. First, Thomas recognized that reality is not a matter of hard facts, but of how people define situations. The traits of any category of people are therefore a matter of social definition. In this way, stereotypes become very real to those who believe them, including those who suffer as a result of them. The box illustrates how some members of minority groups deal with this problem.

Second, if people define a minority group in a negative way, they will act accordingly toward that group, making the definition of the situation real in its consequences. To illustrate, many whites in the United States have historically defined nonwhites as an inferior category of human beings. This resulted in discrimination by which nonwhites were denied equal access to jobs, income, education, and political rights. While not producing *innate* inferiority, of course, this did produce *social* inferiority, constraining many nonwhites to poverty, low-prestige occupations, and poor housing within racially segregated neighborhoods.

Therefore, prejudice and discrimination form a *vicious circle*—a situation that perpetuates itself over time. White people today see that many blacks, Mexican Americans, and Native Americans are socially disadvantaged. All too readily, they may interpret this as evidence that such categories of people have been innately inferior all along—an interpretation William Ryan (1976) described (see Chapter 9) as "blaming the victim." This justifies a new round of prejudice and discrimination. Therefore, the *consequences* of definitions made in the past become *causes* of new definitions that affect the future—a cycle that repeats itself again and again, as graphically illustrated in Figure 11–2.

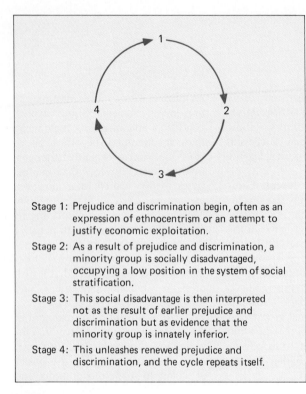

Stage 1: Prejudice and discrimination begin, often as an expression of ethnocentrism or an attempt to justify economic exploitation.

Stage 2: As a result of prejudice and discrimination, a minority group is socially disadvantaged, occupying a low position in the system of social stratification.

Stage 3: This social disadvantage is then interpreted not as the result of earlier prejudice and discrimination but as evidence that the minority group is innately inferior.

Stage 4: This unleashes renewed prejudice and discrimination, and the cycle repeats itself.

Figure 11–2 Prejudice and Discrimination—The Vicious Circle

The self-perpetuating character of prejudice and discrimination can be understood as a vicious circle, as graphically represented in this figure.

MAJORITY AND MINORITY: PATTERNS OF INTERACTION

The patterns of interaction between a minority group and more privileged members of society vary. Commonly, however, they take four major forms.

Pluralism

Pluralism refers to *a state in which all racial and ethnic groups are socially distinct, but have roughly equal social standing.* People may maintain their distinctive social identity as a matter of pride, but they are not forced to be different by prejudice and discrimination. For this reason, pluralism is ideally a stable social pattern involving no social conflict (Newman, 1973).

The ideal of pluralism is expressed in American pride in the fact that people of various racial and ethnic groups have come to our society from all over the world in search of greater opportunity and personal freedom. The laws of the United States also provide considerable freedom for people to maintain their distinct cultural identities. Some degree of pluralism in the United States is easy to see. Large cities contain countless ethnic villages in which people display the cultural traditions of their immigrant ancestors (Greeley, 1971; Gans, 1982). In New York, these include Spanish Harlem, Little Italy, and Chinatown; in Philadelphia, Polish Kensington and Italian South Philly; in Chicago, Vietnamese Little Saigon; and in Los Angeles, Hispanic East Los Angeles. As one resident of a Hispanic neighborhood in Chicago explained, "There are people who come here and live and die and never learn English" (Kiefer, 1984:130).

But the concept of pluralism has only limited application to American society. First, most Americans seek to maintain their racial and ethnic identity only to a point. Few wish to live apart from the rest of society. Therefore, pluralism often takes the form of pride in one's racial or ethnic identity. For example, people may join social clubs based on race or ethnicity, they may participate in cultural festivals, and they may wish for their children to appreciate their cultural heritage.

Second, American society does not always support the wishes of racial and ethnic minority groups to maintain their own way of life. The controversy over prayer in public schools is one important example. In a 1986 national survey, about 60 percent of Americans claimed that religious observances such as reading the Bible and reciting the Lord's Prayer—which reflect only some religious traditions in the United States—should be part of all public school programs (N.O.R.C., 1987:154).

Third, distinctive racial and ethnic identity is often forced on people by others. For example, many communities in the Appalachian Mountains of the eastern United States remain culturally distinctive because their members are snubbed as "hillbillies" and subjected to discrimination that perpetuates their poverty (Sacks, 1986). As we shall see presently, many white ethnic groups have long struggled to enter the American mainstream by gaining more economic opportunity. Similarly, many blacks and Hispanic Americans continue to be socially isolated by prejudice and discrimination on the part of the white majority.

Switzerland, which contains large German, French, and Italian cultural groups, has been relatively successful in maintaining a true pluralism. Swiss com-

Visible evidence of the pluralism of New York City is frequently provided by parades sponsored by various ethnic communities—in this instance, the growing population of Korean Americans.

mitment to pluralism is evident in the official recognition of the languages of all three ethnic groups. Moreover, many Swiss are able to speak more than one of these languages. The key to Switzerland's remarkable success in maintaining pluralism lies in the society's small size in the midst of other large societies that historically shaped its way of life. Furthermore, no segment of the Swiss population is subject to extreme economic disadvantages. Consequently, Swiss society truly values diversity and accords substantial respect and dignity to citizens of various cultural backgrounds (Simpson & Yinger, 1972).

Assimilation

Assimilation is *the process by which members of minority groups gradually modify their ways of life to conform to patterns of the dominant culture.* Assimilation may mean changing one's name and mode of dress, as well as one's values, religion, and language. Americans have long viewed the United States as a melting pot in which various nationalities joined to form an entirely new way of life. The following turn-of-the-century description of the United States by one European immigrant remains influential today:

America is God's Crucible, the great melting-pot where all races of Europe are melting and reforming. Here you stand, good folks, think I, when I see them at Ellis Island [historical entry point for many immigrants in New York], here you stand with your fifty groups, with your fifty languages and histories, and your fifty blood-hatreds and rivalries. But you won't be long like that, brothers, for these are the fires of God . . . Germans and Frenchmen, Irishmen and Englishmen, Jews and Russians, into the Crucible with you all! God is making an American! (Zangwill, 1921:33; orig. 1909)

Many of us can see the process of assimilation at work in our own families as younger people have moved away from the distinctive ethnic traditions of earlier generations. But the melting pot concept is inaccurate. Rather than everyone melting into a new cultural pattern, minorities in the United States have typically adopted the cultural traits of the dominant group. During the last century, immigrants to the United States entered a society dominated by the Anglo-Saxon culture of the earliest settlers, so assimilation typically involved trading their own cultural background for a more Anglicized way of life. They did so to improve their social position and to escape the prejudice and discrimination directed against foreigners (Newman, 1973). Recall from Chapter 1, for example, that many well-known entertainers adopted Anglo names early in their careers.

Sociologists also disagree about the extent to which assimilation has actually occurred in the United States. Some claim that, at least over several generations, assimilation has been extensive. Herbert Gans (1982), for example, suggests that while first-generation immigrants typically retain their traditional culture, distinctive patterns of ethnicity are far less evident among second and subsequent generations. Thus, as Figure 11–3 shows, many Irish and Italian neighborhoods disappeared as members of these ethnic groups gradually dispersed across the city of Philadelphia during this century. Race may be a different matter, however, as this has been far less true among blacks. Evidence that racial or ethnic districts persist has led others to argue that they are still building blocks of American society. In a study of New York, Nathan Glazer and Daniel Moynihan maintain that "ethnicity and race [still] dominate the city, more than ever seemed possible" (1970:ix).

There is truth in both arguments. Some assimilation has certainly occurred during this century. But mi-

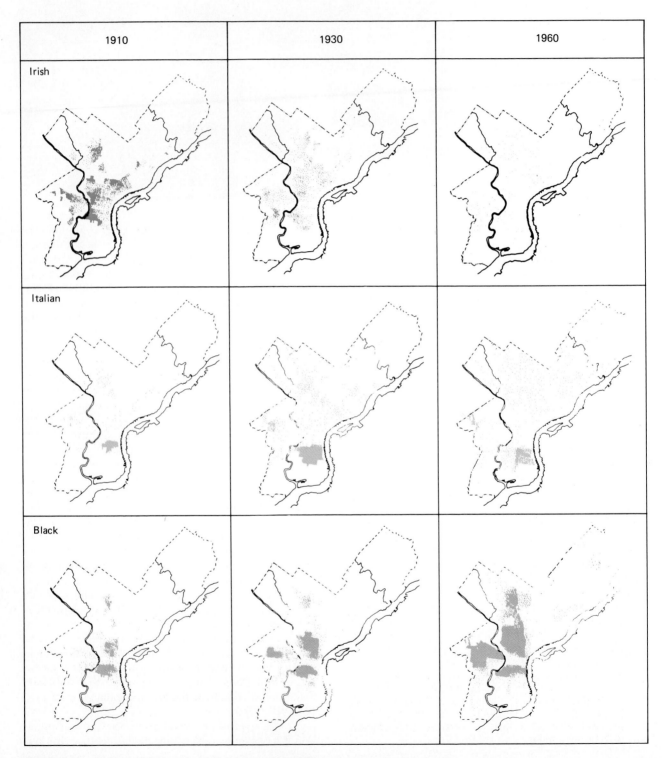

Figure 11–3 Residential Patterns in Philadelphia, 1910–1960

(Wurman & Gallery, 1972)

norities are not likely to disappear from American society—certainly not as long as minority standing is linked to economic disadvantage (Alba, 1985).

As a cultural process, assimilation involves changes in ethnicity but not race. For example, although many of the descendants of Japanese immigrants who came to the United States a century ago do not maintain a traditionally Japanese way of life, they may still have a distinctive racial identity. But it is also possible for racial distinctiveness to change over generations. **Miscegenation** is *the biological process of interbreeding among various racial categories*. Miscegenation is a true melting pot—in the biological sense—that reduces racial distinctiveness. Although opposition to interracial marriage remains strong, as noted earlier, considerable miscegenation has occurred throughout American history.

Miscegenation has been even more common in Latin America, where early European colonization was largely limited to males. Both in and out of marriage, therefore, these European men fathered children born to women of Native American and African ancestry. Thus, in contrast to the North American pattern of defining as "black" all people of mixed race, Latin American societies recognize various categories of racial mixture. In descending order of social prestige, these are whites (Spanish ancestry), *mestizos* (white and Indian ancestry), *mulattoes* (some African ancestry), blacks, and finally, Indians (the native inhabitants of Latin America) (Butterworth & Chance, 1981). Clearly, this status system reflects the fact that the Spanish and other Europeans dominated many Latin American societies in the centuries following colonization.

Segregation

Segregation is *the physical and social separation of categories of people*. Although racial and ethnic groups sometimes voluntarily segregate themselves (such as the Amish, described in the box in Chapter 3), minority groups are more often segregated involuntarily at the wishes of more powerful members of society. Segregation involves any and all aspects of life, including residential neighborhoods, schools, occupations, hospitals, and even cemeteries. In addition, interaction that does occur reflects the social inferiority of the minority group. For instance, some affluent whites have employed nonwhites in their homes as servants, although these people might not be very welcome as guests. Thus while pluralism implies distinctiveness without disadvantage, segregation is based on enforced separation to the detriment of the minority group.

South Africa's system of apartheid (described in the box in Chapter 9) is perhaps the clearest case of racial segregation within any society. Apartheid involves the forcible segregation of the black majority from the white minority that dominates South African society. South Africa is largely two different societies that touch only when blacks provide services for whites. Apartheid is alien to the cultures of Africa. It was created by the European minority it serves, and remains in effect only through the use of considerable (and often brutal) power by the dominant group (Fredrickson, 1981).

Racial segregation has a long history in the United States. When slavery existed, blacks and whites actually lived in closer proximity than they do in most of America today (Hirschman, 1983). But black slaves were treated as objects or beasts of burden without human rights of any kind. After the abolition of slavery in 1865, Jim Crow laws were used to perpetuate the racial caste system, so that—as in South Africa today—blacks and whites were separated in virtually every aspect of life. Black people were forbidden to use white hotels, railroad cars, buses, public restrooms, and even drinking fountains (Woodward, 1974). Until the Supreme Court outlawed segregated schools in 1954, most black children received a separate and unequal education according to law. Other minority groups, including Native Americans, Hispanics, and Asians, received similar treatment from the white majority in various parts of the United States.

Such overt discrimination has been outlawed, but de facto segregation continues within the United States. A generation ago, Karl and Alma Taeuber (1965) described residential segregation in over two hundred American cities, using a numerical index that ranged from zero (indicating that neighborhoods contained blacks and whites in the same proportion as the city as a whole) to 100 (total racial segregation). They found that the average score for the cities studied was 86.2. Research reveals that a majority of blacks in the United States would prefer to live in a racially integrated neighborhood (N.O.R.C., 1987:171). But research also shows that racial segregation in the United States has declined very little in recent decades (Van Valey, Roof, & Wilcox, 1977; Calmore, 1986). Even when minority group members have achieved economic standing equal to that of whites, segregation usually persists (Hwang et al., 1985).

Looking at urban America in general, the white population of suburbs has risen dramatically, while center cities have become increasingly black. The white suburb of Dearborn, Michigan, for instance, has only eighty-three blacks among a population of over ninety thousand, and has legally forbidden "nonresidents" (meaning blacks from nearby Detroit) to use its public parks (DeMott, 1986). Many of the small but growing number of suburban blacks are concentrated in a few areas that often have the same problems of unemployment and poverty as the more visible central-city ghettos (Clark, 1979; Logan & Schneider, 1984; Stahura, 1983, 1986). At the same time, many businesses in black inner-city areas are owned and operated by whites—a pattern that Robert Blauner (1972) has described as *internal colonialism*.

As a type of oppression, segregation often provokes the active resistance of minority groups. The family of Linda Brown, described earlier, successfully used the court system to challenge school segregation. In some cases, the action of even a single individual can have lasting consequences. On December 1, 1955, Rosa Parks was riding a bus in Montgomery, Alabama, sitting in a section designated by law for blacks. When more white passengers boarded the crowded bus, the driver asked four blacks to give up their seats to whites. Three did so, but Rosa Parks was tired and did not believe she should have to stand so that a white man could sit. When she refused to move, the driver left the bus and returned with police, who arrested Parks for violating the racial segregation laws. She was later convicted in court and fined $14. But her action sparked the black community of Montgomery to boycott city buses, ultimately bringing this practice to an end (King, 1969).

Annihilation

Annihilation is *the violent extermination of one category of people by another*. Also known as *genocide*, this extreme form of racism and ethnocentrism opposes virtually all recognized moral standards, but has nonetheless been common in human history.

Annihilation is part of the long history of contact between Europeans and the indigenous population of the Americas. From the sixteenth century on, the Spanish, Portuguese, English, French, and Dutch forcefully established vast colonial empires. The native populations of North and South America, who in many cases initially welcomed the Europeans as friends and equals, were systematically subjugated and killed as the Europeans sought to gain control of their wealth. The Spanish explorer Hernando Cortés (1485–1547) reduced the Aztec capital—site of today's Mexico City—to rubble and slaughtered thousands of Aztecs. Similarly, the God-fearing colonists of early New England exterminated Native Americans, whom they regarded as heathen savages. In the end, diseases introduced by Europeans and outright slaughter resulted in the death of most of this hemisphere's indigenous population (Hardoy, 1975; Cottrell, 1979; Butterworth & Chance, 1981; Matthiessen, 1984).

Many of us were taught that the Europeans brought Christianity and civilization to the New World. The painting "Battle of the Aztecs and the Spaniards" by Mexican artist Diego Rivera is more truthful. In many cases, Europeans attempted to annihilate the Native American population.

The history of annihilation continues into the twentieth century. Unimaginable horror was experienced by Jews during World War II as the Nazi regime took control of much of Europe. Hitler used the Jews as a scapegoat—a relatively powerless group blamed for all the ills of society—inaugurating a reign of terror known as the Holocaust in which some 6 million Jews were killed. Within the last generation, genocide has taken place in other parts of the world. Between 1975 and 1980, for example, the communist regime of Pol Pot in Kampuchea (formerly Cambodia) systematically exterminated people thought to represent capitalist cultural influences. This group included all those who knew any Western language and, in some cases, even people who wore eyeglasses (defined as a capitalist cultural element). Perhaps one-fourth of the population (some 2 million people) perished (Shawcross, 1979).

These four major types of contact between dominant categories of people and minorities can and do exist simultaneously within one society. Americans, for example, are proud to point to patterns of pluralism and assimilation. We are often less willing, however, to recognize the extent to which our society has been built on segregation and annihilation.

The final section of this chapter makes use of these four types of contact to examine the history and present social standing of major racial and ethnic groups in American society.

RACIAL AND ETHNIC VARIATION IN THE UNITED STATES

> *Give me your tired, your poor,*
> *Your huddled masses yearning to breathe free,*
> *The wretched refuse of your teeming shore,*
> *Send these, the homeless, tempest-tossed to me:*
> *I lift my lamp beside the golden door.*

These words by Emma Lazarus, inscribed on the Statue of Liberty, express an ideal belief in the dignity of all people, the right to freedom, and the opportunity to build a better life. But America's golden door has never opened as widely for some as for others. Social inequality has long been entrenched in American society, providing some with social advantages and privileges that others can only dream of attaining. This inconsistency between principles and practice is evident in the history of America's various racial and ethnic groups.

Political regimes sometimes engage in the madness of mass murder. These shoes are silent testimony to the systematic death wrought by the Nazis in World War II. More recently, the Pol Pot regime turned Kampuchea (Cambodia) into "killing fields," murdering some two million people.

White Anglo-Saxon Protestants

White Anglo-Saxon Protestants (WASPs) have historically dominated American society. WASP ancestry is usually English, but sometimes includes Scots and Welsh as well. WASPs are Protestants, and those who are members of the Episcopal Church—derived from the Anglican Church in England—have the highest social standing of all Protestants in the United States (Roof, 1979). WASPs predominated in the early settlement of America; only in the nineteenth century did substantial immigration of people who were not WASPs begin. Although

WASPs are no longer a numerical majority in the United States, there were almost 50 million Americans of English ancestry in 1980—the largest single ethnic or racial category (see Table 11–1). If people of Scottish and Welsh ancestry are added to this figure more than one in four Americans are at least partly WASP.

Historically, WASP dominance reflects the fact that these immigrants were highly skilled and strongly motivated toward achievement by the Protestant work ethic, described in Chapter 4. Also, because they long formed the majority and had the greatest social power, WASPs were not subject to the prejudice and discrimination experienced by other categories of people. In fact, the historical dominance of WASPs has been so great that, as noted earlier, becoming assimilated into American society has largely meant becoming more like the WASPs (Gordon, 1964).

As American society became more ethnically diverse in the nineteenth century, some WASPs directed prejudice and discrimination at new arrivals they defined as undesirable foreigners. Such ethnocentrism, often in the form of organized nativist movements, included efforts to legally halt the rapidly rising rate of immigration. Many wealthier WASPs also began to socially isolate themselves from people they deemed their inferiors. Louis Brandeis, a brilliant Jewish lawyer who finally overcame prejudice to become a justice of the U.S. Supreme Court, recalled that wealthy WASPs in Boston advised their children that "Boston holds nothing for you except heavy taxes and political misrule. When you marry, pick out a suburb to build a house in, join [a country club], and make your life center about your club, your home and your children" (Mumford, 1961:495). Thus the 1880s—the decade in which the Statue of Liberty was erected to welcome immigrants to America—also saw the founding of the first American country club (with virtually all WASP members). Soon afterward, WASPs established various genealogical societies—such as the Daughters of the American Revolution (1890) and the Society of Mayflower Descendants (1894)—and began publishing the *Social Register* (see the box in Chapter 10). These organizations served to socially isolate many wealthy WASPs from newly arrived immigrants (Baltzell, 1964).

After the Great Depression of the 1930s, WASP dominance gradually declined (Baltzell, 1964, 1976). One symbol of this change was the election of John Fitzgerald Kennedy—of Irish-Catholic background—as president of the United States in 1960. Though Kennedy certainly displayed the personal style of the WASP upper class into which his Bostonian family had become assimilated, he still faced considerable prejudice both as an Irish American and as a Roman Catholic.

Although their power has declined, WASPs continue to have great influence in American society. On the average, WASPs are highly educated, work in high-prestige occupations, and enjoy above-average incomes (Neidert & Farley, 1985). The majority of people in the upper-upper class are WASPs (Greeley, 1974; Baltzell, 1979; Roof, 1981). Furthermore, English is the only official language of the United States, and religions other than Protestantism are still viewed as minority religions. Finally, our legal system and conceptions of human rights and responsibilities continue to reflect English origins. In short, America is a socially diverse and changing society, but the continuing importance of white Anglo-Saxon Protestants is unmistakable.

Native Americans

The phrase *Native Americans* refers collectively to the hundreds of distinct peoples who were the original inhabitants of the Americas: Aleuts, Cherokee, Hopi, Sioux, Mohawk, Aztec, and Inca—to name only a few. Thousands of years ago, migrating peoples crossed a land bridge from Asia to North America where the Bering Strait (off the coast of Alaska) is today. Over the centuries, they spread throughout the western hemisphere. When the first Europeans arrived late in the fifteenth century, Native Americans had already inhabited the continent for some thirty thousand years and numbered several million (Dobyns, 1966).

From the outset, contact with Europeans was disastrous for Native Americans. What Europeans ethnocentrically described as bringing civilization to the wilderness was, in practice, the destruction of many ancient civilizations. Exposure to European diseases took a terrible toll among Native Americans, and tens of thousands more were annihilated as Europeans sought wealth and land. By the beginning of this century, the "vanishing Americans" numbered only about 250,000 in the United States (Tyler, 1973).

Use of the term *Indians* to refer to Native Americans is traced to Christopher Columbus (1446–1506), who is said to have mistaken the Antilles in the Caribbean for India. Like other early explorers, Columbus found the indigenous Americans to be a peaceful and generous people (Matthiessen, 1984). The many distinct Native American cultures differed in countless ways, but most stressed sharing of resources and living in harmony with nature. Such values clashed with those of Europeans, whose way of life was more hierarchical, competitive, and aggressive. Although Europeans sometimes defined Native Americans as innocent and childlike, conflict over wealth and land soon led them to demean Native Americans as thieves and murderers, and even as subhuman (Josephy, 1982). Among the early colonial leaders of New England, Roger Williams described Native Americans as "wolves with men's brains," William Bradford termed them "wild men," and Cotton Mather denounced them as sinful "hounds of hell" (Matthiessen, 1984: 3–4). Such strongly negative stereotypes, of course, were an important means by which European colonists justified their often barbarous treatment of these people (Unruh, 1979).

After the Revolutionary War, the new United States government adopted a superficially pluralist approach to Native American societies. The government sought to gain Native American land through treaties. But payment for land was far from fair, and if Native Americans were unwilling to surrender their homelands, white settlers used superior military power to evict them. Thousands of Cherokees, for example, died on a forced march—the Trail of Tears—from their homes in the southeastern United States to segregated reservations in the Midwest. By the early 1800s, few Native Americans remained east of the Mississippi River.

By the 1870s, the United States government was trying to resolve "the Indian problem" through assimilation. But violence did not end, and under this policy, Native Americans lost not only their land, but their culture as well. As dependent wards of the government on reservations, Native Americans were taught English and pressured to abandon their traditional religious beliefs in favor of Christianity. Children were frequently taken from their parents to boarding schools, operated by the Bureau of Indian Affairs, to be resocialized into "Americans." Political power on reservations was given to the minority of Native Americans who supported government policies, and reservation land—defined as common property according to traditional Native American values— was placed under the control of individual families (Tyler, 1973). In the process, whites were able to grab still more land for themselves.

Today the remaining Native American territories are under increasing pressure from outsiders who wish to develop their extensive coal, oil, natural gas, and uranium reserves (Josephy, 1982). Native Americans differ among themselves as to whether they should accept lucrative offers from big corporations for their land. Progressives favor the sale of mining leases, while traditionalists consider mining or any other commercial activity on lands considered sacred to be a desecration.

Since granting Native Americans citizenship in 1924, the government has encouraged them to move from reservations. Many Native Americans have indeed adopted mainstream cultural patterns and, more than any other American minority, they marry outside their own group (Vander Zanden, 1983). Many large cities now have sizeable Native American populations. But in 1980, as shown in Table 11–2, Native American families had incomes significantly below the American average, and had a much lower proportion of college graduates (7.7 percent) than the population as a whole (17.1 percent).

Through in-depth interviews with Native Americans in a western city, Joan Albon (1971) found that many were handicapped by little education, few marketable skills, less than perfect English, and dark skin that provokes prejudice and discrimination. In addition, she noted, Native Americans often lacked the individualistic and competitive values of capitalist America, a result of long dependency on government assistance.

Like other racial and ethnic minorities in the United States, Native Americans have recently begun to reassert their pride in their cultural heritage and to secure greater rights and opportunity for themselves. They have sued the national government for return of lands taken in the past by force, and organizations such as the Pan-Indian American Indian Movement seek dem-

Table 11–2 THE SOCIAL STANDING OF NATIVE AMERICANS, 1980*

	Native Americans	Entire United States
Median Family Income	$16,672	$19,917
Proportion in Poverty	27.5%	12.4%
Median Education (Age 25 and over)	12.2 years	12.5 years
Completion of Four or More Years of College (Age 25 and over)	7.7%	17.1%

SOURCE: U.S. Bureau of the Census.

* The data used in this chapter are the most recent available at the time of publication. Comparisons of all racial and ethnic categories are only possible using data from the 1980 census, but more recent statistics are also included wherever possible.

ocratic control of reservation lands by Native Americans themselves. In some cases, Native Americans have even entered into violent confrontation with federal government officials. Few Native Americans support violence as a means to address grievances, but the vast majority share a profound sense of the injustice that they have endured at the hands of whites (Josephy, 1982; Matthiessen, 1983).

Black Americans

Although blacks accompanied Spanish explorers to the New World in the fifteenth century, the beginning of black history in the United States is usually set at 1619, when a Dutch trading ship brought twenty Africans to Jamestown, Virginia (Holt, 1980). There is some debate as to whether these people arrived as slaves or as indentured servants—people who were obligated to work for a fixed period of time in return for passage across the Atlantic Ocean. In any event, being black in America soon became virtually synonymous with being a slave. In 1661, the first law recognizing slavery was passed in Virginia (Sowell, 1981).

Slavery was extremely profitable for white owners of large farms and plantations. Other whites prospered from the slave trade, which operated legally until 1808. In all, some 10 million Africans were forcibly transported to the western hemisphere; about 400,000 entered the United States (Sowell, 1981). During a voyage of several weeks across the Atlantic Ocean, hundreds of slaves were chained on board small sailing ships as human cargo with barely enough room to move. Filth and disease killed many; others were driven to suicide. Overall, perhaps half the Africans died en route (Tannenbaum, 1946; Franklin, 1967).

Surviving the journey was a mixed blessing: a life of forced servitude as the economic property of white owners. Most often slaves engaged in farming, although some worked in cities at a variety of trades (Franklin, 1967). Work usually lasted from morning until evening, and for up to twenty hours a day during the harvest.

To ensure that slaves worked continuously, the law afforded slave owners whatever discipline they wished. Corporal punishment was widely used. Even the killing of a slave by a white owner rarely brought legal prosecution. Slave families were also divided at the will of white owners, who bought and sold slaves like any other piece of property. Slaves were further controlled by eliminating all opportunities to gain an education and by ensuring that they remained totally dependent on their owner for their basic needs (Sowell, 1981).

Some blacks in both the North and the South were legally free. Such free people of color, as they were called, were often small-scale farmers, skilled workers, or small-business owners (Murray, 1978). But the lives of most black Americans were an obvious contradiction of the principles of equality and freedom on which the United States was founded. The Declaration of Independence states, "We hold these Truths to be self-evident, that all Men are created equal, that they are endowed by their Creator with certain unalienable Rights, that among these are Life, Liberty, and the Pursuit of Happiness. . . ." Most white Americans did not apply these ideals to blacks, however. In the Dred Scott case in 1857, the United States Supreme Court addressed the question "Are blacks citizens?" and answered, "We think they are not, and that they are not included, and were not intended to be included, under the word 'citizens' in the constitution, and can therefore claim none of the rights and privileges which that instrument provides for and secures for citizens of the United States" (Blaustein & Zangrando, 1968:160). Thus arose what Gunnar Myrdal (1944) later called the *American dilemma*: the recognition of individual rights and freedoms and the simultaneous denial of those rights and freedoms to an entire category of Americans. To resolve this dilemma, many whites simply defined blacks as innately inferior.

The Thirteenth Amendment to the Constitution outlawed slavery in the United States in 1865. Subsequently, however, Jim Crow laws were used to maintain the division of American society into two racially based castes (Woodward, 1974). Thus racial segregation persisted despite the end of formal slavery. Especially in the South, whites maintained segregation by using violence against blacks (and some whites) who advocated racial equality. Thousands of blacks were brutally lynched or burned, often on the basis of the flimsiest allegations by whites.

Although racial segregation has continued, the twentieth century has brought dramatic changes to black America. Overwhelmingly concentrated in the South a century ago, thousands of blacks left farming for industrial jobs in northern cities in the decades after World War I. These migrants did find greater economic opportunity in the North, but they also encountered prejudice and discrimination greater than that experienced by white immigrants from Europe arriving at the same time (Lieberson, 1980). In the 1950s, blacks and sympathetic whites launched an attack on racism in America that became a national civil rights movement. A number of important legal battles were won during this period, including ending legal support for racially segregated schools. Civil rights acts passed in the 1960s lessened overt racial discrimination in employment and public accommodations.

Nonetheless, blacks continue to occupy a clearly subordinate position in the American system of social stratification, as shown in Table 11–3. Notice that the median income of black families in 1986 ($17,604) was substantially below that for America as a whole ($29,458). Black families are also three times as likely as white families to be poor. In 1980, median family income

Table 11–3	THE SOCIAL STANDING OF BLACK AMERICANS, 1980 AND 1985–1986	
	Black Americans	Entire United States
Median Family Income	$12,598 ($17,604 in 1986)	$19,917 ($29,458 in 1986)
Proportion in Poverty	29.9% (31.1% in 1985)	12.4% (13.6% in 1985)
Median Education (Age 25 and over)	12.0 years (12.3 years in 1985)	12.5 years (12.6 years in 1985)
Completion of Four or More Years of College (Age 25 and over)	8.4% (10.9% in 1986)	17.1% (19.4% in 1986)

SOURCE: U.S. Bureau of the Census.

Some five thousand lynchings were officially recorded in the United States between 1880 and 1930. Lynch mobs were formed by whites as a means of maintaining dominance over blacks and other minority groups.

for blacks was about 63 percent that of whites; by 1984, however, the proportion had fallen to 56 percent. By 1986, some improvement was noted as the figure rose to 59 percent. Furthermore, about 60 percent of all black households in the United States actually lost purchasing power during the first half of the 1980s (Jacob, 1986).

Part of this problem is that blacks have long been overrepresented in low-paying occupations. Recent changes in the American economy have also seriously hurt black Americans. Since 1980, almost 3 million blue-collar factory jobs—an important source of black employment—have been lost. An additional burden has been the drastic cuts in domestic spending engineered by the Reagan administration, resulting in less opportunity for those who lose factory jobs to get retraining in some other field. Thus unemployment among blacks has remained twice as high as among whites, and among black teenagers the figure exceeds 40 percent (Farley, 1980; Wilson, 1984; Jacob, 1986).

Education is one dimension on which the social standing of black Americans has improved over the last generation. In 1960, the median education for blacks over the age of 25 was 8.2 years, well below the median of 10.9 years for whites. By 1985, however, the gap was much smaller: the median figure for black education was 12.3 years, compared to 12.6 for whites. However, as Table 11–3 shows, blacks were still only about half as likely as whites to complete four years of college. Of particular concern is the fact that in recent years the number of blacks enrolling in college has actually been

Beginning in the mid-1950s, the Civil Rights movement attempted to establish racial equality in the United States. The resistance to change was often fierce, as was evident in the police tactic of turning fire hoses on protesters.

falling. In 1986, only about one-fourth of black high-school graduates continued on to college, compared with about one-third in 1976. A similar pattern of decline holds for graduate study as well (American Council on Education, 1987; *Black Issues in Higher Education*, 1987). It is quite likely that this decline at the level of higher education is one consequence of the economic setbacks already described.

No less distressing is evidence that education may not solve the economic problems of black America. A generation ago, Peter Blau and Otis Duncan (1967) claimed that education does not promote upward social mobility for blacks as much as for whites. Their research showed that better-educated blacks actually had a lower overall social standing in relation to whites with comparable education than blacks with less education had in relation to their white counterparts. This finding suggests that white prejudice and discrimination may actually increase as blacks gain more education, a conclusion supported by recent research (Tienda & Lii, 1987).

Measured in some ways, black occupational gains have been significant in recent years. There are, for example, twice as many black physicians and six times as many black lawyers in the United States as there

were in the 1960s (Vander Zanden, 1983:225). But these gains stand in contrast to the persistent poverty of millions of blacks—especially women and children—who represent an economically desperate underclass in America (Wilson, 1984).

Black Americans have greatly increased their political power, both in terms of number of registered voters and in terms of number of elected officials. Between 1970 and 1985, the total number of black officials increased more than threefold to over five thousand. Black migration to cities, along with white movement to the suburbs, has resulted in black majorities in many large cities, and in 1988, three of the five largest American cities had black mayors. At the national level, however, blacks made fewer political gains. Jesse Jackson became the first black American to win a state presidential primary election in 1984, but after the 1986 elections there were only 23 blacks in the House of Representatives (out of a total of 435) and none of the 100 senators was black. Overall, less than 1 percent of all national political officials are black. Another political problem is that because of their widespread economic problems, blacks generally favor more extensive changes in American society than whites are willing to support. Thus Dianne Pinderhughes (1986) suggests that neither major political party in the United States actually represents black interests very well.

In sum, for more than 350 years, blacks have struggled to gain social equality in America. Slavery ended over a century ago, and overt discrimination has signifi-

The success of Jesse Jackson in the 1988 presidential campaign reflected more than strong support from black citizens. The idea of a president who is a member of a minority group is no longer unthinkable to most Americans.

SOCIAL POLICY

Affirmative Action—Problem or Solution?

Over the entrance to the Supreme Court building in Washington, D.C., is the phrase "Equal Justice Under Law." There is little question that this ideal has often been compromised—or completely ignored—with regard to many American minority groups. One response to this historical pattern is affirmative action, a policy that mandates making special efforts to achieve the goal of equal opportunity for minorities. Affirmative action means, for example, that employers actively encourage applications from minority group members, and carefully monitor hiring and promotion policies to ensure that they do not discriminate, even unintentionally, against minorities. The final goal of affirmative action is to ensure that minority groups are represented in various occupations, educational programs, and other areas of society in proportion to their population size.

The most controversial element of affirmative action is the establishment of quotas to combat the exclusion of minorities. Under a quota system, a fixed number of minority members are ensured favorable treatment regardless of how they stack up against other applicants. A quota system of this kind was at issue in the famous Supreme Court case involving Allan Bakke and the University of California in 1978.

Bakke's applications for admission were rejected by a University of California medical school in 1972 and 1973. The medical school had set aside sixteen places for blacks, Mexican Americans, and Asian Americans. Under this quota system, some minority applicants were admitted with grades and test scores lower than Bakke's. Bakke sued, claiming that he had been discriminated against because he was white. In 1978, the Supreme Court agreed, objecting to the rigid quota system that had been used. But the Court did endorse the *principle* of affirmative action, allowing an applicant's race and ethnicity to be considered in admission decisions.

Advocates of affirmative action claim that this policy is a fair and necessary corrective for historical patterns of discrimination. Everybody who is alive today, they argue, is advantaged or disadvantaged because of privileges accorded or denied to their parents and grandparents. Since past discrimination affects minorities even today, therefore, some special treatment is necessary for those denied opportunity through no fault of their own. Only in this way, defenders suggest, can the vicious circle of prejudice and discrimination be broken.

Opponents of affirmative action agree that minority groups have historically suffered from discrimination, but they see affirmative action as unfair *reverse discrimination*. Why should whites today be penalized, critics ask, for past discrimination for which they were in no way responsible? Opponents also claim that minority groups have largely overcome historical barriers to opportunity, and that those who have made the greatest efforts have made the greatest strides—which is as it should be. Furthermore, some critics claim that giving minorities special treatment inevitably results in the lowering of standards, which is harmful in the long run to all Americans.

As the data below from a national survey show, most Americans do not support the principle of affirmative action on behalf of black Americans:

> Some people think that blacks have been discriminated against for so long that the government has a special obligation to help improve their living standards. Others believe that the government should not be giving special treatment to blacks. (N.O.R.C., 1987:303)

This survey uses numbers 1 through 5 to show the range of opinion in relation to the three categories shown below.

SOURCE: Survey data from N.O.R.C., *General Social Surveys* (Chicago: National Opinion Research Center, 1987), p. 303.

I strongly agree that the government is obligated to help blacks.		I agree with both answers.		I strongly agree that the government shouldn't give special treatment.
1	2	3	4	5
10.2%	10.3%	28.3%	17.4%	30.8%

No Response = 3.0%   Total = 1,466 subjects

cantly declined during this century. Yet research has found that the psychological well-being and overall quality of life for blacks remains below that of whites with comparable economic position (Thomas & Hughes, 1986). Even absent economic deprivation, then, race remains a powerful force in American society. Obviously, the problem is made worse by the fact that, on the average, blacks have a social position well below that of whites. One response has been the controversial government policy of affirmative action, which involves preferential treatment for members of minority groups historically subject to white prejudice and discrimination.

Asian Americans

Although sharing some racial characteristics, Asian Americans represent enormous cultural diversity. As shown earlier in Table 11–1, at the beginning of this decade the largest single category of Asian Americans was of Chinese ancestry (about 800,000 people), followed by those of Filipino ancestry (775,000), and those of Japanese ancestry (about 700,000). Most Asian Americans live in the West. The Chinese and Japanese began migrating to the United States over a century ago; these long-established minority groups are described in detail below. In recent years, large numbers of Koreans, Filipinos, and Vietnamese have immigrated to this country. As a result of high levels of immigration, Asian Americans are now the fastest-growing minority group in the United States. These newer immigrants have changed the face

A "culture of achievement" has propelled many Asian Americans to successfully complete college degrees. During the 1980s college enrollments of this category of Americans rose dramatically.

of western cities; between 1970 and 1983, the Asian-American population of Los Angeles, for example, more than tripled to about 750,000 people (Anderson, 1983). Smaller numbers of new Asian immigrants have also settled across the East and Midwest.

Asian immigrants—especially young people—have attracted both attention and respect in recent years as high achievers. For instance, *Time* magazine recently did a cover story on "Asian-American Whiz Kids" (Brand, 1987). Prominently noted was the fact that many of the best American colleges and universities now have large numbers of Asian-American students. Accounting for 2 percent of all Americans, they represent 20 percent of 1987's freshman class at the Massachusetts Institute of Technology, for example. In California, where they are 7 percent of the population, one of every four students at the University of California at Berkeley is Asian American.

It is important to remember, however, that the American attitude toward Asians has not always been one of pride. In addition, the success of some Asian Americans exists alongside substantial problems for others.

Chinese Americans

Chinese immigration to the United States began about 140 years ago. The California Gold Rush of 1849 fueled a tremendous economic boom in the West. People swarmed into the region in search of easy riches, and new towns and businesses developed virtually overnight. Having a pressing need for cheap labor, whites welcomed Chinese immigrants, most of whom were young, hard-working males willing to take lower-status jobs shunned by whites themselves (Ling, 1971).

When an economic depression came in the 1870s, however, whites were desperate for any kind of work and began competing with the Chinese for jobs. To white workers, both the industriousness of the Chinese and their willingness to work for low wages were threatening. The result was mounting prejudice and discrimination (Boswell, 1986).

The Chinese were legally barred from many occupations and, in some areas, were even forbidden to testify against whites in court (Sowell, 1981; Vander Zanden, 1983). The Chinese lost legal protections just when they needed them most. As fear of the "Yellow Peril" grew, whites directed vicious racist campaigns against the Chinese. In 1877, thousands of whites attacked the Chinese community in San Francisco, injuring people and burning homes and businesses. The entire Chinese populations of some towns were driven away by threat of violence (Lyman, 1971). American society seemed to line up against the Chinese, which explains how the saying about not having "a Chinaman's chance" became part of our folklore (Sung, 1967:56).

On behalf of the white majority, the United States government in 1882 passed the first of a series of laws ending the immigration of Chinese. This brought further hardship because, of the hundred thousand Chinese already in the United States, there were about eighteen males for every female (Hsu, 1971; Lai, 1980). Restricting immigration meant that the wives and children of these men could not join them in the United States, and this sex imbalance caused the Chinese population to fall to about sixty thousand by 1920. This situation greatly enhanced the status of Chinese women who were already in the United States, however. Being in such demand, they were less likely to be submissive to men (Sowell, 1981).

In response to white oppression, some Chinese moved eastward; many more sought the relative safety of urban Chinatowns (Wong, 1971). There Chinese traditions flourished, and kinship networks called *clans* provided financial assistance to individuals and served as political organizations representing the interests of all. With the help of the clans, Chinese could obtain loans to start businesses and find jobs. At the same time, of course, Chinatowns discouraged the learning of the English language and other forms of cultural assimilation.

By the 1940s, hostility toward the Chinese diminished because labor was again in short supply (Lai, 1980). In 1943, President Roosevelt ended the ban on Chinese immigration and extended the rights of citizenship to Chinese Americans born abroad. Many Chinese Americans responded by moving out of Chinatowns and beginning a period of cultural assimilation. In Honolulu, for example, 70 percent of all Chinese people lived in Chinatown in 1900; by the late 1970s, only 20 percent did (Lai, 1980).

After 1950, many Chinese Americans experienced considerable upward social mobility. No longer restricted to such occupations as operating laundries and restaurants, many Chinese Americans now work in high-prestige occupations. Their achievement has been outstanding in fields related to science and technology, in which many Chinese Americans—including three Nobel Prize winners—have excelled (Sowell, 1981). As shown in Table 11–4, the median household income of Chinese Americans in 1980 ($22,559) was above the national

Table 11–4 THE SOCIAL STANDING OF CHINESE AND JAPANESE AMERICANS, 1980

	Chinese Americans	Japanese Americans	Entire United States
Median Family Income	$22,259	$27,354	$19,917
Proportion in Poverty	13.5%	6.5%	12.4%
Median Education (Age 25 and over)	13.4 years	12.9 years	12.5 years
Completion of Four or More Years of College (Age 25 and over)	36.6%	26.4%	17.1%

SOURCE: U.S. Bureau of the Census.

average ($19,917), and Chinese Americans have twice the proportion of college graduates as Americans taken as a whole.

Despite a general record of success, Chinese Americans still contend with serious problems. Overt prejudice and discrimination have lessened considerably, but racial hostility persists. Poverty among Chinese Americans is also above the national average, especially among those who remain within the protective circle of Chinatowns. At the beginning of the 1980s, half of all males in New York's Chinatown still worked in restaurants, while about three-fourths of all females had low-paying jobs in the garment industry. Not surprisingly, the poverty level in Chinatown was twice that for New York as a whole (Sowell, 1981).

Japanese Americans

Japanese immigration to the United States began slowly in the 1860s; only three thousand entered the country by 1890. Japanese immigrants were welcomed to the Hawaiian Islands (which became a state in 1959) as a source of cheap labor on sugar plantations. Although hostility toward Chinese immigrants was strong by 1870, the small number of early Japanese immigrants apparently escaped most anti-Asian prejudice. But later, as a growing number of Japanese immigrants began demanding better pay, whites sought to curb Japanese immigration (Daniels, 1971). In 1908, the United States signed an agreement with Japan limiting male immigration which was seen as a major economic threat, but continuing to allow Japanese female immigration to ease the sex-ratio imbalance. By the early 1920s, however, more restrictive laws all but ended Japanese immigration. At this point, Japanese immigrants faced much the same prejudice and discrimination as the Chinese. In some places, laws mandated segregation and forbade interracial marriage. Foreign-born Japanese were also excluded from United States citizenship until 1952.

But Japanese immigrants differed from the Chinese in two significant ways. First, knowledge of the United States was much more extensive in Japan than in China. Although maintaining their ethnic identity, Japanese immigrants were therefore poised for assimilation when they arrived in the United States (Sowell, 1981). Second, Japanese immigrants were less concentrated in urban areas. In response to white prejudice and discrimination, some Japanese did form defensive enclaves—called Little Tokyos or Little Osakas by immigrants and simply Jap-towns by hostile whites (Daniels, 1971)—but many began farming in rural areas.

Attempts by the Japanese to buy farmland brought a swift reaction from economically threatened whites. In 1913, California passed the first of a series of laws preventing anyone ineligible for citizenship from owning farmland. Since Japanese and Chinese immigrants were denied citizenship at this time, this institutional discrimination was clearly intended to prevent them from entering the lucrative agricultural market. But more basically, such laws were simply racist, as the attorney general of California conceded in 1914 with remarkable candor:

> The fundamental basis of all legislation has been, and is, race undesirability. It seeks to limit [Japanese] presence by curtailing the privileges which they may enjoy here, for they will not come here in large numbers and abide with us if they may not acquire land. (Kitano, 1980:563)

The Japanese responded in two ways. One tactic was for the foreign-born Japanese (called the *Issei*) to place farmland in the names of their American-born children (the *Nisei*), who were automatically United States citizens under the Constitution. Another response was to lease farmland, which many Japanese did with great success.

The Japanese faced an even greater struggle after December 7, 1941, when the nation of Japan destroyed much of the U.S. naval fleet at Hawaii's Pearl Harbor. The rage felt toward Japan was taken out on Japanese living in America. Some feared the Japanese here would commit espionage and sabotage on behalf of Japan. Within a year, President Roosevelt signed Executive Order 9066, an unprecedented act intended to protect the national security of the United States. Areas of the West Coast were designated as military zones from which anyone suspected of disloyalty could be relocated inland. This order was applied to over 110,000 people of Japanese ancestry, representing 90 percent of their total population in the United States.

This policy has been strongly criticized ever since for a number of reasons. First, the act was applied not to individuals, but to an entire *category* of people, not one of whom was ever convicted of any disloyal act. Second, roughly two-thirds of those imprisoned were Nisei—American citizens by birth. But racism was apparently stronger than the concern for the rights of Americans, and the cry "The Japs must go" was raised by liberals and conservatives alike (Kitano, 1985:244). Third, no Japanese were subject to relocation in Hawaii—precisely where the Japanese attack occurred (Kitano, 1980). The likely reason is that there was less anti-Japanese sentiment in Hawaii, with its far larger Asian population. Fourth and finally, although the United States was also at war with Germany and Italy, no comparable action was taken against whites of German and Italian ancestry.

Life within military prison camps—surrounded by barbed wire and armed soldiers—was a great hardship. Until the end of 1944, families were crowded into single rooms, often in buildings that had previously been used for livestock (Fujimoto, 1971; Bloom, 1980). Making matters even worse, relocation demanded selling businesses, homes, and furnishings on short notice for whatever price could be obtained. As a result, almost the entire Japanese-American population was economically devastated.

The internment ended in 1944 when it was declared unconstitutional by the Supreme Court. In 1983, a government commission recommended that all victims of this policy receive compensation of $20,000—a token payment to acknowledge the economic loss and personal suffering endured by Japanese Americans.

After World War II, Japanese Americans made a dramatic recovery. Having lost their traditional businesses, they entered a wide range of new occupations. Because their culture places such a high value on education and hard work, Japanese Americans have enjoyed remarkable success. As shown in Table 11–4, the median income of a Japanese-American household was $27,354 in 1980—more than 30 percent above the national average. In addition, the rate of poverty among Japanese Americans was half the national average, and Japanese Americans have above-average education.

The internment of Japanese Americans during World War II was justified as a matter of national security, but it was more an expression of racism that had long existed in the western United States.

This rapid upward social mobility has been accompanied by considerable cultural assimilation. The third and fourth generations of Japanese Americans (the Sansei and Yonsei) rarely live within residential enclaves, as many Chinese Americans do. Forty percent of the Sansei have married non-Japanese Americans, indicating not only cultural assimilation but biological miscegenation as well (Vander Zanden, 1983). This extensive change has been a mixed blessing because many Japanese traditions, including the ability to speak Japanese, have been lost. But a high proportion of Japanese Americans participate in ethnic associations as a means of maintaining some ethnic identity (Fugita & O'Brien, 1985). Still, many Japanese Americans appear to be caught between two worlds, belonging to neither one. As one man claims, "I never considered myself 100 percent American because of obvious physical differences. Nor did I think of myself as Japanese" (Okimoto, 1971:14).

Hispanic Americans

Although some Hispanic Americans are of purely Spanish descent, most are a combination of Spanish, African, and Native American ancestry. Hispanic Americans also represent a variety of cultures. As noted earlier in Table 11–1, more than half are Mexican Americans, commonly called *Chicanos*. Puerto Ricans are next in population size, followed by Cuban Americans. Many other societies of Latin America are represented by smaller numbers of Hispanic Americans. Because the birth rate among Hispanic Americans is extremely high, their population is currently increasing by almost 1 million a year. On this basis, Hispanic Americans may outnumber blacks in the United States early in the next century (Moore & Pachon, 1985).

Mexican Americans

Some Mexican Americans are descendants of people who lived in a large region of the American Southwest that was part of Mexico prior to the Mexican-American War (1846–1848). Most Mexican Americans, however, immigrated to the United States in recent decades. During the 1970s, immigration from Mexico was greater than from any other country in the world (Fallows, 1983). By 1987, almost 12 million Mexican Americans were recorded as living in the United States, most in the West and the Southwest.

The actual number of Mexican Americans in the United States is certainly much greater than the official figures suggest because large numbers have entered this country illegally. How many people have done so is impossible to determine since undocumented aliens both enter and leave the United States without the knowledge of authorities. But some estimates have placed the actual number of Mexican Americans at twice the official count (Weintraub & Ross, 1982). The rapid increase in the Mexican-American population has reshaped cities such as San Antonio and Los Angeles, where large numbers of Mexican Americans now live. By 1983, the Mexican-American population of Los Angeles was estimated at over 2 million—more than double the number in 1970 (Anderson, 1983).

Prejudice and discrimination against Mexican Americans have long been commonplace. One notable outbreak of hostility was the 1943 "zoot suit riots" in Los Angeles. The term *zoot suit* refers to a mode of dress—long jackets with padded shoulders, porkpie hats, and long watch chains—popular at the time among Mexican-American teenagers. Street fighting between "zooters" and sailors on leave was widely reported in the press as having been instigated by Mexican Americans; in reality, naval officials and local police allowed white sailors to assault not only youths dressed in zoot suits, but any and all Mexican Americans (Kitano, 1985).

The rapidly growing Mexican-American population continues to spark hostility from some whites. Other whites are only too happy to have a source of inexpensive labor, much as whites a century ago benefited from the cheap labor of Japanese and Chinese immigrants.

The fact that many Mexican Americans continue to hold low-paying jobs is reflected in the figures presented in Table 11–5. In 1980, the median family income for Mexican Americans was $14,765. This was about the same as for all categories of Hispanics ($14,712), but well below the national average ($19,917). Family income rose during the 1980s, but the economic standing of Hispanics generally declined in relation to all Americans. In the case of Mexican Americans, the 1987 median family income of $19,326 was about 65 percent of the comparable national figure, down from 74 percent at the beginning of the decade. In 1987, one-fourth of Mexican-American families were classified as poor. This is more than twice the national average, although below the figure for blacks. It also represents a slight increase during this decade, Finally, Mexican Americans have significantly less education than Americans taken as a whole, although a pattern of improvement since 1980 is evident.

Puerto Ricans

Puerto Rico came under United States control at the end of the Spanish-American War in 1898. Citizens of the United States since 1917, Puerto Ricans are able to move freely to and from the mainland (Fitzpatrick, 1980). Most coming to the mainland seek greater economic opportunity.

In 1910, about 500 Puerto Ricans lived in the city of New York; by 1940, this number had increased to about 70,000. After World War II, however, regular airline service between San Juan, the capital of Puerto Rico, and New York City sparked far greater migration.

Almost 40,000 Puerto Ricans came to New York during 1946 alone, and New York's Puerto Rican population had reached 187,000 by 1950 (Glazer & Moynihan, 1970). In the late 1950s, Puerto Rican anthropologist Elena Padilla described the widespread desire to come to the largest city in the United States:

> For years now Puerto Ricans have been hearing about New York City, have read about it in the local papers, heard about it on the radio and seen some of its scenery in the movies. . . . New York is regarded as a place where many Puerto Ricans . . . have improved their conditions of life, their health, and their general welfare. (1958:21)

Life in New York may have been better than on the island, but it was not what most Puerto Ricans had hoped for. By the mid-1960s, about half of all Puerto Ricans in New York were living in poverty (Moore & Pachon, 1985). Today about half of over 2 million Puerto Ricans in the continental United States live within New York's Spanish Harlem. Despite founding various mutual assistance organizations, as other minority groups have done, they still have many social problems. Adjusting to cultural patterns on the mainland—including, for many, learning the English language—is a major challenge, and Puerto Ricans with darker skin encounter especially strong prejudice and discrimination. As a result, migrants to the mainland sometimes return to Puerto Rico, perhaps to migrate again at a later time. During the mid-1970s, in fact, more Puerto Ricans left the mainland than arrived (Sowell, 1981).

Perhaps the ease with which Puerto Ricans can return to Puerto Rico has limited their cultural assimilation relative to other minorities. For instance, about

Table 11–5 THE SOCIAL STANDING OF HISPANIC AMERICANS, 1980 and 1987

	All Hispanics		Mexican Americans		Puerto Ricans		Cuban Americans		Entire United States	
	1980	1987	1980	1987	1980	1987	1980	1987	1980	1987
Median Family Income	$14,712	$19,995	$14,765	$19,326	$10,734	$14,585	$18,245	$26,770	$19,917	$29,458
Proportion in Poverty	23.5%	24.7%	23.3%	24.9%	36.3%	38.1%	13.2%	13.3%	12.4%	10.9%
Median Education (years) (Age 25 or over)	10.8	12.0	9.6	10.8	10.5	12.1	12.2	12.4	12.5	12.7
Completion of Four or More Years of College (Age 25 or over)	7.6%	8.6%	4.9%	5.8%	5.6%	8.0%	16.2%	17.1%	17.1%	19.9%

SOURCE: U.S. Bureau of the Census.

Hispanic Americans represent a majority of the residents of Miami, Florida. In the Little Havana district of that city, Cuban immigrants have blended their traditional cultural patterns with those of the surrounding cultures.

three-fourths of Puerto Rican families on the mainland speak Spanish in the home compared to about one-half of Mexican American families; doing so tends to maintain a strong ethnic identity (Sowell, 1981; Stevens & Swicegood, 1987). It is clear, however, that Puerto Ricans have lower social standing than other Hispanic Americans. This reflects a higher incidence of female-headed households, noted in Chapter 10 to be strongly linked to poverty in America (Reimers, 1984). Table 11–5 shows that in 1987 the median household income for Puerto Ricans was $14,585—about half that for the United States as a whole. Furthermore, throughout the 1980s, poverty has been higher among Puerto Ricans (38.1 percent in 1987) than among all Hispanics (24.7 percent in 1987). In short, Puerto Ricans continue to be the most socially deprived of all Hispanic minority groups.

Cuban Americans

Large numbers of Cubans immigrated to the United States after the 1959 socialist revolution led by Fidel Castro. Special legislation enabled some 400,000 Cubans to enter the United States by 1972 (Pérez, 1980). Most settled in Miami, although the Cuban community in New York now numbers over 50,000. The Cubans who fled Castro's Cuba were generally not the "huddled masses" described on the Statue of Liberty, but highly educated people with careers in business and the profes-

sions. They wasted little time building much the same success that they had enjoyed in Cuba (Fallows, 1983). Table 11–5 shows that the median household income for Cuban Americans in 1987 was $26,770—well above average for all categories of Hispanics, and almost equal to that of Americans as a whole. Similarly, the proportion of Cuban Americans living in poverty is well below that for all Hispanics, although slightly higher than for all Americans. Notice, too, that Cuban Americans have more education, on the average, than other categories of Hispanics.

Cuban Americans have retained much of their traditional culture. Of the categories of Hispanics we have considered, they are the most likely to speak Spanish in their homes; eight out of ten families do so (Sowell, 1981). Cultural distinctiveness surely provokes hostility on the part of some whites. Miami, for example, has gradually been transformed by the large Cuban-American population centered in the Little Havana district. While some whites applaud the economic and social contributions made by this community, others angrily assert that the city has been taken over by outsiders. One bumper sticker put the matter bluntly: "Will the last American to leave Miami remember to bring the flag?"

In 1987, the number of Cuban Americans was estimated to be about 1 million (U.S. Bureau of the Census, 1987). A large proportion of the population increase during this decade followed Fidel Castro's decision in 1980 to allow immigration to the United States through Mariel Harbor. The result was a flotilla of boats, which came to be called the Mariel boat lift, carrying some 125,000 refugees. Several thousand of these immigrants had been released from Cuban prisons and mental hospitals, and this minority was the focus of mass-media accounts, which fueled prejudice toward all Cuban Americans (Clark, Lasaga, & Regue, 1981; Portes, 1984).

About 90,000 of these Cubans settled in the Miami area, while others—especially those with darker skin—entered cities in the Northeast (Pérez, 1980). These recent immigrants are typically poorer and less educated than those who arrived a generation earlier, which has caused friction between them and more established Cuban Americans in Miami (Fallows, 1983). But they, too, are quickly becoming established. By 1986, most had applied for resident status so that their relatives abroad could also be admitted to the United States.

White Ethnic Americans

Despite a century of describing the United States as a melting pot, there is little doubt that ethnicity retains considerable importance among white Americans (Rubin, 1976). In the 1960s, the term *white ethnics* began to be used to recognize the fact that many whites proudly maintain their ethnic heritage. White ethnics are people of European ancestry, although generally not the WASPs described earlier.

The huge wave of immigration from Europe in the nineteenth century greatly increased the social diversity of the United States. Initially, German and Irish immigrants predominated. Italians and Jews from many European societies followed. Despite cultural differences, these Europeans shared the hope that America would offer more political freedom and economic opportunity than they had known in their homelands. In the 1840s, for example, famine in Ireland drove thousands of immigrants to the shores of the United States; two generations later, poor farmers from southern Italy came to share in the wealth being produced by American industrialization. The belief that the streets of America were paved with gold was, however, a far cry from the reality experienced by the vast majority of immigrants. Jobs were not always easy to find, and most demanded hard labor for low wages.

Economic problems were made worse by prejudice and discrimination, which swelled with the increasing tide of immigration. Nativist organizations opposed the entry of more non-WASP Europeans to America, and stirred up prejudice and discrimination against those already here. Newspaper ads seeking workers in the mid-nineteenth century often carried a warning to new arrivals: "None need apply but Americans" (Handlin, 1941:67).

Surely some prejudice and discrimination reflected class—the immigrants were typically poor and often had little command of English. But hostility was also provoked by ethnic differences. This is evident in expressions of prejudice toward even the most distinguished achievers. Fiorello La Guardia was an outstanding mayor of New York between 1933 and 1945. But this son of immigrants, half Italian and half Jewish, was once denounced by President Herbert Hoover in words that reveal unambiguous ethnic hatred:

> You should go back where you belong and advise Mussolini how to make good honest citizens in Italy. The Italians are preponderantly our murderers and bootleggers. . . . Like a lot of other foreign spawn, you do not appreciate the country that supports and tolerates you. (Mann, 1959, cited in Baltzell, 1964:30)

That such a comment would be made by the president of the United States suggests the extent to which ethnic prejudice was rooted in American society. Prejudice and discrimination directed against white ethnics grew as the number of immigrants increased. Figure 11–4 shows the number of immigrants entering the United States by decade. Nativist opposition to the "dilution of WASP America" was greatest between 1880 and 1930, the decades of intensive immigration. In addition, the Bolshevik Revolution in Russia and other political conflicts in Europe after World War I encouraged unrealistic fears of immigrants as political radicals. A "Red Scare" gripped much of the country with deadly effects, as illustrated by the case of two Italian immigrants, Nicola Sacco and Bartolomeo Vanzetti.

Sacco and Vanzetti were political activists accused of robbery and murder in Braintree, Massachusetts, in 1920. Both staunchly maintained their innocence, and the evidence presented against them was far from convincing. But in a climate of fear and prejudice, both men were convicted and executed in 1927 as five hundred police—many armed with machine guns—stood outside the prison. In 1977, on the fiftieth anniversary of their execution, Massachusetts governor Michael Dukakis declared their deaths to have been a tragic injustice (Jackson, 1981).

Nativists were finally victorious. Between 1921 and

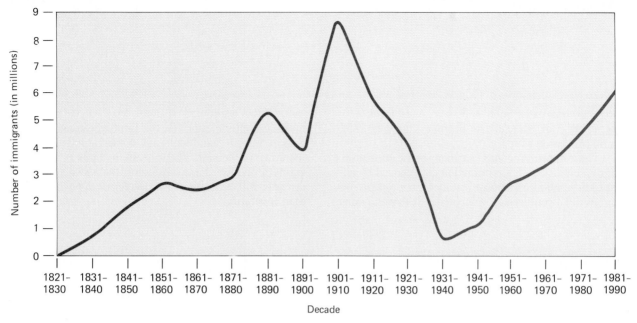

Figure 11–4 Immigration to the United States by Decade
(U.S. Immigration and Naturalization Service)

1968, strict immigration quotas were applied to each foreign country. Immigration from all nations was reduced, but immigration by southern and eastern Europeans—peoples likely to have darker skin and to culturally differ from the dominant WASPs—was restricted the most (Fallows, 1983).

In the face of widespread prejudice and discrimination, many white ethnics followed the pattern of forming ethnic enclaves where opportunity and mutual assistance were available. Often an ethnic minority was able to gain an economic foothold in a specialized trade. Italian Americans, for example, entered the construction industry; Irish Americans often worked in various building trades and civil service occupations; Jews were heavily represented in the garment industry; many Greeks (like the Chinese) worked in the retail food business (Newman, 1973).

With gradual economic prosperity, cultural assimilation accelerated for many white ethnics. Others, however, are still struggling to gain economic security. Many of these, keenly aware of their own plight, resent the greater national attention focused on the problems of other minorities, especially blacks. As one white ethnic Bostonian complained, "I'm working my ass off. My kids don't have a place to swim, my parks are full of glass, and I'm supposed to bleed for a bunch of people on relief" (Schrag, 1969:16).

Despite continuing problems, white ethnics have achieved considerable success over the course of the last century. Many of the descendants of immigrants who labored in sweatshops and lived in overcrowded tenements now have respectable positions—both socially and economically—in American society. No doubt this is the primary reason that ethnic heritage is now a source of pride to many white Americans.

American Minorities: A Hundred-Year Perspective

The United States has been, and still is, a land of immigrants. Immigration during the nineteenth century brought striking cultural diversity to America, which diminished only with the restrictive legislation enacted between 1882 and the 1920s (Easterlin, 1980). For most members of minority groups, the first half of this century brought gradual economic gains and at least some cultural assimilation. In addition, citizenship was eventually extended to Native Americans (1924), foreign-born Chinese Americans (1943), and Japanese Americans (1952). In the 1950s, black Americans organized the civil rights movement in response to centuries of oppression.

As Figure 11–4 shows, immigration has increased once again during the 1980s, but the names, faces, and cultural patterns are different. No longer do most immigrants come from Europe; by 1970, only about one in six did, while most were from Latin America and Asia. In the late 1980s, the countries providing the largest number of immigrants to the United States are Mexico, the Philippines, and Korea. Rather than entering the large cities on the "European" side of the United States, these new immigrants are bringing profound cultural changes to cities in the South and West. As one commentator noted, Los Angeles has become "the new Ellis Island" (Anderson, 1983).

These new immigrants face many of the same problems of prejudice and discrimination experienced by minorities throughout American history. As European immigrants did a century ago, many today struggle to enter the "golden door" of American society without entirely losing their traditional culture. Many have also built racial and ethnic enclaves: the Little Havana and Little Saigon of today stand alongside the Little Italy and Germantown of the past. They also share the hope of immigrants throughout American history that racial and ethnic diversity will be defined as a matter of *difference* rather than *inferiority*.

SUMMARY

1. Race is based on common biological traits. The traditional distinctions among Caucasians, Negroids, and Mongoloids have been undermined by the fact that there are no pure races.

2. Ethnicity is based on a shared cultural heritage, and is subject to change within a generation, while race is not.

3. Race and ethnicity are the bases of membership in minority groups insofar as they result in a distinctive social identity and subordinate position in the system of social stratification.

4. Prejudice is a matter of attitudes—making an unfair generalization or sterotype about a category of people. Racism is a powerful type of prejudice asserting that one race is innately superior or inferior to another.

5. Discrimination is a matter of action—treating various categories of people differently. Both prejudice and discrimination are part of the fabric of American society.

6. Pluralism recognizes social differences based on race and ethnicity, but treats categories of people as socially equal. Although Americans often describe the United States as a pluralistic society, minority groups do not have equal social standing.

7. Assimilation is a process by which minorities gradually adopt the patterns of the dominant culture. Rather than forming part of a true melting pot, immigrants to the United States have typically become more Anglicized.

8. Segregation is the physical and social separation of categories of people. Although some minority groups seek to separate themselves, segregation is typically involuntary.

9. Annihilation is the violent extermination of a category of people. In the history of the Americas, European colonists and settlers annihilated a large proportion of the Native American people. Instances of annihilation have occurred in this century.

10. White Anglo-Saxon Protestants (WASPs) have long dominated American society. WASPs predominated among the original European settlers of America, and continue to enjoy a high social position today.

11. Native Americans—the original inhabitants of the Americas—have been subject to annihilation, segregation, and forced assimilation at the hands of Europeans. Today the social standing of Native Americans is well below the national average.

12. Black Americans endured over two centuries of slavery in America. After 1865, they were rigidly segregated in American society by law. De facto segregation continues to this day. The social standing of blacks is well below the American average.

13. Both Chinese and Japanese Americans have been socially disadvantaged because of their racial and ethnic differences. Today, however, both categories have above-average income and education.

14. Hispanic Americans include many ethnic groups that share a Spanish heritage. Mexican Americans are the largest Hispanic minority, heavily concentrated in the Southwest. Puerto Ricans, most of whom live in New York, are poorer. Cubans, heavily concentrated in Miami, are the most affluent category of Hispanics; their income is only slightly below the national average.

15. White ethnic Americans include non-WASPs of European ancestry. While making gains during the last century, many white ethnics are still struggling for economic security.

16. Immigration has increased in recent years. No longer primarily from Europe, immigrants are now mostly from Latin America and Asia and settle primarily in the South and West.

KEY CONCEPTS

annihilation the violent extermination of one category of people by another

assimilation the process by which members of minority groups gradually modify their ways of life to conform to patterns of the dominant culture

discrimination treating various categories of people differently

ethnicity a cultural heritage shared by a category of people

institutional discrimination patterns of discrimination that are woven into the fabric of society

minority group a category of people defined by physical or cultural traits subject to social disadvantage

miscegenation the biological process of interbreeding among various racial categories

pluralism a state in which all racial and ethnic groups, while socially distinct, have roughly equal social standing

prejudice an unfounded generalization about a category of people

race a category of people with common biological traits passed from generation to generation

racism the belief that one racial category is innately superior or inferior to another

scapegoat one person or category of people unfairly blamed for the troubles of another

segregation the physical and social separation of categories of people

stereotype a description of a category of people that persists even in the face of contrary evidence

SUGGESTED READINGS

This paperback text provides a closer examination of issues raised in this chapter.

Harry H. L. Kitano. *Race Relations*. 3rd ed. Englewood Cliffs, NJ: Prentice-Hall, 1985.

Prejudice and discrimination are central processes of racial and ethnic relations. These two books provide a detailed analysis of both within American society.

George Eaton Simpson and J. Milton Yinger. *Racial and Cultural Minorities: An Analysis of Prejudice and Discrimination*. New York: Plenum, 1985.

Joe R. Feagin and Clairece Booher Feagin. *Discrimination American Style: Institutional Racism and Sexism*. 2nd ed. Malabar, FL: Kreiger, 1986.

Just as cultural patterns cause unity, so can they turn people against one another. This book, by a noted journalist who lived for five years in Jerusalem, explores the Middle Eastern conflict between Arabs and Jews in terms of the stereotypes that carry hatred into the lives of each new generation.

David K. Shipler. *Arab and Jew: Wounded Spirits in a Promised Land*. New York: Times Books, 1986.

The significance of race as it shaped the World War II conflict between the United States and Japan is examined in this book.

John W. Dower. *War Without Mercy: Race and Power in the Pacific War*. New York: Pantheon Books, 1986.

How do factors such as social class and race shape early educational experiences? This study compares a Head Start center in a black working-class neighborhood and a preschool in a white middle-class neighborhood.

Sally Lubeck. *Sandbox Society: Early Education in Black and White America—A Comparative Ethnography*. Philadelphia: Falmer Press/Taylor & Francis, 1985.

This paperback has a format resembling a children's book, but packs powerful lessons about the experience of being different.

Rosabeth Moss Kanter with Barry A. Stein. *A Tale of "O": On Being Different in an Organization*. New York: Harper & Row, 1980.

The mass media have enormous power to shape public attitudes about race and ethnicity. This book focuses on how television has ignored or misrepresented black Americans.

J. Fred MacDonald. *Blacks and White TV: Afro-Americans in Television Since 1948*. Chicago: Nelson-Hall, 1983.

This recent report describes the social and economic standing of blacks in the United States.

James D. Williams, ed. *The State of Black America in 1987*. New York: National Urban League, 1987.

This study focuses on the Mexican-American and Puerto Rican communities in Chicago: not only how they encounter the larger city, but how they interact with each other.

Felix M. Padilla. *Latino Ethnic Consciousness: The Case of Mexican Americans and Puerto Ricans in Chicago*. Notre Dame, IN: University of Notre Dame Press, 1985.

This study argues that, rather than having assimilated, Jews remain a distinctive and vital part of American society.

Calvin Goldscheider. *Jewish Continuity and Change: Emerging Patterns in America*. Bloomington: Indiana University Press, 1986.

CHAPTER 12

Sex and Gender

In 1840, an American couple traveled to London to attend the World Anti-Slavery Convention—a meeting of people opposed to black slavery. Henry Brewster Stanton, an eloquent speaker, was welcomed as a delegate. But Elizabeth Cady Stanton was surprised to be rudely turned away from the convention. Ironically, as a woman, she was barred from a meeting opposed to social inequality!

While in London, Elizabeth Cady Stanton met Lucretia Mott, who had also been excluded from the meeting. They shared their dismay at how people fervently opposed to racial injustice failed to recognize their unfair treatment of women. The two discussed holding a convention of their own; eight years later, the meeting was held in Seneca Falls, New York. The participants described how blacks and women suffered from many of the same patterns of prejudice and discrimination. Like black slaves, women typically could not own property, keep their earnings, enter into business, or vote; neither could they testify in court against their husbands.

In 1865, the Thirteenth Amendment to the Constitution outlawed slavery in the United States. Soon after, Congress extended citizenship to all blacks (Fourteenth Amendment) and the right to vote to black men (Fifteenth Amendment). But suffrage was still denied to women of all races. Thus Elizabeth Cady Stanton and others launched the National Woman Suffrage Association. Finally, in 1920, the Nineteenth Amendment to the Constitution did give women the right to vote (McGlen & O'Connor, 1983; Friedrich, 1984).

Almost seventy years later, although women have made important gains, they are still socially disadvantaged

and men continue to hold a position of relative privilege. This inequality is often thought to reflect innate differences between the sexes, but it is actually a creation of society itself, as this chapter explains. To begin, we shall explore the key concepts of sex and gender.

Sex: A Biological Distinction

Sex refers to *the division of humanity into biological categories of male and female.* As a biological distinction, sex is determined at the moment a child is conceived through sexual intercourse. The female ovum and the male sperm, which join to form a fertilized embryo, each contain twenty-three pairs of chromosomes—biological codes that guide a human being's physical development. One pair of chromosomes determines the child's sex: a mother always contributes an X chromosome; a father may contribute either an X or a Y. If the father contributes an X chromosome, a female embryo (XX) develops, while a father's Y chromosome results in a male embryo (XY).

About six weeks after conception, sex differentiation in a human embryo begins. In males, testicular tissue produces testosterone, a chemical hormone that produces the male genitals. Without testosterone, the embryo develops female genitals. This suggests that nature's basic blueprint is for a female child; only when testosterone is present to alter this plan does a child become male (Offir, 1982:130–131). About 105 males are born for every 100 females, although a higher death rate among males soon results in females being a slight majority (Baker et al., 1980).

At birth, males and females are distinguished by **primary sex characteristics**—*the genitals, used to reproduce the human species.* At puberty in the early teens, when people become capable of reproduction, further biological differentiation takes place in terms of **secondary sex characteristics**—*distinctive physical traits of males and females not directly linked to reproduction.* In order to accommodate pregnancy, giving birth, and nurturing infants, adolescent females develop wider hips, breasts, and soft fatty tissue to provide a reserve supply of nutrition during pregnancy and breast-feeding (Brownmiller, 1984). Males, usually slightly taller and heavier than females from birth, in adolescence typically show more muscular development of the upper body, more extensive body hair, and voices deeper in tone. Note that these are only general differences. Many males are smaller and lighter than many females; some males have less

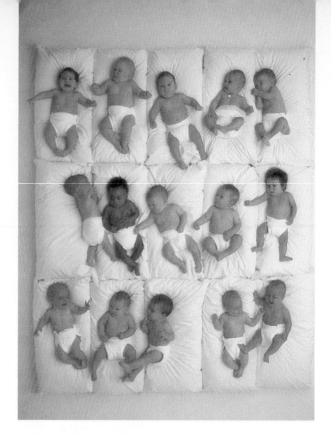

The biological categories of sex—male and female—develop prior to birth. The full significance of being masculine and feminine, however, is not evident among infants; this takes place only as infants grow within a social environment.

body hair than some females; and some males speak in a higher tone than some females do.

Almost everyone is biologically female or male but in rare cases, hormone imbalance before birth results in a *hermaphrodite* (a word derived from Hermaphroditus, the offspring of the mythological Greek gods Hermes and Aphrodite who embodied both sexes). Hermaphrodites have some combination of male and female internal and external genitals. Because our culture is rather intolerant of sexual ambiguity, we often regard hermaphrodites with confusion and even disgust. In contrast, the Navaho look upon hermaphrodites with awe, seeing them as the embodiment of the full potential of both the male and the female. And the Pokot of Eastern Africa are rather indifferent to what they define as a simple biological error (Geertz, 1975).

There are also rare cases of people who choose to change their sex. Sometimes hermaphrodites surgically alter their genitals to gain the appearance (and occasionally the function) of a sexually normal male or female. Other cases involve *transsexuals,* who feel they are one sex when biologically they are the other. Some twenty thousand transsexuals in the United States have surgically changed their sex to escape the sense of being "trapped in the wrong body" (Restak, 1979, cited in Offir, 1982:146).

Sexual Orientation

Sexual orientation refers to *the manner in which people experience sexual arousal and achieve sexual pleasure.* In most living organisms, sexuality is biologically programmed. In human beings, however, sexual orientation is a more complex matter of culture. The norm within virtually all industrial societies is *heterosexuality* (*hetero* is a Greek word meaning "the other of two"), by which a person is sexually attracted to the opposite sex. However, *homosexuality* (*homo* is the Greek word for "the same") by which a person is sexually attracted to the same sex is a common pattern.

All cultures endorse heterosexuality, but many tolerate—and some even encourage—homosexuality. Among the ancient Greeks, for instance, male intellectuals tended to celebrate homosexuality and to view heterosexuality as, at best, necessary for reproduction. (Not coincidentally, this cultural pattern was accompanied by a general disregard for the mental abilities of women.) Researchers have also noted that in a few societies people who do *not* engage in homosexuality have been defined as deviant (Kluckhohn, 1948; Ford & Beach, 1951). But the simple fact that homosexual relations do not permit reproduction explains why no society has been known to endorse only homosexuality.

Most Americans consider homosexuality to be deviant. Toleration of homosexuals—now widely called gay people—has certainly increased considerably during this century. Worth noting is the fact that the American Psychiatric Association removed homosexuality from its listing of mental disorders in 1974. But gays are still subject to both prejudice and discrimination, which has increased somewhat in recent years as the public has associated homosexuality with the feared disease AIDS. As noted in Chapter 8, many states continue to outlaw homosexual activity. It is hardly surprising, then, that many gay people choose to remain "in the closet," that is, avoid public disclosure of their sexual orientation. Heterosexuals can begin to understand what this means only by imagining never speaking about their romances to parents, roommates, or anyone else (Offir, 1982:216). Many organizations of gay people are struggling to overcome inaccurate stereotypes of gay men and gay women (also called lesbians). In fact, gay people vary as much in their personalities and behavior as heterosexuals do.

The pioneering research of Alfred Kinsey (1948, 1953) suggested that only about 4 percent of males and about 2 percent of females are exclusively homosexual. But perhaps 25 percent of Americans have had at least some homosexual experience. This means that the sexual orientations we have described are not mutually exclusive—many people, called *bisexuals*, have some combination of homosexual and heterosexual orientations.

How any person gains a specific sexual orientation is not entirely understood. There is some evidence that sexual orientation is shaped at birth by biological factors. Somewhat more evidence suggests that sexual orientation reflects hormone balance as we grow. Still other research supports the conclusion that sexual orientation is a product of the social environment. Probably none of these factors alone is an adequate explanation of sexual orientation; more likely, all three have some importance. One influential study concluded that attempting to explain homosexuality is futile—just as much as explaining heterosexuality (Bell, Weinberg, & Kiefer-Hammersmith, 1981).

Gender: A Cultural Distinction

Gender refers to *human traits linked by culture to each sex.* Within a society, males are socialized to be masculine, as females are taught to be feminine. Gender is the difference that sex makes within a society, guiding how we are to think of ourselves, how we interact with others, and what position we assume within the system of social inequality. The distinction between the biological fact of sex and the social fact of gender is illustrated by the timeless question of whether either males or females are innately superior. There are certainly biological *differences* between the sexes. Beyond the obvious reproductive differences, males have more muscle in the arms and shoulders, so that the average male can lift more weight than the average female can. Furthermore, males have greater strength over short periods of time. On the other hand, because of the energy they derive from greater body fat, females can outperform males in many tests of long-term endurance. Perhaps more important, females outperform males in life itself. According to the Bureau of the Census, the average life expectancy for males born in 1985 is 71.2 years, while females born the same year can expect to live 78.2 years.

With regard to mental abilities, adolescent males seem to have greater mathematical ability than females, while females outperform males in verbal tasks. Overall, however, research suggests that there is no significant difference in the mental ability of males and females (Maccoby & Jacklin, 1974; Baker et al., 1980; Lengermann & Wallace, 1985).

Biologically, therefore, typical males and females reveal limited differences, but clearly neither sex has an overall natural superiority. However, as we shall presently see, the cultural notion that one sex is superior to the other can and does place one sex in a position of dominance over the other. Like all cultural patterns, the social inequality of males and females may seem so natural that we simply assume it is the inevitable consequence of sex itself. But society rather than biology is at work. This can be seen in several different kinds of research.

An unusual case study. In 1963, a physician was performing a routine penis circumcision on seven-month-old identical twins. Using electrocautery (a surgical technique employing a heated needle), the physician accidentally burned off the penis of one boy. The parents were horrified. After months of medical consultation, they decided to use further surgery and hormone treatments to change the boy's sex, and to raise him as a female.

The child was dressed as a girl, her hair was allowed to grow, and she was treated according to cultural definitions of femininity. At the same time, the brother—an exact biological copy—was raised as a boy.

Because of their different socializations, each child learned a distinctive **gender identity,** which refers to *the ways males and females, within their culture, learn to think of themselves.* In this case, one child learned to think of himself in terms that our culture defines as masculine, while the other child—despite beginning life as a male—soon became feminine. As the twin's mother observed:

> One thing that really amazes me is that [my daughter] is so feminine. I've never seen a little girl so neat and tidy. . . . She is very proud of herself, when she puts on a new dress, or I set her hair. She just loves to have her hair set; she could sit under the dryer all day long to have her hair set. She just loves it. . . . [My daughter] likes for me to wipe her face. She doesn't like to be dirty, and yet my son is quite different. I can't wash his face for anything. . . . She seems to be daintier. (Money & Ehrhardt, 1972:124)

Since these two children were biologically identical at the outset, the differences between them must be the consequences of culture.

The Israeli kibbutzim. Further evidence that society shapes the lives of males and females differently is found in studies of collective settlements in Israel called *kib-*

butzim. The kibbutz (the singular form) intentionally fosters social equality: everyone is expected to share in necessary work, property is held collectively, and everyone has a voice in decision making.

The members of kibbutzim also tend to oppose conceptions of gender that divide the responsibilities of males and females so that one sex can dominate the other. All types of work, including child care, cooking, cleaning, laundry, and caring for the ill, may involve both men and women. Rather than being socialized differently, boys and girls typically are treated alike and, from the first weeks of life, live in dormitories under the care of specially trained personnel.

Within many kibbutzim, however, the patterns of social equality between males and females are not as strong as they once were. Perhaps the desire for sexual equality is simply not as strong among today's members as it once was. Another possibility, suggested by some sociobiologists (see Chapter 3), is that subtle biological dispositions may tend to undermine efforts to establish sexual equality (Tiger & Shepher, 1975). But the kibbutzim certainly demonstrate that cultures have no fixed way of defining what is masculine or what is feminine. Moreover, a society can encourage sexual equality just as it can allow one sex to dominate the other.

Cross-cultural research. Examining gender in many cultures is perhaps the easiest way to see that the significance of the two sexes is created by society. If gender reflects the biological facts of sex, what is defined as masculine and feminine should be much the same in all societies; if gender is cultural, however, these conceptions should be variable.

The best-known research of this kind is the study of gender in three societies of New Guinea by anthropologist Margaret Mead (1963; orig. 1935). In the mountains of New Guinea, Mead observed the Arapesh, among whom males and females typically displayed similar attitudes and behavior. Mead described both Arapesh females and males as cooperative, unaggressive, and sensitive to the needs of others. By American standards, then, both males and females were feminine.

Moving south, Mead then observed the Mundugumor, whose culture of head-hunting and cannibalism was a striking contrast to the gentle ways of the Arapesh. Here Mead also found males and females to be alike, although quite different from the Arapesh. Both Mundugumor males and females were typically selfish, aggressive, and insensitive to other people—masculine, according to American culture.

Finally, Mead traveled west to observe the Tchambuli and found that they considered males and females to have very different personal traits just as Americans do. Yet the Tchambuli reversed our conceptions of gender: females were dominant and rational, while males were submissive and emotional.

Mead's research shows that societies may exaggerate or minimize social differences between males and females. In addition, what one culture defines as masculine may be considered feminine by another. Mead's research is therefore strong support for the conclusion that gender is a variable creation of society.

A broader study of gender in over two hundred preindustrial societies was carried out by George Murdock (1937). Murdock found that most societies defined some tasks as feminine and viewed others as masculine. He also noted that hunting and warfare are usually defined as the responsibilities of males, while home-centered tasks such as cooking and child care are usually defined as tasks for females. No doubt, this pattern has some

The stereotypical American view of females as "the weaker sex" is not shared by many other societies, where women routinely engage in physically demanding labor.

biological basis. Because of their typically greater size and short-term strength, males tend to be responsible for hunting and warfare in preindustrial societies; because females bear children, their activities are likely to be more domestic.

But beyond such general patterns, Murdock found significant differences. Agriculture—the core of preindustrial production—is defined as feminine about as often as it is viewed as masculine. Mostly, however, this is a responsibility of both males and females. With regard to many other tasks, from building shelters to tattooing the body, Murdock discovered considerable variation from culture to culture.

In larger, industrial societies, gender is even more variable. Americans tend to define physically taxing jobs as masculine, but females perform many such tasks in the Soviet Union and China. Noteworthy, too, is the fact that industrialization is usually accompanied by a gradual lessening of social inequality between males and females (Lenski & Lenski, 1987).

All of this evidence suggests that gender is simply too variable to be considered a simple or natural expression of the biological categories of sex. Rather, like many other elements of culture, what it means to be male and female is mostly a creation of society.

Patriarchy and Sexism

Although conceptions of gender are highly variable, a universal pattern is some degree of **patriarchy** (literally, "the rule of fathers"), meaning *a form of social organization in which males dominate females*. Despite the mythical tales of societies dominated by female "Amazons," the pattern of **matriarchy**, which refers to *a form of social organization in which females dominate males*, is not at present part of the human record (Harris, 1977; Kipp, 1980; Lengermann & Wallace, 1985). Bear in mind, however, that most societies are some combination of these two organizational types. Along with a universal tendency toward patriarchy is found significant variation in the relative power and privilege of males and females.

In principle, patriarchy is based on **sexism**, which is *the belief that one sex is innately superior to the other*. Within a patriarchal world, sexism is expressed as the belief that males are innately superior to females and therefore rightly dominate them. As Table 12–1 shows, sexism has much in common with racism, which was discussed in Chapter 11. Just as racism is an ideology supporting white domination of nonwhites, so is sexism

Table 12–1 WAYS IN WHICH SEXISM AND RACISM ARE ALIKE

	Women	Blacks
Link to highly visible personal traits	Secondary sex characteristics.	Skin color.
Assertion of innate inferiority	Women are mentally inferior.	Blacks are mentally inferior.
	Women are irresponsible, unreliable, and emotional.	Blacks are irresponsible, unreliable, and pleasure-seeking.
Assertion that those who are disadvantaged are content with their "proper place" in society	"A woman's place is in the home." All women really enjoy being treated "like a woman."	"Blacks should remain in their place." Blacks are content living just as they do.
Assertion that victims are under the protection of their oppressors	"Men put women on a pedestal."	Whites "take care of" blacks.
Coping strategies on the part of victims	Behavior flattering to men; letting men think they are better even when they are not.	Deferential behavior toward whites; letting whites think they are better even when they are not.
	Hiding one's real feelings.	Hiding one's real feelings.
	Attempting to outwit men.	Attempting to outwit whites.
Barriers to opportunity	Women don't need an education.	Blacks don't need an education.
	Confined to "women's work."	Confined to "black occupations."
	Women should stay out of politics.	Blacks should stay out of politics.
Criticism of those who do not "stay in their place"	Assertive women are "pushy."	Assertive blacks are "uppity."
	Ambitious women are trying to be like men.	Ambitious blacks are trying to be like whites.
	Women as traditional targets of violence by men.	Blacks as traditional targets of violence by whites.

SOURCE: Adapted from Helen Mayer Hacker, "Women as a Minority Group," *Social Forces*, Vol. 30 (October 1951): 60–69; and "Women as a Minority Group: Twenty Years Later," in Florence Denmark, ed., *Who Discriminates Against Women?* (Beverly Hills, CA: Sage, 1974), pp. 124–134.

an ideological defense of males (allegedly the superior sex) dominating females (argued to be natural inferiors of men). Notice, too, that both racism and sexism cause people to distort their own abilities by interpreting *social* privilege or disadvantage as *personal* merit or deficiency.

The liabilities of sexism for females include obvious subordination in the system of social inequality. Society as a whole also pays a high price for maintaining sexism. By limiting the opportunities available to women, it ensures that the full talents and abilities of half the population will never be developed. Males, of course, derive significant benefits from sexism, including a disproportionate share of power and wealth. But they, too, suffer as a consequence of sexism. As Marilyn French (1985) points out, patriarchy demands that males remain in control—not only of women, but also of themselves and the surrounding world. This is a human impossibility, of course, and the effort extracts a high price in terms of accidents, stress, heart attacks, and other diseases that result in higher rates of death among males of all ages. Indeed, the so-called Type A personality—characterized by impatience, drive, and competitiveness, and

known to be linked to heart disease—bears a striking resemblance to what our culture defines as masculine (Ehrenreich, 1983). Furthermore, insofar as males learn to emphasize control over others, they lose the ability to experience intimacy, equality, and trust (French, 1985:323). Finally, when human feelings, thoughts, and actions are rigidly scripted to fit cultural conceptions of gender, people are denied the opportunity to freely express the full range of their humanity. Males are strongly pressured to be assertive, competitive, and in control, which is surely a burden to many. Females are pressured to be submissive and dependent, regardless of their individual personality traits. The box illustrates how rigid conceptions of gender are limiting to human beings.

Is Patriarchy Inevitable?

In technologically primitive societies, patriarchy was initially based on the biological differences of sex. Pregnancy and childbirth limited the range of female participation in society, while their greater height and short-term strength typically allowed males to overpower females.

In industrial societies, however, advanced technology serves to control births just as it enables millions to die at the push of a button. Thus such biological differences would seem to provide little justification for patriarchy.

Still, patriarchy persists in industrial societies, despite being increasingly challenged by both women and men. Sweden, for example, shares with many other industrial societies laws that mandate equal opportunity for males and females in all occupations and that require equal pay for equal work. Swedish culture also supports the idea that housework should be the responsibility of both sexes. Nonetheless, in Sweden as in other societies, women still have primary responsibility for maintaining the household, while most economic and political power is in the hands of males (Haas, 1981).

Since the socialist revolution in 1917, the Soviet Union has officially endorsed sexual equality. Soviet women are heavily represented in many occupations that are defined as masculine in the United States, including physically demanding work in construction and factories. However, Soviet society is dominated by males, who occupy almost all the key positions in the political and economic systems. The Politburo (the key political decision-making body in the Soviet Union) had no women members in 1987; and in the Communist Party (the one official political party), men outnumbered women by three to one. Moreover, as in virtually all societies in the world, occupational positions commonly held by women provide less income and social prestige than those typically held by men. For example, most physicians in the Soviet Union are women, but this profession has a lower social ranking than it has in the United States, where most physicians are males (Mamonova, 1984).

Does the persistence of patriarchy mean that it is inevitable? A few researchers claim that there are biologically based factors that encourage distinctive behavior patterns in the two sexes, and which make the complete eradication of patriarchy difficult, if not impossible (Goldberg, 1974, 1987). Most sociologists, however, are highly skeptical of that claim. The fact that no society has yet eliminated patriarchy does not mean that patriarchy is an inevitable social pattern. To see this, imagine the world of hunting and gathering societies some ten thousand years ago. At that time in human history, there were no large cities, nor a single industrial factory. On the basis of evidence available then, one might well have concluded that industrial societies as we know them were outside the range of cultural possibility (Kipp, 1980:10–11). Today, we are in much the same position

with regard to patriarchy. Although patriarchy has long been part of human history, this pattern is now being widely challenged. Unless one were to accept the idea that some immutable biological forces are at work, there is no reason to assume that patriarchy will remain a part of all human societies in the future.

To understand the remarkable persistence of patriarchy, we now turn to an examination of how gender is deeply rooted in society, from the way children are taught to think of themselves to patterns of social inequality that affect men and women as adults.

GENDER AND SOCIALIZATION

Gender is a fundamental element of the socialization process. From birth until death, human feelings, thoughts, and actions reflect cultural definitions of gender. As they interact with others, children quickly learn that males and females are defined as different kinds of human beings and, by about the age of three or four, they apply this distinction to themselves (Bem, 1981; Kohlberg, 1966, cited in Lengermann & Wallace, 1985:37). Table 12–2 lists the conventional human traits that form the gender identity of males and females in American society.

But the fact that societies assign some human traits to one sex and some to the other does not mean that everyone acts accordingly. In a study of college students,

Table 12–2 TRADITIONAL GENDER IDENTITY

Masculine Traits	Feminine Traits
Dominant	Submissive
Independent	Dependent
Intelligent and competent	Unintelligent and incapable
Rational	Emotional
Assertive	Receptive
Analytical	Intuitive
Strong	Weak
Brave	Timid
Ambitious	Content
Active	Passive
Competitive	Cooperative
Insensitive	Sensitive
Sexually aggressive	Sex object
Attractive because of achievement	Attractive because of physical appearance

"X—A Fabulous Child's Story"

Once upon a time, a baby named X was born. This baby was named X so that nobody could tell whether it was a boy or a girl.

In a children's story by Lois Gould, "X" was given to Mr. and Ms. Jones, a couple carefully screened from thousands of applicants, as an experiment. The Joneses were to follow only one rule: X was not to be socialized as masculine or feminine, but was to learn everything a child could. Assisted by a heavy *Official Instruction Manual*, the Joneses promised to follow this rule as closely as possible. They agreed to take equal turns feeding and caring for X, to spend as much time bouncing as cuddling the baby, and to praise X for being strong just as often as for being sweet. But trouble began almost right away when the Joneses' friends and relatives asked whether X was a boy or a girl.

When the Joneses smiled and said "It's an X!" nobody knew what to say. They couldn't say, "Look at her cute little dimples." And they couldn't say "Look at his husky little biceps!" And they couldn't even say just plain "kitchy-coo." In fact, they all thought that the Joneses were playing some kind of rude joke.

The Joneses were, of course, being quite serious, but all the same, other people became irritated and embarrassed:

"People will think there's something wrong with it!" some of them whispered.

"There *is* something wrong with it!" others whispered back.

And what did baby X think about all the fuss? It simply finished its bottle with a loud and satisfied burp.

Finding toys for X was another problem. The first trip to the toy store brought this immediate question from the store clerk: "Well, now, is it a boy or a girl?" In the storekeeper's mind, footballs and fire engine sets were for boys and dolls and housekeeping sets were for girls. But the Joneses knew that they had to be sure baby X had *all* kinds of toys to play with, including:

a boy doll that made pee-pee and cried "Pa-Pa." And a girl doll that talked in three languages and said "I am the Pres-i-dent of Gen-er-al Motors." They also bought a storybook about a brave princess who rescued a handsome prince from his ivory tower, and another one about a sister and brother who grew up to be a baseball star and a ballet star, and you had to guess which was which.

But the biggest problem came when X was old enough to begin school, where the children were treated according to their sex. Boys and girls lined up separately, played games separately, and, of course, used different bathrooms. The other children had never met an X before, and just *had* to know what its sex really was. But the Joneses had raised X very carefully so that there was no easy answer:

You couldn't tell what X was by studying its clothes; overalls don't button right-to-left, like girl's clothes, or left-to-right, like boy's clothes. And you couldn't tell whether X had a girl's short haircut or a boy's long haircut. And it was very hard to tell by the games X liked to play. Either X played ball very well for a girl, or else X played house very well for a boy.

Larry Bernard (1980) found only about 35 percent of males to be entirely "masculine" and about 41 percent of females as consistently "feminine." About one-fourth of both male and female students scored high on both masculine and feminine attributes. Bernard described the remaining students (about one-third of males and one-fifth of females) as "undifferentiated" because they scored low on both sets of attributes. Thus there is considerable personal diversity among both males and females. But clearly males are encouraged to suppress the feminine side of their humanity as females are taught to suppress their masculine side. In addition, the fact that males have somewhat more difficulty conforming to their ideal gender pattern than females do to theirs suggests that rigid notions of gender may be more burdensome to males than to females (French, 1985).

Just as we are socialized to incorporate gender into our personal identities, so do we learn to act according to cultural conceptions of what is masculine and feminine. **Gender roles** (or sex roles) refers to *attitudes and activities that a culture links to each sex*. Gender roles are the active expression of gender identity. In other

The other children found X a very strange playmate: one day it would ask boys to weave some baskets in the arts and crafts room, and the next day it would ask some girls to go shoot baskets in the gym. But X tried very hard to be friendly to everyone and to do well in school. And X did *very* well in school, winning spelling bees, athletic events, and coming in second in a baking contest (even X's aren't perfect). As other children noticed what a good time X was having in school, they began to wonder if maybe X wasn't having twice as much fun as they were!

From then on, some really funny things began to happen. Susie, who sat next to X in class, suddenly refused to wear pink dresses to school any more. She insisted on wearing red-and-white checked overalls—just like X's. Overalls, she told her parents, were much better for climbing monkey bars. Then Jim, the class football nut, started wheeling his little sister's doll carriage around the football field. He'd put on his entire football uniform, except for the helmet. Then he'd put the helmet *in* the carriage, lovingly tucked under an old set of shoulder pads. Then he'd start jogging around the field, pushing the carriage and singing "Rockabye Baby" to his football helmet. He told his family that X did the same thing, so it must be okay. After all, X was now the team's star quarterback.

But this kind of behavior in the children horrified their parents. And when Peggy started using Joe's hockey skates while Joe enjoyed using Peggy's needlepoint kit, matters went from bad to worse. X was to blame for all this! So the Parents' Association at school demanded that X be identified as a boy or a girl and be forced to act accordingly. A psychiatrist was asked to conduct a full examination and report back to the parents. If, as most suspected, X was found to be a very confused child, it should be expelled from school altogether.

The teachers were puzzled by this; after all, X was one of their very best students. But the school—as well as the Joneses—finally agreed to let X be examined.

The next day the psychiatrist arrived at the school and began a long examination of X while everyone waited anxiously outside. When the psychiatrist finally emerged from the examination room, the results were not what most people expected. "In my opinion," the psychiatrist told them, "young X here is just about the *least* mixed up child I've ever examined!" The doctor explained that by the time that X's sex really mattered, everyone would know what it was.

This, of course, made the Joneses very happy, and delighted the scientists who had begun the experiment in the first place. And later that day, X's friends (dressed in red-and-white checked overalls) came over to X's house to play. They found X in the backyard playing with a new tiny baby.

"How do you like our new baby?" X asked the other children proudly.

"It's got cute dimples," said Jim.

"It's got husky biceps, too," said Susie.

"What kind of baby is it?" asked Joe and Peggy.

X frowned at them. "Can't you tell?" Then X broke into a big mischievous grin. "It's a Y!"

SOURCE: Adapted from Lois Gould, "X: A Fabulous Child's Story," *Ms.*, Vol. 1 (December 1972):74–76, 105–106.

words, because our culture defines males as ambitious and competitive, we expect males to engage in team sports and seek out positions of leadership. Females, culturally defined as self-effacing and emotional, are expected to be good listeners and supportive of other people's needs.

Throughout our lives, we experience social pressure to conform to gender roles. An assertive young girl who loves competitive sports more than dresses and dolls may be tolerated as a "tomboy," but later in life she may be labeled more negatively as "hard" and "mannish." Similarly, a sensitive young boy may be derided as a "sissy," and later be defined as "unmanly" if his deviant pattern persists. In short, gender becomes a blueprint imposed on males and females by all the agents of socialization described in Chapter 5.

Gender and the Family

The first question usually asked about a newborn child is: "Is it a boy or a girl?" This is an important question because the answer involves much more than sex; it

Play may appear to be simply a matter of having fun, but it is also a serious means of teaching children how their culture defines the roles of each sex.

In a patriarchal society, there is little surprise at the fact that most couples express a preference for male children. In one recent national survey, even women favored having sons over daughters: 45 percent wanted a boy and 20 percent preferred a girl, while the remainder had no preference (cited in Lengermann & Wallace, 1985:61). Historically, and in some parts of the world even today, the failure of a woman to have a son has been sufficient cause for her husband to seek another wife.

The distinct worlds of males and females are also based on the different ways in which parents treat male and female children. Research on parental attitudes toward children suggests that both fathers and mothers tend to emphasize physical strength, aggressiveness, and achievement in sons, while expecting daughters to be more delicate, weaker, and less assertive (Witkin-Lanoil, 1984:66–71). Typically, parents convey these expectations in the way they handle children. A recent experiment at an English university involved introducing a series of women to an infant in some cases dressed as a boy and in other cases dressed as a girl. Videotapes revealed that the women typically handled the "female" child tenderly, with frequent hugs and caresses, while the "male" child was treated more aggressively, often being lifted up in the air or bounced on the knee (Bonner, 1984). Research also shows that mothers typically have more physical contact with their male infants than with their female infants (Major, 1981). The message is clear: the female world is one of passivity and emotion, while the male world involves independence and action.

Parents also teach children the importance of gender by encouraging dress and grooming that is appropriately masculine or feminine. In addition, the toys they provide for their children and the ways in which they ask children to help out around the house serve to reinforce the fact that males and females live in distinct, gender-based social worlds.

Gender and the Peer Group

On reaching school age, children begin to interact more intensively outside the family, especially with others their own age. Within the peer group, the blue and pink worlds are further developed. The box on p. 324 provides an illustration of how peer groups shape a young boy's sense of himself as masculine.

As suggested in Chapter 3, children's games provide important cultural lessons. After a year of observing fifth-graders at play, Janet Lever (1978) concluded that the

carries a great deal of significance for the child's entire life.

Sociologist Jessie Bernard, who is introduced in the box, suggests that males and females are born into two different worlds within a single society: the "pink world" of girls and the "blue world" of boys (1981). As Chapters 9, 10, and 11 have shown, people of different social classes and racial and ethnic groups may share physical space but be separated by considerable *social distance*. The social distance between males and females is greater than many people realize.

Jessie Bernard (1903–   )

Now in her eighties, Jessie Bernard continues to produce a new book almost every year, adding to her important contributions to the discipline of sociology. Gender has long been a major focus of her work.

Bernard urges sociologists to in-clude women in their work. In the past, even sociologists critical of the status quo have been guilty of a conventional disregard for women. For example, Karl Marx paid virtually no attention to women in his writings. Bernard believes that giving balanced attention to males and females is harder than it may initially seem. This is because sociology, like many other disciplines, has developed largely under the control of men, so that many familiar sociological issues and concepts have a built-in bias that excludes women.

Consider, for example, the topic of social stratification. As explained in Chapter 10, many sociologists have traditionally defined social classes in terms of income, occupational prestige, and education. But is this definition equally true for males and females? To be within the upper class, a male must have considerable wealth. But this is not necessarily so for a female, whose social class position is derived from her father and, subsequently, her husband. Further, in ranking the prestige of occupations (see Table 10–1), sociologists usually do not even include housework—traditionally the most common activity of women. By defining the concept of occupational prestige so that it applies mostly to males, sociologists have effectively excluded women from sociological research.

In sum, sociologists must use care to ensure that their work addresses both males and females because otherwise sociology is the study of only half of society.

SOURCE: Based on Jessie Bernard, *The Female World* (New York: Free Press, 1981), and personal communication.

peer-group activities of boys and girls differ considerably, providing in each case a distinctive type of socialization. Lever found that boys typically engage in team sports—such as baseball and football—that involve many roles, complex rules, and clear objectives like scoring a run or a touchdown. These games are almost always competitive, producing winners and losers. Such activity among boys reinforces the characteristics of masculinity noted earlier, notably aggression, competition, and remaining in control.

Lever concluded that girls typically play games such as hopscotch or jump-rope in small groups, or simply talk, sing, or dance together. Such activity tends to be spontaneous, involving few formal rules. Just as important, since these games rarely have "victory" as their ultimate goal, girls rarely oppose one another. However, female peer groups do serve to teach the interpersonal skills of communication and cooperation that are the basis for life within the family.

Carol Gilligan's (1982) study of children showed that boys and girls learn to use distinctive patterns of moral reasoning. Boys tend to reason according to rules and principles, so that "rightness" is largely a matter of "playing by the rules." Girls, however, understand morality more in terms of responsibility to other human beings, so that "rightness" lies in maintaining close relationships with others. Clearly, these distinctive patterns of moral reasoning are encouraged by the different kinds of peer-group activity common to boys and girls.

Gender in School

Schools continue the process of placing males and females within distinctive social worlds. One way this is accomplished is through the books children read. In one study, a group of researchers examined a number of books widely used by pre–elementary school children

SOCIOLOGY OF EVERYDAY LIFE

Learning to Be Masculine

By the time I was ten, the central fact in my life was the demand that I become a man. By then, the most important relationships by which I was taught to define myself were those I had with other boys. I already knew that I must see every encounter with another boy as a contest in which I must win or at least hold my own. . . . The same lesson continued [in school], after school, even in Sunday School. My parents, relatives, teachers, the books I read, movies I saw, all taught me that my self-worth depended on my manliness, my willingness to stand up to the other boys. This usually didn't mean a physical fight, though the willingness to stand up and "fight like a man" always remained a final test. But the relationships between us usually had the character of an armed truce. Girls weren't part of this social world at all yet, just because they weren't part of this contest. They didn't have to be bluffed, no credit was gained by cowing them, so they were more or less ignored. Sometimes when there were no grownups around we would let each other know that we liked each other, but most of the time we did as we were taught.

SOURCE: Michael Silverstein, in Jon Snodgrass, ed., *A Book of Readings for Men Against Sexism* (Albion, CA: Times Change Press, 1977), pp. 178–179.

(Weitzman et al., 1972). In most books, males were the focus of attention; with females acknowledged far less frequently. For example, there were more than ten pictures of male children for every picture of female children. Book titles were three times more likely to mention males than to mention females. Thus the researchers concluded that children "are bound to receive the impression that girls are not very important because no one has bothered to write books about them" (1972:1129). The books also presented the lives of males and females in stereotypical ways that favored males. Males engaged in diverse and interesting activities, while females usually stayed in the house. In addition, the females depicted in these books were usually concerned about pleasing males: girls sought the favor of their father and brothers, and women tried to please their husbands. Males were shown actively shaping their lives, while females were shown as passive participants or observers:

> The little boy is constantly in motion, continuously interacting with the world around him. He is *jumping* up to touch the scarecrow next to the cornstalk, *unwrapping* his baseball bat (leaving the mess of paper, string, and box for someone else to clean up), *building* blocks on top of his sled, *reaching* up on tiptoe to touch his father's workbench, and *spraying* the lawn (and himself) with the garden hose. In contrast the little girl relates to each of the objects around her merely by *looking* at them. (Weitzman et al., 1972:1137)

More like dolls than living beings, the girls in these books were mostly attractive and compliant objects, sources of support and pleasure to males.

Within the last decade, the growing awareness that what is learned in childhood can affect people's lives as adults has led to changes in the publishing industry. Today's books for children tend to portray males and females in a more balanced way.

The learning toys made available to children in the early years of school are also likely to reflect cultural expectations of each sex—wheeled toys and building equipment for boys, dollhouses and miniature kitchens for girls. In addition, while boys are often allowed to leave the school building to play, girls are more likely to be asked to remain indoors to assist the teacher with housekeeping chores. Thus even though the formal lessons in reading, writing, and arithmetic may be the same for both sexes, what Raphaela Best (1983) calls "the second curriculum" encourages children to adopt the identity and roles considered appropriate to their sex.

In high school, the curriculum itself begins to reflect the different roles males and females are expected to assume as adults. Instruction in such home-centered skills as nutrition, cooking, and sewing is provided to classes almost entirely composed of females, while classes in woodworking and auto mechanics are still mostly all-male.

Most schools do little to encourage students to question gender stereotypes and to learn skills traditionally associated with the opposite sex. Guidance counselors often steer students into classes that help to prepare them for conventional masculine and feminine roles. Just as students from less privileged social backgrounds

Find My Ball

Sally said, "I want my ball.

My pretty yellow ball.

Who can find it for me?"

Generations of Americans were taught to read by using "Dick and Jane" books that helped to socialize them to conventional gender roles.

may be tacked into vocational rather than academic courses of study, so girls are often advised to take typing and home economics, while boys are directed toward courses such as business math that prepare them for work that will support a family. In college, much the same tracking takes place as males and females are encouraged to pursue different majors. Traditionally, the natural sciences—including physics, chemistry, biology, and mathematics—have been defined as part of the male world. Women have been expected to major in the humanities (such as English), the fine arts (music, dance, and drama), or the social sciences (including anthropology and sociology). Emerging areas of study are also likely to be sex-linked; evidence indicates that learning computer skills, for example, has become a predominantly male activity (Klein, 1984).

Extracurricular activities are also likely to segregate males and females. Here again, attention and financing tend to go to male activities. Mass media coverage of high school and college athletics is extensive for male sports. Many females are enthusiastic players of team sports, but sports programs for females tend to receive less funding and little attention from both students and the mass media. Because of this emphasis on male athletics, many females assume supportive roles as observers or cheerleaders.

In many colleges and universities, the fraternity system (traditionally far stronger than sororities) has long been a bastion of male dominance. Although fraternities have strong defenders, they have come under fire for encouraging sexism and sometimes outright violence against women. One recent report suggests that some fifty instances of gang rapes have been documented in American fraternities in the last several years (cited in A. Merton, 1985). As one professor concedes, "Fraternities are sporting clubs, and their game is women" (1985:60).

Gender and the Mass Media

As indicated in Chapter 5, the mass media are a powerful force in the socialization process. Films, magazines, and especially television have a significant effect on the ways we think and act.

Since it became widespread in the 1950s, television has provided the greatest attention to the dominant category of Americans: white males. Racial and ethnic minorities were virtually absent from television until the early 1970s, and only within the last decade have there been a number of programs in which female characters occupy center stage.

Beyond the *inclusion* of both sexes in television, an important issue is *how* they are portrayed. In general, men play the brilliant detectives, fearless explorers, skilled surgeons, and interesting conversationalists. Males take charge; they give the orders and are portrayed as competent and capable. Women, on the other hand, have mostly been portrayed as reliant on males—less competent and more often the targets of comedy (Busby, 1975). Women have also long been portrayed as sex objects important for little other than their physical attractiveness. These negative stereotypes persist in the 1980s, although there is more programming with interesting and responsible women in major roles.

Like television programming directed at adults, children's programs reinforce gender stereotypes. Linda Busby (1975) found that males were portrayed as active, ambitious, brave, competent, in control of situations, and unlikely to show fear or other emotions. Females, in contrast, were passive, content to be what they were, timid, incapable, and emotional. In recent years, a number of television programs—including *Mister Rogers'*

SHE'S VERY CHARLIE.

Charlie
REVLON

Some recent advertising utilizes reverse sexism in which males are portrayed as the sex objects of successful females. Although the role reversal is new, the use of unrealistic gender stereotypes is very old indeed.

thoritative voiceover in television and radio advertising was almost always male. A recent review of research in this area suggests that this pattern has changed only a little in the 1980s (Courtney & Whipple, 1983).

Erving Goffman (1979) also concluded that advertising conveys cultural ideals of each sex. In his study of ads in magazines and newspapers, Goffman found that men were typically placed in photographs to appear taller than women, implying social superiority. In addition, women were far more likely than men to be shown lying down (on sofas and beds) or, like children, seated on the floor. The expressions and gestures of men conveyed competence and authority; women were more likely to be shown in poses that appeared childlike or implied deference to others.

Advertising not only perpetuates gender stereotypes, but makes use of them to sell products. It encourages the belief that being properly masculine and feminine is largely a matter of what we consume. For example, the really masculine man drives the "right" car or vacations in the "right" place. Similarly, the truly feminine woman buys the kind of clothing and cosmetics that make her look younger and more attractive to males. Moreover, as the box suggests, having successful relationships is often linked to conforming to conventional gender patterns.

Gender and Adult Socialization

Our gender identity and gender roles typically come to feel natural well before we become adults. For this reason, appropriately feminine and masculine attitudes, behavior, and patterns of speech are commonly reinforced in the social interaction of adults (Spender, 1980; Kramarae, 1981).

Pamela Fishman (1977, 1978) conducted research with three young, white, middle-class couples in which they agreed to operate a tape recorder in their apartments for a period of up to two weeks, producing a total of fifty-two hours of taped conversations. Fishman discovered that even in conversation males assume a position of dominance over females. Men were more successful than women in generating conversation. That is, when men began a conversation, women almost always attempted to keep it going; on the other hand, men frequently allowed conversations initiated by women to collapse. This suggests that both males and females think what males have to say is more important. The women were more likely than the men to open conversations

Neighborhood and *Sesame Street*—have won praise for presenting less stereotypical views of the sexes. But some have criticized even these "model" programs for perpetuating traditionally narrow conceptions of gender (Doyle, 1983).

Although gender stereotypes in the mass media have lessened in recent years, commercial advertising has changed less. This is because advertising sells the most products by conforming to widely established cultural patterns. More than a decade ago, Linda Busby (1975) found that television and magazine advertising presented women in the home far more often than in an occupational role. Moreover, women were found primarily in ads for household items such as cleaning products, foods, clothing, and appliances, while men predominated in ads for cars, travel, banking services, industrial companies, and alcoholic beverages. The au-

with remarks like "This is interesting" or "Do you know what?" Fishman interpreted this pattern—also common to the speech of children—as women's way of trying to find out if men really want to hear what they wish to say. Opening a conversation with "This is interesting," for example, makes the claim to the male that he should pay attention to what follows. Beginning with "Do you know what?" is equivalent to stating, "I have something to say; are you willing to listen?"

The women asked about three times more questions than the men did. Since asking a question is a sign of deference to the person whose answer or advice is sought, this pattern, too, reflected the women's subordination to their husbands. Both the men and the women used various "minimal responses" (such as "yeah," "umm,"

and "huh"), but in different ways. For men, such remarks were an expression of minimal interest, as if to say, "I guess I'll continue to listen if you insist on continuing to speak." Women, on the other hand, used minimal responses as a form of "support work," inserting them continually while men spoke as a means of expressing interest and encouraging men to continue the conversation.

Since gender has placed males and females in distinctive social worlds, it is not surprising that in marriage husbands and wives often have considerable difficulty simply communicating with each other. Studies of verbal interaction within marriage have indicated that this problem is commonly cited by both spouses (Komarovsky, 1967; Rubin, 1976, 1983).

SOCIOLOGY OF EVERYDAY LIFE

Advertising—A "Sixty-Second Insult to Women"

In a television commercial, a woman explains to millions of viewers how she looks after her health by taking Geritol vitamin supplements every day. As she finishes, a man walks into the picture, smiles widely at the audience, and exclaims that his wife is so wonderful that "I think I'll keep her!"

A simple statement about vitamins? Maybe, but also a statement about gender: if women are successful in keeping their health and youthful looks, their husbands will "keep them" just as they might keep a dependable automobile. As Keith Melville points out, we can hardly imagine the same commercial with the woman and man playing the opposite parts. In short, the ad is a sixty-second insult to women.

Advertising emphasizes that the value of females lies not in their talents or achievements but in their sexual attractiveness to males. Countless ads, for example, attempt to sell women on the idea that they need

extensive makeup, young-looking skin, hair that stays beautifully in place, or underwear that flatters their figures. Do ads ever suggest that *men* need these things to be successful?

In addition, advertising only occasionally acknowledges the fact that women's participation in the labor force has been steadily increasing: women are still portrayed primarily within the home. So as men wheel and deal in the world of business, women choose laundry detergent, floor wax, and spray starch. As Melville explains:

As portrayed in commercials, women are fanatics about cleanliness. They waltz around the living room in chiffon skirts polishing the furniture. They frantically scrub the sink, or wonder whether the toilet bowl smells.

Commercials attempt to establish impossible standards of cleanliness and beauty in an effort to sell more products. But there is an added message:

failure to live up to these standards means rejection by family and friends:

Guests register their disapproval at scuffed floors; neighbors wrinkle their noses at household odors. And, worst, of all, husbands withdraw their approval. The Wisk ad, for example, shows a husband and wife—on a carefree vacation—getting off the plane in Hawaii. A Hawaiian girl in a hula skirt comes up to greet them, and to put a *lei* around the husband's neck, only to draw back in horror as the mortified wife hears the words "Ring Around the Collar!" There they are, on a romantic vacation, and all of a sudden the wife is threatened with the evidence of her inadequacy—and by a beautiful woman, no less. The wife's reaction is to recoil, distraught and guilty. The ads never suggest that perhaps *he* ought to wash his neck more often.

SOURCE: Adapted from Keith Melville, *Marriage and Family Today*, 2nd ed. (New York: Random House, 1977), pp. 195–196.

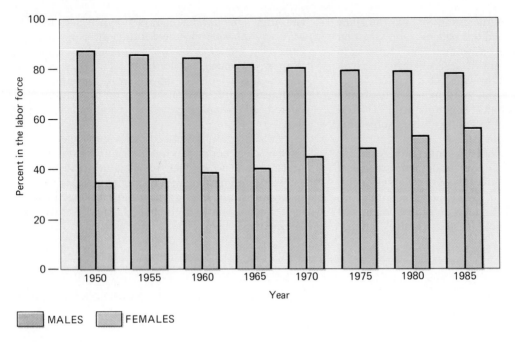

FIGURE 12–1 Men and Women in the American Labor Force
(U.S. Bureau of Labor Statistics)

GENDER AND SOCIAL STRATIFICATION

Gender involves more than how people think and act. The concept of **gender stratification** refers to *the unequal distribution of wealth, power, and privileges between the two sexes*. More specifically, females have less valued resources than males do.

Working Men and Women

In 1987, two-thirds of all Americans over the age of sixteen were in the labor force, which included 77 percent of men and 55 percent of women. In 1900, only about one-fifth of women were in the labor force, but as shown in Figure 12–1, the proportion has increased steadily in recent decades. Furthermore, almost three-fourths of women who work today do so full-time. Thus the traditional view that the world of work is largely male is no longer correct.

Among the many factors associated with this change are the growth of cities, economic expansion,

declining family size, and changes in cultural norms regarding appropriate roles for women. In addition, because economic decline has reduced the income of many Americans during the last fifteen years (see Chapter 10), many families find that wives as well as husbands must work simply to maintain a comfortable standard of living.

A common—although incorrect—belief is that women in the labor force are usually single or, if married, without children. More than half of all married women were working in 1986. In addition, women with children are actually *more* likely to be working than childless women. In 1986, 68 percent of married women with children between six and seventeen years of age were working, as were 54 percent of those with children under six. For divorced women, the comparable figures were 85 percent and 74 percent (U.S. Bureau of the Census, 1987e). The increase in child-care support in many workplaces is one factor allowing women to combine the responsibilities of being a worker and a parent, which is especially important for divorced mothers. Just as important, as noted in Chapter 10, a large number of women are single parents who are poor and cannot afford to give up their incomes.

Gender and Occupations

Although the proportions of the two sexes in the labor force are converging, men and women continue to have different kinds of occupations. According to the U.S. Bureau of Labor Statistics (1987), women have a relatively small range of jobs: almost half of all working women fall within two broad occupational categories. The first is clerical work—29 percent of all working women are secretaries, typists, and stenographers. Because these jobs are considered support positions, it is no surprise that more than 80 percent of clerical workers are female. Jessie Bernard (1981) has described this type of work as the "pink-collar" world of women. It is interesting that a century ago, when few women were in the labor force, clerical positions were held almost exclusively by men and were more prestigious than they are today (Davies, 1979). The second broad category of women's work, accounting for about 18 percent of employed women, is service work, including such occupations as waitresses and other food service employees and nurses and other health service workers.

Of hundreds of specific occupations, almost one-third of the 49 million women in the labor force in 1986 held one of the ten occupations listed in Table 12–3. Each of these job categories—defined as feminine in our culture—contains only a small proportion of males. Thus while more and more women are working, married or single, they remain highly segregated in a narrow segment of the labor force (Roos, 1983; U.S. Bureau of Labor Statistics, 1987).

Men predominate in just about every job category beyond the ten occupations noted in the table. The highest proportion of men are in the trades; for instance, more than 99 percent of brickmasons, stonemasons, metal workers, and heavy equipment mechanics are male. In addition, males are likely to predominate in any job that provides a lot of income, prestige, and power. For example, more than 80 percent of all physicians and lawyers are men, as are more than 60 percent of managers, administrators, and computer specialists, and more than 90 percent of all engineers. In addition, there are virtually no women among the very top executives of America's largest corporations.

In general, then, gender stratification is evident in the fact that males tend to hold powerful occupational positions, while women work at occupations that are relatively powerless. This hierarchy is often apparent in the job setting itself: male physicians work with female nurses, male executives have female secretaries, and male

Table 12–3 THE TEN MOST COMMON JOBS FOR AMERICAN WOMEN, 1986

Occupation	Number of Women Employed	Percent in Occupation Who Are Women
1. Dental hygienist	58,700	99.5
2. Secretary	3,983,000	99.0
3. Dental assistant	165,000	99.0
4. Kindergarten teacher	353,000	98.3
5. Licensed practical nurse	407,000	97.5
6. Private child-care worker	390,000	97.4
7. Receptionist	703,000	97.1
8. Child-care worker	735,000	96.5
9. Household cleaner and servant	502,000	95.3
10. Typist	870,000	95.2

SOURCE: U.S. Bureau of Labor Statistics, *Employment and Earnings*, Vol. 34, No. 1 (January 1987): 179–183.

airline pilots work with female flight attendants. Furthermore, within a single occupation, the greater a job's income and social prestige, the more likely it is to be held by a male. In teaching, for example, women are 98 percent of all kindergarten teachers, 85 percent of teachers in the elementary grades, 55 percent of secondary school teachers, but only 36 percent of professors in colleges and universities (U.S. Bureau of Labor Statistics, 1987). At the top of the pyramid, only 12 percent of all college and university presidents are women, and these women usually preside over smaller institutions, many with an all-female student body (American Council on Education, 1984).

Housework

Just as work outside the home has traditionally been defined as part of the male world, so has housework—maintaining the home and caring for children—been defined as female work. The importance of housework has always been a cultural contradiction; though touted as essential to American life, like other work done by women, it has carried little social prestige (J. Bernard, 1981).

Women's participation in the labor force has

changed the pattern of responsibility for housework very little. Indeed, one estimate indicates that between 1959 and 1983 the hours of housework performed by women declined only slightly, and the proportion of housework shared by men remained virtually the same (Fuchs, 1986). In a typical American household, responsibilities shared by the two sexes tend to be limited to disciplining the children and managing finances. Men engage in a few activities such as home repairs and mowing the lawn; women typically do the daily and time-consuming tasks of shopping, cooking, and cleaning. Not surprisingly, then, many women in the labor force adopt the pattern of working "double days"—doing both paid work and unpaid housework (Schooler et al., 1984; Benokraitis & Feagin, 1986).

The simple fact is that most men endorse women entering the labor force, but few are willing to modify their own gender roles to help women do so (Komarovsky, 1973). Thus only in rare cases such as the Israeli kibbutzim is housework extensively shared. Even in Sweden—a society with a strong belief in the social equality of the sexes—perhaps one in five couples share housework evenly (Haas, 1981).

The controversy about housework lies in the fact that most women do not enjoy it. In a study of women in London, Anne Oakley (1974) found that 70 percent expressed dissatisfaction about doing housework, commonly objecting to the monotony and loneliness of it.

Oakley also found that the average housewife worked 77 hours a week—almost twice the standard workweek. Men have traditionally asserted that housework is natural for females, which is perhaps why it has never warranted pay.

Gender, Income, and Wealth

Because women predominate in low-paying clerical and service jobs and men in the higher-paying positions in business and the professions, men earn much more than women. In 1986, women working full-time had a median income of $16,843, while full-time male workers earned $25,894. Thus men earn in six days what women work ten days to earn, or more simply, for every dollar earned by men, women earn about 65 cents. This income disparity between males and females has diminished only slightly over the last two decades.

Put in different terms, one in five women working full-time earned less than $10,000 in 1986, but this was true for only one in ten men. Only one in five women earned more than $25,000, while one in two men did. Men were also ten times more likely than women to earn more than $75,000 (U.S. Bureau of the Census, 1987e).

Several factors are responsible for the earning disparity between the sexes. First, as already noted, males

Women in the American labor force were historically concentrated in a few occupations, such as garment making, usually under the supervision of males.

and females tend to hold different occupations, and this fact strongly benefits men. Second, a smaller earning increment in favor of men reflects the fact that male workers have somewhat more education than their female counterparts. Third, family-related factors—especially motherhood—disadvantage female workers (Fuchs, 1986). In part, this means that women who are raising children often settle for jobs that pay less, but provide other advantages such as a shorter commuting distance, flexible hours, or child-care services. In addition, pregnancy, childbirth, and raising small children keep many younger women out of the labor force altogether at a time when younger men are likely to be making occupational gains. The obvious result is that men tend to have more seniority in a given job than women do.

Thus differences in earnings for women and men are evident even within the *same* occupational category. As shown in Table 12–4, this ratio varies according to the type of work. In no case, however, do women earn more than three-fourths as much as men do.

Taken together, the three factors noted so far account for about two-thirds of the earnings disparity between women and men. A fourth factor, then, is simple discrimination against women, which accounts for at least one-third of the difference (Pear, 1987). Discrimination may be less harsh today, but this illegal practice remains a major cause of economic disadvantage for working women.

Of course, efforts to bring about economic equity for women must contend with the fact that the two sexes are likely to remain concentrated within different types of jobs for some time to come. In response, advocates of greater fairness are now demanding equal pay for jobs of *comparable worth*, as explained in the box.

Finally, many Americans believe that women own most of the country's wealth, including stocks, bonds, and other interest-earning investments. This inaccurate belief arose from the fact that wives typically outlive their husbands and are therefore thought to end up with most of the wealth. In fact, government statistics (calculated for 1982) show that only 47 percent of all Americans with at least $500,000 in assets were women, although widows were highly represented among them. Among people with more modest wealth ($100,000 or more in assets), only 42 percent were women (U.S. Department of Labor, 1983; U.S. Bureau of the Census, 1985). More recently, in *Forbes* magazine's listing of the four hundred richest Americans in 1987, only fifty-five (14 percent) were women.

Table 12–4   EARNINGS OF FULL-TIME WORKERS 15 YEARS OF AGE AND OVER, 1986

Selected Occupational Categories	Median Income (dollars)		Women's Income as a Percentage of Men's
	Men	Women	
Executives, administrators, and managers	34,962	21,432	61.3
Professional specialties	35,143	23,076	65.6
Technical workers	27,880	19,236	69.0
Sales	26,803	12,956	48.3
Precision production, craft and repair workers	24,281	16,810	69.2
Clerical and other administrative support workers	22,718	15,509	68.3
Transportation workers	21,770	14,310	65.7
Machine operators, assemblers, and inspectors	20,551	12,324	60.0
Service workers	17,332	10,367	59.8
Farming, forestry, and fishing	10,748	8,032	74.7
All occupations	25,256	16,232	64.3

SOURCE: U.S. Bureau of the Census, *Money Income and Poverty Status of Families and Persons in the United States: 1986*, Series P-60, No. 157 (Washington, DC: U.S. Government Printing Office, 1987).

Gender and Education

Women have traditionally been discouraged, if not formally excluded, from higher education in the belief that schooling is unnecessary for homemakers. By the beginning of the 1980s, however, educational disadvantages linked to being female had greatly diminished. In fact, slightly more women than men attend colleges and universities today. Nonetheless, more women than men are part-time students, and women are slightly less likely to complete a college degree than are men. These differences reflect the facts that women marry somewhat earlier than men and receive less financial aid than men do (Marini, 1978; Kaufman, 1982; Moran, 1984).

As noted earlier, men and women often pursue different courses of study in college, although the extent to which parents, friends, and school counselors steer students into a major on the basis of gender has probably declined in recent years. For example, in 1970, only 26 pecent of the bachelor's degrees in science and engineering were awarded to women; by 1980, the proportion

SOCIAL POLICY

Equal Pay for Equal Worth?

In 1963, the federal government passed the Equal Pay Act, which requires that males and females receive the same pay for the same job. In simple terms, this is the doctrine of "equal pay for equal work." But this doctrine is difficult to apply to the American economy because males and females typically hold *different* jobs. This legislation does not actually require that males and females have exactly the same occupations in order to receive the same earnings; therefore, those seeking to reduce economic disparity between the sexes argue that jobs requiring essentially the same skill and effort and having the same level of responsibility should receive the same pay. This is the issue of "equal pay for equal *worth*."

Sociologists now know that determining if the worth of a job is more or less than the pay it provides is quite complex. But sexist attitudes are one factor that can elevate earnings in jobs simply because they are typically held by males. Similarly, jobs commonly held by females are often defined as having lower worth and are rewarded accordingly. Many women across the United States claim that, because of sexism in the workplace, they are being paid less than what their work is worth.

In 1983, for example, Helen Castrilli sued the state of Washington claiming that her job as a hospital secretary was worth as much as many jobs held by men, even though her income was hundreds of dollars a month less. Evidence was presented in this case that state laundry workers (who are mostly female) earned $150 a month less than state truck drivers (who are mostly male), although the two jobs were argued to have equal worth. A federal court judge ruled in Castrilli's favor, ordering the state of Washington to give some 15,500 employees, most of whom were women, almost $1 billion in back pay. In 1985, however, a higher court reversed the ruling on the grounds that the government has no obligation to eliminate economic inequality created by market forces.

Other cases concerned with equal worth are pending, and legislation on this matter is currently before Congress. In the wake of the original decision in the Washington case, more than one hundred cities and states have reviewed their salary scales for inequities. In Los Angeles, for example, clerks and librarians, who are mostly female, are now being paid as much as maintenance workers and gardeners, who are mostly male.

There is as yet no clear procedure for determining the worth of various jobs in the United States, although countries such as Great Britain and Australia do have such laws. As this issue has been debated by courts and by Congress, two sides have emerged.

Proponents of equal-worth laws argue that the value of occupations can be objectively determined, and that jobs performed mostly by females have long been undervalued. Sexism is a powerful force in America, they argue, and women have been systematically denied earnings commensurable with the worth of the work they perform.

Opponents claim that there is no objective way to assess the worth of various occupations other than what employers actually pay their workers. Further, they argue, America is a free-market society and government should not interfere with the way private employers set pay scales.

However this issue is finally resolved, an enormous amount of money is at stake. Comparable-worth standards might mean, for example, that employers would have to pay nonunionized secretaries the same wages they pay unionized truck drivers who just won a hefty pay increase. On a national level, estimates suggest that the adoption of a comprehensive equal-worth law might cost employers more than $300 billion.

SOURCE: Based on U.S. Department of Labor, 1983; Bob Arnold, "Why Can't a Woman's Pay Be More Like a Man's?" *Business Week*, January 26, 1985, pp. 82–83; Jennett Conant, "A Loss for Comparable Worth," *Newsweek*, September 16, 1985, p. 36; Toby L. Parcel, Charles W. Mueller, and Steven Cuvelier, "Comparable Worth and Occupational Labor Market: Explanations of Occupational Earnings Differentials," paper presented to American Sociological Association, New York, 1986.

had risen to 35 percent (Kaufman, 1982). Nevertheless, significant imbalances remain.

Postgraduate education, often a springboard to a high-prestige job, has traditionally been even more of a male preserve. In the past, women who tried to enter graduate schools were often discouraged by professors and university officials, who expected that they would "probably just get married and drop out anyway." No doubt such attitudes persist today, although they are more rarely expressed. But graduate education is now much more open to women. Today, when all areas of study are counted, as many master's degrees are earned by women as by men. In addition, a growing number of women are pursuing programs of study that were until recently virtually all male. For example, in 1970, women received only 750 masters of business administration (MBA) degrees; in 1980, the number exceeded 12,000 (Kaufman, 1982). Even so, men earned more than three-fourths of all such degrees.

Men also continue to receive most of other advanced degrees that lead to high-paying occupations. In 1984, males received two-thirds of all doctorates. Men also received 63 percent of all law degrees (LL.B. and J.D.), 72 percent of all medical degrees (M.D.), and 81 percent of all dental degrees (D.D.S. and D.M.D.) (U.S. Bureau of the Census, 1987g). In a culture that still links high-paying professions (and the drive and competitiveness needed to succeed in them) to being male, women may be discouraged from completing professional education after having enrolled (Fiorentine, 1987). But the proportion of women in professional schools has been rising, so gradual change is likely to continue.

Gender and Politics

Throughout American history, men have had more power than women because of their occupational position, greater income and wealth, and educational advantages. Male dominance is also evident in American political history.

A century ago, women were all but excluded from politics. Virtually no women held elected office. The law barred women from voting in national elections in Canada until 1917, and in the United States until 1920. However, a few women were candidates for political office long before they could vote. The Equal Rights Party supported Victoria Woodhull for the presidency in 1872; perhaps it was a sign of the times that she spent election day in jail in New York City. Table

12–5 describes important events in women's gradual movement into American politics, including the election of Jeannette Rankin to Congress in 1917 as the first woman to hold a national office in the United States. Notice that the first two women to serve as state governors and the first woman to enter the Senate did so only by succeeding their husbands.

The political power of American women has steadily grown. Although there was none of record in 1970, over 10,000 women were directors of federal agencies in 1984 (Schreiner, 1984). In addition, in 1983 more than 1,700 women served as mayors of American cities and towns (Mashek & Avery, 1983). But in higher offices, there has been much less change, although a majority of Americans now claim that they do not object to having a woman even as president. In 1988, 3 of the 50 state governors were women (6 percent); within Congress, 23 of 435 (5 percent) members of the House of Representatives and 2 of 100 senators (2 percent) were women.

Table 12–5 SIGNIFICANT "FIRSTS" FOR WOMEN IN AMERICAN POLITICS

1872	First woman to run for the presidency (Victoria Woodhull) represents the Equal Rights Party.
1917	First woman elected to the House of Representatives (Jeannette Rankin of Montana).
1924	First women elected as state governors (Nellie Tyloe Ross of Wyoming and Miriam Ferguson of Texas); both followed their husbands into office. First woman to have her name placed in nomination for the vice presidency at the convention of a major political party (Lena Jones Spring).
1931	First woman to serve in the Senate (Hattie Caraway of Arkansas); completed the term of her husband upon his death, and was reelected in 1932.
1932	First woman appointed to a presidential cabinet (Frances Perkins, Secretary of Labor); as of 1988, only eight women have been so appointed.
1964	First woman to have her name placed in nomination for the presidency at the convention of a major political party (Margaret Chase Smith).
1972	First black woman to have her name placed in nomination for the presidency at the convention of a major political party (Shirley Chisholm).
1981	First woman appointed to the U.S. Supreme Court (Sandra Day O'Connor).
1984	First woman to be successfully nominated for the vice presidency (Geraldine Ferraro).

SOURCE: Adapted from Sandra Salmans, "Women Ran for Office Before They Could Vote," *New York Times*, July 13, 1984, p. A 11.

Minority Women

Chapter 11 described the social disadvantages of racial and ethnic minorities in American society. Women within minority groups—*minority women*—have a double social disadvantage. First, there is the disadvantage associated with race and ethnicity. This dimension of disadvantage is evident in the fact that in 1986 black women in the labor force full-time earned 88 percent as much as white women; Hispanic women earned about 83 percent as much as white women. Second, there is the disadvantage associated with sex. This dimension of disadvantage is shown by the fact that black women earned 80 percent as much as black men, while Hispanic women earned about 83 percent as much as Hispanic men. Combined, these social disadvantages explain why minority women earn only about half as much as white men (U.S. Bureau of the Census, 1987).

The low income of minority women reflects the fact that they are generally even further down the occupational ladder than white women. Whenever the economy sags, as it did after the early 1970s, minority women are especially likely to experience declining purchasing power and unemployment.

Chapter 10 explained that poverty in the United States is much more common among females than among males. About one-half of poor households are headed by women, in contrast to only 4 percent headed by men. This *feminization of poverty* is especially dramatic among minority women. In 1986, about 28 percent of households headed by white women were poor, but over 50 percent of households headed by black and Hispanic women were poor.

Are Women a Minority Group?

In Chapter 11, a minority group was defined as a category of people with a distinctive social identity who are socially disadvantaged. A reasonable question, in a patriarchal society, is whether all women should be defined as a minority group. Objectively, women must be viewed as a minority group, since cultural conceptions of gender provide a distinctive social identity and women occupy a disadvantaged position in the system of social stratification.

Yet many white women at least do not view themselves as belonging to a minority group (Hacker, 1951; Lengermann & Wallace, 1985). This is partly because, unlike racial and ethnic minorities that are disproportion-ately in the lower social classes, white women are part of families of all social classes. Yet women in any social class typically have less income, wealth, education, and power than men. As Jessie Bernard (1981) points out, women have traditionally gained their social standing through men—initially, their fathers, and later, their husbands.

Another reason that many white women do not consider themselves part of a minority group is that they have been socialized to accept their social position as natural. In other words, a woman who accepts conventional ideas about gender believes that she *should* be submissive and deferential to men and that men *should* have power over her. As noted earlier, such beliefs are a foundation of both sexism and racism in that they justify social inequality.

In sum, some women—especially those who are relatively privileged—may not think of themselves as members of a minority group. Yet as a category of Americans, women have both the distinctive identity and the social disadvantages to be correctly considered as such.

THEORETICAL ANALYSIS OF GENDER

Both the structural-functional and social-conflict paradigms can be used to understand the significance of gender in American society.

Structural-Functional Analysis

The structural-functional paradigm is based on an understanding of society as a complex system containing numerous separate but integrated parts. The significance of any element of society is to be found in its functional contribution to the operation of society as a whole.

As explained in Chapter 4, the earliest human societies were based on hunting and gathering. Within such societies, primitive technology allows only a very limited range of cultural diversity to develop. For this reason, the biological facts of sex take on a great deal of importance. There is no effective means to control reproduction, for example, so that the range of women's activities is limited by frequent pregnancies and the related responsibilities of child care (Lengermann & Wallace, 1985). As a result, social norms that encourage females to center their lives around home and children function to promote societal survival. Thus cultures come to view these activities as feminine.

In addition, both the greater short-term strength of males and the fact that they are not subject to the physical limitations of pregnancy suggest that men should have other responsibilities. Males are typically more successful in capturing game, for example; thus such activities away from the home come to be defined as masculine.

In societies that have limited technology, then, the biological facts of sex and cultural conceptions of gender are likely to be rather closely linked. This is, of course, not a matter of biological necessity but simply a strategy to promote the efficient operation of the society. Most preindustrial societies adopt this strategy for its survival value, and over many generations the sex-based division of labor becomes institutionalized—that is, built into the structure of society and taken for granted.

Industrial technology opens up a vastly greater range of cultural possibilities. Human beings and animals are no longer the primary sources of energy, so the physical strength of males loses much of its earlier significance. Furthermore, the ability to control reproduction provides females with greater choice in shaping their lives.

Under such circumstances, one might expect the traditional conceptions of gender to gradually weaken. Without doubt, this has happened to some degree in all industrial societies, including the United States. But such changes are resisted to the extent that gender has become institutionalized. In other words, without understanding the original reasons for dividing human activities into masculine and feminine worlds, people assume that such patterns are natural.

In addition, as Talcott Parsons (1951, 1954) has explained, gender continues to play an important part in maintaining society—at least in its traditional form. Parsons claimed that gender is an important system of cultural ideas that links males and females within family units that are, in turn, central to the operation of society. For each of the two sexes, a *complementary* set of culturally supported activities is specified. Females serve to maintain the internal operation of the family, managing the household and taking primary responsibility for raising children. Males function to connect the family to the larger world, primarily through their participation in the labor force.

Parsons further explained that individuals are prepared to assume these differing adult responsibilities through the socialization process. Both males and females learn their appropriate gender identity, as well as the skills and attitudes needed to fulfill gender roles. Because their primary societal responsibility is achievement in the labor force, males are socialized to be rational, self-assured, and competitive—a complex of traits that Parsons described as *instrumental*. In order to take primary responsibility for child rearing, females are socialized to display what Parsons termed *expressive* qualities, such as emotion and sensitivity to others. In Parsons's scheme, then, gender identity is learned early in life as the foundation for the gender roles assumed later by adults.

Finally, Parsons claimed that social patterns related to gender are enforced through various means of social control. In part, this social control is internal, as people incorporate cultural definitions of gender into their own identities, so that guilt accompanies violation of these norms. Social control is also external, as when the failure to display the personal traits appropriate to one's sex leads to criticism from others and shame. Parsons also suggested that a powerful form of social control is the belief that failure to adopt culturally approved gender traits will result in the failure to be loved by a member of the opposite sex. In simple terms, women are likely to view a male who flouts cultural standards of masculinity as sexually unattractive. In the same way, unfeminine women risk rejection by men.

Evaluation. Structural-functional analysis emphasizes how masculinity and femininity are culturally defined in complementary fashion. One problem with this approach is its failure to recognize that many women have traditionally worked outside the household, most out of economic necessity. In other words, Parsons's analysis implies only one kind of family as normative—a view that conforms to the lives of men and women today even less than it did in the past. Another common criticism of Parsons's analysis is that what he termed "complementarity" is actually "domination." Is a system of gender functional for society when it confers privileges on one category of people? Finally, as an approach supportive of a gender-based society, Parsons's analysis pays little attention to the personal strains and social costs produced by such a system.

Social-Conflict Analysis

Social-conflict analysis suggests that the relation between males and females is not one of complementarity but rather one of inequality. Gender is seen as benefiting males, while women are a socially disadvantaged minority group (Hacker, 1951, 1974). Like racial and ethnic

"Hire him. He's got great legs."

SEX DISCRIMINATION ISN'T FUNNY.
SUPPORT THE NATIONAL ORGANIZATION FOR WOMEN
28 EAST 56 STREET N.Y.C. 10022

For generations, the evaluation of women in terms of physical appearance instead of job performance contributed to unequal occupational opportunities. By turning the tables, this educational poster helps people see how grossly unfair this practice really is.

minorities, then, females are subject to prejudice and discrimination in a patriarchal society (Collins, 1971; Lengerman & Wallace, 1985). Gender sparks social conflict as males seek to protect their privileges, while females challenge the status quo. Sexist ideology is one important element of this conflict, and includes any ideas that justify "keeping females in their place." As racism has been used to legitimate the oppression of nonwhites, so has the philosophy of sexism been used to devalue women and their activities. Patriarchy can persist only to the extent that males are believed to be innately superior and females are defined as incapable of challenging males in the labor force, in politics, or even in the home. Patriarchy derives additional power from both the law and, especially in the family, violence directed against women (F. Klein, 1982).

As noted in earlier chapters, the social-conflict paradigm draws heavily on the ideas of Karl Marx. Marx's writings—like those of most social scientists until re-

cently—focused almost exclusively on men, but his friend and colleague Friedrich Engels extensively addressed the issue of gender. Engels linked the origins of gender inequality to the historical formation of social classes (1902; orig. 1884).

Although women and men in hunting and gathering societies typically engaged in different activities, the contributions of both sexes were viewed as vital. A successful hunt may have brought males great prestige, but since most of the society's food was vegetation gathered by women, females had great importance as well (Leacock, 1978). As horticulture and agriculture made possible a productive surplus, however, the custom of sharing all goods gave way to the idea of private property—to Marx and Engels the basis of social classes. At this point, males gained power over females. Accumulating more goods than necessary for survival, males became concerned with passing on their wealth to their true offspring. They solved this problem by creating monogamous marriage and the family. These institutions allowed men to identify their own offspring and ensure that their property would be passed on to them. But forming families depended on men's ability to engage the services of women for bearing and raising children. This led to the creation of the male world of work and the home-centered world of the female.

Engels claimed that capitalism furthered male domination. First, capitalism created far more wealth, which is still owned mostly by men. Second, the capitalist economy expanded as women were defined as consumers and socialized to seek personal fulfillment through buying various products. Third, in order for males to work in factories, females have to maintain the home. Thus capitalism exploits males by paying them low wages for their labor, but women work for no wages at all (Eisenstein, 1979; Barry, 1983; Jagger, 1983; Vogel, 1983).

According to social-conflict analysis, those who suffer social disadvantages are likely to act to change society. As we shall see presently, this is indeed the case among many women and men. But as William Goode (1983) points out, men are less likely than women to recognize gender as a matter of social conflict. As subordinates, Goode suggests, women are well aware that men have the power to shape their lives. But men, who are less influenced by women, often fail to see that gender matters. Men also think that they are not personally responsible for a patriarchal society; thus they fail to see that patriarchy can persist only so long as individuals conform to its demands. Moreover, prejudice and discrimination are commonly experienced by women; men, on the other hand, tend to view anyone's success or failure simply as a matter of personal merit. Finally, men emotionally identify with women as lovers, wives, mothers, and daughters. They define their role as protecting females and providing for their needs, so that they see themselves as benevolent despots. For all these reasons, many men are hurt and confused by women's claims of being victimized.

Evaluation. Social-conflict analysis stresses the domination of society by males. In doing so, it minimizes the extent to which males and females live together cooperatively in families. Furthermore, the assertion that capitalism is the basis of gender stratification has been challenged by those who point out that even socialist societies are strongly patriarchal.

FEMINISM

In the 1960s, the popular soul artist Aretha Franklin sang, "I know that a woman's duty is to help and love a man, and that's the way it was planned." But on a hit record in 1985, Franklin asserts that "Sisters are doin' it for themselves" and tells the man she loves, "I know that you got your daddy's way, but your daddy's way was yesterday. Time has moved on and things have changed; ladies' priorities rearranged."

One arrangement of priorities that has profoundly affected the lives of women and men in the last two decades is **feminism**—*the support for the social equality of the sexes, leading to opposition to patriarchy and sexism.* Feminism is not new to America; as described at the beginning of this chapter, women such as Elizabeth Cady Stanton and Lucretia Mott began what is often described as the first wave of feminism in the 1840s when they drew parallels between the oppression of non-whites and the oppression of women (Randall, 1982). The major objective of the women's movement at that time was gaining the right to vote. But after suffrage was achieved in 1920, many other disadvantages for women persisted. This is the context in which the second wave of feminism arose in the 1960s.

Central Feminist Ideas

In general terms, feminism involves a new and different view of ourselves and society. Feminism—like the sociological perspective—involves stepping back from conventional social patterns to gain a keener awareness of what is taken for granted. Also like the sociological perspective, feminism is a way to link *personal* experiences to the operation of *society*. In other words, how we think of ourselves (gender identity), how we act (gender roles), and our place in society (gender stratification) represent the power of society over us.

But feminism is also decidedly critical, challenging conventional ideas about the two sexes, especially the masculine values of power and control that dominate a patriarchal society. For example, our culture defines masculinity largely in terms of power over others. In contrast, femininity is defined largely in terms of altruism—selflessly responding to the needs of other people, especially males. In short, feminism holds that only by critically examining the values and ideas of American culture can women expect to gain importance and dignity equal to men's.

Feminism is also committed to the "reintegration of humanity" (French, 1985:443). As this chapter has explained, cultural ideas about gender serve to divide the full range of human qualities into two distinct spheres—the male world of rationality and competition, and the female world of emotions and cooperation. Feminism challenges the assertion that masculine traits are inherently more important than feminine traits. Furthermore, it claims that *all* human beings are capable of developing *all* of these traits. Therefore, feminism represents a process of resocialization in which all human beings have the opportunity to develop and express the full range of their human potential.

Feminism also provides a criticism of gender stratification, challenging, for example, restrictions that keep women from obtaining as much income and education as men have and undertaking the most rewarding occupations. Feminism seeks to reorganize society so that the half of the population that is female does not leave decision making to the half that is male—whether in the privacy of the home or in the public world of national politics. One step in this direction would be passage of the Equal Rights Amendment (ERA), a proposed addition to the United States Constitution that states simply:

> Equality of rights under the law shall not be denied or abridged by the United States or any State on account of sex.

A final area of feminist concern is human sexuality. In a patriarchal society, sexual relationships between men and women are often an expression of male power (Millet, 1970; J. Bernard, 1973). This is reflected in the widespread pattern of sexual harassment. On many college campuses, for example, about one-third of female students report unwanted sexual advances from their male teachers (Dziech & Weiner, 1984). Another recent survey found that about one-fourth of female college students had been victims of rape—often what is commonly called date rape—in which male students force themselves on women in the course of spending an evening together (Sweet, 1985). Surveys of men and women in the workplace also indicate that a majority of both sexes believe sexual harassment is a serious problem (Loy & Stewart, 1984).

More generally, feminism supports the right of females to control their own sexuality and reproduction. This is why feminists have advocated the right of women to obtain birth control information—which was illegal in some states even a generation ago. In addition, most feminists support a woman's right to choose to have children or to terminate a pregnancy. Feminism is not *in favor of* abortion, but claims that the decision to bear children should be made by women themselves rather than by men—as husbands, physicians, and legislators. In addition, many feminists support the struggle by gay people to overcome prejudice and discrimination within a culture dominated by heterosexuality. Such social disadvantages are even greater in the case of lesbians than gay men, because lesbians violate not only the cultural norm of heterosexuality, but also the norm that men should control the sexuality of women (Deckard, 1979; Barry, 1983; Jagger, 1983).

Resistance to Feminism

As one might expect, feminism has been strongly resisted by both men and women who accept the dominant cultural ideas about gender. Many males oppose feminism for the same reasons that many whites have historically opposed social equality for nonwhites: they do not want to lose privileges linked to patriarchy. Many other men, including those who are neither rich nor powerful, are uneasy about a social movement that appears to threaten an important basis of their status and self-respect: their masculinity. Men who have been socialized to be strong and dominant can understandably feel threatened by the feminist challenge that men can also be gentle and warm (Doyle, 1983). Many other men, however, support feminist ideas. Some simply object to an entire category of human beings being treated unequally in American society. Others find in feminism encouragement for de-

More than a century after the original women's movement in the United States, a "second wave" of feminism sought to reduce gender-based inequality. Although considerable progress has been made, American society still provides no explicit guarantees of equal rights under the law for both sexes.

veloping themselves more fully—the opportunity, in the words of army recruiters, to "be all that you can be."

Some women, as well, are uneasy about feminism. For example, women who have centered their lives around their husbands and children may perceive feminism as a threat to all they believe is important. More accurately, however, feminism simply seeks to give women a greater choice in life.

Finally, many people's fears about feminism are based on incorrect images of what feminism is. Feminism does not seek to set men and women against each other. Rather, believing that patriarchy has long fostered social conflict, feminism seeks to eliminate the element of power from human relationships. Nor are the vast majority of feminists man-haters, as unreasonable critics sometimes suggest.

Widespread support for at least some feminist ideas can be inferred from the fact that two-thirds of American adults endorse the Equal Rights Amendment (N.O.R.C., 1983:199). But the fact that the ERA—first proposed in Congress in 1923—has yet to be ratified shows that resistance to feminism is strong, at least among male legislators.

Variations within Feminism

In theory and in practice, feminism is highly variable. People who describe themselves as feminists advance different criticisms of patriarchy and propose different alternatives to the status quo. Three distinct variants of feminism are often noted, although the distinctions among them are far from clear-cut, and each is continually changing as feminist thinking develops (Barry, 1983; Jagger, 1983; Stacey, 1983; Vogel, 1983).

Liberal feminism accepts the basic organization of American society, but seeks to ensure that females have the same rights and opportunities as males. Liberal feminism endorses the Equal Rights Amendment, and stresses the need to eliminate the prejudice and discrimination that have historically limited women's opportunities. Liberal feminism supports reproductive freedom for all women. While accepting the family as a central social institution, liberal feminism advocates the availability of maternity leave and child care for women who wish to work. A striking fact is that over one hundred nations of the world guarantee maternity leaves for all working women, but the United States has no such policy that applies to all working women (Hewlett, 1986).

Socialist feminism is based on the ideas of Karl Marx and Friedrich Engels, and links the social disadvantages of women primarily to the capitalist economic system. Thus while socialist feminists endorse the reforms sought by liberal feminism, they view these as inadequate. Socialist feminists claim that only a socialist revolution can provide significant equality for all men and women. (Further discussion of socialism is found in Chapter 18.)

Radical feminism endorses the reforms sought by liberal feminism, but also views them as inadequate by themselves. Neither do radical feminists consider socialist revolution to be an adequate means to end patriarchy. Rather, they believe patriarchy can be ended by nothing short of the elimination of gender itself. This does not mean, of course, that males and females will not differ biologically in terms of sex, but rather that culture should not define sex in terms that divide human capacities into masculine and feminine worlds. In short, radical feminists seek a gender-free society.

GENDER IN THE TWENTY-FIRST CENTURY

Predictions about the future are, at best, a matter of informed speculation. Just as economists disagree about the likely inflation rate a year from now, there is little consensus among sociologists as to the future state of our society. But to conclude this chapter, some general comments will be made about the future of gender in American society.

Recall, first, the position of American women more than a century ago. Husbands controlled property within most marriages, women were barred from most areas

Since the emergence of feminism in the United States, some people have feared sexual equality. As this 1869 Currier and Ives drawing suggests, males may fear the loss of privileges that are the basis of their masculine identity.

of the labor force, and no women were able to vote. Although women are socially disadvantaged today, the movement toward greater equality has been striking and seems certain to persist.

Many factors have contributed to this change. Perhaps most important, industrialization has served to expand the participation of women in society. Industrialization has both broadened the range of human activity and shifted the nature of work from physically demanding tasks that favored male strength to jobs that demand thought and imagination. In addition, medical technology has placed reproduction under human control so that women's lives are no longer as limited by unwanted pregnancies.

In addition, many women and men have made deliberate efforts to lessen the power of patriarchy. Feminism seeks to end the limitations imposed on people by a society that assigns activities and forms of self-expression simply on the basis of sex. As these efforts continue, the social changes in the twenty-first century may be even greater than those we have already witnessed.

At the same time, there is strong opposition to the changes advocated by feminism. As structural-functional analysis explains, gender is an important foundation of personal identity, of family life, and also of the operation of our entire society. Therefore, we should expect efforts to change cultural ideas about the two sexes to provoke considerable anxiety, fear, and resistance.

On balance, it seems that radical change in American society's view of gender is not likely in the near future. Yet the movement toward a society in which males and females enjoy more equal rights and opportunities is likely to continue.

SUMMARY

1. Sex is a biological concept; human beings are male or female from the moment of conception. Rare cases of hermaphrodites combine the biological traits of both sexes. Transsexuals are people who deliberately alter their sex through surgery.

2. Heterosexuality is the dominant sexual orientation in virtually all societies of the world. Homosexuality characterizes a small proportion of the American population. Sexual orientation is not always clear-cut, however; many people are bisexual.

3. Gender refers to the human traits attached to each sex by culture. Gender varies across cultures and over time.

4. Patriarchy exists to some extent in all societies. Male dominance has been defended by sexism, just as racial dominance has been defended by racism.

5. The socialization process links personal identity to gender (gender identity), and teaches males and females to engage in distinctive activities (gender roles). All the major agents of socialization—family, peer groups, schools, and the mass media—reinforce cultural definitions of what is masculine and feminine.

6. Gender stratification imposes numerous social disadvantages on women. Since the late 1970s, most women have been in the paid labor force. But a majority of working women are clerical workers or service workers. Housework also remains a feminine activity.

7. On the average, women earn about 65 percent as much as men do because of a number of factors, including discrimination. This has led to the demand that all workers be paid fairly for the worth of their job.

8. The historical exclusion of women from higher education has significantly lessened. Women are now a slight majority of all college students, and receive half of all master's degrees granted. Most doctorates and professional degrees, however, are still received by men.

9. The number of women in politics has increased sharply in recent decades. Still, the vast majority of national officials are men.

10. Minority women have greater social disadvantages than white women. Overall, minority women earn only half as much as white men. More than 50 percent of households headed by minority women are poor. Because of their distinctive social identity and social disadvantages, *all* women can be considered as a minority group.

11. Structural-functional analysis explains that assigning distinctive activities to males and females in preindustrial societies was a functional strategy for societal survival. In industrial societies, where the survival value of such a strategy no longer operates, long-established cultural norms related to gender are slow to change. Moreover, Talcott Parsons claimed that complementary gender roles increase the social integration of the family.

12. Social-conflict analysis explains that society places males in a position of dominance over females. Friedrich Engels linked gender stratification to the development of social classes. Engels claimed that capitalism increased male dominance by devaluing females as homemakers who work for no pay.

13. Feminism is the belief in the social equality of the sexes, and the organized opposition to patriarchy and sexism. Feminism challenges the cultural pattern of dividing human capabilities into masculine and feminine traits, and seeks the elimination of the historical social disadvantages faced by females.

14. Because gender is a foundation of American society, feminism has met with strong resistance. Although two-thirds of Americans express support for the Equal Rights Amendment, this legislation—first proposed in Congress in 1923—has yet to become part of the Constitution.

KEY CONCEPTS

feminism the support for the social equality of the sexes, leading to opposition to patriarchy and sexism

gender human traits linked by culture to each sex

gender identity the ways males and females, within their culture, learn to think of themselves

gender roles (sex roles) attitudes and activities that a culture links to each sex

gender stratification the unequal distribution of wealth, power, and privileges between the two sexes

matriarchy a form of social organization in which females dominate males

patriarchy a form of social organization in which males dominate females

primary sex characteristics the genitals, used to reproduce the human species

secondary sex characteristics distinctive physical traits of males and females not directly linked to reproduction

sex the division of humanity into biological categories of male and female

sexism the belief that one sex is innately superior to the other

sexual orientation the manner in which people experience sexual arousal and achieve sexual pleasure

---

SUGGESTED READINGS

The first of these texts provides a straightforward discussion of sexuality and sexual orientation. The second presents a detailed introduction to the concept of gender.

David A. Shultz. *Human Sexuality.* 3rd ed. Englewood Cliffs, NJ: Prentice-Hall, 1988.

Patricia Madoo Lengermann and Ruth A. Wallace. *Gender in America: Social Control and Social Change.* Englewood Cliffs, NJ: Prentice-Hall, 1985.

Gender is one foundation of personal identity. Essays in this book explain how being female becomes the core of a feminine "self."

Mary Jo Deegan and Michael Hill, eds. *Women and Symbolic Interaction.* Winchester, MA: Allen & Unwin, 1987.

This book is a fascinating account of American discomfort with sexuality, documenting many historical misconceptions that have shaped attitudes toward sex.

John Money. *The Destroying Angel: Sex, Fitness & Food in the Legacy of Degeneracy Theory, Graham Crackers, Kellogg's Corn Flakes, & American Health History.* Buffalo: Prometheus, 1985.

Homosexuality has long been ignored by scholars, as it has by the general public. This collection of essays from the journal *Signs* is a rich and varied consideration of homosexuality among women.

Estelle B. Freedman, Barbara C. Gelpi, Susan L. Johnson, and Kathleen M. Weston. *The Lesbian Issue: Essays from SIGNS.* Chicago: University of Chicago Press, 1985.

In this classic, the author explains the importance of gender by arguing that males and females live within different, socially constructed worlds. She also maintains that sociology itself must change if it wishes to accurately understand the lives of women.

Jessie Bernard. *The Female World.* New York: Free Press, 1981.

Here are two useful books on masculinity. The first is a collection of essays exploring masculinity from many points of view. The second focuses on men in American society since 1950.

Harry Brod, ed. *The Making of Masculinity: The New Men's Studies.* Winchester, MA: Allen & Unwin, 1987.

Barbara Ehrenreich. *The Hearts of Men: American Dreams and the Flight from Commitment.* Garden City: Anchor/Doubleday, 1983.

Sociologists have a keen interest in the links between gender and work, which are well introduced in this book.

Paula England and George Farkas. *Households, Employment, and Gender: A Social, Economic and Demographic View.* Hawthorne, NY: Aldine de Gruyter, 1986.

This paperback provides an excellent overview of sexism in many forms.

Nijole V. Benokraitis and Joe R. Feagin. *Modern Sexism: Blatant, Subtle, and Covert Discrimination.* Englewood Cliffs, NJ: Prentice-Hall, 1986.

Because two of three poor adults in America are women, the feminization of poverty is a growing social problem. Essays in this book consider the issue in both American and world contexts.

Barbara C. Gelpi, Nancy C. M. Hartsock, Clare C. Novak, and Myra H. Strober. *Women and Poverty.* Chicago: University of Chicago Press, 1986.

A thorough discussion of the history of patriarchy, the significance of gender in today's society, and feminism is found in the following:

Marilyn French. *Beyond Power: On Women, Men, and Morals.* New York: Summit Books, 1985.

This book helps to explain why feminism has remained so controversial, and why many people oppose its goals.

Janice Doane and Devon Hodges. *Nostalgia and Sexual Difference: The Resistance to Contemporary Feminism.* New York: Methuen, 1987.

Finally, this book criticizes the direction of the women's movement in the United States and offers a program for improving the social standing of women.

Sylvia Ann Hewlett. *A Lesser Life: The Myth of Women's Liberation in America.* New York: Warner Books, 1986.

CHAPTER 13

Aging
and the Elderly

Every morning I wake up in pain. I wiggle my toes. Good. They still obey. I open my eyes. Good. I can see. Everything hurts, but I get dressed. I walk down to the ocean. Good. It's still there. Now my day can start. About tomorrow I never know. After all, I'm eighty-nine. I can't live forever. (Myerhoff, 1980:1)

These words introduce us to the life of Basha, a central character in anthropologist Barbara Myerhoff's widely praised study of aging Jews in Venice Beach—a seaside community in Southern California. To Basha, the ocean and her own impending death are edges that frame each of her remaining days.

Living alone, Basha has considerable difficulty with daily routines that most of us take for granted. She values independence above all, yet she finds washing, dressing, cooking, cleaning a small apartment, and providing for her daily medical needs exhausting. The telephone is a vital link to others; yet on days when her fingers swell with arthritis, even using the telephone dial is painful.

There is no longer a neighborhood grocery store. Basha can travel to a supermarket by bus, but the steps of the bus are high and often the driver will not allow her to bring along her wheeled shopping cart. And she faces the constant problem of living on a small fixed income: $320 a month.

Once a week, Basha speaks by telephone with her daughter, who is a lawyer. Her daughter's work is a source of pride to them both, yet Basha is often aware that this achievement has created a social distance between them. Basha could accept an invitation to live with her daughter's family. Yet their way of life is very different from her own, and to join them would mean sacrificing the self-sufficiency she values so highly.

This chapter completes our exploration of social inequality by examining a rapidly growing segment of Americans: the elderly. Many older Americans face the problems of prejudice and discrimination and the ever-present dangers of poverty described in earlier chapters. In addition, we shall see that while the process of aging is certainly linked to biological changes, the reality of being old is very much shaped by society.

The Graying of American Society

An important revolution is reshaping American society. This is a quiet revolution, which is only occasionally described in the mass media, but its changes are likely to be dramatic.

Simply put, the number of elderly Americans—people aged sixty-five and over—is increasing more than twice as fast as the population as a whole. In 1900, half of all Americans were under twenty-three years of age and only 4 percent of the population was over sixty-five. As shown in Figure 13–1, however, American society has steadily become older. In 1980, the median age of Americans passed thirty, and about 11 percent of the population was over the age of sixty-five. By 1985, elderly Americans outnumbered teenagers by more than 2 million. By the year 2030—within the lifetime of most readers of this book—the median age of all Americans will be approaching forty and almost one in five people will be over the age of sixty-five (Bouvier, 1980; Soldo, 1980).

Two major developments have set the stage for the graying of America. The first is the baby boom that began in the late 1940s as Americans enthusiastically settled into family life after World War II. Before this era ended about 1960, some 75 million babies were born. The birth rate has declined since then; therefore, this unusually large cohort of Americans (who first gained attention by forging the youth culture of the 1960s) will continue to shape American society as they reach old age. The second cause is the steadily increasing life expec-

tancy of Americans. Males born in 1900 could expect to live, on the average, only about forty-eight years; females could expect to live about fifty-one years. As noted in Chapter 12, American males born in 1985 can expect to live 71.2 years; the life expectancy of females has increased to 78.2 years. The life expectancy of Americans has been increasing because a rising standard of living and medical advances have all but eliminated many infectious diseases such as smallpox, diphtheria, and measles, which killed many young people early in the century. More recently, medicine has also made great strides in combating cancer and heart disease, typical afflictions of the elderly (Wall, 1980). Today, not only are more Americans living to the age of sixty-five, but they are living well beyond. In fact, the fastest-growing segment of the elderly population is people over the age of seventy-five, who are expected to account for one in eight Americans by the year 2050 (Barberis, 1981; Hallowell, 1985).

The effects of this rapid increase in the elderly population are evident even now and will soon be tremen-

Figure 13–1 The Graying of American Society

(Soldo, 1980)

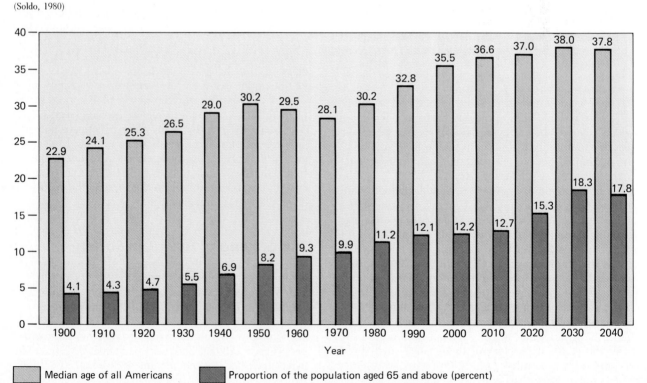

Median age of all Americans

Proportion of the population aged 65 and above (percent)

People over the age of sixty-five, who already outnumber teenagers in the United States, will represent about one in five Americans by 2030.

dous. As long as people over the age of sixty-five are expected to retire from the labor force, the proportion of nonworking Americans will sharply increase. In the years to come, ever-greater demands will be placed on social resources and programs that provide support for the nonworking elderly.

Consider, for example, the Social Security system, which is a major source of retirement income for millions of Americans. This system operates on a simple principle: people who are working pay taxes on their earnings, which are used to support those who have retired. The danger, of course, lies in a growing imbalance between workers and nonworkers. In 1960, there were about five workers for every person receiving benefits. By 1980, this ratio had dropped to almost three to one. But by the year 2030, government projections indicate, one person will be receiving benefits for every *two* paying into the system, so that current financing problems are likely to become much worse (Barberis, 1981; Newman & Matzke, 1984). The strength of the Social Security system has already been undermined, and the need for new reforms is currently being debated in Congress and throughout the country. Providing for the needs of a rapidly increasing elderly population is a challenge that will require action now if older Americans are to have a financially secure future.

The elderly are also major consumers of medical care, accounting for one-fourth of all health expenditures. They are more likely than other Americans to require the services of physicians and hospitalization, and they use one-quarter of all prescription drugs (Butler, 1975). At the same time, physicians and hospitals have traditionally directed relatively little attention to the needs of the elderly (Hallowell, 1985). Unless steps are taken to ensure that the medical needs of tens of millions of additional older people can be met—meaning in many cases providing medical care that the elderly can *afford*—

our society will face a crisis of truly monumental proportions in the next century.

Perhaps most important, the elderly will become much more common in everyone's daily experience. Americans are now accustomed to a considerable degree of age segregation. Young people have few intimate associations with old people, and their ideas about the elderly are often inaccurate. In the twenty-first century, when the elderly population of the United States is twice what it is now, young people will have far more direct contact with elderly people in their family, neighborhood, and elsewhere. Indeed, as the proportion of the elderly in American society rises, many more adults will face the responsibilities of caring for aging parents (Gelman, 1985). In addition, the expectation that old age will be a greater portion of their own lives will give younger people good reason to want to understand the process of aging. Thus the graying of American society means not only that the elderly segment of society will become larger, but also that the presence of more elderly people will affect the attitudes and life experiences of everyone.

GROWING OLD: BIOLOGY AND CULTURE

The importance of the graying of America is reflected in the development of a relatively new field of social science. **Gerontology** (a term derived from the Greek word *geron*, meaning "an old person") is *the study of aging and the elderly*. Gerontology is concerned not only with the physical process of aging, but also with how old age is culturally defined.

The human life cycle is certainly based on the biological process of aging. But the reality of any stage of life depends on how a society defines aging and socially structures personal experience. In all societies, people of different ages may be defined as different kinds of people. Americans distinguish children, adolescents, and adults from one another, and expect certain personal traits and types of behavior from people in each category. But this is not true of every society. As Chapter 5 explained, Margaret Mead (1961; orig. 1928) found that the Samoan Islanders barely recognized adolescence; Philippe Ariès (1965) argued that childhood as we know it did not exist in medieval Europe. Therefore, fully understanding old age—or any stage of life—requires consideration of both the biological facts of aging and how they are perceived in a social context.

Biological Changes

From the moment of birth to the moment of death, our bodies are constantly changing. In youth-oriented American society, however, we tend to attach positive significance to biological changes that occur earlier in life and to define later physical changes in negative terms. Growing children and maturing adolescents receive more responsibility, diplomas, and additional legal rights to reward their progress. But few people are congratulated for getting old. We commiserate with those approaching old age, and make jokes about their supposed physical and mental decline. In other words, we assume that after a certain point in the life cycle, people cease growing *up* and being to grow *down*.

Certainly old age involves physical problems for many people, but Americans generally exaggerate the extent to which the elderly are physically different from younger people (Harris, 1976). Gerontological research helps to separate the facts of aging from cultural stereotypes.

Gray hair, wrinkles, loss of height and weight, and an overall decline in strength and vitality are part of the aging process that begins in middle age for most Americans (Colloway & Dollevoet, 1977). After about the age of fifty, bones tend to become more brittle, and falls that might be of little consequence earlier in life can result in disabling injuries. Such injuries may take much longer to heal in the elderly than in the young. A substantial proportion of the elderly are also subject to illnesses such as arthritis that can limit their physical activity, and to serious life-threatening conditions such as heart disease and cancer. Recently, considerable public attention has been focused on Alzheimer's disease, a devastating disability that currently afflicts some 3 million Americans representing about 7 percent of the population over the age of sixty-five. The box describes the effects of this cruel and incurable disease.

The sensory abilities—taste, sight, touch, smell, and especially hearing—are likely to diminish with age. While only about 5 percent of all middle-aged people have visual impairments, about 10 percent of the elderly do. Hearing problems are even more common, increasing in frequency from about 15 percent of middle-aged people to almost one-third of the elderly. Such impairments are also somewhat more common among men than women (U.S. National Center for Health Statistics, 1987a). The declining ability to taste and smell can cause changes in eating habits that frequently result in health problems related to poor nutrition (Eckholm, 1985).

But the physical disabilities associated with aging vary greatly within the elderly population. As noted in Chapter 10, physical health is related to social class; those who have been able to afford a healthful environment and extensive medical care throughout their lives fare far better than those with fewer social privileges. In addition, as more and more Americans are aware, people can contribute to their own good health at all ages through regular exercise, careful attention to diet, and avoidance of health hazards such as cigarette smoking.

Disability and disease increase with age and include life-threatening conditions such as heart disease and cancer, as well as less serious disabilities such as arthritis and diabetes. The greater health problems of older people are reflected in the fact that 70 percent of Americans who die are over the age of sixty-five. On the other hand, the vast majority of the elderly are not disabled by physical diseases. Only about one in ten reports having trouble walking, and roughly one in twenty requires the intensive care provided by a hospital or nursing home. No more than 1 percent of the elderly are bedridden. Not surprisingly, then, about 70 percent of people over the age of sixty-five assess their health as "good" to "excellent," while 30 percent state their overall condition to be "fair" or "poor" (U.S. National Center for Health Statistics, 1987).

Psychological Changes

Nor do most elderly people suffer from mental or psychological problems, as is widely assumed. Samuel Johnson, the famous eighteenth-century observer of British society, once observed, "There is a wicked inclination in most people to suppose an old man decayed in his intellect. If a young or middle-aged man, when leaving a company, does not recollect where he laid his hat, it is nothing; but if the same inattention is discovered in an old man, people will shrug their shoulders and say, 'His memory is going'" (cited in Berger, 1983:544). Johnson's point is that our interpretations of human behavior are colored by cultural assumptions about the various stages of life.

Until fairly recently, most psychologists agreed that changes in intelligence over the life cycle followed a simple rule: "What goes up must come down" (Baltes & Shaie, 1974). Some even claimed that mental decline can begin as early as twenty-five (Wechsler, 1972). Today, however, more psychologists suspect that mental decline among the elderly is simply a myth, and that

CLOSE-UP

Alzheimer's Disease—A Case of Dying Twice

. . . your memory is gone, it's dead. I don't know what's missing. Your thoughts become a void, and then there's nothing.

These words were spoken by a woman experiencing the initial stages of Alzheimer's disease. Only fifty-three years of age, her mind is slowly dying. As the disease progresses, she will experience increasing loss of memory, disorientation, and perhaps hallucinations. Ultimately, she will completely lose touch with the world around her—not knowing where she is, the time, or even if it's day or night. She may not even recognize people in her own family. At this point, unable to engage in social interaction, she will have experienced social death. As the second, biological, death approaches, she will lose control of her body as well, ultimately entering a coma from which she will not recover.

This is the cruel tragedy of Alzheimer's disease, which, along with other dementia-producing diseases, currently affects over 6 million Americans and causes several hundred thousand deaths annually. As the elderly population has increased, the incidence of diseases of this type has soared to about ten times the level at the beginning of this century. In

the past, the symptoms of Alzheimer's disease were often thought to be simply the results of old age. But medical research has gradually come to the realization that this disorder—named after Alois Alzheimer, a German physician who pioneered investigation of the illness in the early years of this century—is actually a physical deterioration of nerve fibers in the brain. At this point, however, only small gains have been made in understanding the disease. There is now hope, but there is currently no cure.

The agony of Alzheimer's disease affects not only the victim but family members and friends as well. Initially, a victim may experience only mild loss of memory (which, in itself, is certainly no sure indication of having the disease). But as the disease intensifies, the victim becomes increasingly helpless, which places more and more of a burden on others. Family members must painfully watch the victim lose the ability to work, perform simple household tasks, and interact with others.

Worse still, there is the ever-present danger that victims may unintentionally cause injury to themselves or other people. Families must learn to take unusual precautions. Confusion operating water faucets may cause a victim to become scalded in

the shower; consequently, water temperatures must be fixed at a lower range. Automobiles must be disabled to ensure that a victim will not aimlessly and dangerously attempt to drive. Even stairways may become a deadly danger requiring the installation of protective gates.

The burdens of care only increase with time. Even the strongest family members eventually recognize that they cannot cope with the constant attention that the Alzheimer's victim requires. The solution is usually institutional care; the expense (as much as several thousand dollars a month) provides yet another crippling blow.

But perhaps the greatest pain for families is their own helplessness in the face of the gradual death of a loved one, coupled with the fact that the victim may not even be able to respond to their efforts. The wife of an Alzheimer's victim in San Diego recalled, "One day my husband threatened to leave home because he wanted to go off to call his wife. He cried and begged me to let him call 'Lil.' I told him I was Lil—it was devastating."

SOURCE: Based on Matt Clark, "A Slow Death of the Mind," *Newsweek*, December 3, 1984, pp. 56–62; and Congress of the United States, *Losing A Million Minds: Confronting the Tragedy of Alzheimer's Disease and Other Dementias* (Washington, DC: U.S. Government Printing Office, 1987).

---

some dimensions of intelligence may actually *increase* as one ages.

Resolving this controversy depends on clearly defining the concept *intelligence*. Some measures of intelligence emphasize what psychologists call *sensorimotor coordination*, which involves, for example, the ability to arrange a series of objects to match a drawn figure.

Such measures do show a steady decline after midlife. Similarly, tests that involve the learning of new material and those that focus on speed of mental performance reveal lower scores for the elderly, especially those beyond the age of seventy (Schaie, 1980). On the other hand, scores of tests that make use of present knowledge show little or no decline with age. Still other measures of intelligence, such as verbal ability and numerical skills, appear to rise with advancing age (Baltes & Schaie, 1974). Bear in mind that any measure of intelligence is affected by the education and social class of the subject. In some cases, these factors have a greater impact on measures of intelligence than a subject's age (Botwinick, 1977; Riegel, 1977).

Psychological research has also shown, contrary to widespread belief, that the personality changes little as people grow old. An exception to this pattern is that the elderly tend to become somewhat more introverted—concerned with their own thoughts and feelings. But in most respects, people who knew one another as children will recognize much the same personality traits in one another when they have grown old (Neugarten, 1971, 1972, 1977).

Aging and Culture

What age is viewed as old depends, in part, on the age of the viewer. A teenager may feel old in relation to a brother still in grammar school, but young in relation to a sister who already has a career and children. Forty may seem over the hill until we have reached that age. And a ninety-year-old may regard a retired person of seventy as a mere youngster.

More objectively, what age is old depends on the average life expectancy in a particular society. This, in turn, is related to the society's overall standard of living and its technological ability to control disease and other threats to human life. Throughout most of human history, people's lives were quite short by current American standards. Teenagers married and had children, those in their twenties were middle-aged, and people became old by about thirty. Reaching the age of forty was rare until the late Middle Ages, when a rising standard of living and technological advances began to provide the means to control infectious diseases that were common killers of people of all ages (Mahler, 1980; Cox, 1984).

Even today, there is great variation in life expectancy among the societies of the world. In much of the industrialized northern hemisphere—including the United States, Canada, the societies of Western Europe, the Soviet Union, and Japan—the average life span is about seventy years. As a consequence, individuals are not usually regarded as old until they reach their mid-sixties. On the other hand, in many societies—primarily in the less industrialized and poor nations of the southern hemisphere—life expectancy is considerably less. In the

poorest societies, people expect to live perhaps forty years—about the same as in Europe during the Middle Ages.

One society, Abkhasia in the southwestern Soviet Union, is an unusual case. Although the Abkhasians lack the advanced technology associated with industrialization, a large number of them have been reported as living to the age of one hundred and even beyond. Such claims may be exaggerated, but the life span of the Abkhasians does appear to be quite a bit longer than that typical of preindustrial societies, as the box explains.

The Elderly: A Comparative View

Like race, ethnicity, and sex, age is one basis for assigning people a different rank in the social hierarchy in virtually all societies. **Age stratification** is *the unequal distribution of wealth, power, and privileges among people of different*

In less developed societies, life expectancy is often shorter than it is in the United States. Although not old enough to be considered elderly by American standards, this Somalian woman has physical traits associated with advanced age.

Growing (Very) Old in Abkhasia

Anthropologist Sula Benet was sharing wine and conversation with a man in Tamish, a small village in the Republic of Abkhasia in the southwest corner of the Soviet Union. She judged the man to be about seventy, and raising her glass, she offered a toast to his long life. "May you live as long as Moses," she exclaimed. The gesture of goodwill fell rather flat: Moses lived to be a hundred and twenty, but Benet's friend was already a hundred and nineteen.

An outsider—even an open-minded anthropologist—might be skeptical about the longevity of the Abkhasians. In one village of twelve hundred examined by Benet, for example, almost two hundred people claimed to be at least eighty-one, and many were quite a bit older. Systematic research has not been carried out since 1954, but at that time, 2.5 percent of all Abkhasians were over ninety—a proportion more than six times as high as that in the United States.

To her surprise, Benet found that any misrepresentation of age among the Abkhasians was likely to be a matter of *understatement*. For example, one man claimed to be ninety-five, but his daughter (who was eighty-one) produced a birth certificate indicating his actual age was one hundred and eight. Why the deception? In this case, because the man was soon to be married. As another man (of a hundred and four) explained with a wink, "A man is a man until he is one hundred, you know what I mean. After that, well, he is getting old."

What is the Abkhasian secret of long life? The answer most certainly is *not* the advanced medical technology in which Americans place so

Cultural patterns as well as diet contribute to the longevity of the Abkhasians. This man is reported to be 123 years old.

much faith; physicians are rarely used in Abkhasia. Nonetheless, health among all Abkhasians—including the very old—is remarkable by our standards.

One possible explanation is genetic: centuries of grueling warfare may have favored the survival of those with robust physical traits, but there is no available evidence to test this hypothesis. A more likely cause is diet. Abkhasians eat few saturated fats (which are associated with heart disease) and use no sugar, but consume large amounts of fresh fruits and vegetables. They also drink no coffee or tea (but lots of buttermilk and low-alcohol wine). Few Abkhasians use tobacco. In addition, Abkhasians are active: work and regular exercise are part of the lives of those of all ages.

Benet suggests, however, that the primary cause of Abkhasian longevity

may be cultural. Abkhasian culture is based on a clear and consistent set of values and norms. All Abkhasians enjoy a strong sense of belonging and find great significance in their lives. Old people are therefore active and valued members of society—a healthful situation that contrasts sharply with our own cultural patterns. As Benet explains: "The old [in the United States], when they do not simply vegetate, out of view and out of mind, keep themselves 'busy' with bingo and shuffleboard." In these words lies the sharpest contrast between Abkhasian society and our own. The Abkhasians have no word for old people, nor is the idea of retirement part of their society. The elderly have great prestige; they are respected for their wisdom and make decisions that affect all members of their families. According to Benet:

> The extraordinary attitude of the Abkhasians—to feel needed at 99 or 110—is not an artificial, self-protective one; it is a natural expression, in old age, of a consistent outlook that begins in childhood. . . .
>
> Abkhasians expect a long and useful life and look forward to old age with good reason: in a culture which so highly values continuity in its traditions, the old are indispensable in their transmission. The elders preside at important ceremonial occasions, they mediate disputes and their knowledge of farming is sought. They feel needed because, in their own minds and everyone else's, they are. They are the opposite of burdens: they are highly valued resources.

SOURCE: Based on Sula Benet, "Why They Live to Be 100, or Even Older, in Abkhasia," *The New York Times Magazine*, December 26, 1971, pp. 3, 28–29, 31–34.

ages. In practice, however, age stratification varies considerably from one society to another. In general, the position of the elderly in the social hierarchy reflects a society's level of technological development. In agrarian societies, the elderly have a relatively high social ranking; but growing old involves a loss of social standing in societies that are technologically primitive as well as in those that are technologically the most advanced (Lenski & Lenski, 1987).

As described in Chapter 4, hunting and gathering societies lack the technological ability to produce a surplus of food and are typically nomadic. This confers great importance on physical strength and stamina. As their strength and energy decline so that they become less productive, the elderly are seen as an economic burden because they continue to consume resources. Therefore, they tend to be less valued members of technologically primitive societies (Sheehan, 1976).

Pastoral, horticultural, and agrarian societies have the technological means to domesticate animals and cultivate crops. Such societies are able to produce a material surplus, and individuals often accumulate considerable property over a lifetime. Because of their greater wealth,

the elderly—chiefly elderly males in patriarchal societies—have considerable power over younger people. This is **gerontocracy**—*a form of social organization in which the elderly have the most wealth, power, and privileges*. Old people, particularly old men, are feared and honored by their families because of their wealth and power. They usually remain active members of society until they die.

In addition, societies at this level of technological development commonly have a rich folk life that changes very slowly. The elderly are respected as those who best know the traditional wisdom and rituals, and they play an important part in transmitting those cultural elements from generation to generation (Sheehan, 1976). Moreover, the tendency of such societies to practice ancestor worship as part of their religious beliefs links power and prestige to old age.

Industrialization is associated with a loss of social power and prestige among the elderly because people leave the land and the family to obtain work in urban industrial centers. Children still expect to inherit property from their parents, but their livelihoods usually depend much more on their own earning power. Furthermore,

The power and prestige of elders in preindustrial societies is based on wisdom accumulated over a lifetime. This is often passed on to the young through rituals such as storytelling.

because the pace of technological development is rapid, cultural patterns change quickly, resulting in a discontinuity in the life experience of various generations. Skills and attitudes that served one generation soon become outdated, so that the wisdom of the elderly is often devalued as irrelevant by younger people. Then, too, tradition is less important in industrial societies, so the elderly do not enjoy much respect for maintaining traditional values and rituals (Atchley, 1982).

In industrial societies such as the United States and Canada, economic and political leaders are usually middle-aged specialists. In the most rapidly changing areas of the economy such as the high-tech fields, key executives are often quite young. Lacking the skills currently demanded in the marketplace, older workers may be defined as outdated and put out to pasture. One consequence of this is the tendency of older people to predominate in many traditional occupations (such as barbers, tailors, and seamstresses) and occupations that typically involve little activity (such as night security guards) (Kaufman & Spilerman, 1982). In addition, the tremendous productivity of industrial societies means that the work of everyone is not necessary—another reason that the elderly and the very young are often assigned nonproductive roles in industrial societies (Cohn, 1982).

The generation gap characteristic of industrial societies is reflected in changes in the organization of families. The *extended family*, including the elderly, younger adults, and their offspring, is common in preindustrial societies. With industrialization, however, *nuclear families*, composed of parents and their children, predominate. Older people live with their children in only about 20 percent of American households, but this pattern is gaining acceptance among Americans (N.O.R.C., 1987:207). At the beginning of this century, most elderly people who lived with their adult children were considered to be the head of the household. But this is now rare: today aged parents are usually dependent on their sons and daughters (Dahlin, 1980).

In some industrial societies—especially Japan—cultural values rooted in the agrarian past still support a high (although declining) social position for the elderly (Harlan, 1968; Treas, 1979; Yates, 1986). Japan's Shinto religion, for example, encourages veneration of the elderly. This is reflected in the fact that more than three-fourths of the elderly in Japan live with their adult children and play an important part in family life (Palmore, 1982). Elderly Japanese are also far more likely than elderly Americans to remain in the labor force, and the oldest employees in Japanese corporations typically

Japan is distinctive among industrialized societies in that the elderly are accorded high prestige and respect by younger family members.

receive the greatest respect. Still, in general, growing old in industrial societies brings at least some loss in social importance (Cowgill & Holmes, 1972).

TRANSITION AND PROBLEMS IN GROWING OLD

As explained in Chapter 5, all stages of the human life cycle involve personal change. Individuals must unlearn self-concepts and social patterns that are no longer applicable to their lives and simultaneously learn to cope with new circumstances. Of all stages of life, however, old age probably presents the greatest personal challenges because of biological decline and diminished social standing.

Although elderly Americans experience less physical disability than the cultural stereotype suggests, physical decline is indeed an important part of old age and can cause considerable emotional stress. Pain, loss of activity, dependence on others, and reminders of our mortality can be sources of frustration, self-doubt, and even depression. Since American culture so highly values youth, physical vitality, and good looks, changes in physical capabilities and physical appearance can threaten the self-esteem of older people. And the elderly must face the fact that physical decline has no cure and is a prelude to ultimate death.

Psychologist Erik Erikson (1963, 1980) described old age as a stage of life in which individuals experience the tension of "integrity versus despair." However much they may still be learning and achieving, the elderly must face the fact that their lives are nearing an end.

Thus old age involves reflection about one's past, which can bring either satisfaction or regret. Erikson claims that maintaining high self-esteem in the face of physical and social decline, and accepting mistakes as well as successes, can make old age a time of personal integrity. Otherwise, old age may be a time of despair—a dead end without positive meaning.

As noted earlier, personality usually changes little over the course of a lifetime. Research suggests that certain personality types are more likely than others to find personal well-being in old age, just as in their earlier years. In a seven-year study of people in their seventies, Bernice Neugarten (1971) identified four different personality types, which have variable success in adjusting to old age.

People with *disintegrated and disorganized personalities*—the fewest subjects in Neugarten's research—were almost entirely unable to adjust to old age. Severe psychological problems, in some cases existing for years, prevented them from living day to day without help from others. Many survived only because of support from sympathetic families or by living in hospitals or nursing homes. Understandably, people in this situation experienced old age with considerable despair.

Those with *passive-dependent personalities* sought help with daily life whether or not they actually needed it. Their level of activity was typically quite low—in some cases bordering on withdrawal—and their satisfaction was likewise relatively low.

Those with *defended personalities* lived independently, but feared advancing age. They shielded themselves from the reality of old age by fighting bravely to stay healthy, physically fit, and youthful. While their health concerns were certainly reasonable, their failure to accept the reality of aging was a source of personal stress and unhappiness.

Most of Neugarten's subjects, however, had *integrated personalities* and were quite successful in adapting to old age. These people displayed a high level of dignity and self-confidence in the face of advancing age. They accepted their situation, so the reality of growing old did not dampen their basic optimism.

Americans overwhelmingly doubt that the elderly can be happy: one national survey found that only about 1 percent of Americans under sixty-five thought that elderly people could yet experience the best years of their lives (Harris, 1976). Certainly some elderly people share this view, but most have a much more positive outlook. Neugarten's research indicates that, whatever the personal adjustments required, growing old is not the singularly unpleasant experience it is made out to be in familiar stereotypes. The experience of growing old is highly variable, and people who have adapted successfully to changes earlier in life are usually satisfied with themselves later on (Palmore, 1979a).

This fact is all the more significant when we consider that growing old often presents people with major challenges, as we shall now describe.

Social Isolation

Being alone is a common source of anxiety to people of all ages; most Americans consider social isolation to be an especially serious problem among the elderly (Harris, 1976). The extent of social isolation is actually less than we might assume; still, most elderly people must adjust to more social isolation than they were used to earlier in life. Retirement closes off one source of social activity, physical problems may limit opportunities to be out and about, and American society does not generally favor elderly people living with their adult children. Our cultural emphasis on the new and improved also encourages negative stereotypes of the elderly as senile and "over the hill," serving to discourage young people from maintaining social contact with old people.

But probably the most important factor that creates a sense of social isolation among the elderly is the death of important peers. And few human experiences generate as much stress, frustration, and loneliness as the death of a spouse. The widowed elderly must adjust to the loss of a person with whom, in many cases, they spent most of their adult lives. The difficulties of adjusting to this loss are suggested by the fact that some surviving spouses choose not to live at all: one study of elderly men noted a sharp increase in the incidence of death, sometimes by suicide, in the six-month period following the death of their wives (Benjamin & Wallis, 1963).

Social isolation is more common among elderly women in the United States (Uhlenberg, 1979). This is because women usually live longer than men, and they are also typically younger than their husbands to begin with. Table 13–1 shows that in 1985 three-fourths of elderly men lived with their spouses, twice the proportion of elderly women that did so. Almost 40 percent of elderly women were living alone, compared to about 14 percent of elderly men. This is one important reason that mental health is generally not as good among elderly women as among elderly men in North America (Chappell & Havens, 1980).

Table 13–1	LIVING ARRANGEMENTS OF THE ELDERLY, 1985	
	Males	Females
Living alone	14.4%	39.6%
Living with spouse	74.0	36.9
Living with other relatives	7.4	17.8
Living with nonrelatives	2.9	2.0
Living in nursing home	1.3	3.7

SOURCE: Calculations by the author, based on data from the U.S. Bureau of the Census.

At the same time, even those who are living alone often continue to receive social support from their families. Although only a small percentage of elderly Americans live with their adult children, Ethel Shanas (1979) found that more than half of all elderly people in her research lived within a ten-minute travel time of at least one child, and over three-fourths claimed that they had seen at least one of their children during the preceding week. Only 10 percent said they had not seen a child within the past month. To many elderly people accustomed to considerable social activity, loneliness may be a problem. But the family can serve to lessen social isolation.

Elderly women typically outlive their husbands, which is likely to be stressful. This may produce social isolation, but it also provides opportunities to forge new social ties and engage in new activities.

Retirement

For most Americans, identity is based largely on occupation. Thus retirement from paid work can spark an identity crisis, involving the loss of income and social prestige, and also a major element of self (Chown, 1977). At the extreme, retirement can render life virtually meaningless. Margaret Clark, for example, interviewed one retired man who talked about his life in the past tense: "I was a waiter *in my life*" (1972:134).

Retirement is almost always accompanied by a loss of social prestige. Some organizations make deliberate efforts to ease this transition. Colleges and universities, for instance, often confer the title of "professor emeritus" on retired faculty members. Those holding this status are typically permitted to use college libraries, are given parking privileges and mail service, are allowed to attend faculty meetings, and sometimes are even provided with office space so that they may continue their research.

For other people, new activities minimize the personal disruption caused by retirement and provide a continuing source of social prestige (Rose, 1968). Participation in various voluntary organizations is common among the elderly. One such organization is the American Association of Retired People (AARP), which has over 15 million members past the age of fifty. There are more than three thousand local chapters across the United States, each providing a range of recreational activities and supporting political action that benefits elderly Americans.

Although an accepted fact of life in the United States today, retirement actually became common in industrial societies only during the last century (Atchley, 1982). In contrast, people in preindustrial societies usually work until they are incapacitated or simply choose not to. But advancing technology has reduced the need for workers and placed a premium on up-to-date skills. Retirement permits younger workers, presumably with the latest knowledge and training, to predominate in the labor force.

Currently, sixty-five is widely viewed as the proper age for retirement in the United States. This is somewhat arbitrary, of course; Japan, for example, has linked retirement to the age of fifty-five, although most Japanese work longer (Kii, 1979; Palmore, 1982). Given the vast differences in the interests and capacities of older people, an important and controversial issue is whether a society should formally recognize *any* specific age as the point of retirement. For example, in 1988, Ronald Reagan, who was seventy-seven, became the oldest person to ever serve as president of the United States. Politics may be an unusual case; Americans have often elected older people to high office. But if we entrust national leadership to a man in his late seventies, should we consider someone that age too old for other productive work?

In the 1960s, most workers were forced to retire at sixty-five. This policy of **mandatory retirement**—*formal regulations requiring people to retire from their occupational work at a specified age*—was a consequence of legislation and pension programs that had increased the financial security of retired Americans. During the 1970s, however, Congress curtailed mandatory retirement: policies that require retirement before the age of seventy cannot be adopted by companies that employ twenty or more workers, and most federal employees are now exempt from mandatory retirement. In 1987, Congress acted to eliminate mandatory retirement entirely, subject to approval by a majority of the states. This position has sparked considerable controversy, as the box explains.

Retirement in the United States has traditionally been far more common among men than among women. As noted in Chapter 12, only within the last decade have a majority of women been in the labor force. Elderly women who have spent their lives as homemakers have no precise point of retirement, although perhaps the departure of the last child from home may serve as a rough parallel. Even lifelong homemakers, however, must adjust to their husband's retirement and presence in the home, which has been called the "husband underfoot syndrome" (Mitchell, 1972). But if women must adjust to their husbands' retirement, they may also enjoy helping their husbands become engaged in new activities (Keating & Cole, 1980). As the proportion of women in the labor force continues to rise, however, retirement will increasingly be an issue of great concern to both sexes.

Limited Economic Resources

For most Americans, retirement results in a significant decline in income. At the same time, many elderly people face increasing expenses for medical care, household help, and upkeep and utilities for aging homes. Only a small proportion of elderly Americans have significant savings or pension plans; most depend on Social Security (C.E.D., 1981). As a result, the likelihood of living in poverty jumps considerably at the age of sixty-five. Figure

13–2 shows the proportion of all Americans living in poverty in 1986 by age. As noted in Chapter 10, children are the most likely of all age categories to be poor, and the incidence of poverty declines with age. The elderly, however, represent a reversal of this general pattern.

Still, the proportion of poor elderly people has declined from about 35 percent in 1960 to 12.4 percent in 1986 (U.S. Bureau of the Census, 1970, 1987). The decline is due mostly to improved pension benefits won by many workers and to increases in Social Security benefits.

Elderly Americans are not a socially homogeneous category of people: members of racial and ethnic minority groups are the most economically disadvantaged elderly Americans. For example, in 1986, the poverty rate among elderly Hispanics (22.5 percent) was twice the rate for elderly whites (10.7 percent); elderly blacks (31.0 percent) are even more likely to be poor.

The significant difference in income between American males and females continues into old age. In 1986, men aged sixty-five and over who were working

Figure 13–2 Poverty Across the Life Cycle, 1986

(U.S. Bureau of the Census)

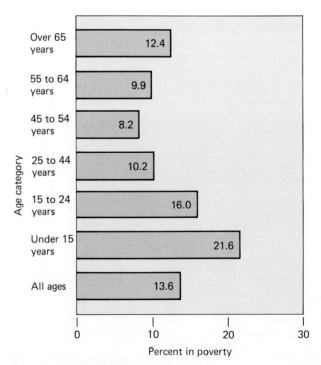

SOCIAL POLICY

Mandatory Retirement

During this century, legislation and pension programs created to increase financial security after retirement from the labor force often specified the age of retirement as sixty-five. By the 1960s, most workers were subject to rigid mandatory retirement regulations. Subsequent legislation has greatly curtailed mandatory retirement policies, but this issue has been hotly debated in the 1980s.

Proponents of mandatory retirement point to the policy's advantages. First, since the performance of at least some older workers can be expected to decline, linking retirement to a specific age protects an organization from less competent employees. Note that if all workers of a given age retire together, being forced to retire causes little loss of face. And in some occupations, mandatory retirement may be crucial to public safety: pilots for major commercial airlines, for example, are required to retire at the age of sixty; similarly, police in New York City must retire at sixty-three. Second, absent a fixed retirement age, employers must evaluate the performance of all older employees—a time-consuming and extremely expensive procedure. Moreover, older workers could reasonably demand that such evaluations be applied to workers of *all* ages. Third, any performance evaluations are subject to abuse. Minority group members, for example, could be removed from jobs with the allegation that they were simply not measuring up. A single age-based retirement policy has the benefit of treating all workers in a uniform manner. Fourth, since the training and skills required in many jobs change fairly rapidly in industrial societies, mandatory retirement policies help to speed the replacement of older workers (many, presumably, with outdated skills) by younger workers who are (again, presumably) more appropriately trained. Fifth and finally, mandatory retirement policies allow all workers to know when they will retire so they can plan accordingly; in other words, such programs have the benefit of making retirement a predictable event.

Opponents of mandatory retirement policies present opposing arguments. First, as a condition of age rather than individual performance, mandatory retirement categorically discriminates against an entire segment of the labor force. Such discrimination is just as unethical as denying blacks, women, or any other category of people the opportunity to work. Second, a number of studies suggest that older workers actually perform very well in relation to younger workers (Harris, 1976; Dunlop, 1983). In Japan, for example, the proportion of elderly people in the labor force (almost 50 percent) is twice that of the United States, underlining the productive potential of older workers (Atchley, 1982). Thus, forcing older workers to retire is a waste of human resources. Third, retirement creates many problems for elderly people: financial hardship as well as the loss of prestige and social identity. Allowing the elderly to continue working if they wish to do so increases their financial security (reducing the need for social welfare programs) and also their personal satisfaction. Fourth, mandatory retirement policies treat all older people alike, despite the fact that the elderly are an extremely variable category of people. It would be more reasonable, opponents claim, to let individuals decide for themselves when to retire on the basis of their own health, financial situation, and interests. Fifth and finally, mandatory retirement policies are especially harmful to women in the labor force, many of whom began working later in life. Being forced to retire at age sixty-five greatly reduces women's career opportunities as well as their ability to build up retirement benefits through pension programs.

Since many workers wish to retire by the age of sixty-five, the proportion of workers affected by mandatory retirement policies is not large. Nonetheless, the valve of a retirement policy that recognizes the legitimate concerns of employers and the differing needs and abilities of older workers, is obvious.

full-time had a median income of $27,326. In contrast, the median income of elderly women working full-time was $17,180. This indicates that elderly females who work full-time earn about 63 percent as much as their male counterparts, a disparity slightly greater than that noted in Chapter 12 (65 percent) for all workers. Table 13–2 also provides the median income for all elderly men and women, whether working or not. Counted here is all income, including wages and salaries (for workers), Social Security, pensions, and income from any investments. Since nonworking people are included, income figures are lower: $11,544 for men and $6,425 for women. Comparing these numbers shows that the income of all elderly women is only about 56 percent that of all elderly men. This means that economic disadvantages faced by women increase somewhat in old age.

In general, then, growing old increases the likelihood of being poor for all Americans, but especially for minority groups such as Hispanics, blacks, and all women.

The poverty of the elderly is sometimes hard to perceive. Pride and a desire for the dignity of independent living lead many elderly people to hide financial problems even from their own families. It is often difficult for people who have provided for themselves for years to admit that they can no longer do so, even though it is usually no fault of their own. Furthermore, as already noted, some elderly people become socially isolated, confined to their homes by physical limitations and fear of violence on the streets. For these reasons, elderly Americans may suffer economic disadvantages very privately. The elderly poor in rural areas are often among the most socially isolated people in the United States.

Growing old is often accompanied by a decrease in income. The elderly poor, however, are people likely to have been poor throughout their lives—namely, women and minorities.

Abuse of the Elderly

During the 1980s, Americans have become increasingly aware of violence within the family: sexual abuse of children, physical assaults on women, and also abuse of the elderly. Abuse of older people can take many forms, including passive neglect, verbal and emotional abuse, financial exploitation, and even physical assault. As with all forms of family violence, the extent of this practice is difficult to determine. Government studies, however, estimate that more than 1 million elderly Americans—about 4 percent—are abused every year, and that one in ten of the elderly are victimized at some time (Clark, 1986). More disturbing still is the conclusion that the incidence of abuse has increased since the beginning of the decade (cited in Bruno, 1985:75).

Studying this problem is understandably difficult because many elderly people are reluctant to talk about their victimization. Although the causes of elderly abuse

Table 13–2	EARNINGS AND TOTAL INCOME OF ELDERLY MEN AND WOMEN, 1986	
	Median Annual Income from Full-time Work (workers only)	Median Total Income for All Elderly (working and nonworking)
Males, 65 and over	$27,326	$11,544
Female, 65 and over	$17,180	$ 6,425

SOURCE: U.S. Bureau of the Census.

are complex, one important fact is that more and more American adults face the responsibility—financial as well as emotional—of caring for elderly parents. This is especially difficult since both male and female adults typically are in the labor force. The reality of one or two aging parents can mean a tremendous commitment of time and energy or the financial burden of $25,000 or more annually for nursing-home care. Little wonder, that even in Japan—where caring for aging parents at home is traditional—more and more adult children find that they simply can't cope with the problem (Yates, 1986). Abuse appears to be most common in families with a very old parent suffering from serious health problems. The children are faced with long-term demands that they cannot easily meet, despite their good intentions (Douglass, 1983; Gelman, 1985).

In sum, only some of the problems and transitions of growing old are caused by physical decline. Problems of social isolation, adjustment to retirement, limited economic resources, and abuse from family members are really *social* problems. The next section of the chapter suggests why society shapes the lives of the elderly in this way.

THEORETICAL ANALYSIS OF AGING

Various theories explain the experiences of elderly people in American society. They have been developed from the major theoretical paradigms in sociology that have been used in other chapters.

Disengagement Theory

Disengagement theory *relates the disengagement of elderly people from positions of social responsibility to the orderly operation of society.* Disengagement theory was an early attempt to explain how and why society defined the elderly differently from younger people. Making use of the ideas of Talcott Parsons—the most influential architect of the structural-functional paradigm—Elaine Cumming and William Henry (1961) based disengagement theory on the biological reality of human decline and eventual death. Society must devise some means to persist, they reasoned, even though it ultimately loses each of its individual members. This is accomplished

by the orderly transfer of various statuses and roles from elderly people to those who are younger. In this way, patterns of status and role remain largely stable, although the people holding the statuses and roles change over time. If incompetence or death were the only basis for this changing of the guard, there would be considerable social disruption because many jobs would be left vacant. Thus industrial societies arrange for statuses and roles to be transferred to younger people while older people are still functioning productively.

Disengagement theory also states that this process benefits elderly people themselves. As people's physical capacities diminish, they presumably welcome relinquishing some of the pressures of performing occupational tasks. Furthermore, elderly people enjoy greater freedom of behavior; they are usually not expected to abide as rigidly by cultural norms as they were in middle age. Thus we are likely to define unusual behavior on the part of older people as harmless eccentricity rather than as a socially dangerous form of deviance. Disengagement also provides the opportunity—health and finances permitting, of course—for the elderly to engage in personally satisfying activities of their own choosing (Palmore, 1979b).

This need for old people to disengage from society applies primarily to industrial societies. Because of rapid social change, the continuous replacement of older workers by younger workers functions to keep the skills and training of workers as up-to-date as possible. In preindustrial societies, as noted earlier, social change is far slower, so the elderly are defined as wise rather than as obsolete. Of course, preindustrial societies are also less productive and must rely on the work of all their members. Thus in preindustrial societies, the elderly do not typically disengage from social life as much as they do in industrial societies.

Evaluation. Disengagement theory provides one explanation of an important pattern in American society: defining elderly people as socially marginal. But this approach can be criticized for ignoring the fact that many elderly people do not wish to disengage. As we have noted, for many old people, growing old is associated with numerous problems—including loss of social prestige, social isolation, and limited economic resources. Furthermore, social norms that encourage disengagement do not reflect the fact that the elderly differ widely in terms of their ability and interest in continuing to be productive members of society.

Activity Theory

Activity theory (sometimes called *substitution theory*) *relates a high level of social activity to personal satisfaction in old age.* Developed largely in reaction to disengagement theory, activity theory draws heavily on the social-interaction paradigm (Friedman & Havighurst, 1954). This approach stresses that individuals build a sense of self and a social identity based on their statuses and roles in society. Consequently, old age characterized by disengagement may produce little satisfaction in many elderly people.

Cultural norms may encourage old people to disengage from society, but activity theory suggests that the elderly will usually try to remain socially active by substituting new activities for those they lose. The implication is that elderly people do not differ in any significant way from younger adults; they evaluate themselves according to the same cultural norms. American culture has traditionally emphasized the value of being productive. Therefore, the elderly are likely to find the absence of activity and responsibility just as unsatisfying as a younger adult would. Of course, some elderly people welcome some degree of disengagement. Therefore, activity theory suggests that old age must be viewed as a highly variable stage of life, reflecting the distinctive needs, interests, and physical abilities of particular individuals.

Research in support of activity theory has indeed found that personal satisfaction in old age is related to a person's level of activity (Havighurst, Neugarten, & Tobin, 1968; Neugarten, 1977; Palmore, 1979a). In general, this research indicates that old people who maintain high activity levels are the most satisfied with their lives. But this research also stresses the extent of individual variability: not everyone seeks the same level of social activity in old age, and for a relatively small proportion of elderly people, inactivity brings the greatest happiness.

Evaluation. Activity theory is an important response to disengagement theory because it focuses attention on the elderly themselves rather than on the needs of society. But this approach can be criticized for providing little understanding of how elderly people can remain active when this may cause problems for others. Furthermore, those elderly who suffer from severe disabilities or are poor may be unable to maintain high levels of social activity. But activity theory's assertion that the elderly generally do find greater personal satisfaction in leading active lives appears to be well supported.

Social-Conflict Analysis

The social-conflict approach emphasizes the importance of age stratification by which older and younger people compete for resources in society. As noted earlier, Americans in their middle years enjoy the greatest social privileges, while the elderly are typically subjected to various social disadvantages (Phillipson, 1982). Would the elderly be as willing to disengage from society as disengagement theory suggests if younger people were unable to force them out to pasture?

The social-conflict approach, derived from the ideas of Karl Marx, offers many helpful insights into the social standing of the elderly in industrial-capitalist societies such as the United States. Recall, for example, the theory of deviance developed by Steven Spitzer (1980), which was presented in Chapter 8. Spitzer argued that since a capitalist society is based on the pursuit of individual profits, the people whose activities are most economically productive are the most highly valued. Conversely, people who either cannot or choose not to be economically productive are likely to be defined as members of socially deviant problem populations. Spitzer characterizes those who have the potential to actively challenge the capitalist system (such as unemployed minority-group members or political radicals) as *social dynamite*. Those who also make little productive contribution but pose no political threat to capitalism he describes as *social junk*. The elderly are members of the latter category. In other words, capitalist societies tend to define human value in terms of what people *do* (as producers), rather than in terms of what they *are* (as human beings). Elderly people are socially devalued as nonproducers, but not feared because they are nonthreatening (Spitzer, 1980; Phillipson, 1982).

Furthermore, the belief that elderly people are less productive workers, but costly because their salaries and wages are typically higher than those of younger counterparts, makes them undesirable from an employer's point of view. Since younger workers are readily available, employers have historically sought to replace the elderly with these less costly workers (Atchley, 1982).

Social-conflict analysis also stresses the importance of social stratification *within* the elderly population. Social class, race, ethnicity, and sex are the basis of social inequality among the elderly as well as within society as a whole. Elderly people in the higher social classes enjoy far more social advantages than other elderly Americans: they have more economic security, better medical care, and greater options for personally satisfying activity in later life. As noted in Chapter 11, elderly members of racial and ethnic minority groups typically have fewer social choices than do elderly WASPs. Women—who become an increasing majority of the elderly with advancing age—continue to suffer the social disadvantages of sexism. Like females at all stages of life, elderly women have fewer financial resources than their male counterparts.

Evaluation. The most important contributions of social-conflict analysis are pointing out patterns of age stratification, and the importance capitalist societies attach to being occupationally productive. An additional strength is emphasizing that some categories of the elderly (those in minority groups) are especially likely to be socially disadvantaged. This approach may be criticized, however, for implying that the elderly fare better in non-capitalist societies. There is some evidence to support this view (Treas, 1979), but certainly industrialization itself is largely responsible for the relatively low social standing of elderly people.

AGEISM

Earlier chapters explained the importance of *ideology* in justifying social inequality. Sociologists have coined the term **ageism** to refer to *the belief that one age category is superior or inferior to another.* In industrial societies, ageism tends to favor young adults and middle-aged people, while subjecting both the very young and very old to social disadvantages.

Like racism and sexism, ageism bases negative beliefs about categories of people on highly visible physical characteristics. As innately inferior, they deserve their social inferiority. Such people are expected to remain in their place and to allow others to make decisions that affect their lives. Thus ageism uses the alleged immaturity of adolescents and the senility of elderly people to justify denying them full human rights and social dignity. Contending that old people are not capable of being fully independent, younger people subject them to condescension, often talking down to them as if they were children (Kalish, 1979).

Familiar negative stereotypes portray the elderly as helpless, confused, resistant to change, and generally unhappy (Butler, 1975). More subtle expressions of ageism include intended compliments—such as "My, but you certainly don't look your age!"—which implies that most elderly people fall short of standards of appearance that are based on youth, yet applied to everyone. Even supposedly positive stereotypes of the elderly are sometimes subtle denials of the full range of their humanity. Sentimental views of little old ladies and gentlemen as charmingly eccentric ignore the fact that the aged are complex individuals with distinct personalities and long years of experience and accomplishment.

Like many forms of prejudice, ageism may have some foundation in fact. Certainly there are some old people (as there are young people) who are mentally impaired, overly dependent, dirty, or practically anything else. But ageism makes unwarranted generalizations about an entire category of people, most of whom do not conform to the stereotypes. As indicated earlier in this chapter, most elderly people do not suffer from severe physical or mental disabilities, and in most crucial respects are very much like everyone else. Research has shown, for example, that elderly people in good health can and do enjoy satisfying sexual relationships. Some younger people find this fact surprising, even grotesque, since stereotypes suggest that anyone with gray hair and wrinkles is devoid of sex appeal.

As we found in the discussion of sexism in Chapter 12, the mass media play a part in perpetuating negative stereotypes. In this case, the most widespread criticism is that elderly men—and especially elderly women—have long been excluded from mass media presentations. Moreover, studies indicate that while negative stereotyping of the elderly is not as extensive as in the case of women, television and the print media have contributed to ageism in American society (Kubey, 1980; Buchholz & Bynum, 1982). In the last few years, television has

Television is beginning to reflect the fact that the viewing audience—target of the TV ads—is becoming older. Programs such as "Golden Girls" are likely to be more common in the future.

Claude Pepper: Champion of the Elderly

Most Americans probably reach a career peak by their fifties, but Claude Pepper—eighty-eight years of age and still going strong—has never enjoyed so much power and influence. At ten, Pepper knew he was going to be a senator; he succeeded in winning a place in the Senate for fourteen years, then spent another twenty as a member of the House of Representatives. He has always made programs for people the center of his agenda, and no one in America speaks more forcefully—or acts more effectively—on behalf of the elderly.

An elderly woman spots Pepper on a Miami sidewalk and throws her arms around his neck. "I just want to thank you," she says, "for what you are doing for us."

Claude Pepper has done quite a bit for the less advantaged. He was a major force behind the first minimum wage law in American history, and helped to establish the World Health Organization in the 1940s. But nothing is as important to him as legislation addressing the needs of the elderly. "They deserve much," he asserts bluntly, "and need much. I am helping them."

As a state official in Florida early in his career, Pepper sponsored a bill to allow anyone over the age of sixty-five to fish without a license. More recently, federal legislation that greatly limited mandatory retirement regulations was largely his doing. "The only mandatory retirement," he claims, "is when you can't do the work anymore."

Claude Pepper has learned first-hand the difficulties of growing old. After his parents were all but ruined by the Great Depression of the 1930s, he took them into his own home. They remained until his father's death in 1945. At her death in 1961, his mothers was eighty-four. Pepper also lost his wife to cancer in 1979. He has health problems of his own: he wears trifocal glasses and is almost deaf without two hearing aids; one of his heart valves is synthetic, and he wears a pacemaker in his chest to regulate his heartbeat.

But none of this has interfered with his level of activity, which often involves eighteen-hour days. Indeed, he remains one of the most popular and influential members of Congress. He is as alert and articulate as ever, rarely using notes when he delivers powerful speeches against ageism, which he considers no less harmful than sexism and racism. He believes that the circumstances of the elderly in the United States have improved during his lifetime, and is convinced that as the elderly population steadily increases, the problems of growing old will command more and more attention.

What about his own plans? Claude Pepper concedes that he will someday retire, and even states, "I've set the year." Then, waiting long enough to pique his listener's curiosity, he adds through his smile, "The year 2000. But I reserve the right to change my mind."

SOURCE: Based on Ed Magnuson, "Champion of the Elderly," *Time*, Vol. 121, No. 117 (April 25, 1983): 21–23, 26, 29.

included more and more elderly people—some portrayed in very positive terms—which no doubt means that networks recognize the elderly as a rapidly growing segment of the audience. People aged fifty and over are now estimated to buy more than 40 percent of all consumer goods, a fact that has surely not escaped the attention of television advertisers (Hoyt, 1985).

Perhaps, as some research suggests, negative stereotypes about the elderly are declining. One reason could be that Americans are not as preoccupied with work as they were in the past, and so are less likely to devalue elderly people as nonproductive. A more important reason is the fact that the number of elderly people in American society is rapidly growing, and most of the elderly have a positive view of themselves. Surely, this represents a powerful force that can be expected to undermine negative stereotypes (Tibbitts, 1979).

Another important reason for the decline in negative stereotypes is that, like other socially disadvantaged categories of people, the elderly themselves have actively sought to improve their position in American society. Probably the major national figure in what has become known as the Gray Power movement is Claude Pepper, who has spent most of the last forty years as a member of Congress from Florida representing the interests of elderly people across the United States. Pepper is a living example of the fact that the elderly are capable of making a contribution to American society: in 1988, he was the oldest member of Congress at the age of eighty-eight. The box on p. 360 provides a closer look at this "champion of the elderly."

Activism among the elderly is not limited to a few people in high office. As noted earlier, the millions of older Americans in the American Association of Retired Persons are a strong political force opposing ageism. The Gray Panthers, founded by Maggie Kuhn in 1972, have also been a highly visible political force. This organization and its founder are described in the box below.

Are the Elderly a Minority Group?

This chapter has shown that, as a category of Americans, the elderly do face social disadvantages. But sociologists differ as to whether old people should be called a minority group in the same way as, say, blacks, Hispanics, or

---

PROFILE

Maggie Kuhn: Leader of the Gray Panthers

Alex Comfort, a physician-writer interested in the process of growing old, once suggested that no medicine could help old people more than a change in the negative ways in which Americans view old age. This observation is the basis of the work of Maggie Kuhn, one of the foremost advocates of change in our cultural attitudes toward the elderly. After many years of working as a church administrator, Kuhn concluded that the church—like many other institu-

tions in American society—did not positively address the elderly's needs and potentials. Many religious organizations, she found, maintain a policy of mandatory retirement and support rest homes in which the elderly lead unproductive lives. Her response, in 1972, was to form the Gray Panthers, an organization of both older and younger adults with the goal of creating change.

Kuhn's approach to the problems of growing old in America can be described as militant. She recognizes that the view of the elderly as having little value is deeply rooted in our way of life and that efforts to create change will be met with resistance. She maintains that our conventional views about the elderly are harmful, not only to the elderly themselves, but also to society as a whole. Ageism in all forms undermines the self-confidence of those growing old, encouraging them to withdraw from society into lives that lack purpose. In the process, society loses one of its greatest resources: people who have a lifetime

of wisdom and experience to offer their fellow citizens. Kuhn is waging a campaign to reinstate the historical view of the elderly as societal elders who can perhaps make their greatest social contribution in the later years of life.

More specifically, the Gray Panthers have strongly opposed the policy of mandatory retirement, as well as physical and social segregation of even a small proportion of the elderly in rest homes. The Gray Panthers also oppose, as a type of age segregation, retirement communities in which private homes are restricted to the elderly. Adequate medical care for the elderly is another important item on the Gray Panther agenda.

The overriding goal of the Gray Panthers, however, is to encourage Americans to consider old age—in Maggie Kuhn's words—not as "a defeat, but a victory; not a punishment, but a privilege."

SOURCE: Based on Dieter Hessel, ed., *Maggie Kuhn on Aging* (Philadelphia: The Westminster Press, 1977).

women. Briefly outlining this debate will show the similarities and the differences between the elderly and other categories of people that earlier chapters termed minority groups.

Almost three decades ago, Leonard Breen (1960) asserted that the elderly are a minority group. He noted that they have a clear social identity based on the ascribed status of being old, and that they are typically subject to prejudice and discrimination. In addition, as we have already noted, the elderly are often socially isolated, denied equal opportunity for jobs, and are more likely than middle-aged Americans to be poor (Eitzen, 1980; Levin & Levin, 1980; Barrow & Smith, 1983).

Other sociologists, however, are not convinced that the elderly qualify as a minority group because they differ in some important respects from women and racial and ethnic minorities. Gordon Streib (1968) points out that membership in minority groups is usually both permanent and exclusive. To illustrate, a person is black, Hispanic, or female throughout the life cycle, and this status precludes being part of the dominant category of white males. Being elderly, however, is an open status because people are elderly for only part of their lives and everyone who has the good fortune to live long enough grows old.

This means that the elderly are a highly heterogeneous category of people including males and females, people of different races and ethnicities, and members of all social classes. In other words, they are not likely to think of themselves primarily as old people. On the contrary, while being aware of their age, the elderly commonly think of themselves in terms of their sex, race, ethnicity, and social class. Females, of course, are also members of various races, ethnicities, and social classes, which is one reason many women do not think of themselves as belonging to a minority group.

Streib also claims that the social disadvantages faced by the elderly are not as substantial as those experienced by the categories of people we described as minority groups in earlier chapters. For example, the elderly have never been deprived of the right to own property, to vote, or to hold office, as blacks and women have been. In fact, older men—and to a much smaller extent, older women—exercise considerable political control over American society. Streib adds that some elderly people suffer from economic disadvantages, but this is not primarily a result of old age. Rather, most of the elderly poor are women and members of racial and ethnic minorities, who are more likely to be poor *at any age*. Streib believes, in short, that "the poor grow old" rather than "the old grow poor," although advancing age in itself does increase the likelihood of poverty to some extent (Butler, 1975).

Taking a moderate position in this debate, Arnold Rose (1968) suggests that the way of life of the elderly should be considered a *subculture* since old people are a socially distinctive category who do not meet the more demanding criteria of a minority group. Rose argues that subcultures are typically built on two foundations: an affinity of interests that leads people to interact with one another and a tendency to be excluded from many other social settings. The elderly have numerous physical and social experiences in common; they are also what sociologists call an *age cohort*—people of roughly the same generation who have lived through much the same period of history and whose lives have been shaped by many of the same historical events and social changes. But Rose also claims that other factors actively link the elderly to the rest of society—such as family and neighborhood relationships and continuing participation in the labor force—reducing the social distance between the generations.

Another alternative would be to emphasize the great diversity of the elderly. Because growing old is an experience of all categories of Americans, an enormous range of social variation is found among the elderly. Perhaps, therefore, the elderly should simply be considered a *segment* of the American population.

DEATH AND DYING

To every thing there is a season,
And a time for every matter under heaven:
A time to be born and a time to die . . .

These well-known lines from the Book of Ecclesiastes in the Bible convey basic truths of human existence: the fact of birth and the inevitability of death. Yet, as much as life itself, death is subject to striking variation across human history. The final section of this chapter briefly examines the changing character of death—the final stage in the process of growing old.

Historical Patterns of Death

Throughout most of human history, death was a common element of most people's experience. In technologically primitive hunting and gathering societies, for example,

The centrality of death to medieval society in Europe is evident in much of the art of that period. This painting, "The Triumph of Death" by Pieter Brueghel, makes the point with chilling realism.

the fact of birth carried little assurance of remaining alive for very long; in many societies, uncertainty about the survival of newborns was so great that infants were not even named until they reached several years of age (Herty, 1960). Those who survived infancy became members of societies with a very low standard of living by contemporary measures, so that illness caused by poor nutrition, accidents, and natural catastrophes such as drought or famine combined to make life far less certain that it is in our society today.

As agricultural technology allowed societies to grow in size and establish permanent settlements, new life-threatening dangers served to keep death within the common experience of everyone. Herds of animals in close proximity to human settlements were a dangerous source of infectious diseases. In addition, cities growing in size and density had little effective means to dispose of human waste, with life-threatening unsanitary conditions the inevitable result. Until about the seventeenth century, rapidly spreading plagues and other transmittable diseases sometimes wiped out much of the population of entire cities. Finally, preindustrial societies were not nearly as productive as industrial societies. Therefore, when a population rose to the point where everyone's well-being was threatened, a common practice was to deliberately kill the least productive members of society. Most com-

monly, this meant engaging in *infanticide*—the killing of newborn infants—and *geronticide*—the killing of the elderly (Newman & Matzke, 1984).

As Chapter 19 explains in detail, the explosive urban growth caused by the Industrial Revolution initially increased death rates among people of all ages. By the beginning of the twentieth century, however, a rising standard of living coupled with advancing medical technology had all but eliminated many common causes of death throughout the life cycle.

During the Middle Ages, death was so common to the social experience of everyone that it was regarded as a natural and inevitable part of life. Beyond the fact that death could and did strike frequently and often without warning, strong religious beliefs defined death as simply one element in a divine plan for human existence. To illustrate, historian Philippe Ariès describes how Sir Lancelot, one of King Arthur's fearless Knights of the Round Table, made ready for his own death when he believed himself mortally wounded:

> His gestures were fixed by old customs, ritual gestures which must be carried out when one is about to die. He removed his weapons and lay quietly upon the ground. . . . He spread his arms out, his body forming a cross . . . in such a way that his head faced east toward Jerusalem. (1974:7–8)

As societies gradually gained the ability to control many causes of death, attitudes about death began to change. Death was no longer an everyday experience: children rarely died at birth, and accidents and disease killed far fewer younger adults. Except in times of war or other catastrophes, people came to see dying as something quite out of the ordinary, at least through most of the life cycle. The result, of course, was the linkage of death to old age. In 1900, about one-third of all deaths in the United States occurred before the age of five, another one-third occurred before the age of fifty-five, so that only one-third of Americans died in what was then defined as old age. By the mid-1970s, however, more than 80 percent of Americans died when they were past the age of fifty-five (Atchley, 1983).

The Modern Separation of Life and Death

As death has become less common to everyday experience, it has also come to be defined as unnatural. Religious beliefs that define both life and death as part of a divine plan have declined in importance in the modern world. Just as important, modern Americans have a strong faith in the ability of medical technology to overcome disease and even the physical deterioration of old age. If the conditions of their lives made our ancestors ready to accept their own deaths, modern society has fostered in us a desire for immortality. In this sense, then, death has become separated from life.

In addition, death and dying are now often physically removed from public life. The clearest evidence of this is the fact that many Americans have never seen a person die. While our ancestors typically died at home, the usual locations for death today are hospitals and, to a lesser extent, rest homes (Ariès, 1974). Even in hospitals, the process of dying is typically separated from the process of healing: dying patients are commonly segregated in a special part of the hospital, and hospital morgues are usually located well out of sight of patients and visitors alike (Sudnow, 1967). Finally, to the extent that the elderly are socially isolated from others in American society, death is further removed from the lives of most of the population.

The historical pattern of accepting death has now been largely replaced by one of fear and anxiety about dying. There is some evidence, however, that the fear of death is less pronounced in elderly people than in younger people. For some elderly people who suffer from severe and painful disabilities, death may not be feared at all, but welcomed as an end to suffering. More generally, however, the greater acceptance of death among the elderly reflects the fact that they are able to look back on many years of life and recognize that the future promises them relatively little. In addition, the elderly are typically socialized toward greater acceptance of death by the deaths of family members and peers (Kalish, 1976, cited in Atchley, 1983). Generally, however, Americans have a strong avoidance of death and commonly feel considerable discomfort even discussing the subject. This has unfortunate consequences for dying people, who feel socially isolated from friends and relatives who are unable to face up to the reality of their impending death. Furthermore, since few Americans die at home, hospital personnel—rather than family members and friends—often attend the dying.

Bereavement

Chapter 5 described the process by which people commonly become resigned to their own death. Elizabeth Kübler-Ross (1969) claims that people initially react with denial, but gradually become resigned to and finally accept their death. Adjustment to death, of course, rarely involves only the dying person; those who are especially close to that person are also faced with the need for adjustment. *Bereavement* refers to the experience of loss as the consequence of the death of another.

Some of the experiences of bereavement may parallel the stages of dying described by Kübler-Ross. Those close to a terminally ill patient, for example, may initially deny the reality of death, only gradually coming to the stage of acceptance. This is a significant parallel because the attitudes of those around them have an important effect on the adjustment of the dying person. In other words, people who are able to accept the impending death can help the dying person to do the same; in contrast, a dying person may have difficulty accepting death if surrounded by relatives and friends who deny the reality of the entire process.

One recent development intended to provide support to dying people is the *hospice*. Unlike a hospital, a hospice does not attempt to cure disease; rather, only people close to death are admitted to such a facility. The hospice provides medical care intended to minimize pain and suffering as much as possible and attempts to provide the dying person with dignity and comfort. Hospices also encourage family members to become involved with the dying person to prevent the social isolation

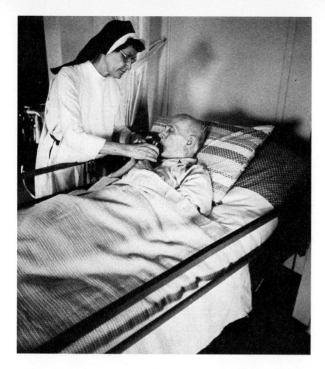

Hospices, a fairly recent innovation in medical care, attempt to provide physical comfort and emotional support to people who are dying. This New York hospice also helps family members face the impending death of a loved one.

that commonly accompanies terminal illness. Many patients die in the hospice; others wish to return home prior to death. The hospice staff helps to prepare dying people to die at home and family members to make this process as comfortable as possible (Stoddard, 1978).

People who understand and accept the death of a loved one are likely to experience less intense bereavement. Moreover, grief is lessened if survivors feel that their relationship with the dying person was completed. This means simply that they did not deny the inevitability of the death, and took whatever opportunity was available to speak with the dying person to provide a closure to their relationship. Family and friends who have done this are likely to be able to provide comfort and support to one another after the death of the loved one (Atchley, 1983).

But even under the most favorable circumstances, the experience of bereavement may persist for some time. In addition to profound grief, survivors typically experience social disorientation because the dead person was an important point of reference in their own lives. As suggested earlier, among the elderly—especially elderly women—the loss of a spouse is perhaps the most common and difficult bereavement.

In the future, we can expect that the rapidly increasing proportion of Americans over the age of sixty-five will cause changes in the way death is understood. As Americans gain greater experience in interacting with old people, it seems likely that death will cease to be the social taboo it has been through most of this century. The result may well be beneficial to young and old alike.

SUMMARY

1. From 4 percent in 1900, the elderly now represent more than 11 percent of American society and will be approaching 20 percent by the year 2030. This growing proportion of elderly people will have many significant consequences for American society.

2. Gerontology is the study of aging and the elderly. It is concerned with biological and psychological changes in old age, as well as with how aging is defined within a culture.

3. Growing old is accompanied by a greater frequency of disease and disability. However, the extent of disability among the elderly is commonly exaggerated by younger people.

4. Growing old does not result in overall loss of intelligence. Moreover, psychological research suggests that the personality changes little with advancing age.

5. The age at which people are defined as old has

varied historically: until several centuries ago, old age began at about thirty. In poorer societies of the world today, life expectancy is several decades less than in North America.

6. The elderly have a relatively high social ranking in agrarian societies. In industrial societies, however, they have a much lower social ranking.

7. A common problem of growing old is social isolation owing to such factors as retirement, physical disability, and the deaths of friends and often one's spouse. However, for most elderly people, family members provide considerable social support.

8. Retirement requires the elderly to make many adjustments. Although traditionally a problem faced primarily by men, the increasing participation of women in the labor force makes this a concern of both sexes.

9. Many elderly people must contend with limited eco-

nomic resources. Since 1960, however, poverty among the elderly has dropped significantly. Even so, elderly women and elderly members of other minority groups are especially likely to be poor.

10. Disengagement theory suggests that the elderly disengage from positions of social responsibility prior to the likely onset of disability and death. In this way, statuses and roles are transferred from the elderly to younger people in an orderly way.

11. Activity theory suggests that all people base their social identity on their statuses and roles. Thus people who maintain a high level of social activity are likely to experience greater personal satisfaction in old age.

12. Social-conflict analysis views patterns of age stratification as a reflection of the dominant position of middle-aged people. Further, the emphasis on economic productivity in capitalist societies results in devaluing those who are less productive, including the elderly.

13. Ageism refers to the belief that one age category is superior to another. Ageism serves to justify patterns of age stratification.

14. While some consider the elderly to be a minority group, the fact that the elderly represent both sexes and all races, ethnicities, and social classes suggests otherwise.

15. Historically, confronting death was a common experience. Today, however, the large majority of Americans who die are elderly. This has resulted in the separation of death from life, reflected in the segregation of dying people and the ordinary person's discomfort with the subject of death.

KEY CONCEPTS

activity theory (substitution theory) a theory that relates a high level of social activity to personal satisfaction in old age

ageism the belief that one age category is superior or inferior to another

age stratification the unequal distribution of wealth, power, and privileges among people of different ages

disengagement theory a theory that relates the disengagement of elderly people from positions of social responsibility to the orderly operation of society

gerontocracy a form of social organization in which the elderly have the most wealth, power, and privileges

gerontology the study of aging and the elderly

mandatory retirement formal regulations requiring people to retire from their occupational work at a specified age

SUGGESTED READINGS

These two advanced texts provide a fuller account of issues related to aging and the elderly.

Harold Cox. *Later Life: The Realities of Aging.* 2nd ed. Englewood Cliffs, NJ: Prentice-Hall, 1988.

Robert C. Atchley. *Aging: Continuity and Change.* 2nd ed. Belmont, CA: Wadsworth, 1987.

The human experience of growing old is vividly portrayed in this comparison of elderly communities in the United States and England. This book offers insights into how the transitions of aging can be made easier and even enjoyable.

Doris Francis. *Will You Still Need Me, Will You Still Feed Me, When I'm 84?* Bloomington, IN: Indiana University Press, 1984.

This book focuses on very old people, who are the fastest-growing segment of the elderly American population.

Ira Rosenwaike, with the assistance of Barbara Logue. *The Extreme Aged in America: A Portrait of an Expanding Population.* Westport, CT: Greenwood Press, 1985.

The government recognizes that the aging of the American population will have broad and powerful consequences. This Senate report examines the consequences of the graying of America with regard to issues such as the family, the economy, retirement, and health.

U.S. Senate Committee on Aging. *Aging America: Trends and Projections, 1985–86 Edition.* Washington, DC: U.S. Government Printing Office, 1986.

The first of these books is regarded as the "bible" for people facing the task of caring for someone with Alzheimer's disease or other dementing illnesses in which mental abilities are reduced. The second is a short congressional publication describing Alzheimer's disease and the government's response to this national problem.

Nancy L. Mace and Peter V. Rabins. *The 36-Hour Day: A Family Guide to Caring for Persons with Alzheimer's Disease, Related Dementing Illnesses, and Memory Loss in Later Life.* New York: Warner Books, 1984.

Congress of the United States. *Losing a Million Minds: Confronting the Tragedy of Alzheimer's Disease and Other Dementias.* Washington, DC: U.S. Government Printing Office, 1987.

These books take an applied approach to health-care problems for the elderly for those with an interest in this area of public policy.

Edgar F. Borgatta and Rhonda J. V. Montgomery. *Critical Issues on Aging Policy: Linking Research and Values.* Newbury Park, CA: Sage Publications, 1987.

Nancy N. Eustis, Jay N. Greenberg, and Sharon K. Patten. *Long-Term Care for Older Persons: A Policy Perspective.* Monterey, CA: Brooks/Cole, 1984.

Here is a new edition of a Pulitzer Prize winner that criticizes America's approach to aging and the elderly and provides extensive suggestions for reform.

Robert N. Butler. *Why Survive? Being Old in America.* New York: Harper and Row, 1985.

This historical study centered in Boston examines work, retirement, and various social problems among older people.

Brian Gratton. *Urban Elders: Family, Work, and Welfare Among Boston's Aged, 1890–1950.* Philadelphia: Temple University Press, 1986.

Social isolation is often a problem among the elderly. This book describes how patterns of friendship are distinctive among older people, but also emphasizes variation in relationships among older people.

Sarah H. Matthews. *Friendships Through the Life Course: Oral Biographies in Old Age.* Newbury Park, CA: Sage, 1986.

Can the elderly be considered a "leisure class"? This analysis of national survey data investigates volunteer work among older Americans.

Susan Maizel Chambré. *Good Deeds in Old Age: Volunteering by the New Leisure Class.* Lexington, MA: Lexington Books/D.C. Heath, 1987.

This book presents a social-conflict approach to the problems of the elderly.

Chris Phillipson. *Capitalism and the Construction of Old Age.* London: Macmillan, 1982.

All facets of death and dying are considered here, from the common death of pets to the uncommon death of children. There is also extensive coverage of the health-care profession, including the emerging hospice movement.

Jack B. Kamerman. *Death in the Midst of Life: Social and Cultural Influences on Death, Grief, and Mourning.* Englewood Cliffs, NJ: Prentice-Hall, 1988.

CHAPTER 14

Family

Louise and Ben Sprecher seem to have it made. Next to their spacious home in Beverly Hills, California, is a swimming pool in which their grandchildren often enjoy spending an afternoon. Tennis is another favorite pastime, and the Sprechers also enjoy ski vacations in Europe. Active enough as individuals to have separate telephones in their home, the Sprechers have been happily married for forty-three years.

Sarah Bentham was nine when her mother left their home in Toronto, Canada. Shortly afterward, her father invited another woman and her two children to move in. Sarah painfully recalls the shame she felt at the presence of this woman: "She's got a foul mouth and she was really awful to us kids. She'd curse us and she'd call us the most awful, terrible names. When she got drunk, she'd be even worse. She'd knock us down and kick us while she was screaming at us."

Brian Batey is a sixteen-year-old boy whose family life has revolved around the courts. His mother—an evangelical Christian—and his father—who is gay—divorced in 1976. Initially, custody of Brian was awarded to Betty Lou Batey. But, in 1982, a new court ruling specified that Brian would live with his father, Frank. Subsequently, his mother put Brian into hiding; after nineteen months, the boy surrendered himself. For this, the court imposed a fine and a short jail sentence on his mother. Courts then placed Brian in a foster home pending resolution of legal appeals by both parents. In 1986, Frank Batey, living in Palm Beach, California, with a male lover, finally won the long court

Brian Batey, whose turbulent family life is described here, is shown in one of the last photos taken with his father, Frank Batey (right), and Craig Corbett (left).

battle for Brian's custody. A year later, a court cleared Betty Lou Batey of any wrongdoing in the case. But Brian's plight soon intensified, when his father died from AIDS. Brian demanded to remain with Craig Corbett, his father's lover. Betty Lou Batey opposed this plan, however, so that Brian's future once again became a matter for the courts to decide.

The Ortega family lives in a modest neighborhood in New Orleans. Juan and Margarita, married for twelve years, have four children. A year ago, when they purchased their present house, Juan's widowed mother accepted an offer to join them. Since finding a new job in the area, one of Margarita's cousins is also staying with the Ortegas until he can locate a home of his own. The house has barely enough room for everyone, but the family enjoys sharing many daily activities.

Sixteen-year-old Lydia Brown lives in a poor neighborhood in Atlantic City, New Jersey. A year ago, she learned that she was pregnant, yet she had no desire to marry. After the birth of her son, Franklin, she became eligible for support from the county welfare department, which gave her the financial resources to move out of her mother's home. She has no regrets about the birth of her child: "Franklin is mine. He needs me and loves me. It makes me feel good to have this child, and I try to do the best I can for him."

These vignettes suggest the diversity of family life in America, a fact that has not always been recognized.[°] As recently as the early 1980s, a stereotype of the American family was widely supported by the mass media and even textbooks. This was the American Dream family, with a father who worked, a mother who was a housewife, and one or more well-scrubbed children. This family was portrayed as financially comfortable, living in a world with no hint of poverty, racial and ethnic diversity, or serious family problems. Men were the "natural" leaders and breadwinners, women the "natural" homemakers.

Today, more aware of social diversity and social inequality, Americans are less likely to assume that the family has one ideal form. The conventional family of working husband, housewife, and children still exists, of course, but represents only about one in ten house-

holds. In fact, no single set of characteristics can accurately describe today's American family. This chapter, then, will examine both the general traits of family forms and the ways in which families vary.

One point on which there is little disagreement is the importance of the family: in the United States and in every other society, the family is a major social institution. Recall from Chapter 4 that a *social institution* is a major structural part of society that addresses one or more of its basic needs. Other social institutions, including the educational system, the religious system, the political system, and the economic system, are discussed in subsequent chapters of this book. All social institutions have many important consequences—both positive and negative—for society as a whole.

Kinship: Basic Concepts

Kinship refers to *social relationships based on blood, marriage, or adoption.* In small preindustrial societies, people typically rely on all of their kin for a wide variety of needs. In industrial societies, however, people distinguish between *distant relatives*, among whom there is usually little social contact, and *close relatives*, who make up the social group commonly called the *family*.

Definitions of the family vary considerably around the world, but in basic terms, the **family** is *a social group of two or more people related by blood, marriage, or adoption who live together.* Family life tends to be cooperative; families are typically primary groups in which members share economic resources and day-to-day responsibilities. As Chapter 6 explained, the family is often the most important primary group in our lives. In industrial societies, people first live within a **family of orientation**—*the family into which a person is born, and which provides intensive early socialization.* Later in life, a person lives within a **family of procreation**—*a family within which people have or adopt children of their own.* In most societies of the world, families result primarily from **marriage,** which is *a socially approved relationship involving both economic cooperation and sexual activity.* As we shall see, patterns of marriage show striking variation around the world. At present in the United States, however, marriage can unite only one male and one female. The importance of marriage as the basis for procreation is evident in the traditional attachment of the label of *illegitimacy* to children born out of wedlock. However, this norm has weakened considerably in recent years.

[°] The description of the Sprecher family appears in Elias (1984); the Bentham family (the name and location are fictitious) is described in Rubin (1976:54); the Batey family is described in Peterson (1984), *The New York Times*, 1987, and various other news reports; the portrait of the Ortega family is fictitious; the description of the Brown family is based on facts presented in Russell (1984).

But even these few generalizations cannot be applied to all families in the United States today. For example, an unmarried couple and their children are likely to think of themselves as a family, although this pattern may provoke disapproval from some Americans. A divorced parent and a child separated by a court custody ruling also commonly view themselves as part of one family. Many gay male and lesbian couples, possibly living with the children of one or both partners, also consider themselves to be a family, although they cannot marry under current American laws. Sometimes communal groups of unrelated people who choose to live together for a period of time and share resources consider themselves a family.

THE FAMILY IN CROSS-CULTURAL PERSPECTIVE

Virtually all societies recognize families (Murdock, 1945). But families are universal only in the most general sense because there are important dimensions of cross-cultural variation.

As noted in earlier chapters, industrial societies recognize the **nuclear family**—composed of *one or, more commonly, two parents and children*. Because the nuclear family is typically based on marriage, it is also often called the *conjugal family*. In the preindustrial societies that contain most of the world's population, however, the common form is the **extended family,** which includes *parents, children, and other kin*. This is also called the *consanguine family*, meaning that it is based on blood ties. Extended families often include grandparents, aunts, uncles, and other kin.

Although extended families have always existed in the United States, the nuclear family has always been the predominant form in American society (Laslett, 1978; Degler, 1980). Nuclear families tend to become especially pronounced as industrialization progresses because productive work is located away from the home. Thus children typically grow up to leave families (of orientation); they move out to pursue careers and form new families (of procreation). Such geographical movement, as well as social mobility, makes extended families difficult to maintain.

Extended families have not vanished from American society, however. Some ethnic groups, including Hispanic Americans, continue to favor extended families. And about one in seven elderly people live with relatives other than a spouse, thereby forming extended families.

Marriage Patterns

Cultural norms regulate whom a person may marry. To varying degrees, many societies observe the norm of **endogamy**, or *marriage between people of the same*

In modern industrial societies such as Canada and the United States, members of extended families usually do not live together. However, they may assemble for family rituals such as weddings, funerals, or family reunions.

CROSS-CULTURAL COMPARISON

Polygyny Among the Mormons

In 1856, two converts to the Mormon religion, John Vance and Lucy Stone, were married in England. Four years later, they moved to Utah in the United States, the center of Mormon settlement. Ellen Johnson, a friend of Lucy's, accompanied them; a year later, she, too, married John Vance. In 1868, Vance took Susan Porter as his third wife. Vance divided his time among all his wives, spending a night with each one, but never retiring before he had kissed *all* his wives and children good night.

Founded in 1830 in New York State by Joseph Smith, the Church of Jesus Christ of Latter-Day Saints—or more simply, the Mormons—gradually moved west to escape the hostility generated by their unconventional religious beliefs. Of all Mormon doctrines, none drew more criticism than the practice of polygyny, which Mormons call *plural marriage*.

Although probably practiced a decade earlier, polygyny was officially sanctioned by the Mormons in 1852, when they settled in the Utah territory. The Mormons claimed that plural marriage was the will of God and a necessary step toward restoring true Christianity. They also pointed to biblical precedent: some ancient Hebrew men, including Abraham, David, Solomon, and Moses, had more than one wife. Moreover, noting that polygyny was widely endorsed by other cultures of the world, the Mormons maintained that it eliminated the evil of prostitution and reduced the chances that a husband would divorce a wife of many years in order to marry a younger and more attractive woman.

The expense of supporting many wives (and even more children) was high; for this reason, not many Mormon males could afford to practice polygyny. For those who could, however, plural marriages were often successful, although not without jealousy and conflict among a man's various wives.

Officially, the Mormon Church discontinued the practice of polygyny in 1890—one of the conditions demanded by the federal government for admitting Utah to the Union. Today, polygyny violates official church doctrine as well as state law, but estimates suggest that between ten thousand and thirty thousand people live within plural marriages—one legal marriage and others performed by a local church.

SOURCE: Based on Kimball Young, *Isn't One Wife Enough?* (New York: Henry Holt and Company, 1954); Gary L. Bunker and Davis Bitton, *The Mormon Graphic Image, 1834–1914* (Salt Lake City: University of Utah Press, 1983); and "Polygamy Spreading Despite Laws" (UPI news story), *Mt. Vernon News*, April 24, 1985, p. 20.

---

social group or category—that is, of the same tribe, race, religion, or social class. Other societies endorse the contrasting pattern of **exogamy**, *marriage between people of different social groups or categories*. Either pattern may be seen as beneficial. By uniting people of similar backgrounds, endogamy encourages group solidarity and helps to maintain traditional values and norms. On the other hand, exogamy may forge useful alliances with other groups and is likely to encourage cultural diffusion. Although exogamy is becoming more common in the United States, endogamous norms persist. For instance, only a tiny fraction of American marriages are racially mixed, and many religious groups continue to favor marriage to "one of our own."

In all industrial societies, both law and cultural norms prescribe a form of marriage called **monogamy**—*marriage that joins one female and one male*. Because of widespread divorce and remarriage, however, many

Americans actually engage in a pattern of *serial monogamy*, a series of monogamous marriages.

In preindustrial societies, a more common marital pattern is **polygamy**—*marriage that unites three or more people*. Polygamous marriage creates an extended family composed of two or more nuclear families linked by the person with more than one spouse. Polygamy takes two forms. By far the more common form is **polygyny**—*marriage that joins one male with more than one female*. Typically, a man must have considerable wealth in order to support several wives and children. In societies that endorse this marital pattern, therefore, few males actually have several wives, and those who do enjoy great social prestige (Ember & Ember, 1985). In the United States, polygyny is a violation of law, although, historically, followers of the Mormon religion have endorsed this practice, as the box explains. **Polyandry**—*marriage that joins one female with two or more males*—is extremely rare in the world, existing only in a few societies, apparently because of a shortage of women.

Worldwide, monogamy is the most common marital pattern. Although only about one-fourth of all societies consider this to be the *only* proper form of marriage, most societies endorse this pattern (Murdock, 1965). Even in Islamic nations, in which men may have up to four wives, the limited number of females means that most marriages are monogamous.

Residential Patterns

Societies of the world also differ in the way families typically establish a residence. In industrial societies, the predominant pattern is **neolocality** (meaning "new place")—*a residential pattern in which a married couple lives apart from the parents of both spouses.* While sometimes newlyweds live with the parents of one spouse, the American cultural norm appears to be "Honor thy mother and father—but get away from them" (Blumstein & Schwartz, 1983:26). In preindustrial societies, however, other residential patterns provide both economic security and mutual protection. **Patrilocality** (meaning "place of the father") is *a residential pattern in which a married couple lives with or near the husband's family.* This pattern is the most common around the world (Murdock, 1965). **Matrilocality** (meaning "place of the mother") is *a residential pattern in which a married couple lives with or near the wife's family.* This is a rare pattern limited to the few societies in which families define their daughters as more important economic assets than their sons (Ember & Ember, 1971, 1985).

Patterns of Descent

Descent refers to the way in which kinship is traced over generations, and provides the answer to the basic question: To whom am I related? Industrial societies recognize a pattern of **bilateral descent** (two-sided descent)—*a practice linking children in kinship to the families of both parents.*

In preindustrial societies, however, two other patterns of descent predominate. The more common is **patrilineal descent,** *the practice of tracing kinship only through males.* This means that the father's side of the family, but not the mother's, is defined as kin. In such cases, property is passed across the generations only to males. Less common is **matrilineal descent,** *the practice*

of tracing kinship only through females. Here, only the mother's side of the family is defined as kin, with property passing from mothers to daughters. In general, patrilineal descent is found in pastoral and agrarian societies in which males produce most valued resources. Similarly, in horticultural societies in which women are the primary breadwinners, matrilineal descent is common (Haviland, 1985:476).

Patterns of Authority

The marital patterns that predominate in the world—polygyny, patrilocality, and patrilineal descent—reflect the fact that all world societies are, to some varying degree, *patriarchal.* Wives and mothers have considerable power in many societies, but no society is known to be clearly matriarchal. In industrial societies such as the United States, males are usually the heads of households, just as they dominate most areas of social life. More egalitarian family patterns are gradually evolving, especially as more and more women enter the labor force. But the status of wife still has a lower social standing than that of husband, just as the children of unmarried women still contend with the stigma of being illegitimate. As noted in Chapter 12, most families still prefer male children, and most children are given their father's last name.

THEORETICAL ANALYSIS OF THE FAMILY

Following the pattern of earlier chapters, different theoretical approaches will be used to provide valuable insights about the family.

Functions of the Family

The structural-functional paradigm directs attention to several important social functions performed by the family. Taken together, they suggest why the family is sometimes described as the backbone of society.

Socialization

As explained in Chapter 5, the family is the first and most important agent in the socialization process. The personalities of each new generation are shaped within the family, so that, ideally, children grow to be well-integrated and contributing members of the larger society (Parsons & Bales, 1955). In industrial societies, of course, peer groups, schools, churches, and the mass media are also important in the socialization of children. But this remains the primary function of the family. The family also contributes to the continuing socialization of people throughout the life cycle. Adults learn and change within marriage, and as anyone with children knows, parents learn as much from their children as their children learn from them.

Regulation of Sexual Activity

Every culture places some restrictions on sexual behavior. Sexual intercourse is a personal matter to those involved, but as the basis of human reproduction and inheritance, it is also a matter of considerable social importance.

All societies enforce some type of **incest taboo,** meaning *cultural norms that forbid sexual relations or marriage between certain kin.* Exactly which kin are subject to the incest taboo is culturally variable. Most Americans consider sexual relations with a parent, grand-parent, sibling, aunt, or uncle to be both immoral and unnatural. But such sexual relations have been con-doned—or even encouraged—in some cultures. Brother-sister marriages, for example, were common among the ancient Egyptian, Inca, and Hawaiian nobility; and male nobles of the Azande in eastern Africa are reported to marry their daughters (Murdock, 1965). Some societies forbid sexual relations with cousins, while others do not; in our own society, Catholic religious beliefs prohibit marriage between first cousins, while Jewish religious beliefs do not (Murphy, 1979). Further, about as many states prohibit this practice as allow it. Therefore, the incest taboo may be universal, but it is also quite variable among societies.

The significance of the incest taboo is primarily social rather than biological. Contrary to common as-sumptions, sexual activity between close relatives does not, in itself, produce mental or physical abnormalities in offspring. As Robert Murphy (1979) points out, it is society, not nature, that punishes incest. Indeed, only human beings—who live within a world of culture rather than instinct—observe an incest taboo. Why? Primarily because the incest taboo serves to maintain family life. First, it minimizes sexual competition within families by restricting legitimate sexual access to spouses. Second, the incest taboo forces people to marry outside of their

immediate family. This results in alliances that provide political and economic advantages to some families, and strengthens social ties among all members of society.

Social Placement

From a biological point of view, of course, the family is not necessary for people to have children. Within families, however, children are born not only as biologi-cal beings, but also as *members of society.* Many important social statuses—including race, ethnicity, religion, and social class—are ascribed at birth through the family. This explains society's long-standing concern that chil-dren be born of socially sanctioned marriages. Legitimate birth, especially when parents are of similar social posi-tion, allows for the stable transmission of social standing from parents to children and clarifies inheritance rights.

Material and Emotional Security

In ideal terms, the family protects and supports its mem-bers physically, emotionally, and often financially from birth until death. The family is usually a person's most important primary group, and family members generally have intense and enduring relationships with one an-other. This concern for one another's welfare seems to engender an important sense of self-worth and security in each individual; indeed, people living in families tend to be healthier than those who live alone.

However, the intense character of family ties also means that families have the ability to undermine the individual's self-confidence, health, and well-being. This

Families provide people with their initial placement in society. The life of each person shown here was shaped by virtue of being born (or marrying) a Kennedy. From left to right are Rose, Edward (Teddy), Rosemary, Joseph P., Jr., Joseph P., Sr., Eunice, Jean, John F., Robert, Patricia, and Kathleen.

fact has become clear as researchers have studied patterns of family violence and, especially, child abuse.

Social Inequality and the Family

The social-conflict paradigm also recognizes the importance of the family in the operations of society, but it emphasizes how the family perpetuates patterns of social inequality. Rather than providing benefits to everyone, in other words, the family helps to maintain the social dominance of certain categories of people.

As explained in Chapter 12, Friedrich Engels (1902; orig. 1884) linked the development of the family in human history to the emergence of private property in horticultural and early agrarian societies. Ever since, the family has served to concentrate wealth in the hands of a small proportion of the population through inheritance, as property is passed from one generation to the next. As noted in Chapter 10, about half of the four hundred richest Americans received their great wealth primarily through inheritance (*Forbes*, 1987). There is a significant degree of social mobility from generation to generation within industrial societies, but the social position ascribed to a person at birth usually does not change very much over the person's lifetime. Similarly, patterns of social inequality among the various racial and ethnic groups described in Chapter 11 are perpetuated through the operation of the family. This is due, of course, to endogamy, by which people in a disadvantaged category of the population commonly marry others in the same category, so that patterns of social inequality continue across the generations.

Engels also pointed out that the family serves to perpetuate the social dominance of males over females, which is the essence of patriarchy. He considered marriage to be the arena of an important class antagonism by which females have been socially (and often legally) defined as the property of males. A century ago in the United States, wives were typically unable to keep their own earnings; anything they earned belonged to their husbands as heads of the household. This pattern has largely been eliminated, but the domination of wives by husbands continues in other ways. For example, as noted in Chapter 12, women continue to bear major responsibility for housework and child rearing, in spite of the fact that most women are now in the labor force (Haas, 1981; Schooler et al., 1984; Fuchs, 1986). Although this family pattern certainly provides considerable benefits to men, they, too, are disadvantaged in the

sense that they have less opportunity to share in the personal satisfaction and growth that come from interaction with children.

This link between the traditional family and social inequality is related to a number of conflicts and changes that will be explored presently, such as violence against women, divorce, and the growing number of women who choose to raise their children outside of marriage.

Other Theoretical Analyses

Both structural-functional and social-conflict analyses view the family in broad terms as a major structural component of society. Other sociological approaches explore the experience of family life.

Symbolic-interaction analysis suggests that marriage and family life are perceived differently by various family members. The power of gender in society means that females and males learn to have different expectations and perceptions of family life (Bernard, 1982). Similarly, parents and children typically have different perceptions of the family because of their distinctive positions in it. For example, children usually perceive their parents only as their mother and father, with little understanding of them as sexual partners. In addition, the experiences and perceptions of all family members change over time. Two people's expectations as they exchange their wedding vows usually change considerably when they confront the daily realities of married life. A change in the role of one spouse—such as a wife entering law school—is likely to alter the roles of other family members. Thus the symbolic-interaction approach points to the inadequacy of describing marriage and the family in terms of any rigid characteristics.

Social-exchange analysis views interaction as a process of negotiation in which people exchange socially valued resources and advantages (Blau, 1964). This approach is especially useful for understanding the process of mate selection. In courtship, a person typically assesses the likely advantages and disadvantages of taking another person as a spouse. Physical attractiveness is one important dimension of exchange in courtship. In patriarchal societies around the world, beauty has long been an important commodity offered by women on the marriage market. This, no doubt, explains why females have traditionally been more concerned with their physical appearance—and more sensitive about revealing their age—than males. Physically unattractive males, on the other hand, may succeed in marrying very attractive women if they can offer the women a high income (Melville, 1983). New patterns of social exchange are emerging, however, as more women enter the labor force and become less dependent on men to support them and their children.

THE LIFE COURSE OF THE TYPICAL AMERICAN FAMILY

Family life is not static. Sociologists commonly recognize four distinct stages that together make up the life course of the family. The first stage is courtship; the second is the subsequent period of settling in to the realities of married life; the third, for most couples at least, is raising children; the fourth is the later years of marriage after the children have left home to form families of their own.

Courtship

In preindustrial societies, extended families are an important economic asset. Marriage is thus considered too important to be left to the choice of the individuals involved (Stone, 1977; Haviland, 1985). *Arranged marriages* represent an alliance between two extended families that will affect the social standing of them both. Parents often arrange marriages for their children at a very early age. A century ago in India, for example, some children were married as early as five years of age, and half of all females were married by the age of fifteen (Mayo, 1927; Mace & Mace, 1960).

In industrial societies, the declining importance of extended families provides more individual choice in courtship. In recent decades, the age of couples at first marriage has been rising: in 1987, the median age for females was 23.6 years, and for males, 25.8 (U.S. Bureau of the Census, 1987c). Thus marriage usually concludes a long period of dating. This process generally begins as group dating, in which several girls and boys interact together. In time, this gives way to couple dating. In the United States today, courtship is often a period of sexual experimentation, and many couples also live together before deciding to marry.

American culture places an enormous amount of emphasis on *romantic love*—the experience of affection and sexual passion toward another person—as the basis for marriage. The American distaste for arranged mar-

In industrial-capitalist societies, marriage is primarily based on personal feelings of love. Luis Alberto Acuña's painting "Rural Love" testifies to the fact that romantic love is hardly a modern phenomenon. Its importance has simply increased.

riages is, of course, a reflection of this exaltation of romantic love. For us, marriage without love is difficult to imagine, and the mass media—in stories from "Cinderella" to contemporary paperback romance novels—present romantic love as the keystone of a successful marriage. It is not surprising, then, that the vast majority of Americans believe romantic love is the single most important element in courtship (Roper, 1974).

Romantic love was well established early in the Middle Ages among the nobility. However, it was not the basis for marriage—far more practical considerations of social standing guided choices of marital partners. Rather, courtly love was an expression of the feudal ideal by which knights pledged themselves in service to noblewomen whom they revered from a distance but were ineligible to marry. Noblewomen, in return, praised the bravery and dedication of these men. But such love was not supposed to develop into an intimate personal relationship (Beigel, 1951). Over time, however, romantic love grew in importance as the basis of marriage.

Romantic love has the useful consequence of being a strong incentive to leave one's original family of orientation to form a new family of procreation. Moreover, romantic love is typically most intense when people first marry, and may therefore carry a newly married couple through the difficult period of adjusting to the realities of married life (Goode, 1959). But romantic love also presents some problems. Based on feelings, it is a less stable foundation for marriage than social and economic considerations. Disappointed romantic expectations contribute to marriage conflicts, which often end in divorce. Furthermore, as "Cinderella" and countless other folktales suggest, romantic love can draw together people of different social backgrounds. Although this is rare, romantic love can be a truly revolutionary force when marriages guided solely by the heart challenge racial, ethnic, religious, and social class boundaries. But keep in mind that, even in fairy tales, well-to-do parents are unlikely to approve of their children marrying a poor servant such as Cinderella.

Indeed, sociologists have long recognized that Cupid's arrow is aimed by society more than individualistic Americans like to think. Most married couples are about the same age, and of the same race, religion, and social class. This pattern is called **homogamy** (literally, "like marrying like"), meaning *marriage between people with the same social characteristics.*

Homogamy is explained in a number of ways. First, people who share important social characteristics tend to cluster together in neighborhoods, schools, and other settings, which means we interact most intensively with others socially like ourselves. Second, socialization within a particular social context encourages similar tastes and interests, so that others we find attractive are likely to have the same social backgrounds that we have. Third, parents and peers often discourage a person from marrying an outsider. In some cases, this influence is subtle; in others, it is more heavy-handed. Traditional Jews, for example, strongly oppose the marriage of their children to non-Jews. If a son or daughter should do so, parents may engage in the ritual of "sitting shiva," in which people gather to lament the loss of a loved one. Typically used in the case of death, the ritual is employed in this case to signify that by marrying an outsider, the child has undergone social death and may no longer be considered a family member.

In sum, "falling in love" is actually a shorthand expression for a host of social forces that guide the courtship process. Perhaps by exaggerating the importance of romantic love, we reassure ourselves that even in the midst of powerful social forces, we are nonetheless making a personal choice.

Settling In: Ideal and Real Marriage

Given the importance of marriage in any society, we should not be surprised that cultures often sustain highly idealized images of married life. Consider the following account of a thirty-one-year-old woman, married eleven years and the mother of three children:

> When I got married, I suppose I must have loved him, but at the time, I was busy planning the wedding and I wasn't thinking about anything else. I was just thinking about this big white wedding and all the trimmings, and how I was going to be a beautiful bride, and how I would finally have my own house. I never thought about problems we might have or anything like that. I don't know even if I ever thought much about him. Oh, I wanted to make a nice home for Glen, but I wasn't thinking about how anyone did that or whether I loved him enough to live with him the rest of my life. I was too busy with my dreams and thinking about how they were finally coming true. (Rubin, 1976:69)

One does not have to read very closely between the lines to see that for this woman family life has fallen short of earlier ideals. Such disappointment is a common result of idealizing marriage and the family. Especially for women—who, more than men, are socialized to view marriage as the key to their future happiness—the pleasures of marriage are likely to be accompanied by disenchantment. During courtship, couples usually spend a limited amount of time together and often see each other only at their best. If one person is tired, ill, or depressed, a date can be postponed. Moreover, research suggests that romantic love often involves a considerable degree of fantasy—people fall in love with others, not necessarily as they are, but as they want them to be (Berscheid & Hatfield, 1983). Within marriage, however, spouses see each other more regularly and realistically, for better or for worse. Further, only after marriage does a couple usually confront the day-to-day challenges of maintaining a shared household. This sobering range of less-than-romantic responsibilities includes paying monthly bills, managing new relationships with in-laws, and performing mundane tasks such as shopping, cooking, and cleaning. In short, there is much truth in the assertion that you learn a great deal about marriage—and your spouse—only *after* the wedding.

Newly married couples may also have to make sexual adjustments. Several generations ago, American cultural norms endorsed sexual activity only after marriage and, no doubt, some people married simply for

Table 14—1 FREQUENCY OF SEXUAL ACTIVITY AMONG MARRIED COUPLES

Years Together	Sexual Frequency (times per month)			
	1 or less	1–4	4–12	12 or more
0–2	6%	11%	38%	45%
2–10	6	21	46	27
10 or more	16	22	45	18

SOURCE: Adapted from Philip Blumstein and Pepper Schwartz, *American Couples* (New York: William Morrow, 1983), p. 196.

this reason. But by 1980, about 80 percent of unmarried males and almost 70 percent of unmarried females reported having sexual intercourse by the age of nineteen (Zelnick & Kanter, 1980). While some Americans observe the traditional norm of premarital virginity, the majority no longer do so.

Despite premarital experience, sexuality can prove disappointing in marriage. Through the romantic haze of falling in love, people may anticipate marriage as an extended sexual honeymoon, and experience some dismay and even self-doubt when marital sex becomes less than an all-consuming passion. As Table 14–1 shows, marital sexual activity declines over time; even so, about 70 percent of married people claim to be satisfied with the sexual dimension of their marriages (Blumstein & Schwartz, 1983).

Research also indicates that couples who report the greatest overall satisfaction with their marriages are likely to report having the most satisfying sexual relationships. Such findings do not mean that sex is the key to marital bliss, but simply that good sex and good relationships go together (Hunt, 1974; Tavris & Sadd, 1977; Blumstein & Schwartz, 1983). Of course, sexual satisfaction is a highly relative concept based on highly variable individual needs and desires.

Infidelity—sexual activity outside marriage—is another area in which the reality of marriage may not square with the American cultural ideal. Traditional marriage vows "to forsake all others" appear to be strong norms (N.O.R.C., 1987:238). About 73 percent of American adults claimed that sex outside of marriage is "always wrong," and another 16 percent thought infidelity was "almost always wrong." About 8 percent stated that infidelity was "wrong only sometimes," while the remainder either did not consider infidelity to be wrong at all or gave no response. Even so, a large proportion of married people in the United States do engage in extramarital sex. Some forty years ago, Alfred Kinsey and his associates (1948, 1953) estimated that about half of all married men and one-fourth of all married women had experienced extramarital sex. Since then, the percentage has remained relatively stable for men, but increased somewhat for women—especially younger wives. This may reflect a decline in the double standard that has long winked at male adultery while condemning females for the same activity. In addition, as more women enter the labor force, they experience much more regular contact with men (Hunt, 1974; Offir, 1982; Thompson, 1984; Saunders & Edwards, 1984). However, research has yet to take account of the effect on infidelity of the AIDS crisis.

Child Rearing

The birth of a child brings significant change to a marriage as new demands are made on each spouse's attention, time, and energy. One thirty-year-old father described how the birth of his son had disrupted his marriage:

> Those first two years were almost perfect. . . . But when the baby was born everything began to change; it sort of all fell apart. It seemed [my wife] was busy with him all the time. And I felt like I didn't count anymore . . . and I got resentful of Danny, then I felt terrible. What kind of father am I to feel resentful at a little kid like that? But I couldn't help how I felt. (Rubin, 1983:61)

Although they often face the birth of children with ambivalence, virtually all Americans believe that a family should contain a least one child, but not more than three to four, as the results of a national survey shown in Table 14–2 indicate (N.O.R.C., 1987:234). This represents quite a change from family patterns two centuries ago, when *eight* children was the American average (Newman & Matzke, 1984). As in all preindustrial societies in which production is based on human labor, large families were considered an economic asset. Furthermore, with few women in the labor force, having children was widely regarded as a wife's duty. Birth control technology was crude at best, so that wives often became pregnant whether they wanted to or not. Finally, a large number of births reflected the reality of infant mortality: as late as 1900, about one-third of American children died before adolescence (Wall, 1980).

Table 14—2 THE IDEAL NUMBER OF CHILDREN FOR AMERICANS

Number of Children	Proportion of Respondents
0	1.0%
1	1.6
2	50.4
3	24.4
4	12.6
5	1.7
6 or more	1.4
As many as you want	4.8
No response	2.0

SOURCE: N.O.R.C., *General Social Surveys, 1972–1987* (Chicago: National Opinion Research Center, 1987), p. 234.

With industrialization, children became less of an economic asset. Most Americans do not become financially independent until at least the age of eighteen (and some not until their mid-twenties), and the expense of raising a child can be staggering. A recent estimate placed the cost of rearing one child to the age of eighteen at over $140,000, to which another $50,000 to $160,000 would have to be added if the child goes to college (Urban Institute, cited in Schreiner, 1984).

Today most American women are in the labor force and therefore want responsibility for fewer children. Birth control technology is far more effective and available, and has reduced the number of unplanned pregnancies. Furthermore, a great reduction in infant mortality has lessened parents' desire to have large families. Together, these factors explain the steadily declining American birth rate during this century to about two children per family today.

Still, given the vital importance of raising children, it is surprising that American society does so little to prepare us for parenthood. Before gaining the privilege and responsibility to operate a car, for example, people must demonstrate they have the necessary skills. Yet there is no comparable measure of fitness to be a parent. Certainly we acquire useful lessons from our family of orientation, but children often learn little of family life from a parent's point of view (Macionis, 1978; Pollak & Wise, 1979). Therefore, most new parents learn directly from their own successes and mistakes.

As suggested in Chapter 12, American culture still considers women to be natural mothers because a "maternal instinct" is supposed to exist in all women. Besides being scientifically unfounded and sexist, such a supposition ignores the numerous and often conflicting roles of American wives and mothers in today's complex society. For instance, in 1986, 55.4 percent of all American women were in the labor force, and the proportion of working women with children under eighteen years of age was higher still: 62.4 percent (U.S. Bureau of Labor Statistics, 1987). In most cases, these women are providing income crucial to their families' welfare. Other women are exercising their growing freedom to pursue personally satisfying and lucrative careers, just as some men do. But unlike most men, wives and mothers who work outside the home usually also bear the traditional responsibility for raising children and doing housework. Some American men are enlarging their roles as parents, of course, but most continue to resist sharing responsibility for household tasks that our culture has long defined as exclusively feminine (Radin, 1982).

As more women join men in the labor force, public attention has focused on what are called *latchkey kids*—children with working parents who are left to fend for themselves for a good part of the day. There are perhaps 6 million such children in America today. Defenders of the traditional American family such as Phyllis Schlafly (1984) contend that many working mothers are indulging their material desires at the expense of their dependent sons and daughters. Husbands and fathers are not usually subject to this criticism because their work income is assumed to be necessary to support their families. But exactly the same holds for most working mothers (Keni-

Although parenting in American society remains primarily a mother's responsibility, many fathers are discovering the pleasures of extensive involvement in child rearing.

ston, 1985). Indeed, as suggested in earlier chapters, an important irony is that as more women have entered the labor force, more households headed by women are poor (Cahan, 1985). Chapter 10 described this pattern as the feminization of poverty: over half of all poor families in the United States are households headed by women.

Perhaps because parenting competes with other personal interests and needs, more couples are choosing to delay childbirth or to have no children at all. In 1960, 12.6 percent of women aged twenty-five to twenty-nine who had ever been married had no children; by 1986, this proportion had risen to 27.3 percent (U.S. Bureau of the Census, 1987a). The likely reasons are that many working women have low-paying jobs and cannot support children, others wish to use their income to gain more education, while still others want to become established in a career before assuming the responsibilities of parenthood (Blumstein & Schwartz, 1983).

The Family in Later Life

The increasing life expectancy of Americans means that, barring divorce, couples are likely to remain married for a long time. By about the age of fifty, most have completed the major task of raising children. The remaining years of marriage are often described as the *empty nest* because, as at the beginning of marriage, couples have no children living in their households.

The departure of children, just like their birth, brings important changes to a family. Although couples must make serious adjustments, their relationship typically becomes closer and more satisfying (Kalish, 1982). Perhaps the best description of a healthy marrige at this stage of life is *companionship*. Years of living together may have diminished a couple's sexual passion for each other, but their mutual understanding and commitment are likely to have increased.

Personal contact with children usually continues, since most older adults live within a short distance of at least one of their children (Shanas, 1979). People's incomes usually peak in late middle age, and the expenses of child rearing are diminished. Thus at this stage in family life, parenting may involve helping children make large purchases (a car or a house) and, of course, periodically baby-sitting for new grandchildren.

Retirement, discussed in Chapter 13, represents another important change in family life. In marriages in which the wife was a homemaker and the husband worked outside the home, retirement means spouses will be spending far more time together. This is often a source of pleasure to both spouses, but it may cause dramatic changes in established routines. Sometimes wives find the presence of retired husbands an intrusion, as illustrated by one wife's blunt reaction: "I may have married him for better or worse, but not for lunch" (Kalish, 1982:96). Today, of course, retirement is more commonly experienced by both husbands and wives. Therefore, this final stage of family life provides the opportunity for spouses to pursue many new activities, often together, to the enjoyment of both.

The final, and most difficult, transition in married life involves the death of a spouse. Because women typically live longer than men do, and usually marry men older than themselves, men are likely to die as husbands while women are likely to die as widows. The bereavement and loneliness that accompany the death of a spouse can be extremely challenging. This experience may be even more difficult for men, since women are usually the more socially oriented partner in a marriage and widowers typically have fewer friends than widows. Moreover, men who have spent their lives in traditional masculine roles must adjust to the new and unfamiliar responsibility of housework (Berardo, 1970).

THE VARIETY OF AMERICAN FAMILIES

Earlier chapters of this book have explained that social class, race and ethnicity, and gender are powerful forces shaping the lives of Americans. Each shapes the family, producing considerable variety in marriage and family life.

Social Class

As described in Chapter 10, social class accounts for vast differences in standard of living. This affects a family's financial security, range of choices and opportunities, and patterns of interaction among family members.

Of course, affluence is no guarantee of personal happiness, nor does it automatically ensure a successful family life. Even so, the economic advantages enjoyed by more affluent American families permit a far greater sense of security in an uncertain world. In a study of working-class families, Lillian Rubin (1976:33) reports the following observations of a working-class housewife:

Social class, race, and ethnicity all shape families, just as they shape the lives of family members.

"I guess I can't complain. He's a steady worker; he doesn't drink; he doesn't hit me. That's a lot more than my mother had, and she didn't sit around complaining and feeling sorry for herself, so I sure haven't got the right." Rubin found that being a steady worker, not excessively drinking, and refraining from violence were the three attributes most frequently mentioned by working-class women as positive qualities in a husband. In contrast, Rubin reports, these attributes were never mentioned in evaluations of marriages by middle-class women, who were more concerned with intimacy, sharing, and communication with their husbands. Working-class women value these things, too, but recognize that they are secondary to the more basic need for economic and physical security.

Social scientists have also documented the negative effects on family life of unemployment (Brenner, 1976). Unemployment is a more common experience among families with fewer resources and can generate destructive fears and anxieties. A thirty-year-old man recalls the family turmoil caused by the loss of his job: "Right after our first kid was born, I got laid off . . . and I didn't have much in the way of skills to get another job with. My unemployment [payments] ran out pretty quick, and Sue Ann couldn't work because of the baby . . . so we moved in with my folks. We lived there for about

a year. What a mess. My mom and Sue Ann just didn't get along" (Rubin, 1976:73). If money cannot buy happiness, its absence can certainly introduce strains and pressures into the lives of both parents and children.

Social class also affects the relationship between spouses. Elizabeth Bott (1971) found that working-class couples tended to adhere to a *segregated-marriage network*, in which husband and wife carried out many daily tasks and leisure activities separately. Wives tended to spend time in the home, often in the company of other women. When not at work, husbands usually remained away from the home in the company of other men. Husbands also dominated wives in working-class marriages, making major family decisions on their own.

Bott's middle-class subjects, however, formed what she called a *joint-marriage network*. These husbands and wives were less rigid in dividing tasks into "men's work" and "women's work," and generally passed leisure time together, often in the home with other couples. Although here again, men had the upper hand, such couples were somewhat more egalitarian in family decision making.

Certainly, class has an important influence on married life. But such patterns are sometimes more complex than Bott's conclusions suggest. For example, middle-class couples with two-career marriages may spend little time together. This resembles the working-class pattern, although the underlying causes are clearly somewhat different.

Research also indicates that spouses of higher social class tend to be relatively more open and expressive with each other (Komarovsky, 1967; Rubin, 1976). Of course, such differences are relative and conceal much variety in couples of all social backgrounds. But this general pattern reflects the fact that working-class Americans are also likely to have less education than their middle-class counterparts, as well as jobs that place less emphasis on verbal skills. In addition, social class involves somewhat differing patterns of socialization. As noted in Chapter 5, working-class children are somewhat more likely than middle-class children to learn to embrace conventional gender roles and also to value obedience rather than critical self-expression (Rubin, 1976; Kohn, 1977).

Rigid adherence to gender roles means that husbands and wives lead very different lives and are likely to share fewer common interests. Furthermore, as Lillian Rubin (1976) explains, males who grow up with conventionally masculine ideas of self-control that stifle emotional expressiveness may become tight-lipped about their personal feelings as adults. On the other hand, wives strictly socialized to be feminine tend to express themselves more openly. In a sense, then, many husbands and wives speak different languages and seek out members of their own sex as confidants, while experiencing frustration in attempting to communicate with each other.

Ethnicity and Race

As Chapter 11 indicated, ethnicity and race are linked to many dimensions of difference within American society. The family is a good illustration of this fact.

Among many Hispanic Americans, for example, extended families persist and are the basis of strong ties of loyalty and mutual support. Hispanic-American parents who adhere to traditional cultural norms also exercise considerable control over the courtship of their children, seeing marriage as an alliance between two extended families rather than as a union based on romantic love. Hispanic families are also notable for relatively pronounced adherence to conventional gender roles. *Machismo*—meaning masculine strength, daring, and sexual prowess—is strongly emphasized. The double standard, by which males are encouraged to engage in sexual activities outside marriage while females are expected to enter

marriage as virgins and remain faithful to their husbands afterward, is also strong.

Assimilation into the larger American culture is gradually altering these traditional patterns, however. Puerto Ricans who have migrated to New York, for example, are unlikely to maintain the strong extended families found in Puerto Rico. Moreover, especially among Hispanic families in higher social classes, the traditional authority of males over females has diminished (Fitzpatrick, 1971; Moore & Pachon, 1985).

Black American families have been the focus of considerable attention during the last two decades. Blacks are about three times as likely as whites to be poor, and as noted in Chapter 11, the income for black households in 1986 was only 57 percent that of white households (U.S. Bureau of the Census, 1987c). Thus the family patterns of many black Americans are shaped by poverty. Poverty is closely linked to families headed by women. As shown in Figure 14–1, women were the heads of 41.8 percent of black households in 1986, compared to 13.0 percent of white households (U.S. Bureau of the Census, 1987c). For all races, there has been a significant increase in female-headed households in recent decades, but this increase has been greater among blacks than whites. Figure 14–2 shows that female-headed households are most prevalent among the poor for both blacks and whites, but are especially common among poor blacks. Just as striking is the fact that roughly two-thirds of first children are born to black women who are unmarried, and in the majority of cases, the mothers are poor (Hogan & Kitagawa, 1985).

How to explain these facts is a matter of considerable debate among sociologists (Rainwater & Yancey, 1967). A generation ago, Daniel Patrick Moynihan (1965) published a major, and quite controversial, report in which he claimed that the black family was in crisis. Moynihan called particular attention to the fact that in 1960 over 20 percent of black households had no adult male to serve as husband and father, in comparison to less than 5 percent of white households. He linked this pattern to a number of social problems, including births out of wedlock, poverty, welfare dependency, and crime. He suggested that this crisis would escalate as many people who experienced financial and cultural deprivation in childhood dropped out of school and subsequently formed "broken" families of their own. Once established, the cycle of poverty would be perpetuated from generation to generation.

In the liberal climate of the 1960s, Moynihan's research was hotly criticized, not so much because of the facts he presented as because of how he chose to interpret them. He downplayed the fact that most black families then (as now) included both parents. More important, his description of female-headed black families

Figure 14–1 Composition of White Families and Black Families, 1986

(U.S. Bureau of the Census)

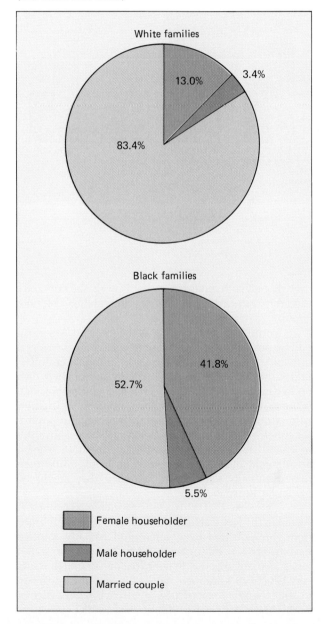

as a "tangle of pathology" struck many critics as a subtle expression of prejudice against both women and blacks. In other words, critics asked, would Moynihan have been so quick to apply the label *pathological* to a black single-parent family headed by a male or to a white single-parent family headed by a female? Moynihan was also criticized for implying that this type of family was the *cause*—rather than the *consequence*—of poverty and other problems. William Ryan (1976), whose "blaming the victim" thesis was presented in Chapter 10, forcefully responded that claiming the black family was the cause of black poverty was simply blaming poor blacks for their own victimization. In Ryan's view, the one-parent pattern of many black families is explained by the fact that blacks living in a white society are more likely to be poor and to suffer from prejudice and discrimination.

Moynihan's report also provoked a debate about the history of the black family. Moynihan viewed the instability of the black family as a legacy of slavery and its forcible separation of black families. But more recent research challenges this conclusion, showing that the growing proportion of black families headed by women emerged during black migration to cities after 1940. At that time, half of all blacks lived in cities; by 1980, the proportion was over 80 percent. Entering the city with few industrial skills, and further disadvantaged by racial prejudice and discrimination, blacks faced an economic crisis of monumental proportions. Forced to work in low-paying, unskilled jobs and constantly in danger of unemployment, many poorer blacks could not attain the financial security necessary to maintain a family, although some managed to fare better (Gutman, 1976). Thus some scholars trace the disintegration of the black family to the enormous economic disadvantages rooted in historical racism (Wilson, 1984).

Pronounced economic disadvantages, then, appear to have caused a transformation of the black family within the last fifty years. And the decline of traditional industries during the 1980s has continued to hit black families hard. But the problem in many black families is not the absence of fathers as much as widespread poverty among both sexes. More than half of all black children currently grow up in poverty. Moreover, the rise in motherhood among poor teenagers suggests that Moynihan was right to fear an expanding cycle of poverty among women and their children (Ladner, 1986). However, research also shows that although some have lost hope, many poor blacks are still striving valiantly to overcome their extraordinary social and economic disadvantages (Stack, 1975; Cherlin & Furstenberg, 1983).

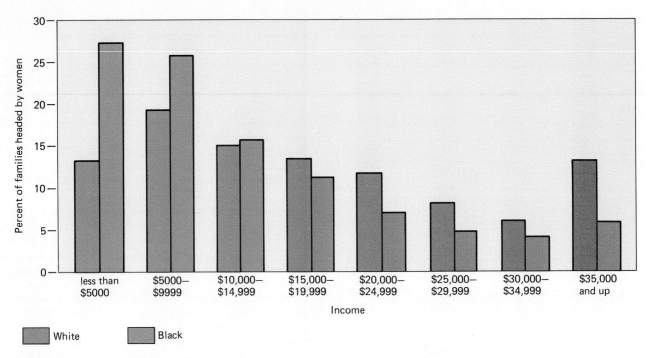

Figure 14–2 The Feminization of Poverty

(Wilson, 1984)

Gender

Even within categories of the population defined by social class, ethnicity, and race, the way in which American culture defines males and females affects marriage and the family. Sociologist Jessie Bernard (1982) argues that every marriage is, in fact, two different marriages: a female marriage and a male marriage.

In patriarchal societies, religion, law, and social custom all enforce the authority of men over women and children. During the last century, the extent of male domination of the family has diminished, yet even today few marriages are the union of two equal partners.

Mirra Komarovsky (1973, 1976) found, for example, that the male was typically dominant in the ideal marriage envisioned by most college seniors of both sexes. She noted, too, that even men who claimed to believe in sexual equality did not want to marry a woman who might upstage them. On the other hand, because females are socialized to defer to males, many women actually seek a husband they consider to be their superior. No doubt, this is why men are expected to be older than the women they marry, as well as taller. Furthermore,

even though both spouses commonly work, the husband's career is assumed to have more importance (McRae, 1986).

Surprising, in this light, is the fact that American culture promotes the idea that marriage is more beneficial for women than for men (Bernard, 1982). At countless bridal showers, women congratulate one of their own on her impending marriage; yet at bachelor parties men bemoan the loss of one of their number to his new wife. Consider, too, the contrast between the positive stereotype of the carefree bachelor and the negative stereotype of the old maid and spinster. In short, women are thought to eagerly pursue a husband, while men may eventually settle down, although they are in no particular hurry to do so.

The view that marriage is favorable to women is rooted in the fact that because they were largely excluded from the industrial labor force until recently, women have had to rely on husbands for financial security. But Jessie Bernard suggests that, in reality, marriage is not very beneficial to women. She notes that in comparison to single women, married women have poorer mental health and more passive attitudes toward life, and report greater personal unhappiness. Men, she claims, are the beneficiaries of marriage. In relation to single men, married men generally live longer, have better mental health, and report greater personal happiness. Moreover, after divorce, far more women than men report happier lives, which is one reason that women are less likely than men to remarry. Bernard (1982:24) concludes that there is no better guarantor of long life, health, and happiness for men than a wife well socialized to perform the "duties of a wife," willing to devote her life to taking care of him, providing, even enforcing, the regularity and security of a well-ordered home.

Bernard is not saying that marriage must be unhealthy for women. The problem, she claims, is the "anachronistic way in which marriage is structured today," with husbands dominating wives and constraining them to tedious work within the home. Under these circumstances, as the box suggests, men reap considerable advantages from marriage, while women have reason to be at the forefront of the effort to reform marital patterns in American society.

Recent research based on a national random sample of married couples helps us to see the connections between gender, power, and happiness in marriage (Ross, Mirowsky, & Huber, 1983; Mirowsky & Ross, 1984). Four different marital patterns were found to be linked to depression in marriage.

In the first type of marriage, only the husband is employed while the wife does all the housework and child rearing. Both husband and wife approve of these conventional gender roles. As shown in Figure 14–3, this arrangement produces a moderate level of depression in the wife, whose status as homemaker carries little social prestige, even though this is her preferred role. The husband fares somewhat better psychologically because of the power and prestige he derives from income-producing employment.

In the second pattern, both the husband and the wife have a job, but she still does all the housework and child rearing. She works out of economic necessity, although both she and her husband would prefer that she stay home. In this case, as Figure 14–3 shows, depres-

SOCIOLOGY OF EVERYDAY LIFE

"I Want a Wife!"

Judy Syfers, who is a married woman, is aware that marriage generally benefits men more than women. Let's be fair, she suggests, "I, too, want a wife!"

I am a wife. Not long ago a male friend of mine appeared on the scene fresh from a recent divorce. He is obviously looking for another wife. As I thought about him while ironing one evening, it suddenly occurred to me that I, too, would like to have a wife.

I want a wife who will work and send me to school so that I can become economically independent. And while I am going to school I want a wife to take care of the children. I want a wife to keep track of the children's doctor and dentist appointments. And to keep track of mine too. I want a wife to make sure my children eat properly and are kept clean. I want a

wife who will wash the children's clothes and keep them mended.

I want a wife who will take care of *my* physical needs. I want a wife who will keep my house clean. A wife who will pick up after me. I want a wife who will keep my clothes clean, ironed, mended, replaced when need be, and who will see to it that my personal things are kept in their proper place so that I can find what I need the minute I need it. I want a wife who cooks the meals, a wife who is a *good* cook. I want a wife who will plan the menus, do the necessary grocery shopping, prepare the meals, serve them pleasantly, and then do the cleaning up while I do my studying. I want a wife who will care for me when I am sick and sympathize with my pain and loss of time from school.

When I meet people at school whom

I like and want to entertain, I want a wife who will have the house clean, will prepare a special meal, serve it to me and my friends, and not interrupt when I talk about the things that interest me and my friends.

And I want a wife who knows that sometimes I need a night out by myself.

I want a wife who is sensitive to my sexual needs, a wife who makes love passionately and eagerly when I feel like it, a wife who makes sure that I am satisfied. And, of course, I want a wife who will not demand sexual attention when I am not in the mood for it.

My, God, who *wouldn't* want a wife?

SOURCE: Abridged from Judy Syfers, "I Want a Wife," *Ms.*, December 1979, p. 144.

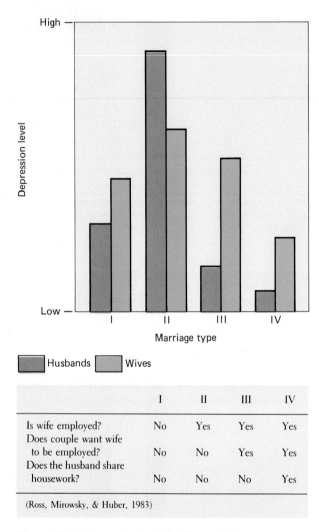

	I	II	III	IV
Is wife employed?	No	Yes	Yes	Yes
Does couple want wife to be employed?	No	No	Yes	Yes
Does the husband share housework?	No	No	No	Yes

(Ross, Mirowsky, & Huber, 1983)

Figure 14–3   Depression in Four Types of Marriages

sion is greater for the wife, and much greater for the husband. The wife has two demanding jobs, one (or both) of which she does not want. The husband, believing that he should be able to support his family, suffers from being unable to do so. Notice that this is the only marital pattern in which husbands have poorer mental health than wives.

In the third marital pattern, both husband and wife are happy that the wife has a job, which provides psychological benefits for her even though she is still responsible for all the housework. The husband benefits even more: the greater family income reduces the chance that his unemployment or any other unexpected setback will result in financial hardship for the family.

In the fourth pattern, both husband and wife are happy to be working outside the home and they also share most family responsibilities. This pattern provides the greatest psychological benefits to both husbands and wives because sharing household responsibilities reduces tensions that arise when a working wife is expected to take sole responsibility for housework and children. The fourth pattern is gradually becoming more common in American society, although it is still quite rare.

This research supports Jessie Bernard's (1982) contention that egalitarian marriages tend to be happier for both husbands and wives than other marital arrangements. The results of this study also support Bernard's conclusion that men generally benefit from marriage more than women do: in three of the four marital patterns, husbands show less depression than wives. In the face of such evidence, we may wonder why conventional and unequal marriages persist. Apparently, changing long-established cultural definitions of the two sexes is a difficult and gradual process despite the fact that both men and women may well benefit from doing so.

TRANSITION AND PROBLEMS IN FAMILY LIFE

Ann Landers, one of the best-known observers of the American scene, recently commented that "One marriage out of twenty is wonderful, four are good, ten are tolerable, and five are pure hell" (Landers, 1984). We have already seen that the reality of family life often falls far short of the ideal; but in some cases, the reality involves problems serious enough to threaten family life itself.

Divorce

Figure 1–1 showed changes in the divorce rate—the number of divorces for every one thousand people over the age of fifteen—during the last century. During this time, the divorce rate has increased about tenfold. Put in other terms, by the 1970s, the proportion of marriages in the United States that were expected to end in divorce was estimated to be approaching one-half, and has declined only slightly since then. The United States has the highest divorce rate in the world, and American marriages are now as likely to be ended by divorce as by death (Cherlin, 1981; Kitson & Raschke, 1981; Weitzman, 1985).

This high divorce rate is partly a reflection of the fact that the United States also has the highest marriage rate in the world; simply put, people who do not marry cannot become divorced. But the marriage rate has remained relatively stable during the last century, while the divorce rate has dramatically increased—a pattern that is related to a number of broader changes in American society (Huber & Spitze, 1980; Kitson & Raschke, 1981). First, in the past, families were both larger and more central to social and economic life. Today, both parents and children spend much of their lives individually, in schools, in workplaces, and in various recreational settings. Second, as noted earlier, Americans view romantic love as the basis of marriage. But the passion of sexual attraction usually subsides with time, so that spouses may end one marriage in favor of a relationship that will renew excitement and romance. This pattern is reflected in the fact that men who divorce often remarry women considerably younger than themselves. Third, increasing participation in the labor force has reduced the extent to which women are financially dependent on husbands. In other words, growing economic equality between the sexes may generate strains within conventional marriages. Fourth, in marriages in which both parents work outside the home, child rearing can be a considerable burden. The birth of children has been shown to stabilize many marriages (Waite, Haggstrom, & Kanouse, 1985), but divorce still typically occurs during the first eight years of marriage, when many couples have young children. Fifth, a century ago, divorce bore a powerful negative stigma. Today, although many people still consider marriage rather than divorce to be "normal," being divorced is far less a basis of deviance (Thornton, 1985; Gerstel, 1987). Practically speaking, divorces are also easier to obtain. In the past, courts required spouses seeking a divorce to demonstrate that one or both had violated important cultural norms—such as engaging in adultery or physical or mental abuse of the other. Today, however, most states allow a couple to divorce if they believe that their marriage has failed. To many Americans, such changes have made divorce *too* easy (N.O.R.C., 1987:237). But the emotional and financial costs of ending a marriage remain high.

Who Divorces?

Young people, especially teenagers, are likely to have less emotionally and financially stable marriages. People in lower social classes, too, are more likely to divorce because of financial strains. In addition, divorce is more likely among couples who have different social backgrounds, which creates tensions that may be difficult to resolve. People previously divorced also tend to show higher divorce rates, partly because problems often follow them from one marriage to another. Finally, people who are geographically mobile and lose the stabilizing support of family and friends are also more likely to divorce (Yoder & Nichols, 1980; Booth & White, 1980; Glenn & Shelton, 1985).

Problems of Divorce

Divorce is not necessarily a problem; sometimes it is a transition that benefits all parties. But even in the best of situations, ending a marriage brings as much change as beginning one. Commonly, however, divorce is fraught with disappointment and frustration, if not outright hostility. Divorced people may also feel a sense of personal failure, loneliness, a need to reorganize friendships ("Were they really *my* friends or my spouse's?") and to adjust their relations with parents and other family members who had grown accustomed to seeing them as part of a couple.

Another serious problem, especially for women, is financial hardship. In a recent study, Lenore Weitzman (1985) found that in the year after a divorce, women suffer a 73 percent *reduction* in their standard of living while men experience a 42 percent *increase* in their standard of living. Weitzman claims that this is due to recent reforms in divorce laws. The traditional laws under which the man provided his ex-wife with alimony and child support (since mothers generally retain custody of children) have changed so that ex-husbands generally pay less than in the past. In addition, courts often require homes to be sold so that marital assets can be evenly divided. For the woman—especially if she does not work—this usually means a marked reduction in housing quality. Finally, ex-wives commonly lose other forms of financial security, such as insurance policies, pension programs, and credit that remain with ex-husbands. Weitzman also noted that older women who have not been in the labor force face special problems, since they generally lack job skills and experience.

Another common complication is child custody. About half of American children under the age of eighteen are likely to experience the divorce of their parents (Bumpass, 1984; Weitzman, 1985). The practice of awarding custody to mothers is a reflection of the conventional belief that women are better parents than men are. Recently, however, a small but growing proportion of fathers have sought to gain custody of their children. Another trend is toward *joint custody*, in which children live primarily in the home of one parent but regularly spend time with the other parent, or in which the children's time is divided more or less evenly between the two parents. Joint custody may be difficult if the divorced parents do not live near each other or are unable to get along, but it does have the advantage of keeping the children in regular contact with both parents (Roman & Haddad, 1978; Cherlin & Furstenberg, 1983).

A related problem is financial support for children of divorced parents. Typically, fathers earn more income than mothers, but mothers retain custody of children. Financial support for the children is commonly ordered by courts, yet perhaps half of all children of divorced parents do not receive the financial support to which they are legally entitled. This situation, which Lenore Weitzman (1985) calls "an epidemic of nonsupport," has led to federal legislation mandating that parents who fail to fulfill this obligation will have the payments withheld from their earnings.

About three in five divorces dissolve families with children (Furstenberg, 1984). Conventional wisdom suggests that divorce is hardest on the children. Certainly, divorce often tears children from familiar surroundings and confronts them with disturbing changes. Moreover, children may feel somehow responsible for the divorce of their parents. At the same time, recent research on the long-term effects of divorce on children is more positive: children who experience family breakup appear to fare far better than those who remain in a family torn by tension or violence (Zill, 1984). In the past, many parents believed in staying together for the sake of the children, but this no longer appears to be true of troubled families: 70 percent of adults now believe that, while difficult for everyone in a family, divorce is preferable to maintaining an intact family fraught with conflict (Black, 1984). Ideally, of course, children fare best in the absence of both divorce and family conflict.

Remarriage

Most people who divorce remarry. Men, who generally benefit from marriage more than women do, are somewhat more likely to marry again. When divorce occurs later in life, remarriage is much more common among men than women. This is mostly because males readily marry women younger than themselves; older women, on the other hand, have less to offer in a culture that values women largely on the basis of youthful attractiveness.

Common sense suggests that what people learn from failed first marriages should make their subsequent marriages more successful. Yet remarriages are even *more* likely to end in divorce. One reason is that people who have already been through a divorce will be prepared to end another unsatisfactory marriage. In addition, the first divorce may have been caused by attitudes or behavior that will undermine a subsequent marriage as well.

Subsequent marriages are often more complex than original marriages, especially when children from first marriages are included. Remarriage often creates *blended families*, composed of both biological parents and stepparents, so that children may have two, one, or no parents in common. Because the biological parents of at least some children in blended families reside in other households, there is some disagreement as to who is and is not a part of the child's nuclear family (Furstenberg, 1984). Blended families also subject children to new relationships: an only child, for example, may suddenly find she has two older brothers. Such factors help to explain why research indicates that remarriages involving children are characterized by greater internal stress and conflict; under such circumstances, the likelihood of divorce increases (Kalmuss & Seltzer, 1984).

Violence in the Family

Although the ideal family is a haven from the dangers of the larger world, Americans are finally confronting the disturbing reality of **family violence**—*emotional, physical, or sexual abuse of one family member by another.* According to sociologist Richard J. Gelles:

> The family is the most violent group in society with the exception of the police and the military. You are more likely to get killed, injured, or physically attacked in your home by someone you are related to than in any other social context. In fact, if violence were a communicable disease, the government would consider it an epidemic. (Cited in Roesch 1984:75)

Gelles is here describing the underworld of family life, a sinister problem hidden or ignored for centuries, but which is finally receiving public attention. The facts are chilling, and in some cases, almost incredible. Yet public awareness is the first step toward curtailing a problem that victimizes millions of adults and children.

Spouse Abuse

> I guess the first time he hit me was when we had been married about eight years. I'd gone to my music lesson and had arranged for a babysitter to take the children to a school fair. When my husband got home from work the house was dark and no one was there. This enraged him, and in the driveway when I arrived, he greeted me with a punch in the kidneys. I doubled over. I didn't even know what I'd done. We never talked afterward. I swallowed my pain and tried to forget.

This incident took place in a fashionable suburb of Philadelphia in a family with plenty of money, beautiful children—and a lot of violence (Saline, 1984).

The common stereotype of spouse abuse involves a lower-class man who now and then drinks too much, loses control, and beats up his wife. In fact, spouse abuse exists among *all* social classes, races, and ethnic groups, though financial problems and unemployment can make the problem worse. Furthermore, as the example above suggests, in many families violence occurs without apparent explanation. Because the vast majority of cases are never reported to officials, the actual incidence of spouse abuse is not known. But perhaps 2 million cases occur each year, and about 5 percent of all couples experience serious spouse abuse at some time (Straus, 1980). Most victims are women, but not all: about 300,000 husbands are beaten each year by their wives (O'Reilly, 1983). Government statistics show that 20 percent of homicides each year occur within the family, and they often involve knives and guns. Some four thousand wives die each year at the hands of husbands, ex-husbands, or unmarried household partners. Overall, women are more likely to be injured by a family member than they are to be mugged or raped by a stranger or injured in an automobile accident. Not surprisingly, about one-third of police activities involve family violence, and one in five police officers killed on duty is attempting to resolve a family conflict (O'Reilly, 1983).

Marital rape is a type of spouse abuse that has attracted attention in recent years. Historically, wives were considered to be the property of their husbands, so that a man could not be legally charged with raping his wife. By the mid-1980s, however, one-third of the states had enacted laws allowing husbands to be charged with rape just as any other person might be. In a few other states, husbands remain legally protected from such

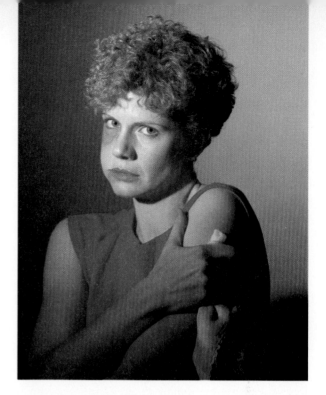

American society has reluctantly come to the realization that the family can be a dangerous place; this is especially true for women, with something approaching two million victims of spouse abuse each year.

prosecution; in most states, a marital rape charge is permissible only under specific circumstances such as after legal separation (Russell, 1982; O'Reilly, 1983; Margolick, 1984).

Women who are physically abused have traditionally had few options. They may want to leave home, but many—especially those with children and without much money—have nowhere to go. Moreover, most wives are committed to their marriages, and believe (however unrealistically) that they can help abusive husbands to change. Some, unable to understand their husbands' violence, blame themselves. Other women, who were raised in violent families, simply expect assault as part of family life. The trap of family violence is suggested by the finding that one-fourth of women who had entered a metropolitan hospital after attempting suicide had been reacting to family violence (Stark & Flitcraft, 1979).

There is reason to hope that the problem of spouse abuse can be brought under control. A decade ago, the law tended to regard domestic violence as a private concern of families. Now, without first seeking separation or divorce, a woman can obtain court protection to ensure that abuse will be punished. Medical personnel are also more aware today of the telltale signs of spouse violence and are likely to report such cases to police.

Communities across North America are establishing domestic shelters that provide counseling as well as a temporary home for women and children driven from their homes by violence. First established in Pasadena, California, in 1964, almost one thousand such shelters now exist (although this is still far short of the three thousand *animal* shelters in the United States). Some men and women who abuse their partners are also joining self-help groups in an effort to understand and control their own behavior.

Child Abuse

As an adult, "Deirdre" will never be able to forget the sexual abuse she suffered as a child. Her stepfather regularly separated her from other members of the family and, often in a parked car, forced her to have oral sex with him. Her mother was sick at the time, and the stepfather warned her that telling of their sexual relationship would cause her mother to die. "I believed him," she recalls. "I thought my mother would die and I would be left with this man." (Watson, 1984)

As this incident suggests, the vicious nature of child abuse lies in adults' use of power and trust to victimize children. Thus, beyond the violence involved, the trust that is the core of family relationships is undermined (Magnuson, 1984). As with spouse abuse, the full extent of child abuse and neglect is not known, but a recent government estimate suggests that 2 million children are abused each year, including several thousand who die as a result (U.S. House of Representatives, 1987). In addition, family violence is a major reason that tens of thousands of children run away from home every year.

Because children typically do not reveal their suffering to others, they often grow up believing that they are somehow to blame for their own victimization. The initial abuse, coupled with years of guilt, can leave lasting emotional scars that prevent people abused as children from forming healthy relationships as adults.

About 90 percent of all child abusers are men, but they do not conform to the common stereotype. As one man who entered a therapy group reported, "I kept waiting for all the guys with raincoats and greasy hair to show up. But everyone looked like regular middle class people" (Lubenow, 1984). However, abusers are likely to have one trait in common: being abused themselves as children. Researchers have found that violent behavior within close personal relationships—like other social patterns—is learned (Gwartney-Gibbs, Stockard, & Bohmer, 1987). Therefore, along with legal protection for victims, treatment programs for victims and offenders alike may help to reduce this serious social problem.

ALTERNATIVE FAMILY FORMS

Over the course of the last century, American society has embraced greater freedom of family living. This is certainly more true for some family forms than for others, but marriage and the family now represent a range of legitimate lifestyles.

One-Parent Families

As shown in Figure 14–4, of all families with children under eighteen years of age in 1970, 88.9 percent had two parents in the household. By 1987, this proportion had fallen to 79.9 percent. This reflects a rapid growth of one-parent families, which now contain about one-fifth of all American children. Such families—in which the single parent is about four times more likely to be female than male—are sometimes created by divorce, but more and more they are being formed by women and men who desire parenthood without marriage. A significant number of Americans who choose this family form are financially independent women, a segment that has grown since a majority of women are now in the labor force (Kantrowitz, 1985). Others—including an increasing number of teenagers who become mothers—are far from financially secure. Some estimates suggest as many as 40 percent of all females in the United States will become pregnant as teenagers, and most will decide to raise their children (Wallis, 1985). The proportion of one-parent families is almost three times as high among blacks (47.3 percent) as among whites (16.6 percent). But this gap is closing: the rate of increase of one-parent families is now higher for whites than for blacks (Besharov, Quin, & Zinsmeister, 1987).

There has certainly been a significant decline in the negative stigma attached to being born out of wedlock. Even so, in a recent national survey about 60 percent of Americans claimed that a woman should not become pregnant if she does not plan to raise the child with its biological father (Kelley, 1984).

Most research supports the conclusion that growing up in a one-parent family does not necessarily have negative effects on children. But families with one parent—especially if that parent is female—are more likely than two-parent families to be poor. Poverty, rather than the absence of the other parent, is probably the major reason that children raised in one-parent families are somewhat more likely to have lower income as adults and to divorce or have children outside of marriage themselves (Mc-

Lanahan, 1985; Weisner & Eiduson, 1986). However, some research does suggest that, regardless of economic circumstances, growing up in a single-parent family is linked to lower educational and occupational achievement (Mueller & Cooper, 1984). Such inconsistent results point to the need for continuing research about this emerging family form.

Figure 14–4 Single-Parent Families in the United States, 1970 and 1987

(U.S. Bureau of the Census)

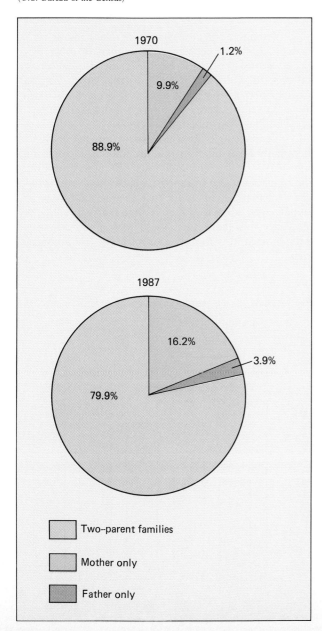

1970

1.2%

9.9%

88.9%

1987

16.2%

3.9%

79.9%

☐ Two-parent families

☐ Mother only

■ Father only

The pattern of "children having children" is most common among the socially disadvantaged, with the burden falling primarily on the young mother. The responsibility of parenting decreases the likelihood of her completing high school or securing a job that will support a family.

Cohabitation

The term **cohabitation** refers to the *sharing of a household by an unmarried couple.* Even a generation ago, terms such as "shacking up" and "living in sin" indicated that cohabitation was widely viewed as deviant. Yet the number of cohabiting couples in the United States has increased sharply: from about 500,000 in 1970 to 2.3 million by 1988, representing about 4 percent of all couples (U.S. Bureau of the Census, 1987d). Although still illegal in some states, living together has become a popular way to test a serious relationship and, at the same time, save the expense of maintaining a second residence. One study of Lane County, Oregon, found that the proportion of married couples who cohabited before their marriage rose from about one in eight in 1970 to over one-half by 1980, which seems to be about the norm nationwide (Gwartney-Gibbs, 1986).

For many people, cohabitation does not imply as much commitment as marriage. As one woman of twenty-four who recently married her live-in partner of five years stated, "For me, [marriage] was deciding to make a real commitment. When we were living together I felt I could walk out at any time" (Clancy & Oberst, 1985). As this example suggests, cohabitation usually lasts only several years; at that point, couples typically either marry or split up. Furthermore cohabiting seems to lead to marriage in only about 40 percent of all cases, and only rarely do cohabiting couples have children (Blumstein & Schwartz, 1983; Macklin, 1983).

Whatever their level of personal commitment, however, court decisions indicate that long-term unmarried partners may have a claim on each other's property. In other words, as cohabitation has gained legitimacy as a family form in American society, the legal distinction between this pattern and marriage has become less clear.

Gay Male and Lesbian Couples

Romantic love between people of the same sex has long been scorned by the heterosexual-based norms of American culture, and gay male and lesbian couples continue to be barred from legal marriage. Even so, most gay men and lesbians form long-term, committed partnerships they themselves honor as marriages and view as the basis of families (Bell, Weinberg, & Kiefer-Hammersmith, 1981).

Gay male and lesbian couples reveal many of the same patterns of interpersonal dynamics that heterosexual couples do (Blumstein & Schwartz, 1983). They enter relationships with romantic ideals and then adjust to day-to-day realities; they share the strains of financial and household responsibilities; and, like heterosexual people, they must deal with conventional cultural values that favor so-called masculine attributes more than what our culture defines as feminine. Some of these couples also raise children—usually the offspring of previous heterosexual relationships, but the technique of artificial insemination has given women the option to have children without a male partner.

Homosexual couples face decided legal disadvantages, and often family opposition as well. Many gay men and lesbians feel compelled to keep their relationships secret to minimize prejudice and discrimination. Partners must therefore turn to each other for all the emotional, spiritual, and material support that heterosexual couples can find elsewhere. Obviously, the strains placed on any bond between two people are greatly increased in such a situation. Yet, despite these disadvantages, many partnerships between lesbians and gay men appear to be strong, resilient, and long-lasting.

Singlehood

As noted earlier, Americans are more likely to marry than any other people in the world: throughout this century, about 95 percent of Americans have been married at some point in their lives. Thus, for most people, singlehood is only a transitional phase. In recent decades, however, more Americans have been deliberately choosing the freedom and independence of living alone, remaining both single and childless.

This increase is shown in Figure 14–5. In 1950, only about one household in ten contained a single person. By 1987, however, this proportion was approaching one in four: a total of 21 million single adults. Of course, most will marry at some point in their lives, but an increasing number will deliberately choose not to do so.

Perhaps the greatest change is evident among young women. In 1960, 28 percent of women aged twenty to twenty-four were single; by 1987, the proportion was 60 percent. Certainly the key to this trend is greater participation in the labor force; for those women who are financially secure, taking a husband is a matter of choice rather than financial necessity.

Yet the single life is not always a matter of choice. Especially for women in midlife, another factor comes into play: a lack of available men. Because our culture discourages women from marrying partners much younger than themselves (while encouraging men to do so), middle-aged women who do wish to marry find the odds stacked against them. In 1986, there were 121 unmarried women aged forty to forty-four for every 100 unmarried men (U.S. Bureau of the Census, 1987d).

Figure 14–5 Single Adults in the United States, 1950–1987

(U.S. Bureau of the Census)

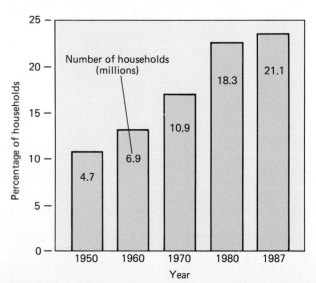

NEW REPRODUCTIVE TECHNOLOGY AND THE FAMILY

We have already explained that the development of industrial technology has influenced family life during the last several centuries. In recent years, medical advances generally referred to as *new reproductive technology* have had a direct impact on many families. In the future, such technological advances promise even more widespread benefits, but society will also have to confront difficult ethical issues surrounding the creation and manipulation of life itself.

In Vitro Fertilization

A decade ago in England, the birth of Louise Brown marked the world's first "test-tube" baby. Since then, several thousand people have been conceived in this way. This number is expected to rise rapidly, so that by the beginning of the next century, 2 or 3 percent of the population of industrial societies will be the result of "new birth technologies" (Vines, 1986; Ostling, 1987).

Technically speaking, "test-tube" babies are the result of the process of *in vitro fertilization*, a name derived from the fact that the union of the male sperm and the female ovum occurs "in glass" rather than in a woman's body. This complex medical procedure often begins with the use of drugs to stimulate the production of more than the usual single egg in each ovary during a woman's reproductive cycle. Eggs are surgically "harvested" from the ovaries, and combined with sperm in a laboratory dish. Successful fusion of eggs and sperm results in embryos, which are replaced in the womb of the mother-to-be. Embryos need not be placed in the woman who provided the eggs, however. Nor must they be implanted immediately; rather, they may be frozen for use at a later time.

The benefits of *in vitro* fertilization are twofold. First, although only about one in five couples who cannot normally conceive children can be helped in this way, this process has enabled many couples who could not otherwise do so to become parents. Second, looking to the future, many medical experts believe that new birth technologies have the potential to greatly reduce the incidence of birth defects. In other words, by genetically screening sperm and eggs, medical specialists can reasonably predict the birth of healthy children (Vines, 1986).

Ethical Issues

Not surprisingly, the new reproductive technology has sparked heated debate. In basic terms, medical technology now provides control over life itself that would have been unthinkable only a few generations ago. The result is a classic example of "cultural lag" (see Chapter 3), in which society has yet to catch up to the moral implications of this new power.

One problem is that, as in most cases of technological advance, some people benefit while others do not. In the United States, new reproductive technology is part of a health-for-profit system. Thus the high cost of *in vitro* fertilization—currently over $5,000 for a single attempt—ensures that only a minority of Americans can even consider this procedure. Beyond financial concerns, medical experts have also claimed the right to restrict their practice to people whom they define as potentially constituting a proper "family." In most cases, *in vitro* fertilization has been made available only to women who are both under forty years of age and part of a heterosexual couple. This means that single women and older women, as well as lesbian couples, have so far been excluded from the practice. The social values that guide the application of such scientific procedures are evident in the recent comment of one physician: "I would be most unwilling to set up a one-parent family, even in the case of a frozen embryo thawed after the husband's death. But at least then the embryo was conceived in love, albeit in the laboratory . . ." (Vines, 1986:27).

Other ethical problems are raised by the new reproductive technology. One controversial issue is *surrogate motherhood*, in which one woman bears a child for another. Surrogate motherhood can take two forms. The first type involves joining the ovum and sperm produced by a couple and implanting the embryo that is formed into the body of another woman, who gives birth to the child. Such a practice allows a woman unable to carry a baby to term to utilize a second woman—her surrogate—in order to create a child that is the biological offspring of her husband and herself. The second type involves an agreement between a woman and a couple that the woman will bear a child for the couple by having her own ovum artificially fertilized by the man's sperm.

Both cases of surrogate motherhood raise difficult issues about who the parents are. This is especially true in the latter case since—legal agreements notwithstanding—the surrogate mother is giving birth to her own biological offspring. The "Baby M" case that gained national attention in 1987 showed clearly how complex such matters can become; a tangled court case was needed to resolve the issue of maternity. Despite the fact that surrogate motherhood can provide some couples with the child they desire, the idea of giving birth for profit has been widely described as unethical.

Perhaps the most outspoken party in the controversies surrounding new reproductive technologies has been the Catholic Church. The Church has recently condemned *all* new reproductive technology as reducing human life to an object subject to human manipulation, as the box below explains.

SOCIAL POLICY

Are New Reproductive Technologies Immoral?—The Catholic Church's View

Americans tend to applaud technological advances, believing that they will significantly benefit humanity. New reproductive technologies—including *in vitro* fertilization and genetic research—have been defended as allowing more women who want children to conceive, and as promising to drastically reduce birth defects.

The Catholic Church, however, has recently condemned any and all such practices. No child, a recent report concludes, should be "conceived as the product of an intervention of medical or biological techniques." Rather than serving humanity, the Church claims, such techniques treat human life as nothing more than an object of research. In light of the Nazi genetic experiments of the 1930s and 1940s, the Church claims reasonable grounds for fearing that new reproductive technologies could encourage efforts to produce genetic "superhumans."

Such concerns have led Vatican officials to seek an end to all research using human embryos. Although many scientists claim that this research could produce useful results, the Church maintains that results can never justify manipulation of an embryo—a human life—in a laboratory. The Church has strong political support in this controversy; in America,

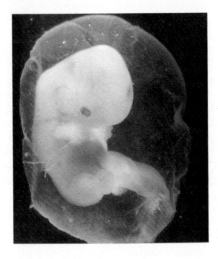

half the states currently restrict such practices, as do many European societies.

The Church also opposes the application of new reproductive technologies to assist infertile couples who wish to have children. It argues that *in vitro* fertilization separates the act of procreation from the loving union of two parents, an argument that is an extension of the Church's long-established prohibition of artificial contraception. Once reproduction is separated from human sexuality, birth is in danger of becoming a business rather than a family concern.

Many people agree with the Church's opposition to genetic research and practices such as surrogate motherhood. But fewer are willing to accept sexual intercourse between husband and wife as the only moral means to conceive children. Since many loving couples cannot conceive in this way, opponents argue, artificial insemination (in which a husband's sperm is used to fertilize an ovum directly in the wife's womb) or *in vitro* fertilization are of obvious value. Moreover, critics point out, this prohibition strikes hardest against Catholics who have been influenced by the Church to view Catholic families as incomplete without children.

No doubt some Catholics will ignore the Church's recent pronouncements, as many have overlooked earlier prohibitions against artificial birth control. But few people—whether Catholics or not—can easily dismiss the Church's concern that what is technologically possible may not always be morally permissible.

SOURCES: Based on Congregation for the Doctrine of the Faith, *Instruction on Respect for Human Life in Its Origin and on the Dignity of Procreation: Replies to Certain Questions of the Day* (Vatican City, 1987); also Richard N. Ostling, "Technology and the Womb," *Time*, Vol. 129, No. 12 (March 23, 1987):58–59; and Kenneth L. Woodward, "Rules for Making Love and Babies," *Newsweek*, Vol. 109, No. 12 (March 23, 1987):42–43.

THE FAMILY IN THE TWENTY-FIRST CENTURY

American family life has changed dramatically in recent decades, and new reproductive technology promises even greater changes in the future. This has led some observers to wonder if the family may gradually disappear. Indeed, controversy continues to arise between advocates of traditional family values and proponents of new family forms and greater personal choice (Berger & Berger, 1983).

This chapter suggests four general conclusions about the family as we approach the next century. The first is that the traditional view that marriage lasts "till death do us part" is no longer realistic. As noted earlier, divorce terminates as many marriages today as death. The divorce rate has stabilized in the 1980s, but it is unlikely that marriage will regain the stability characteristic of the 1950s. Because a growing proportion of women are able to support themselves, the traditional form of marriage appeals to fewer and fewer of them. Men, too, are beginning to embrace change. Yet the higher divorce rate of the last several decades may signify a transformation of marriage rather than an end. In the majority of cases, divorce leads to remarriage, suggesting that marriage is hardly discredited in Americans' eyes. Furthermore, as women's roles—and men's—change, we can expect that new forms of family life will emerge, forms that may prove not only more stable but more satisfying.

The second conclusion is that family life in the twenty-first century is likely to be understood as pluralistic rather than monolithic. Significant changes in this regard are the increasing numbers of cohabiting couples, one-parent families, and blended families created from remarriage after divorce. Each of these relational forms is accompanied by problems as well as satisfactions, yet there is little reason to believe that they represent a threat to basic American family values. Likewise, although they are likely to increase in popularity, singlehood and childless marriage will probably be chosen by only a small minority of the population.

The third conclusion is the notable decline in the importance of American males in child rearing. Certainly many fathers today are becoming more involved in the rearing of their children. At the same time, however, the increasing number of women raising children outside of marriage either because of divorce or single motherhood means that more and more American children are growing up without fathers. As noted earlier, most research suggests that the absence of fathers is not directly and significantly detrimental to children. But there is little doubt that the absence of husbands and fathers from families is an important factor in the feminization of poverty in American society.

Fourth and finally, the impact of new reproductive technology will become evident during the next century. It is possible, of course, that opposition will greatly limit such developments. On the other hand, new forms of reproduction might also substantially alter the traditional meanings of parenthood. At the very least, this new technology will provoke continued reflection about family life within American society.

Despite all the changes that have affected the American family, a large majority of Americans report that they are happy both as partners and as parents (Cherlin & Furstenberg, 1983). Marriage and family life may be an area of social controversy, but the family is likely to remain the foundation of our society for some time to come.

SUMMARY

1. Societies are built on kinship; in industrial societies, the family is composed of close relatives. Family forms vary considerably across cultures, as they have varied across history.

2. Historically, nuclear families have predominated in American society. As is generally the case in industrial societies, marriage in the United States is monogamous. Most preindustrial societies of the world, however, allow polygamy, of which there are two types: polygyny and polyandry.

3. Cross-culturally, families also differ in residential patterns. Although industrial societies favor neolocality, patrilocality is more common throughout the world, while a few cultures have matrilocal households. Similarly, industrial societies recognize bilateral descent, while preindustrial societies tend to be either patrilineal or matrilineal.

4. Structural-functional analysis points to four major functions of the family: socialization of the young, regulation of sexual activity, social placement, and providing emotional support.

5. Social-conflict theory draws attention to the fact

that the family serves to perpetuate social inequality in terms of social classes, ethnic and racial groups, and gender.

6. Symbolic-interaction analysis highlights the dynamic nature of family life. The reality of family living differs for different family members, and members' interactions shape and reshape the family over time.

7. The life course of the family begins with the process of courtship. In contrast to the United States, most societies do not allow romantic love to guide the choice of a mate. Despite our emphasis on romantic love, however, most American marriages are homogamous; marked social differences between spouses are uncommon.

8. When couples settle into marriage, they may find the reality quite different from the cultural ideal. Spouses often discover that they have much to learn about each other as well as about married life. Sexual infidelity, although still a violation of cultural norms, is probably experienced at some time by a majority of married men and a large minority of married women.

9. The vast majority of married couples have children, although family size is smaller today than in the past. Industrialization is linked to smaller families because in this form of social organization children are an economic liability, large numbers of women are in the labor force, advanced birth control technology is available, and infant mortality is low. Delaying childbirth or deciding to have no children at all are more common in American society today.

10. In later life, marriage changes as children leave home to form families of their own. Retirement often affects the relationship between spouses. The final stage of marriage begins with the death of one spouse, usually the husband.

11. In American society, social class affects family life by providing some families with more options and financial security than others. Patterns of marital activities and communication also show variation by social class.

12. Ethnicity and race also affect families. Hispanic families often maintain extended families and adhere to more conventional gender roles. Black families differ primarily as a result of the lower overall income of black Americans; the proportion of families headed by women is more than three times higher for blacks than for whites. In addition, roughly two-thirds of first children are born to black mothers who are not married.

13. Gender affects family dynamics. Husbands continue to dominate the vast majority of families. Furthermore, research suggests that marriage provides more benefits to men than to women.

14. The divorce rate today is ten times what it was a century ago; almost one-half of current marriages will end in divorce. Most people who divorce—especially men—remarry. Subsequent marriages, however, are more likely to end in divorce than first marriages. Remarriage often creates blended families that include children from previous marriages.

15. Family violence emerged as a major public issue in the 1980s. Both spouse abuse and child abuse are far more widespread than is commonly recognized. Abuse of wives reflects cultural patterns that give males power over females. Most adults who abuse family members were themselves abused as children.

16. American family life has become increasingly varied. One-parent families have increased rapidly in recent years. Cohabitation has also become more widespread. Gay men and lesbians cannot legally marry, but commonly form long-lasting relationships. Singlehood is also increasingly common. For many, this is a matter of choice, while for others—especially older women—the lack of available men is responsible.

17. The rapid change in American families has sparked considerable controversy. Present research suggests that divorce will continue to end close to half of all marriages, family life will continue to take many diverse forms, new reproductive technology may alter patterns of parenting, and fathers will have less importance in child rearing because of their absence from many families.

KEY CONCEPTS

bilateral descent a practice linking children in kinship to the families of both parents

cohabitation sharing of a household by an unmarried couple

endogamy marriage between people of the same social group or category

exogamy marriage between people of different social groups or categories

extended family (consanguine family) a family composed of parents, children, and other kin

family a social group of two or more people related by blood, marriage, or adoption who live together

family of orientation the family into which a person is born, and which provides intensive early socialization

family of procreation a family within which people have or adopt children of their own

family violence emotional, physical, or sexual abuse of one family member by another

homogamy marriage between people with the same social characteristics

incest taboo cultural norms that forbid sexual relations or marriage between certain kin

kinship social relationships based on blood, marriage, or adoption

marriage a socially approved relationship involving both economic cooperation and sexual activity

matrilineal descent the practice of tracing kinship only through females

matrilocality a residential pattern in which a married couple lives with or near the wife's family

monogamy a form of marriage that joins one male and one female

neolocality a residential pattern in which a married couple lives apart from the parents of both spouses

nuclear family (conjugal family) one or, more commonly, two parents and children

patrilineal descent the practice of tracing kinship only through males

patrilocality a residential pattern in which a married couple lives with or near the husband's family

polyandry a form of marriage that joins one female with more than one male

polygamy a form of marriage that unites three or more people

polygyny a form of marriage that joins one male with more than one female

SUGGESTED READINGS

This textbook offers an overview of marriage and the family.

Keith Melville. *Marriage and Family Today*. 4th ed. New York: Random House, 1987.

This wide-ranging study of pairing in American society is based on questionnaires and interviews obtained from some six thousand couples. It is both an excellent example of sociological research and a source of fascinating insights.

Philip Blumstein and Pepper Schwartz. *American Couples: Money, Work, Sex*. New York: Pocket Books, 1985.

Two-career marriages are becoming more and more common in American society. The first of these books argues that economic power is strongly related to domestic power for women, as it is for men. The second is a fascinating account of marriages in which women have more economic power than their husbands.

Rosanna Hertz. *More Equal Than Others: Women and Men in Dual-Career Marriages*. Berkeley, CA: University of California Press, 1986.

Susan McRae. *Cross-Class Families: A Study of Wives' Occupational Superiority*. New York: Oxford University Press, 1986.

Based on interviews with couples, this book reveals how different religious backgrounds affect marriages and childrearing.

Egon Mayer. *Love and Tradition: Marriage Between Jews and Christians*. New York: Plenum Press, 1985.

This historical account is one of the most influential studies of the black family in America.

Herbert G. Gutman. *The Black Family in Slavery and Freedom: 1750–1925*. New York: Pantheon Books, 1976.

How much does having a child change your life? The first book listed below explores the consequences of pregnancy and childrearing for thirty working women. The second presents the experience of parenting from a father's point of view.

Constance S. Pond. . . . *And Along Comes Baby: What Happens When the Working Woman Becomes Pregnant*. Lanham, MD: University Press of America, 1986.

Charlie Lewis. *Becoming a Father*. Philadelphia: Open University Press, 1986.

One consequence of the "graying of America" is that more people have the experience of being grandparents. This is among the first pieces of research on this topic of growing importance.

Andrew J. Cherlin and Frank F. Furstenberg, Jr. *The New American Grandparent: A Place in the Family, a Life Apart*. New York: Basic Books, 1986.

This policy-oriented study argues that divorce is currently beneficial to men financially, while being a source of economic hardship to women and children.

Lenore Weitzman. *The Divorce Revolution: The Unexpected Social and Economic Consequences for Women and Children in America*. New York: Free Press, 1985.

CHAPTER 15

Education

Now, what I want is, Facts. Teach these boys and girls nothing but Facts. Facts alone are wanted in life. Plant nothing else, and root out everything else. You can only form the minds of reasoning animals upon Facts; nothing else will ever be of any service to them. This is the principle upon which I bring up my own children, and this is the principle upon which I bring up these children. Stick to Facts, sir!

Thus Charles Dickens introduced readers to his character Thomas Gradgrind in the mid-nineteenth-century novel *Hard Times* (1854). Dickens went on to describe—with evident disapproval—the mechanical educational system that had emerged in England as a result of the Industrial Revolution. Teachers such as Mr. Gradgrind, enemies of creativity and imagination, were intent on filling the children in their charge with nothing but cold, hard facts. Dickens clearly recognized that education does not exist in isolation from the rest of society; he saw that the schools in England's new age of industry and capitalism were molding children to resemble the machines that many would operate as adults.

As Dicken's insight shows, the institution of education is an important part of the socialization process. Throughout life, we learn a great deal from our families, peer groups, religious leaders, and the mass media. But much learning takes place within the system of formal

education. In general, **education** is defined as *the various ways in which knowledge—including factual information and skills, as well as cultural norms and values—is transmitted to members of society.* One important part of the broad process of education is **schooling**—*formal instruction under the direction of specially trained teachers.*

399

EDUCATION IN CROSS-CULTURAL PERSPECTIVE

Living in a technologically advanced society at the end of the twentieth century, we take for granted the idea that children can expect to spend much of the first eighteen years of their life in school. Yet schooling has been widespread in the Western world only for the last few centuries, and even today the vast majority of young people in many societies of the world receive little or no schooling.

As explained in Chapter 4, for most of history, human society was based on the primitive technology of hunting and gathering. In such societies, the family was the central social institution; just as there were no governments or churches, there was no formally organized system of schooling. The knowledge and skills needed in adult life were taught to children by family members (Lenski & Lenski, 1987).

In more technologically advanced agrarian societies—which are common in many parts of the world today—people engage in a wide range of specialized crafts and trades. In each case, experienced practitioners teach their skills to novices. But schooling that is not directly linked to the world of work is generally available only to wealthy people: the English word *school* is, in fact, derived from a Greek word meaning "leisure." In ancient Greece, renowned teachers such as Socrates, Plato, and Aristotle instructed aristocratic males in both philosophy and science. The famous Chinese philosopher Confucius was also a teacher to the privileged few (Rohlen, 1983).

During the Middle Ages, the church provided schooling for a somewhat larger part of the population, and established the first colleges and universities (Ballantine, 1983). But schooling remained largely a privilege of the ruling elites in both Western Europe and North America until the Industrial Revolution.

The United States was the first nation to embrace the principle of mass education. In part, this was a means to forge a literate citizenry able to participate in the political process. Perhaps more important, the industrializing American economy demanded a labor force with at least the basic skills of reading and writing and a bit of arithmetic. The subsequent growth of bureaucracy in the United States and other industrial societies signaled the birth of an economy based on paperwork as well as machines, so that schooling became all the more important.

Early in the twentieth century, laws in all states required children to attend school. Away from the larger cities, one-room schoolhouses served the needs of children of many grade levels, who were all taught by one teacher.

By 1850, almost half of Americans between the ages of five and nineteen were enrolled in school. By the early decades of the twentieth century, every state had **mandatory education laws**—*the legal requirement that children receive a minimum of formal education* (typically to the age of sixteen or completion of the eighth grade). Table 15–1 shows that by the middle of this century, one-third of Americans over the age of twenty-five had completed high school; by the mid-1960s, a majority of adults had done so. Today, over 70 percent of American adults have at least a high-school education, and about one-fifth have completed four years of college.

Only a very small proportion of Americans today are officially classified as illiterate. Much the same is true of other industrial societies, including Great Britain, the Soviet Union, and Japan. In most agrarian societies of the world, however, most people can neither read nor write. Part of the explanation for this world pattern is that nonindustrial societies are typically terribly poor: average income is only 5 or 6 percent of that in the United States. Faced with basic survival problems associated with widespread poverty, these societies do not have the resources to easily expand educational opportunities beyond a small proportion of elites. Moreover, the schooling that does exist is usually of low quality, so children do not learn as much or as rapidly as their counterparts in richer societies (Hayneman & Loxley, 1983).

Even so, there have been some striking educational success stories in poor societies. Before the 1960 revolution that brought the Castro regime to power, schooling in Cuba was limited to a small elite. Since that time, however, Cuba has made a determined effort to provide some formal education to everyone and now claims to have virtually eliminated illiteracy. Similarly, the illiteracy rate in Nicaragua—a nation that, like Cuba, has embraced socialist principles—is rapidly approaching that of richer industrial societies. Such cases suggest that even in poor societies educational achievement is possible if the government defines it as a high social priority.

Industrial societies provide extensive schooling for their populations, but not in exactly the same way, as the following brief descriptions of formal education in Great Britain, Japan, and the Soviet Union will show.

Schooling in Great Britain

As noted in Chapter 9, the legacy of Great Britain's feudal past is evident in British society today. During the Middle Ages, schooling was a privilege largely limited to the nobility. Members of the nobility typically studied classical subjects, since they had little need for the practical skills related to earning a living. Thus schools and colleges contained people of much the same privileged background.

Table 15–1 EDUCATIONAL ACHIEVEMENT IN THE UNITED STATES, 1910–1987*

Year	High School Graduates	College Graduates	Median Years of Schooling
1910	13.5%	2.7%	8.1
1920	16.4	3.3	8.2
1930	19.1	3.9	8.4
1940	24.1	4.6	8.6
1950	33.4	6.0	9.3
1960	41.1	7.7	10.5
1970	55.2	11.0	12.2
1980	68.7	17.0	12.5
1987	75.6	19.9	12.7

SOURCE: National Center for Education Statistics and U.S. Bureau of the Census, 1987.

* For persons twenty-five years of age and over.

As the Industrial Revolution created the need for an educated labor force, schooling gradually included a larger proportion of the British people. Moreover, working people successfully demanded that the British educational system be opened to them. Today, British children are legally required to attend school until the age of sixteen.

All the same, traditional social distinctions continue to shape British education. Many wealthy families send their children to what the British call *public schools*, which are, in American terms, private boarding schools. These are out of the financial reach of most British families, who send their children to state-supported day schools, just as most families in the United States do. All British schools teach academic subjects to students, but the elite public schools also have the important function of socializing children from wealthy families into a distinctive way of life. These children learn the patterns of speech, mannerisms, and social graces that distinguish members of the upper class from other Britons.

As late as 1950, a college education was limited to a very small elite in Great Britain. During the 1960s and 1970s, however, the British greatly expanded their university system (Sampson, 1982). Much like children in the United States, British children compete for places in the university system by taking examinations during their high-school years. In contrast to the United States, however, the British government generally pays the tuition and living expenses of those who are successful. Even at the university level, however, social background is important: a disproportionate number of well-to-do children attend Oxford and Cambridge, the British universities with the highest social prestige (roughly comparable to Yale, Harvard, and Princeton in the United States). Not surprisingly, graduates of Oxford and Cambridge are likely to go on to powerful positions in business and government. This is illustrated by the fact that seventeen of the twenty-one members of the original cabinet formed by Prime Minister Margaret Thatcher were graduates of Oxford or Cambridge, and all twenty-one had attended elite public schools (Pfaff, 1980).

Schooling in Japan

Historically, schooling in Japan was limited to the privileged few, only becoming widespread after the enactment of mandatory education laws in 1872. Although influenced by China, European societies, and the United States (which occupied Japan after World War II), the

University Entrance Exams: A Japanese Obsession

Pick up any of Japan's national news magazines in February and March and you will find university examinations to be lead stories, surpassing in popular interest for the moment even political scandals, economic problems, and gossip about movie stars. From the end of New Year festivities to the beginning of the new school year in April, an inordinate amount of attention is given to the trials and tribulations of the three-quarters of a million adolescents hoping to enter university. What makes this 1 percent of the population so fascinating is that their individual destinies are being shaped to a remarkable extent by just a few hours of test taking. The competition is se-

vere and the preparations are grueling. Ominous labels have been coined to express this concern. It is the time of the "examination hell" (juken jigoku). Students are enlistees in an "examination war" (juken senso). Twelve years of schooling culminate in this moment, which is a crucial turning point in the life cycle of most Japanese. Like other such moments, the whole nation undergoes the experience vicariously each year.

It is midnight. Families, friends, and even interested observers stand shivering in the cold on some campus waiting for the university officials to post the names of the successful candidates

for admission on large, flood-lit bulletin boards. There is much nervous chatter, and the sense of excitement is heightened by the fact that so many are braving the cold just to learn the results as soon as possible. The lists begin to go up. Flash bulbs pop, journalists scurry around, the people stand on tiptoe to search for names they know. Shouts of happy surprise are heard. Others remain intently searching, and some turn and silently disappear from the scene. . . .

SOURCE: Thomas P. Rohlen, *Japan's High Schools* (Berkeley: University of California Press, 1983), pp. 77–78.

Japanese educational system remains in many ways unique (Rohlen, 1983).

Schooling in Japan reflects the strong cultural value of group solidarity. In the lower grades, students are treated as a group in which competition is discouraged. Schooling also stresses respect for elders and others in positions of authority (Benedict, 1974). Like the British, the Japanese make use of competitive examinations for admission to universities. Americans are familiar with the Scholastic Aptitude Tests (SATs), which are used for college admissions. In the United States, however, even students with low SAT scores can expect to be admitted to some college—especially if their families do not require financial aid to offset tuition costs. But in Japan, test scores literally make or break the college aspirations of young people, rich and poor alike. Therefore, students face these examinations with the utmost seriousness, and parents often enlist the services of tutors to supplement their children's regular classroom study (Rohlen, 1983). So important are these examinations to the Japanese that awaiting the outcome is an ordeal for students and their families and a source of suspense and fascination for the general public, as the box explains.

Despite criticism for placing almost unbearable pressure on adolescents, the Japanese educational system

produces impressive results. In a number of academic areas—most notably mathematics and science—Japanese students outdistance students of all other industrial societies, including the United States (Hayneman & Loxley, 1983; Rohlen, 1983). Apparently, Japanese cultural traditions, linked to an examination system that demands high achievement in order to enter a university, strongly motivate Japanese students to learn.

Schooling in the Soviet Union

Before the socialist revolution of 1917, Russia was an agrarian society in which schooling was limited to a small elite. In the 1930s, the Soviet Union adopted mandatory education laws. Political unrest and the costs and social disruption of World War II slowed educational programs, yet by the end of the 1940s, half of all young people in the Soviet Union were in school. The Soviets have had to contend with the problem of forging a national educational system in a culturally diverse nation that is physically larger than any other country in the world. By 1975, however, the Soviets claimed that virtually all children were enrolled in school (Ballantine, 1983; Matthews, 1983).

As in all societies, Soviet schooling reflects social needs and important cultural values. Universal schooling has been viewed by the Soviets as a key component of their quest to become an industrial power. In addition, socialist principles have shaped the development of Soviet education. Like other major parts of Soviet society, the educational system is highly standardized and under the direction of the central government (Grant, 1979). Furthermore, according to official Soviet policy, children of both sexes and all ethnic backgrounds have equal educational opportunity. The United States, too, professes equal opportunity. And like the United States, the Soviet Union does not fully realize this ideal. Although access to higher education is roughly the same for women as for men, Soviet women remain overrepresented in areas of study (such as education and medicine) that have relatively low social prestige, while men dominate higher-prestige studies (such as agriculture and engineering). Similarly, although the Soviets have made considerable strides toward providing equal access to higher education for their many ethnic groups, some still fare better than others (Avis, 1983).

The Soviets also view schooling as a means to teach what they hold are the proper norms and values of socialist living (Matthews, 1983; Tomiak, 1983). Like the British and the Japanese, the Soviets use competitive examinations to admit the most academically able students to higher education. But the support of officials of the Communist Party can play an important part in any student's acceptance or rejection by institutions of higher learning (Ballantine, 1983).

As noted in Chapter 9, Soviet society is characterized by lesser differences of wealth than are found in the United States. This fact, along with government payment of most educational costs, suggests that young people in the Soviet Union probably have more equal educational opportunity regardless of their family background than is the case in the United States. Even so, children from privileged families in the Soviet Union (those including members of the Communist Party) tend to enter schools that provide general academic training, while children from less privileged backgrounds tend to enroll in vocational schools geared to careers in various trades (Matthews, 1983). Furthermore, as in the United States, the children who receive the most privileged educations tend to have the greatest opportunities later on. In short, although the Soviet Union does provide substantial educational opportunity for students from families with little wealth or power, opportunity is by no means equal for all (Avis, 1983).

According to official policy, both males and females receive equal educational opportunities in the Soviet Union. As in the United States, however, this ideal is not fully realized in practice.

This brief look at the educational systems in three different societies suggests an important conclusion: schooling is shaped by the larger society. Societies generally adopt mandatory education laws as a consequence of industrialization. Furthermore, the operation of the educational system typically reflects historical patterns (as the case of Great Britain illustrates), cultural patterns (seen clearly in the Japanese educational system), and the character of the political system (as is evident in the Soviet Union).

Schooling in the United States

Industrialization is linked to the expansion of schooling in the United States; the American educational system has also been shaped by distinctive cultural values.

In comparison to our mother country, Great Britain, the United States has historically placed greater cultural emphasis on widespread political participation. Such democratic ideals encouraged the expansion of formal education; in Thomas Jefferson's view, formal education would give the American people the ability to "read and understand what is going on in the world" (cited in Honeywell, 1931:13). In practice, of course, political rights were long restricted to white males, and even today are not extended equally to women, gay people, and other minority groups. But however imperfectly these democratic ideals were applied, the United States was one of the first nations to enact mandatory education laws and has long had a larger proportion of its people attending colleges and universities than other industrial societies (Rubinson, 1986).

Formal education in the United States is linked to the cultural value of equal opportunity. In one national survey, 80 percent of respondents stated that education was an "extremely important" avenue to future success; only 1 percent dismissed it as of little importance (Gallup, 1982). Consider the fact that only eight of the thirty-nine men who have served as president of the United States did not graduate from college; this has been true of only four presidents since the Civil War and only one in this century (Harry Truman).

Historically, of course, educational opportunity has not been equally available to all: women were effectively excluded from higher education until this century, and even today a college education is commonplace only among the higher social classes. But for nearly a century, Americans have supported a policy of universal primary and secondary schooling financed by public taxes. In addition, public funds have long been used to support state colleges and universities so that higher education is available to a larger proportion of the American population. The ideal is that all Americans should have the opportunity to achieve as much as their individual talents and efforts allow.

The American cultural value of practicality has also shaped formal education in the United States. This means that schooling tends to emphasize those studies that have a direct bearing on people's lives and, especially, their occupations. The noted educational philosopher John Dewey (1859–1952) was perhaps the foremost advocate of the idea that schooling should have practical consequences. In contrast to the traditionalist emphasis on teaching a fixed body of knowledge to each generation of students, Dewey (1968; orig. 1938) endorsed *progressive education* that reflected people's changing concerns and needs.

George Herbert Mead, the architect of the symbolic-interaction paradigm in sociology and Dewey's friend, echoed these sentiments, claiming that "any education that is worthy of the name [provides] the solution to problems that we all carry with us" (1938:52). Further, Mead claimed that "whatever is stored up, without immediate need, for later occasion, for display, or to pass examinations is mere information [with] no enduring place in the mind" (1906:395). Reflecting this practical emphasis in American education, today's college students tend to select major areas of study with an eye toward their future job worth. Figure 15–1 shows recent trends; note especially the rapid growth in the study of computer science in the midst of America's high-tech revolution.

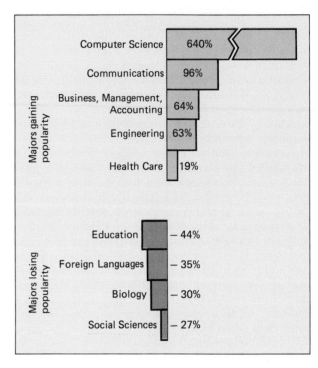

Figure 15–1 Changes in Bachelor's Degrees Conferred, 1985–1986 Compared to 1975–1976

(National Center for Education Statistics, 1980, 1987)

THE FUNCTIONS OF FORMAL EDUCATION

Structural-functional analysis directs attention to the ways in which education maintains the integration and stability of society over time. As one of the major agents in the lifelong socialization process, formal education helps people to participate in the larger social order.

Socialization

As we have seen, all societies transmit their way of life from one generation to the next. In technologically simple societies, the transmission function is assumed by the family. As societies become more technologically advanced, however, numerous social institutions emerge to play a part in the socialization process. Especially in industrial societies, the family can no longer provide all the learning needed by the young. Formal education, because it makes use of specially trained personnel, can provide a wide range of general learning as well as specialized knowledge and training.

Beginning in primary school, children learn the basic language and mathematical skills indispensable to an industrial society. This learning is gradually expanded throughout secondary school and, for some, in college as well. Because industrial societies change rapidly, formal education teaches students not only facts (which may become obsolete), but also how to learn so that they will be able to adapt to unanticipated changes in the future.

Schools transmit cultural values and norms as well. In some cases, students receive explicit instruction in the American way of life (in civics classes, for example). Other important cultural lessons are learned in more subtle ways—sometimes by how the classroom itself operates. Teachers often foster competition among students with questions such as "Who can solve this math problem?" As the box suggests, one child's success is often at the expense of another child. Thus children learn early the cultural importance of competition. Norms are also learned in schools, which place considerable importance on punctuality, displaying respect for school officials, and generally obeying the rules. Athletic programs, too, teach not only the values of competition and personal achievement, but also the norms of fair play.

Formal education also has a political component. As noted earlier, the Soviets see formal education as a means to teach socialist principles to the young. While our political values differ, the same process occurs in American schools. Classroom teaching commonly explains the advantages of political democracy and a free-market economy, while patriotism is fostered through regular rituals such as saluting the flag and singing "The Star-Spangled Banner."

Social Integration

Schooling helps to forge a population into a unified society. Teaching approved values and norms fosters conformity and discourages deviance. This function is especially important in societies such as the United States in which large numbers of people are immigrants with diverse cultural backgrounds.

Not surprisingly, mandatory education laws were established in the United States at the same time that millions of immigrants were entering this country. The integrative function of formal education is no less important today, because, as noted in Chapter 11, millions of immigrants are still entering the United States, mostly from Latin America and Asia. In 1984, the majority of students in more than half of the twenty largest school districts in the United States were members of racial and ethnic minority groups, and their numbers are likely to increase in the future (Boyer, 1984).

Social Placement

Formal education helps to channel young people into culturally approved statuses and roles that contribute to the ongoing life of society. The purpose of this screening and selection process is to identify and develop the varying talents and abilities of individuals. For this reason, ideally at least, schools evaluate students' performance in terms

SOCIOLOGY OF EVERYDAY LIFE

In the Classroom: A Lesson in American Culture

Boris had trouble reducing "12/16" to the lowest terms, and could only get as far as "6/8." The teacher asked him quietly if that was as far as he could reduce it. She suggested he "think." Much heaving up and down and waving of hands by the other children, all frantic to correct him. Boris pretty unhappy, probably mentally paralyzed. The teacher, quiet, patient, ignores the others and concentrates with look and voice on Boris. She says, "Is there a bigger number that you can divide into the two parts of the fraction?" After a minute or two, she becomes more urgent, but there is no response from Boris. She then turns to the class and says, "Well, who can tell Boris what the number is?" A forest of hands appears, and the teacher calls Peggy. Peggy says that four may be divided into the numerator and the denominator.

SOURCE: Jules Henry, *Culture Against Man* (New York: Vintage Books, 1963), pp. 295–296.

of achievement rather than social background. This means, in practice, that the "best and the brightest" are encouraged to pursue the most challenging and advanced studies, while students of more modest abilities are guided into educational programs and occupations suited to their talents. The educational system, therefore, has the function of increasing the extent to which American society is a meritocracy: a society in which social position is a reflection of personal ability and effort.

Obviously, this is of special importance to people who begin life with social disadvantages based on ascribed characteristics such as sex, race, ethnicity, and social class. Formal education has long been considered an important avenue of upward social mobility in American society (Hurn, 1978).

Cultural Innovation

Educational systems create as well as transmit culture. Schools stimulate intellectual inquiry and critical thinking and provide a stable environment in which new ideas develop.

Today, for example, most college professors not only teach but engage in research that leads to discoveries and reevaluation of conventional ideas. Research in the humanities, the social sciences, and the natural sciences is changing attitudes and patterns of life throughout American society. Medical research, carried on largely in major universities, has helped to dramatically increase the average life expectancy of Americans, and research by sociologists and psychologists has helped us to better take advantage of this longevity. In sum, formal education fosters cultural innovation even as it maintains important traditions.

Latent Functions of Formal Education

The discussion so far has concentrated on the widely recognized manifest functions of formal education. Formal education has latent functions as well, which usually go unrecognized. One such function is child care. Because of the rising number of one-parent families and two-career marriages, schooling functions to relieve parents of some child-care duties. Moreover, since our culture recognizes a long period of adolescence, students often attend schools well into their twenties. This also has the effect of keeping many young people out of competition for positions in the labor force.

Another latent function of schools is to establish social relationships that can have lasting importance. High schools, colleges, and universities bring together people of marriageable age. We should hardly be surprised that many people meet their future spouse in schools.

More generally, social ties formed in the course of schooling can be of considerable value later on. Affiliation with a particular school is frequently the basis of lasting social networks. While the opportunities and advantages of such networks vary according to the social position of those involved, at the very least, friendships formed in school often remain important long after graduation.

FORMAL EDUCATION AND SOCIAL INEQUALITY

Social-conflict analysis explains how formal education reflects and perpetuates patterns of social inequality. The educational system of every society is strongly linked to its system of social stratification. As we just noted, structural-functional analysis suggests that schooling enhances meritocracy by linking social placement to individual talents and abilities. Social-conflict analysis emphasizes the extent to which schooling perpetuates social inequality based on sex, race, ethnicity, and social class.

Both the extent and content of formal education differ greatly among various categories of people. Throughout the world, for instance, schooling has long been considered to be more important for males than for females. As Chapter 12 described, this is less true in the United States today than in the past, but females and males are still encouraged to study conventionally feminine and masculine subjects. Schools also reinforce the values of dominant racial and cultural groups, to the disadvantage of minorities. In addition, well-to-do Americans have much more educational opportunity than the poor.

Social Control

Social-conflict analysis views formal education as a means of social control that encourages people to accept the status quo with its inherent inequities. Because this process is often unrecognized, sociologists use the term **hidden curriculum** to refer to *important cultural lessons* *of schooling that are usually not explicitly acknowledged.* Samuel Bowles and Herbert Gintis (1976) point out that public education was expanded late in the nineteenth century, when American capitalists needed a docile, disciplined, and minimally educated work force. Mandatory education laws ensured that immigrants with diverse cultural backgrounds would learn the English language as well as cultural values supportive of capitalism. Moreover, compliance, punctuality, and discipline were—and still are—an important part of the hidden curriculum of American schools, the intention being to produce adult workers unlikely to threaten the capitalist system.

Testing and Social Inequality

Here is a question of the kind typically used to measure the intelligence and academic ability of American school-age children:

> Painter is to painting as _____ is to sonnet.
>   Answers: (a) driver
>   (b) poet
>   (c) priest
>   (d) carpenter

The correct answer is (b) *poet*: a painter creates a painting as a poet creates a sonnet. Notice that the ability to demonstrate logical reasoning in this case depends entirely upon knowing the meaning of the terms used. Unless students know that a sonnet is a form of poetry, they are unlikely to answer the question correctly. Someone with a well-to-do Western European cultural background is likely to have the knowledge required by such tests. But the same student might not score as well on an intelligence test devised by a Native American Hopi of the Southwest! The fact is that most standardized tests used in the United States reflect America's dominant culture and thus unfairly place some categories of people at a disadvantage.

Intelligence tests—first developed at the beginning of this century, as formal education was becoming widespread—inevitably have a cultural orientation. While partly a matter of innate mental capacity, intelligence also reflects learning within a particular cultural environment. Thus any measure of intelligence actually assesses mastery of a particular culture, although most societies that use such tests contain a considerable degree of cultural variation in their populations. In the United States, tests designed by white, affluent educators are likely to have at least some bias in favor of white, affluent test takers.

Mandatory education laws developed during an era of rapid industrialization and immigration in the United States. Schooling served to teach American culture and also to instill the discipline demanded of workers in an industrial-capitalist society.

Intelligence tests are biased in yet another way. The most widely used intelligence quotient (IQ) tests measure intelligence in terms of logical capacities, such as the ability to analyze complex facts and understand spatial relationships. They overlook other dimensions of human awareness and creativity, including intuition and artistic ability. Thus the validity of intelligence tests has long been a matter of controversy; some claim tests do not actually measure what they are supposed to measure.

Tracking and Social Inequality

In spite of the deficiencies of standardized tests, many schools in the United States and elsewhere use them as the basis for **tracking**—*categorically assigning students to different types of educational programs.* Tracking (or *streaming*, as the practice is called in Great Britain) has been part of schooling in the United States since the end of the Civil War and is used today in some primary and virtually all secondary schools (Persell, 1977).

Schools generally justify tracking as a way to give students of different academic abilities formal education appropriate to their particular needs. Tracking, of course, also affects the duration of schooling, since college preparatory tracks lead students into higher education, while vocational tracks prepare them for jobs immediately after graduation.

In principle, tracking permits every child—regardless of social background—to display innate talents and to receive the education or training that these talents merit. But according to social-conflict analysis, tracking actually undermines the meritocratic operation of schools. A considerable body of research (which has influenced court decisions) indicates that social background is a decisive factor in how students are tracked (Bowles & Gintis, 1976; Persell, 1977; Davis & Haller, 1981; Oakes, 1982). Sociologist Jeannie Oakes (1985) asserts that almost all students have the capacity to succeed in any educational program, but tracking—based on "scientific" testing—has the effect of defining half of all students as below average. In practice, students from privileged social backgrounds (who in the United States are disproportionately white) are likely to be placed in higher tracks, while those from less privileged backgrounds (disproportionately members of minority groups) are likely to be placed in lower tracks. In both cases, a student's track is unlikely to change over the course of schooling.

Students in higher tracks typically receive a richer education. They usually have better teachers who put more effort into classes, show more respect for students, and are more likely to encourage them to be creative and actively involved in their own learning. Those in lower tracks encounter greater use of memorization, classroom drill, and other unstimulating teaching techniques. Furthermore, regimentation—including an emphasis on punctuality and respect for those in authority—is more pronounced in lower tracks.

Needless to say, tracking can have a major impact on students' self-concept. People who spend years in higher tracks tend to see themselves as bright and able. Spending years in a lower track greatly reduces the self-esteem of other students. The box describes an eleven-year-old who is fighting to maintain a positive image of himself in the face of continuous signals to the contrary from his school. If students like Ollie Taylor finally accept the school's definition of themselves as "dumb," the process of the self-fulfilling prophecy—described in Chapter 11—is set in motion. Believing that they are intellectually inferior, students will behave accordingly (Bowles & Gintis, 1976; Persell, 1977; Rosenbaum, 1980; Oakes, 1982, 1985).

Inequality among Schools

American schools reveal considerable variation: private schools differ in many ways from public schools, and public schools also vary from place to place.

Public and Private Schools

In 1985, almost 90 percent of American students in primary and secondary grades were attending state-funded

CLOSE-UP

What Tracking Did to Ollie Taylor

The only thing that matters in my life is school and there they think I'm dumb and always will be. I'm starting to think they're right. Hell, I know they put all the Black kids together in one group if they can, but that doesn't make any difference either. I'm still dumb. Even if I look around and know that I'm the smartest in my group, all that means is that I'm the smartest of the dumbest, so I haven't got anywhere at all, have I? I'm right where I always was. Every word those teachers tell me, even the ones I like most, I can hear in their voice that what they're really saying is "All right you dumb kids. I'll make it as easy as I can, and if you don't get it then, you'll never get it. Ever." That's what I hear every day, man. From every one of them. Even the other kids talk that way to me too.

SOURCE: Thomas J. Cottle, "What Tracking Did to Ollie Taylor," *Social Policy*, Vol. 5, No. 2 (July–August 1974), pp. 22–24.

Most American children who receive a privately funded education attend parochial schools operated by the Catholic Church. Parochial schools combine religious teaching with academic instruction—a practice forbidden in public schools by the Constitution.

public schools. The remainder—some 6 million young people—were in private schools. During the 1980s, private-school enrollments have increased, often at the expense of public-school enrollments (U.S. Bureau of the Census, 1986c).

A majority of students receiving private education attend schools affiliated with Christian religious organizations. In most cases, these are *parochial schools* operated by the Catholic Church, which rapidly built a school system in the latter part of the nineteenth century as millions of Catholic immigrants entered the predominantly Protestant United States. In recent years, other religious schools have been established by Protestants with fundamentalist religious views. These *Christian schools*—like parochial schools—are attractive to parents who want their children's schooling to include instruction in specific religious beliefs. Some parents also favor such private schools because they believe that the academic and disciplinary standards in public schools have been declining (Zigli, 1984). Furthermore, recent efforts to desegregate public schools have been unpopular with some Americans, leading them to place their children in racially homogeneous religious schools. As might be expected, this is more common among white than black Americans.

In addition, a relatively small number of American private schools enroll students mostly from the upper classes. These prestigious and expensive *preparatory schools* send many of their graduates to equally prestigious and expensive private universities. They not only provide a strong academic program, but also inculcate the mannerisms, attitudes, and social graces of the highest social classes. "Preppies" are likely to maintain lifelong social networks with other graduates of their school that provide numerous social advantages.

Since families must pay the costs of private education, American students in private schools tend to be economically advantaged. Research suggests that private schools teach students more effectively than public schools do. Two influential reports (Coleman, Hoffer, & Kilgore, 1981; Coleman & Hoffer, 1987) indicate that students in private schools show higher rates of academic achievement than public-school students with similar social backgrounds. Private schools appear to generate no greater interest in learning than do public schools, but class size is often smaller than in public schools. Another advantage is more academically demanding and stringent disciplinary policies that result in a safer and more orderly learning environment. In general, graduates of private schools are more likely than public-school graduates to complete college and subsequently enter high-paying occupations.

Inequality in Public Schooling

Funds allocated to public schools across the United States vary considerably. In 1985, per-student expenditures ranged from a high of $8,000 in Alaska to a low of about $2,300 in Utah (U.S. Bureau of the Census, 1987g). Within states, funding also varies by specific locality. Generally, schools in wealthy, largely white suburbs have far greater financial resources than schools in central cities, where financially disadvantaged minority students predominate.

An important study of educational inequality in public schools was completed in 1966 by a team of researchers headed by James Coleman. The researchers studied four thousand public schools across the United States and used survey data provided by more than 645,000 students. They found that the vast majority of students in the United States attended schools that were racially segregated. Although illegal since 1954, racial segregation persists because, especially at the primary level, the racial composition of schools mirrors that of local neighborhoods, which are typically racially homogeneous. This is one reason that busing—the transportation of students of one race to schools attended primarily by students of another race—has been adopted by many American cities. This controversial policy seeks to equalize educational opportunities, although critics point to the high cost of such programs and the fact that they undermine the concept of neighborhood schools.

The Coleman report also found that white students generally had a better educational environment than nonwhite students. Overall, predominantly white schools were better funded and had fewer students per class, more laboratories in sciences and foreign languages, more library books, and more extracurricular programs. White students also showed significantly more academic achievement than nonwhite students did.

Surprisingly, however, this research found only a weak relationship between the amount of funding available to a school and the academic achievement of its students. The researchers pointed out that available funds are only one of the many factors that shape a school's learning environment, and suggested that the attitudes of teachers as well as the influence of students' families and peer groups may have a greater impact on academic achievement. In other words, since a large proportion of nonwhite children are poor, these students suffer from economic and cultural disadvantages that are reflected in their academic performance. Supporting this conclusion, Christopher Jencks (1972) claims that even if educa-

Busing—a policy to lessen educational disparities by transporting some children to schools out of their neighborhoods—has been extremely controversial. In Boston and other cities, busing plans required extensive police protection.

tional opportunity were equalized for all American students, academic performance would still be markedly unequal because some students have far greater social advantages than others.

The conclusion is clear: schools alone cannot overcome the broad patterns of social inequality in American society. Therefore, educational reform would not be enough to provide every young American with equal educational opportunities. Apparently, this could be accomplished only by lessening the highly unequal distribution of wealth, power, and privilege in American society as a whole.

Unequal Access to Higher Education

The proportion of Americans who have attended college has risen steadily over the course of this century. Government support for higher education (especially for military veterans after World War II) and the onset of the space race in the 1950s were important factors that drew more and more people into the college classroom. Because Americans strongly link higher education to occupational achievement, about 85 percent of parents with children in primary or secondary school claim that they would like to send their children to college (Gallup, 1982). Yet, in the mid-1980s, less than half of high-school graduates were enrolled in college and, as noted earlier, only about one-fifth of Americans over the age of twenty-five were college graduates.

So parents' educational aspirations for their children clearly exceed the education these children actually receive. Some high-school students, of course, do not wish to continue their education, despite encouragement from their parents to do so. Moreover, the intellectual demands of the college curriculum discourage some students with limited abilities. Yet most American children wish to attend college, and the completion of a college program is well within the ability of the vast majority of students.

The most crucial factor affecting access to higher education is money. Unlike primary and secondary education, which is available free of tuition to everyone, higher education must be purchased, and the costs are indeed high. Even at state colleges and universities (which are partly supported by public funds), tuition is usually at least several thousand dollars a year; and in 1988, the tuition at the most expensive private colleges and universities was about $18,000 dollars a year. In addition, although room and board may be included in tuition costs, students face extra costs for books and other necessary supplies.

In some respects, unequal access to higher education in the United States has greatly diminished: as noted in Chapter 12, females and males now have about the same opportunity to attend college. Yet family income continues to greatly affect any person's chances to attend college (Mare, 1981). Figure 15–2 shows, by family income, the proportion of Americans aged eighteen to twenty-four who were in college in 1985. A majority (53.8 percent) of Americans from families earning more than $50,000 a year were in college; the proportion whose families earned under $10,000 a year was less than one-third as large (15.4 percent) (U.S. Bureau of the Census,

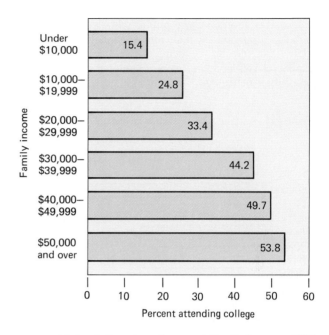

Figure 15–2   College Attendance and Family Income, 1985 (Includes people between 18 and 24 years of age)

(U.S. Bureau of the Census, 1987)

1987g). Most colleges offer needy students some financial aid, but not enough for most of them to afford to enroll. This problem has become worse in the 1980s. During a decade of declining income for many Americans, college costs have soared: between 1980 and 1987, expenses at public colleges and universities went up about 60 percent and those of private schools about 80 percent (Evangelauf, 1987).

Minorities, typically with below-average incomes, find attending college more and more difficult. Figure 15–3 shows that whites are overly represented in relation to minorities at every stage in American education from high school to graduate school—a trend that became more pronounced in the 1980s. For example, the number of black students on American college campuses has declined, much more dramatically in the case of males than of females (Collison, 1987).

For those who do enroll in an institution of higher education, patterns of social inequality often determine both the type and the quality of schooling. People of limited financial means are likely to attend public community colleges and other government-supported schools because they charge lower tuitions than private colleges and universities. Certainly many students receive an excellent education in these public schools. But private schools, supported by high tuitions and endowments, often offer greater academic advantages—including smaller classes and professors considered to be at the top of their fields. Also, in most cases at least, a degree

Figure 15-3 Educational Achievement of Whites and Minorities

(Higher Education Research Institute, 1982)

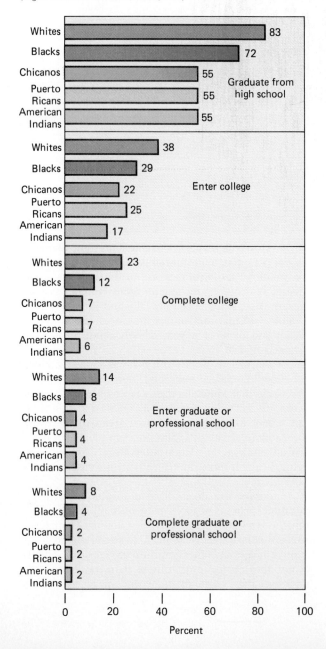

from a private college or university confers greater social prestige than one from a state-supported institution.

A degree from the most prestigious of these private institutions—such as one of the eight Ivy League universities (Harvard, Yale, Princeton, Columbia, Cornell, Dartmouth, Brown, and Pennsylvania)—is likely to impress potential employers and ensure admission to social networks containing many powerful people. More generally, graduates of private institutions have higher-prestige and higher-paying occupations than graduates of state institutions (Monk-Turner, 1983; Useem & Karabel, 1986).

Two or three generations ago, the majority of students in private colleges and universities were white, male, and wealthy. Some of these schools formally excluded females, and many had informal quota policies limiting the number of other minorities. Today equal-opportunity policies and more available financial aid have opened these institutions to a broader segment of the American population. They are still elite schools, of course, but they are relatively less exclusive in terms of social background and relatively more exclusive in terms of academic entrance requirements (Baltzell, 1976). Even so, they remain beyond the financial reach of most Americans.

Whatever kind of college a person attends, higher education is an investment that brings expanded social opportunities, personal satisfaction, often a better job, and greater lifetime income. As Table 15–2 shows, eighteen-year-old males who do not finish high school can expect to earn, on the average, about $600,000 by age sixty-four. For each increasing level of educational achievement—high-school diploma, some college, college degree—there is a corresponding increase in lifetime earnings. Male college graduates can expect to earn almost twice as much over a lifetime as men who do not complete high school. Among women, the financial gains of education are even greater, but at each level of educational achievement, women earn considerably less than men. Indeed, Table 15–2 shows that the lifetime earnings of a female college graduate are less on average than those of a man who did not complete high school! While a sound financial investment, education clearly does not overcome the earning liability of being female in the work world.

Of course, the higher earnings of college graduates are not due to education alone, since college students are likely to come from relatively well-to-do families with all the attendant social and economic advantages. In addition, investing in a college education involves more than the cost of tuition and related expenses. The

Table 15–2 EDUCATION AND LIFETIME EARNINGS

	Lifetime Earnings*	
Education	Males	Females
Less than 12 years	$601,000	$211,000
High school graduate	861,000	381,000
Some college	957,000	460,000
College graduate (4 years)	1,190,000	523,000

SOURCE: U.S. Bureau of the Census, 1984.

* Figures reflect earnings up to age sixty-four, in constant 1981 dollars.

time a person spends in school could otherwise be spent earning an income. But the lifelong financial advantages of a college degree more than make up for this early loss of earnings.

Credentialism

Sociologist Randall Collins (1979) has called the United States a *credential society*, meaning that Americans have come to view diplomas and degrees as evidence of ability to hold a job or perform specialized social roles. Ascribed characteristics such as social class still have a powerful effect on a person's life chances; but as modern societies have become more technologically advanced, culturally diverse, and socially mobile, credentials have assumed some of the importance once attached to family background.

Credentialism, then, is *the requirement that a person hold an advanced degree as a condition of employment in many occupations.* Structural-functional analysis suggests that credentialism reflects the need of a technologically complex society to fill challenging occupations with well-trained people. In contrast, social-conflict analysis points to the fact that credentials often bear little relation to the specific skills and responsibilities jobs demand. An insurance agency, for example, may require a college degree of all applicants for managerial positions; yet the company is likely to provide a comprehensive training program for new employees all the same. Someone with no college degree may have managerial talent and experience, but be excluded for lacking the necessary credentials.

Therefore, Collins (1979) argues, degrees are indeed important, but for reasons other than those usually claimed. One important latent function of higher education is the teaching of cultural norms consistent with an industrial-capitalist economy, as well as the manners and attitudes common to members of high-prestige occupational groups. In other words, employers can reasonably expect a college graduate to fit into their organization. Advanced degrees also represent a considerable investment of time and money and therefore are likely to be held by people who are already socially privileged. Thus credentials serve a gate-keeping function insofar as they ensure that powerful and lucrative occupations are restricted to a rather small segment of the population.

Such inequality of opportunity is legitimated by the belief that advanced education is necessary to meet the demands of the high-prestige positions typically held by people of high social class. In short, the belief that men and women become physicians and lawyers because they are intelligent enough to earn the required advanced degrees tends to conceal the fact that such people have the social privileges—including the time and money—essential to obtain the necessary degrees in the first place.

Finally, the emphasis on credentials in American society has led some to suggest that many Americans are actually overeducated. **Overeducation** refers to *a situation in which workers have more formal education than their occupations require.* There is little question that the development of many new specialized jobs in the American economy has increased the need for higher education. But research indicates that educational achievement has actually outpaced what the labor force demands (Berg, 1970; Rumberger, 1981). Why are Americans so intent on gaining more and more education if their jobs do not require it? As Val Burris (1983) suggests, making credentials the key to obtaining jobs pressures Americans to become more educated. Burris notes that about one-fifth of the American labor force has more formal education than their jobs require, and one consequence of this overeducation is that many people are dissatisfied in their jobs.

PROBLEMS IN AMERICAN EDUCATION

For the last few decades, the quality of education in America has been the subject of debate. As shown in Table 15–3, a recent national survey found that only 10 percent of Americans gave their public schools an

Table 15–3 GRADING AMERICA'S PUBLIC SCHOOLS

Rating	Proportion of Respondents
A	10%
B	32
C	35
D	11
FAIL	4
Don't know	8

SOURCE: George H. Gallup, "The 16th Annual Gallup Poll of the Public's Attitudes Toward Public Schools," *Phi Delta Kappan*, Vol. 66 (September 1984), p. 25.

These figures reflect the responses of a national sample of American adults to the question: Students are often given the grades A, B, C, D, and FAIL to denote the quality of their work. Suppose the public schools themselves, in this community, were graded in the same way. What grade would you give the public schools here—A, B, C, D, or FAIL?

A rating, while half graded their schools at the C level or below (Gallup, 1984). Critics of the educational system have pointed to violence as a serious problem in many schools. More generally, many students are passive, with little motivation to learn. In addition, academic standards at all levels of education have declined in recent decades. Given the importance of formal education to American society, these problems demand thoughtful study.

School Discipline

Many Americans suspect that schools no longer enforce discipline—a prerequisite for even basic education. These fears are supported by some disturbing facts. A decade ago government statistics showed that several hundred thousand students and at least one thousand teachers were physically assaulted on school grounds every year. Moreover, at the end of the last decade, three of every four teachers who were members of the National Educational Association stated that discipline was a major problem in their classrooms (McGrath, 1984).

Such disorder is not necessarily the fault of the schools. Schools reflect the larger society of which they are a part, and American society as a whole is relatively violent. As noted in Chapter 8, communities that contain high concentrations of the desperately poor are especially prone to this problem (Blau & Blau, 1982). When a community itself is characterized by a high level of violence, its schools are likely to confront disciplinary prob-

lems. Nevertheless, schools do have the power to effect change for the better.

At the beginning of this decade, for example, Thomas Jefferson High School in Los Angeles was plagued by violence, drug abuse, and vandalism. In 1982, Francis Nakano became principal of the school and set out to improve discipline and the school's view of itself. The school was refurbished to improve its physical appearance, but more important, Nakano and his staff held students personally responsible for any disruptions that occurred in school. Leaders of student gangs, who were at the center of much of the violence, were informed that violence would be suppressed by whatever means necessary. These changes brought a remarkable turnaround: Jefferson High is now getting on with the business of education (McGrath, 1984).

Examples of this kind of change can be found throughout the country. The key to success appears to lie in firm policies directed at enforcing discipline, supported by parents of students and, when necessary, law enforcement officials (Burns, 1985). Schools cannot be expected to solve problems of violence that have roots deep in American society itself (Reed, 1983). But they can broaden their power to control violence by forming alliances with parents and community leaders.

Bureaucracy and Student Passivity

A problem more specific to schools themselves is pervasive *student passivity*—a lack of active participation in learning. This problem is not confined to any particular type of school, but is commonly found in both public and private schools and at all grade levels (Coleman, Hoffer, & Kilgore, 1981). Student passivity does not imply that students are not interested in schooling as a means of getting the credentials that open many doors later in life. Rather, for many, education has become nothing but a means to other ends, one more hurdle to be cleared, rather than a stimulating and satisfying end in itself.

On the face of it, education would seem a wonderful opportunity. In medieval Europe, children assumed many adult responsibilities before they become teenagers; in the early decades of American history, children often worked long hours in factories, on farms, and in coal mines for little pay. Today, in contrast, the major responsibility faced by most young people under the age of sixteen is to study their own human heritage: to learn the effective use of language, to master the manipulation of numbers, and to acquire knowledge and skills that will enhance their comprehension and enjoyment of the surrounding world. Yet the startling fact is that many students do not perceive the opportunities provided by schooling as a privilege, but rather as a series of endless tasks and assignments that have little intrinsic value. In short, students are bored. While some of this problem undoubtedly lies within students themselves, much of the responsibility for the pervasive passivity of American students must be placed on the educational system.

In the nineteenth century, much American schooling took place in one-room schoolhouses; schooling was thus the responsibility of local communities and subject to considerable variation across the country. Even for much of this century, outside large urban areas, formal education was conducted in relatively small schools where teachers and students had considerable personal interaction. To reduce the costs of maintaining many local schools, and also to allow more effective governmental supervision of school curricula, small local schools were gradually merged into large regional institutions. In other words, our schools reflect the high level of bureaucratic organization found throughout American society. While this type of organization may make sense in terms of cost and efficiency, it may well have a negative effect on administrators, teachers, and students.

After studying high schools across the United States, Theodore Sizer (1984) acknowledged that the bureaucratic structure of American schools may be necessary to meet the massive educational demands of today's larger and more complex society. Yet he found six serious problems that result from the bureaucratic structure of American high schools (1984:207–209).

Bureaucracy fosters *uniformity*, which often ignores the cultural variation found within countless local communities. It is also *insensitive* to the needs and interests of individual students as well as to school personnel. In addition, like most systems, American schools are preoccupied with various *numerical ratings* of performance. School officials endlessly discuss attendance rates, dropout rates, and scores on achievement tests, and often overlook dimensions of schooling that are difficult to quantify, such as the creativity of students and the energy and enthusiasm of teachers. Similarly, school systems tend to define an adequate education in terms of the number of days (or even minutes) per year that students are inside a school building rather than the school's contribution to students' personal development.

In today's bureaucratic system of schooling in the United States, students often show greater interest in learning in less formal settings.

Bureaucratic schools also have *rigid expectations* of all students. Fifteen-year-olds, for example, are expected to be in the tenth grade, and eleventh-grade students are expected to score at a certain level on a standardized verbal achievement test. Thus the high-school diploma rewards a student for going through the educational system in the proper amount of time and in the proper sequence of activities. Rarely are exceptionally bright and motivated students allowed to graduate early. Likewise, the system demands that students who have learned little in school graduate with their class.

In schools, the *rigid division of labor* typical of bureaucracies takes the form of specialized personnel. High-school students learn English from one teacher, receive guidance from another, and are coached in math by others. No one school official interacts with the "full" student as a complex human being. Students experience this division of labor as a continual shuffling among rigidly divided fifty-minute periods throughout the school day.

The highly bureaucratized school system is—in principle as well as in practice—opposed to giving students *responsibility* for their own learning. Similarly, teachers have little leeway in what and how they teach their classes; bureaucratic inertia makes school curricula resistant to innovation. Standardized policies dictating what is to be taught and how long the teaching should take tend to render teachers as passive and unimaginative as their students.

Of course, many factors have advanced the bureaucratic character of American schools. Among them, Sizer points to the effectiveness of uniform schooling in minimizing the social disruption, rapid change, and increase in the school population wrought by the high rate of immigration and urban growth a century ago. The number of children in our school systems has exploded over time; the entire student population of America in 1911 is equal to the enrollment in only the school system of New York City today. American cultural values are also at work: we tend to believe that the most effective way to accomplish any task is to formulate a system, and for better or worse, that is precisely what secondary education is in the United States today.

Since bureaucracy discourages initiative and creativity, students become passive. The solution, drawing on the discussion in Chapter 7, is to *humanize bureaucracy*. In this case, Sizer claims, Americans must humanize their schools. He recommends eliminating rigid class schedules, reducing class size, and training teachers more broadly so that they can become more fully involved in the lives of their students. Most radically perhaps, Sizer would make graduation from high school depend on what a student has learned rather than on the length of time spent in school.

Student Passivity in College

Consider the following observations of a bright and highly motivated freshman at a high-quality four-year college:

> I have been disappointed in my first year at college. Too many students do as little work as they can get away with, take courses that are recommended by other students as being "gut" courses, and never challenge themselves past what is absolutely necessary. It's almost like thinking that we don't watch professors but we watch television. (Forrest, 1984:10)

As this comment suggests, the pattern of student passivity common in primary and secondary schools continues into college. Sociologists have done little research on the college classroom—a curious fact considering how much time they spend there. One study carried out by David Karp and William Yoels (1976), based on the symbolic-interaction paradigm, shows that the patterns of interaction in the college classroom are remarkably predictable and involve little initiative and creative thinking on the part of most students.

Karp and Yoels systematically observed classes and conducted a survey of students at a coeducational university. They included various disciplines in their research, and studied both small (under forty students) and large (over forty students) classes. Although the small classes were characterized by slightly more student participation, in no case were more than a few students active. In small classes, only four or five students typically made more than one comment during a class period, and these few students were responsible for three-fourths of all interaction in the class. In larger classes, only two or three students were active participants; their discussion accounted for more than half of all class interaction. These results contradict the familiar argument that smaller classes encourage extensive student participation: in classes of *all* sizes, the vast majority of students are passive.

Karp and Yoels also found that students themselves became irritated when one of their number was especially active in a class discussion. More than 60 percent of both male and female students reported that they were annoyed by students who "talked too much."

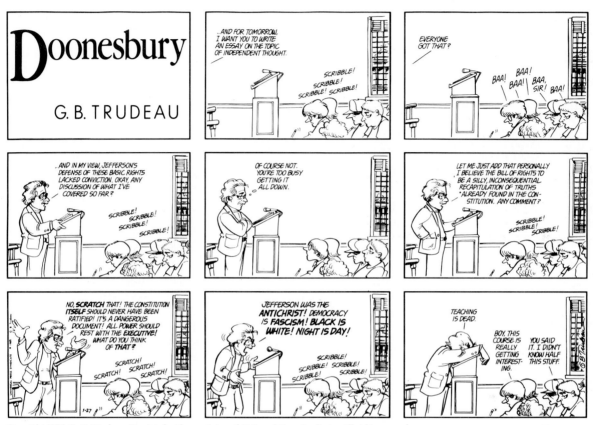

The sex of the instructor affected the extent of active student participation. In classes taught by men with roughly equal proportions of male and female students, male students were responsible for about 75 percent of all class discussion; with women as instructors, female student participation rose from 25 percent to 42 percent, while male participation slipped from 75 percent to 58 percent. Many female students are apparently more comfortable in a class taught by a female instructor. Why? Perhaps because female instructors were as likely to direct specific questions to female students as to male students, while male teachers were more than twice as likely to direct questions to male students. Gender is, therefore, part of the interpersonal dynamics of the class.

Students provided Karp and Yoels with numerous explanations of their passivity in the classroom; these are listed in Table 15–4. Notice that students tend to explain passivity in terms of their *own* shortcomings, which might be interpreted as a case of the victims of a bureaucratized educational system blaming themselves. Long before reaching college, Karp and Yoels suggest, students are taught to see instructors as the "experts" who will provide the "truth." Thus they do not expect knowledge to emerge from classroom discussion or debate, and view their proper role as passively listening and taking notes. According to Karp and Yoels, these attitudes explain why only 10 percent of class time in college is devoted to class discussion. Students also know that instructors generally come to class ready to deliver carefully prepared lectures. Favoring a lecture format in order to present a great deal of material in each class, instructors can ill afford to allow much time for class discussion (Boyer, 1987). During any lecture, they usually direct a few questions to the class; but early in each course, students identify a few of their number who will always be eager to respond and let them take care of all the answers. Taken together, these facts encourage passivity on the part of the majority of college students.

Table 15–4 STUDENT EXPLANATIONS OF CLASSROOM PASSIVITY

	Males		Females	
	Percent	Rank	Percent	Rank
I had not done the reading assignment	80.9	1	76.3	2
The feeling that I didn't know enough about the subject matter	79.6	2	84.8	1
The large size of the class	70.4	3	68.9	4
The feeling that my ideas were not well enough formulated	69.8	4	71.1	3
The course simply isn't meaningful to me	67.3	5	65.1	5
The chance that I would appear unintelligent in the eyes of the teacher	43.2	6	41.4	7
The chance that I would appear unintelligent in the eyes of other students	42.9	7	45.4	6
The small size of the class	31.0	8	33.6	8
The possibility that my comments might negatively affect my grade	29.6	9	24.3	9
The possibility that other students might not respect my point of view	16.7	10	12.5	11
The possibility that the teacher might not respect my point of view	12.3	11	12.5	10

SOURCE: David A. Karp and William C. Yoels, "The College Classroom: Some Observations on the Meaning of Student Participation," *Sociology and Social Research*, Vol. 60, No. 4 (July 1976), p. 108.

Academic Standards and Quality of Education

Pervasive student passivity is not a matter of public controversy, perhaps because bureaucratic organization and its effects on individual initiative have become an accepted part of all social life in the United States. In recent decades, however, the public has become alarmed by reports that the academic quality of American education has seriously declined.

The most recent comprehensive study of the academic quality of American education was prepared by the National Commission on Excellence in Education in 1983. The report, called *A Nation at Risk*, found that the quality of American education has indeed deteriorated, and described the seriousness of the problem in strong language:

> If an unfriendly foreign power had attempted to impose on America the mediocre educational performance that exists today, we might well have viewed it as an act of war. As it stands, we have allowed this to happen to ourselves. (1983:5)

Numerous facts support this conclusion. The average scores on standardized achievement tests began to decline in the early 1960s. Perhaps the most widely recognized measure of secondary school achievement is the Scholastic Aptitude Test (SAT), commonly called the college boards. The decline in scores for both the mathematical and verbal parts of this test has been significant in the past two decades, although scores rebounded slightly in the 1980s. In the early 1960s, average scores for American students were about 500 on the mathematical test and 480 on the verbal test; in 1987, the respective averages were 476 and 430 (Fiske, 1987). Many explanations for this trend have been advanced, especially the fact that a broader segment of the population has been taking college boards in recent years (Owen, 1985). But this explains only some of the decline; more generally, American education itself has suffered a setback.

The report also noted with alarm the extent of **functional illiteracy,** meaning *the lack of basic reading and writing skills needed for everyday life*. About 13 percent of all American children complete secondary school without learning to read or write very well, if at all. Among young people in minority groups, the report suggested, the proportion may be as high as 40 percent. The box provides a closer look at this American problem.

Schooling attempts to teach more than basic skills, however. High-order thinking is also an important goal of formal education. Yet the commission's report claimed that "nearly 40 percent of 17-year-olds cannot draw inferences from written material; only one-fifth can write a persuasive essay; and only one-third can solve mathematical problems requiring several steps" (1983:9).

The report recommended strong medicine to cure the poor performance of our schools. It strongly advocated

Functional Illiteracy: A National Problem

Imagine not being able to read the labels on cans of food, the instructions for assembling a child's toy, the dosage on a medicine bottle, or even the information on your own paycheck. This is the experience of *functional illiteracy*—the inability to read and write well enough to carry out everyday activities.

When schooling became virtually universal among Americans, the United States government confidently concluded that illiteracy was all but eliminated from American society. In recent years, however, the extent of functional illiteracy—even among high-school graduates—has come as a shocking revelation. According to estimates made by some researchers—now acknowledged as roughly accurate by the government—some 26 million American adults read and write at no more than a fourth-grade level. Another 45 million have only eighth-grade language skills. Overall, about one-fourth of all American adults are functionally illiterate, and the proportion is higher among the elderly and among many minority groups.

Functional illiteracy is a complex social problem. One source of functional illiteracy is the educational system: our schools tend to pass children from one grade to the next even though their level of learning is woefully deficient. Another source is community indifference to local schools: parents and teachers do not work together toward improving children's learning. Still another source is the home: millions of children grow up with illiterate parents who do not give them the opportunity or the encouragement to learn language skills.

Functional illiteracy means not only being out of touch—it often means being out of work. Finding and keeping a good job is extremely difficult for those who lack reading and writing skills.

Functional illiteracy is estimated to cost our society more than $100 billion a year. This cost represents the loss of productivity by workers who do not properly perform their jobs, the fact that people who cannot read and write well enough to obtain jobs do not work at all (and thus often end up on public welfare or in prison), and accidents that are caused by the failure to understand written instructions in the home or on the job.

Correcting this national problem requires one approach for the young and another for the old. The American public must demand that children not be permitted to graduate from school until they have learned basic language abilities. For adults, the answer is more complex since many feel deep shame at their plight and avoid disclosing their need for help. Once such people are identi-fied, however, they must be provided with adequate adult education programs; currently, such programs are available for only a small proportion of those who need assistance.

American society is one of the richest and most powerful nations on earth, yet more than a dozen other societies have a more literate population than we do. Functional illiteracy is more than a national disgrace, however; it is a personal disaster. The suffering experienced by the tens of millions of Americans who cannot read and write should certainly be sufficient cause to do something about this problem.

SOURCE: Based on Jonathan Kozol, "A Nation's Wealth," *Publisher's Weekly*, May 24, 1985, pp. 28–48; *Prisoners of Silence: Breaking the Bonds of Adult Illiteracy in the United States* (New York: Continuum, 1980); and *Illiterate America* (Garden City, NY: Doubleday, 1985).

more stringent educational requirements: all students should be required to enroll in several years of English, mathematics, social studies, general science, and computer science courses. The report also urged schools at all educational levels to raise academic standards and cease tolerating students' failure to learn necessary material. A third recommendation was that students spend more time in school. A fourth set of recommendations had to do with improving teaching: teachers' salaries should be raised to attract better people into the profession, teacher training should be improved, and teachers should be allowed time to enrich their own education through further study and research. In sum, *A Nation at Risk* concludes that educators must ensure that schools meet the expectations of the American people. At the same time, however, we must all be prepared to bear the costs of good schools.

RECENT ISSUES IN AMERICAN EDUCATION

Ideas about formal education have changed over time, reflecting both criticism of the bureaucratic character of schooling in the United States and the changing needs of American society. Many new ideas have taken the form of alternatives to established schools.

Alternative Types of Schooling

The rigid system of schooling described by Charles Dickens at the beginning of this chapter developed largely as a result of changes in society itself: the rise of an industrial economy and the accompanying demand for skilled, but highly disciplined and compliant, workers. Although there have been continual challenges to the traditional educational system—most notably in the ideals of progressive education advanced by John Dewey and George Herbert Mead—schoolrooms have not changed very much. Indeed, the increasing bureaucratization of society has replaced small local schools with large, highly standardized educational systems. Thus schooling has the effect of making students passive objects of a teaching process rather than active learners. One response to this problem has been the development of alternative approaches to schooling.

The Free School

The **free school philosophy** is *an educational philosophy in which students are encouraged to pursue their own interests in a creative way, within a nonhierarchical and noncompetitive learning environment*. This view of education has its roots in the progressive education movement early in this century, and it gained popularity in the 1960s.

In general, free schools reject the rigid standardization that characterizes traditional school systems, believing instead that teachers and students should shape the educational process according to the needs of distinct individuals (Ballantine, 1983). Thus schooling may take place in classrooms, outdoors, or in any setting that supports learning. Instruction need not follow any particular model, and a wide range of learning materials may be used. Free schools minimize the formality and hierarchy that characterize relationships betweeen teachers and students in the traditional school in order to encourage more egalitarian interaction. The human qualities of intuition, emotion, and open expression of personality differences are valued rather than dismissed or repressed. Free schools also try to minimize the traditional separation of school officials from parents and the community by joining the outside world and the classroom.

Traditional education attempts to impose knowledge on students, who often become passive as a consequence. In contrast, the free school approach attempts to elicit the active involvement of students in their own education by placing maximum value on individual creativity. In short, while traditional education emphasizes the process of adult-centered *teaching*, the free school approach emphasizes the process of student-centered *learning*.

Competition among students is less important in such an environment because students are (ideally) self-motivated and self-expressive, and success is based on the interests and desires of individuals. Free schools do not transform individual differences into a hierarchy in which some students are called "gifted" and others are defined as "slow learners."

Proponents of free schools believe that these educational principles enhance learning and discourage student passivity. Critics counter that this type of schooling is "soft" and does not place sufficient academic demands on students. Whatever the merits of free schools may be, they involve only a small minority of children in the United States.

Home Schooling

Some parents—often sympathetic to the philosophy of free schooling—undertake the schooling of their children at home. Although, as suggested earlier, education was carried out within the family through most of human history, this pattern is rare today. American parents who wish to educate their children at home must contend with mandatory education laws. Most states allow home schooling only under extraordinary circumstances, although a few are relatively lenient.

Home education presents a considerable challenge to parents. It requires a great deal of time, so the possibility of work outside the home for the teaching parent is virtually eliminated. Furthermore, parents may find that they lack the ability to teach at least some parts of a basic school curriculm effectively. Nonetheless, many families find that home schooling is an effective way of giving their children the education they consider most appropriate.

Schooling for the Disabled

Laws mandating a minimum education not only require children to attend school, they also express the obligation of our society to provide a basic education to everyone.

Yet millions of young people in the United States receive little or no education because they have various types of mental and physical disabilities. Because a highly bureaucratized system of mass education does not readily meet the needs of such children, many have been defined as uneducable.

Providing an education for disabled children requires overcoming several problems. Children with physical disabilities may have difficulty getting to and from school, and the interiors of many school buildings contain stairs and other obstacles for those who must use crutches or wheelchairs. At least some children who are mentally retarded or who suffer from emotional problems require extensive personal attention from teachers with specialized training. For such reasons, mentally and physically disabled children often have received a public education only because of the persistent efforts of parents and other concerned citizens.

Recently, however, there has been a trend to **mainstreaming**—*the integration of disabled students into the educational program as a whole*. Mainstreaming is an alternative to segregated special education classes containing only disabled students. One advantage of mainstreaming is that it allows disabled children to partake of the widest possible educational experiences within the limits of their abilities. Another is that disabled children learn how to interact more extensively with other

The policy of mainstreaming allows students with physical disabilities to take advantage of broader educational opportunities.

children, and, just as important, other children learn how to interact with people who are disabled. A significant problem of mainstreaming is its expense: it often necessitates changes in physical facilities, as well as enlisting teachers who are capable of meeting the special needs of disabled children.

Adult Education

Traditionally, schooling has been confined to children and adolescents. In the last several decades, however, a growing proportion of the adult population has enrolled in school, some of them returning after a considerable period of time.

By the beginning of the 1980s, over 21 million adults in the United States were enrolled in school—more than ever before in history. About one-third of these people are between twenty-four and thirty-five. But some of the oldest Americans have not outgrown their desire for education: around 4 percent of all adults in school are over the age of sixty-five. In general, adult students are a fairly privileged segment of the population. Most are white, and they typically earn more than $25,000 a year.

Why do adults return to school? There are as many specific reasons as there are students, but usually the motivation is work-related. Many pursue areas of study that are directly linked to occupations in which they are already working. Almost one-fourth of adult education students are studying business; about another one-fourth are enrolled in course work in health and engineering (National Center for Education Statistics, 1983). Others return to school to get a high-school diploma or college degree because they recognize its occupational advantages. Still others go back to school simply in search of intellectual stimulation.

Education in the Computer Age

The final bell has already rung at Benjamin Franklin Junior High in Ridgewood, New Jersey, yet some students are reluctant to go home. This may sound unusual, and it is. The explanation for this intense student interest is Benjamin Franklin's computer science program. George Mamunes is completing a program that will graphically display every part of the human heart; Pam Miller is developing a program that simulates the operation of a nuclear reactor; Meilin Wong is debugging a business management program; Jim McGuire is developing a video game of his own. What makes this schoolroom scene unusual is explained by teacher Bob Muller: "No one told [the students] they have to be here. They're not usually doing assignments. They're experimenting. They're letting their imaginations run free" (Golden, 1982:51).

This chapter has emphasized the many links between the educational system and other parts of society. Just as the Industrial Revolution had a major impact on formal education in the nineteenth century, schooling in the United States is now being transformed by another technological revolution—the computer.

The computer is already playing a part in virtually every occupation in American society. It stands to reason then that a familiarity with computers should be part of the educational program. The American population appears to be convinced of the importance of learning to use computers: a national survey found that 86 percent of respondents believed that computers and instruction in their use will be available to all students by the beginning of the next century (Gallup, 1983). The United States appears to be well on the way to reaching that goal; in 1985, over 90 percent of American public schools were using personal computers in instructional activity (U.S. Bureau of the Census, 1987g). Other industrial societies share America's enthusiasm for computers in schools: the Soviet Union began requiring computer education in its high schools in 1985 (Alexander, 1985).

The advantages of using computers in school are not limited to learning job-related skills. Computers may also improve the nature of schooling itself. In many subjects, computers have the capacity to interact with students—that is, they react directly to students' input. Moreover, computers allow students to progress at their own pace. For disabled students unable to write with pencil and paper, computers may permit an easier formal education. Perhaps most important of all, the introduction of computers into our schools—in some cases, as early as kindergarten—has sparked a new passion for learning among many students. The effect of computers on learning is a topic that is commanding increasing attention in research. Initial studies suggest that computer-assisted instruction can significantly increase the speed at which students learn and the amount of information that they retain (Fantini, 1986).

The use of computers in the schools has its dangers as well. Computers will never have the personal insight into the needs of individual students that a qualified and motivated human teacher has. Moreover, the computer is of little value in many areas of traditional education. As one educator critically noted, "There's a whole world of real problems, of human problems, which is essentially being ignored." Another teacher fears that students will be "out of touch with certain springs of human identity and creativity, which belong to the full use of language rather than mathematical and symbolical codes" (Golden, 1982:56).

Because computers are a significant financial investment, school districts in wealthy areas had the lion's share of the roughly 500,000 computers in American schools in 1985. Yet in many school districts, parents are so eager for their children to join in the high-tech revolution that they help raise money to purchase computers. Business, too, has been getting into the act: legislation currently provides generous tax benefits for computer manufacturers who donate machines for educational use (Golden, 1982).

Certainly the introduction of computers into American education will not solve many of the problems that plague our schools. Yet there is little doubt that computers will significantly shape the American educational system of the twenty-first century.

SUMMARY

1. Education is a major social institution for transmitting knowledge and skills, as well as cultural norms and values, to young people. Education in preindustrial societies occurs informally within the family; industrial societies develop formal systems of schooling.

2. The United States was among the first societies to develop a system of compulsory mass education, which reflected both our democratic political ideals and the needs of the industrial-capitalist economy. Our educational system has also been shaped by such cultural values as practicality, efficiency, and competitive individualism.

3. Structural-functional analysis suggests that schooling contributes to socialization, promotes social integration and appropriate social placement, and encourages cultural innovation. Other, latent functions of schooling include child care and forging lasting personal relationships.

4. Social-conflict analysis points out that the opportunity for formal education is unequally distributed among Americans. This approach also explains that schooling is a means of social control, instilling the discipline that produces compliant adult workers.

5. Standardized testing measures intelligence and aptitude as they are related to cultural patterns, which vary within the population. Since most tests are designed by majority group members, minorities taking these tests may be at a disadvantage.

6. While allegedly based on individual talents, tracking is also strongly related to students' social background. Tracking provides greater educational resources to more privileged people and thereby perpetuates patterns of social inequality.

7. The great majority of Americans attend state-funded public schools. Most privately funded schools are affiliated with religious organizations. A very small proportion of American young people—generally of privileged social background—attend private preparatory schools.

8. School districts across America vary in the amount of resources allocated per student. Although research has shown that spending money does not guarantee educational quality, schools in affluent areas are likely to provide a richer education than schools in poorer areas.

9. Today, only one-fifth of Americans over the age of twenty-five are college graduates. Most Americans attend state-funded institutions; private colleges and universities are usually much more expensive and enroll students from more well-to-do families. A college degree is likely to greatly increase lifetime earnings.

10. America has been described as a credential society. By requiring degrees for higher-paying occupations, employers are able to ensure that workers have learned norms and attitudes appropriate to the business setting. Further, since degrees are expensive, those able to afford higher education are also more likely to ultimately obtain the most desirable occupations.

11. Americans are critical of their public schools. Especially in poor neighborhoods, violence is a highly visible problem. Generally, the bureaucratic character of American schools has fostered widespread student passivity.

12. Declining academic standards are a major educational problem in America, reflected in lower average scores on academic achievement tests and functional illiteracy among a significant proportion of high-school graduates.

13. Various alternative approaches to education have been advanced as a means to improve the educational system. Free schools emphasize individual creativity in an egalitarian and cooperative environment. A few parents use home schooling to better meet the educational needs of their children.

14. Mentally and physically disabled children traditionally have been schooled in special classes or not at all. In recent years, mainstreaming has afforded handicapped students with greater educational opportunities.

15. A growing proportion of students in the United States are adults, who often return to school after some time. They usually engage in study directly related to their occupational work.

16. For many students, computers are a source of more effective learning. Computers are not suitable for teaching all kinds of subjects, however, and they are currently more likely to be found in wealthier school districts.

KEY CONCEPTS

credentialism the requirement that a person hold an advanced degree as a condition of employment in many occupations

education the various ways in which knowledge—including factual information and skills, as well as cultural norms and values—is transmitted to members of society

free school philosophy an educational philosophy in which students are encouraged to pursue their own interests in a creative way, within a nonhierarchical and noncompetitive learning environment

functional illiteracy the lack of basic reading and writing skills needed for everyday life

hidden curriculum important cultural lessons of schooling that are usually not explicitly acknowledged

mainstreaming the integration of disabled students into the educational program as a whole

mandatory education laws the legal requirement that children receive a minimum of formal education

overeducation a situation in which workers have more formal education than the performance of their occupations requires

schooling formal instruction under the direction of specially trained teachers

tracking categorically assigning students to different types of educational programs

SUGGESTED READINGS

This textbook is a good resource for the sociological analysis of education.

Jeanne H. Ballantine. *The Sociology of Education*, 2nd ed. Englewood Cliffs, NJ: Prentice-Hall, 1989.

For a scholarly book to top the best-seller list is rare indeed. But this conservative critique of education captured the attention of Americans.

Allan Bloom. *The Closing of the American Mind: How Higher Education Has Failed Democracy and Impoverished the Souls of Today's Students.* New York: Simon & Schuster, 1987.

The following two books provide a comparative look at schooling in two major industrial societies of the world.

J. J. Tomiak, ed. *Soviet Education in the 1980s.* London: Croom Helm, 1983.

Thomas P. Rohlen. *Japan's High Schools.* Berkeley: University of California Press, 1983.

In recent years, the educational system of the United States has been the subject of considerable criticism and debate. The first book listed below is a recent governmental report on American education; the second is a critical appraisal of American education by a man who has spent his life in administrative positions within many levels of schools; the third, also by a longtime educator, suggests a number of educational reforms.

The National Commission on Excellence in Education. *A Nation at Risk: The Full Account.* Cambridge, MA: USA Research, 1984.

Theodore R. Sizer. *Horace's Compromise: The Dilemma of the American High School.* Boston: Houghton Mifflin, 1984.

Mario D. Fantini. *Regaining Excellence in Education.* Columbus, OH: Merrill, 1986.

The following two books explain how and why the educational system in the United States perpetuates social inequality.

Samuel Bowles and Herbert Gintis. *Schooling in Capitalist America: Educational Reform and the Contradictions of Economic Life.* New York: Basic Books, 1976.

Jeannie Oakes. *Keeping Track: How High Schools Structure Inequality.* New Haven, CT: Yale University Press, 1985.

A critical analysis of standardized testing, focusing on the Scholastic Aptitude Test (SAT) commonly used in college admissions procedures in the United States, is the following:

David Owen. *None of the Above: Behind the Myth of Scholastic Aptitude.* Boston: Houghton Mifflin, 1985.

Here is an in-depth look at how social class, race and ethnicity, and gender affect schooling in America.

Carl A. Grant and Christine E. Sleeter. *After the School Bell Rings.* Philadephia: Falmer Press/Taylor & Francis, 1986.

Another useful study of how class and culture affect early schooling is found in this comparison of a white preschool and a black Head Start center.

Sally Lubeck. *Sandbox Society: Early Education in Black and White America—A Comparative Ethnography.* Philadephia: Falmer Press/Taylor & Francis, 1985.

The startling extent of functional illiteracy in the United States, its causes, and its consequences are the focus of this book by a well-known social critic.

Jonathan Kozol. *Illiterate America.* Garden City, NY: Anchor/Doubleday, 1985.

This book reports on a detailed study of a Baptist Christian school in Chicago, suggesting that such schools more closely resemble total institutions than do public schools.

Alan Peshkin. *God's Choice: The Total World of a Fundamentalist Christian School.* Chicago: University of Chicago Press, 1986.

The undergraduate college in American society is the focus of these two books. The first is a historical analysis of the college scene, with important implications for the present. The second is the critical report of the Carnegie Foundation on higher education in the United States based on information provided by both students and faculty.

Helen Lefkowitz Horowitz. *Campus Life: Undergraduate Cultures from the End of the Eighteenth Century to the Present.* New York: Alfred A. Knopf, 1987.

Ernest L. Boyer. *College: The Undergraduate Experience in America.* Prepared by the Carnegie Foundation for the Advancement of Teaching. New York: Harper & Row, 1987.

CHAPTER 16

Religion

Anthropologist Elenore Smith Bowen was gradually adjusting to life in a technologically primitive society in western Africa. As she sat down to begin her dinner one evening, a storm was in the dark night air. Loud, frightened voices rose from the village around her, speaking of a "fire" in the marketplace. Stepping outside to take a look, Bowen saw no smoke rising from the marketplace and tried to calm the others. But a moment later she was aghast to see

> —at treetop level down by the market, . . . a ball of light moving slowly and steadily through the air. There was a gasp and sighing from the people about me. It went out, not failing or dimming, just extinguished. Ihugh [the son of the village leader] stepped forward. "Witches," he spoke the word softly. "My father must be told of this."

> Another ball of light followed. We stared at it in silence. It too went out, all at once, absolutely. (1964:40)

Fearfully, Ihugh asked Bowen to accompany him to his father's hut on the far side of the marketplace, in the belief that witches would avoid foreigners. Other villagers, uneasy about their own safety, preferred to remain where they were. The two made the trip uneventfully and gave Ihugh's father their report. As she returned home, Bowen's mind raced with possible explanations of what she had seen. She had heard stories of strange lights of this kind. Most Americans and Europeans understood such things in scientific terms, describing them as extremely rare—but perfectly natural—electrical phenomena. But in the villagers' culture, the balls of light were the unmistakable work of witches—persons with awesome power derived from supernatural forces.

RELIGION: BASIC CONCEPTS

Human beings have the capacity to define objects and events in their surrounding world in various ways. For much of human history (and in some societies today), people understood the operation of the universe largely through belief in spirits that were responsible for birth, death, and the success or failure in human endeavors. Before the Industrial Revolution, Europeans also defined many social patterns as an expression of divine will. Gradually, however, science emerged as a different world view, one that attempts to explain the natural world—including human society—through systematic observation. But the supernatural has hardly been eclipsed by science. For one thing, the more our scientific knowledge advances, the more awesome and mysterious our vast universe seems. Even more important, science cannot address the vital issue of the meaning of human existence.

As French sociologist Emile Durkheim pointed out early in this century, questions about "all sorts of things which surpass the limits of our knowledge" are the basis of the social experience we call religion (1965:62; orig. 1915). Durkheim noted that human beings have long attached two very different kinds of significance to objects, events, and experiences. That which is understood as **profane** (or "secular") includes *all the ordinary elements of everyday life*. In contrast, what Durkheim called the **sacred** refers to *that which is defined as extraordinary, inspiring a sense of awe, reverence, and even fear*. The distinction between the profane and the sacred has been the foundation of religious belief throughout human history. Therefore, **religion** can be defined basically as *a system of beliefs and practices built upon the recognition of the sacred*.

Because religion deals with that which transcends everyday experience, its validity can be assessed by neither common sense nor science. Religion is a matter of **faith:** *belief that is not based on scientific evidence*. To illustrate, in the New Testament of the Bible, Christians are said to "walk by faith, not by sight" (II Corinthians 5:7), and faith is described as "the conviction of things not seen" (Hebrews 11:1).

Matters of faith vary greatly throughout the world. Nothing is considered to be either sacred or profane by everyone on earth; anything *can* be defined as coming under either category. Most books, for example, fall within the realm of the profane; but the Torah (the first five books of the Hebrew Bible or Old Testament) is defined as sacred by Jews, as is the entire Bible by Christians and the Koran by Muslims. Likewise, most cities are defined as part of the profane world, but Jerusalem is considered sacred by Christians, Muslims, and Jews.

Durkheim claimed that what is sacred is "set apart and forbidden" (1965:62). By this he meant that profane things are understood in terms of their everyday usefulness, but what is defined as sacred is separated from everyday life and evokes a reverent response (O'Dea & Aviad, 1983). For instance, Muslims demand that people remove their shoes before entering a mosque—a sacred place of worship that is not to be symbolically defiled by shoes that have touched the profane ground outside.

The sacred is usually addressed through **ritual,** defined as *formal, ceremonial behavior*. Holy communion is the central ritual for most Christians; the wafer and wine consumed during communion are never defined as food—they are sacred symbols of the body and blood of Christ.

Religion and Sociology

The idea of applying the sociological perspective to religion may generate some uneasiness, especially in those who are strongly religious. Sociologists have good reason to study religion, however, for religious beliefs and practices are central elements of virtually every culture on earth. But because religion is concerned with the sacred, approaching it in a secular manner as one might study social stratification or the family may seem irreverent to some people.

Sociology does not pass judgment on religion as an element of human experience, however, nor can it determine whether a particular religion is right or wrong. Neither does sociological analysis suggest that religion in general is either good or bad. As we shall see, while sociological analysis shows that religion has many important consequences for the operation of society, some sociologists have interpreted these consequences as positive, others have viewed them as negative, and still others have regarded them in a neutral manner. In all cases, however, sociological analysis is limited to the *conse-*

The boundary between the sacred and the profane is marked for Muslims by the practice of removing shoes—which touch the profane ground—before entering a sacred shrine.

Emile Durkheim (1858–1917)

Emile Durkheim is widely regarded as one of the most influential figures in the development of sociology, and was the first formally recognized sociologist in France. His studies of suicide (Chapter 1) and deviance (Chapter 8) are sociological classics, but his study of religion is perhaps the most noteworthy of his diverse contributions to sociology.

All of Durkheim's work was con-cerned with social integration—the means by which the lives of distinct individuals fuse to form a cohesive society. Examining many sources of social integration, Durkheim concluded that religion was the strongest of them all. His interest in religion may have been rooted in his own biography: he was born into a family whose men had for generations been rabbis, and he initially studied to become a rabbi himself. Although he later lost his personal religious beliefs, he expressed an interest in religion in his sociological work for the remainder of his life.

Like many social thinkers of his time, Durkheim recognized that religion, which had been a unifying force in medieval Europe, was declining in strength. This fact raised a troubling question: Did the decline of religion mean the breakup of society? Durkheim's answer to this question was both simple and profound. He recognized society as a power greater than any individual; thus religious experience is essentially the awareness of society. Indeed, he believed that conceptions of the sacred express the power of society in comprehensible terms. Thus Durkheim concluded not only that the origins of religious belief are social, but also that religious belief actually celebrates the power of society. Therefore, the decline of traditional religion is not a sign of impending chaos. On the contrary, Durkheim believed that people might come to respect the power of their society—a source of unity and meaning—just as they had participated in traditional religions.

SOURCE: Based on Emile Durkheim, *The Elementary Forms of Religious Life* (New York: Basic Books, 1965; orig. 1915); and *Moral Education: A Study in the Theory and Application of the Sociology of Education* (New York: Free Press, 1973; orig. 1925). This discussion also draws on Lewis A. Coser, *Masters of Sociological Thought: Ideas in Historical and Social Context* (New York: Harcourt Brace Jovanovich, 1971), pp. 136–139.

quences of religion for society; the *validity* of any religious doctrine is a matter of faith, and therefore cannot be evaluated sociologically. For this reason, sociologists, like other people, have various religious orientations: some are not very religious, while others participate in a wide variety of religions.

THEORETICAL ANALYSIS OF RELIGION

Whatever their personal religious beliefs, all sociologists agree that religion is an important dimension of social life. Several approaches to the sociological analysis of religion reflect the use of different theoretical paradigms.

The Functions of Religion

Emile Durkheim (introduced in the box), one of the most influential nineteenth-century sociologists, contributed to the development of sociology's structural-functional paradigm. He viewed society as a complex system of many interdependent parts that remains relatively stable over long periods of time. As such, he emphasized, society has a life and power of its own beyond the lives of the individual members who collectively created it. Durkheim thus considered society itself to be "godlike." Unlike its individual members, society does not die, and its power to shape the lives of any one of us often evokes a sense of reverence and awe; society also demands the submission of individuals to its values and norms. Thus, according to Durkheim (1965; orig.

1915), society itself is the foundation of the sacred, so that as people develop religious beliefs, they celebrate society's awesome power.

People are able to understand the power of their society, Durkheim continued, by transforming specific, everyday objects into sacred symbols. The sacred, then, symbolizes the collective immortality of individually mortal beings. Among technologically primitive societies, Durkheim found that the power of society is typically represented by a **totem**—*an object, usually an element of the natural world, that is imbued with sacred qualities.* An animal or a plant may be used as a sacred representation of the entire society—the basis of the society's name and group identity, and the focus of ritual that reinforces the bonds that join people together.

In Durkheim's view, whether or not divine powers exist, religious beliefs and practices arise as a part of culture to reflect the power of society. He identified several major functions of religion for the operation of society.

Social Cohesion

Religion promotes social cohesion, uniting members of a society through shared values and norms. In simple societies, the totem is the visible symbol of this unity. In the United States, the American flag serves much the same purpose, symbolizing "one nation, under God, indivisible." Furthermore, all American currency is inscribed with the words "In God We Trust," implying a collective unity based on belief.

Of course, religion can be *dysfunctional* by causing division within a society or by generating conflict between societies. During the early Middle Ages, for example, religious beliefs motivated European Christians to organize the Crusades against Muslims in the East. For their part, Muslims sought to defend their faith against invading Christians. Conflict among Muslims, Jews, and Christians is the source of much political instability in the Middle East today, and the citizens of Northern Ireland are divided into two armed camps on the basis of adherence to Protestant or Catholic religious beliefs.

Social Control

Every society develops various ways of promoting the social conformity that stabilizes its way of life. Many cultural norms—especially the morally significant norms described in Chapter 3 as *mores*— are given sacred legitimacy by religious beliefs. In medieval Europe, social patterns were widely considered to be the will of God, and monarchs often claimed to be ruling by divine right. In today's Iran, the Ayatollah Khomeini justifies his leadership in a similar fashion. Although few other modern political leaders invoke religion in such an explicit way to exert social control, many publicly ask for the blessing of God on their work, and this action encourages their fellow citizens to see their leadership as both right and just.

Meaning and Purpose

In the face of death, disease, natural catastrophes, and numerous human failings, life can seem hopelessly vulnerable, chaotic, and meaningless. Religious beliefs offer people the comforting sense that many human experiences—from birth to death—have a greater purpose. Strengthened by such beliefs, human beings are less likely to collapse with despair when confronted by life's uncertainties and calamities and more likely to continue making an active contribution to the general social welfare.

In a basic sense, then, religion provides a means to address the ultimate questions of life and death to which neither common sense nor science can provide answers. Durkheim's analysis of the functions of religion does not imply that any particular religious beliefs are valid or invalid. Certainly, the world contains countless religious beliefs, many of them contradictory; what one person holds as a matter of faith, another may consider absurd. But insofar as religious beliefs are shared within a society, social cohesion, social stability, and a sense of meaning and purpose result.

The Social Construction of the Sacred

Over the past two decades, sociologist Peter Berger has made an important contribution to the sociological analysis of religion. Berger's ideas are guided by the symbolic-interaction paradigm, which views society as the ongoing creation of human interactions using cultural symbols. "Society," he asserts, "is a human product and nothing but a human product, that yet continuously acts back upon its producer" (1967:3). In other words, society with all its components, including religion, is a reality constructed by interacting human beings that acts back upon its creators.

In Berger's view, religion is a social construction like other parts of society, but one that involves the special quality of the sacred. Members of society learn the meaning of the sacred through ritual, including religious services, saying grace before meals, and taking sacred oaths as part of various legal proceedings. Berger explains that the primary reason societies construct the sacred is to legitimate and stabilize patterns of social life. Because society is a human creation, it is inherently precarious and subject to disruption. If, however, many important events in everyday life are placed within a "cosmic frame of reference," the fallible, transitory creations of human beings gain "the semblance of ultimate security and permanence" (1967:35–36).

In this way, marriage, for example, is defined as *holy* matrimony, giving great authority to culturally approved mating patterns. Similarly, violations of cultural norms that regulate sexual activity may be defined as *sin*. Symbols of the sacred are especially useful in life-threatening situations, and come to the fore in times of social turmoil, war, and natural disaster. Even people who are otherwise not very religious may pray when confronting the death of loved ones, and soldiers have long gone to war "with God on their side." Through the social creation of the sacred, human life is lifted above the ultimate reality of death, so that society—if not its individual members—becomes immortal.

Berger points out, however, that the ability of the sacred to legitimate and stabilize society rests on one major condition: *the socially constructed character of the sacred must go unrecognized.* The conception of holy matrimony would lose power over us if we were to understand that we as members of society had created it in the first place. Similarly, faced with the threatening reality of disaster or death, human beings could draw little strength from sacred beliefs if they saw them as merely a human device for coping with tragedy. For this reason, no doubt, members of every society avoid confronting the fact that they have created the sacred just as they have created the rest of society.

Religion and Social Inequality

The social-conflict paradigm has also offered an analysis of religion, derived in large measure from the ideas of Karl Marx. Marx saw religion as a form of ideology, legitimating the status quo and diverting people's attention from social problems and inequities. Thus, if religion stabilizes society, this is *dysfunctional* because only radical social change can eliminate striking patterns of social inequality.

Marx emphasized the ways in which a society's dominant religion is ideological, protecting the interests of the powerful while limiting the social advantages of the majority. In England, where Marx spent his later life, the monarch has traditionally been crowned by the head of the Church of England—a clear illustration of the close alliance between religious and political elites. Thus, Marx claimed, opposing the political status quo often means challenging the church—and, by implication, God as well. Because they are socialized to accept existing society as morally just, Marx believed that people are blinded to the fact that they can—and should—act to forge a more humane society in which the privileges of the few are not obtained at the expense of the many. In one of Marx's best known statements, he offered a stinging criticism of religion as "the sigh of the oppressed creature, the sentiment of a heartless world, and the soul of soulless conditions. It is the opium of the people" (1964:27; orig 1848). In Marx's view, the Christian religion that predominated in the capitalist European societies of his time lulled the socially disadvantaged into accepting their suffering by promising rewards in a world to come. In contrast, Marx believed that the working population should actively oppose their oppression under capitalism and attempt to establish a just society in this world.

Certainly Marx's analysis of the role of religion in maintaining patterns of social inequality had a great deal of validity in his own time, and in many respects still does. Consider as illustration the fact that virtually all the major religions of the world have long reflected and encouraged male dominance of social life, as the box on p. 432 explains.

During Marx's lifetime, the powerful Christian nations of Western Europe used the "conversion of heathens" as one justification for colonial exploitation of less technologically advanced societies in Africa, Asia, and the Americas. In the United States, major churches in the South pronounced white domination of blacks through slavery consistent with God's will. Until well into the twentieth century, many of these same churches supported racial segregation and other forms of racial injustice.

But there is another side to religion, one that promotes social change. A major example of how religious ideas can promote change was developed by Max Weber (1958; orig. 1904–1905). As Chapter 4 explained in detail, Weber shared many of Marx's ideas about how social conflict can promote change. Yet he viewed the rise of industrial-capitalist societies as not just the product

Religion and Patriarchy

Historically, religion has played a significant part in the persistence of patriarchy in human societies around the world. This is evident in passages from many of the sacred writings of major world religions.

The Koran—the sacred text of Islam—clearly asserts that males are to have social dominance over women:

> Men are in charge of women. . . . Hence good women are obedient. . . . As for those whose rebelliousness you fear, admonish them, banish them from your bed, and scourge them. (cited in Kaufman, 1976:163)

Christianity—the dominant religion of the Western world—has also supported patriarchy. Although Mary, the mother of Jesus, is highly revered within Christianity, the New Testament contains the following passages:

> A man . . . is the image and glory of God; but woman is the glory of man. For man was not made from woman, but woman from man. Neither was man created for woman, but woman for man. (I Corinthians 11:7–9)

> As in all the churches of the saints, the women should keep silence in the churches. For they are not permitted to speak, but should be subordinate, as even the law says. If there is anything they desire to know, let them ask their husbands at home. For it is shameful for a woman to speak in church. (I Corinthians 14:33–35)

> Wives, be subject to your husbands, as to the Lord. For the husband is the head of the wife as Christ is the head of the church. . . . As the church is subject to Christ, so let wives also be subject in everything to their husbands. (Ephesians 5:22–24)

Judaism, too, has traditionally supported patriarchy. Male Orthodox Jews include the following words in daily prayer:

> Blessed art thou, O Lord our God, King of the Universe, that I was not born a gentile. Blessed art thou, O Lord our God, King of the Universe, that I was not born a slave. Blessed art thou, O Lord our God, King of the Universe, that I was not born a woman.

Historically, the major religions have also excluded women from the clergy, but this is currently an issue of controversy. Islam continues to exclude women from such positions, as does the Roman Catholic Church. Many Protestant denominations, however, have embraced the practice of ordaining women. Although Orthodox Judaism still upholds the traditional prohibition against women rabbis, Reform Judaism has had women serving as rabbis for some years now, and in 1985, the first woman assumed the position of rabbi in the Conservative denomination of Judaism.

---

of social conflict, but also as the consequence of a particular world view that predominated among early Calvinists. In Weber's terms, the "Protestant ethic" was a rational and highly disciplined approach to life that was transformed into the "spirit" of capitalism.

Marx's sweeping criticism of religion also ignored the ways in which religion has promoted greater social equality. In the nineteenth century, for example, some American religious groups played an extremely important part in the movement to abolish slavery. In this century, religious Americans of all races have made notable contributions toward increased racial equality in the United States. Both leaders and the rank and file of numerous religious groups were active participants in the civil rights movement of the 1950s and 1960s; perhaps the most outstanding American in this regard was Martin Luther King, Jr., a minister. During the 1960s and 1970s, many clergy were active in the movement to end the war in Vietnam and, more recently, some have supported revolutionary change in Latin America and elsewhere. Some American churches today are offering controversial asylum to refugees from El Salvador, Nicaragua, Guatemala, and other politically unstable countries to our south. In general, Marx did not foresee the extent to which religious groups would promote social change in the twentieth century. *Liberation theology*, an important recent theological movement that is supported by many Christians in the United States and elsewhere, fuses Christian principles with many of Marx's own ideas about social justice, as the box explains.

CROSS-CULTURAL COMPARISON

Liberation Theology

Christianity has long addressed the suffering of the oppressed people of the world, traditionally through efforts to strengthen the faith of the believer in a better life to come—an approach to social justice inconsistent with the ideas of Karl Marx. In recent years, however, some religious leaders and theologians have embraced Marx's emphasis on social justice in *this* world. One major result has been the liberation theology movement.

Liberation theology first developed in the late 1960s within the Roman Catholic Church in Latin America. In simple terms, liberation theology begins with the established teaching of the Catholic Church that Christianity offers liberation from human sin. What is new—and controversial—is the additional assertion that the church has a responsibility to help people liberate themselves from the abysmal poverty that is widespread in technologically undeveloped societies commonly called the Third World. Although there is substantial variation on many points among advocates of liberation theology, the movement is based on three general principles.

First, human suffering exists in the world on a scale that is barely imaginable by the relatively secure and comfortable populations of rich societies such as the United States. Worldwide, some 80 percent of all humanity lives from day to day on only 20 percent of the world's resources; the

inevitable results include high rates of infant mortality, widespread disease, poor nutrition, and alarming levels of starvation. Liberation theology is based, first of all, on the recognition of this reality of human suffering.

Second, according to liberation theologists, human suffering on such a massive scale is inconsistent with Christian moral principles. In simple terms, the gross social inequalities found in today's world contradict the Christian belief in the unity of all humankind. Thus liberation theology claims that such a state violates God's vision for humanity.

Third, liberation theology asserts that, as an expression of faith and conscience, Christians must act to relieve this suffering. Practical strategies must be formulated to bring about change, which usually entails political action.

Many liberation theologians have adopted a Marxist analysis of the social problems of the world. Poverty, they assert, is not a transitory problem that has arisen only recently; rather it is deeply rooted in the structure of many Third World societies in which wealth is controlled by a small proportion of the population. More broadly, the concentration of the world's wealth within a small portion of all societies makes the suffering of most of humankind inevitable.

Thus a growing number of men and women within the Roman Catholic Church have allied themselves

with the poor in a political struggle against the ruling powers in Latin American societies. The costs of doing so have been high. A number of church members have been killed in the widespread violence that engulfs much of that region. In 1980, for example, Oscar Arnulfo Romero, the archbishop of San Salvador (capital of El Salvador), was gunned down inside his church while celebrating mass. Since then, a number of other church leaders have met a similar fate.

Liberation theology has also met with resistance within the Catholic Church. Pope John Paul II has strongly opposed the mixing of politics with traditional church doctrine and has forbidden church officials to participate in political conflicts. The Vatican believes that liberation theology represents a fundamental danger to the Catholic faith because it diverts attention from the otherworldly concerns of Christianity and embroils the church in political controversy. Nonetheless, the liberation theology movement—in principle and in practice—continues in Latin America, fueled by the belief that both Christian faith and a sense of human justice demand efforts to change the plight of the world's poor.

SOURCE: Based, in part, on Leonard and Clodovis Boff, *Salvation and Liberation: In Search of a Balance Between Faith and Politics* (Maryknoll, NY: Orbis Books, 1984).

Religion does not always support the status quo. Martin Luther King, Jr. and other members of the clergy, both black and white, have been in the forefront of the Civil Rights movement in the United States.

TYPES OF RELIGIOUS ORGANIZATION

Since at least the time of the early Christians within the Roman Empire, religious people have faced the problem of living within a world that seems indifferent to religious ideals. This tension between religion and society is at the heart of the distinction between a church and a sect made some fifty years ago by Ernst Troeltsch (1931).

Church and Sect

Drawing on ideas formulated by his teacher Max Weber, Troeltsch described a **church** as *a general type of formal religious organization that is well integrated into the larger society*. A church tends to be well established in a society and typically persists for a long period of time. It usually includes all members of a family, often over many generations. Its stability is enhanced by bureaucratic organization. Church officials are formally ordained and placed within a hierarchy of offices, where

they formally enact various church policies and regulations.

Although all religion is concerned primarily with the realm of the sacred, churches accept the profane society. Churches tend to address what is right and just in abstract terms, but typically ignore specific social arrangements that are inconsistent with such principles. For example, a church may advance the idea that all human beings are brothers and sisters, but remain silent about laws that deny equal rights to people of a particular race or social class. This practice minimizes conflict between the church and the political state (Troeltsch, 1931; Johnstone, 1983; O'Dea & Aviad, 1983).

The general qualities of a church are found within two kinds of actual religious organizations. An **ecclesia** is *a churchlike religious organization that is formally allied with the state*. There have been many ecclesias in human history: for centuries, the Catholic Church was formally allied with the Roman Empire and the Anglican Church has long been the official Church of England; Confucianism was the state religion in China until early in this century; and Islam is the official religion of Pakistan and Iran today. As official religions, ecclesias are likely to claim all people in a society as members. Often such membership is a matter of law, with little toleration of religious differences within a population. Because there is no separation between church and state, an ecclesia is a clear case of religious accommodation to the larger society.

Another type of church is a **denomination**: *a churchlike religious organization that recognizes religious pluralism*. Denominations do not form alliances with the state; rather, they typically exist within societies that formally separate church and state. In the United States, for example, there are many Christian denominations, including Catholics, Baptists, Methodists, and Lutherans. In each case, members of a denomination may strongly hold religious beliefs while recognizing the right of other people to hold beliefs that differ from their own.

Distinct from churches are sects. A **sect** is defined as *a general type of informal religious organization that is not well integrated into the larger society*. Sects typically lack the rigid hierarchy found within established churches. While churches emphasize formal ritual, sects tend to exalt personal experience and emotion. Thus the members of churches tend to be relatively passive during religious services, singing or verbally responding only as called for in a formally organized service, but the members of sects are often highly spontaneous and active, perhaps rejoicing in the perceived presence of God.

Patterns of leadership also differ between churches and sects. Church leadership is a matter of formal office, as in the cases of priests, rabbis, and ministers. Leadership in sects, however, is often based on **charisma**—*extraordinary personal qualities that can turn an audience into followers.* Leaders of sects often provoke strong emotional responses from others, so that they are viewed by the membership as divinely inspired. Generally, the leaders of sects are critical of established religion for having lost the true path; consequently, sects typically seek to *restore* religious beliefs and practices from the past in a pure form (Stark & Bainbridge, 1979).

Also unlike churches, sects seldom seek an accommodation with the established society. In extreme cases, they are hostile to the larger society, sometimes withdrawing completely so that they may practice their religion without interference from outsiders. This suggests that sects often see the larger society as representing evil and misunderstanding, in contrast to the enlightenment and salvation offered by their own beliefs and practices. The Amish, described in a box in Chapter 3, provide an example of a sect that has long sought to remain apart from the larger society (Hostetler, 1980). Sects also typically view their own beliefs as the only true religion and often display intolerance toward those whose religious beliefs differ. Unlike churches, in other words, sects do not usually endorse the doctrine of religious pluralism.

Because sects are typically not long established, their membership depends heavily on outsiders joining their ranks. For this reason, many sects advocate the active recruitment, or *proselytizing,* of new members. This leads to **conversion,** which means *a personal transformation based on new religious beliefs.* Members of Jehovah's Witnesses, for example, are encouraged to spread their religious beliefs among others in the hope of attracting new members.

Churches and sects also differ somewhat in their social composition. As well-established religious organizations, many churches count people of high social standing among their members. As marginal religious organizations in the view of the dominant culture, sects often attract people of lower social position. Moreover, the sect's openness to new members and promise of personal salvation and fulfillment may be especially appealing to people who perceive themselves as social outsiders.

Sects generally form as breakaway groups from established churches or other religious organizations: sects,

Because churches are typically quite formal, behavior during a worship service is relatively passive and subdued. The more informal organization of sects reflects the value placed on personal experience of the divine presence, which often generates strong emotion among members.

then, are the result of religious *schism* (Stark & Bainbridge, 1979). With little formal structure, sects are typically not as stable and long-lived as churches, and many are founded only to soon disappear. But some sects endure, often becoming more churchlike over time. Both the Puritans and the Quakers who originally settled in seventeenth-century America were members of break-

away sects in England. Several centuries later, both evolved into churches in the United States. This changing status of religious organizations suggests that the terms *church* and *sect* should be used as conceptual ideals; any religious organization should be described as being churchlike or sectlike to some degree.

Cult

A **cult** is *a religious movement that has little or nothing in common with other religious organizations in a particular society*. Whereas a sect is typically formed by schism from an established religious organization, a cult represents something almost entirely new. Cults typically originate when a leader who claims some special understanding of divine truth organizes followers into a movement. One example is the early Church of Jesus Christ of Latter-Day Saints (the Mormons), organized by Joseph Smith in New York State in 1830. While including many established Christian principles, Mormonism was initially more of a cult insofar as it embraced unconventional religious ideas, including the practice of plural marriage as described in Chapter 13. Today, of course, the Mormons are no longer a cult, having abandoned such practices to become an established church.

Cults are also the result of the diffusion of religious ideas from a society in which they are conventional to a society where they have no precedent. An example of a cult formed in the United States in this way is Transcendental Meditation (TM), which embodies many Hindu religious ideas introduced to America when Maharishi Mahesh Yogi came to California from India in the late 1950s. During the 1970s, TM attracted perhaps 500,000 followers, although its popularity has declined considerably since then (Bainbridge & Jackson, 1981). Another example of a transplanted religious movement that became an American cult is the Unification Church, which developed in Korea and was brought to the United States in 1959 by the electrical-engineer-turned-religious-leader Sun Myung Moon. Beginning in the late 1940s, Moon received what he believed were messages from God that he was the returned Jesus Christ (Lofland, 1977:3). On the basis of this belief, he successfully forged a religious movement among Koreans and, subsequently, Americans. Membership in the Unification Church in the United States probably numbers about two thousand (Bromley & Shupe, 1979; Harper, 1982).

Cults tend to be even more at odds with established society than sects. In many cults, membership extends

Growing alienation from society as a whole, coupled with the power of an unstable charismatic leader, led to the 1978 tragedy in Jonestown, Guyana. On the order of Jim Jones, over nine hundred of his followers drank Kool-aid laced with cyanide, thus ending one of the most bizarre cases of religious behavior.

beyond religious beliefs to an entire *lifestyle* that involves a radical change in self-identity. For this reason, cults are often accused of brainwashing new members into renouncing their past lives. People who are cut off from their families and friends may experience a cult as a total institution (described in Chapter 5). While there is little doubt that some cults have effected significant change in people, most people who seek to learn about cults do not ultimately become members, and evidence suggests that those who do suffer no psychological harm (Barker, 1981; Kilbourne, 1983).

Although cults involve greater personal transformation, they are like sects in that they rely heavily on charismatic leadership. Most cults form and disperse rather quickly, with little public notice. Others, however, gradually adopt a bureaucratic social organization and become more established. As already noted, this is the history of the Mormons, now an established church reported to be the most rapidly growing religious organization in America (Stark, 1984). In general, if and when a cult becomes more established, it typically seeks accommodation with society, and public hostility consequently declines.

RELIGION IN HISTORY

Religion is found within every society of the world. At the same time, like the family and other social institutions, religion shows considerable historical and cross-cultural variation.

Religion in Preindustrial Societies

Religion was a part of human life even before the beginning of recorded history. At least forty thousand years ago, our human ancestors held religious beliefs and engaged in religious rituals.

Religious ideas varied among early hunting and gathering societies. But common to this period of human history was **animism,** which is *the belief that objects in the natural world are endowed with consciousness and can affect human lives.* For example, even today some technologically primitive peoples view trees, oceans, mountains, and the wind as spiritual forces responsible for events within human societies. Furthermore, since hunting and gathering societies are characterized by little social complexity, religious life exists entirely within the family. In some such societies, the status of *shaman* is assigned to a religious leader, but this is not a full-time specialized activity.

The belief in a divine power responsible for the creation of the world arose only gradually as human beings gained the technological skills of horticulture and agriculture. Such societies commonly believed that a supernatural power created the world and was actively present in it. In this way, a cultural system of morality was supported by the recognition of the sacred. At the same time, religion gradually emerged from the family as a social institution often fused with politics: leaders of society were frequently regarded as both kings and priests, as in the case of the Egyptian pharoah or the early Chinese emperors.

Religion in Industrial Societies

Long before the Industrial Revolution, religion emerged as a distinct social institution, as evidenced by the church in medieval Europe. But the Industrial Revolution brought a growing emphasis on science as a path toward human understanding. When people were distressed, they increasingly turned to practitioners of science—such as physicians—to provide the assistance they had earlier sought from religious leaders. As a result, religious beliefs became less pronounced than they were in medieval times.

But science did not eliminate religion from industrial societies. On the contrary, religion persists because science cannot address issues of ultimate meaning in human life. *How* this world works is a scientific matter, in other words; but *why* we and the rest of the universe

exist at all is a question about which science has nothing to say. Therefore, as will be explained presently, not only have many traditional religions persisted during the twentieth century, but new religions have also emerged. In short, whatever the benefits of science, religion retains a unique ability to address important dimensions of human existence.

The fact that religion and science represent powerful but distinct ways of viewing the universe has sometimes fostered an uneasy relationship between the two. In recent years, many Americans have become aware of this tension in terms of the controversy surrounding the origin of humanity. As the box explains, this debate puts scientific "facts" about human evolution in opposition to religious "beliefs" commonly termed *creationism.*

This gold sarcophagus of the Pharaoh Tutankhamon suggests the extent to which rulers of ancient agrarian societies were worshipped as gods.

The Creation Debate

"In the beginning God created the heavens and the earth." So begins the book of Genesis in the Bible, the sacred text of millions of Christian and Jewish believers. According to a literal interpretation of Genesis, life on earth began on the third day of creation when God created vegetation; on the fifth and sixth days, God created all forms of animal life—most importantly, human beings, fashioned in God's own image.

In 1859, the English scientist Charles Darwin published *On the Origin of Species*, in which he applied biological knowledge based on the logic of science to the origin of humanity. In Darwin's theory of human evolution, the world was not created in the form we find today; rather, all living things changed over time as a consequence of biological evolution (described in Chapter 3). Human beings did not emerge in the initial creation of the earth, but evolved over millions of years from lower forms of animal life.

Darwin's theory of evolution was immediately controversial. What many considered to be a great contribution to science, others saw as an attack against centuries-old sacred be-liefs. On the face of it, Darwin's scientific explanation of human evolution was a total contradiction of a literal reading of biblical creation: after all, if human beings took billions of years to evolve, they could not have been created when the earth was formed. This apparent contradiction remains at the center of the *creation debate*.

A major event in the course of this controversy took shape in the little town of Dayton, Tennessee, in 1925. At that time, a new state law forbade the teaching of "any theory that denies the story of the Divine Creation of man as taught in the Bible, and to teach instead that man descended from a lower order of animals." This law became the topic of discussion one afternoon in Doc Robinson's drugstore. As a fierce debate developed, John Thomas Scopes, a science teacher in the local high school, confirmed that he had, on occasion, taught evolution in the Dayton school. Scopes agreed to stand charged with the crime in order to test this law.

Public interest in the eleven-day trial that followed was heightened by the presence of two great trial lawyers of the day. William Jennings Bryan (three-time presidential candidate) was a fundamentalist Christian leading a national campaign against evolutionary science; he enthusiastically agreed to serve as prosecutor in the case. Clarence Darrow—perhaps the most renowned criminal lawyer in the country—agreed to defend the teacher in what came to be known as the Scopes Monkey Trial.

The trial proved to be one of Clarence Darrow's finest performances, while Bryan—aging, ill, and only days from death—was able to do little for the creationist cause. Yet the community applauded when Scopes was found guilty and fined $100. On appeal, his conviction was reversed on a technical matter, perhaps to prevent the case from reaching the U.S. Supreme Court. Thus the Tennessee law forbidding the teaching of evolution was not repealed until 1967. In 1968, the U.S. Supreme Court struck down all such laws on the grounds that they violated the constitutional prohibition against establishing government-supported religion.

But this decision did not end the controversy. To get around the Court's ruling, creationists adopted

WORLD RELIGIONS

There are thousands of different religions in the world today. Many are found in only limited geographical areas and have very few adherents. Others, which can be termed *world religions*, have millions of followers spread throughout the world. The six world religions described in the following discussion represent some 2.5 billion people—more than half of the earth's population. The size and geographical distribution of these regions are shown in Table 16–1.

Christianity

Christianity is the largest religion in the world: about 1 billion people, or roughly one-fifth of the world's population, identify themselves as Christians. Most live in Europe and North America; about two-thirds of the people

a different line of attack: if the teaching of evolution could not be barred from the schools, then creationism should be introduced into science classes for balance. To do so, however, creationism was stripped of its obvious religious qualities and *creation science* was born.

Creation science attempts to support traditional creationist beliefs as found in Genesis with scientific facts. Creation science had some initial success. The legislatures of California, Arkansas, and Louisiana required that creation science be included in school curricula. All such laws, however, were struck down by the courts in 1985 as violating the constitutional separation of church and state. In addition, creation science was declared to be without scientific merit.

This judgment is based on the fact that science has a provisional character—all theories are accepted only insofar as they are consistent with empirical evidence. Thus while the theory of evolution has continually changed as new facts have emerged from research, creation science does not recognize the possibility of being falsified. One judge concluded that

creation science is religion rather than science, "dogmatic, absolutist and never subject to revision."

Nonetheless, many Americans believe in the literal truth of the biblical account of creation. In a recent national poll, 44 percent of Americans endorsed the creation science belief that God created human beings in their present form within the last ten thousand years. Only 9 percent of respondents held to a nonreligious evolutionary view that humanity evolved from lower forms of life over millions of years, with God having no part in the process. However, 38 percent of Americans endorsed the mixed view that evolution is a scientific fact, but that God has directed the process. The remaining 9 percent claimed to have no knowledge of how human beings came to be (Severo, 1982).

Thus Americans remain quite divided over the creationism question even today. But are science and religion truly in conflict here? Not according to many leading scientists and church leaders. John S. Spong, the Episcopal bishop of Newark, New Jersey, claimed that scientists and biblical scholars alike must recognize the

"enormous amount of evidence" that humanity was not created in the last ten thousand years. He added that the findings of the poll presented above were a "sorry reflection" on the teaching of science in America.

The point is, as indicated in Chapter 2, religion and science represent *two distinct ways of knowing* that conform to different standards of truth and address different kinds of questions. Science is based on observable facts and thus deals only with events within the natural world; religion is a matter of faith that focuses on the supernatural world. Thus even though scientific evidence overwhelmingly supports the general theory of evolution, God's role in human creation will forever be a matter of faith and not of scientific fact.

SOURCE: Based on Harry Nelson and Robert Jermain, *Introduction to Physical Anthropology*, 3rd ed. (St. Paul, MN: West, 1985), pp. 22–24; Stephen J. Gould, "Evolution as Fact and Theory," *Discover*, May 1981, pp. 35–37; Ronald L. Numbers, "Creationism in 20th-Century America," *Science*, Vol. 218, No. 5 (November 1982): 538–544; Richard Severo, "Poll Finds Americans Split on Creation Idea," *New York Times*, August 29, 1982, p. 22. Professor J. Kenneth Smail of Kenyon College also contributed ideas to this discussion.

in the United States and Canada claim Christianity as their religion. The tremendous influence of Christianity in the Western World is indicated by the fact that the Western calendar is based on the birth of Christ. Sizable Christian populations exist throughout the rest of the world, largely as a result of colonization by Westerners in the past.

Christianity began as a Middle-Eastern cult. With roots in Judaism, early Christianity could perhaps be called a sect, but it was actually more new than a continu-

ation of what had gone before. As is true of many cults, Christianity grew out of people's response to the personal charisma of Jesus of Nazareth, who challenged the established society of the time. Jesus was not a political revolutionary, however; he counseled political accommodation to the Roman Empire, admonishing his followers to "Render therefore to Caesar things that are Caesar's" (Matthew 22:21). But the power of Christ's message to believers was the hope of overcoming the world and its inevitable decay in an eternal life to come. Such hope—

Table 16–1 ESTIMATED SIZE AND GEOGRAPHICAL DISTRIBUTION OF SIX WORLD RELIGIONS

Location	Religion					
	Christianity	Islam	Hinduism	Buddhism	Confucianism	Judaism
North and Central America	260,925,000	1,581,000	310,000	330,000	100,000	7,612,000
South America	197,642,000	405,000	635,000	240,000	58,000	739,000
Europe and the Soviet Union	334,467,000	20,201,000	440,000	240,000	440,000	4,110,000
Asia	103,741,000	378,100,000	458,600,000	248,770,000	157,500,000	4,291,000
Africa	147,400,000	153,220,000	850,000	15,000	2,000	230,000
Oceania	18,781,000	87,000	325,000	24,000	18,000	74,000
Total	1,062,956,000	553,594,000	461,160,000	249,619,000	158,118,000	17,056,000

SOURCE: *The World Almanac and Book of Facts 1986* (New York: Newspaper Enterprise Association, 1986), p. 336.

central to this faith—is also the basis of a proper life on earth, in which people are joined in Christian love.

Christianity also challenged the Roman Empire's **polytheism,** meaning *religious beliefs recognizing many gods.* Like Judaism, from which it developed, Christianity is an example of **monotheism**, *religious beliefs recognizing a single divine power.* Christianity, however, has a unique view of the Supreme Being as the sacred Trinity: God the Father, the Creator; Jesus Christ, the Son of God and the Redeemer; and the Holy Spirit, a Christian's personal experience of God's presence.

The basis of the belief in Jesus' divinity lies in the final events of his life on earth. He was tried and sentenced to death in Jerusalem as a perceived threat to the established political leaders. Jesus endured a cruel execution by crucifixion, from which the cross became the sacred symbol of Christianity. According to Christian belief, Jesus was resurrected—that is, he rose from the dead—and this was viewed by his followers as evidence that he was indeed the Son of God.

The relative peace created by the Roman Empire allowed the Apostle Paul and others to travel widely, spreading Christianity throughout the Mediterranean region. Although Christians were initially subjected to persecution, in the fourth century Christianity became an ecclesia—the officially recognized religion of the Roman Empire. Thus what had begun as a cult was transformed into an established church.

Soon afterward, Rome declined, although the eastern part of the empire, based in the city of Constantinople (now Istanbul, Turkey), continued until the fifteenth century. A religious division in the eleventh century resulted in two centers of Christianity: the Roman Catholic Church based in Rome and the Orthodox Church in Constantinople.

Further divisions within Christianity took place toward the end of the Middle Ages, when religious leaders such as Martin Luther (1483–1546) protested many of the religious doctrines of the established church. The Reformation in Europe ushered in a period of increasing religious pluralism in which numerous Protestant denominations emerged within Christianity. More than a dozen Protestant denominations—the Baptists and Methodists are the two largest—command sizable followings in the United States; these and others are also found in other parts of the world.

In sum, Christianity is one of the oldest world religions, and the one that has most influenced Western civilization. Initially, a cult outside of established society, Christianity gradually became well integrated into many societies. Divisions over the course of two millennia have produced the many variants of Christianity we know today. Yet all base their religious doctrines on the belief that a historical figure named Jesus of Nazareth was the Son of God sent to reform human society and to offer everlasting life to those who accept him as their personal savior (Smart, 1969; Kaufman, 1976; Stavrianos, 1983).

Islam

Islam is the second largest religion in the world, with more than 500 million followers called Muslims (or Moslems). Islam is the dominant religion in most of the

Middle East and North Africa; a majority of Arabs are Muslims. In addition, sizable Muslim populations are found throughout the world, including about 1.5 million in North America.

Islam is based on the life of Muhammad, who was born in the city of Mecca (in western Saudi Arabia) about the year 570. To Muslims, Muhammad was a prophet, not a divine being as Jesus is regarded by Christians. Muhammad's role was to record the word of Allah, the God of Islam. The Koran, a book of Muhammad's writings, is sacred to Muslims as the word of God. In Arabic, the word *Islam* means both "submission" and "peace," and the Koran teaches that through submission to Allah an individual finds inner peace. Muslims express this personal devotion in a daily ritual of five prayers.

Islam spread rapidly after the death of Muhammad, and divisions arose within the religion as they did within Christianity. But the Koran directs all believers to pray, to fast at specified times, to journey at least once to Mecca (the sacred city of Muhammad's birth), and to seek justice in the world. Like many other religions, Islam claims that all people are accountable to God for their deeds on earth; those who have lived obediently will be rewarded in heaven, while unbelievers will suffer infinite punishment.

Muslims also recognize an obligation to defend their faith against all threats. In some cases, this tenet of Islam has been used to justify holy wars against unbelievers (in roughly the same way that medieval Christians joined the Crusades in military opposition to the Muslims). This concern has been recently evident as Muslims—most notably in Iran—have attempted to rid their society of Western social influences they regard as morally compromising (Kaufman, 1976; Martin, 1982).

Muslims carefully study the Koran—often committing much of it to memory—as part of the discipline of their faith.

Finally, like most religions, Islam is linked to the domination of women by men. In the view of many Westerners, Muslim women are among the most socially restrained people on earth. Muslim women do lack many personal freedoms enjoyed by Muslim men, but we should bear in mind that patriarchy was well established in the Middle East long before the birth of Muhammad. Furthermore, some defenders argue that Islam actually elevated the social position of women to at least some degree by limiting the practice of polygyny so that no man can have more than four wives.

Hinduism

Hinduism is probably the oldest of the world religions, with roots in the Indus Valley some twenty-five hundred years before the common era. Over thousands of years, Hinduism and Indian society have become so intertwined that one cannot easily be described apart from the other. For this reason, unlike Christianity and Islam, Hinduism has not readily diffused to other societies (Schmidt, 1980).

Indeed, most of the 500 million Hindus live in India and Pakistan, but small numbers live in other parts of the world. In North America, for example, Hindus number about a quarter of a million.

Hinduism is also unlike Christianity and Islam in that it is not linked to the life of a single person. Nor does Hinduism have an officially recognized book of writings comparable to the Bible or the Koran. Not surprisingly, Hindu beliefs and practices vary widely. In general, however, Hindus believe that the moral force of the universe makes demands on all people, responsibilities termed *dharma*. Upholding the traditional caste system of social stratification, as described in Chapter 9, is one part of dharma.

Also central to Hinduism is the concept of *karma*, a belief in the spiritual progress of each person's soul. Every human action has a direct spiritual consequence; proper living causes moral improvement, while improper living results in moral decline. Karma also involves reincarnation, a belief that a new birth follows each death, so that one is reborn into a spiritual state corresponding to the moral quality of one's previous life. Unlike Christianity and Islam, Hinduism proclaims no ultimate justice at the hands of a supreme god; but through the cycle of rebirth, each person may be said to reap exactly what is sown. The ultimate state of paradise—the Hindu concept of *nirvana*—is spiritual perfection in which the soul is spared the need for further rebirth.

India's Ganges River is sacred to Hindus, who believe that bathing in its waters is spiritually purifying. During the Kumbh Mela, millions make a pilgrimage to participate in this ritual.

Strictly speaking, Hinduism is neither monotheistic nor polytheistic. There is an element of monotheism in the Hindu view of the universe as a single moral system, but Hindus may perceive this moral order in any part of the natural world. Hindus also engage in highly variable rituals. Many are carried out privately, including, for example, ritual cleansing following contact with a person of lower caste. Still other rituals are massive public events, such as the *Kumbh Mela*, which takes place every twelve years. At this time millions of Hindus go on a pilgrimage to the Ganges River—a major sacred symbol—to bathe in the ritually purifying waters. The last such event, in 1977, involved some 10 million people.

Hinduism is unlike most other world religions in many respects and is based on doctrines quite unfamiliar to most Westerners. The marked variety of Hindu practice reflects the fact that Hinduism has been interwoven into the daily lives of people living in countless Indian villages over more than four thousand years. To each Hindu, however, this religion is a powerful force offering both explanation and guidance in life (Pitt, 1955; Sen, 1961; Embree, 1972; Kaufman, 1976; Schmidt, 1980).

Buddhism

Buddhism emerged in India some five hundred years before the common era. Today about 250 million people, almost all of whom live in Asia, are adherents of the Buddhist religion. This religion resembles Hinduism in some ways, but differs in that its inspiration is the life of one individual.

About 563 B.C.E., Siddhartha Gautama was born to a high-caste Indian family. At the age of twenty-nine, he claimed that his preoccupation with spiritual matters had led him to a radical personal transformation. After additional years of travel and meditation, Gautama reached what Buddhists describe as *bodhi*, or enlightenment. Through his understanding of the essence of life, Gautama became a Buddha.

Overcome by his personal charisma, many followers spread Buddha's teachings—the *dhamma*—across India. During the third century B.C.E, Buddhism was embraced by the ruler of India, who sent missionaries to spread the religion throughout Asia. Thus Buddhism became a world religion.

To Buddhists, all existence is suffering. Without denying the possibility of pleasure, Buddhists believe that human joy is merely transitory. This belief emerged in Buddha's own travels within a society rife with poverty. But Buddhism does not view wealth as a solution to suffering. On the contrary, materialism is seen as a barrier to spiritual development. In the quest for spiritual peace, then, Buddhists reject any form of material pleasure. If Buddhism does suggest an answer to world problems, it is radical personal change toward more spiritual being.

Like Hinduism, Buddhism claims that each subsequent life reflects the spiritual state of previous lives. The person who attains full enlightenment ceases to be reborn; only in this way can one be liberated from the suffering of the world. Buddhism also shares with Hinduism the belief that day-to-day human acts have spiritual consequences, and that every human activity is either wholesome (leading to spiritual improvement) or unwholesome (resulting in spiritual decline). In this way, like Hinduism, Buddhism recognizes justice in the world without a singular god of judgment.

In sum, Buddhism shares with Christianity and Islam an origin in the life of a charismatic teacher. But in doctrine, Buddhism is much closer to Hinduism because it is based on the conception of a highly ordered moral universe without a high god and belief in the process of individual spiritual development over many lifetimes (Schumann, 1974; Thomas, 1975).

Confucianism

From about 200 B.C.E. until the beginning of this century, Confucianism was an ecclesia—the official religion of China (McGuire, 1987). Although Confucianism has weakened greatly since the 1949 revolution that initiated the People's Republic of China, over 150 million people are followers of this religion and many more are influenced by its teachings.

As in the case of most world religions, the doctrine of Confucianism was largely shaped by a single person, K'ung-Fu-tzu, known to Westerners as Confucius. Confucius is believed to have lived between 551 and 479 B.C.E. and shared with Buddha a deep concern for the problems and suffering he found in the world around him. But while Buddhism encourages a spiritual withdrawal from the world, Confucius taught that personal salvation is to be attained by living within the world according to specific principles of moral conduct. In this way, Confucianism became fused with the traditional culture of China. As in the case of Hinduism, this close association between religious thought and a single society resulted in little diffusion of the religion beyond the society's borders.

In the simplest terms, Confucianism is based on the concept of *jen*, or humaneness. In practice, this means that morality should always take precedence over self-interest. Especially within the family, individuals' lives should reflect loyalty and concern for others. From personal loyalty arises strong families; these, in turn, are the basis of a sound society. Unlike Jesus and Buddha, Confucius did not direct attention to the future and away from this world; rather, he taught that moral living is based on studying the past.

Without a clear concept of the sacred, Confucianism is arguably not a religion at all but rather a disciplined study of Chinese cultural history. Indeed, compared to many cultures, the Chinese have traditionally maintained a rather skeptical attitude toward the supernatural.

Perhaps Confucianism is best described as a disciplined and scholarly way of life, but one that shares with religion a body of beliefs and practices that strive for goodness and produce social unity (Kaufman, 1976; Schmidt, 1980).

Judaism

Judaism is a world religion with over 17 million adherents. The majority of Jews live in North America, with much of the remainder divided between Europe and the Middle East.

Like Confucianism, Judaism is eminently historical: Jews of today regard the past as a source of guidance in the present and for the future. For Jews, the past extends back to the ancient cultures of Mesopotamia and Egypt almost four thousand years before the common era. At this time, the Jews, led by Abraham, their earliest great ancestor, were animistic; that is, they believed that objects within the natural world had a spiritual existence. But this belief was to change after Jacob, Abraham's grandson, led his people to Egypt.

Under Egyptian rule, the Jews endured centuries of slavery. In the thirteenth century before the common era, a turning point came as Moses, the adopted son of an Egyptian princess, was called by God to lead the Jews out of Egypt. The exodus is commemorated by Jews today in the ritual of Passover. At this time, Judaism became monotheistic, recognizing a single, all-powerful God.

A distinctive element of Judaism is the *covenant*—a special relationship with God by which Jews became a "chosen people." The covenant is in the form of law, and centers on the Ten Commandments revealed to Moses by God. Jews regard the Bible (or, in Christian terms, the Old Testament) as both their history and the laws that all Jews must follow. Of special importance are the first five books of the Bible (Genesis, Exodus, Leviticus, Numbers, and Deuteronomy), designated as the *Torah*. This word is roughly equivalent to the English words "teaching" and "law." In contrast to Christianity's central concern with personal salvation, therefore, Judaism emphasizes moral behavior within this world.

Like Christianity, Judaism has undergone internal divisions based on interpretations of doctrine (Lazerwitz & Harrison, 1979). Orthodox Jews (including more than 1 million Americans) strictly observe traditional beliefs and practices, including forms of dress, segregation of men and women at religious services, and consumption

Chanukah is an important Jewish ritual of commemoration that serves to teach young Jews their long and rich history.

of only kosher foods. On the basis of such unconventional practices, Orthodox Judaism can be considered relatively sectlike. In the mid-nineteenth century, many Jews sought greater accommodation to the larger society, leading to the formation of the more churchlike Reform Judaism (now including over 400,000 Americans). More recently, a third segment—Conservative Judaism (about 1.7 million Americans)—has established a middle ground between the other two categories.

All Jews, however, maintain a keen awareness of their cultural history and the fact that their ancestors have historically been subjected to considerable prejudice and discrimination. Jews endured centuries of slavery in Egypt, conquest by Rome, and persecution in Europe and elsewhere. The denial of equal political rights and economic opportunity to European Jews was accompanied by forcible residential segregation in areas of cities that came to be called *ghettos*.

Jewish emigration to America began in the mid-1600s. As large numbers arrived in the final decades of the nineteenth century during the Great Immigration, prejudice and discrimination, commonly referred to as *anti-Semitism*, increased. During the twentieth century, anti-Semitism reached its height when Jews experienced the most horrific persecution in modern times—the Holocaust, in which some 6 million of them were systematically annihilated by the Nazis during the 1930s and 1940s. The killing was so unbelievably extensive and methodical that many Americans and Europeans initially refused to recognize it for what it was: genocide (Abzug, 1985).

In sum, one of the oldest world religions, Judaism has changed considerably over thousands of years. Like Christianity and Islam, Judaism recognizes a single God; but like Hinduism and Confucianism, Judaism is not strongly otherworldly. Rather, this religion emphasizes moral directives for life within this world. The history of Judaism also serves as a grim reminder of the extent to which religious minorities have been the target of hatred and outright slaughter in human history (Bedell, Sandon, & Wellborn, 1975; Holm, 1977; Schmidt, 1980; Seltzer, 1980; B. Wilson, 1982; Eisen, 1983).

RELIGION IN THE UNITED STATES

American society has experienced remarkable changes in the last 350 years. In the minds of some at least, the Industrial Revolution, universal education, and the embrace of science and technology have called into doubt the survival of traditional religion (Collins, 1982). Yet there is ample evidence that religion remains a central element in American social life.

Religious Affiliation

National surveys reveal that about 90 percent of Americans identify with a particular religion (N.O.R.C., 1983; Gallup, 1984). Formal affiliation with a religious organization, however, characterizes only about 60 percent of the population—a proportion that has remained relatively stable over the last fifty years (Gallup, 1984; U.S. Bureau of the Census, 1985). One notable pattern is a somewhat lower rate of religious affiliation in western states, where higher geographical mobility seems to discourage membership in religious organizations (Welch, 1983; Gallup, 1984).

The United States has no official religion; the separation of church and state is mandated by the First Amendment to the Constitution. But the Christian-Judaic tradition certainly dominates American culture, so that members of other religions (and those with no religion) may often feel like "outsiders." As Table 16–2 indicates, about 65 percent of Americans claim to be Protestants, Catholics account for about 25 percent, and less than 2 percent identify themselves as Jews.

This variation—as well as denominational variation among Protestants—makes American society appear to be religiously pluralistic. As Figure 16–1 suggests, however, a single religious affiliation predominates within most geographic regions of the United States. New England, urban areas of the Midwest, and the Southwest are largely Catholic. The southern states are overwhelmingly Baptist, while Lutherans predominate in the northern plains states. Members of the Church of the Latter-Day Saints (Mormons) are heavily concentrated in and around Utah. In only a few areas (shown in the figure with no color) does no one religion represent at least one-fourth of the population. Therefore, although American society as a whole is, indeed, pluralistic, from the point of view of an individual anywhere in America, one religious affiliation is likely to stand out.

Religiosity

In general terms, **religiosity** is *the importance of religion in a person's life*. The fact that many more Americans identify with a religion than are actually affiliated with one points to a problem that has long concerned researchers: religiosity varies according to how it is measured. Many years ago, Charles Glock (1959, 1962) suggested that religiosity involves many distinct dimensions. *Experiential* religiosity refers to a person's inward emotional tie to a religion. *Ritualistic* religiosity refers to ritual activity such as prayer and church attendance. *Ideological* religiosity concerns belief in religious doctrine. *Consequential* religiosity has to do with how evident religious beliefs are in a person's overall daily behavior. *Intellectual* religiosity refers to the extent of a person's knowledge of the history and beliefs of a particular religion. Clearly, any one person is probably more religious in some ways than in others, underlining the difficulty of measuring a complex concept such as religiosity.

How religious, then, are Americans? Almost everyone in the United States (95 percent) claims to believe in a divine power of some kind and, as we have seen, 90 percent of Americans identify with a specific religion. Moreover, 84 percent claim to feel "closeness" to God (N.O.R.C., 1987:140). In terms of experiential religiosity, Americans do seem to be a religious people.

Americans appear to be less religious, however, in ideological terms: only about 70 percent, for instance, claim to believe in a life after death. Americans score even lower on dimensions of ritualistic religiosity. For example, only about half of American adults claim to pray at least once a day (N.O.R.C., 1987:139), and only about 35 percent attend religious services on a weekly or almost-weekly basis (N.O.R.C., 1987:132).

American religiosity is, therefore, an ambiguous matter. Because belief in God is normative within American culture, for many people such a claim may be simply a matter of conformity. Similarly, people can have various motives for attending religious services, not all of which are, strictly speaking, religious. For some, religious organizations provide a sense of identity and belonging, a means of serving the community, or a source of social prestige. We may safely conclude, then, that most Americans are only marginally religious, although a large minority are deeply religious. This conclusion is supported

Table 16–2 RELIGIOUS IDENTIFICATION AMONG AMERICANS, 1987*

Religion	Proportion Indicating Preference
Protestant denominations	64.8%
Baptist	21.8
Methodist	9.9
Lutheran	5.7
Presbyterian	5.3
Episcopalian	2.1
All others, or no denomination	20.0
Catholic	24.2
Jewish	1.4
Other or no answer	2.5
No religious preference	7.1

SOURCE: N.O.R.C., *General Social Surveys, 1972–1987* (Chicago: National Opinion Research Center, 1987), p. 130–131.

* Based on a national sample of persons aged 18 or over.

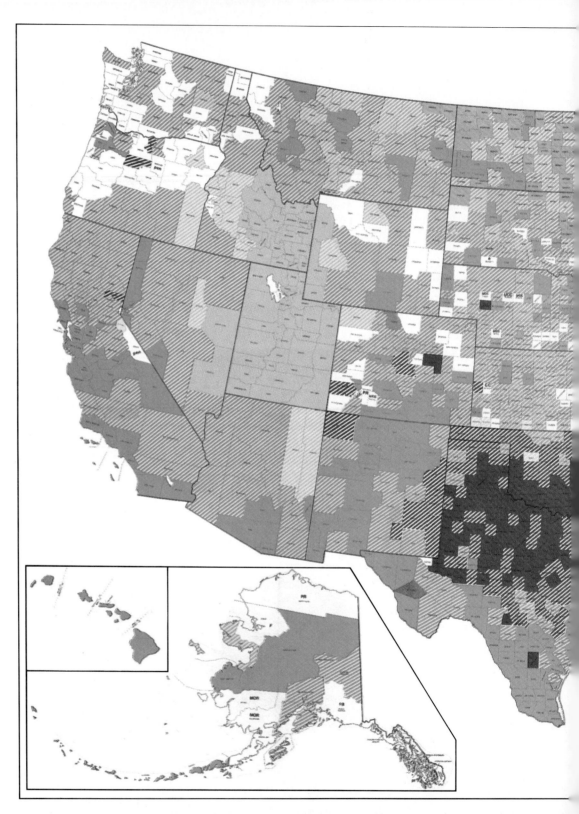

Figure 16–1 Major Denominations by Counties of the United States, 1980

(Glenmary Research Center)

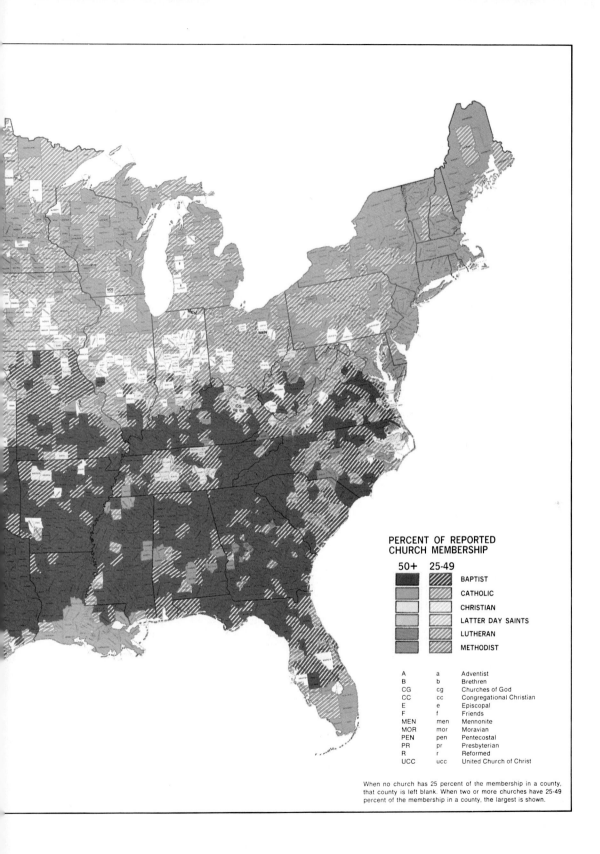

PERCENT OF REPORTED
CHURCH MEMBERSHIP

50+	25-49	
		BAPTIST
		CATHOLIC
		CHRISTIAN
		LATTER DAY SAINTS
		LUTHERAN
		METHODIST

A	a	Adventist
B	b	Brethren
CG	cg	Churches of God
CC	cc	Congregational Christian
E	e	Episcopal
F	f	Friends
MEN	men	Mennonite
MOR	mor	Moravian
PEN	pen	Pentecostal
PR	pr	Presbyterian
R	r	Reformed
UCC	ucc	United Church of Christ

When no church has 25 percent of the membership in a county,
that county is left blank. When two or more churches have 25-49
percent of the membership in a county, the largest is shown.

447

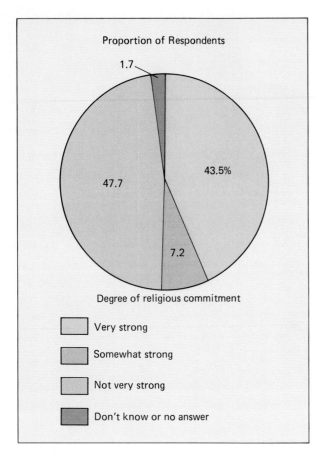

Proportion of Respondents

1.7

43.5%

47.7

7.2

Degree of religious commitment

☐ Very strong

☐ Somewhat strong

☐ Not very strong

☐ Don't know or no answer

Figure 16–2 The Strength of American Religious Beliefs, 1983

(National Opinion Research Center, 1983:97)

by the results of a survey of American adults, illustrated in Figure 16–2.

Patterns of belief are also quite variable among different religious organizations. In a classic study, Rodney Stark and Charles Glock (1968) assessed the religiosity of various Christian organizations, some more churchlike and others more sectlike. Table 16–3 provides the results of their research. Among churchlike denominations, Catholics appear to be generally more religious than Protestants. Notice, too, considerable variation in terms of religiosity among Protestant denominations. Members of sectlike religious organizations, however, show much higher religiosity than either Catholics or other Protestants.

Correlates of Religious Affiliation

Religious affiliation is related not only to religiosity, but to other familiar social patterns as well.

Social Class

Although there are differences in social class within every religious category, religious affiliation is generally linked to social class. Table 16–4 presents the relative standing of the members of major religious groups in the United States during the mid-1970s (Roof, 1979). Of all the categories included in the table, Jews have the highest overall social standing in terms of income, occupational prestige, and educational attainment. Among Protestant denominations, Episcopalians and Presbyterians have higher social position than Methodists, Lutherans, and Baptists. In general, Catholics occupy a middle position in the class structure of America. In the lowest position are members of various Christian sects.

Several factors account for these differences. As noted earlier, churchlike religious organizations tend to have members of higher social standing. The Protestant denominations that rank highest in Table 16–4 are those whose members are primarily of Northern European background, many of whose ancestors came to the United States many generations ago. Thus they have encountered the least prejudice and discrimination and have had the greatest time to establish themselves socially. Roman Catholics, on the other hand, are likely to be more recent immigrants to the United States (Johnstone, 1983). And as suggested previously, sects tend to attract people of somewhat lower social standing.

Jews have relatively high social standing despite the fact that many came to the United States within the last century, often with little wealth, and frequently had to confront anti-Semitism from some members of the Christian majority. Sometimes people explain Jewish success by asserting that Jews are likely to work in banks and other financial positions. This is not true, however: in New York, Jews represent half of all college graduates, but only 2 percent of banking officials (Schaefer, 1979). More accurately, Jewish culture has long placed great value on education, which reflects the historical importance of religious study. Thus, although a large proportion of Jews began life in the United States in poverty, an intense desire for learning often led to the extensive formal education of children, so that the social position of many—although certainly not all—Jews rose in a generation or two.

Table 16–3 RELIGIOUS BELIEFS OF CHRISTIAN CHURCHES AND SECTS

	Congre-gational	Methodist	Episco-palian	Disciple of Christ	Presby-terian	American Lutheran	American Baptist	Missouri Synod Lutheran	Southern Baptist	Sects	Total Protestant	Roman Catholic
Percentage endorsing statement												
I know God really exists, and I have no doubts about it.	41	60	63	76	75	73	78	81	99	96	71	81
Jesus is the divine Son of God, and I have no doubts about it.	41	54	59	74	72	74	76	93	99	97	69	86
Percentage claiming statement to be "completely true"												
Jesus was born of a virgin.	21	34	39	62	57	66	69	92	99	96	57	81
Jesus walked on water.	19	26	30	62	51	58	62	83	99	94	50	71
Miracles actually happened just as the Bible says they did.	28	37	41	62	58	69	62	89	92	92	57	74
There is a life beyond death.	36	49	53	64	69	70	72	84	97	94	65	75
The devil actually exists.	6	13	17	18	31	49	49	77	92	90	38	66

SOURCE: Based on data from Rodney Stark and Charles Y. Glock, *American Piety: The Nature of Religious Commitment:* Vol. 1, *Patterns of Religious Commitment* (Berkeley, CA: University of California Press, 1968), pp. 33–34; 36–37.

Table 16—4 RELIGION AND SOCIAL CLASS IN THE UNITED STATES*

| | Dimension of Social Stratification | | |
Religion	Family Income (dollars)	Relative Occupational Prestige	Education (years)
Jews	14,350	50.0	13.7
Protestants	10,120	45.9	11.7
Episcopalians	14,100	48.4	13.6
Presbyterians	13,200	49.0	13.1
Congregationalists	12,045	47.3	12.7
Methodists	10,085	46.2	12.0
Lutherans	10,400	45.1	11.6
Baptists	9,245	45.8	11.0
Sects	8,080	45.7	10.5
Catholics	10,820	43.8	11.7

SOURCE: Based on data from Wade Clark Roof, "Socioeconomic Differentials Among White Socioreligious Groups in the United States," *Social Forces*, Vol. 58 (September 1979), pp. 280–289.

* Survey data collected during the mid-1970s.

Ethnicity and Race

Around the world, religion is strongly linked to ethnicity. Many world religions are found predominantly within a single geographical region, in some cases, within a single society. Islam, for example, is concentrated in the Arab cultures of the Middle East, and Hinduism is virtually synonymous with Indian culture, as Confucianism is with the culture of China. In other cases, however, the links between religion and ethnicity are less strong. Christianity is widely spread throughout numerous cultures, as is Judaism.

Within American society, we often speak of Anglo-Saxon Protestants, Irish Catholics, Russian Jews, and Greek Orthodox. This reflects the fact that many of the societies from which immigrants came had one predominant religion. Still, virtually every American ethnic group contains at least some religious diversity. Americans of English ancestry, for instance, are not only members of many Protestant denominations, but are Roman Catholics, Jews, and members of other religions as well.

Religion has long been an important element in black society. After arrival in the western hemisphere, most blacks became Christians—the dominant religion in the Americas—but fused Christian belief and practice with elements of African religions. For this reason, and

in reaction to the harsh discipline of slavery, black Christianity was—by white standards—highly emotional and spontaneous. These qualities have persisted in many (although not all) black religious organizations today (Frazier, 1965; Roberts, 1980). In spite of its obvious contradiction of Christian ideals, racial segregation has traditionally been found in Christian churches as in other areas of American life. Historically, American blacks have either attended all-black churches or worshiped in segregated sections of white churches.

In the wake of emancipation, the church came to play a central role in the black communities of America. As blacks gradually migrated from the rural South to the industrial cities of the North, the church responded to problems of dislocation, prejudice, and poverty. A number of major black leaders—including Ralph Abernathy, Martin Luther King, Jr., and Jesse Jackson—have led political movements from their positions as religious officials.

Political Attitudes

Two decades ago, Charles Glock and Rodney Stark (1965) examined links between religiosity and political attitudes in Great Britain and France. Politically speaking, British society can be divided into supporters of the Tory Party (who are politically conservative and generally of higher social class) and supporters of the Labour Party (who are politically liberal and generally of lower social standing). Glock and Stark found that Tories were more religious than Labourites: they were almost twice as likely to attend church, and were also more likely to believe in life after death. The same pattern was found in France: more politically conservative people were much more likely to engage in religious activity than more liberal people.

Looking at the United States, Protestants tend to be more conservative than Catholics. Consequently, Protestants are more likely to support the Republican Party, while Catholics have historically been Democrats. Jews, too, have traditionally supported the Democratic party (J. Wilson, 1978; Gallup, 1982). Consistent with their European research, Glock and Stark (1965) found that, among Protestants, the more conservative Republicans attended church more frequently than did the more liberal Democrats.

Keep in mind, however, that religion and politics are complex, and we cannot assume that religion alone accounts for political atittudes. Protestant conservatism certainly reflects the fact that Protestants historically have enjoyed a privileged social position in American society. More liberal Catholics and Jews, on the other hand, have traditionally been religious and ethnic minorities with lower social standing. Similarly, the long-standing political activism of black churches represents not only Christian ideals but historical patterns of prejudice and discrimination as well.

RELIGION IN A CHANGING SOCIETY

All societies change over time. Just as patterns of social inequality, family life, and formal education have changed, so, too, has religious life in the United States, and it will continue to do so.

Secularization

One of the most important—and controversial—patterns of social change is **secularization:** *the decline in the influence of religion.* Secularization is commonly associated with modern, technologically advanced societies; in fact, this term is derived from the Latin word meaning "the present age" (Cox, 1971; O'Dea & Aviad, 1983).

Conventional wisdom holds that secularization reflects the increasing importance of science to human understanding during the last several centuries. In essence, secularization involves a shift from a religious understanding of the world (based on faith in what *cannot* be directly proved) to a scientific understanding (based on knowledge about what *can* be directly proved). To illustrate, imagine Sir Isaac Newton (1642–1727) sitting under an apple tree observing apples falling to the ground. Had he followed the mode of thought that dominated Europe during the Middle Ages, Newton might have asserted—on the basis of faith—that objects fall to the ground according to the will of God. But Newton lived in an age when human beings were beginning to use the logic of science to understand the natural world. Thus his observations ultimately led him to formulate the law of gravity.

Today most Americans do not understand illness, for example, as the work of a divine power; when ill, we are more likely to consult a physician (whose knowledge is based on science) than a church leader (whose knowledge is based on faith). In practice, then, secularization means the diminishment of religion's sphere of influence. Theologian Harvey Cox elaborates:

The world looks less and less to religious rules and rituals for its morality or its meanings. For some, religion provides a hobby, for others a mark of national or ethnic identification, for still others an esthetic delight. For fewer and fewer does it provide an inclusive and commanding system of personal and cosmic values and explanations. (1971:3)

If Cox is correct, should we expect that at some point religion will completely disappear? Not according to many sociologists (Hammond, 1985; McGuire, 1987). Recall that the vast majority of Americans continue to profess a belief in God. Furthermore, two-thirds of Americans are affiliated with a religious organization today, a proportion that is actually twice as high as in 1900 and four times as high as in 1850. Furthermore, church attendance has remained steady in recent decades (Hout & Greeley, 1987). Also, we shall see presently that American society has recently experienced a growth in many types of religious activity.

Therefore, secularization is not a linear process that will ultimately eliminate religion. More accurately, secularization is an uneven process of change in which a decline in some aspects of religion may be accompanied by an increase in others. Nor does everyone agree about the consequences of secularization. Some associate it with a lamentable decline in traditional American values. Others, however, view secularization as liberation from the all-encompassing beliefs of the past, so that people now take greater responsibility for what they choose to believe. In addition, secularization has brought the practices of many religious organizations more in line with widespread social attitudes. The Catholic Church, for example, has abandoned Latin in religious services in favor of commonly spoken languages, and many religions have recently allowed the ordination of women.

Secularization, then, can be interpreted as either moral advance or moral decline. But what does the future hold for religion? On this score, the fears of some that religion may disappear are almost certainly unfounded, as we shall now explain.

Civil Religion

While some analysts of the secularization process have pointed to a decline in traditional religious beliefs, others have suggested that secularization involves the replacement of old forms of religion with new ones (McGuire, 1987). One emerging pattern of belief and practice is what Robert Bellah (1975) has called **civil religion,** meaning *a quasi-religious loyalty binding individuals to their society*. The term *civil* refers to the ordinary life of citizens of a political state; yet the ties of citizenship have many religious qualities.

A vast majority of people in the United States, for example, associate the American way of life with what is good and believe that American involvement in the world is beneficial to other countries. In contrast, most Americans believe that communism as a political system represents evil (N.O.R.C., 1983, 1987). Civil religion also includes many forms of ritual. Before the opening of sporting events, spectators rise for the playing of the national anthem. Furthermore, public parades held throughout the year (including New Year's Day, Memorial Day, the Fourth of July, Labor Day, Thanksgiving Day, and Christmas) encourage the patriotic submission of individuals to the goals of the nation. Much like the cross to Christians and the Star of David to Jews, the flag serves as a sacred symbol that is treated with reverence and respect.

Furthermore, the human reaction to patriotic events has much in common with our response to religion. Participants in a patriotic celebration often feel the same sense of reverence and awe experienced by those at religious rituals. The explanation lies in Durkheim's insight that at such events individuals experience their collective identity—the power of their society.

Civil religion is not a specific religious doctrine; indeed, the political doctrine of separation of church and state is so well established in the United States that it could not be. Moreover, references to God in political life are usually general enough to be consistent with the great majority of established religions. Yet civil religion is based on the incorporation of many elements of traditional religion within the political system of a secular society. The fact that Americans exhibit such a strong belief in the goodness of their society (based more on faith than on clear scientific evidence) suggests the continuing importance of religion today.

Religious Revival in America

As already noted, religiosity as measured by belief in God and church attendance has changed little in recent decades. But several important changes have occurred in the commitment of Americans to religion. On the one hand, adherence to traditional churchlike organizations has declined, yet on the other hand, many newer forms of religious activity have increased. This suggests

that secularization may be a self-limiting process: as established religions decline, the timeless human need for meaning and security results in the rise of new forms of religious activity (Stark & Bainbridge, 1981).

Religious Fundamentalism

During the last several decades, the proportion of Americans affiliated with established churchlike organizations has declined. However, a growing proportion have become members of sectlike organizations (Jacquet, 1984). This reflects a general increase in **religious fundamentalism,** defined as *conservative religious organizations that seek to restore what are viewed as fundamental elements of religion.* Because the United States is a predominantly Protestant society, the growing significance of fundamentalism is most evident among Protestants; yet, on a smaller scale, fundamentalism is increasingly evident among Roman Catholics and Jews as well.

Fundamentalism came to the attention of many Americans when conservative Christian organizations visibly supported Ronald Reagan for president in 1980. But fundamentalism has actually been growing in importance throughout this century (Bromley & Shupe, 1984). Religious fundamentalism emerged in response to the process of secularization in America. As more and more Americans enrolled in schools (described in Chapter 15), scientific thinking appeared to be replacing traditional religious beliefs. In addition, the widespread discussion of Darwin's theory of evolution was evidence to many people of the dangers to religion inherent in science. Further, the influence of rapidly growing cities was reshaping American culture, and traditions were further threatened by the arrival of millions of immigrants from around the world.

Religious fundamentalism has sought to maintain traditional religious beliefs in this climate of rapid change. To counteract the perceived evils of secularization, fundamentalists seek to restore religious purity to religious organizations whose doctrine they believe has been eroded. Especially important among fundamentalist Christians is the literal message of the Gospels (the first four books of the New Testament), viewed as the path to true religion (Johnstone, 1983).

In general, fundamentalist Christianity is distinctive in three ways. First, believing that many of the more established clergy have embraced incorrect interpretations of the Bible, fundamentalists stress literal interpretation of Scripture. In terms of the creationism debate described earlier, for example, fundamentalists claim that God created the world literally according to the account in Genesis. Second, fundamentalists tend to be less tolerant of religious diversity than are members of more established religious organizations. They are inclined to view their own beliefs as the only true religion, while pointing out the error in other beliefs. Third, fundamentalism has a sectlike emphasis on the personal experience of religion. In contrast to the reserve and self-control common within more established religious organizations, fundamentalism often seeks to propagate "good old-time religion" through rituals that take the form of spiritual revivals. Furthermore, to fundamentalists, being "saved" is a personal experience that is expected to be clearly evident in the lives of those who are "born again" through the process of conversion.

Just as every religious organization is considered to be a church or a sect in variable degree, the label *fundamentalist* applies to some religious organizations more than to others. Generally, however, Christian organizations such as Pentecostals, Southern Baptists, Seventh-Day Adventists, and the Assembly of God are widely regarded as embracing religious fundamentalism. The exact number of people in the United States who can accurately be described as religious fundamentalists is a matter of informed estimate. Operationalizing the concept of fundamentalist to include people who interpret the Bible literally and who claim to have been born again, Gallup (1982) estimated that some 27 million adults (16 percent of the American population over the age of sixteen in 1982) are fundamentalist Christians.

Fundamentalism has long been strong in rural America. As described earlier, the trial of John Scopes in Tennessee in 1925 rallied those who wished to suppress the teaching of scientific evolution in the public schools. Yet this trial turned out to be an embarrassment for the fundamentalist cause, and the movement entered a period of decline. In the 1950s, however, fundamentalism became more visible once again, linked to the anti-communist sentiment that swept America at the beginning of the cold war with the Soviet Union (Hunter, 1985).

During the 1980s, fundamentalism has broadened its support of political conservatism in the form of what is often called the New Christian Right (Viguerie, 1981; Speer, 1984; Ostling, 1985). Jerry Falwell, a fundamentalist preacher who helped bring this religious movement to national attention, described its goals:

I am seeking to rally together the people of this country who still believe in decency, the home, the family, morality, the free enterprise system, and all the great ideals that are the cornerstone of this nation. Against the growing tide of permissiveness and moral decay that is crushing our society, we must make a sacred commitment to God Almighty to turn this nation around immediately. (Falwell, 1980, cited in Speer, 1984:20)

In 1987, Falwell claimed to be retiring from political life in order to return to his church in Lynchburg, Virginia. But he and other fundamentalist leaders continue to oppose what they see as a "liberal agenda," including the Equal Rights Amendment, the legal right of women to choose to have an abortion, the civil rights of homosexuals, and the free availability of pornography. They have also sought to return prayer to American public schools. Moreover, they have criticized the American educational establishment for allegedly fostering a morally permissive climate of secular humanism in the schools, and charged that the mass media color their presentations with liberal sentiments (Hunter, 1983).

Christian fundamentalism in the United States has expanded its educational efforts beyond the doors of the church. Some 450 fundamentalist Bible colleges exist in the United States, along with 18,000 fundamentalist Christian schools. In addition, fundamentalist organizations publish about 275 periodicals to spread their message (Hunter, 1985). Even more important, in recent years, fundamentalist Christianity has made increasing use of the most powerful medium of communication in the United States: television.

The Electronic Church

The mass media have become an important means of generating religious excitement and gaining converts to fundamentalist religion. Religious fundamentalism has spread from small local congregations to radio and television audiences across the nation through what is commonly called the *electronic church* dominated by prime-time preachers (Hadden & Swain, 1981).

At the beginning of the 1980s, some 1,400 radio stations and 60 television stations (including a growing number of cable television channels) in the United States were owned and operated by religious organizations, and hundreds more carry some religious programs. Aided by their electronic churches, religious leaders such as Jimmy Swaggart, Oral Roberts, and Robert Schuller have become better known to Americans than all but a few clergymen of the past. It is likely that about 5 percent of the national television audience (some 15 million Americans) are regular viewers of religious television,

Is it religion or is it big business? Heritage, USA—a "Christian theme park" in Fort Mill, South Carolina—became a centerpiece of Jim and Tammy Bakker's empire.

while perhaps 20 percent (some 60 million) watch at least some religious programming every month (Martin, 1981; Gallup, 1982; Ostling, 1986).

The use of the mass media brought a financial windfall in the form of solicited contributions to many religious organizations, which far more than offsets the high costs of a television-based ministry. Broadcasting in 3,200 stations in half the countries in the world, Jimmy Swaggart's viewers responded to his requests for contributions with some $180 million in 1986, which has enabled Swaggart to strengthen his religious organization with a bible college.

At the moment, the best-known and most controversial of the televangelists are Jim and Tammy Bakker, who began their religious television career in 1965 hosting a children's puppet show. Within a decade, they had founded the *PTL Club*, and begun development of the 2,300-acre Heritage, USA, Christian theme park in South Carolina. By the beginning of the 1980s, they were drawing six-figure salaries supplemented by large expense accounts. In 1987, however, they fell from grace when Jim Bakker confessed to unethical personal conduct. The public then learned that the pair's income had skyrocketed to over $1 million a year, and various federal agencies began investigating alleged wrongdoing at PTL.

In the wake of the PTL scandal, support for all television preachers dropped dramatically. Public con-

cern—which extends far beyond the PTL—is that televangelism has reached empire proportions in terms of both popularity and financial resources. At the same time, unlike most large businesses, these religious organizations remain largely under the control of single charismatic leaders (and their families), whose use of power and resources is accountable to virtually no one (Hull, 1987; Ostling, 1987). As of 1988, no formal charges of improper conduct had been lodged against any other such organization. However, Americans remain reasonably wary about whether televangelists are concerned with raising moral standards or simply cash.

The popularity of media-based ministries, the growth of cults and sects, and the adherence of millions more Americans to traditional religious organizations together indicate that secularization is unlikely to eliminate religion from the modern world (Stark & Bainbridge, 1981; Bateson & Ventis, 1982; Hunter, 1985). The apparent limits to the secularization process reflect the character of modern society as much as the appeal of any religious leaders. In a complex world of rapid social change, many people long for a more secure sense of individual identity and purpose. Moreover, the social anonymity of life in a modern industrial society can generate personal feelings of isolation.

Science has simply been unable to provide answers to the most central human needs and questions, especially in an era when the world sometimes seems to be on the brink of annihilation. Moreover, sometimes (as in the case of nuclear armaments) scientific technology has only increased anxiety about the future of the human species. Religion—especially many of the smaller-scale new religions—provides a social setting in which the individual can experience meaningful membership and direction (Barker, 1981). No wonder, then, that many people still turn to religion for a sense of security and hope (Cox, 1977; Johnstone, 1983).

SUMMARY

1. Religion is a major social institution based on the distinction between the sacred and the profane. Not subject to scientific assessment, religion is a matter of faith, and involves various forms of ritual behavior.

2. Sociology can analyze religion as a social phenomenon, but the discipline makes no claims as to the ultimate truth or falsity of any religious beliefs.

3. Emile Durkheim argued that religion is an expression of the power of society over individuals. His structural-functional analysis suggests that religion promotes social cohesion, social control, and provides meaning and purpose to life.

4. Using the symbolic-interaction paradigm, Peter Berger has explained how religious beliefs are generated in social interaction. Berger emphasizes the importance of religious beliefs as a source of individual meaning and security.

5. Using the social-conflict paradigm, Karl Marx pointed out that religion supports patterns of social inequality. But religious ideals have also motivated some people to seek greater equality within society.

6. Churches are a general type of formal religious organization that is well integrated into the larger society. Two types of churches are ecclesias and denominations.

7. Sects are a general type of informal religious organization that is not well integrated into the larger society. Sects generally emerge as the result of religious division and are often characterized by charismatic leadership.

8. Cults are religious organizations based on new beliefs and practices that have little in common with other religions within a particular society.

9. Technologically primitive human societies were generally animistic; more complex societies developed a distinct religious institution. Patterns of religious belief are highly variable throughout the world today.

10. Followers of six major world religions—Christianity, Islam, Hinduism, Buddhism, Confucianism, and Judaism—represent about half of all humanity. These six religions, which have had great importance in human history, differ considerably in patterns of belief and practice.

11. Most American adults identify with a religion; about 60 percent have a formal religious affiliation, with the largest number belonging to various Protestant denominations.

12. The religiosity of the American population varies according to how this concept is operationalized. The vast majority of Americans claim to believe in God, but only about half engage in daily prayer and just about four in ten adults attend religious services regularly.

13. Religious affiliation is related to social stratification as well as to ethnicity and race. Further, in the United States and elsewhere, religion is linked to political attitudes.

14. Secularization is an important dimension of social change involving the diminishing importance of religion. A controversial topic of study, secularization is seen by some as a breakdown of traditional morality and by others as a form of liberation and source of greater tolerance. Few doubt that religion has declined in importance in Western societies over the last several centuries, but many traditional religious organizations persist in America and newer forms of religion have increased in popularity.

15. Civil religion is a quasi-religious belief by which people profess loyalty to their society, often in the form of patriotism.

16. The growth of religious fundamentalism—often in the form of religious sects—suggests the limits of the historical process of secularization. Fundamentalist Christianity stresses literal interpretation of the Bible, is relatively intolerant of religious diversity, and emphasizes the personal experience of the power of religion. Many fundamentalist Christian organizations have actively supported conservative political goals in the United States.

17. Despite the historical process of secularization, the persistence of religion suggests its unique ability to address timeless questions about human experiences and needs.

KEY CONCEPTS

animism the belief that objects in the natural world are endowed with consciousness and can affect human lives

charisma extraordinary personal qualities that can turn an audience into followers

church a general type of formal religious organization that is well integrated into the larger society

civil religion a quasi-religious loyalty binding individuals to their society

conversion a personal transformation based on new religious beliefs

cult a religious movement that has little or nothing in common with other religious organizations in a particular society

denomination a churchlike religious organization that recognizes religious pluralism

ecclesia a churchlike religious organization that is formally allied with the state

faith belief that is not based on scientific evidence

monotheism religious beliefs recognizing a single divine power

polytheism religious beliefs recognizing many gods

profane that which is defined as an ordinary element of everyday life

religion a system of beliefs and practices built upon the recognition of the sacred

religiosity the importance of religion in a person's life

religious fundamentalism conservative religious organizations that seek to restore what are viewed as fundamental elements of religion

ritual formal, ceremonial behavior

sacred that which is defined as extraordinary, inspiring a sense of awe, reverence, and even fear

sect a general type of informal religious organization that is not well integrated into the larger society

secularization the decline in the influence of religion

totem an object, usually an element of the natural world, that is imbued with sacred qualities

---

SUGGESTED READINGS

This text provides an overview of a sociological analysis of religion.

Meredith B. McGuire. *Religion: The Social Context.* 2nd ed. Belmont, CA: Wadsworth, 1987.

Challenging the view that the church has been only a conservative force in the world, this book argues that there has also been a progressive character to Brazil's Catholic Church.

Scott Mainwaring. *The Catholic Church and Politics in Brazil, 1916–1985.* Stanford, CA: Stanford University Press, 1986.

The growth of new religious movements in recent decades is examined in this paperback, which offers an explanation of people joining unconventional religious organizations.

Irving Hexham and Karla Poewe. *Understanding Cults and New Religions.* Grand Rapids, MI: Wm. B. Eerdmans, 1986.

The creationist controversy continues to attract widespread attention. The first of these paperbacks presents the case for creation science; the second argues that creationism is an invalid abuse of science.

Duane T. Gish. *Evolution: The Fossils Say NO!* 3rd ed. San Diego, CA: Creation-Life Publishers, 1980.

Philip Kitcher. *Abusing Science: The Case Against Creationism.* Cambridge, MA: MIT Press, 1983.

Here is a well-written and illustrated survey of major world religions:

Walter Kaufman. *Religion in Four Dimensions: Existential and Aesthetic, Historical and Comparative.* New York: Reader's Digest Press, 1976.

The first of these books examines the extermination of European Jews during World War II, and explains how the reality of the Holocaust was difficult for many Americans to accept. The second, written by a sociologist who survived the Holocaust, tries to explain why some Christians risked their lives to save Jews.

Robert H. Abzug. *Inside the Vicious Heart: Americans and the Liberation of Nazi Concentration Camps.* New York: Oxford University Press, 1985.

Nechama Tec. *When Light Pierced the Darkness: Christian Rescue of Jews in Nazi-Occupied Poland.* New York: Oxford University Press, 1986.

As a consequence of increased emigration, the religious diversity of American society is increasing. This book, a report on five Islamic communities, provides insights into a religion generally unknown in the United States.

Yvonne Yazbeck Haddad and Adair T. Lummis. *Islamic Values in the United States: A Comparative Study*. New York: Oxford University Press, 1987.

Religion has long played a major part in the social relations between the sexes. This collection of ten essays examines both the ideal and the real social position of women in Islamic societies.

Freda Hussain, ed. *Muslim Women*. New York: St. Martin's Press, 1984.

The history of black religious movements, especially those promising a "deliverance" to black Americans, is presented in this recent book:

Wilson Jeremiah Moses. *Black Messiahs and Uncle Toms: Social and Literary Manipulations of a Religious Myth*. University Park, PA: The Pennsylvania State University Press, 1986.

This book, by a noted historian, explores the extent and importance of religious diversity in American society.

R. Laurence Moore. *Religious Outsiders and the Making of Americans*. New York: Oxford University Press, 1986.

The first of these books focuses on the fusion of Christianity and conservative politics that emerged in the 1980s. The second suggests the future of evangelicalism by studying young people preparing to lead such religious organizations.

David G. Bromley and Anson Shupe. *New Christian Politics*. Macon, GA: Mercer University Press, 1984.

James Davison Hunter. *Evangelicalism: The Coming Generation*. Chicago: University of Chicago Press, 1987.

This collection of essays explores the process of secularization:

Philip E. Hammond, ed. *The Sacred in a Secular Age: Toward Revision in the Scientific Study of Religion*. Berkeley, CA: University of California Press, 1985.

CHAPTER 17

Politics
and Government

For fourteen years beginning in 1920, the United States Constitution outlawed the manufacture, sale, and transportation of all alcoholic beverages. American cultural values, rooted in conservative Protestant religious beliefs, had long deplored the use of alcohol as a morally dangerous form of self-indulgence that "obliterates fear of the Lord," and ministers had condemned drunknness as "a sin which excludes from heaven" (Kobler 1973:54).

Many Americans supported these views in principle. Yet, from colonial days on, consumption of alcohol was an integral part of everyday social life in this country, common among children as well as adults. George Washington and Thomas Jefferson, for example, officially opposed strong drink, but both privately consumed wine and rum. Physicians routinely prescribed alcohol for ailments of all kinds. And distilleries, taverns, and overseas trade in alcohol were thriving elements of the American economy.

During the nineteenth century, an antiliquor movement began to gain strength in the United States as a result of patterns of social change. Agrarian America was being transformed by the Industrial Revolution, and tens of millions of immigrants from European nations were entering America's burgeoning cities. By the beginning of this century, the temperance movement came to represent not only hostility to alcohol, but also fear and anger directed toward immigrants, who were viewed as a threat to established cultural patterns. The Irish were widely regarded as whiskey drinkers; wine was perceived as the common beverage among Italians; and German communities could scarcely be imagined apart from their breweries and taverns. In the American mind, the vices of the urban dance halls, houses of prostitution, and saloons were all too easily reduced to two causes: immigrants and their alcohol.

After World War I, legal action began to limit both immigration and the use of alcohol. As described in Chapter 11, laws passed during the 1920s drastically reduced immigration—especially from countries of Southern and Eastern Europe, whose cultural patterns were most at odds with those of predominantly Anglo-Saxon America. And 1920 saw the adoption of the Eighteenth Amendment to the Constitution outlawing intoxicating liquor everywhere in the United States.

Many Americans rejoiced at the onset of Prohibition. But this "noble experiment," in President Woodrow Wilson's words, was unpopular among other segments of American society. Understandably, many immigrants reacted indignantly to what they saw as outright prejudice against themselves. In many places, the manufacture and sale of beer and hard liquor simply went underground—netting fortunes for bootleggers, ironically including many ambitious ethnic Americans like Al Capone. Prohibition did not end until 1933, when the Eighteenth Amendment was repealed under the administration of President Franklin Roosevelt (Kelley, 1982).

The story of Prohibition contains numerous sociological lessons, among them that a society's way of life is rarely a simple matter of cultural patterns embraced by all. On the contrary, standards of morality depend largely on which categories of people have more power than others, and what sorts of laws the powerful find to their liking. An important social institution, then, is **politics:** *the organized way in which power is distributed and decisions are made within a society.*

POWER AND AUTHORITY

Only someone living in complete isolation could make decisions with complete disregard for how others might respond. Early in this century, the German sociologist Max Weber (1978; orig. 1921) recognized this fact by defining **power** within society as *the likelihood of achieving desired ends in spite of possible resistance from others.* Power is a fundamental part of social life that springs from many sources. In human history, surely the most basic form of power is sheer force—physical or psychological coercion used to achieve one's ends. But no society can long exist if social power is expressed only in this way. Force may produce compliance, but always does so by generating fear or, in extreme cases, terror. An enduring society, on the other hand, is based on engineering significant agreement among its members on proper goals (in the form of cultural values) and the proper means of attaining them (in the form of cultural norms). Thus, considering ways in which power might be perceived in terms of justice rather than coercion, Weber defined **authority** as *power widely perceived as legitimate rather than coercive.*

To illustrate, imagine that a teacher assigns a term paper to a class. The assignment may be greeted by groans, but students usually do the work according to the teacher's directions. Certainly the teacher can coerce a reluctant student with the threat of a poor grade; the system of grading is one element of a teacher's power. Yet in most cases, coercion of this kind is not necessary because most students have learned to see the teacher's power as legitimate. In making the assignment, the teacher is conforming to classroom norms, just as students are when they complete the work. Power used in ways consistent with social norms is perceived as legitimate and is thus transformed into authority.

On the other hand, a teacher who attempts to use the threat of a poor grade to obtain sexual favors from a student does so without the support of cultural norms. Such a teacher is exercising coercive power rather than authority. In short, the norms underlying authority bind not only those who comply, but also those who issue the command.

Weber described three ways in which power is commonly transformed into authority. Each represents an ideal case; any actual situation is likely to be some combination of the three.

Traditional Authority

The first is by fusing power with tradition. Weber claimed that **traditional authority** is *power legitimated by respect for long-established cultural patterns.* Traditional authority is most pronounced in preindustrial societies because there change is slow. The power of the Chinese emperors of antiquity was legitimated by tradition, as was the rule of nobility in medieval Europe. In such cases, leaders exercise authority to the extent that, over a long period of time, a cultural system supporting their rule becomes well established. Put simply, hereditary monarchs continue to rule because they have always done so. Some traditional leaders even claimed a divine right to rule, asserting that their power was both natural and God-given. Weber added that people exercising traditional authority are rarely constrained by detailed rules and regulations. Their subjects are expected to obey them as a matter of personal loyalty to members of families whose power has become accepted as legitimate over many generations.

Traditional authority typically declines as a society becomes industrialized. Hannah Arendt (1963) pointed out that industrialization increases cultural diversity so that tradition is a less effective justification for power today than it was in the past. Several European societies still reveal a feudal heritage by recognizing the traditional authority of a royal family, but in most cases, real political power has shifted to commoners who are elected to office. The United States has little heritage of traditional authority at the national level. While American presidents may imply that they serve the will of God, none would dare claim to have been placed in office as a direct consequence of divine will. At the same time, however, some upper-class American families—such as the Roosevelts,

Kennedys, and Rockefellers—have so long played a role in politics that they have gained a limited measure of traditional authority (Baltzell, 1964).

But traditional authority has not disappeared from industrial societies. Patriarchy, the traditional domination of females by males, persists in the United States, although subject to increasing challenge. In American society and elsewhere, the power of parents over their young children is perhaps the clearest case of traditional authority. Such authority is rooted in the traditional status of parents; children are expected to obey even if they do not agree with—or fully understand—a parental command. Thus when children ask *why* they should obey, a parent sometimes replies curtly, "Because I said so!"

Rational-Legal Authority

As explained in Chapters 4 and 7, Weber viewed bureaucracy as a distinctive characteristic of modern industrial societies. Bureaucracy is supported by a rational view of the world in which long-established customs and practices gradually give way to formal rules and regulations, often in the form of law. Thus Weber defined **rational-legal authority** (sometimes called *bureaucratic authority*) as *power legitimated by legally enacted rules and regulations.*

Rationally enacted rules underlie most authority in the United States today. Teachers in college classrooms have some measure of traditional legitimacy, but their authority rests primarily on holding specific positions that operate according to rules and regulations of bureaucratic colleges and universities. In the same way, the bureaucratic authority of political leaders is not a personal quality, but lies in their offices—the statuses they occupy in the social structure. Thus while a queen may always be a queen, a president who leaves office enjoys a generous pension but loses presidential authority.

In contrast to traditional authority, bureaucratic authority stresses achievement over ascribed characteristics. An officeholder presumably exercises rational-legal authority on the basis of talent or special training, not on the basis of birth or family ties. A king's brother, for example, is always a prince; but brothers and sisters of American presidents rarely attract much public notice, and exercise no authority unless they, too, hold office.

In principle, bureaucratic rules and regulations apply to all members of an organization: even the author-

The rational-legal authority of the police officer is symbolized by the uniform (the ideal of impersonal enforcement) and the badge (the symbol of government). However, the fact that most police officers are armed indicates that the state will resort to force when necessary to secure compliance.

ity of the American presidency is subject to law. This fact was at the heart of the Watergate crisis in the early 1970s. Unlawful actions were taken to advance Richard Nixon's successful 1972 campaign for reelection. Subsequently, a number of top government officials, including Nixon himself, attempted to conceal those activities. But when evidence was amassed that Nixon had exceeded the legal limits of presidential authority, he resigned from office rather than face almost certain impeachment by the House of Representatives.

Charismatic Authority

Weber was intrigued by *charisma*, defined in Chapter 16 as extraordinary personal qualities that turn an audience into followers. He defined **charismatic authority** as *power legitimated through extraordinary personal abili-*

ties that inspire devotion and obedience. Unlike traditional and rational-legal authority, charismatic authority does not emanate from an inherited or achieved social status. Charisma has no link to an individual's position in society; it is an element of individual personality. But the end result is the same: power exercised by charismatic people is likely to be viewed, at least by some, as legitimate.

All societies contain people whom others consider to be especially forceful, creative, and personally magnetic. In modern societies, these include famous artists, entertainers, and political leaders, as well as more obscure people who are admired mainly by their friends. Some people use their charisma to enhance traditional or rational-legal authority, as, for instance, American presidents like Franklin Roosevelt and Ronald Reagan. But Weber noted that people may also use their charisma to challenge traditional customs and established organizations. As noted in Chapter 16, for example, the leadership of religious cults—which introduce new beliefs and practices into a society—is often based on personal charisma.

Thus charismatic authority is not constrained by conventional cultural norms. Indeed, people with charismatic authority may make their own rules, as if drawing on a higher power. This transcendent legitimacy is perhaps most evident in religious leaders from the Buddha and Jesus of Nazareth to the Ayatollah Khomeini. As different as these three may be, all preached an alternative to established cultural patterns and inspired their followers to transform the existing social order. The revolutionary effects of charismatic authority have also contributed to many political changes in the world: Vladimir Lenin led the revolution against the Russian czar, Mahatma Gandhi led the struggle to free India from British rule, and Martin Luther King, Jr., led the civil rights movement in the United States until he was assassinated in 1968.

Patriarchy still limits women's opportunities to assume formal positions of political power. For this reason, they have commonly expressed personal charisma within the arts, the family, and other social contexts defined as feminine. Nonetheless, personal charisma has enabled some women to gain considerable power in national affairs, as the careers of Indira Gandhi of India and Margaret Thatcher of the United Kingdom demonstrate. Perhaps the most fascinating example of a charismatic woman in politics during this century is the Argentinian Eva Peron, whose life is described in the box.

Because charismatic authority is tied to a single personality rather than to a formal organization, charismatic movements face the inevitable problem of sustaining themselves once their charismatic leader is gone. Weber argued that the long-term survival of a charismatic movement requires the **routinization of charisma**: *the transformation of charismatic authority into some combination of traditional and bureaucratic authority.* Chris-

Charismatic leaders are strong personalities; not surprisingly, they differ greatly from one another. India's Mahatma Gandhi spread a message of nonviolent resistence, while Nazi leader Adolph Hitler thrust a troubled world into war.

Evita: Charisma and Argentine Politics

In the strongly patriarchal culture of Argentina, women play little role in national politics. Yet one of the most influential leaders in that nation's history was Eva Peron—a woman whose personal charm, energy, and ambition earned her power and fame at home and abroad as the incomparable Evita.

Born poor in a small rural village in 1919, Eva Maria Duarte had important personal assets: she was intelligent, beautiful, a talented actress, and possessed a magnetic and forceful personality. As a young woman, she moved to Buenos Aires, Argentina's capital, and soon gained a wide following as a radio and film star. In the eyes of her detractors, she used other people, including numerous men with whom she had affairs, as rungs on the social ladder she climbed to the very top.

A turning point in Eva Duarte's life came when she met and entranced Juan Peron, a powerful figure in the Argentine army. He was elected vice president of the nation, but the turbulent political climate of the time soon turned his fortunes downward and he was forced from office and jailed in 1945. It was then that Eva came into her own as his public defender. She was a brilliant speaker at public gatherings; her charisma and ability to play up her poor background swayed the masses into a political movement that soon secured Peron's release from prison and election to the presidency. Within days, Eva Duarte and Juan Peron formally celebrated the advantages of their alliance by getting married.

As First Lady of Argentina, Eva Peron lacked the bureaucratic authority of her husband, but her charisma was overpowering. She won the hearts and minds of millions of the country's poor (whom she called *los descamisados,* or "the shirtless"), while reaping wealth for herself.

As charismatic leaders often are, Eva Peron was highly controversial. Although popular with the working class, she was opposed by the middle and upper classes as an unprincipled social climber who threatened their more established power. After the end of World War II, she toured Europe in an effort to build alliances between Argentina and other right-wing countries, notably Italy and Spain.

By the early 1950s, Eva Peron had become synonymous with Argentina. Her ambition remained unsatisfied, and she worked behind the scenes to secure the vice presidency for herself. But she was stopped by something against which her charisma was powerless—her own failing health. Stricken by uterine cancer, she rapidly declined, dying in 1952. But even after her death, Eva Peron's mystique persisted in Argentine politics. To her devoted followers, death had transformed her into a saint—*Santa Evita.*

SOURCE: Based, in part, on Nicholas Fraser and Marysa Navarro, *Eva Peron* (New York: Norton, 1980).

---

tianity, for example, began as a cult based on the personal charisma of Jesus of Nazareth. But Christianity persisted after the death of Jesus, gradually becoming established as the Roman Catholic Church, now based on a combination of traditional and bureaucratic authority. Of course, the routinization of charisma is by no means assured. Most charismatic movements disintegrate when the inspirational leader departs. The nineteenth-century Oneida community in upstate New York, a Christian sect established by a charismatic clergyman named John Humphrey Noyes, declined once Noyes left the community.

POLITICS IN HISTORICAL PERSPECTIVE

Technologically primitive hunting and gathering societies contain little specialized social activity beyond that which distinguishes male activities from female ones. With minimal material wealth, such societies need to make very few decisions concerning allocation of resources. Operating much like one large family, they usually have a single leader, generally a male who exhibits unusual strength, hunting skill, or personal charisma. But this person occupies no organizational position, and therefore has only modest power over others. After all, the leader has few resources with which to reward his supporters and can do little to punish those who ignore or challenge his leadership. In short, the leader in such a society may enjoy special prestige, but he has no more wealth and only slightly more power than anyone else (Lenski & Lenski, 1987).

Agrarian societies have far more specialized human activity and produce a material surplus. As social inequality develops, the majority of people become subject to control by a small elite. Politics emerges as a social institution distinct from family life. With the elite controlling a primitive bureaucracy, Weber's rational-legal form of authority comes into play. If elites maintain social dominance over generations, they may also acquire traditional authority. Gradually, then, political leadership becomes a specialized position in society. The power of leaders grows as the political organization increases in size and scope, leading to the formation of the **political state**—*a formal government exercising control over a society and claiming the legitimate use of coercion to support its rule.* A government is not the only source of political power within a society, of course, as political revolutions over the course of human history attest. Yet government is distinguished from other centers of power through its claim of legitimacy, based on one or more of the principles Weber described.

Initially, the power of the state is limited by technology; even a few centuries ago, communication and the transportation of armies and supplies across great distances was slow and uncertain. Forging a political state within geographical regions containing many distinct cultural groups often presented additional difficulties. For these reasons, the earliest political empires—such as Mesopotamia in the Near East some five thousand years ago—were generally composed of many small *city-states* (Stavrianos, 1983). This political form was also found among the ancient Greeks and persisted in Europe until the nineteenth century. A present-day example is Vatican City, the center of the Roman Catholic Church, which is a politically independent city-state inside Rome. Not all historical city-states remained small, however. Some developed an unusually effective political organization that made possible the formation of a vast empire—such as that controlled by Rome for some five hundred years beginning about the first century B.C.E. By today's standards, however, such governments were inefficient and cumbersome; the inability to effectively control its vast empire was one reason Rome eventually collapsed.

Within the last several centuries, political organiza-

Vatican City, within the Italian city of Rome, is the best known example of a contemporary city-state.

tion throughout the world has taken the form of the *nation-state.* Currently, there are almost two hundred different nation-states. They differ, of course, in countless ways depending on their cultures and levels of technological development.

POLITICAL SYSTEMS

Four major political systems can be distinguished in nation-states today. All of these political systems have one characteristic in common, however: governments attempt to legitimate their power so that at least most of the population believes that the particular political system is good.

Monarchy

Monarchy is *a type of political system in which power is passed from generation to generation within a single family.* Monarchy is a very old form of government;

the Bible, for example, tells of great kings such as David and Solomon. In terms of Weber's analysis, monarchy is legitimated primarily by tradition. In Great Britain, the current royal family (as well as many members of the traditional aristocracy) can trace their ancestry back through centuries of nobility. In some cases, of course, these men and women were aided by personal charisma; in all cases, a governmental organization served their interests. But the most important reason that royal families retained their authority is that monarchy was deeply rooted in the culture.

During the medieval period, most agrarian societies from Britain to China took the form of *absolute monarchy*, in which hereditary rulers claimed a virtual monopoly of power. Such absolute power was often strengthened by the monarch's assertion of a divine right to rule. Chinese emperors were widely regarded as gods themselves. Monarchy remained widespread into the early twentieth century. In 1910, the funeral of Great Britain's King Edward VII brought leaders of some seventy nations to London. More than fifty were royalty; worth noting is that the American president Theodore Roosevelt, with no royal rank, was placed at the end of the long funeral procession (Baltzell, 1964).

During this century, however, national leadership gradually shifted from hereditary nobility to elected officials. Even in European societies in which royal families are still found—including Great Britain, Norway, Sweden, Belgium, Denmark, and the Netherlands—monarchs have none of the absolute power they enjoyed in the past. The governments of these nations take the form of a *constitutional monarchy*, in which the royal ruler is the symbolic head of state, but the government operates according to a constitution. The actual heads of government are typically elected prime ministers. In short, in some nations of the world, the nobility may reign, but elected officials now rule (Roskin, 1982).

Democracy

More common than monarchy in the modern world is **democracy**: *a political system in which power is exercised by the people as a whole.* Of course, this does not mean that every member of society participates directly in decision making; this would be possible only in a very small political entity. In most cases, a *representative democratic* system places governmental authority in the hands of elected leaders. Thus, in principle at least, everyone shares political power through the process of democratic

elections. In reality, however, democracy rarely involves the participation of the entire adult population. In the 1984 presidential election, for example, just over half of all eligible Americans cast a vote.

Democratic political systems are usually found in industrial societies that are relatively rich by world standards (Hannan & Carroll, 1981). As noted in earlier chapters, industrial societies have a highly specialized economy that demands a literate populace. Thus increasing education is historically linked to broader participation in the political system. In addition, industrial societies contain a wide range of formal organizations, most of which seek to advance their interests within the political arena. Consequently, in contrast to the high concentration of power found in the absolutist monarchies common to agrarian societies, industrial societies have a more complex and diffuse political system.

The traditional legitimation of power typical of monarchy gives way in democratic political systems to rational-legal patterns of authority. This means that democratic leaders are chosen through a rational process of election involving at least two competing candidates. Leaders exercise the authority of the office to which they are elected. Thus democracy and rational-legal authority are linked in much the same way as monarchy and traditional authority are.

Democratic governments are far more bureaucratic than any monarchy in the past. But although bureaucracy is necessary to carry out the extensive activities of democratic governments, there is an inherent antagonism between democracy and bureaucracy. The political system of the United States, for example, includes some 3 million employees of the federal government—surely one of the largest bureaucracies in the world—and almost 14 million employees in over eighty thousand local governments. The great majority of these bureaucratic employees were not elected by the people: choosing bureaucrats this way would be both undesirable and impractical, given the need for specially trained people to manage government agencies. Indeed, most Americans lack the time and interest required to understand the full operation of our complex political system. As a result, much day-to-day decision making is done by career bureaucrats in an undemocratic way (Scaff, 1981; Edwards, 1985; Etzioni-Halevy, 1985).

Most Americans view democracy as a fairer and more egalitarian system of government than monarchy, but democratic political systems are not inherently egalitarian. Leaders are only a small proportion of the population. Although, in principle, they represent everyone, leaders in the United States hardly represent the population in a descriptive sense. Women—a numerical majority of the population—are grossly underrepresented among our leaders, as are members of virtually all minority groups. Moreover, as is evident from published tax returns, high government officials are among the richest of all Americans. So while the American population as a whole may share significant political power, actual decision making in the United States is carried out by professional bureaucrats and—in the highest positions of power—a small, wealthy elite.

Two Versions of Freedom

Distinctions between the East and the West are familiar to any observer of the political scene today. The East is represented by the Soviet Union and the nations of Eastern Europe. The West is identified with the United States, Canada, Western Europe, and other allied nations such as Japan. Although strikingly different in operation, both types of societies describe their people as free.

One primary difference between the two regions is *economic*—an issue that will be explored in depth in Chapter 18. Western societies operate under the free-market principles of capitalism, while Eastern societies have socialist economies that are largely under the control of the government. In every society, economics exerts a strong influence on politics, and these two different economic systems promote quite different political systems.

In Western societies such as the United States, freedom is defined in terms of personal *liberty*—involving not only the right to vote, but also the ability to act in one's own interest with minimal interference from the government. Such liberty is, of course, the basis of capitalism as well as of political democracy. As Chapter 18 explains, however, capitalism fosters considerable inequality of wealth, which is the fundamental criticism of Western societies by their Eastern counterparts. In other words, critics claim that Western societies are neither free nor truly democratic because various segments of the population have vastly different economic power. As long as the rich in the United States hold the lion's share of wealth and other social resources, they will impose their will on others. Moreover, critics argue, the fact that all people can vote has little practical significance. Voting is unlikely to change the reality that important resources such as housing, education, and health care are enjoyed in abundance by some and denied to others who desperately need them.

In contrast to the Western emphasis on personal liberty, Eastern societies define freedom as ensuring that all the people are provided with necessary resources such as jobs, housing, education, and medical care. In other words, such societies embrace the goal of economic *equality* among their people. Eastern societies with socialist economic systems are undemocratic in the sense that their people do not have the right to elect political leaders representing opposing political parties, nor can they freely act in their own interests. But most such governments claim to be democratic because they are responsive to the needs of their people. It is only because their goal is to provide all citizens with roughly equal social resources that socialist governments must be extensively involved in people's personal lives. This provokes criticism from Westerners, who believe that government infringement on personal liberties undermines any claim to be providing freedom.

The contrast between capitalist and socialist societies suggests that political liberty and economic equality are incompatible. Western efforts to promote political liberty seem to increase economic inequality, while socialist governments seem to promote economic equality only at the cost of limiting personal liberty. This dilemma is the subject of continuing debate among politicians and intellectuals alike, and as Chapter 18 describes, many societies have attempted to forge social institutions that promote both political liberty and economic equality.

Despite sharp arguments about these two ap-

The Berlin Wall provides stark evidence that divergent political systems do not always coexist peacefully. Since East Germany erected the wall in 1961, Berlin has been a single city divided by differing versions of freedom and justice.

proaches to defining freedom, few people in the East or the West have had the opportunity to objectively evaluate the relative merits of either type of political system. Capitalist societies socialize their members to emphasize the positive consequences of personal liberty and to downplay the problems associated with social inequality. They typically see differences in wealth as the result of differences in personal merit rather than as the consequence of social institutions. And in socialist societies, people are socialized to emphasize the benefits of greater equality and encouraged to accept the pervasive presence of government in their lives as a necessary means to that end.

Authoritarianism and Totalitarianism

Authoritarianism refers to *the exclusion of the majority from political participation, although with little governmental intervention in people's lives.* Since no society actually involves all its people in the daily activities of government, all political systems are authoritarian to some degree. We have noted that political decision making in the United States is carried out by millions of government officials who are not directly accountable to the population, and by top elected leaders who are typically men of great wealth. But because virtually all Americans over the age of eighteen have the right to vote, the political system of the United States is not actually very authoritarian.

The term *authoritarian* is more correctly used to characterize political systems in which the population has little or no institutionalized means to voice an opinion. Absolute monarchies are therefore highly authoritarian, although they are rare in the world today. Authoritarian political systems in this century more commonly take the form of military juntas and other dictatorships. These include the regime of Juan and Eva Peron in Argentina during the 1940s and 1950s, the recently overthrown dictatorships of Ferdinand Marcos in the Philippines and the Duvalier family in Haiti, as well as the military junta that rules Chile.

Political control of a population is even greater in cases of governmental **totalitarianism,** meaning *the exclusion of the majority from free political participation coupled with extensive governmental intervention in people's lives.* While authoritarian governments have existed throughout history, totalitarianism has emerged only within the last century as governments have gained the technological means to rigidly control the lives of citi-

zens. For this reason, absolute monarchies in the past may have been authoritarian, but they certainly lacked the ability to become totalitarian. By the time the Nazis rose to power in Germany, leading to World War II, the technological resources were available to support totalitarianism. In recent decades, advanced electronic technology—including electronic surveillance and computers for storing vast amounts of information—has greatly increased the potential for government manipulation of a large population.

In principle, leaders of totalitarian governments often claim to represent the will of the people, but in practice, the government seeks to manipulate people's attitudes and actions to reflect the will of the government. Thus such governments permit no opposing centers of power. Citizens are not free to join together for political purposes: indeed, totalitarianism is most effective in a society that is socially atomized. The government also typically limits the ability of its citizens to freely disseminate information: in the Soviet Union, for example, both telephone directories and copying machines are generally unavailable to the public. Further, the government may encourage citizens to report the unpatriotic activities of others. In the recent past, for instance, children were instructed to report disloyalty on the part of even their own parents in the People's Republic of China. As Timothy Garton Ash put it, in totalitarian societies, "wherever two or three are gathered together, there the party-state desires to be" (1983:8).

Socialization in totalitarian societies is thus intensely political—a process that critics have suggested involves not just obedience but also thought control. Political messages and pictures of leaders are often prominently displayed in public, serving as a constant reminder that each citizen is to provide total support to the state. The mass media present only official information favorable to the government, rather than providing a forum for a number of different political viewpoints, as they do in democratic societies (Arendt, 1958; Kornhauser, 1959; Friedrich & Brzezinski, 1965; Nisbet, 1966).

Totalitarian governments span the political spectrum from the far right (e.g., Nazi Germany) to the far left (e.g., the Soviet Union). Americans are socialized to view all socialist societies as totalitarian. True, socialism does involve greater governmental regulation of the economy, but socialism (a type of economic system) and totalitarianism (a quality of political systems) are not synonymous. The Reagan administration has charged the Sandinista regime in Nicaragua with being totalitarian in part simply because it has a largely socialist econ-

Nicaragua: Assessing a Revolution

Nicaragua is a small nation in Central America with a population of roughly 3 million (about equal to Los Angeles) and a land area about equal to that of Mississippi. In 1979, revolutionary guerillas toppled dictator Anastasio Somoza Debayle, whose father had established an authoritarian political dynasty in Nicaragua in the 1930s with the support of the United States.

At the time the Somoza family seized power in Nicaragua, their military forces killed Augusto César Sandino, a national hero to many Nicaraguans. In his honor, the Nicaraguan revolutionaries adopted the name Sandinistas.

Current public opinion about the Sandinistas is divided. To some long opposed to the Somoza dictatorship, the Sandinistas are a legitimate "people's government" that has improved the lives of Nicaraguans in many ways. Others who also deplored the Somoza dictatorship are dismayed that the Sandinista regime has not lived up to the democratic principles it embraced at the outset of the revo-

lution. Still others follow the position held by the Reagan administration, which opposed the revolution as establishing a Marxist totalitarian state in Nicaragua much the same as Castro's Cuba. This administration urged American aid to counterrevolutionaries (the *contras*) fighting the Sandinista government.

Initially, the Sandinista regime enjoyed the support of over three-fourths of the Nicaraguan population. In part, this reflected widespread hatred of Somoza. But the Sandinistas also won favor by distributing land more widely, expanding schools to increase literacy, making health care more available in rural areas, and improving the social position of women.

The popularity of the Sandinistas appears to have declined during the 1980s to perhaps 40 or 50 percent of the population. Certainly, economic problems are severe: by some accounts, runaway inflation and soaring foreign debt have caused a substantial drop in personal standards of living. More generally, however, crit-

ics charge that Nicaragua is gradually becoming a totalitarian state.

The Sandinista government acknowledges that greater social equality has been achieved by infringement of personal liberties, and that political repression does exist in Nicaragua today. The few independent newspapers are subject to government censorship, for example, although an underground press circulates widely among the people and radio stations broadcasting from neighboring Costa Rica and Honduras provide daily criticisms of government policies. Furthermore, local Sandinista "defense committees" are widely seen as ignoring basic rights to privacy and free speech. The Sandinistas claim that current limitations on personal liberty are necessary because the country is being threatened by a counterrevolutionary army supported by the United States. These *contras* consist of diverse groups with varying political goals: some fight to force the government to become more democratic, while others—previous supporters of

omy. Yet, as the box explains, this assertion is debatable. Furthermore, Sweden, one of several Western nations today whose economy has many socialist qualities, is also one of the most politically democratic societies on earth. On the other hand, some societies with capitalist economies, such as Chile and South Africa, exercise sufficient control over the lives of most of their citizens to be considered totalitarian.

A century and a half ago, in his famous book *Democracy in America* (1969; orig. 1834–1840), the brilliant Frenchman Alexis de Tocqueville pointed out that all modern governments had the potential to become totalitarian because they were growing in size and scope

and becoming involved in an ever-greater portion of their citizens' lives. Tocqueville believed that the danger of totalitarianism could be minimized if citizens formed numerous voluntary associations as centers of power apart from the government.

THE AMERICAN POLITICAL SYSTEM

The founding of the United States was one of the boldest political experiments in human history. Part of the British Empire in the eighteenth century, the American colonies

measure of political opposition, the government has "traveled far down the road toward totalitarianism." In considering this assessment, it should be remembered that the revolution is barely a decade old. Even the United States took years to adopt a democratic constitution after defeating the British in its revolution. But the Sandinistas staunchly refuse to allow any independent survey of political opinion in the country, although conducting polls for themselves. Further, their control of the mass media and the military means that, as one commentator put it, "if they have opened a door to freedom, they have kept all the keys."

Although political campaigns and elections are held in Nicaragua, in the view of many critics that government has become increasingly totalitarian.

SOURCE: Based on Mario Vargas Llosa, "In Nicaragua," *The New York Times Magazine*, April 28, 1985, pp. 37–42, 44–46, 76–77, 81–83, 92–94; and Jill Smolowe, "Sidetracked Revolution," *Time*, Vol. 127, No. 13 (March 31, 1986): 22–24; John Borrell, "Nicaragua: At War with Itself," *Time*, Vol. 130, No. 20 (November 16, 1987): 41–42; and Stephen Kinzer, "The Door Is Open, but Sandinistas Keep the Keys," *The New York Times*, November 22, 1987, p. 2.

Somoza—fight to regain their dominant position in Nicaraguan society.

After a tour of Nicaragua, Peruvian political analyst Mario Vargas Llosa (1985) concluded that while the Sandinista regime still tolerates some

fought a revolutionary war to establish an independent American political system. In 1789, George Washington was elected the first president, and Congress met for the first time in New York—the nation's first capital.

Early American political leaders sought to replace the British monarchy with a democratic political system. In the years since, the commitment of Americans to democratic principles has remained strong, although our political system has become vastly larger and more complex. The American version of democracy, of course, differs from other democracies around the world, reflecting our particular history, economy, and cultural traditions.

Culture, Economics, and Politics

American culture has traditionally valued hardy individualists—strong, skilled, self-reliant people who compete with one another to achieve success commensurate with their abilities and effort. Such values are, of course, the foundation of the capitalist economic system, suggesting the close relationship between these two societal institutions.

Individualism, or extensive personal liberty, is formally recognized in the Bill of Rights, which guarantees the individual's right to act without undue interference from government. Most Americans would probably agree with the nineteenth-century philosopher and poet Ralph Waldo Emerson's observation that "the government that governs best is the government that governs least."

At the same time, virtually all Americans acknowledge that government is necessary for some purposes, including maintaining a national defense, overseeing the operation of schools, and maintaining law and order. Consequently, as the United States has become a larger and more complex society, government has also grown, and quite dramatically.

In 1789, the federal budget was a mere $4.5 million; as shown in Table 17–1, by 1986 the federal budget had passed the $1 trillion mark. Similarly, in the early nineteenth century, only a few thousand people (outside the armed forces) were employed by the federal government; today this figure exceeds 3 million.

Two causes of this striking growth are the historical increases in both the geographical size and the population of the United States. But these are not the only causes.

Table 17–1 THE GROWTH OF UNITED STATES GOVERNMENT SPENDING

Year	Federal Government Expenditure (In Millions of Dollars; Unadjusted for Inflation)	Government Expenditure as Proportion of Gross National Product
1795	6	
1800	11	
1810	9	
1820	18	
1830	25	
1840	20	
1850	44	
1860	56	
1870	411	
1880	334	2.4
1890	403	2.4
1900	567	2.8
1910	676	2.0
1920	6,649	6.9
1930	4,058	3.7
1940	6,361	9.1
1950	39,485	13.9
1960	92,492	18.3
1970	193,743	20.1
1980	576,500	33.5
1986	1,030,300	24.5

SOURCE: U.S. Bureau of the Census and U.S. Bureau of Economic Analysis.

Table 17–2 THE ROLE OF GOVERNMENT: A NATIONAL SURVEY, 1987

QUESTION: Some people think that the government in Washington is trying to do too many things that should be left to individuals and private businesses. Others disagree and think that the government should do even more to solve our country's problems. Still others have opinions in between. What do you think?

I strongly agree that the government should do more.		I agree with both answers.		I strongly agree that government is doing too much.
1	2	3	4	5
14.3%	13.9%	37.5%	14.9%	13.9%

Don't know, no answer: 5.5%

SOURCE: N.O.R.C., *General Social Surveys, 1972–1987* (Chicago: National Opinion Research Center, 1987), p. 303.

The numbers 1 to 5 indicate the range of opinions across the three categories.

Early in the nineteenth century, there was roughly one government employee for each eighteen hundred persons in the United States; today the corresponding ratio is one employee for every eighty persons. The expanding range of governmental responsibilities accounts for much of this growth. In the past, most Americans had little direct contact with the federal government. Often the presence of the federal government in communities was limited to the local post office. But changes such as universal education, civil rights legislation to provide more equal opportunities for all Americans, safety standards to protect consumers and workers, and the need for a larger and more complex system of national defense have all resulted in government growth. Today a majority of Americans depend in a direct way on the federal government for at least part of their income (Caplow et al., 1982). State and local governments have also grown as they address the needs of various segments of the population such as the elderly, students, and veterans (Devine, 1985).

Although few Americans wish to return to the minimal government we had in the eighteenth century, many believe that government does too many things that people could do for themselves. The results of a national survey, presented in Table 17–2, indicate that more than one-third of Americans think that government is "doing too much," while less than one-fourth claim that government "should do more." Slightly more than one-third take a middle position, apparently believing that government should do more of some things and less of others.

Political Parties

Since the beginning of the last century, Americans have banded together to form **political parties,** *political organizations in which people of similar attitudes and interests influence the political process*. Even before the United States was officially founded, the merits of political parties were hotly debated. Some, including Thomas Jefferson, believed that parties representing different political positions would ensure that social power would never become concentrated in the hands of any one group. Most others, however, feared that parties would generate political conflict that would tear the new nation apart. Perhaps for this reason political parties are not mentioned at all in the U.S. Constitution (Hilsman, 1985).

Yet, from the outset, Americans confronted important differences of opinion among themselves that gradually became the basis of political parties. Several political parties came and went in the early years of the republic until, on the eve of the Civil War, the two major parties we know today—the Republicans and the Democrats—were established (Burnham, 1983).

Thus the United States is a two-party system, meaning that virtually all political candidates represent either the Democratic Party or the Republican Party. There have been recent exceptions to this rule, however. In the 1968 presidential election, the American Independent Party led by George Wallace gained over 13 percent of the popular vote. In the 1988 presidential election, a wide range of minor parties, including the Libertarian Party, the Populist Party, the Communist Party, the Workers League, and the Prohibition Party, ran candidates, but none gained a significant share of the vote.

Functions of Political Parties

Political parties have persisted in American society because of the important societal functions they perform.

Promoting political pluralism. Political parties provide one source of political *pluralism*, meaning that they form many independent centers of power that prevent the concentration of power in one segment of the population. In contrast, the Nazi regime in Germany several decades ago ruthlessly eliminated opposing political parties, and the Communist Party in the Soviet Union today likewise tolerates no organized political opposition.

Increasing political involvement. Parties provide an organized structure that draws the population into the political process. They articulate different points of view about controversial social issues and formulate specific policies and programs. Thus they serve as reference groups that help Americans to identify their needs and interests, while encouraging active participation in the achievement of social goals.

Selection of political candidates. Political parties are responsible for selecting candidates to run for office. In this way, they are a part of the system by which elected officials are held accountable to the people they purport to represent. Although candidates seeking reelection (commonly called *incumbents*) have advantages unavailable to their opponents, no one can be assured of reelection without renomination by the party and subsequent support by the voters. Political candidates represent the opinions of their supporters to a significant extent, and political campaigns allow public debate of important issues, further engaging the public in the political process.

Forging political coalitions. Parties provide a means by which supporters of various interests and issues unite to increase their greater political power. The two major political parties of the United States are unusual in world context in that they represent a broad range of political interests rather than a single segment of the population. Although at times in American history minor political parties have arisen to represent only a single issue, most failed to gain widespread support.

Maintaining political stability. Political parties promote political stability by maintaining relatively consistent positions on a number of issues. Thus, although particular candidates come and go, parties provide continuity of political values over time (Wolfinger, Shapiro, & Greenstein, 1980; Irish, Prothro, & Richardson, 1981; Burnham, 1983).

The Political Spectrum in America

Many Americans identify themselves politically as either liberal or conservative. Others prefer to describe themselves as moderates or middle-of-the-roaders. Still others do not readily describe themselves in political terms at all. These labels are associated with certain political attitudes and establish an individual's place on what is commonly called the *political spectrum*, which ranges from extreme liberalism on the left to extreme conservatism on the right. Historically, the Republican Party has been somewhat more conservative and the Democratic Party has been somewhat more liberal.

But general labels such as *liberal* and *conservative* confound two distinct dimensions of political attitudes. *Economic issues* have to do with the extent of economic opportunity available to all Americans and with patterns of economic inequality. *Social issues* refer to matters of morality and the extent to which all categories of Americans have equal legal rights.

Economic Issues

A century ago, American society was experiencing a major transformation wrought by industrialization, the rise of corporate businesses of unparalleled size, and the entrance of millions of immigrants into the cities. The industrial age brought fabulous wealth to the few people who owned industrial factories, but the vast majority of Americans earned little economic reward from long hours of work in factories or on small family farms across the nation.

By the time the Great Depression began in 1929, there was mounting evidence that the immense wealth produced by American capitalism was being distributed in a highly unequal fashion, so that most people had limited financial security. The election of Democrat Franklin Delano Roosevelt in 1932 brought a major change in the character of American government. Previously, the proper responsibilities of government were perceived as limited to such matters as printing currency, financing internal improvements such as roads, and maintaining the armed forces. Government intervention in the economy was slight and sporadic. Roosevelt's New Deal, however, directly involved government in economic matters. The federal government expanded the availability of electricity, regulated the stock market, provided guarantees for bank savings, and in numerous other ways increased the financial security of the American people. In 1935, the Social Security system was established, requiring that all workers and employers make financial contributions from their earnings to provide retirement income to the elderly. Similarly, the Works Project Administration and Civilian Conservation Corps created jobs and income for millions of out-of-work Americans (Friedrich, 1982).

The use of government power to affect the economic well-being of the population was a sharp and controversial departure from the past. Then, as today, the Democratic Party tended to support more extensive government involvement in the economy than the Republican Party. Economic liberals (likely to be Democrats) believe that such policies are the proper responsibility of government. Economic conservatives (likely to be Republicans), in contrast, hold that government should not interfere with the operation of the so-called free economy (Burnham, 1983).

As part of President Franklin Roosevelt's New Deal, the Work Projects Administration (WPA) created jobs by employing artists to paint murals on public buildings. This one, in San Francisco's Coit Tower, depicted Americans at work at a time of catastrophic unemployment.

Social Issues

A second dimension of the political spectrum involves attitudes on various social issues ranging from the legal standing of racial and ethnic minorities, women, and homosexuals to moral questions such as abortion and the use of the death penalty. Social liberals support equal rights and opportunities for all segments of American society. They typically favor individual choice regarding abortion and oppose the death penalty because it has historically been applied disproportionately to members of minority groups. Social conservatives support traditional distinctions among various segments of the population and tend to oppose the civil rights and women's movements. Social conservatives usually condemn abortion as a moral wrong and favor the death penalty as a morally necessary response to the most serious crimes.

In general, the Democratic Party is more socially liberal and the Republican Party is more socially conservative. Yet both social liberals and social conservatives tend to support government activity that supports their aims. As social liberals, for example, Democrats have supported an Equal Rights amendment (ERA) to the Constitution as a means of reducing traditional patriarchy. Many socially conservative Republicans, however, oppose this change, believing that the government should not undermine cultural conceptions of gender. On the other hand, social conservatives believe that the government *should* enact legislation forbidding abortion. Social liberals, in contrast, believe that the government has no business becoming involved in personal decisions of this kind.

Political concepts of liberal and conservative are indeed complex, and to make matters more complicated still, individuals may hold attitudes on economic issues that do not parallel their attitudes on social issues. Probably for this reason, a large proportion of Americans do not readily call themselves either liberals or conservatives.

Researchers thus rely on a wide range of indirect evidence to describe how the American population is spread across the two dimensions of the political spectrum. Political scientists Michael Barone and Grant Ujifusa (1981) have categorized American political attitudes as shown in Figure 17–1. They estimate that 10 percent of Americans are liberal on both economic and social issues, while more than one-third are conservative in both respects. The majority of Americans hold mixed political views: 25 percent are economically conservative and socially liberal; 30 percent are economically liberal and socially conservative.

	SOCIAL ISSUES		
	Liberal	Conservative	Total
Liberal	10%	30%	40%
Conservative	25%	35%	60%
Total	35%	65%	100%

Figure 17–1 The Political Attitudes of Americans

(Barone & Ujifusa, 1982:1)

Generally speaking, well-to-do Americans are conservative on economic issues, reflecting their desire to protect their considerable wealth. But because their high social standing makes them sufficiently socially secure to favor change regarding social issues, privileged Americans tend to be social liberals. Americans of low social position, on the other hand, tend to be economic liberals and social conservatives. Their economic liberalism is an expression of their desire to obtain more economic security. But because they have less social prestige, Americans of lower social position tend to be conservative on social issues. They tend to take pride in conforming to conventional cultural patterns and commonly disapprove of those—such as gay people and cohabiting couples—who do not adhere to established American mores (Nunn, Crocket, & Williams, 1978; Erikson, Luttbeg, & Tedin, 1980; Syzmanski, 1983; Humphries, 1984). These general patterns vary somewhat according to race, ethnicity, and sex. Regardless of social standing, for instance, black Americans are likely to be socially liberal and, since the New Deal era, strongly Democratic.

Because they, too, have often been poor and the targets of social prejudice, most ethnic minorities have been economically liberal and have supported the Democratic Party, which they perceived as offering more opportunity for economic advancement. There is evidence, however, that by midcentury this pattern was breaking down because ethnicity had become a far less powerful force in American politics (Knoke & Felson, 1974). Even today, however, Hispanic Americans (long overly represented among the poor) and Jews (historically an oppressed minority group) continue to provide strong support for the Democratic Party.

In recent years, some political observers have discerned a "gender gap" in American politics. There is evidence that women are somewhat more likely to hold liberal attitudes than men, although the extent of this difference is probably not very great. In the 1984 presidential election, for example, a majority of both women and men voted for conservative Republican Ronald Reagan, although support for Reagan was more pronounced among men (64 percent) than among women (55 percent) (Thomas, 1984).

In general, the Democratic Party has traditionally represented more liberal political attitudes on both economic and social issues than the Republican Party. But since an individual's political attitudes toward economic and social issues may not be consistently liberal or conservative, self-identification as a Democrat or a Republican is not as strong as one might expect. In this respect, the United States differs from most European democracies, in which most people identify strongly with one political party (Wolfinger, Shapiro, & Greenstein, 1980). Even so, well-to-do Americans tend to support the Republican Party, while less privileged Americans lean toward the Democratic Party.

Table 17–3 presents the results of a national survey in which American adults indicated their party affiliation (N.O.R.C., 1987). More than half of all Americans (50.3 percent) identified themselves—at least to some degree—as Democrats; the corresponding figure for Republicans was about one-third (36.9 percent); 12 percent claimed no preference for either major party. In this sense, the Democrats are the majority party in the United States. Only a small proportion of the respondents, however, indicated a strong commitment to either party: 18.4 percent in the case of the Democrats, 10.3 percent in the case of the Republicans. Thus in any election a large proportion of Americans may swing from one party to another, which explains why in the last ten presidential elections the Republicans have captured the White House as often as the Democrats.

One likely reason for the lack of strong party support in the United States is that, despite some real differences, the two major parties have very much in common. Both parties, for example, support the capitalist economic system, strong national defense, and the principles on which the United States Constitution is based. In addition, since Roosevelt's New Deal, both parties have supported some measure of government involvement both in the American economy and in promoting social change.

Another consequence of the general similarity between the two major parties is that those who desire radical change in American society are not likely to support either major party. Some Americans are politically on the far left, seeking to establish a socialist economy; others are on the far right, advocating the virtual abolition of government intervention in the American economy. Because these views are so at odds with the established American political system, political candidates who promote radical social change have received very little political support from the population as a whole.

In this regard, the United States differs from most democracies, in which political parties represent a wider range of political positions. In England, for example, the Labour party (on the left) and the Conservative Party (on the right) differ from one another more than the two major parties in the United States. In addition, Sweden, the Netherlands, Switzerland, Belgium, and Israel all have a host of political parties that represent voters across a wide political spectrum (Roskin, 1982).

Special-Interest Groups

In 1985, President Reagan proposed a major tax-reform program that, he claimed, would make the tax system both more simple and more fair. One proposed change was a limitation on the amount of expenses that people could deduct for dining and entertaining while engaging

Table 17–3 POLITICAL PARTY IDENTIFICATION IN THE UNITED STATES, 1987

Party Identification	Proportion of Respondents
Democrat	50.3%
Strong Democrat	18.5
Not very strong Democrat	20.9
Independent, close to Democrat	10.9
Republican	36.9
Strong Republican	10.3
Not very strong Republican	17.1
Independent, close to Republican	9.5
Independent	11.4
Other Party, No Response	1.4

SOURCE: N.O.R.C., *General Social Surveys, 1972–1987* (Chicago: National Opinion Research Center, 1987), p. 88.

in business. Almost immediately, the restaurant industry reacted with a vengeance: eliminating the tax-deductible business lunch, it contended, would put tens of thousands of restaurant workers out of their jobs and drastically reduce the profits of this sector of the economy.

The restaurant industry is just one example of a **special-interest group**: *a political alliance of people who share an orientation with regard to a particular economic or social issue.* Any voluntary association (described in Chapter 6) is a special-interest group to the extent that it seeks political influence. The array of special-interest groups in the United States is thus truly vast, representing virtually all businesses and professions, religions, and racial and ethnic groups. Tocqueville described the United States as a nation of joiners, and there is probably no society in the world in which special-interest groups are so numerous.

Labor unions, professional associations, and religious groups are examples of established special-interest organizations that regularly monitor government activity and mobilize their members when legislation that may affect their interests is proposed. Sometimes a special-interest group forms as a grass-roots reaction to an emerging political debate. Many local organizations composed of people seeking a nuclear freeze emerged in this way during the 1980s as both the United States and the Soviet Union embarked on a military buildup.

Many special-interest groups make use of *lobbyists*—people who earn their living by representing the interests of one group or another to members of Congress and other national political officials. In 1984, there were some seventy-two hundred registered lobbyists in the United States—twice as many as a decade earlier (Sheler, 1985).

Societies in which special-interest groups flourish are generally those with relatively weak political parties. In most European societies, for example, political parties rather than special-interest groups are the primary means of influencing governmental policy. But in societies such as the United States in which relatively few people are strongly committed to political parties, special-interest groups are a common means of advancing political aims (Burnham, 1983).

The Agenda of Special-Interest Groups

In the United States, the most powerful special-interest groups are concerned with economic issues. Big business, with its tremendous wealth, is unquestionably one of the major powers in the American political system. The

In recent years, Vietnam veterans have organized into a special-interest group to gain belated recognition for their sacrifices in fighting an unpopular war.

five largest oil companies in the United States, for example, have combined assets valued at over $200 billion (Magnet, 1985). Since in American society money provides access to political power, the oil companies are able to exert great influence on the political process.

Labor unions are another powerful interest group concerned primarily with economic issues. The political power of organized labor comes from the financial and voter support provided to candidates by millions of union members across the United States. The American Federation of Labor–Congress of Industrial Organizations (AFL-CIO) is the nation's largest labor union, with some 14 million members. As you might expect, while big business directs most of its financial support to officials and candidates of the Republican Party, the AFL-CIO channels most of its support to Democrats.

Farming is another sector of the American economy that attempts to influence the political system. Farmers have a direct stake in government because for many years Washington has guaranteed price supports for certain crops. When the Soviet Union invaded Afghanistan in 1980, President Jimmy Carter responded by stopping the shipment of American grain to the USSR. Grain producers, who were financially hurt by the action, exerted strong pressure through such organizations as the Farm Bureau to end the embargo a year later.

Other special-interest groups are concerned with broader social issues. Prominent examples of socially oriented special-interest groups are the National Organization of Women (NOW), numerous consumer-protection organizations such as those headed by Ralph Nader, environmentalist groups such as the Sierra Club, and the American Civil Liberties Union (ACLU). The ACLU, one of the most active special-interest groups of this kind, was instrumental in bringing about the landmark Supreme Court decision in *Brown v. Board of Education of Topeka* that outlawed school segregation in 1954 (discussed in Chapter 11). Generally, the ACLU is perceived as a socially liberal organization, but there are special-interest groups to represent all social positions. The National Rifle Association, widely viewed as a socially conservative organization, has some 2 million members nationwide and has spent millions of dollars opposing legislation that would restrict the private ownership of firearms.

Religious organizations attempt to influence public opinion and government legislation on a variety of social issues, including controversies such as abortion and school prayer. Although most established churches tend to maintain a low political profile, conservative Christian organizations are likely to remain active in politics during the 1990s.

Political Action Committees

Many special-interest groups exert political influence by providing votes and money directly to political parties. But the weakening of political parties in the United States has been accompanied by the rise of **political action committees** (PACs), *organizations formed by special-interest groups, independent of political parties, to pursue a specific political aim through raising and spending money.* The most common strategy employed by political action committees is channeling funds directly to candidates who are likely to support their interests.

The first political action committees were formed by labor organizations during the early years of Roose-

velt's New Deal. But it was the passage of legal reforms limiting direct contributions to candidates in the early 1970s that brought PACs to the forefront of American politics. The Federal Elections Campaign Act of 1971 formally granted the right of special interests, including business and labor, to form PACs, and their number has subsequently grown rapidly. In the early 1970s, about six hundred PACs were operating; by mid-1987 the number was over forty-five hundred (Sabato, 1984; Jones & Miller, 1985; Federal Election Commission, 1987).

The success of PACs is directly related to their ability to raise money (Walker, 1983). Usually, the largest spenders are concerned with economic issues. But PACs also represent special-interest groups concerned with social issues, including the National Organization of Women (NOW), which seeks to advance the equality of women, and the National Conservative Political Action Committee (NCPAC), which opposes abortion and seeks to restore traditional values to American society.

Because of the rapid increase in the cost of running for office, candidates are typically happy to accept financial support from political action committees. Between 1972 and 1987, fifty-one U.S. senators each received more than $1 million from PACs. Although candidates for the House of Representatives tend to receive somewhat less money, they got one-third of all contributions from PACs during the 1986 campaign (Berke, 1987). PAC contributions to political candidates totaled about $127 million for the 1986 elections. This has sparked a lively controversy, as the box explains.

Politics and the Individual

In principle, the American political system is based on the direct participation of the population as a whole. But how do individuals become liberals, conservatives, or independents in the first place? And to what extent do Americans actually make use of their right to participate in the political system?

Political Socialization

John F. Kennedy was the only president in this century to raise young children in the White House. One can easily imagine Kennedy referring to his children as "good little Democrats." But no one, of course, is born with any particular political orientation. Political attitudes are learned, like all other elements of culture, through the socialization process. As discussed in Chapter 5, the

SOCIAL POLICY

Political Action Committees: A Democratic Trend?

The fact is that the Political Action Committees movement is a *reform movement itself*. It is a straightforward way in which many individuals make small contributions and work in concert to achieve ends in which they believe. It is the antithesis of backroom politics.

Senator Richard Lugar,
Indiana

I think that it is time to declare that the government of the United States is not up for sale. . . . Let's plan controls on these PACs.

Walter Mondale,
former vice president

As the number of political action committees has increased and the public has grown aware of the vast amount of money they pour into the American political system, PACs have become the subject of a heated controversy. Are these organizations an expression of American political democracy, or do they threaten our democratic system?

Supporters of political action committees claim that there is little danger—or even little that is new—in PACs. They point out that Americans have traditionally provided financial support for political organizations and candidates. The recent growth of PACs stems from legislation that curbed large donations made directly to candidates by wealthy individuals. Now millions of Americans—many through their unions or places of employment—can contribute a small amount of money to support an organization seeking to advance some political aim. Therefore, supporters claim, PACs have actually increased the level of participation in the political process. Supporters also argue that since thousands of PACs represent a wide range of political opinion, the influence of any one PAC is scarcely sinister. PAC contributions are also said to have opened politics to people who do not have the personal resources to run for office in an age of immensely costly campaigns. Finally, PAC supporters claim that contributions—currently limited to $5,000 per candidate in any election—are not intended to buy the influence of politicians, but rather to provide necessary support for those leaders people believe already represent their political beliefs.

Opponents of PACs charge that the game of American politics is now being played according to a new "golden rule": Those with the gold are likely to rule. Together, the thousands of PACs make enormous contributions to political candidates—some of whom have received millions of dollars—with at least the expectation that recipients will not bite the hand that feeds them. Moreover, PACs representing companies doing business with the government have contributed to politicians who influence the awarding of government contracts. How, then, critics charge, can these contributions *not* affect politicians' behavior? Opponents also point out that most PAC contributions go to incumbents, whose enormous war chests often discourage challengers from entering a political contest. Finally, although PACs represent diverse segments of society, the enormous power they wield often works against the best interests of the American people as a whole. Legislation to protect consumers, for example, has been effectively curbed by PACs representing corporations that would be affected by such laws.

PACs representing big business are most numerous in American society, although the earliest PACs were formed by labor unions. At least some of the outrage about PACs is simply due to the fact that PACs representing conservative economic and social issues have begun to outnumber other PACs. As President Ronald Reagan observed:

I'm a little amused that suddenly our opponents have developed a real conscience about political action committees. I don't remember them being that aroused when the only ones that you knew about were on their side. Now they're on our side and they want to do away with them.

SOURCE: Based on Larry J. Sabato, *PAC Power: Inside the World of Political Action Committees* (New York: Norton, 1984); Jeffrey E. Sheler, "Is Congress for Sale?" *US News and World Report*, Vol. 96, No. 21 (May 28, 1984): 47–50; Richard L. Berke, "51 Senators List $1 Million in Aid," *The New York Times*, August 10, 1987, p. A17.

family, schools, and the mass media are especially important agents of socialization. Each typically influences the learning of political attitudes.

The family is probably the strongest single influence on anyone's political attitudes. Children generally adopt the political attitudes of their parents. In many cases, the social composition of the neighborhood reinforces what is learned at home, since people of the same race and social class (and hence political orientation) tend to cluster in neighborhoods. By the time children are in elementary school, they are likely to have a lasting identification with their parents' political affiliation (Knoke & Felson, 1974; Burnham, 1983).

As described in Chapter 15, schools teach the dominant political values of their culture. In daily routines such as reciting the Pledge of Allegiance, students affirm support of their country ("I pledge allegiance to the flag of the United States of America . . .") and come to believe that its political system is good (". . . one nation, under God, with liberty and justice for all"). In addition, schools encourage the development of discipline and respect for those in positions of authority, which has the effect of strengthening patriotism (Bowles & Gintis, 1976). In much the same way, the mass media—including what any society presents as "news"—typically reinforces the established political system (Gans, 1980).

Not everyone learns conventional political attitudes, however. Some children learn to challenge the American political and economic systems. During the 1960s—a period of significant social upheaval in the United States—many young people expressed disenchantment with the more conventional values of their parents, as captured in the political slogan "Don't trust anyone over thirty." Such dissatisfaction among young people has greatly diminished in recent years, yet some segments of American society still provide greater support for the status quo than others.

Generally speaking, the degree of support for the political system is associated with how well American society meets the individual's needs, especially for economic opportunity. Thus those who are poor, who are unable to find employment, or who otherwise believe that society has not offered them a fair shake have traditionally expressed less support for the American political system (Zipp, 1985; Pinderhughes, 1986).

Voter Apathy

Many Americans idealistically describe their democratic political system as government "of the people, by the people, and for the people." In reality, however, the United States is a society of *voter apathy*. A smaller proportion of eligible people vote in the United States than in virtually all other democratic societies. In addition, this proportion of Americans is actually lower today than it was a century ago. In the 1984 presidential election, just over half of all eligible voters went to the polls.

Who is and is not likely to vote in the United States? Historically, sex has been of major importance. Women only gained the franchise in 1920, and for decades they voted in lower proportions than men. In 1986, however, women were slightly more likely than men to vote. Age, race and ethnicity, and social class also have long affected voting patterns. In general, the likelihood of voting increases dramatically with age. In the 1986 congressional election, for example, about one-fifth of those between eighteen and twenty-four voted, but almost 60 percent of Americans over forty-five did so. In 1986, about 47 percent of all eligible whites claimed to have voted, compared to about 43 percent of eligible blacks and only 24 percent of eligible Hispanics. Americans with high incomes, prestigious occupations, and high levels of formal education are significantly more likely to vote than are other Americans (Wolfinger & Rosenstone, 1980; U.S. Bureau of the Census, 1987i).

Research has suggested a number of likely explanations of voter apathy. First, at any given time, millions of Americans are sick or otherwise disabled, and millions more are away from home and have made no arrangement to submit an absentee ballot. Second, people must register in advance in order to vote, and must reregister whenever they move from one election district to another. Third, registration and voting require the ability to read and write. As noted in Chapter 15, perhaps 65 million American adults are functionally illiterate, and many are presumably embarrassed to ask for help in registering and voting.

But these factors explain only some voter apathy. Undoubtedly, the most important reason for low voter turnout is that many Americans simply lack the motivation to participate in the political system. This conclusion is supported by the fact that voting levels have dropped even though traditional barriers to voting—such as literacy tests and poll taxes—have been eliminated in recent decades and, since 1971, Americans between the ages of eighteen and twenty-one have had the right to vote.

What lies behind this lack of motivation is a matter of some speculation. Many conservative analysts claim that voter apathy reflects the fact that Americans are by and large content with their political system and see little need to become personally involved. Apathetic voters, then, would appear to be simply *indifferent* to politics. Radical political analysts counter that many Americans are deeply dissatisfied with society, but believe that elections are unlikely to result in significant change for the better. Apathetic voters are thus described as *alienated* from politics. For this reason, the argument goes, many Americans choose to participate in other forms of political activity such as protests, strikes, and work stoppages to demonstrate their dissatisfaction with the political system.

No doubt, each of these explanations contains some measure of truth. In a political system dominated by two parties that have much in common, many Americans may believe that the choices between candidates are not very significant. With more political parties representing a wider range of political opinion, perhaps Americans would have a greater incentive to vote (Zipp & Smith, 1982; Zipp, 1985).

THEORETICAL ANALYSIS OF POWER IN SOCIETY

For at least half a century, both sociologists and political scientists have sought answers to several basic questions about power in the United States: How is power distributed in American society? Who makes important political decisions? In whose interest are these decisions made?

Political power is one of the most difficult issues to study scientifically. Decision making is a complex process that often occurs informally behind closed doors. Important decision makers do not usually welcome the scrutiny of social scientists as they go about their business. In addition, theories about political power are difficult to isolate from the political beliefs of social researchers themselves. In the course of conducting research, American social scientists have developed two competing models of power in the United States. Each model is as much an evaluation as a description of American society.

The Pluralist Model

The pluralist model, which shares some ideas with the structural-functional paradigm in sociology, emphasizes the ways in which a political system functions to meet the needs of the entire society. Formally, the **pluralist** **model** is *an analysis of politics emphasizing the dispersion of power among many competing interest groups.*

The most basic assertion of the pluralist model is that in any large society there are likely to be many (or plural) centers of power. Many different groups and organizations have some degree of power, and each of them seeks somewhat different political goals. No group or organization is believed to have sufficient power to obtain all its goals; many, however, operate as *veto groups*, meaning that they are capable of keeping competing organizations from achieving all of their goals.

Government officials, of course, have considerable power to shape society; yet they are responsible to a wide range of competing special-interest groups. Key decisions, therefore, are not made by any one organization or group of people; society operates as an overall result of numerous decisions made by different people in different places. Power is further dispersed throughout the population by the democratic electoral system through which voters express their individual political interests.

The pluralist model also points out that power has many sources—including wealth, political office, social prestige, and personal charisma. Only in exceptional cases, pluralists argue, are all these sources of power available to the same people. Moreover, the United States is a strikingly diverse society of different races, ethnicities, religions, occupations, and political beliefs. These segments of the population may not have equal power, but each is large and powerful enough to have some voice in the political process.

Because numerous groups and organizations have sufficient power to serve as veto groups, American politics is a complex matter of negotiation and compromise within which no interest group can expect to receive all it seeks. At the same time, these negotiations bridge the differences among various power centers, minimizing conflict and encouraging agreements that are acceptable to all (Dahl, 1961, 1982).

In general, the implications of the pluralist model are that American society is democratic in practice as well as in principle because it grants at least some political power to virtually everyone. Pluralists assert that not even the most powerful Americans can always get their way, and even the least powerful are able to band together to ensure that their political interests are addressed.

The best-known research in support of the pluralist model has focused on decision making in the city of New Haven, Connecticut. In one study, Nelson Polsby (1959) found that key decisions in different areas of the city's politics—including urban renewal, nominations of political candidates, and the educational system—were made by different people. Thus Polsby concluded that power is fairly widely dispersed in that city. Moreover, he found that few members of the New Haven upper class—people listed in that city's *Social Register*—had major positions of economic leadership, a finding consistent with the view that no one segment of society is all-powerful.

Echoing Polsby's conclusions, Robert Dahl (1961) noted that early in New Haven's history a small segment of the population apparently did control the political system, but power subsequently became more dispersed. Thus, Dahl claimed, in New Haven "virtually no one, and certainly no group of more than a few individuals, is entirely lacking in [power]" (1961:228).

The Power-Elite Model

The power-elite model, closely allied with the social-conflict paradigm in sociology, contends that power is heavily concentrated within American society. The **power-elite model**, therefore, is *an analysis of politics emphasizing the concentration of power among the rich.*

This analysis begins by pointing to the marked social stratification of American society. C. Wright Mills (1956), who introduced the term *power elite* into sociology's vocabulary, argued that because the upper class (described in Chapter 10) has most of society's wealth and

The term military-industrial complex *implies that government and economic elites are largely one and the same. Although the Pentagon and the president don't always agree—the B-1 bomber shown here was canceled by Jimmy Carter—the government is the biggest customer of American industry.*

social prestige, its members are the key decision makers on the political scene.

The power elite are largely the "super-rich" of American society: families who often forge alliances in corporate boardrooms and at the altar. Thus these powerful people share many of the same goals and interests and join together to ensure that their political agenda is put into practice.

The power elite is viewed as controlling the three major sectors of American society—the economy, the government, and the military. According to Mills, elites in any of these three areas of society are likely to circulate into positions of power in the others. Alexander Haig, for example, is a retired army general who served as secretary of state under Ronald Reagan, was a presidential candidate in 1988, and has also held various top positions in private business. A large majority of political leaders in the administrations of Reagan and other recent presidents entered public life from powerful and highly paid positions in private business—to which they typically returned in time (Brownstein & Easton, 1983). In his final speech as president almost thirty years ago, Dwight Eisenhower warned that a *military-industrial complex*, led by a small group of extremely powerful people, had acquired unparalleled control over American society.

According to the power-elite model, American democratic principles do not actually count for much in practice since power is concentrated in the hands of a few. Whereas pluralists claim that various centers of power serve as checks and balances on one another, the power-elite model suggests that those at the top have no real opposition.

One of the earliest studies of political power, conducted by Robert and Helen Lynd in 1937, provided support for the power-elite model. The Lynds extensively studied Muncie, Indiana (which they called Middletown, to suggest that this city was in many ways typical of the United States), and were struck by how many dimensions of city life were dominated by a single family. The pervasive power of the Ball family, who had built their fortune on the manufacture of glass canning jars, was evident even to the casual observer: their name appeared on many of Muncie's local institutions, including the bank, the college, the hospital, and the department store. The Balls were also financially involved in dozens of other businesses and charities. Thus, in Muncie, a single family appeared to be at the center of what Mills called a power elite.

A major study of Atlanta, Georgia, carried out by Floyd Hunter (1963), also provided support for the

Table 17–4 THE PLURALIST AND POWER-ELITE MODELS: A COMPARISON

	Pluralist Model	Power-Elite Model
How is power distributed in the United States?	Highly dispersed.	Highly concentrated.
How many centers of power exist?	Many, each with a limited scope.	Few, with power that extends to many areas.
How do centers of power relate to one another?	They represent different political interests and thus provide checks on one another.	They represent the same political interests and face little opposition.
What is the relation between power and the system of social stratification?	Some people have more power than others, but even minority groups can organize to gain power. Wealth, social prestige, and political office are rarely combined.	Most people have little power and the upper class dominates society. Wealth, social prestige, and political office are commonly combined.
What is the importance of voting?	Voting provides the public as a whole with a political voice.	Voting cannot create significant political change.
What, then, is the most accurate description of the American political system?	A pluralist democracy.	An oligarchy—rule by the wealthy few.

power-elite model. Hunter concluded that Atlanta's political life was dominated by about forty people who held top positions in the city's economy.

Contrasting the Two Models

Table 17–4 provides a summary of major differences between the pluralist and power-elite models of power in American society. Clearly, the view of politics based on the studies of Muncie and Atlanta differs sharply from that emerging from the New Haven research. Perhaps there is a real difference in the politics of American cities. More likely, however, the differences in results reflect how the researchers chose to interpret the facts. G. William Domhoff, who has described the political system of the United States in terms consistent with the power-elite model (1967, 1971, 1979), recently re-examined many of the materials that Robert Dahl (1961) used in his original study of New Haven and reached very different conclusions from Dahl's (Domhoff, 1983). Domhoff suggests that cities can be described as "growth machines" in which wealthy landowners attempt to control the political system as much as they can in order to encourage the economic growth that brings them personal profits.

On balance, research on the distribution of power in American society does appear to give greater support to the power-elite model. Even Robert Dahl (1982)—one of the stalwart supporters of the pluralist model—has recently conceded that the great inequality of wealth in America, as well as the barriers to equal opportunity faced by minority groups, are basic flaws in America's quest for a truly pluralist democracy.

This does not mean that pluralism is entirely lacking in American politics, however. We must simply face up to the fact that our political system is not as democratic as we may want to believe. Americans have the right to vote, in other words, but the choices available to them are likely to be those acceptable to the most powerful segments of American society (Bachrach & Baratz, 1970). Republican and Democratic leaders may offer different approaches to helping the poor, for example, but no major-party politician has ever suggested radically redistributing wealth or abolishing the capitalist system.

At the same time, even the most powerful members of our society do not always get their way. As long as rank-and-file Americans continue to form associations with political purposes, there will be a significant element of pluralism. For example, although Domhoff has argued extensively that power is concentrated among the business leaders of American cities, he points out that in his own city of Santa Cruz, California, residents of local neighborhoods have joined forces with university students to successfully oppose business interests in virtually every major decision regarding urban development in the last decade (Domhoff, 1984).

The United States has a history of violent conflict between workers and police. Especially in the late nineteenth century and early twentieth century, police power was routinely used to break strikes and uphold the control of the workplace by owners, as in this strike by miners in Illinois.

In sum, both the pluralist and the power-elite models of social power offer insights into the American political system. In a society characterized by marked social inequality, some people certainly have much more power than others; yet the size and social diversity of American society ensure that no one segment of the population can completely dominate the political system.

POWER BEYOND THE RULES

Politics is inevitably a matter of disagreement about goals and the means to achieve them. Yet all political systems attempt to resolve controversy within a system of rules. In the United States, the basic rules of the political system are found in the Constitution and its twenty-six amendments. Other specific norms, in the form of rules and regulations, are attached to every office in our political system from the presidency to the county tax assessor. But sometimes political power exceeds—or even seeks to do away with—established practices.

Corruption and Machine Politics

To some, the term *politician* is synonymous with leadership; to others, the word suggests a wheeler-dealer whose goal is simply self-enrichment. Powerful people may be no less ethical than anyone else, but their mischief is likely to have more serious consequences for society as a whole. As noted in Chapter 8, white-collar crime generally involves far more public harm than street crime, although elite criminals are far less likely to suffer criminal sanctions.

Historically, one visible example of corruption among powerful people involves political machines in American cities. A **political machine** is *an organization that seeks virtually complete control of the political system within a local area.* The most notorious of all political machines was Tammany Hall, the Democratic administration of New York City during the nineteenth century. Because of the extensive power of machine politicians, their possibilities for personal gain were virtually limitless. If they knew where a city planned to build a new park, for example, they could buy worthless land for little money and then reap enormous profits. Although laws now prohibit such use of inside information, charges of political corruption are still common in political life.

Whatever their faults, the political machines of the past did provide some advantages for Americans with little power. As noted in the opening to this chapter, immigrants who filled the cities of the nineteenth and early twentieth centuries were generally ignored by established political leaders. Political machines often gave members of minority groups some benefits in exchange for their votes (Mann, 1963; Spates & Macionis, 1987). But after the New Deal programs of the Roosevelt administration provided more federal government assistance to the poor, urban political machines gradually declined in the United States.

Revolution

Every political system attempts to transform its power into legitimate authority, as already discussed. In some cases, however, political systems become defined as illegitimate by such a significant number of their citizens that radical political change results. **Political revolution** is *the overthrow of one political system as part of the effort to establish another.*

Political revolution is quite different from reform. While reform involves change *within the system* consistent with established political rules, revolution implies change *of the system itself.* In addition, although efforts toward reform often involve conflict, they rarely produce violence. When one set of leaders overthrows another—an event commonly called a *coup d'état*—some violence may occur, but it is limited. A revolution, in contrast, involves popular opposition to an established political system so that widespread violence is the likely result. The Sandinista revolution against the authoritarian dictator Somoza involved years of widespread violence. On the other hand, some revolutions—such as the overthrow of the authoritarian Marcos regime in the Philippines in 1986—have been relatively free of violence.

Many Americans tend to associate revolution with efforts to establish a socialist political system. Revolutions can occur within any type of political system, however, and have a wide range of outcomes. The American Revolution, for example, ended the control of the American colonies by the British monarchy and resulted in a democratic government. The French revolutionaries of 1789 also overthrew a monarch and summarily executed many members of the feudal aristocracy, but in a few years monarchy returned in the person of Napoleon. Early in this century, the Russian Revolution replaced a system of monarchy with a socialist government based on the ideas of Karl Marx. Following the death of dictator Francisco Franco in 1975, Spain experienced a mostly peaceful political revolution that resulted in a democratic government.

Nonetheless, several general patterns tend to characterize revolutionary societies (Tocqueville, 1955, orig. 1856; Davies, 1962; Brinton, 1965; Skocpol, 1979; Lewis, 1984).

Rising expectations. Although common sense might suggest that revolution is more likely under conditions of extreme deprivation and oppression, history shows that revolutions are actually more likely when people's lives are improving. Social improvements stimulate the desire for an even better life, and such rising expectations may outpace reality. As Crane Brinton has pointed out, revolutions are typically "not started by down-and-outers, by starving, miserable people"; rather, they are "born of hope and their philosophies are formally optimistic" (1965:250).

Inequality and social conflict. Revolutionary societies are typically highly stratified. Disadvantaged people perceive themselves as unjustly deprived, with little chance for improving their lot within the prevailing political system. Sometimes advantaged segments of society lose faith in their own claims of legitimacy and thus become vulnerable to attack from below.

Nonresponsiveness of the old government. Revolutions are likely when an existing political system is unable or unwilling to change, especially to meet the demands of powerful segments of society (Tilly, 1986). For example, monarchies or dictatorships in largely agrarian societies may be unable to meet the demands of a rising middle class based on industry and trade. Thus a new and increasingly powerful segment of society may find revolution an attractive path toward greater power for themselves.

Radical leadership by intellectuals. Thomas Hobbes observed that the center of political rebellion in seventeenth-century England was the universities, a pattern that was repeated during the American political unrest of the 1960s. A successful revolution is likely to be led by an opposition that is not only militarily strong, but also has a well-expressed justification for revolt. Intellectuals are important for formulating convincing principles to support revolution. In a general sense, intellectuals function as a revolutionary special-interest group that expresses the varied grievances of segments of the population and unites diverse opposition to the existing political system into a single revolutionary movement.

Establishing a new legitimacy. The successful overthrow of the old political system does not ensure the long-term success of a revolution. Revolutionary movements may be unified primarily by the hatred of the past government. Once the initial objective of political overthrow is accomplished, divisions within the revolutionary movement may intensify. Even more important, a new political regime faces the task of legitimating its authority, which involves developing new processes of political socialization. In the short run, revolutionary regimes face the danger of *counterrevolution* led by past leaders attempting to regain control of the society—a situation now occurring in Nicaragua. To counter this danger, a revolutionary regime often eliminates the past leadership through exile or execution.

In general, the consequences of revolution cannot be defined as either good or bad. Certainly revolution involves a radical disruption of established social patterns, in at least some instances widespread death and destruction occur, and new governments are certain to be subject to political criticism both within and beyond the society in question. Historically, however, revolutions have launched many nations—including the United States, France, the Soviet Union, and China—into positions of world prominence. Recent revolutions in Cuba, Vietnam, and Nicaragua remain controversial, reminding us that revolution—like established politics—always evokes disagreement and conflict.

Terrorism

In recent years, the world has been plagued by acts of **terrorism**: *the use of violence or the threat of violence* *in pursuit of political goals.* Like revolution, terrorism is generally understood to be political action entirely outside the rules of most established political systems. Paul Johnson (1981) offers three useful insights about terrorism.

First, terrorism elevates violence to a legitimate political tactic—rather than a necessary evil, as in the case of war. Thus terrorists reject standards of morality recognized by most cultures by engaging in violent intimidation. They also ignore (or are excluded from) established channels of political negotiation.

Second, although also used by democratic political systems, terrorism is especially compatible with totalitarian governments as a means of sustaining fear and intimidation among their populations. This was true of both the left-wing Stalinist regime in the Soviet Union and the right-wing Nazi regime in Germany.

Third, extensive civil liberties make democratic societies especially vulnerable to terrorism. Therefore, the fear of terrorism may provoke the suspension of civil liberties. After the Japanese attack on Pearl Harbor that brought the United States into World War II, for example, the fear that Japanese Americans might engage in terrorism resulted in imprisoning over 100,000 Japanese-American citizens for the duration of the war.

During the 1980s, terrorism around the world has increased in frequency and severity. Terrorists have seized embassies and consulates of over fifty nations; kidnapped (and sometimes subsequently murdered) hundreds of political officials, business leaders, and even teachers; and killed Olympic athletes, as well as several world leaders (Jenkins, 1982). Even the pope was the target of a terrorist attack in 1981.

Although many nations have fallen victim to terrorism, about one-third of all recent terrorist acts have been directed against the United States (Jenkins, cited in Church, 1985:27). In 1983, terrorists bombed the American embassy and marine barracks in Beirut, Lebanon, killing 258 Americans. In 1985, Lebanese terrorists seized an American airliner departing from Athens, killing one American serviceman and holding the crew and passengers hostage for up to seventeen days. And 1988 began with eight Americans in terrorist captivity in the Middle East.

Much of the terrorism directed against Americans have been staged by Islamic extremists who regard the United States as an evil force in their part of the world. The box explains how terrorism is part of the international tension between the Islamic world and the United States.

How should a democratic nation such as the United

States respond to terrorist acts? The immediate difficulty is identifying those responsible for the terrorism. Since terrorist groups are typically shadowy organizations with no formal connection to any established state, targeting reprisals is often impossible. Yet as terrorism expert Brian Jenkins points out, "Threats of retaliation that aren't carried out create unfulfilled expectations that lead to the conclusion that America is impotent. It also encourages other terrorist groups, who begin to realize that this can be a pretty cheap way to wage war on the United States" (cited in Whitaker, 1985:29). On the other hand, a forceful military response to terrorism may only serve to broaden violence and risk confrontation with other governments.

A final consideration is that terrorism is not limited to groups opposing established governments. An additional form is *state terrorism,* in which political conflict involves a government using violence against various groups. State terrorism has long existed in the world. During the French Revolution, for instance, the government executed perhaps seventeen thousand people who, for various reasons, were defined as opponents of the state (Stohl & Lopez, 1984). Violent political repression has also been used by the American government, particularly as part of intense conflict with labor organizations during the late nineteenth and early twentieth century. State terrorism remains widespread in the world today, notably in the case of "death squads" used by various Latin American governments to keep their populations in a state of intimidation and compliance.

The state, of course, generally has far greater ability

An indelible image of the Vietnam War was this public execution of a Viet Cong fighter by the Saigon chief of police. This event demonstrated that government officials, as well as those who seek to topple them, can employ brutality to advance their own ends.

Behind the Face of Terror: Shi'ites of the Middle East

They led the uprising that brought Iran's Ayatollah Ruhollah Khomeini to power in 1979. Since then, some of their number claimed responsibility for the bombings of the American embassy and marine headquarters in Beirut in 1983, and the hijacking of an American airliner and subsequent kidnapping of Americans in 1985. They are the Shi'ites, whose members led a campaign of terror against Israel and the United States that captured headlines throughout the 1980s.

After its founding in the seventh century, the Islamic religion (see Chapter 16) divided into several distinct groups. The Shi'ites are a minority group within Islam—representing about 20 percent of all Muslims—who are among the poorest people in the Middle East.

In Iran, where Shi'ites are over 90 percent of the population, the 1979 revolution brought a sense of hope for a better standard of living. But the overthrow of Shah Mohammad Reza Pahlavi also reflected fundamentalist Islamic opposition to Western influences the shah had encouraged. Since the revolution, the more radical Shi'ites have sought to eliminate Western culture from the entire Middle East.

The terrorism practiced by extremist Shi'ites is modeled on the Islamic tradition of holy war against people who threaten their way of life. Indeed, Jihad—the name taken by some Islamic terrorist groups—means "holy war" in Arabic, and Islamic beliefs promise a heavenly reward to those who die participating in such an endeavor. In this light, suicidal acts of terror carried out by religious zealots are more easily understood.

The Shi'ites believe that the United States had the major responsibility for establishing the state of Israel in the Middle East and, more generally, for undermining the Islamic way of life. Thus what may appear to be isolated acts of violence are actually expressions of religion-based political conflict. Terrorism has proved a successful strategy by which small numbers of poorly armed people can—for a time, at least—hold the most powerful nation in the world at bay.

SOURCE: Based in part on "Shiites: At the Cutting Edge of Islamic Revolution," *US News and World Report*, Vol. 99, No. 1 (July 1, 1985): 25–28; and "The Roots of Fanaticism," *Time*, Vol. 125, No. 25 (June 24, 1985): 25.

to force compliance than any particular political group does. But the distinction between group and state terrorism is based on more than the number of soldiers and guns that are involved. As explained in this chapter, the state also claims it is using force *legitimately*, and is usually able to convince at least much of the population of the rightness of its actions. When groups engage in political violence, in other words, they do so as terrorists; when governments engage in political violence, they are merely "maintaining law and order." For this reason, no doubt, the study of terrorism has long focused on groups rather than on governments. But from the point of view of those who oppose a government, the state can be the ultimate terrorist. Like all political behavior, then, terrorism involves not just action but definitions of what is just.

SUMMARY

1. Politics is a major social institution involving the organization of power in society. Political systems attempt to foster the perception that their power is legitimate rather than coercive. Authority—power viewed as legitimate—is derived from tradition, rationally enacted rules and regulations, and personal charisma.

2. Traditional authority predominates in preindustrial societies; industrial societies legitimize power through bureaucratic organizations and law. Charismatic authority arises in all societies and may become routinized into traditional or rational-legal authority.

3. Technologically primitive societies have no distinct political system. With the creation of a material surplus, however, a formally organized political system emerges as part of the historical process of institutional specialization.

4. Monarchy based on traditional authority has been common in human history. Over the last several centuries, many monarchies have been transformed into democratic political systems based on rational-legal authority and extensive bureaucracy.

5. Democracy is a type of political system in which power is widely shared within a population. Democracies typically make use of extensive government bureaucracy.

6. Authoritarian political systems exclude the population from political participation, but do not rigidly control their lives. Totalitarian political systems, based on advanced technology, exclude the populace from free political participation and also exercise control over people's everyday lives.

7. The American government has grown dramatically over the last two centuries, reflecting both population increase and wider government involvement in society.

8. Since the early nineteenth century, political parties have played a central role in the American political system. The Republican Party is somewhat more conservative, and the Democratic Party more liberal.

9. The political spectrum—from extreme liberalism on the left to extreme conservatism on the right—is actually composed of two distinct types of issues: economic and social. The former involve the degree of government regulation of the economy; the latter involve the extent to which all segments of the population should enjoy rights and opportunities.

10. Special-interest groups represent segments of the population and attempt to influence the political process. Lobbyists advance the goals of such groups.

11. In recent decades, political action committees—formed by special-interest groups—have gained increasing importance in funding political campaigns. This development has been accompanied by a decline in the importance of political parties.

12. Individuals learn political attitudes through the process of socialization. Yet many Americans do not readily describe themselves in political terms, nor are they strongly allied with one political party. Moreover, no more than half of the eligible population makes use of its right to vote.

13. The pluralist model holds that political power is widely dispersed; the power-elite model holds that political power is concentrated in a small, wealthy segment of American society.

14. Political machines, traditionally important in urban politics, declined in importance when the federal government expanded its role in American society.

15. Political revolution involves the radical transformation of a political system. Historically, political revolutions have met with varied success, and successful revolutions have established widely varying political systems.

16. Terrorism uses deliberate violence in pursuit of political aims. Although attention has long focused on group terrorism, state terrorism is potentially far more powerful.

KEY CONCEPTS

authoritarianism the exclusion of the majority from political participation, although with little governmental intervention in people's lives

authority power that is widely perceived as legitimate rather than coercive

charismatic authority power legitimated through extraordinary personal abilities that inspire devotion and obedience

democracy a type of political system in which power is exercised by the people as a whole

monarchy a type of political system in which power is passed from generation to generation within a single family

pluralist model an analysis of politics emphasizing the dispersion of power among many competing interest groups

political action committee (PAC) an organization formed by a special-interest group, independent of political parties, to pursue a specific political aim through raising and spending money

political machine an organization that seeks virtually complete control of the political system within a local area

political parties political organizations in which people of similar attitudes and interests influence the political process

political revolution the overthrow of one political system as part of the effort to establish another

political state a formal government exercising control over a society and claiming the legitimate use of coercion to support its rule

politics the organized way in which power is distributed and decisions are made within a society

power the likelihood of achieving desired ends in spite of possible resistance from others

power-elite model an analysis of politics emphasizing the concentration of power among the rich

rational-legal authority (also **bureaucratic authority**) power legitimated by legally enacted rules and regulations

routinization of charisma the transformation of charis-

matic authority into some combination of traditional and bureaucratic authority

special-interest group a political alliance of people who share an orientation with regard to a particular economic or social issue

terrorism the use of violence or the threat of violence in pursuit of political goals

totalitarianism the exclusion of the majority from free political participation coupled with extensive governmental intervention in people's lives

traditional authority power that is legitimated through respect for long-established cultural patterns

---

SUGGESTED READINGS

A general text dealing with politics and society is the following:

> Anthony M. Orum. *Introduction to Political Sociology: The Social Anatomy of the Body Politic*. 2nd ed. Englewood Cliffs, NJ: Prentice-Hall, 1983.

The first paperback listed below provides an overview of political systems and controversies currently found in Latin America; the second examines the interplay of politics and Islam in the Middle East.

> Martin C. Needler. *An Introduction to Latin American Politics*. 2nd ed. Englewood Cliffs, NJ: Prentice-Hall, 1983.

> Daniel Pipes. *In the Path of God: Islam and Political Power*. New York: Basic Books, 1984.

A classic analysis of politics and society is the following paperback, based on a journey made by a French aristocrat through the United States in the early 1830s. Many of Tocqueville's insights about the American political system remain as valuable today as they were when he wrote them.

> Alexis de Tocqueville. *Democracy in America*. Garden City, NY: Doubleday/Anchor Books, 1969; orig. 1834–1840.

A good analysis of Max Weber's thinking on politics and society is this paperback.

> David Beetham. *Max Weber and the Theory of Modern Politics*. New York: Polity Press/Basil Blackwell, 1985.

This analysis of the current political system in Nicaragua was written by an early supporter of the Sandinistas who resigned from the regime because of increasing government censorship.

> Omar Cabezas. *Fire from the Mountain: The Making of a Sandinista*. Kathleen Weaver, trans. New York: Crown, 1986.

This book provides an analysis of the impact of political action committees on American politics.

> Larry J. Sabato. *PAC Power: Inside the World of Political Action Committees*. New York: Norton, 1984.

The following books provide a good overview of the pluralist and power-elite models of social power in the United States. The first is a pluralist analysis; the other two describe the American power elite.

> Robert A. Dahl. *Dilemmas of Pluralist Democracy: Autonomy and Control*. New Haven, CT: Yale University Press, 1982.

> C. Wright Mills. *The Power Elite*. New York: Oxford University Press, 1956.

> G. William Domhoff. *Who Rules America Now? A View of the 80s*. Englewood Cliffs, NJ: Prentice-Hall, 1983.

The history of American music is a rich source of information about political protest. This book combines history, illustrations, and music spanning two centuries of American politics.

> Pete Seeger and Bob Reiser. *Carry It On! A History in Song and Picture of the Working Men and Women of America*. New York: Simon & Schuster, 1985.

These two books provide analyses of political revolution in historical and cross-cultural perspective.

> Theda Skocpol. *States and Revolutions: A Comparative Analysis of France, Russia, and China*. Cambridge (UK): Cambridge University Press, 1979.

> Jack A. Goldstone, ed. *Revolutions: Theoretical, Comparative, and Historical Studies*. New York: Harcourt Brace Jovanovich, 1986.

These two books are a good starting point for the study of terrorism. The first examines a wide range of examples of national and international terrorism. The second is a collection of essays about state terrorism in various societies of the world.

> Paul Wilkinson. *Terrorism and the Liberal State*. 2nd ed. New York: New York University Press, 1986.

> Michael Stohl and George A. Lopez, eds. *The State as Terrorist: The Dynamics of Governmental Violence and Repression*. Westport, CT: Greenwood Press, 1984.

CHAPTER 18

The Economy
and Work

One day Deng Xiaoping decided to take one of his grandsons to visit Mao Zedong.

"Call me Granduncle," Mao offered warmly.

"Oh, I certainly couldn't do that, Chairman Mao," the awestruck child replied.

"Why don't you give him an apple?" suggested Deng to Mao.

No sooner had Mao done so than the boy took a healthy bite out of it, and happily chirped, "Oh, thank you, Granduncle."

"You see," said Deng, smiling, "what incentives can achieve."

This story is popular in the city of Beijing (Peking), the capital of the People's Republic of China (cited in Iyer, 1984:26). Mao Zedong led the revolution that established China as a socialist society in 1949. After Mao's death in 1976, Deng Xiaoping was the nation's leader until he relinquished some of his power in 1987. During his decade of rule, China experienced a transformation that may again change the face of the world's most populous nation.

Under Mao's leadership, China was a highly regimented society in which the state rigidly controlled the economy. In the countryside, the state told China's 800 million peasants what and how much to grow, and when to plant and harvest. Peasants sold their crops to the state for fixed prices. In China's cities, the government closely supervised factories, so that all workers were treated alike, with similar working conditions and fixed wages.

This economic system allowed for only small differences of income within the population. It also fostered low productivity, and any economic gains were offset by population growth. The result was that the standard of living of the Chinese people hardly advanced at all. In short, fixed wages kept income equal, but gave people little incentive to do more work than was absolutely necessary or to devise innovations that would increase productivity.

All this began to change under the leadership of Deng Xiaoping. Deng's new economic policies, applied first to rural areas, provided incentives for people to become more productive. Farm production over a specified quota could be sold to the state for a premium price—or to anyone else for as much money as the farmer could get. Farmers were also allowed to cultivate extra land for their own use, selling whatever they grew for their personal profit. They could pool their money to invest in farm machinery—from tractors to airplanes for crop dusting—and keep for themselves any profits resulting from the greater productivity.

The consequences of these new policies have been nothing short of spectacular. Since 1978, agricultural production has more than doubled, and so has the average income of farmers. Similar economic reforms have taken place, although more slowly, in the cities. Large industries are still tightly controlled by the state, but employees who previously received little more than official thanks for contributing to production increases now enjoy large cash bonuses. As a result, Chinese industrial production rose by about 50 percent between 1978 and 1983. Limited private enterprise in cities has also received the blessing of the state. In more and more cities, small privately owned stores do a thriving business, and city streets bustle with traders hawking all kinds of merchandise, from food to electronics to trendy Western-style clothing.

Deng Xiaoping's economic reforms have gradually changed the social texture of China—exaggerated in one recent commentary as a transformation "from Marx to Mastercard" (P.B.S., 1985). Only a few years ago, public photographs of Mao and political messages on billboards encouraged the population to work collectively. Today Mao's likeness is rarely seen, and political slogans that were clearly collective ("Sacrifice for socialism") are now individualistic ("To get rich is glorious") (Iyer, 1985:56).

There is another side to this reform program, however. Greater productivity has also sparked a growing economic gap between the newly rich "haves" and the "have-nots." Furthermore, traditional Marxists describe the cultural values accompanying the new economic freedom—a growing interest in Western fashions and music, as well as an emphasis on self-interest at the expense of collective responsibility—as "bourgeois decadence" (Iyer, 1984, 1985).

The transformation of Chinese society during the last decade provides an especially clear illustration of how the economy can shape other dimensions of social life. This chapter examines the economy as a social institution, the variations among the economies of different societies, and the consequences of these differences.

WHAT IS THE ECONOMY?

The **economy** is *a social institution that organizes the production, distribution, and consumption of goods and services*. Goods and services include just about any material object or human activity that has value. *Goods* are elements of material culture ranging from basic commodities (such as food, clothing, and shelter) to relatively luxurious items (such as automobiles and swimming pools). *Services* are elements of nonmaterial culture in the form of activities that benefit others (such as the work of religious leaders, physicians, police officers, and telephone operators). Through the economy, all goods and services are distributed throughout society in an organized way to be consumed by the population.

Goods and services are valued because they satisfy basic survival needs or because they make human life easier, more interesting, or more aesthetically pleasing. Although the natural world seems rich enough to satisfy the material needs of everyone, most societies operate on the assumption of scarcity so that people compete with one another for limited goods and services. Most people in American society must work to acquire these commodities, and what they own is also important for their self-concept and public identity. Goods and services are unequally distributed within American society and all other societies, as Chapters 9 and 10 explained, although not to the same degree.

Most people take the complex economy for granted, however, only rarely considering how a book or a pair of jeans makes its way to them in the first place, or how such items reflect their culture's system of values. Like other aspects of social life, the economy varies according to time and place.

The complex economies of modern industrialized societies have resulted from centuries of technological innovation and social change. As Chapter 4 explained, in technologically simple societies of the past, material

The economic reforms in the People's Republic of China instituted by Deng Xiaoping are significantly changing Chinese society. The extensive regimentation of the past is giving way to greater individualism, which many Chinese equate with acquiring consumer goods.

production was largely confined to what people immediately consumed. These small nomadic social groups lived off the land—hunting game, gathering vegetation, and making rudimentary clothing, tools, and shelters. As the only social institution, the family was responsible for producing, distributing, and consuming all goods and services. In short, economic activity was simply a part of family life.

The Agricultural Revolution

Through centuries of cultural innovation and diffusion, the use of plows and animal power led to the emergence of agriculture. Because agrarian societies are ten to twenty times more productive than hunting and gathering societies, people produce much more than they can consume. Freed from the continual need to gather food, individuals assumed specialized economic roles, producing complex crafts, tools, and dwellings within larger permanent settlements. Trading networks linked many settlements through the exchange of food and other goods (Jacobs, 1970). Overall, then, four factors—agricultural technology, productive specialization, permanent settlements, and trade—combined to create a revolutionary expansion of the economy.

As noted in previous chapters, this economic expansion also involved an increase in social inequality. Unlike relatively egalitarian hunting and gathering societies, societies in which agriculture and trade flourish have been marked by a concentration of wealth in the hands of a small elite. Greater productivity, in other words, does not necessarily mean a better standard of living for everyone.

In such agrarian societies, specialization of economic roles means that the economy becomes distinct from family life. Even so, economic activity usually stays close to the home. In medieval Europe, for instance, most people were farmers working nearby fields. In cities of that era, the home itself was often the workplace—an economic pattern called *cottage industry*. Goods produced at home were commonly sold in outdoor markets.

In England and America three centuries ago, an urban home might have included several rooms used as a bakery, under the direction of the husband, who held the status of master baker. His wife usually helped him, but the pronounced patriarchy of the times placed her in a clearly subordinate position. In addition, the household typically included several male apprentices working for wages as they developed their skills, and young men and women working as servants. Therefore, although not of a single family, all members of the household worked within relationships that were quite personal (Laslett, 1984).

The Industrial Revolution

Beginning in mid-eighteenth-century England, industrial machines brought revolutionary changes to the economies of Western societies. Industrialization involved four major changes in production.

Energy. From the earliest hunting and gathering societies throughout the agrarian period, energy was produced by human beings and animals. Perhaps the onset of industrialization can be traced to the year 1765, when James Watt applied a steam engine to the production of material goods. Steam increased the power of muscles a hundred-fold, making possible the operation of many large machines.

Factories. Steam power and large equipment quickly rendered the system of cottage industry obsolete. Thus centralized workplaces apart from the home came into existence. Because factories were large and impersonal, economic activity became further distinct from the family.

Manufacturing and mass production. Before the emergence of factories, most people worked to produce raw materials, such as wool and wood. Factories changed the focus of the economy from *producing* raw materials to *manufacturing* them into salable products. For example, factories turned wool into clothing and lumber into furniture. Small-scale cottage industry continued to provide some manufactured goods, but the new technology of the factories allowed products to be mass-produced so that they were available to far more people.

Specialization. In the cottage-industry system, a single worker fashioned a product from beginning to end. This required great skill, acquired only through years of apprenticeship. In the factory, however, many workers created a single product, and most highly specialized jobs required little skill. Typically, an industrial worker repeated a single task thousands of times during the course of a single working day, year after year. So while specialization in factories increased overall productivity, it also reduced the skill level of the average worker (Warner & Low, 1947).

Women in the Factories of Lowell, Massachusetts

The American textile industry began in 1822 in the Massachusetts town of Lowell—named for Francis Cabot Lowell, the ancestor of the prominent Cabot and Lowell families in Boston today, who had brought with him from England the plans for a textile factory.

About 75 percent of the Lowell workers were women. Factory owners employed large numbers of women for two reasons. First, they worked for about $2 to $3 a week—roughly half the going wage rate for men at that time. Second, by employing women from families that had been in New England for several generations, ethnically prejudiced factory owners avoided hiring newly arriving male immigrants, who were also willing to work for low wages.

Women came to work in the Lowell factory from all over New England. Although wages were low in relation to those paid to men, they were higher than what women could earn in the few other occupations

(such as teaching and household service) that were open to them.

Because most of the women were unmarried, the Lowell factory provided dormitory-type housing and meals, for which a worker's wages were reduced about one-third. Dormitories were managed in a clearly paternalistic fashion. Women were

subject to curfews and, as a condition of employment, were required to attend church services regularly. Any conduct that did not meet the moral standards of the company (such as bringing men to their rooms or staying out beyond curfew) brought disciplinary action against the offender. By supervising the workers' lives in such detail and penalizing them for infractions of the rules, factory owners limited the workers' ability to organize among themselves to increase their bargaining power. With a workday of almost thirteen hours, the Lowell employees had good reason to seek improvements in their working conditions. Yet any open criticism of the factory, or even the possession of "radical" literature, could result in a worker losing her job and perhaps being barred from employment elsewhere.

SOURCE: Based on Benita Eisler, *The Lowell Offering: Writings by New England Mill Women 1840–1845* (Philadelphia and New York: J. B. Lippincott Company, 1977).

The Industrial Revolution changed not only the nature of production, but also society as a whole. Greater productivity gradually raised the standard of material comforts by introducing countless new products and services into an expanding market. These benefits were far from equally shared, of course. People who owned the factories often made vast fortunes, while the majority of industrial workers remained perilously close to poverty. As skills declined, most workers had only their labor to sell to factory owners. Furthermore, they worked not in their own homes but in factories owned and controlled by strangers. The box illustrates the relative powerlessness of industrial workers by describing the lives of women working in New England textile mills early in the nineteenth century.

The Postindustrial Society

The profound social changes that accompanied industrialization in Europe and North America cannot be overestimated. Traditional social patterns were disrupted as people from far-flung rural areas uprooted themselves and migrated to industrial cities. Although workers had little power during the early period of industrialization, the growth of labor unions in the twentieth century has greatly multiplied the power of the individual worker. Furthermore, governments have gradually enacted legislation to regulate the operation of industry, improve working conditions, and extend political rights to a larger segment of the population.

In other words, industrialization itself is a changing

process. Over the course of this century, increasingly sophisticated machinery has reduced the need for human labor in manufacturing. At the same time, expanding bureaucracy has increased the need for workers in clerical and managerial positions. As Robert Heilbroner (1985:48) points out, at the end of the nineteenth century, the American economy had one manager for every thirteen industrial workers, but by the mid-1980s, there was one manager for every two workers. In America today, vast service industries—such as public relations, advertising, banking, and real estate—employ a growing proportion of the labor force. In recent decades, computer technology has created a host of new occupations requiring ever more specialized skills. Large industrial cities, once the core of the American economy, now face economic problems as new high-technology industries proliferate in the suburbs and across America's Sunbelt. Daniel Bell (1976), therefore, has described a **postindustrial economy** as *an economy based on services and high technology.*

Sectors of the Economy

Most economies today, whether fully industrialized or not, are composed of three parts, or *sectors.* Which sector of the economy dominates depends on historical patterns of technological development.

The **primary sector** is *that part of the economy that generates raw materials directly from the natural environment.* Economic activities in the primary sector include agriculture, animal husbandry, fishing, forestry, and mining. The primary sector dominates the economies of preindustrial agrarian societies. Early in American history, for example, most working Americans engaged in agriculture and other primary-sector activities. Today, however, less than 5 percent of the American labor force is employed in the primary sector. The economies of developing nations of the world such as India, however, are still dominated by the primary sector.

The **secondary sector** refers to *that part of the economy that transforms raw materials into manufactured goods.* A predominantly secondary-sector economy is found in societies that have achieved full industrialization, such as the United States during the first half of this century. Such economic activity includes, for instance, the refining of petroleum and the manufacture of wood into furniture and metals into tools, building materials, and automobiles. In societies that are beginning to industrialize—such as Yugoslavia and Greece—

The primary sector of the economy generates raw materials such as oil and gas from the natural environment.

The secondary sector of the economy transforms raw materials into manufactured goods. In mature industrial societies, an increasing amount of production is performed by robots—a case of machines creating machines.

The tertiary sector of the economy generates services rather than goods. Most jobs in the American economy are now in this sector.

the secondary sector of the economy has grown to roughly the same size as the primary sector. In the United States today, about one-third of the labor force works in the secondary sector.

The **tertiary sector** is *that part of the economy that generates services rather than goods.* Extremely small in preindustrial economies, the tertiary sector grows with industrialization until it becomes the dominant economic sector in postindustrial societies such as the United States. More than 60 percent of the American labor force is now employed in a wide range of service occupations, including secretarial and clerical work and positions in food service, sales, law, advertising, and teaching.

The terms *primary, secondary,* and *tertiary* do not imply a ranking of inherent importance. All three types of economic activity make a significant contribution to a society's economic well-being. The terms simply reflect the fact that the three sectors typically develop in sequence as an economy becomes increasingly complex.

COMPARATIVE ECONOMIC SYSTEMS

Most economies today can be described in terms of two ideal models: *capitalism* and *socialism*. The economies of the world vary greatly, however, and no society has an economy that is purely capitalist or purely socialist. These two models, then, represent two ends of a spectrum on which an actual economy can be placed. Most societies have mixed economies, containing both capitalist and socialist elements, although one type of economic pattern usually predominates.

Capitalism

Capitalism is *an economic system in which natural resources, as well as the means of producing goods and services, are privately owned.* An ideal capitalist economy has three distinctive features—unrestricted rights to private property, the pursuit of maximum personal profit, and free-market competition based on consumer sovereignty.

Private ownership of property. In principle, a capitalist economy supports the right of individuals to own virtually anything. These rights are enacted into law—that is, upheld by the power of the state—so that violating property rights is not only morally wrong but criminal.

All societies recognize some right of private property, at the very least including small personal possessions. The more capitalist an economy is, however, the more extensive private ownership of wealth-producing property becomes. Factories, retail businesses, real estate, and even a society's crucial natural resources may be privately owned.

Pursuit of personal profit. A capitalist society encourages people to maximize personal profit—that is, to act in ways that acquire for them the greatest amount of private property, even at the expense of others. Of course, the cultural goal of amassing private property is embraced by some people more than others and, for most people, does not guide behavior within primary groups such as the family. In general, however, capitalism views a selfish orientation as natural and simply a matter of "doing business."

Capitalist societies also defend the pursuit of personal profit on practical grounds. The Scottish economist Adam Smith (1723–1790), whose ideas were influential in the development of capitalist economies, claimed that the individual's pursuit of profit has a practical advantage for all of society. Smith argued that such self-centered goals actually lead an entire society to "wealth and prosperity" (1937:508; orig. 1776).

Free competition and consumer sovereignty. Adam Smith's defense of private property and personal profit is based on a third characteristic of capitalist economies—free competition and consumer sovereignty. Free competition means that, in principle, the economy operates without interference from the government. In this way, the state assumes what is often called a *laissez-faire* (a French expression meaning roughly "to leave alone") approach to the economy. In the absence of a "guiding hand" from government, Smith argued, a freely competitive economy regulates itself by the "invisible hand" of consumer sovereignty. In the marketplace, he asserted, consumers benefit by comparing products in terms of quality and price and then buying those goods and services that provide the greatest value. Producers, competing with one another for sales, know that the greatest profits go to those who produce the highest-quality goods and services at the lowest possible price. Therefore, they attempt to be as efficient as possible, embracing technological advances in production that will ultimately benefit consumers even more. Producers and consumers are likely to be motivated by personal gain more than by concern for others. Yet, according to Smith, the whole society benefits because production becomes more efficient, technology advances, and consumers enjoy ever-increasing value. In short, the classic defense of capitalism rests on the conclusion that from narrow self-interest comes the greatest good for the greatest number of people. In other words, even without a captain, the actions of individual crew members who are motivated by self-interest are sufficient to ensure that the ship will remain on course (Albrecht, 1983:47).

The United States is the leading capitalist society, yet the guiding hand of government regulates the American economy to some extent. Not all productive property in the United States is privately owned. The U.S. Postal Service, the Amtrak railroad system, the Tennessee Valley Authority (a large electrical utility company), and the Nuclear Regulatory Commission (which conducts atomic research and produces nuclear materials) are all owned and operated by the federal government. In some cases, the federal government will assume partial or total control of privately owned businesses in order to prevent their collapse. This bailout approach led the government to become involved in Amtrak and, for a time, the Chrysler Corporation. State and local governments are also involved in numerous large business organizations, including the Port Authority of New York and New Jersey, the Los Angeles Department of Water and Power, and San Francisco's Bay Area Rapid Transit (BART) system (Herman, 1981). The government also regulates economic activity in a host of other ways: through laws setting minimum wage levels and safety standards for the workplace, antitrust laws affecting mergers of large corporations, price supports for farm products, Social Security and welfare payments, student loans, and veterans' benefits. Local governments also intervene in the

No society could survive without extensive cooperation among workers. Capitalist societies, however, encourage motives of self-interest, while socialist societies foster a greater sense of collective responsibility.

economy by, for example, controlling rents or utility costs within a city. In addition, roughly 17 percent of the American labor force is employed by local, state, or federal government (U.S. Bureau of the Census, 1987g).

Socialism

Socialism is *an economic system in which natural resources, as well as the means of producing goods and services, are collectively owned.* In ideal terms, a socialist economy is based on the antithesis of each of the three characteristics of capitalism described above.

Collective ownership of property. An economy is socialist to the extent that it limits the rights to private property, especially property used in producing goods and services. Socialist economies reflect the belief that productive property should provide goods and services for the whole society and therefore should be collectively owned. Housing, for example, is a social resource needed by everyone. A socialist society should therefore ensure that housing is available to everyone instead of treating it as a private commodity to be traded in the marketplace for the enrichment of those who produce it.

Private ownership of productive property is the basis of social classes—the target of criticism by such socialist thinkers as Karl Marx. Since productive property generates wealth, an economy that places productive property in private hands invariably confers great wealth and privilege on owners at the expense of the majority of people. Furthermore, the ownership of productive property also provides power to shape the lives of working employees. In contrast to capitalism, socialism regards social classes as a destructive force within society, and therefore seeks to legally regulate private ownership of property.

Pursuit of collective goals. The individualistic pursuit of personal profit is also at odds with the collective orientation of socialism. Cultural values and norms in the strictest socialist societies define such self-serving behavior as immoral and often as illegal. Socialist values and norms encourage individuals to seek personal satisfaction through contributing to the prosperity and well-being of society as a whole.

Government control of the economy. Socialism rejects the idea that the economy is self-regulating on the basis of free competition. It rejects a laissez-faire approach in favor of placing some or all sectors of the economy under government control. For this reason, a socialist economy is often described as a *command economy* or a *centrally controlled economy*. In a socialist system, government attempts to ensure that the needs of the whole population—for food, housing, transportation, and various consumer goods—are met in an equitable manner. From a socialist point of view, individuals acting on the basis of narrow self-interest are unlikely to generate this result. Indeed, an economy that operates like a ship without a captain can be expected to flounder or—worse still—be destroyed on the rocks. In the absence of the guiding hand of government, the economy will experience spasms of growth and recession, and ultimately collapse with the onset of serious depression. Moreover, continuous inflation and unemployment are likely to adversely affect millions of people. In short, pure socialism considers Adam Smith's "invisible hand"—the profit motive of consumers and producers—an inadequate regulator of a whole society's well-being.

Socialism challenges the assertion that through their purchasing power consumers are able to guide the activities of capitalist producers. Consumers often do not have the information necessary to make objective evaluations of the performance and potential dangers of various products. On the contrary, producers manipulate consumers through commercial advertising, creating artificial needs to increase their own profits instead of meeting the genuine needs of consumers. For this reason, commercial advertising plays little, if any, part in a purely socialist economy. Just as important, capitalist producers are far more concerned with affluent consumers than with the poor, so a free-market economy is unlikely to solve social problems such as unemployment and poverty (Pryor, 1985). From a socialist point of view, only government—committed to serving the needs of all members of society in an equitable manner—can accomplish such goals.

The Soviet Union, Eastern European societies, and some societies in Asia, Africa, and Latin America pattern their economies on the socialist ideal, and place almost all wealth-generating property under government control (Gregory & Stuart, 1985). In the Soviet Union, the most powerful socialist society in the world, private ownership of productive property is virtually nonexistent. Eastern European societies have been under the political control of the Soviet Union since the end of World War II in 1945. Even so, their economies are not all alike. The economies of Bulgaria, Czechoslovakia, and East Germany, for example, are tightly controlled by the government. In Poland and Hungary, on the other hand, a limited market system coexists with a centralized economy (Rakowska-Harmstone, 1978; Gregory & Stuart, 1985).

In Yugoslavia, the only Eastern European nation that is not under the political domination of the Soviet Union, the government sets broad economic policies, but large businesses are collectively operated by their own employees according to what the Yugoslavs call *worker self-management*. Moreover, small businesses with no more than six employees—representing about 20 percent of all businesses—are allowed to operate privately in the belief that they do not generate enough wealth to cause excessive social inequality.

Socialism and Communism

Americans often mistakenly equate the term *socialism* with the term *communism*. In fact, **communism** is an unrealized ideal, *an economic and political system in which all property is collectively owned and all members of society have economic and social equality.* Karl Marx viewed socialism as a transitory stage on the path toward a communist society in which the social inequality and social conflict caused by social classes would be eliminated, along with government. Although in some socialist societies today, dominant political parties describe themselves as communist, in none of them has this ideal been achieved.

As described in Chapters 9 and 10, social stratification involves differences of power as well as wealth. Even if a socialist economy succeeds in abolishing privately owned productive property, government officials still have more power than other people. Full social equality requires, therefore, that once the state has achieved economic equality, it must itself be eliminated. A truly communist society would have a socialist economy in which the guiding hand of the central government would disappear to allow an equal and cooperative association of all people. In Marx's view, a communist society would resemble the earliest egalitarian human societies, except that its technology would be far more advanced. In the absence of inequality and exploitation, all people would contribute to society according to their personal abilities and receive from society according to their personal needs. In this way, rigid productive specialization could be abandoned so that all people could freely and fully develop all the dimensions of their interests and abilities.

Marx would have been the first to agree that such a society is a *utopia* (from the Greek words meaning "not a place") that exists nowhere in the world. Indeed, his writings provide only a vague description of true communism. Yet Marx considered communism a worthy goal, and would certainly have regarded existing "Marxist" societies such as the Soviet Union as a far cry from his communist ideal.

Democratic Socialism

In many Western European democracies—including Great Britain, Sweden, and Italy—historical patterns of capitalism have been integrated with socialist policies through elections rather than revolution. These societies now practice **democratic socialism:** *a political and economic system in which free elections and a market economy coexist with government efforts to minimize social inequality.* A number of key industries and services, such as mining, transportation, health care, and education, are likely to be owned by the government, and privately owned industry may be subject to extensive regulation. High taxation (aimed especially at the rich) provides funds for social welfare programs to help the less advantaged members of society.

Despite efforts by Margaret Thatcher's government to restore traditional capitalism in Great Britain, about 10 percent of the economy remains nationalized. Great Britain also has a far more expansive social welfare program than is found in the United States. Its National Health Service, for example (described in Chapter 19), defines health care as the right of all citizens rather than as a commodity available only to those who can afford to purchase it in a free-market system.

In 1981, a socialist government was elected in France. About 12 percent of French businesses—including all but one television station—became state-owned. Italy and Sweden also have predominantly capitalist economies in which about 12 percent of all businesses are under state control (Roskin, 1982; Gregory & Stuart, 1985).

Relative Advantages of Capitalism and Socialism

Capitalism and socialism shape the lives of billions of people throughout the world. In each case, advocates readily point to the advantages of the economic system and tend to ignore the drawbacks. Moreover, assessing these economic systems is difficult since nowhere can

they be precisely and objectively compared. In any society, the performance of the economy—whatever its mix of capitalism and socialism—is affected by additional factors. For example, different historical and cultural patterns produce different social goals and working practices and affect perceptions of the importance of work. Working hours and the size and composition of the labor force are also highly variable from one society to the next. In addition, societies have varying natural resources and levels of technological development, as well as different patterns of trade and political alliances. Finally, the economies of some societies are burdened by the destructive effects of war (Gregory & Stuart, 1985). Despite all these complicating factors, however, some comparisons are possible.

Productivity

Table 18–1 compares economic performance for a number of societies with predominantly capitalist and predom-

Table 18–1 ECONOMIC PERFORMANCE OF CAPITALIST AND SOCIALIST ECONOMIES, 1984

	Per Capita GNP (U.S. dollars)
Predominantly Capitalist Economies	
Austria	8,892
Belgium	8,372
Canada	13,100
Denmark	10,990
France	9,510
Greece	3,613
Japan	10,410
West Germany	11,020
Great Britain	8,270
United States	15,380
Unweighted average	9,956
Predominantly Socialist Economies	
Czechoslovakia	8,298
East Germany	9,769
Hungary	7,277
Poland	6,159
Soviet Union	7,266
Yugoslavia	2,071
Unweighted average	6,807

SOURCE: U.S. Arms Control and Disarmament Administration. *World Military Expenditures and Arms Transfers, 1986* (Washington, DC: Government Printing Office, 1987), Table 1, pp. 59–100.

The productivity of capitalist societies is suggested by the overwhelming presence of corporate power in central cities, for example, the Ginza district in Tokyo. But since social equality is a primary concern of socialist societies, Moscow reveals no central business district. Rather, Red Square and the Kremlim convey a sense of the importance of government.

inantly socialist economies. "Gross National Product" (or GNP) refers to the total value of all goods and services produced annually by the economy; the "Per Capita" (or per person) values allow comparisons among societies with labor forces of different sizes. Each society, of course, uses a different currency system so original GNP and income figures have been converted into U.S. dollars.

Among the societies with predominantly capitalist economies in 1984, the United States had the highest per capita GNP ($15,380), while Greece had the lowest ($3,613). Obviously, there is considerable variation in GNP among these predominantly capitalist societies, reflecting complicating factors noted at the outset of this section. For all ten societies, the *unweighted* average (meaning the fact that the countries are not of equal size has been ignored) is $9,956: this is a crude measure of the value of goods and services produced by a worker each year in the average predominantly capitalist society.

Per capita GNP also varies significantly among societies with predominantly socialist economies. In 1984, East Germany had the highest economic output per worker ($9,769), while Yugoslavia had the lowest ($2,071). Overall, however, these socialist economies produced somewhat less than did their capitalist counterparts. A worker in the average socialist society produced $6,807 worth of goods and services in 1984—only about two-thirds as much as a worker in the average capitalist society. The comparison between East and West Germany is of particular interest, since this is a case of a single society that was divided at the end of World War II into two parts—one capitalist and one socialist. In 1984, per capita GNP in socialist East Germany was about 88 percent that of capitalist West Germany.

Distribution of Income

Productivity, however, is not the only economic concern. How wealth is distributed in a population is also important. Table 18–2 compares the extent of income inequality in several societies with predominantly capitalist and predominantly socialist economies. The income ratios presented compare the income of people near the top of the income hierarchy with the income of people near the bottom.*

---

* More specifically, income ratio is derived by dividing the 95th percentile income by the 5th percentile income.

Table 18–2 DISTRIBUTION OF INCOME IN CAPITALIST AND SOCIALIST ECONOMIES

	Income Ratio
Predominantly Capitalist Economies	
United States (1968)	12.7
Canada (1971)	12.0
Italy (1969)	11.2
Sweden (1971)	5.5
Great Britain (1969)	5.0
Unweighted average	9.3
Predominantly Socialist Economies	
Soviet Union (1966)	5.7
Czechoslovakia (1965)	4.3
Hungary (1964)	4.0
Bulgaria (1963–1965)	3.8
Unweighted average	4.5

SOURCE: Adapted from P. J. D. Wiles, *Economic Institutions Compared* (New York: Halsted Press, 1977), as cited in Paul R. Gregory and Robert C. Stuart, *Comparative Economic Systems*, 2nd ed. (Boston: Houghton Mifflin, 1985), p. 503.

Of the five predominantly capitalist societies listed in Table 18–2, the United States had the greatest income inequality: an income ratio of 12.7 means that a rich American's income is almost thirteen times that of a poor American. The American income ratio was closely followed by those of Canada (12.0) and Italy (11.2). Both Sweden (5.5) and Great Britain (5.0) have much less income inequality, which is perhaps to be expected since they have incorporated socialist principles into traditionally capitalist economies. The unweighted average shows that a rich person has more than nine times the income of a poor person in a predominantly capitalist society.

Although the predominantly socialist societies also vary among themselves, their unweighted average ratio is 4.5, indicating roughly half the inequality of income characteristic of more capitalist societies. These ratios reflect the fact that collective ownership of productive property produces more egalitarian societies, while private ownership of productive property seems to concentrate income in the hands of a few. The greater income disparity in capitalist societies is the basis of a long-standing moral controversy. In 1984, for example, the Roman Catholic bishops in the United States released a report that was highly critical of economic inequality in the

United States. The box presents some of their arguments.

This comparison of economic performance in predominantly capitalist and predominantly socialist societies leads to an important general conclusion: A capitalist society is relatively more productive, but also generates greater social inequality; a socialist society can boast of greater social equality, but is relatively less productive. These facts help to clarify recent developments in the People's Republic of China. Under Mao Zedong's leadership, China held to a socialist economic system that kept economic inequality to a minimum, but at the price of low productivity. Deng Xiaoping showed that the personal incentives provided by a market system would increase productivity, though the price has been increasing economic inequality (Schell, 1984; Iyer, 1984, 1985).

Economics and Politics

As Chapter 17 explained, a society's economic system significantly shapes its political life. Capitalism depends on the freedom to pursue individual interests with minimal interference from the state. Consumers seeking the greatest value may buy what they wish; producers seeking the greatest profits may market what they wish. In this way, Adam Smith maintained, an invisible hand guides the economy. Clearly capitalism requires a great deal of personal liberty in the marketplace. From a socialist point of view, such freedom is an obstacle to collective goals. Opponents of the recent introduction of capitalist policies into the Chinese economy, for example, claim that capitalist practices are leading to increased selfishness and economic inequality.

Predominantly socialist societies define the goal of government as maximizing economic and social *equality*. Doing so requires considerable government intervention in the economy, and thus in the lives of all citizens. In this way, the economy is thought to more effectively address the needs of all people for such basic things as adequate housing, education, and health care. From the capitalist point of view, however, this kind of government intervention undermines any claim by socialist societies to being democratic.

As noted in Chapter 17, humanity has yet to devise a means to completely resolve the timeless antagonism between the goals of personal liberty and economic equality. The democratic socialist societies of Western Europe, however, have attempted to lessen this antagonism by combining capitalist and socialist principles.

SOCIAL POLICY

Is Capitalism Immoral?—The Catholic Church's View

The needs of the poor must take priority over the desires of the rich; and the rights of workers over the maximization of profits.
Pope John Paul II, 1984

For two thousand years, the Roman Catholic Church has judged economic policies according to religious standards, and during the last century, a number of popes have explicitly criticized capitalism. In 1891, while stating that private property was "in accordance with the law of nature," Pope Leo III asserted that the proper purpose of wealth is to meet the needs of all humanity, not just a small elite. In 1931, Pope Pius XI claimed that while government should not rigidly control the economy, workers should be permitted to participate in economic decision making. Pope John XXIII stated in 1963 that all people have a right to private property, but also to a basic education, safe working conditions, and a host of other social welfare programs providing "food, clothing, shelter, rest, [and] medical care." The comment by Pope John Paul II noted above therefore continues a long tradition of concern about some of the social consequences of capitalism.

A recent statement on American capitalism by the 290 Roman Catholic bishops of the United States has become controversial. While supporting capitalism in principle, the report criticizes two serious shortcomings of the American economy. First, the bishops find the distribution of income in the United States to be morally troubling. They point out that despite our high economic productivity, at least 15 percent of Americans live in poverty. Moreover, during the 1980s, the ranks of the poor have sharply increased. In addition, they note that the richest fifth of the population enjoys as much income as everyone else combined. To remedy this problem, the bishops suggest that, in the short run, social welfare programs be expanded and, in the long run, American society find a way to distribute wealth more equitably.

Second, the bishops are concerned about unemployment, which stood at 6.2 percent in 1988, after approaching 10 percent in the early 1980s. Unemployment is not only a cause of economic suffering, the bishops note; it also imposes damaging personal stress and social isolation. The bishops claim that the unemployment rate should be no more than 5 percent, and suggest using government-sponsored programs to create jobs and train workers. Special attention, they add, is required to eliminate barriers to employment that handicap women and other minority groups.

While the bishops' report has enjoyed support from many Catholics and non-Catholics, some people have criticized its conclusions. Elmo Zumwalt, a retired admiral who is now a corporate executive, commented, "I came away with a feeling that these are well-meaning people who really don't understand our capitalist system." The major criticism of the report is that further government intervention in the economy will probably reduce productivity, thereby undercutting the economic growth that can provide more wealth and more jobs. Furthermore, in the eyes of some critics, the bishops' call for expanded social welfare programs only repeats an approach that failed in the 1960s. Rather than seeing capitalism as the cause of poverty and economic inequality, opponents of the bishops' position believe that capitalism—unfettered by government regulation and expensive social welfare programs—will prove to be the solution to these problems, both in the United States and around the world.

On one side of the issue, then, are those who claim that American capitalism has generated morally troublesome social inequality and therefore requires major redirection by government. On the other side are those who believe that capitalism is the greatest wealth-producing system ever known and is capable of solving social problems—if allowed to operate on its own terms.

SOURCE: Based on "U.S. Bishops' Pastoral Letter on Catholic Social Teaching and the U.S. Economy," *Origins*, Vol. 14, No. 22/23 (November 15, 1984): 337–383; also John Greenwald, "Am I My Brother's Keeper?" *Time*, Vol. 124, No. 22 (December 26, 1984): 80–82; "The Church and Capitalism," *Businessweek* (November 12, 1984): 104–107, 110, 112.

THE AMERICAN ECONOMIC SYSTEM

The United States has a predominantly capitalist economy that generates characteristically high productivity. Indeed, the overall standard of living in the United States is matched by few societies anywhere in the world. At the same time, economic inequality in America is also considerable in relation to other industrial societies. This general picture provides the foundation for a closer look at the operation of the American economy.

Work in the Postindustrial Economy

In 1987, roughly 121 million Americans were part of the labor force—about two-thirds of all Americans over the age of sixteen. As shown in Table 18–3, sex and race are related to participation in the labor force. Across all racial and ethnic categories, a larger proportion of American men (76.0 percent) than women (56.7 percent) had income-producing jobs. As noted in Chapter 12, however, this gap has steadily diminished in recent decades. The percentage of black men who are in the labor force is somewhat less than the percentage of white men, while black women are somewhat more likely to be employed than are white women.

Age also affects labor force participation. As shown in Figure 18–1, labor force participation rises rapidly for both men and women in their early twenties. Women's participation subsequently remains below that for men during childbearing years. In the last few years, however, the proportion of women in their forties and

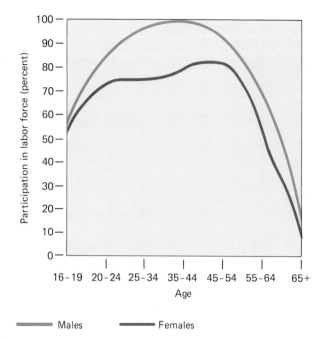

Figure 18–1 Participation in the Labor Force by Age and Sex, 1987

(U.S. Bureau of Labor Statistics, 1988)

early fifties in the labor force has risen sharply. For both men and women, labor force participation declines rapidly after the age of fifty-five, and only a small proportion of either sex continues to work after reaching age sixty-five.

The Decline of Agricultural Work

At the beginning of the twentieth century, the United States was still a largely rural society with almost 40 percent of the labor force engaged in farming. By 1950, however, this proportion had fallen to about 10 percent, and by 1988, to under 3 percent. Figure 18–2 graphically illustrates this rapid decline. The change reflects the diminished role of the primary sector in the American economy. Even so, the American economy produces more agricultural products than ever—far more, in fact, than the population consumes. A century ago, a typical farmer produced food for five people. Agricultural productivity has increased so much that today a single farmer produces food for seventy-five. This dramatic increase in productivity is the result of new types of crops, pesticides that provide higher yields, larger and more sophisti-

Table 18–3 PARTICIPATION IN THE LABOR FORCE BY SEX AND RACE, 1987

Category of the Population	In the Labor Force	
	Number (millions)	Percent
Males (aged 16 and over)	66.2	76.2
White	57.8	76.8
Black	6.5	71.1
Females (aged 16 and over)	53.7	56.0
White	45.5	55.7
Black	6.5	58.0

SOURCE: U.S. Bureau of Labor Statistics. *Employment and Earnings,* Vol. 35, No. 1 (January 1988), pp. 161–162.

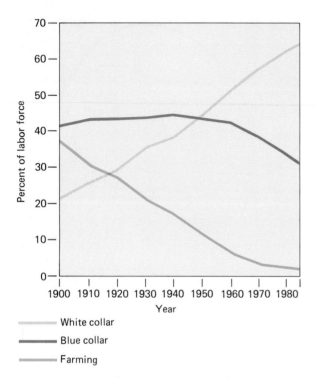

White collar
Blue collar
Farming

Figure 18–2 The Changing Pattern of Work in the United States, 1900–1985

(U.S. Bureau of the Census)

Thousands of families were forced to leave the farm during the 1980s. Such events represent not only a loss of animals and equipment, but also of a way of life.

cated farm equipment, and advances in farming techniques. At the same time, the average American farm has doubled in size since 1950 to about 455 acres today. The largest farms, now under the control of corporate agribusinesses, are many times that size. This means that only a very small percentage of all farms were responsible for most U.S. farm output.

Although both large-scale and small-scale farming were highly profitable during the 1970s, an economic crisis during the 1980s has threatened the American tradition of the family farm. Lower demands from abroad for American agricultural products, coupled with declining land prices and mounting debts, have pushed many smaller farms into bankruptcy: some twenty thousand farms were forced to sell out between 1981 and 1985 (Greenwald, 1985). Many other smaller farms remain in operation only because families are able to earn supplementary income from nonagricultural occupations. Thus, while agricultural productivity has reached an unprecedented level during this century, farming gives full-time employment to only a small and declining proportion of Americans.

Blue-Collar to White-Collar Work

The color of a person's work shirt has traditionally been a shorthand indicator of occupational status (and thus of overall social standing) in American society, as discussed in Chapters 9 and 10. People who earned their living through physical labor—operating machinery, building houses, delivering the mail—often wore tough blue work shirts identifying them as members of the working class. People who earned their living primarily through mental effort and working with other people—clerical workers, salespeople, managers, and the members of various professions—wore crisp white shirts that served as a badge of membership in the middle class.

The industrialization of the American economy drew many people into blue-collar occupations. By 1900, as shown in Figure 18–2, over 40 percent of working Americans had blue-collar jobs—roughly twice the proportion with white-collar jobs. This pattern held until the 1950s, when the expansion of the service-oriented tertiary sector of the economy triggered a white-collar revolution. By 1985, almost two-thirds of employed Americans held white-collar jobs, while blue-collar occupations accounted for only about one-third of the labor force.

Although a useful shorthand distinction, the terms *blue-collar* and *white-collar* do not adequately represent the complexity of the American labor force. Especially today, numerous occupations do not fit neatly into either category (is a computer repairer blue-collar or white-collar?), and blue-collar workers such as carpenters often earn more money than, say, white-collar clerks. Furthermore, since both the blue shirt and the white shirt are typical male attire, this distinction overlooks the so-called pink-collar occupations such as domestic work and food service jobs that have traditionally employed women.

Another problem is that, while people commonly link white-collar jobs and the service sector of the economy, not all service-sector jobs are white-collar. Furthermore, many service jobs provide little income and social prestige—witness the growing number of Americans who serve hamburgers in fast-food restaurants (Carey, 1981).

Professions

Professional work has increasing importance in the emerging postindustrial economy of the United States. In everyday conversation, a wide range of full-time work is called *professional*—as when we speak of a professional exterminator or a professional tennis player. As distinct from *amateurs*, professionals engage in a particular activity for a living, and they presumably have above-average skills and qualifications.

More precisely, a **profession** is *a white-collar occupation with high social prestige that requires considerable formal education*. In the past, professional standing was limited to a few occupations, principally medicine, law, and the ministry (W. Goode, 1960). Today, however, any occupation may be described as more or less professional to the extent that it has the following four characteristics (Ritzer, 1972: 56–60).

Theoretical knowledge. Unlike occupations involving only technical skills, professionals claim to have a theoretical understanding of their field based on extensive formal training and informal interaction with others in their profession. Anyone, for instance, can learn first-aid skills, but a physician makes the professional claim of having a theoretical understanding of human health and illness.

Self-regulated training and practice. While most workers are subject to on-the-job supervision, professionals enjoy a high degree of autonomy, ideally working independently rather than as salaried employees of large organizations (Zald, 1971). Professional training is regulated by formal organizations (called *professional associations*) that are composed of people in the profession. Formal degrees and other certificates are required of those who wish to practice within the profession. Professional associations also demand adherence to a formal code of ethics, but without subjecting their membership to day-to-day supervision.

Authority over clients. Because of their extensive formal and informal education, professionals claim to have knowledge that no one outside their profession can fully understand. For this reason, while most occupations deal with *customers* who direct the transaction, professionals deal with *clients* who they assume lack the knowledge to critically evaluate the service being performed. Thus the typical professional is in a position of power over the client.

Orientation to community rather than to self-interest. Professionals emphasize the altruism of their work; they profess to be serving the needs of clients and the community as a whole, rather than seeking simply personal enrichment. Most business executives readily admit to seeking financial gain for their work. The work of a minister, on the other hand, is generally seen as a contribution to the well-being of others. For their efforts, professionals receive positive recognition in the form of high social prestige. In practice, of course, most professionals also enjoy a high income.

Beyond the traditional professions of medicine, law, and the ministry are a number of other occupations that can be described as *new professions*—including architecture, college teaching, psychiatry, social work, and accountancy—because they approximate the four characteristics presented above. With the development of many new service occupations in America's postindustrial economy, many more occupations have attempted to gain professional standing—a process that is termed *professionalization*.

The members of an occupational category typically attempt to gain public recognition as professionals in several ways (Ritzer, 1972). First, they begin to use a new name to describe their occupation, both to suggest that they employ special, theoretical knowledge in their work and to overcome the public's previous view of them as having nonprofessional standing. In this way, for example, government administrators become "public policy analysts." Second, members of the occupation form a professional association that formally attests to their individual skills. Third, the professional association adopts a code of ethics that, like those of the traditional professions, emphasizes the contribution the occupation makes to the community. Finally, professional association seeks to legally restrict the practice of the occupation to associa-

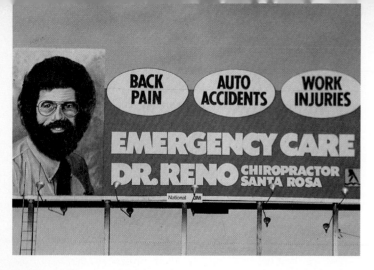

Because professionals have traditionally claimed to serve the community rather than just themselves, the American Medical Association prohibits members from advertising their services. However, not all medical professionals, including chiropractors, share this policy.

tion members. They may also take part in a public relations campaign to win acceptance of their professional standing.

Not all occupational categories are likely to become publicly recognized as professions; most don't even seek this status. In marginal cases, the term *paraprofessional* is used to describe occupations, such as medical technician, with some claim to professional standing but lacking the extensive theoretical education required in the established professions.

Trends in Workplace Inequality

Chapter 9 cited the growth of white-collar occupations as one reason for the widespread—if misleading—view of the United States as a middle-class society. Since the prestige of white-collar work now applies to two-thirds of the labor force, it is tempting to conclude that the United States has indeed become overwhelmingly middle-class. However, although the emerging postindustrial economy has transformed the nature of work, patterns of social inequality have changed very little.

Work within the American economy can be described in terms of two labor markets (Edwards, 1979). In relation to the blue-collar/white-collar distinction noted earlier, the issue here is less the kind of work a person does than the benefits the work provides.

The **primary labor market** includes *occupations that provide extensive benefits to workers*. This segment contains primarily white-collar occupations including the professions and higher management positions in business and other formal organizations. People working in the primary labor market enjoy *extrinsic benefits*, meaning that they receive high income and considerable job security. They also give various *intrinsic benefits*, mean-

ing that their work is personally challenging and satisfying. These occupations, which require a broad education rather than specialized training, also offer good opportunity for advancement. Workers who obtain additional education, for example, are likely to be promoted. Other workers often advance simply as a result of increasing seniority.

A somewhat less privileged segment of this category is the *subordinate primary labor market*, which includes white-collar work in lower management and retail sales, as well as the most skilled office work and blue-collar work. These jobs may offer lower pay, but labor unions often provide workers with job security. On the other hand, the work is often repetitive and routine and demands specific skills more than a general education.

The **secondary labor market** includes *occupations that provide minimal benefits to workers*. In this segment of the American labor force are found the least skilled blue-collar workers, along with white-collar workers in low-prestige clerical positions. Jobs in the secondary labor market usually provide few extrinsic rewards: income is considerably lower than among workers in the primary labor market, and workers have far less job security. Workers have little opportunity for advancement, even if they gain more education or training. In these dead-end jobs, which are usually not unionized and lack even a seniority system, a worker's income and job security may not improve even after years of employment. Not surprisingly, workers in the secondary labor market are most likely to experience alienation and distress (Mottaz, 1981; Kohn & Schooler, 1982).

As Richard Edwards (1979) points out, a large proportion of the new service jobs in the emerging postindustrial economy involve the same kind of unchallenging tasks, low wages, and poor working conditions that characterized manufacturing jobs in factories a century ago. Today's secondary labor market workers therefore tend to measure the value of their job solely in terms of the income it provides rather than in terms of personal satisfaction (Gruenberg, 1980). In the box, two workers—one holding a traditional blue-collar job in a factory and the other a low-status white-collar position—describe their occupations in very similar terms.

Although the emerging postindustrial economy has increased productivity and created somewhat more leisure time for workers, it has had little effect on the patterns of social inequality. Generally, the traditionally advantaged segments of American society—the middle and upper classes, whites, and males—are overrepresented in the primary labor market. Blacks, women,

SOCIOLOGY OF EVERYDAY LIFE

Low-Status Industrial and Service Jobs—Much the Same

Mike Lefevre is an industrial worker in a Chicago steel mill. He is aware that jobs such as his are declining in America. He also explains that he finds little personal satisfaction in his work.

I'm a dying breed. A laborer. Strictly muscle work . . . pick it up, put it down, pick it up, put it down. We handle between forty and fifty thousand pounds of steel a day. (Laughs) I know it's hard to believe—from four hundred pounds to three- and four-pound pieces. It's dying.

. . . It's hard to take pride in a bridge you're never gonna cross, in a door you're never gonna open. You're mass-producing things and you never see the end of it. (Muses) I worked for a trucker one time. At least I could see the truck depart loaded. In a steel mill, forget it. You don't see where nothing goes.

I got chewed out by my foreman once. He said, "Mike, you're a good worker but you have a bad attitude." My attitude is that I don't get excited about my job. I do my work but I don't say whoopee-doo. The day I get excited about my job is the day I go to a head shrinker. How are you gonna get excited about pullin' steel? How

are you gonna get excited when you're tired and want to sit down?

It's not just the work. Somebody built the pyramids. Somebody's going to build something. Pyramids, Empire State Building—these things just don't happen. There's hard work behind it. I would like to see a building, say, the Empire State, I would like to see on one side of it a foot wide strip from top to bottom with the name of every bricklayer, the name of every electrician, and all the names. So when a guy walked by, he could take his son and say, "See, that's me over there on the forty-fifth floor, I put the steel beam in." Picasso can point to a painting. What can I point to? Everybody should have something to point to.

Heather Lamb is also a Midwestern worker, employed in the newer service sector of the American economy. Her work as a long-distance telephone operator provides little more autonomy and personal satisfaction than Mike Lefevre finds in the steel mill.

It's a strange atmosphere. You're in a room about the size of a gymnasium, talking to people thousands of miles away. You come in contact with at least thirty-five an hour. You can't exchange any ideas with them. They don't know you, they never will. You

feel like you might be missing people. You feel like they put a coin in the machine and they've got you. You're there to perform your service and go. You're kind of detached.

. . . A big thing is not to talk with a customer. If he's upset, you can't say more than "I'm sorry you've been having trouble." If you get caught talking with a customer, that's one mark against you. You can't help but want to talk to them if they're in trouble or they're just feeling bad or something. For me it's a great temptation to say, "Gee, what's the matter?" You don't feel like you're really that much helping people.

. . . It's a hard feeling when everyone's in a hurry to talk to somebody else, but not to you. Sometimes *you* get a feeling of need to talk to somebody. Somebody who wants to listen to you other than "Why didn't you get me the right number?"

It's something to run into somebody who says "It's a nice day out, operator. How's your day, busy?" You're so thankful for these people. You say, "Oh yes, it's been an awful day. Thank you for asking."

SOURCE: Studs Terkel, *Working* (New York: Pantheon Books, 1974), 1–2, 65, 66, 69. (Copyright © 1974 by Pantheon Books, a Division of Random House, Inc.

---

and other disadvantaged categories of people are found largely in the secondary labor market.

Self-Employment

Early in American history, work was mostly a matter of *self-employment*. Before the growth of bureaucratic organizations, people earned a living more or less independently. In rural areas, farms were family owned and

operated, while in the cities, self-employed workers owned small businesses or sold their skills and labor on the open market. While no precise data are available, C. Wright Mills (1951) estimated that in the early nineteenth century about 80 percent of the American labor force was self-employed. By 1870, however, the proportion of self-employed American workers had fallen to about one-third of the labor force, and by 1940, to about one-fifth.

Government statistics indicate that only about 8 percent of the labor force was self-employed in 1987. Among the shrinking number of agricultural workers, however, self-employment is still pronounced. In 1987, about half of all men and one-third of all women working in agriculture were self-employed (U.S. Bureau of Labor Statistics, 1988).

The self-employed have a variety of occupations. Lawyers, physicians, and other professionals have always been strongly represented among the self-employed because they possess the special education and skills that enable them to make a living without working for any organization. The majority of self-employed workers, however, are not professionals. They include owners of small businesses, plumbers, carpenters, free-lance writers and artists, and long-distance truck drivers. As these examples suggest, the self-employed may have white-collar or blue-collar jobs, although the latter are more common.

Because our culture has always celebrated the value of independence, self-employment is attractive to many Americans. There are no time clocks to punch, no inflexible routines, and no supervision. In addition to being their own boss, the self-employed have the potential—although it is rarely realized—of earning a great deal of money. Small-business owners are more privileged than their employees, however: they typically have higher incomes, more social prestige, and find greater personal satisfaction in their work. These differences are related not only to owning a business, but also to being older and more educated than employees; they are probably also related to the fact that most small-business owners are white males.

Self-employed people also face special problems. They are particularly susceptible to fluctuations in the economy, and lack the pensions and subsidized health-care plans that benefit many employees of large organizations. Perhaps one-third of small businesses do not survive for a period of five years (Form, 1982).

Unemployment

To the vast majority of people, work is the major source of necessary income. As noted earlier, work can be a source of personal satisfaction and social prestige, and is always an important piece of personal identity. Unemployment, therefore, often causes not only financial hardship, but also serious social and psychological problems (Riegle, 1982).

Some unemployment is characteristic of all societies. Few young people entering the labor force find a job immediately; some workers temporarily leave the labor force while seeking a new job or as the result of a labor strike; others suffer from long-term illnesses; and still others who are illiterate or totally without skills are unable to perform useful work. Yet regardless of their mix of capitalism and socialism, in all societies unemployment is also caused by the operation of the economy itself: workers lose their jobs because of economic recession, because their occupations have become obsolete, and because the businesses they worked for closed down in the face of import competition. In recent years, for example, the growth of high-technology industries exists alongside increased unemployment rates among relatively advantaged workers in many traditional blue-collar occupations (Kasarda, 1983).

In societies with predominantly capitalist economies such as the United States, unemployment rates rarely dip below 5 percent of the labor force. In fact, this level of unemployment is now viewed by public policymakers as natural and is even described as "full employment." Only when the unemployment rate rises above about 8 percent is there widespread recognition of an "unemployment problem" (Albrecht, 1983). In contrast, societies with predominantly socialist economies consider work to be each person's right and obligation, so the government may create jobs to keep the unemployment rate low. Even so, unemployment is a continuing problem in societies with socialist economies as well.

In 1988, almost 7 million people over the age of sixteen were unemployed—about 6.2 percent of the work force. This represents a decline in unemployment since 1982—the year of the highest annual unemployment rate (9.7 percent) since the Great Depression ended in the early 1940s. But in good times and bad, American culture embraces the mistaken idea that anyone who really wants to work can do so. Thus the unemployed may be harshly judged as unmotivated people who refuse to take advantage of this land of opportunity.

The problems of unemployment are more common to workers in the secondary labor market than to those in the primary labor market. Figure 18–3 shows the official unemployment rate for various segments of the American population in 1987 (U.S. Bureau of Labor Statistics, 1988). The unemployment rate was more than twice as high among blacks (13.0 percent) as among whites (5.3 percent), largely reflecting the fact that blacks have long been concentrated in the secondary labor market (DiPrete, 1981). All categories of teenagers have high

This mural, painted as part of the Work Projects Administration (WPA) during the 1930s, poignantly portrays the experience of unemployment as undermining self-worth as well as financial security.

unemployment, but this problem is far more pronounced among blacks (34.7 percent) than among whites (14.4 percent). Even among college graduates, who tend to have jobs in the primary labor market, unemployment among blacks (11.4 percent) was twice the rate among whites (5.1 percent). For both blacks and whites, women had about the same level of unemployment as men had in 1987. This is a new development, since before 1981 unemployment among women was consistently higher than among men. In 1976, for example, the male unemployment rate was 7.2 percent, while the rate for females was 8.6 percent. The turnaround is explained by the fact that the economic recession of the early 1980s hit male-dominated blue-collar industrial jobs especially hard.

Official U.S. unemployment rates are based on monthly national surveys. Aside from a certain amount of random error inevitable in any survey, these statistics probably understate unemployment for two reasons. First, in order to be officially unemployed, a person must be actively seeking work. Especially during economic recessions, many people become discouraged after failing to find a job for a long time and simply stop looking. Such people are not counted among the unemployed even though their joblessness is not voluntary. Second, many people who are unable to find jobs for which they are qualified take "lesser" employment, as, for example, a former college professor who drives a

Figure 18–3 Official Unemployment Rate among Various Categories of Americans, 1987

(U.S. Bureau of Labor Statistics, 1988)

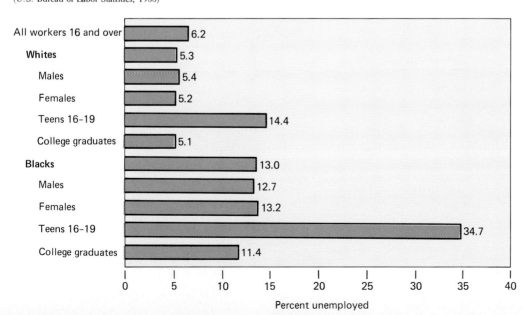

507

taxi while seeking a new teaching position. Other people settle temporarily for part-time jobs. Although the government considers such people to be employed, they are more accurately described as *underemployed*. Official statistics may also overstate unemployment in some instances. Many people counted as unemployed may actually have some income from odd jobs or illegal activity. Overall, however, the actual level of unemployment at any time is probably several percentage points above the official figure.

The Underground Economy

The American economy is a complex system in which transactions are formally recorded on sales slips, annual reports, and income tax returns. Yet a sizable segment of our economy operates informally without written records. The **underground economy** is *all economic activity that involves income or the exchange of goods and services that is not reported to the government.*

On a small scale, the underground economy operates in many familiar ways: children sell lemonade in front of their homes; teenagers baby-sit for parents in their neighborhoods; a family makes some extra money by holding a garage sale. All such activities generate income that, if not reported to the government as required by law, becomes part of the underground economy. People also exchange goods or services according to the age-old system of barter in order to avoid paying taxes. Another large segment of the underground economy involves income from criminal activity, especially from the sale of illegal drugs. Of course, illegal income from crimes such as prostitution, bribery, theft, illegal gambling, and loan-sharking also goes unreported. In addition, some economic activity occurs "under the table" because people wish to avoid time-consuming official paperwork. As Betty Lou Valentine (1978) points out, however, the poor often turn to "hustling" and other activities within the underground economy simply in order to make ends meet.

The single largest segment of the underground economy, however, is legal income unreported on income tax forms. Self-employed persons such as carpenters, physicians, and owners of small businesses may understate their incomes; waiters, waitresses, and other service workers may not report all their income from tips. Such relatively small omissions and misrepresentations on individual income tax returns add up to billions of dollars within the underground economy (Simon & Witte, 1982).

Illegal activities such as prostitution are part of the underground economy, whose income goes unreported and untaxed.

Exactly how big is the underground economy? There is no way of knowing because of the lack of record keeping. However, estimates suggest that roughly 10 percent of all economic activity in the United States is unreported (Gutmann, cited in Simon & Witte, 1982: xii). In 1986, the gross national product of the United States was about $4.2 trillion. During that year, then, the underground economy probably amounted to over $400 billion—more than the combined GNP of all the Scandinavian countries.

The underground economy distorts the official economic indicators (such as the unemployment rate) used to design and implement various government programs and services. More important, hidden economic activity deprives the government of revenues used to fund such activities.

Corporations

The core of today's capitalist economies are corporations. A **corporation** is *an organization that is recognized by law as having rights apart from those of its members*. In a real sense, of course, any organization exists only in terms of the decisions and activities of its members. When an organization becomes legally incorporated, however, it is regarded by law as an entity unto itself able to enter into contracts and own property. Of the perhaps 16 million businesses in the United States in the mid-1980s, about 3.2 million were incorporated (U.S. Internal Revenue Service, 1987). The great size and wealth of the largest American corporations gives them social power far greater than this number suggests.

Although corporations today also include nonprofit organizations, legal incorporation developed about a century ago largely to benefit the profit-seeking owners of large businesses. Corporate law is, of course, quite complex, but for our purposes it is sufficient to point out that incorporation affords capitalists two major benefits. First, because the profits of an incorporated business are owned by the corporation itself, the individuals who operate the corporation are able to protect their personal wealth from lawsuits arising from business debts or harm to consumers. Second, under the tax laws of the United States, corporate profits have not been taxed as heavily as personal profits. Although this was somewhat changed by tax-code reform in 1987, owners who incorporate usually still keep more of the money their business earns.

Chapter 9 explained that many corporations are owned by large numbers of stockholders rather than by single families. This dispersion of corporate ownership has often been viewed as spreading wealth by making many Americans small-scale capitalists. Moreover, as Ralf Dahrendorf (1959) has pointed out, the day-to-day operation of a corporation is typically supervised by white-collar executives who are responsible to the stockholders. In practice, however, a great deal of corporate stock is owned by a small number of the corporations' top executives. Such major stockholders are part of a small economic elite, which owns and operates the richest and most powerful American businesses. Thus the legal process of incorporation has not substantially changed the operation of large businesses in the United States (Useem, 1980).

Economic Concentration

Profit-making corporations in the United States range in size from tiny businesses owned and operated by one or two self-employed people to veritable giants such as the major automobile manufacturers, which employ hundreds of thousands of people in the United States and abroad. About half are relatively small, with total assets worth less than $100,000. But the significance of corporations to the American economy lies in the size of the few very largest.

The first truly giant American corporation was the United States Steel Corporation, formed in 1901 from the merger of several steel producers. Under the leadership of industrialist J. P. Morgan, U.S. Steel produced two-thirds of American steel in the early decades of the twentieth century. Its billion-dollar assets at the time would have paid for the operation of the federal government for almost two years (Baltzell, 1964; Fusfeld, 1982). In subsequent years, U.S. Steel grew even larger because of its ability to buy almost any other corporation it wished to own.

Indeed, throughout this century, the growth of corporations in general has resulted in a staggering, and increasing, concentration of economic power in a small number of corporations that operate on a national and international scale. In 1968, for example, the 100 largest manufacturing corporations controlled more productive assets than the 200 largest firms in 1950 (Fusfeld, 1982). Of more than 3 million American corporations in 1985, 281 had total assets exceeding $1 billion. The total assets of these 281 corporations represented two-thirds of *all* American corporate assets. These corporations also earned almost 70 percent of *all* corporate profits in 1985 (U.S. Bureau of the Census, 1987e).

Table 18–4 presents the twenty largest corporations in the United States in 1986, ranked by sales. At the top of the list is General Motors, a manufacturer of motor vehicles. GM had over $100 billion in sales and more than $72 billion in total assets. The magnitude of GM's sales is more easily understood by noting that 100 billion represents far more money than any of the fifty states collected in taxes during that year. Indeed, it is more than half as much as they *all* collected. Moreover, GM had more employees than the combined total of governments in states all along the West Coast, including Alaska and Hawaii. As this pattern of economic

Table 18—4 THE 20 LARGEST INDUSTRIAL CORPORATIONS IN THE UNITED STATES, 1986 (RANKED BY SALES)

Corporation	Product	Sales ($ billions)	Assets ($ billions)	Number of Employees
1. General Motors	Motor vehicles	102.8	72.6	876,000
2. Exxon	Oil refining	69.9	69.5	102,000
3. Ford Motor	Motor vehicles	62.7	37.9	382,274
4. International Business Machines (IBM)	Office equipment	51.3	57.8	403,508
5. Mobil	Oil refining	44.9	39.4	127,400
6. General Electric	Electronics	35.2	34.6	359,000
7. American Telephone & Telegraph (AT&T)	Electronics	34.1	38.9	316,900
8. Texaco	Oil refining	31.6	34.9	51,978
9. E. I. du Pont de Nemours	Chemicals	27.1	26.7	141,268
10. Chevron	Oil refining	24.4	34.6	51,095
11. Chrysler	Motor vehicles	22.5	14.5	115,074
12. Philip Morris	Tobacco products	20.7	17.6	111,000
13. Amoco	Oil refining	18.3	23.7	46,775
14. RJR Nabisco	Tobacco and food products	17.0	17.0	124,617
15. Shell Oil	Oil refining	16.8	26.2	32,641
16. Boeing	Aerospace	16.3	11.1	118,500
17. United Technologies	Aerospace	15.7	11.1	193,500
18. Procter & Gamble	Chemicals	15.4	13.1	74,500
19. Occidental Petroleum	Oil and food products	15.3	17.5	51,353
20. Atlantic Richfield	Oil refining	14.6	17.5	26,600

SOURCE: Adapted from "The Fortune 500 Largest U.S. Industrial Corporations," *Fortune*, Vol. 115, No. 9 (April 27, 1987), pp. 364, 390–408. © 1987 Time Inc. All rights reserved.

concentration suggests, a few large corporations control many American markets. Table 18–5 provides several examples of major markets in which three or four corporations predominate.

Conglomerates and Other Corporate Linkages

Economic concentration has resulted in the formation of **conglomerates**: *giant corporations composed of many smaller corporations*. Conglomerates arise as corporations seek to increase their profits by entering new markets. In some cases, a corporation creates a new company; more often, it buys a company that is already established in a particular market. Diversifying its operations in this way protects the corporation from potentially declining profits in its original market. Coca-Cola, the soft-drink producer, now produces not only a wide range of soft drinks and fruit drinks, but also coffee, bottled water,

feature films, and television programs. Beatrice Foods is a corporate "umbrella" containing over fifty smaller corporations, that produce well-known products such as Reddi-Wip, Wesson cooking oils, Peter Pan peanut butter, Hunt's foods, Tropicana fruit juices, La Choy foods, Orville Redenbacher popping corn, Max Factor cosmetics, Playtex clothing, and Samsonite luggage (Beatrice, 1985).

Beyond forming conglomerates, corporations are connected in other ways. Although less common today than earlier in this century, they may be joined through ownership by extremely wealthy families. For example, when Pittsburgh banking magnate Richard K. Mellon died in 1970, his family reportedly owned a controlling interest in six major corporations (Fusfeld, 1982). Today corporations are more often linked through the ownership of corporate stock by other corporations. Because they can legally own property in much the same way individuals do, corporations invest heavily in one another. In addition, large American corporations routinely engage

Table 18–5 ECONOMIC CONCENTRATION IN MAJOR MARKETS OF THE AMERICAN ECONOMY

Market	Leading Corporations	Percent of Market
Television	NBC ABC CBS	80–90
Aircraft	Boeing McDonnell-Douglas General Dynamics	80–90
Auto tires/tubes	Goodyear Firestone Uniroyal	70–80
Drugs	American Home Products Merck Pfizer Lilly	70–80
Motor vehicles	General Motors Ford Chrysler	70–75
Chemicals	Du Pont Union Carbide Dow Monsanto	60–70
Soaps and household products	Procter & Gamble Colgate Lever	60–70
Dairy products	Borden National Dairy Carnation	60–70
Iron and steel	U.S. Steel Bethlehem Armco Republic	50–60
Oil refining	Exxon Mobil Texaco	40–50

SOURCE: Adapted from Daniel R. Fusfeld, *Economics: Principles of Political Economy* (Glenview, IL: Scott, Foresman, 1982), p. 356. Copyright © 1982 by Scott, Foresman and Company. Reprinted by permission.

in joint ventures when doing so is in their collective financial interest (Herman, 1981).

Another type of linkage among corporations is the **interlocking directorate:** *a corporate linkage created when members of one corporation's board of directors become members of other corporations' boards.* Such formal interconnections give corporations access to insider informa-

tion about one another. When it was founded in 1901, for example, the U.S. Steel Corporation was linked in this way to over one hundred other corporations. Interlocking directorates are less extensive today, partly because antitrust laws make direct linkages of this kind illegal if the corporations involved are in competition with one another. Yet direct linkages persist among noncompeting corporations that share common interests—for example, a corporation that produces tractors may share directors with one that produces tires. Furthermore, competing corporations may be indirectly linked when, for example, a member of General Motor's board of directors joins a member of Ford's board of directors on the board of a third corporation.

Research reveals that interlocking directorates remain an important trait of the corporate economy (Marlios, 1975; Herman, 1981; Scott & Griff, 1985). Beth Mintz and Michael Schwartz (1981) found that General Motors is linked through board-of-director memberships to twenty-nine major corporations. The members of these boards, in turn, serve on the boards of almost seven hundred other corporations. Mintz and Schwartz also note that extensive formal linkages among corporations are heavily centered in major banks and insurance companies, which seek to protect the financial well-being of American corporations as a whole.

Finally, Gwen Moore (1979) has described how *social networks* (described in Chapter 6) also link members of the corporate elite. In addition to their association on boards of directors, in other words, corporate executives participate in wide-ranging social networks that they use to exchange various types of valuable information. As Michael Useem (1979) has noted, such networks also enhance the influence of corporate leaders within political, social, and charitable organizations.

These various types of linkages among corporations do not necessarily oppose the public interest, but they are a means by which corporations can engage in illegal activity. Price-fixing, for instance, is legal in much of the world (the Organization of Petroleum Exporting Countries—OPEC—meets regularly to try to set oil prices), but not in the United States. Legal restraints have not always prevented some large corporations from attempting to enrich themselves through price-fixing, however. In the late 1950s, faced with a declining demand for their products, the largest electronics corporations entered into an illegal conspiracy to avoid a drastic loss of profits. The episode was finally discovered, and twenty-nine corporations were convicted of illegal business practices and fined a total of almost $2 million.

As noted in Chapter 8, however, powerful individuals often escape punishment for such white-collar crimes. In this case, only seven of the people who actually broke the law served short jail sentences (Smith, 1970; Fusfeld, 1982).

Competition and the American Economy

In principle, businesses in a capitalist economy operate independently within a competitive market. In practice, however, the *competitive sector* is limited to smaller businesses and self-employed people. The large corporations at the core of the American economy are part of the *noncompetitive sector*. Corporations are not truly competitive because, first, they are so widely linked to one another that they do not operate independently, and second, many major markets within the American economy are dominated by a small number of corporations.

Ideally, any corporation would maximize profits by achieving a **monopoly,** meaning *the domination of a market by a single producer.* A producer in this situation is able to dictate prices and thereby generate enormous profits. A century ago, the federal government recognized the danger of monopolies to the public welfare and limited them by law, beginning with the Sherman Anti-Trust Act of 1890.

Such legislation has effectively eliminated true monopolies; however a pattern of limited competition remains that is termed **oligopoly,** or *the domination of a market by a few producers.*

A tendency toward oligopoly is inherent in the industrial-capitalist economy. Entering the automobile manufacturing market today, for example, would take an investment of billions of dollars. Over past decades, entry costs have become higher and higher as existing automobile manufacturers have protected themselves against the risks of competition by merging to form ever-larger corporations. In short, big business seeks to *limit* competition in order to minimize risk to its profits.

Controlling competition also means that corporations offer products that are quite similar to one another. In addition, large corporations spend billions of dollars annually on advertising. The power of the mass media to shape consumer behavior further protects corporate profits.

Finally, the model of ideal capitalism suggests that government intervention in the economy should be minimal. But the power of large corporations is so great—

and the level of actual competition among them so low—that government regulation is often the only means to protect the public interest. In most cases, however, government can hardly be described as an adversary of large corporations. First, the government is the single biggest customer of large corporations (Madsen, 1980). In addition, because large corporations are the core of the American economy, the failure of any one of them could disrupt the entire economy. Recognizing this, the government sometimes acts to bolster a struggling corporation—as when it gave $1.5 billion in loan guarantees to the Chrysler Corporation in the late 1970s when the company was facing bankruptcy. In sum, corporations tend to work together—with considerable help from the government—to make the entire economy more stable and, of course, to make themselves more profitable.

CORPORATIONS AND THE WORLD ECONOMY

As corporations in the United States and other capitalist societies have grown in size and power, they have spilled across national boundaries. Trade has historically served to tie together many diverse cultures, but never before has so much economic activity spanned the globe. Indeed, the largest corporations now view the entire world as one vast marketplace.

The term **multinational corporation** (or *transnational corporation*) designates *a large corporation that operates in many different nations.* A multinational corporation typically both produces and markets its products in several countries. Beatrice Foods, for example, is a multinational corporation, with factories in thirty countries that produce products sold in over one hundred.

Several multinationals are internationally owned—Unilever and Shell, for instance, have both British and Dutch owners. But the vast majority of multinationals have owners in a single nation, most often the United States (Gilpin, 1975). Most large American corporations are multinational to a variable degree. Exxon, for instance, is heavily multinational, earning roughly three-fourths of its profits outside the United States through the production, refining, and sale of petroleum products in about one hundred countries. General Motors is also a multinational, but on a smaller scale: about one-fourth of its profits are earned through foreign operations in a dozen countries (Madsen, 1980).

Corporations become multinational in pursuit of

The expansion of Western multinational corporations has changed patterns of consumption throughout the world, even in distant places such as New Guinea.

their primary goal: making money. About three-fourths of the world's population lives in nonindustrialized societies, and much of the planet's resources are found there. Therefore, worldwide operations provide access to larger markets, less costly labor, and more raw materials. Becoming international also allows corporations to lower their tax liabilities and to move money from country to country, further profiting from the changing value of various currencies.

Multinationals and Development

The overall consequences of capitalist expansion to the poor societies of the Third World are controversial, as Chapter 22 explains in detail. One side of the argument is that multinationals are the key to world economic development (Rostow, 1978; Madsen, 1980; Berger, 1986). In the face of staggering social problems such as poverty and hunger, multinationals unleash the great productivity of the capitalist economic system. For instance, the Exxon corporation alone is more productive than almost any of the roughly one hundred *nations* that make up the Third World. During the 1980s, Exxon's annual sales have averaged several times the combined gross national product of all seven nations of Central America.

Defenders of multinationals, therefore, claim that corporate expansion can spark the economic development of the world's poor societies. First, multinationals provide a needed source of employment. Just as important are the kinds of jobs that are introduced. In nonindustrial-

ized societies, most people work in the primary sector of the economy. Multinationals, however, introduce jobs in the secondary (manufacturing) and tertiary (service) sectors of the economy. Second, multinationals introduce new technology—especially manufacturing techniques—that accelerates economic growth. Therefore, multinationals provide short-term advantages by paying wages and taxes, and stimulate long-term development for societies that need it most.

Multinationals and Underdevelopment

Critics of multinational expansion base their opposition on another characteristic of capitalism: unequal distribution of income and wealth (Vaughan, 1978; Wallerstein, 1979; Delacroix & Ragin, 1981; Bergesen, 1983). The operation of capitalist corporations, critics argue, benefits the few rather than the many—both within poor societies and in the world as a whole.

First, with regard to employment, a considerable amount of multinational investment in poor societies is *capital-intensive*, meaning that machinery rather than labor is used, so few jobs are created. Moreover, the presence of tremendously powerful multinationals often inhibits the growth of *labor-intensive* local industries, which would increase employment. Second, although it is true that multinationals introduce new technology to poor societies, they do so for their own benefit with little advantage to the larger population. This is because foreign-owned corporations typically produce expensive consumer goods that are exported back to rich societies,

CROSS-CULTURAL COMPARISON

Multinationals and the Third World: The Case of Baby Formula

What has become known as the "baby food scandal" began in 1973 in press reports about the harmful consequences of baby formula widely sold by Nestlé, a Swiss multinational corporation. Physicians working in health-related organizations were alarmed by the rising incidence of malnutrition among African babies. They claimed that the problem was partly due to the marketing practices of Nestlé, which encouraged a dangerous use of its product.

Advertising by Nestlé promoted baby formula over breast milk, even though mother's milk is far better for a child. To make matters worse, Nestlé's formula is difficult to use correctly in poor societies. This is because the formula must be prepared with clean water in a sterilized bottle. It must also be fed to a baby in sufficient quantities to ensure proper nutrition. While this is easy enough for parents in industrial societies, poor

Africans often lack reliable cooking equipment and safe drinking water. Moreover, baby formula is expensive. Enough formula to nourish a single child can cost as much as one-third of a poor family's income.

Nonetheless, African radio advertising, posters, and loudspeaker-equipped vehicles all touted Nestlé's product. The corporation also employed hospital nurses as salespeople to encourage formula use, and provided free samples to new mothers. However, many mothers gave their infants formula that had become contaminated. In addition, because of the high cost of Nestlé's formula, many mothers were forced to dilute it, greatly reducing its nutritional value. Noting the consequences to infants, one pair of physicians concluded that "undoubtedly, the increase of malnutrition in the young baby and the many deaths which occur from this must have some rela-

tionship to the increased misuse of artificial feeding."

Health organizations can do little to counteract the marketing power of multinationals in such cases. The advertising budget of the Nestlé Corporation, for example, is much greater than the annual funds available to the World Health Organization, a Swiss organization that attempts to address such problems.

In the wake of the baby food scandal, a number of multinationals, including Nestlé, adopted advertising guidelines intended to reduce dangerously improper use of their products. Yet this incident illustrates the potential for harm that powerful multinational corporations—concerned with profit rather than with social welfare—represent in the Third World.

SOURCE: Based on Susan George, *How the Other Half Dies: The Real Reasons for World Hunger* (Totowa, NJ: Rowman & Allanheld, 1977), pp. 152–154.

---

rather than food and other necessities that the national economy lacks.

Critics also argue that the multinationals use poor nonindustrial societies as a market for products that are detrimental to the well-being of the population, especially with regard to nutrition. Critics claim, for example, that the presence of multinationals has often damaged local food production and, moreover, that the processed foods corporations find it profitable to produce are typically poor substitutes for the traditional foods produced locally. Mary Kay Vaughan (1978:8) notes with dismay the growing number of Mexicans who now consume Hostess Twinkies and Pepsi-Cola in place of their more nutritious traditional foods. As described in the box, perhaps the greatest controversy in this regard has surrounded the sale of baby formula in Third World societies.

Some critics believe not only that multinationals have harmed the populations of Third World societies,

but also that world capitalism is fostering a global division between the "have" and "have-not" nations (Wallerstein, 1974, 1979; Frank, 1980, 1981). Historically, they claim, the rise of capitalism was accelerated by *colonialism*, by which European societies colonized most of the rest of the world to gain both raw materials and markets for goods manufactured at home. This initiated a pattern of *dependency*, by which poor societies exported their raw materials and became dependent on rich societies for manufactured goods and various skills and services. Because the income from exporting raw materials was typically far less than that needed to purchase more expensive manufactured goods abroad, these societies became progressively poorer. Rather than developing the economies of the Third World, in short, capitalism is argued to have *underdeveloped* them.

The growth of multinational corporations is seen as an extension of this historical pattern, a form of *neoco-*

lonialism (or "new colonialism"). The only difference is that rich societies are no longer concerned with direct political control of the world. But rich capitalist societies such as the United States do attempt to ensure that governments abroad will allow the operation of multinationals. Reflecting on the fact that direct political colonization has been replaced by economic neocolonialism during the twentieth century, one defender of multinationals asserted, "We are not without cunning. We shall not make Britain's mistake. Too wise to govern the world, we shall simply own it" (cited in Vaughan, 1978:20).

Global Corporations:
The Future of Economics and Politics

The twentieth century has been a period of remarkable economic change. Socialist economic systems, in varying form derived largely from the theories of Karl Marx, now supply the needs of more than one-fourth of all humanity. Centuries older, capitalism has reached an advanced stage of development in the economies of the United States, Canada, Western Europe, and Japan.

In recent decades, perhaps the most notable economic issue has been the rapid growth in size and number of capitalist multinational corporations spanning much of the globe. Some estimates suggest that by the end of this century multinational corporations will be the most powerful economic force on earth, with three hundred of them accounting for as much as 90 percent of world economic production (Idris-Soven, Idris-Soven, & Vaughan, 1978).

Certainly the continuing growth of multinational corporations will be accompanied by major political changes. Perhaps, as some defenders of multinationals suggest, the nation-state will gradually wither away—not because of the emergence of communism, as Marx imagined, but because corporations will efficiently manage global affairs (Madsen, 1980). Or maybe, as critics fear, multinationals will gain still more of the world's wealth by encouraging the governments of poorer nations to use increasingly repressive tactics to neutralize the aspirations of their people for a better standard of living (Vaughan, 1978).

The future is unclear. Claims that capitalism will eventually improve the world's standard of living are met with claims that wealth is becoming more and more concentrated in the hands of a few. Today roughly 10 percent of the world's population, living in the world's richest societies, enjoys the benefits of about half the world's total economic production (Madsen, 1980). If this remains the case, the division between the few who are rich and the many who are poor is likely to carry the price of world instability and widespread violence.

SUMMARY

1. The economy is a major social institution by which goods and services are produced, distributed, and consumed. Although part of all societies, the economy may operate in many different ways.

2. In the technologically least developed societies, economic activity is subsumed within family life. In agrarian societies, however, the economy becomes distinct from the family. Industrialization results in significant expansion of the economy, based on new sources of energy, factories, mass production, and specialization. In a postindustrial economy, most workers are involved in the production of services rather than goods.

3. The primary sector of the economy generates raw materials; the secondary sector manufactures various goods; the tertiary sector produces services. In preindustrial societies, the primary sector predominates; the secondary sector is of greatest importance in industrial societies; the tertiary sector predominates in postindustrial societies.

4. The economies of today's industrial societies may be described in terms of two ideal models. Capitalism is based on private ownership of productive property and the pursuit of personal profit in a market characterized by free competition and consumer sovereignty. Socialism is based on collective ownership of productive property and the pursuit of collective well-being through government control of the economy.

5. The United States has one of the most capitalist economies in the world, although government involvement in the economy is widely evident. Many Western European societies have developed a democratic socialism, with greater government involvement in their economies. The Soviet Union and the societies of Eastern Europe have predominantly socialist economies, in which economic activity is planned and regulated directly by the government.

6. Predominantly capitalist economies are generally more productive and thus provide a higher overall stan-

dard of living. However, predominantly socialist economies generate less social inequality.

7. The proportion of the American labor force engaged in agriculture has declined sharply during this century. Blue-collar jobs have also steadily declined, while white-collar work has grown in importance. Today about two-thirds of the labor force are white-collar workers, while about one-third are blue-collar workers.

8. Professions are a category of white-collar work based on theoretical knowledge, occupational autonomy, authority over clients, and an emphasis on community service. The traditional professions were principally medicine, law, and the ministry. In recent decades, however, many more occupations have gained professional standing.

9. In the primary labor market, occupations provide substantial extrinsic benefits in terms of earnings and job security, and also the intrinsic benefit of job satisfaction. In the secondary labor market, workers enjoy fewer extrinsic benefits and almost no intrinsic benefits. Many service occupations today involve work that is low-paying and routine, like many of the industrial jobs of the past.

10. Today fewer than one in ten workers is self-employed. Although most professionals are in this category, the majority of self-employed workers have blue-collar occupations.

11. In all societies, some proportion of the labor force is unable or unwilling to work at any given time. However, the operation of the economy itself generates unemployment. Capitalist societies tend to regard an unemployment rate of 5 or 6 percent as full employment. Socialist societies emphasize each individual's right to a job, but they, too, experience unemployment.

12. The underground economy represents about 10 percent of all economic activity in the United States, and includes most criminal activity as well as legal activities whose income is unreported on income tax forms.

13. Corporations are the core of the American economy; the few largest corporations account for most corporate assets and profits. Conglomerates are giant corporations that produce and market diverse products through many smaller corporations. Corporations are also linked through ownership by wealthy families, joint ventures, interlocking directorates, and informal social networks among executives.

14. Smaller businesses represent the competitive sector of the American economy. Large corporations, however, dominate many markets in the noncompetitive sector.

15. Multinational corporations have grown in number and size during this century. Defenders of multinationals claim their productivity is the key to economic development in poor societies of the world. But critics see multinationals as causing the underdevelopment of the Third World while enriching industrialized societies.

KEY CONCEPTS

capitalism an economic system in which natural resources, as well as the means of producing goods and services, are privately owned

communism a utopian economic and political system in which all property is collectively owned and all members of society have economic and social equality

conglomerates giant corporations composed of many smaller corporations

corporation an organization that is recognized by law as having rights apart from those of its members

democratic socialism a political and economic system in which free elections and a market economy coexist with government efforts to minimize social inequality

economy a social institution that organizes the production, distribution, and consumption of goods and services

interlocking directorate a corporate linkage created when members of one corporation's board of directors become members of other corporations' boards

monopoly the domination of a market by a single producer

multinational corporation (or **transnational corporation**) a large corporation that operates in many different nations

oligopoly the domination of a market by a few producers

postindustrial economy an economy based on services and high technology

primary labor market occupations that provide extensive benefits to workers

primary sector that part of the economy that generates raw materials directly from the natural environment

profession a white-collar occupation with high social prestige that requires considerable formal education

secondary labor market occupations that provide minimal benefits to workers

secondary sector that part of the economy that transforms raw materials into manufactured goods

socialism an economic system in which natural resources, as well as the means of producing goods and services, are collectively owned

tertiary sector that part of the economy that generates services rather than goods

underground economy all economic activity that involves income or the exchange of goods and services that is not reported to the government

SUGGESTED READINGS

In this book, one of sociology's best contemporary thinkers examines capitalism and its consequences for social life. Of special note is a chapter (6) on capitalism and world economic development.

Peter L. Berger. *The Capitalist Revolution: Fifty Propositions about Prosperity, Equality, and Liberty.* New York: Basic Books, 1986.

This textbook focuses on work in American society, with an emphasis on patterns of conflict within the workplace.

George Ritzer and David Walczak. *Working: Conflict and Change.* 3rd ed. Englewood Cliffs, NJ: Prentice-Hall, 1986.

The first of these books is a sociological classic that explores the emergence of a postindustrial society. The second, published a decade later, argues that manufacturing remains crucial to the American economy and to the ability to develop high-wage service occupations.

Daniel Bell. *The Coming of Post-Industrial Society: A Venture in Social Forecasting.* New York: Harper Colophon, 1976.

Stephen S. Cohen and John Zysman. *Manufacturing Matters: The Myth of the Post-Industrial Economy.* New York: Basic Books, 1987.

This book offers a useful discussion of the controversy surrounding the charge that women receive less pay than men do for work of the same value.

Frances C. Hunter. *Equal Pay for Equal Worth: The Working Woman's Issue of the Eighties.* New York: Praeger, 1986.

Although widely thought to benefit from high pay and strong unions, construction workers, it is argued in this book, have been suffering economic decline in recent years.

Marc L. Silver. *Under Construction: Work and Alienation in the Building Trades.* Albany, NY: State University of New York Press, 1986.

This book describes the developing economic crisis of rural America.

Larry W. Waterfield. *Conflict and Crisis in Rural America.* New York: Praeger, 1986.

Although farming has received some attention in recent decades, the role of the one million American women in farming is rarely studied. This book describes farmwork, household work, and community life among farm women today.

Rachel Ann Rosenfeld. *Farm Women: Work, Farm, and Family in the United States.* Chapel Hill, NC: University of North Carolina Press, 1985.

The first of these books is a comparative study of one important dimension of the economy—attitudes toward work. Included is an extensive discussion of the changing Japanese labor force. The second book compares the automobile industries in Europe, Japan, and the United States.

Tomotsu Sengoku. *Willing Workers: The Work Ethics in Japan, England, and the United States.* Westport, CT: Quorum Books, 1985.

David Marsden, Stephen Wood, and Paul Willman. *The Car Industry: Labour Relations and Industrial Adjustment.* New York: Tavistock, 1985.

This is a recent book by two sociologists who have made extensive study of linkages among American corporations.

Beth Mintz and Michael Schwartz. *The Power Structure of American Business.* Chicago: University of Chicago Press, 1985.

Working people in the United States have historically struggled for a greater voice in political affairs and a higher standard of living. The first of these books is a collection of brief essays on a variety of labor organizations that have influenced the lives of working Americans. The second is an examination of labor unions in the present.

Paul Buhle and Alan Dawley, eds. *Working for Democracy: American Workers from the Revolution to the Present.* Urbana, IL: University of Illinois Press, 1985.

Richard B. Freeman and James L. Medoff. *What Do Unions Do?* New York: Basic Books, 1984.

The following two books provide contrasting views of the operation of multinational corporations. The first suggests that multinationals will have a growing, positive influence in the world; the second criticizes multinationals for contributing to the growing problem of world hunger.

Axel Madsen. *Private Power: Multinational Corporations for the Survival of Our Planet.* New York: William Morrow, 1980.

Immanuel Wallerstein. *The Capitalist World-Economy.* New York: Cambridge University Press, 1979.

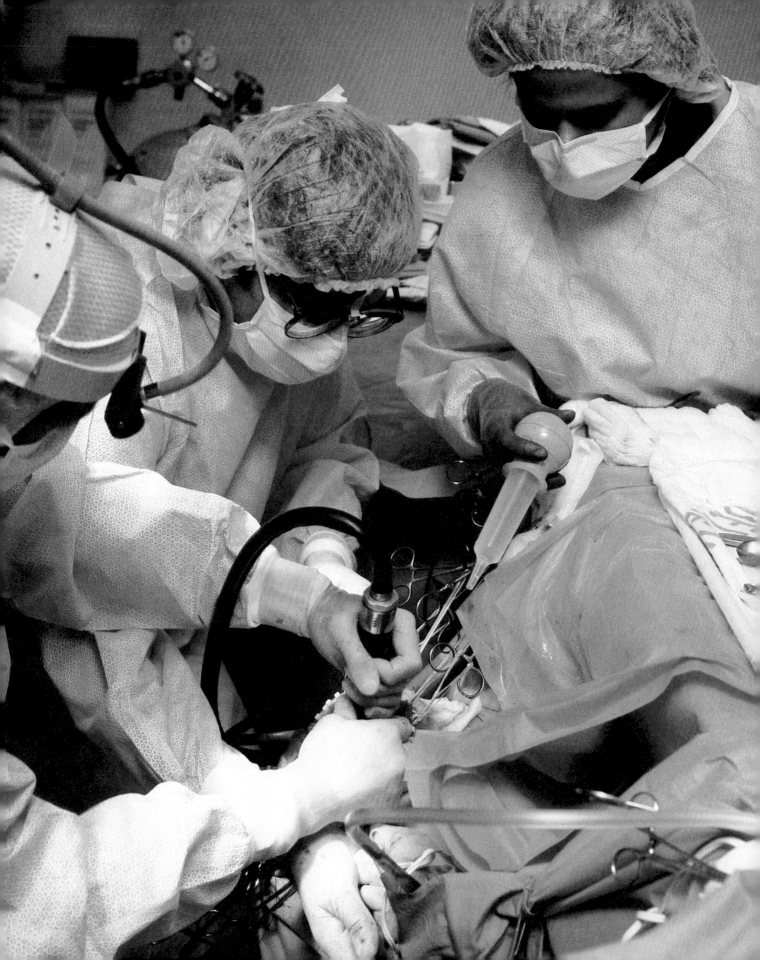

CHAPTER 19

Health and Medicine

At the age of seventy-three, Emily Gilbert was suffering from Alzheimer's disease—a degeneration of the nervous system that causes gradual loss of all mental and physical abilities and, ultimately, death. She was in pain, and knew that there was no medical cure for her illness. The future would bring only suffering to her and to her seventy-six-year-old husband.

With enough presence of mind to recognize one means of escape, Emily Gilbert begged her husband Roswell to end her life. As she slept on their flowered sofa, Roswell Gilbert placed a gun to his wife's head and pulled the trigger. Thinking that she might still be alive, he reloaded the gun and fired again. Gilbert made no attempt to conceal or deny what he had done. Under Florida law, he was convicted of first-degree murder and was sentenced to life imprisonment. As of 1988, he had served two years in prison.

Not surprisingly, the Gilbert case sparked a heated controversy. Was Roswell Gilbert's act a mercy killing or deliberate murder? Gilbert claimed that he "did what he had to do," which he maintained was not a crime, but simply the only way to end his wife's suffering. The Gilberts' daughter also defended his action, pointing to her parents' fifty-one years of devoted marriage. The prosecution, however, claimed that the killing was an "act of convenience" that solved Roswell Gilbert's problem, but not his wife's (Barber, 1985:3A; Kelley, 1985:2A).

The controversy surrounding the case of Emily and Roswell Gilbert illustrates how issues of life and death, and of health and medicine, often involve far more than the narrow concerns of particular patients and physicians. These important social issues raise moral and legal questions about individual rights and the role of the state in extremely personal situations.

More broadly, patterns of health are themselves products of society. Indeed, ethical problems surrounding death have become widespread in the United States as technological advances have allowed most Americans to live to old age, when debilitating diseases may kill them slowly and often painfully. In short, patterns of health and health care—in the United States and throughout the world—are shaped by other dimensions of social life.

WHAT IS HEALTH?

Common sense suggests that health is simply the absence of disease. Taking a more sociological viewpoint, however, the World Health Organization states that health is not only the absence of disease, but "a state of complete physical, mental, and social well-being" (1946:3). Such an approach to health underscores the major theme of this chapter—*health is as much a social as a biological issue.* Of course, probably no one on earth enjoys *complete* physical, mental, and social well-being. Therefore, we can more usefully define **health** as *a state of relative physical, mental, and social well-being.* While including the commonsense idea that health is the absence of disease, this definition also directs attention to the importance of society in shaping patterns of health.

Health and Society

Like all dimensions of human life, patterns of health arise within society. The health of any population is shaped by its dominant culture, its characteristic technology, and its social structure.

Health is related to a society's cultural patterns. While everyone agrees that death is extremely unhealthy, most other concepts of health are strongly tied to norms and values that vary from culture to culture. This means that those who are well and those who are ill are distinguished according to standards of physical, mental, social, and moral well-being that are common enough to be defined as normal. For this reason, René Dubos (1980; orig. 1965) points out, early in this century the contagious skin disease yaws was so common among people in tropical Africa that it was considered normal.

In every society, what most people view as morally good is also defined as healthy, and that which is deplored as morally bad is viewed as unhealthy. Some Americans, for example, still view homosexuality as both sinful and sick, although such attitudes are no longer supported by the medical establishment. Americans also tend to define as normal our competitive, achievement-oriented way of life, although this produces stress that is linked to perhaps two-thirds of all physician visits and most heart disease—the leading cause of death in the United States (Wallis, 1983). Moreover, people who do not live up to the standards of our culture's Protestant work ethic—either out of personal preference or as a result of social inequality—may find themselves stigmatized as unhealthy (Waxman, 1983). Obviously, then, dominant ideas about what constitutes good health are forms of social control, encouraging members of a society to abide by cultural norms.

Like all aspects of culture, standards of health change over time. Many Americans may be surprised to learn that at the beginning of this century prominent physicians deplored higher education for women as an unhealthy strain on the female brain, and defined masturbation as both a moral weakness and a detriment to health (Smith Rosenberg & Rosenberg, 1984; Money, 1985). At this time, too, cigarette smoking was culturally acceptable—even fashionable—behavior; some cigarette manufacturers even touted smoking as a *benefit* to health. In recent years, however, public attitudes about smoking have become negative and smokers are fast acquiring a deviant status.

Health is related to a society's technology and social resources. Cultural definitions of health are linked to a society's level of technological development and the social resources available to meet the needs of its population. All humans require at least some food and shelter to live; beyond survival, different standards of health reflect the availability of goods and services. Although malnutrition, poor sanitation, occupational hazards, and infectious diseases were commonplace in American history, industrialization greatly raised the standard of living so that norms of health also changed dramatically. In the world's least technologically sophisticated societies, health is quite poor by American standards, but this is taken for granted as the norm since such societies are incapable of supplying the goods and services that permit higher health standards. In the poorest societies of the Third World, half of all children born each year do not survive infancy, and those who do typically live twenty fewer years than the average American (George, 1977; Harrison, 1984).

Health is related to social inequality. In virtually every society on earth, the resources that promote personal well-being are unequally distributed. As discussed in Chapter 18, societies with government-controlled socialist economies strive for social and economic equality, and attempt to make good health equally accessible to everyone. Societies with capitalist economies, stressing individual liberty and the competitive marketplace, generate more economic and social inequality and view health as a commodity that must be purchased to the extent that a person's financial resources allow. Not surprisingly, the physical, mental, and emotional health of wealthier Americans is typically far better than that of poor Americans—a pattern that is evident throughout the life cycle.

Historical Patterns of Health

One of the clearest indications of the link between health and society is the pronounced change in patterns of health over the course of history. Important social changes such as the development of agriculture, the growth of cities, and the emergence of scientific medicine have had a major impact on patterns of health.

Health in Early Societies

A major concern in the earliest hunting and gathering societies, as explained in Chapter 4, was ensuring an adequate supply of food. In areas of relative abundance, patterns of health were more favorable, but the primitive technology of hunting and gathering societies greatly limited their ability to generate a healthful environment. As Gerhard and Jean Lenski (1987) point out, because infants typically must be breast-fed for several years, a food shortage or the birth of another child to a nursing mother sometimes meant that at least one child would be abandoned. Children fortunate enough to survive infancy were continuously subject to injuries or illnesses with which they had little power to cope. Perhaps half of all members of hunting and gathering societies died before reaching the age of twenty, and few lived past forty.

Health in Agrarian Societies

The technological advances associated with the development of agriculture increased the supply of food and other resources. Yet marked social inequality meant that better health was enjoyed by only part of the population. Elites benefited from the production of greater wealth, but peasants and slaves typically were accorded crowded, unsanitary shelter. Hunger, hard work, and frequent abusive treatment took their toll on the majority. Their patterns of health were poor—in some cases, even worse than among hunting and gathering societies.

Patterns of health in developing cities were typically worse than in the countryside owing to the combination of high population concentration and the virtual absence of sanitation. Even rich urbanites in medieval Europe lived amid human waste and other refuse, and as cities grew, dangers to health became worse (Mumford, 1961). Although efforts to restrict the environmental pollution in European cities date from the fourteenth century, they had little effect—as described in the box. The spread of infectious disease, including the plague, periodically wiped out sizable portions of the population. Overall, those who survived childhood in medieval times did not have a life expectancy much longer than that of their ancestors thousands of years earlier.

Health in Industrial Societies

The Industrial Revolution brought great changes in health patterns. As Chapter 20 explains in detail, the emergence of factories in the mid-eighteenth century sparked the rapid growth of industrial cities across Europe

In general, poorer Americans have poorer health. One reason is that the poor can afford only the less costly public care of crowded outpatient clinics.

and, subsequently, North America. When millions of people flooded into cities from the countryside, sanitation problems were exacerbated. As always, the economic elite enjoyed better nutrition, housing, and physical safety than other segments of the population. Even the more fortunate industrial workers lived in tenements that were both crowded and unsanitary. City streets were filthy and rife with crime. Factories freely and continuously fouled the air with smoke, which was not viewed as a threat to health until well into the twentieth century. Accidents in the workplace were common, since worker safety was a minor concern to early industrialists.

During the nineteenth century, however, patterns of health in Western Europe and North America began to improve. This change is often attributed to medical advances, but in fact, the death rate in Western Europe and in North America declined *before* many important medical advances took place (Illich, 1976; McKeown, 1979; Mahler, 1980). The improvement in health was actually due to the rising standard of living—including better nutrition and housing—associated with industrialization.

During the second half of the nineteenth century, rapid advances in scientific medicine improved health even further, especially in the cities, where poor sanitation had made infectious diseases commonplace. Early researchers soon realized how closely human health is linked to the physical environment. In 1854, John Snow examined residential patterns of cholera victims in London and traced the source of this disease to contaminated drinking water (Mechanic, 1978). Within several decades, cholera was known to be transmitted by bacteria, leading to the development of protective vaccines. Such discoveries also curbed the age-old practice of discharging raw sewage into rivers used for drinking water. By the early decades of the twentieth century, death rates from infectious diseases had sharply declined in Western societies.

This dramatic improvement in the patterns of health in industrialized societies has continued during this century, as Table 19-1 demonstrates. Influenza and pneumonia were the leading causes of death in 1900, accounting for roughly one-fourth of all deaths. Today these diseases account for fewer than 3 percent of all deaths in the United States. Other infectious diseases that were among the leading killers in 1900—including tuberculosis, stomach and intestinal diseases, diseases of early infancy, and diphtheria—are no longer major threats to health. At the same time, heart disease, cancer, and cerebrovascular diseases such as stroke have become more serious threats to health, causing the deaths of almost 60 percent of Americans today. To some extent, the increases in these diseases can be attributed to changing patterns of social life. Americans today make more

SOCIETY IN HISTORY

The Unheavenly Medieval City

The streets of medieval towns were generally little more than narrow alleys, the over-hanging upper stories of the houses nearly meeting, and thus effectually excluding all but a minimum of light and air. . . . In most continental towns and some English ones, a high city wall further impeded the free circulation of the air. The main streets might be roughly paved with [cobblestones], the rest of the streets, or rather alleys, would be totally unpaved. Rich citizens might possess a court yard in which garbage was collected and occasionally removed to the suburbs, but the usual practice was to throw everything into the streets, including the garbage of slaughter houses and other offensive trades. [Laws] against this practice were quite ineffective, as were the regulations ordering citizens to [clean] the street in front of their houses. Filth of every imaginable description accumulated indefinitely in the unpaved streets and in all available space and was trodden into the ground. The water would be obtained either from wells or springs, polluted by the gradual percolation through the soil of the accumulated filth, or else from an equally polluted river. In some towns, notably London, small streams running down a central gutter served at once as sewers and as water supply. The dwelling houses of the well-to-do would be of timber, or timber-framed upon a foundation of brick or stone. Even these, as picturesque as they appear to a modern eye, seem to have been designed to admit a minimum of light and air. The dwellings of the poor were mere hovels, built of unseasoned wood and with tiny windows. . . . Thousands of Londoners dwelt in cellars or horrible overcrowded tenements.

SOURCE: M. C. Buer, *Health, Wealth, and Population in the Early Days of the Industrial Revolution* (New York: Howard Fertig, 1968; orig. 1926), p. 77.

This woodcut of life in nineteenth-century London reveals the plight of the poor in the cities that grew up after the Industrial Revolution. Not surprisingly, the health of such people was extremely poor.

Table 19-1 THE CHANGING CAUSES OF DEATH IN THE UNITED STATES

The Ten Leading Causes of Death in 1900
1. Influenza and pneumonia
2. Tuberculosis
3. Stomach and intestinal diseases
4. Heart disease
5. Cerebral hemorrhage
6. Kidney disease
7. Accidents
8. Cancer
9. Diseases of early infancy
10. Diphtheria

The Ten Leading Causes of Death in 1987
1. Heart disease
2. Cancer
3. Cerebrovascular diseases
4. Accidents
5. Lung disease (noncancerous)
6. Influenza and pneumonia
7. Diabetes
8. Suicide
9. Cirrhosis and related liver disease
10. Artery disease

SOURCE: Information for 1900 is from William C. Cockerham, *Medical Sociology*, 2nd ed. (Englewood Cliffs, NJ: Prentice-Hall, 1986), p. 24; information for 1987 is from U.S. National Center for Health Statistics, *Monthly Vital Statistics Report*, Vol. 36, No. 3 (June 22, 1987): Table 6.

use of work-saving devices that reduce healthful physical activity, and are also more likely to smoke cigarettes than they were at the beginning of this century. The American diet is also heavily based on meat and eggs, resulting in an average intake of some 60 percent more cholesterol than is recommended by the American Heart Association. Consequently, we have a significantly higher rate of heart disease than the Japanese, for example, whose diet is based largely on fish (Wallis, 1984).

Another important fact underlying patterns of American health is that precisely because people are *less* likely today to die from infectious diseases, they are *more* likely to die from chronic diseases (such as heart disease and cancer) associated with advancing age. As noted in Chapter 13, average life expectancy in the United States has greatly increased since 1900. At that time, perhaps one-third of all Americans died of infectious diseases before reaching adolescence (Wall, 1980), so that a male could expect to live only forty-eight years and a female about fifty-one years. For Americans born in 1985, the figures are seventy-one years for males and seventy-eight years for females. Living longer, in sum, typically means dying of chronic illnesses such as heart disease, cancer, and stroke rather than of the infectious diseases common in the past.

World Health Today

Earlier chapters described the striking poverty that characterizes Third World societies. Even in the wealthier nations of the Third World, personal income is only about one-fifth as much as in the United States and Canada (see Table 10-4). As a result, overall health in Third World societies is far poorer than in industrial societies.

A general indicator of this low state of health is the relatively short life expectancy. On the average, people in Third World societies can expect to live less than sixty years, ten years below the average in industrial societies (Mahler, 1980). In Africa, the figure is barely fifty, and in the poorest societies in the world—such as Kampuchea and Ethiopia—it is only about forty.

Hundreds of millions of poor people around the world experience the cruel reality of continuous hunger. As explained in the box, ill health is the result not only of insufficient food, but also of consuming only a single

CROSS-CULTURAL COMPARISON

The Consequences to Health of Hunger in the Third World

The widespread famine in Africa during the last several years has made the image of starving children familiar to Americans. Some of the children shown in photographs and television documentaries appear bloated, while others have shriveled to little more than skin drawn tightly over bones. As Susan George explains, these disparate images reflect two different medical consequences of hunger.

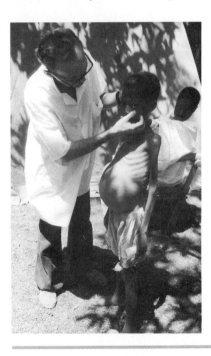

Children with bloated bodies suffer from protein deficiency. In West Africa, this condition is commonly described by the word *kwashiorkor,* which literally means "one-two." This term is derived from the common practice by which African mothers abruptly wean a first child upon the birth of a second. Mother's milk is an important source of protein for young children living in poverty. Without it, they may get no nutritious food at all. Children with shriveled bodies, on the other hand, suffer from a deficiency of both protein and calories. In both cases, however, children usually do not die of starvation. Rather, their weakened physical state in an unhealthy environment makes them vulnerable to death from stomach ailments such as gastroenteritis or childhood diseases like measles. The death rate from measles is one thousand times greater in parts of Africa than in North America, where measles is rarely fatal.

Serious medical problems linked to protein, vitamin, or mineral deficiencies are also caused by diets heavily based on a single food. Some 3 million people in the Third World suffer from goiter—a debilitating diet-related disease of the thyroid gland. Pellagra—a disease common to peo-

ple who consume only corn—is equally serious, frequently leading to madness. Similarly, those who depend on processed rice are prone to beri-beri.

In short, Susan George concludes, a host of diseases that are virtually unknown to Americans are a common experience of life—and death—in much of the Third World.

SOURCE: Based, in part, on Susan George, *How the Other Half Dies: The Real Reasons for World Hunger* (Totowa, NJ: Rowman and Allanheld, 1977), pp. 11–12.

kind of food. Poverty also usually means an unsanitary environment and a lack of sanitary water, so infectious diseases are common. The leading causes of death in the United States in 1900—such as influenza, pneumonia, and tuberculosis—are still serious health problems in nonindustrialized societies. Parasites such as hookworms, tapeworms, and roundworms also cause widespread suffering (Harrison, 1984; Newman & Matzke,

1984). While a majority of Americans die in old age from heart disease and cancer, then, most people in the Third World die from infectious and parasitic diseases that kill throughout the life cycle. For the Third World as a whole, Paul Harrison (1984) estimates that 10 percent of children die before their first birthdays; in the poorest societies of the world, half of all children do not survive into adulthood. Susan George (1977) points out that the children of the Third World die at about the same rate as European children did in 1750.

Improving health within the Third World represents a monumental challenge for two reasons. First, poor health and poverty are linked in a vicious circle. Poverty is a breeding ground for disease, which then undermines the ability of people to be economically productive (Harrison, 1984). As explained in Chapter 18, because of the continuing concentration of wealth and power in the industrialized societies, there is little basis for optimism that the desperate poverty typical of the Third World today will be eliminated in the foreseeable future. Thus the prognosis for improving the physical, mental, and social well-being of the world's poorest people is bleak.

The second reason for pessimism is that the medical technology used to control many infectious diseases causes the populations of poor societies to dramatically increase. Given existing patterns of economic inequality, poor societies do not have the resources to ensure the well-being of even their current populations, so population growth is only likely to increase poverty. As a result, the gains in health produced by medical advances are often negated by increased disease fueled by rampant poverty.

Still, human beings do have the ability to alter the worldwide economic and political patterns that currently perpetuate poor health among so much of the world's population.

HEALTH IN THE UNITED STATES

In comparison to citizens of nonindustrialized nations, Americans enjoy very favorable patterns of health. At the same time, some categories of Americans are far healthier than others.

Social Epidemiology: The Distribution of Good Health

Patterns of health are the focus of social epidemiology, which is *the study of the distribution of disease or relative health in a society's population*. Initially, social epidemiology was primarily concerned with the origin and spread of epidemic diseases, illustrated by the cholera research of John Snow noted earlier. Today social epidemiology has broadened its focus to include explaining how all patterns of health are linked to the physical and social environment (Cockerham, 1986). For example, a social epidemiologist might examine the incidence of heart disease among people who engage in different types of occupations. For sociologists, research in social epidemiology involves relating patterns of health to such variables as age, sex, and social inequality.

Age and Sex

During this century, a rising standard of living and advances in medical care have greatly reduced the death rate for Americans of almost every age. The only exception to this pattern are young adults, who suffer more accidental deaths, often involving automobiles. Barring a world holocaust such as nuclear war, therefore, a child born in the United States today has a better than 75 percent chance of living to the age of sixty-five (U.S. Bureau of the Census, 1987g). Indeed, as Chapter 13 explained, most Americans now live well past the age of sixty-five, so that the elderly make up about 12 percent of the population (see Figure 13-1).

American females have somewhat better patterns of health than American males. Females are slightly less likely than males to die before or immediately after birth, an initial health advantage that must be considered biological rather than social. From childhood on, socialization of children into gender roles also favors the health of females. Males are encouraged to be more competitive and aggressive, and thus are the primary victims of accidents, acts of violence, and suicide. Throughout life, masculinity in America is linked to competition for occupational success, repression of emotion, and other hazardous behaviors such as smoking and alcohol consumption. The long-term result is that, while almost 85 percent of all female children born in the United States today can expect to live to age sixty-five, this is true of only about 73 percent of male children. In short, while patterns of gender inequality in the United States provide males with more privileges, conventionally masculine patterns of behavior also entail greater health risks.

Social Inequality and Poverty

The research findings of social epidemiologists show that patterns of health are strongly related to social class. Table 19-2 shows that Americans' perceptions of their own health are related to income. Almost 80 percent of Americans who had an income over $35,000 evaluated their health as excellent or very good, a claim made

Table 19–2 ASSESSMENT OF PERSONAL HEALTH BY INCOME, 1986

Family Income	Excellent	Very Good	Good	Fair	Poor
Under $10,000	26.6%	22.6%	29.2%	14.4%	7.2%
$10,000–$19,999	32.0	26.7	27.2	9.8	3.9
$20,000–$34,999	43.1	28.7	21.5	5.3	1.3
$35,000 and over	50.8	29.0	16.6	2.7	0.9

SOURCE: U.S. National Center for Health Statistics, *Current Estimates from the National Health Interview Survey United States, 1986*, Series 10, No. 164 (Washington, DC: Government Printing Office, 1987), Table 70, p. 116.

by not quite half of those earning less than $10,000. On the other side of the coin, while only about 4 percent of high-income people described their own health as fair or poor, more than 20 percent of the poorest Americans described their health in such negative terms. The link between poverty and poor health is strengthened by the fact that the elderly are slightly overrepresented among the American poor. But generally, the health of Americans is clearly linked to income level.

For no category of Americans is the death rate among newborns as high as it is in many Third World societies. But American children born into poverty are almost 50 percent more likely to die during the first year of life than those born into more privileged families (Gortmaker, 1979). Throughout the life cycle, the health of the poor remains worse, on the average (Doyal, 1981). Figure 19-1 shows the average number of days of medical

disability—that is, when usual activities like going to school or work are suspended because of poor health—for Americans with different levels of family income. People whose family income was over $35,000 had an average of about ten days of disability in 1986; those with income under $10,000 had nearly three times as many days of disability.

As indicated in Chapter 11, nonwhite Americans generally have a lower overall social position and are therefore more likely than whites to live in poverty. As a consequence, their patterns of health are considerably less favorable. Blacks are more likely than whites to die in infancy, spend more time suffering from illness as adults, and typically die about five years sooner.

Table 19-3 shows the average life expectancy for American children born in 1985. Among whites, life expectancy is over seventy-five years. Nonwhites, however, can expect to live only about seventy-one years. Sex is a more powerful factor than race, however: on the average, nonwhite females born in 1985 can expect to outlive white males, although they are not expected to outlive white females. Table 19-3 also indicates that while about 73 percent of white males born in 1985

Figure 19-1 Average Number of Days of Medical Disability by Income, 1986

(U.S. National Center for Health Statistics, 1987)

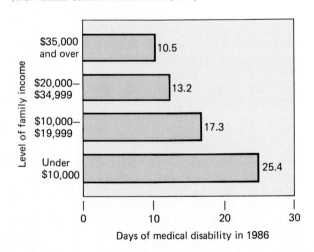

Days of medical disability in 1986

Table 19–3 LIFE EXPECTANCY FOR AMERICAN CHILDREN BORN IN 1985

	Males	Females	Both Sexes
Whites	71.8 (73%)	78.7 (85%)	75.3
Nonwhites	67.2 (60%)	75.2 (76%)	71.2
All races	71.2	78.2	74.7

SOURCE: U.S. Bureau of the Census, 1987.

Figures in parentheses indicate the chances of living to age 65.

can expect to live to age sixty-five, only about 60 percent of black males can expect to do so. The comparable chances of living to age sixty-five for women are about 85 percent for whites and 76 percent for nonwhites.

In the United States today, as throughout history here and around the world, poverty means that people are likely to live in a crowded and unsanitary environment that breeds infectious diseases. Tuberculosis, for example, is now a rare cause of death in the United States. But black Americans, who are three times more likely than whites to be poor, are four times as likely to die from tuberculosis. The poor also suffer from the effects of nutritional deficiencies. As suggested in Chapter 10, perhaps 45 million people—roughly 20 percent of all Americans—do not have a sufficient income to ensure a healthful diet. Just as important, the poor are often unable to purchase the medical care that more privileged Americans take for granted. As a result, while rich Americans are likely to live long enough to die of chronic illnesses such as heart disease and cancer, poor Americans are more likely to die earlier in life from infectious diseases and illnesses related to poor nutrition.

Poverty also breeds social stresses that can make areas containing a high concentration of poor people dangerously violent. Frustration and despair have long been commonplace in many of America's urban ghettos, in which the poor—often the black poor—are confined. Since blacks are among the most socially disadvantaged of all Americans, violence is a serious health hazard in predominantly poor and black inner-city areas. Among black males between the ages of fifteen and twenty-four, the leading cause of death is not disease or accident but homicide. Indeed, over 5,000 black Americans were killed by other black Americans in 1986—a number almost equal to the total deaths among black soldiers during the entire Vietnam War. According to a report by the U.S. Bureau of Justice Statistics, the odds of dying as a result of homicide are 1 in 369 for white women, and 1 in 131 for white men. For black women, however, the odds are 1 in 104, and for black men, a staggering 1 in 21 (Langan & Innes, 1985).

Of course, even the most privileged Americans are not immune to illness. In fact, the ability to indulge in a rich diet and to avoid physical work takes a toll on the rich in terms of higher death rates from heart disease (Fuchs, 1974; Wallis, 1984). At the same time, however, the United States is a society in which wealth buys health—in the form of better nutrition, a safer home environment, greater freedom from the stresses caused by financial worries, and more extensive medical

care. The fact that affluent people live longer and suffer from fewer illnesses than other Americans is clear evidence that health is closely related to how a society operates.

Environmental Pollution

Other issues besides the central matter of unequal access to good health have received widespread attention in recent years. Industrialization has benefited Americans by raising their standard of living and fostering advanced medical technology. At the same time, however, industrialization endangers the health of everyone by polluting the environment.

Air pollution caused by automobiles and industry is now a well-known threat to health. Especially in large cities, the air often contains unsafe levels of pollutants. In Los Angeles, for example, the air is considered to be a threat to human health about half the days of the year. Thus the consequences of modern technology are both beneficial and hazardous.

Industrial wastes—the subject of increasing public concern—may pose an even more serious threat to health. For more than half a century, industries across the United States have been disposing of poisonous chemicals in often haphazard fashion. Some companies have been caught pouring highly toxic substances into rivers and streams or into the local sewage system. Others have put steel drums filled with dangerous chemical wastes in dumps or buried them underground. Over time, these containers begin to leak into the surrounding soil and groundwater. One recent inspection of toxic waste sites by the U.S. Environmental Protection Agency found that almost half of these sites were poisoning groundwater.

National attention was drawn to the problem of toxic wastes in 1980, when the residents of Love Canal, near Niagara Falls, New York, found that the deadly chemical dioxin was seeping up from an old petrochemical dump. In 1983, the entire town of Times Beach, Missouri, had to be abandoned because oil contaminated with dioxin had been sprayed on its roads.

There are now more than 375,000 hazardous waste sites across the United States, at least 10,000 of which pose an immediate threat to public health. Between 1980 and 1985, however, only six of the most serious sites were improved by the U.S. Environmental Protection Agency. In the process of economic development, Americans may have mortgaged the health of future generations (Magnuson, 1985).

Nuclear power is a major technological advance that some hope can provide inexpensive energy without depleting finite resources such as coal and oil. In 1987, one hundred nuclear reactors in the United States were producing about 17 percent of the electricity consumed by Americans. These facilities pose two major environmental problems. First, in the event of a major malfunction, the meltdown of a nuclear reactor's core could release enough radiation into the atmosphere to kill people for hundreds of miles around, in the same manner as fallout from an atomic bomb. Accidents involving nuclear reactors have occurred since they first began operating in the early 1950s. Serious malfunctions occurred at reactors near Ottawa, Canada (1952), near Liverpool, England (1957), and at the Three Mile Island facility near Harrisburg, Pennsylvania (1979). After the most serious accident to date—a meltdown of the reactor core at the Chernobyl nuclear plant near Kiev in the Soviet Union in 1986—radiation escaping into the atmosphere spread throughout much of the world (Greenwald, 1986). The short-term death toll was thirty, but long-term health hazards of radiation exposure will no doubt kill many more in the years to come. The Soviets responded to this accident by evacuating almost 100,000 people from an eighteen-mile radius around the reactor for an indefinite period of time.

A second serious problem is the disposal of waste products from nuclear power plants, which remain highly radioactive for hundreds of thousands of years. Already some nuclear wastes have been known to leak from sealed storage containers. No current means of disposing of nuclear waste can eliminate the danger of radioactive contamination of the environment in the future.

Cigarette Smoking

A generation ago, cigarette smoking was socially acceptable. Despite some early evidence of the dangers of smoking, most Americans were unaware of the extent to which cigarettes harm health. Today cigarette smoking is recognized as the leading preventable cause of illness and death among Americans and is rapidly becoming defined as a mild form of social deviance.

Cigarette smoking in the United States became common only in this century. Almost no cigarettes were smoked in 1900; by 1986, some 580 billion were smoked each year. Extensive advertising by cigarette manufacturers (banned from television and radio in 1971) certainly helped to increase the number of smokers early in this century.

Quitting smoking is often difficult because cigarette smoke contains physically addictive nicotine. People can also develop a psychological dependence on cigarettes,

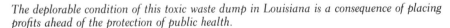
The deplorable condition of this toxic waste dump in Louisiana is a consequence of placing profits ahead of the protection of public health.

since smoking may be a means of coping with stress. This is suggested by the fact that the Americans most likely to smoke are the unemployed, those who are divorced or separated, and people in the military services. Adult males (30 percent) are more likely to smoke than adult females (24 percent). In addition, men and women with blue-collar occupations are more likely to smoke than their white-collar counterparts. Finally, for both sexes, increasing education is associated with a sharp decline in smoking (U.S. Center for Disease Control, 1987).

The first evidence of the health risks of smoking appeared in the 1930s, when medical researchers noted a sharp rise in smoking-related diseases such as lung cancer. This was roughly twenty years after cigarette smoking began to significantly increase in the United States. We know today that people generally must smoke cigarettes for about twenty years before lung cancer will develop. Not until the 1960s, however, did the government begin a systematic study of the dangers of smoking. In part, this greater concern about the health hazards of smoking was stimulated by increases in lung cancer among women, who began smoking in large numbers during the 1940s. By the mid-1960s, government reports were linking cigarette—as well as cigar and pipe smoking—to a variety of diseases, including heart disease; cancer of the mouth, throat, and lungs; and other lung diseases, including bronchitis and emphysema. Roughly 350,000 Americans—about seven times the number killed during the entire Vietnam War—die each year as a direct result of cigarette smoking. Smokers also experience more frequent minor illnesses than nonsmokers do. Pregnant women who smoke increase the likelihood of spontaneous abortion and prenatal death, and recent research indicates that nonsmokers who are exposed to cigarette smoke face a higher risk of smoking-related diseases (Shephard, 1982).

Tobacco was a $25 billion industry in the United States in 1986. The tobacco industry still maintains that because the precise link between cigarettes and disease has not been specified, the health effects of smoking remain "an open question" (Rudolph, 1985). But the American tobacco industry is not breathing as easily today as it once did. Laws mandating a smoke-free environment are rapidly increasing in number. Recent legal changes have threatened the traditional invulnerability of cigarette producers to lawsuits brought by people (or their survivors) who have suffered health problems from smoking. On the other hand, cigarette manufacturers are now selling more of their products in the Third World, where regulation of tobacco sales and advertising and antismoking sentiments are less pronounced. In the United States, however, an increasing number of smokers are taking advantage of the fact that about ten years of not smoking will give them about the same patterns of health as lifelong nonsmokers. In 1970, about 37 percent of American adults smoked cigarettes. By 1986, the proportion of cigarette smokers was 26 percent, and it continues to decline.

Sexually Transmitted Diseases

Although vital to the species, sexual activity has always been associated with the transmission of a number of diseases. References to what are commonly called *venereal diseases* (from Venus, the Roman goddess of love) are found in the Old Testament of the Bible. American culture has traditionally taken an ambivalent view of sex as a source of pleasure and a means of procreation on the one hand, and as a sinful act on the other. Consequently, Americans have sometimes viewed venereal diseases not only as illnesses, but also as punishments for immorality.

During the 1980s, sexually transmitted diseases have become a major national concern. In part, this is because the American population had become much more sexually active in the decades after 1950, a change often tagged the *sexual revolution*. In the 1950s, perhaps two-thirds of males and one in ten females reported having premarital sexual intercourse. By the beginning of the 1980s, the comparable figures had risen somewhat for males to about three-fourths and soared for females to about two-thirds. But most of the concern about this increase stems from the fact that sex has now become potentially deadly. Traditional venereal diseases persist, as an exception to the general pattern of decline among infectious diseases during this century. But it is AIDS (acquired immune deficiency syndrome) that has sparked a *sexual counter-revolution* that is causing individuals to reexamine their values and behavior and forcing public officials to confront difficult issues (Kain, 1987; Kain & Hart, 1987).

Gonorrhea and Syphilis

Two long-established venereal diseases are gonorrhea and syphilis, each of which is caused by a microscopic organism almost always transmitted by sexual contact. If untreated, gonorrhea can eventually cause sterility, while syphilis can damage the major organs of the body, causing blindness, mental disorders, and even death. In the past, American culture severely stigmatized victims of gonorrhea and syphilis, both of which were thought to be the "wages of sin" and were associated with social outcasts such as prostitutes. Both diseases, however, are now easily cured with penicillin, an antibiotic drug in widespread use since the 1940s. Therefore, they do not represent a serious health problem in the United States today.

Genital Herpes

In the early 1980s, genital herpes began to receive widespread public attention. This disease is far less serious than gonorrhea and syphilis because its symptoms vary from none at all to periodic (although painful) blisters on the genitals, accompanied by fever and headache. This disease is currently incurable, however. Although genital herpes is never fatal to adults, women with active genital herpes can transmit the disease to newborn children, to whom it may be fatal. For this reason, such women may give birth by cesarean section.

Estimates suggest that perhaps 20 million Americans are infected with the genital herpes virus. While evenly divided among females and males, victims of genital herpes are typically young, well educated, and have above-average incomes (Leo, 1982). Growing concern about herpes in the 1980s has undoubtedly changed sexual patterns in American society. During the sexual revolution of the 1960s, traditional cultural beliefs opposing sexual activity before marriage weakened considerably. In the last decade, however, the fear that casual sex may lead to incurable genital herpes has encouraged Americans to be far more cautious about their sexual conduct.

AIDS

A far more serious disease that has spread rapidly during the 1980s is acquired immune deficiency syndrome, or AIDS. Although cases of AIDS may have occurred as early as the 1960s, this disease was identified only in 1981, and it has since become a major health concern. At present, AIDS is incurable and fatal. Some twenty-thousand new cases of AIDS were reported during 1987, pushing the national total by mid-1988 to over sixty-five thousand; more than half of these people have already died.

AIDS is caused by a human immunodeficiency virus or, in medical shorthand, HIV. Within the body, the virus can attack white blood cells, which are the core of the immune system through which the body protects itself against infections. As white blood cells are destroyed, a person with AIDS becomes vulnerable to a wide range of other infectious diseases that eventually cause death. Technically, then, AIDS kills people by rendering them unable to fight off common infections.

In 1988, estimates put the number of Americans infected with HIV at roughly 1.5 million. Infection with HIV and having AIDS are not the same, although this medical puzzle is far from resolved at present. The majority of infected persons show no symptoms, and are probably not even aware of their infection. Symptoms of AIDS—or a number of other HIV complications—typically do not appear for at least a year, and more often it takes five years or longer to develop symptoms. Within about five years, perhaps 25 percent of infected persons will develop AIDS; the proportion of infected people who eventually develop AIDS is still uncertain. However, conservative estimates place the number of Americans with the active disease at 270,000 by 1991, and the number may end up closer to 400,000. Whatever the precise figure, AIDS clearly represents a catastrophic development—potentially the most serious epidemic of modern times.

Among infected persons, HIV has been isolated in a number of bodily fluids, although it is most likely to be transmitted through blood and semen. This means that AIDS is *not* spread through casual contact with an infected person, including shaking hands, hugging, or even social kissing. There is no known case of the virus being spread through coughing and sneezing, from sharing such items as towels, dishes, or telephones, or through water in a bath, pool, or hot tub. AIDS is a deadly disease, but it is also hard to get. There is no danger of becoming infected by donating blood, and testing of blood supplies means that blood transfusions are now virtually safe.

During the 1980s, AIDS has remained heavily concentrated among specific categories of Americans. About two-thirds of persons with AIDS are homosexual and bisexual males. This led to the initial conception of AIDS as a gay men's disease. There are two reasons that gay men have been at the center of the AIDS epidemic. First, many gays practice anal intercourse, by which semen and blood can readily come into contact, easily transmitting the virus. Second, as noted in Chapter

2, early in this decade some gay men were quite promiscuous, having hundreds of sexual partners a year. As the AIDS epidemic developed, however, promiscuity greatly declined (McKusick et al., 1985).

HIV is less easily spread through heterosexual intercourse, but heterosexuals are also vulnerable, and their risk is likely to increase with time. Currently in the United States, only 4 percent of AIDS cases are thought to have been caused by heterosexual contact (although, infected in various ways, heterosexuals account for about 20 percent of all persons with AIDS). However, in central Africa (where the disease is suspected to have originated) and other poor societies, heterosexuals are already the disease's primary victims.

Intravenous drug users who share needles are the second high-risk category, accounting for about 17 percent of persons with AIDS. The risk here is high, of course, because needles can readily pass the virus from one person directly into the bloodstream of another. Intravenous drug users are of added significance because they are the major path by which the virus has begun to spread within the heterosexual population. In some cases, infected women pass the virus to their newborn children. In other cases, prostitutes who are drug abusers infect heterosexual men.

Because AIDS was initially so closely linked to gay men and intravenous drug users—two deviant categories in American society—there was little public response to the disease. For more than five years, the Reagan administration remained virtually silent on the matter, and some people went so far as to suggest that AIDS was a form of "divine vengeance" against people who deserved their fate. Conservative commentator Patrick Buchanan, who served as a White House staff writer, claimed in 1983 that homosexuals had "declared war on nature, and now nature is exacting an awful retribution" (cited in Clark et al., 1985:20). Such antigay prejudice, coupled to ignorance about how AIDS is and is not transmitted, applied an isolating stigma to persons with the disease, as the box illustrates.

In recent years, however, the public perception of AIDS has begun to change. In part, this is because many more people now know a person with AIDS, someone who may not be in a stigmatized category. The public has also become aware that victims include some five hundred children who were infected either at birth or through past blood transfusions. Perhaps even more linked to the change in public opinion, is the fact that no one is sure how far the virus has spread. There is

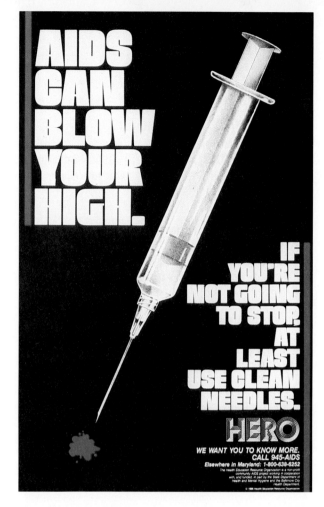

More attention is being paid to intravenous drug abuse as a means of transmitting the AIDS virus because, first, drug abusers are a difficult population to educate to the dangers of this deadly disease, and second, drug abusers have been spreading the virus into the heterosexual population.

as yet no evidence of a massive "breakout" into the general population, but the long period between infection and when symptoms appear makes the disease difficult to track. In simple terms, people with AIDS *now* are those who were infected with HIV *years ago*. Until comprehensive testing programs are carried out, the future dimensions of this health crisis will remain uncertain.

By anyone's reckoning, however, AIDS will place an unprecedented burden on the American health-care system. The costs of treating a person with AIDS already exceed $150,000, an amount that will surely rise as new treatments are developed. By 1985, the national medical bill for AIDS was about $5 billion, a figure that will triple by 1991. Beyond the direct medical costs, lost earnings and productivity will amount to tens of billions more. Government health programs, private insurance, and personal savings are likely to meet only a small fraction of this total. There is little doubt, then, that AIDS represents both a medical and a social problem of monumental proportions.

Ethical Issues Surrounding Death

There are many important ethical issues involved with health and medicine in American society. A number of these are related to death; they arise largely as a result of technological changes that give human beings greater control over life itself.

When is a person dead?   Common sense suggests that death occurs when breathing and heartbeat stop. Advancing medical technology, however, has rendered this view of death obsolete. Today a heart that has stopped beating can be revived or replaced, just as breathing can be sustained by artificial means. To complicate matters fur-

ther, both heartbeat and breathing may continue in the absence of any brain activity. Today, then, life and death are often difficult to distinguish. Medical and legal consensus in the United States now generally defines death as an irreversible state involving no response to stimulation, no movement or breathing, no reflexes, and no indication of brain activity (Ladd, 1979; Wall, 1980).

Do people have a right to die?   When the death of a terminally ill person depends on a human decision, who should assume this responsibility? This issue came to national attention in 1975, when twenty-one-year-old Karen Ann Quinlan fell into an irreversible coma after mixing tranquilizers and alcohol. Physicians assured Quinlan's parents that their daughter had no hope for recovery. Four months later, the Quinlans sought to remove her from the respirator that was keeping her alive. A New Jersey court stated, however, that they had no right to make such a decision. When this court ruling was reversed by the state supreme court in 1976, Karen Ann Quinlan's respirator was disconnected. Even

---

SOCIOLOGY OF EVERYDAY LIFE

Social Isolation: The Stigma of AIDS

During the winter of 1984, Robert Doyle began to experience a severe shortness of breath and soon after was coughing up blood from his lungs. Fearing that he had contracted tuberculosis, the thirty-two-year-old construction worker entered a hospital in Baltimore and learned that his illness was far worse: he had pneumonia brought on by AIDS.

Doctors treated Doyle's pneumonia. They could do little else for him, however, and so attempted to place him in a nursing home or hospice. All institutions contacted refused to admit Doyle after learning that he had AIDS. Doyle's two brothers also shunned him, and the man with whom he had been sexually involved demanded that he move out of their

apartment. With only months to live, Robert Doyle had no money and no place to die.

Ultimately, he was able to secure a room in a rundown hotel. Members of the hotel staff were afraid of his disease, however, and refused to enter his room. Too weak to move about on his own, Doyle had to survive on food that hotel employees left on the floor outside his door.

Doyle's plight became the subject of a newspaper article that inspired a stranger to offer him a place in her home. Within two days, however, the woman's fear for her own health and that of her children put Doyle back on the streets. An elderly couple then offered Doyle shelter, but threatening telephone calls and vandal-

ism—presumably the work of neighbors—ended his stay after two weeks. Finally, Doyle was able to find a home with three other adults, one of whom was also a victim of AIDS. Soon afterward, however, he returned to the hospital to die.

What is all too typical about Robert Doyle's story is the extent to which unfounded fears can transform a victim of a deadly disease into a social outcast. Combating AIDS will involve not only medical research, but also coming to terms with the social dimensions of this epidemic.

SOURCE: Based on Jean Seligmann and Nikke Finke Greenberg, "Only Months to Live and No Place to Die," *Newsweek*, August 12, 1985, p. 26.

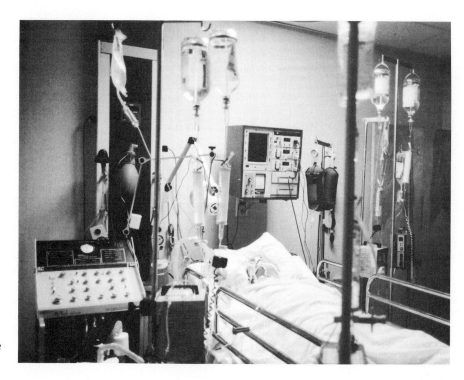

The heroic treatment of dying patients is controversial. Some Americans believe in prolonging life at all costs, while others argue that an artificially extended life has little value.

so, Quinlan lived for another nine years. In 1985, never having regained consciousness and weighing only seventy pounds, Quinlan finally stopped breathing.

Some ten thousand Americans are currently in the same kind of permanent vegetative state as Karen Ann Quinlan was (Wallis, 1986). A recent presidential commission (1983) provided a number of guidelines concerning the rights of such people to die. The commission noted, first, that physicians and hospitals have the general responsibility to protect the patient's life rather than helping to end it. The commission also asserted that physicians must explain all the medical options available to patients, or to family members when patients are incapacitated. At the same time, the commission recognized the right of terminally ill patients to refuse heroic treatment that may extend their lives without giving them any hope of recovery.

The commission also concluded that physicians should honor any patient's *living will*, a personal statement indicating a desire or refusal to be given heroic treatment in the case of terminal illness. Laws in most, but not all, states currently support this principle. In the absence of a living will, or if the patient is a newborn child, physicians and hospitals have the responsibility to provide any treatment that can be expected to sustain life. If treatment is deemed to be futile, however, another person—usually a parent or other close family member—may decide, in consultation with physicians, to refuse further treatment. In all decisions, however, the paramount concern should be the interests of the patient, not the interests of other family members.

What about mercy killing? *Mercy killing* is the common term for **euthanasia:** *assisting in the death of a person who is suffering from a painful and incurable disease.* Euthanasia (derived from the Greek words meaning "an easy death") poses an ethical dilemma, since it combines an act that directly or indirectly causes the death of another person—which cultural norms view as a serious crime—with the presumed motive of kindness toward the one who dies. Although the patient's right to die has increasing support in the United States, assisting in the death of another person is a more ethically complex and socially controversial matter, as illustrated by the shooting of Emily Gilbert by her husband, described at the beginning of this chapter.

Those who view life as always preferable to death, no matter what suffering living may entail, rule out euthanasia entirely. Those who take the view that under some circumstances death is preferable face the practical problem of determining just when the life of another person is no longer worth living. After requesting physicians to revive the heart of her dying father, one daughter recently said, "I'm glad they brought him back. He was old, but that doesn't mean he should stop living. He was still alive, and as long as he's alive, he should be saved." In another case, however, a daughter insisted that physicians not prolong the life of her ninety-eight-year-old mother: "If my mother's heart stopped beating, I don't want them pounding on her chest and destroying her body any more than it was. For what? Revive her for another day or another two weeks?" (cited in Kleiman, 1985:11).

These contrasting views are both compelling, and illustrate the difficulty faced by family members who must decide whether to sustain the life of a loved one—even though heroic treatment may be painful—or to allow the person to die with dignity. In many cases, treatment costs are an additional, if unspoken, concern. A single attempt to revive a patient whose heart has stopped may cost $1,500. Two weeks of heroic lifesaving efforts may add up to tens of thousands of dollars. Such expenses may be beyond the resources of a family, thereby adding the family's welfare to the factors that must be weighed in reaching a decision regarding heroic treatment.

Guidelines for dealing with dying patients are only gradually becoming established. At present, Americans widely support the concept of *passive* euthanasia, illustrated by the case of Karen Ann Quinlan, in which family members and physicians decide to forgo heroic treatment of a terminally ill person. Americans are far less supportive of *active* euthanasia, illustrated by Roswell Gilbert's shooting of his wife. In such cases, there is always the possibility that actively causing the death of another—even a person who is suffering and certain to die—may be a means of resolving a situation that has become impossible for *others* to bear.

HEALTH CARE

Practiced in every society, **health care** may be defined as *deliberate activity directed toward improving health*. Throughout most of human history, health care was a responsibility of the family. In more socially complex societies, health care develops into **medicine**, *a social institution concerned with combating disease as a means to improve health*. Medicine emerges as a distinct social institution when some people within a society assume formal, specialized roles as healers. In societies that have not yet industrialized, medicine involves traditional knowledge about the healing properties of certain plants, often combined with astute insights into the emotional and spiritual needs of the ill (Ayensu, 1981). Sometimes dismissed by ethnocentric Americans as simply witch doctors, traditional healers—from herbalists to acupuncturists—do indeed improve human health, in spite of facing some of the greatest health problems in the world.

In industrialized societies, medicine has become the province of highly trained and legally licensed specialists, including physicians and other technicians. Although family members still treat one another's minor illnesses, Americans associate health care primarily with medical treatment from specialists in their professional offices or in hospitals.

Medicine in the United States, as well as in most other industrialized societies, is based on the logic of science. This has only been the case for about one hundred years, however, as we shall now explain.

The Rise of Scientific Medicine

American health care today is dominated by *scientific medicine*, meaning that the logic of science is applied to medical research and the treatment of disease and injury. In colonial America, however, medicine was an open field in which many categories of people, including herbalists, druggists, midwives, and even ministers, practiced. During the 1700s, perhaps one in every six hundred Americans was engaged in some form of medical work—about the same proportion as today—but there was no consensus about how this work should be done (Stevens, 1971). Even the few who had received formal medical training in Europe had very limited medical knowledge by today's standards, and often it was less reliable than the knowledge possessed by traditional healers such as herbalists and midwives. Furthermore, lack of anesthesia made surgery a terrible ordeal, and because of their ignorance and use of unsanitary instruments, physicians and surgeons killed perhaps as many patients as they saved.

Gradually, however, as medical specialists learned more about human anatomy, physiology, and biochemistry, medicine became scientific. Medical doctors were able to establish themselves as self-regulating, service-oriented professionals (see Chapter 18) whose theoretical knowledge and complex skills were beyond the grasp of the ordinary person.

Early in the nineteenth century, medical societies were organized across the United States. Each licensed practitioners according to its own medical standards, claiming to represent the legitimate approach to medical care. To train licensed practitioners, medical schools were also founded: the four in 1800 increased to more than four hundred by the end of the century. The number of hospitals also grew rapidly in the second half of the nineteenth century, mostly in larger cities (Stevens, 1971).

The final transformation of scientific medicine into a profession began with the founding of the American Medical Association (AMA) in 1847. The scientific model of medicine had gained widespread acceptance because of its success in tracing the cause of life-threatening diseases to bacteria and viruses and its use of vaccines to increase human resistance to disease. But alternative approaches—many of which stressed the importance of nutrition and the social environment in promoting human health—still had many defenders.

The AMA version of scientific medicine finally triumphed in the early twentieth century. By 1910, state licensing boards certified only physicians who had passed state medical examinations proving their competence in standardized medical knowledge approved by the AMA (Starr, 1982). Many medical schools—especially those with a less scientific orientation—were forced to close in the face of declining enrollments, and the practice of medicine became largely restricted to people holding the M.D. degree. Once American medical care came under the firm control of the AMA, the occupational standing of physicians with M.D. degrees rose dramatically until medicine became perhaps the most prestigious profession in the United States. In the process, physicians obtained a virtual monopoly in medicine and became among the highest-paid Americans, earning an average of about $120,000 in 1985.

Some adherents of alternative medical approaches—such as osteopathic physicians—saw the writing on the wall and gradually accepted scientific medicine. Originally, the work of osteopaths was based on the manipulation of the skeleton and muscles. Today, however, osteopaths (with D.O. degrees) treat illness much as medical doctors (with M.D. degrees) do. But other medical practitioners—such as chiropractors, her-

bal healers, and midwives—held to their traditional practices, and as a result, their work became defined as a fringe area of the medical profession. With far less social prestige and income than physicians, such practitioners of alternative medicine today have only a small, if devoted, following among Americans (Gordon, 1980).

The rise of scientific medicine also influenced the kinds of people likely to become physicians. Many medical colleges established in rural areas during the nineteenth century had provided medical training to people of modest financial means. Such colleges, however, were often prime targets of the AMA because of their allegedly deficient standards and facilities. Some of these medical schools were indeed inadequate from the viewpoint of scientific medicine, but they were the only means of ensuring that rural Americans had access to any medical care at all. In contrast, the medical training required by the AMA and state licensing boards was (and remains) extremely time-consuming and expensive so that medicine became a profession mostly of the well-to-do. Furthermore, women were discouraged from becoming physicians just as the AMA denigrated more traditional forms of health care in which females had long played a large role. Some medical schools did provide training to women and black Americans, but with little public support or financial resources, few of these schools survived. As the number of medical schools in the United States tumbled to only seventy-seven by 1950, the number of blacks and women in medicine declined as well, and remained quite low until recently (Starr, 1982; Huet-Cox, 1984).

In sum, as the AMA established physicians as scientific professionals, it simultaneously restricted the practice of medicine to those who were welcomed by a few elite and often discriminatory medical schools, and, of course, who could afford the high costs of a medical education. In practice, this meant that medicine became dominated by white males, most of whom were from privileged families in urban areas (Stevens, 1971; Starr, 1982). This explains the American shortage of physicians in rural areas, as well as the lack of women and other minorities in the ranks of physicians.

Holistic Medicine

Although the approach to health represented by scientific medicine became dominant early in this century, criticisms from outside the medical establishment persisted. One alternative that has been regaining support among

Americans in recent decades is **holistic medicine,** which is *a medical orientation that seeks to improve health by taking account of the whole person as well as the physical and social environment.*

Holistic medicine is a reaction to scientific medicine's tendency to focus on diseases and injuries rather than on a person's overall health. From the point of view of holistic medicine, the medical establishment's emphasis on drugs, surgery, artificial organs, and high technology has transformed physicians into narrow specialists concerned with symptoms rather than people, and with disease rather than health. Without denying that drugs and surgery are sometimes necessary, holistic medicine endorses a broader approach to health that seeks to understand a person's entire life and environment. Therefore, holistic medicine finds full expression in the teamwork of a wide variety of trained personnel—including physicians, physical therapists, nutritionists, counselors, clergy, and even acupuncturists and teachers of meditation—who seek to improve the physical, mental, and social well-being of their clients. Of course, the many medical organizations that describe themselves as holistic vary considerably. In general, however, the

holistic approach to health care includes the following major concerns (Gordon, 1980).

Patients are people. Holistic practitioners are concerned with the symptoms of disease, but also with the ways in which each person's environment and way of life may encourage or inhibit health. A full understanding of any client demands paying attention to the person's social and physical environment. The likelihood of illness is known to increase under conditions of stress caused, for example, by the death of a family member, intense competition at work, poverty, or social isolation (Duhl, 1980). Therefore, the holistic approach to health encourages stress-free and supportive social relationships that increase individual well-being. Holistic health practitioners are also actively concerned with environmental pollution and other dangers to public health.

Responsibility, not dependency. Holistic medicine places primary responsibility for health on individuals themselves. Conventional medicine tends to view the dynamics of health as so complex that only professional physicians can understand them. This fosters a sense of dependency in patients. While holistic medicine recognizes that experts must assume immediate control of a crisis situation, holistic health-care practitioners generally define their role as helping people to recognize their own ability to engage in health-promoting patterns of behavior (Ferguson, 1980). The holistic approach attempts to take an *active* approach to pursuing health, in contrast to scientific medicine's *reactive* approach to disease.

Personal treatment environment. Conventional medicine has shifted the location of health care away from the familiar setting of the home to impersonal offices and hospitals. These professional settings are disease-oriented rather than health-oriented, and reinforce uninformed reliance on medical experts. While recognizing that hospitalization may be necessary for the treatment of severe illness, holistic medicine maintains that, whenever possible, health care should take place in personal and relaxed settings. Many holistic health centers attempt to foster such an environment, and many holistic practitioners offer assistance in the familiar setting of the home.

Optimum health for all. The holistic approach to health care attempts to promote the highest possible level of well-being for everyone. Beyond treating illness, the holistic approach assists people who are "well" to realize "a state of extraordinary vigor, joy, and creativity" (Gordon, 1980:17).

Although Americans generally accept scientific medical treatment, a wide range of other approaches claim to enhance health. Acupuncture, derived from Chinese folk medicine, cures illness through puncturing the skin with carefully placed needles.

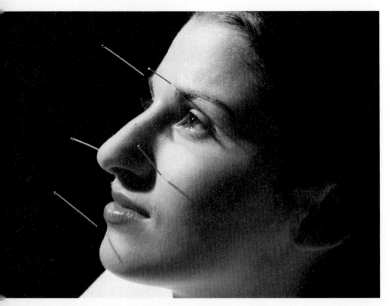

The principles of holistic health care are intended to reestablish the more personal social ties that united healers and patients before the rise of scientifically trained specialists. The AMA currently recognizes more than fifty specialized areas of medical practice. Over the course of this century, a growing proportion of new M.D.'s have entered these high-paying specialties rather than family practice, which is more concerned with the patient in the holistic sense. Holistic medicine is clearly committed to the World Health Organization's definition of health as "a state of complete physical, mental, and social well-being."

The Economics of Medical Care

Industrial societies today equate health care with professional medical care, which is extremely expensive. Thus all industrialized societies have developed some type of government policy to help people meet these costs. Although each society does this somewhat differently, characteristic patterns of medical care in industrialized societies today are linked to the two main types of economic systems described in Chapter 18.

Medical Care in Socialist Economies

In societies with predominantly socialist economies—such as the Soviet Union, Poland, and Cuba—the government provides a wide range of social welfare benefits to the population, including medical care. In spite of many differences among them, all socialist societies agree on one fundamental principle: Medical care is a *right* of all citizens that the government provides, in more or less equal fashion, regardless of a person's financial circumstances. People do not pay directly for services provided by physicians and hospitals; the government uses public funds to pay medical costs. Medical facilities are typically owned and operated by the government, and practitioners receive salaries as government employees.

The Soviet Union. In the Soviet Union, for example, no citizen pays directly for medical care. At the same time, however, the costs of government-provided medical care have the effect of reducing the average person's income (Fuchs, 1974; Knaus, 1981). Hospitals and clinics are owned and operated by the government. People do not choose a physician, as in the United States, but simply report to public health facilities near their homes.

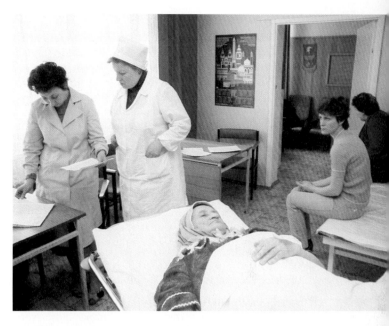

Socialist principles hold that medical care is a right of everyone. In practice, Soviet citizens contend with a rigidly bureaucratic medical system that has come under attack for being inefficient and impersonal.

Compared to their counterparts in the United States, Soviet physicians do not have high prestige or income. With a typical income of about $3,600 a year in 1980, Soviet physicians were paid only an average salary, about the same as that of skilled industrial workers. Beyond socialist attempts at economic equality, this relatively low income reflects the fact that about 70 percent of Soviet physicians are female, compared to about 18 percent in the United States. Like the United States, the Soviet Union is a patriarchal society in which occupations held largely by females tend to be allocated fewer social resources (Knaus, 1981).

The Soviet system of medical care has been mostly successful in meeting the basic needs of a large population. It is also rigidly bureaucratic, however, and has been criticized for providing highly standardized and impersonal medical care. For instance, one drawback of the Soviet system is its apparent inability to embrace the holistic approach to health noted earlier.

China. The socialist People's Republic of China, while beginning to industrialize, is still a largely poor and agrarian society. The task of attending to the health of China's enormous population—now more than 1 billion—is truly monumental. The traditional healing arts, including acupuncture and the use of medicinal herbs, are still the most accessible types of health care in China, where holistic concern for the interplay of mind and body has been a cultural trait for thousands of years (Sidel & Sidel, 1982b; Kaptchuk, 1985). However, industrialization is increasing the importance of science and specialization within Chinese medicine. The recent introduction of limited capitalism to China has resulted in some degree of privately purchased medical care, but every citizen is still accorded free medical care in government-operated facilities. China's so-called barefoot doctors, whose basic medical knowledge is comparable to that of American paramedics, have brought at least some elements of modern medicine to the millions of peasants who live in the many remote rural villages of China.

Medical Care in Capitalist Economies

Societies with mostly capitalist economies generally limit government welfare programs, including those concerned with health. They expect citizens to largely provide for themselves according to their own resources and personal preferences. As described in Chapter 18, predominantly capitalist societies such as the United States have pronounced patterns of economic inequality. If health were purely a commodity sold to the highest bidder in the marketplace, a large segment of the population would be able to purchase little if any medical care. As a result, every capitalist society provides some type of government assistance in securing medical care. Most of these nations—with the noteworthy exception of the United States—have comprehensive programs that provide some benefits to the entire population. In Western Europe, particularly in societies that have adopted democratic socialism, health-care programs administered by the government were established about a century ago (Starr, 1982).

Sweden.   Sweden instituted a comprehensive and compulsory system of health care administered by various government agencies in 1891. Today the Swedish program is financed through taxes, which are among the highest in the world. Thus most physicians derive their income not from fees collected directly from patients, but from salaries paid by the government. Hospitals are typically government agencies, not private profit-making organizations. Because this system of medical care resembles that found in socialist societies, it is often described as **socialized medicine:** *a health-care system in which*

most medical facilities are owned and operated by the government, and most physicians are government employees who receive salaries rather than fees directly from patients.

Great Britain.   A program of socialized medicine has also existed in Great Britain since 1948, growing out of a medical insurance program begun in 1911. Some physicians and hospitals operate privately, however. While all British citizens are entitled to medical care provided by the National Health Service, those who have the necessary financial means may purchase more extensive care from private practitioners. Thus all British citizens do not have equal access to medical care, which is reflected in the fact that those with higher incomes tend to suffer less from disease than those who are poorer (Doyal, 1981). The British National Health Service does ensure, however, that at least basic medical care is provided to all segments of the population.

Canada.   All Canadians have government-funded access to hospitalization and physician services. But physicians operate privately, rather than as government employees, so that the Canadian system is not really a case of socialized medicine. Physicians also have the right to work entirely outside of the government-funded system, charging whatever fees they wish to patients able and willing to pay for private medical care. Few physicians do so, however. Fees for all health-care services are paid by the federal government and the governments of the ten Canadian provinces according to schedules that are set annually in consultation with associations of medical professionals (Grant, 1984; Vayda & Deber, 1984).

Japan.   Physicians in Japan also operate privately, but the costs of medical care are paid through a combination of private insurance systems and a government program. As described in Chapter 7, large Japanese businesses take a broad interest in the welfare of their employees. Many corporations provide medical care for their workers as a benefit of employment. For those who are not covered by such privately funded programs, the government sponsors medical insurance that covers 70 percent of all costs, and the elderly pay nothing at all (Vogel, 1979).

Despite their differences, the medical-care systems of most capitalist societies other than the United States provide at least three major benefits. First, basic medical care is available to everyone regardless of income. Second, because the costs of treating a major illness are often beyond the financial means of even well-to-do people, government programs protect citizens against the financial ruin that could result from serious illness. Third, by providing at least some medical care with little or no direct costs to individuals, such government programs encourage people to make regular use of medical facilities even when they are healthy, which is an important means of preventing illness.

The Economics of Medical Care in the United States

The United States is unique among the industrialized societies of the world in that the federal government has established no program to ensure that all Americans are able to meet the costs of basic medical care. The federal government does assist some categories of Americans in paying certain medical expenses, but the American medical-care system is primarily a private, profit-making industry in which more money buys better care. Thus the United States is characterized by a **direct-fee system:** *a medical-care system in which patients pay directly for services provided by physicians and hospitals.*

Income is more unequally distributed in the United States than in the Western European nations that have adopted the principles of democratic socialism. This income inequality, combined with the absence of a comprehensive national medical-care program, means that poor Americans have far less access to medical care than other Americans do. Although the United States is richer than any European society, in some respects our health is worse than that of Europeans. For example, the mortality rate for infants in the first year of life is higher in the United States than in almost any Western European society, and the death rate for forty-five-year-old men is about twice as high in the United States as it is in Sweden (Fuchs, 1974; United Nations, 1983).

There are three major reasons that a national health-care program has not developed in the United States. First, Americans have traditionally opposed government intervention into the economy and into supposedly private matters such as personal health. A century ago, when European societies were initiating national medical-care plans, the federal government played only a small role in American society. Second, although the government role in American society has increased greatly in the last fifty years, no organized social movement or political party in the United States has strongly promoted a national program of medical care for all. Such programs emerged in European societies largely

as the result of demands made by organized labor and socialist political parties. Americans, however, have traditionally mistrusted socialist ideas and policies; even among the American working class, support for socialism has been minimal. Although labor unions were organized in the United States as early as the end of the nineteenth century, they have never made government-supported medical care a very high priority. Instead, American unions attempted—with considerable success—to win health-care benefits from employers. Third, the American Medical Association and the private insurance industry, both powerful special-interest groups, have effectively opposed a national health-care program (Starr, 1982).

Because of the technological sophistication of American medicine, the costs of medical care today are extremely high. As shown in Figure 19-2, expenditures for medical care increased over forty-fold between 1950 and 1987, from a little over $12 billion to almost $500 billion. In other terms, while we spent about 4 percent

Figure 19-2 The Increasing Cost of Medical Care in the United States

(U.S. Bureau of the Census, 1970, 1987)

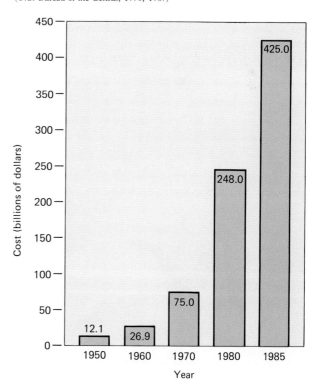

of gross national product on medical care in 1950, by 1987, medical care was absorbing 11 percent of GNP. In the absence of a program of socialized medicine or comprehensive federal health insurance, how do Americans pay for their medical care?

Private insurance programs. In 1985, 136 million Americans, or about 57 percent of the population, received some medical-care benefits from the employer or labor union of a family member. Another 45 million Americans (19 percent) purchased some amount of private coverage. Most large-scale programs such as Blue Cross and Blue Shield do not pay all medical costs, but overall, about three-fourths of the American population has some private medical insurance (U.S. Bureau of the Census, 1987f; Health Insurance Association of America, 1987).

Public insurance programs. In 1965, Congress enacted legislation providing limited medical benefits to specific categories of Americans. Medicare provides partial coverage of medical costs primarily for Americans over sixty-five. In 1987, almost 38 million Americans, or about 16 percent of the population, were covered by Medicare. Medicaid, a medical insurance program for the poor, provided benefits to almost 22 million Americans, or about 9 percent of the population, in 1985. After World War II, the U.S. Veterans Administration granted veter-

ans free medical care in government-operated hospitals. About 10 million Americans, or roughly 4 percent of the population, receive VA benefits. In all, then, about 25 percent of Americans receive some medical-care benefits from the government, but most of these people are also included in the private insurance programs already discussed.

Health Maintenance Organizations. In recent years, an increasing number of Americans are coping with the rising costs of health care by joining a **health maintenance organization** (HMO): *a formal organization that provides comprehensive medical care for which subscribers pay a fixed fee.* In 1986, there were 626 HMOs in the United States providing medical care to over 27 million members, or almost 12 percent of the American population. HMOs vary in terms of costs and benefits, but virtually none provide full coverage of medical costs. However, since the cost of HMO membership is not based on how many services a person uses, these organizations have a financial interest in keeping their subscribers healthy. Consequently, many HMOs have adopted the principles of holistic medicine described earlier in this chapter, which emphasize the importance of promoting health rather than treating illness (Ginsburg, 1983).

Overall, then, more than 85 percent of Americans have some medical-care program. In most cases, these are privately funded, with the government providing

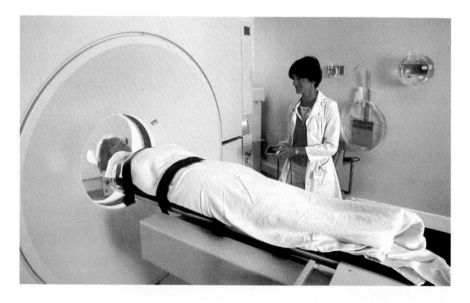

Technological advances in medical care such as the CAT scan offer significant benefits, but they have also contributed to the soaring cost of medical care in the United States.

some care to specific (mostly low-income) segments of the population. But this combination approach falls short of meeting the medical-care needs of the population. Consider, first, that perhaps 50 million Americans have medical programs that do not pay enough of the costs of a major illness for people to survive it financially. Thus a major illness threatens millions of Americans—including many who think of themselves as middle class—with financial ruin. Second, no program covers all medical needs. Most private insurance programs, as well as Medicare and Medicaid, exclude many medical services, such as dental care (Eve, 1984). Third, and most seriously, over 30 million Americans (about 13 percent of the population) have no medical insurance at all. Since most of these people are quite poor, they can neither afford to become ill nor afford to purchase the medical care they need to remain healthy. This situation has been described as "the inverse care law," which means that those Americans who need health care the most are least likely to get it (Tutor, 1971, cited in Grant, 1984).

THEORETICAL ANALYSIS OF HEALTH AND MEDICINE

Each of the major theoretical paradigms in sociology provides a means of organizing and interpreting the facts and issues presented in this chapter.

Structural-Functional Analysis

As described in earlier chapters, sociology's structural-functional paradigm is based on an image of society as a complex system that is internally well-integrated and stable. Talcott Parsons (1951) suggested that the good health of its members is critical to a society's functioning. Illness is dysfunctional, meaning that it undermines the ability of individuals to contribute to the operation of society.

The Sick Role

Perhaps the most important concept in the structural-functional analysis of health is that of the **sick role,** referring to *patterns of behavior that are socially defined as appropriate for those who are ill*. As developed by Talcott Parsons, the sick role has the following four characteristics.

A *sick person is exempted from routine responsibilities.* In daily life, people are expected to perform a variety of social roles—for example, student, parent, employee. The more serious the illness is perceived to be, the more likely it is that the sick person's social responsibilities will be relaxed or suspended entirely. But people cannot define themselves as ill; assuming the sick role usually depends on the assessment of a person's health by recognized medical experts.

A *person's illness is not deliberate.* People are not normally regarded as responsible for their own illness. Rather, illness is something that happens to someone. For this reason, the failure of ill people to fulfill responsibilities associated with routine social roles does not lead to punishment.

A *sick person must want to be well.* The first two characteristics depend on the fact that a person does not want to be ill. Those suspected of feigning illness in order to escape the responsibility of routine social roles or to receive special attention from others are not entitled to assume a socially recognized sick role.

A *sick person must seek competent help.* Simply wanting to become well is not sufficient. An ill person must seek whatever assistance is available and cooperate with health-care practitioners.

One important limitation of this useful analysis of the social foundation of health and illness is that the sick role concept is more easily applied to the wealthy and middle classes than to the poor. But since illness is a common consequence of poverty, poor health may be taken for granted by an impoverished person with little hope of ever being cured. Moreover, as already indicated, many poor Americans simply cannot afford effective health care; nor can many poor people afford not to work, even when they are ill.

The Physician's Role

In the United States and other industrial societies, the physician's role as primary provider of medical care is shaped in relation to the sick role of the patient. Because the sick role contains the expectation that those suffering from illness want to become well and will seek competent help to do so, people who are ill typically seek the services of a physician. The primary responsibility of the physician is to cure illness. In some cases, of course, this may not be possible, but both physician and patient initially share the expectation that the illness will be cured. If the physician is subsequently unable to cure the patient's illness, the physician-patient relationship is likely to be weakened.

In Talcott Parsons's view, a physician-patient relationship is usually hierarchical, with the physician having a position of power over the patient. The physician's power is based on the cultural norm that those who are ill must cooperate with physicians, and is further strengthened by the fact that the physician has knowledge unavailable to the patient. Physicians not only expect patients to comply with their requests, but also routinely ask for personal information that the patient may possibly share with no one else. Parsons notes that this information is provided to the physician only to assist in the treatment process; physicians may not make any other use of it.

Worth noting is the fact that Parsons's view of the physician's role applies only to the model of conventional, scientific medicine described earlier, in which physicians react to disease instead of working with patients on a regular basis to promote health. Treatment-oriented physicians almost always assert authority over the patient. Holistic-health–oriented physicians, on the other hand, tend to foster a more egalitarian partnership in which patients are encouraged to take considerable responsibility for their own health.

Symbolic-Interaction Analysis

The symbolic-interaction paradigm views social life as an ongoing process in which different human beings come to perceive reality in different terms. The reality of health, then, has much to do with how we define any situation.

Subjective Perceptions of Health

The importance of subjective perceptions of health is revealed by a personal experience of British sociologist Ann Holohan. In the office of a physician for what she assumed to be treatment for a breast infection, Holohan was told that she might have cancer and should enter the hospital for a biopsy. She was still in a state of shock minutes later when she left the physician's office and reentered the outside world:

It seemed incredible that nothing had changed—the sun was still shining, the road sweeper gathering the leaves. I sat in my car [and] immense waves of panic engulfed me. I drove blindly home and recall very little of the actual journey. . . . Yet I was no "sicker" than before my consultation. All that had changed was the possibility of a medical label for my symptom. (1977, cited in Cockerham, 1982:95).

Later Holohan learned that she did not have cancer. But simply the perception that she might be ill was sufficient to make the disease real enough to affect her behavior. Medical experts have long noted the existence of *psychosomatic* physical disorders, in which physical illness is caused or aggravated by the person's state of mind (Hamrick, Anspaugh, & Ezell, 1986).

The Social Construction of Illness

Subjective perceptions of health, of course, reflect internalized social definitions. Labels such as *cancer* or *AIDS* and their powerful connotations arise as part of the process of the social construction of reality, as described in Chapter 6. Thus any state of health or illness is subject to highly variable interpretations within different social settings. In a society where most people are suffering from the effects of hunger, a rather sickly child may be considered comparatively healthy. Similarly, Americans have been slow to recognize as unhealthful such widespread patterns of behavior as smoking and eating rich foods.

The "expert opinions" of medical professionals also vary according to nonmedical factors in the larger social environment. David Mechanic (1978) has pointed out that during periods of low worker productivity in the Soviet Union, physicians are less generous in acknowledging that the health-related complaints of workers are serious enough to excuse them from their jobs. Similarly, soldiers' symptoms that may be defined as legitimate illness during peacetime may not qualify as such in times of war. And college students have been known to ignore symptoms of possible illness just before a vacation, but more readily report to the infirmary before a difficult examination for which they are not prepared. This final illustration suggests how people may try to use medical experts to legitimate their claim to assuming the sick role in order to be excused from routine expectations. Whether or not a person is defined as sick, then, depends on a process of social negotiation with others as much as on any objective symptoms.

The symbolic-interaction paradigm's strength is that it emphasizes the relativity of the concepts of sickness and health. At the same time, this approach has the drawback of minimizing objective standards of well-being. Certain physical states and injuries do indeed cause very concrete changes in human capacities, however they are socially defined. Even if people in poor societies define themselves as healthy in relation to one another, they are nevertheless not healthy by world standards.

Social-Conflict Analysis

Relative differences in patterns of health and access to medical care are major concerns of social-conflict analysis, which focuses on patterns of social inequality and conflict. Social-conflict analysis has been used to develop three major criticisms of capitalist societies with regard to health.

Unequal Access to Medical Care

Health is a foundation of social life. Yet by defining medical care as a commodity to be purchased, capitalist societies limit the access of those with limited financial means to good health. As already noted, this problem is more serious in the United States than in other capitalist societies that have instituted national medical-care programs. Some critics of the American medical system —including some members of Congress—therefore advocate expanding the role of government in providing medical care to the American population. Vested interests—especially the medical establishment—continue to oppose any such program.

More radical critics claim that no government-sponsored medical-care plan can eliminate all the health-related consequences of social inequality in capitalist societies, for the heart of the problem is the class system itself. The strikingly unequal distribution of income and wealth in American society makes the goal of equal medical care for the entire population unreachable. Only a significant redistribution of economic resources can be expected to make medical care more equally available (Bodenheimer, 1977; Navarro, 1977).

Medical Care and the Profit Motive

The above criticisms view medical care itself in positive terms, questioning only its unequal distribution throughout the population. But some social-conflict theorists criticize capitalist medical care itself as just another big business. Physicians, hospitals, and producers of drugs and medical supplies together make up an industry that has hundreds of billions of dollars in sales each year (Ehrenreich, 1978). These critics suggest that the quest for ever-increasing profits leads to questionable medical practices, including performing unnecessary tests and surgery and overprescribing certain drugs (Kaplan et al., 1985). To give some idea of the saturation of the United States with medical drugs, Americans consume some 20,000 tons of aspirin per year—roughly 225 pills per person on the average—though it is known that the overuse of aspirin causes a number of ailments such as stomach bleeding (Gordon, 1980). Moreover, some drugs are addictive, while others may cause a variety of adverse reactions. Perhaps 1 million Americans enter a hospital each year because of an adverse reaction to a medical drug (Illich, 1976). Some very profitable medical products have also been found to cause widespread suffering. The Dalkon shield, for example, is a contraceptive intrauterine device that the A. H. Robins Company continued to sell even after evidence indicated that it caused

The dominant position of scientific medicine in American society has been criticized for encouraging excessive reliance on drugs.

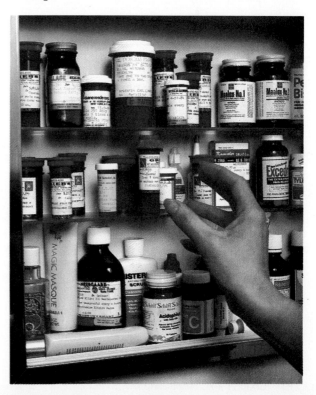

life-threatening illness in thousands of women (Perry & Dawson, 1985).

Some 25 million surgical operations were performed in the United States in 1985. Determining how many were unnecessary is obviously difficult, but three-fourths of all surgery is elective, meaning that the operation is not a response to a medical emergency but a decision made with the presumed intention of increasing a patient's long-term health. But growing evidence suggests that the decision to perform surgery reflects the

SOCIETY IN HISTORY

Medical Science and Social Control: The Case of Victorian Women

A century ago, the social relationship between the sexes was changing in the United States, as it continues to change today. Medical science was far from neutral about this change. Under the control of males, American medicine was generally a conservative force seeking to perpetuate traditional patterns of sexual inequality.

In general, medical opinion held that conventional gender distinctions were a natural and inevitable reflection of human biology. Females were simply weaker than males, with smaller skulls and brains and less muscular potential. Even more important, physicians pronounced males naturally rational and intellectual, while females were dominated by their emotions and hypersensitive nervous systems.

Consequently, medical science supported the idea that women's proper role centered on childbearing and the home. As one physician wrote in 1890, the physical condition of women is "as if the Almighty, in creating the female sex, had taken the uterus and built up a woman around it" (cited in Smith-Rosenberg & Rosenberg, 1984:13). Furthermore, women who did not have children were thought to have a higher incidence of both physical and mental illness and a shorter life span.

Medical science of the times also opposed the growing demands by women for a formal education. Physicians argued that intellectual pursuits damaged a woman's health, rendering her weak and sickly and increasing the likelihood of sterility or of bearing unhealthy children. Writing about the educated woman in 1901, one gynecologist asserted, "She may become highly cultured and accomplished and shine in society, but her future husband will discover too late that he has married a large outfit of headaches, backaches, and spine aches, instead of a woman fitted to take up the duties of life" (cited in Smith-Rosenberg & Rosenberg, 1984:16). Edward H. Clarke, a Harvard faculty member and an influential physician whose writings widely circulated within the medical community well into this century, likewise argued strongly that the education of women would result in their inability to be mothers: "If she puts as much force into her brain education as a boy, the brain or the special apparatus [meaning the reproductive system] will suffer" (cited in Bollough & Voght, 1984:30).

In the same manner, physicians opposed efforts by women to take control of their own sexuality. The American medical establishment promoted the view that females had no interest in sexual activity other than as a means of having children; they had neither the desire nor the ability to achieve orgasm. Males, on the other hand, were believed to require sexual intercourse concluded by orgasm in order to prevent the buildup of dangerous levels of nervous energy. Male orgasms unimpeded by contraceptive devices such as condoms had health benefits for women, physicians asserted. Sexual intercourse would cause nervous disease in women unless semen were "bathing the female reproductive organs" (cited in Smith-Rosenberg & Rosenberg, 1984:19). Until well into the twentieth century, in fact, the American Medical Association and other medical societies opposed both contraception and abortion as practices that could lead to physical and mental illness in women.

Conventional medical opinion did not go unchallenged, of course. Martha Carey Thomas, president of Bryn Mawr College, said early in this century that while these ideas were widespread, they were "pseudo-scientific." She was not alone in concluding that men who held such attitudes toward women were themselves "pathological, blinded by neurotic mists of sex, unable to see that women form one-half of the kindly race of normal, healthy human creatures in the world" (cited in Bollough & Voght, 1984:34).

interests of surgeons and hospitals as well as the medical needs of patients (Illich, 1976). Some estimates suggest that, at the very least, 10 percent of all elective surgery in the United States could safely be refused or deferred, saving patients more than $1 billion each year. More important, since about one in every two hundred cases of elective surgery results in the death of the patient (because surgery is itself dangerous), perhaps thirteen thousand lives could be saved annually (Sidel & Sidel, 1982a).

From the social-conflict point of view, improving the performance of the American health-care system would involve moving toward the model of socialized medicine, in which health, not profit, is a primary importance.

Health Care as Social Control

Social-conflict analysis also views medical care as a means of social control. Americans have long considered science a means of obtaining objective truth, which is why the scientific model of medicine dominates our understanding of health. Yet, despite the fact that science declares itself to be politically neutral, there is ample evidence that scientific medicine has taken sides in important social issues. The political biases of scientific medicine include resisting the development of government health-care programs. Medical science also has a long history of racial and sexual discrimination, using so-called scientific facts to promote the interests of wealthy white males, who dominate the medical profession (Leavitt, 1984). The box provides several illustrations of scientific medicine's historical support for sexism. Such practices de-

creased considerably as American females and nonwhites achieved greater social equality, but critics contend that there are still social and political biases in the American medical establishment (Zola, 1978; Brown, 1979).

Even today, scientific medicine is criticized as a means of maintaining inequality based on social class. Scientific medicine tends to explain illness largely in terms of bacteria, viruses, or other biological processes rather than in terms of social patterns such as wealth and poverty. From a scientific point of view, in other words, poor people become ill because of poor sanitation, unhealthy diet, and stress, despite the fact that the underlying cause of all these ills may be poverty. Therefore, critics charge, scientific medicine depoliticizes the issue of health in the United States by reducing social and political issues to matters of biological process.

The social-conflict paradigm can certainly be criticized for minimizing the improvements in American health brought about by scientific medicine. Yet this analysis has the strength of showing that scientific medicine is not as wholly positive as most Americans tend to believe.

Despite their different emphases, sociology's three major theoretical paradigms together demonstrate that health and health care are very much social issues. The famous French scientist Louis Pasteur (1822–1895) spent much of his life studying how bacteria cause disease. Just before his death, however, he is reported to have remarked that health depends much less on bacteria than on the social environment in which bacteria operate (Gordon, 1980:7). Explaining Pasteur's insight is sociology's contribution to human health.

SUMMARY

1.   Health is a social and biological issue. Health reflects the extent and distribution of resources in a society. Culture shapes definitions of health, and cultural patterns promote or inhibit health. Cultures shape health care as well.

2.   Through most of human history, health has been relatively poor by contemporary American standards. Dramatic improvement occurred in Western Europe and North America in the nineteenth century because of a rising standard of living, initially due to industrialization, and later to medical advances.

3.   Both the rising standard of living and medical advances curtailed infectious diseases that were the major killers at the beginning of this century. Today most Americans die in old age of heart disease, cancer, or stroke.

4.   In the Third World, patterns of health are extremely poor. Poverty produces poor sanitation and hunger, so that in the poorest nations of the world half of all people born do not survive into adulthood. Average life expectancy is about twenty years less than that in the United States.

5.   In the United States, three-fourths of all children

born today can expect to live to at least age sixty-five. Throughout the life cycle, however, females have relatively better health than males. Similarly, better health characterizes those of higher social position.

6. Industrialization has raised the American standard of living, thus improving health. But environmental pollution—especially from industrial wastes—is a growing problem that threatens the future health of Americans.

7. Cigarette smoking increased during this century to become the greatest preventable cause of death in the United States. But in the face of mounting evidence of the health hazards of smoking and the decreasing social tolerance of smokers, cigarette consumption is now declining.

8. Sexually transmitted diseases are a health issue growing in importance. In the early 1980s, the spread of genital herpes began to transform patterns of sexuality. This change has been reinforced by the spread of AIDS, a fatal and incurable disease.

9. Advancing medical technology has created a growing number of ethical issues surrounding death and the rights of the dying. The ability to artificially sustain life means that death is often a matter of human decision making.

10. Over time, health care was transformed from a family concern to the responsibility of trained specialists. In the United States, health care became dominated by the model of scientific medicine in this century.

11. Holistic medicine is an alternative to the model of conventional, scientific medicine. It is concerned with promoting health, rather than treating disease, through personal knowledge of patients and their environment. It also encourages people to assume responsibility for their own health instead of depending on medical specialists.

12. Socialist societies define medical care as a right. Government-controlled medical-care systems attempt to provide equal benefits to all people.

13. Capitalist societies view medical care as a commodity to be purchased, although most capitalist governments are involved in medical care through programs of socialized medicine or national health insurance.

14. The United States is the only industrialized society with no comprehensive medical-care program. Americans purchase medical care through a direct-fee system. Most Americans have private health insurance, and government insurance or membership in health maintenance organizations help many others to pay the rising costs of medical care. However, one in five Americans does not have adequate means to pay for all medical care.

15. A major contribution of the structural-functional analysis of health is the concept of the sick role, through which people who are ill are typically excused from routine social responsibilities while being expected to cooperate with physicians.

16. The symbolic-interaction paradigm shows that health is largely a matter of subjective perception and social definition.

17. Social-conflict analysis is concerned with the unequal distribution of health and medical care. It criticizes American medical care for its overreliance on drugs and surgery, and for its overemphasis on the biological rather than the social causes of illness.

KEY CONCEPTS

direct-fee system a medical-care system in which patients pay directly for services provided by physicians and hospitals

euthanasia (also **mercy killing**) assisting in the death of a person who is suffering from a painful and incurable illness

health a state of relative physical, mental, and social well-being

health care deliberate activity directed toward improving health

health maintenance organization (HMO) a formal organization that provides comprehensive medical care for which subscribers pay a fixed fee

holistic medicine a medical orientation that seeks to improve health by taking account of the whole person as well as the physical and social environment

medicine a social institution concerned with combating disease as a means to improve health

sick role patterns of behavior that are socially defined as appropriate for those who are ill

social epidemiology the study of the distribution of disease or relative health in a society's population

socialized medicine a health-care system in which most medical facilities are owned and operated by the government, and most physicians are government employees who receive salaries rather than fees collected directly from patients

SUGGESTED READINGS

The first of these books is a paperback text that provides a more detailed look at many of the issues raised in this chapter. The second is a collection of essays about medical sociology by a woman long recognized as an expert in the field.

Howard Schwartz. *Dominant Issues in Medical Sociology.* 2nd ed. New York: Random House, 1987.

Renée C. Fox. *Essays in Medical Sociology.* 2nd ed. New Brunswick, NJ: Transaction, 1987.

The history of the medical establishment in the United States makes for fascinating reading. The first of these books details the emergence of the medical profession. The second provides an account of the changing relations between physicians and patients.

Paul Starr. *The Transformation of American Medicine.* New York: Basic Books, 1982.

Edward Shorter. *Bedside Manners: The Troubled History of Doctors and Patients.* New York: Simon & Schuster, 1985.

The history of medicine is also a tale of conflict between males and females. The first of these books explains how women were systematically excluded from the emerging medical establishment. The second examines how the female occupation of midwifery was gradually replaced by the male specialty of obstetrics.

Regina Markell Morantz-Sanchez. *Sympathy and Science: Women Physicians in American Medicine.* New York: Oxford University Press, 1985.

Jane B. Donegan, *Women & Men Midwives: Medicine, Morality, and Misogyny in Early America.* Westport, CT: Greenwood Press, 1985.

Health and medicine show significant variation from society to society. The first of these books written by an American physician, provides a look at health care in the Soviet Union. The second is a collection of essays examining some of the wide variation of approaches to health and medicine within African societies.

William A. Knaus. *Inside Russian Medicine: An American Doctor's First-Hand Report.* New York: Everest House, 1981.

Brian M. de Toit and Ismail H. Abdalla, eds. *African Healing Strategies.* New York: Trado-Medic, 1985.

Few issues reveal the interplay of medicine and social ethics as much as abortion. The first book explains how and why patterns of abortion differ in the United States and Great Britain. The second, based on interviews of obstetricians and gynecologists, reveals how ethical issues are becoming legal ones as well.

Colin Francome. *Abortion Practice in Britain and the United States.* Winchester, MA: Allen and Unwin, 1986.

Jonathan B. Imber. *Abortion and the Private Practice of Medicine.* New Haven, CT: Yale University Press, 1986.

Complex ethical questions about medically prolonging life and accepting death are examined in this book. Adopting the general position that living longer is not necessarily living better, the author asks if we should—or can afford to—provide unlimited medical care for aging people.

Daniel Callahan. *Setting Limits: Medical Goals in an Aging Society.* New York: Simon and Schuster, 1987.

Here are two recent books concerned with the AIDS epidemic. The first provides an overview of the character and the extent of the problem. The second is a collection of essays by specialists that provide detailed information on various aspects of the disease.

David Black. *The Plague Years: A Chronicle of AIDS, the Epidemic of Our Time.* New York: Simon and Schuster, 1986.

Inge B. Corless and Mary Pittmann-Lindeman. *AIDS: Principles, Practices, and Politics.* New York: Hemisphere Publishing Co., 1987.

A general source of information about health, medicine, and women in American society is the following:

Judith Walzer Levitt. *Women and Health in America.* Madison, WI: University of Wisconsin Press, 1984.

This book tells the story of legal claims based on women's use of the Dalkon shield, a birth control device marketed by A. H. Robins in the early 1970s.

Susan Perry and Jim Dawson. *Nightmare: Women and the Dalkon Shield.* New York: Macmillan, 1985.

This collection of short articles is a good introduction to the holistic approach to health care.

Arthur C. Hastings et al., eds. *Health for the Whole Person: The Complete Guide to Holistic Medicine.* Boulder, CO: Westview Press, 1980.

CHAPTER 20

Population and Urbanization

The first light of dawn shone softly on the mud-brick houses in Catal Hüyük (pronounced Sha-tal Hoo-yook) in what is now Turkey. One of the earliest known cities, Catal Hüyük covered approximately thirty acres (about five square blocks of today's New York) and had a population of perhaps six thousand. This technologically simple society used pieces of flint and sulphur to build fires for light, heat, and cooking. From inside their houses, people could see little of the morning light, because homes were clustered together, each with a single door through the roof reached by a ladder.

In such early settlements, most people practiced small-scale planting and raised sheep. A few traded pottery and fabrics in the surrounding region. At this point in human history—the dawning of civilization some eight thousand years ago—life was short by today's standards: not many people lived beyond their thirties (Hamblin, 1973).

Early permanent settlements such as Catal Hüyük had little in common with such great cities of today as New York, Toronto, or Tokyo. For one thing, the settlements were small both in physical size and in population. Indeed, on the entire earth at that time lived perhaps 20 million people—about as many as found in the largest *cities* of the world today. But these early city dwellers were rare in their own time, for permanent settlements like Catal Hüyük contained only a tiny fraction of the world's population.

The world that emerged during the last eight millennia is beyond the comprehension of our ancestors who lived in such settlements as Catal Hüyük. This chapter examines two dimensions of social change that have had a major impact on human societies: population growth and urbanization. Both have played a central part in forming a world vastly larger in terms of population—now over 5 billion people, a growing proportion of whom live in cities of unprecedented size.

DEMOGRAPHY: THE STUDY OF POPULATION

As Chapter 3 explained, the human species in its present biological form has lived on earth for about forty thousand years. Until about eight thousand years ago—when Catal Hüyük and a few other early cities appeared—the population of the entire earth was quite small and vulnerable to disease and natural disaster. Ironically, perhaps, the world population is now so large and growing so rapidly that some people claim humanity is falling victim to its own fertility.

How this has come about is the focus of the discipline of **demography,** *the study of human population.* Demography (from the Greek words for "description of people") is closely related to sociology, but its primary concern is the quantitative description of population. Demographers study population characteristics such as size, age and sex composition, people's movements from one geographic area to another, and the causes of change in any of these factors. Demography is more than a numbers game, however. It also poses crucial questions about the consequences of population growth, and is thus an exploration of the quality of human life.

Several basic variables are the foundation of demographic analysis.

Fertility

Any study of human population must be concerned with how many people are born. A fundamental concept used by demographers is **fertility,** which is *the incidence of childbearing in a society's population.* Of course, only females of childbearing age—from first menstruation (typically in the early teens) to menopause (usually in the late forties)—are capable of giving birth to children. During some thirty years, then, a woman has the potential to bear well over twenty children. But most women's *fecundity,* or potential number of children, is far greater than their actual number of children owing to health and financial concerns as well as cultural norms.

The measure of fertility most commonly used by demographers is the **crude birth rate:** *the number of live births in a given year for every thousand people in a population.* Demographers calculate crude birth rate by dividing the number of live births in a given year by the total population of a society, then multiplying the result by 1,000. In the United States, there were some 3.7 million live births in 1986 within a total population of about 243 million (U.S. Bureau of the Census, 1987h). Dividing the first number by the second and multiplying the result by 1,000 produces a crude birth rate of 15.3: there were 15.3 live births for every thousand people in the United States in 1986.

Such birth rates are called "crude" because they are calculated on the basis of total population, including males, children, and women past their childbearing years. Thus comparing the crude birth rates of two societies is sometimes misleading, since one society may have a higher proportion of females of childbearing age than another. A crude birth rate also does not reflect the fact that birth rates are likely to differ among people of different races, ethnicities, and religions. But this crude measure of fertility has the advantage of being easy to calculate, and it does provide a good indication of a

About 3.7 million babies were born in the United States in 1986. This number has declined in recent years, in part because people are waiting longer to have children.

society's overall fertility. Table 20–1 shows that the crude birth rates of the United States and other technologically advanced societies are relatively low in world context.

Mortality

Population size is also affected by **mortality,** which is *the incidence of death in a society's population.* The most commonly used measure of mortality is the **crude death rate:** *the number of deaths in a given year for every thousand people in a population.* The crude death rate is calculated in much the same way as the crude birth rate: the number of deaths in a given year is divided by the total population, and the result is multiplied by

1,000. In 1986, there were 2.1 million deaths within the total United States population of 243 million. Dividing the first number by the second and multiplying the answer by 1,000 yields a crude death rate of 8.7. Table 20–1 also provides a comparison of crude death rates in societies around the world. The data show that the crude death rate for the United States is low by world standards.

Another widely used measure of mortality is the

Table 20–1 FERTILITY AND MORTALITY RATES AMONG WORLD SOCIETIES, 1985

	Crude Birth Rate	Crude Death Rate	Infant Mortality Rate
North America			
United States	16	9	10
Canada	15	7	8
Europe			
Belgium	12	12	10
Denmark	10	12	8
France	14	10	9
Spain	11	8	9
United Kingdom	13	12	10
U.S.S.R.	19	11	31
Latin America			
Chile	24	6	22
Cuba	18	6	17
Haiti	36	13	107
Mexico	32	6	42
Puerto Rico	19	7	15
Nicaragua	44	9	69
Africa			
Algeria	42	10	80
Cameroon	44	17	128
Egypt	40	11	105
Ethiopia	44	23	168
Nigeria	46	18	127
South Africa	33	10	86
Asia			
Afghanistan	47	23	182
Bangladesh	44	17	140
India	33	12	101
Israel	23	7	13
Japan	12	6	6
Vietnam	34	9	59

SOURCE: U.S. Bureau of the Census, *World Population Profile: 1985* (Washington, DC: Government Printing Office, 1986), Table 3, pp. 29–33.

infant mortality rate: *the number of deaths within the first year of life for each thousand live births in a given year*. The infant mortality rate is calculated by dividing the number of deaths of children under one year of age by the number of live births during the same year and multiplying the result by 1,000. In 1986, there were 38,000 infant deaths and about 3.7 million live births in the United States. Dividing the first number by the second and multiplying the result by 1,000 produces an infant mortality rate of 10.3. Like the other demographic variables already described, the infant mortality rate is a general statistic concealing the fact that infant mortality varies considerably among different segments of the American population. Over the last several decades, for instance, infant mortality among poor Americans has been twice as high as among the well-to-do (Stockwell, Swanson, & Wicks, 1987).

The infant mortality rate is a general measure of the overall quality of life of any society or any segment of a society. Table 20–1 shows that the infant mortality rates for the United States, Canada, and other rich, technologically advanced societies are considerably lower than those for poor societies with less technological development.

The infant mortality rate has a large impact on any society's **life expectancy,** which is *how long a person, on the average, can expect to live*. American males born in 1985 can expect to live almost 71.2 years, while females can expect to live 78.2 years. In many poor societies of the Third World in which death at childbirth or in infancy is common, life expectancy is often about twenty years less.

Migration

Population size is a function of more than fertility and mortality because people move from one place to another, both within and between societies. In some cases, migration is involuntary, as illustrated by the forcible transport of some 10 million Africans to the western hemisphere as slaves (Sowell, 1981). The motives for more common voluntary migration are often described in terms of *push-pull factors*. Poverty in many rural villages in poor societies of the world is an important push factor, just as the perception of greater opportunity in cities can be a powerful pull factor. As will be explained later in this chapter, migration is a major cause of the rapid growth today of many cities in the Third World. In other cases, people are motivated by religious or political oppression to seek greater freedom elsewhere—a factor related to much migration to the United States. In still other cases, people are seeking a more agreeable climate—a factor related to the migration of many Americans to the Sunbelt in recent decades.

Thus demographers define **migration** as *the movement of people into and out of a specified territory*. The rate at which people move into a territory is described as the *in-migration rate*—in statistical terms, the number of people entering a territory for every thousand people in the total population. The rate of movement out of a territory is called the *out-migration rate*—the number of people leaving a territory for every thousand people in the total population. Because any territory is likely to experience both types of migration simultaneously, demographers describe the difference between in-migration and out-migration as the *net-migration rate*.

Population Growth

Fertility, mortality, and migration affect the population size of any society. Generally speaking, fertility and mortality are the most important. Because fertility and mortality have opposing consequences for population size, demographers subtract the crude death rate from the crude birth rate in order to arrive at the *natural growth rate* of a population. Using the birth and death rates presented above, the natural growth rate of the American population in 1986 was 6.6 per thousand (15.3 crude birth rate minus 8.7 crude death rate), or 0.66 percent annually. This growth rate is low in relation to the overall world growth rate of about 1.6 percent. Indeed, the population of the United States has been growing at a very low rate in recent years, primarily because the crude birth rate has been extremely low.

Figure 20–1 shows that the rates of population growth in the industrialized regions of the world—including Europe (0.5 percent), North America (0.9 percent), and Oceania (1.2 percent)—are well below the world average. In contrast, annual rates of population growth are at or above the world average in regions commonly labeled as Third World—including Asia (1.5 percent), Latin America (2.3 percent), and Africa (3.0 percent). If the current rate of population growth in Africa remains constant, that continent's population will double in roughly twenty-four years. The fact that the poorest regions of the world have the highest rates of population growth is deeply troubling to many population experts. Poor societies typically lack the resources necessary to

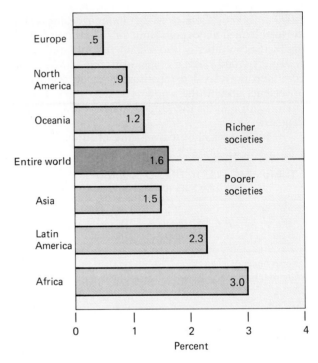

Figure 20–1 Annual Rate of Population Growth by World Region, 1985–1990

(U.S. Bureau of the Census, 1986.)

support the populations they have now, much less the far larger populations they are likely to have in the future.

Population Composition

In addition to studying changes in population size, demographers describe the composition of a society's population at one point in time. A simple variable of this kind is the **sex ratio**, which is *the number of males for every hundred females in a given population*. In 1986, the sex ratio of the population of the United States was 95.2, meaning that there were 95.2 males for every 100 females in the population as a whole. The major reason that the sex ratio is lower than 100 in most societies is that, as indicated in Chapter 12, females typically live longer than males.

A more complex representation of the composition of a population is the **age-sex pyramid**: *a graphic representation of the age and sex of a population*. Figure 20–2 presents the age-sex pyramid for the population of the

United States in 1986. The figure has two sides, graphically showing the number of males of varying ages on the left and the corresponding number of females on the right. The general pyramid shape is primarily the result of the fact that the chances of death increase as people age. For every age category beyond about age thirty, females outnumber males in the American population—a pattern that becomes more and more pronounced with advancing age. The bulge in the pyramid among those between the ages of fifteen and thirty-nine reflects the fact that from the late 1940s to the late 1960s, the United States experienced a particularly high crude birth rate—commonly known as the baby boom. The contraction at the base of the pyramid shows that this period was followed by a baby bust: a sharp decline in the birth rate. From a peak of 25.3 in 1957, the crude birth rate dropped to 15.3 in 1986.

The bulges and contractions in an age-sex pyramid

Figure 20–2 Age-Sex Population Pyramid for the United States, 1986

(U.S. Bureau of the Census, 1987)

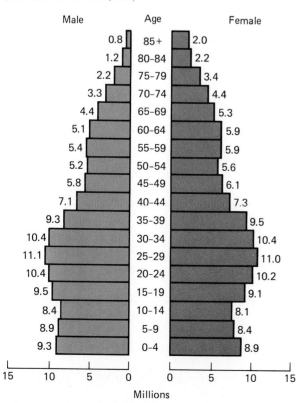

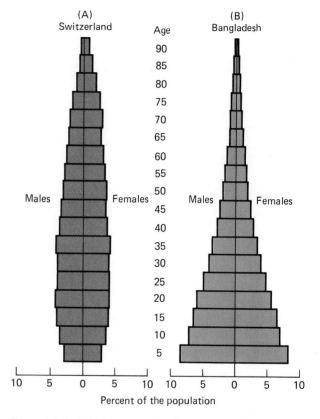

Figure 20–3 The Demographic Composition of Switzerland and Bangladesh

(Newman & Matzke, 1984).

provide a quick summary of the demographic history of a society. Even more important, the age and sex composition today is used to predict future population patterns. Figure 20–3 provides age-sex pyramids for Switzerland and Bangladesh. The relatively boxlike pyramid for Switzerland shows that Swiss society has long had low birth rates, and the contraction of the pyramid under age ten indicates that in recent years the Swiss birth rate has become even lower. With fewer females being born to enter their childbearing years a generation hence, the *natural* population growth of Switzerland is likely to be low. (Keep in mind that migration is not included here—a factor that has increased the Swiss population.) The low natural population increase of Switzerland is typical of industrialized societies.

Bangladesh presents a dramatic contrast. The extremely wide base of this pyramid reveals a very high

Bangladesh is a poor country that is struggling to meet the needs of a large population. With its continuing high birth rate, the population problem is likely to become more serious in the future.

birth rate. The sharp point toward the top of the pyramid reflects high death rates among those beyond what Americans would call middle age. Bangladesh's high birth rate, typical of nonindustrialized societies, bodes ill for the future. The majority of females in Bangladesh have yet to enter their childbearing years. When they do—unless measures are taken to limit births—the population of Bangladesh will explode, placing an even greater strain on already deficient social resources.

HISTORY AND THEORY OF POPULATION GROWTH

Historically, human societies had high birth rates because, without advanced technology, people were a major source of productive power. In addition, before the development of effective means of birth control a century ago, attempts to limit births were uncertain at best. Death rates were also high because people lacked the ability to control disease. With fertility and mortality more or less in balance, population growth in most societies was fairly low. As shown in Figure 20–4, the population of the entire world in the first century C.E. was only about 250 million—more than ten times greater than at the dawning of civilization (about 6000 B.C.E.), yet only comparable to the population of North America today. In Europe, population grew slowly during the Middle

Ages, although gains were periodically erased by outbreaks of disease that took a frightening toll in human lives, such as the Black Death that swept across much of Western Europe in the mid-fourteenth century.

Roughly 250 years ago, however, the population of the earth began to rise sharply, as shown in Figure 20–4, reaching 1 billion by about 1850. Forty thousand years of human reproduction were necessary to bring world population to the 1 billion mark. Yet in 1930—

Figure 20–4 The Growth of World Population

From a level of some 20 million around 6000 B.C.E., world population reached 1 billion by the year 1850. Today over 5 billion people live on the earth. The world's population at the beginning of the twenty-first century is projected to be over 6 billion.

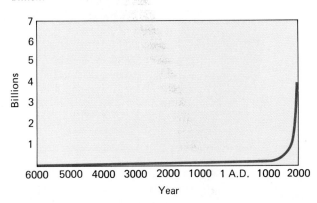

less than a century later—a second billion had been added to the earth's population. In other words, not only did population itself increase, but the *rate* of growth also rose sharply. A third billion was added by about 1962—only an additional thirty-two years—and a fourth billion by 1974—a scant twelve years later. More recently, the rate of world population growth slowed somewhat, but the 5 billion mark was reached in mid-1987. In no previous century had the world's population even doubled. In the twentieth century, however, it has increased about *fourfold*.

Demographic projections are always a matter of informed guesswork. Current projections are that world population will exceed 6 billion early in the twenty-first century, probably reaching the 8 billion mark by the year 2025 (Gupte, 1984; Russell, 1984). There is little wonder, then, that the size of the world's population has become a matter of urgent concern.

Malthusian Theory

Attempts to explain the rapid population growth that began a few centuries ago and to understand its effects on human life stimulated the development of demography. One early and influential demographer was Thomas Robert Malthus (1766–1834), an English clergyman and economist, whose theory of population growth predicted impending social chaos. Malthus (1926; orig. 1798) realized that world population in the late eighteenth century was increasing at a faster and faster rate. He explained this as the result of a high birth rate, reflecting the timeless passion between the sexes. Thus he expected that population would increase according to what mathematicians call a geometric progression, as illustrated by the series of numbers 2, 4, 8, 16, 32, and so on. Following this pattern, Malthus concluded, world population would soon reach numbers beyond human comprehension.

Malthus thought food production would also increase, but only in arithmetic progression, as illustrated by the series of numbers 2, 3, 4, 5, 6, and so on. This was because, despite technological innovations in agriculture, the land available for farming would always be limited. Thus Malthus was led to a conclusion as obvious as it is troubling: the world would face an increasing shortage of food leading ultimately to widespread starvation.

Malthus believed that two kinds of factors might limit population growth: *positive checks*, including disease and war; and *preventive checks*, including artificial means of birth control, sexual abstinence, and delayed marriages. Because of his religious beliefs, Malthus rejected artificial birth control. Furthermore, he believed that people were only likely to abstain from sex or marry later when faced with widespread famine. For this reason, his view of the future was pessimistic indeed, earning him the title of the "dismal parson."

Had Malthus's analysis been precisely accurate, many of us would not be here today. Indeed, as predictions about the future of humanity often are, Malthus's analysis turned out to be flawed in several respects. First, by the middle of the nineteenth century, the birth rate in Europe began to drop, so that population growth was not as rapid as he had feared. As industrialization proceeded, children became less of an economic asset and more of an economic liability. In addition, despite the continuing formal objections of the Roman Catholic Church and others who share Malthus's religious views, artificial methods of birth control became widespread, further limiting population increase. Second, Malthus underestimated the human capacity to generate more food and other basic resources. Advances in irrigation, fertilizers, and pesticides have greatly increased the productivity of farmers, and industrial technology has resulted in unforeseen increases in the production of other goods. Third, Malthus overlooked the important fact that people's experience of famine and other shortages of material resources depends on their position in society. Thus Karl Marx (1967; orig. 1867) sharply criticized Malthus for attributing to a "law of nature" human suffering that was, in Marx's view, the result of the capitalist economy.

Yet we cannot entirely dismiss Malthus's dire prediction. First, many necessary resources such as habitable land and clean water are certainly finite. The same technology that has boosted economic productivity has also created new and threatening problems, such as environmental pollution described in Chapter 19. Twentieth-century advances in health technology have also been responsible for greatly lowering the death rate around the world, thus stimulating an unprecedented increase in world population.

Second, we must not narrowly judge the effects of the world's huge and increasing population in terms of the quality of life in North America—perhaps the richest region of the world. Population growth is currently highest in the poorest societies of Africa, Asia, and Latin America. The catastrophic starvation of people in northern Africa that shocked the world in the early 1980s shows only too clearly that resources in many societies are already strained to the breaking point. Perhaps one-fourth of the world's people remain in jeopardy.

Third, although the rate of population increase has unquestionably been far below that feared by Malthus, in the long run at least, *no rate of population growth is acceptable* (Ehrlich, 1978). Whether population grows quickly or slowly, in other words, the limited water, food, and land cannot sustain indefinite growth.

Demographic Transition Theory

Malthus's rather crude analysis has been superseded in recent decades by **demographic transition theory:** *the thesis that population patterns are linked to a society's level of technological development.*

Demographic transition theory links demographic patterns to three distinct stages of technological development, as shown in Figure 20–5. In *Stage 1,* typical of preindustrial agrarian societies, birth rates are high, both because children are a valuable source of human labor and because there are no effective means of birth control. Death rates, too, are high, owing to the generally low standard of living and the absence of advanced medical technology—a situation in which infectious diseases are commonplace, as described in Chapter 19. Under these conditions, population increase is very gradual. This explains the world's modest population increase for thousands of years before the Industrial Revolution began in eighteenth-century Europe.

Stage 2, the beginning of the demographic transition, coincides with industrialization. Advancing technology expands food supplies and provides effective means of combating disease. Birth rates remain high, but death rates fall sharply, with rapid population growth the predictable result. Not surprisingly, Malthus devel-

oped his ideas about population growth when English society was at this stage of technological development during the century or so following the onset of the Industrial Revolution.

In *Stage* 3, a society has a fully developed industrial economy. With a higher standard of living, and the considerably higher costs of raising children, large families are an economic liability rather than an asset. More women begin to work outside of the home. Sophisticated technology makes effective birth control widely available. Birth rates begin to fall into line with low death rates, producing, once again, a rough balance of fertility and mortality with only slow population growth. This has been the case in Western industrial societies for much of this century.

Demographic transition theory certainly provides more grounds for optimism than does Malthusian theory. While Malthus foresaw a runaway population increase, demographic transition theorists foresee technological development creating both a lower rate of population growth and more material resources to sustain the population.

However, one controversy surrounding demographic transition theory is its implication that all societies of the world will follow the path of development of European societies over the last few centuries. Technological development has not occurred uniformly throughout the world. Thus, although societies in North America and Western Europe fall within Stage 3, the majority of the world's people live in societies that are in Stage 2 of high population growth. Therefore, the world today can be divided into two very different categories: industrial societies in which population growth is low, and less technologically developed societies in which population growth is producing problems whose seriousness we are only beginning to grasp.

World Population Today

Living amid low population growth and a high standard of living, Americans have little direct experience of the population problems common to most of the world. Demographic transition theory suggests how and why population patterns differ within the world today.

Industrialized Societies

At the beginning of the Industrial Revolution, Western Europe and North America had high rates of population

Figure 20–5 Demographic Transition Theory

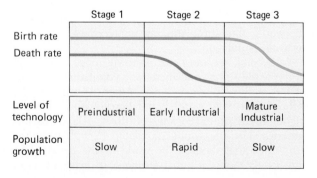

growth—about 3 percent annually. Population growth declined as industrialization continued, and has remained below 1 percent annually in the United States since 1970. The United States, Canada, and other mature industrial societies are all in Stage 3 of demographic transition theory, characterized by low population growth. Indeed, in recent years, the United States and most societies in Western Europe have fallen below the population replacement level of 2.1 births per woman, a point often described as **zero population growth,** or *the level of reproduction that maintains population at a steady state.* Indeed, in several European societies, a *natural decrease* in population has already been noted. This decline in the birth rate has led some analysts to suggest that a *second demographic transition* is under way by which, at most, Europe's population will increase slightly during the next several generations (van de Kaa, 1987). The population of the United States is still relatively young—with a median age of 31.8 in 1986—so for at least several decades population growth will continue. Yet as the median age of Americans rises during

the next century (discussed in Chapter 13), the point of zero population growth may be reached.

The higher costs of raising children, the increasing proportion of women in the labor force, and the growing numbers of people who choose to marry at a later age or to remain childless are contributing factors. The use of contraceptives by married American women has also increased within the last generation, to about two-thirds of women in the childbearing years. An especially notable pattern is the dramatic increase in voluntary sterilization—now the most common form of birth control in the United States. American Catholics, whose religious doctrine continues to prohibit the use of any form of artificial birth control, no longer differ from other religious categories of Americans in their use of artificial birth control (Westoff & Jones, 1977; Moore & Pachon, 1985). Since the legalization of abortion in 1973, the number of pregnancies terminated in this manner has steadily increased—to some 1.3 million in 1983 (Ellerbrock et al., 1987). Poor Americans still tend to have somewhat larger than average families and, as noted in

The birthrate in France dropped so low that the government turned to advertising to encourage citizens to have children. The ad implies that babies are becoming so rare that this one can remark: "It appears that I am a sociocultural phenomenon." At the bottom right is added, "France needs children."

Il paraît que je suis un phénomène socio-culturel.

LA FRANCE A BESOIN D'ENFANTS.

Chapter 10, the largest category of poor people in the United States is children. Yet, in world context, population growth in this and other relatively rich industrial societies is of minor concern compared to the much more rapid population growth in poor societies.

Nonindustrialized Societies

Few societies today remain completely untouched by the technological advances related to industrialization. In terms of demographic transition theory, only a handful of very small, isolated societies remain within Stage 1, with high birth rates, high death rates, and relatively low overall population growth. Many societies with predominantly agrarian economies have begun to industrialize, thus entering Stage 2 with high population growth. Furthermore, across Latin America, Africa, and Asia, gradual advances in medical technology (often imported from industrialized societies) have sharply reduced death rates while birth rates remain high. As shown in Figure 20–6, these regions have long accounted for most of the earth's population, and about 80 percent of the world's population growth in this century has also been in poor societies collectively known as the Third World. By the beginning of the next century, poor societies are expected to contain about three-fourths of the 6 billion people on earth (Piotrow, 1980).

Birth rates remain high within Third World societies for many of the same reasons they were high everywhere on earth for thousands of years. In agrarian societies, children are important economic assets, often working eight or ten hours a day to contribute to their families' income. Parents also typically look to their children for economic support in old age. In light of the economic value of children and high mortality among infants and children, parents understandably wish to have large families. Throughout the Third World, about four or five children is average for a family; in rural areas, the number is often higher (The World Bank, 1984).

The social position of women is also a crucial factor in today's population picture. As discussed in previous chapters, gender inequality is still strong in agrarian societies, where cultural patterns strictly enforce male authority. Although females in such societies play an important role in economic production, bearing and raising children are still considered their primary responsibilities. Thus in Latin America, for example, most women understand contraception, but a combination of economic need, traditional patriarchy, and Roman

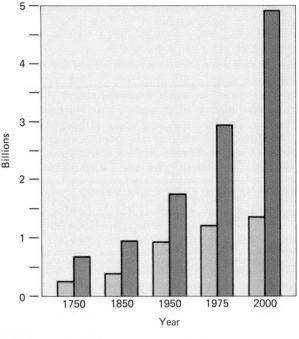

Figure 20–6 Population Distribution, Industrial and Nonindustrial Societies, 1750–2000

(Piotrow, 1980)

Catholic doctrine greatly inhibits their use. Across the continent of Africa, on the other hand, women in poor villages often know little about effective forms of birth control, a fact directly linked to that continent's higher overall fertility (Salas, 1985). Asia represents a mixed case. In many Asian countries, women are completely without effective contraception, while in others—including India and China—bold programs to control birth rates have been launched by the government. The box provides a closer look at the current situation in China, the world's most populous society and one in which the government takes a heavy hand in family planning.

The connection between the social standing of women and population growth involves much more than contraception. There is a practical realization that women allowed no alternative to the traditional roles of child rearing and homemaking are likely to have the greatest number of children, thus fueling world popula-

CROSS-CULTURAL COMPARISON

Birth Control in China

Many Third World governments have recently responded to rapid population growth with a variety of programs aimed at reducing family size. In the People's Republic of China—which entered the 1980s with more than 1 billion people (then almost one-fourth of the world's population)—the government adopted a heavy-handed approach in the desperate struggle to limit fertility.

The problem is simple to see, yet difficult to solve. More than half the Chinese people are under thirty, raising the specter of a baby boom without parallel in human history. To avoid this demographic nightmare, in 1979 the Chinese government developed a tough new policy designed to limit the country's population to 1.2 billion by the end of this century. To accomplish this, Chinese couples are expected to have no more than one child.

Family planning has become defined as each couple's social responsibility. Local teams of family planning officials strongly encourage couples to delay childbirth or, if they have a child already, to submit to sterilization or abort subsequent pregnancies. A broad program of incentives also encourages one-child families. Couples who have only one child receive financial rewards and can expect their child to be given priority in school enrollment and, later, in employment and housing. Reduced pay punishes those who have more children.

China has had some success in limiting its population growth: the 2.0 percent annual growth rate during the

Population policies often have unanticipated consequences. By limiting families to a single child on which parents and grandparents lavish attention, many Chinese are worried that they are raising a generation of "little emperors."

1960s dropped to 1.8 percent by 1980. But the new policies have spawned a number of problems. First, as Chapter 18 explained, China has also recently begun a program of incentives to encourage greater economic growth. In the countryside, farmers who grow more now earn more—making larger families to work the fields more profitable. Thus popula-

tion control and economic growth now work at cross purposes in rural areas. Second, widespread sterilization in China has raised the suspicion that many people underwent surgery against their will. The third problem is perhaps the most dismaying: female infanticide—a long-established pattern in male-dominated Chinese society—may be unintentionally encouraged by the one-child policy. Chinese cultural tradition gives to sons the responsibility of caring for elderly parents. Daughters, on the other hand, serve their husband's parents. Since there is no national retirement program, few Chinese couples wish to face old age without a son. Thus most hope their one child will be a boy. In at least some cases, first-born girls are killed so that the couple may try again for a male. Although infanticide is a crime in China, some rural areas contain as many as five boys for each girl—suggesting that this age-old practice is far from eradicated.

Without doubt, the Chinese government's ambitious plan to curtail population growth is generating great social strains. Yet the alternative appears even worse: at the present rate of growth, the population would double about the year 2025, causing a significant decline in an already struggling society's standard of living.

SOURCE: Based on Melinda Beck, "An Unwanted Baby Boom," *Newsweek*, April 30, 1984, p. 47; *World Development Report 1984* (New York: Oxford University Press, 1984); and "China's Program: 'Voluntary, not Coercive,'" *Popline*, Vol. 7, No. 2 (February 1985): 3.

tion growth. Women given the opportunity to gain a formal education and more economic power not only contribute to their society's economic development, but also have fewer children. Research has shown, for example, that in Sudan (Africa) and Colombia (South America) women with seven years of schooling had half as many children as those without any education. As they gain an education, women not only become more aware of contraception, but actually wish to have smaller families, which greatly reduces birth rates (Ross, 1985; Salas, 1985).

Efforts to control population growth have met with some success: in many Third World societies, average family size fell by over 20 percent between 1975 and 1985. The decline is expected to continue until the end of this century, although at a slower rate (Salas, 1985). But birth rates remain relatively high in world perspective, and this factor, coupled with declining death rates, means that rapid population growth throughout the Third World will continue.

Actually, *most* population growth in the Third World is due to declining death rates. Advances in scientific medicine, nutrition, and sanitation began to reduce the death rates in Europe and North America soon after the onset of the Industrial Revolution. This technology was gradually exported to Third World countries, so that by the end of World War I, a sharp decline in death rates began in Latin America, Africa, and Asia. Inoculations against infectious diseases, antibiotics, and insecticides reduced the death rates with stunning effectiveness. Malaria, for example, was a savage killer in many parts of the world. In Sri Lanka, a malaria epidemic was responsible for perhaps half of all deaths in the mid-1930s. In 1946, however, Sri Lanka (then the British colony of Ceylon) began to use the insecticide DDT to kill malaria-carrying mosquitoes. Within a decade, this highly successful program cut the death rate in half (Ehrlich, 1978). There is good reason to rejoice at such an achievement, but the long-run effect was a dramatic increase in Sri Lanka's population.

By the standards of richer societies, infant mortality and average life expectancy remain quite unfavorable throughout the Third World. Yet they have improved dramatically over the course of this century. More children survive to adulthood—in the process, of course, having more children of their own. The current annual growth rate of about 2 percent will double the population of Asia in only thirty-five years; a 3 percent growth rate will double the population of Africa in only twenty-four years. Newly instituted birth control programs in such areas of the world are an attempt to limit the sharp increase in population growth resulting from successful

In developing nations, children are an economic asset because their labor provides much-needed household income. This situation contributes to high fertility rates in such areas.

programs of "death control" several generations ago (Piotrow, 1980).

The Importance of Demography

The statistical picture of changing population generated by demography is vital to understanding how and why the earth is gaining unprecedented population. Only in this way can humankind address many pressing problems.

The technological advances that caused the populations of Europe and North America to grow during the past centuries simultaneously provided better standards of living. Today, however, technological advances are stimulating unprecedented population growth in societies that do not have the productive capacity to cope with their present populations, much less with what the next century is likely to bring. Population growth is therefore clearly linked to the world economic patterns discussed in Chapter 18. While a small proportion of humanity lives in rich societies that are, in world context, *over*developed economically, the majority face at best an uncertain future. The picture is made even bleaker by the fact that population is growing fastest in the poorest societies of the world.

At present, the problems of feeding a hungry world are overwhelming. The next century promises even greater problems of housing, educating, and employing billions of people. For years, many members of rich societies have felt complacently isolated from the harsh realities of life in the Third World. The rising tide of terrorism during the 1980s—much of it carried out by members of poor societies who perceive the rich industrialized societies as the cause of their problems—has made Americans more aware of the widespread frustration and anguish in the world. The peace of the entire planet may ultimately depend on resolving many of the economic and social problems of poor, overly populated countries and on bridging the widening gulf between the have and have-not societies of the world. After describing the population growth of recent decades as "a great wave," one official of the United States government concluded:

> I see the world population movement as the effort to construct a breakwater—a structure that will stop the wave and prevent it from engulfing and sweeping away centuries of human development and civilization. (cited in Gupte, 1984:323)

URBANIZATION: THE GROWTH OF CITIES

At the dawning of human civilization in the Middle East some eight thousand years ago, widely scattered settlements such as Çatal Hüyük—described at the beginning of this chapter—each contained only a few thousand people. Taken together, early city dwellers were a tiny fraction of the earth's population. Today each of the largest cities in the world contains roughly the earth's entire population at the time of Çatal Hüyük. The future promises to bring further dramatic changes, as many cities in the world become larger still.

Population increase has certainly been a significant cause of social change. But just as important is **urbanization**: *humanity's increasing concentration within limited geographical areas called cities*. Urbanization not only changes the distribution of population within a society; it also transforms many patterns of social life.

The Evolution of Cities

Cities are a relatively recent development in the long course of human history. Although members of our biological species have inhabited this planet for some 2 million years, human beings first created permanent settlements only about ten thousand years ago. For most of human history, people lived in small groups that survived by hunting animals and gathering vegetation in the wild. As described in Chapter 4, hunting and gathering peoples were constantly on the move in search of food. While some migrating groups periodically returned to favored locations, no settlements were occupied permanently. About ten thousand years ago, however, two major factors set the stage for the *first urban revolution*: the emergence of permanent settlements.

The first factor was *ecological*: as glaciers began to melt at the end of the last ice age, warm and fertile soil drew people to particular regions of the earth. The second was *technological*: about the same time, humans began to develop the technology to raise animals and crops, giving rise to the horticultural and pastoral societies described in Chapter 4. Applied in ecologically favorable areas, advancing technology permitted people to produce a surplus, far more food than most hunters and gatherers had known. Raising crops and animals required people to remain in one place, just as hunting and gathering previously demanded continual movement (Lenski &

Lenski, 1982). Furthermore, a material surplus freed some people from food production, allowing them to build shelters, make tools and clothing, and serve as religious leaders. A surplus of food, then, raised the standard of living above the subsistence level and gave human beings the opportunity to create labor-saving devices and numerous other material artifacts that were not easily transportable. Thus the founding of urban settlements was truly revolutionary because it was the beginning of social life characterized by productive specialization.

The First Cities

Human beings developed permanent settlements gradually, and it is difficult to say precisely when this form of settlement warranted the term *city*. Some archaeologists suggest that Jericho, a settlement to the north of the Dead Sea in disputed land currently occupied by Israel, could be called the first city. About 8000 B.C.E., Jericho had an estimated population of six hundred—barely a small town by contemporary standards—but the presence of thick walls suggests the organized work of specialists that gave Jericho an urban character (Kenyon, 1957; Hamblin, 1973; Spates & Macionis, 1987).

Archaeological evidence shows that, following Jericho, somewhat larger permanent settlements developed in the Middle East, including Catal Hüyük in present-day Turkey. About 4000 B.C.E., numerous cities were flourishing in the Fertile Crescent region between the Tigris and Euphrates rivers in present-day Iraq and, soon afterward, along the Nile River in Egypt. Some of these cities contained perhaps fifty thousand people and became the centers of urban empires whose economic and military power spread over large regions. These urban empires were distinguished by highly complex social structures featuring a pronounced division of labor and rigid patterns of social stratification. Leaders who served as both kings and priests wielded absolute power over lesser nobility, administrators, artisans, soldiers, and farmers. Slaves, captured in frequent military campaigns, provided the labor used to build the urban empires' characteristically monumental architecture such as the pyramids of Egypt (Wenke, 1980; Stavrianos, 1983; Lenski & Lenski, 1987).

Cities also originated independently in at least three other ecologically favorable areas of the world. Several large and complex cities existed in the Indus River region of present-day Pakistan about 2500 B.C.E. Chinese cities are believed to date from at least 2000 B.C.E. In Central

Early urban settlements in Latin America often took the form of ceremonial centers. Shown here is the Pyramid of the Sun at Teotihuacán, near Mexico City.

and South America, urban centers can be traced back to about 1500 B.C.E. Significant urbanization in North America, however, did not begin until the arrival of European settlers in the sixteenth century (Lamberg-Karlovsky, 1973; Change, 1977; Coe & Diehl, 1980).

Preindustrial Cities in Europe

European urbanization began about 1800 B.C.E. on the Mediterranean island of Crete, probably as a result of the expanding trade between cities in the Middle East. Urbanism gradually spread throughout Greece—resulting in more than one hundred city-states, of which Athens is by far the most famous. Especially during its Golden Age—from about 500 B.C.E. to the beginning of the Peloponnesian War in 431 B.C.E.—Athens stood apart as a historical example of the positive potential of urban life. The Athenians, numbering some 300,000 in an area of roughly one square mile, developed many elements of culture that are still central to the Western way of life, including philosophy, the arts, the principles of democracy, and an emphasis on physical—as well as mental—fitness, symbolized by the Olympic games (Mumford, 1961; Carlton, 1977; Stavrianos, 1983).

The achievements of Athenian society cannot be overestimated, but Athenian glory—like that of earlier cities—was built largely on the labor of slaves, who accounted for perhaps one-third of the population. Their democratic principles notwithstanding, Athenian males denied the rights of citizenship to Athenian females and to foreigners in their midst (Mumford, 1961; Gouldner, 1965).

As the brilliant Greek civilization faded, the city

of Rome, with roughly 1 million inhabitants, became the center of a growing empire. By the first century C.E., the Roman Empire encompassed much of northern Africa, Europe, and the Middle East. Like that of the Greeks, the urban civilization of the Romans profoundly shaped later Western culture in terms of language, arts, and technological innovations. Yet, unlike Athens, Rome extended its cultural influence primarily through the use of imperialistic military power. In addition to almost continual military campaigns, Rome transformed the brutal killing of human beings—usually slaves from its subject territories—into public spectacles that were more popular than football is with us today (Mumford, 1961). In the striking contrast between these two early forms of European urbanism, we can see how very different cultural forces produce distinctive cities (Spates & Macionis, 1987).

By the fifth century C.E., the Roman Empire was in disarray, a victim of its own gargantuan size, internal corruption, and militaristic appetite. During the millennium between the Athenian Golden Age and the decline of Rome, numerous cities—including London, Paris, and Vienna—were founded all across Europe. The fall of the Roman Empire, however, initiated a period of urban decline and stagnation throughout Europe. Cities that had once contained between 50,000 and 100,000 people became mere towns of perhaps half that size. These medieval towns, containing perhaps 10 percent of the European population, were typically walled for protection against competing warlords who battled one another for territory and power.

After the eleventh century, a revival of trade sparked by the Christian Crusades to the Middle East breathed new life into European cities such as Venice and Florence. First in southern Europe and then gradually in the north, cities slowly but steadily grew as trade expanded once again.

Since most economic activity still occurred in the home, the preindustrial cities of Europe were not divided into commercial, residential, and manufacturing districts as our cities are today. The narrow, winding, and usually filthy streets of London, Brussels, and Florence—suited to pedestrian traffic and a slow pace of life—were typically teeming with people from all walks of life: artisans, merchants, priests, peddlers, jugglers, nobles, and servants emptying slop jars into gutters. The preeminence of the Christian religion in medieval life was signified by the cathedrals that dominated the architecture of European cities. Other buildings were rarely more than two or three stories high. The small scale of these cities—intensi-

fied by their enclosure within walls—produced in the visitor little of the awe aroused by the monumental temples of ancient Rome or the towering commercial skyscrapers of present-day New York.

Social life was surprisingly personal by our standards; the majority of people living in a medieval city had at least some personal knowledge of one another (Sjoberg, 1965). Family ties were strong, and those who practiced a particular trade or shared religious and ethnic traditions clustered together in distinctive urban neighborhoods or quarters. At the same time, the social hierarchy of nobility, priests, merchants, and impoverished workers was extremely rigid. Females had few legal rights, and ethnic and religious minorities were often forcibly restricted to certain districts of the city. Jews, for example, were targets of extensive prejudice and discrimination in an era when the Roman Catholic Church was the dominating social force. First in Venice, and subsequently throughout most of Europe, Jews were confined to a limited area of the city known as the *ghetto*.

Industrial-Capitalist Cities in Europe

In many respects, the walled medieval city was a world unto itself. But the small scale of urban living was to change with the flowering of industrial capitalism after about 1700.

Throughout the Middle Ages, steadily increasing commerce filled the pockets of an expanding urban middle class or bourgeoisie (a French word literally meaning "of the town"). Although, as noted in earlier chapters, a hereditary nobility exists to this day in many European societies, by the late Middle Ages the balance of power was shifting to the bourgeoisie because of its commercial wealth. The European colonization of much of the rest of the world beginning in the fifteenth century also immeasurably bolstered the economies of Europe.

A *second urban revolution* occurred in Europe—and subsequently in North America—as the economic power unleashed by industrial technology reached unprecedented heights beginning in the eighteenth century. As shown in Table 20–2, the populations of European cities began to soar during this period. In part, this was due to natural population growth, as noted earlier in this chapter. Just as important, however, was migration from rural areas to the expanding industrial cities as Europeans sought a better standard of living. The population of all German cities, for example, was roughly 2.5 million at the beginning of the nineteenth century. A century later, this figure had increased over *five-fold* to

Table 20–2 POPULATION GROWTH IN SELECTED INDUSTRIAL CITIES OF EUROPE (IN THOUSANDS)

City	Year			
	1700	1800	1900	1987
Amsterdam	172	201	510	679
Berlin	100	172	2,424	3,055
Lisbon	188	237	363	807
London	550	861	6,480	6,768
Madrid	110	169	539	2,119
Paris	530	547	3,330	2,118
Rome	149	153	487	2,826
Vienna	105	231	1,662	1,489

SOURCE: Based on data from Tertius Chandler and Gerald Fox, *3000 Years of Urban History* (New York: Academic Press, 1974), pp. 17–19; and *The Statesman's Year-Book 1987–1988*, 124th ed. (New York: St. Martin's Press, 1987).

13 million. Likewise, during the nineteenth century, Paris grew from 500,000 to over 3 million, and the population of London soared from about 800,000 to 6.5 million (A. Weber, 1963, orig. 1899; Chandler & Fox, 1974).

Cities changed in other ways as well. Commerce—but one dimension of life in the medieval city—became the dominant cultural element in the industrial-capitalist city. This was evident in the changing physical shape of cities: the irregular street pattern of the medieval city gave way to broad, straight streets able to accommodate a vastly larger flow of commercial traffic and, in time, motor vehicles. Lewis Mumford (1961) explains that the city was divided into regular-sized lots so that land became a commodity to be bought and sold as part of the expanding capitalist economy. Moreover, the cathedral as a focal point was displaced by a central business district of offices, banks, and retail stores. Steam and electricity soon powered trolleys that crisscrossed European cities, and advancing technology made possible ever-higher buildings—monuments to the power of the capitalist economy.

Urban social life was also transformed. As cities grew, they also became more impersonal, crowded, unsanitary, and dangerous. Work in the home was replaced by daily travel to large, anonymous factories and bureaucratic commercial offices (Laslett, 1984). Industrial pollution filled the air: London fog at its worst was a deadly killer. Crime rates rose. Men, women, and children who worked long hours in factories for little pay suffered greatly, while the small number of industrialists lived in grand style. To make matters worse, cities were unable to absorb the tremendous influx of people drawn by the promise of a better life.

Table 20–2 shows that European cities continued to grow during the twentieth century. In response to the political demands of workers for a better standard of living, legislation mandated minimal dwelling standards. Public services—including water, sewage, and electricity—gradually improved workers' living conditions further. Today poverty remains the daily plight of millions of city dwellers, but the wealth produced by industrialization is largely responsible for the better life that has been the historical attraction of the city.

American Cities

Although Native Americans have lived in North America for tens of thousands of years, they established few permanent settlements. Cities in North America were a product of European colonization beginning in the sixteenth century. The Spanish made an initial settlement at St. Augustine, Florida, in 1565, and the English founded Jamestown, Virginia, in 1607. Both settlements remained quite small, however, so that one should probably begin the story of American urbanization with the founding of New Amsterdam (later called New York) in 1624 by the Dutch. Today the United States is one of the most urban societies in the world: more than three-fourths of all Americans live in urban places that make up only about 16 percent of the land area of the United States. The corporate-based economy, national political system, mass media, colleges and universities, and most other elements of American life are largely city-based. The beginnings of this remarkable transformation of a wilderness into an urban civilization are found in the colonial era.

Colonial Settlement: 1624–1800

American urban history began as Europeans arrived on the eastern edge of a vast, unknown territory. The Dutch settlement of New Amsterdam at the tip of Manhattan Island (1624) and the English Puritan settlement of Boston (1630) were initially small villages. In their early years, they resembled medieval European cities, with narrow, winding streets that are still evident in lower Manhattan and downtown Boston. New Amsterdam was

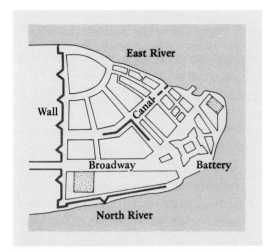
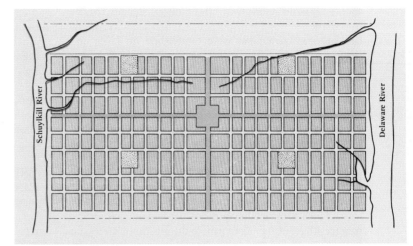

Figure 20–7 The Street Plans of Colonial New Amsterdam and Philadelphia

The plan of colonial New Amsterdam, shown on the left, reflects the preindustrial urban pattern of walls enclosing a city of narrow, irregular streets. Colonial Philadelphia—founded fifty years later—reflects the industrial urban pattern of accessible cities containing wide, regular streets to facilitate economic activity.

also walled on the north, on the site of today's Wall Street. Boston was the largest colonial city in 1700 with a population of only seven thousand.

Other American cities founded in the seventeenth century included Newport, Rhode Island (1639), Charles Town (later Charleston), South Carolina (1680), and Philadelphia (1680). By the final decades of the century, Philadelphia had adopted a gridlike street pattern to facilitate commercial activities. Figure 20–7 contrasts the regular physical design of Philadelphia with the irregular design of New Amsterdam, founded some fifty years earlier.

American cities grew slowly during the eighteenth century, remaining small enough so that residents lived within a network of personal relationships. Without the industrial technology to allow rapid movement, colonial cities were cities of pedestrians.

At this point, the United States was far from an urban society. In 1790, the government's first census counted roughly 4 million Americans. As shown in Table 20–3, only about 5 percent of them lived in urban places.

Urban Expansion: 1800–1860

Early in the nineteenth century, dozens of new cities were formally established from coast to coast. This urban expansion was the result of transportation routes that opened the American West. The National Road (now Interstate 40) linked Baltimore to the Ohio Valley in 1818; a decade later, the Baltimore and Ohio Railroad made the transportation of people and products far more efficient. The Erie Canal (1825) connected New York to the Great Lakes, sparking the development of cities

Table 20–3 THE URBAN POPULATION OF THE UNITED STATES, 1790–1986

Year	Population (millions)	Percent Urban
1790	3.9	5.1
1800	5.3	6.1
1820	9.6	7.3
1840	17.1	10.5
1860	31.4	19.7
1880	50.2	28.1
1900	76.0	39.7
1920	105.7	51.3
1940	131.7	56.5
1960	179.3	69.9
1980	226.5	73.7
1986	243.8	76.6

SOURCE: U.S. Bureau of the Census.

such as Buffalo, Cleveland, and Detroit. Because of the importance of water transportation at this point in American history, most cities were established on lakes and rivers.

By 1860, about one-third of Americans lived in urban places, and cities were coming to dominate the American way of life. What some greeted as progress and modernization, however, others mourned as the passing of a traditional agrarian life, based on self-reliance. During this period of American history, rural-urban tensions were pronounced: many urbanites adopted negative stereotypes of "ignorant country cousins," while rural residents criticized the rising number of "untrustworthy city slickers" in the United States (Callow, 1969).

The Industrial Revolution that began early in the nineteenth century transformed the northern states far more than the states in the largely agricultural South. Thus urbanization was primarily a northern development. By 1850, for example, the population of New York City was about ten times greater than that of Charleston. This division of the United States into the industrial-urban North and the agrarian-rural South was one underlying cause of the Civil War (Schlesinger, 1969).

The Metropolitan Era: 1860–1950

As industrialization had sparked an urban revolution in Europe, so it did in North America, reaching full intensity after the Civil War. Millions of Americans migrated from rural areas to cities whose factories offered greater economic opportunity. In the final decades of the nineteenth century, in fact, the population of almost half of rural America actually declined (Glaab, 1963). As was explained in Chapter 11, during this period cities also absorbed tens of millions of immigrants, primarily from Europe. Table 20–4 shows the rapid growth that characterized many American cities during the final decades of the nineteenth century.

By the beginning of the twentieth century, New York boasted some 4 million residents. Chicago, a city of only 100,000 in 1860, was approaching the 2 million mark in 1900. The city of the early nineteenth century became the twentieth-century **metropolis**—*a very large city that socially and economically dominates a broad urban area.* Cities at the core of *metropolitan areas*, became huge commercial, manufacturing, and residential centers influencing numerous smaller cities and towns in the surrounding region.

Furthermore, industrial technology changed the physical shape of American cities. Until about 1850, few buildings exceeded three or four stories. By the 1880s, however, steel girders and mechanical elevators made building over ten stories possible. In 1930, the Empire State Building in New York became an urban wonder, a true "skyscraper" reaching 102 stories into the clouds. Transportation technology also enabled cities to expand outward, allowing the movement of people and goods

Table 20–4 POPULATION GROWTH IN SELECTED AMERICAN CITIES, 1870–1986

City	Population (in thousands)						
	1870	1890	1910	1930	1950	1970	1986
Baltimore	267	434	558	805	950	905	753
Boston	251	448	671	781	801	641	574
Chicago	299	1,100	2,185	3,376	3,621	3,369	3,010
Dallas	7	38	92	260	434	844	1,004
Detroit	80	206	466	1,569	1,850	1,514	1,086
Los Angeles	6	50	319	1,238	1,970	2,812	3,259
Milwaukee	71	204	374	578	637	717	605
New Orleans	191	242	339	459	570	593	555
New York*	942	2,507	4,767	6,930	7,892	7,896	7,263
Philadelphia	674	1,047	1,549	1,951	2,072	1,949	1,643
St. Louis	311	452	687	822	857	622	426
San Francisco	149	299	417	634	775	716	749

SOURCE: U.S. Bureau of the Census.
* Population figures for New York in 1870 and 1890 reflect that city as presently constituted.

In every society, cities magnify and enhance cultural patterns. "Tenement Flats," a painting by Millard Sheets, suggests that American cities reveal both the promise and problems of American society.

far more efficiently than was possible in the pedestrian cities of the colonial era (Warner, 1962).

But, as in Europe, the wealth produced by industrial technology was concentrated among the industrialist elite, while millions of poor urbanites—particularly newly arrived immigrants—lived in appalling poverty. Because of rapid population growth, most industrial cities in the United States faced a serious housing shortage. Tenement housing was developed at this time as a means of packing the greatest number of people into the smallest amount of land area.

At the end of World War I, a majority of Americans for the first time lived in urban places. The industrial cities of the United States continued to grow until about 1950. The rural-urban controversy that had simmered throughout the nineteenth century was now all but over: America was, and would remain, an urban society.

Urban Decentralization: 1950–Present

Residents of New York, Chicago, or Atlanta in the early twentieth century may well have imagined that the growth of American cities would never cease. In only a few generations, the population of the largest American cities had soared into the millions, and most other cities had greatly increased in size. Yet, since about 1950, while the proportion of Americans living in urban areas has continued to increase, many people have moved away from the central cities in a process known as *urban decentralization* (Edmonston & Guterbock, 1984). As

Table 20–4 shows, the largest cities of the Northeast and Midwest have stopped growing and, in many cases, have actually *lost* population in recent decades. Although slowly growing again in the last few years, New York, for example, has lost almost 630,000 people since 1950.

Suburbs and central cities.   Urban decentralization is closely tied to the growth of **suburbs:** *the urban area beyond the political boundaries of a city.* Some people have always lived on the fringes of cities. But the numbers increased late in the nineteenth century as railroad lines radiating outward from a city's center enabled people to live outside the city limits and commute to work "downtown." Not surprisingly, the first people able to do so were relatively rich; some even maintained country homes along with their town houses (Baltzell, 1979). In an age of enormous immigration, many Americans were motivated by intolerance to escape from the social diversity of the central city to high-prestige and socially homogeneous suburbs. These trendsetters inspired other less wealthy Americans to view a single-family house on its own piece of leafy suburban ground as part of their American Dream.

The economic boom that followed World War II placed this dream within the grasp of many more people as automobiles opened outlying areas not served by railroads. With a long war over, Americans eagerly returned to family life, sparking the baby boom described earlier in this chapter. Since central cities contained little space for new housing construction, suburban areas blossomed almost overnight. The government provided a helping hand, guaranteeing bank loans for the purchase of housing, thereby placing a single-family home within the reach of a far larger segment of the population. Unlike the suburban growth of the late nineteenth century, few postwar suburbs were the exclusive domain of the well-to-do. Indeed, beginning with Levittown—built on potato fields of New York's Long Island in the late 1940s—many suburban developments contained thousands of inexpensive, prefabricated look-alike houses (Wattel, 1958). With a home at last within their financial reach, urban Americans flocked to the suburbs in unprecedented numbers, so that by 1970 more Americans lived in the suburbs than in the central cities.

Business followed consumers out of the city. The suburban mall—today's equivalent of Main Street in the nineteenth-century small town—became the site of most retail shopping by 1970 (Rosenthal, 1974; Tobin, 1976; Geist, 1985). The building of the interstate highway system during the postwar period also encouraged industry to move to the suburbs. Old industrial districts near

Urban Renewal: Benefits for Whom?

Government renewal has its roots in the New Deal proclaimed by President Franklin Delano Roosevelt in the early 1930s. In the wake of the Great Depression, Roosevelt sought to assist hundreds of thousands of Americans facing the loss of their homes through bank foreclosures. His administration also devised policies to spark the construction of new housing—including low-rent housing for the poor—in cities across the United States.

The housing shortage and deterioration of inner cities that followed World War II were addressed by the Housing Act of 1949. This program involved three basic steps. First, local city governments seized rundown urban neighborhoods through the right of eminent domain—meaning that owners were compensated for their property, but had no choice except to sell to the city. Second, the city sold these properties to private developers, who rebuilt the area. Third, developers subsequently sold the properties to private owners.

An additional element of early urban renewal was building public housing projects to provide more housing for low-income people, including those displaced by the demolition of condemned neighborhoods. In many cases, the government also subsidized rents of low-income tenants. By 1985, there were about 1.5 million public housing units in the United States. Typically built in highrise fashion, these massive low-income projects soon became the residences of the poorest people in the city (most of them members of minority groups) in which vandalism and other forms of crime were rampant. Indeed, the social problems in public housing have become so great that some projects have been closed down.

In response to the limited success of public housing projects, more recent programs have placed single-family houses within the reach of more low-income and moderate-income people through government guarantees of mortgage loans and financial assistance in meeting mortgage payments. But a lot of the homes purchased by poor people under these programs were in need of expensive repairs. Unable to afford these repairs, many poor people soon left the houses they had purchased, so that the gov-

ernment had to repay the bank loans and assume ownership of undesirable houses. By the mid-1970s, the federal government owned 500,000 such houses.

Clearly, the record of urban renewal in the United States is mixed. Defenders point out that such programs have rebuilt many inner-city districts. Some even claim that urban renewal has been an important factor in the urban renaissance noted since the 1970s. In addition, rather than having the government take direct responsibility for building and managing millions of housing units, urban renewal programs are credited for giving private business a major role.

Critics of urban renewal have other arguments. First, because the responsibility for redevelopment was handed over to private interests seeking profits, new construction in the neighborhoods that were demolished during the 1950s and 1960s was targeted mostly for businesses and more well-to-do residents. In other words, although intended to provide more housing for the poor, urban renewal actually benefited the rich. In fact, critics charge, urban renewal has *re-*

the central city became expensive (because of high taxes and crime) and inconvenient for heavy truck traffic. This explains why today's cities are surrounded by commercial parks containing both industry and offices.

The rapid growth of suburbs created financial problems for the older central cities of the Northeast and Midwest. Population loss reduced their tax revenues. Moreover, the central cities have lost relatively affluent people, who pay more taxes, to the suburbs, while having to finance increasingly expensive social programs for the poorer people who have remained behind (Gluck & Meis-

ter, 1979). The predictable result was the gradual decay of central cities after about 1950 (Sternlieb & Hughes, 1983). To many white Americans, the deteriorating inner city became synonymous with low-quality housing, crime, and high concentrations of the unemployed, the poor, and the nonwhite. This perception fueled even further "white flight." Thus the suburbs have remained largely white, while the populations of central cities have become increasingly nonwhite (Clark, 1979; Logan & Schneider, 1984; Stahura, 1986).

The government response to the economic decline

Baltimore harbor has been given new life by urban planner James Rouse. Such places are visually exciting and full of wonderful shops and restaurants. But renewal of this kind—typical of the United States—does little to address the day-to-day problems of the neediest Americans.

duced the number of urban housing units available to low-income people. Second, critics claim that urban renewal resulted in the destruction of many low-income neighborhoods whose only problem was that they did not conform to the typically mid-dle-class standards of urban planners. Thus thriving communities were demolished, disrupting the lives of many urbanites who had difficulty finding comparably priced housing elsewhere. Moreover, the public projects intended to provide housing for those who were displaced have generally fared badly. A third criticism pertains to more recent programs that encourage the purchase of houses by low-income urbanites. These programs have paid rich dividends to speculators, who often profited by selling poor people substandard homes that were later found to be in need of major repairs. Once again, critics conclude, the benefits were not received by those for whom they were intended.

To sum up, inner-city areas in the United States have rebounded since the initiation of urban renewal programs, and the overall quality of urban housing is better today than it was a generation ago. However, there is little doubt that urban renewal programs have done far less than intended for those urbanites who need help the most—the poor.

SOURCE: Based on Jane Jacobs, *The Death and Life of Great American Cities* (New York: Random House, 1961); Scott Greer, *Urban Renewal and American Cities* (Indianapolis: Bobbs-Merrill, 1965); Robert L. Green, *The Urban Challenge: Poverty and Race* (Chicago: Follett, 1977); and Herbert J. Gans, *The Urban Villagers: Group and Class in the Life of Italian-Americans* (New York: Free Press, 1982).

of the central cities was **urban renewal**—*governmental programs intended to revitalize cities.* Usually involving substantial funding from the federal government, many inner cities have been successfully rebuilt. Yet improvements have mostly benefited the business community rather than providing housing needed by low-income residents. The box reviews the controversy surrounding urban renewal.

Snowbelt and Sunbelt. A second trend related to the decentralization of American cities is the migration of population from the Snowbelt of the Midwest and Northeast to the Sunbelt of the South and West. In 1940, the Snowbelt contained almost 60 percent of all Americans. After 1975, as Figure 20–8 shows, the Sunbelt passed the Snowbelt in overall population. By 1986, the Sunbelt contained 54.6 percent of all Americans. This substantial regional migration has further eroded the population of older Snowbelt cities, contributing to their distress in recent decades.

In contrast, Sunbelt cities are now growing rapidly. This demographic shift is clearly evident in a comparison

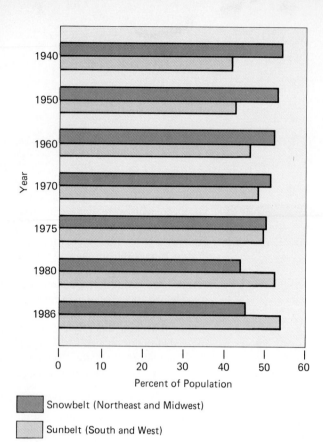

1940
1950
1960
1970
1975
1980
1986

Year

0   10   20   30   40   50   60

Percent of Population

■ Snowbelt (Northeast and Midwest)

□ Sunbelt (South and West)

Figure 20–8 The Regional Population of the United States, 1940–1986

(U.S. Bureau of the Census)

made the Sunbelt cities financially stronger than Snowbelt cities. But the great sprawl of the typical Sunbelt city is not without drawbacks. Movement across such a city is difficult, especially for those who cannot afford to maintain automobiles. Without a highly concentrated downtown, Sunbelt cities also lack the urban intensity one experiences in New York or Chicago. Indeed, Los Angeles is often criticized as a vast cluster of suburbs with no well-defined center.

Urban regions. The decentralization of American cities has produced vast urban regions. The Bureau of the Census (1986d) recognized 261 urban regions in the United States in 1985, each termed a *metropolitan statistical area* (MSA). All MSAs contain a city with at least fifty thousand people and densely populated surrounding counties. In effect, the Census Bureau's designation sug-

of the ten largest cities in the United States in 1986 with those of 1950, as shown in Table 20–5. In 1950, only two of the top ten (Los Angeles and San Francisco) were in the Sunbelt; while in 1986, six were. The four Snowbelt cities that remain on the list have all lost substantial population in the interim. Just as the twentieth century opened with tremendous urban growth in the North and Midwest, the twenty-first century will open with rapid urban growth in the South and West.

Unlike their older, Snowbelt counterparts, newer cities of the Sunbelt grew *after* the onset of urban decentralization—which is the key to their rapid population increase. By the beginning of this century, Snowbelt cities were enclosed by a ring of politically independent suburbs. Outward migration thus was at the expense of the central city. Newer Sunbelt cities were not encased by suburbs, so they have simply expanded. (Chicago, for example, covers 228 square miles; Houston covers over 565.) Many Sunbelt cities have successfully annexed towns and unincorporated settlements that lay in their paths—a course of action strongly resisted by long-established suburbs in the Snowbelt (Gluck & Meister, 1979). By enlarging the tax base, this physical expansion has

Table 20–5 THE TEN LARGEST CITIES IN THE UNITED STATES, 1950 AND 1986

1950		
Rank	City	Population
1	New York	7,892,000
2	Chicago	3,621,000
3	Philadelphia	2,072,000
4	Los Angeles	1,970,000
5	Detroit	1,850,000
6	Baltimore	950,000
7	Cleveland	915,000
8	St. Louis	857,000
9	Boston	801,000
10	San Francisco	775,000

1986		
Rank	City	Population
1	New York	7,263,000
2	Los Angeles	3,259,000
3	Houston	3,009,530
4	Chicago	3,009,340
5	Philadelphia	1,643,000
6	Detroit	1,086,000
7	San Diego	1,015,000
8	Dallas	1,004,000
9	San Antonio	914,000
10	Phoenix	894,000

SOURCE: U.S. Bureau of the Census.

gests that in an era of decentralization, the urban population is often better described in terms of regions than cities. Not surprisingly, all of the fifty fastest-growing MSAs are located in the Sunbelt.

The largest of these MSAs, in which more than 1 million people live, are called *consolidated metropolitan statistical areas* (CMSAs). In 1985, there were 21 CMSAs, the largest of which included New York and adjacent urban areas in Long Island and northern New Jersey, with a population of about 18 million. Next in size was the CMSA in Southern California that includes Los Angeles, Riverside, and Anaheim, with a population of over 13 million.

Many of these urban regions have grown so large that they have come into contact with one another. For example, the CMSA centered on New York is but one part of a four-hundred-mile supercity extending from southern New England to northern Virginia. In the early 1960s, French geographer Jean Gottmann (1961) first used the term **megalopolis** to designate *a vast urban region containing a number of cities and their surrounding suburbs*. A megalopolis is composed of hundreds of politically independent cities and suburbs, but from an airplane at night, the lights of a megalopolis make it look like one continuous city. Other American megalopolises are the eastern coast of Florida, much of Southern California, and the urban strip extending from Cleveland to Chicago. In the future, many additional urban regions will emerge, especially in the Sunbelt, where urban growth is currently most rapid.

Rural Life versus Urban Life

The sociological importance of rapid urban growth since the Industrial Revolution lies in understanding how and why life in cities differs from that in rural areas.

Ferdinand Toennies

In the late nineteenth century, the German sociologist Ferdinand Toennies (1855–1936) contrasted two types of social organization—one typical of rural areas, the other characteristic of industrial cities (1963; orig. 1887). **Gemeinschaft** (a German word meaning roughly "community") is *a type of social organization characterized by strong social solidarity based on tradition and predominantly personal relationships*. In Toennies's view, people who lived in the rural villages common in Europe and North America before the Industrial Revolution were strongly bound to one another by ties of kinship, neighborhood, and friendship. *Gemeinschaft*, then, describes any social setting in which people form what is, more or less, a single primary group.

In contrast, **gesellschaft** (a German word meaning roughly "association") is *a type of social organization characterized by weak social solidarity resulting from cultural pluralism and predominantly impersonal social relationships*. In a *gesellschaft*, people rarely act with the well-being of everyone in mind. Instead, they are motivated largely by self-interest. City dwellers, Toennies suggested, have little common identity and few collective goals. Like a vast secondary group, they tend to see others as a means of achieving their own individual goals. In general, then, Toennies believed that the growth of cities was causing a marked changed in the character of social life as the long-lasting personal ties that bound people in the countryside gave way to temporary and largely impersonal ties in the city.

Georg Simmel

Toennies's analysis was extended by another German sociologist, Georg Simmel. Like Toennies, Simmel saw urban life as distinctive and sought to understand how the city shapes the individual's attitudes and orientation toward others (1964; orig. 1905). Because the city contains so many people, objects, and events in a limited area, Simmel argued, the urbanite can become overwhelmed by all the stimulation. Consequently, city people typically develop what Simmel called a *blasé attitude*. By this he meant that they learn to be selective about their responses, tuning out much of what goes on around them and focusing their attention only on what they

As Simmel points out, urbanites tend to respond selectively to their environment. For many Americans, tuning out the poor and homeless is a response to feeling powerless to help.

deem important. Of course, city dwellers are not without sensitivity and compassion for other human beings. It is simply that the social intensity of the city would soon overwhelm anyone who did not adopt a degree of indifference toward at least most other people.

The Chicago School

The first university in the United States to embrace the discipline of sociology was the University of Chicago. Like Toennies and Simmel, sociologists in the midst of this rapidly growing metropolis at the turn of the century were interested in urban life. Under the leadership of Robert Ezra Park, introduced in the box, several generations of American sociologists carried out a detailed exploration of the emerging American metropolis.

Louis Wirth

In 1938, Louis Wirth (1897–1952) published a highly influential essay that encapsulated many of the ideas developed by what has come to be known as the Chicago School of American sociology. Wirth noted three characteristics of cities that make urban social life distinctive: *large population size*, *dense settlement*, and *social diversity*. Echoing ideas expressed earlier by Toennies and Simmel, Wirth argued that these characteristics make urban life typically impersonal, superficial, and transitory. As one of perhaps millions, a city resident usually has some contact with many more people than a rural dweller does. But a city resident knows a large portion of these people for what they do—driving the school bus, managing the office at work, working in the grocery store—rather than for who they are. Urban social relationships are also usually formed on the basis of self-interest. A shopper, for example, sees a grocer as a source of needed food. The grocer, in turn, sees the shopper as a source of business. At times, of course, such people may exchange greetings and idle conversation, but this is not the main reason they interact in the first place. This limited personal involvement with others and the great social diversity of the urban environment—where people of many different backgrounds and interests mingle in public—make city dwellers more tolerant of social differences than rural residents are. Social mores are often vigorously enforced in rural communities, but the socially diverse population of a city shares no single moral code (Wilson, 1985).

Like the ideas of Toennies and Simmel (but not

Robert Park), Wirth's ideas about the city seem on balance to be rather negative. Indeed, the rapid urbanization of European and North American society was deeply troubling to many early sociologists—as well as others—because the personal ties and traditional morality of rural life appeared to be lost in the anonymous rush of the city.

Evaluation. From today's vantage point, the consequences of urbanization seem more complex and open to interpretation. To some degree, urban settings do appear to lack the strong sense of community found in rural areas. At the same time, there is a danger of exaggerating the degree of social cohesion in rural life: social conflict has long been a feature of the countryside as well as the city. And the fact that urbanites tend to treat most people impersonally does not mean that they lack close, personal relationships altogether. The greater public anonymity found in cities means that some people "walk lonely in the crowd," but it also means greater privacy, which is welcomed by many other people (Keller, 1968; Cox, 1971; Macionis, 1978; Wellman, 1979; Lee et al., 1984).

Moreover, while introducing distinct patterns to social life, the city does not neutralize important social factors discussed in earlier chapters. Herbert Gans (1968) criticized Wirth's uniform view of urban social life by pointing out that people of different social classes, races, and ethnicities lead distinctive lives in cities. Gans notes, for example, that "urban villages," based on highly personal social ties among people sharing a religious or ethnic background, are common to American cities, and are not well represented in Wirth's analysis. The lives of rich and poor people in cities are, of course, quite distinct as well. Thus the city has a general social character, but people respond to urban life according to their particular cultural patterns and the social resources at their command.

Urban Ecology

Sociologists' interest in the city goes beyond describing the general qualities of urban life. Recall from Chapter 3 that cultural ecology examines ways in which cultural patterns are related to the physical environment. **Urban ecology** is *the analysis of the interplay of physical and social dimensions of urban life*. The crucial contribution of urban ecology is revealing the city to be both a physical and a social setting, each of which affects the other.

Urban settlements tend to arise in certain geographic locations, for example. The earliest cities were established in the region of the Tigris and Euphrates rivers in the Middle East, mainly because fertile soil favored agricultural production. Defense was also a high priority when preindustrial cities relied on the natural environment for self-protection. Athens was originally situated on an outcropping of rock, while Paris and Mexico City were first established on islands. After the Industrial Revolution, as more and more importance was placed on economics, cities were typically founded near rivers and natural harbors to facilitate trade. Eventually, advancing technology that allowed the movement of goods over great distances permitted cities to be established in a wider range of geographical areas. Salt Lake City, Utah, for instance, was built on the arid salt flats of the western high plains and now has a population of roughly 165,000.

Urban ecology is also concerned with the physical design of cities, and several models of city structure explain the use of physical space in industrial cities.

PROFILE

Robert Ezra Park (1864–1944)

I suspect that I have actually covered more ground, tramping about in cities in different parts of the world, than any other living man. (1950:viii)

Robert Ezra Park, one of the founders of sociology in the United States, appropriately described his work in these words. During the course of almost thirty years at the University of Chicago, his central interest was the city, which he sought to understand primarily by direct, systematic observation of urban life.

Park's work was unquestionably influenced by European sociologists such as Ferdinand Toennies and Georg Simmel (with whom Park had studied in Germany). Yet he directed the Chicago School toward a different approach to understanding the city, favoring direct observation over the armchair theorizing that characterized European sociology of the time. Thus several generations of sociologists at the University of Chicago set out to directly observe virtually every part of their city.

From these observations, Park came to understand the city as a highly ordered setting in which many distinctive regions (such as ethnic communities, vice areas, and industrial districts) develop and change in relation to one another. In short, Park understood the city as a complex social organism containing numerous distinctive but interrelated parts.

Living in Chicago as that city was becoming a great metropolis, Park was also intrigued by the waves of people continually drawn from rural areas. He gradually came to believe that the city's magnetic appeal lay in its ability to provide an unparalleled range of social diversity:

The attraction of the metropolis is due in part to the fact that in the long run every individual finds somewhere among the varied manifestations of city life the sort of environment in which he expands and feels at ease; he finds, in short, the moral climate in which his particular nature obtains the stimulations that bring his innate dispositions to full and free expression. It is, I suspect, motives of this kind . . . which drove many, if not most, of the young men and young women from the security of their homes in the country into the big, booming confusion and excitement of city life. (1967:41, orig. 1925)

Thus while some early sociologists viewed the city rather negatively, Park was fascinated by it—which, no doubt, motivated him to personally explore cities throughout the world. Park believed cities were growing primarily because they offered a more desirable way of life—the possibility of greater human freedom than could be found elsewhere.

SOURCE: Based on Robert E. Park, "The City: Suggestions for the Investigation of Human Behavior in the Human Environment," in Robert E. Park and Ernest W. Burgess, *The City* (Chicago: University of Chicago Press, 1967; orig. 1925), pp. 1–46; and Robert E. Park, *Race and Culture* (Glencoe, IL: Free Press, 1950).

The concentric zone model. In 1925, Ernest W. Burgess, a student and colleague of Robert Park, advanced what became known as the *concentric zone model* of city structure. Burgess suggested that the various uses of land in Chicago and several other American cities formed a series of concentric zones. At the center of the city, Burgess observed, is the central business district, which spills into a ring of factories. Beyond this commercial center are rings of residential areas that become more expensive with greater distance from the noise and pollution of the city's center.

The sector model. In 1939, Homer Hoyt expanded the scope of Burgess's research by investigating a larger number of cities. He noted that distinctive areas of cities often grew outward in wedge-shaped sectors, perhaps along a train or trolley line. Hoyt noted, too, that the most desirable neighborhoods are not always at great distance from downtown. San Franciscans, for example, have long prized neighborhoods such as Nob Hill with breathtaking views of San Francisco Bay and the Golden Gate Bridge.

The multiple-nuclei model. Chauncey Harris and Edward Ullman (1945) added still more to the ecological analysis of American cities. Reflecting the accelerating urban decentralization, they argued that mature industrial cities were coming to have a number of different centers of business and manufacturing, as well as numerous distinctive neighborhoods.

Distinct activities become spatially segregated for two major reasons. First, some activities are antagonistic to others. Few people wish to live close to industrial areas, for example, and owners of fashionable retail shops usually want to distance themselves from urban slums and pornography and vice areas such as Boston's Combat Zone. Thus the complexity and diversity of city activity yields a mosaic of urban districts whose distinctiveness is typically ensured through the operation of legal zoning codes. Second, as a city expands, the outer fringe offers the least expensive land. Thus industry often prefers outlying industrial parks to older, congested inner-city areas. Similarly, the automobile vastly increases the mobility of the urban population, so that suburbs have grown and retail businesses have clustered together far from the central city.

Social area analysis. More recently *social area analysis* has been used to study how the population of a city spreads into distinctive residential areas. This is done by determining what factors people in specific neighborhoods have in common. Research conducted in industrial cities in the United States and elsewhere suggests that three factors are of the greatest importance: *family form*, including marital status and family size; *social standing*, based on income and prestige; and *race and ethnicity* (Shevky & Bell, 1955; Johnston, 1976).

Simply put, these factors can explain a great deal about how the population of any city is dispersed into distinctive areas. In part, they influence people's choices. The rich generally seek out high-prestige neighborhoods and shun low-income people. Those with children are drawn to areas offering larger apartments or single-family houses and good local schools. Members of a particular ethnic group may cluster together. On the other hand, the poor and members of some minority groups live in distinctive areas because they *lack* a choice.

An integrated analysis. Because each of the models described above provides some understanding of the city, the best work in urban ecology has integrated them all. Brian Berry and Philip Rees (1969) argue that the factor of family form acting alone, tends to disperse population in concentric zones, supporting the model advanced by Ernest Burgess. That is, families with few children tend to live closer to the city's center, while those with more children tend to live farther away. Differences of social standing Berry and Rees argue, tend to generate the sector-shaped districts described by Homer Hoyt. Racial and ethnic differences promote the clustering of socially distinctive people at various points throughout the city, supporting Harris and Ullman's multiple-nuclei model and the findings of social area analysis.

While showing the value of each ecological model, Berry and Rees caution that urban ecology provides only an idealized picture that does not precisely describe any real city. Also keep in mind that ecologists have often minimized the extent to which urban development is guided by some people more than others. That is, powerful business interests have been instrumental in turning American cities into "growth machines" in pursuit of profits (Molotch, 1976; Feagin, 1983). Remember, too, that urban ecology is based on studies of American cities during a limited historical period. In other words, cities in industrial societies today differ in many respects from preindustrial cities of the past, as well as from present-day cities that are only beginning to industrialize. Similarly, Berry and Rees's results have been confirmed by some research in other societies (Borukhov, Ginsberg, & Werczberger, 1979), but no model is likely to account for the full variety of urban patterns throughout the world.

Third World Urbanization

Twice in human history the world has experienced a revolutionary development of cities. The first urban revolution spanned thousands of years after about 8000 B.C.E., when cities first appeared on earth. The second urban revolution began about 1750 as the Industrial Revolution sparked rapid growth of cities in Europe and subsequently in North America.

A *third urban revolution* is taking place today, but not within the industrial societies of the world, where roughly 75 percent of the population already are city dwellers. Unprecedented urban growth is now under way in the Third World, in which only about 30 percent of the people live in cities (Spates & Macionis, 1987).

In 1950, there were just seven cities in the world with a population over 5 million, and only two of these were in the Third World. By 1985, twenty-six cities had more than 5 million residents, and eighteen were in the Third World (Fornos, 1986). Moreover, by the end of this century, some Third World cities are expected to dwarf nearly all of the largest cities in industrialized societies.

Table 20–6 gives the populations of the world's ten largest urban areas—cities and their densely populated surroundings—in 1981 and estimates for the year 2000. At the beginning of the 1980s, six of the ten largest urban areas were located in industrialized societies. By the beginning of the next century, however, only four of the top ten (the megalopolis made up of Tokyo and Yokohama, and that composed of Osaka, Kobe, and Kyoto in Japan; Seoul, South Korea; and New York) will be in industrialized societies. The rest will be in less economically developed societies of the Third World. These urban areas will not only be among the world's largest, but they will also contain a staggering number of inhabitants. Relatively rich societies such as Japan may be able to provide for urban populations approaching 30 million, but the same may not be true for less developed societies such as Mexico and Brazil.

Causes of Rapid Third World Urbanization

To understand this third urban revolution, recall that many nonindustrial societies are now entering the high-growth stage of demographic transition. Declining death

Table 20—6 THE WORLD'S TEN LARGEST URBAN AREAS, 1981 AND 2000

1981	
Urban Area	Population (in millions)
New York, U.S.	16.5
Tokyo-Yokohama, Japan	14.4
Mexico City, Mexico	14.0
Los Angeles–Long Beach, U.S.	10.6
Shanghai, China	10.0
Buenos Aires, Argentina	9.7
Paris, France	8.5
Moscow, U.S.S.R.	8.0
Beijing, China	8.0
Chicago, U.S.	7.7

2000	
Urban Area	Population (in millions)
Tokyo-Yokohama, Japan	30.0
Mexico City, Mexico	27.9
São Paulo, Brazil	25.4
Seoul, South Korea	22.0
Bombay, India	15.4
New York, U.S.	14.7
Osaka-Kobe-Kyoto, Japan	14.3
Tehran, Iran	14.3
Rio de Janeiro, Brazil	14.2
Calcutta, India	14.1

SOURCE: 1981 data from various reports of the United Nations; 2000 data from U.S. Bureau of the Census, *World Population Profile: 1985* (Washington, DC: Government Printing Office, 1986), Table 12, pp. 51–52.

rates caused by improved health-related technology are stimulating a population explosion in Latin America, Africa, and Asia. But the rate of population growth is actually twice as great in urban areas as in rural areas because millions of people have been migrating from the countryside to cities in search of a higher standard of living. Jobs, health care, education, and a host of other advantages such as running water and electricity are more readily available in cities. In addition, the establishment of capitalism in poor societies has been linked to the seizure of land by elites, leaving peasants little choice but to migrate toward cities (London, 1987).

As always, this migration is motivated by people's

Mexico City, like other rapidly expanding cities of the Third World, is surrounded by shantytowns. But even these settlements provide a better standard of living than most rural areas—an important cause of migration to the cities.

perception of *relative* advantages. Cities may provide more opportunities than rural areas, but they do not offer a panacea for the massive problems generated by rapid population growth and poverty. Currently bursting at the seams, many Third World cities are simply unable to meet the needs of much of their population. Every day, for example, thousands of rural people flock to Mexico City—even though more than 10 percent of this city's residents have no running water in their homes, more than 15 percent have no sewage facilities, only about half the trash and garbage produced each day can be processed, and people are choked by the exhaust from millions of cars that jam the streets and by smoke from factories. Air pollution is estimated to cause the deaths of 100,000 people each year, including some 30,000 children (Friedrich, 1984). Like major cities throughout Latin America, Africa, and Asia, Mexico City is surrounded by wretched shantytowns—settlements in which people construct makeshift homes from all kinds of discarded materials. Major earthquakes in 1985 devastated large sections of Mexico City and increased the numbers of homeless. Even the city dumps are home to thousands of the poorest people, who pick through the waste hoping to find enough of value to ensure their survival for another day.

The Future of Third World Cities

The problems now facing Third World cities seem to defy solution. Yet the future looks bleaker still if these cities increase their population as dramatically as the figures presented in Table 20–6 suggest. Early in the twenty-first century, half the population of the Third World is expected to be living in cities, and the end of this remarkable urban growth is nowhere in sight. What hope, if any, is there of relieving the terrible plight of most of the people in these emerging megacities?

Chapter 18 suggested two different answers to this question. Some have postulated that as the Third World finally undergoes industrialization (as Western Europe and North America did two centuries ago), greater productivity will gradually raise the standard of living and population growth will subside. Others claim that Third World societies are unlikely to experience much economic progress as long as they continue to export so many of their valuable resources to the rich societies of the world.

Jane Jacobs (1984) argues that Third World cities must break their trading ties with technologically advanced cities in rich societies and instead build trading networks among themselves. Only in this way, she maintains, can their economies develop beyond their present state of providing only raw materials and inexpensive labor to wealthy corporate interests located in rich societies such as the United States. But other social analysts believe even this may not be enough. The wealth produced in Third World societies is currently concentrated in a small segment of the population. Thus revolutionary change within these societies may also be necessary to ensure that the basic needs of most people are met (Gilbert & Gugler, 1983). Whatever the final course of events, much of the drama of overpopulation in the Third World will be played out in the cities.

The Historical Importance of Cities

Americans have historically been ambivalent about the city. Thomas Jefferson, as he was about to assume the presidency in 1800, described the city as a "pestilence to the morals, the health and the liberties of man" (cited in Glaab, 1963:52). Almost a century later, Rudyard Kipling visited Chicago and wrote, "Having seen it, I urgently desire never to see it again. It is inhabited by savages" (cited in Rokove, 1975:22). Many others, of course, have celebrated the city throughout human history.

Why do cities provoke such spirited and divergent responses in human beings? Probably the answer lies in the city's ability to encapsulate and intensify human culture. Cities have been the setting for the greatest human achievements (in the tradition of classical Athens) and the greatest human failings (recall the violence of classical Rome). For over 350 years, American society has become progressively urbanized, motivated by Aristotle's belief that cities provide the opportunity to live the good life. Still, many of our worst social problems—poverty, crime, racial tensions, environmental pollution—are most clearly evident in our cities. In short, the city is a complex interweaving of noble accomplishments and wretched shortcomings.

As we approach the twenty-first century, the greatest test of urban living will occur in societies of the Third World. Cities such as Mexico City, São Paulo, and Bombay will contain almost unimaginable numbers of people. Throughout history, the city has been the most effective means of improving the standard of living of the world's population: why else would so many people have been drawn continuously to cities? But will cities in poor societies be able to meet the needs of their vastly larger and poorer populations in the next century? The answer to this question is likely to affect the lives of us all.

SUMMARY

1.   Fertility and mortality, reflected in crude birth rates and crude death rates, respectively, are major components of population growth. In relation to the world as a whole, fertility, mortality, and population growth in North America are relatively low.

2.   Migration is another key demographic concept, especially important to understanding the historical growth of cities.

3.   Demographers are also concerned with describing the composition of a population. Age-sex pyramids provide a convenient means to do so, and also offer a basis for projecting future population patterns.

4.   Historically, world population grew slowly because high birth rates were largely offset by high death rates. About 1750, however, a demographic transition began as world population started to rise sharply, primarily because of declining death rates.

5.   Contrary to Malthus's ominous predictions, demographic transition theory holds that technological advance results in gradually declining birth rates. This has happened in industrialized societies, where population growth is now relatively low. In the Third World, however, declining death rates coupled with continued high birth rates are swelling population to unprecedented levels.

6.   Many factors are related to the current rapid population growth in the Third World. Research has shown that lowering birth rates and improving economic productivity are both closely linked to improving the social position of women.

7.   World population is expected to reach 8 billion—almost twice its current level of 5 billion—by the year 2025. If this projection is correct, social problems related to poverty may overwhelm many Third World societies in which population growth is now greatest.

8.   Like population growth, urbanization has historically transformed much of the world. The first urban revolution began with the appearance of cities after 8000 B.C.E.; by the start of the Christian era, cities had emerged in all regions of the world.

9.   While all members of preurban societies were continually preoccupied with the search for food, cities permitted the development of a wide range of productive specialization.

10.   Preindustrial cities were typically small by contemporary standards. They were characterized by small buildings and narrow, winding streets, personal social ties, and rigid patterns of social inequality.

11.   A second urban revolution began about 1750 as the Industrial Revolution caused rapid urban growth in Europe. A greater emphasis on economics produced wide, regular streets and greater social anonymity. Social inequality persisted, although in time the overall standard of living of the population increased.

12.   Urbanism came to North America with European settlers. A string of small cities dotted the Atlantic coastline by 1700 and grew steadily throughout the colonial era. During the first half of the nineteenth century, hundreds of new urban settlements were established from coast to coast.

13. After the Civil War, industrialization attracted rural Americans and millions of immigrants to cities. By the early decades of the twentieth century, a majority of Americans lived in urban places, and the largest cities had become metropolitan centers with millions of inhabitants.

14. In recent decades, the urban population of the United States has become decentralized. The growth of the suburbs is one dimension of this change. In addition, newer, rapidly growing Sunbelt cities have typically expanded to cover a far larger geographical area than is typical of the older, Snowbelt cities.

15. This decentralization has generated vast urban areas that the Census Bureau terms metropolitan statistical areas (MSAs), and even larger consolidated metropolitan statistical areas (CMSAs). As these urban areas expand, they may form a megalopolis—a vast urban sprawl.

16. During the rapid urbanization of Europe in the nineteenth century, early sociologists contrasted rural and urban social life. Ferdinand Toennies suggested that the personal and enduring relationships of *gemeinshaft*, characteristic of rural life, gave way to impersonal and transitory relationships of *gesellschaft* in the city. Georg Simmel further claimed that because of the overstimula-

tion of the city, urbanites typically develop a blasé attitude toward much of what occurs around them.

17. At the University of Chicago, sociologist Robert Park saw cities positively, as settings that allowed greater social freedom. Another Chicago School sociologist, Louis Wirth, suggested that the size, density, and social heterogeneity of the urban population generated an environment characterized by impersonality, self-interest, and tolerance.

18. Urban ecology studies the interplay of the physical and social environment of the city. The concentric zone, sector, multiple-nuclei, and social area models each provide a partial understanding of urban structure.

19. A third urban revolution is occurring today within societies of the Third World. By the beginning of the twenty-first century, most of the world's largest urban areas will be in the Third World.

20. The rapid urbanization in the Third World is due to enormous population growth and to migration from the countryside by people looking for a better life. Cities do provide a relatively higher standard of living, but the widespread poverty in Third World societies is already the cause of massive urban social problems.

KEY CONCEPTS

age-sex pyramid a graphic representation of the age and sex of a population

crude birth rate the number of live births in a given year for every thousand people in a population

crude death rate the number of deaths in a given year for every thousand people in a population

demographic transition theory the thesis that population patterns are linked to a society's level of technological development

demography the study of human population

fertility the incidence of childbearing in a society's population

gemeinschaft a type of social organization characterized by strong social solidarity based on tradition and predominantly personal relationships

gesellschaft a type of social organization characterized by weak social solidarity resulting from cultural pluralism and predominantly impersonal relationships

infant mortality rate the number of deaths within the

first year of life for each thousand live births in a given year

life expectancy how long a person, on the average, can expect to live

megalopolis a vast urban region containing a number of cities and their surrounding suburbs

metropolis a very large city that socially and economically dominates a broad urban area

migration the movement of people into and out of a specified territory

mortality the incidence of death in a society's population

sex ratio the number of males for every hundred females in a given population

suburbs the urban area beyond the political boundaries of a city

urban ecology analysis of the interplay of physical and social dimensions of urban life

urbanization humanity's increasing concentration within limited geographical areas called cities

urban renewal governmental programs intended to revitalize cities

zero population growth the level of reproduction that maintains population at a steady state

SUGGESTED READINGS

The following is a readable introduction to demography, which discusses the links between population and numerous sociological topics, including aging, urbanization, and economic development:

John R. Weeks. *Population: An Introduction to Concepts and Issues.* 3rd ed. Belmont, CA: Wadsworth, 1986.

These two books, both by noted population experts, describe the current state of world population and include straightforward statements of what must be done to limit population increase.

Rafael M. Salas. *Reflections on Population.* New York: Pergammon Press, 1984.

Werner Fornos. *Gaining People, Losing Ground: A Blueprint for Stabilizing World Population.* Washington, DC: The Population Institute, 1986.

How can the needs of rapidly increasing urban populations in poor societies be met? This books reports on efforts by the United Nations to attack urban problems in a number of Asian societies.

G. Shabbir Cheema, ed. *Reaching the Urban Poor: Project Implementation in Developing Countries.* Boulder, CO: Westview Press, 1986.

The interrelationship of demographic and economic issues, with special attention to the Third World, is explored in this recent report.

World Development Report 1986. Published for the World Bank. New York: Oxford University Press, 1986.

A textbook that provides a historical and contemporary analysis of cities in North America and throughout the world is the following:

James L. Spates and John J. Macionis. *The Sociology of Cities.* 2nd ed. Belmont, CA: Wadsworth, 1987.

The following paperback is a classic, although quite long, account of urban history that emphasizes how cities are shaped by historical and cultural forces:

Lewis Mumford. *The City in History.* New York: Harcourt, Brace and World, 1961.

Like all elements of human culture, cities vary around the world. The 21 essays in this book focus on cities in the Middle East, and include case studies of Cairo, Beirut, and Jerusalem.

Abdulaziz Y. Saqqaf, ed. *The Middle East City: Ancient Traditions Confront a Modern World.* New York: Paragon House, 1987.

The policies of the Reagan administration have had a significant impact on America's cities during the 1980s. The following collection of essays draws on a wide range of material to examine this issue:

George E. Peterson and Carol W. Lewis, eds. *Reagan and the Cities.* Washington, DC: Urban Institute Press, 1986.

This account of the history of Philadelphia provides insights into the making of urban America.

Sam Bass Warner, Jr. *The Private City: Philadelphia in Three Periods of Its Growth.* 2nd ed. Philadelphia: University of Pennsylvania Press, 1987.

The history of American cities is a story of industry, and also of staggering social problems. The first of these books explains how and why welfare programs were crucial in early-nineteenth-century Philadelphia. The second examines the "female city" that has often been neglected by urban historians, with a focus on the lives of women in early New York.

Priscilla Ferguson Clement. *Welfare and the Poor in the Nineteenth-Century City: Philadelphia, 1800–1854.* Cranbury, NJ: Associated University Presses, 1985.

Christine Stansell. *City of Women: Sex and Class in New York, 1789–1860.* New York: Knopf, 1987.

Crime has long been a special concern of city dwellers. This collection of essays investigates the variation in crime rates from one community to another, and suggests several approaches to controlling urban crime.

Albert J. Reiss, Jr., and Michael Tonry. *Communities and Crime.* Chicago: University of Chicago Press, 1987.

This collection of essays presents an analysis of the decline of the inner city in the United States.

Paul E. Peterson, ed. *The New Urban Reality.* Washington, DC: The Brookings Institution, 1985.

This book, by a newspaper journalist, provides a wide variety of interesting insights about suburban life in the United States, including how the proliferation of shopping malls has affected American culture.

William Geist. *Toward a Safe and Sane Halloween and Other Tales of Suburbia.* New York: Time Books, 1985.

An account of the history of suburban growth in the United States is found in this book by a well-known historian.

Kenneth T. Jackson. *Crabgrass Frontier: The Suburbanization of the United States.* New York: Oxford University Press, 1985.

Jane Jacobs, a widely known urbanist, prepared this analysis of the role of cities in the world economy.

Jane Jacobs. *Cities and the Wealth of Nations.* New York: Random House, 1984.

CHAPTER 21

Collective Behavior and Social Movements

Thank you for calling Procter and Gamble concerning the malicious and completely false stories about our company trademark. For the past four and one half years, false stories have been circulating around the country that Procter and Gamble is linked to Satanism. There is absolutely no truth to these stories; they are total fabrications. Our moon and stars trademark has been used for more than one hundred years by the Procter and Gamble Company. The thirteen stars commemorate the original thirteen colonies, and the man in the moon was a popular design used by artists in the 1800s. The design is simply a pictorial way of identifying Procter and Gamble products.

This recorded message from the Procter and Gamble Company was connected to a toll-free telephone in 1985. For 103 years, Procter and Gamble had used the symbol of a moon and thirteen stars as a company logo on such familiar products as Crest toothpaste, Comet cleanser, and Tide laundry detergent. In 1979, however, a rumor began circulating linking the symbol to a Satanic religion. No one knows how the rumor got started; nor was there ever a shred of evidence to substantiate it. Yet, unable to dispel the rumor, the company decided in mid-1985 to remove the logo from all its products (Koenig, 1985).

This story may seem amusing, but rumors often involve more serious issues and can have powerful and

lasting consequences. In November 1985, two couples—one a black woman and a black man, and the other a white woman and a black man—moved into an all-white neighborhood in southwest Philadelphia. Rumors spread through the neighborhood that one couple had purchased

their house for less than its actual value through an affirmative action program. Long-term residents became afraid that the neighborhood was "going black." Soon an angry mob of whites gathered outside the newcomers' homes, chanting racial slurs and threats, which caused the mayor to declare a local state of emergency. After fleeing to the safety of a friend's home, the black couple announced their intention to move. Even so, their house was subsequently burned. The interracial couple—despite serious vandalism of their home—bravely declared their intention to stay (Infield, 1985; Storck, 1985).

Rumors and mobs are two examples of what sociologists call **collective behavior**: *actions, thoughts, and emotions that involve large numbers of people and that do not conform to established social norms.* Collective behavior can take many forms, any of which can be viewed as either positive or negative in its consequences. Fashions and fads, panics, riots, crowds, mass hysteria, public opinion, and social movements aimed at bringing about change—these are examples of collective behavior. To some degree, all examples of collective behavior—from a new form of clothing that captivates or shocks the public for a time to demonstrations at a nuclear test site that result in protesters being dragged off by the police—deviate from the norms and values usually observed by a majority of a society's population. For this reason, collective behavior is linked to the general process of social change.

COLLECTIVE BEHAVIOR

Although collective behavior has been a fundamental element of society for thousands of years, sociologists find it among the most difficult topics of study. Because collective behavior was long thought to be an unusual or even gravely aberrant part of social life, sociologists were late in giving it the attention they focused on more established social patterns such as social stratification and family life. Only since the tumultuous decade of the 1960s, with its great social unrest and numerous social movements in the United States, have sociologists undertaken extensive research into the various types of collective behavior (Weller & Quarantelli, 1973; G. Marx & Wood, 1975; Turner & Killian, 1987).

The second obstacle to the sociological study of collective behavior is the rather bewildering array of social phenomena the subject encompasses. Various types of collective behavior have different characteristics and

consequences. Fashions in clothing, for example, usually involve only variations on normative styles of apparel, while mob behavior, which can involve destruction of property and loss of human life, is likely to directly challenge the law.

The third problem is that collective behavior often involves large numbers of people who usually do not know one another. In contrast to established social patterns such as family life, rumors, for example, seem to come out of nowhere. The Procter and Gamble Company was never able to determine how or why the rumor linking it to so-called Satanic practices originated. Similarly, there may be no obvious way to explain a crowd of people observing the arrest of a drunken driver and suddenly erupting in a riotous rampage.

Finally, collective behavior is difficult to study because it often involves a spontaneous expression of emotion and in many cases is of short duration. The fact that family life is a well-established and enduring social pattern partly accounts for the extensive study it has received. But rumors, riots, and fashions tend to arise and dissipate quickly, which is hardly conducive to systematic sociological research. By making use of accounts provided by various observers and participants, however, sociologists have achieved considerable success in explaining such events in terms of larger patterns of social life.

The social framework within which collective behavior occurs is a **collectivity**—*a large number of people who have limited interaction with one another and who do not share well-defined and conventional norms.* Crowds are examples of *localized collectivities* in which people are in physical proximity to one another. Rumors and fashion, on the other hand, are examples of *dispersed collectivities* in which people influence one another although physically separated (Turner & Killian, 1987). In general, collectivities can be distinguished from social groups, discussed in Chapter 7, on the basis of three characteristics:

Limited social interaction. Members of social groups interact directly with one another, often over a considerable period of time. Localized collectivities such as mobs involve limited and temporary interaction among their members, while people who are part of a dispersed collectivity such as a fad may have no direct interaction with one another at all.

Unclear social boundaries. Who is—and who is not—a member of a social group is usually fairly clear. People engaged in collective behavior, however, usually lack a sense of membership. Localized crowds may share an interest (such as rooting for a sports team or watching a despondent person standing on a ledge high above the street), but with little sense of meaningful social unity. Those involved in dispersed collectivities, such as a public that has opinions on some important social issue, have even less sense of shared membership.

Weak and unconventional norms. Behavior in social groups is typically regulated by social norms that are widely recognized. A new group, such as a college debating club, is likely to adopt social norms commonly observed by other such groups. Some collectivities operate according to established social norms, as in the case of people traveling on the same airliner; even then, however, they usually form and disband without developing much social structure. Other collectivities—such as jubilant or angry fans who destroy property while leaving a sports event—rather spontaneously develop decidedly unconventional social norms (Weller & Quarantelli, 1973; Turner & Killian, 1987).

Crowds

One of the most important concepts in the study of collective behavior, a **crowd** is defined as *a temporary gathering of people who share some common focus of attention and often influence one another.*

Crowds have been found in all but the smallest and most technologically simple human societies, but they are more commonplace in large industrialized societies. As historian Peter Laslett (1984) suggests, large crowds of some twenty-five thousand people were limited in medieval Europe to major military engagements, but such crowds are now a regular occurrence at football stadiums and even registration halls of large universities. Herbert Blumer (1969) has identified four distinct types of crowds, partly defined by different levels of emotional intensity.

Casual crowds involve little, if any, interaction. Examples are people gathered on the beach or on a street corner to observe an automobile accident. Because people have only a passing awareness of one another, few social patterns are typical of casual crowds beyond the momentary sharing of an interest.

Conventional crowds would include people attending an auction, a lecture, or a funeral. Unlike a casual crowd, a conventional crowd is typically the result of deliberate planning. Although people may not interact very much, they do so according to recognized norms

appropriate to the situation. This is why such crowds are described as conventional.

Expressive crowds form around events that have emotional appeal to crowd members—religious revivals, professional wrestling matches, and the New Year's celebration that draws hundreds of thousands of people to New York's Times Square. People join expressive crowds for enjoyment or emotional and spiritual support, and within the crowd they may be spontaneous and exuberant. The emotional energy generated by expressive crowds can be exhilarating, at times even intoxicating. Thus expressive crowds are not as formally organized as conventional crowds, and behavior that is acceptable in expressive crowds—shouting, crying, laughing— would be frowned upon in more conventional social situations.

Acting crowds engage in violent and destructive action. The emotions that unite an acting crowd are more powerful than those of an expressive crowd, reaching feverish intensity that provokes participants to unrestrained action. As a result, acting crowds may violate cultural norms by, for example, physically attacking other people. In the summer of 1985, some sixty thousand soccer fans assembled near Brussels, Belgium, to watch the European Cup Finals, involving teams from Italy and Great Britain. About forty-five minutes before the game was to begin, British fans—many of whom were reportedly intoxicated—began to taunt Italians sitting beyond a fence in the next section of the stadium. The two sides began to throw bottles and rocks at each other. Suddenly, British fans surged toward the Italians, tearing down the fence in a human wave. As an estimated 400 million television viewers watched in horror, a rampaging mob trampled hundreds of helpless spectators. Within minutes, thirty-eight people were dead and another four hundred injured (Lacayo, 1985).

This example, also illustrates how a crowd can change from one type to another. Spectators at a soccer match are often a conventional crowd. They may cheer and boo, but they are otherwise relatively passive and interact little with one another. In this case, however, a conventional crowd became an expressive crowd. Eventually, hostile emotions transformed some spectators into an acting crowd that rampaged into an adjoining section of the stadium.

Protest crowds are a fifth type of crowd that can be added to the four identified by Blumer. Protest crowds involve people engaged in a variety of actions—including strikes, boycotts, sit-ins, and protest marches—whose purpose is to advance some political goal (McPhail &

Casual crowds gather in pleasant public places. In New York City, a favorite spot is the steps of the Public Library.

Conventional crowds, such as people attending a funeral, typically act according to well-defined cultural norms.

Protest crowds played an important part in bringing down the Marcos regime in the Philippines in 1986.

Expressive crowds can often be found at sports events. American fans are almost as active as the athletes on the playing field.

Soccer fans at the 1985 European Cup finals in Brussels turned into a violent acting crowd. Before police were able to restore order, thirty-eight people had died.

Wohlstein, 1983). For example, in the midst of a bitter strike that had been going on for months, workers from more than a dozen states marched through the streets of Austin, Minnesota, in 1986 in an effort to call attention to what they contended were unfair practices by the Hormel meatpacking company. Hormel, facing financial problems, had attempted to cut workers' wages and benefits, and the workers decided to publicly challenge the company's policies.

Protest crowds vary in their emotional energy, resembling conventional crowds in some cases, and engaging in violence in others. Many public marches and demonstrations that were part of the civil rights movement during the 1950s and 1960s, for example, were peaceful. However, sometimes in response to aggressive police tactics, a protest was transformed into a violent confrontation.

Mobs, Riots, and Panics

The most violent type of acting crowd is a **mob**, defined as *a highly emotional crowd united by the common purpose of some specific violent or destructive action*. A mob is actually a highly emotional "acting" crowd directed toward conscious and deliberate violence. Mobs typically dissipate quickly, since they have limited objectives. In some cases, mob behavior reflects the intentions of effective leaders, who encourage unity of purpose in mob members.

Lynching is one of the most notorious examples of mob behavior in the United States. In the wake of the Civil War, black Americans freed from slavery gained new political rights and economic freedoms that challenged the traditional social patterns by which whites had ruthlessly dominated them, especially in the South. In an effort to maintain white domination, the terrorist lynch mob emerged as a highly effective form of social control. Blacks who questioned white superiority—or who were simply suspected of doing so—were put to death by vengeful whites, generally by hanging and sometimes by being burned alive. Blacks became all-purpose scapegoats. Any event that disturbed the white community was sufficient to direct suspicion and violence toward them, whether or not they had anything to do with the event in question. The box describes the law of "Judge Lynch."

SOCIETY IN HISTORY

Mob Violence: "Judge Lynch" as American Justice

In September 1892, several members of the white Woodruff family of Quincy, Mississippi, became ill and suspected that the water in their well had been poisoned. A number of white residents of Quincy decided that a black man named Benjamin Jackson may have poisoned the Woodruffs' well. Jackson was promptly arrested by police, along with his wife and his mother-in-law.

Before his trial could begin, a crowd of some two hundred whites demanded that Jackson be released to them so he could be lynched. The police complied, and Jackson was promptly hanged. A formal investigation was held to determine the possible involvement of Jackson's wife and her mother in the alleged poisoning.

The investigation found no evidence that they (or Jackson himself) had been involved in a crime of any kind, and a jury ordered that the two women be released. When they returned to their home, however, they, too, were seized by a mob and promptly hanged. At this point, the mob began a search for another black man, Rufus Bigley, whose name had been mentioned during the legal investigation. Within a short time, he was hanged as well.

This account is typical of thousands of lynchings in the United States. The term *lynching* is derived from the activities of Charles Lynch, a Virginia colonist who attempted to maintain law and order before the establishment of formal courts. As applied in the nineteenth and twentieth centuries, however, the word meant terrorism and murder outside the legal system.

Lynchings such as those described here were chronicled by Ida B. Wells, a black woman who courageously opposed lynching in her newspaper, *The Free Speech*, in Memphis, Tennessee. Her efforts served only to provoke local whites into forcing the closing of her paper. As Wells noted, the tragedy of widespread lynching was surpassed only by the apparent indifference of whites to this perversion of justice and basic human decency.

SOURCE: Based on Ida B. Wells-Barnett, *On Lynchings* (New York: Arno Press and The New York Times, 1969; orig. 1892), pp. 48–49; also Walter White, *Rope and Faggot* (New York: Arno Press and The New York Times, 1969; orig. 1929).

Lynch mobs were most active in the United States between about 1880 and 1930, although murders caused by mobs have occurred since then. During that fifty-year period, approximately five thousand lynchings were officially recorded; no doubt, many more actually occurred. The states of the Deep South—where the abolition of slavery left an agrarian economy that still depended on a cheap and docile black labor force—accounted for most of these murders. But lynchings took place in virtually every state of the Union, and were directed against members of all minority groups. On the western frontier, Mexican and Asian Americans were frequent targets of lynch mobs. As lynching became more common, whites sometimes lynched other whites, accounting for perhaps 25 percent of all lynchings. Only about one hundred females are known to have been victims of lynch mobs, and almost all of them were black (White, 1969, orig. 1929; Grant, 1975).

Less structured and unified than a mob is a **riot,** a situation that results when *a crowd explodes into undirected violent and destructive behavior.* Unlike a mob, a riot usually has no single focus for its emotional power. In some cases, riots occur when long-standing anger is triggered into spontaneous action by some apparently minor event (Smelser, 1962). People may then engage in more or less dispersed acts of violence against property or persons in the vicinity. While a mob action usually ends when a specific violent goal has been achieved (or decisively prevented), a rioting crowd usually disperses only when the participants in the collective outburst run out of steam or are gradually brought under control by community leaders or police.

Riots have erupted throughout American history as a way of expressing a collective sense of injustice. Many riots, for example, involved industrial workers expressing outrage at their working conditions; Chicago's Haymarket Riot in 1888 typified the violent decades in American labor history. Rioting has also been commonplace among prisoners protesting injustices of the penal system. In 1987, for instance, Cuban prisoners rioted in Georgia and Louisiana detention centers to challenge allegedly unfair treatment by the federal government. Throughout American history, race riots have occurred with striking regularity. In the early twentieth century, large crowds of whites violently attacked black people in large cities such as Chicago and Detroit. In the summer of 1965, one of the most destructive urban riots in American history was triggered by alleged brutality on the part of two Los Angeles police officers arresting a black man for drunken driving. The five-day riot that followed resulted in thirty-four deaths, hundreds of injuries, thousands of arrests, and millions of dollars' worth of property damage. During the summers of the late 1960s, and sporadically since then, riots have occurred in the black ghettos of many American cities as seemingly trivial events triggered violent expressions of anger at continuing prejudice and discrimination.

Some riots, however, result from positive feelings—such as the high spirits characteristic of crowds of young people who flock to resort areas around the United States during the annual college spring break. In March 1986, for example, the exuberance of vacationing students in Palm Springs, California, erupted into a riot that resulted in over a hundred arrests when crowds of young men began throwing rocks and bottles at passing cars and stripping the clothing off terrified women (DeMott, 1986).

Another type of acting crowd event is a **panic,** which occurs when *a crowd is provoked into seemingly irrational and often self-destructive behavior by some perceived threat.* A familiar example of a panic situation is a fire in a crowded theater that causes members of the audience to flee in hysteria, trampling one another and blocking the exits so that few are actually able to escape.

Theories of Crowd Dynamics

How can the often unconventional behavior of crowds be explained? Over the last century, social scientists have developed several different theories.

Contagion Theory

Developed by French sociologist Gustave Le Bon (1841–1931), contagion theory was one of the first systematic explanations of crowd behavior. Le Bon (1960, orig. 1895) maintained that crowds can exert a hypnotic influence on their members. In the anonymity of a crowd, people can lose their individual identities, surrendering their personal will and sense of responsibility to a collective mind. The crowd takes on a life of its own, indifferent to social norms and other social restraints. Le Bon claimed that a crowd's individual members become unreasoning automatons guided by contagious emotional forces within the crowd. A particular emotion—Le Bon cited fear and hate as common examples—resonates throughout the crowd, building in intensity. Participants ultimately become hypnotized by a single-minded determination to satisfy this emotion through an outburst of unrestrained action. Conventional social restraints are overwhelmed by the energy that bonds each member of a crowd to all others. The predictable result, Le Bon concluded, is destructive violence.

Le Bon's assertion that crowds are characterized by anonymity, suggestibility, and emotional contagion remains largely accepted today, and seems to apply to mobs and riots in contemporary American society. But there is little support for the idea that a crowd takes on a mind of its own entirely apart from the thoughts and intentions of participants. Crowds may facilitate the release of emotions people would otherwise restrain, but they do not create these emotions. Participating in a crowd may have encouraged white Philadelphians in 1985 to use violence to try to evict black newcomers from their neighborhood in the incident described earlier. But this racist action was not created by a crowd; racism was already present in the minds of the people involved.

Convergence Theory

Convergence theory accepts the idea that crowds are united in action, but rejects Le Bon's contention that crowds develop a mind of their own once people have come together. It suggests, instead, that the unity of crowds is the result of a factor that precedes the formation of the crowd itself—like-minded individuals being drawn together by some common attitude or interest. In the Philadelphia incident, for example, the crowds that formed can be understood as the convergence of people who shared an attachment to their traditionally white neighborhood, who feared or opposed the presence of black residents, and who had a propensity for violent action.

Participation in a crowd may encourage people to engage in behavior that would be restrained by social norms in most other settings. But the fact that people in a crowd act in similar ways is more a consequence of the characteristics of individuals than a creation of the crowd itself. This suggests that, in many cases at least, crowd behavior is not irrational, as Le Bon maintained, but rather the result of rational decision making on the part of participants (Berk, 1974). The members of a protest crowd, then, are not motivated by emotional forces as much as by a rational desire to achieve some specific goal.

Emergent-Norm Theory

Additional insights into crowd behavior are found in emergent-norm theory. Ralph Turner and Lewis Killian (1987) agree that crowds are not the irrational collectivity described by Le Bon; they also argue that while similar interests may draw some people to a particular crowd, no crowd is completely understood as the convergence of like minds. In most cases, Turner and Killian maintain, crowds are initially collections of people with somewhat mixed interests and motives. In conventional and casual crowds, the norms that guide behavior are generally conventional and understood well in advance. But the more unstable types of crowds—expressive, acting, and protest crowds—tend to be normatively ambiguous, so that norms that guide behavior often emerge within the situation. Such emergent norms are likely to be initiated by a few leaders, and quickly adopted by others. The result is mildly or radically unconventional behavior. For example, one person at a rock concert holds up a lit cigarette lighter to signal praise for the performers, and others follow suit; or a few people in an angry street crowd throw bricks through store windows, and a riot ensues. In the infamous tavern rape in New Bedford, Massachusetts, in 1983, one man initially assaulted a twenty-one-year-old woman who had come into the bar to buy cigarettes, then raped her on the floor. For about an hour and a half, five other men repeatedly raped the woman. The perpetrators were cheered on by many others, who apparently accepted this brutality as a collective norm in that context. No one in the bar expressed allegiance to conventional norms against rape by calling the police (*Time*, March 5, 1984).

Like any social gathering, a crowd is likely to generate pressure toward conformity. But this does not mean that everyone in a crowd agrees with the norms that may emerge or behaves accordingly. While some people in a crowd assume positions of leadership and others become their lieutenants or rank-and-file followers, still others remain relatively inactive bystanders (Weller & Quarantelli, 1973; Zurcher & Snow, 1981).

In sum, Turner and Killian explain that crowd behavior is not as chaotic and irrational as contagion theory suggests, nor is it as purposeful and rational as convergence theory implies. In any crowd, some outcomes are clearly more likely than others, but collective goals typically emerge as the situation unfolds. Even in crowds that are intensely emotional, Killian and Turner argue, decision making can and does occur. To someone watching a subsequent news story, frightened people clogging the exits of a theater may seem to be victims of irrational panic. Yet choosing to flee in that life-threatening situation can also be viewed as a rational alternative to death by fire (1972:10). Similarly, it is easy to assume that an episode of racial conflict was a simple expression of racism on the part of some participants. In many cases, however, crowd behavior may actually be more complex, motivated partly by norms that arose within the particular setting.

Crowds, Politics, and Social Change

In early American history, the hostility of most colonists toward Great Britain increased dramatically after the Boston Massacre and the Boston Tea Party. The first occurred in March of 1770 when a number of Bostonians, angry at the domination of their lives by the British, confronted a British soldier who, in panic, called for more troops. The clash between British soldiers and the citizens of Boston—five of whom died as a result—greatly increased support for American independence. Three years later, in angry reaction to British taxation policies, Bostonians gathered in a protest meeting. Soon afterward, some of their number dressed up as Indians and dumped tea carried by British commercial ships into Boston harbor (Kelley, 1982). At the time, the British and their colonial supporters certainly viewed this event as a deplorable mob action. Yet most American colonists, and most Americans since, have regarded the confrontations that led to the Boston Massacre and the Boston Tea Party as legitimate protest against injustice—patriotic demonstrations that helped pave the way for a new, more democratic society.

Because they are linked to social changes, crowds have often sparked controversy. As a result, defenders of the established social order have long feared and hated

To defenders of Israel, participants in the West Bank unrest are unprincipled rioters. To supporters of the Palestinians, however, they are legitimate freedom fighters protesting the occupation of their land by a foreign power.

crowds. For example, Gustave Le Bon's negative view of crowds was common among his fellow aristocrats, who would have widely agreed that "crowds are only powerful for destruction" (1960:18; orig. 1895). But what these aristocrats viewed as *destructive* crowd behavior was probably viewed as *constructive* action by others who did not enjoy their social privileges. In general, those unsympathetic to the political aims of crowds have tended to discredit them as mobs and riots in defiance of law and order. On the other hand, those who approve of the political aims of crowds may support such collective action as the voice of the people speaking out against a flawed system.

But few would deny that crowds have long played a crucial role in both creating and opposing social change. Throngs of Roman subjects rallying to the words of the Sermon on the Mount by Jesus of Nazareth, traditional weavers joining together to destroy new industrial machinery that was making their skills obsolete, thousands of marchers carrying banners and shouting slogans either for or against a law permitting abortion—countless such instances across the centuries show that crowds are an important means by which people have challenged or supported established power structures (Rudé, 1964; Canetti, 1978).

Rumor

Collective behavior is not limited to people in physical proximity to one another. Sociologists use the term **mass behavior** to refer to *collective behavior among people dispersed over a wide geographical area*. A common example of mass behavior is rumor.

Rumor is *unsubstantiated information spread informally, often by word of mouth*. The validity of a rumor is typically difficult to assess. Rumor has probably always been an element of human social life, but the means of transmitting rumors have changed dramatically within the last century. Through most of human history, rumors were spread through face-to-face communication. In industrial societies, however, telephones, computers, and the mass media have greatly increased the speed with which rumors spread, as well as enlarged the number of people who may become involved.

Rumors tend to thrive in a climate of *ambiguity*: they arise and spread most effectively when large numbers of people lack definitive information about some topic of interest. If there is widespread suspicion that the pronouncements of authorities are untruthful, rumors are

especially likely to emerge. Rumors tend to provide information that *clarifies a situation* about which substantiated facts are largely unavailable (Shibutani, 1966; Rosnow & Fine, 1976). Rumors also *arise easily*. In the absence of substantiated facts about a topic of interest, virtually anyone can start or spread a rumor. Different rumors about a certain situation form competing conceptions of reality. Rumors are also *changeable*. As they circulate, they may be altered in the telling, so that a number of variations on a single rumor add to the confusion. Generally, some details take on greater importance as a rumor is spread from person to person, while others are lost as unimportant. For example, in a rumor concerning a confrontation between political demonstrators and police, people sympathetic to the demonstration's goals are likely to emphasize details placing responsibility for any violence on the police and to ignore those attaching blame to the demonstrators. Those with opposing political views, of course, do just the opposite. Finally, rumors are typically *difficult to stop*. Once a rumor begins to circulate, the number of people who are aware of it tends to increase in geometric progression as each person spreads the rumor to several others. Although some rumors dissipate with time, others persist for years. Rumors can be effectively stopped only when clear, substantiated information is widely disseminated. Even then, there is no guarantee that everyone will accept such information as fact.

In recent years, for example, rumors about acquired immune deficiency syndrome, or AIDS—a disease discussed in Chapter 19—have mistakenly asserted that someone can acquire AIDS through casual contact with an AIDS victim or through sharing an AIDS victim's dishes, towel, or toilet. Medical experts have publicized information contradicting such rumors and thereby helped decrease unfounded fears about the disease. But since medical science still does not fully understand this disease, some people continue to believe rumors rather than medical pronouncements, and persist in ostracizing the victims of AIDS.

Rumor, founded or unfounded, can trigger the formation of crowds or other collective action. During the urban disturbances of the 1960s, numerous rumor-control centers were established in major American cities to counter the potentially explosive effects of rumors. In other cases, rumors simply fade away as people lose interest in the subject. The box describes the rumored death of Beatle Paul McCartney, which persisted in the face of contrary evidence for years.

A concept closely related to rumor is *gossip*, which

The Rumored Death of Beatle Paul McCartney

The Beatles—John Lennon, Paul McCartney, George Harrison, and Ringo Starr—were probably the most celebrated rock band in the world until their breakup in 1970. Their fame also spawned one of the most widespread rumors of the time: the alleged death of Paul McCartney.

Although perhaps beginning as early as 1967, this rumor spread rapidly in 1969 after a Detroit radio station announced several curious "facts":

1. Played backward, the phrase "Number 9, Number 9, Number 9" from the song "Revolution 9" on the Beatles' White Album (*The Beatles*) becomes "Turn me on, dead man!"
2. At the end of the song "Strawberry Fields Forever," from the album *Magical Mystery Tour*, filtering out background noise reveals a voice saying "I buried Paul!"
3. In a picture inside this album, John, George, and Ringo wear red carnations, while Paul's carnation is black.

This was sufficient to launch the rumor that McCartney had died. Immediately millions of people across the United States began to carefully inspect Beatle albums for other clues

of McCartney's demise. Not surprisingly, plenty were found including these:

4. The cover of the *Sgt. Pepper's Lonely Hearts Club Band* album shows a grave with yellow flowers arranged in the shape of Paul's bass guitar.
5. On the inside of this album, McCartney wears an armpatch with the letters "OPD," which were interpreted to mean "Officially Pronounced Dead."
6. On the back cover of this album, three Beatles face forward while McCartney turns his back.

At one point, a report in the University of Michigan newspaper provided the details of McCartney's alleged death, even presenting a photograph of a bloodied head said to be his. The story claimed that the Beatle had been decapitated in an automobile crash early in November of 1966 and had been secretly replaced by a double.

Paul McCartney is, of course, very much alive to this day. It is likely that the Beatles intentionally provided at least some of the clues to encourage the interest of their fans.

This incident illustrates how

quickly rumors may arise, and persist when those who contradict them are not trusted. In the cultural climate of distrust toward the mass media of the late 1960s, many young people were prepared to believe that an event such as McCartney's death would be concealed by powerful interests. In other words, they were at least willing to entertain the possibility that he was dead despite all evidence to the contrary. Therefore, when McCartney himself denied the rumor in a *Life* magazine interview in 1969, this establishment publication was seen by the distrustful youth subculture as an unreliable source. Indeed, thousands of readers noticed that, on the opposite side of the page presenting McCartney's picture, there was an advertisement for a particular automobile. Holding the page up to the light showed a car across McCartney's chest blocking his head!

Clearly, situations involving ambiguity and distrust are likely to fuel rumors—despite efforts to provide the facts.

SOURCE: Based on Ralph L. Rosnow and Gary Alan Fine, *Rumor and Gossip: The Social Psychology of Hearsay* (New York: Elsevier, 1976), pp. 14–20.

is rumor about the personal affairs of other people. As Charles Horton Cooley (1962, orig. 1909) points out, rumor tends to involve issues or events of interest to a large segment of the public, while gossip is of interest only to those who have some personal knowledge of the people in question. Gossip, then, tends to be localized, while rumors may readily spread throughout an entire society.

Gossip can be an effective means of informal social control as other people become aware that they are the topic of praise or scorn. People may also engage in gossip to elevate their own standing in a social group. Through gossiping about others, a person may gain status by demonstrating access to insider information not available to other members of the group. In addition, to the extent that the gossip is damaging to its target, those who spread the information are able to feel a sense of social superiority since, presumably, what applies to the target of the gossip does not apply to them. At the same time, however, because gossiping is often viewed as disreputable, those who gossip may be viewed adversely by others.

Public Opinion

As noted in Chapter 5, *public opinion* refers to the attitudes of people throughout a society toward one or more controversial issues. Although we often speak about *the* public, as if everyone were concerned about the same things and able to express an opinion on them, most societies actually contain many publics. Widely dispersed individuals are united into a public by their shared interest in air pollution, handguns, abortion, sports, the opposite sex, the same sex, foreign relations, and thousands of other debated issues and activities. Members of a public share a particular interest or concern, but may well be divided by their opinions about it. The term *public issue* thus refers to important matters on which people do not agree (Lang & Lang, 1961; Turner & Killian, 1987).

Members of a public usually share social characteristics that sensitize them to particular issues and help shape their opinions about them. As Chapter 17 noted, for example, the political attitudes of Americans tend to vary according to age, sex, race and ethnicity, religion, and social class. For example, the public supporting a Republican candidate tends to be more affluent and white than the public supporting a Democratic candidate, since the Democratic Party has traditionally represented the interests of working-class and nonwhite Americans more than the Republican Party has (Burnham, 1983).

Most people simultaneously belong to several publics because of their wide range of social characteristics, personal interests, and social affiliations. At the same time, ignorance or lack of interest excludes some people from the public holding an opinion on any issue. Although the proportion varies from issue to issue, usually at least 10 percent of the American population has no opinion on a particular public concern. A public also tends to grow larger or smaller over time as people's interest in a particular issue waxes and wanes or dies out completely when the issue is resolved or no longer seems relevant. Interest in the position of women in American society was strong during the years of the women's suffrage movement and waned after women won the right to vote in 1920. In recent decades, a second wave of feminism has once again created a public with strong opinions for and against changes in social patterns related to the two sexes.

Some publics have more social influence than others because wealth and power are unequally distributed throughout a society. Many well-funded special-interest groups in the United States (described in Chapter 17) are able to shape public policy although they represent only a small minority of Americans. Physicians, for example, have enormous influence on health-care policy even though they represent only about 2 percent of the American population. Publics whose members have high positions in the social hierarchy have the financial means, prestige, social contacts, and special access to the mass media that help promote their opinions, no matter how small their numbers may be. Not surprisingly, the most influential publics are likely to be primarily white, Protestant, and male. National surveys reveal that about two-thirds of the American people support the Equal Rights Amendment that would provide equality under the law to males and females (N.O.R.C., 1983). But ERA has not been enacted into law—partly, at least, because the vast majority of public officials in the United States are male.

Locally and nationally, socially prominent people serve as *opinion leaders* who both reflect and shape public opinion. Husbands and fathers have traditionally been the shapers of opinion within families, and on the national level prominent males such as President Ronald Reagan and newscaster Dan Rather are influential. More generally, the high social status of many physicians, lawyers, entertainers, and athletes in the United States causes other Americans to emulate their tastes and attitudes.

Gauging the opinion of various publics is especially important in capitalist democracies such as the United States and Canada, where political leaders try to win the support of voters and businesses attempt to win the allegiance of customers. Public opinion polls (described in Chapter 2) are an important means by which public attitudes are measured. Of course, both political and business leaders also attempt to shape public opinion. In other words, political campaigns attempt to manipulate as much as respond to the electorate. In the same way, stimulating consumption is crucial to the growth of any capitalist economy. In 1985, almost $100 billion was spent by businesses on advertising, about 75 percent of it in the mass media (U.S. Bureau of the Census, 1987g).

Many famous entertainers are opinion leaders. Jesse Jackson's 1988 presidential campaign was boosted by television star Bill Cosby.

Propaganda. Political leaders, special-interest groups, and businesses all attempt to influence public tastes and attitudes through the use of **propaganda:** *information presented with the intention of shaping public opinion.* Although the term *propaganda* has negative connotations, the information conveyed by propaganda is not necessarily false. Like rumor, propaganda can be a variable combination of truth and falsehood. What turns information into propaganda is the intention with which it is presented: rather than encouraging broad, critical reflection on an issue, propaganda aims at winning people to a particular viewpoint. Political speeches, commercial advertising, and public relations efforts by professional associations, labor unions, and religious organizations are all likely to include propaganda.

Mass Hysteria

Mass hysteria refers to *a situation in which people in a wide area respond to some perceived threat with anxious or frantic behavior.* Mass hysteria need not be based on fact. It is likely to arise when large numbers of people *think* they are confronted with a threatening situation over which they have little control. In other words, un-

founded fears based on learning that one's children are attending school with a child who has AIDS may spark mass hysteria in a community just as much as the very real danger of an approaching hurricane. Furthermore, the irony is that people in the grip of mass hysteria are likely to act in ways that make the situation worse rather than better. At the extreme, mass hysteria involves chaotic flight and other panic reactions. If a disturbance should cause the formation of crowds, the element of emotional contagion can make mass hysteria even stronger. People who see others in fear may become more afraid themselves; realizing the ineffectiveness of their actions may provide more grounds for hysteria and panic.

On the night before Halloween in 1938, CBS radio broadcast a dramatization of H. G. Wells's novel *War of the Worlds* (Cantril, Gaudet, & Herzog, 1947; Koch, 1970). From a New York studio, a small group of actors presented a program of "live dance music" heard by an estimated 10 million Americans from coast to coast. The program was interrupted to report that explosions on the surface of the planet Mars had been followed by the appearance of a mysterious cylinder embedded in the ground near a farmhouse in New Jersey. The program then switched to an "on-the-scene reporter" who presented a chilling account of giant monsters equipped with death-ray weapons emerging from the cylinder. An "eminent astronomer," played by Orson Welles, provided scientific substantiation that Martians had begun a full-scale invasion of Earth.

Although at the beginning, middle, and end of the program an announcer identified the broadcast as a fictitious dramatization, subsequent research indicated that about one-fourth of the radio audience believed the program to be factual. By the time the show was over, thousands of Americans were in a panic—gathering in the streets to spread news of the "invasion" and flooding telephone switchboards with warning calls to friends and relatives. Among those who simply jumped into their cars and fled were a college senior and his roommate:

My roommate was crying and praying. He was even more excited than I was—or more noisy about it anyway; I guess I took it out in pushing the accelerator to the floor. . . . After it was all over, I started to think about that ride, I was more jittery than when it was happening. The speed was never under 70. I thought I was racing against time. . . . I didn't have any idea exactly what I was fleeing from, and that made me all the more afraid. (Cantril, Gaudet, & Herzog, 1947:52).

Mass hysteria, then, is a situation in which panic tends to build on itself in a vicious circle. The box provides details of another outstanding example of mass hysteria, this one based on entirely fictitious accounts of the presence of witches in colonial Massachusetts in the late seventeenth century.

SOCIETY IN HISTORY

The Witches of Salem, Massachusetts

Perhaps the best-known instance of mass hysteria in early American history centered on allegations that witches were present in Salem, Massachusetts, a village some fifteen miles north of Boston, during most of 1692. One of the longer episodes of mass hysteria on record, this "witch scare" dramatically disrupted the lives of the Puritan settlers.

Historians locate the beginning of this episode in the home of Salem minister Samuel Parris. Parris owned a female slave named Tituba, brought to the Massachusetts Bay Colony from Barbados and reputed to be skilled in black magic. A group of young girls met regularly to listen to Tituba spin tales that were, no doubt, beyond the bounds of conventional conversation in this small and devoutly pious community. Before long, two of the youngest girls began to exhibit exceedingly strange behavior—writhing about on the ground in apparent convulsions. These bi-

zarre symptoms were soon displayed by other young girls throughout the village. Horrified parents concluded that their children were bewitched.

The powerful clergy of Salem demanded that the girls identify those responsible for this "Satanic" outbreak. Initially, the girls singled out Tituba and two other older women as witches. Brought to trial, Tituba provided a chilling and detailed account of beliefs about the "underworld" that she had learned in her youth, and suggested that many people in Salem were indeed practicing witchcraft. Pressed to identify still others, the girls spewed forth names and the jail soon overflowed with suspects awaiting trial. The fear of being named a witch became as much a source of panic as the alleged presence of the witches themselves. As a result, few people were willing to come to the aid of the accused, lest they too be labeled as witches. By the end of the summer of 1692, twenty people

convicted of witchcraft had been executed. Two others died while in prison awaiting trial.

The witchcraft hysteria eventually began to fade as questions arose about the validity of the girls' accusations. No doubt, the young girls had become keenly aware of the new and unaccustomed power they now had over their quite patriarchal Puritan colony. Undaunted by the consequences of their actions, they began to accuse far too many people they had never even met. Even more important, while their early accusations had been made against the female slave Tituba and other "outsiders," they now directed suspicion toward some of the founding fathers of the community who had the power to fight back. Only then, almost as quickly as they had invaded Salem, were the witches gone.

SOURCE: Based on Kai T. Erikson, *Wayward Puritans: A Study in the Sociology of Deviance* (New York: John Wiley & Sons, 1966), pp. 141–150.

Fashions and Fads

Fashions and fads are two additional types of collective behavior among people dispersed over a large geographical area. A **fashion** is *a social pattern favored for a time by a large number of people.* In contrast to more established social norms, fashion is subject to continual change and, at the extreme, may last only a matter of months. Fashion characterizes the arts (including painting, music, drama, and literature), automobiles, language, architecture, business practices, and public opinion. The most widely recognized example of fashion, however, is clothing and other dimensions of personal appearance.

In preindustrial societies, as Lyn Lofland (1973) points out, clothing and other forms of personal adornment reflect traditional styles that change little over the course of many years. Different categories of people—males and females, adults and children, and members of various social classes—typically wear distinctive clothes and hairstyles to visibly indicate their social position.

In industrial societies, style gives way to fashion for two reasons. First, traditions weaken as a society industrializes, so people are more willing to embrace new social patterns. Indeed, in the United States today, the phrase *old-fashioned* generally has a negative meaning, while *new* and *up-to-date* are terms of approval. Second, as noted in Chapters 9 and 10, industrial societies have a relatively high degree of social mobility. People's changing social position is likely to be symbolized by their selection of clothing, automobile, and housing, and also to be reflected in their patterns of speech and points of view. As German sociologist Georg Simmel (1971, orig. 1904) pointed out, people use fashions to shape their presentations of self, seeking approval and prestige. According to Simmel, affluent people are usually the trend-setters, since they have the money to spend on changeable luxuries that advertise their position of privilege. In this way, Thorstein Veblen (1953, orig. 1899) linked fashion to *conspicuous consumption*—the practice of spending money in ways that display one's wealth to others. Many less affluent people, lacking the financial means to buy exactly what the influential rich can afford, are likely to purchase less expensive copycat items. As a particular fashion moves downward in society, it loses its prestige, and affluent people eventually move on to a new fashion. In this way, many fashions that are born at the top of the social hierarchy—on the Fifth Avenues and Rodeo Drives of the rich—decline to mass popularity in bargain stores across the country.

Especially in recent decades, however, some American fashions have originated among people of lower social position and been adopted by those who are more affluent. The best-known illustration of the upward movement of fashion is blue jeans, or dungarees (from a Hindi word referring to a coarse and inferior fabric). Blue jeans were first worn by people who did manual labor. But over the years more affluent people—including social activists who identified with the socially disadvantaged—began to wear jeans as a political symbol. Jeans became the uniform of political activists in the civil rights and antiwar movements in the 1960s and, gradually, of a large part of the college population across the country. As *radical chic* became a fashion adopted by the rich, public schools began to allow students to wear jeans to class. More recently, less durable and much more expensive designer jeans became fashionable among Americans of all political persuasions.

A **fad** is *a somewhat unconventional social pattern that is embraced enthusiastically by a large number of people, although for only a short period of time.* Fads—sometimes called *crazes*—are commonplace in the United States and Canada. In the late 1950s, for example, two young entrepreneurs in California produced a brightly colored plastic version of a toy popular in Australia: a three-foot wooden hoop swung around the body by gyrating the hips. Hula hoops soon became a national craze, although now they can be found mainly in people's attics and in flea markets. Streaking—a fad of the early 1970s—involved running naked in public. More recent fads have included the Rubik's cube puzzle and the Cabbage Patch dolls that American children prized above all others for about a year.

Fads and fashions are obviously similar. Both involve dispersed collectivities adopting some distinctive social patterns for a relatively short period of time. But fads and fashions do differ in several respects (Blumer, 1968; Turner & Killian, 1987). Fads are truly passing fancies—enthusiasms that capture the mass imagination for a brief time, then burn out. Fashions, however, reflect fundamental human values and social patterns that evolve over time: love, work, health, power, social status, and sexual attractiveness. A fashion, then, builds on what precedes it and influences what follows it, becoming incorporated into a society's dominant culture. As a fad, streaking came out of nowhere and soon vanished. As a fashion, however, blue jeans came out of the rough mining camps of Gold Rush California and are walking every street in the United States today. Because fashions have more historical continuity and ties to convention than fads, the word *fashionable* is generally a compliment, while the word *faddish* is a mild insult.

SOCIAL MOVEMENTS

Crowds, rumors, fashions, and other forms of collective behavior discussed thus far are usually of short duration and only occasionally have lasting consequences for society as a whole. Social movements are far more deliberate and long-lasting forms of collective behavior.

A **social movement** is *long-term organized activity that encourages or discourages some dimension of social change.* Social movements are distinguished from other types of collective behavior by a combination of three characteristics: a higher degree of internal organization; a typically longer duration, perhaps over many years; and a deliberate attempt to shape the organization of society itself.

Social movements may develop around any public issue. In recent years, many homosexual Americans—supported by heterosexuals sympathetic to their political aims—have organized in pursuit of political and social opportunities equal to those of the heterosexual majority. This social movement has already succeeded in having legislation passed in several major cities barring various forms of discrimination based on a person's sexual preference. However, like any social movement that challenges established social patterns, the gay rights movement has sparked a *countermovement*—an organized effort to block, in this case, greater political and social rights for gay people. Almost all public issues that attract widespread attention are likely to become the basis for social movements in favor of change and countermovements that oppose change (Lo, 1982).

Types of Social Movements

Several sociologists have classified social movements according to various criteria (Aberle, 1966; Cameron, 1966; Blumer, 1969). One dimension of difference is *breadth*: some focus only on individuals or a category of a population, while others seek to involve society as a whole. A second dimension of difference is *depth*: some social movements attempt only superficial change in individuals or society, while others pursue more extensive transformations. Combining these two dimensions produces

Social movements address controversial issues. Many men and women have rallied for equal rights for homosexuals, while other Americans support a countermovement that opposes this goal.

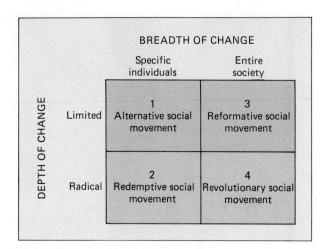

BREADTH OF CHANGE

	Specific individuals	Entire society
Limited	1 Alternative social movement	3 Reformative social movement
Radical	2 Redemptive social movement	4 Revolutionary social movement

(DEPTH OF CHANGE)

Figure 21–1 Four Types of Social Movements

(Aberle, 1966)

four types of social movements, shown in Figure 21–1.

Alternative social movements desire limited change in some individuals by convincing them to discard specific attitudes and behaviors in favor of alternatives. Planned Parenthood, for example, is part of the social movement in the United States concerned with population growth. It encourages individuals of childbearing age to take the possible consequences of their sexual activity more seriously by consistently using birth control technology.

Redemptive social movements also focus on some individuals, but attempt to bring about radical change in their lives. For example, fundamentalist Christian religions that seek new members through the process of conversion—described in Chapter 16—are redemptive social movements. Their goal is change so radical that a person is described as being "born again."

Reformative social movements attempt to bring about limited social change in society as a whole. The holistic health-care movement, described in Chapter 19, is a reformative social movement that seeks to modify health-care practices throughout American society. Reformative social movements generally work within the system, with the goal of accomplishing moderate social change through the political process. They can be progressive (seeking to change some aspect of society into a new form) or reactionary (countermovements seeking to preserve some aspect of present society or to return to social

patterns that existed in the past). In the ongoing debate about abortion in the United States, both the movement in favor of legalized abortion and that opposed to it are reformative social movements.

Revolutionary social movements attempt to bring about a revolutionary transformation of society as a whole. They reject existing social institutions in favor of radically new alternatives. Revolutionary social movements in the American colonies in the eighteenth century and in Czarist Russia in the early twentieth century led to the overthrow of existing regimes and introduced new political systems. The American and Russian revolutions have since served as models for successful revolutionary movements in France, China, Cuba, the Philippines, and elsewhere. Although for most Americans today, the word *revolution* is associated with the ultraradical left, revolutionary social movements also emerge among the ultraconservative right. The John Birch Society and the political organization headed by Lyndon LaRouche each claim that the United States is extensively influenced by socialists, and therefore seek to radically change American social institutions (Broyles, 1978; *Time*, April 21, 1986).

Theories of Social Movements

Since social movements are a highly organized type of collective behavior that endures over a long period of time, sociologists find them somewhat easier to explain than fleeting cases of collective behavior such as mobs and mass hysteria. Several social theories offer insights into how and why social movements arise.

Deprivation Theory

Deprivation theory maintains that social movements arise when large numbers of people feel deprived of things they consider necessary to their well-being. Those who believe that they lack the income, working conditions, political rights, or social dignity they deserve can be expected to engage in organized collective behavior to bring about a more just state of affairs (Morrison, 1978; Rose, 1982).

The emancipation of black Americans from slavery at the end of the Civil War seemed to signal an end to white domination. In the South, however, the economic prosperity of many white farmers depended on low-cost black labor. Whites therefore felt threatened by the apparent rise in the social position of blacks. They were especially likely to feel deprived when the economy was performing poorly. The result was various social movements designed to keep black Americans "in their place." (Dollard et al., 1939). These efforts supported legal reforms such as Jim Crow laws, which rigidly segregated blacks and whites in public settings, and organizations such as the Ku Klux Klan, which spawned terrorist mobs to reinforce racial inequality. By keeping blacks down, these white people were able to hold on to some of their advantages and privileges. Blacks, of course, had long experienced an even greater sense of deprivation in a largely racist white society, and thus had even more to gain from organizing in opposition to the status quo. But they had relatively little opportunity to do so in the face of overwhelming white power. Not until well into the twentieth century were blacks able to successfully organize for racial justice.

The deprivation approach is also found in Karl Marx's expectation that deprived industrial workers would eventually organize in opposition to capitalism. As described in Chapter 4, Marx claimed that capitalism deprived workers economically and politically, by giving them low wages and little social power, and psychologically, by alienating them from their own creative potential. While no socialist revolution has occurred in the United States, labor unions and various political organi-

zations of workers have arisen in an effort to address the sense of deprivation experienced by working-class Americans.

As noted in Chapter 7, deprivation is a relative concept (Stouffer et al., 1949; Merton, 1968). In other words, regardless of their level of deprivation in absolute terms—meaning their actual amount of money and power—people tend to evaluate themselves relative to the situation of some category of other people. **Relative deprivation** is a *perceived disadvantage based on comparisons with what other people have or some other standard.* Relative deprivation obviously arises if people use others in a more favorable position as a reference group, thinking that "there's no reason that *we* shouldn't have what *they* have." People also feel relatively deprived to the extent that they imagine how their lives could be more satisfying than they actually are.

More than a century ago, Alexis de Tocqueville (1955, orig. 1856) examined the social uprising that became the French Revolution. Why, he asked, did revolution occur in France rather than in neighboring Germany, where the peasants were, in absolute terms, far more deprived? Tocqueville's answer was that, as bad as their plight was, German peasants had known nothing but feudal servitude and thus had no basis for feeling deprived. French peasants, on the other hand, had expe-

The Ku Klux Klan reached its peak of power in the decades after the Civil War and continues even now with its program to maintain white supremacy.

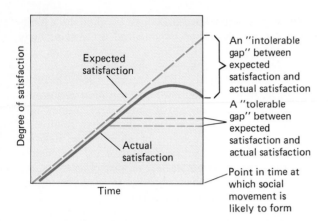

Figure 21–2 Relative Deprivation and Social Movements

In this diagram, the solid line represents a rising standard of living over time. The dotted line represents the expected standard of living, which is typically somewhat higher. Davies describes the difference between the two as "a tolerable gap between what people want and what they get." If the standard of living suddenly drops in the midst of rising expectations, however, this gap grows to an intolerable level. At this point, social movements can be expected to form. (Davies, 1962)

rienced steady improvement in their lives and were aware that society did not have to be the way it was. Able to imagine still further improvements, they experienced a keen sense of relative deprivation. Tocqueville concluded that "steadily increasing prosperity, far from tranquilizing the population, everywhere promoted a spirit of unrest" (1955:175; orig. 1856).

Echoing Tocqueville's insight, James C. Davies (1962) has stressed the link between the birth of social movements and *rising expectations*. As life gets better, in other words, people quickly take the improvements for granted and look to the future for even more. If the standard of living stops improving—or worse, suddenly begins to drop—people are likely to experience a pronounced sense of relative deprivation. Thus, as illustrated in Figure 21–2, social movements aimed at changing society are most likely to occur when an extended period of improvement in the standard of living is followed by a shorter period of declining circumstances.

Evaluation. Deprivation theory is generally viewed as basically sound, and this approach explains why common sense is not always a good predictor of discontent. But this approach also has shortcomings. Within any society,

at least some discontent is likely to be found among most segments of the population at all times. How, then, can we explain the fact that social movements emerge among some categories of people and not others? Deprivation theory's usual answer involves circular reasoning: social movements are caused by deprivation, the only evidence for which is the formation of a social movement. But the validity of this approach can only be demonstrated by establishing the presence of relative deprivation independent of the formation of social movements (Jenkins & Perrow, 1977).

Mass-Society Theory

William Kornhauser's mass-society theory (1959) suggests that social movements are formed by people who feel socially isolated and personally insignificant within the masses of large, complex societies. Lacking significant social attachments to others through family, work, or neighborhood, such people are likely to feel powerless. Under these circumstances, social movements can be attractive, offering a sense of belonging and conferring greater meaning on a person's life. The significance of social movements, from this point of view, lies not so much in their goal of changing society as in the opportunity they offer to people to escape from their intolerable isolation. Areas in which families or neighborhoods are weak are likely to have many people who can readily be mobilized into a social movement; where there is strong social integration, on the other hand, social movements are unlikely.

Like the ideas of Gustave Le Bon discussed earlier, Kornhauser's view of social movements is conservative and negative, regarding them as psychologically motivated groups prone to deviance. Kornhauser also suggests that social movements contain people who are easily manipulated by leaders into active subversion of democratic principles. He asserts that support for social movements embracing political ideas—from the far right to the far left—is typically greatest among people who otherwise have the fewest memberships in social groups.

Evaluation. The strength of Kornhauser's theory is that it links characteristics of "joiners" to qualities found in both social movements and the larger society. Yet response to mass-society theory has been mixed. In part, criticism has been on practical grounds: in research, how does one define or measure the extent of a "mass society"? Partly, too, criticism has been a matter of principle: this theory tends to view a well-integrated society in positive terms, despite the fact that such a society is likely to have pronounced racial or class inequality.

Research provides mixed support for this approach. The Nazi movement in Germany, for instance, appears to have recruited mostly people who were *not* socially isolated (Lipset, 1963; Oberschall, 1973). Similarly, people who took to the streets in the urban riots of the 1960s typically had extensive ties to the community (Tilly, Tilly, & Tilly, 1975). There is also evidence that young people who join religious cults do not have particularly weak family ties (Wright & Piper, 1986). On the other hand, Frances Piven and Richard Cloward (1977) argue that a dramatic breakdown of routine social patterns does contribute to social movements among poor people. And Bert Useem's (1985) study of the New Mexico State Penitentiary showed an increase in protest activity by inmates after the suspension of prison programs that had promoted social ties among them. Useem further claims that the absence of social ties was responsible for the chaotic and violent nature of the insurgency among those prisoners.

Structural-Strain Theory

One of the most influential approaches to understanding the emergence of social movements was developed by Neil Smelser (1962). Smelser's structural-strain theory identifies six social conditions that contribute to the formation of a social movement. In simple terms, the more that these factors are present, the greater the likelihood that a social movement will develop. Smelser's theory also offers some hypotheses about why collective behavior sometimes takes the form of a relatively unorganized mob or riot, and at other times takes the highly organized form of a social movement.

The antiwar movement, and particularly organized opposition to nuclear weapons, in the United States and Western Europe during the 1980s illustrates each of the six factors of Smelser's theory.

1. *Structural conduciveness.* The theory argues that social movements are rooted in society itself. Social structure conducive to the emergence of a social movement includes any social patterns that set the stage for significant social problems. The antiwar movement exists because of the possibility of war in the world, especially the dangerous political and military opposition between the United States and the Soviet Union that has existed since World War II. In addition, for a social movement to emerge, social structure must allow for active political opposition. The greater toleration of political dissent in the West explains the more extensive antiwar organization there than in the more repressive Soviet Union and East European countries.

2. *Structural strain.* The emergence of social movements is encouraged by strains within society, including any patterns of social conflict or the failure of reality to meet expectations. The antiwar movement was sparked by the inconsistency between the expected function of government—to provide protection and security to citizens—and the reality of warlike rhetoric and a massive buildup of nuclear as well as conventional arms that generated widespread anxiety.

3. *Growth and spread of an explanation.* A needed step toward organized collective behavior is developing a clear statement of the problem, its causes, likely consequences, and what can be done to make matters better. If this is not done well, people are likely to express their dissatisfaction in a disorganized way. At the least, they will formulate no clear response; at best, they may engage in rioting. A well-formulated analysis of a situation, spread throughout the society, encourages a well-organized social movement. The fact that most Americans apparently accept the idea that the world is, and will remain, a dangerous place has certainly inhibited a widespread antiwar movement in the United States. In Western Europe, however, a growing number of citizens came to think that governments were unable or unwilling to end the arms race, and that it was up to people themselves to reduce the danger of war through direct political action. This explanation became the moral justification of the antiwar movement.

4. *Precipitating factors.* Social movements are often a long time in the making. At some point, however, an event may precipitate the onset of collective action. The rapid increase in the nuclear stockpiles of both superpowers—now totaling more than 50,000 warheads—was a general cause of growing antiwar organization among Americans and Europeans. More specifically, the introduction of intermediate-range nuclear missiles to Western Europe by the Reagan administration in 1983 precipitated extensive antiwar demonstrations and swelled the ranks of antiwar organizations.

5. *Mobilization for action.* Once precipitating factors have focused widespread concern on a public issue, collective action is likely to take place: committee meetings, leafleting, fund-raising, lobbying, and demonstrations. In the wake of the 1980s military buildup and the increasingly hawkish rhetoric by superpower leaders, tens of

The social movement opposing the use of nuclear weapons has attracted supporters all over the world who believe that people can pressure their governments to end the arms race.

thousands of people joined the nuclear freeze movement. This international movement sought to halt the arms race as a first step in gradually reducing nuclear arsenals. In Western Europe, where American missiles had been introduced, large protest rallies were frequent and widespread.

6. *Lack of social control.* The direction and consequences of any social movement are partly determined by the responses of various established authorities, including political officials and police. Powerful repression on the part of the state can weaken a social movement, as a lack of social control can allow it to grow. Of course, should leaders initiate changes demanded by a social movement, the movement is likely to weaken along with its reason for existing. The antiwar movement somewhat declined as a first summit between President Reagan

and General Secretary Gorbachev raised new hopes of world peace. Subsequent failure to reach firm agreement on arms reduction led to renewed mobilization, however. In 1987, the two superpowers did agree to eliminate intermediate-range missiles from Europe. This has led to a sharp decline in antiwar activity, no doubt with some sense of success among movement leaders. The threat of nuclear war remains, however, so that the antiwar movement will certainly continue.

Neither Western European officials nor leaders of the American government have ever attempted to use the force of the state to quash the antiwar movement. The description of the Polish Solidarity movement, presented in the box, is sufficient to remind us that state power can effectively oppose most social movements even after they have gained considerable support.

Evaluation. A strength of Smelser's approach is that it shows how a combination of social factors may encourage or inhibit collective behavior. Structural-strain theory also explains that collective behavior may take the form of organized social movements or more spontaneous mob action or rioting. Of course, the theory is complex and offers only a general indication of how particular combinations of factors may influence specific situations. Furthermore, Smelser's theory is certainly incomplete, ignoring, for example, the important role of resources in the success or failure of a social movement (Oberschall, 1973; Jenkins & Perrow, 1977; McCarthy & Zald, 1977).

Resource-Mobilization Theory

Resource-mobilization theory adds an important consideration: social movements cannot be successful—or even get started—unless they have necessary resources, including money, human labor, office and communications facilities, social contacts with influential people and the mass media, and a positive public image. This approach points out that the fate of any social movement depends on organizing effectively to attract resources and mobilize people to act. Rosa Parks—the black woman who refused to give up her seat on a public bus to a white man (described in Chapter 11)—was instrumental in beginning the bus boycott in Montgomery, Alabama, largely because she was already involved in civil rights networks in that city and thus could attract resources (Killian, 1984).

Outsiders as well as insiders can play a crucial role in supplying and developing a social movement's resources (McCarthy & Zald, 1977). People with social disadvantages often lack the money, contacts, leadership skills, and organizational know-how that a successful movement requires. Absorbed in meeting their daily needs, they may feel isolated from one another and unsure of how to develop and unite their skills and energies. Often sympathetic outsiders with more money, education, and leisure may fill the resource gap. Thus well-to-do whites, including many college students, played an important part in the black civil rights movement in the 1960s, and many affluent white women and men have taken a leading role in the American women's movement.

People are motivated to join a social movement to the degree that they and the organization have consistent understandings of events. In practice, this means that new recruits are in social networks of present members. Such people are also likely to have few social ties to the movement's opponents. Social networks are therefore an important means of attracting people who can provide loyalty as well as money and labor to a social movement (Snow, Zurcher, & Ekland-Olson, 1980; Snow, Rochford, Jr., Worden, & Benford, 1986).

There was little governmental response to the AIDS epidemic when it began in the United States in the early 1980s. To a large extent, the responsibility of developing educational programs was assumed by the gay communities in several large cities. As the number of persons with AIDS rapidly increased, however, more resources were forthcoming from state and local governments. And as public concern about AIDS rose after 1985, the federal government began to provide more and more funding for fighting the disease. Also important has been the financial and public relations support provided by members of the entertainment industry. In short, the ability to attract extensive resources has transformed the movement seeking an end to this deadly disease from a small and uncertain beginning to a national coalition of political leaders, educators, and medical personnel.

Evaluation. The strength of resource-mobilization theory is its recognition that resources as well as discontent are necessary to the success of a social movement. This theory also points out the likely interplay between any social movement and other groups and organizations that can provide or withhold valuable resources. One problem with the theory, however, is the implication that successful social movements can develop among relatively powerless segments of American society only if outside resources are available. Aldon Morris (1981) has demonstrated that the black civil rights movement of the 1950s and 1960s was supported largely by black people and resources within the black community. Furthermore, there is ample evidence that powerful members of society often oppose any effort to challenge the status quo. Some powerful whites certainly did provide valuable resources to the black civil rights movement in the United States. But white elites typically attempted to limit the success of this social movement (McAdam, 1982, 1983).

In general, then, the success or failure of a social movement is a political struggle involving challengers and supporters of the status quo. If established political forces or countermovements are strong and united, a movement seeking social change is likely to fail. If, on the other hand, they are weak or divided, the opportunities for success increase.

The four major theories of social movements each

Solidarity: Protest in Poland

At the end of World War II, Poland came under the political control of the Soviet Union, whose army had occupied much of the country while advancing against Germany. In the late 1940s, the Soviet Union established a socialist economic system in Poland under a Polish government controlled from Moscow. Loss of national independence and the continuing Soviet presence in Polish society were crucial factors underlying the formation of the Polish workers' movement commonly known as Solidarity in the late 1970s.

The first major confrontation between Polish workers and Soviet-backed authorities erupted in 1956, as the economy experienced a severe recession. Workers protesting low wages, poor working conditions, high prices, and housing shortages flooded the streets of the city of Poznan, and fighting resulted in over fifty deaths before the government ended the insurgency.

Discontent simmered through the 1960s. In 1970, government-announced increases in food prices precipitated further demonstrations and protests—this time led by shipyard workers in the city of Gdansk, where one protesting worker named Lech Walęsa gradually rose to leadership that would bring him world attention. As protests swept the country, the government again responded harshly, and more Polish workers died at the hands of the military.

Limited reforms during the 1970s—including a freeze on prices—demonstrated the effectiveness of worker protests and sparked rising expectations of a better standard of living and greater political freedom. Opposition to the government, including numerous underground newspapers, intensified during the late 1970s as the state of the Polish economy steadily worsened. The workers gained support and legitimacy from many of Poland's intellectuals and from the influential Catholic Church. As the seeds of Solidarity began to flower, a decision was made not to oppose Soviet domination of Poland in an outright fashion. Instead, workers would attempt to gain control over working conditions by forming trade unions independent of the government. The people's sense of political strength and unity was heightened after Polish Cardinal Karol Wojtyla became Pope John Paul II of the Roman Catholic Church and visited his native land to great public acclaim in the summer of 1979. By the end of that year, crowds of sympathetic Poles were listening to Solidarity's public demands for free trade unions, the right to strike, and freedom of speech. Solidarity had become both a social movement and an officially established organization representing some 10 million Polish workers. Family members included, Solidarity now involved a majority of Poles.

The powerful force of rising expectations and Solidarity's specific demands were more than the Polish

---

point to different elements of the process by which social movements are likely to form. Table 21–1 presents a summary of these theories.

Stages in Social Movements

The duration of any social movement clearly depends on the effectiveness of its organizational foundation. Some social movements in recent years deliberately avoided extensive organization. One example was the Yippie movement of the 1960s, an outgrowth of the hippie movement. The Yippies embraced a "do your own thing" philosophy that was hostile to rigid organizational practices (Hoffman, 1968), and the movement consequently dissolved within a few years. On the other hand, the black civil rights movement, the women's movement, and the gay rights movement are all supported by well-established organizations, which has contributed to their longevity.

While every social movement is in some ways unique, most move through certain defined stages. Sociologists have pointed out four general stages in the life course of a typical social movement (Blumer, 1969; Mauss, 1975; Tilly, 1978).

Stage 1: Emergence. Social movements are typically provoked by the perception that all is not well, although each theory already discussed describes this dissatisfaction in somewhat different terms. Some social movements—

Solidarity reached the peak of its power in 1980 and was soon suppressed by the Polish government. But in 1988 worker protests renewed demands for a greater voice in political affairs.

at the shipyards at Gdansk, could force even more concessions. Solidarity had already gained far more power than the government ever imagined it could.

As illegal strikes spread in 1981, the Polish government acted decisively to cripple Solidarity. First, telephone communication was suspended to inhibit further organization. Then the government declared a state of martial law. Polish troops, and the ever-present fear of an invasion by the Soviet army, finally brought Solidarity to its knees. In the years since then, the attention of the world has turned to other matters. Yet the ideals represented by Solidarity continue as a source of great hope, frustration, and conflict in Polish society.

government was prepared to meet, cope with, and certainly more than the Soviets were prepared to tolerate. The government attempted to diffuse protest by granting minor concessions, but these only served to support the belief that the Solidarity movement, led by Wałęsa and the workers

SOUCE: Based on Timothy Garton Ash, *The Polish Revolution: Solidarity* (New York: Charles Scribner's Sons, 1983); also Denis MacShane, *Solidarity: Poland's Independent Trade Union* (Nottingham, UK: Spokesman, 1981).

such as the civil rights and women's movements—are born of widespread dissatisfaction. Still others emerge when a small group attempts to increase public awareness of some issue—a process often described as *agitation*—with the intention of building grass-roots support. This process is illustrated by the nuclear freeze movement in the 1980s.

Stage 2: Coalescence. After a social movement emerges, the next state typically involves the coalescence of a number of individuals into an organization that actively enters public life. This includes developing leadership, formulating policies and tactics, building positive morale, and recruiting new members. At this stage, the social movement may engage in collective action—such

as a rally or demonstration—to promote public awareness of its cause and to gain recognition as an established political force. The mass media are usually of considerable importance for carrying the movement's message to the entire society. The movement may also seek to form alliances with other organizations to gain the resources needed for success.

Stage 3: Bureaucratization. Once established, a social movement is likely to develop many of the characteristics of formal organization described in Chapter 7. Initially, success may depend on the personal abilities of a few leaders. In time, however, bureaucratic organization replaces personal ties as the means of holding the movement together. Of course, a social movement may or may not succeed in becoming established in this way. Many activist organizations on college campuses during the late 1960s were based on the charismatic qualities of individual leaders. Avoiding formality as a matter of principle and politics, most of these movements did not endure for long. On the other hand, the National Organization for Women (NOW) provides a steady voice on behalf of the women's movement. Bureaucratization can sometimes hinder the success of a social movement, however. In a review of social movements in recent American history, Frances Piven and Richard Cloward (1977) note that leaders can be so preoccupied with building a formal organization that they neglect their responsibility to encourage sentiments of insurgency among movement members. In this way, Piven and Cloward claim, the radical edge of protest can be lost.

Stage 4: Decline.   Social movements are inherently dynamic, so they typically reach a point of decline. Frederick Miller (1983) has suggested four general reasons for the decline of social movements.

First, a social movement may be so successful in accomplishing its goals that it has no further reason to exist—as, for example, the women's suffrage movement that in 1920 won American women the right to vote. Successes of this kind are rare, however, because few social movements have a single specific goal. The women's movement today has many goals, and gaining one victory often leads to new demands.

Second, a social movement may fail because of poor leadership, loss of interest in its goals within the larger society, the exhausting of available resources, re-

Radical youth burst on the American scene in 1968 with a message of anger and frustration. But without a well-defined internal structure, many of these organizations soon disappeared.

Table 21-1   THEORIES OF SOCIAL MOVEMENTS: A SUMMARY

Deprivation Theory	People join as a result of experiencing relative deprivation. Social movement is a means of seeking change that brings participants greater benefits. Social movements are especially likely when rising expectations are frustrated.
Mass-Society Theory	People who lack established social ties are easily mobilized into social movements. Periods of social breakdown are likely to spawn social movements. Social movement is a means of gaining a sense of belonging and social participation.
Structural-Strain Theory	People join because of their shared concern about the inability of society to operate as they believe it should. The growth of a social movement reflects many factors, including a belief in its legitimacy and some precipitating event that provokes action.
Resource-Mobilization Theory	People may join for all of the reasons noted above and also because of social ties to existing members. The success or failure of a social movement depends largely on the resources available to it. Also important is the extent of opposition to its goals within the larger society.

pression by established authorities, or bureaucratization. Some people attracted by the excitement often generated in the early stages of a social movement may lose interest when formal organization replaces personal relationships and activities and responsibilities become increasingly routine. Fragmentation resulting from internal conflicts over goals and tactics is also fairly common. Students for a Democratic Society (SDS), for example, was an organization that developed out of the civil rights and antiwar movements of the 1960s. It fragmented when some members decided to pursue more radical social action, often involving violence, and other members reverted to supporting traditional political parties. As this example suggests, fragmentation may cause one social movement to decline while simultaneously giving rise to other social movements.

Third, a social movement may decline because its leaders are coopted by the established power structure, which may offer them money, prestige, and other rewards that divert them from pursuing the goals of the social movement. This process of "selling out" is one example of the iron law of oligarchy, noted in Chapter 7, by which Robert Michels (1949, orig. 1911) claimed that organizational leaders are likely to use their positions to enrich themselves. For example, Jerry Rubin—one of the better-known political activists of the late 1960s— used his celebrity standing as a rebel to build a career in the New York financial world. On the other hand, there are cases of people who left lucrative, high-prestige occupations to become active in social movements. Cat Stevens—a famous rock star of the 1970s—has become a Muslim, changed his name to Yusuf Islam, and now seeks to promote the spread of the Islamic religion.

Fourth, a social movement may decline as the result of repression. This means simply that the establishment opposed by the movement has the power to frighten away participants, to discourage new recruits, or—in extreme cases—to subject leaders to imprisonment or violence. Often the state reacts in this way to social movements that are considered to be revolutionary in their goals. The government of South Africa, for example, has banned the African National Congress (ANC), a political organization that seeks to overthrow the government-supported system of apartheid. Anyone suspected of involvement in this organization is subject to arrest. One of this movement's leaders, Nelson Mandela, has been in prison for more than twenty-five years.

Beyond the reasons for decline noted by Miller, a fifth possibility is that a social movement may become established. This does not mean that it is entirely success-

Despite violent suppression by the white government, many black South Africans support the African National Congress— a social movement seeking an end to apartheid.

ful, although social movements that become established do typically realize some of their goals. Rather, it means that a social movement loses its distinctive character as an opposition organization at the margins of political life and becomes part of the system. For example, the American labor movement is now largely established; its leaders control vast sums of money and resemble the tycoons of business they opposed in earlier decades. Another example is the consumer movement. Led by Ralph Nader and a host of volunteers called Nader's Raiders during the 1960s, the consumer movement entered the 1980s as an established lobbying organization in Washington, D.C. Not surprisingly, when a social movement becomes established, at least some people are likely to charge its leadership with selling out.

Figure 21–3 provides a graphic summary of the various stages of social movements.

Social Movements and Social Change

Because social movements are generally based upon important public issues, they attempt to encourage—or inhibit—some dimension of social change. Of course, social movements have various degrees of success in

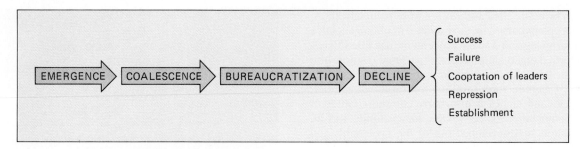

Figure 21–3 Stages in the Lives of Social Movements

achieving their goals. The goal of racial equality in the United States, although far from realized, has progressed—demonstrating the relative success of the civil rights movement and the relative failure of white supremacist countermovements such as the Ku Klux Klan.

The success of many social movements in American history may be overlooked to the extent that the changes they provoked are now taken for granted. Early labor movements, for example, eventually brought an end to child labor in American factories. Limited working hours, safer working conditions, and the legal right to collectively bargain with employers are also the fruits of various social movements supported primarily by working people. Legislation protecting the environment is another area in which social movements have been successful during this century. In recent decades, widespread and unregulated pollution of the environment has come under the scrutiny of various watchdog agencies of the federal and local governments, although certainly the goal of a healthful environment has yet to be reached.

The American women's movement also has yet to attain its goal of total equality under the law for men and women, but its achievements in extending the legal rights and social opportunities of American women are great enough that many young people are all but ignorant of the extent of social inequities that existed in the recent past.

Social movements and social change are deeply interrelated. Efforts to extend the rights of workers were themselves sparked by the Industrial Revolution and the rise of capitalism in Western Europe and North America. In the same way, the social gains made by various segments of the American population—including women, racial and ethnic minorities, and gay people—represent broad changes in American society that have provoked various countermovements attempting to preserve the "traditional American way of life." Especially in large and complex societies, social change is a continuous process that is both the cause and the consequence of social movements.

SUMMARY

1. Collectivities differ from social groups in their limited social interaction among participants, unclear social boundaries, and weak and often unconventional social norms.

2. Crowds are a common and important type of collective behavior. Five major types are casual crowds, conventional crowds, expressive crowds, acting crowds, and protest crowds.

3. Mobs and riots are types of crowd behavior involving emotional intensity and violence. While mobs usually

have a specific focus for their activity, rioting is typically undirected destructiveness.

4. Contagion theory claims that crowds are inherently anonymous, suggestible, and subject to emotional contagion. Convergence theory suggests that the behavior of crowds is a consequence of the characteristics of people within them. Emergent-norm theory states that crowds develp their own social structure.

5. Crowd behavior has historically been linked to social change. Crowd activity is either destructive or construc-

tive, depending on the political orientation of the observer.

6. Rumor is a type of collective behavior that thrives in a climate of ambiguity. Rumors are concerned with public issues, while gossip, a closely related concept, involves information about personal affairs that is of more localized interest.

7. Public opinion involves different positions on issues of general social importance. Americans with greater wealth and power are likely to be opinion leaders. On any public issue, a significant proportion of the population has no opinion. Public opinion is also subject to change over time.

8. Mass hysteria is a type of collective behavior in which people anxiously respond to a perceived threat—real or imagined. It often involves an increasing spiral of panic in which hysteria leads to ineffective action, which, in turn, causes hysteria to build further.

9. Fashion is a characteristic of industrial societies related to efforts to gain social prestige. A fad is distinguished from a fashion as typically being less conventional, having less continuity over time, and involving greater enthusiasm.

10. A social movement is a distinctive type of collective behavior that is highly organized, is of relatively long duration, and involves deliberate efforts to change or discourage change.

11. Alternative social movements attempt to make limited changes in particular individuals; redemptive social movements seek extensive change in individuals. Reformative social movements are efforts to change society in a limited way; revolutionary social movements desire a radically reorganized society.

12. Deprivation theory explains social movements as a response to perceived deprivation. The concept of relative deprivation suggests that deprivation is not perceived in absolute terms, but in relation to some variable standard of reference.

13. Mass-society theory suggests that people are likely to join social movements to gain a sense of belonging and social participation. In addition to seeking social change, then, social movements provide a means of meeting personal needs.

14. Structural-strain theory explains the development of social movement as a cumulative consequence of six factors. Important among them are strain caused by the failure of society to perform as people think it should and the emergence of a generalized explanation of events that favors some course of action in response to a social problem.

15. Resource-mobilization theory emphasizes that the success or failure of a social movement depends greatly on the availability of resources such as money, human labor, and alliances with other organizations. In addition, people with considerable money and leisure time have the ability to be active in social movements and often provide much of the necessary resources.

16. Social movements typically proceed through four consecutive stages. Emergence involves recognition of a public issue as important; coalescence represents the social movement's entry into public life as an active organization; bureaucratization refers to a social movement's increasingly formal organization over time. Finally, many social movements die as a result of their success, failure, the cooptation of their leaders, repression, or becoming established.

17. Social movements cannot be separated from the process of social change. The success of social movements in promoting social change is found in many characteristics of society that have come to be taken for granted. In addition, social change also sparks social movements. Social movements and social change are therefore deeply interrelated.

KEY CONCEPTS

collective behavior actions, thoughts, and emotions that involve large numbers of people and that do not conform to established social norms

collectivity a large number of people who have limited interaction with one another and who do not share well-defined and conventional norms

crowd a temporary gathering of people who share some common focus of attention and often influence one another

fad a somewhat unconventional social pattern that is embraced enthusiastically by a large number of people, although for only a short period of time

fashion a social pattern favored for a time by a large number of people

mass behavior collective behavior among people dispersed over a wide geographical area

mass hysteria a situation in which people in a wide area respond to some perceived threat with anxious or frantic behavior

mob a highly emotional crowd united by the common purpose of some specific violent and destructive action

panic a situation that occurs when a crowd is provoked into seemingly irrational and often self-destructive behavior by some perceived threat

propaganda information presented with the intention of shaping public opinion

relative deprivation a perceived disadvantage based on comparisons with what other people have or some other standard

riot a situation that results when a crowd explodes into undirected violent and destructive behavior

rumor unsubstantiated information spread informally, often by word of mouth

social movement long-term organized activity that encourages or discourages some dimension of social change

SUGGESTED READINGS

These two books provide further reading on topics covered in this chapter.

Ralph H. Turner and Lewis M. Killian. *Collective Behavior.* 3rd ed. Englewood Cliffs, NJ: Prentice-Hall, 1987.

Mayer N. Zald and John D. McCarthy, eds. *Social Movements in an Organizational Society.* New Brunswick, NJ: Transaction, 1987.

This recent book is one of the few academic examinations of gossip, including supermarket tabloids and various types of "idle talk."

Jack Levin and Arnold Arluke. *Gossip: the Inside Scoop.* New York: Plenum Press, 1987.

This book describes how rumors have adversely affected large American corporations, from Procter and Gamble to McDonald's.

Fredrick Koenig. *Rumor in the Marketplace: The Social Psychology of Commercial Hearsay.* Dover, MA: Auburn House, 1985.

A collective-behavior classic is this story of the 1938 *War of the Worlds* broadcast.

Howard Koch. *The Panic Broadcast: Portrait of an Event.* Boston: Little, Brown, 1970.

This examination of Chicano protest in the western United States focuses on the various ways in which people express their suffering and how this may or may not provoke an effective response.

John C. Hammerback, Richard J. Jensen, and José Angel Gutierrez. *A War of Words: Chicano Protest in the 1960s and 1970s.* Westport, CT: Greenwood Press, 1985.

Various theories of social movements are applied to decades of black protest movements in the United States in this book.

Doug McAdam. *Political Process and the Development of Black Insurgency.* Chicago: University of Chicago Press, 1982.

These two books examine political movements of the 1960s and 1970s. The first provides a history of Students for a Democratic Society, a central force in the political events of that turbulent period. The second book examines which Americans were involved in organizing against the Vietnam War.

James Miller. *"Democracy in the Streets" from Port Huron to the Siege of Chicago.* New York: Simon and Schuster, 1987.

Nancy Zaroulis and Gerald Sullivan. *Who Spoke Up? American Protest against the Vietnam War 1963–1975.* New York: Holt, Rinehart and Winston, 1985.

This collection of essays explores a wide range of social movements in recent American history.

Jo Freedman, ed. *Social Movements of the Sixties and Seventies.* New York: Longman, 1983.

This book provides an insider's account of the rise of ACORN (Association of Community Organizations for Reform Now), a recent social movement of national significance.

Gary Delgado. *Organizing the Movement: The Roots and Growth of ACORN.* Philadelphia: Temple University Press, 1986.

This book describes one of the most stunning examples of collective behavior in recent years: the mass suicide of some 900 members of a sect called the People's Temple in Jonestown, Guyana.

John R. Hall. *Gone from the Promised Land: Jonestown in American Cultural History.* New Brunswick, NJ: Transaction, 1987.

Here is a personal account of a teenager's experiences during the Cultural Revolution in China that took place between 1966 and 1969—which has been dubbed a mass movement out of control.

Gao Yuan. *Born Red: A Chronicle of the Cultural Revolution.* Stanford, CA: Stanford University Press, 1987.

Unlike political leaders with big bankrolls, most people concerned with political change must mobilize extensive popular support. This book describes the role of social workers in community change.

Karen S. Haynes and James S. Mickelson. *Affecting Change: Social Workers in the Political Arena*. New York: Longman, 1986.

An analysis of the rise of the Solidarity social movement in Poland is contained in this recent study.

Timothy Garton Ash. *The Polish Revolution: Solidarity*. New York: Charles Scribner's Sons, 1983.

These two books provide a look at social movements in world perspective, with special attention to the Third World.

Robert P. Weller and Scott E. Guggenheim, eds. *Power and Protest in the Countryside: Studies of Rural Unrest in Asia, Europe, and Latin America*. Durham, NC: Duke Press Policy Studies, 1982.

John Walton. *Reluctant Rebels: Comparative Studies of Revolution and Underdevelopment*. New York: Columbia University Press, 1984.

CHAPTER 22

Social Change and Modernity

Thornton Wilder's play *Our Town* begins with a description of the fictional town of Grover's Corners, New Hampshire, in the early summer of 1901:

Well, I'd better show you how our town lies. [Pointing] Up here is Main Street. Polish Town's across the tracks, and some [Canadian] families. [Points again] Over there is the Congregational Church; across the street's the Presbyterian. Methodist and Unitarian are over there. Baptist is down in the holla' by the river. Catholic Church is over beyond the tracks.

Here's the Town Hall and the Post Office combined; jail's in the basement. . . . Along here's a row of stores. Hitching posts and horse blocks in front of them. . . . Here's the grocery store and here's Mr. Morgan's drugstore. Most everybody in town manages to look into these two stores once a day. . . . Nice town, y'know what I mean? Nobody very remarkable ever came out of it, s'far as we know. The earliest tombstones in the cemetery up there on the mountain say 1670–1680—they're Grovers and Cartwrights and Gibbes and Herseys—same names as are around here now. . . . Over there are some Civil War veterans. Iron flags on their graves. . . . New Hampshire boys . . . had a notion that the Union ought to be kept together, though they'd never seen more than fifty miles of it themselves. . . . There are a hundred and twenty-five horses in Grover's Corners . . . and now they're bringing in these automobiles, the best thing to do is to just stay home. Why, I can remember when a dog could sleep all day in the middle of Main Street and nothing come along to disturb him. . . . Everybody locks their house doors now at night. Ain't been any burglars in town yet, but everybody's heard about 'em.

You'd be surprised, though—on the whole, things don't change much around here. (1957:6–7, 65, 79–80; orig. 1938)

In 1901, the majority of Americans lived in rural areas and small towns such as Grover's Corners. The entire country's population was only about 76 million—the same as that of the five largest states today. Many Americans never traveled more than a few miles from where they were born. Their lives began and ended within a small, familiar sphere of experience; the rest of the world was largely unknown. Yet the United States was on the verge of a number of changes that would greatly expand the size and complexity of American society. At the same time, from the point of view of any particular individual, the world itself would seem increasingly small.

Mass communications were in their infancy at the turn of the century. Most newspapers reported only local events, and the first telephones linked only people within a single town. Not until 1915 were coast-to-coast calls possible from a few major cities. Shortly afterward, the radio became commonplace. Television was introduced a generation later in 1939. Nationwide television networks began operation only in 1951.

Changes in transportation also steadily expanded people's awareness of the surrounding world. For thousands of years, transportation had been a matter of animal power, limiting an average day's journey to a distance of perhaps fifty miles. The railroad moved goods and people more efficiently, but it was the automobile that forever changed the way Americans think about distance—attracting both praise as a technological wonder and scorn as a threat to the independent world of the small town. The airplane, pioneered by the Wright brothers and others in the first years of this century, eventually linked the entire world, just as the automobile linked the nation. The first airplane crossed the Atlantic Ocean in 1919, and air travel became increasingly common after World War II.

The advantage of hindsight shows changes in American society—and throughout the world—during the twentieth century to be nothing less than staggering.

In an age of malls filled with thousands of strangers, the idea that people dropped by a local store just to say hello—or for a friendly game of checkers—is all but forgotten.

This chapter provides a detailed look at the process of social change and some of its consequences, both positive and negative. Social change has resulted in what sociologists call *modernity* in industrialized societies such as the United States. Modernity represents a profound transformation of traditional, preindustrial societies, at once providing solutions to age-old problems and creating problems beyond the imagination of people living centuries ago.

WHAT IS SOCIAL CHANGE?

The complex organization of human social life has been the focus of this entire book. Some previous discussions have examined relatively *static* social patterns, including values and norms, statuses and roles, social stratification and social institutions. Other discussions have focused on *dynamic* forces that recast human consciousness, human skills, and human needs—including technological innovation, the development of formal organizations, the growth of cities, social conflict, and the emergence of social movements. All of these are closely linked to **social change,** meaning *transformation of culture and social institutions over time that is reflected in the life patterns of individuals.* The process of social change has four general characteristics.

Social change is universal but variable. Few dimensions of human experience remain the same over time. But although every society is affected by social change, all do not change at the same rate. As noted in Chapter 4, hunting and gathering societies changed little over thousands of years. Gerhard and Jean Lenski (1987) point out that a society's rate of social change typically increases as technology advances. This is because new technology expands the range of human possibilities. In addition, the more cultural elements already present in a society, the greater the overall consequences of a single invention, owing to the greater number of new combinations of elements.

Furthermore, not all cultural elements change at the same rate. The concept of *cultural lag* developed by William Ogburn (1964) refers to the fact that material culture usually changes faster than nonmaterial culture (see Chapter 3). As noted in Chapter 19, for example, the rapid development of medical devices to prolong the life of seriously ill people (elements of material culture) has outpaced our ability to clearly define "death" (an element of nonmaterial culture).

Social change is both intentional and unplanned. Especially in industrial societies, many dimensions of social change are deliberately encouraged. Scientists continually seek more effective forms of energy and medical technology, for example. On the other hand, there is usually only a limited understanding of the consequences of such changes. When the automobile appeared in the United States early in this century, few could have foreseen the way it would reshape American society. There may be little surprise in the fact that people now travel in a single day distances that required weeks or months a century ago. But who could have predicted how the car would change American family patterns and the shape of urban America?

Social change is often controversial. Anyone is likely to find some good and some bad in any example of social change. In the case of the automobile, most Americans undoubtedly appreciate the mobility that cars provide. At the same time, however, a nation with over 175 million motor vehicles now finds that auto exhaust is a major cause of air pollution, and almost 50,000 Americans die in automobile accidents each year.

Of course, any transformation of society is likely to be supported by some and opposed by others. The Industrial Revolution, for example, was welcomed by capitalists, who saw advanced technology and factories as a means of earning greater profits. But many workers, fearful of losing their jobs to machines, had good reason to oppose "progress." More recently, the development of nuclear power has sparked controversy in American society. Some people see it as a source of inexpensive energy that will not deplete such natural resources as oil and coal. Others, however, view the near disaster at Pennsylvania's Three Mile Island in 1979 and the catastrophic accident at the Chernobyl nuclear plant in the Soviet Union in 1986 as adequate evidence that nuclear reactors are not only a source of radioactive waste but also an immediate threat to public safety. Apart from technology, changing social patterns involving relations between blacks and whites, between men and women, and between gays and "straights" have also become controversial public issues.

Social changes differ in duration and consequences. Once introduced, some social changes are of passing importance, but others endure for generations. The least important are fads such as Cabbage Patch dolls, which tend to dissipate quickly with little long-term effect on society. But Americans are still coming to terms with some powerful technological advances such as television,

which recently celebrated its fiftieth birthday. At this point, we can only imagine how the computer revolution will transform the entire world in generations to come. Like the automobile and television, computers are likely to have both positive and negative long-range effects, providing new kinds of jobs while eliminating old ones, and allowing easier processing of information while reducing personal privacy.

Sources of Social Change

Previous chapters have suggested that causes of social change are found both inside and outside a society. As advanced technology in communication and transportation increasingly links the societies of the world, and advancing industrialization affects the ecosystem of the entire planet, change in one place begets change elsewhere.

Cultural Processes

Culture is a dynamic system into which human beings continually introduce new elements, just as they abandon others. As noted in Chapter 3, new cultural elements appear through several basic processes. *Invention*—including mechanical devices, ideas, and patterns of behavior—contributes to the reshaping of society. Since the 1940s, research in the area of rocket propulsion has produced increasingly sophisticated vehicles for space flight. By the mid-1980s, Americans had come to take voyages of the space shuttle almost for granted. Then the 1986 *Challenger* disaster reminded us how fragile innovative technology can be.

Discovery occurs when people recognize existing elements of the world or begin to understand them in a new way. Medical advances are largely a matter of gaining a greater understanding of the operation of the human body. The fact that the average life expectancy of Americans today is decades longer than it was at the beginning of this century is partly due to the incorporation of scientific discoveries into our social patterns.

Diffusion creates social change as cultural elements spread from one society to another through trade, immigration, and mass communication. As Ralph Linton (1937) pointed out, many cultural elements we view as "100 percent American" were actually created elsewhere (see the box in Chapter 3). Turn-of-the-century immigration made the United States a cultural melting pot. A new wave of immigration in the 1980s, largely from

Latin America and Asia, is bringing countless cultural changes to American society—clearly evident in the sights, smells, and sounds of cities across the country (Fallows, 1983; Muller & Espenshade, 1985). In a similar way, American computer technology is rapidly bringing change to many societies of the Third World.

Social Structure

Another major source of social change is tension and conflict within the structure of society itself. Perhaps the most influential theory linking social structure and social change was formulated by Karl Marx, as described in Chapters 4 and 9. Marx claimed that social class is the basis of conflict between unequally advantaged segments of the population, and that this conflict provides the energy for social change. In industrial-capitalist societies, Marx maintained, social conflict between capitalists who own and control factories and other centers of production and workers who provide the productive labor to run them generates continual pressure toward social change. Marx predicted this pressure would ultimately transform capitalist societies into socialist societies. So far, this outcome has been more rare than Marx would have wished. But he was quite right in foreseeing that social conflict arising from patterns of inequality—involving social class, race, and gender—would result in marked social change in all societies of the world, including the United States. As described in Chapter 21, social movements may emerge out of the experience of deprivation by some segment of the population. The labor, civil rights, women's, and gay rights movements all developed in this manner, and each has brought changes to American society.

Ideas

Max Weber was aware that complex transformations of society could never be accounted for by any single factor, as explained in Chapter 4. Weber acknowledged the importance of social conflict in transforming societies. But while Marx linked social change to the process of material production, Weber maintained that nonmaterial elements of culture such as ideas and beliefs also encourage social change. One example of the power of ideas is personal charisma (described in Chapters 16 and 17),

The National Aeronautics and Space Administration (NASA) had a record of remarkable achievement, but the tragic explosion of the space shuttle Challenger *on January 28, 1986— after twenty-four successful shuttle flights—raised troubling questions about whether NASA had pushed the space program too quickly.*

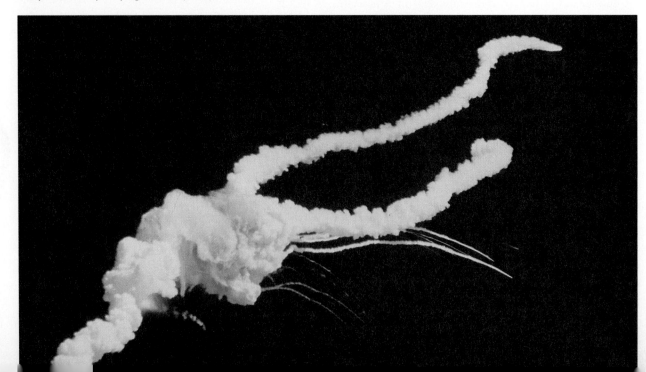

which Weber viewed as a means by which extraordinary people can truly change the world. But perhaps Weber's clearest statement of this theory is his analysis of the connection between Protestantism and the rise of industrial capitalism. After noting that industrial capitalism developed primarily in the areas of Western Europe in which the Protestant work ethic was strong, Weber (1958) concluded that the disciplined and rational world view embraced by Calvinist Protestants helped encourage such social change.

The importance of ideas in the process of social change is also evident in the development of social movements. As explained in Chapter 21, a crucial element in the emergence of a social movement is a general understanding of the *wrongness* of society as it exists and the *rightness* of a proposed course of social change (Smelser, 1962). Thus, for example, the gay rights movement in the United States has gained strength from the belief that homosexual Americans have wrongly been deprived of opportunities, and that the rights of lesbians and gay men should be equal to those enjoyed by the heterosexual majority. Of course, opposition to the gay rights movement remains strong among many Americans—which indicates the power of ideas to inhibit, as well as to advance, social change.

Ideas always have consequences that, to a varying degree, support or oppose the status quo. This is why, as noted in earlier chapters, *ideology* is the organization of ideas in defense of the interests of some segment of society.

The Natural Environment

Human societies and their natural environments are interrelated, so that change in either one is likely to result in change in the other.

In North America, for example, many traditional Native American cultures emphasized preserving the natural environment, while most European colonizers believed in changing nature to suit human purposes. The newcomers confronted a virtual wilderness, but they systematically cut down forests to provide space and materials for building, established towns, extended roads in all directions, and dammed rivers as a source of water and energy. Initially, of course, patterns of settlement were strongly influenced by the natural environment. As noted in Chapter 20, for example, most American cities were founded on navigable waterways. But, over time, nature was reshaped to suit the purposes of American culture. In the early seventeenth century, Manhattan

Island was covered with woods and streams. Today, as the center of the city of New York, it is twenty-two square miles of almost unbroken concrete and commercial buildings reaching thousands of feet into the sky. Such human construction not only reveals the American determination to master the natural environment, but also suggests the central importance of economic activity in American society. Our industrial way of life has brought enormous benefits, but it has also caused dangerous environmental pollution. Depletion and erosion of valuable farmland are other consequences of this aggressive approach to the natural environment. In turn, depleted nature has fewer resources to offer human society.

Inherent cyclical changes in the natural environment also affect human life—in some cases, ending entire societies. A thriving civilization in ancient India was destroyed about 1500 B.C.E. as the waters of the Indus River gradually rose. Four centuries later, the complex civilization on the island of Crete perished as a result of devastating earthquakes (Hamblin, 1973; Stavrianos, 1983). As any resident of the Gulf Coast knows, social life today is periodically disrupted by tropical storms, hurricanes, and tornadoes. In 1985, a major storm flooded a large area of Bangladesh, resulting in some ten thousand deaths; a major earthquake killed perhaps twice as many people in Mexico City; and drought in central Africa brought death to many thousands and devastated the way of life of millions more.

Population

Demographic pressures (described in Chapter 20) are also linked to social change. One part of this picture is the escalating demands placed on the natural environment by an increasing population. In many geographically small countries—notably the Netherlands and Japan—social patterns have long been influenced by limited physical space. The United States and Canada have not had to contend with such severe geographical limitations. Yet population growth has also changed North American societies as people have become concentrated within expanding urban areas. Many small towns—which in the past shared the characteristics of Thornton Wilder's fictional Grover's Corners—have been swamped by the vast urban sprawl. Urbanization causes changes in small-town life that are likely to be controversial, as the box on p. 616 illustrates.

Profound social changes also result from the shifting composition of a society's population. Chapter 13 described some consequences of the aging of the Ameri-

SOCIOLOGY OF EVERYDAY LIFE

Change in Rural America: The Invasion of the City Slickers

Historically, population growth in the United States has gone hand in hand with the expansion of cities. Urban growth affects not only city residents, but also people living in the Grover's Corners of America, as small towns are drawn into the orbit of expanding cities. While some small-town residents may applaud this change, others resist it.

When city people move to the country, Noel Perrin explains, they bring with them "a series of unconscious assumptions. It might be better for rural America if they brought a few sticks of dynamite. . . ."

Take a typical example. Mr. and Mrs. Nice are Bostonians. They live a couple of miles off Route 128 in a four-bedroom house. He's a partner in an ad agency; she has considerable talent as an artist. For some years they've had a second home in northern New Hampshire. The kids love it up there in Grafton County.

For some years, too, both Nices have been feeling they'd like to simplify their lives. They look with increasing envy on their New Hampshire neighbors, who never face a morning traffic jam, or an evening one, either; who don't have a long drive to the country on Friday night and a long drive back on Sunday; who aren't cramped into a suburban lot; who live in harmony with the natural rhythm of the year; who think the rat race is probably some minor event at a county fair.

One Thursday evening Don Nice says to Sue that he's been talking to the other partners, and they've agreed there's no reason he can't do some of his work at home. If he's in the office Wednesday and Thursday every week, why the rest of the time he can stay in touch by telephone. Sue, who has been trapped all year as a Brownie Scout leader and who has recently had the aerial snapped off her car in Boston, is delighted. She reflects happily that in their little mountain village you don't even need to lock your house, and there is no Brownie troop.

So the move occurs. In most ways Don and Sue are very happy. They raise practically all their own vegetables the first year; Sue takes up cross-country skiing. Don personally splits some of the wood they burn in their new woodstove.

But there are some problems. The first one Sue is conscious of is the school. It's just not very good. It's clear to Sue almost immediately that the town desperately needs a new school building—and also modern playground equipment, new school buses, more and better art instruction at the high school, a different principal. Don is as upset as Sue when they discover that only about 40 percent of the kids who graduate from that high school go on to any form of college. The rest do native things like becoming farmers, and mechanics, and joining the Air Force. An appalling number of the girls marry within twelve months after graduation. How are Jeanie and Don, Jr., going to get into good colleges from this school? . . . Pretty soon Sue and Don join an informal group of newcomers in town who are working to upgrade education. All they want for starters is the new building ($5.6 million) and a majority of their kind on the school board.

As for Don, though he really enjoys splitting the wood—in fact, next year he's planning to get a chainsaw and start cutting a few trees of his own—he also likes to play golf. There's no course within twenty miles. Some of the nice people he's met in the education lobby feel just as he does. They begin to discuss the possibility of a nine-hole course. The old farmer who owns the land they have in mind seems to be keeping only four or five cows on it, anyway. Besides, taxes are going up, and the old fellow is going to have to sell, sooner or later. (Which is too bad, of course. Don and Sue both admire the local farmers, and they're sincerely sorry whenever one has to quit.)

Over the next several years, Don and Sue get more and more adjusted to rural living—and they also gradually discover more things that need changing. For example, the area needs a good French restaurant. And it needs a *much* better airport. At present there are only two flights a day to Boston, and because of the lack of sophisticated equipment, even they are quite often canceled. If Don wants to be sure of getting down for an important meeting, he has to drive. Sue would be glad of more organized activities for the kids. There's even talk of starting a Brownie troop.

In short, if enough upper-middle-class people move to a rural town, they are naturally going to turn it into a suburb of the nearest city. For one generation it will be a nice and truly rustic suburb, with real farms dotted around it, and real natives speaking their minds at town meeting. Then as the local people are gradually taxed out of existence (or at least out of town), one more piece of rural America has died.

SOURCE: Noel Perrin, "Rural Area: Permit Required," *Country Journal*, April 1980, pp. 34–35.

can population. In 1987, people over sixty-five accounted for about 12 percent of all Americans, almost three times their proportion at the beginning of this century. By the year 2030, this proportion is expected to be over one in five (Bouvier, 1980; U.S. Bureau of the Census, 1984). The Social Security system will require extensive reform in order to help meet the income needs of millions more elderly people. Health-care services and medical knowledge about problems confronting the elderly will have to be improved, and conventional attitudes toward the elderly are likely to change as more and more Americans enter this stage of life (Barberis, 1981).

Migration between and within societies creates change through cultural diffusion, but also through fluctuations in the sheer numbers of people living in certain areas. Between roughly 1870 and 1930, a great wave of foreign immigrants and rural Americans swelled the industrial cities in the United States. Thousands of rural communities declined as metropolises burgeoned, and the United States became, for the first time, a predominantly urban society. Today many small towns and rural areas of the Sunbelt are rapidly urbanizing because of the migration of industries and people from the Snowbelt states.

MODERNITY

One of the central ideas in the study of social change is **modernity,** defined as *patterns of social organization linked to industrialization.* In everyday usage, the word designates the present in relation to the past. As used sociologically, however, modernity is a catch-all term for the social patterns that emerged in the wake of the Industrial Revolution that began in Western Europe in the late eighteenth century. Thus broad patterns of social change since the Industrial Revolution make up the process of *modernization.* Peter Berger (1977) has noted four general characteristics of modernization.

1. *The decline of small traditional communities.* Berger suggests that a characteristic of modernity is "the progressive weakening, if not destruction, of the concrete and relatively cohesive communities in which human beings have found solidarity and meaning throughout most of history" (1977:72). For thousands of years, from the camps of hunters and gatherers to the rural villages of early North American settlers, humans lived in small-scale settlements where family and neighbors answered

basic needs. Each person had a well-defined place in a world based on tradition—sentiments and beliefs passed from generation to generation. While membership in small primary groups certainly limited the range of personal experience, it had the simultaneous effect of conferring a strong sense of identity, belonging, and purpose. Such small and isolated communities still exist in many societies, including the United States, but they are not typical of industrialized societies. The scale of social life has been broadened by population growth and advanced forms of communication and transportation, and the family is no longer its unrivaled center. As Talcott Parsons (1966) noted, much of modern life is carried out within social institutions that are distinct from the family—including religion, the political system, the economy, and the educational system.

2. *The expansion of personal choice.* In traditional preindustrial societies, people typically see life as shaped by forces beyond human control—whether gods, spirits, or simply fate. More accurately, of course, this traditional conception of fate reflects the limited range of choices available to members of preindustrial societies. Each person lives largely according to traditional social patterns strictly enforced in formal and informal ways by the family and the local community.

As the power of tradition declines, people in modern societies come to view their lives as a series of options or personal choices, which Peter Berger describes as the process of *individualization.* Perhaps the clearest illustration of individualization is American society's recognition of multiple lifestyles representing alternatives that any person may choose to adopt or reject. In Berger's view, this recognition of alternatives is based on a crucial willingness to embrace change. In modern societies, he claims, people readily imagine that "things could be other than what they have been" (1977:77).

3. *Increasing diversity in patterns of belief.* In preindustrial societies, religious beliefs and other elements of tradition tend to enforce conformity at the expense of diversity and change. Modernization promotes a more rational, scientific world view, however, so that cultural norms and values become more variable. Furthermore, the growth of cities, expansion of impersonal, formal organizations, and mix of migrants from other places all foster in modern societies a diversity of belief and behavior far beyond what is typical of traditional societies.

Chapter 16 described the historical decline of the importance of religion termed *secularization.* Secularization does not, of course, involve abandoning religious

Oil production has brought great wealth and encouraged modernization in many Middle Eastern societies. Some people benefit greatly, but others have resisted what they see as the undermining of traditional cultural patterns.

beliefs. On the contrary, religion continues to be a powerful force in American society and in other industrial societies around the world. Although support for many of the more established churches has declined in the United States in recent decades, other forms of religious activity such as fundamentalism have grown and prospered (Stark & Bainbridge, 1981; Johnstone, 1983). Taking the longer historical view, however, there is little doubt that religion has less impact on everyday life in the United States and elsewhere today than it had before the Industrial Revolution (Laslett, 1984).

4. *Future orientation and growing awareness of time.* Berger suggests that time has special significance to members of modern societies in two ways. First, modern societies are oriented more toward the future than the past. In preindustrial societies where tradition is strong, people look to the past for guidance. In modern societies, where industrialization has weakened tradition, people tend to look to the future in the hope that new inventions and discoveries will make life better. For this reason, modern societies readily embrace many social changes

that are resisted in traditional preindustrial societies. Second, in modern societies, specific units of time are an important foundation of everyday life. Clocks began to appear in Europe only late in the Middle Ages. As the Industrial Revolution progressed, the importance of time increased to the point where people now claim that "Time is money!" Not surprisingly, then, virtually all activities are deliberately scheduled to begin and end at a specific hour and minute—a pattern that contrasts sharply with the preindustrial practice of measuring time according to the day or the season. Berger adds that wearing a wristwatch is one of the most widespread symbols of becoming modern in societies that are beginning to industrialize.

In sum, Peter Berger sees modernization as human emancipation from tightly knit social communities in which traditional religious beliefs provided each person with a strong sense of belonging but little individual freedom. In modern societies, people have far more autonomy with regard to beliefs and actions; on the other side of the coin, the social ties that bind each person to others are typically less personal and enduring.

Explaining Modernity

Modernization is one of the causes of sociology itself. As noted in Chapter 1, sociology emerged in the nineteenth century in the societies of Western Europe that were experiencing the most rapid social change after the Industrial Revolution. To a large degree, the ideas of many early European sociologists—and the American sociologists who followed them—were attempts to describe and explain the rise of modern society and its consequences for human beings.

Toennies: The Loss of Community

The German sociologist Ferdinand Toennies, who is introduced in the box, developed one of the most influential accounts of the rise of modernity, which is discussed at length in Chapter 20. Like Peter Berger, whose ideas he influenced, Toennies maintained that modernization involved the progressive loss of human community, or *gemeinschaft*, based on personal ties that provide a sense of group membership and loyalty. Industrialization and the rise of capitalism introduced a "strictly business" emphasis on facts, efficiency, specialization, and cost effectiveness. Such cultural patterns gradually made tra-

Ferdinand Toennies (1855–1936)

Ferdinand Toennies was born in the German countryside to a wealthy family able to provide him with an extensive education. Along with his colleagues George Simmel and Max Weber, Toennies was instrumental in establishing sociology as an academic discipline in Germany.

His work reveals a deep concern with the quality of life in modern societies, most evident in his influential book *Gemeinschaft and Gesellschaft*. During Toennies's lifetime, Germany and other European countries were changing rapidly in the wake of the Industrial Revolution. His work is largely a reaction to a world becoming more and more impersonal.

Toennies's writings suggest that traditional societies are the foundation of virtues such as morality and honor, while modernization erodes people's sense of community and interpersonal responsibility. But he did not simplistically maintain that modern society was "worse" than societies of the past. While critical of expanding individualism, Toennies also celebrated the rational, scientific thinking associated with modern society. Rather than advocating a return to social patterns of the past, he looked to the future with the hope that some form of socialism would encourage collective responsibility (a quality of traditional societies) while advancing scientific research and individual rights (qualities of modern societies).

SOURCE: Based on Werner J. Cahnman and Rudolf Heberle, "Introduction," in *Ferdinand Toennies on Sociology: Pure, Applied, and Empirical* (Chicago: University of Chicago Press, 1971), pp. vii–xxii.

---

ditional European and North American societies more rootless and impersonal and weakened social solidarity— a state Toennies termed *gesellschaft* (1963; orig. 1887).

Thornton Wilder's fictional town of Grover's Corners, New Hampshire, illustrates the qualities of *gemeinschaft* in villages and towns of preindustrial Europe and North America: small size and population, so that "most everybody" had some contact during the day; a hardworking, slow-moving way of life in which "nobody very remarkable" stood out from the rest and in which people were bound together by kinship, church, and neighborhood. In an era when mass communications and rapid transportation did not exist, such highly cohesive communities were largely worlds unto themselves.

Of course, such communities had their inevitable tensions and conflicts. In Grover's Corners, for instance, the Polish families and their Catholic Church were "over beyond the tracks," segregated from Protestant families. But Toennies believed that the traditional ties of gemeinschaft cause people to "remain essentially united in spite of all separating factors" (1963:65).

In modern societies characterized by greater gesell-schaft, according to Toennies (1963:65), people are "essentially separated in spite of united factors." We have only to consider the social life of the cities in which most Americans live to appreciate the applications of Toennies's insights: bank tellers who refuse to cash a check unless one has the proper identification; high rates of crime against people and property; people refraining from eye contact on the streets; residential areas in which neighbors are virtual strangers who change from one year to the next; large numbers of people seeking counseling to overcome their sense of isolation and meaninglessness. The relative rootlessness of American society is demonstrated in Table 22–1, which shows that over 40 percent of Americans changed their residence between 1980 and 1985—moving on as jobs required, or in search of something new and better.

Of course, the qualities of gemeinschaft are not totally absent from modern life. But, particularly in large cities, the indifference of most people to those outside their immediate circle that disturbed Toennies in the 1880s still has alarming consequences today, as the box on p. 621 illustrates.

Table 22–1 MOVING ON IN MODERN AMERICA

Region	Residence in 1985				
	Same House as 1980	Different House than in 1980	Different House Same County	Different County Same State	Different State
Northeast	66.9%	31.3%	18.8%	7.3%	5.2%
Midwest	60.9	38.3	22.9	9.1	6.3
South	56.0	42.4	21.5	9.8	11.0
West	49.6	47.2	25.9	9.8	11.5
Total US	58.3	39.9	22.1	9.1	8.7

SOURCE: U.S. Census Bureau, "Current Population Reports: P–20, Population Characteristics, No. 420," *Geographical Mobility: 1985* (Washington, D.C.: Government Printing Office, 1987), Table 12, p. 38.

Durkheim: The Division of Labor

The French sociologist Emile Durkheim was also well aware that profound social changes were occurring in nineteenth-century Europe and North America. Durkheim's analysis of the rise of modernity is based on the increasing **division of labor**—meaning *highly specialized economic activity*—that accompanies industrialization (1964b; orig. 1893). Durkheim formulated two contrast-ing, ideal types of social organization similar to those used by Toennies—one based on social likeness, the other on social difference. **Mechanical solidarity** refers to *social bonds typical of small preindustrial societies, based on the perception that people are alike and belong together.* In societies with strong mechanical solidarity, the division of labor is minimal, so that people engage in many of the same activities and share traditional social patterns. Durkheim described this solidarity as *mechani-*

George Tooker's painting "The Subway" depicts a common problem of modern life: weakening social ties may leave us strangers to one another, anxious about who and what we are.

Modernity and Impersonality: The Death of Kitty Genovese

A common criticism of modern society is that people are so caught up in their own lives that they fail to recognize any responsibility for the well-being of others. In March of 1964, an event in New York City brought this issue to national attention. Returning from her job late at night, Kitty Genovese was attacked and stabbed to death in the parking lot near her apartment building. While initial news reports treated this as simply one more crime common to large cities, subsequent investiga-

tion revealed the chilling fact that *almost forty of Genovese's neighbors had watched while she was repeatedly attacked over a period of one-half hour without coming to her assistance. No one called the police until after she had died.*

When this fact became known, the nation shamefully asked whether American society was losing its sense of neighborly responsibility and basic human decency. While many of the people who had witnessed this crime later expressed regret about their inac-

tion, all claimed that—at the time—they simply did not want "to get involved."

While events of this kind do not occur every day, they are frequent enough to raise troubling questions about how a sense of personal responsibility for the welfare of others can be maintained in a world that has come to value privacy and that often places more importance on personal concerns than on community needs.

---

cal because people's likeness to one another convinces them that they belong together and unites them more or less automatically. Mechanical solidarity has essentially the same social characteristics as Toennies's *gemeinschaft.*

Toennies's view of modernization as the transformation of gemeinschaft to gesellschaft is paralleled in Durkheim's work as the transformation of mechanical solidarity to **organic solidarity**: *social bonds typical of large industrial societies, based on the interdependence of people who engage in specialized activities.* In other words, the pronounced division of labor in industrialized societies means that an individual engages in only one of many diverse activities, depending on others to meet a wide range of other human needs. Organic solidarity has essentially the same social characteristics as Toennies's concept of gesellschaft.

Despite obvious similarities, Durkheim and Toennies interpreted the significance of modernity somewhat differently. Toennies described the modern world of gesellschaft as the *loss* of social solidarity—the gradual change from the "natural" and "organic" rural patterns of the past to the "artificial" and "mechanical" urban patterns of the present. Durkheim, however, emphasized that the village and city ways of life are equally natural for the human species. Therefore, he reversed Toennies's use of the terms *organic* and *mechanical*, applying the term *organic* to the social solidarity characteristic of mod-

ern life and using the term *mechanical* to refer to traditional social patterns. Durkheim viewed modernization as a *change* in the basis of social solidarity—from bonds based on likeness (kinship and neighborhood) to economic interdependence (based on the division of labor). Thus Durkheim's view of modernity is both more complex and more positive than that of Toennies.

Nonetheless, Durkheim recognized that economic interdependence means that although people need each other, they do not necessarily agree on matters of morality. As cultural patterns become more diverse, Durkheim feared, modern societies would be increasingly vulnerable to **anomie**: *a condition of weak and conflicting cultural norms that provide little moral guidance to individuals.* In such a state, society continues to operate, as people depend on one another to meet their various needs. But they simultaneously tend toward *ego-centrism* (placing their own needs above those of others), and are likely to embrace any of a wide range of lifestyles.

Weber: Rationalization

Max Weber's emphasis on the importance of ideas and beliefs in creating social change led him to view modernity as the progressive replacement of tradition by a rational world view.

A strong traditional orientation often results in resistance to change. "Truth" in traditional societies, Weber

The extensive specialization and impersonality of modern industrial society is evident in the frequent use of the telephone directory to locate people who can provide various goods and services.

claimed, is "that which has always been" (1978:36; orig. 1921). Modern societies, on the other hand, are characterized by deliberate calculation of the most efficient means to reach a desired goal. Efficiency encourages the adoption of new social patterns insofar as innovation allows goals to be achieved more readily. Thus, as Peter Berger (1977) noted, modern societies tend to look to the future and view social life as a range of options to be evaluated in terms of their consequences.

In much the same way that Toennies and Durkheim described the progressive weakening of tradition, Weber asserted that modern society had become "disenchanted." By this he meant that a rational world view had rendered calculable and predictable what earlier societies had considered to be a matter of divine will or fate (Coser, 1977:233). Without denying the continued presence of organized religion in modern society, Weber stressed how secularization had turned modern humanity away from the gods and toward rational systems of thought, including science.

Perhaps the clearest evidence of a rational world view is the emergence in modern society of bureaucracy. While traditional social organization is based on personal loyalties and adherence to past practices, bureaucracy involves deliberately creating policies intended to accomplish large-scale tasks efficiently. As described in Chapter 7, formal organizations attempt to maximize efficiency by operating according to rules and regulations so that people interact in an atmosphere of deliberate impersonality.

Also like Toennies and Durkheim, Weber did not embrace modern society uncritically. Indeed, his view of modernity is the most negative of the three. Weber recognized that while science could produce technological wonders, it was incapable of providing answers to the most basic questions about the meaning and purpose of human existence. Just as important, he feared that rationalization—especially in formal organizations—would result in the dehumanization of society as people's lives became increasingly regulated by impersonal bureaucratic organizations.

Marx: Capitalism

Karl Marx's view of modernity differs considerably from those of the other social thinkers noted so far. While they examined social change with an eye toward shifting patterns of moral consensus and social stability, Marx stressed the importance of social conflict. To Marx, modern society was synonymous with capitalism, an economic system produced by the class struggle toward the end of the feudal era of European history. As explained in Chapter 4, Marx claimed that the bourgeoisie emerged in medieval Europe as a social class intent on wresting control of society from the traditional nobility. The bourgeoisie was finally successful when the Industrial Revolution placed a powerful new productive system under its control.

Marx did not deny that the rise of modernity involved the decline of small-scale communities (as described by Toennies), an increasing division of labor (as noted by Durkheim), and the emergence of a rational world view (as described by Weber). Indeed, he emphasized that all three of these factors were necessary for capitalism to flourish. Capitalism, he maintained, draws population from rural areas and small towns into an ever-growing market system centered in the cities; specialization is the foundation for the operation of factories; and rationality is most clearly expressed in modern society's unending quest for greater and greater profits.

As earlier chapters have made clear, Marx was a relentless critic of capitalist society. Yet his vision of modernity contained a crucial element of optimism. Unlike Weber, who pessimistically viewed modern society as an "iron cage" of bureaucracy, Marx believed that social conflict within capitalist social systems would produce revolutionary social change, ultimately leading to the establishment of an egalitarian communist society. This, he claimed, would rid the world not only of social conflict, but also of dehumanization, which he traced to the exploitation of the many by the few. So, while Marx's evaluation of modern capitalist society was highly negative, his vision of the future optimistically assumed both human freedom and a greater sense of human community.

Two Interpretations of Modernity

The rise of modernity was clearly a complex process involving many different dimensions of social change, described in previous chapters and summarized in Table 22–2. These various dimensions of social change are drawn together in two general interpretations of modern society—as a *mass society* and as a *class society*.

Modernity as Mass Society

One important interpretation of modernity emphasizes the ways in which the Industrial Revolution has led to the formation of large-scale mass societies (Dahrendorf, 1959; Kornhauser, 1959; Nisbet, 1966, 1969; Baltzell, 1968; Stein, 1972; Berger, Berger, & Kellner, 1974). The term **mass society** refers to *an industrial society characterized by extensive bureaucracy that fosters social atomization and feelings of personal isolation.* The mass-society approach to modernity—which draws upon the ideas of Ferdinand Toennies, Emile Durkheim, and Max Weber—has two parts. First, the small scale of life common to preindustrial societies has been lost. Industrial societies are typically large and internally complex, with extensive cultural diversity and impersonal bureaucracy. Second, since the Industrial Revolution, the state has expanded so that now government takes responsibility for tasks (such as social welfare programs and defense) that in the past were informally carried out by families and neighbors. The modern state has addressed many social problems—including poverty and discrimination—but the price paid has been the increasing regulation of human lives by distant and impersonal bureaucracies.

The increasing scale of social life. Traditional small-scale societies of Europe and North America before the Industrial Revolution contained countless rural villages and small towns. Each of these approximated Toennies's concept of gemeinschaft, involving extensive face-to-face communication and little anonymity. Because there was little personal privacy, gossip was an informal, yet highly effective, means of social control. Cultural values in these small-scale communities were relatively homogeneous, forming the basis of the mechanical solidarity described by Durkheim. Limited population, social isolation, and the power of established religion all fostered uniformity of belief and behavior. In England until the year 1690, for example, the law demanded that everyone attend church and partake in the Christian practice of Holy Communion (Laslett, 1984). Similarly, most of the early colonies in New England did not recognize any right of religious dissent. Because social differences were the basis for legal prosecution, subcultures and countercultures were rare indeed. Cultural uniformity, coupled to a strong embrace of tradition, permitted only a slow rate of social change. As described in Chapter 9, patterns of social inequality in small-scale societies of the past were based largely on ascription, which curtails social mobility.

The specialization of economic activity, urbanization, and rapid population growth that accompanied the Industrial Revolution greatly increased the scale of social life. In larger-scale societies, while an individual is still likely to know a few other people intimately, most ac-

Table 22–2 TRADITIONAL AND MODERN SOCIETIES: DIMENSIONS OF DIFFERENCE

	Social Characteristics Associated with Traditional Society	Social Characteristics Associated with Modern Society
Scale of Life		
	Small scale; population typically small and widely dispersed (rural villages and small towns)	Large scale; population typically large and concentrated (cities)
Social Structure		
Status and role	Few statuses, most ascribed; few specialized roles	Many statuses, some ascribed and some achieved; many specialized roles
Relationships	Typically primary; little anonymity and privacy	Typically secondary; considerable anonymity and privacy
Communication	Face-to-face	Face-to-face communication supplemented by extensive mass media
Social control	Informal gossip	Formal police and legal system
Social stratification	Rigid patterns of social inequality; little mobility	Fluid patterns of social inequality; considerable social mobility
Gender patterns	Pronounced patriarchy; few women in the paid labor force	Declining patriarchy; increasing number of women in the paid labor force
Family	Extended family as the primary means of socialization and economic production	Nuclear family retains some socialization function, but is a unit of consumption rather than production
Religion	Religion is basis of world view; little religious pluralism	Religion weakens with the rise of science; extensive religious pluralism
Education	Formal schooling limited to elites	Basic schooling becomes universal, with growing proportion receiving advanced education
State	Small-scale government; little state intervention into society	Large-scale government; considerable state intervention into society
Economy	Based on agriculture; limited manufacturing within the home; little white-collar work	Based on advanced industrial mass production; factories become center of production; increasing white-collar work
Health	High birth and death rates; limited life expectancy because of low standard of living and primitive medical technology	Low birth and death rates; greater life expectancy because of higher standard of living and advanced medical technology
Cultural Patterns		
Values	Homogeneous; sacred character; few subcultures and countercultures	Heterogeneous; secular character; many subcultures and countercultures
Norms	High moral significance; little tolerance of diversity	Variable moral significance; high tolerance of diversity
Orientation	Present linked to past	Present linked to future
Technology	Preindustrial; human and animal energy	Industrial; advanced energy sources
Social Change		
	Slow; change evident over many generations	Rapid; change evident within a single generation

quaintances are known solely in terms of their functions (for example, as the "doctor" or as the "gas station attendant"). The remainder of the population is merely part of an anonymous mass. Face-to-face communication still exists, of course, but the formally organized mass media (including newspapers, television, and radio) grow in importance. Formalization is evident in numerous other aspects of social life as large organizations assume responsibilities once undertaken informally by family, friends, and neighbors: universal public education greatly extends the scope of learning; police, lawyers, and courts supervise a vast system of social control; and strangers at the Red Cross and government welfare agencies offer impersonal charity to the needy.

Mass communication and transportation contribute to the weakening of traditional cultural values, as an increasingly mobile and informed public becomes exposed to a wide range of cultural values and norms. Inevitably, people who observe world events on television news, encounter immigrants from around the world in urban settings, and travel across the country and to distant nations develop a greater tolerance of cultural diversity and come to value individual rights and freedom of choice. Subcultures and countercultures flourish in mass societies. Socially disadvantaged segments of the population—females and racial and ethnic minorities—gain broader participation in society, including the right to vote. These greater opportunities, coupled to an expanding economy, stimulate social mobility.

The rise of the state. In the small-scale societies of Europe before the Industrial Revolution, government was largely in the hands of the local nobility. All of England, for example, was under the formal rule of a single royal family, but lacking efficient means of communication and transportation, the monarch could not exercise effective control over the whole society.

Steadily, however, the centralized government grew in size and importance. As noted in Chapter 17 (see Table 17–1), the federal government of the United States was quite small when Americans won their independence from England. In all, the government managed to operate on only about $6 million in 1795—an amount the federal government spent every three days in 1988. As the size of the state has increased, government has entered areas of social life in which it was not initially active: regulating wages and working conditions, educating the future work force, providing financial assistance in times of unemployment and illness. In the process, of course, taxes have steadily increased, so that the average American now works four months of the year to earn the money to pay for the expanded services of government.

At the same time, political decision making has become centered in large bureaucracies that often leave people in local communities with the sense that they have little power over their own lives. The United States government now demands, for example, that schools have standardized educational programs, that streets be maintained in a specific fashion, and that businesses keep extensive records of their operations. While such regulations certainly provide benefits, they also depersonalize human decision making and limit the autonomy of individuals and local communities.

In sum, mass-society theory views the consequences of the transformation from small-scale to large-scale social life in both positive and negative terms. Modern societies provide a greater emphasis on individual rights, greater toleration of social differences, and a higher standard of living than was typical of traditional societies in the past. But mass societies are also characterized by some degree of what Emile Durkheim called *anomie*. Their size and complexity mean that people often feel powerless amidst massive bureaucracies. As noted in Chapter 17, although the American political system now grants every citizen over the age of eighteen the right to vote, only about half of all eligible voters participated in recent presidential elections. This fact suggests that the political system—like many dimensions of large-scale societies—often leaves the individual with the feeling that no one person can make a difference.

Overall, this interpretation of modernity tends to view the small scale of life in the past favorably. For this reason, mass-society analysis has considerable attraction for social and economic conservatives, who support strong conventional morality and oppose extensive government regulation of social life.

Modernity as Class Society

The class-society interpretation of modernity is based largely on the ideas of Karl Marx. The term **class society** refers to *an industrial society in which capitalism has generated pronounced social stratification.* This interpretation accepts the fact that modern societies have assumed a mass scale, yet claims that the heart of modernization has been the expansion of the capitalist economy. Furthermore, patterns of social inequality and social conflict remain pronounced in capitalist societies, even if those patterns are not precisely the same as in the past (Miliband, 1969; Habermas, 1970; Polenberg, 1980; Blumberg, 1981; Harrington, 1984).

Capitalism. According to Marx, the increasing scale of nineteenth-century social life in Europe and North America was not simply a product of the Industrial Revolution, but reflected the expansionist goals inherent in capitalism. The capitalist system is based on the quest for ever-increasing profits, and therefore seeks constant increase in both production and consumption. In fact, Marx considered the Industrial Revolution itself an important stage in the expansion of the capitalist economic system.

Because it reflects the profit motive rather than

established traditions, Marx claimed, capitalism effectively undermined the "feudal ties" that provided social cohesion to small-scale communities in the past. Instead, capitalism emphasized "naked self-interest," which justifies each person's efforts to gain as much wealth as possible, even at the expense of the well-being of others (1972:337; orig. 1848). Just as important, in order for capitalists to exploit the working majority effectively, human beings had to be viewed impersonally as commodities—a source of labor for the expanding industrial-capitalist economy. Thus capitalism gradually eroded traditional morality, which conceived of individuals of all social classes as people with souls valued by God, and replaced it with a view of human beings as cogs in the social machinery of modernity. The scientific method also challenged traditional beliefs, legitimating the power and wealth of capitalists. In preindustrial Europe, the rule of nobility was based on traditional conceptions of obligation and responsibility supported by religion. Science has increasingly challenged the influence of religion in modern society, but a scientific outlook shares with religion the ability to legitimate the status quo because it maintains that technical advances continually improve social life (Habermas, 1970). In this way, class-society theory claims, science invents or discovers panaceas for social problems—such as poor health among much of the population—rather than changing the social patterns that largely created the problems in the first place.

The logic of science and the expanding scale of modern society are nowhere more evident than in the growth of private business. Businesses utilize the logic of science in claiming that efficiency "demands" continual growth. As described in Chapter 18, corporations in industrial-capitalist societies have reached enormous size and control almost unimaginable wealth. Not satisfied with the profits that can be earned in their own countries, they are now expanding throughout the world as multinationals. From the class-society point of view, the expanding scale of life is the inevitable consequence of capitalism.

The persistence of social inequality. Mass-society theory emphasizes the ways in which modernity has gradually lessened the sharp and rigid social distinctions that characterized traditional preindustrial societies. The class-society approach, however, maintains that modernity has only superficially changed the patterns of social inequality. Despite the rise in the average standard of living, in other words, modern capitalist societies are still sharply stratified with most wealth held by a small

elite. Recall from Chapter 10, for example, that the richest 5 percent control more than half of all wealth in the United States. As Paul Blumberg (1981) notes, the rising standard of living in the United States during this century has not altered the fact that a very small minority still controls most of the wealth, while a significant minority continues to live in poverty.

And what of the expanding state, which mass-society theory portrays as a means of addressing problems related to social inequality? According to Marx, the state in a capitalist society usually defends the wealth and social privileges of capitalists, the most powerful social class. Class-society theory thus claims that the greater political rights and economic benefits enjoyed by the majority of working Americans today are not expressions of government benevolence, but rather were won through political struggle. As described in Chapter 21, many gains made by underprivileged segments of American society—including blue-collar workers, members of minority groups, women, and gay people—resulted from social movements that encountered considerable resistance from powerful supporters of the status quo. Throughout the 1980s, in the name of efficiency and a free-market system, conservative political leaders have attempted to curtail funding for government programs that benefit less privileged Americans (Harrington, 1984; Jacob, 1986). Not surprisingly, then, the class-society interpretation of modernity enjoys widespread support among social and economic liberals who favor greater equality for all categories of people and desire more extensive regulation of the capitalist marketplace.

In sum, class-society theory interprets the rise of modernity very differently from mass-society theory, as summarized in Table 22–3. Rather than emphasizing the expanding scale of social life and the rise of large formal organizations, this approach stresses the expansion

Table 22–3 TWO INTERPRETATIONS OF MODERNITY: A SUMMARY

	Key Process of Modernization	Key Effects of Modernization
Mass-society theory	Industrialization Growth of bureaucracy	Increasing scale of life; rise of the state and other formal organizations
Class-society theory	Rise of capitalism	Expansion of capitalist economy; persistence of social inequality

of capitalism. Moreover, in place of mass-society theory's emphasis on the alleviation of social problems linked to social inequality, the class-society approach emphasizes the persistence of patterns of social inequality. Indeed, as the industrial-capitalist economic system matures, an increasing proportion of economic power in the United States is held by a few extremely large corporations. Instead of the moral relativism that underlies Durkheim's anomie, then, class-society theory sees widespread *alienation*—the concept used by Marx to indicate that the majority of people have little real power to affect their own lives.

The Individual in Modern Society

Mass-society theory and class-society theory focus primarily on broad patterns of social change since the Industrial Revolution. But they also offer valuable insights into how modernity affects the lives of individuals.

Mass Society: Problems of Identity

In the large-scale societies of the modern world, individuals have become liberated from the tightly knit small communities of the past. They have greater privacy and greater freedom to express their individuality in the form of various lifestyles. At the same time, mass society theory points out, social diversity, weaker social cohesion, and rapid social change in modern societies make the development of individual identity a difficult matter (Wheelis, 1958; Riesman, 1970; Berger, Berger, & Kellner, 1974).

Chapter 5 explained how every person develops a social identity through interaction with other people.

This process involves incorporating cultural values, beliefs, and meanings into a distinct personality. Small, homogeneous, and slowly changing societies of the past provided a stable social foundation for the development of personal identity, and a clear, although narrow, road map for an individual's life experience. For example, in the traditional small-scale Amish communities that still exist in the United States and Canada (see the box in Chapter 3), a clearly defined way of life permits relatively few personal choices. As a result, people know what being Amish means—that is, how to think and behave—and what is natural and right about living as they do. Of course, not everyone born into an Amish community readily embraces such a rigidly prescribed way of life, but Amish people typically have little difficulty in establishing a clear personal identity (Hostetler, 1980).

Large, culturally diverse, and rapidly changing societies, on the other hand, provide the individual with such a bewildering range of options that the social world often feels less like a firm foundation than like shifting sands. Greater autonomy in choosing one's pattern of life means greater likelihood of losing one's way. When right and wrong, good and bad, beautiful and ugly, are relative rather than absolute concepts, the modern individual gains creative freedom at the expense of the security that tradition's limited alternatives once provided.

David Riesman (1970; orig. 1950) has described modernization in terms of its effects on **social character,** defined as *personality patterns that are shared by large numbers of people within a society.* In other words, social character refers to personality traits typical among people living in the same society at the same point in history. Riesman describes the social character of preindustrial societies as **tradition-directedness,** meaning *rigid person-*

Growing up in a society of rapidly changing and inconsistent cultural patterns promotes problems of personal identity. A growing number of Americans—and especially younger people—find support and solutions in counseling groups.

ality patterns involving conformity to traditional ways of living. People who live in small, slowly changing societies, in other words, build their lives on what has persisted for many generations. Because what is "good" is equivalent to "what has always been," tradition-directedness manifests itself as cultural conservatism. Tradition-directed people tend to think and act alike, but their conformity is not a simple effort to mimic one another. Rather, lives are alike because everyone draws on the same cultural foundation, which is held to be the one proper way to live. In the case of the Amish—who thrive within tradition-directed enclaves of American society—a rigidly prescribed life is simply "submission to the will of God" (Hostetler, 1980:172).

In culturally diverse and rapidly changing industrial societies, a rigid personality is a liability. Personal adaptability is highly prized. Thus Riesman describes social character in large-scale modern societies as **other-directedness,** meaning *highly flexible personality patterns involving openness to change, often through imitating the behavior of others.* Other-directed people develop an identity that, like the society around them, tends toward inconsistency and change. Other-directed individuals try different identities on for size and, as Chapter 6 explains, engage in various "performances" as they move through different social situations (Goffman, 1959). The average American's performances at school or work are often quite different from those evident at home, in church, or at a party. Such a shifting personality would mark a person as untrustworthy in a traditional society, but personal flexibility and the ability to fit in are valued personal traits in modern societies (Wheelis, 1958).

Adherence to peer values and norms—including fashions and fads, as discussed in Chapter 21—is a prominent example of other-directedness in American society. People of one's own generation, not one's elders, are the most important role models in societies that value what is up-to-date rather than what is traditional. But basing the self on changing social surroundings can lead to the identity crisis so familiar to Americans today. "Who Am I?" is a nagging question throughout the life cycle of many people. In the sociological view, this personal problem is a reflection of the inherent inconsistency of society itself.

Class Society: Problems of Meaningful Participation

Class-society theory maintains that modern society's promise of greater individual freedom is undermined by the persistence of social inequality. While modern society may be characterized by greater moral relativism—meaning that what is right or wrong is often a matter of widespread disagreement—it continues to place some categories of people in positions of clear disadvantage. The unequal distribution of wealth and power, discussed in Chapters 9 and 10, means that some people have far more opportunities than others. As we saw in Chapter 11, the members of racial and ethnic minority groups experience both prejudice and discrimination that limit their social opportunities. Similarly, as Chapter 12 explained, females—half the population in modern societies—have a wider range of social participation in modern societies than in traditional societies, but continue to experience the barriers of sexism. Elderly people as well are subject to patterns of prejudice and discrimination, described in Chapter 13 as *ageism*. Thus, rather than suffering from the consequence of too much freedom, as the theory of mass society suggests, a majority of people in American society continue to be denied the opportunity to participate fully in social life and to enjoy its benefits in a manner equal to that of young, white, well-to-do males.

Despite the fact that industrialization has increased social mobility, modern societies continue to be dominated by elites, while a significant proportion of the population lives in poverty. Consequently, demands for greater participation in decision making are arising on many fronts. Workers, for example, are seeking greater power in the workplace, consumers are pressing for more control over the marketplace, and citizens are attempting to make government more responsive to their needs (Toffler, 1981).

On a world scale, the expanding scope of industrial capitalism has placed an increasing proportion of the earth's population under the influence of multinational corporations. As described in Chapter 18, this process has resulted in the concentration of about half the world's wealth in the richest societies, which contain only about 10 percent of the world's people (Madsen, 1980). Given these circumstances, class-society theorists ask, is it any wonder that throughout the poor societies of Latin America, Africa, and Asia people are seeking more power to shape their own lives?

Problems of this kind led Herbert Marcuse (1964) to challenge Max Weber's description of modern society as rational. Marcuse saw modern society as irrational because it fails to meet the basic needs of many people. While modern capitalist societies produce unparalleled wealth, poverty remains the daily plight of millions of people (in world context, billions). Moreover, the advance of technology has not afforded people greater control over their own lives. On the contrary, the power to make key decisions affecting the entire world is concentrated more than ever in the hands of a few. Not only do most people suffer from the inability to participate in meaningful decision making, but the threat of nuclear annihilation now hangs over the entire globe. Despite the fact that technology is widely viewed as a means of *solving* the world's problems, Marcuse claimed, technology is more accurately understood as a *cause* of these problems. In short, class-society theory criticizes modern societies for having reduced the extent to which people control their own lives.

Modernity and Progress

The cultures of most industrial societies closely link modernity to the idea of *progress*—moving toward a goal that is assumed to be good. As noted in Chapter 3,

Especially in light of enormous productive capacity, we can well ask why societies still fail to provide for the basic needs of so many people.

Americans tend to embrace the notion of progress, believing that the present is better than the past, and that the future will be better still.

This chapter has already suggested that equating modernity with progress is simplistic because it ignores the complexity of social change. What we define as progress depends on our underlying values: social changes that seem progressive or good from one point of view appear regressive or bad from another. And few people would view as positive *all* of the many different social changes that modernization entails.

One of the most significant consequences of modernization is the recognition of basic human rights. The idea that people have rights simply by virtue of being human, rather than because of their social position, is a distinctly modern idea reflected in such influential documents as the American Declaration of Independence and the United Nations' Declaration of Human Rights (Berger, Berger, & Kellner, 1974). Historically, the concepts of human rights and human dignity—the assertion of the value of all people—can be seen as successors to the concept of honor in preindustrial society, as the box on p. 630 explains.

In principle, most Americans support the idea that individuals should have considerable autonomy in shaping their own lives. Yet social diversity—the inevitable result of freedom of choice—continues to be a source of tension and conflict in American society. The family is one area of increasing social diversity. In modern societies, the traditional extended family has declined, and the nuclear family is assuming quite varied forms. As described in Chapter 14, an increasing number of Americans are choosing to remain single, to live together outside of marriage, to have children without marrying, or to form partnerships with members of their own sex. To those who support the greatest amount of individual choice, changes of this kind are progress. But those who value traditional family patterns as the backbone of society tend to view these developments with despair (Wallis, 1985).

The consequences of modernization are controversial in many other ways. Although most Americans define greater social equality as progress, the rich still seek to maintain their wealth and privileges. Again, although many Americans applaud the fact that women and other minorities have improved their social standing, these improvements did not happen without political conflict and are still controversial.

Even technological advance cannot be considered a clear instance of progress. Without doubt, technological

Traditional Honor and Modern Dignity

Honor occupies about the same place in contemporary usage as chastity. An individual asserting it hardly invites admiration, and one who claims to have lost it is an object of amusement rather than sympathy.

In the view of Peter Berger, Brigitte Berger, and Hansfried Kellner (1974), honor is one of the leftovers from our feudal heritage that is inconsistent with the organization of modern societies. The concept of *honor* refers to thoughts and actions that conform to traditional cultural norms. Honor, then, cannot be separated from the rigid patterns of social hierarchy that characterize traditional societies. According to the aristocratic principles of the European Middle Ages, members of the nobility acted honorably insofar as they carried out their feudal obligations to their social inferiors and displayed proper respect for their peers. Similarly, people of low social position could claim to be honorable to the extent that they carried out their responsibilities to their superiors and abided by community norms in their relations with those who occupied the same station in the social order.

At each level of traditional society, past and present, men have had a position of dominance over women. Therefore, honor demands that men treat women according to cultural norms, which generally means displaying a fatherly and protective attitude and, of course, not "taking advantage" of women. For their part, women are honorable when they abide by the norms of deference toward men of their own social position (although men of a lower social position may be correctly treated with indifferent courtesy). Nonconformity to hierarchical norms is punished by defining the nonconformer as "dishonorable," a powerfully deviant label by which one becomes "separated from the basic norms that govern human life" (1974:87).

In modern societies, however, cultural norms are weaker and variable, and patterns of social inequality are more fluid. While the concept of honor survives among members of traditional ethnic groups and within hierarchical occupations such as the military, it has far less significance for most members of modern societies.

Modernization involves greater concern for people *as individuals*, which is expressed in the concept of *dignity*. While honor cannot be separated from social position, dignity is based on the belief that any and all human beings have inherent value. In practice, then, recognizing the dignity of other people means becoming indifferent to all patterns of social (and even biological) inequality and treating all people in an equally respectful manner.

In American society today, for example, many women object to being treated *as women* rather than as individuals. The traditional practices of a man holding open a door for a woman and paying for a meal they share are increasingly defined as an affront to the dignity of women, who can certainly do these things for themselves, just as men can.

In sum, honor is an important element of culture in traditional societies where individuals gain a sense of security from the social hierarchy and a sense of self-worth from cultural conformity. In modern societies, cultural diversity and rapid social change render all social arrangements somewhat suspect. As a result, human beings are now argued to have self-worth apart from the structures of society, which is the essence of dignity.

SOURCE: Based on Peter Berger, Brigitte Berger, Hansfried Kellner, *The Homeless Mind: Modernization and Consciousness* (New York: Vintage Books, 1974), pp. 83–96.

---

innovation is responsible for improving the lives of Americans in many ways—we have more rapid transportation, more efficient and extensive communications, and a greater ability to combat disease. But advanced technology has also been responsible for an unprecedented threat to the natural environment and, in the form of nuclear weapons, to the future of all humanity.

In sum, Alvin Toffler suggests that those who study social change "must resist the temptation to be seduced by straight lines" (1981:129). By this he means that social change does not proceed in a predictable, linear fashion. Present society is in some ways a direct extension of the past, but in other ways reveals unexpected developments. Because social change is as uncertain as it is complex, modernity cannot be simply equated with progress.

MODERNIZATION IN WORLD PERSPECTIVE

Thus far, this chapter has focused on the process of modernization that has already transformed the industrialized societies of Europe and North America. In recent decades, striking social changes have taken place as well in the traditional societies of Latin America, Africa, and Asia that contain about two-thirds of the world's population. Two theoretical approaches offer different interpretations of the process of modernization now occurring in the Third World. As will be readily seen, these approaches are closely related to the theories of mass society and class society that have already been described.

Modernization Theory

In simple terms, **modernization theory** is *an approach to global change maintaining that traditional societies will gradually be transformed by industrialization to resemble Europe and North America.* Modernization theory begins by distinguishing two general types of societies in the world: rich, industrial societies containing roughly one-fifth of the earth's population, and poor, preindustrial societies in which the rest of humanity currently is found. These are, of course, crude categories, since each includes many different societies and enormous cultural diversity. But this distinction usefully points to a simple world reality: people in industrial societies are generally well off, while the problems of population growth, poverty, and hunger are heavily concentrated in preindustrial societies. Recall from Table 10–4 that average personal income in preindustrial societies is typically only a small fraction of that of industrial societies such as the United States and Canada. Furthermore, as Chapter 20 explained, the most rapid population growth is currently in poor societies of Latin America, Africa, and Asia. For the foreseeable future, then, the world is likely to remain divided between "have" and "have not" societies.

Historical Perspective

How did this striking pattern of world stratification come about? Modernization theory explains that, centuries ago, virtually the *entire* world was poor by contemporary standards. But economic expansion in the late Middle Ages accelerated in Western Europe, leading to the Industrial Revolution that soon transformed European and North American societies. The distribution of newly produced wealth was far from equal, of course, but industrial technology was so productive that gradually the standard of living of even the relatively disadvantaged was raised.

A related question is why did industrialization transform only part of the world? Based largely on Max Weber's analysis of Protestantism and capitalism (discussed in Chapter 4), modernization theory points out that exploiting the potential of new technology depends on perceiving advantages in doing so. In simple terms, modernization requires casting aside a traditional world view. Insofar as poor societies of the world remain tradition-directed in David Riesman's terms, they are unlikely to embrace advanced technology or other changes that could improve their lives.

Rostow's Stages of Modernization

Over time, however, progressive influences from industrial societies can be expected to begin the modernization process worldwide. Walt W. Rostow (1978), perhaps the most influential proponent of this approach, has suggested that modernization involves four general stages.

1. *Traditional stage.* Initially, strongly traditional societies are likely to have cultural values that oppose any technological innovation. Because existing technology is rather primitive, limited productivity results in a low standard of living. In some cases, however, medical technology introduced from more technologically advanced societies may reduce the death rate from infectious diseases: while obviously beneficial in terms of saving lives, this contributes to high population growth. The poorest societies of the world, such as Bangladesh, are at this initial stage of development.

2. *Take-off stage.* As economic specialization gradually increases, a market economy begins to flourish. People no longer produce simply for their own consumption, but to engage in profitable trade. This sparks a greater achievement orientation on the part of individuals, so that tradition is weakened. This was the state of Great Britain in the early 1800s, the United States about 1840, and poorer nations such as Thailand today. Rostow argues that economic "take-off" in the Third World now depends on progressive influences—including foreign aid, introduction of advanced technology and investment capital, and schooling abroad—provided by rich nations.

3. *Drive to technological maturity.* At this point, "take-off" has occurred and a nation is able to sustain a growing

From the point of view of modernization theory, developing societies abandon a traditional world view in favor of rational, change-oriented cultural patterns. In the process, traditional and modern contrasts are often striking.

industrial economy. The United States reached this point by about 1880, and this stage characterizes nations such as Mexico, India, and the People's Republic of China in the 1980s. As industrialization proceeds, many of the familiar characteristics of modernity will appear: growing cities, declining population growth as birth rates drop, extensive productive specialization, impersonal relationships, mass education, and growing concern for individual rights. Traditional patriarchy is also likely to decline, although, as the box explains, modernization subjects women to new disadvantages.

4. *High mass consumption.* This represents the final point at which the fruits of modernization are realized. An industrial society now has mass consumption of a wide range of consumer goods and services. The United States entered this stage early in this century, and other industrial nations such as Japan and the Soviet Union achieved high mass consumption by about 1950. Now reaching this level of development are rapidly modernizing societies such as Taiwan and South Korea.

Evaluation. Modernization theory has had considerable support within the discipline of sociology (cf. Parsons, 1966; W. Moore, 1977, 1979; Bauer, 1981). Perhaps more important, this approach has guided the foreign policy of the United States and other industrial nations for decades. Economic assistance and the introduction of Western culture around the world, government officials claim, will push traditional societies toward the industrial development that has so benefited rich nations.

Powerful defenders notwithstanding, criticism of modernization theory has grown in recent years. First, modernization theory tends to view technological advance and economic development as unambiguously pos-

itive. As we have already explained, modernization cannot be simplistically equated with progress. Second, this approach implies that there is but one "road to modernity" that all societies of the world will follow. Critics maintain that cultural differences alone challenge the notion that poor nations of the world will follow the same course of modernization that today's rich nations pursued (Gusfield, 1972; Meyer, Boli-Bennet, & Chase-Dunn, 1975). Furthermore, such a narrow view of modernization implies that "development" is the same as "Westernization," making rich societies the standard by which the rest of the world should be judged. Third, modernization theory is criticized for being ahistorical—that is, failing to recognize that the conditions that accelerated industrialization centuries ago for some societies do not exist today. As explained in the next section, Europe and North America industrialized from a position of global strength, while today's preindustrial societies are weak by world standards. Fourth, foreign aid and other assistance to poor nations is rarely a case of rich-nation altruism. Commonly, any "help" is provided to ensure political stability and to foster the growth of multinational corporations, thereby advancing the interests of rich societies. Fifth and finally, modernization theory is criticized for placing the *causes* of world poverty in poor societies themselves—the practice of "blaming the victim" noted in Chapter 10. Similarly, the *solutions* to world poverty are argued to be found in the rich societies.

Overall, there is considerable evidence that development has occurred in many societies of the world according to the modernization theory model. But this approach remains controversial because it seems to defend the interests of rich societies, while ignoring issues of power and conflict in the world. From such concerns has emerged a second approach to global inequality: world-system theory.

World-System Theory

World-system theory is *an approach to global change that links any society's development to its place in a world economic system.* The foundation of this approach is the assertion that, with the rapid growth of capitalism, the world's nations have become linked into a global economic system (Wallerstein, 1974, 1979, 1983). *Core societies* of the world system are those where the Industrial Revolution occurred early and which now have powerful capitalist economies and a high standard of living. Cen-

CROSS-CULTURAL COMPARISON

The Effects of Modernization on Women in Traditional Societies

Modernization is generally thought to advance the social position of women in traditional societies in Latin America, Africa, and Asia. The onset of modernization does tend to weaken the strongly patriarchal values and norms of traditional societies where males have almost total dominance over females and women's lives are usually limited to the home. Women gain some measure of dignity as greater rights and freedoms are accorded to everyone, including greater opportunities for formal education and employment.

There is another side to this picture, however. In a study of the position of women in a poor rural district of Bangladesh, Sultana Alam discovered several ways in which modernization undermines the security of women in traditional societies.

First, as modernization provides greater occupational opportunities in the cities, men from rural areas may migrate to urban areas, leaving women and children to fend for themselves.

Second, as modern cultural values erode the traditional strength of the extended family and sense of responsibility for neighbors, women who are abandoned, divorced, or widowed may have difficulty finding economic assistance. In the past, for example, a Bangladeshi woman's family would readily reabsorb her if she found herself alone. Today this is less common. Widespread poverty is part of the problem, since people who can scarcely provide for themselves are unlikely to welcome the responsibility of feeding yet another person.

Third, one of the new ideas introduced into traditional societies by modernization is the sexualization of women. In traditional Bangladesh, although a woman might be viewed as an attractive sexual partner, she also had value and status as a sister, wife, and mother. Today, under the influence of Western mass media images, the emphasis on sexuality has increased so that Bangladeshi women are more likely to be viewed merely as sex objects. This tends to encourage males (who are usually considerably older than their wives) to desert an aging spouse in favor of a younger woman. Like their counterparts in the industrialized societies of the West, Bangladeshi women now have to contend with a form of sexism that emphasizes sexual attractiveness at the expense of ability and other personal qualities.

Overall, then, modernization cannot be described as simply advancing the social position of women. Like all social changes, it benefits women in some ways, but also introduces problems for women that were largely unknown in traditional societies.

SOURCE: Based on Sultana Alam, "Women and Poverty in Bangladesh," *Women's Studies International Forum*, Vol. 8, No. 4 (1985), pp. 361–371.

---

tered on the United States, this core also includes the nations of Western Europe and Japan. At the other extreme are *peripheral societies*—most of the nations of Latin America, Africa, and Asia—which have a low standard of living. The world system operates so that rich societies are becoming richer while poor societies are becoming poorer (Vaughan, 1978; Barney, 1980).

Historical Perspective

World-system theory argues that the economic development of some societies of the world has been—and continues to be—at the expense of other societies. Initially, this pattern of global exploitation took the form of *colonialism*, in which European nations seized political and economic control of much of the world beginning in the late fifteenth century. The rapid economic development of European nations that followed was largely due to looting the resources of their colonies. Today's pattern of "have" and "have not" societies began to take shape as some nations developed only as others were intentionally underdeveloped.

Colonialism gradually weakened as core societies proved unable to politically control their global empires. In Latin America, colonization declined in the nineteenth century; in Africa, many nations won independence only some thirty years ago. But the demise of colonization has not ended the world system. On the contrary, as Chapter 18 explains, global domination now takes the form of economic *neocolonialism*. This means that multinational corporations based in core societies continue to exploit the resources, labor, and markets of peripheral societies. In short, the world system continues to operate to the advantage of a small proportion of the world's population.

Dependency and Underdevelopment

World-system theory maintains that global poverty cannot be explained by lack of natural resources, labor, or organizational skills in poor societies themselves. Nor is a traditional world view, as emphasized by modernization theory, the real problem. More accurately, massive poverty is the result of the operation of a world economic system that prevents—or actually reverses—the economic development of most nations. With little economic resources of their own, poor societies end up being *dependent* on rich societies in several respects (Frank, 1980, 1981; Delacroix & Ragin, 1981; Bergesen, 1983).

1. *Narrow, export-oriented economies.* The economies of poor societies are not well diversified, as those in rich societies are. Historically, European colonization imposed an economy based on exporting a few raw materials from each colony, a pattern that persists today. Consequently, poor societies depend on rich societies to buy their crucial exports, which are generally sold at low prices. At the same time, poor societies must buy many, more expensive manufactured goods from rich societies.

2. *Multinational corporations.* During this century, the economic power of core societies has become concentrated in corporations that cast a long shadow over much of the world. These profit-seeking businesses draw heavily from the economic resources of a peripheral society, while inhibiting development of locally owned industries. Of course, multinationals also attempt to expand their markets in poor societies, funneling wealth back to rich societies.

3. *Internal stratification.* With the onset of colonization, foreign powers set up local elites to represent their interests. In an age of neocolonialism, capitalist investment also produces a small, Westernized elite with much the same role. This elite is able to politically and economically dominate a poor society through support from powerful core societies—including foreign aid and the presence of military bases. The result is ensuring the "stability" of the society as a host country for multinational corporations. Thus the power structure of poor societies is distorted by the interests of rich societies.

4. *Foreign debt.* During the 1970s and 1980s, a global debt crisis emerged as poor societies that owed enormous

In Guatemala City, becoming "modern" is closely tied to consuming products produced by multinational corporations owned by the richer nations.

sums of money to the rich nations were increasingly unable to make their debt payments. In part, this form of dependency reflects unequal trade relations, as noted above: cheap exports coupled to expensive imports. In addition, the debt crisis resulted from peripheral societies borrowing money from core societies to finance their economic development. But poor societies typically have little control over their own economies, and are highly dependent on income from a few raw materials whose prices often fluctuate unpredictably. The result is that loans often cannot be repaid, furthering the pattern of dependency.

The overall consequence of the world system is that modernization has been limited to only some societies. Over past centuries, the world's resources have become concentrated in a few rich societies, to the disadvantage of most of the world. Thus, while modernization theory implies that the standard of living worldwide is likely to *converge* as poor societies eventually industrialize, world-system theory claims that the economic power of "haves" and "have not" can be expected to *diverge* even further.

Evaluation. World-system theory provides a powerful challenge to the conventional wisdom of modernization theory. The greatest strength of this theory is that, instead of treating each society of the world as an independent case, it forces the examination of global patterns of power and conflict.

However, this approach has also drawn criticism. First, the assertion that rich societies are responsible for world poverty may be simplistic. World cultural patterns vary greatly: some societies embrace change readily, while others remain staunchly traditional. In all cases, critics claim, there are predictable consequences for modernization. Second, critic P. T. Bauer (1981) suggests that world-system theory may be more an expression of Western guilt about world poverty than a factual analysis, since contact with rich societies cannot be shown to have been clearly harmful to the Third World. Indeed, societies such as Japan, Singapore, and South Korea have all prospered from extensive contact with rich nations—even to the point of competing effectively with the United States. On the other hand, many of the poorest nations of the world are remote places that have had little contact with the West. Third, the governments of poor societies must take some responsibility for thwarting development. Population control and improving the status of women are known to aid development, but they have not always been high priorities. In some cases, loans have been used to construct "showplace" airports or fashionable urban centers rather than to finance economic projects that would provide long-term benefits to the population as a whole. Fourth and finally, the policy implications of world-system theory are not well developed. This approach suggests that poor societies end Western contact, and perhaps nationalize foreign industries. But the full implication of world-system theory would seem to be world revolution directed at ending the capitalist system—to some a worthy end, but certainly a goal opposed by the United States and many other powerful capitalist societies.

Looking to the Future

Social change is a process as controversial as it is complex, as variable as it is universal. At the beginning of this century, a majority of people in even the most technologically advanced societies lived in relatively small settlements with a limited range of experience. The world today is vastly different in ways that few people alive then could have imagined. We now discuss the relationships among nations in much the same way that people a century ago considered the expanding ties among towns and cities.

The twentieth century has been an era of unparalleled human achievement. Yet solutions to many of the timeless problems of human existence—including finding meaning in life, poverty, and tensions both within and among societies—are as elusive as ever. One source of optimism as we approach the twenty-first century is the fact that recent decades have also brought a greater understanding of human society.

SUMMARY

1. In every society, social change is continuous, although with varying speed and consequences. Social change is usually intentional and unplanned, and always controversial.

2. Some social change is caused by the cultural processes of invention and discovery within a society, and some by the process of cultural diffusion from one society to another. Social change can also be caused by social structure—tensions and conflicts within society itself. Ideas can also encourage or inhibit social change. Finally, the natural environment and population dynamics contribute to social change.

3. Modernity refers to the social consequences of industrialization. Peter Berger notes that the general characteristics of modernity are the weakening of small traditional communities, the expansion of personal choice, increasing diversity in patterns of belief, and a keener awareness of time, especially the future.

4. Ferdinand Toennies described modernization as the transition from gemeinschaft to gesellschaft. In his view, this process involves the progressive loss of community and the growing emphasis on individuality.

5. For Emile Durkheim, modernization involved an expanding division of labor in productive activity. Mechanical solidarity, based on common activities and shared beliefs, gradually gives way to organic solidarity, in which interdependent people engage in different activities. While Durkheim sought to illuminate the continu-

ing integration of modern society through specialization, he was concerned that modern societies were vulnerable to anomie—a condition of weak and conflicting cultural norms.

6.   Max Weber described the rise of modernity as the replacement of traditional patterns of thought by rationality. He feared that rational organization would dehumanize modern society.

7.   Karl Marx's view of modernity was shaped by the triumph of capitalism over feudalism. Because capitalist societies were fraught with social conflict, he anticipated revolutionary change to a more egalitarian socialist society.

8.   Mass-society theory emphasizes the growing scale of modern life, and the fact that within modern societies government and other formal organizations carry out many social tasks performed informally by the family and neighbors in traditional societies.

9.   Class-society theory considers the development of capitalism central to the process of modernization, and stresses the persistence of social inequality in modern societies.

10.   Mass-society theory explains that individuals in modern societies typically experience changing personal identities and sometimes have difficulty finding significance in their lives. This happens because of the consider-

able cultural diversity and rapid social change in modern societies.

11.   Class-society theory describes the modern problem of gaining a sense of meaningful participation in society as a consequence of capitalism's concentration of power and material resources in the hands of the few.

12.   Americans commonly link modernity to the idea of social progress. This simplified view overlooks the fact that social changes perceived as good from one point of view may be perceived as bad from another. In addition, social change is highly complex; from virtually any point of view, modernity has produced consequences that are both good and bad.

13.   In world context, some societies are rich and technologically advanced, while others are poor and largely traditional. Modernization theory argues that the traditional poor societies of the Third World will gradually come to resemble the societies of Europe and North America as they industrialize.

14.   World-system theory argues that modernization greatly depends on a society's position in the emerging world economic system. Poor societies cannot be expected to follow the same path of modernization as rich societies did because their development is inhibited by their economic dependency on rich societies.

KEY CONCEPTS

anomie a condition of weak and conflicting cultural norms that provide little moral guidance to individuals

class society an industrial society in which capitalism has generated pronounced social stratification

division of labor highly specialized economic activity

mass society an industrial society characterized by extensive bureaucracy that fosters social atomization and feelings of personal isolation

mechanical solidarity social bonds typical of small preindustrial societies, based on the perception that people are alike and belong together

modernity patterns of social organization linked to industrialization

modernization theory an approach to global change maintaining that traditional societies will gradually be transformed by industrialization to resemble Europe and North America

organic solidarity social bonds typical of large industrial societies, based on the interdependence of people who engage in specialized activities

other-directedness highly flexible personality patterns involving openness to change, often through imitating the behavior of others

social change transformation of culture and social institutions over time that is reflected in the life patterns of individuals

social character personality patterns that are shared by large numbers of people within a society

tradition-directedness rigid personality patterns involving conformity to traditional ways of living

world-system theory an approach to global change that links any society's development to its place in the world economic system

SUGGESTED READINGS

This paperback textbook provides an overview of the topic of social change in world perspective.

Daniel Chirot. *Social Change in the Modern Era*. New York: Harcourt Brace Jovanovich, 1986.

This paperback, by a sociologist widely known for his accounts of social change, presents ideas about how to humanize the world of the twenty-first century.

Alvin Toffler. *The Third Wave*. New York: Bantam Books, 1981.

The following books are both highly readable and filled with interesting insights about the modern world.

Peter Berger, Brigitte Berger, and Hansfried Kellner. *The Homeless Mind: Modernization and Consciousness*. New York: Vintage Books, 1974.

Peter L. Berger. *Facing Up to Modernity: Excursions in Society, Politics, and Religion*. New York: Basic Books, 1977.

Grasping the implications of modernity is difficult without a basis for comparison. The following paperback by a social historian presents a detailed look at life in England before the Industrial Revolution.

Peter Laslett. *The World We Have Lost: England Before the Industrial Age*. 3rd ed. New York: Charles Scribner's Sons, 1984.

The modern problem of controlling human technology is best illustrated by the nuclear arms race. This recent paperback examines both the causes and the consequences of the growing number of nuclear weapons.

Lester R. Kurtz, with Robert D. Benford and Jennifer E. Turpin. *The Nuclear Cage: A Sociology of the Arms Race*. Englewood Cliffs, NJ: Prentice-Hall, 1988.

This book examines recent transformations in the medical-care system of the United States, especially the role of physicians in encouraging and opposing change.

John Colombotos and Corrine Kirchner. *Physicians and Social Change*. New York: Oxford University Press, 1986.

Even small events rarely have consequences that are entirely predictable; major events never do. This book examines many kinds of change in American society—including attitudes toward sexuality, sex roles, and homosexuality—that were the legacy of World War II.

John Costello. *Virtue Under Fire: How World War II Changed Our Social and Sexual Attitudes*. Boston: Little, Brown, 1986.

This book takes a popular-culture approach to social change in the United States, exploring the transformations in roadside architecture over the course of the twentieth century.

Chester H. Liebs. *Main Street to Miracle Mile: American Roadside Architecture*. Boston: New York Graphic Society/ Little, Brown, 1985.

The rising rate of immigration has resulted in the introduction of many new cultural patterns to American society. This book is a collection of essays that describe current immigration, many social changes it has introduced, and the controversy it has sparked.

Nathan Glazer, ed. *Clamor at the Gates: The New American Immigration*. San Francisco: ISC Press, 1985.

Social change in world context is the focus of the following two collections of articles. The first presents material based heavily on modernization theory, while the second is grounded in world-system theory.

Cyril E. Black, ed. *Comparative Modernization: A Reader*. New York: Free Press, 1976.

Albert Bergesen, ed. *Crises in the World System*. Beverly Hills, CA: Sage Publications, 1983.

These two paperbacks provide contrasting views of global relationships. The first is a conservative analysis of patterns of world inequality; the second is a collection of essays written by one of the most influential architects of world-system theory.

P. T. Bauer. *Equality, the Third World, and Economic Delusion*. Cambridge, MA: Harvard University Press, 1981.

Immanuel Wallerstein. *The Politics of the World-Economy: The States, the Movements, and the Civilizations*. Cambridge, UK: Cambridge University Press, 1984.

This book examines social change in traditional societies with a focus on music: how Western music is influencing traditional musical patterns in a number of countries.

Bruno Nettl. *The Western Impact on World Music: Change, Adaptation, and Survival*. New York: Schirmer Books, 1985.

This government report provides a comprehensive and largely pessimistic look at the future of the world as we approach the beginning of the twenty-first century. Special attention is given to problems associated with the natural environment and population growth.

Gerald O. Barney. *The Global 2000 Report to the President of the U.S.: Entering the 21st Century*. Vol. 1: *The Summary Report*. New York: Pergamon Press, 1980.

Glossary

absolute poverty a state of deprivation of social resources that is life-threatening

achieved status a social position that is assumed voluntarily and that reflects a significant measure of personal ability and effort

activity theory (*also* **substitution theory**) a theory that relates a high level of social activity to personal satisfaction in old age

ageism the belief that one age category is superior or inferior to another

age-sex pyramid a graphic representation of the age and sex of a population

age stratification the unequal distribution of wealth, power, and privileges among people of different ages

agrarian society a society that engages in large-scale agriculture based on the use of plows drawn by animals

animism the belief that objects in the natural world are endowed with consciousness and can affect human lives

annihilation the violent extermination of one category of people by another

anomie a condition of weak and conflicting cultural norms that provide little moral guidance to individuals

anticipatory socialization the process of social learning directed toward assuming a desired status and role in the future

ascribed status a social position that is received at birth or involuntarily assumed at a later point in the life course

assimilation the process by which members of minority groups gradually modify their ways of life to conform to patterns of the dominant culture

authoritarianism the exclusion of the majority from political participation, although with little governmental intervention in people's lives

authority power that is generally perceived as legitimate rather than coercive

bilateral descent a practice linking children in kinship to the families of both parents

blue-collar jobs occupations that involve mostly manual labor

bureaucracy an organizational model rationally designed to perform complex tasks efficiently

bureaucratic authority *see* **rational-legal authority**

bureaucratic inertia the tendency of bureaucratic organizations to persist over time

bureaucratic ritualism preoccupation with organizational rules and regulations as ends in themselves rather than as the means to organizational goals

capitalism an economic system in which natural resources, as well as the means of producing goods and services, are privately owned

capitalists those who own factories and other productive enterprises

caste system a system of social stratification based almost entirely on ascription

cause and effect a relationship between two variables in which change in one (the independent variable) causes change in another (the dependent variable)

charisma extraordinary personal qualities that can turn an audience into followers

charismatic authority power legitimated through extraordinary personal abilities that inspire devotion and obedience

church a general type of formal religious organization that is well integrated into the larger society

civil religion a quasi-religious loyalty binding individuals to their society

class consciousness the recognition by workers of their unity as a social class in opposition to capitalists and to capitalism itself

class society an industrial society in which capitalism has generated pronounced patterns of social stratification

class system a system of social stratification in which individual achievement is of considerable importance

cohabitation sharing of a household by an unmarried couple

collective behavior actions, thoughts, and emotions that involve large numbers of people and that do not conform to established social norms

collectivity a large number of people who have limited interaction with one another and who do not share well-defined and conventional norms

communism a utopian economic and political system in which all property is collectively owned and all members of society have economic and social equality

concept an abstract idea that represents some element of the world

concrete operational stage Piaget's term for the level of human development characterized by the use of logic to understand objects or events, but not in abstract terms

conglomerates giant corporations composed of many smaller corporations

conjugal family *see* **nuclear family**

consanguine family *see* **extended family**

control the ability to neutralize the effect of one variable so that the relationship among other variables can be more precisely determined

conversion a personal transformation based on new religious beliefs

corporation an organization that is recognized by law as having rights apart from those of its members

correlation a relationship between two (or more) variables in which they vary together with no demonstrated relationship of cause and effect

counterculture cultural patterns that are strongly at odds with the dominant culture

credentialism the requirement that a person hold an advanced degree as a condition of employment in many occupations

crime the violation of norms that have been formally enacted into criminal law

crimes against property (*also* **property crimes**) crimes that involve theft of property belonging to others

crimes against the person (*also* **violent crimes**) crimes against people that involve violence or the threat of violence

criminal justice system the formal process by which society reacts to alleged violations of the law through the use of police, courts, and punishment

criminal recidivism subsequent offenses by people previously convicted of crimes

crowd a temporary gathering of people who share some common focus of attention and often influence one another

crude birth rate the number of live births in a given year for every thousand people in a population

crude death rate the number of deaths in a given year for every thousand people in a population

cult a religious movement that has little or nothing in common with other religious organizations in a particular society

cultural ecology a theoretical paradigm that explores the interrelationship of human culture and the physical environment

cultural integration the principle that the various parts of a cultural system are extensively interrelated

cultural lag inconsistencies within a cultural system resulting from the unequal rates at which different cultural elements change

cultural relativism the practice of judging any culture by its own standards

cultural transmission the process by which culture is passed from one generation to the next

cultural universals traits found within all human cultures

culture the beliefs, values, behavior, and material objects shared by a particular people

culture shock the personal disorientation that may accompany entry into an unfamiliar social world

deductive logical thought a logical process that begins with general ideas that generate specific hypotheses subject to scientific evaluation

democracy a type of political system in which power is exercised by the people as a whole

democratic socialism a political and economic system in which free elections and a market economy coexist with government efforts to minimize social inequality

demographic transition theory the thesis that population patterns are linked to a society's level of technological development

demography the study of human population

denomination a churchlike religious organization that recognizes religious pluralism

dependent variable a variable that is changed by another (independent) variable

deterrence reducing criminal activity by instilling the fear of being punished

deviance the recognized violation of cultural norms

direct-fee system a medical-care system in which patients pay directly for services provided by physicians and hospitals

discrimination treating various categories of people differently

disengagement theory a theory that relates the disengagement of elderly people from positions of social responsibility to the orderly operation of society

division of labor highly specialized economic activity

dramaturgical analysis the analysis of social interaction in terms of theatrical performance

dyad a social group with two members

ecclesia a churchlike religious organization that is formally allied with the state

economy a social institution that organizes the production, distribution, and consumption of goods and services

education the various ways in which knowledge—including factual information and skills, as well as cultural norms and values—is transmitted to members of society

ego Freud's designation of the conscious attempt to balance the plea-sure-seeking drives of the human organism and the demands and realities of society

empirical evidence what we can observe or otherwise verify with our senses

endogamy marriage between people of the same social group or category

ethnicity a cultural heritage shared by a category of people

ethnocentrism the practice of judging another culture by the standards of our own culture

ethnomethodology the study of the everyday, commonsense understandings that people have of the world around them

euthanasia (*also* **mercy killing**) assisting in the death of a person who is suffering from a painful and incurable illness

exogamy marriage between people of different social groups or categories

experiment a method of sociological investigation that seeks to specify cause-and-effect relationships among variables

expressive leadership leadership that emphasizes the collective well-being of the members of a social group

extended family (*also* **consanguine family**) a family composed of parents, children, and other kin

fad a somewhat unconventional social pattern that is embraced enthusiastically by a large number of people for a very short period of time

faith belief that is not based on scientific evidence

false consciousness the belief that the shortcomings of individuals themselves, and not society, are responsible for many of the personal problems that people experience

family a social group of two or more people related by blood, marriage, or adoption who live together

family of orientation the family into which a person is born, and which provides intensive early socialization

family of procreation a family within which people have or adopt children of their own

family violence emotional, physical, or sexual abuse of one family member by another

fashion a social pattern favored for a time by a large number of people

feminism the support for the social equality of the sexes, leading to opposition to patriarchy and sexism

feminization of poverty a trend by which females represent an increasing proportion of the poor

fertility the incidence of childbearing in a society's population

folkways norms that have little moral significance and about which greater personal discretion is allowed

formal operational stage Piaget's term for the level of human development characterized by highly abstract thought and the ability to imagine alternatives to reality

formal organization a large, secondary group that is formally organized to facilitate achieving its goals

free school philosophy an educational philosophy in which students are encouraged to pursue their own interests in a creative way, within a nonhierarchical and noncompetitive learning environment

functional illiteracy the lack of basic reading and writing skills needed for everyday life

gemeinschaft a German word meaning a type of social organization characterized by strong social solidarity based on tradition and predominantly personal relationships

gender human traits linked by culture to each sex

gender identity the ways males and females, within their culture, learn to think of themselves

gender roles (*also* **sex roles**) attitudes and activities that a culture links to each sex

gender stratification the unequal distribution of wealth, power, and privileges between the two sexes

generalized other G.H. Mead's term for widespread cultural norms and values that are used as a reference in evaluating ourselves

gerontocracy a form of social organization in which the elderly have the most wealth, power, and privileges

gerontology the study of aging and the elderly

gesellschaft a German word meaning a type of social organization characterized by weak social solidarity resulting from cultural pluralism and predominantly impersonal relationships

Hawthorne effect distortion in research caused by the awareness of subjects that they are the focus of study

health a state of relative physical, mental, and social well-being

health care deliberate activity directed toward improving health

health maintenance organization (HMO) a formal organization that provides comprehensive medical care for which subscribers pay a fixed fee

hidden curriculum important cultural lessons of schooling that are usually not explicitly acknowledged

holistic medicine a medical orientation that seeks to improve health by taking account of the whole person as well as the physical and social environment

homogamy marriage between people with the same social characteristics

horticultural society a society that cultivates plants using hand tools

"humanizing bureaucracy" efforts to develop human potential in the belief that this is the primary resource of any formal organization

hunting and gathering society a society that uses simple technology to hunt animals and gather vegetation

hypothesis a theoretical statement of the relationship between any facts or variables

id Freud's designation of the human being's basic needs

ideal culture social patterns consistent with cultural values and norms

ideal type an abstract description of any social phenomenon in terms of its essential characteristics

ideology ideas that reflect and support the interests of some category of a population

incest taboo cultural norms that forbid sexual relations or marriage between certain kin

income occupational wages or salaries and earnings from investments

independent variable a variable that causes change in another (dependent) variable

inductive logical thought a logical process that begins with specific observations that are linked together into a general theory

industrial society a society that uses sophisticated machinery powered by natural fuels to produce material goods

infant mortality rate the number of deaths within the first year of life for each thousand live births in a given year

ingroup a social group with which individuals identify and toward which they feel a sense of loyalty

institutional discrimination patterns of discrimination that are woven into the fabric of society

instrumental leadership leadership that emphasizes the completion of tasks by a social group

intergenerational social mobility change in the social position of children in relation to that of their parents

interlocking directorate a corporate linkage created when members of one corporation's board of directors become members of other corporations' boards

interview questions administered personally to the subject by the researcher

intragenerational social mobility change in social position occurring during a person's lifetime

juvenile delinquency the violation of legal standards by children or adolescents

kinship social relationships based on blood, marriage, or adoption

labeling theory the assertion that deviance and conformity are the result of the process by which individuals are defined or labeled by others

language a system of symbols with standard meanings that allows members of a society to communicate with one another

latent functions the unrecognized and unintended consequences of any social pattern

life expectancy how long a person, on the average, can expect to live

looking-glass self Cooley's term for a conception of self derived from the responses of others to us

macro-level orientation a concern with large-scale patterns that characterize society as a whole

mainstreaming the integration of disabled students into the educational program as a whole

mandatory education laws the legal requirement that children receive a minimum of formal education

mandatory retirement formal regulations requiring people to retire from their occupational work at a specified age

manifest functions the recognized and intended consequences of any social pattern

marriage a socially approved relationship involving both economic cooperation and sexual activity

mass behavior collective behavior among people dispersed over a wide geographical area

mass hysteria a situation in which people in a wide area respond to some perceived threat with anxious or frantic behavior

mass media channels of communication directed toward a vast audience within a society

mass society an industrial society characterized by extensive bureaucracy that fosters social atomization and feelings of personal isolation

master status a status that has exceptionally great significance for shaping a person's entire life

material culture tangible elements of culture such as clothing and cities

matriarchy a form of social organization in which females dominate males

matrilineal descent the practice of tracing kinship only through females

matrilocality a residential pattern in which a married couple lives with or near the wife's family

mean the arithmetic average of a series of numbers, calculated by dividing the sum by the number of cases

measurement the process of determining the value of a variable in a specific case

mechanical solidarity social bonds typical of small preindustrial societies, based on the perception that people are alike and belong together

median the value that occurs midway in a series of numbers

medicalization of deviance viewing as medical matters patterns of behavior previously understood in moral terms

medicine a social institution concerned with combating disease as a means to improve health

megalopolis a vast urban region containing a number of cities and their surrounding suburbs

mercy killing see **euthanasia**

meritocracy a system of social stratification in which rewards are matched to personal merit

metropolis a very large city that socially and economically dominates a broad urban area

micro-level orientation a concern with small-scale patterns of social interaction within specific settings

migration the movement of people into and out of a specified territory

minority group a category of people defined by physical or cultural traits subject to social disadvantage

miscegenation the biological process of interbreeding among various racial categories

mob a highly emotional crowd united by the common purpose of some specific violent and destructive action

mode the value that occurs most often in a series of numbers

modernity patterns of social organization linked to industrialization

modernization theory an approach to global change maintaining that traditional societies will gradually be transformed by industrialization to resemble Europe and North America

monarchy a type of political system in which power is passed from generation to generation within a single family

monogamy a form of marriage that joins one male and one female

monopoly the domination of a market by a single producer

monotheism religious beliefs recognizing a single divine power

mores norms that have great moral significance, the violation of which is usually met with a vigorous reaction

mortality the incidence of death in a society's population

multinational corporation (also **transnational corporation**) a large corporation that operates in many different nations

neolocality a residential pattern in which a married couple lives apart from the parents of both spouses

nonmaterial culture intangible elements of culture such as values and norms

nonverbal communication communication using body movements, gestures, and facial expressions rather than spoken words

norms rules and expectations by which a society guides the behavior of its members

nuclear family (also **conjugal family**) one or, more commonly, two parents and children

objectivity the state of complete personal neutrality in conducting research

oligarchy the rule of the many by the few

oligopoly the domination of a market by a few producers

operationalizing a variable specifying exactly what is to be measured in assigning a value to a variable

organic solidarity social bonds typical of large industrial societies, based on the interdependence of people who engage in specialized activities

other-directedness highly flexible personality patterns involving openness to change, often through imitating the behavior of others

outgroup a social group with which individuals do not identify and toward which they feel a sense of competition or opposition

overeducation a situation in which workers have more formal education than the performance of their occupations requires

panic a situation that occurs when a crowd is provoked into seemingly irrational and often self-destructive behavior by some perceived threat

participant observation a method of sociological investigation involving the systematic observation of people while taking part in their activities, usually in a natural setting

pastoral society a society whose livelihood is based on the domestication of animals

patriarchy a form of social organization in which males dominate females

patrilineal descent the practice of tracing kinship only through males

patrilocality a residential pattern in which a married couple lives with or near the husband's family

peer group people with common interests and social position who are usually of the same age

personality the organized system of personal thoughts, feelings, and behavior

plea bargaining a process of legal negotiation in which the prosecution agrees to reduce the charge against a defendant in exchange for a guilty plea

pluralism a state in which all racial and ethnic groups, while socially distinct, have roughly equal social standing

pluralist model an analysis of politics emphasizing the dispersion of power among many competing interest groups

political action committee (PAC) an organization formed by a special-interest group, independent of political parties, to pursue a specific political aim through raising and spending money

political machine an organization that seeks virtually complete control of the political system within a local area

political parties political organizations in which people of similar attitudes and interests influence the political process

political revolution the overthrow of one political system as a part of the effort to establish another

political state a formal government exercising control over a society and claiming the legitimate use of coercion to support its rule

politics the organized way in which power is distributed and decisions are made within a society

polyandry a form of marriage that joins one female with more than one male

polygamy a form of marriage that unites three or more people

polygyny a form of marriage that joins one male with more than one female

polytheism religious beliefs recognizing many gods

population all people about whom research gathers information

positivism the assertion that science, rather than any other type of human understanding, is the path to knowledge

postindustrial economy an economy based on services and high technology

power the likelihood of achieving desired ends in spite of possible resistance from others

power-elite model an analysis of politics emphasizing the concentration of power among the rich

prejudice an unfounded generalization about a category of people

preoperational stage Piaget's term for the level of human development in which language and other symbols are first used

presentation of self the ways in which individuals, in various settings, attempt to create specific impressions in the minds of others

primary group a typically small social group in which relationships are both personal and enduring

primary labor market occupations that provide extensive benefits to workers

primary sector that part of the economy that generates raw materials directly from the natural environment

primary sex characteristics the genitals, used to reproduce the human species

profane that which is defined as an ordinary element of everyday life

profession a white-collar occupation with high social prestige that requires considerable formal education

proletariat those who provide the labor necessary for the operation of factories and other productive enterprises

propaganda information presented with the intention of shaping public opinion

public opinion the attitudes of people throughout a society about one or more controversial issues

qualitative research research based heavily on subjective interpretation

quantitative research research that emphasizes analysis of numerical data

questionnaire a series of questions or items to which subjects are asked to respond

race a category of people with common biological traits passed from generation to generation

racism the belief that one racial category is innately superior or inferior to another

rational-legal authority (*also* **bureaucratic authority**) power legitimated by legally enacted rules and regulations

rationality deliberate, matter-of-fact calculation of the most efficient means to accomplish any particular goal

rationalization of society the change from tradition to rationality as the characteristic mode of human thought

real culture actual social patterns that are typically only an approximation of ideal cultural norms

reference group a social group that serves as a point of reference for individuals in evaluation and decision making

rehabilitation reforming the offender so that subsequent offenses will not occur

relative deprivation a perceived disadvantage based on comparisons with what other people have or some other standard

relative poverty a state of deprivation of social resources in relation to some standard of greater privilege

reliability the quality of consistency in measurement

religion a system of beliefs and practices built upon the recognition of the sacred

religiosity the importance of religion in a person's life

religious fundamentalism conservative religious organizations that seek to restore what are viewed as fundamental elements of religion

replication the process by which a study is repeated by other researchers

research method a strategy for carrying out research in a systematic way

resocialization socialization at odds with past social experiences that may radically alter the individual's personality

retribution subjecting an offender to suffering comparable to that caused by the offense itself as an act of social revenge

retrospective labeling the interpretation of a person's past in terms that are consistent with a present deviant label

riot a situation that results when a crowd explodes into undirected violent and destructive behavior

ritual formal, ceremonial behavior

role patterns of behavior corresponding to a particular status

role conflict incompatibility among the roles corresponding to two or more statuses

role set a number of roles attached to a single status

role strain incompatibility among roles corresponding to a single status

routinization of charisma the transformation of charismatic authority into some combination of traditional and bureaucratic authority

rumor unsubstantiated information spread informally, often by word of mouth

sacred that which is defined as extraordinary, inspiring a sense of awe, reverence, and even fear

sample a representative part of a population

Sapir-Whorf hypothesis the assertion that people perceive the world only in terms of symbols provided by their language

scapegoat one person or category of people unfairly blamed for the troubles of another

schooling formal instruction under the direction of specially trained teachers

science a logical system that bases knowledge on facts that are derived from direct, systematic observation

secondary analysis a method of sociological investigation involving the independent analysis of data originally collected by other researchers

secondary group a typically large and impersonal social group based on some special interest or activity

secondary labor market occupations that provide minimal benefits to workers

secondary sector that part of the economy that transforms raw materials into manufactured goods

secondary sex characteristics distinctive physical traits of males and females not directly linked to reproduction

sect a general type of informal religious organization that is not well integrated into the larger society

secularization the decline in the influence of religion

segregation the physical and social separation of categories of people

self the individual's awareness of being a distinct entity in the midst of society

sensorimotor stage Piaget's term for the level of human development in which the world is experienced only through the senses in terms of physical contact

sex the division of humanity into biological categories of male and female

sex ratio the number of males for every hundred females in a given population

sex roles *see* **gender roles**

sexism the belief that one sex is innately superior to the other

sexual orientation the manner in which people experience sexual arousal and achieve sexual pleasure

sick role patterns of behavior that are socially defined as appropriate for those who are ill

social alienation the experience of powerlessness in social life

social change transformation of culture and social institutions over time that is reflected in the life patterns of individuals

social character personality patterns that are shared by large numbers of people within a society

social conflict struggle among segments of society over valued resources

social-conflict paradigm a theoretical framework based on the view of society as a system characterized by social inequality and social conflict that generate social change

social construction of reality the process by which individuals creatively shape reality through social interaction

social control the process by which members of a culture encourage conformity to cultural norms

social dysfunctions the undesirable consequences of any social pattern

social epidemiology the study of the distribution of disease or relative health in a society's population

social functions the consequences of any social pattern for the operation of society

social group two or more people who have a high degree of common identity and who interact on a regular basis

social institution a major structural part of society that addresses one or more of its basic needs

social marginality exclusion from social activity as an "outsider"

social mobility changes in the social position of individuals within a system of social stratification

social movement long-term organized activity that encourages or discourages some dimension of social change

social network a web of social ties that links people, but with less common identity and less social interaction than are typical of a social group

social stratification a system by which categories of people within a society are ranked in a hierarchy

social structure relatively stable patterns of social behavior

socialism an economic system in which natural resources, as well as the means of producing goods and services, are collectively owned

socialization a lifelong process, based on social interaction, by which individuals develop their human potential and learn the patterns of their culture

socialized medicine a health-care system in which most medical facilities are owned and operated by the government, and most physicians are government employees who receive salaries rather than fees collected directly from patients

society people who interact with one another within a limited territory and who share a culture

sociobiology a theoretical paradigm that seeks to explain cultural patterns as the product, at least in part, of biological causes

sociocultural evolution the process of social change resulting from gaining new cultural elements, particularly technology

socioeconomic status a composite social ranking based on various dimensions of social inequality

sociology the scientific study of society and the social activity of human beings

special-interest group a political alliance of people who share an orientation with regard to a particular economic or social issue

status a recognized social position that an individual occupies within society

status consistency consistency of social ranking with regard to various dimensions of social inequality

status set all the statuses a particular person holds at a given time

stereotype a description of a category of people that persists even in the face of contrary evidence

stigma a powerful negative social label that radically changes a person's social identity and self-concept

structural-functional paradigm a theoretical framework based on the view of society as a system of many different parts that work together to generate relative stability

structural social mobility social mobility on the part of large numbers of people that is due primarily to changes in society itself, rather than to the efforts and abilities of individuals

subculture cultural patterns that differ from the dominant culture in some distinctive way

substitution theory see **activity theory**

suburbs the urban area beyond the political boundaries of a city

superego Freud's designation of the presence of culture within the individual in the form of internalized values and norms

survey a method of sociological investigation in which individuals provide responses to a series of items or questions

symbol anything that carries a particular meaning recognized by members of a culture

symbolic-interaction paradigm a theoretical framework based on the view of society as a highly variable product of continuous interaction of individuals in various settings

technology the application of cultural knowledge to the task of living in a physical environment

terrorism the use of violence or the threat of violence in pursuit of political aims

tertiary sector that part of the economy that generates services rather than goods

theoretical paradigm a fundamental image of society that guides sociological thinking

theory an explanation of the relationship between two or more specific facts

Thomas theorem the assertion that situations that are defined as real are real in their consequences

total institution a setting in which individuals are isolated from the rest of society and controlled and manipulated by an administrative staff

totalitarianism the exclusion of the majority from free political participation coupled to extensive governmental intervention in people's lives

totem an object, usually an element of the natural world, that is imbued with sacred qualities

tracking categorically assigning students to different types of educational programs

tradition sentiments and beliefs about the world that are passed from generation to generation

traditional authority power that is legitimated through respect for long-established cultural patterns

tradition-directedness rigid personality patterns involving conformity to traditional ways of living

transnational corporation see **multinational corporation**

triad a social group with three members

underground economy all economic activity that involves income or the exchange of goods and services that is not reported to the government

urban ecology analysis of the interplay of physical and social dimensions of urban life

urban renewal governmental programs intended to revitalize cities

urbanization humanity's increasing concentration within limited geographical areas called cities

validity the quality of measurement afforded by actually measuring what one intends to measure

values culturally defined standards of desirability, goodness, and beauty that serve as broad guidelines for social life

variable a concept that has a value that varies from case to case

verstehen a German word meaning the effort to learn how individuals in a particular social setting understand their own actions

victimless crimes violations of law in which there are no readily apparent victims

wealth the total amount of money and valuable goods that any person or family controls

white-collar crime crimes committed by people of high social position in the course of their occupations

white-collar jobs occupations that involve mostly mental activity and skills not identified with manual labor

world-systems theory an approach to global change that links any society's development to its place in the world economic system

zero population growth the level of reproduction that maintains population at a steady state

References

ABERLE, DAVID F. *The Peyote Religion Among the Navaho.* Chicago: Aldine, 1966.

ABRAHAMSON, MARK, and VALERIE J. CARTER. "Tolerance, Urbanism and Region." *American Sociological Review.* Vol. 51, No. 2 (April 1986):287–294.

ABZUG, ROBERT H. *Inside the Vicious Heart: Americans and the Liberation of Nazi Concentration Camps.* New York: Oxford University Press, 1985.

ADLER, FREDA, and HERBERT M. ADLER. "Female Delinquency: Minor Girls and Major Crimes." In Delos H. Kelly, ed., *Deviant Behavior: Readings in the Sociology of Deviance.* New York: St. Martin's Press, 1979:523–536.

ADORNO, T. W., et al. *The Authoritarian Personality.* New York: Harper Brothers, 1950.

ADRIAANSENS, HANS P. M. "The Conceptual Dilemma: Towards a Better Understanding of the Development of Parsonian Action Theory." *British Journal of Sociology.* Vol. 30, No. 1 (March 1979):5–24.

AKERS, RONALD L., MARVIN D. KROHN, LONN LANZA-KADUCE, and MARCIA RADOSEVICH. "Social Learning and Deviant Behavior." *American Sociological Review.* Vol. 44, No. 4 (August 1979):636–655.

ALBA, RICHARD D. *Italian Americans: Into the Twilight of Ethnicity.* Englewood Cliffs, NJ: Prentice-Hall, 1985.

ALBON, JOAN. "Retention of Cultural Values and Differential Urban Adaptation: Samoans and American Indians in a West Coast City." *Social Forces.* Vol. 49, No. 3 (March 1971):385–393.

ALBRECHT, WILLIAM P., JR. *Economics.* 3rd ed. Englewood Cliffs, NJ: Prentice-Hall, 1983.

ALEXANDER, CHARLES P. "Playing Computer Catch-Up." *Time.* Vol. 125, No. 15 (April 15, 1985):84–85.

ALEXANDER, JEFFREY C. *The Modern Reconstruction of Classical Thought: Talcott Parsons, Theoretical Logic in Sociology,* Vol. 4. London: Routledge & Kegan Paul, 1984.

ALLPORT, GORDON W. *The Nature of Prejudice.* Garden City, NY: Anchor Books, 1958.

AMERICAN COUNCIL ON EDUCATION, as reported in "Number of Black Students Still Falling, Study Finds." *The Chronicle of Higher Education.* Vol. XXXIV, No. 11 (November 11, 1987):2.

AMERICAN COUNCIL ON EDUCATION. "Senior Women Administrators in Higher Education: A Decade of Change, 1975–1983." Washington, DC: 1984.

AMERICAN SOCIOLOGICAL ASSOCIATION. "Code of Ethics." Washington, DC: 1984.

ANDERSON, DANIEL R., and ELIZABETH PUGZLES LORCH. "Look at Television: Action or Reaction?" In Jennings Bryant and Daniel R. Anderson, eds., *Children's Understanding of Television: Research on Attention and Comprehension.* New York: Academic Press, 1983:1–33.

ANDERSON, HARRY. "Fuming Over College Costs." *Newsweek* (May 18, 1987):66–68, 70, 72.

ANDERSON, KURT. "The New Ellis Island." *Time.* Vol. 121, No. 24 (June 13, 1983):18–22, 24–25.

ANG, IEN. *Watching Dallas: Soap Opera and the Melodramatic Imagination.* London: Methuen, 1985.

ARENDT, HANNAH. *Between Past and Future: Six Exercises in Political Thought.* Cleveland, OH: Meridian Books, 1963.

ARENDT, HANNAH. *The Origins of Totalitarianism.* Cleveland, OH: Meridian Books, 1958.

ARIÈS, PHILIPPE. *Centuries of Childhood: A Social History of Family Life.* New York: Vintage Books, 1965.

ARIÈS, PHILIPPE. *Western Attitudes Toward Death: From the Middle Ages to the Present.* Baltimore, MD: The Johns Hopkins University Press, 1974.

ASCH, SOLOMON. *Social Psychology.* Englewood Cliffs, NJ: Prentice-Hall, 1952.

ATCHLEY, ROBERT C. *Aging: Continuity and Change.* Belmont, CA: Wadsworth, 1983; also 2nd ed., 1987.

ATCHLEY, ROBERT C. "Retirement as a Social Institution." *Annual Review of Sociology.* Vol. 8. Palo Alto, CA: Annual Reviews, Inc., 1982:263–287.

AVIS, GEORGE. "Access to Higher Education in the Soviet Union." In J. J. Tomiak, ed., *Soviet Education in the 1980s.* London: Croom Helm, 1983:199–239.

AYENSU, EDWARD S. "A Worldwide Role for the Healing Powers of Plants." *Smithsonian.* Vol. 12, No. 8 (November 1981):87–97.

BABBIE, EARL. *The Practice of Social Research.* Belmont, CA: Wadsworth, 1983.

BACHRACH, PETER, and MORTON S. BARATZ. *Power and Poverty.* New York: Oxford University Press, 1970.

BAINBRIDGE, WILLIAM SIMS, and DANIEL H. JACKSON. "The Rise and Decline of Transcendental Meditation." In Bryan Wilson, ed., *The Social Impact of New Religious Movements.* New York: The Rose of Sharon Press, 1981:135–158.

BAKER, MARY ANNE, CATHERINE WHITE BERHEIDE, FAY ROSS GRECKEL, LINDA CARSTARPHEN GUGIN, MARCIA J. LIPETZ, and MARCIA TEXLER SEGAL. *Women Today: A Multidisciplinary Approach to Women's Studies.* Monterey, CA: Brooks/Cole, 1980.

BALES, ROBERT F. "The Equilibrium Problem in Small Groups." In Talcott Parsons et al., eds., *Working Papers in the Theory of Action.* New York: Free Press, 1953:111–115.

BALES, ROBERT F., and PHILIP E. SLATER. "Role Differentiation in Small Decision-Making Groups." In Talcott Parsons and Robert F. Bales, eds., *Family, Socialization and Interaction Process.* New York: Free Press, 1955:259–306.

BALLANTINE, JEANNE H. *The Sociology of Education: A Systematic Analysis.* Englewood Cliffs, NJ: Prentice-Hall, 1983.

BALTES, PAUL B., and K. WARNER SCHAIE. "The Myth of the Twilight Years." *Psychology Today.* Vol. 7, No. 10 (March 1974):35–39.

BALTZELL, E. DIGBY. *Philadelphia Gentlemen: The Making of a National Upper Class.* Philadelphia, PA: University of Pennsylvania Press, 1979; orig. 1958.

BALTZELL, E. DIGBY. *The Protestant Establishment: Aristocracy and Caste in America.* New York: Vintage, 1964.

BALTZELL, E. DIGBY. "The Protestant Establishment Revisited." *The American Scholar*. Vol. 45, No. 4 (Autumn 1976):499–518.

BALTZELL, E. DIGBY. *Puritan Boston and Quaker Philadelphia*. New York: Free Press, 1979.

BALTZELL, E. DIGBY, ed. *The Search for Community in Modern America*. New York: Harper & Row, 1968.

BANFIELD, EDWARD C. *The Unheavenly City Revisited*. Boston, MA: Little, Brown, 1974.

BARASH, DAVID. *The Whispering Within*. New York: Penguin Books, 1981.

BARBER, BEN. "Guilty Verdict in 'Mercy Killing.'" *USA Today* (May 10, 1985):3A.

BARBERIS, MARY. "America's Elderly: Policy Implications." *Population Bulletin*. Vol. 35, No. 4 (January 1981), Population Reference Bureau.

BARKER, EILEEN. "Who'd Be a Moonie? A Comparative Study of Those Who Join the Unification Church in Britain." In Bryan Wilson, ed., *The Social Impact of New Religious Movements*. New York: The Rose of Sharon Press, 1981:59–96.

BARNEY, GERALD O. *The Global 2000 Report to the President of the U.S.: Entering the 21st Century*. Vol. 1: *The Summary Report*. New York: Pergamon Press, 1980.

BARONE, MICHAEL, and GRANT UJIFUSA. *The Almanac of American Politics*. Washington, DC: Barone and Co., 1981.

BARROW, GEORGE M., and PATRICIA A. SMITH. *Aging, the Individual, and Society*. 2nd ed. St. Paul, MN: West, 1983.

BARRY, KATHLEEN. "Feminist Theory: The Meaning of Women's Liberation." In Barbara Haber, ed., *The Women's Annual 1982–1983*. Boston, MA: G. K. Hall, 1983:55–78.

BATESON, C. DANIEL, and W. LARRY VENTIS. *The Religious Experience: A Social-Psychological Perspective*. New York: Oxford, 1982.

BAUER, P. T. *Equality, the Third World, and Economic Delusion*. Cambridge, MA: Harvard University Press, 1981.

BEATRICE COMPANY, INC. *Annual Report 1985*. Chicago: Beatrice, 1985.

BECKER, HOWARD S. *Outsiders: Studies in the Sociology of Deviance*. New York: Free Press, 1966.

BEDELL, GEORGE C., LEO SANDON, JR., and CHARLES T. WELLBORN. *Religion in America*. New York: Macmillan, 1975.

BEIGEL, HUGO G. "Romantic Love." *American Sociological Review*. Vol. 16, No. 3 (June 1951):326–334.

BELL, ALAN P., MARTIN S. WEINBERG, and SUE KIEFER-HAMMERSMITH. *Sexual Preference: Its Development in Men and Women*. Bloomington, IN: Indiana University Press, 1981.

BELL, DANIEL. *The Coming of Post-Industrial Society: A Venture in Social Forecasting*. New York: Harper Colophon, 1976.

BELLAH, ROBERT N. *The Broken Covenant*. New York: Seabury, 1975.

BELLAH, ROBERT N., RICHARD MADSEN, WILLIAM M. SULLIVAN, ANN SWIDLER, and STEVEN M. TIPTON. *Habits of the Heart: Individualism and Commitment in American Life*. New York: Harper & Row, 1985.

BELSKY, JAY, RICHARD M. LERNER, and GRAHAM B. SPANIER. *The Child in the Family*. Reading, MA: Addison-Wesley, 1984.

BEM, SANDRA LIPSITZ. "Gender Schema Theory: A Cognitive Account of Sex-Typing." *Psychological Review*. Vol 88, No. 4 (July 1981): 354–364.

BENEDICT, RUTH. *The Chrysanthemum and the Sword: Patterns of Japanese Culture*. New York: New American Library, 1974; orig. 1946.

BENJAMIN, BERNARD, and CHRIS WALLIS. "The Mortality of Widowers." *The Lancet*. Vol. 2 (August 1963):454–456.

BENOKRAITIS, NIJOLE, and JOE FEAGIN. *Modern Sexism: Blatant, Subtle and Overt Discrimination*. Englewood Cliffs, NJ: Prentice-Hall, 1986.

BERARDO, F. M. "Survivorship and Social Isolation: The Case of the Aged Widower." *The Family Coordinator*. Vol. 19 (January 1970):11–25.

BERG, IVAR. *Education and Jobs: The Great Training Robbery*. New York: Praeger, 1970.

BERGER, BRIGITTE, and PETER L. BERGER. *The War Over the Family: Capturing the Middle Ground*. Garden City, NY: Anchor/Doubleday, 1983.

BERGER, KATHLEEN STASSEN. *The Developing Person Through the Lifespan*. New York: Worth, 1983.

BERGER, PETER L. *The Capitalist Revolution: Fifty Propositions About Prosperity, Equality, and Liberty*. New York: Basic Books, 1986.

BERGER, PETER L. *Facing Up to Modernity: Excursions in Society, Politics, and Religion*. New York: Basic Books, 1977.

BERGER, PETER L. *Invitation to Sociology*. New York: Anchor Books, 1963.

BERGER, PETER L. *The Sacred Canopy: Elements of a Sociological Theory of Religion*. Garden City, NY: Doubleday & Company, Inc., 1967.

BERGER, PETER, BRIGITTE BERGER, and HANSFRIED KELLNER. *The Homeless Mind: Modernization and Consciousness*. New York: Vintage Books, 1974.

BERGER, PETER L., and HANSFRIED KELLNER. *Sociology Reinterpreted: An Essay on Method and Vocation*. Garden City, NY: Anchor Books, 1981.

BERGER, PETER L., and THOMAS LUCKMANN. *The Social Construction of Reality: A Treatise in the Sociology of Knowledge*. Garden City, NY: Anchor, 1967.

BERGESEN, ALBERT, ed. *Crises in the World-System*. Beverly Hills, CA: Sage Publications, 1983.

BERK, RICHARD A. *Collective Behavior*. Dubuque, IA: Wm. C. Brown, 1974.

BERKE, RICHARD L. "51 Senators List $1 Million in Aid." *The New York Times* (August 10, 1987):A17.

BERNARD, JESSIE. *The Female World*. New York: Free Press, 1981.

BERNARD, JESSIE. *The Future of Marriage*. New Haven, CT: Yale University Press, 1982; orig. 1973.

BERNARD, LARRY CRAIG. "Multivariate Analysis of New Sex Role Formulations and Personality." *Journal of Personality and Social Psychology*. Vol. 38, No. 2 (February 1980):323–336.

BERRY, BRIAN L., and PHILIP H. REES. "The Factorial Ecology of Calcutta." *American Journal of Sociology*. Vol. 74, No. 5 (March 1969):445–491.

BERSCHEID, ELLEN, and ELAINE HATFIELD. *Interpersonal Attraction*. 2nd ed. Reading, MA: Addison-Wesley, 1983.

BESHAROV, DOUGLAS J., ALISON QUIN, and KARL ZINSMEISTER. "A Portrait in Black and White: Out-of-Wedlock Births." *Public Opinion*. Vol. 10, No. 1 (May/June 1987):43–45.

BEST, RAPHAELA. *We've All Got Scars: What Boys and Girls Learn in Elementary School*. Bloomington, IN: Indiana University Press, 1983.

BINGHAM, AMY. "Division I Dilemma: Making the Classroom a Priority for Athletes." *The Kenyon Journal*. Vol. II, No. 3 (November 1986):2.

BLACK, GORDON S., INC., Rochester, NY. National poll reported in *USA Today*. (a: December 31, 1984:6A; b: December 20, 1984:5D).

Black Issues in Higher Education. "Black Graduate Students Decline." Vol. 4, No. 8 (July 1, 1987):1–2.

BLAU, JUDITH R., and PETER M. BLAU. "The Cost of Inequality: Metropolitan Structure and Violent Crime." *American Sociological Review*. Vol. 47, No. 1 (February 1982):114–129.

BLAU, PETER M. *Exchange and Power in Social Life*. New York: Wiley, 1964.

BLAU, PETER M., and OTIS DUDLEY DUNCAN. *The American Occupational Structure*. New York: John Wiley, 1967.

BLAUNER, ROBERT. *Racial Oppression in America*. New York: Harper & Row, 1972.

BLAUSTEIN, ALBERT P., and ROBERT L. ZANGRANDO. *Civil Rights and the Black American*. New York: Washington Square Press, 1968.

BLOOM, LEONARD. "Familial Adjustments of Japanese-Americans to Relocation: First Phase." In Thomas F. Pettigrew, ed., *The Sociology of Race Relations*. New York: Free Press, 1980:163–167.

BLUM, ALAN, and GARY FISHER. "Women Who Kill." In Delos H. Kelly, ed., *Criminal Behavior: Readings in Criminology*. New York: St. Martin's Press, 1980:291–301.

BLUMBERG, ABRAHAM S. *Criminal Justice*. Chicago: Quadrangle Books, 1970.

BLUMBERG, PAUL. *Inequality in an Age of Decline*. New York: Oxford University Press, 1981.

BLUMER, HERBERT G. "Collective Behavior." In Alfred McClung Lee, ed., *Principles of Sociology*. 3rd ed. New York: Barnes & Noble Books, 1969:65–121.

BLUMER, HERBERT G. "Fashion." In David L. Sills, ed., *International Encyclopedia of the Social Sciences*. Vol. 5. New York: Macmillan and Free Press, 1968:341–345.

BLUMSTEIN, PHILIP, and PEPPER SCHWARTZ. *American Couples*. New York: William Morrow, 1983.

BODENHEIMER, THOMAS S. "Health Care in the United States: Who Pays?" In Vicente Navarro, ed., *Health and Medical Care in the U.S.: A Critical Analysis*. Farmingdale, NY: Baywood Publishing Co., 1977:61–68.

BOGARDUS, EMORY S. "Comparing Racial Distance in Ethiopia, South Africa, and the United States." *Sociology and Social Research*. Vol. 52, No. 2 (January 1968):149–156.

BOLLOUGH, VERN, and MARTHA VOGHT. "Women, Menstruation, and Nineteenth Century Medicine." In Judith Walzer Leavitt, ed., *Women and Health in America*. Madison, WI: The University of Wisconsin Press, 1984:28–37.

BONNER, JANE. Research presented in "The Two Brains." Public Broadcasting System telecast, 1984.

BOOTH, ALAN, and LYNN WHITE. "Thinking About Divorce." *Journal of Marriage and the Family*. Vol. 42, No. 3 (August 1980):605–616.

BORUKHOV, ELI, YONA GINSBERG, and ELIA WERCZBERGER. "The Social Ecology of Tel-Aviv: A Study in Factor Analysis." *Urban Affairs Quarterly*. Vol. 15, No. 2 (December 1979):183–205.

BOSWELL, TERRY E. "A Split Labor Market Analysis of Discrimination Against Chinese Immigrants, 1850–1882." *American Sociological Review*. Vol 51, No. 3 (June 1986):352–371.

BOTT, ELIZABETH. *Family and Social Network*. New York: Free Press, 1971; orig. 1957.

BOTWINICK, JACK. "Intellectual Abilities." In James E. Birren and K. Warner Schaie, eds., *Handbook of the Psychology of Aging*. New York: Van Nostrand Reinhold, 1977:580–605.

BOULDING, ELISE. *The Underside of History*. Boulder, CO: Westview Press, 1976.

BOUVIER, LEON F. "America's Baby Boom Generation: The Fateful Bulge." *Population Bulletin*. Vol. 35, No. 1 (April 1980), Population Reference Bureau.

BOWEN, ELENORE SMITH. *Return to Laughter*. Garden City, NY: Doubleday, 1964.

BOWEN, EZRA. "The Worst of Two Worlds." *Time*. Vol. 126, No. 17 (October 28, 1985):64.

BOWERS, WILLIAM J., and GLENN L. PIERCE. "The Illusion of Deterrence in Isaac Ehrlich's Research on Capital Punishment." *The Yale Law Journal*. Vol. 85 (December 1975):187–208.

BOWKER, LEE H. *Corrections: The Science and the Art*. New York: Macmillan, 1982.

BOWLES, SAMUEL, and HERBERT GINTIS. *Schooling in Capitalist America: Educational Reform and the Contradictions of Economic Life*. New York: Basic Books, 1976.

BOYER, ERNEST L. *College: The Undergraduate Experience in America*. Prepared by The Carnegie Foundation for the Advancement of Teaching. New York: Harper & Row, 1987.

BOYER, ERNEST L. "The Test of Growing Student Diversity." *The New York Times Magazine* (November 11, 1984):63.

BRAITHWAITE, JOHN. " 'The Myth of Social Class and Criminality' Reconsidered." *American Sociological Review*. Vol. 46, No. 1 (February 1981):36–57.

BRAND, DAVID. "The New Whiz Kids." *Time*. Vol. 130, No. 9 (August 31, 1987):42–46, 49, 51.

BREAULT, K. D. "Suicide in America: A Test of Durkheim's Theory of Religious and Family Integration, 1933–1980." *American Journal of Sociology*. Vol. 92, No. 3 (November 1986):628–656.

BREEN, LEONARD Z. "The Aging Individual." In Clark Tibbitts, ed., *Handbook of Social Gerontology*. Chicago: University of Chicago Press, 1960:145–162.

BRENNER, HARVEY. *Estimating the Social Costs of National Economic Policy: Implications for Mental and Physical Health and Criminal Aggression*. Joint Economic Committee, 94th Congress, October 26, 1976.

BRINTON, CRANE. *The Anatomy of Revolution*. New York: Vintage Books, 1965.

BROMLEY, DAVID G., and ANSON D. SHUPE, JR. *"Moonies" in America: Cult, Church, and Crusade*. Beverly Hills, CA: Sage, 1979.

BROMLEY, DAVID G., and ANSON D. SHUPE, JR. *New Christian Politics*. Macon, GA: Mercer University Press, 1984.

BROPHY, BETH. "Middle-Class Squeeze." *U.S. News & World Report* (August 18, 1986):36–41.

BROWN, CLAUDE. "Manchild in Harlem." *The New York Times Magazine*. (September 16, 1984):36–41, 44, 54, 76, 78.

BROWN, E. RICHARD. *Rockefeller Medicine Men: Medicine and Capitalism in America*. Berkeley, CA: University of California Press, 1979.

BROWNMILLER, SUSAN. *Femininity*. New York: Linden Press, Simon and Schuster, 1984.

BROWNSTEIN, RONALD, and NINA EASTON. *Reagan's Ruling Class: Portraits of the President's Top One Hundred Officials*. New York: Pantheon, 1983.

BROYLES, J. ALLEN. "The John Birch Society: A Movement of Social Protest of the Radical Right." In Louis E. Genevie, ed., *Collective Behavior and Social Movements*. Itasca, IL: F. E. Peacock, 1978:338–345.

BRUNN, STANLEY D., and JACK F. WILLIAMS. *Cities of the World: World Regional Urban Development*. New York: Harper & Row, 1983.

BRUNO, MARY. "Abusing the Elderly." *Newsweek* (September 23, 1985):75–76.

BUCHHOLZ, MICHAEL, and JACK E. BYNUM. "Newspaper Presentation of America's Aged: A Content Analysis of Image and Role." *The Gerontologist*. Vol. 22, Number 1 (February 1982):83–88.

BUMPASS, L. "Children and Marital Disruption: A Replication and Update." *Demography*. Vol. 21, No. 1 (February 1984):71–82.

BUNKER, STEPHEN G. "Modes of Extraction, Unequal Exchange, and the Progressive Underdevelopment of an Extreme Periphery: The Brazilian Amazon, 1600–1980." *American Journal of Sociology*. Vol. 89, No. 5 (March 1984):1017–1064.

BURAWOY, MICHAEL, and JÁNOS LUKÁCS. "Mythologies of Work: A Comparison of Firms in State Socialism and Advanced Capitalism." *American Sociological Review*. Vol. 50, No. 6 (December 1985):723–737.

BURCH, ROBERT. Testimony to House of Representatives Hearing in "Review: The World Hunger Problem." October 25, 1983, Serial 98–38.

BURGESS, ERNEST W. "The Growth of the City." In Robert E. Park and Ernest W. Burgess, eds., *The City*. Chicago: University of Chicago Press, 1925:47–62.

BURNHAM, WALTER DEAN. *Democracy in the Making: American Government and Politics*. Englewood Cliffs, NJ: Prentice-Hall, 1983.

BURNS, JAMES A. "Discipline: Why Does It Continue To Be a Problem? Solution Is in Changing School Culture." *National Association of Secondary School Principals Bulletin*. Vol. 69, No. 479 (March 1985):1–47.

BURRIS, VAL. "The Social and Political Consequences of Overeducation." *American Sociological Review*. Vol. 48, No. 4 (August 1983):454–467.

BUSBY, LINDA J. "Sex Role Research on the Mass Media." *Journal of Communications*. Vol. 25 (Autumn 1975):107–131.

BUTLER, ROBERT N. *Why Survive? Being Old in America*. New York: Harper & Row, 1975.

BUTTERWORTH, DOUGLAS, and JOHN K. CHANCE. *Latin American Urbanization*. Cambridge (UK): Cambridge University Press, 1981.

CAHAN, VICKY. "The Feminization of Poverty: More Women Are Getting Poorer." *Business Week*. No. 2878 (January 28, 1985):84–85.

CALLOW, A. B., Jr., ed. *American Urban History*. New York: Oxford University Press, 1969.

CALMORE, JOHN O. "National Housing Policies and Black America: Trends, Issues, and Implications." In *The State of Black America 1986*. New York: National Urban League, 1986:115–149.

CAMERON, WILLIAM BRUCE. *Modern Social Movements: A Sociological Outline*. New York: Random House, 1966.

CANETTI, ELIAS. *Crowds and Power*. New York: The Seabury Press, 1978.

CANTOR, MURIAL G., and SUZANNE PINGREE. *The Soap Opera*. Beverly Hills, CA: Sage Publications, 1983.

CANTRIL, HADLEY, HAZEL GAUDET, and HERTA HERZOG. *Invasion from Mars: A Study in the Psychology of Panic*. Princeton, NJ: Princeton University Press, 1947.

CAPLOW, THEODORE, and HOWARD M. BAHR. "Half a Century of Change in Adolescent Attitudes: Replication of a Middletown Survey by the Lynds." *Public Opinion Quarterly*. Vol. 43 (1979):1–17.

CAPLOW, THEODORE, et al. *Middletown Families*. Minneapolis, MN: University of Minnesota Press, 1982.

CAPUTO, PHILIP. *A Rumor of War*. New York: Holt, Rinehart and Winston, 1977.

CAREY, MAX L. "On Occupational Employment Growth Through 1990." *Monthly Labor Review*. Vol. 104, No. 8 (August 1981):42–55.

CARLTON, ERIC. *Ideology and Social Order*. London: Routledge & Kegan Paul, 1977.

C.E.D. *See* COMMITTEE FOR ECONOMIC DEVELOPMENT.

CENTER ON BUDGET AND POLICY PRIORITIES. *Smaller Slices of the Pie: The Economic Growing Vulnerability of Poor and Moderate Income Americans*. Washington, DC: 1985.

CERNKOVICH, STEPHEN A., and PEGGY C. GIORDANO. "A Comparative Analysis of Male and Female Delinquency." In Delos H. Kelly, ed., *Criminal Behavior: Readings in Criminology*. New York: St. Martin's Press, 1980:112–129.

CHAGNON, NAPOLEON A. *Yąnomamö*. 3rd ed. New York: Holt, Rinehart and Winston, 1983.

CHANDLER, TERTIUS, and GERALD FOX. *3000 Years of Urban History*. New York: Academic Press, 1974.

CHANGE, KWANG-CHIH. *The Archaeology of Ancient China*. New Haven, CT: Yale University Press, 1977.

CHAPPELL, NEENA L., and BETTY HAVENS. "Old and Female: Testing the Double Jeopardy Hypothesis." *The Sociological Quarterly*. Vol. 21, No. 2 (Spring 1980):157–171.

CHARON, JOEL M. *The Meaning of Sociology*. Palo Alto, CA: Mayfield, 1982.

CHERLIN, ANDREW. *Marriage, Divorce, Remarriage*. Cambridge, MA: Harvard University Press, 1981.

CHERLIN, ANDREW, and FRANK F. FURSTENBERG, JR. "The American Family in the Year 2000." *The Futurist*. Vol. 17, No. 3 (June 1983):7–14.

CHILDREN'S DEFENSE FUND. *A Children's Defense Budget: An Analysis of the President's FY 1986 Budget and Children*. Washington, DC: 1985.

CHIROT, DANIEL. *Social Change in the Modern Era*. New York: Harcourt Brace Jovanovich, 1986.

CHOWN, SHEILA M. "Morale, Careers and Personal Potentials." In James E. Birren and K. Warner Schaie, eds., *Handbook of the Psychology of Aging*. New York: Van Nostrand Reinhold, 1977:672–691.

CHURCH, GEORGE J. "The Dilemma of Retaliation." *Time*. Vol. 125, No. 25 (June 24, 1985):27.

CLANCY, PAUL, and GAIL OBERST. "First Comes Love, Then Comes Live-In." *USA Today* (March 28, 1985):1A, 2A.

CLARK, CURTIS B. "Geriatric Abuse: Out of the Closet." In *The Tragedy of Elder Abuse: The Problem and the Response*. Hearings before the Select Committee on Aging, House of Representatives, July 1, 1986, pp. 49–50.

CLARK, JUAN M., JOSE I. LASAGA, and ROSE S. REGUE. *The 1980 Mariel Exodus: An Assessment and Prospect: Special Report*. Washington, DC: Council for Inter-American Security, 1981.

CLARK, MARGARET. "An Anthropological View of Retirement." In Frances M. Carp, ed., *Retirement*. New York: Behavioral Publications, 1972.

CLARK, MATT. "A Slow Death of the Mind." *Newsweek*. (December 3, 1984):56–62.

CLARK, MATT, et al. "Aids." *Newsweek* (August 12, 1985):20–24, 26–27.

CLARK, THOMAS A. *Blacks in Suburbs*. New Brunswick, NJ: Rutgers University Center for Urban Policy Research, 1979.

CLINARD, MARSHALL B. *Cities with Little Crime: The Case of Switzerland*. Cambridge (UK): Cambridge University Press, 1978.

CLINARD, MARSHALL, and DANIEL ABBOTT. *Crime in Developing Countries*. New York: Wiley, 1973.

CLOWARD, RICHARD A., and LLOYD E. OHLIN. *Delinquency and Opportunity: A Theory of Delinquent Gangs*. New York: Free Press, 1966.

COAKLEY, JAY J. *Sport in Society: Issues and Controversies*. 3rd ed. St. Louis, MO: C. V. Mosby, 1986.

COCKERHAM, WILLIAM C. *Medical Sociology*. 2nd ed. Englewood Cliffs, NJ: Prentice-Hall, 1982; 3rd ed. 1986.

Coe, Michael D., and Richard A. Diehl. *In the Land of the Olmec*. Austin, TX: University of Texas Press, 1980.

Cohen, Albert K. *Delinquent Boys: The Culture of the Gang*. New York: Free Press, 1971; orig. 1955.

Cohn, Richard M. "Economic Development and Status Change of the Aged." *American Journal of Sociology*. Vol. 87, No. 2 (March 1982):1150–1161.

Coleman, James, et al. *Equality of Educational Opportunity* ("The Coleman Report"). U.S. Department of Health, Education, and Welfare. Washington, DC: U.S. Government Printing Office, 1966.

Coleman, James S., and Thomas Hoffer. *Public and Private High Schools: The Impact of Communities*. New York: Basic Books, 1987.

Coleman, James, Thomas Hoffer, and Sally Kilgore. *Public and Private Schools: An Analysis of Public Schools and Beyond*. Washington, DC: National Center for Education Statistics, 1981.

Coleman, John R. "Diary of a Homeless Man." *New York Magazine*. (February 21, 1983):26–35.

Coleman, Richard P., and Bernice L. Neugarten. *Social Status in the City*. San Francisco, CA: Jossey-Bass, 1971.

Coleman, Richard P., and Lee Rainwater. *Social Standing in America*. New York: Basic Books, 1978.

Collins, Randall. "A Conflict Theory of Sexual Stratification." *Social Problems*. Vol. 19, No. 1 (Summer 1971):3–21.

Collins, Randall. *The Credential Society: An Historical Sociology of Education and Stratification*. New York: Academic Press, 1979.

Collins, Randall. *Sociological Insight: An Introduction to Nonobvious Sociology*. New York: Oxford University Press, 1982.

Collins, Randall. *Weberian Sociological Theory*. Cambridge (UK): Cambridge University Press, 1986.

Collison, Michele N-K. "More Young Black Men Choosing Not to Go to College." *The Chronicle of Higher Education*. Vol. XXXIV, No. 15 (December 9, 1987):A1, A26.

Colloway, N. O., and Paula L. Dollevoet. "Selected Tabular Material on Aging." In Caleb Finch and Leonard Hayflick, eds., *Handbook of the Biology of Aging*. New York: Van Nostrand Reinhold, 1977:666–708.

Comfort, Alex. "Sexuality in Later Life." In James E. Birren and R. Bruce Sloane, eds., *Handbook of Mental Health and Aging*. Englewood Cliffs, NJ: Prentice-Hall, 1980:885–892.

Committee for Economic Development (C.E.D.). "Reforming Retirement Policies." New York: 1981.

Comte, Auguste. *Auguste Comte and Positivism: The Essential Writings*. Gertrud Lenzer, ed. New York: Harper Torchbooks, 1975.

Conrad, Peter, and Joseph W. Schneider. *Deviance and Medicalization: From Badness to Sickness*. Columbus, OH: Merrill, 1980.

Cooley, Charles Horton. *Human Nature and the Social Order*. New York: Schocken Books, 1964; orig. 1902.

Cooley, Charles Horton. *Social Organization*. New York: Schocken Books, 1962; orig. 1909.

Coser, Lewis A. *Masters of Sociological Thought: Ideas in Historical and Social Context*. 2nd ed. New York: Harcourt Brace Jovanovich, 1977.

Cottrell, John, and the Editors of Time-Life. *The Great Cities: Mexico City*. Amsterdam: 1979.

Counts, G. S. "The Social Status of Occupations: A Problem in Vocational Guidance." *School Review*. Vol. 33 (January 1925):16–27.

Courtney, Alice E., and Thomas W. Whipple. *Sex Stereotyping in Advertising*. Lexington, MA: D. C. Heath, 1983.

Cowgill, Donald, and Lowell Holmes. *Aging and Modernization*. New York: Appleton-Century-Crofts, 1972.

Cox, Harold. *Later Life: The Realities of Aging*. Englewood Cliffs, NJ: Prentice-Hall, 1984.

Cox, Harvey. *Turning East: The Promise and Peril of the New Orientalism*. New York: Simon and Schuster, 1977.

Cox, Harvey. *The Secular City*. Rev. ed. New York: Macmillan, 1971; orig. 1965.

Cuff, E. C., and G. C. F. Payne, eds. *Perspectives in Sociology*. London: George Allen and Unwin, 1979.

Cumming, Elaine, and William E. Henry. *Growing Old: The Process of Disengagement*. New York: Basic Books, 1961.

Currie, Elliott. *Confronting Crime: An American Challenge*. New York: Pantheon, 1985.

Cutright, Phillip. "Occupational Inheritance: A Cross-National Analysis." *American Journal of Sociology*. Vol. 73, No. 4 (January 1968):400–416.

Dahl, Robert A. *Dilemmas of Pluralist Democracy: Autonomy vs. Control*. New Haven, CT: Yale University Press, 1982.

Dahl, Robert A. *Who Governs?* New Haven, CT: Yale University Press, 1961.

Dahlin, Michael. "Perspectives on Family Life of the Elderly in 1900." *The Gerontologist*. Vol. 20, No. 1 (February 1980):99–107.

Dahrendorf, Ralf. *Class and Class Conflict in Industrial Society*. Stanford, CA: Stanford University Press, 1959.

Damon, William. *Social and Personality Development*. New York: W. W. Norton, 1983.

Daniels, Roger. "The Issei Generation." In Amy Tachiki et al., eds., *Roots: An Asian American Reader*. Los Angeles: UCLA Asian American Studies Center, 1971:138–149.

Dannefer, Dale. "Adult Development and Social Theory: A Reappraisal." *American Sociological Review*. Vol. 49, No. 1 (February 1984):100–116.

Davies, James C. "Toward a Theory of Revolution." *American Sociological Review*. Vol. 27, No. 1 (February 1962):5–19.

Davies, Margery. "A Woman's Place Is at the Typewriter: The Feminization of the Clerical Labor Force." In Zillah R. Eisenstein, ed., *Capitalist Patriarchy and the Case for Socialist Feminism*. New York: Monthly Review Press, 1979:248–266.

Davies, Mark, and Denise B. Kandel. "Parental and Peer Influences on Adolescents' Educational Plans: Some Further Evidence." *American Journal of Sociology*. Vol. 87, No. 2 (September 1981):363–387.

Davis, Kingsley. "Extreme Social Isolation of a Child." *American Journal of Sociology*. Vol. 45, No. 4 (January 1940):554–565.

Davis, Kingsley. "Final Note on a Case of Extreme Isolation." *American Journal of Sociology*. Vol. 52, No. 5 (March 1947):432–437.

Davis, Kingsley, and Wilbert Moore. "Some Principles of Stratification." *American Sociological Review*. Vol. 10, No. 2 (April 1945):242–249.

Davis, Sharon A., and Emil J. Haller. "Tracking, Ability, and SES: Further Evidence on the 'Revisionist-Meritocratic Debate.'" *American Journal of Education*. Vol. 89 (May 1981):283–304.

Deckard, Barbara Sinclair. *The Women's Movement: Political, Socioeconomic, and Psychological Issues*. 2nd ed. New York: Harper & Row, 1979.

DeFleur, Melvin. "Diffusing Information." *Social Science and Modern Society*. Vol. 25, No. 2 (January/February 1988):72–81.

Degler, Carl. *At Odds: Women and the Family in America From the Revolution to the Present*. New York: Oxford University Press, 1980.

DELACROIX, JACQUES, and CHARLES C. RAGIN. "Structural Blockage: A Cross-national Study of Economic Dependency, State Efficacy, and Underdevelopment." *American Journal of Sociology*. Vol. 86, No. 6 (May 1981):1311–1347.

DEMOTT, JOHN S. "Shop Here, but Don't Stop Here." *Time*. Vol. 127, No. 10 (March 10, 1986):46.

DEMOTT, JOHN S. "Wreaking Havoc on Spring Break." *Time*. Vol. 127, No. 14 (April 7, 1986):29.

DEVINE, JOEL A. "State and State Expenditure: Determinants of Social Investment and Social Consumption Spending in the Postwar United States." *American Sociological Review*. Vol. 50, No. 2 (April 1985):150–165.

DEWEY, JOHN. *Experience and Education*. New York: Collier Books, 1968; orig. 1938.

DICKENS, CHARLES. *The Adventures of Oliver Twist*. Boston, MA: Estes and Lauriat, 1886; orig. 1837–1839.

DICKENS, CHARLES. *Hard Times*. New York: W. W. Norton, 1966; orig. 1854.

DIPRETE, THOMAS A. "The Professionalization of Administration and Equal Employment Opportunity in the U.S. Federal Government." *American Journal of Sociology*. Vol. 93, No. 1 (July 1987):119–140.

DIPRETE, THOMAS A. "Unemployment over the Life Cycle: Racial Differences and the Effect of Changing Economic Conditions." *American Journal of Sociology*. Vol. 87, No. 2 (September 1981):286–307.

DOBSON, RICHARD B. "Mobility and Stratification in the Soviet Union." *Annual Review of Sociology*. Vol. 3. Palo Alto, CA: Annual Reviews, Inc., 1977:297–329.

DOBYNS, HENRY F. "An Appraisal of Techniques with a New Hemispheric Estimate." *Current Anthropology*. Vol. 7, No. 4 (October 1966):395–446.

DOERNER, WILLIAM R. "In the Dead of the Night." *Time*. Vol. 127, No. 17 (April 28, 1986):28–31.

DOLLARD, JOHN, et al. *Frustration and Aggression*. New Haven, CT: Yale University Press, 1939.

DOMHOFF, G. WILLIAM. "The Growth Machine and the Power Elite: A Theoretical Challenge to Pluralists and Marxists Alike." Paper presented to the American Political Science Association. Washington, DC: 1984.

DOMHOFF, G. WILLIAM. *The Higher Circles: The Governing Class in America*. New York: Vintage, 1971.

DOMHOFF, G. WILLIAM. *The Powers That Be: Processes of Ruling Class Domination in America*. New York: Vintage, 1979.

DOMHOFF, G. WILLIAM. *Who Rules America?* Englewood Cliffs, NJ: Prentice-Hall, 1967.

DOMHOFF, G. WILLIAM. *Who Rules America Now? A View of the 80s*. Englewood Cliffs, NJ: Prentice-Hall, 1983.

DONOVAN, VIRGINIA K., and RONNIE LITTENBERG. "Psychology of Women: Feminist Therapy." In Barbara Huber, ed., *The Women's Annual 1981: The Year in Review*. Boston: G. K. Hall, 1982:211–235.

DOUGLASS, RICHARD L. "Domestic Neglect and Abuse of the Elderly: Implications for Research and Service." *Family Relations*. Vol. 32 (July 1983):395–402.

DOYAL, LESLEY, with IMOGEN PENNELL. *The Political Economy of Health*. London: Pluto Press, 1981.

DOYLE, JAMES A. *The Male Experience*. Dubuque, IA: Wm. C. Brown, 1983.

DUBOS, RENÉ. *Man Adapting*. New Haven, CT: Yale University Press, 1980; orig. 1965.

DUHL, LEONARD J. "The Social Context of Health." In Arthur C. Hastings et al., eds., *Health for the Whole Person: The Complete Guide to Holistic Medicine*. Boulder, CO: Westview Press, 1980: 39–48.

DUNLOP, DONALD P. *Mandatory Retirement Policy: A Human Rights Dilemma?* 2nd ed. A report from the Compensation Research Centre of the Conference Board in Canada, 1983.

DURKHEIM, EMILE. *The Division of Labor in Society*. New York: Free Press, 1964a; orig. 1895.

DURKHEIM, EMILE. *The Elementary Forms of Religious Life*. New York: Free Press, 1965; orig. 1915.

DURKHEIM, EMILE. *The Rules of Sociological Method*. New York: Free Press, 1964b; orig. 1893.

DURKHEIM, EMILE. *Selected Writings*. Anthony Giddens, ed. Cambridge (UK): Cambridge University Press, 1972.

DURKHEIM, EMILE. *Suicide*. New York: Free Press, 1966; orig. 1897.

DZIECH, BILLIE WRIGHT, and LINDA WEINER. *The Lecherous Professor: Sexual Harassment on Campus*. Boston, MA: Beacon Press, 1984.

EASTERLIN, RICHARD A. "Immigration: Economic and Social Characteristics." In *Harvard Encyclopedia of American Ethnic Groups*. Cambridge, MA: Harvard University Press, 1980: 476–486.

ECKHOLM, ERIK. "Malnutrition in Elderly: Widespread Health Threat." *The New York Times* (August 13, 1985):19–20.

ECKHOLM, ERIK. "Pygmy Chimp Readily Learns Language Skill." *The New York Times* (June 24, 1985):A1, B7.

ECKMAN, PAUL. *Telling Lies: Clues to Deceit in the Marketplace, Politics, and Marriage*. New York: W. W. Norton, 1985.

EDMONSTON, BARRY, and THOMAS M. GUTERBOCK. "Is Suburbanization Slowing Down? Recent Trends in Population Deconcentration in U.S. Metropolitan Areas." *Social Forces*. Vol. 62, No. 4 (June 1984):905–925.

EDWARDS, DAVID V. *The American Political Experience*. 3rd ed. Englewood Cliffs, NJ: Prentice-Hall, 1985.

EDWARDS, HARRY. *Sociology of Sport*. Homewood, IL: Dorsey Press, 1973.

EDWARDS, RICHARD. *Contested Terrain: The Transformation of the Workplace in the Twentieth Century*. New York: Basic Books, 1979.

EHRENREICH, BARBARA. *The Hearts of Men: American Dreams and the Flight from Commitment*. Garden City, NY: Anchor, 1983.

EHRENREICH, JOHN. "Introduction." In John Ehrenreich, ed., *The Cultural Crisis of Modern Medicine*. New York: Monthly Review Press, 1978:1–35.

EHRLICH, PAUL R. *The Population Bomb*. New York: Ballantine Books, 1978.

EISEN, ARNOLD M. *The Chosen People in America: A Study of Jewish Religious Ideology*. Bloomington, IN: Indiana University Press, 1983.

EISENSTEIN, ZILLAH R., ed. *Capitalist Patriarchy and the Case for Socialist Feminism*. New York: Monthly Review Press, 1979.

EITZEN, D. STANLEY. *Social Problems*. Boston: Allyn and Bacon, 1980.

EKMAN, PAUL, WALLACE V. FRIESEN, and JOHN BEAR. "The International Language of Gestures." *Psychology Today*. (May 1984):64–69.

ELIAS, MARILYN. "What Keeps Couples Together?" *USA Today* (October 19, 1984):1D, 2D.

ELKIN, FREDERICK, and GERALD HANDEL. *The Child and Society: The Process of Socialization*. 4th ed. New York: Random House, 1984.

ELKIND, DAVID. *The Hurried Child: Growing Up Too Fast Too Soon*. Reading, MA: Addison-Wesley, 1981.

ELLERBROCK, TEDD, et al. "Abortion Surveillance, 1982–1983."

CDC Surveillance Summaries, February 1987. Vol. 37, No. 1. Atlanta: Center for Disease Control.

ELLIOT, DELBERT S., and SUZANNE S. AGETON. "Reconciling Race and Class Differences in Self-Reported and Official Estimates of Delinquency." *American Sociological Review.* Vol. 45, No. 1 (February 1980):95–110.

EMBER, CAROL, and MELVIN M. EMBER. *Anthropology.* 4th ed. Englewood Cliffs, NJ: Prentice-Hall, 1985.

EMBER, MELVIN, and CAROL R. EMBER. "The Conditions Favoring Matrilocal versus Patrilocal Residence." *American Anthropologist,* Vol. 73, No. 3 (June 1971):571–594.

EMBREE, AINSLIE T. *The Hindu Tradition.* New York: Vintage Books, 1972.

ENGELS, FRIEDRICH. *The Origin of the Family.* Chicago: Charles H. Kerr and Company, 1902; orig. 1884.

ERIKSON, ERIK H. *Childhood and Society.* New York: W. W. Norton, 1963; orig. 1950.

ERICKSON, ERIK H. *Identity and the Life Cycle.* New York: W. W. Norton, 1980.

ERIKSON, KAI T. *Everything in Its Path: Destruction of Community in the Buffalo Creek Flood.* New York: Simon and Schuster, 1976.

ERIKSON, KAI T. *Wayward Puritans: A Study in the Sociology of Deviance.* New York: John Wiley, 1966.

ERIKSON, ROBERT S., NORMAN R. LUTTBERG, and KENT L. TEDIN. *American Public Opinion: Its Origins, Content, and Impact.* 2nd ed. New York: Wiley, 1980.

ESMAN, MILTON J. "The Politics of Bilingualism in Canada." *Political Science Quarterly.* Vol. 97, No. 2 (Summer 1982):233–253.

ETZIONI, AMITAI. *A Comparative Analysis of Complex Organization: On Power, Involvement, and Their Correlates.* Revised and enlarged ed. New York: Free Press, 1975.

ETZIONI-HALEVY, EVA. *Bureaucracy and Democracy: A Political Dilemma.* Rev. ed. Boston: Routledge & Kegan Paul, 1985.

EVANGELAUF, JEAN. "Student Financial Aid Reaches $20.5 Billion, but Fails to Keep Pace with Rising College Costs, Study Finds." *The Chronicle of Higher Education.* Vol. XXXIV, No. 14 (December 2, 1987):A33, A36.

EVE, SUSAN BROWN. "Age Strata Differences in Utilization of Health Care Services among Adults in the United States." *Sociological Focus.* Vol. 17, No. 2 (April 1984):105–120.

FALK, GERHARD. Personal communication, 1987.

FALLOWS, JAMES. "Immigration: How It's Affecting Us." *The Atlantic Monthly.* Vol. 252 (November 1983):45–52, 55–62, 66–68, 85–90, 94, 96, 99–106.

FANTINI, MARIO D. *Regaining Excellence in Education.* Columbus, OH: Merrill, 1986.

FARLEY, REYNOLDS. "The Long Road: Blacks and Whites in America." *American Demographics.* Vol. 2, No. 2 (February 1980):11–17.

FARRELL, MICHAEL P., and STANLEY D. ROSENBERG. *Men at Midlife.* Boston, MA: Auburn House, 1981.

FEAGIN, JOE. *The Urban Real Estate Game.* Englewood Cliffs, NJ: Prentice-Hall, 1983.

FEATHERMAN, DAVID L., and ROBERT M. HAUSER. *Opportunity and Change.* New York: Academic Press, 1978.

FEDERAL ELECTION COMMISSION. *Federal Election Commission Record.* Vol. 13, No. 8 (August 1987).

FERGUSON, TOM. "Medical Self-Care: Self Responsibility for Health." In Arthur C. Hastings et al., eds., *Health for the Whole Person: The Complete Guide to Holistic Medicine.* Boulder, CO: Westview Press, 1980:87–109.

FERGUSSON, D. M., L. J. HORWOOD, and F. T. SHANNON. "A Proportional Hazards Model of Family Breakdown." *Journal of Marriage and the Family.* Vol. 46, No. 3 (August 1984):539–549.

"Final Report of the Commission on the Higher Education of Minorities." Los Angeles, CA: Higher Education Research Institute, 1982.

FINKELSTEIN, NEAL W., and RON HASKINS. "Kindergarten Children Prefer Same-Color Peers." *Child Development.* Vol. 54, No. 2 (April 1983):502–508.

FIORENTINE, ROBERT. "Men, Women, and the Premed Persistence Gap: A Normative Alternatives Approach." *American Journal of Sociology.* Vol. 92, No. 5 (March 1987):1118–1139.

FISCHER, CLAUDE S. *The Urban Experience.* 2nd ed. New York: Harcourt Brace Jovanovich, 1984.

FISCHER, CLAUDE S., et al. *Networks and Places: Social Relations in the Urban Setting.* New York: Free Press, 1977.

FISHER, ELIZABETH. *Woman's Creation: Sexual Evolution and the Shaping of Society.* Garden City, NY: Anchor/Doubleday, 1979.

FISHMAN, PAMELA M. "Interactional Shitwork." *Heresies: A Feminist Publication on Art and Politics.* Vol. 2 (May 1977):99–101.

FISHMAN, PAMELA M. "The Work Women Do." *Social Problems.* Vol. 25, No. 4 (April 1978):397–406.

FISKE, EDWARD B. "One Language or Two: The Controversy over Bilingual Education in America's Schools." *The New York Times.* (November 10, 1985), Section 12:1, 45.

FISKE, EDWARD B. "Steady Gains Achieved by Blacks on College Admission Test Scores." *The New York Times* (September 23, 1987):A1, D30.

FITZPATRICK, JOSEPH P. *Puerto Rican Americans: The Meaning of Migration to the Mainland.* Englewood Cliffs, NJ: Prentice-Hall, 1971.

FITZPATRICK, JOSEPH P. "Puerto Ricans." In *Harvard Encyclopedia of American Ethnic Groups.* Cambridge, MA: Harvard University Press, 1980: 858–867.

Forbes. "The 400 Richest People in America." Special Issue. Vol. 140, No. 9 (October 26, 1987).

FORD, CLELLAN S., and FRANK A. BEACH. *Patterns of Sexual Behavior.* New York: Harper & Row, 1951.

FORM, WILLIAM. "Self-Employed Manual Workers: Petty Bourgeois or Working Class?" *Social Forces.* Vol. 60, No. 4 (June 1982):1050–1069.

FORNOS, WERNER. "Growth of Cities Is Major Crisis." *Popline.* Vol. 8, No. 3 (March 1986):4.

FORREST, HUGH. "They Are Completely Inactive . . ." *The Gambier Journal.* Vol. 3, No. 4 (February 1984):10–11.

FRANK, ANDRE GUNDER. *Crisis: In the World Economy.* New York: Holmes & Meier, 1980.

FRANK, ANDRE GUNDER. *Reflections on the World Economic Crisis.* New York: Monthly Review Press, 1981.

FRANKLIN, JOHN HOPE. *From Slavery to Freedom: A History of Negro Americans.* 3rd ed. New York: Vintage Books, 1967.

FRAZIER, E. FRANKLIN. *Black Bourgeoisie: The Rise of a New Middle Class.* New York: Free Press, 1965.

FREDRICKSON, GEORGE M. *White Supremacy: A Comparative Study in American and South African History.* New York: Oxford University Press, 1981.

FRENCH, MARILYN. *Beyond Power: On Women, Men, and Morals.* New York: Summit Books, 1985.

FRIEDMAN, EUGENE A., and ROBERT J. HAVIGHURST. *The Meaning of Work and Retirement.* Chicago: University of Chicago Press, 1954.

FRIEDRICH, CARL J., and ZBIGNIEW BRZEZINSKI. *Totalitarian Dicta-*

torship and Autocracy. 2nd ed. Cambridge, MA: Harvard University Press, 1965.

FRIEDRICH, OTTO. "Braving Scorn and Threats." Time. Vol. 125, No. 30 (July 23, 1984):36–37.

FRIEDRICH, OTTO. "F.D.R.'s Disputed Legacy." Time. Vol. 119, No. 5 (February 1, 1982):20–26, 30, 33–38, 43.

FRIEDRICH, OTTO. "A Proud Capital's Distress." Time. Vol. 124, No. 6 (August 6, 1984):26–30, 33–35.

FRIEDRICH, OTTO. "United No More." Time. Vol. 129, No. 18 (May 4, 1987):28–37.

FUCHS, VICTOR R. "Sex Differences in Economic Well-Being." Science. Vol. 232 (April 25, 1986):459–464.

FUCHS, VICTOR R. Who Shall Live. New York: Basic Books, 1974.

FUGITA, STEPHEN S., and DAVID J. O'BRIEN. "Structural Assimilation, Ethnic Group Membership, and Political Participation among Japanese Americans: A Research Note." Social Forces. Vol. 63, No. 4 (June 1985):986–995.

FUJIMOTO, ISAO. "The Failure of Democracy in a Time of Crisis." In Amy Tachiki et al., eds., Roots: An Asian American Reader. Los Angeles: UCLA Asian American Studies Center, 1971:207–214.

FURSTENBERG, FRANK F., JR. "The New Extended Family: The Experience of Parents and Children after Remarriage." Paper presented to the Changing Family Conference XIII: The Blended Family. University of Iowa, 1984.

FUSFELD, DANIEL R. Economics: Principles of Political Economy. Glenview, IL: Scott, Foresman, 1982.

GAGLIANI, GIORGIO. "How Many Working Classes?" American Journal of Sociology. Vol. 87, No. 2 (September 1981):259–285.

GALLUP, GEORGE H. "The 14th Annual Gallup Poll of the Public's Attitudes toward the Public Schools." Phi Delta Kappan. Vol. 64 (September 1982):37–50.

GALLUP, GEORGE H. "The 15th Annual Gallup Poll of the Public's Attitudes toward the Public Schools." Phi Delta Kappan. Vol. 65 (September 1983):33–47.

GALLUP, GEORGE H. "The 16th Annual Gallup Poll of the Public's Attitudes toward the Public Schools." Phi Delta Kappan. Vol. 66 (September 1984):23–38.

GALLUP, GEORGE, JR. Religion in America. Princeton, NJ: Princeton Religion Research Center, 1982.

GALLUP, GEORGE, JR. Religion in America: The Gallup Report. Report No. 222. Princeton, NJ: Princeton Religion Research Center, March 1984.

GALLUP OPINION INDEX. "Religion in America, 1977–78," Report 145 (January 1978); and "Religion in America," Report 184 (January 1981).

GANS, HERBERT J. Deciding What's News: A Study of CBS Evening News, NBC Nightly News, Newsweek and Time. New York: Vintage, 1980.

GANS, HERBERT J. People and Plans: Essays on Urban Problems and Solutions. New York: Basic Books, 1968.

GANS, HERBERT J. The Urban Villagers: Group and Class in the Life of Italian-Americans. New York: Free Press, 1982; orig. 1962.

GARDNER, R. ALLEN, and BEATRICE T. GARDNER. "Teaching Sign Language to a Chimpanzee." Science. Vol. 165, 1969:664–672.

GARFINKEL, HAROLD. "Conditions of Successful Degradation Ceremonies." American Journal of Sociology. Vol. 61, No. 2 (March 1956):420–424.

GARFINKEL, HAROLD. Studies in Ethnomethodology. Cambridge (UK): Polity Press, 1967.

GARTON ASH, TIMOTHY. The Polish Revolution: Solidarity. New York: Charles Scribner's Sons, 1983.

GEERTZ, CLIFFORD. "Common Sense as a Cultural System." The Antioch Review. Vol. 33, No. 1 (Spring 1975):5–26.

GEIST, WILLIAM. Toward a Safe and Sane Halloween and Other Tales of Suburbia. New York: Times Books, 1985.

GELMAN, DAVID. "Who's Taking Care of Our Parents?" Newsweek (May 6, 1985):61–64, 67–68.

GEORGE, SUSAN. How the Other Half Dies: The Real Reasons for World Hunger. Totowa, NJ: Rowman & Allanheld, 1977.

GERSTEL, NAOMI. "Divorce and Stigma." Social Problems. Vol. 43, No. 2 (April 1987):172–186.

GERTH, H. H., and C. WRIGHT MILLS, eds. From Max Weber: Essays in Sociology. New York: Oxford University Press, 1946.

GESCHWENDER, JAMES A. Racial Stratification in America. Dubuque, IA: Wm. C. Brown, 1978.

GEST, TED. "Are White-Collar Crooks Getting Off Too Easy?" U.S. News & World Report. Vol. 99, No. 1 (July 1, 1985):43.

GIBBONS, DON C. Delinquent Behavior. 3rd ed. Englewood Cliffs, NJ: Prentice-Hall, 1981.

GIBBONS, DON C., and MARVIN D. KROHN. Delinquent Behavior. 4th ed. Englewood Cliffs, NJ: Prentice-Hall, 1986.

GIDDENS, ANTHONY. Sociology: A Brief but Critical Introduction. New York: Harcourt Brace Jovanovich, 1982.

GIELE, JANET ZOLLINGER. "Women's Work and Family Roles." In Janet Zollinger Giele, ed., Women in the Middle Years: Current Knowledge and Directions for Research and Policy. New York: John Wiley and Sons, 1982:115–150.

GILBERT, ALAN, and JOSEF GUGLER. Cities, Poverty, and Development. New York: Oxford University Press, 1983.

GILBERT, DENNIS, and JOSEPH A. KAHL. The American Class Structure: A New Synthesis. 3rd ed. Homewood, IL: The Dorsey Press, 1987.

GILLETT, CHARLIE. The Sound of the City: The Rise of Rock and Roll. New York: Pantheon, 1983.

GILLIGAN, CAROL. In a Different Voice: Psychological Theory and Women's Development. Cambridge, MA: Harvard University Press, 1982.

GILPIN, ROBERT. U.S. Power and the Multinational Corporation: The Political Economy of Foreign Direct Investment. New York: Basic Books, 1975.

GINSBURG, PAUL B. "Market-Oriented Options in Medicare and Medicaid." In Jack B. Meyer, ed., Market Reforms in Health Care: Current Issues, New Directions, Strategic Decisions. Washington, DC: American Enterprise Institute for Public Policy Research, 1983:103–118.

GLAAB, CHARLES N. The American City: A Documentary History. Homewood, IL: Dorsey Press, 1963.

GLASER, DANIEL, and MAX S. ZEIGLER. "Use of the Death Penalty v. Outrage at Murder." Crime and Delinquency. Vol. 20, No. 4 (October 1974):333–338.

GLASS, DAVID V., ed. Social Mobility in Britain. London: Routledge & Kegan Paul, 1954.

GLAZER, NATHAN, and DANIEL P. MOYNIHAN. Beyond the Melting Pot. 2nd ed. Cambridge, MA: M.I.T. Press, 1970.

GLENN, CHARLES L., and FRANMARIE KENNEDY-KEEL. "Commentary." Education Week. Vol. V, No. 21 (February 5, 1986):21.

GLENN, NORVAL D., and BETH ANN SHELTON. "Regional Differences in Divorce in the United States." Journal of Marriage and the Family. Vol. 47, No. 3 (August 1985):641–652.

GLOCK, CHARLES Y. "On the Study of Religious Commitment." Religious Education. Vol. 62, No. 4 (1962):98–110.

GLOCK, CHARLES Y. "The Religious Revival in America." In Jane

Zahn, ed., *Religion and the Face of America*. Berkeley, CA: University of California Press, 1959:25–42.

GLOCK, CHARLES Y., and RODNEY STARK. *Religion and Society in Tension*. Chicago: Rand McNally, 1965.

GLUCK, PETER R., and RICHARD J. MEISTER. *Cities in Transition*. New York: New Viewpoints, 1979.

GLUECK, SHELDON, and ELEANOR GLUECK. *Unraveling Juvenile Delinquency*. New York: Commonwealth Fund, 1950.

GOFFMAN, ERVING. *Asylums: Essays on the Social Situation of Mental Patients and Other Inmates*. Garden City, NY: Anchor, 1961.

GOFFMAN, ERVING. *Encounters: Two Studies in the Sociology of Interaction*. Indianapolis, IN: Bobbs-Merrill, 1961.

GOFFMAN, ERVING. *Gender Advertisements*. New York: Harper Colophon. 1979.

GOFFMAN, ERVING. *Interactional Ritual: Essays on Face to Face Behavior*. Garden City, NY: Anchor, 1967.

GOFFMAN, ERVING. *The Presentation of Self in Everyday Life*. Garden City, NY: Anchor, 1959.

GOFFMAN, ERVING. *Stigma: Notes on the Management of Spoiled Identity*. Englewood Cliffs, NJ: Prentice-Hall, 1963.

GOLDBERG, STEVEN. *The Inevitability of Patriarchy*. New York: William Morrow and Co., 1974.

GOLDBERG, STEVEN. Personal communication, 1987.

GOLDEN, FREDERIC. "Here Come the Microkids." *Time*. Vol. 119, No. 18 (May 3, 1982):50–56.

GOLDSBY, RICHARD A. *Race and Races*. 2nd ed. New York: Macmillan, 1977.

GOLDSEN, ROSE K. *The Show and Tell Machine: How Television Works and Works You Over*. New York: Delta, 1978.

GOLDSMITH, H. H. "Genetic Influences on Personality from Infancy." *Child Development*. Vol. 54, No. 2 (April 1983):331–355.

GOODE, WILLIAM J. "Encroachment, Charlatanism, and the Emerging Profession: Psychology, Sociology and Medicine." *American Sociological Review*. Vol. 25, No. 6 (December 1960):902–914.

GOODE, WILLIAM J. "The Theoretical Importance of Love." *American Sociological Review*. Vol. 24, No. 1 (February 1959):38–47.

GOODE, WILLIAM J. "Why Men Resist." In Arlene S. Skolnick and Jerome H. Skolnick, *Family in Transition*. 4th ed. Boston, MA: Little, Brown, 1983:201–218.

GORDON, JAMES S. "The Paradigm of Holistic Medicine." In Arthur C. Hastings et al., eds., *Health for the Whole Person: The Complete Guide to Holistic Medicine*. Boulder, CO: Westview Press, 1980:3–27.

GORDON, MILTON M. *Assimilation in American Life*. New York: Oxford University Press, 1964.

GORING, CHARLES BUCKMAN. *The English Convict: A Statistical Study*. Montclair, NJ: Patterson Smith, 1972; orig. 1913.

GORTMAKER, STEVEN L. "Poverty and Infant Mortality in the United States." *American Journal of Sociology*. Vol. 44, No. 2 (April 1979):280–297.

GOTTMANN, JEAN. *Megalopolis*. New York: Twentieth Century Fund, 1961.

GOULDNER, ALVIN. *The Coming Crisis of Western Sociology*. New York: Avon Books, 1970b.

GOULDNER, ALVIN. *Enter Plato*. New York: Free Press, 1965.

GOULDNER, ALVIN. "The Sociologist as Partisan: Sociology and the Welfare State." In Larry T. Reynolds and Janice M. Reynolds, eds., *The Sociology of Sociology*. New York: McKay, 1970a:218–255.

GRANOVETTER, MARK. "The Strength of Weak Ties." *American Journal of Sociology*. Vol. 78, No. 6 (May 1973):1360–1380.

GRANT, DONALD L. *The Anti-Lynching Movement*. San Francisco, CA: R and E Research Associates, 1975.

GRANT, KAREN R. "The Inverse Care Law in the Context of Universal Free Health Insurance in Canada: Toward Meeting Health Needs Through Public Policy." *Sociological Focus*. Vol. 17, No. 2 (April 1984):137–155.

GRANT, NIGEL. *Soviet Education*. New York: Pelican Books, 1979.

GRAY, ROBERT. *A History of London*. London: Hutchinson, 1978.

GREELEY, ANDREW M. *Ethnicity in the United States: A Preliminary Reconnaissance*. New York: John Wiley, 1974.

GREELEY, ANDREW M. *Why Can't They Be Like Us? America's White Ethnic Groups*. New York: E. P. Dutton, 1971.

GREENWALD, JOHN. "Deadly Meltdown." *Time*. Vol. 127, No. 19 (May 12, 1986):38–44, 49–50, 52.

GREENWALD, JOHN. "The New Grapes of Wrath." *Time*. Vol. 125, No. 4 (January 28, 1985):66–67.

GREGORY, PAUL R., and ROBERT C. STUART. *Comparative Economic Systems*. 2nd ed. Boston, MA: Houghton Mifflin, 1985.

GRIFFIN, LARRY J., MICHAEL E. WALLACE, and BETH A. RUBIN. "Capitalist Resistance to the Organization of Labor Before the New Deal: Why? How? Success?" *American Sociological Review*. Vol. 51, No. 2 (April 1986):147–167.

GRISWOLD, WENDY. "The Fabrication of Meaning: Literary Interpretation in the United States, Great Britain, and the West Indies." *American Journal of Sociology*. Vol. 92, No. 5 (March 1987):1077–1117.

GRUENBERG, BARRY. "The Happy Worker: An Analysis of Educational and Occupational Differences in Determinants of Job Satisfaction." *American Journal of Sociology*. Vol. 86, No. 2 (September 1980):247–271.

GUPTE, PRANAY. *The Crowded Earth: People and the Politics of Population*. New York: W. W. Norton, 1984.

GUSFIELD, JOSEPH R. "Tradition and Modernity: Misplaced Polarities in the Study of Social Change." *American Journal of Sociology*. Vol. 72, No. 4 (January 1972):351–362.

GUTMAN, HERBERT G. *The Black Family in Slavery and Freedom, 1750–1925*. New York: Pantheon Books, 1976.

GWARTNEY-GIBBS, PATRICIA A. "The Institutionalization of Premarital Cohabitation: Estimates from Marriage License Applications, 1970 and 1980." *Journal of Marriage and the Family*. Vol. 48, No. 2 (May 1986):423–434.

GWARTNEY-GIBBS, PATRICIA A., JEAN STOCKARD, AND SUSANNE BOHMER. "Learning Courtship Aggression: The Influence of Parents, Peers, and Personal Experiences." *Family Relations*. Vol. 36, No. 3 (July 1987):276–282.

HAAS, LINDA. "Domestic Role Sharing in Sweden." *Journal of Marriage and the Family*. Vol. 43, No. 4 (November 1981):957–967.

HABERMAS, JÜRGEN. *Toward a Rational Society: Student Protest, Science, and Politics*. Jeremy J. Shapiro, trans. Boston, MA: Beacon Press, 1970.

HACKER, HELEN MAYER. "Women as a Minority Group." *Social Forces*. Vol. 30 (October 1951):60–69.

HACKER, HELEN MAYER. "Women as a Minority Group: 20 Years Later." In Florence Denmark, ed., *Who Discriminates Against Women*. Beverly Hills, CA: Sage, 1974:124–134.

HADDEN, JEFFREY K., and CHARLES E. SWAIN. *Prime Time Preachers: The Rising Power of Televangelism*. Reading, MA: Addison-Wesley, 1981.

HAGAN, JOHN, A. R. GILLIS, and JOHN SIMPSON. "The Class Structure of Gender and Delinquency: Toward a Power-Control Theory of Common Delinquent Behavior." *American Journal of Sociology*. Vol. 90, No. 6 (May 1985):1151–1178.

HAGAN, JOHN, and PATRICIA PARKER. "White-Collar Crime and Punishment: The Class Structure and Legal Sanctioning of Securities Violations." *American Sociological Review*. Vol. 50, No. 3 (June 1985):302–316.

HAGAN, JOHN, JOHN SIMPSON, and A. R. GILLIS. "Class in the Household: A Power-Control Theory of Gender and Delinquency." *American Journal of Sociology*. Vol. 92, No. 4 (January 1987):788–816.

HALLOWELL, CHRISTOPHER. "New Focus on the Old." *The New York Times Magazine* (December 15, 1985):42, 44, 48, 50, 109–111.

HAMBLIN, DORA JANE. *The First Cities*. New York: Time-Life, 1973.

HAMMOND, PHILIP E. "Introduction." In Philip E. Hammond, ed., *The Sacred in a Secular Age: Toward Revision in the Scientific Study of Religion*. Berkeley, CA: University of California Press, 1985:1–6.

HAMRICK, MICHAEL H., DAVID J. ANSPAUGH, and GENE EZELL. *Health*. Columbus, OH: Merrill, 1986.

HANDLIN, OSCAR. *Boston's Immigrants 1790–1865: A Study in Acculturation*. Cambridge, MA: Harvard University Press, 1941.

HANEY, CRAIG, CURTIS BANKS, and PHILIP ZIMBARDO. "Interpersonal Dynamics in a Simulated Prison." *International Journal of Criminology and Penology*. Vol. 1 (1973):69–97.

HANNAN, MICHAEL T., and GLENN R. CARROLL. "Dynamics of Formal Political Structure: An Event-History Analysis." *American Sociological Review*. Vol. 46, No. 1 (February 1981):19–35.

HARDOY, JORGE E. "Two Thousand Years of Latin American Urbanization." In Jorge E. Hardoy, ed., *Urbanization in Latin America: Approaches and Issues*. Garden City, NY: Anchor Books, 1975.

HAREVEN, TAMARA K. "The Life Course and Aging in Historical Perspective." In Tamara K. Hareven and Kathleen J. Adams, eds., *Aging and Life Course Transitions: An Interdisciplinary Perspective*. New York: Guilford Press, 1982:1–26.

HARLAN, WILLIAM H. "Social Status of the Aged in Three Indian Villages." In Bernice L. Neugarten, ed., *Middle Age and Aging: A Reader in Social Psychology*. Chicago: University of Chicago Press, 1968:469–475.

HARLOW, HARRY F., and MARGARET KUENNE HARLOW. "Social Deprivation in Monkeys." *Scientific American*. Vol. 207 (November 1962):137–146.

HARPER, CHARLES L. "Cults and Communities: The Community Interfaces of Three Marginal Religious Movements." *Journal for the Scientific Study of Religion*. Vol. 21, No. 1 (March 1982):26–38.

HARRINGTON, MICHAEL. *The New American Poverty*. New York: Penguin Books, 1984.

HARRIS, CHAUNCEY D., and EDWARD L. ULLMAN. "The Nature of Cities." *The Annals*. Vol. 242 (November 1945):7–17.

HARRIS, LOUIS, and ASSOCIATES. *The Myth and Reality of Aging in America*. Washington, DC: National Council on Aging, 1976.

HARRIS, MARVIN. *Cows, Pigs, Wars and Witches: The Riddles of Culture*. New York: Vintage Books, 1975.

HARRIS, MARVIN. *Cultural Anthropology*. 2nd ed. New York: Harper & Row, 1987.

HARRIS, MARVIN. "Why Men Dominate Women." *New York Times Magazine* (November 13, 1977):46, 115–123.

HARRISON, PAUL. *Inside the Third World: The Anatomy of Poverty*. 2nd ed. New York: Penguin Books, 1984.

HAVIGHURST, ROBERT J., BERNICE L. NEUGARTEN, and SHELDON S. TOBIN. "Disengagement and Patterns of Aging." In Bernice L. Neugarten, ed., *Middle Age and Aging: A Reader in Social Psychology*. Chicago: University of Chicago Press, 1968:161–172.

HAVILAND, WILLIAM A. *Anthropology*. 4th ed. New York: Holt, Rinehart and Winston, 1985.

HAYNEMAN, STEPHEN P., and WILLIAM A. LOXLEY. "The Effect of Primary-School Quality on Academic Achievement Across Twenty-nine High- and Low-Income Countries." *American Journal of Sociology*. Vol. 88, No. 6 (May 1983):1162–1194.

HEALTH INSURANCE ASSOCIATION OF AMERICA. *1986–1987 Source Book of Health Insurance Data*. Washington, DC: 1987.

HEILBRONER, ROBERT L. *The Making of Economic Society*. 7th ed. Englewood Cliffs, NJ: Prentice-Hall, 1985.

HERITAGE, JOHN. *Garfinkel and Ethnomethodology*. Cambridge (UK): Polity Press, 1984.

HERMAN, EDWARD S. *Corporate Control, Corporate Power: A Twentieth Century Fund Study*. New York: Cambridge University Press, 1981.

HERTY, ROBERT. "The Collective Representation of Death." In *Death and the Right Hand*. Aberdeen: Cohen and West, 1960:84–86.

HEWLETT, SYLVIA ANN. *A Lesser Life: The Myth of Women's Liberation in America*. New York: William Morrow, 1986.

HILSMAN, ROGER. *The Politics of Governing America*. Englewood Cliffs, NJ: Prentice-Hall, 1985.

HIRSCHI, TRAVIS. *Causes of Delinquency*. Berkeley, CA: University of California Press, 1969.

HIRSCHI, TRAVIS, and MICHAEL GOTTFREDSON. "Age and the Explanation of Crime." *American Journal of Sociology*. Vol. 89, No. 3 (November 1983):552–584.

HIRSCHMAN, CHARLES. "America's Melting Pot Reconsidered." *Annual Review of Sociology*. Vol. 9. Palo Alto, CA: Annual Reviews, Inc., 1983:397–423.

HIRSCHMAN, CHARLES, and MORRISON G. WONG. "Socioeconomic Gains of Asian Americans, Blacks, and Hispanics: 1960–1976." *American Journal of Sociology*. Vol. 90, No. 3 (November 1984):584–607.

HODGE, ROBERT W., DONALD J. TREIMAN, and PETER H. ROSSI. "A Comparative Study of Occupational Prestige." In Reinhard Bendix and Seymour Martin Lipset, eds., *Class, Status, and Power: Social Stratification in Comparative Perspective*. 2nd ed. New York: Free Press, 1966:309–321.

HOFFMAN, ABBIE. *Revolution for the Hell of It*. New York: The Dial Press, 1968.

HOGAN, DENNIS P., and EVELYN M. KITAGAWA. "The Impact of Social Status and Neighborhood on the Fertility of Black Adolescents." *American Journal of Sociology*. Vol. 90, No. 4 (January 1985):825–855.

HOLM, JEAN. *The Study of Religions*. New York: The Seabury Press, 1977.

HOLT, THOMAS C. "Afro-Americans." In *Harvard Encyclopedia of American Ethnic Groups*. Cambridge, MA: Harvard University Press, 1980:5–23.

HONEYWELL, ROY J. *The Educational Work of Thomas Jefferson*. Cambridge, MA: Harvard University Press, 1931.

HOOK, ERNEST B. "Behavioral Implications of the XYY Genotype." *Science*, Vol. 179 (January 12, 1973):139–150.

HOSTETLER, JOHN A. *Amish Society*. 3rd ed. Baltimore: Johns Hopkins University Press, 1980.

HOUT, MICHAEL, and ANDREW M. GREELEY. "The Center Doesn't Hold: Church Attendance in the United States, 1940–1984." *American Sociological Review*. Vol. 52, No. 3 (June 1987):325–345.

HOYT, HOMER. *The Structure and Growth of Residential Neighborhoods in American Cities*. Washington, DC: Federal Housing Administration, 1939.

HOYT, MARY FINCH. "The New Prime Time." *USA Weekend* (December 13–15, 1985):4.

HSU, FRANCIS L. K. *The Challenge of the American Dream: The Chinese in the United States*. Belmont, CA: Wadsworth, 1971.

HUBER, JOAN, and GLENNA SPITZE. "Considering Divorce: An Expansion of Becker's Theory of Marital Instability." *American Journal of Sociology.* Vol. 86, No. 1 (July 1980):75–89.

HUET-COX, ROCIO. "Medical Education: New Wine in Old Wine Skins." In Victor W. Sidel and Ruth Sidel, eds., *Reforming Medicine: Lessons of the Last Quarter Century.* New York: Pantheon Books, 1984:129–149.

HULL, JON D. "The Rise and Fall of 'Holy Joe.'" *Time.* Vol. 130, No. 5 (August 3, 1987):54–55.

HULS, GLENNA. Personal communication, 1987.

HUMPHRIES, HARRY LEROY. *The Structure and Politics of Intermediary Class Positions: An Empirical Examination of Recent Theories of Class.* Unpublished Ph.D. dissertation. Eugene, OR: University of Oregon, 1984.

HUNT, MORTON. *Sexual Behavior in the 1970s.* Chicago: Playboy Press, 1974.

HUNTER, FLOYD. *Community Power Structure.* Garden City, NY: Doubleday, 1963; orig. 1953.

HUNTER, JAMES DAVISON. *American Evangelicalism: Conservative Religion and the Quandary of Modernity.* New Brunswick, NJ: Rutgers University Press, 1983.

HUNTER, JAMES DAVISON. "Conservative Protestantism." In Phillip E. Hammond, ed., *The Sacred in a Secular Age.* Berkeley, CA: University of California Press, 1985:50–66.

HURN, CHRISTOPHER. *The Limits and Possibilities of Schooling.* Boston: Allyn and Bacon, 1978.

HWANG, SEAN-SHONG, STEVEN H. MURDOCK, BANOO PARPIA, and RITA R. HAMM. "The Effects of Race and Socioeconomic Status on Residential Segregation in Texas, 1970–80." *Social Forces.* Vol. 63, No. 3 (March 1985):732–747.

HYMAN, HERBERT H., and CHARLES R. WRIGHT. "Trends in Voluntary Association Memberships of American Adults: Replication Based on Secondary Analysis of National Sample Survey." *American Sociological Review.* Vol. 36, No. 2 (April 1971):191–206.

IDRIS-SOVEN, AHAMED, ELIZABETH IDRIS-SOVEN, and MARY K. VAUGHAN. "Introduction." In Ahamed Idris-Soven et al., eds., *The World as a Company Town: Multinational Corporations and Social Change.* The Hague: Mouton Publishers, 1978:1–11.

ILLICH, IVAN. *Medical Nemesis: The Expropriation of Health.* New York: Pantheon Books, 1976.

INFIELD, TOM. "Two Decades of Transition and Tension." *The Philadelphia Inquirer* (November 24, 1985):1-A, 20-A.

INTERFAITH ACTION FOR ECONOMIC JUSTICE. "End Results: The Impact of Federal Policies Since 1980 on Low Income Americans." Washington, DC: 1984.

IRISH, MARIAN D., JAMES W. PROTHRO, and RICHARD J. RICHARDSON. *The Politics of American Democracy.* 7th ed. Englewood Cliffs, NJ: Prentice-Hall, 1981.

IRWIN, JOHN. *Prison in Turmoil.* Boston, MA: Little, Brown, 1980.

IYER, PICO. "Capitalism in the Making." *Time.* Vol. 123, No. 18 (April 30, 1984):26–31, 35.

IYER, PICO. "The Second Revolution." *Time.* Vol. 126, No. 12 (September 23, 1985):42–46, 51, 55–56.

JACKSON, BRIAN. *The Black Flag: A Look at the Strange Case of Nicola Sacco and Bartolomeo Vanzetti.* Boston, MA: Routledge & Kegan Paul, 1981.

JACOB, JOHN E. "An Overview of Black America in 1985." In James D. Williams, ed., *The State of Black America 1986.* New York: National Urban League, 1986:i–xi.

JACOBS, DAVID. "Inequality and Police Strength." *American Sociological Review.* Vol. 44, No. 6 (December 1979):913–925.

JACOBS, JANE. *Cities and the Wealth of Nations.* New York: Random House, 1984.

JACOBS, JANE. *The Economy of Cities.* New York: Vintage, 1970.

JACOBS, PATRICIA A., MURIEL BRUNTON, and MARIE M. MELVILLE. "Aggressive Behavior, Mental Subnormality, and the XYY Male," *Nature.* Vol. 208, No. 5017 (December 25, 1965):1351–1352.

JACQUET, CONSTANT H., JR., ed., *Yearbook of American and Canadian Churches, 1983.* Nashville, TN: Abingdon Press, 1984.

JAGGER, ALISON. "Political Philosophies of Women's Liberation." In Laurel Richardson and Verta Taylor, eds., *Feminist Frontiers: Rethinking Sex, Gender, and Society.* Reading, MA: Addison-Wesley, 1983.

JANIS, IRVING. *Victims of Groupthink.* Boston, MA: Houghton Mifflin, 1972.

JENCKS, CHRISTOPHER. "Genes and Crime." *The New York Review* (February 12, 1987):33–41.

JENCKS, CHRISTOPHER, et al. *Inequality: A Reassessment of the Effect of Family and Schooling in America.* New York: Basic Books, 1972.

JENKINS, BRIAN M. "Statements About Terrorism." In *International Terrorism, The Annals of the American Academy of Political and Social Science.* Vol. 463 (September 1982). Beverly Hills, CA: Sage Publications:11–23.

JENKINS, J. CRAIG, and CHARLES PERROW. "Insurgency of the Powerless: Farm Worker Movements (1946–1972)." *American Sociological Review.* Vol. 42, No. 2 (April 1977):249–268.

JOHNSON, PAUL. "The Seven Deadly Sins of Terrorism." In Benjamin Netanyahu, ed., *International Terrorism.* New Brunswick, NJ: Transaction Books, 1981:12–22.

JOHNSTON, R. J. "Residential Area Characteristics." In D. T. Herbert and R. J. Johnston, eds., *Social Areas in Cities. Vol. 1: Spatial Processes and Form.* New York: Wiley, 1976:193–235.

JOHNSTONE, RONALD L. *Religion in Society: A Sociology of Religion.* 2nd ed. Englewood Cliffs, NJ: Prentice-Hall, 1983.

JONES, DAVID A. *History of Criminology: A Philosophical Perspective.* Westport, CT: Greenwood Press, 1986.

JONES, RUTH S., and WARREN E. MILLER. "Financing Campaigns: Macro Level Innovation and Micro Level Response." *The Western Political Quarterly.* Vol. 38, No. 2 (June 1985):187–210.

JOSEPHY, ALVIN M., JR. *Now That the Buffalo's Gone: A Study in Today's American Indians.* New York: Alfred A. Knopf, 1982.

KAELBLE, HARTMUT. *Social Mobility in the 19th and 20th Centuries: Europe and America in Comparative Perspective.* New York: St. Martin's Press, 1986.

KAHN, ALFRED J., and SHIELA B. KAMERMAN. *Child Care: Facing the Hard Choices.* Dover, MA: Auburn House, 1987.

KAIN, EDWARD L. "A Note on the Integration of AIDS Into the Sociology of Human Sexuality." *Teaching Sociology.* Vol. 15, No. 4 (July 1987):320–323.

KAIN, EDWARD L., and SHANNON HART. "AIDS and the Family: A Content Analysis of Media Coverage." Presented to National Council on Family Relations, Atlanta, 1987.

KALISH, RICHARD A. *Late Adulthood: Perspectives on Human Development.* 2nd ed. Monterey, CA: Brooks/Cole, 1982.

KALISH, RICHARD A. "The New Ageism and the Failure Models: A Polemic." *The Gerontologist.* Vol. 19, No. 4 (August 1979):398–402.

KALMUSS, DEBRA, and JUDITH A. SELTZER. "Continuity of Marital Behavior in Remarriage: The Case of Spouse Abuse." Unpublished paper. November 1984.

KAMINER, WENDY. "Volunteers: Who Knows What's in It for Them." *Ms.* (December 1984):93–94, 96, 126–128.

KANTER, ROSABETH MOSS. "All That Is Entrepreneurial Is Not Gold." *The Wall Street Journal* (July 22, 1985):18.

KANTER, ROSABETH MOSS. *The Change Masters: Innovation and*

Entrepreneurship in the American Corporation. New York: Simon and Schuster, 1983.

KANTER, ROSABETH MOSS. *Men and Women of the Corporation.* New York: Basic Books, 1977.

KANTER, ROSABETH MOSS, and BARRY A. STEIN. "The Gender Pioneers: Women in an Industrial Sales Force." In R. M. Kanter and B. A. Stein, eds., *Life in Organizations.* New York: Basic Books, 1979:134–160.

KANTER, ROSABETH MOSS, and BARRY STEIN. *A Tale of "O": On Being Different in an Organization.* New York: Harper & Row, 1980.

KANTROWITZ, BARBARA. "Mothers on Their Own." *Newsweek* (December 23, 1985):66–67.

KAPLAN, ERIC B., et al. "The Usefulness of Preoperative Laboratory Screening." *Journal of the American Medical Association.* Vol. 253, No. 24 (June 28, 1985):3576–3581.

KAPTCHUK, TED. "The Holistic Logic of Chinese Medicine." In Shepard Bliss et al., eds., *The New Holistic Health Handbook.* Lexington, MA: The Steven Greene Press/Penguin Books, 1985:41.

KARP, DAVID A., and WILLIAM C. YOELS. "The College Classroom: Some Observations on the Meaning of Student Participation." *Sociology and Social Research.* Vol. 60, No. 4 (July 1976):421–439.

KASARDA, JOHN D. "Entry-Level Jobs, Mobility, and Urban Minority Employment." *Urban Affairs Quarterly.* Vol. 19, No. 1 (September 1983):21–40.

KATZ, ZEV. "Patterns of Social Mobility in the U.S.S.R." Cambridge, MA: Center for International Studies, Massachusetts Institute of Technology, 1973.

KAUFMAN, POLLY WELTS. "Women and Education." In Barbara Haber, ed., *The Women's Annual, 1981: The Year in Review.* Boston, MA: G. K. Hall and Company, 1982:24–55.

KAUFMAN, ROBERT L., and SEYMOUR SPILERMAN. "The Age Structures of Occupations and Jobs." *American Journal of Sociology.* Vol. 87, No. 4 (January 1982):827–851.

KAUFMAN, WALTER. *Religions in Four Dimensions: Existential, Aesthetic, Historical and Comparative.* New York: Reader's Digest Press, 1976.

KEATING, NORAH C., and PRISCILLA COLE. "What Do I Do with Him 24 Hours a Day? Changes in the Housewife Role After Retirement." *The Gerontologist.* Vol. 20, No. 1 (February 1980):84–89.

KELLER, SUZANNE. *The Urban Neighborhood.* New York: Random House, 1968.

KELLEY, JACK. "Births Out of Wedlock Opposed." *USA Today* (December 31, 1984):6A.

KELLEY, JACK. "Roswell Gilbert, 097753." *USA Today* (August 16, 1985):2A.

KELLEY, ROBERT. *The Shaping of the American Past. Vol. 2: 1865 to the Present.* 3rd ed. Englewood Cliffs, NJ: Prentice-Hall, 1982.

KENISTON, KENNETH. "Working Mothers." In James M. Henslin, ed., *Marriage and Family in a Changing Society.* 2nd ed. New York: Free Press, 1985:319–321.

KENYON, KATHLEEN. *Digging Up Jericho.* London: Ernest Benn, 1957.

KERBO, HAROLD R. *Social Stratification and Inequality: Class Conflict in the United States.* New York: McGraw-Hill, 1983.

KERCKHOFF, ALAN C., RICHARD T. CAMPBELL, and IDEE WINFIELD-LAIRD. "Social Mobility in Great Britain and the United States." *American Journal of Sociology.* Vol. 91, No. 2 (September 1985):281–308.

KESSLER, RONALD C., and PAUL D. CLEARY. "Social Class and Psy-

chological Distress." *American Sociological Review.* Vol. 45, No. 3 (June 1980):463–478.

KIEFER, MICHAEL. "New Faces Old Dreams." *Chicago.* Vol. 33, No. 3 (March 1984):127–135.

KII, TOSHI. "Recent Extension of Retirement Age in Japan." *The Gerontologist.* Vol. 19, No. 5 (October 1979):481–486.

KILBOURNE, BROCK K. "The Conway and Siegelman Claims Against Religious Cults: An Assessment of Their Data." *Journal for the Scientific Study of Religion.* Vol. 22, No. 4 (December 1983):380–385.

KILLIAN, LEWIS M. "Organization, Rationality and Spontaneity in the Civil Rights Movement." *American Sociological Review.* Vol. 49, No. 6 (December 1984):770–783.

KING, MARTIN LUTHER, JR. "The Montgomery Bus Boycott." In Walt Anderson, ed., *The Age of Protest.* Pacific Palisades, CA: Goodyear, 1969:81–91.

KINSEY, ALFRED, et al. *Sexual Behavior in the Human Female.* Philadelphia: W. B. Saunders, 1953.

KINSEY, ALFRED, et al. *Sexual Behavior in the Human Male.* Philadelphia: W. B. Saunders, 1948.

KIPP, RITA SMITH. "Have Women Always Been Unequal?" In Beth Reed, ed., *Towards A Feminist Transformation of the Academy: Proceedings of the Fifth Annual Women's Studies Conference.* Ann Arbor, MI: Great Lakes Colleges Association, 1980:12–18.

KITANO, HARRY H. L. "Japanese." In *Harvard Encyclopedia of American Ethnic Groups.* Cambridge, MA: Harvard University Press, 1980:561–571.

KITANO, HARRY H. L. *Race Relations.* 3rd ed. Englewood Cliffs, NJ: Prentice-Hall, 1985.

KITSON, GAY C., and HELEN J. RASCHKE. "Divorce Research: What We Know; What We Need to Know." *Journal of Divorce.* Vol. 4, No. 3 (Spring 1981):1–37.

KITTRIE, NICHOLAS N. *The Right To Be Different: Deviance and Enforced Therapy.* Baltimore, MD: The Johns Hopkins University Press, 1971.

KLEIMAN, DENA. "Changing Way of Death: Some Agonizing Choices." *The New York Times* (January 14, 1985):1, 11.

KLEIN, FREDA. "Violence Against Women." In Barbara Haber, ed., *The Women's Annual, 1981: The Year in Review.* Boston, MA: G. K. Hall and Company, 1982:270–302.

KLEIN, SUSAN SHURBERG. "Education." In Sarah M. Pritchard, ed., *The Women's Annual, Number 4, 1983–1984.* Boston, MA: G. K. Hall and Company, 1984:9–30.

KLEUGEL, JAMES R., and ELIOT R. SMITH. *Beliefs About Inequality: Americans' Views of What Is and What Ought to Be.* New York: Aldine de Gruyter, 1986.

KLUCKHOHN, CLYDE. "As An Anthropologist Views It." In Albert Deutch, ed., *Sex Habits of American Men.* New York: Prentice-Hall, 1948.

KNAUS, WILLIAM A. *Inside Russian Medicine: An American Doctor's First-Hand Report.* New York: Everest House, 1981.

KNOKE, DAVID, and RICHARD B. FELSON. "Ethnic Stratification and Political Cleavage in the United States, 1952–1968." *American Journal of Sociology.* Vol. 80, No. 3 (November 1974):630–642.

KOBLER, JOHN. *Ardent Spirits: The Rise and Fall of Prohibition.* New York: G. P. Putnam's Sons, 1973.

KOCH, HOWARD. *The Panic Broadcast: Portrait of an Event.* Boston, MA: Little, Brown, 1970.

KOENIG, FREDRICK. *Rumor in the Market Place: The Social Psychology of Commercial Hearsay.* Dover, MA: Auburn House, 1985.

KOHLBERG, LAWRENCE, and CAROL GILLIGAN. "The Adolescent as Philosopher: The Discovery of Self in a Postconventional World." *Daedalus.* Vol. 100 (Fall 1971):1051–1086.

KOHN, MELVIN L. *Class and Conformity: A Study in Values*. 2nd ed. Homewood, IL: The Dorsey Press, 1977.

KOHN, MELVIN L., and CARMI SCHOOLER. "Job Conditions and Personality: A Longitudinal Assessment of Their Reciprocal Effects." *American Journal of Sociology*. Vol. 87, No. 6 (May 1982):1257–1283.

KOMAROVSKY, MIRRA. *Blue Collar Marriage*. New York: Vintage Books, 1967.

KOMAROVSKY, MIRRA. "Cultural Contradictions and Sex Roles: The Masculine Case." *American Journal of Sociology*. Vol. 78, No. 4 (January 1973):873–884.

KOMAROVSKY, MIRRA. *Dilemmas of Masculinity: A Study of College Youth*. New York: W. W. Norton, 1976.

KORNHAUSER, WILLIAM. *The Politics of Mass Society*. New York: Free Press, 1959.

KOZOL, JONATHAN. *Illiterate America*. Garden City, NY: Anchor/Doubleday, 1985a.

KOZOL, JONATHAN. "A Nation's Wealth." *Publisher's Weekly* (May 24, 1985):28–30.

KOZOL, JONATHAN. *Prisoners of Silence: Breaking the Bonds of Adult Illiteracy in the United States*. New York: Continuum, 1980.

KRAMARAE, CHERIS. *Women and Men Speaking*. Rowley, MA: Newbury House, 1981.

KRISBERG, BARRY, and IRA SCHWARTZ. "Rethinking Juvenile Justice." *Crime and Delinquency*, Vol. 29, No. 3 (July 1983):333–364.

KUBEY, ROBERT W. "Television and Aging: Past, Present, and Future." *The Gerontologist*. Vol. 20, No. 1 (February 1980):16–35.

KÜBLER-ROSS, ELISABETH. *On Death and Dying*. New York: Macmillan, 1969.

LACAYO, RICHARD. "Blood in the Stands." *Time*. Vol. 125, No. 23 (June 10, 1985):38–39, 41.

LADD, JOHN. "The Definition of Death and the Right to Die." In John Ladd, ed., *Ethical Issues Relating to Life and Death*. New York: Oxford University Press, 1979:118–145.

LADNER, JOYCE A. "Teenage Pregnancy: The Implications for Black Americans." In James D. Williams, ed., *The State of Black America 1986*. New York: National Urban League, 1986:65–84.

LAI, H. M. "Chinese." In *Harvard Encyclopedia of American Ethnic Groups*. Cambridge, MA: Harvard University Press, 1980:217–233.

LAMAR, JACOB V., JR. "Redefining the American Dilemma." *Time*. Vol. 126, No. 19 (November 11, 1985):33, 36.

LAMBERG-KARLOVSKY, C. C., and MARTHA LAMBERG-KARLOVSKY. "An Early City in Iran." In *Cities: Their Origin, Growth, and Human Impact*. San Francisco: Freeman, 1973:28–37.

LANDERS, ANN. Syndicated Column: *The Dallas Morning News* (July 8, 1984):4F.

LANE, DAVID. "Social Stratification and Class." In Erik P. Hoffman and Robbin F. Laird, eds., *The Soviet Polity in the Modern Era*. New York: Aldine, 1984:563–605.

LANG, KURT, and GLADYS ENGEL LANG. *Collective Dynamics*. New York: Thomas Y. Crowell, 1961.

LANGAN, PATRICK A., and CHRISTOPHER A. INNES. *The Risk of Violent Crime*. Special Report from the Bureau of Justice Statistics. Washington, DC: U.S. Government Printing Office, 1985.

LASLETT, BARBARA. "Family Membership, Past and Present." *Social Problems*. Vol. 25, No. 5 (June 1978):476–490.

LASLETT, PETER. *The World We Have Lost: England Before the Industrial Age*. 3rd ed. New York: Charles Scribner's Sons, 1984.

LAZERWITZ, BERNARD, and MICHAEL HARRISON. "American Jewish Denominations: A Social and Religious Profile." *American Sociological Review*. Vol. 44, No. 4.(August 1979):656–666.

LEACOCK, ELEANOR. "Women's Status in Egalitarian Societies: Implications for Social Evolution." *Current Anthropology*. Vol. 19, No. 2 (June 1978):247–275.

LEAVITT, JUDITH WALZER. "Women and Health in America: An Overview." In Judith Walzer Leavitt, ed., *Women and Health in America*. Madison, WI: University of Wisconsin Press, 1984:3–7.

LE BON, GUSTAVE. *The Crowd: A Study of the Popular Mind*. New York: The Viking Press, 1960; orig. 1895.

LEE, BARRETT A., R. S. OROPESA, BARBARA J. METCH, and AVERY M. GUEST. "Testing the Decline of Community Thesis: Neighborhood Organization in Seattle, 1929 and 1979." *American Journal of Sociology*. Vol. 89, No. 5 (March 1984):1161–1188.

LEMERT, EDWIN M. *Human Deviance, Social Problems, and Social Control*. 2nd ed. Englewood Cliffs, NJ: Prentice-Hall, 1972.

LEMERT, EDWIN M. *Social Pathology*. New York: McGraw-Hill, 1951.

LENGERMANN, PATRICIA MADOO, and RUTH A. WALLACE. *Gender in America: Social Control and Social Change*. Englewood Cliffs, NJ: Prentice-Hall, 1985.

LENIHAN, JEFF. "Minorities Shut Out On All Sports Levels." *The Plain Dealer* (May 10, 1987):1-C, 12-C.

LENSKI, GERHARD. *Power and Privilege: A Theory of Social Stratification*. New York: McGraw-Hill, 1966.

LENSKI, GERHARD, and JEAN LENSKI. *Human Societies: An Introduction to Macrosociology*. 3rd ed. New York: McGraw-Hill, 1978; also 4th ed., 1982; also 5th ed., 1987.

LENZ, MARY. "Business Insecurity: Advisors Ease Culture Shock." *The Dallas Times-Herald* (July 9, 1984):1C, 2C.

LEO, JOHN. "The New Scarlet Letter." *Time*. Vol. 120, No. 5 (August 2, 1982):62–66.

LEONARD, EILEEN B. *Women, Crime, and Society: A Critique of Theoretical Criminology*. New York: Longman, 1982.

LESTER, DAVID. *The Death Penalty: Issues and Answers*. Springfield, IL: Charles C. Thomas, 1987.

LEVER, JANET. "Sex Differences in the Complexity of Children's Play and Games." *American Sociological Review*. Vol. 43, No. 4 (August 1978):471–483.

LEVIN, JACK, and WILLIAM C. LEVIN. *Ageism: Prejudice and Discrimination Against the Elderly*. Belmont, CA: Wadsworth, 1980.

LEVINSON, DANIEL J., with CHARLOTTE N. DARROW, EDWARD B. KLEIN, MARIA H. LEVINSON, and BRAXTON MCKEE. *The Seasons of a Man's Life*. New York: Alfred A. Knopf, 1978.

LEWIS, FLORA. "The Roots of Revolution." *The New York Times Magazine* (November 11, 1984):70–71, 74, 77–78, 82, 84, 86.

LEWIS, OSCAR. *The Children of Sanchez*. New York: Random House, 1961.

LEWONTIN, R. C., STEVEN ROSE, and LEON J. KAMIN. *Not In Our Genes: Biology, Ideology, and Human Nature*. New York: Pantheon, 1984.

LIAZOS, ALEXANDER. "The Poverty of the Sociology of Deviance: Nuts, Sluts and Preverts." *Social Problems*. Vol. 20, No. 1 (Summer 1972):103–120.

LIEBERSON, STANLEY. *A Piece of the Pie: Black and White Immigrants Since 1880*. Berkeley, CA: University of California Press, 1980.

LIEBOW, ELLIOT. *Tally's Corner*. Boston, MA: Little, Brown, 1967.

LIN, NAN, WALTER M. ENSEL, and JOHN C. VAUGHN. "Social Resources and Strength of Ties: Structural Factors in Occupational Status Attainment." *American Sociological Review*. Vol. 46, No. 4 (August 1981):393–405.

LING, PYAU. "Causes of Chinese Emigration." In Amy Tachiki et al., eds., *Roots: An Asian American Reader*. Los Angeles: UCLA Asian American Studies Center, 1971:134–138.

LINK, BRUCE G., FRANCIS T. CULLIN, JAMES FRANK, and JOHN F. WOZNIAK. "The Social Rejection of Former Mental Patients: Understanding Why Labels Matter." *American Journal of Sociology*. Vol. 92, No. 6 (May 1987):1461–1500.

LINK, BRUCE G., BRUCE P. DOHRENWEND and ANDREW E. SKODOL. "Socio-Economic Status and Schizophrenia: Noisome Occupational Characteristics As A Risk Factor." *American Sociological Review*. Vol. 51, No. 2 (April 1986):242–258.

LINTON, RALPH. "One Hundred Percent American." *The American Mercury*. Vol. 40, No. 160 (April 1937):427–429.

LINTON, RALPH. *The Study of Man*. New York: D. Appleton-Century, 1937.

LIPSET, SEYMOUR MARTIN. *Political Man: The Social Bases of Politics*. Garden City, NY: Doubleday Anchor Books, 1963.

LIPSET, SEYMOUR MARTIN, and REINHARD BENDIX. *Social Mobility in Industrial Society*. Berkeley, CA: University of California Press, 1967.

LIPSET, SEYMOUR MARTIN, MARTIN TROW, and JAMES COLEMAN. *Union Democracy: The Inside Politics of the International Typographical Union*. New York: Free Press, 1977; orig. 1956.

LISKA, ALLEN E. *Perspectives on Deviance*. 2nd ed. Englewood Cliffs, NJ: Prentice-Hall, 1987.

LISKA, ALLEN E., and MARK TAUSIG. "Theoretical Interpretations of Social Class and Racial Differentials in Legal Decision Making for Juveniles." *Sociological Quarterly*. Vol. 20, No. 2 (Spring 1979):197–207.

LITSKY, FRANK. "Baseball Consultant Hired to Find Minority Jobs." *International Herald Tribune* (June 15, 1987):21.

LO, CLARENCE Y. H. "Countermovements and Conservative Movements in the Contemporary U.S." *Annual Review of Sociology*. Vol. 8. Palo Alto, CA: Annual Reviews, Inc., 1982:107–134.

LOFLAND, JOHN. *Doomsday Cult: A Study of Conversion, Proselytization, and Maintenance of Faith*. New York: Irvington Publishers, 1977; orig. 1966.

LOFLAND, LYN. *A World of Strangers*. New York: Basic Books, 1973.

LOGAN, JOHN R., and MARK SCHNEIDER. "Racial Segregation and Racial Change in American Suburbs, 1970–1980." *American Journal of Sociology*. Vol. 89, No. 4 (January 1984):874–888.

LOGAN, RAYFORD W. "Charles Richard Drew." In Rayford W. Logan and Michael R. Winston, eds., *Dictionary of American Negro Biography*. New York: W. W. Norton, 1982:190–192.

LONDON, BRUCE. "Structural Determinants of Third World Urban Change: An Ecological and Political Economic Analysis." *American Sociological Review*. Vol. 52, No. 1 (February 1987):28–43.

LONG, EDWARD V. *The Intruders: The Invasion of Privacy by Government and Industry*. New York: Frederick A. Praeger, 1967.

LORD, WALTER. *A Night to Remember*. Rev. ed. New York: Holt, Reinhart, and Winston, 1976.

LOW, W. AUGUSTUS, and VIRGIL A. CLIFT. "Charles Richard Drew." *Encyclopedia of Black America*. New York: McGraw-Hill, 1981:325–326.

LOY, PAMELA HEWITT, and LEA P. STEWART. "The Extent and Effects of Sexual Harassment of Working Women." *Sociological Focus*. Vol. 17, No. 1 (January 1984):31–43.

LUBENOW, GERALD C. "A Troubling Family Affair." *Newsweek* (May 14, 1984):34.

LYMAN, STANFORD. "Strangers in the City: The Chinese in the Urban Frontier." In Amy Tachiki et al., *Roots: An Asian American Reader*. Los Angeles: UCLA Asian American Studies Center, 1971:159–187.

LYND, ROBERT S. *Knowledge For What? The Place of Social Science in American Culture*. Princeton, NJ: Princeton University Press, 1967.

LYND, ROBERT S., and HELEN MERRELL LYND. *Middletown: A Study in Modern American Culture*. New York: Harcourt, Brace & World, 1956; orig. 1929.

LYND, ROBERT S., and HELEN MERRELL LYND. *Middletown in Transition*. New York: Harcourt, Brace & World, 1937.

MACCOBY, ELEANOR EMMONS, and CAROL NAGY JACKLIN. *The Psychology of Sex Differences*. Palo Alto, CA: Stanford University Press, 1974.

MACE, DAVID, and VERA MACE. *Marriage East and West*. Garden City, NY: Doubleday (Dolphin), 1960.

MACIONIS, JOHN J. "Are We Familiar or Intimate? Marriage as a Primary Relationship." Presentation, Annual Meeting of the American Sociological Association. Chicago, 1977.

MACIONIS, JOHN J. "Intimacy: Structure and Process in Interpersonal Relationships." *Alternative Lifestyles*. Vol. 1, No. 1 (February 1978):113–130.

MACIONIS, JOHN J. "The Search for Community in Modern Society: An Interpretation." *Qualitative Sociology*. Vol. 1, No. 2 (September 1978):130–143.

MACIONIS, JOHN J. "A Sociological Analysis of Humor." Presentation to the Texas Junior College Teachers Association, Houston, 1987.

MACLIN, ELEANOR D. "Nonmarital Heterosexual Cohabitation: An Overview." In Eleanor D. Macklin and Roger H. Rubin, eds., *Contemporary Families and Alternative Lifestyles: Handbook on Research and Theory*. Beverly Hills, CA: Sage, 1983:49–74.

MADSEN, AXEL. *Private Power: Multinational Corporations for the Survival of Our Planet*. New York: William Morrow, 1980.

MAGNET, MYRON. "The Fortune 500 Special Report: The Dollar Dampens the Profit Party." *Fortune*. Vol. 111, No. 9 (April 29, 1985):252–258, 260, 262, 265–286.

MAGNUSON, ED. "Champion of the Elderly." *Time*. Vol. 121, No. 117 (April 25, 1983):20–23, 26, 29.

MAGNUSON, ED. "Child Abuse: The Ultimate Betrayal." *Time*. Vol. 122, No. 5 (September 5, 1984):20–22.

MAGNUSON, ED. "A Problem That Cannot Be Buried." *Time*. Vol. 126, No. 15 (October 14, 1985):76–78, 83–84.

MAHLER, HALFDAN. "People." *Scientific American*. Vol. 243, No. 3 (September 1980):67–77.

MAJOR, BRENDA. "Gender Patterns in Touching Behavior." In Clara Mayo and Nancy M. Henley, eds., *Gender and Nonverbal Behavior*. New York: Springer-Verlag, 1981:15–37.

MALTHUS, THOMAS ROBERT. *First Essay on Population 1798*. London: Macmillan, 1926; orig. 1798.

MAMONOVA, TATYANA. *Women and Russia*. Boston, MA: Beacon Press, 1984.

MANGAN, J. A., and ROBERTA J. PARK. *From Fair Sex to Feminism: Sport and the Socialization of Women*. London: Frank Cass, 1987.

MANN, ARTHUR. "When Tammany Was Supreme." In William L. Riordon. *Plunkitt of Tammany Hall*. New York: E. P. Dutton, 1963:vii–xxii.

MARCUSE, HERBERT. *One-Dimensional Man*. Boston, MA: Beacon Press, 1964.

MARE, ROBERT D. "Change and Stability in Educational Stratification." *American Sociological Review*. Vol. 46, No. 1 (February 1981):72–87.

MARGOLICK, DAVID. "Rape in Marriage is No Longer Within the Law." *The New York Times* (December 13, 1984):6E.

MARINI, MARGARET MOONEY. "The Transition to Adulthood: Sex Differences in Educational Attainment and Age at Marriage." *American Sociological Review*. Vol. 43, No. 4 (August 1978):483–507.

MARLIOS, PETER. "Interlocking Directorates and the Control of Corporations: The Theory of Bank Control." *Social Science Quarterly*. Vol. 56, No. 3 (December 1975):425–439.

MARSDEN, PETER. "Core Discussion Networks of Americans." *American Sociological Review*. Vol. 52, No. 1 (February 1987):122–131.

MARSHALL, R., C. B. KNAPP, M. H. LIGGET, and R. W. GLOVER. *Employment Discrimination: The Impact of Legal and Administrative Remedies*. New York: Praeger, 1978.

MARTIN, RICHARD C. *Islam: A Cultural Perspective*. Englewood Cliffs, NJ: Prentice-Hall, 1982.

MARTIN, WILLIAM. "The Birth of a Media Myth." *The Atlantic*. Vol. 247, No. 6 (June 1981):7, 10, 11, 16.

MARX, GARY T., and JAMES L. WOOD. "Strands of Theory and Research in Collective Behavior." In Alex Inkeles, et al., eds., *Annual Review of Sociology*. Vol. 1. Palo Alto, CA: Annual Reviews, Inc., 1975:363–428.

MARX, KARL. *Capital*. Friedrich Engels, ed. New York: International Publishers, 1967; orig. 1867.

MARX, KARL. Excerpt from "A Contribution to the Critique of Political Economy." In Karl Marx, and Friedrich Engels. *Marx and Engels: Basic Writings on Politics and Philosophy*. Lewis S. Feuer, ed. Garden City, NY: Anchor Books, 1959:42–46.

MARX, KARL. *Karl Marx: Early Writings*. T. B. Bottomore, ed. New York: McGraw-Hill, 1964a.

MARX, KARL. *Karl Marx: Selected Writings in Sociology and Social Philosophy*. T. B. Bottomore, trans. New York: McGraw-Hill, 1964.

MARX, KARL. "Theses on Feuerbach." In Robert C. Tucker, ed., *The Marx-Engels Reader*. New York: Norton, 1972:107–109; orig. 1845.

MARX, KARL, and FRIEDRICH ENGELS. "Manifesto of the Communist Party." In Robert C. Tucker, ed., *The Marx-Engels Reader*. New York: W. W. Norton, 1972:331–362; orig. 1848.

MASHEK, JOHN W., and PATRICIA AVERY. "Women Politicians Take Off the White Gloves." *U.S. News & World Report* (August 15, 1983):41–42.

MATHEWS, TOM. "Lennon's Alter Ego." *Newsweek*. (December 22, 1980):34–35.

MATTHEWS, MERVYN. "Long Term Trends in Soviet Education." In J. J. Tomiak, ed., *Soviet Education in the 1980s*. London: Croom Helm, 1983:1–23.

MATTHIESSEN, PETER. *Indian Country*. New York: Viking Press, 1984.

MATTHIESSEN, PETER. *In the Spirit of Crazy Horse*. New York: Viking Press, 1983.

MATZA, DAVID. *Delinquency and Drift*. New York: John Wiley, 1964.

MAUSS, ARMAND L. *Social Problems of Social Movements*. Philadelphia, PA: Lippincott, 1975.

MAYO, KATHERINE. *Mother India*. New York: Harcourt, Brace and Co., 1927.

McADAM, DOUG. *Political Process and the Development of Black Insurgency, 1930–1970*. Chicago: University of Chicago Press, 1982.

McADAM, DOUG. "Tactical Innovation and the Pace of Insurgency." *American Sociological Review*. Vol. 48, No. 6 (December 1983):735–754.

McCARTHY, JOHN D., and MAYER N. ZALD. "Resource Mobilization and Social Movements: A Partial Theory." *American Journal of Sociology*. Vol. 82, No. 6 (May 1977):1212–1241.

McCOY, CRAIG R. "Who Was John Africa?" *The Philadelphia Inquirer Magazine* (January 12, 1986):18–28.

McGLEN, NANCY E., and KAREN O'CONNOR. *Women's Rights: The Struggle for Equality in the Nineteenth and Twentieth Centuries*. New York: Praeger Publishers, 1983.

McGRATH, ELLIE. "Preparing to Wield the Rod." *Time*. Vol. 121, No. 4 (January 23, 1984):57.

McGUIRE, MEREDITH B. *Religion: The Social Context*. 2nd ed. Belmont, CA: Wadsworth, 1987.

McKEOWN, THOMAS. *The Role of Medicine: Dream, Mirage, or Nemesis?* Princeton, NJ: Princeton University Press, 1979.

McKUSICK, LEON, et al. "Reported Changes in the Sexual Behavior of Men at Risk for AIDS, San Francisco, 1982–84—the AIDS Behavioral Research Project." *Public Health Reports*. Vol. 100, No. 6 (November–December 1985):622–629.

McLANAHAN, SARA. "Family Structure and the Reproduction of Poverty." *American Journal of Sociology* Vol. 90, No. 4 (January 1985):873–901.

McPHAIL, CLARK, and RONALD T. WOHLSTEIN. "Individual and Collective Behaviors Within Gatherings, Demonstrations, and Riots." *Annual Review of Sociology*. Vol. 9. Palo Alto, CA: Annual Reviews, Inc., 1983:579–600.

McRAE, SUSAN. *Cross-Class Families: A Study of Wives' Occupational Superiority*. New York: Oxford University Press, 1986.

McROBERTS, HUGH A., and KEVIN SELBEE. "Trends in Occupational Mobility in Canada and the United States: A Comparison." *American Sociological Review*. Vol. 46, No. 4 (August 1981):406–421.

MEAD, GEORGE HERBERT. *Mind, Self, and Society*. Charles W. Morris, ed. Chicago: University of Chicago Press, 1962; orig. 1934.

MEAD, GEORGE HERBERT. *Philosophy of the Act*. Charles W. Morris, ed. Chicago: University of Chicago Press, 1938.

MEAD, GEORGE HERBERT. "The Teaching of Science in College." *Science*. Vol. 24 (1906):390–397.

MEAD, MARGARET. *Coming of Age in Samoa*. New York: Dell, 1961; orig. 1928.

MEAD, MARGARET. *Sex and Temperament in Three Primitive Societies*. New York: William Morrow, 1963; orig. 1935.

MECHANIC, DAVID. *Medical Sociology*. 2nd ed. New York: Free Press, 1978.

MELTZER, BERNARD N. "Mead's Social Psychology." In Jerome G. Manis and Bernard N. Meltzer, eds., *Symbolic Interaction: A Reader in Social Psychology*. 2nd ed. Boston, MA: Allyn & Bacon, 1977:15–27; also 3rd ed., 1978.

MELVILLE, KEITH. *Marriage and Family Today*. 3rd ed. New York: Random House, 1983.

MERTON, ANDREW. "Return to Brotherhood." *Ms.* (September 1985):60, 62, 64–65, 121–122.

MERTON, ROBERT K. "Discrimination and the American Creed." In *Sociological Ambivalence and Other Essays*. New York: The Free Press, 1976:189–216.

MERTON, ROBERT K. "Social Structure and Anomie." *American Sociological Review*. Vol. 3, No. 6 (October 1938):672–682.

MERTON, ROBERT K. *Social Theory and Social Structure*. New York: Free Press, 1968.

MEYER, JOHN W., JOHN BOLI-BENNETT, and CHRISTOPHER CHASE-DUNN. "Convergence and Divergence in Development." In Alex Inkeles et al., eds., *Annual Review of Sociology*. Vol. 1. Palo Alto, CA: Annual Review, 1975:223–246.

MICHELS, ROBERT. *Political Parties*. Glencoe, IL: Free Press, 1949; orig. 1911.

MILGRAM, STANLEY. "Behavioral Study of Obedience." *Journal of Abnormal and Social Psychology*. Vol. 67, No. 4 (1963):371–378.

MILGRAM, STANLEY. "Group Pressure and Action Against a Person." *Journal of Abnormal and Social Psychology*. Vol. 69, No. 2 (August 1964):137–143.

MILGRAM, STANLEY. "Some Conditions of Obedience and Disobedience to Authority." *Human Relations*. Vol. 18 (February 1965):57–76.

MILIBAND, RALPH. *The State in Capitalist Society*. London: Weidenfield and Nicolson, 1969.

MILLER, ARTHUR G. *The Obedience Experiments: A Case of Controversy in Social Science*. New York: Praeger, 1986.

MILLER, FREDERICK D. "The End of SDS and the Emergence of Weatherman: Demise Through Success." In Jo Freeman, ed., *Social Movements of the Sixties and Seventies*. New York: Longman, 1983:279–297.

MILLER, WALTER B. "Lower Class Culture as a Generating Milieu of Gang Delinquency." In Marvin E. Wolfgang, Leonard Savitz, and Norman Johnston, eds., *The Sociology of Crime and Delinquency*. 2nd ed. New York: John Wiley, 1970:351–363; orig. 1958.

MILLET, KATE. *Sexual Politics*. Garden City, NY: Doubleday, 1970.

MILLS, C. WRIGHT. *The Power Elite*. New York: Oxford University Press, 1956.

MILLS, C. WRIGHT. *The Sociological Imagination*. New York: Oxford University Press, 1959.

MILLS, C. WRIGHT. *White Collar: The American Middle Classes*. New York: Oxford University Press, 1951.

MINTZ, BETH, and MICHAEL SCHWARTZ. "Interlocking Directorates and Interest Group Formation." *American Sociological Review*. Vol. 46, No. 6 (December 1981):851–869.

MINTZ, BETH, and MICHAEL SCHWARTZ. *The Power Structure of American Business*. Chicago: University of Chicago Press, 1985.

MIROWSKY, JOHN. "The Psycho-Economics of Feeling Underpaid: Distributive Justice and the Earnings of Husbands and Wives." *American Journal of Sociology*. Vol. 92, No. 6 (May 1987):1404–1434.

MIROWSKY, JOHN, and CATHERINE ROSS. "Working Wives and Mental Health." Presentation to the American Association for the Advancement of Science. New York, 1984

MITCHELL, WILLIAM L. "Lay Observations on Retirement." In Frances M. Carp, ed., *Retirement*. New York: Behavioral Publications, 1972:199–217.

MOLNAR, STEPHEN. *Human Variation: Races, Types, and Ethnic Groups*. 2nd ed. Englewood Cliffs, NJ: Prentice-Hall, 1983.

MOLOTCH, HARVEY. "The City as a Growth Machine." *American Journal of Sociology*. Vol. 82, No. 2 (September 1976):309–333.

MOLOTCH, HARVEY L., and DEIRDRE BODEN. "Talking Social Structure: Discourse, Domination, and the Watergate Hearings." *American Sociological Review*. Vol. 50, No. 3 (June 1985):273–288.

MONEY, JOHN. *The Destroying Angel: Sex, Fitness & Food in the Legacy of Degeneracy Theory, Graham Crackers, Kellogg's Corn Flakes & American Health History*. Buffalo, NY: Prometheus Books, 1985.

MONEY, JOHN, and ANKE A. EHRHARDT. *Man and Woman, Boy and Girl*. New York: New American Library, 1972.

MONK-TURNER, ELIZABETH. "Sex, Educational Differentiation, and Occupational Status: Analyzing Occupational Differences for Community and Four-Year Entrants." *The Sociological Quarterly*. Vol. 24, No. 3 (July 1983):393–404.

MOORE, GWEN. "The Structure of a National Elite Network." *American Sociological Review*. Vol. 44, No. 5 (October 1979):673–692.

MOORE, JOAN, and HARRY PACHON. *Hispanics in the United States*. Englewood Cliffs, NJ: Prentice-Hall, 1985.

MOORE, WILBERT E. "Modernization as Rationalization: Processes and Restraints." In Manning Nash, ed., *Essays on Economic Development and Cultural Change in Honor of Bert F. Hoselitz*. Chicago: University of Chicago Press, 1977:29–42.

MOORE, WILBERT E. *World Modernization: The Limits of Convergence*. New York: Elsevier, 1979.

MORAN, MARY. "Student Financial Assistance: Next Steps to Improving Education and Economic Opportunity for Women." Washington, DC: American Council on Education, 1984.

MORRIS, ALDON. "Black Southern Sit-in Movement: An Analysis of Internal Organization." *American Sociological Review*. Vol. 46, No. 6 (December 1981):744–767.

MORRISON, DENTON E. "Some Notes Toward Theory on Relative Deprivation, Social Movements, and Social Change." In Louis E. Genevie, ed., *Collective Behavior and Social Movements*. Itasca, IL: F. E. Peacock, 1978:202–209.

MOTTAZ, CLIFFORD J. "Some Determinants of Work Alienation." *The Sociological Quarterly*. Vol. 22, No. 4 (Autumn 1981):515–529.

MOYNIHAN, DANIEL. *The Negro Family: The Case for National Action*. Office of Policy Planning and Research, United States Department of Labor. Washington DC: U.S. Government Printing Office, 1965.

MUELLER, DANIEL P., and PHILIP W. COOPER. "Children of Single Parent Families: How Do They Fare as Young Adults?" Presentation to the American Sociological Association. San Antonio, Texas, 1984.

MULLER, PETER O. "The Transformation of Bedroom Suburbia into the Outer City: An Overview of Metropolitan Structural Change Since 1947." Paper presented to "Suburbia Reexamined" Conference, Hofstra University, 1987.

MULLER, THOMAS, and THOMAS J. ESPENSHADE. *The Fourth Wave: California's Newest Immigrants*. Washington, DC: The Urban Institute Press, 1985.

MUMFORD, LEWIS. *The City in History: Its Origins, Its Transformations, and Its Prospects*. New York: Harcourt, Brace & World, 1961.

MURDOCK, GEORGE P. "The Common Denominator of Cultures." In Ralph Linton, ed., *The Science of Man in World Crisis*. New York: Columbia University Press, 1945:123–142.

MURDOCK, GEORGE P. "Comparative Data on the Division of Labor by Sex." *Social Forces*. Vol. 15, No. 4 (May 1937):551–553.

MURDOCK, GEORGE PETER. *Social Structure*. New York: Free Press, 1965; orig. 1949.

MURPHY, ROBERT F. *An Overture to Social Anthropology*. Englewood Cliffs, NJ: Prentice-Hall, 1979.

MURRAY, PAULI. *Proud Shoes: The History of an American Family*. New York: Harper & Row, 1978.

MYERHOFF, BARBARA. *Number Our Days*. New York: Simon and Schuster, 1980.

MYRDAL, GUNNAR. *An American Dilemma: The Negro Problem and Modern Democracy*. New York: Harper and Brothers, 1944.

NATIONAL CENTER FOR EDUCATION STATISTICS. *Digest of Education Statistics 1983–84*. Washington, DC: U.S. Government Printing Office, 1983.

NATIONAL COMMISSION ON EXCELLENCE IN EDUCATION. *A Nation at Risk*. Washington, DC: U.S. Government Printing Office, 1983.

NATIONAL INSTITUTE OF MENTAL HEALTH. *Television and Behavior: Ten Years of Scientific Progress and Implications for the Eighties*. 2 Vols. Washington, DC: U.S. Government Printing Office, 1982.

NAVARRO, VICENTE. "The Industrialization of Fetishism or the Fetishism of Industrialization: A Critique of Ivan Illich." In Vicente Navarro, ed., *Health and Medical Care in the U.S.: A Critical Analysis*. Farmingdale, NY: Baywood Publishing Co., 1977:38–58.

NEIDERT, LISA J., and REYNOLDS FARLEY. "Assimilation in the United States: An Analysis of Ethnic and Generation Differences in Status and Achievement." *American Sociological Review.* Vol. 50, No. 6 (December 1985):840–850.

NEUGARTEN, BERNICE L. "Grow Old with Me. The Best Is Yet to Be." *Psychology Today.* Vol. 5 (December 1971):45–48, 79, 81.

NEUGARTEN, BERNICE L. "Personality and Aging." In James E. Birren and K. Warren Schaie, eds., *Handbook of the Psychology of Aging.* New York: Van Nostrand Reinhold, 1977:626–649.

NEUGARTEN, BERNICE L. "Personality and the Aging Process." *The Gerontologist.* Vol. 12, No. 1 (Spring 1972):9–15.

NEW HAVEN *Journal-Courier.* "English Social Structure Changing." November 27, 1986.

NEWMAN, JAMES L., and GORDON E. MATZKE. *Population: Patterns, Dynamics, and Prospects.* Englewood Cliffs, NJ: Prentice-Hall, 1984.

NEWMAN, WILLIAM M. *American Pluralism: A Study of Minority Groups and Social Theory.* New York: Harper & Row, 1973.

New York Times, The. "Judge Acquits Mother of Stealing Her Son." May 19, 1987:A20.

NIELSEN, JOHN. "Rising Racism on the Continent." *Time.* Vol. 125, No. 6 (February 6, 1984):40–41, 44–45.

NISBET, ROBERT. "Sociology as an Art Form." In *Tradition and Revolt: Historical and Sociological Essays.* New York: Vintage Books, 1970.

NISBET, ROBERT A. *The Sociological Tradition.* New York: Basic Books, 1966.

NISBET, ROBERT A. *The Quest for Community.* New York: Oxford University Press, 1969.

N.O.R.C. *General Social Surveys, 1972–1983: Cumulative Codebook.* Chicago: National Opinion Research Center, 1983.

N.O.R.C. *General Social Surveys, 1972–1987.* Chicago: National Opinion Research Center, 1987.

NUNN, CLYDE Z., HARRY J. CROCKETT, JR., and J. ALLEN WILLIAMS, JR. *Tolerance for Nonconformity.* San Francisco, CA: Jossey-Bass Publishers, 1978.

OAKES, JEANNIE. "Classroom Social Relationships: Exploring the Bowles and Gintis Hypothesis." *Sociology of Education.* Vol. 55, No. 4 (October 1982):197–212.

OAKES, JEANNIE. *Keeping Track: How High Schools Structure Inequality.* New Haven, CT: Yale University Press, 1985.

OAKLEY, ANNE. *The Sociology of Housework.* New York: Random House/Pantheon Books, 1974.

OBERSCHALL, ANTHONY. *Social Conflict and Social Movements.* Englewood Cliffs, NJ: Prentice-Hall, 1973.

O'DEA, THOMAS F., and JANET O'DEA AVIAD. *The Sociology of Religion.* 2nd ed. Englewood Cliffs, NJ: Prentice-Hall, 1983.

OFFIR, CAROLE WADE. *Human Sexuality.* New York: Harcourt Brace Jovanovich, 1982.

OGBURN, WILLIAM F. *On Culture and Social Change.* Chicago: University of Chicago Press, 1964.

OKIMOTO, DANIEL. "The Intolerance of Success." In Amy Tachiki et al., eds., *Roots: An Asian American Reader.* Los Angeles: UCLA Asian American Studies Center, 1971:14–19.

O'REILLY, JANE. "Wife Beating: The Silent Crime." *Time.* Vol. 122, No. 10 (September 5, 1983):23–24, 26.

OSTLING, RICHARD N. "God and Money." *Time.* Vol. 130, No. 5 (August 3, 1987):48–49.

OSTLING, RICHARD N. "Jerry Falwell's Crusade." *Time.* Vol. 126, No. 9 (September 2, 1985):48–52, 55, 57.

OSTLING, RICHARD N. "Power, Glory—And Politics." *Time.* Vol. 127, No. 7 (February 17, 1986):62–69.

OSTLING, RICHARD N. "Technology and the Womb." *Time.* Vol. 129, No. 12 (March 23, 1987):58–59.

OSTRANDER, SUSAN A. "Upper Class Women: The Feminine Side of Privilege." *Qualitative Sociology.* Vol. 3, No. 1 (Spring 1980):23–44.

OSTRANDER, SUSAN A. *Women of the Upper Class.* Philadelphia, PA: Temple University Press, 1984.

OUCHI, WILLIAM. *Theory Z: How American Business Can Meet the Japanese Challenge.* Reading, MA: Addison-Wesley, 1981.

OWEN, DAVID. *None of the Above: Behind the Myth of Scholastic Aptitude.* Boston, MA: Houghton Mifflin, 1985.

PADILLA, ELENA. *Up from Puerto Rico.* New York: Columbia University Press, 1958.

PALMORE, ERDMAN. "Advantages of Aging." *The Gerontologist.* Vol. 19, No. 2 (April 1979b):220–223.

PALMORE, ERDMAN. "Predictors of Successful Aging." *The Gerontologist.* Vol. 19, No. 5 (October 1979a):427–431.

PALMORE, ERDMAN. "What Can the USA Learn from Japan About Aging?" In Steven H. Zarit, ed., *Readings in Aging and Death: Contemporary Perspectives.* New York: Harper & Row, 1982:166–169.

PAMPEL, FRED C., KENNETH C. LAND, and MARCUS FELSON. "A Social Indicator Model of Changes in the Occupational Structure of the United States: 1947–1974. *American Sociological Review.* Vol. 42, No. 6 (December 1977):951–964.

PARCEL, TOBY L., CHARLES W. MUELLER, and STEVEN CUVELIER. "Comparable Worth and Occupational Labor Market: Explanations of Occupational Earnings Differentials." Paper presented to the American Sociological Association, New York, 1986.

PARENTI, MICHAEL. *Inventing Reality: The Politics of the Mass Media.* New York: St. Martin's Press, 1986.

PARKIN, FRANK. *Class Inequality and Political Order.* New York: Praeger, 1971.

PARKINSON, C. NORTHCOTE. *Parkinson's Law and Other Studies in Administration.* New York: Ballantine Books, 1957.

PARSONS, TALCOTT. *Essays in Sociological Theory.* New York: Free Press, 1954.

PARSONS, TALCOTT. *The Social System.* New York: Free Press, 1964; orig. 1951.

PARSONS, TALCOTT. *Societies: Evolutionary and Comparative Perspectives.* Englewood Cliffs, NJ: Prentice-Hall, 1966.

PARSONS, TALCOTT, and ROBERT F. BALES, eds. *Family, Socialization and Interaction Process.* New York: Free Press, 1955.

PARSONS, TALCOTT, and EDWARD SHILS, eds. *Toward a General Theory of Action.* Cambridge, MA: Harvard University Press, 1951.

PARSONS, TALCOTT, and NEIL J. SMELSER. *Economy and Society: A Study in the Integration of Economic and Social Theory.* New York: Free Press, 1965; orig. 1956.

P.B.S. (PUBLIC BROADCASTING SYSTEM). "Adam Smith in the New China—From Marx to Mastercard." Television broadcast, June 12, 1985.

PEAR, ROBERT. "Women Reduce Lag in Earnings, But Disparities With Men Remain." *The New York Times* (September 4, 1987): 1, 7.

PÉREZ, LISANDRO. "Cubans." In *Harvard Encyclopedia of American Ethnic Groups.* Cambridge, MA: Harvard University Press, 1980:256–260.

PERRY, SUSAN, and JIM DAWSON. *Nightmare: Women and the Dalkon Shield.* New York: Macmillan, 1985.

PERSELL, CAROLINE HODGES. *Education and Inequality: A Theoretical and Empirical Synthesis.* New York: Free Press, 1977.

PETER, LAURENCE J., and RAYMOND HULL. *The Peter Principle: Why Things Always Go Wrong.* New York: William Morrow, 1969.

PETERS, THOMAS J., and ROBERT H. WATERMAN, JR. *In Search of*

Excellence: Lessons From America's Best-Run Companies. New York: Warner Books, 1982.

PETERSON, NORMA. "Coming to Terms With Gay Parents." *USA Today* (April 30, 1984):3D.

PFAFF, WILLIAM. "Reflections: Aristocracies." *The New Yorker* (January 14, 1980):70, 72–78.

PHILLIPSON, CHRIS. *Capitalism and the Construction of Old Age.* London: The Macmillan Press, 1982.

PHYSICIAN TASK FORCE ON HUNGER IN AMERICA. "Hunger Reaches Blue-Collar America." Report issued 1987.

PINDERHUGHES, DIANNE M. "Political Choices: A Realignment in Partisanship Among Black Voters?" In James D. Williams, ed., *The State of Black America 1986.* New York: National Urban League, 1986:85–113.

PINES, MAYA. "The Civilization of Genie." *Psychology Today.* Vol. 15 (September 1981):28–34.

PIOTROW, PHYLLIS T. *World Population: The Present and Future Crisis.* Headline Series 251 (October 1980). New York: Foreign Policy Association.

PIRANDELLO, LUIGI. "The Pleasure of Honesty." In *To Clothe the Naked and Two Other Plays.* New York: Dutton, 1962:143–198.

PITT, MALCOLM. *Introducing Hinduism.* New York: Friendship Press, 1955.

PIVEN, FRANCES FOX, and RICHARD A. CLOWARD. *Poor People's Movements: Why They Succeed, How They Fail.* New York: Pantheon, 1977.

PLOMIN, ROBERT, and TERRYL T. FOCH. "A Twin Study of Objectively Assessed Personality in Childhood." *Journal of Personality and Social Psychology.* Vol. 39, No. 4 (October 1980):680–688.

POLENBERG, RICHARD. *One Nation Divisible: Class, Race, and Ethnicity in the United States Since 1938.* New York: Pelican Books, 1980.

POLLACK, OTTO, and ELLEN S. WISE. *Invitation to a Dialogue: Union and Separation in Family Life.* New York: SP Medical and Scientific Books, 1979.

POLSBY, NELSON W. "Three Problems in the Analysis of Community Power." *American Sociological Review.* Vol. 24, No. 6 (December 1959):796–803.

POMER, MARSHALL I. "Labor Market Structure, Intragenerational Mobility, and Discrimination: Black Male Advancement Out of Low-Paying Occupations, 1962–1973." *American Sociological Review.* Vol. 51, No. 5 (October 1986):650–659.

PORTES, ALEJANDRO. "The Rise of Ethnicity: Determinants of Ethnic Perceptions Among Cuban Exiles in Miami." *American Sociological Review.* Vol. 49, No. 3 (June 1984):383–397.

PORTES, ALEJANDRO, and SASKIA SASSEN-KOOB. "Making It Underground: Comparative Material on the Informal Sector in Western Market Economies." *American Journal of Sociology.* Vol. 93, No. 1 (July 1987):30–61.

PREMACK, DAVID. *Intelligence in Ape and Man.* Hillsdale, NJ: Lawrence Erlbaum Associates, 1976.

PRESIDENT'S COMMISSION FOR THE STUDY OF ETHICAL PROBLEMS IN MEDICINE AND BIOMEDICAL AND BEHAVIORAL RESEARCH. *Deciding to Forego Life-Sustaining Treatment.* Washington, DC: U.S. Government Printing Office, 1983.

PRYOR, FREDERIC L. *A Guidebook to the Comparative Study of Economic Systems.* Englewood Cliffs, NJ: Prentice-Hall, 1985.

QUINNEY, RICHARD. *Class, State and Crime: On the Theory and Practice of Criminal Justice.* New York: David McKay, 1977.

RADIN, NORMA. "Primary Caregiving and Role-Sharing Fathers." In Michael E. Lamb, ed., *Nontraditional Families: Parenting and Child Development.* Hillsdale, NJ: Lawrence Erlbaum Associates, 1982:173–204.

RAINWATER, LEE, and WILLIAM L. YANCEY. *The Moynihan Report and the Politics of Controversy.* Cambridge, MA: M.I.T. Press, 1967.

RAKOWSKA-HARMSTONE, TERESA. "Eastern European Communism in the Seventies." In Morton A. Kaplan, ed., *The Many Faces of Communism.* New York: Free Press, 1978:194–227.

RANDALL, VICKI. *Women and Politics.* London: Macmillan Press, 1982.

RECKLESS, WALTER C. "Containment Theory." In Marvin E. Wolfgang, Leonard Savitz, and Norman Johnstone, eds., *The Sociology of Crime and Delinquency.* 2nd ed. New York: John Wiley, 1970:401–405.

RECKLESS, WALTER C., and SIMON DINITZ. "Pioneering with Self-Concept as a Vulnerability Factor in Delinquency." *Journal of Criminal Law, Criminology, and Police Science.* Vol. 58, No. 4 (December 1967):515–523.

REED, RODNEY J. "Administrator's Advice: Causes and Remedies of School Conflict and Violence." *National Association of Secondary School Principals Bulletin.* Vol. 67, No. 462 (April 1983):75–79.

REID, SUE TITUS. *Crime and Criminology.* 3rd ed. New York: Holt, Reinhart and Winston, 1982.

REIMAN, JEFFREY H. *The Rich Get Richer and the Poor Get Prison: Ideology, Class, and Criminal Justice.* 2nd ed. New York: John Wiley & Sons, 1984.

REIMERS, CORDELIA W. "Sources of the Family Income Differentials Among Hispanics, Blacks, and White Non-Hispanics." *American Journal of Sociology.* Vol. 89, No. 4 (January 1984):889–903.

REMOFF, HEATHER TREXLER. *Sexual Choice: A Woman's Decision.* New York: Dutton/Lewis, 1984.

RIDGEWAY, CECILIA L. *The Dynamics of Small Groups.* New York: St. Martin's Press, 1983.

RIEGEL, KLAUS F. "History of Psychological Gerontology." In James E. Birren and K. Warner Schaie, eds., *Handbook of the Psychology of Aging.* New York: Van Nostrand Reinhold, 1977:70–102.

RIEGLE, DONALD W., JR. "The Psychological and Social Effects of Unemployment." *American Psychologist.* Vol. 37, No. 10 (October 1982):1113–1115.

RIESMAN, DAVID. *The Lonely Crowd: A Study of the Changing American Character.* New Haven, CT: Yale University Press, 1970; orig. 1950.

RITZER, GEORGE. *Man and His Work: Conflict and Change.* New York: Appleton-Century-Crofts, 1972.

RITZER, GEORGE. *Sociological Theory.* New York: Knopf, 1983.

ROBERTS, J. DEOTIS. *Roots of a Black Future: Family and Church.* Philadelphia, PA: The Westminster Press, 1980.

ROESCH, ROBERTA. "Violent Families." *Parents.* Vol. 59, No. 9 (September 1984):74–76, 150–152.

ROETHLISBERGER, F. J., and WILLIAM J. DICKSON. *Management and the Worker.* Cambridge, MA: Harvard University Press, 1939.

ROHLEN, THOMAS P. *Japan's High Schools.* Berkeley, CA: University of California Press, 1983.

ROKOVE, MILTON L. *Don't Make No Waves, Don't Back No Losers.* Bloomington, IN: Indiana University Press, 1975.

ROMAN, MEL, and WILLIAM HADDAD. *The Disposable Parent: The Case for Joint Custody.* New York: Holt, Rinehart and Winston, 1978.

ROOF, WADE CLARK. "Socioeconomic Differentials Among White Socioreligious Groups in the United States." *Social Forces.* Vol. 58, No. 1 (September 1979):280–289.

ROOF, WADE CLARK. "Unresolved Issues in the Study of Religion and the National Elite: Response to Greeley." *Social Forces.* Vol. 59, No. 3 (March 1981):831–836.

Roos, Patricia. "Marriage and Women's Occupational Attainment in Cross-Cultural Perspective." *American Sociological Review.* Vol. 48, No. 6 (December 1983):852–864.

Roper Organization. *The Virginia Slims American Women's Public Opinion Poll.* New York, 1974.

Rose, Arnold M. "The Subculture of the Aging: A Topic for Sociological Research." In Bernice L. Neugarten, ed., *Middle Age and Aging: A Reader in Social Psychology.* Chicago: University of Chicago Press, 1968:29–34.

Rose, Jerry D. *Outbreaks.* New York: Free Press, 1982.

Rosenbaum, James E. "Track Misperceptions and Frustrated College Plans: An Analysis of the Effects of Tracks and Track Perceptions in the National Longitudinal Survey." *Sociology of Education.* Vol. 35, No. 2 (April 1980):74–88.

Rosenthal, Jack. "The Rapid Growth of Suburban Employment." In Lois H. Masotti and Jeffrey K. Hadden, eds., *Suburbia in Transition.* New York: New York Times Books, 1974:95–100.

Roskin, Michael G. *Countries and Concepts: An Introduction to Comparative Politics.* Englewood Cliffs, NJ: Prentice-Hall, 1982.

Rosnow, Ralph L., and Gary Alan Fine. *Rumor and Gossip: The Social Psychology of Hearsay.* New York: Elsevier, 1976.

Ross, Catherine E., John Mirowsky, and Joan Huber. "Dividing Work, Sharing Work, and In-Between: Marriage Patterns and Depression." *American Sociological Review.* Vol. 48, No. 6 (December 1983):809–823.

Ross, Susan. "Education: A Step Ladder to Mobility." *Popline.* Vol. 7, No. 7 (July 1985):1–2.

Rossides, Daniel W. *The American Class System.* Boston, MA: Houghton Mifflin, 1976.

Rostow, Walt W. *The World Economy: History and Prospect.* Austin, TX: University of Texas Press, 1978.

Rowe, David C. "Biometrical Genetic Models of Self-Reported Delinquent Behavior: A Twin Study." *Behavior Genetics.* Vol. 13, No. 5 (1983):473–489.

Rowe, David C., and D. Wayne Osgood. "Heredity and Sociological Theories of Delinquency: A Reconsideration." *American Sociological Review.* Vol. 49, No. 4 (August 1984):526–540.

Rubin, Beth A. "Class Struggle American Style: Unions, Strikes and Wages." *American Sociological Review.* Vol. 51, No. 5 (October 1986):618–631.

Rubin, Lillian B. *Intimate Strangers: Men and Women Together.* New York: Harper & Row, 1983.

Rubin, Lillian Breslow. *Worlds of Pain: Life in the Working-Class Family.* New York: Basic Books, 1976.

Rubinson, Richard. "Class Formation, Politics, and Institutions: Schooling in the United States." *American Journal of Sociology.* Vol. 92, No. 3 (November 1986):519–548.

Rudé, George. *The Crowd in History: A Study of Popular Disturbances in France and England, 1730–1848.* New York: John Wiley & Sons, 1964.

Rudolph, Barbara. "Tobacco Takes a New Road." *Time.* Vol. 126, No. 20 (November 18, 1985):70–71.

Rumberger, Russell. *Overeducation in the U.S. Labor Market.* New York: Praeger, 1981.

Russell, Diana E. H. *Rape in Marriage.* New York: Macmillan, 1982.

Russell, Don. "Atlantic City's Unwed Mothers." *The Sun.* Vol. 6, No. 98 (September 5, 1984):1, 4.

Russell, George. "The Fall of a Wall Street Superstar." *Time.* Vol. 128, No. 21 (November 24, 1986):71, 74.

Russell, George. "People, People, People." In *Time.* Vol. 124, No. 6 (August 6, 1984):24–25.

Ryan, William. *Blaming the Victim.* Rev. ed. New York: Vintage, 1976.

Rytina, Joan Huber, William H. Form, and John Pease. "Income and Stratification Ideology: Beliefs About the American Opportunity Structure." *American Journal of Sociology.* Vol. 75, No. 4 (January 1970):703–716.

Sabato, Larry J. *PAC Power: Inside the World of Political Action Committees.* New York: Norton, 1984.

Sacks, Howard L. Letter to the author, 1986.

Sagan, Carl. *The Dragons of Eden.* New York: Ballantine, 1977.

Salas, Rafael M. "The State of World Population 1985: Population and Women." *Popline.* Vol. 7, No. 7 (July 1985):4–5.

Saline, Carol. "Bleeding in the Suburbs." *Philadelphia.* Vol. 75, No. 3 (March 1984):81–85, 144–151.

Sampson, Anthony. *The Changing Anatomy of Britain.* New York: Random House, 1982.

Sampson, Robert J. "Urban Black Violence: The Effects of Male Joblessness and Family Disruption." *American Journal of Sociology.* Vol. 93, No. 2 (September 1987):348–382.

Sapir, Edward. *Selected Writings of Edward Sapir in Language, Culture, and Personality.* David G. Mandelbaum, ed. Berkeley: University of California Press, 1949.

Sapir, Edward. "The Status of Linguistics as a Science." *Language.* Vol. 5 (1929):207–214.

Saunders, Janice Miller, and John N. Edwards. "Extramarital Sexuality: A Predictive Model of Permissive Attitudes." *Journal of Marriage and the Family.* Vol. 46, No. 4 (November 1984):825–835.

Scaff, Lawrence A. "Max Weber and Robert Michels." *American Journal of Sociology.* Vol. 86, No. 6 (May 1981):1269–1286.

Schaefer, Richard T. *Racial and Ethnic Groups.* Boston: Little, Brown, 1979.

Schaie, K. Warner. "Intelligence and Problem Solving." In James E. Birren and R. Bruce Sloane, eds., *Handbook of Mental Health and Aging.* Englewood Cliffs, NJ: Prentice-Hall, 1980:262–284.

Scheff, Thomas J. *Being Mentally Ill: A Sociological Theory.* 2nd ed. New York: Aldine, 1984.

Schell, Orville. "A Reporter At Large: The Wind of Wanting To Go It Alone." *The New Yorker.* Vol. 59, No. 49 (January 23, 1984):43–85.

Schlafly, Phyllis. "Mothers, Stay Home; Your Kids Need You." *USA Today* (May 30, 1984):10A.

Schlesinger, Arthur. "The City in American Civilization." In A. B. Callow, Jr., ed., *American Urban History.* New York: Oxford University Press, 1969:25–41.

Schmidt, Roger. *Exploring Religion.* Belmont, CA: Wadsworth, 1980.

Schooler, Carmi, Joanne Miller, Karen A. Miller, and Carol N. Richtand. "Work for the Household: Its Nature and Consequences for Husbands and Wives." *American Journal of Sociology.* Vol. 90, No. 1 (July 1984):97–124.

Schrag, Peter. *Out of Place in America.* New York: Random House, 1969.

Schreiner, Tim. "A Revolution That Has Just Begun." *USA Today* (May 29, 1984):4D.

Schreiner, Tim. "Your Cost to Bring Up Baby: $142,700." *USA Today* (October 19, 1984):1D.

Schumann, Hans Wolfgang. *Buddhism: An Outline of Its Teachings and Schools.* Wheaton, IL: The Theosophical Publishing House, Quest Books, 1974.

Schur, Edwin M. *Labeling Women Deviant: Gender, Stigma, and Social Control.* Philadelphia: Temple University Press, 1983.

SCHWARTZ-NOBEL, LORETTA. *Starving in the Shadow of Plenty.* New York: McGraw-Hill, 1981.

SCOTT, JOHN, and CATHERINE GRIFF. *Directors of Industry: The British Corporate Network, 1904–1976.* New York: Blackwell, 1985.

SCOTT, W. RICHARD. *Organizations: Rational, Natural, and Open Systems.* Englewood Cliffs, NJ: Prentice-Hall, 1981.

SELLIN, THORSTEN. *The Penalty of Death.* Beverly Hills, CA: Sage Publications, 1980.

SELTZER, ROBERT M. *Jewish People, Jewish Thought: The Jewish Experience in History.* New York: Macmillan, 1980.

SEN, K. M. *Hinduism.* Baltimore, MD: Penguin, 1961.

SENGOKU, TAMOTSU. *Willing Workers: The Work Ethics in Japan, England, and the United States.* Westport, CT: Quorum Books, 1985.

SENNETT, RICHARD, and JONATHAN COBB. *The Hidden Injuries of Class.* New York: Vintage, 1973.

SHANAS, ETHEL. "Social Myth as Hypothesis: The Case of the Family Relations of Old People." *The Gerontologist.* Vol. 19, No. 1 (February 1979):3–9.

SHAW, CLIFFORD R., and HENRY D. McKAY. *Juvenile Delinquency in Urban Areas.* Chicago: University of Chicago Press, 1972; orig. 1942.

SHAWCROSS, WILLIAM. *Sideshow: Kissinger, Nixon and the Destruction of Cambodia.* New York: Pocket Books, 1979.

SHEEHAN, TOM. "Senior Esteem as a Factor in Socioeconomic Complexity." *The Gerontologist.* Vol. 16, No. 5 (October 1976):433–440.

SHEEHY, GAIL. *Passages: Predictable Crises of Adult Life.* New York: E. P. Dutton, 1976.

SHELDON, WILLIAM H., EMIL M. HARTL, and EUGENE McDERMOTT. *Varieties of Delinquent Youth.* New York: Harper, 1949.

SHELER, JEFFERY L. "Lobbyists Go for It." *U.S. News & World Report.* Vol. 98, No. 23 (June 17, 1985):30–34.

SHEPHARD, ROY J. *The Risks of Passive Smoking.* London: Croom Helm, 1982.

SHERRID, PAMELA. "Hot Times in the City of London." *U.S. News & World Report* (October 27, 1986):45–46.

SHEVKY, ESHREF, and WENDELL BELL. *Social Area Analysis.* Stanford, CA: Stanford University Press, 1955.

SHIBUTANI, TAMOTSU. *Improvised News: A Sociological Study of Rumor.* Indianapolis, IN: Bobbs-Merrill, 1966.

SHIPLER, DAVID K. *Russia: Broken Idols, Solemn Dreams.* New York: Penguin Books, 1984.

SIDEL, RUTH, and VICTOR W. SIDEL. *The Health Care of China.* Boston, MA: Beacon Press, 1982b.

SIDEL, VICTOR W., and RUTH SIDEL. *A Healthy State: An International Perspective on the Crisis in United States Medical Care.* Rev. ed. New York: Pantheon, 1982a.

SILBERMAN, CHARLES E. "Race, Culture, and Crime." In Delos H. Kelly, ed. *Criminal Behavior: Readings in Criminology.* New York: St. Martin's Press, 1980:103–111.

SILLS, DAVID L. "The Succession of Goals." In Amitai Etzioni, ed., *A Sociological Reader on Complex Organizations.* 2nd ed. New York: Holt, Rinehart and Winston, 1969:175–187.

SIMMEL, GEORG. "Fashion." In Donald N. Levine, ed., *Georg Simmel: On Individuality and Social Forms.* Chicago: University of Chicago Press, 1971; orig. 1904.

SIMMEL, GEORG. "The Mental Life of the Metropolis." In Kurt Wolff, ed., *The Sociology of Georg Simmel.* New York: Free Press, 1964:409–424; orig. 1905.

SIMMEL, GEORG. *The Sociology of Georg Simmel.* Kurt Wolff, ed., New York: Free Press, 1950:118–169.

SIMON, CARL P., and ANN D. WITTE. *Beating the System: The Underground Economy.* Boston, MA: Auburn House, 1982.

SIMON, DAVID R., and D. STANLEY EITZEN. *Elite Deviance.* Boston, MA: Allyn & Bacon, 1982; also 2nd ed., 1986.

SIMPSON, GEORGE EATON, and J. MILTON YINGER. *Racial and Cultural Minorities: An Analysis of Prejudice and Discrimination.* 4th ed. New York: Harper & Row, 1972.

SINGER, DOROTHY. "A Time to Reexamine the Role of Television in Our Lives." *American Psychologist.* Vol. 38, No. 7 (July 1983):815–816.

SINGER, JEROME L., and DOROTHY G. SINGER. "Psychologists Look at Television: Cognitive, Developmental, Personality, and Social Policy Implications." *American Psychologist.* Vol. 38, No. 1 (July 1983):826–834.

SIPES, RICHARD G. "War, Sports and Aggression: An Empirical Test of Two Rival Theories." *American Anthropologist.* Vol. 75, No. 1 (January 1973):64–86.

SIZER, THEODORE R. *Horace's Compromise: The Dilemma of the American High School.* Boston, MA: Houghton Mifflin, 1984.

SJOBERG, GIDEON. *The Preindustrial City.* New York: Free Press, 1965.

SKOCPOL, THEDA. *States and Social Revolutions: A Comparative Analysis of France, Russia, and China.* Cambridge (UK): Cambridge University Press, 1979.

SKOLNICK, ARLENE. *The Psychology of Human Development.* New York: Harcourt Brace Jovanovich, 1986.

SLATER, PHILIP E. "Contrasting Correlates of Group Size." *Sociometry.* Vol. 21, No. 2 (June 1958):129–139.

SLATER, PHILIP. *The Pursuit of Loneliness.* Boston, MA: Beacon Press, 1976.

SMART, NINIAN. *The Religious Experience of Mankind.* New York: Charles Scribner's Sons, 1969.

SMELSER, NEIL J. *Theory of Collective Behavior.* New York: Free Press, 1962.

SMILGAS, MARTHA. "The Big Chill: Fear of AIDS." *Time.* Vol. 129, No. 7 (February 16, 1987):50–53.

SMITH, ADAM. *An Inquiry into the Nature and Causes of The Wealth of Nations.* New York: The Modern Library, 1937; orig. 1776.

SMITH, DOUGLAS A., and CHRISTY A. VISHER. "Street-Level Justice: Situational Determinants of Police Arrest Decisions." *Social Problems.* Vol. 29, No. 2 (December 1981):167–177.

SMITH, RICHARD AUSTIN. "The Incredible Electrical Conspiracy." In Marvin E. Wolfgang et al., eds., *The Sociology of Crime and Delinquency.* 2nd ed. New York: John Wiley and Sons, 1970:529–548.

SMITH, ROBERT ELLIS. *Privacy: How to Protect What's Left of It.* Garden City, NY: Anchor Press/Doubleday, 1979.

SMITH-ROSENBERG, CAROL, and CHARLES ROSENBERG. "The Female Animal: Medical and Biological Views of Woman and Her Role in Nineteenth Century America." In Judith Walzer Leavitt, ed., *Women and Health in America.* Madison, WI: University of Wisconsin Press, 1984:12–27.

SNOW, DAVID A., E. BURKE ROCHFORD, JR., STEVEN K. WORDEN, and ROBERT D. BENFORD. "Frame Alignment Processes, Micromobilization, and Movement Participation." *American Sociological Review.* Vol. 51, No. 4 (August 1986):464–481.

SNOW, DAVID A., LOUIS A. ZURCHER, JR., and SHELDON EKLAND-OLSON. "Social Networks and Social Movements: A Macrostructural Approach to Differential Recruitment." *American Sociological Review.* Vol. 45, No. 5 (October 1980):787–801.

SNOWMAN, DANIEL. *Britain and America: An Interpretation of Their Culture 1945–1975.* New York: Harper Torchbooks, 1977.

SOLDO, BETH J. "America's Elderly in the 1980s." *Population Bulle-*

tin. Vol. 35, No. 4 (November 1980), Population Reference Bureau.

SOWELL, THOMAS. *Ethnic America*. New York: Basic Books, 1981.

SPATES, JAMES L. "Counterculture and Dominant Culture Values: A Cross-National Analysis of the Underground Press and Dominant Culture Magazines." *American Sociological Review*. Vol. 41, No. 5 (October 1976b):868–883.

SPATES, JAMES L. "Sociological Overview." In Alan Milberg, ed., *Street Games*. New York: McGraw-Hill, 1976a:286–290.

SPATES, JAMES L. "The Sociology of Values." In Ralph Turner, ed., *Annual Review of Sociology*. Vol. 9. Palo Alto, CA: Annual Reviews, 1983:27–49.

SPATES, JAMES L., and JOHN J. MACIONIS. *The Sociology of Cities*. 2nd ed. Belmont, CA: Wadsworth, 1987.

SPATES, JAMES L., and H. WESLEY PERKINS. "American and English Student Values." *Comparative Social Research*. Vol. 5. Greenwich, CT: Jai Press, 1982:245–268.

SPEER, JAMES A. "The New Christian Right and Its Parent Company: A Study in Political Contrasts." In David G. Bromley and Anson Shupe, eds., *New Christian Politics*. Macon, GA: Mercer University Press, 1984:19–40.

SPEIZER, JEANNE J. "Education." In Barbara Haber, ed., *The Women's Annual 1982–1983*. Boston: G. K. Hall, 1983:29–54.

SPENDER, DALE. *Man Made Language*. London: Routledge & Kegan Paul, 1980.

SPITZER, STEVEN. "Toward a Marxian Theory of Deviance." In Delos H. Kelly, ed., *Criminal Behavior: Readings in Criminology*. New York: St. Martin's Press, 1980:175–191.

SRINIVAS, M. N. *Social Change in Modern India*. Berkeley, CA: University of California Press, 1971.

STACEY, JUDITH. *Patriarchy and Socialist Revolution in China*. Berkeley: University of California Press, 1983.

STACK, CAROL B. *All Our Kin: Strategies for Survival in a Black Community*. New York: Harper & Row, 1975.

STACK, STEVEN. "Publicized Executions and Homicide, 1950–1980." *American Sociological Review*. Vol. 52, No. 4 (August 1987):532–540.

STAHURA, JOHN M. "Determinants of Change in the Distribution of Blacks Across Suburbs." *Sociological Quarterly*. Vol. 24, No. 3 (Summer 1983):421–433.

STAHURA, JOHN M. "Suburban Development, Black Suburbanization and the Black Civil Rights Movement Since World War II." *American Sociological Review*. Vol. 51, No. 1 (February 1986):131–144.

STAPLES, BRENT. "Where Are the Black Fans?" *New York Times Magazine* (May 17, 1987):26–34, 56.

STARK, EVAN, and ANN FLITCRAFT. "Domestic Violence and Female Suicide Attempts." Presentation to American Public Health Association, New York, 1979.

STARK, RODNEY. "The Rise of a New World Faith." *Review of Religious Research*. Vol. 26, No. 1 (September 1984):18–27.

STARK, RODNEY, and WILLIAM SIMS BAINBRIDGE. "Of Churches, Sects, and Cults: Preliminary Concepts for a Theory of Religious Movements." *Journal for the Scientific Study of Religion*. Vol. 18, No. 2 (June 1979):117–131.

STARK, RODNEY, and WILLIAM SIMS BAINBRIDGE. "Secularization and Cult Formation in the Jazz Age." *Journal for the Scientific Study of Religion*. Vol. 20, No. 4 (December 1981):360–373.

STARK, RODNEY, and CHARLES Y. GLOCK. *American Piety: The Nature of Religious Commitment*. Berkeley, CA: University of California Press, 1968.

STARR, PAUL. *The Social Transformation of American Medicine*. New York: Basic Books, 1982.

STAVRIANOS, L. S. *A Global History: The Human Heritage*. 3rd ed. Englewood Cliffs, NJ: Prentice-Hall, 1983.

STEIN, MAURICE R. *The Eclipse of Community: An Interpretation of American Studies*. Princeton, NJ: Princeton University Press, 1972.

STEPHENS, JOHN D. *The Transition from Capitalism to Socialism*. Urbana, IL: University of Illinois Press, 1986.

STERNLIEB, GEORGE, and JAMES W. HUGHES. "The Uncertain Future of the Central City." *Urban Affairs Quarterly*. Vol. 18, No. 4 (June 1983):455–472.

STEVENS, GILLIAN, and GRAY SWICEGOOD. "The Linguistic Context of Ethnic Endogamy." *American Sociological Review*. Vol. 52, No. 1 (February 1987):73–82.

STEVENS, ROSEMARY. *American Medicine and the Public Interest*. New Haven, CT: Yale University Press, 1971.

STOCKWELL, EDWARD G., DAVID A. SWANSON, and JERRY W. WICKS. "Trends in the Relationship Between Infant Mortality and Socioeconomic Status." *Sociological Focus*. Vol. 20, No. 4 (October 1987):319–327.

STODDARD, SANDOL. *The Hospice Movement: A Better Way to Care for the Dying*. Briarcliff Manor, NY: Stein and Day, 1978.

STOHL, MICHAEL, and GEORGE A. LOPEZ, eds. *The State as Terrorist: The Dynamics of Governmental Violence and Repression*. Westport, CT: Greenwood Press, 1984.

STONE, LAWRENCE. *The Family, Sex and Marriage in England 1500–1800*. New York: Harper & Row, 1977.

STORCK, DOROTHY. "Neighborhood with No Pride." *The Philadelphia Inquirer* (November 24, 1985):B–1.

STOUFFER, SAMUEL A., et al. *The American Soldier: Adjustment During Army Life*. Princeton, NJ: Princeton University Press, 1949.

STRAUS, MURRAY. "Wife-Beating: How Common and Why?" In Murray A. Straus and Gerald T. Hotaling, eds., *The Social Causes of Husband-Wife Violence*. Minneapolis: University of Minnesota Press, 1980:23–36.

STREIB, GORDON F. "Are the Aged a Minority Group?" In Bernice L. Neugarten, ed., *Middle Age and Aging: A Reader in Social Psychology*. Chicago: University of Chicago Press, 1968:35–46.

SUDNOW, DAVID N. *Passing On: The Social Organization of Dying*. Englewood Cliffs, NJ: Prentice-Hall, 1967.

SUMNER, WILLIAM GRAHAM. *Folkways*. New York: Dover, 1959; orig. 1906.

SUNG, BETTY LEE. *Mountains of Gold: The Story of the Chinese in America*. New York: Macmillan, 1967.

SUTHERLAND, EDWIN H. "White Collar Criminality." *American Sociological Review*. Vol. 5, No. 1 (February 1940):1–12.

SUTHERLAND, EDWIN H., and DONALD R. CRESSEY. *Criminology*. 3rd ed. Philadelphia: J. B. Lippincott, 1930; 8th ed. 1970; 10th ed. 1978.

SWEET, ELLEN. "Date Rape: The Story of an Epidemic and Those Who Deny It." *Ms./Campus Times* (October 1985):56–59, 84–85.

SYZMANSKI, ALBERT. *Class Structure: A Critical Perspective*. New York: Praeger, 1983.

SYZMANSKI, ALBERT. *The Logic of Imperialism*. New York: Praeger, 1981.

SZASZ, THOMAS S. *The Manufacture of Madness: A Comparative Study of the Inquisition and the Mental Health Movement*. New York: Dell, 1961.

SZASZ, THOMAS S. *The Myth of Mental Illness: Foundations of a Theory of Personal Conduct*. New York: Harper & Row, 1970; orig. 1961.

TAEUBER, KARL, and ALMA TAEUBER. *Negroes in Cities*. Chicago: Aldine, 1965.

TAJFEL, HENRI. "Social Psychology of Intergroup Relations." *Annual Review of Psychology*. Palo Alto, CA: Annual Reviews, 1982:1–39.

TANNENBAUM, FRANK. *Slave and Citizen: The Negro in the Americas*. New York: Vintage Books, 1946.

TAVRIS, CAROL, and SUSAN SADD. *The Redbook Report on Female Sexuality*. New York: Delacorte Press, 1977.

TAVRIS, CAROL, and CAROLE WADE. *The Longest War: Sex Differences in Perspective*. 2nd ed. New York: Harcourt Brace Jovanovich, 1984.

THEEN, ROLF H. W. "Party and Bureaucracy." In Erik P. Hoffmann and Robbin F. Laird, eds., *The Soviet Polity in the Modern Era*. New York: Aldine, 1984:131–165.

THEODORSON, GEORGE A., and ACHILLES G. THEODORSON. *A Modern Dictionary of Sociology*. New York: Barnes and Noble Books, 1969.

THIO, ALEX. *Deviant Behavior*. 2nd ed. Boston: Houghton Mifflin, 1983.

THOITS, PEGGY A. "Self-labeling Processes in Mental Illness: The Role of Emotional Deviance." *American Journal of Sociology*. Vol. 91, No. 2 (September 1985):221–249.

THOMAS, EDWARD J. *The Life of Buddha as Legend and History*. London: Routledge & Kegan Paul, 1975.

THOMAS, EVAN. "Every Region, Every Age Group, Almost Every Voting Bloc." *Time*. Vol. 124, No. 21 (November 19, 1984):42, 45.

THOMAS, MELVIN E., and MICHAEL HUGHES. "The Continuing Significance of Race: A Study of Race, Class, and Quality of Life in America, 1972–1985." *American Sociological Review*. Vol. 51, No. 6 (December 1986):830–841.

THOMAS, W. I. "The Relation of Research to the Social Process." In Morris Janowitz, ed., *W. I. Thomas on Social Organization and Social Personality*. Chicago: University of Chicago Press, 1966:289–305; orig. 1931.

THOMPSON, ANTHONY PETER. "Emotional and Sexual Components of Extramarital Relations." *Journal of Marriage and the Family*. Vol. 46, No. 1 (February 1984):35–42.

THORNBERRY, TERRANCE, and MARGARET FARNSWORTH. "Social Correlates of Criminal Involvement: Further Evidence on the Relationship Between Social Status and Criminal Behavior." *American Sociological Review*. Vol. 47, No. 4 (August 1982):505–518.

THORNTON, ARLAND. "Changing Attitudes Toward Separation and Divorce: Causes and Consequences." *American Journal of Sociology*. Vol. 90, No. 4 (January 1985):856–872.

THUROW, LESTER C. "A Surge in Inequality." *Scientific American*. Vol. 256, No. 5 (May 1987):30–37.

TIBBITTS, CLARK. "Can We Invalidate Negative Stereotypes of Aging?" *The Gerontologist*. Vol. 19, No. 1 (February 1979):10–20.

TIENDA, MARTA, and DING-TZANN LII. "Minority Concentration and Earnings Inequality: Blacks, Hispanics, and Asians Compared." *American Journal of Sociology*. Vol. 93, No. 1 (July 1987):141–165.

TIGER, LIONEL, and JOSEPH SHEPHER. *Women in the Kibbutz*. New York: Harcourt Brace Jovanovich, 1975.

TILLY, CHARLES. "Does Modernization Breed Revolution?" In Jack A. Goldstone, ed. *Revolutions: Theoretical, Comparative, and Historical Studies*. New York: Harcourt Brace Jovanovich, 1986:47–57.

TILLY, CHARLES. *From Mobilization to Revolution*. Reading, MA: Addison-Wesley, 1978.

TILLY, CHARLES, LOUISE TILLY, and RICHARD TILLY. *The Rebellious Century, 1830–1930*. Cambridge, MA: Harvard University Press, 1975.

TIME. "The Crime That Tarnished a Town." Vol. 123, No. 10 (March 5, 1984):19.

TIME. "Sudden Exposure: Lyndon LaRouche Explains It All." Vol. 127, No. 16 (April 21, 1986):32.

TITTLE, CHARLES R., and WAYNE J. VILLEMEZ. "Social Class and Criminality." *Social Forces*. Vol. 56, No. 22 (December 1977):474–502.

TITTLE, CHARLES R., WAYNE J. VILLEMEZ, and DOUGLAS A. SMITH. "The Myth of Social Class and Criminality: An Empirical Assessment of the Empirical Evidence." *American Sociological Review*. Vol. 43, No. 5 (October 1978):643–656.

TOBIN, GARY A. "Suburbanization and the Development of Motor Transportation: Transportation Technology and the Suburbanization Process." In Barry Schwartz, ed., *The Changing Face of the Suburbs*. Chicago: University of Chicago Press, 1976.

TOCQUEVILLE, ALEXIS DE. *Democracy in America*. Garden City, NY: Doubleday Anchor Books, 1969; orig. 1834–1840.

TOCQUEVILLE, ALEXIS DE. *The Old Regime and the French Revolution*. Stuart Gilbert, trans. Garden City, NY: Doubleday Anchor Books, 1955; orig. 1856.

TOENNIES, FERDINAND. *Community and Society*. New York: Harper & Row, 1963; orig. 1887.

TOFFLER, ALVIN. *The Third Wave*. New York: Bantam Books, 1981.

TOMIAK, JANUSZ. "Introduction." In J. J. Tomiak, ed., *Soviet Education in the 1980s*. London: Croom Helm, 1983:vii–x.

TREAS, JUDITH. "Socialist Organization and Economic Development in China: Latent Consequences for the Aged." *The Gerontologist*. Vol. 19, No. 1 (February 1979):34–43.

TREIMAN, DONALD J. "Industrialization and Social Stratification." In Edward O. Laumann, ed., *Social Stratification: Research and Theory for the 1970s*. Indianapolis: Bobbs-Merrill, 1970.

TROELTSCH, ERNST. *The Social Teaching of the Christian Churches*. New York: Macmillan, 1931.

TUMIN, MELVIN M. *Social Stratification: The Forms and Functions of Inequality*. 2nd ed. Englewood Cliffs, NJ: Prentice-Hall, 1985.

TUMIN, MELVIN M. "Some Principles of Stratification: A Critical Analysis." *American Sociological Review*. Vol. 18, No. 4 (August 1953):387–394.

TURNER, RALPH H., and LEWIS M. KILLIAN. *Collective Behavior*. 3rd ed. Englewood Cliffs, NJ: Prentice-Hall, 1987.

TYGIEL, JULES. *Baseball's Great Experiment: Jackie Robinson and His Legacy*. New York: Oxford University Press, 1983.

TYLER, S. LYMAN. *A History of Indian Policy*. Washington, DC: United States Department of the Interior, Bureau of Indian Affairs, 1973.

TYREE, ANDREA, MOSHE SEMYONOV, and ROBERT W. HODGE. "Gaps and Glissandos: Inequality, Economic Development, and Social Mobility in 24 Countries." *American Sociological Review*. Vol. 44, No. 3 (June 1979):410–424.

UHLENBERG, PETER. "Older Women: The Growing Challenge to Design Constructive Roles." *The Gerontologist*. Vol. 19, No. 3 (June 1979):236–241.

UNITED NATIONS. *Demographic Yearbook 1983*. New York: United Nations, 1983.

UNNEVER, JAMES D., CHARLES E. FRAZIER, and JOHN C. HENRETTA. "Race Differences in Criminal Sentencing." *The Sociological Quarterly*. Vol. 21, No. 2 (Spring 1980):197–205.

UNRUH, JOHN D., JR. *The Plains Across*. Urbana: University of Illinois Press, 1979.

U.S. BUREAU OF THE CENSUS. *Fertility of American Women: June 1986*. P-20, No. 421. Washington, DC: U.S. Government Printing Office, 1987a.

U.S. BUREAU OF THE CENSUS. *The Hispanic Population in the United*

States: March 1986 and 1987 (Advance Report). Washington, DC: U.S. Government Printing Office, 1987b.

U.S. BUREAU OF THE CENSUS. *Household and Family Characteristics: March 1985*. P-20, No. 411. Washington, DC: U.S. Government Printing Office, 1986a.

U.S. BUREAU OF THE CENSUS. *Households, Families, Marital Status, and Living Arrangements: March 1987*. P-20, No. 417. Washington, DC: U.S. Government Printing Office, 1987c.

U.S. BUREAU OF THE CENSUS. *Marital Status and Living Arrangements: March 1986*. P-20, No. 418. Washington, DC: U.S. Government Printing Office, 1987d.

U.S. BUREAU OF THE CENSUS. *Money Income and Poverty Status of Families and Persons in the United States: 1985*. Washington, DC: U.S. Government Printing Office, 1986b.

U.S. BUREAU OF THE CENSUS. *Money Income and Poverty Status of Families and Persons in the United States: 1986*. P-60, No. 157. Washington, DC: U.S. Government Printing Office, 1987e.

U.S. BUREAU OF THE CENSUS. *Projections of the Population of the United States by Age, Sex, and Race: 1983 to 2080*. P-25, No. 952. Washington, DC: U.S. Government Printing Office, 1984.

U.S. BUREAU OF THE CENSUS. *Receipt of Selected Noncash Benefits: 1985*. P-60, No. 155. Washington, DC: U.S. Government Printing Office, 1987f.

U.S. BUREAU OF THE CENSUS. *School Enrollment—Social and Economic Characteristics of Students: October 1985*. P-20, No. 409. Washington, DC: U.S. Government Printing Office, 1986c.

U.S. BUREAU OF THE CENSUS. *State and Metropolitan Area Data Book 1986*. Washington, DC: U.S. Government Printing Office, 1986d.

U.S. BUREAU OF THE CENSUS. *Statistical Abstract of the United States 1970*. 91st ed. Washington, DC: U.S. Government Printing Office, 1970.

U.S. BUREAU OF THE CENSUS. *Statistical Abstract of the United States 1985*. 105th ed. Washington, DC: U.S. Government Printing Office, 1985.

U.S. BUREAU OF THE CENSUS. *Statistical Abstract of the United States 1986*. 106th ed. Washington, DC: U.S. Government Printing Office, 1986e.

U.S. BUREAU OF THE CENSUS. *Statistical Abstract of the United States 1987*. 107th ed. Washington, DC: U.S. Government Printing Office, 1987g.

U.S. BUREAU OF THE CENSUS. *United States Population Estimates and Components of Change: 1970 to 1986*. P-25, No. 1006. Washington, DC: U.S. Government Printing Office, 1987h.

U.S. BUREAU OF THE CENSUS. *Voting and Registration in the Election of 1986*. P-20, No. 414. Washington, DC: U.S. Government Printing Office, 1987i.

U.S. BUREAU OF JUSTICE STATISTICS. *Capital Punishment, 1985*. Washington, DC: U.S. Government Printing Office, 1986.

U.S. BUREAU OF LABOR STATISTICS. *Employment and Earnings*. Vol. 34, No. 10 (October 1987). Washington, DC: U.S. Government Printing Office, 1987.

U.S. BUREAU OF LABOR STATISTICS. *Employment and Earnings*. Vol. 35, No. 1 (January 1988). Washington, DC: U.S. Government Printing Office, 1988.

U.S. CENTER FOR DISEASE CONTROL. *Smoking Tobacco and Health: A Fact Book*. Washington, DC: U.S. Government Printing Office, 1987.

U.S. COMMISSION ON CIVIL RIGHTS. *Twenty Years After Brown: The Shadows of the Past*. Washington, DC: U.S. Government Printing Office, 1974.

U.S. DEPARTMENT OF LABOR. *Time of Change: 1983 Handbook on Women Workers*. Bulletin 298. Washington, DC: U.S. Government Printing Office, 1983.

U.S. EDUCATION DEPARTMENT. Center for Statistics. *Digest of Educational Statistics 1985–86*. Washington, DC: U.S. Government Printing Office, 1986.

USEEM, BERT. "Disorganization and the New Mexico Prison Riot of 1980." *American Sociological Review*. Vol. 50, No. 5 (October 1985):677–688.

USEEM, MICHAEL. "Corporations and the Corporate Elite." In Alex Inkeles et al., eds., *Annual Review of Sociology*. Vol. 6. Palo Alto, CA: Annual Reviews, 1980:41–77.

USEEM, MICHAEL. "The Social Organization of the Corporate Business Elite and Participation of Corporate Directors in the Governance of American Institutions." *American Sociological Review*. Vol. 44, No. 4 (August 1979):553–572.

USEEM, MICHAEL, and JEROME KARABEL. "Pathways to Corporate Management." *American Sociological Review*. Vol. 51, No. 2 (April 1986):184–200.

U.S. FEDERAL BUREAU OF INVESTIGATION. *Crime in the United States 1986*. Washington, DC: U.S. Government Printing Office, 1987.

U.S. FEDERAL BUREAU OF PRISONS. *Statistical Report Fiscal Year 1986*. Washington, DC: U.S. Government Printing Office, 1987.

U.S. HOUSE OF REPRESENTATIVES, SELECT COMMITTEE ON CHILDREN, YOUTH, AND FAMILIES. *Abused Children in America: Victims of Official Neglect*. Washington, DC: U.S. Government Printing Office, 1987.

U.S. INTERNAL REVENUE SERVICE. *Statistics of Income Bulletin*. Vol. 6, No. 4 (Spring). Washington, DC: U.S. Government Printing Office, 1987.

U.S. NATIONAL CENTER FOR EDUCATION STATISTICS. *The Condition of Education: 1986 Edition Statistical Report*. Washington, DC: U.S. Government Printing Office, 1987.

U.S. NATIONAL CENTER FOR EDUCATION STATISTICS. *Projections of Education Statistics to 1992–93*. Washington, DC: U.S. Government Printing Office, 1985.

U.S. NATIONAL CENTER FOR HEALTH STATISTICS. *Current Estimates From the National Health Interview Survey United States, 1986*. Vital and Health Statistics, Series 10, No. 164. Washington, DC: U.S. Government Printing Office, 1987a.

U.S. NATIONAL CENTER FOR HEALTH STATISTICS. *Monthly Vital Statistics Reports*. Vol. 36, No. 3 (June 22, 1987b).

VALENTINE, BETTY LOU. *Hustling and Other Hard Work*. New York: Free Press, 1978.

VAN DE KAA, DIRK J. "Europe's Second Demographic Transition." *Population Bulletin*. Vol. 42, No. 1 (March 1987). Washington, DC: Population Reference Bureau.

VAN DEN HAAG, ERNEST, and JOHN P. CONRAD. *The Death Penalty: A Debate*. New York: Plenum Press, 1983.

VANDER ZANDEN, JAMES W. *American Minority Relations*. 4th ed. New York: Alfred A. Knopf, 1983.

VAN VALEY, T. L., W. C. ROOF, and J. E. WILCOX. "Trends in Residential Segregation." *American Journal of Sociology*. Vol. 82, No. 4 (January 1977):826–844.

VATZ, RICHARD E., and LEE S. WEINBERG. *Thomas Szasz: Primary Values and Major Contentions*. Buffalo, NY: Prometheus Books, 1983.

VAUGHAN, MARY KAY. "Multinational Corporations: The World as a Company Town." In Ahamed Idris-Soven et al., eds. *The World as a Company Town: Multinational Corporations and Social Change*. The Hague: Mouton Publishers, 1978:15–35.

VAYDA, EUGENE, and RAISA B. DEBER. "The Canadian Health Care System: An Overview." *Social Science and Medicine*. Vol. 18, No. 3 (1984):191–197.

VEBLEN, THORSTEIN. *The Theory of the Leisure Class.* New York: The New American Library, 1953; orig. 1899.

VIGUERIE, RICHARD A. *The New Right: We're Ready to Lead.* Falls Church, VA: The Viguerie Company, 1981.

VINES, GAIL. "Whose Baby is it Anyway?" *New Scientist.* No. 1515 (July 3, 1986):26–27.

VOGEL, EZRA F. *Japan as Number One: Lessons for America.* Cambridge, MA: Harvard University Press, 1979.

VOGEL, LISE. *Marxism and the Oppression of Women: Toward a Unitary Theory.* New Brunswick, NJ: Rutgers University Press, 1983.

VOLD, GEORGE B., and THOMAS J. BERNARD. *Theoretical Criminology.* 3rd ed. New York: Oxford University Press, 1986.

VON HIRSH, ANDREW. *Past or Future Crimes: Deservedness and Dangerousness in the Sentencing of Criminals.* New Brunswick, NJ: Rutgers University Press, 1986.

VONNEGUT, KURT, JR. "Harrison Bergeron." In *Welcome to the Monkey House.* New York: Delacorte Press/Seymour Lawrence, 1968:7–13; orig. 1961.

WAITE, LINDA J., GUS W. HAGGSTROM, and DAVID E. KANOUSE. "The Consequences of Parenthood for the Marital Stability of Young Adults." *American Sociological Review.* Vol. 50, No. 6 (December 1985):850–857.

WALKER, JACK L. "The Origins and Maintenance of Interest Groups in America." *The American Political Science Review.* Vol. 77, No. 2 (June 1983):390–406.

WALL, THOMAS F. *Medical Ethics: Basic Moral Issues.* Washington, DC: University Press of America, 1980.

WALLERSTEIN, IMMANUEL. *The Capitalist World-Economy.* New York: Cambridge University Press, 1979.

WALLERSTEIN, IMMANUEL. "Crises: The World Economy, The Movements, and the Ideologies." In Albert Bergesen, ed., *Crises in the World-System.* Beverly Hills, CA: Sage Publications, 1983:21–36.

WALLERSTEIN, IMMANUEL. *The Modern World-System: Capitalist Agriculture and the Origins of the European World-Economy in the Sixteenth Century.* New York: Academic Press, 1974.

WALLIS, CLAUDIA. "AIDS: A Growing Threat." *Time.* Vol. 126, No. 6 (August 12, 1985):40–47.

WALLIS, CLAUDIA. "Children Having Children." *Time.* Vol. 126, No. 23 (December 9, 1985):78–82, 84, 87, 89–90.

WALLIS, CLAUDIA. "To Feed or Not to Feed?" *Time.* Vol. 127, No. 13 (March 31, 1986):60.

WALLIS, CLAUDIA. "Hold the Eggs and Butter." *Time.* Vol. 123, No. 13 (March 26, 1984):56–63.

WALLIS, CLAUDIA. "Stress: Can We Cope?" *Time.* Vol. 121, No. 23 (June 6, 1983):48–54.

WARNER, SAM BASS, JR. *Streetcar Suburbs.* Cambridge, MA: Harvard University and M.I.T. Presses, 1962.

WARNER, W. LLOYD, and J. O. LOW. *The Social System of the Modern Factory.* Yankee City Series, Vol. 4. New Haven, CT: Yale University Press, 1947.

WARNER, W. LLOYD, and PAUL S. LUNT. *The Social Life of a Modern Community.* New Haven, CT: Yale University Press, 1941.

WATSON, JOHN B. *Behaviorism.* Rev. ed., New York: W. W. Norton, 1930.

WATSON, RUSSELL. "A Hidden Epidemic." *Newsweek* (May 14, 1984):30–36.

WATTEL, H. "Levittown: A Suburban Community." In William Dobriner, ed., *The Suburban Community.* New York: G. P. Putnam's Sons, 1958:287–313.

WAXMAN, CHAIM I. *The Stigma of Poverty: A Critique of Poverty Theories and Policies.* 2nd ed. New York: Pergamon Press, 1983.

WEBER, ADNA FERRIN. *The Growth of Cities.* New York: Columbia University Press, 1963; orig. 1899.

WEBER, MAX. *Economy and Society.* G. Roth and C. Wittich, eds. Berkeley, CA: University of California Press, 1978.

WEBER, MAX. *General Economic History.* Frank H. Knight, trans. New York: Collier Books, 1961; orig. 1919–1920.

WEBER, MAX. *Max Weber: Essays in Sociology.* H. H. Gerth and C. Wright Mills, eds. and trans., New York: Oxford University Press, 1946.

WEBER, MAX. *The Protestant Ethic and the Spirit of Capitalism.* New York: Charles Scribner's Sons, 1958; orig. 1904–1905.

WECHSLER, D. *The Measurement and Appraisal of Adult Intelligence.* 5th ed. Baltimore, MD: Williams and Wilkins, 1972.

WEINTRAUB, SIDNEY, and STANLEY R. ROSS. *"Temporary" Alien Workers in the United States: Designing Policy from Fact and Opinion.* Boulder, CO: Westview Press, 1982.

WEISNER, THOMAS S., and BERNICE T. EIDUSON. "The Children of the 60s as Parents." *Psychology Today* (January 1986):60–66.

WEITZMAN, LENORE J. *The Divorce Revolution: The Unexpected Social and Economic Consequences for Women and Children in America.* New York: Free Press, 1985.

WEITZMAN, LENORE J., DEBORAH EIFLER, ELIZABETH HODAKA, and CATHERINE ROSS. "Sex-Role Socialization in Picture Books for Preschool Children." *American Journal of Sociology.* Vol. 77, No. 6 (May 1972):1125–1150.

WELCH, KEVIN. "Community Development and Metropolitan Religious Commitment: A Test of Two Competing Models." *Journal for the Scientific Study of Religion.* Vol. 22, No. 2 (June 1983):167–181.

WELLER, JACK M., and E. L. QUARANTELLI. "Neglected Characteristics of Collective Behavior." *American Journal of Sociology.* Vol. 79, No. 3 (November 1973):665–685.

WELLFORD, CHARLES. "Labeling Theory and Criminology: An Assessment." In Delos H. Kelly, ed., *Criminal Behavior: Readings in Criminology.* New York: St. Martin's Press, 1980:234–247.

WELLMAN, BARRY. "The Community Question: Intimate Networks of East Yorkers." *American Journal of Sociology.* Vol. 84, No. 5 (March 1979):1201–1231.

WELLS, RICHARD H., and J. STEVEN PICOU. *American Sociology: Theoretical and Methodical Structure.* Washington, DC: University Press of America, 1981.

WENKE, ROBERT J. *Patterns of Prehistory.* New York: Oxford University Press, 1980.

WESTOFF, CHARLES F., and ELISE F. JONES. "The Secularization of U.S. Catholic Birth Control Practices." *Family Planning Perspective.* Vol. X, No. 5 (Sept./Oct. 1977):203–207.

WHEELIS, ALLEN. *The Quest for Identity.* New York: W. W. Norton, 1958.

WHITAKER, MARK. "Ten Ways to Fight Terrorism." *Newsweek* (July 1, 1985):26–29.

WHITE, RALPH, and RONALD LIPPITT. "Leader Behavior and Member Reaction in Three 'Social Climates.'" In Dorwin Cartwright and Alvin Zander, eds., *Group Dynamics.* Evanston, IL: Row, Peterson, 1953:586–611.

WHITE, WALTER. *Rope and Faggot.* New York: Arno Press and The New York Times, 1969; orig. 1929.

WHORF, BENJAMIN LEE. "The Relation of Habitual Thought and Behavior to Language." In *Language, Thought, and Reality.* Cambridge: The Technology Press of M.I.T./New York: Wiley, 1956:134–159; orig. 1941.

WHYTE, WILLIAM FOOTE. *Street Corner Society*. 3rd ed. Chicago: University of Chicago Press, 1981; orig. 1943.

WHYTE, WILLIAM H., JR. *The Organization Man*. Garden City, NY: Anchor, 1957.

WILLIAMS, ROBIN M., JR. *American Society: A Sociological Interpretation*. 3rd ed. New York: Alfred A. Knopf, 1970.

WILSON, ALAN B. "Residential Segregation of Social Classes and Aspirations of High School Boys." *American Sociological Review*. Vol. 24, No. 6 (December 1959):836–845.

WILSON, BRYAN. *Religion in Sociological Perspective*. New York: Oxford University Press, 1982.

WILSON, CLINTY C., II, and FÉLIX GUTIÉRREZ. *Minorities and Media: Diversity and the End of Mass Communication*. Beverly Hills, CA: Sage Publications, 1985.

WILSON, EDWARD O. *On Human Nature*. New York: Bantam Books, 1978.

WILSON, EDWARD O. *Sociobiology: The New Synthesis*. Cambridge, MA: Belknap Press of the Harvard University Press, 1975.

WILSON, JAMES Q., and RICHARD J. HERRNSTEIN. *Crime and Human Nature*. New York: Simon and Schuster, 1985.

WILSON, JOHN. *Religion in American Society: The Effective Presence*. Englewood Cliffs, NJ: Prentice-Hall, 1978.

WILSON, LOGAN. *American Academics Then and Now*. New York: Oxford University Press, 1979.

WILSON, THOMAS C. "Urbanism and Tolerance: A Test of Some Hypotheses Drawn from Wirth and Stouffer." *American Sociological Review*. Vol. 50, No. 1 (Feb. 1985):117–123.

WILSON, WILLIAM JULIUS. "The Black Underclass." *The Wilson Quarterly*. Vol. 8 (Spring 1984):88–99.

WINN, MARIE. *Children Without Childhood*. New York: Pantheon Books, 1983.

WIRTH, LOUIS. "Urbanism As A Way of Life." *American Journal of Sociology*. Vol. 44, No. 1 (July 1938):1–24.

WITKIN-LANOIL, GEORGIA. *The Female Stress Syndrome: How to Recognize and Live with It*. New York: Newmarket Press, 1984.

WOLFGANG, MARVIN E., and FRANCO FERRACUTI. *The Subculture of Violence: Towards an Integrated Theory in Criminology*. Beverly Hills, CA: Sage Publications, 1982.

WOLFGANG, MARVIN E., ROBERT M. FIGLIO, and THORSTEN SELLIN. *Delinquency in a Birth Cohort*. Chicago: University of Chicago Press, 1972.

WOLFINGER, RAYMOND E., and STEVEN J. ROSENSTONE. *Who Votes?* New Haven, CT: Yale University Press, 1980.

WOLFINGER, RAYMOND E., MARTIN SHAPIRO, and FRED I. GREENSTEIN. *Dynamics of American Politics*. 2nd ed. Englewood Cliffs, NJ: Prentice-Hall, 1980.

WONG, BUCK. "Need for Awareness: An Essay on Chinatown, San Francisco." In Amy Tachiki et al., eds., *Roots: An Asian American Reader*. Los Angeles: UCLA Asian American Studies Center, 1971:265–273.

WOODALL, MARTHA. "Segregation Being Ended, Clayton Says." *Philadelphia Inquirer* (November 20, 1984):1A, 8A.

WOODWARD, C. VANN. *The Strange Career of Jim Crow*. 3rd rev. ed. New York: Oxford University Press, 1974.

THE WORLD BANK. *World Development Report 1984*. New York: Oxford University Press, 1984.

WORLD HEALTH ORGANIZATION. *Constitution of the World Health Organization*. New York: World Health Organization Interim Commission, 1946.

WRIGHT, ERIK OLIN, and BILL MARTIN. "The Transformation of the American Class Structure, 1960–1980." *American Journal of Sociology*. Vol. 93, No. 1 (July 1987):1–29.

WRIGHT, STUART A., and ELIZABETH S. PIPER. "Families and Cults: Familial Factors Related to Youth Leaving or Remaining in Deviant Religious Groups." *Journal of Marriage and the Family*. Vol. 48, No. 1 (February 1986):15–25.

WRONG, DENNIS H. "The Oversocialized Conception of Man in Modern Sociology." *American Sociological Review*. Vol. 26, No. 2 (April 1961):183–193.

YATES, RONALD E. "Growing Old in Japan; They Ask Gods for a Way Out." *Philadelphia Inquirer* (August 14, 1986):3A.

YODER, JAN D., and ROBERT C. NICHOLS. "A Life Perspective: Comparison of Married and Divorced Persons." *Journal of Marriage and the Family*. Vol. 42, No. 2 (May 1980):413–419.

YOUNGMAN, HENNY. "That Don't Look Jewish to Me." *VIS a VIS*. Vol. 1, No. 2 (April 1987):136.

ZALD, MAYER N. *Occupations and Organizations in American Society*. Chicago: Markham, 1971.

ZANGWILL, ISRAEL. *The Melting Pot*. New York: Macmillan, 1921; orig. 1909.

ZASLAVSKY, VICTOR. *The Neo-Stalinist State: Class, Ethnicity, and Consensus in Soviet Society*. Armonk, NY: M. E. Sharpe, 1982.

ZEITLIN, IRVING M. *The Social Condition of Humanity*. New York: Oxford University Press, 1981.

ZELNICK, MELVIN, and JOHN F. KANTER. "Sexual Activity, Contraceptive Use, and Pregnancy Among Metropolitan-Area Teenagers: 1971–1979." *Family Planning Perspectives*. Vol. 12, No. 5 (September–October 1980).

ZIGLI, BARBARA. "Enrollment: What's the Score?" *USA Today* (December 20, 1984):D1.

ZILL, NICHOLAS. National survey conducted by Child Trends, Inc., Washington, DC, 1984. Reported by Marilyn Adams. "Kids Aren't Broken by the Breakup." *USA Today* (December 20, 1984):5D.

ZIMBARDO, PHILIP G. "Pathology of Imprisonment." *Society*. Vol. 9 (April 1972):4–8.

ZIPP, JOHN F. "Perceived Representativeness and Voting: An Assessment of the Impact of 'Choices' vs. 'Echoes.'" *The American Political Science Review*. Vol. 79, No. 1 (March 1985): 50–61.

ZIPP, JOHN F., and JOEL SMITH. "A Structural Analysis of Class Voting." *Social Forces*. Vol. 60, No. 3 (March 1982):738–759.

ZOLA, IRVING KENNETH. "Medicine as an Institution of Social Control." In John Ehrenreich, ed., *The Cultural Crisis of Modern Medicine*. New York: Monthly Review Press, 1978:80–100.

ZURCHER, LOUIS A., and DAVID A. SNOW. "Collective Behavior: Social Movements." In Morris Rosenberg and Ralph Turner, eds., *Social Psychology: Sociological Perspectives*. New York: Basic Books, 1981:447–482.

Acknowledgments

Photographs

Chapter 1: **xxii** Paul Fusco/Magnum Photos. **2** Suzanne Szasz/ Photo Researchers. **4** Four By Five. **5** Catherine Ursillo/Photo Researchers. **8** Frank Siteman/Taurus Photos (top); George Bellerose/Stock, Boston (bottom). **9** United Nations Photo by Gaston Guarda. **12** New York Public Library. **13** The Pierpont Morgan Library (left); Frederick Lewis Photographs (right). **17** New York Public Library Picture Collection. **18** The Bettmann Archive. **19** Philip Jon Bailey/The Picture Cube. **22** Harvey Barad/Photo Researchers. **23** AP/Wide World Photos, Inc. (top left); Ken Regan/ Camera 5 (middle); Peter Miller/Photo Researchers (bottom).

Chapter 2: **28** United Nations Photo. **30** Rene Burri/Magnum Photos. **35** Ray Pfortner/Peter Arnold, Inc. **36** The Institute for Intercultural Studies, Inc. **39** H.E. Edgerton. **41** T. Campion/ Sygma. **42** Philip G. Zimbardo. **45** Michal Heron (left); L. Morris-Nantz (right). **51** Craig Aurness/Woodfin Camp & Associates (top); A. Baum/Monkmeyer Press (bottom). **56** Sotheby's.

Chapter 3: **60** S. Asad/Peter Arnold, Inc. **62** Napoleon A. Chagnon. **64** The Associated Press/AP PhotoColor (top); Topham/The Image Works (bottom); Mark & Evelyne Bernheim/Woodfin Camp & Associates (right). **67** E. Rubert/Language Research Center. **70** The Picture Cube. **72** Miro Vintoniv/Stock, Boston. **74** Detroit Institute of Art. **75** Tom Hollyman/Photo Researchers. **76** Mark Richards/Picture Group. **81** UPI/Bettmann Newsphotos. **83** Paolo Koch/Rapho/Photo Researchers. **85** Randy Matusow/ Monkmeyer.

Chapter 4: **90** Kotoh/Leo de Wys. **93** Courtesy of the Lenskis; photo by Will Owens. **94** Four By Five. (left); John Hiney/ Photo Researchers (right). **95** James R. Holland/Stock, Boston. **96** Robert Frerck/Woodfin Camp & Associates. **99** U.S. Air Force Photo/Photo Researchers. **102** Brown Brothers. **104** The Bettmann Archive/BBC Hulton Picture Library. **107** Sygma. **108** New York Public Library Picture Collection. **111** Private collection. **112** Harvard University News Office. **115** Four By Five. (left); Jeffrey Foxx/ United Nations (top); M. Reichenthal/The Stock Market (middle).

Chapter 5: **120** © Henley & Savage. **123** Lew Merrim/Monkmeyer Press (top); Mimi Forsyth/Monkmeyer Press (left); Cary Wolinsky/Stock, Boston (right). **124** UPI/Bettmann Newsphotos. **125** Harry F. Harlow, University of Wisconsin Primate Laboratory. **126** Mary Evans/Sigmund Freud Copyrights; courtesy of W.E. Freud. **128** Elizabeth Crews. **130** Courtesy of University of Chicago Archives. **132** L. Morris/Nantz (left); Randy Duchaine/The Stock Market (middle); Martin Rogers/Woodfin Camp & Associates (right). **139** Prado Museum, Madrid. **140** Tomas Sennet/Magnum Photos.

Chapter 6: **148** United Nations Photo/Nicole Toutounji. **149** Henry Holt and Company. © 1985 by Michael Hague. **152** Carolyn A. McKeone/Photo Researchers. **155** David Woo/Stock, Boston. **157** Matthew Naythons/Stock, Boston. **158** Mark Antman/The Image Works. **160** David C. Bitters/The Picture Cube (left); Charles Gupton/Stock, Boston (middle); Four by Five (right). **162** David Johnson, *Time* Magazine, April 22, 1985, p. 59. **165** Painting of "The Fight of Carnival and Lent" by Peter Brueghel; Art Resource. **166** Jan Halaska/Photo Researchers. **167** CBS Photograph (top); Ken Sax/Shooting Star (bottom). **169** The Museum of Modern Art/Film Stills Archive (top); Paramount Pictures Corporation (bottom).

Chapter 7: **172** Tom Tracy/The Stock Market. **173** Mark Antman/The Image Works. **175** Prentice-Hall. **179** William Vandivert. **182** Owen Franken/Stock, Boston. **184** Hazel Hankin/Stock, Boston. **185** Alex Webb/Magnum Photos. **187** Lester Sloan/ Woodfin Camp & Associates. **189** Yoram Kahana/Shooting Star. **190** The Metropolitan Museum of Art; George A. Hearn Fund, 1956. **191** Joseph Nettis/Photo Researchers. **192** AP/Wide World Photos. **193** Julie Houck. **196** Ethan Hoffman/Archive Pictures, Inc.

Chapter 8: **200** Pana-Vue. **202** L.L.T. Rhodes/Taurus Photos. **203** UPI/Bettmann Newsphotos. **206** Jean-Marie Simon/Taurus Photos. **208** Roger Marschutz/Fotofolio (left); Courtesy of PepsiCo Inc. (right). **210** UPI/Bettmann Newsphotos. **212** Charles Ledford/ Gamma-Liaison. **213** Bill Bachman/Photo Researchers. **218** William Strode/Woodfin Camp & Associates (left); Leonard Lessin/ Peter Arnold (right). **219** UPI/Bettmann Newsphotos. **225** David Austen/Stock, Boston. **227** Richard Kalvar/Magnum Photos. **230** Wally McNamee/Woodfin Camp & Associates.

Chapter 9: **234** Steve McCurry/Magnum Photos. **235** Ken Marschall; collection of Joseph M. Ryan. **238** William Campbell/*Time* Magazine. **239** Bruce Coleman Inc. (left); Neal Preston/Camera 5 (right). **243** F. Hibon/Sygma. **244** Art Resource. **246** Alan Carey/ The Image Works. **247** Jacques M. Chenet/Woodfin Camp & Associates. **248** New York Public Library.

Chapter 10: **254** Ulrike Welsch/Photo Researchers. **255** Ray Elllis/Photo Researchers. **261** C. Vergara/Photo Researchers. **262** Movie Star News. **265** Chuck Fishman/Woodfin Camp & Associates. **267** Mark Sherman/Bruce Coleman, Inc. (left); Jeffrey D. Smith/Woodfin Camp & Associates (right). **270** Tyrone Hall/ Stock, Boston (left); Alex Webb/Magnum Photos (right). **272** Collection, The Museum of Modern Art, New York; gift of Edward M. M. Warburg. **273** Kenneth Murray/Photo Researchers. **275** Eugene Gordon.

Chapter 11: 280 Bill Anderson/Monkmeyer. 281 Don White/ *Time* Magazine. 282 John Pitkin. 286 Sam Dennison, *Scandalize My Name: Black Imagery in American Popular Music* (New York: Garland Publishing, 1982), p. 46. 291 Katerina Thomas/Photo Researchers. 294 Kenyon College. 295 Raymond Depardon/ Magnum Photos (top); Wally McNamee/Woodfin Camp & Associates (bottom). 299 UPI/Bettmann Newsphotos. 300 Bob Adelman (top); Peter Blakely/Picture Group (bottom). 302 Thomas Hopker/ Woodfin Camp & Associates. 305 Library of Congress. 307 Randy Taylor/Sygma.

Chapter 12: 312 Campion/Sygma. 313 Library of Congress. 314 Michel Tcherevkoff/The Image Bank. 317 P.B. Kaplan/Photo Researchers. 322 Richard Hutchings/Photo Researchers (top); Jim Weiner/Photo Researchers (bottom). 323 Courtesy of Pennsylvania State University. 325 New York Public Library Picture Collection. 326 Courtesy of Revlon. 330 Library of Congress. 336 Courtesy of National Organization for Women. 338 AP/Wide World Photos. 339 Library of Congress.

Chapter 13: 342 Ruth and John Park/The Stock Market. 345 Jonathan T. Wright/Bruce Coleman Inc. 348 Michael S. Yamashita/ Woodfin Camp & Associates. 349 Eve Arnold/Magnum Photos. 350 N.R. Farbman, LIFE Magazine; © 1947, 1975 Time Inc. 351 Bruno J. Zehnder/United Nations. 353 Peter Menzel/Stock, Boston. 356 Will McIntyre/Photo Researchers. 359 AP/Wide World Photos. 360 Jose Fernandez/Woodfin Camp & Associates. 361 AP/Wide World Photos. 363 Scala Art Resource. 365 Abraham Menashe/Photo Researchers.

Chapter 14: 368 Willie L. Hill/The Image Works. 369 UPI/ Bettmann Newsphotos. 372 Farrell Grehan/Photo Researchers. 374 Marcus Adams/Woodfin Camp & Associates. 376 Luis Alberto Acuña. 379 Four By Five. 381 Four By Five (left); Ellan Young/Photo Researchers (right). 389 Will & Deni McIntyre/ Photo Researchers. 391 Gale Zucker/Stock, Boston. 394 Petit-Format/Nestle/Science Source/Photo Researchers.

Chapter 15: 398 Katerina Thomas/Photo Researchers. 399 Addison Gallery of American Art, Phillips Academy, Andover, Massachusetts. 400 TVA/Hine, Photo Researchers. 403 Tass from Sovfoto. 407 The Bettmann Archive. 409 Mark Mittelman/Taurus Photos. 410 Owen Franken/Liaison Agency. 415 Richard Hutchings/Photo Researchers. 417 Copyright 1985 G.B. Trudeau. Reprinted with permission of Universal Press Syndicate. All rights reserved. 419 Michael Grecco/Stock, Boston. 421 Will McIntyre/Photo Researchers.

Chapter 16: 426 Mehmet Biber/Photo Researchers. 428 Cary Wolinsky/Stock, Boston. 429 New York Public Library. 434 AP/ Wide World Photos. 435 Donald Dietz/Stock, Boston (top); Karen Kasmauski/Wheeler Pictures (bottom). 436 Gamma-Liaison. 437 Art Resource. 441 R. & S. Michaud/Woodfin Camp & Associates. 442 Peter Menzel/Wheeler Pictures. 444 Jan Lukas/Photo Researchers. 454 David Burnett/Contact Press Images, Woodfin Camp & Associates.

Chapter 17: 458 Owen Franken/Stock, Boston. 461 B. Daemmrich/Stock, Boston. 462 AP/Wide World Photos (left and right). 463 UPI/Bettmann Newsphotos. 464 Georg Gerster/Photo Researchers. 466 AP/Wide World Photos. 469 Claude Urraca/ Sygma. 472 Ellis Herwig/Stock, Boston. 475 Bettye Lane/Photo Researchers. 480 Peter Menzel/Stock, Boston. 482 The Bettmann Archive. 484 AP/Wide World Photos.

Chapter 18: 488 Kit Luce/International Stock Photo. 490 Catherine LeRoy/*Time* Magazine. 492 National Archives. 493 Chuck O'Rear/Woodfin Camp & Associates (top); Kevin Horan/Stock, Boston (middle); Richard Hutchings/Photo Researchers (bottom). 495 Richard Hutchings/Photo Researchers. 498 Marcello Bertinetti/Photo Researchers (top); Gilda Schiff/Photo Researchers (bottom). 504 Ellis Herwig/Stock, Boston. 507 Ellis Herwig/Stock, Boston. 508 Eric Kroll/Taurus Photos. 513 Gamma-Liaison.

Chapter 19: 518 Martin M. Rotker/Taurus Photos. 521 Joseph Nettis/Photo Researchers. 523 The Bettmann Archive. 524 WHO photo by J. Marquis (left); WHO photo (right). 528 Susan Leavines/ Photo Researchers. 531 Jacques M. Chenet/Woodfin Camp & Associates. 533 Ken Karp. 536 Lawrence Fried. 537 James Pozarik/Gamma-Liaison. 540 Larry Mulvehill/Photo Researchers. 543 Ray Ellis/Photo Researchers.

Chapter 20: 548 Julie Houck/Stock, Boston. 550 Hella Hammid/ Photo Researchers. 554 Bernard Wolff/Photo Researchers. 557 N. Maceschal/The Image Bank 559 Anderson/Gamma-Liaison. 560 United Nations Photo. 562 Monkmeyer Press. 567 National Museum of American Art, Smithsonian Institution Transfer from the U.S. Department of the Interior, National Park Service. 569 George Hall, Woodfin Camp & Associates. 571 Jan Lukas/Photo Researchers. 573 The University of Chicago Library. 576 Paul Conklin/Monkmeyer Press.

Chapter 21: 580 Scott Thode/International Stock Photo. 581 AP/ Wide World Photos. 584 Taurus Photos (top left); Mark Mittelman/ Taurus Photos (top right); Barbara Kirk/The Stock Market (center); UPI/Bettmann Newsphotos (bottom left); UPI/Bettmann Newsphotos (bottom right). 588 AP/Wide World Photos. 592 AP/Wide World Photos. 595 Randy Taylor/Sygma (top): Tannenbaum/Sygma (bottom). 597 Steve Liss/Gamma-Liaison. 600 Tannenbaum/Sygma. 603 UPI/Bettmann Newsphotos. 604 Perry C. Riddle. 605 W. Campbell/Sygma.

Chapter 22: 610 Lou Jones. 612 Tom Hollyman/Photo Researchers. 614 David Welcher/Sygma. 618 Jean Gaumy/Magnum Photos. 619 Bildarchiv Preussischer Kulturbesitz. 620 Whitney Museum of American Art. 622 Frieda Leinwand/Monkmeyer Press. 627 Joan Menschenfreund/Taurus Photos. 629 Wally McNamee/ Woodfin Camp & Associates. 632 Robert Azzi/Woodfin Camp & Associates. 634 Chris Brown/Gamma-Liaison.

Figures

Fig. 1–2 Adapted from Jay J. Coakley, *Sport in Society: Issues and Controversies*, 3rd ed. (St. Louis: Times Mirror/Mosby College Publishing, 1986), pp. 151–153.

Fig. 2–2 Adapted with permission from Walter L. Wallace, ed. *Sociological Theory, An Introduction* (New York: Aldine de Gruyter, 1969). Copyright © 1969 by Walter L. Wallace.

Fig. 4–1 Adapted from Gerhard Lenski and Jean Lenski, *Human Societies: An Introduction to Macrosociology*, 5th ed. (New York: McGraw-Hill, 1987), p. 68.

Fig. 4–3 Adapted from Talcott Parsons, *Societies: Evolutionary and Comparative Perspectives* (Englewood Cliffs, N.J.: Prentice-Hall, 1966), p. 28.

Fig. 5–1 Suggested by Howard L. Sacks, Kenyon College.

Fig. 7–1 Adapted from Solomon Asch, *Social Psychology* (Englewood Cliffs, N.J.: Prentice-Hall, 1952), pp. 452–453.

Fig. 10–2 Based on data from the Federal Reserve Board, as reported by Stephen J. Rose, *The American Profile Poster* (New York: Pantheon, 1986), p. 31, Table 30.

Fig. 10–4 Lester C. Thurow, "A Surge in Inequality," *Scientific American*, Vol. 256, No. 5 (May 1987), p. 32. Copyright © 1987 by Scientific American, Inc. All rights reserved.

Fig. 11–1 Based on Robert K. Merton, "Discrimination and the American Creed," *Sociological Ambivalence and Other Essays* (New York: Free Press, 1976), pp. 189–216.

Fig. 11–3 Richard Saul Wurman and John Andrew Gallery, *Man-Made Philadelphia: A Guide to Its Physical and Cultural Environment* (Cambridge: The Massachusetts Institute of Technology Press, 1972). © Group for Environmental Education.

Fig. 13–1 Based on data from Beth Soldo, "America's Elderly in the 1980s," *Population Bulletin*, Vol. 35, No. 4 (November 1980). Population Reference Bureau.

Fig. 14–2 Adapted from William Julius Wilson, "The Black Underclass," *The Wilson Quarterly*, Vol. 8 (Spring 1984), p. 94. Copyright 1984 by the Woodrow Wilson International Center for Scholars.

Fig. 14–3 Adapted from Catherine E. Ross, John Mirowsky, and Joan Huber, "Dividing Work, Sharing Work, and In-Between: Marriage Patterns and Depression," *American Sociological Review*, Vol. 48, No. 6 (December 1983), p. 819.

Fig. 16–1 Glenmary Research Center, Atlanta, Georgia.

Fig. 17–1 Adapted from Michael Barone and Grant Ujifisa, *The Almanac of American Politics, 1982* (Washington, D.C.: Baron and Company, 1981), p. iii.

Fig. 20–3 Adapted from James L. Newman and Gordon E. Matzke, *Population: Patterns, Dynamics, and Prospects* (Englewood Cliffs, N.J.: Prentice-Hall, 1984), p. 65.

Fig. 20–6 Adapted from Population Reference Bureau, as presented in Phyllis T. Piotrow, *World Population: The Present and Future Crisis*, Headline Series 251 (New York: Foreign Policy Association, 1980).

Fig. 21–1 Adapted from David F. Aberle, *The Peyote Religion Among the Navaho* (Chicago, Aldine, 1966), p. 316.

Fig. 21–2 Adapted from James C. Davies, "Toward a Theory of Revolution," *American Sociological Review*, Vol. 27, No. 1 (February 1962), p. 6.

Index

SUBJECT INDEX